The Civil War Day by Day
AN ALMANAC
1861–1865

Other Works by E. B. Long

Co-Author
The Civil War Digest (with Ralph G. Newman)
As Luck Would Have It (with Otto Eisenschiml)

Editor
Personal Memoirs of U. S. Grant
History of the Civil War by James Ford Rhodes (new edition)
Stonewall Jackson and the American Civil War
by George F. R. Henderson (modern abridgment)
Compiler and Annotator, "General Section,"
Civil War Books, Vol. II, edited by
James I. Robertson, Jr.

The Civil War Day by Day

AN ALMANAC
1861-1865

E. B. LONG

with Barbara Long

Foreword by Bruce Catton

A DA CAPO PAPERBACK

Library of Congress Cataloging in Publication Data

Long, E. B. (Everette Beach), 1919–
  The Civil War day by day.

  (A Da Capo paperback)
  Reprint. Originally published: Garden City, N.Y.:
Doubleday, 1971.
  Bibliography: p.
  1. United States—History—Civil War, 1861–1865—
Chronology. I. Long, Barbara, 1921–   . II. Title.
468.3.L6   1985]   973.7'02'02   85-10356
ISBN 0-306-80255-4 (pbk.)

Maps by Barbara Long
Designed by Joseph P. Ascherl

This Da Capo Press paperback edition of *The Civil War Day by Day: An Almanac
1861-1865* is an unabridged republication of the edition published in New York in
1971. It is reprinted by arrangement with Doubleday & Co.

Published by Da Capo Press, Inc.
A Subsidiary of Plenum Publishing Corporation
233 Spring Street, New York, N.Y. 10013

DEDICATION

I am humbly grateful to the countless mentors I have had along the way in my studies in the field of Civil War history. I wish they all could be named. I dedicate this volume to them, and especially to: Ray Allen Billington, Bruce Catton, the late William B. Hesseltine, the late Allan Nevins, and Ralph G. Newman.

CONTENTS

LIST OF MAPS

following page 562

FOREWORD

In all the vast collection of books on the American Civil War there is no book like this one. It has been needed for a long time, both by the student and by the man who simply likes to read about the Civil War, but until now no one had the dedication or the encyclopedic knowledge to produce it. Here it is, at last—an almanac, or day-by-day recital of the events of the war, running from the end of 1860 down to the close of the conflict, written by Professor E. B. Long of the University of Wyoming.

This almanac grew out of two things—Professor Long's years of work as director of research for *The Centennial History of the Civil War,* and his lifelong study of the war both as an amateur and as a professional. For the Centennial History alone, Professor Long compiled the unimaginable total of nine million words of notes. This compilation grew out of some nine years of full-time study, and that in turn was built on many earlier years of all-embracing research. If there was a battlefield in the Civil War that this man has not visited personally, I do not know where it is; if there is an important collection of papers shedding light on the war that he has not examined, it would be hard to name it. It is no exaggeration whatever to say that this man knows more facts about the Civil War than any other man who ever lived.

To know a subject thoroughly, of course, is one thing; to put the results of that knowledge into lucid prose of manageable compass is something else again. One does not need to examine many pages of this almanac to realize that Professor Long has succeeded admirably in the second task. Crammed to the margins of each page with facts, this book is never soporific. It is for the casual reader as well as for the specialist; it can even, as a matter of fact, be read straight through as a narrative, in which the dramatic and heart-stirring events of America's greatest time of trial pass before the eye on a day-to-day basis.

A book like this has been needed for a long time, but up to now no one was able to write it. It should have a long life, and no one will ever need to do it again. It belongs on the somewhat restricted shelf of Civil War books that will be of permanent value. Professor Long has taken on an important job and he has done it admirably.

BRUCE CATTON

PREFACE

History is not just the mountain peaks of spectacular events, transcendent personalities, or shattering battles. History is all events, all time, all people everywhere.

The historian faces an awesome task. He must attempt to grasp this multitudinous welter of happenings large and small and mold it into a continuity that may be understood and assimilated by the reader. No historian can dig deeply enough or has space enough; the frustrations of writing any history are appalling, terrifying, and humbling.

Several approaches have been partially successful in overcoming the physical limits of the printed page, the time limits of the reader, and the limits of authors who must make the foredoomed attempt to embrace their subject completely.

Many of the histories of the American Civil War conceived in the normal narrative pattern are very capably done. A few are masterful, such as Bruce Catton's *Centennial History of the Civil War,* to which this is a companion and, I hope, a supplemental volume.

No one, no matter what method he uses, can encompass the entire course of those five years of our nation's greatest crisis. One form, however, that can add at least a measure of factual depth, I believe, is an almanac, a day-by-day chronological recounting. By this means a portion of the underlying pattern of occurrences, some impress of the so-called lesser affairs, the trails up to and away from the cataclysms can be traced.

In preparing this book I have eschewed the traditional straight factual chronology of events. I have attempted to present them in a simple narrative framework to try to give some concept of integration and significance, while trying to maintain brevity and clarity. I realize the drawbacks of this method, but I hope this volume will at least partially fulfill a need.

The format of *The Civil War Day by Day* is simple. It covers many events of the Civil War era from the late fall of 1860 into early 1866, with the main concentration on 1861–65. The text is divided into years, months, and days. Major political developments or battles are marked by headlines so that the reader can, if he chooses, easily use this volume as the usual chronology or listing of principal happenings. Each year and month has a brief introduction designed to set the scene as it appeared to those of the time, who, after all, did not know what was coming next. It was my original intention that these interstices should have been longer and more interpretive as to the emotional feelings of the people and more expressive of their fears, questions, and uncertainties.

Following the chronology or main body of the book are sections giving brief statistical data on the population of the nation at the time of the war, the armies, casualties, and the economics of the period. There is also a section on the naval blockade by the North and Southern attempts to evade it. For obvious reasons the blockade could not be mentioned in the entry for each day, yet its presence was continually felt. After these pages examining the people and men of war is the Research Bibliography for *The Centennial History of the Civil War*. As space allowed use of only a little more than half of this bibliography in Bruce Catton's series, I feel it worth while to list it here in full. Countless additional volumes, articles, and monographs, not listed, were examined, though not used specifically.

Special maps for this book by Barbara Long are designed to give the reader a general orientation and the location of principal battles, cities, and geographical features pertaining to the war. It proved an impossibility to incorporate all the places mentioned in the text. The maps clearly are not intended to provide detailed coverage of individual battles.

The primary index is by date rather than by page number, in order to give the reader ready knowledge of when an event occurred. A brief alphabetical supplemental index giving page numbers is a key to the sections of facts and figures.

In recording most scouts and expeditions that extended over a period of time, only the first day is generally mentioned.

I am keenly aware of controversies over spellings. For the most part I have adopted the spellings of communities as they were in the Civil War period, when these can be determined.

In a volume as replete with facts and specifics as this, errors are inevitable despite my earnest efforts to be accurate. Vigilant readers will apprise me of any mistakes. On some points, it must be remembered, even informed, expert opinions may vary and the truth remain ever elusive.

This volume has been in preparation for a good many years. Early versions served as an outline for my research notes for Bruce Catton's *Centennial History of the Civil War*. It is my desire that this almanac may also serve the reader in the same manner—as an outline for his Civil War study and thought.

The Civil War was more than just the sum of what happened militarily in Virginia and along the rivers of the West, even adding what went on in Washington and Richmond. It was all that transpired from the coast of France to the waters of Japan, from Indian fighting in California and in the Pacific Northwest to bank robbery in Vermont and raids off the coast of Maine. Military events alone numbered some 10,455, not considering naval actions, with countless other scraps that did not find their way into official records. Men fought men in all the forgotten woods, valleys, fields, and hamlets just as determinedly and sometimes just as disastrously for those present as at Gettysburg, Vicksburg, Atlanta, or any of the other "big battles" of the war.

The Civil War was a whole made up of nearly infinite but interrelated parts. An acknowledgment of that relationship seems vital to analysis or comprehension of history. I hope that this book has achieved at least some of this interrelation. It is realized there will be those who will quarrel with the selection of secondary activities and the weight given to major ones. Unfortunately, no work can provide all the details of each and every battle, movements of regiments, and similar information. Neither can all the political, social, homefront, and emotional aspects be sufficiently probed. This book is not intended to supplant specialized narrative studies, and it cannot be an inclusive compendium of all knowledge of the period. It is intended to be a guide and reminder to the advanced scholar, and to furnish the beginner and the occasional reader of Civil War literature with useful guideposts.

History is made by people. The leaders must be heard and their words applied to the actions of the time, and the actions to the words. Yet, where possible, the people must be heard as well. When all are blended together with the sweep of time, we have the story of our lives, as well as the story of the lives of those of more than a century ago. If this book has contributed even modestly to the knowledge and over-all understanding of yesterday, and therefore today, I am content.

E. B. LONG

Laramie, Wyoming
1971

1860

NOVEMBER, 1860

It was election time—with four major candidates, four major political parties. The issues were monumental: they included the expansion of slavery into the territories; to what extent could the Federal government control the rights of citizens and states? There was great emotionalism, much heat and distortion, and some thought.

Sectionalism had intruded into the campaign. The Democratic party had split down the middle at the Charleston Convention and had two candidates—John C. Breckinridge of Kentucky, representing primarily the deep South Democrats, largely a sectional party; and Stephen A. Douglas of Illinois, representing Northern and border-state Democrats and some from the lower South, also something of a sectional party. The Republicans, founded in 1854, had Abraham Lincoln of Illinois and were distinctly a Northern sectional party. The Constitutional Unionists, comprised of old-time Whigs and other factions, offered John Bell of Tennessee and their viewpoints of strict constitutional liberty.

Following custom of the day the candidates made few, if any, regular campaign speeches, with the exception of the dynamic Douglas, who toured extensively, spoke often and with deep emotion. The other candidates allowed spokesmen to represent them and meanwhile loosed quantities of pamphlets, printed political speeches, and statements. As election day drew near it became reasonably clear that the split in the Democrats would mean the election of a Republican. There were no organized opinion polls but that outcome seemed probable, especially in view of the electoral system. And if Mr. Lincoln became President-elect, what would follow? South Carolina had threatened secession upon election of *any* Republican and it might come with the naming of Mr. Douglas as well. Could that really happen? If so, would other states follow? Was the question as ominous as it appeared, or was it just politics?

November 6, Tuesday
ABRAHAM LINCOLN ELECTED PRESIDENT OF THE UNITED STATES.

Abraham Lincoln was elected sixteenth President of the United States, with Hannibal Hamlin of Maine his Vice-President. The Republican ticket of Lincoln and Hamlin received 1,866,452 votes and 180 electoral votes in 17 of the 33 states. The Northern Democratic ticket of Stephen A.

Douglas of Illinois and Herschel V. Johnson of Georgia drew 1,376,957 votes, but only 12 electoral votes, 9 from Missouri and 3 of the New Jersey votes. John C. Breckinridge of Kentucky and Joseph Lane of Oregon on the Southern Democratic ticket received 849,781 votes from 11 of the 15 slave states, for 72 electoral votes. Constitutional Unionists John Bell of Tennessee and Edward Everett of Massachusetts drew 588,879 votes, for 39 electoral votes in Kentucky, Tennessee, and Virginia. Because of fusion tickets and sectional difficulties, none of the candidates was on every ballot in all 33 states. While Lincoln was thus a minority President in the popular vote with just over a third of the ballots, he did receive a majority of the electoral votes, 180 to 123 for the other three candidates combined. Douglas' poor electoral showing but high popular vote was due in part to the fact that he was the leading opponent to Lincoln in the populous North, where in some states Douglas and Lincoln were quite close.

While all results showed sectional voting to some extent, those of Lincoln and Breckinridge were the most pronounced. Only Bell carried his home county in the voting. Lincoln carried all the free states but none of the slave states. While trying to play down the radical label, the Republicans had been considered radical in the entire slave state area. In New Jersey Lincoln had four electoral votes to three for Douglas.

Mr. Lincoln spent the day in Springfield seeing visitors and receiving reports by telegraph. By 10 P.M. victory seemed near, but there was still doubt—until Pennsylvania came in Republican. As the victory was confirmed the President-elect visited the Watson Saloon, where a hundred female voices sang, "Ain't you glad you joined the Republicans? Joined the Republicans, Ain't you glad you joined the Republicans, down in Illinois?" At Democratic headquarters gloom set in. In Mobile, Alabama, Douglas was in the office of the Mobile *Register* arguing with its editor that the results did not mean secession. But the senator's attitude was described as "hopeless."

For the Senate the voters decided that the Republicans would have 29 seats to 37 in opposition. In the House there would be 108 Republicans to 129 others. But soon, with secession, and some realignment, the Republicans would gain workable margins.

November 7, Wednesday

At Charleston, South Carolina, the palmetto flag was raised in defiance of the election of Lincoln. That city's authorities arrested a Federal officer for trying to transfer supplies from the Charleston Arsenal to Fort Moultrie. Business was largely suspended and crowds filled the streets to read the bulletin boards. Some cheered for a Southern Confederacy. A judge told his court, "So far as I am concerned, the Temple of Justice raised under the Constitution of the United States is now closed. If it shall never again be opened I thank God that its doors have been closed before its altar has been desecrated with sacrifices to tyranny." Indignation meetings were held in many Southern communities and victory meetings in many Northern communities. At Springfield congratulations poured in to Lincoln at his State House office.

November 8, Thursday

"The tea has been thrown overboard, the revolution of 1860 has been initiated," stated the Charleston, S.C., *Mercury* in commenting on the election.

November 9, Friday

In the last few months of his administration, President James Buchanan faced a dilemma. He was opposed to secession but felt powerless to prevent it. His Cabinet was split pro- and anti-secession. Gen. Winfield Scott had given advice which included setting up four nations out of the present United States. On Nov. 9 the President, nearly seventy, called a Cabinet meeting to plan the State of the Union message. Mr. Buchanan asked the opinion of his Cabinet on responses to the threat of secession. The President himself proposed a general convention of the states, as provided by the Constitution, to plan some sort of compromise. Sec. of State Lewis Cass of Michigan spoke in favor of the Union, condemning secession and advocating the use of force. Att. Gen. Jeremiah Sullivan Black of Pennsylvania also strongly opposed secession and favored sending a force to Charleston. Postmaster General Joseph Holt of Kentucky opposed secession but was not in favor of a convention. Howell Cobb of Georgia, Secretary of the Treasury, thought disunion necessary, desirable, and legal. Jacob Thompson, Secretary of the Interior from Mississippi, said any show of force by the government would move Mississippi to disunion. Sec. of War John B. Floyd of Virginia was opposed to secession at this time because he thought the Lincoln administration would fail. Sec. of the Navy Isaac Toucey of Connecticut favored the constitutional convention.

The papers of the nation were taking their stand, their editorial comment a reflection of their section and politics. However, the New York *Tribune* led important journals in proposing that the "erring sisters" be allowed to go in peace: "We hope never to live in a republic whereof one section is pinned to the residue by bayonets."

November 10, Saturday

The legislature of South Carolina passed a law calling for a convention to meet at Columbia Dec. 17 to consider the question of secession from the Union. U. S. Senators James Chesnut, Jr., and James H. Hammond of South Carolina resigned their seats in the Senate. South Carolina was now in the forefront of the secession movement, with other deep South states following, while middle South and border states were waiting and watchful. In Springfield Mr. Lincoln was still reluctant to speak as he wrote, "I could say nothing which I have not already said, and which is in print, and open for the inspection of all. To press a repetition of this upon those who *have* listened, is useless; to press it upon those who have *refused* to listen, and still refuse, would be wanting in self-respect, and would have an appearance of sycophancy and timidity, which would excite the contempt of good men, and encourage bad ones to clamor the more loudly." A clamor there was, but on both sides. While Mr. Lincoln remained silent, many talked in print or in loud voices. Secession was now inevitable; go, and good riddance! No, others said, secession can never be.

November 12, Monday
The financial market in New York experienced heavy selling with a sharp drop in prices.

November 13, Tuesday
The legislature of South Carolina resolved to raise ten thousand volunteers for defense of the state.

November 14, Wednesday
Georgia Congressman Alexander H. Stephens, known for his conservative views, spoke to the Georgia legislature at Milledgeville, saying, "Good governments can never be built up or sustained by the impulse of passion. . . ." While the avowed principles of the President-elect were in "antagonism to our interests and rights" and would "subvert the Constitution under which we now live," the South must not be hasty, he said. He was opposed to secession and called upon the South to stand upon the Constitution and "Let the fanatics of the North break the Constitution, if such is their fell purpose." At Springfield the influx of politicians seeking office either for themselves or others was rapidly increasing.

November 15, Thursday
Maj. Robert Anderson, First Artillery, received special orders to proceed to Fort Moultrie at Charleston Harbor and relieve Bvt. Col. John L. Gardner in command. Maj. Anderson was a native of Kentucky, a graduate of West Point, had seen service in Mexico, and was considered an able officer.

U. S. Navy Lieut. T. A. Craven informed Washington that due to the

"deplorable condition of affairs in the Southern States" he was proceeding
to take moves to guard Fort Taylor at Key West and Fort Jefferson
on Dry Tortugas, Fla., from possible seizure. (Fort Taylor and the
Key West area later became a vital coaling station for the Federal Navy
and blockading squadron.)

November 16, Friday

President-elect Lincoln wrote a Missouri editor, "I am not at liberty
to shift my ground—that is out of the question." Meanwhile, the question
of Cabinet posts in the new administration became of increasing interest.
The relatively young Republican party was tasting its first victory and
the spoils would be many.

November 18, Sunday

The legislature of Georgia voted a million dollars to arm the state.
A newspaper reporter said Mr. Lincoln appeared undisturbed by the
news from the South and still felt secession would not be attempted.

November 20, Tuesday

President Buchanan, trying to find a course among the troubling storms,
had been consulting his Cabinet frequently, conferring with Winfield
Scott, and preparing his message to Congress. On Nov. 17 he had asked
Att. Gen. Jeremiah Sullivan Black a number of questions. On Nov. 20
Black submitted his opinions. The Attorney General told the President
that the states were subject to the laws of the United States while in
the Union; that the President could collect duties and protect public
property despite resistance, and that it was his duty to do so. The
President could not take action with troops against elements which opposed the government only with talk, and law enforcement must be
through the courts. The government could repel aggression but could
not wage an offensive war against a state; it could act only on the
defensive.

The major subjects of the day in Washington and elsewhere were no
longer slavery and its expansion, but the right of secession and the use
of Federal coercion. The right of secession was denied, but the Federal
government could do little in advance to stop it without recognizing
secession, under Black's opinion. The South believed in the right of secession and any Federal efforts to oppose it would be coercion. Some
Northerners, at least, believed that any secession movement could legally
be put down by force. Mr. Lincoln kept trying to affirm quietly that
the states would be left alone to control their own affairs, but few in
the South believed it. There was discussion of constitutional points, law,
arguments over technicalities, but little of substance was being done to
halt the drift accelerating disunion.

November 21, Wednesday

President-elect Lincoln journeyed to Chicago to meet with the future Vice-President Hannibal Hamlin. They discussed Cabinet posts during the next five days.

November 23, Friday

Maj. Robert Anderson, newly in command at Fort Moultrie on the edge of Charleston Harbor, reported that when the outworks were completed, the fort, appropriately garrisoned, would be capable of "making a very handsome defense." But the present garrison was so weak as to invite attack, which was being "openly and publicly threatened." If beleaguered, they could not hold out long. Fort Sumter, ungarrisoned, on a shoal in the harbor, was incomplete but work was proceeding on mounting of guns and he said it "is the key to the entrance of this harbor." He favored garrisoning Fort Sumter at once, as he did Castle Pinckney, which commanded the city of Charleston. Anderson was trying to avoid a clash but said, "Nothing, however, will be better calculated to prevent bloodshed than our being found in such an attitude that it would be madness and folly to attack us." Anderson reported a settled determination in Charleston to leave the Union. "The clouds are threatening, and the storm may break upon us at any moment." He repeated his call for reinforcements. (He was to repeat this request often.)

The forts had been left in a state of general stagnation. Sand dunes had piled up around Fort Moultrie so that cows could walk right in. Fort Sumter, begun in 1829, remained incomplete. Castle Pinckney was small and near the city, occupied by just an ordnance sergeant and his family. After all, the whole Federal Army numbered a little over sixteen thousand men, mostly on the western frontier.

November 26, Monday

Mr. and Mrs. Lincoln left Chicago for Springfield. Many visitors awaited them at home in the Illinois capital.

DECEMBER, 1860

The election of Abraham Lincoln in November had not solved anything; it appeared to have quickened tempers, increased concern, and perhaps even pushed secession over the brink. But could the nation actually be broken up? South Carolina said it could and would be, and others in the deep South seemed to agree. How much intent and how much just talk was there? What would the new President do in the spring of 1861? He had said little publicly before or after election. Did he have a policy? The old President, Buchanan, still had three months to serve and a Congress to face. Would he, or could he, do anything to avert trouble? Congress would gather the first part of the month and the President would report on the State of the Union. It appeared that Buchanan opposed secession but did not feel he had the power to coerce a state to remain if it wished to depart. His Cabinet was badly split, his critics many. His party had practically overlooked him in the nominations and campaign. Yet he was still President and still trying to do his job as he saw it. What action would Congress take, if any? And how about the Federal forts in Charleston Harbor? Maj. Anderson at Fort Moultrie, calling for reinforcements, suggested defending Federal property from Fort Sumter. South Carolina was gathering state troops, beginning to arm and build defenses.

December 1, Saturday

Florida's legislature was specially convened to consider the issues of the hour.

December 3, Monday

The second session of the Thirty-sixth Congress of the United States convened in Washington. Although a lame-duck affair, it showed surprising life, at least in its volubility about the crisis of the day.

December 4, Tuesday

PRESIDENT REPORTS ON STATE OF THE UNION.

President James Buchanan sent his message on the State of the Union to Congress. He found the "state" not too good. Regarding abolition, "The long-continued and intemperate interference of the Northern people with the question of slavery in the Southern States has at length produced its natural effects." He said that the slave states should be let alone. The states were sovereign and their rights could not be interfered with. At the same time he told the South, "the election of any one of our fellow-citizens to the office of President does not of itself afford just cause for dissolving the Union." Secession in this instance was unjustifiable. No overt or dangerous act had been committed by the President-elect. "The day of evil may never come unless we shall rashly bring it upon ourselves. Secession is neither more nor less than revolution." Calling for calmness and deliberation, the President said he believed slavery was on the way out. As to the forts in South Carolina, Mr. Buchanan believed that aside from execution of the laws the Executive had no authority to decide relations of the Federal government and South Carolina, but if there was any attempt to take the forts by force they would be defended. He proposed a constitutional amendment recognizing the right of property in slaves where it existed and protecting this right in the territories until they should be admitted with or without slavery as their constitutions might prescribe. Fugitive slaves should be returned. Here the President was suggesting remedies no one could live with. Both sides were disappointed by the message: the North because the President opposed secession but proposed no way to meet it; the South because he condemned secession.

This same day the House of Representatives named a special Committee of Thirty-three, one member from each state, to study the condition of the country.

December 5, Wednesday

In Springfield, Ill., President-elect Lincoln read a summary of the President's message to Congress and expressed displeasure that Buchanan placed responsibility for secession on the free states.

December 8, Saturday

Secretary of the Treasury Howell Cobb of Georgia resigned. Formerly a strong unionist, he had come to believe that the election of a Republican justified secession and had dissented with Buchanan's message to Congress. "The evil has now passed beyond control, and must be met by each and all of us, under our responsibility to God and our country," Cobb wrote Buchanan. Cobb was succeeded for about a month by Philip F. Thomas of Maryland. This marked the first break in Buchanan's Cabinet. A delegation of South Carolina congressmen called upon Mr. Buchanan and said that if reinforcements were going to Charleston it would be a sure way to bring about what he wanted to avoid. They asked for negotiations with South Carolina commissioners to consider the turning over of Federal property to the state. The President asked for a memorandum.

December 10, Monday

The South Carolina delegation in Washington spoke again with the President, presenting a memorandum saying that the state would not attack or molest the United States forts in Charleston Harbor prior to the act of secession and, they hoped, until an offer had been made to negotiate for an amicable arrangement between the state and the United States, provided no reinforcements should be sent to the forts. The delegation received the impression that no change would be made by the Federals in the military situation at Charleston. For their part, state authorities would try to prevent any premature collision. This interview later became a subject of dispute.

The President also moved to prepare the limited military resources of the nation for possible action. Maj. Anderson reported every day or two from Charleston. Abraham Lincoln, in Springfield, wrote Sen. Lyman Trumbull, "Let there be no compromise on the question of *extending* slavery. If there be, all our labor is lost, and, ere long, must be done again. . . . The tug has to come & better now, than any time hereafter."

December 11, Tuesday

At Fort Moultrie Maj. Don Carlos Buell, sent by the War Department to Charleston, prepared for Maj. Anderson a memorandum of verbal instruction given Buell by Sec. of War Floyd. Floyd pointed out that he had refrained from sending reinforcements in order to avoid a collision and that he felt South Carolina would not attempt to seize the forts. Anderson was not to take up any position which could be construed as hostile in attitude, but he was to hold possession of the forts and, if attacked, defend his position. He was authorized to put his command into any fort in order to increase its power of resistance if attacked or threatened with attack. A tour of the forts and Charleston convinced Buell that Fort Sumter would be seized. Furthermore, Moultrie would be taken unless Sumter was occupied. There apparently was talk of transferring Anderson's command from Fort Moultrie to Fort Sumter.

President-elect Lincoln wrote Congressman William Kellogg, as he had others, to "Entertain no proposition for a compromise in regard to the *extension* of slavery. The instant you do, they have us under again. . . ." He added, "You know I think the fugitive slave clause of the constitution ought to be enforced—to put it on the mildest form, ought not to be resisted."

December 12, Wednesday

Sec. of State Lewis Cass of Michigan resigned because the President refused to reinforce the Charleston forts. Now two Cabinet members had quit, but they were of opposite viewpoints. The resignation upset Buchanan as Cass still had considerable political influence, and Buchanan felt the Secretary had shifted his opinion since the message to Congress. In Springfield Lincoln was holding conferences in regard to his Cabinet appointments—this day with Francis P. Blair, Jr., of St. Louis, a powerful political figure. At Washington some twenty-three bills and resolutions purporting to solve the crisis were submitted to the House Committee of Thirty-three, which was seeking some plan of compromise. Eventually there were thirty or forty plans, including some calling for dual Presidents, and for splitting the country into districts.

December 13, Thursday

Seven senators and twenty-three representatives from the South issued a manifesto which urged secession and the organization of a Southern

Confederacy. President-elect Lincoln continued to write letters advising against compromise of any sort on slavery extension.

December 14, Friday

The Georgia legislature issued a call to South Carolina, Alabama, Florida, and Mississippi for delegates to be appointed to a convention to consider a Southern Confederacy.

December 15, Saturday

President-elect Lincoln wrote a confidential letter to Congressman John A. Gilmer of North Carolina in which he again expressed his reasons for not making any new statements, as they might be misinterpreted. He said further, "I never have been, am not now, and probably never shall be, in a mood of harassing the people, either North or South." But he was inflexible on the question of slavery extension in the territories: "You think slavery is right and ought to be extended; we think it is wrong and ought to be restricted. For this, neither has any just occasion to be angry with the other."

December 17, Monday

SOUTH CAROLINA SECESSION CONVENTION MEETS.

In the Baptist church of Columbia, S.C., the state capital, the Convention of the People of South Carolina gathered. President D. F. Jamison of Barnwell stated, "It is no less than our fixed determination to throw off a Government to which we have been accustomed, and to provide new safeguards for our future security. If anything has been decided by the elections which sent us here, it is, that South Carolina must dissolve her connection with the [Federal] Confederacy as speedily as possible." Proceeding to list grievances, Jamison went on, "Let us be no longer duped by paper securities. Written Constitutions are worthless, unless they are written, at the same time, in the hearts, and founded on the interests of the people; and as there is no common bond of sympathy or interest between the North and South, all efforts to preserve this Union will not only be fruitless, but fatal to the less numerous section." That evening a resolution stated "That it is the opinion of this Convention that the State of South Carolina should forthwith secede from the Federal Union, known as the United States of America." Another resolution called for a committee to draft such an ordinance. The question on secession passed 159 to nothing, and, in effect, South Carolina was out of the Union. However, the convention adjourned to Charleston due to the prevalence of smallpox at Columbia.

In Washington President Buchanan, faced with dissolution of his Cabinet, named Att. Gen. Jeremiah S. Black of Pennsylvania as Secretary of State to replace resigned Lewis Cass.

December 18, Tuesday

Reconvening in Charleston, the South Carolina Convention met in Institute Hall, with committee work taking most of the day. At Raleigh, N.C., commissioners from Alabama and Mississippi arrived to discuss the situation and the state senate passed a bill to arm the state.

In Washington the Senate passed a resolution that a special committee of thirteen members "inquire into the present condition of the country, and report by bill or otherwise." Sen. John J. Crittenden of Kentucky, basically a strong unionist, presented his "Crittenden Compromise." Referred to the new Committee of Thirteen, the Compromise proposed several amendments to the Constitution: 1. Slavery should be prohibited in all territories north of 36° 30′, the old Missouri Compromise line, and slavery should not be interfered with by Congress south of that line. When admitted as a state, a territory should be admitted with or without slavery as the state constitution provided. 2. Congress could not abolish slavery in places under its exclusive jurisdiction. 3. Congress could not abolish slavery within the District of Columbia so long as it existed in nearby states or without consent of the inhabitants or without just compensation. 4. Congress had no power to prohibit or hinder transportation of slaves from one state to another. 5. Congress should have power to provide that the United States pay to the owner full value of fugitive slaves when officers were prevented from arresting the fugitives. 6. No future amendment should affect the five preceding articles, nor the sections of the Constitution permitting slavery, and no amendment should be made which would give Congress power to abolish or interfere with slavery in states where state laws permitted it. Crittenden felt revival of the Missouri Compromise line, probably the main feature of the plan, would prevent any expansion at all, while, on the other hand, the Republicans could not accept any slavery expansion in the territories and the South could not accept limitation.

December 19, Wednesday

At Charleston various motions and resolutions and speeches were made at the South Carolina Convention. Leaders of the state were also declaring that no more Federal soldiers should be sent to the harbor forts. A representative from Mississippi was making speeches in Baltimore outlining the intentions of the states which proposed to secede.

December 20, Thursday

THE UNION IS DISSOLVED.

"*We, the People of the State of South Carolina, in Convention assembled, do declare and ordain, and it is hereby declared and ordained, That the Ordinance adopted by us in Convention on the twenty-third day* of May, in the year of our Lord one thousand seven hundred and eighty-eight, whereby the Constitution of the United States of America was ratified, and also all Acts, and parts of Acts, of the General Assembly of this State, ratifying amendments of the said Constitution are hereby repealed; and that the union now subsisting between South Carolina and other States, under the name of 'The United States of America' is hereby dissolved." By vote of 169 to nothing the convention had severed the ties of Union and the act so long spoken of was done.

In the evening the formal signing took place in Institute Hall, while Charleston went wild with joy and expectation. It was a warm, bright, cloudless day; the streets had been filled from afternoon on. Placards announced the news, church bells rang, cannons roared, the governor and public officials appeared. However, Judge James Louis Petigru, a highly respected pro-Union citizen of Charleston, spoke out: "I tell you there is a fire; they have this day set a blazing torch to the temple of constitutional liberty, and, please God, we shall have no more peace forever." But Edmund Ruffin, a Virginia secessionist present, wrote that when everyone had signed and South Carolina was proclaimed "to be a free and independent country, the cheers of the whole assembly continued for some minutes, while every man waved or threw up his hat, & every lady waved her handkerchief. . . . In the streets there had been going on popular demonstrations of joy, from early in the afternoon. Some military companies paraded, salutes were fired, & as night came on, bonfires, made of barrels of rosin, were lighted in the principal streets, rockets discharged, & innumerable crackers fired by the boys. . . . I hear the distant sounds of rejoicing, with music of a military band, as if there was no thought of ceasing.—" Another observer said, "The whole heart of the people had spoken." Swiftly the news spread elsewhere.

President Buchanan was attending a wedding reception in Washington when South Carolina Congressman Laurence Keitt came in, crying, "Thank God! Oh, thank God!" Told the news quietly, the President looked stunned, fell back, and grasped the arms of his chair. Buchanan left at once.

Earlier in the day President Buchanan had named prominent Washington attorney and Democratic leader Edwin M. Stanton, originally from Ohio, Attorney General to succeed J. S. Black, who had become Secretary of State. It was the first major role for Stanton, a man whose name was to become both famous and infamous in the years to come. In the Senate Vice-President Breckinridge named the Committee of Thirteen to look into the condition of the country. It included Senators Jefferson Davis of Mississippi and Robert Toombs of Georgia, Stephen A. Douglas of Illinois, William H. Seward of New York, and Ben Wade of Ohio. Thus many shades of opinion from secessionist to Radical were included. At Springfield President-elect Lincoln received the news of secession calmly.

13

December 21, Friday

The news was common now as the telegraph clicked out the message and the people and the press reacted. In much of the deep South public meetings approved the secession of South Carolina, while in the North there was incredulous resentment that the expected had really happened. Others wondered—what next? In Washington the four South Carolina congressmen formally withdrew from the House of Representatives, their letter being presented on Monday, Dec. 24. In Springfield Mr. Lincoln wrote Democratic leader Francis P. Blair, Sr., that "According to my present view if the forts [at Charleston] shall be given up before the inaugeration [sic], the General [Scott] must retake them afterwards." He wrote similarly to Congressman Elihu B. Washburne.

December 22, Saturday

Secessionist and Union meetings continued in the wake of the rupture of the nation. The South Carolina Convention named three commissioners to deal with the United States in regard to Federal property. The convention also passed a resolution that Forts Moultrie and Sumter, Castle Pinckney, and the Charleston Arsenal should now "be subject to the authority and control" of the state, and "that the possession of said forts and arsenal should be restored to the State of South Carolina."

Abraham Lincoln wrote Georgia Congressman Alexander H. Stephens that he wished to assure him that the Republican administration would not interfere with slavery in the South either directly or indirectly: "The South would be in no more danger in this respect, than it was in the days of Washington. I suppose, however, this does not meet the case. You think slavery is *right* and ought to be extended; while we think it is *wrong* and ought to be restricted. That I suppose is the rub."

December 24, Monday

The South Carolina Convention at Charleston passed a Declaration of Immediate Causes of secession, stating that the Union was declared in the Constitution to be an equal Union of the states and that each state had separate control over its institutions, including the right of slavery. "We affirm that these ends for which this Government was instituted have been defeated, and the Government itself has been made destructive of them by the action of the non-slaveholding States." They claimed the non-slaveholding states had "assumed the right of deciding upon the propriety of our domestic institutions; . . ." In an address to the people of the slaveholding states, the convention reported its reasons for dissolving South Carolina's connection with the Union and contended that the Northern states had overthrown the Constitution and "It is no longer a free Government, but a despotism." They would have preferred to remain in the old

Union but "we, of the South, are at last driven together by the stern destiny which controls the existence of nations." The address called for a Confederacy of slaveholding states in order to maintain independence and to work out their own destinies.

Gov. Pickens of South Carolina issued a proclamation declaring the state separate, independent, free, and sovereign. Alabama citizens elected delegates to a state convention and the governor ordered the legislature convened Jan. 14.

In the House of Representatives the letter of resignation of the South Carolina representatives was laid on the table with the names retained on the roll. Thus the secession of the state was not recognized. In the Senate William H. Seward of New York proposed an amendment to the Constitution that Congress should never interfere with slaves in the states; that jury trial be given fugitive slaves and that state constitutions having personal liberty laws in opposition to the Federal Constitution be revised.

It was Christmas Eve in a sadly torn nation.

December 25, Tuesday

"Another Christmas has come around in the circle of time but it is not a day of rejoicing. Some of the usual ceremonies are going on, but there is a gloom on the thoughts and countenance of all the better portion of our people." So wrote a diarist in Camden, Arkansas.

December 26, Wednesday

FEDERAL GARRISON TRANSFERS FROM FORT MOULTRIE TO FORT SUMTER.

By 8 P.M. of the evening of the day after Christmas, Maj. Robert Anderson had completed the transfer of his small garrison from Fort Moultrie on the shoreline of Charleston Harbor to Fort Sumter on a rock shoal in the harbor itself. The move was justified by Anderson in that he felt he had tangible evidence that Fort Moultrie would be forcibly taken by South Carolinians: "The step which I have taken was, in my opinion, necessary to prevent the effusion of blood. . . ." He spiked the guns and destroyed the carriages and later said, "I was certain that if attacked my men must have been sacrificed, and the command of the harbor lost." South Carolina and other Southern areas were outraged; overt action had, in their minds, been taken by the United States in violation of promises of the President that no change in position would be made. Sec. of War Floyd opposed the shift as against orders, but Anderson had interpreted his instructions differently, and under them had merely transferred his force. The move had been made with skill and secrecy, confounding the secessionists. Anderson began immediately to mount guns and strengthen Fort Sumter. He still faced the question of a small garrison, short supplies, and the danger of attack. In Washington the

15

commissioners from South Carolina arrived to discuss the forts and relations with the United States.

December 27, Thursday

Maj. Anderson raised his flag on Fort Sumter and South Carolina troops occupied Castle Pinckney and Fort Moultrie at Charleston. The U. S. Revenue Cutter *William Aiken* surrendered to state forces. Georgia and Alabama offered troops to South Carolina if needed. In a conference with President Buchanan, a group of Southern representatives protested the shift of troops to Fort Sumter. According to one report, the President said it had been against his orders and policy. But he delayed taking any action on the request to return the garrison to Fort Moultrie. The Cabinet met frequently these last few days of December. Sec. of War Floyd strongly advocated removing the entire Federal garrison from Charleston Harbor, on grounds that Anderson had violated pledges of the government. Thompson sided with Floyd, while Holt, Black, and Stanton opposed Floyd's plan. Buchanan had been surprised by Maj. Anderson's transfer and regretted it. He felt it would move other states to join South Carolina before compromise measures could be brought out of the Senate. Buchanan had been hopeful of confining secession to South Carolina.

December 28, Friday

President Buchanan received the commissioners of the state of South Carolina for the only time, and as "private gentlemen." He could not recognize them as commissioners of a sovereign power. The commissioners declared they must have redress for the moving of Anderson's force before entering upon negotiations. They insisted also upon withdrawal of all troops from Charleston. The commissioners pressed the President for a decision but he insisted upon time. Gen. Winfield Scott wrote the Secretary of War opposing evacuation of Fort Sumter and favoring sending reinforcements and supplies, along with armed vessels, to support the fort. President Buchanan was beginning to stiffen in his position. Cabinet meetings continued. Stanton and Floyd almost came to blows over Fort Sumter. Meanwhile, public meetings and the press were clamorous on all sides of the issues facing the nation.

December 29, Saturday

SECRETARY OF WAR FLOYD RESIGNS.

For some time it had been clear that Sec. of War John B. Floyd, former governor of Virginia, would have to leave the Cabinet. He had caused difficulty with his strong pro-Southern viewpoint in the South Carolina crisis and at the same time there had turned up an apparent defalcation of $870,000 of Indian-trust bonds in the Interior Department.

For the bonds Floyd had substituted acceptances to various army contractors. There was a charge of attempting to ship heavy guns from Pittsburgh to the South and seeing to it that small arms reached the Southern arsenals. The facts and Floyd's guilt, or lack of it, were then and still are debated. Historians long placed full blame on Floyd, partly because of his own later attitude, but other authorities then and now felt Floyd had simply been imprudent in the bond matter and had exaggerated his own role in allegedly helping the South obtain arms. At any rate, there was no longer any chance of his staying in the Cabinet. Buchanan had requested his resignation Dec. 23. Floyd's proposal to remove Federal troops from Charleston had been about the last straw. He based his resignation letter on the refusal of the Administration to correct Anderson's shifting of forts. As to the shipping of heavy guns from Pittsburgh, there seems some substantiation of Floyd's guilt, but the plan was prevented after his resignation.

As the year ended, President-elect Lincoln was working on his Cabinet appointments, still greeting and talking with visitors, and denying any idea of compromise.

December 30, Sunday

South Carolina troops seized the Federal Arsenal at Charleston, completing their occupation of all Federal property in the area except Fort Sumter. This news further shocked Buchanan, who was threatened with even more Cabinet resignations unless he took additional pro-Union steps. He and his advisers were discussing the reply to the South Carolina commissioners. Sec. of State Black and Att. Gen. Stanton drafted a document of advice to the President. They pointed out that the President had denied the right of secession and therefore could not recognize the commissioners; negotiation over the Federal forts at Charleston was impossible and they could not be given up; the President had the right to defend those forts; there was no violation of orders by Anderson in moving his garrison; warships should be sent to Charleston. Gen. Scott again wrote the President asking permission to send 250 troops and arms and stores to Fort Sumter.

Abraham Lincoln conferred in Springfield with Simon Cameron, Pennsylvania politician, who was one of the leading candidates for a major Cabinet post.

December 31, Monday

President James Buchanan replied to the commissioners from South Carolina. He said it was his duty to have Congress define the relations between the Federal government and South Carolina. He denied any pledge to preserve the status of the forts, and, after all, the authorities of South Carolina had seized Fort Moultrie after Anderson left. He could not and would not withdraw troops from Charleston. The troops were merely defending what was left of Federal property. Postmaster General Joseph Holt was named acting Secretary of War to replace Floyd. Orders were issued by the President to the War and Navy departments that ships, troops, and stores were to sail for Fort Sumter.

The Senate Committee of Thirteen reported that they had not been able to reach any agreement on a general plan of adjustment or compromise. All the plans, the Crittenden Compromise, Seward's proposal, and the many others, had been defeated in the committee. In fact, only the Crittenden plan had received serious study.

Sen. Judah P. Benjamin of Louisiana said of the compromises, "You do not propose to enter into our States, you say, and what do we complain of? You do not pretend to enter into our States to kill or destroy our institutions by force. Oh, no. . . . You propose simply to close us in an embrace that will suffocate us. . . . The day for adjustment has passed. . . . We desire, we beseech you, let this parting be in peace . . . you can never subjugate us; you can never convert the free sons of the soil into vassals, paying tribute to your power; and you never, never can degrade them to the level of an inferior and servile race. Never! Never—" Confusion in the galleries and loud applause.

The year was ended, but the crisis remained, stark, apparently inevitable, and completely unsolved.

1861

"The year begins with feelings of enmity & apprehensions," wrote an Episcopal minister. At least the question that there would be serious trouble had been answered. South Carolina *had* seceded; the Federal government *was* opposing it, though hard put to determine what form that opposition would take. It was more than probable that other deep South states, at least, would follow South Carolina. Compromise was still looked for by many, but Congress had thus far failed; the President-elect opposed compromise. Neither side appeared willing to accept any real settlement. The basic issue of the crisis at this point had changed from a political one of the rights of the Southern states versus the greater power of the Northern states, and from such issues as expansion of slavery, to one of secession itself. While a few talked of armed conflict and there was a building up of state forces in Charleston Harbor, war did not yet appear inevitable, necessary, or even probable to most observers. It seemed unlikely that one state, or even a few, could oppose the might of the Federal government for long.

JANUARY, 1861

Several issues had been solved as the new year began, but their solution only made things darker. At Charleston Maj. Anderson was safe for the moment with his garrison at Fort Sumter, but time would run out unless he were reinforced or resupplied. In the harbor the state forces worked with great energy and none too great skill at building fortifications and readying Fort Moultrie for possible action. South Carolina was setting up a government as a sovereign power, complete with a Cabinet. Other states of the deep South were meeting, contemplating secession. Talk of a new Southern Confederacy was growing daily. In Washington Buchanan's reorganized Cabinet was strengthening the President's stand against secession, and troops and supplies were ordered to sail for Fort Sumter. Congress still debated possible compromises with little success. In Springfield, Ill., the President-elect was busy with Cabinet choices and the politics of organizing a new administration. At the same time, Mr. Lincoln, violently opposed to secession, was publicly silent, but privately writing that there should be no compromise over slavery expansion. South Carolina had broken the dam of events; now the waters would begin to rush.

January 1, Tuesday

New Year's Day and gloomy in Washington. At the White House there was the usual reception, colorful and gay on the surface, but on the surface only. Southerners attending wondered if this was their farewell. Charles P. Stone was named Colonel of Staff and Inspector General of the District of Columbia. At Charleston preparations for war continued with organization of troops, night patrols, guarding of wharfs and vessels, and general mobilization.

January 2, Wednesday

The commissioners of South Carolina sent the President an arrogant letter replying to Buchanan's rejection of their demands. "You have resolved to hold by force what you have obtained through our misplaced confidence, and by refusing to disavow the action of Major Anderson, have converted his violation of orders into a legitimate act of your executive authority." They added, "If you choose to force this issue upon us, the State of South Carolina will accept it, . . ." They said their mission was for peace and negotiation, but it had been rejected. The President read the letter at an important Cabinet meeting but declined to receive it officially due to its nature. Incensed, the almost entirely reorganized Cabinet agreed with the President that reinforcements should be sent to Fort Sumter. However, Gen. Scott preferred sending a fast merchant steamer with troops and supplies rather than a warship, as this would ensure secrecy and might be more successful. Buchanan reluctantly agreed. The U.S.S. *Brooklyn* had been ordered to be ready at Norfolk.

Col. Charles P. Stone was named to organize the militia of the District of Columbia and defend the capital.

South Carolina troops seized old Fort Johnson in Charleston Harbor, no longer an active military base. It was reported in the press that President-elect Lincoln had received letters threatening violence at the inauguration.

January 3, Thursday

Sen. Crittenden proposed to the Senate that his compromise plan, which never got out of committee, be submitted to a public referendum. This unusual idea received some support but Republicans were opposed. Congressmen from fourteen border and mid-South states met and appointed a committee to consider compromise plans. The South Carolina commissioners left Washington for Charleston, their mission a failure. The War Department canceled the order to remove guns from Pittsburgh to Southern forts; the order had been issued by former Sec. of War Floyd. Meanwhile, rumors spread of armed bands being organized to capture Washington.

Elsewhere, the Delaware legislature rejected proposals that their state join the South, after hearing from a Mississippi representative. The State Convention of Florida assembled at Tallahassee. Georgia state troops seized Fort Pulaski near the mouth of the Savannah River. A strong fort planned for a large garrison, Pulaski was manned only by an ordnance sergeant and a civilian. The state had decided to take over this important post before there was any danger of Federal occupation.

January 4, Friday

It was becoming the practice, now, for the deep Southern states to seize Federal forts and arsenals. Alabama took over the U. S. Arsenal at Mount Vernon, Ala. Some citizens observed a fast day proclaimed earlier by President Buchanan. Salmon P. Chase, prominent Republican from Ohio, arrived in Springfield at the invitation of Mr. Lincoln; the main subject, of course, was a discussion of Cabinet appointments.

January 5, Saturday

The merchant vessel *Star of the West* left New York for Fort Sumter with supplies and 250 troops. The ship had been substituted for the naval vessel *Brooklyn* on advice of Gen. Scott. Senators from Georgia, Alabama, Mississippi, Louisiana, Texas, Arkansas, and Florida held a caucus in Washington, advising their states to secede and form a Southern Confederacy. Meanwhile, the fear of attack in Washington had lessened due to defense measures taken. Fort Washington, below the capital on the Maryland side of the Potomac, was garrisoned by a small force.

The South Carolina Convention adjourned subject to recall. The senate of Missouri resolved that the Committee on Federal Relations report a bill calling for a state convention.

Alabama moved again. This time troops took possession of Forts Morgan and Gaines at the entrance to Mobile Bay, vital points for the protection of Mobile.

January 6, Sunday

The Apalachicola, Fla., Arsenal was taken over by the state of Florida, again with no opposition. A pro-Union mass meeting, like many on both sides, was held in Chicago. Mayor Fernando Wood of New York proposed that if the Union were dissolved New York should become a free city, trading with both North and South. Gov. Thomas H. Hicks of Maryland strongly opposed secession in a message to the people. Lincoln, in Springfield, was concerned about the possibility of having as a Cabinet member Simon Cameron, Pennsylvania politician with a somewhat unfavorable reputation in certain quarters.

January 7, Monday

Fort Marion at St. Augustine, taken by Florida troops, was added to the list of seized Federal properties. Most of these had been unmanned or, at best, occupied by an ordnance sergeant and/or caretaker. The Mississippi State Convention began deliberating at Jackson and the Alabama State Convention at Montgomery. It seemed only a matter of days before other "Gulf Squadron" states of the deep South would join South Carolina in secession. Gov. John Letcher of Virginia in a message to the legislature at Richmond criticized the action of South Carolina, but opposed allowing Federal troops to cross Virginia to coerce any Southern state. He called for a national convention. At Washington the House of Representatives passed a resolution approving Maj. Anderson's shift from Fort Moultrie to Fort Sumter. A special session of the Tennessee legislature met.

The venerable John J. Crittenden spoke for his Compromise in the U. S. Senate. He saw wrong on both sides and strongly opposed secession.

"I am for the Union; but, my friends, I must be also for the equal rights of my State under this great Constitution and in this great Union." He proclaimed that residents of his state of Kentucky had as much right to take slaves into the territories as those who were opposed had a right to go without them.

January 8, Tuesday

Sec. of the Interior Jacob Thompson of Mississippi, last Southerner in the Cabinet, resigned because of Buchanan's policies. He felt, also, that he had been kept in the dark as to Fort Sumter plans. But Thompson and others, learning of the sailing of *Star of the West,* telegraphed Charleston she was coming. Chief Clerk Moses Kelly filled out the term as Acting Secretary of the Interior.

President Buchanan sent a depressing special message to Congress. He felt the present situation was beyond Executive control and he commended the question to Congress, saying, "let us pause at this momentous point and afford the people, both North and South, an opportunity for reflection. . . . Let the question be transferred from the political assemblies to the ballot box," before the crisis ended in war. He called for prompt action by Congress. He advocated the Compromise of Crittenden, dividing the territories along the old Missouri Compromise line.

At Pensacola, Fla., Federal troops fired during the night upon about twenty men who had approached Fort Barrancas. The party fled.

January 9, Wednesday

Star of the West FAILS TO RELIEVE FORT SUMTER.
MISSISSIPPI BECOMES SECOND STATE TO SECEDE.

At Jackson, Miss., the State Convention voted 84 to 15 to secede. Several opponents changed their votes when the overwhelming majority sentiment was expressed. A measure offered by a Whig anti-secessionist to attempt to settle things within the Union had been previously rejected 78 to 21. As the vote to secede passed, "A great wave of excitement swept the audience, and grave and dignified men, swayed by a common impulse, joined in the deafening applause. In an instant the hall was a scene of wild tumult" and outside a shout went up. An immense blue silk banner with a single white star was carried through the crowd. This flag was said to have inspired the patriotic song of the South, "Bonnie. Blue Flag." Comedian Harry Macarthy composed the verses. A second state had joined South Carolina.

At Charleston the scene was different. About midnight of Jan. 8 *Star of the West* arrived off Charleston Harbor with men and supplies for Fort Sumter. At daylight the vessel under Capt. John McGowan crossed the bar and steamed up the main channel toward the fort. A steamer ahead of them fired rockets and signal lights. About a mile and three fourths from Forts Sumter and Moultrie a masked battery on the north end of Morris Island opened upon the Federal vessel. Most of the shots missed, but a ricochet struck in the fore-chains. Lieut. Charles R. Woods, commanding the troops on *Star of the West,* said that, being unable to get to the fort, they had to turn about before they were cut off. The vessel pulled out of the harbor undamaged, and headed back for New York.

The first shots had been fired in Charleston Harbor and many considered them the first serious shots of the war, though there was actually no war yet. The flag on *Star of the West* was answered by running up the garrison flag at Fort Sumter. The men manned the parapets, ready for action. Some officers at the fort were incensed that Maj. Anderson did not let them fire; there was chagrin that the relief ship had turned away so readily. But the officers varied in their opinions. Anderson did protest to Gov. Pickens the firing of two batteries, Morris Island and Fort Moultrie, upon an unarmed vessel bearing the U.S. flag. Pickens replied that the sending of reinforcements would be considered a hostile act as South Carolina was independent now, and that attack must be repelled. Anderson immediately sent messages north. Charleston itself was in an uproar; it seemed for a moment that real war had come and many people welcomed it. But when it was over Fort Sumter was still in Federal hands and the problem remained much as it had been, only more agitated.

January 10, Thursday

FLORIDA IS THIRD STATE TO SECEDE.

At Tallahassee the Florida State Convention passed an ordinance of secession 62 to 7. Two Federal forts had already been seized and passage was expected; Florida was the third of the United States to depart. This same day the Federal garrison was transferred from Barrancas Barracks at Pensacola to Fort Pickens on Santa Rosa Island in the harbor. Lieut. A. G. Slemmer had been expecting attack at Barrancas, where prowlers had been about. He immediately began to put Fort Pickens in defensive shape, anticipating assault even there.

Maj. Anderson at Fort Sumter was told by Washington to act strictly on the defensive but to defend his position, as preparations of a military nature and great agitation continued at Charleston in wake of the *Star of the West* incident. In Louisiana state troops seized the U. S. Arsenal and Barracks at Baton Rouge and Forts Jackson and St. Philip, strategically located on the Mississippi below New Orleans near the river mouths. Citizens of Smithville and Wilmington, N.C., occupied Fort Johnston Jan. 9 and Fort Caswell Jan. 10, a move repudiated a few days later by authorities.

William H. Seward accepted the post of Secretary of State in the

Cabinet being formed; it had long been expected he would be a major figure in the Lincoln administration.

Warning that the nation was being carried into war, Sen. Jefferson Davis of Mississippi called upon the Senate to act. "Senators, we are rapidly drifting into a position in which this is to become a Government of the Army and Navy in which the authority of the United States is to be maintained, not by law, not by constitutional agreement between the States, but by physical force; and you will stand still and see this policy consummated?" If secession was necessary, it was a quarrel not of the South's making and if allowed to separate peacefully, there need be no difficulty.

January 11, Friday

ALABAMA SECEDES FROM THE UNION.

A fourth state departed from the United States. By vote of 61 to 39 the Alabama State Convention at Montgomery adopted an ordinance of secession, joining South Carolina, Mississippi, and Florida. The vote against secession was considerably larger than in previous votes of other states, but many of those who felt bound in principle to oppose secession stated that now that the issue had been decided they would support their state. There had been considerable debate in the convention, especially over a proposed referendum. Northern Alabama, particularly, had strong pockets of anti-secession sentiment. But again, as elsewhere, that night in Montgomery the streets were crowded, rockets blazed, firecrackers popped, and people shouted. The Southern Cross and the Lone Star were the emblems of the time, displayed in illuminated transparencies.

South Carolina again demanded the surrender of Fort Sumter and was summarily refused by Maj. Anderson. Louisiana troops took possession of the U. S. Marine Hospital below New Orleans. In the North the legislature of New York adopted strong pro-Union resolutions. Stanch unionist John A. Dix of New York was appointed Secretary of the Treasury to succeed Philip F. Thomas.

To Republican Congressman James T. Hale of Pennsylvania, President-elect Lincoln wrote that he had won an election and "Now we are told in advance, the government shall be broken up, unless we surrender to those we have beaten, before we take the offices." He added, "if we surrender, it is the end of us, and of the government."

Mass meetings continued North and South. Former Sec. of War Floyd in Richmond urged opposition to coercion, while a Federal judge in Mobile announced from the windows of his courtroom that the U. S. Court for the South District of Alabama was "adjourned forever."

January 12, Saturday

Mississippi representatives in Congress withdrew from the House, while back home artillery was ordered to Vicksburg to help control shipping on the Mississippi. *Star of the West* arrived in New York after its failure at Charleston. Florida state troops took over Barrancas Barracks, Fort Barrancas, Fort McRee, and the Pensacola Navy Yard. At the same time they demanded the surrender of Fort Pickens, which was refused.

Senator Seward of New York in an important address in the Senate said, "The alarm is appalling; for the Union is not more the body than liberty is the soul of the nation. . . . A continuance of the debate on the constitutional power of Congress over the subject of slavery in the Territories will not save the Union. The Union cannot be saved by proving that secession is illegal or unconstitutional." He dreaded civil war and added, "I do not know what the Union would be worth if saved by the use of the sword." He proposed that slavery be left alone where it existed and under control of the states, but opposed slavery in the territories. The Ohio legislature pledged its support to the Union. An abolitionist meeting in Rochester, N.Y., was broken up by pro-Union sympathizers.

January 13, Sunday

Gov. Pickens of South Carolina asked Washington for $3000 due him as former Minister to Russia; the Treasury sent him a draft on the Charleston Subtreasury, already taken over by the state.

Two envoys arrived in Washington. One, Lieut. J. Norman Hall, carried messages from Maj. Anderson regarding the demand for the surrender of Fort Sumter and Anderson's refusal. The other, J. W. Hayne, Attorney General of South Carolina, represented the governor and demanded surrender of the fort. Thus there seemed to be a sort of temporary truce set up between Anderson and Gov. Pickens, until Anderson could get further instructions. This truce embarrassed Buchanan, but he later claimed this arrangement ended Feb. 5 with Washington informing the South Carolina commissioner that Fort Sumter would not be surrendered under any circumstances. Each side appeared to misunderstand the other in this matter.

January 14, Monday

The House of Representatives Committee of Thirty-three, like the Senate Committee of Thirteen, was unable to agree on any compromise proposals. In fact, they were unwilling to act for or against. Finally Chairman Thomas Corwin of Ohio was authorized to report the main proposals to the House. On Jan. 14 Corwin submitted a proposed constitutional amendment which would protect slavery where it existed, and rule out any other amendment concerning slavery except by approval of the slaveholding states. Also he proposed repeal of the personal liberty laws, and execution of the fugitive slave laws, but urged admitting fugitive slaves to jury trials. Others of the committee opposed this report. Little came of it except that the amendment protecting slavery was passed by Congress but never ratified by the states.

Louisiana state troops seized Fort Pike, La., near New Orleans. Federal troops garrisoned Fort Taylor at Key West, Fla., in a move that perhaps prevented seizure, and provided the Union with a vital base for supplying and coaling blockaders and other vessels throughout the war. Without such bases on the Atlantic and Gulf coasts, the blockade and many military operations would have been impossible.

January 15, Tuesday

Demands that Fort Pickens be surrendered to Florida were refused by the Federal commander once more. Talk was increasing throughout the South of a new confederation of Southern states and plans were being laid for a convention.

January 16, Wednesday

The Crittenden Compromise was effectually killed in the U. S. Senate. The Senate adopted a resolution that the Constitution "needs to be obeyed rather than amended." Six Southern senators who refused to vote and the votes of Republicans defeated Crittenden once more. For most of the month the Senate had been debating compromise in general with many fine words, many ideas, and some heat, but no working conclusion had been reached. The Arkansas legislature completed a bill calling for a referendum on secession.

January 18, Friday

President Buchanan named Joseph Holt of Kentucky as Secretary of War to succeed John B. Floyd, who had resigned under fire. Holt, a strong supporter of the Union, had been Postmaster General and effective in bolstering the President's position. The U. S. Army garrisoned Fort Jefferson on Dry Tortugas, Fla., off Key West. Though not as useful as Key West, the fort became famous as a prison for political prisoners during the Civil War. Florida again requested the surrender of Fort Pickens and again was turned down. The legislature of Massachusetts offered the President aid in men and money in order to maintain the authority of the nation.

January 19, Saturday

GEORGIA CONVENTION PASSES ORDINANCE OF SECESSION.

Georgia became the fifth state to depart from the Union as its State Convention at Milledgeville voted 208 to 89 in favor of an ordinance of secession. Prior to the election of Lincoln it appeared that a majority of Georgians favored the Union to some extent. But the election, the secession of South Carolina and other deep South states had swayed many.

There still, however, was a strong moderate group led by Alexander H. Stephens, Herschel V. Johnson, and Benjamin H. Hill opposing secession. Such men as Howell Cobb, Thomas R. R. Cobb, and Francis S. Bartow led the secessionists. Again the great throng outside the hall, the thundering cannon, the illumination at night, and the cheers. Moves to postpone placing the ordinance into effect were defeated. But despite the celebration there were many, particularly from the uplands and interior, who doubted the wisdom of the step.

While the Mississippi legislature called for a convention of representatives from the seceding states, the Virginia General Assembly passed a resolution inviting the states to send representatives to a peace convention in Washington Feb. 4, and Tennessee invited slaveholding states to another convention.

January 20, Sunday

Forces of Mississippi took Fort Massachusetts and the other installations on Ship Island in the Gulf off Mississippi. Two other groups had visited the island and demanded its surrender, but they had left. This time Ship Island, potentially important as a staging and supply point, was finally taken over by the secessionists.

January 21, Monday

FIVE SENATORS WITHDRAW.

In a dramatic and moving scene in the United States Senate, five senators from Florida, Alabama, and Mississippi left the chamber. Their farewell speeches showed reluctance, determination, sorrow, and disappointment. David L. Yulee indicated his path lay with his state of Florida; Stephen R. Mallory of Florida tearfully called for reason and justice over party and passion; Clement C. Clay, Jr., of Alabama, pointed to the years of trial that had led to the present crisis; Benjamin Fitzpatrick of Alabama acknowledged his loyalty to his sovereign state. Then rose Jefferson Davis of Mississippi. Because of the secession of his state "my functions are terminated here." "I concur in the action of the people of Mississippi, believing it to be necessary and proper, and should have been bound by their action if my belief had been otherwise. . . . I am sure I feel no hostility to you, Senators from the North. I am sure there is not one of you, whatever sharp discussion there may have been between us, to whom I cannot now say, in the presence of my God, I wish you well; . . . Mr. President, and Senators, having made the announcement which the occasion seemed to me to require, it only remains for me to bid you a final adieu." Ill, having passed a sleepless night, Davis gravely gave his farewell to the Senate he had served so well. Unshed tears were in his voice, which at first faltered. He was listened to in deep silence, broken by some applause, which Davis depreciated. "Inexpressibly sad he left the chamber, with but faint hope," his wife wrote. That night she heard him pray for peace.

Rumors continued to fly everywhere; this time the Brooklyn Navy Yard was to be attacked. In Boston abolitionist Wendell Phillips addressed the Congregational Society, said he was a disunion man, was glad that the Southern states were leaving, and that he hoped all the slave states would leave and soon. The New York legislature in a series of resolutions pledged to support the Union.

January 22, Tuesday

Wisconsin's legislature supported the New York pro-Union moves, as did other states. New York authorities seized guns in private warehouses intended for Georgia.

January 23, Wednesday

Massachusetts voted its approbation of the Federal Union, following the New York stand.

January 24, Thursday

Georgia state troops took over the U. S. Arsenal at Augusta, complete with its supply of arms. From Fort Monroe, Va., Federal reinforcements sailed for Fort Pickens, Fla. The Pennsylvania legislature pledged its support of the Union. The North Carolina legislature voted to hold a state convention, but submitted the question to the people.

January 25, Friday

In Kentucky the legislature urged a national convention.

January 26, Saturday

LOUISIANA IS SIXTH STATE TO SECEDE.

There had been considerable change of feeling in Louisiana after the election of Lincoln and the secession of other Southern states. Now, at Baton Rouge, the Louisiana State Convention voted for an ordinance of secession 113 to 17. The sixth state had left the Union and it was probable Texas would follow. At the moment that appeared to be the limit to secession, at least until further developments brought a change. New Orleans business was almost at a standstill and the talk of war increased as forts and arsenals in the state were seized. The ordinance of secession was signed with gold pens given each member, and there was the usual approval in the streets. Still, New Orleans and the coast had traded extensively with the North and it had taken radical shifts in opinion to bring the state to this decision.

At Savannah, Ga., the Oglethorpe Barracks and Fort Jackson were appropriated by state troops.

January 28, Monday

President-elect Lincoln was preparing his inaugural address and making plans to leave Springfield, Ill. Louisiana state troops took possession of Fort Macomb, not far from New Orleans.

January 29, Tuesday

Kansas was admitted to the Union by Congress as the thirty-fourth state. The Wyandotte Constitution prohibited slavery and the state was largely Union in sentiment. In New Orleans the U. S. Revenue Cutter *Robert McClelland* was surrendered to state authorities despite orders from Washington to defend the vessel and the flag.

January 30, Wednesday

At Mobile the U. S. Revenue Cutter *Lewis Cass* was surrendered to Alabama officers. Abraham Lincoln left Springfield to visit his stepmother, Sarah Bush Lincoln, in Coles County, Illinois.

January 31, Thursday

As the first month of 1861 ended, and with the crisis immensely aggravated since the secession of South Carolina in December, seizures of Federal property in the deep South continued. The U. S. Branch Mint and Customs House at New Orleans were taken, as was the U. S. Revenue Schooner *Washington*.

FEBRUARY, 1861

The events of January and even the preceding December had tumbled one after the other until many felt both frustration and confusion. Six states had actually declared themselves out of the United States and Texas was about to join them. Questions proliferated. Were they actually gone and for how long? Could anything be done? What about this convention called for early February at Montgomery, Ala.? What about the so-called Peace Convention soon to gather in Washington? What about President Buchanan? Would or could he do anything in the month left of his term? And then what about his successor—Abraham Lincoln of Illinois? Would he take immediate action or would he wait? He had not said much publicly since his election. Where did he really stand? While the non-slave states were firm for the Union there were eight other slave states on the "border" or in the "mid-South." Would they follow their sisters of the Gulf Squadron or would they wait?

Perhaps Mr. Lincoln would speak out en route to Washington or at least before the inaugural. Perhaps there was just a lot of fiery talk from the more determined Southerners and maybe this secession business would pass away. Let the South go, cried some on both sides; no, others shouted, mostly in the North. Secession was the natural right of a sovereign state! No, the Union was indivisible! Neither one was right; why couldn't there be a compromise?

February 1, Friday

TEXAS CONVENTION VOTES FOR SECESSION.

The Convention of the State of Texas voted 166 to 7 in favor of secession. Assembling in Austin Jan. 28, the convention expressed perhaps only part of the opinion of citizens of that sparsely settled state, but it provided, in accordance with the legislature requirements, for an election by the people and set it for Feb. 23. In actual fact the seventh and last of the first group of states to secede had left the Union. Now it would take something further to bring about a decision in the eight other slave states.

At Springfield President-elect Lincoln privately wrote William H. Seward, "I say now, however, as I have all the while said, that on the territorial question—that is, the question of extending slavery under the national auspices,—I am inflexible." He opposed any compromise "which *assists* or *permits* the extension of the institution on soil owned by the nation." President Buchanan appointed Horatio King of Maine as Postmaster General to succeed Joseph Holt, who had become Secretary of War.

February 2, Saturday

President-elect Lincoln wrote that he already had his inaugural address "blocked out" but was holding it subject to revision.

February 4, Monday

CONVENTION OF SECEDED STATES MEETS IN MONTGOMERY, ALABAMA.

"Be it remembered that on the fourth day of February, in the year of our Lord one thousand eight hundred and sixty-one, and in the Capitol of the State of Alabama, in the city of Montgomery, at the hour of noon, there assembled certain deputies and delegates from the several independent Southern States of North America, to wit: Alabama, Florida, Georgia, Louisiana, Mississippi, and South Carolina; . . ." Thus read the official record of the convention of the seceded states that was to become the first session of the Provisional Congress of the Confederate States of America. The thirty-seven delegates named Howell Cobb of Georgia President of the Convention. He told the assemblage: "The separation is perfect, complete, and perpetual. The great duty is now imposed upon us of providing for these States a government for their future security and protection." And they got to work rapidly with a minimum of debate and dissension.

In Washington Judah Benjamin and John Slidell, senators from Louisiana, withdrew from the U. S. Congress to go with their state, already represented at Montgomery. The electoral vote for President as approved by Congress read: Abraham Lincoln 180, John C. Breckinridge 72, John Bell 39, and Stephen A. Douglas 12. In Springfield talk and negotiations over Cabinet appointments went on as Lincoln conferred with various individuals and delegations.

As the secessionists met at Montgomery, so in Washington the Peace Convention called by Virginia convened. There were eventually 131 members representing 21 states. None of the seceded states were represented and many of the delegates were elderly, but among them were many national leaders including former President John Tyler, who presided. At least it was a try and there was much debate by this honest, sincere, generally middle-of-the-road gathering.

February 5, Tuesday

The Buchanan administration announced to the South Carolina commissioner that under no circumstances would Fort Sumter be surrendered. In the President's eyes this ended the unofficial truce at Charleston set up January 13.

Two conventions were meeting. At Washington John Tyler told the Peace Convention that "the eyes of the whole country are turned to this assembly, in expectation and hope." He called for a triumph of patriotism over party and for rescuing the nation.

In Montgomery Alexander Stephens of Georgia presented the rules of the convention of the seceded states and they were adopted. Christopher Memminger of South Carolina presented a resolution calling for formation of "a Confederacy of the States which have seceded from the Federal Union." A committee was named to report a plan for a provisional government.

February 6, Wednesday

The Lincolns held a farewell reception at their home in Springfield, Ill., with a large attendance, including politicians from many sections who had been flocking to the Illinois capital.

February 7, Thursday

The Choctaw Indian Nation declared its adherence to the Southern states. While in Montgomery the Committee of Twelve, headed by Christopher Memminger, named to frame a provisional government, reported to the convention of seceded states. The convention, in secret session, immediately took up a discussion of the report.

February 8, Friday

CONFEDERATE CONSTITUTION ADOPTED.

Late in the evening in the Alabama Capitol at Montgomery the convention of seceded states unanimously adopted the Provisional Constitution of the Confederate States. The Constitution was mainly based on that of the United States with a few significant differences, and a few changes that political scientists then and since have discussed. The primary change was that the right to own slaves was spelled out more completely than in the U. S. Constitution. Each state was acting "in its sovereign and independent character," although no right of secession was stated, just implied. In a modification of the British system, Cabinet officers were to have seats on the floors of both houses in order to discuss measures; duties or taxes on imports to promote or foster industry were prohibited; importation of slaves was prohibited; the President could approve a portion of an appropriation bill or disapprove an appropriation in the same bill, which prevented riders tacked on to legislation; terms of President and Vice-President were six years and the President was not eligible for reelection. The fugitive slave clause of the United States was slightly strengthened and slavery in any territories of the Confederacy was protected. Thus the Confederacy was an operating country with a Provisional Constitution submitted to the states. The next order of business would be a Provisional President and Vice-President. Thus far harmony, wisdom, and patriotism had prevailed, for there was little of the fire-eater apparent in the deliberations or in the Constitution.

Operating under orders of Gov. Henry M. Rector of Arkansas, state troops seized the U. S. Arsenal at Little Rock, the Federal garrison of Capt. James Totten evacuating under force. In Washington President Buchanan approved a loan of $25,000,000 for current expenses and redemption of treasury notes. President-elect Lincoln was making plans for stops at various cities en route to Washington and moved from his home into a hotel.

February 9, Saturday

JEFFERSON DAVIS ELECTED PROVISIONAL PRESIDENT OF THE
CONFEDERACY: ALEXANDER STEPHENS NAMED VICE-PRESIDENT.

Who was to be President of the new Confederacy? For several days there had been extensive discussion and private electioneering at Montgomery, Ala., among the delegates to the secession convention. To avoid a contest on the floor it was thought necessary to agree on the man beforehand. Names considered included William Lowndes Yancey, Howell Cobb, Robert Toombs, Alexander H. Stephens, Robert Barnwell Rhett, and Jefferson Davis. During the night of the eighth, various state delegations met. Georgia withdrew her candidate Toombs in face of the decision of most states for Davis. Jefferson Davis of Mississippi, former Secretary of War and U.S. senator, rated as a moderate among secessionists, was unanimously chosen Provisional President of the Confederate States of America, subject to an election. Georgia presented Alexander Stephens, long-time U.S. representative and former Whig leader, for Vice-President. He, too, was chosen unanimously. There were a few doubts about Stephens, for it seemed to some he had always been a unionist at heart. The Confederacy now had leaders representing the old Democrats and the old Whigs rather than the more rabid secessionists. Davis and Stephens pleased many in the mid-South and border states not yet out of the Union. The time was to come when citizens of the South and historians alike would condemn both Davis and Stephens. But at the moment they seemed wisely selected.

With deliberate and careful proceedings the convention at Montgomery had chosen their leaders under a sense of responsibility instead of the usual raucousness of politics. They were in a hurry through necessity, but not so much that they could not do their job. The provincial-appearing capital of Alabama was crowded with visitors, some of them more openly enthusiastic than the delegates. The leaders, for the most part, wanted the mildest possible break with the past and the Union, and there was even the feeling that the North, not the South, had actually broken away from the spirit and purpose of the founders of the United States.

In addition to choosing its leaders, the Provisional Congress of the Confederacy declared all laws of the United States in force as long as they were not inconsistent with the Constitution of the Confederacy.

In Tennessee voters rejected the proposal to call a convention to consider secession by 68,282 to 59,449. Off Pensacola, Fla., U.S.S. *Brooklyn* arrived with reinforcements for Fort Pickens, but did not land them because of an agreement with Florida authorities that the military situation would not be altered by either side.

February 10, Sunday

At the plantation home of Brierfield in Warren County, Miss., not far from Vicksburg, former U.S. senator Jefferson Davis, now commander of the state forces of Mississippi, was helping his wife Varina prune rosebushes. A messenger arrived from Vicksburg bearing the telegram from Montgomery naming Mr. Davis President of the new nation. Reportedly Davis was stunned by the news. He had not sought or wanted such a position; his aim had been a high military command in the Confederacy. That evening the message of acceptance was sent to Montgomery and plans were made to leave at once for the capital.

February 11, Monday

TWO PRESIDENTS DEPART.

From Springfield, Ill., President-elect Abraham Lincoln of the United States of America departed on a long trip to Washington and inauguration. From Brierfield Plantation on the Mississippi, President-elect Jefferson Davis of the Confederate States of America departed on a long trip to Montgomery, Ala., and inauguration.

More than a thousand citizens gathered in the early morning drizzle at the Great Western Station in Springfield to hear Mr. Lincoln, at times shaken with emotion, surrounded by the party of family, secretaries, dignitaries, and army officers. "Here I have lived a quarter of a century, and passed from a young to an old man. . . . I now leave, not knowing when, or whether ever, I may return, with a task before me greater than that which rested upon Washington. Without the assistance of that Divine Being, who ever attended him, I cannot succeed. With that assistance I cannot fail. Trusting in Him, who can go with me, and remain with you, and be every where for good, let us confidently hope that all will yet be well. To His care commending you, as I hope in your prayers you will commend me, I bid you an affectionate farewell."

As the train rolled slowly eastward across Illinois and Indiana, several stops were made for the President-elect to greet enthusiastic crowds. At Indianapolis he was met by Gov. Oliver P. Morton, and a huge procession of some twenty thousand escorted Mr. Lincoln to the Bates House. At the hotel he told the throng, "It is your business to rise up and preserve the Union and liberty, for yourselves, and not for me." He said he opposed invasion or coercion of a state but that enforcement of the laws and holding of Federal property were not coercion. He spoke of those who in his words believed the Union not a regular marriage "but only a sort of free-love arrangement."

At Brierfield Plantation Jefferson Davis bid farewell to family and plantation slaves before taking a boat alone for Vicksburg and eventually Montgomery, Ala., via Jackson, Miss., Chattanooga, and Atlanta. The trip was difficult due to lack of a direct railroad, poor traveling accommodations, and the haste with which the journey was made. In Vicksburg the Confederate President-elect made the first of many brief speeches declaring he had struggled earnestly to maintain the Union and the "constitutional equality of all the States." But "our safety and honor required us to dissolve our connection with the United States. I hope that our separation may be peaceful. But whether it be so or not, I am ready, as I always have been, to redeem my pledges to you and the South by shedding every drop of my blood in your cause. . . ."

In a simple, unprepared ceremony at Montgomery, Alexander H. Stephens of Georgia was inaugurated Provisional Vice-President of the Confederate States of America. In its speed to get things moving, the convention or Provisional Congress had decided not to await the arrival of the President-elect. Stephens, a small, sallow, emaciated wisp of a man with chronically poor health, took the oath upon his own birth date but declined to make any policy statement. At Austin, Tex., the State Convention voted in favor of formation of a Southern Confederacy and elected seven delegates to Congress.

February 12, Tuesday

Jefferson Davis traveled from Vicksburg to Jackson, Miss., where he resigned as major general of the Mississippi state forces, and is reported to have stated that war "could" result from secession. Crowds were reported large and enthusiastic on the route and Mr. Davis made about twenty-five brief stops in his passage to Montgomery.

President-elect Lincoln left Indianapolis in the morning, headed toward Cincinnati with several stops in between. This was his fifty-second birthday. He called for the people to be true to themselves and the Constitution. At the Burnet House in Cincinnati and the huge reception for him, he seemed to ramble. He did say, "I hope that while these free institutions shall continue to be in the enjoyment of millions of free people of the United States, we will see repeated every four years what we now witness." He added, "I hope that our national difficulties will also pass away." He told a group of German-Americans he would wait until the last moment before expressing himself on his course of action.

At Montgomery the Provisional Congress of the Confederacy provided for a Peace Commission to the United States and also assumed authority to deal with questions of the forts in dispute. Acting Postmaster General Horatio King, named by President Buchanan in January, became Postmaster General for the last month of the old administration. Arkansas state forces seized the U.S. ordnance stores at Napoleon, Ark.

February 13, Wednesday

While in Washington the official count of presidential electoral votes made the election of Lincoln official, the President-elect was addressing the Ohio state legislature in Columbus. In one of his most puzzling speeches Mr. Lincoln said, "I have not maintained silence from any want of real anxiety. It is a good thing that there is no more than anxiety, for there is nothing going wrong. It is a consoling circumstance that when we look out there is nothing that really hurts anybody. We entertain different views upon political questions, but nobody is suffering anything." Far to the south Mr. Davis was continuing his own journey.

In Richmond the Virginia State Convention assembled to consider the question of secession. A majority of the delegates were believed to be unionists, at least at this time.

February 14, Thursday

In the morning Lincoln left Columbus for Pittsburgh, making brief speeches at several points en route.

February 15, Friday

The President-elect of the new Confederacy drew nearer to his new capital of Montgomery. President-elect Lincoln, pursued by rain on his own trip, spoke at length at Pittsburgh, continuing as he had at Columbus: "there is really no crisis except an *artificial* one! . . . If the great American people will only keep their temper, on both sides of the line, the troubles will come to an end, . . ." He arrived in Cleveland during a snowstorm. The roar of artillery and the crowd greeted him. Again he said, "I think that there is no occasion for any excitement. The crisis, as it is called, is altogether an artificial crisis. . . ."

The Peace Conference at Washington had been droning on, but this day a committee presented its resolutions. The Conference at large began lengthy discussions of these proposals. Various officers of the Army and Navy were beginning to decide their allegiance, and Raphael Semmes, outstanding naval officer, resigned to join the Navy of the new Confederacy.

February 16, Saturday

"THE MAN AND THE HOUR HAVE MET"—PRESIDENT DAVIS ARRIVES IN MONTGOMERY.

A deeply tired and concerned Jefferson Davis arrived in Montgomery, Ala., to accept the post of Provisional President of the new Confederacy. Upon arrival he told his greeters, "The time for compromise has now passed, and the South is determined to maintain her position, and make all who oppose her smell Southern powder and feel Southern steel if coercion is persisted in. . . . We ask nothing, we want nothing; we have no complications."

That evening at the Exchange Hotel, William Lowndes Yancey, a stirring orator proclaimed in memorable words that the country had found the statesman, the soldier, and the patriot to lead them: "The man and the hour have met." Mr. Davis said, "It may be that our career will be ushered in in the midst of a storm; it may be that, as this morning opened with clouds, rain, and mist, we shall have to encounter inconveniences at the beginning; but, as the sun rose and lifted the mist, it dispersed the clouds and left us the pure sunshine of heaven. So will progress the Southern Confederacy, and carry us safe into the harbor of constitutional liberty and political equality. . . ."

Mr. Lincoln continued his triumphal and slow way east from Cleveland into New York State. The jam of people was denser than ever. In his remarks the President-elect said, "you, as a portion of the great American people, need only to maintain your composure."

At San Antonio, Tex., the U. S. Arsenal and Barracks were seized by state troops.

February 17, Sunday

A somewhat quieter day, with President-elect Lincoln in Buffalo and President-elect Davis in Montgomery, preparing for his inaugural on the morrow.

February 18, Monday

JEFFERSON DAVIS INAUGURATED PRESIDENT OF THE CONFEDERACY.

In front of the state Capitol at Montgomery, Jefferson Davis of Mississippi was inaugurated Provisional President of the Confederate States of America. To the enthusiastic throng he spoke encouragement. To his wife he wrote, "The audience was large and brilliant. Upon my weary heart was showered smiles, plaudits, and flowers; but, beyond them, I saw troubles and thorns innumerable. We are without machinery, without means, and threatened by a powerful opposition; but I do not despond, and will not shrink from the task imposed upon me." To the crowd he said, "Our present political position has been achieved in a manner unprecedented in the history of nations. It illustrates the American idea that governments rest on the consent of the governed, and that it is the right of the people to alter or abolish them at will whenever they become destructive of the ends for which they were established." The original purpose of the Union had been perverted, Mr. Davis said. The South had labored to preserve the government of their fathers and had no "interest or passion to invade the rights of others, . . ." He hoped to avoid war but if the "lust of dominion should cloud the judgment or inflame the ambition of those States, we must prepare to meet the emergency and maintain, by the final arbitrament of the sword, the position which we have assumed among the nations of the earth." Reunion was neither practicable nor desirable. However, the Confederate government was the same as that of the Constitution in principle. "Obstacles may retard, but they can not long prevent, the progress of a movement sanctified by its justice and sustained by a virtuous people."

It was a balmy and sunny day and Davis rode in a carriage up the hill to the Capitol, tall, slight, but straight, with his sharply defined features set in deep thought as he received the cheers of the throng and heard the bands play "Dixie." After the inauguration a levee, more bands, fireworks, banners, and a salute of a hundred guns. All people seemed to join in, Negroes included. Eyes were wet when the new President bowed his head in tears after solemnly, earnestly intoning "So help me God," hand on the Bible. It was a time of high resolve, of great hopes, of emotional outpouring, and of challenge and wonder as well. Many, including the new President, had their grave doubts but, on this day at least, events had culminated and a new nation was fully on its way —but its direction, its future, its confirmation was uncertain.

Mr. Lincoln proceeded through New York State from Buffalo to Albany with the same cheering throngs as before. Politicians joined the train to speak with the President-elect. The cars halted often but the speeches were brief. To a joint session of the New York legislature he said, "It is true that while I hold myself without mock modesty, the humblest of all individuals that have ever been elevated to the Presidency, I have a more difficult task to perform than any one of them."

At San Antonio, Tex., Bvt. Maj. Gen. David E. Twiggs surrendered U.S. military posts in the Department of Texas to the state. He said he did it in the face of the threat of force, but in Washington his move was regarded as treason.

February 19, Tuesday

In Montgomery President Davis went to work to form his Cabinet. It took some days but the final results were—Secretary of State, Robert Toombs of Georgia; Secretary of the Treasury, Christopher G. Memminger of South Carolina; Secretary of War, LeRoy Pope Walker of Alabama; Secretary of the Navy, S. R. Mallory of Florida; Attorney General, Judah P. Benjamin of Louisiana; and Postmaster General, J. H. Reagan of Texas. (There was no Interior Department as in the United States.) Only Mallory and Reagan would remain in their posts until the end, although Benjamin stayed on in several different jobs. The Cabinet has been highly criticized by some, but others point out that, considering the circumstances and the difficulty of their tasks, most of these men were highly qualified and strove mightily to reap what they could for the embryo nation.

The Lincolns left Albany for New York City escorted by dignitaries. Again, brief stops and brief speeches. It was estimated that a quarter of a million people greeted him in New York as Mr. Lincoln rode to the Astor House. To a crowd he admitted that he had been avoiding a position on the issues in speaking or writing. He said he believed this a proper policy until the time should come when he could speak officially.

The U.S. paymaster's office at New Orleans was seized by Louisiana troops. Col. Carlos A. Waite at Camp Verde, Tex., took over nominal command of U.S. posts in the state, even though they had been surrendered the day before by Gen. Twiggs. But the damage had been done; post after post would soon fall or be abandoned.

February 20, Wednesday

The press of public life crowded in on both Mr. Davis and Mr. Lincoln. At Montgomery President Davis had hardly a moment even to write to his wife. In New York City President-elect Lincoln conferred with individuals and groups, met Mayor Fernando Wood. Replying to the mayor, he said, "There is nothing that can ever bring me willingly to consent to the destruction of this Union, . . . So long, then, as it is possible that the prosperity and the liberties of the people can be preserved in the Union, it shall be my purpose at all times to preserve it." Vice-President-elect Hannibal Hamlin of Maine arrived in New York and dined with the Lincolns. Later Mr. Lincoln attended the new opera by Verdi, *Un Ballo in Maschera*.

The Provisional Congress of the Confederacy authorized the President to make contracts in order to buy and manufacture matériel of war. The Confederate Navy Department was officially established.

February 21, Thursday

In Texas the U.S. property at Brazos Santiago was seized and Federals abandoned Camp Cooper. The Confederate Congress declared navigation of the Mississippi River free and open, and officially declared established the executive departments of the government. President Davis named Stephen R. Mallory of Florida Secretary of the Navy.

The Lincoln party left New York for Philadelphia in the morning. At almost every depot there was a brief halt.

Included in the appearances were short talks to the New Jersey senate and General Assembly at Trenton. The group arrived in Philadelphia late in the afternoon for the usual tumultuous reception. At the end of the evening's festivities Mr. Lincoln was warned of a reported plot to assassinate him when he passed through Baltimore. At the moment he refused to change plans. In reply to the mayor of Philadelphia, Mr. Lincoln did say, "I do not mean to say that this artificial panic has not done harm. That it has done much harm I do not deny," but he hoped to be able to restore peace and harmony.

February 22, Friday

"I have never had a feeling politically that did not spring from the sentiments embodied in the Declaration of Independence," Mr. Lincoln said in the Washington's Birthday celebration at Independence Hall in Philadelphia. "It was that which gave promise that in due time the weights should be lifted from the shoulders of all men, and that *all* men should have an equal chance." He observed that there "is no need of bloodshed and war," and there would be none unless they were forced upon the government. From Philadelphia Mr. Lincoln journeyed to Harrisburg, where he spoke again, this time on preserving peace if it could be done "consistently with the maintenance of the institutions of the country."

The President-elect had now made his speeches, many of them unimportant and some that appeared downright astonishing when he spoke of nothing going wrong. Southern papers were quick to jump on his words about an "artificial crisis." After all, the Confederacy was not a phantom. Behind the scenes at Philadelphia there was concern over Mr. Lincoln's safety.

At the Jones House in Harrisburg, Lincoln learned that plans for the trip to Washington had been revised to attempt to avoid any possible difficulty in pro-Southern Baltimore. Leaving the hotel, Lincoln and Ward Hill Lamon, old-time friend and unofficial bodyguard, boarded a special train, leaving the remainder of the party to come on as planned.

In Charleston the people celebrated Washington's Birthday just as they had in Philadelphia. Gov. Pickens spoke and there were parades of military companies. Far out in San Francisco a mass meeting declared itself in support of the Union.

February 23, Saturday

PRESIDENT-ELECT LINCOLN ARRIVES IN WASHINGTON.

President-elect Lincoln, with Ward Hill Lamon and detective Allan Pinkerton, traveled from Harrisburg through Philadelphia and Baltimore and arrived in Washington at 6 A.M. There was no trouble; the revised travel plans had been kept secret. Mr. Lincoln arrived in Washington to be greeted by Illinois representative Elihu Washburne. After conferring with William H. Seward at Willard's Hotel, Mr. Lincoln called upon President Buchanan and the Cabinet at the White House. Visitors began to flock into the hotel, including an Illinois group led by Sen. Stephen A. Douglas. In the evening the Peace Convention delegates called, among others. It had been an exhausting trip from Springfield and the President-elect now faced an even more trying time.

The voters of Texas approved secession 34,794 to 11,235 in the referendum ordered by the legislature and the secession convention.

February 25, Monday

President-elect Lincoln attended a reception in both the House and Senate at the Capitol and visited the Supreme Court. In Montgomery President Davis was attempting to take in hand the situation at Charleston, sending out messengers and making inquiries.

February 26, Tuesday

The Peace Convention still meeting in Washington began voting on the resolutions or amendments it would advocate. Mr. Lincoln was embroiled in conferences over Cabinet posts and with political leaders. Camp Colorado, Tex., was abandoned by Federal authorities.

February 27, Wednesday

President Davis in Montgomery named three Confederate commissioners to Washington to attempt negotiations with the Federals. He chose Martin J. Crawford, John Forsyth, and A. B. Roman. In Washington the Peace Convention sent the results of its deliberations to Congress. Six constitutional amendments were proposed. First amendment—that involuntary servitude be prohibited north of 36° 30′; that in land south of that line slavery could exist while such area was a territory and Congress could not hinder it; that upon admittance as a state it could come in with or without slavery as its state constitution provided. Second amendment— no further territory should be acquired except through treaty and by consent of four fifths of the Senate. Third amendment—that Congress could not regulate, abolish, or control slavery in the states or territories. Fourth amendment—fugitive slave provisions of the Constitution should be enforced and Congress should not interfere. Fifth amendment—that the foreign slave trade be prohibited. Sixth amendment—there should be compensation for loss of fugitives from labor in certain cases. There was much dissatisfaction with the results and they never stood a chance in Congress. The Peace Convention had not even been too peaceful, with much bickering and dissatisfaction among its members.

From Charleston Gov. Pickens wrote President Davis, "we feel that our honor and safety require that Fort Sumter should be in our possession at the very earliest moment." In Washington Lincoln was listening not only to politicians about appointments, but to others, such as Sen. Douglas and border-state men, pleading for conciliation or compromise. In the House proposal after proposal was voted down. A plan for a constitutional convention lost; the Crittenden proposal finally lost; an amendment not to interfere with slavery lost, but was reconsidered the next day.

February 28, Thursday

The Missouri State Convention met at Jefferson City to consider secession. In Montgomery the Confederate Congress authorized a domestic loan of $15,000,000. The United States Territory of Colorado was formed. At Charleston Maj. Robert Anderson, commanding the Federal garrison at Fort Sumter, was in almost daily telegraphic communication with Washington. Congress, nearing the end of its session, was crammed with last-minute business. The House passed and sent to the Senate the amendment of Thomas Corwin of Ohio as devised by the Committee of Thirty-three and approved by President-elect Lincoln, that slavery could not be interfered with by the Federal government in states where it already existed. This move was described by some as a "harbinger of peace." North Carolina voters turned down a state convention on secession by 651 votes, thus showing strong pro-Union sentiment.

MARCH, 1861

It was a time of both fearful tension and some hopeful waiting. The nation that existed a year before had been partially divided; seven states had apparently successfully left the Union and set up a new government in the South. And now that these states of the lower South had temporarily, at least, made their exit, what would come next? Events seemed in suspension, although the crisis remained grave. In Washington the old administration of President Buchanan marked time before giving way to new faces, new personalities, and a new party in power for the first time. In Washington, too, the new President awaited his inauguration on March 4, and conferred with political leaders. It was not yet quite time to face the whole question.

In the nascent Confederate States of America there was the confusion and uncertainty of setting up a new nation, but there also was the confidence brought by the first success. Could and would their nation be enlarged by admission of other of the slave states? Could they avoid military conflict and succeed in confirming their secession? Could they receive foreign recognition, so necessary to their economic life? Would the new administration leave them alone? What would Abraham Lincoln say in his inaugural address about the policy of the new leaders of the United States? Many questions, indeed, and few answers.

March 1, Friday

The Confederate States of America assumed control of military affairs at Charleston, S.C., where the problem of Fort Sumter remained very much unsolved. President Davis named P. G. T. Beauregard to command the area. Maj. Robert Anderson, commanding the small Federal garrison, at Fort Sumter, told Washington that events were arriving at a point where further delay on the decision to evacuate or reinforce would be impossible. At the moment the Federals had friendly relations with the South Carolinians and provisions were allowed. At the same time extensive Confederate works were being built at various points around the harbor and troops were training and drilling. Sec. of War Joseph Holt ordered Brig. Gen. David E. Twiggs dismissed from the U. S. Army "for his treachery to the flag of his country" in having surrendered military posts and Federal property in Texas to state authorities. In Washington President

Lincoln conferred with various political leaders and offered the War Department secretaryship to Simon Cameron, long-time Pennsylvania politician. Cameron accepted. There was mounting concern in the capital over possible military attack, rioting, or even assassination during the forthcoming inauguration.

March 2, Saturday

The Provisional Confederate Congress meeting in Montgomery, Ala., provided for the admission of Texas to the Confederacy. As the Thirty-sixth U. S. Congress wound up its work, a number of measures were approved by President Buchanan. Two new territories, Nevada and Dakota, were set up. Dakota included what later became North and South Dakota and much of Wyoming and Montana. A $10,000,000 loan was authorized and the Morrill Tariff Act approved, which substituted specific for ad valorem duties and also increased some duties from 5 to 10 per cent, especially on wool and iron. Also receiving approval was a joint resolution to amend the Constitution. This provided that "no amendment shall be made to the Constitution which will authorize or give Congress the power to abolish or interfere within any State with the domestic institutions thereof, including that of persons held to labor or service by said State." This proposed amendment was never approved by the states. The Senate rejected a proposal of John J. Crittenden of Kentucky to adopt the constitutional amendment submitted by the Peace Convention of Feb. 27. Thus the Senate declared itself against the Peace Convention resolutions. It was Crittenden's last major effort in Congress to bring about peace; from now on he devoted his efforts to controlling, as he saw it, the purposes of the war.

The Federal Revenue Cutter *Henry Dodge* was seized by Texas state authorities at Galveston. In Washington President-elect Lincoln was having problems with Cabinet appointments. There was opposition to Salmon P. Chase as Secretary of the Treasury and William H. Seward wrote Lincoln asking permission to withdraw from his Cabinet position.

In a message to Congress, President Buchanan said troops had been ordered to Washington for the purpose of preserving peace and order and defended his action.

March 3, Sunday

President-elect Lincoln had a full day in Washington, giving a dinner for his new Cabinet, visiting the Senate, and conferring on appointments. Army commander Gen. Winfield Scott wrote William H. Seward that he believed it impracticable to relieve Fort Sumter. Meanwhile, the Army went ahead with preparations to protect the inaugural ceremonies set for March 4. At Charleston Brig. Gen. Pierre Gustave Toutant Beauregard assumed command of Confederate troops around Charleston Harbor.

March 4, Monday

INAUGURATION OF LINCOLN.

Abraham Lincoln of Illinois was inaugurated sixteenth President of the United States. Never before or since was a President ushered into office facing the crisis of the nation split asunder. In fact, these were no longer states united. The right of the states to secede was the major issue.

In the morning President Buchanan and his Cabinet met at the Capitol to examine final bills. Sec. of War Holt informed the President that he had word from Maj. Anderson that without twenty thousand reinforcements Fort Sumter could not be held or supplied. Holt indicated he would inform the President-elect. Mr. Lincoln, at Willard's Hotel, asked William H. Seward to remain in the prospective Cabinet, received notables, and went over the inaugural address. President Buchanan and Mr. Lincoln left the hotel shortly after noon in partly cloudy weather with temperatures in the fifties and drove in an open carriage to the Capitol. Troops lined the streets, and windows along Pennsylvania Avenue were watched by riflemen. Artillery was posted in the grounds of the Capitol, where some thirty thousand persons had gathered.

The Senate was called to order and Hannibal Hamlin of Maine sworn in as Vice-President by outgoing Vice-President John C. Breckinridge while President Buchanan and Mr. Lincoln watched. The weather cleared as the President came out on the special platform on the portico of the Capitol about 1 P.M. According to a story now considered true, when the President-elect arose to speak, he could not find a place for his hat and Sen. Douglas reached out and held Mr. Lincoln's hat during the ceremonies. The address that followed had been prepared some weeks before in Springfield, although there had been some recent changes.

There was no need for apprehension on the part of the Southern people, the new President said, because of the ascension of a Republican administration. He reiterated he had no intention of interfering with the institution of slavery where it existed. He had no objection to the proposed amendment forbidding Federal interference with slavery and added that each state had the right to control its domestic institutions. Somehow the President's words seemed a little late, what with secession an accomplished fact. He said a disruption of the Federal Union "is now formidably attempted" but "the Union of these States is perpetual." He argued that the Union could not be dissolved and that any secession resolves and ordinances were void, and further, that acts of violence against the authority of the United States were "insurrectionary or revolutionary. I therefore consider that, in view of the Constitution and the laws, the Union is unbroken; and, to the extent of my ability, I shall take care, as the Constitution itself expressly enjoins upon me, that the laws of the Union be faithfully executed in all the States." He added that there need be no bloodshed or violence and there would not be any "unless it is forced upon the national authority. . . . In *your* hands, my dissatisfied fellow countrymen, and not in *mine,* is the momentous issue of civil war. The government will not assail *you.* You can have no conflict, without being yourselves the aggressors. *You* have no oath registered in Heaven to destroy the government, while *I* have the most solemn one to 'preserve, protect and defend' it. . . . Though passion may have strained, it must not break our bonds of affection. The mystic chords of memory, streching [sic] from every battle-field, and patriot grave, to every living heart and hearthstone, all over this broad land, will yet swell the chorus of the Union, when again touched, as surely they will be, by the better angels of our nature." But those most concerned with the sentiments of this almost poetic address were not there. They were busy building their own nation, based on their rights as they saw them. Much of the address followed the policy of the previous Buchanan administration and no special compromise, concession, or plan was proposed to deal with secession.

After the half-hour speech Chief Justice Roger B. Taney administered the oath of office, the marine band played, and the procession moved off to the White House. In the evening the President attended the inaugural ball at the Patent Office, returning to the White House about one in the morning.

Reaction to the inaugural address was about as expected. Justice John A. Campbell of the Supreme Court, soon to join the Confederacy, called it a *"stump* speech not an inaugural message" and "incendiary." The *Arkansas True Democrat* proclaimed, "If declaring the Union perpetual means coercion, then LINCOLN'S INAUGURAL MEANS WAR!" The Montgomery *Weekly Advertiser* proclaimed that the address meant "War. War, and nothing less than war, will satisfy the Abolition chief." The Charleston *Mercury:* "A more lamentable display of feeble inability to grasp the circumstances of this momentous emergency, could scarcely have been exhibited." While many in the North applauded, there was dissatisfaction also. The New York *Herald* said the country is "no Wiser than it was Before." But the New York *Tribune* said, "Every word of it has the ring of true metal."

At any rate, the thing had been done, and safely. There was also the colorful procession of former Presidents, judges, clergy, foreign ministers, members of Congress, Republican leaders, governors and former governors, legislators, military officers, veterans of the Revolution and of 1812, young ladies representing the thirty-four states of the Union riding in a float—and over it all the unrelenting and yet somehow unapproachable fact that the new President presided over only part of a nation.

The new Cabinet had been decided on—Secretary of State, William H. Seward of New York; Secretary of the Treasury, Salmon P. Chase of

Ohio; Secretary of War, Simon Cameron of Pennsylvania; Secretary of the Navy, Gideon Welles of Connecticut; Secretary of the Interior, Caleb Blood Smith of Indiana; Postmaster General, Montgomery Blair of Maryland; and Attorney General, Edward Bates of Missouri. Three members, Seward, Chase, and Bates, had been leading candidates for the Republican presidential nomination, and even Cameron and Smith had been vaguely mentioned. The Cabinet represented diverse factions of the new Republican party and diverse opinions on the issues of the day. Political deals had entered into the appointment of Cameron and Smith.

In Montgomery the Committee on the Confederate Flag reported to Congress and the first Stars and Bars flew over the Alabama state Capitol, serving now as the Confederate Capitol. Moving to St. Louis the Missouri State Convention, aiming at secession, gathered. The Confederate Congress confirmed the appointment of Stephen Mallory of Florida as Secretary of the Navy, but only after some discussion.

March 5, Tuesday

Maj. Anderson's message of Feb. 28, which arrived at the War Department in Washington on March 4, had presented the Lincoln administration with an immediate crisis. Anderson said that reinforcements probably could not be thrown into Fort Sumter before limited supplies ran out, and that it would take at least twenty thousand men to do the job. The President conferred with Lieut. Gen. Scott, who concurred with Maj. Anderson. The issue would have to be faced, probably within six weeks. Meanwhile, Mr. Lincoln had other problems, including the host of delegations and individuals crying for posts and favors. He did hold his first Cabinet meeting and the Senate in special session confirmed the Cabinet nominations.

March 6, Wednesday

While the immediate excitement of the inauguration in Washington was over, the crowds of office seekers and political hangers-on remained, interfering seriously with the more pressing affairs of state facing President Lincoln. In Montgomery the Confederate Congress was engrossed with such issues as postage, rail transportation, light ships, the lighthouse bureau, liquor control, registration of vessels, Indian agents, and the like. They also confirmed nomination of John Reagan of Texas as Postmaster General. Congress was working hard and putting in long hours with a reported minimum of lengthy debate, but most of the sessions were secret.

At a meeting of military and naval officials in Washington, Gen. Scott said the Army could do no more about the relief of Fort Sumter, and that it was now a naval problem. Also in Washington the three commissioners of the Confederacy were attempting to open relations with the new administration.

March 7, Thursday

Two more points in Texas, Ringgold Barracks and Camp Verde, were abandoned by Federal forces. In Washington President Lincoln conferred with Cabinet members on supplying Fort Sumter. In St. Louis the Missouri Convention was showing strong pro-Union sentiment: among the subjects discussed were a national convention, the Crittenden Compromise as a basis of action, and the proposition that the Southern states had no excuse for seceding.

March 8, Friday

While the Lincolns were holding a large public reception in the White House, the three Confederate commissioners in Washington were presenting their terms on which hostilities might be avoided. Martin J. Crawford, John Forsyth, and A. B. Roman were trying to reach Sec. of State Seward through Supreme Court Justice John A. Campbell. They also were in contact with pro-Southern and peace-minded figures of importance in Washington.

March 9, Saturday

The Federal Cabinet met with the President to consider the Fort Sumter situation. In a lengthy session, they debated whether to evacuate or reinforce and resupply, or just what to do. Time was running out. The consensus seemed to be that evacuation was necessary. To Gen. Scott the President wrote asking how long Anderson could maintain his position without fresh supplies or reinforcements and whether the Army could supply or reinforce the fort.

The Confederate Congress at Montgomery authorized issuance of treasury notes up to a million dollars. Congress also set up an army for the Confederate states. In St. Louis the Committee on Federal Relations of the Missouri Convention pointed out the errors of both sides and declared there was no cause to compel Missouri to dissolve her connection with the Union.

March 11, Monday

The Confederate Congress unanimously adopted the Constitution of the Confederacy and by the end of April seven states had ratified it. Brig. Gen. Braxton Bragg assumed command of Confederate forces in Florida.

In Washington Gen. Winfield Scott answered Lincoln's questions as to Sumter: it was uncertain how long Maj. Anderson could hold out; the Army could not reinforce Fort Sumter within many months and it would require a fleet of war vessels, transports, five thousand regulars, and twenty thousand volunteers. President Lincoln was still very much involved in making appointments.

March 12, Tuesday
Fort McIntosh, Tex., was abandoned by Federal troops. In Britain the newspapers and public were rapidly taking sides regarding recognition of the Confederacy.

March 13, Wednesday
Alabama ratified the Confederate Constitution. President Lincoln told Seward not to see the Confederate commissioners, as such procedure would be admitting that the Southern states were out of the Union, a proposition the President could not now and never would officially accept. Mr. Lincoln conferred with former naval officer Gustavus Vasa Fox on plans for possibly resupplying Fort Sumter.

March 14, Thursday
The Federal Cabinet met once more on the crisis at Fort Sumter and also considered appointments. Louisiana received the thanks of the Confederate Congress for turning over $536,000 taken from the former U. S. Mint in New Orleans.

March 15, Friday
In an important Cabinet meeting President Lincoln requested the written opinions of members on whether or not to provision Fort Sumter. He asked, "Assuming it to be possible to now provision Fort-Sumpter [sic], under all the circumstances, is it wise to attempt it?" Seward was opposed unless it could be done peaceably, for "I would not provoke war in any way *now*." Chase approved, unless it would bring about war. Cameron thought it unwise because of the opinion of military men that it was "perhaps, now impossible to succor that fort, substantially, if at all." Welles was opposed both on military and political grounds. Smith added his opposition to relief as did Bates, while Blair was opposed to evacuation, and favored Gustavus Vasa Fox's plan for provisioning. The President postponed his decision. Meanwhile, in Texas Federals withdrew from still another post, Camp Wood. In Montgomery the Confederate Congress was busy completing its work of setting up a functioning national government and laying plans for possible conflict.

March 16, Saturday
The Confederate Provisional Congress adjourned at Montgomery, its work for the most part well done. President Davis, following the wishes of Congress, named William Lowndes Yancey, Pierre A. Rost, and A. Dudley Mann as commissioners to Britain to attempt to negotiate for

recognition. Georgia ratified the Confederate Constitution and far to the southwest pro-Confederates declared Arizona out of the Union. In Washington Lincoln received the written opinions of his Cabinet members as to Fort Sumter, which he had requested in the Cabinet meeting of March 15. From Fort Sumter itself Maj. Anderson was reporting almost daily, giving details of his own defensive plans and those of the Confederates virtually surrounding him.

March 17, Sunday

Federal troops at Camp Hudson, Tex., gave up their post to state authorities.

March 18, Monday

Aging hero Sam Houston, governor of Texas, refused to take an oath of allegiance to the new Confederacy because he did not believe that secession necessarily meant adherence to the new nation. Now deposed, he quietly left his office and on March 29 refused to support any move of Federal forces to reestablish him as governor. It was the last major act of the frontier leader's public life.

President Davis wrote Gov. Pickens of South Carolina about their mutual concern for the defense of the coasts around Charleston. Beauregard's command would be enlarged to include the Beaufort area. Davis doubted if "the enemy would retire peaceably from your harbor." Of course, the Confederate President preferred that Maj. Anderson and the Federals leave peaceably with Fort Sumter undamaged.

At Washington President Lincoln continued to be intensely perturbed over Fort Sumter. Conferences and discussion were prolonged, and the President drafted a memorandum listing the points in favor of withdrawing the troops and the objections. At the same time the President appointed Charles Francis Adams, scion of the famous Massachusetts Adams family, as Minister to Britain on Seward's suggestion, and named William L. Dayton Minister to France, among other appointments. Adams, not yet an admirer of Lincoln, was to prove one of the most capable and skillful diplomats ever to serve the United States.

Down at Pensacola, Fla., Gen. Bragg forbade passage of further supplies to Fort Pickens and the Federal squadron offshore as a result of Fort Pickens' being reinforced. The Arkansas State Convention at Little Rock had defeated a move toward secession 39 to 35 and now unanimously adopted a resolution to provide for an election in August when voters would choose between secession or Federal cooperation.

March 19, Tuesday

Three more forts in Texas were surrendered by Federal troops: Forts Clark, Inge, and Lancaster.

March 20, Wednesday

The list of relinquished Federal property in Texas increased; today it was Fort Brown and Fort Duncan. A harassed President Lincoln now found that his sons Willie and Tad had the measles. At Mobile U.S.S. *Isabella,* loaded with supplies for the fleet at Pensacola, was seized. Some of the correspondence between Sec. of State Seward and the Confederate commissioners in Washington was released to the public.

March 21, Thursday

Former naval officer Gustavus Vasa Fox visited Charleston and Fort Sumter on behalf of President Lincoln. He talked to Maj. Anderson and Confederate leaders. Fox remained convinced that the fort could be relieved by sea. Louisiana ratified the Confederate Constitution.

March 23, Saturday

Fort Chadbourne, Tex., was abandoned by Federals. The state of Texas ratified the Confederate Constitution.

March 25, Monday

Rumors and reports from Charleston were thick; the crisis was not only mounting but becoming somewhat muddled. Col. Ward Hill Lamon, acting as a messenger for the Federal government, conferred with Gov. Pickens and Gen. Beauregard.

March 26, Tuesday

President Lincoln met long with his Cabinet and others on both appointments and the growing crisis.

March 28, Thursday

President Lincoln submitted some fifty appointments to the Senate before it adjourned and held his first state dinner. That night Gen. Scott told the President that he recommended evacuation of both Fort Sumter and Fort Pickens. Gov. Pickens told the South Carolina Convention that six hundred men would be needed to hold the Charleston Harbor forts.

March 29, Friday

"I desire that an expedition, to move by sea, be got ready to sail as early as the 6th of April next" to attempt to resupply and perhaps reinforce Fort Sumter—President Lincoln had made his decision after many opinions and consultations. Forts Sumter and Pickens would be held. The Cabinet had reversed its stand—Seward was still against trying to hold the fort; Chase and Welles were in favor of holding and reinforcing; Smith was still in favor of evacuation; Blair remained in favor of holding on, and Bates wrote, "I think the time is come either to evacuate or relieve it." Thus opinion was in large part changed. Where previously the vote had been five to two against holding on, it was now three to two in favor, with Bates hedging and Cameron not recorded. Mississippi ratified the Confederate Constitution.

March 31, Sunday

President Lincoln ordered a relief expedition prepared to go to Fort Pickens, Fla. At the same time it was rumored in Washington that Fort Sumter would be evacuated. So at least did the Confederate commissioners believe after their contacts with Seward through Justice John A. Campbell. Lincoln, of course, had made his decision to maintain Federal hold on the fort.

In Texas, Fort Bliss was yielded by the Federals.

APRIL, 1861

It was still a time of waiting, of less hopeful waiting. The fact that two nations now existed where previously there had been one could not be ignored. The issue had to be faced, but how? Opinions and feelings were many, varying in degree and emphasis. Would there soon come a crisis that would force decisions? What about Fort Pickens at Pensacola, Fla., and Fort Sumter in Charleston Harbor, S.C.? Federal troops still garrisoned these, but were they not within Confederate territory? What about the slave states that had not yet seceded: Virginia, Maryland, Delaware, Tennessee, Kentucky, Arkansas, Missouri, and North Carolina?

The seven-state Confederacy was acting very much like a nation, complete with government, President, Constitution, people, and territory. At Washington President Lincoln must try to mold and shape a new administration elected by a new party. He must see to a Cabinet of diverse and ambitious men, must fill jobs with the party faithful, must decide what to do about these forts, what to do about the seceded states he could not recognize as departed. How far would the people back the new President? For the Confederacy at the moment the picture was clearer; there was much to do to solidify the new country, possibly gain new states, foreign recognition, and go about living. But perhaps it would not be that easy.

April 1, Monday

President Lincoln was still much involved with various Federal appointments, compiling lists, and writing memoranda. He signed an order to fit out U.S.S. *Powhatan,* upon the advice of Sec. of State Seward, to go to sea at the earliest possible moment under sealed orders which were apparently issued unknown to the Navy Department. It became a confused situation in which *Powhatan* was kept out of the Fort Sumter expedition. The vessel was now to be used to reinforce Fort Pickens in Florida.

This same day Seward sent Mr. Lincoln "Some thoughts for the President's consideration." The "thoughts" were really policies for the President to follow and virtually suggested that Seward be allowed to act as a prime minister in carrying out foreign policy and actions against the Confederacy. He advised changing the question from one of slavery to Union or disunion. He would terminate the Federal occupation of Fort Sumter, but maintain the other forts. At the same time Seward proposed demanding "explanations" for alleged hemispheric interference from Spain, France, Great Britain, and Russia, and suggested sending agents into Canada, Mexico, and Central America to create a "spirit of independence." If satisfactory "explanations" were not received from Spain and France, he would ask Congress to declare war, hoping this would reunite the nation. The President drafted a reply, but it is not clear whether it was given to Seward or not. He probably did discuss the paper orally. Mr. Lincoln could not see the distinction between Fort Sumter and Fort Pickens. As to handling policy, the President tactfully affirmed that he, not Seward, was President.

April 2, Tuesday

The Federal President visited the Washington Navy Yard and military barracks.

April 3, Wednesday

The Cabinet of President Lincoln met to discuss the Fort Sumter crisis and the President sent Allan B. Magruder to Richmond to arrange possible talks between Lincoln and Virginia unionists. At Morris Island in Charleston Harbor a Confederate battery fired on the American schooner *Rhoda H. Shannon.* The South Carolina State Convention ratified the Constitution of the Confederate States 114 to 16.

April 4, Thursday

The Virginia State Convention meeting in Richmond rejected 89 to 45 a motion to pass an ordinance of secession and submit it to the people. In Washington President Lincoln held a secret meeting with John B. Baldwin, Virginia unionist, in which he reportedly considered exchanging Virginia's loyalty for the surrender of Fort Sumter. The President also informed Gustavus Vasa Fox that the expedition to Fort Sumter would be sent, and drafted a letter, signed by Sec. of War Cameron, to Maj. Robert

Anderson that "the expedition will go forward, . . ." The President hoped that Anderson could hold out until April 11 or 12, when the expedition would attempt to provision the fort, and if there was resistance "will endeavor also to reinforce you." It was desired that Anderson hold out, but the decision would be up to him.

April 5, Friday

Federal forces gave up Fort Quitman, Tex., another in a long series of such actions. Secretary of Navy Welles ordered U.S.S. *Powhatan, Pawnee, Pocahontas,* and Revenue Cutter *Harriet Lane* to provision Fort Sumter, but *Powhatan* had already headed for Fort Pickens.

April 6, Saturday

PRESIDENT LINCOLN INFORMS SOUTH CAROLINA ATTEMPT TO BE MADE TO SUPPLY FORT SUMTER.

President Lincoln sent State Department Clerk Robert S. Chew to Charleston, S.C., to deliver to Gov. Pickens the message that an attempt would be made to supply Fort Sumter with provisions only, and that if there was no resistance, no reinforcement would be made. Capt. Theodore Talbot, who had just returned from Fort Sumter, accompanied Chew. Mr. Lincoln also learned that the plans to reinforce Fort Pickens, Fla., with Regular Army troops had not been carried out. The Federal naval commander had refused because of lack of direct orders canceling an agreement of the Buchanan administration not to land troops. A special messenger was instructed by Washington at once to carry orders for the landing of troops. Sec. of State Seward was directed by the President to restore *Powhatan* to the expedition to Fort Sumter, but it was too late to countermand its orders to go to Fort Pickens. The President conferred with governors of Indiana, Ohio, Maine, and Pennsylvania, and once more with Virginia unionists. He was still seeking ways out of the dilemma, while at the same time taking aggressive action to retain Fort Sumter.

April 7, Sunday

Naval Lieut. John L. Worden left Washington for Fort Pickens, carrying specific orders for the landing of troops by the Navy. At Pensacola, Confederate commander Braxton Bragg asked Sec. of War Leroy Pope Walker for permission to fire upon any reinforcements to Pickens. Walker at Montgomery replied April 8 that Bragg should resist and that an attack on Pensacola itself was expected.

At Charleston Gen. Beauregard told Maj. Anderson that no further intercourse between Fort Sumter and the city would be permitted. Virginia unionist John Minor Botts, former congressman, conferred with President Lincoln on means of keeping Virginia in the Union.

April 8, Monday

State Department Clerk R. S. Chew arrived in Charleston and read to Gov. Pickens President Lincoln's message that Fort Sumter would be resupplied but not reinforced unless there was resistance. Gov. Pickens read the message to Gen. Beauregard, military commander for the Confederates. All military forces of the South in the Charleston area were ordered to their stations. During the night there was a false alarm that war had started at Charleston. In Washington Sec. of State Seward unofficially informed the Confederate commissioners in the capital that the United States had a peaceful policy and would defend its possessions only when attacked. The commissioners wired Pickens that they thought Sumter would be evacuated. From New York the Revenue Cutter *Harriet Lane* departed for Fort Sumter, carrying relief supplies.

April 9, Tuesday

Steamer *Baltic,* with naval agent Gustavus V. Fox aboard, sailed from New York for Fort Sumter. In Washington, despite the increasingly tense situation regarding the forts, President Lincoln devoted time to political appointments. At Charleston the *Mercury* proclaimed that the resupplying of Fort Sumter meant war.

April 10, Wednesday

From Montgomery Sec. of War Walker telegraphed Confederate commander Beauregard at Charleston that if he were certain Fort Sumter was to be supplied "you will at once demand its evacuation, and if this is refused proceed, in such manner as you may determine, to reduce it." U.S.S. *Pawnee* left Hampton Roads for relief of Fort Sumter.

President Lincoln conferred with a representative of the Chiriqui Improvement Company regarding colonization of Negroes. Chiriqui was a prospective coal mining area in what is now Panama, near the Costa Rican border.

At Charleston military preparations continued with the newly constructed Confederate floating battery moved out of dock and anchored near Sullivan's Island. Troops were moving into the various forts, batteries, and earthworks virtually surrounding Fort Sumter. Lieut. Worden had arrived at Pensacola, Fla., with his message from President Lincoln to land troops to reinforce Fort Pickens. He obtained permission from Gen. Bragg to visit the fort.

April 11, Thursday

SURRENDER OF FORT SUMTER DEMANDED BY CONFEDERATES.

A small boat with a white flag pushed off from a Charleston wharf and proceeded to Fort Sumter. Three men were aboard—Col. James Chesnut, until recently a U.S. senator; Capt. Stephen D. Lee, who had resigned from the U. S. Army; and Lieut. Col. A. R. Chisolm, representative of South Carolina's Gov. Pickens. In midafternoon these officers delivered to Maj. Robert Anderson a message from Gen. Beauregard that the Confederate states "can no longer delay assuming actual possession of a fortification commanding the entrance of one of their harbors, and necessary to its defense and security. I am ordered by the Government of the Confederate States to demand the evacuation of Fort Sumter. . . ." For an hour Anderson discussed the situation with his officers, and then replied to Beauregard that he refused to evacuate. As the representatives of Beauregard left, Maj. Anderson asked if there would be any further notice before opening fire. Col. Chesnut said there would probably be such notice. Anderson said that he would be starved out in a few days if not battered to pieces. Receiving the report of his emissaries, Beauregard wired Sec. of War Walker at Montgomery, giving Anderson's reply. Walker wired back, "Do not desire needlessly to bombard Fort Sumter. If Anderson will state the time at which, as indicated by him, he will evacuate, and agree that in the mean time he will not use his guns against us unless ours should be employed against Fort Sumter, you are authorized thus to avoid the effusion of blood. . . ."

In Washington President Lincoln conferred with Gov. Thomas H. Hicks of Maryland regarding the uncertain condition of his state. Meanwhile, guards in Washington were increased and a company of troops paraded at the Capitol. The three Confederate commissioners left Washington, satisfied that they could do little more, and feeling they had been falsely led by Seward and the Federal government.

April 12, Friday
FORT SUMTER FIRED UPON AND REPLIES. WAR BEGINS!

At 11 P.M. the night of April 11 Beauregard's messengers, Chesnut, S. D. Lee, and Chisolm, returned to Maj. Anderson at Fort Sumter, prompted by the telegram of Confederate Sec. of War Walker expressing a wish to avoid firing if Anderson would state time at which, due to lack of supplies, he would have to evacuate. They reached Fort Sumter at 12:45 A.M., April 12, and at 3:15 A.M. received Anderson's reply. The major said he would evacuate on the fifteenth at noon if he did not receive additional supplies or further orders from his government. Anderson added that he would not fire unless fired upon. These terms were obviously unsatisfactory to the Confederates as it was common knowledge supplies and possibly reinforcements were coming, probably along with further orders. The officers had to refuse Anderson's proposal and notified him in writing that Confederate batteries would open in an hour's time. They proceeded to Fort Johnson, arriving at 4 A.M.

At 4:30 A.M. the signal shot was fired from the post of Capt. George S.

James at Fort Johnson, with other batteries opening according to previous orders. Capt. James gave the order and, probably, one Henry S. Farley actually fired the signal shot that arched in the night sky over Charleston Harbor. Edmund Ruffin, Virginia agriculturalist and fiery Confederate, did not, apparently, fire the first real shot, despite the legend. He did fire the first shell from columbiad No. 1 of the iron battery at Cummings Point on Morris Island. The rotation of fire, which was followed, brought this battery into action late. But it matters little; the signal shot did it and the war guns spoke.

For a while, until near 7 A.M., the forty-eight guns of Fort Sumter were silent, and then some of them replied, manned by eighty-five officers and men and some of the forty-three workmen employed in the fort. Opposing the Federal garrison were well over four thousand Confederates and seventy or more guns. Of course, only part of the Union guns could be handled at once due to the small garrison. Three times, at least, the barracks of the fort caught fire, throwing thick black clouds of smoke skyward, but the fires were extinguished each time. The men at the guns suffered little from the Confederate fire, but could not man the open top tier due to the accurate vertical fire of the enemy. All day the Confederate bombardment was constant and heavy. The issue was never in doubt. By night rain and darkness closed in on the beleaguered fort. Only a few minor injuries had been suffered by the men.

For the Confederates it was said a thrill went through the city of Charleston—the issue had been met. Crowds of people watched from the battery and many others perched on rooftops for a better view. A teenager said, "a perfect sheet of flame flashed out, a deafening roar, a rumbling deadening sound, and the war was on." Out at sea the vessels of the Federal relieving fleet could be seen. Would they attempt to come in? While some cheered, others prayed, and some did both.

Miles away at Fort Pickens, Fla., Federal troops were landed on Santa Rosa Island to reinforce the garrison of the fort at the entrance to Pensacola Bay. The Navy carried out the mission after being given special orders by Lieut. Worden, who had come from Washington. Due to the location of Fort Pickens, the Confederates in Pensacola were unable to prevent the landings. The issue there had now been solved and Fort Pickens was to remain in Northern hands, a constant threat to the South on the Gulf Coast.

April 13, Saturday

FORT SUMTER SURRENDERS.

After thirty-four hours of bombardment Fort Sumter was forced to surrender to the Confederates. There was hope by some and fear by others that the Federal squadron offshore would enter into the fray, land troops and supplies and that Fort Sumter would remain in Federal hands. While

U.S.S. *Baltic,* U.S.S. *Pawnee,* and *Harriet Lane* had arrived, they found the war had begun and were unable to complete their mission of rescue.

Inside Fort Sumter on the morning of April 13 the last rice was cooked and served with pork, and fire reopened. But the supply of artillery cartridges was severely limited. A few minor wounds occurred and again the barracks and officers' quarters were ablaze. This time the fire was unextinguishable and the powder magazine was threatened. Artillery fire from the fort was cut down due to lack of cartridges. At one o'clock the flagstaff fell, but amid the storm of shot the Union banner was replaced. Inexplicably former U.S. senator Louis T. Wigfall of Texas appeared at the fort with a white flag and unofficially discussed surrender. Maj. Anderson agreed that the time for surrender had come and the white flag replaced the Stars and Stripes on the battered flagstaff. Aides of Beauregard arrived and stated that Wigfall's visit was unofficial, but after some discussion the surrender stood, occurring about two-thirty in the afternoon.

The Confederate fire on this second day of bombardment had been more accurate than on the twelfth. While injury to the fort was considerable, it was not yet undefendable. But the lack of men and want of provisions, artillery cartridges, and supplies forced the decision. Maj. Anderson felt, correctly, that his men had done their duty and that he had followed orders, for without relief there was no hope.

Offshore the Federal fleet had made no movement and Maj. Anderson at Fort Sumter had been unable to communicate even with flags due to lack of the proper code. Onshore the Confederates at the guns and the citizen observers were cheered by their success, and sympathy was openly expressed for Maj. Anderson and his gallant garrison. One observer wrote, "Thank God the day has come—thank God the war is open, and we will conquer or perish." The cheers of the Southern soldiers and citizens were loud—victory was theirs.

The human cost had been light indeed. Some four thousand shells had been fired in Charleston Harbor and not a human being killed. Only a few were slightly injured, mainly by falling bricks. The only known fatality was one horse—Confederate. But a New York paper later put it soberly: "The curtain has fallen upon the first act of the great tragedy of our age."

Elsewhere, Lieut. Worden, who had carried the orders to the U. S. Navy to land Federal troops at Fort Pickens at Pensacola, Fla., was seized by Confederate authorities near Montgomery, Ala., on his way back to Washington. But Fort Pickens had been reinforced and the harbor was now blockaded.

In Washington there was no confirmed report yet from Charleston but it was believed shots had been fired. President Lincoln told a group of Virginia commissioners that he considered it his duty to "hold, occupy, and possess, the property, and places belonging to the Government," but beyond that there would be no invasion or use of force against the people. However, he said, "I shall hold myself at liberty to re-possess, if I can," places like Fort Sumter if taken from Federal control. In far-off Texas, Fort Davis was abandoned by Federal troops.

April 14, Sunday

FORMAL SURRENDER OF FORT SUMTER.

With colors flying, drums beating, and fifty guns firing in salute, the sturdy, fatigued, and defeated garrison of Fort Sumter marched out of their bastion and boarded vessels which would take them north. But the scene of victory and defeat was marred at the surrender ceremony by the accidental explosion of a pile of cartridges. The blast killed one Federal private outright, another was mortally wounded, and four others injured, one seriously. A large crowd aboard various small and large vessels watched the ceremony at the fort in the excitement of victory. Throughout Charleston it was a holiday to celebrate the evacuation and in the churches special services of thanksgiving were held. Gov. Pickens of South Carolina told a crowd, "We have met them and we have conquered."

The news was now spreading over the land, uniting hearts and making those uncertain declare themselves. The sides had been chosen and the issue joined; it was time now for fresh decisions and preparation for action. In Washington President Lincoln officially heard the news. The Cabinet approved his call for 75,000 militia and a special session of Congress to meet July 4. Sen. Stephen A. Douglas conferred with Mr. Lincoln and pledged his support of the Union despite political differences. The Cabinet and Mr. Lincoln met for a long night session. In Montgomery Jefferson Davis and his Cabinet were slowly getting the news and were likewise deliberating as to their next moves. President Davis expressed thankfulness that no blood had been shed, and stated that separation was not yet necessarily final. The wild rejoicing in the South culminated at Charleston and Montgomery. Some felt that this victory would prevent further war; others feared the real struggle had not yet begun.

Maj. Robert Anderson was to say, "Our Southern brethren have done grievously wrong, they have rebelled and have attacked their father's house and their loyal brothers. They must be punished and brought back, but this necessity breaks my heart."

On Van Dusen's Creek, near Mad River, Calif., Federal troops skirmished with Indians.

April 15, Monday

As excitement increased among the peoples of the now warring nations, President Lincoln at Washington publicly issued a proclamation declaring that an insurrection existed, calling out seventy-five thousand militia from the various Northern states and convening Congress in special session on

July 4. Immediately the strongly Northern states wired back their acceptance of the call for troops; Kentucky and North Carolina as quickly refused. In North Carolina state troops seized Fort Macon, an unmanned Federal fort. The President's proclamation excited much ill feeling in the border areas of Missouri, Kentucky, Maryland, Virginia, and North Carolina, as well as some support.

Throughout North and South papers continued to scream the news, writers penned flaming editorials, and public gatherings sang patriotic songs, heard flamboyant speakers. All the same, it was hard to comprehend that war had actually begun.

April 16, Tuesday

As more Northern states responded to President Lincoln's call for militia, Virginia officially refused. North Carolina state troops seized Forts Caswell and Johnston. In the Indian Territory Federal troops were converging on Fort Washita near the Texas line from other frontier posts. The main question for the immediate future seemed to be the border and upper South slave states that were still officially in the Union—Virginia, North Carolina, Kentucky, Missouri, Tennessee, Arkansas, Maryland, and Delaware. The action at Fort Sumter would certainly cause several of these states to make their decision; perhaps four or more would go with the South. After all, Gov. John Letcher of Virginia had told President Lincoln that his state would not furnish troops "for any such use or purpose as they have in view." The governor was opposed to what he called the subjugation of the Southern states.

April 17, Wednesday

VIRGINIA CONVENTION VOTES FOR SECESSION.

Militia and volunteers were being raised in Northern states in response to the President's call and in reaction to Fort Sumter. Steps were taken in Washington to protect the Federal capital. But in Baltimore, Md., secessionists held a large meeting, and both Missouri and Tennessee refused to furnish their quotas of militia to the United States. At the same time all the non-slaveholding states had responded.

In Richmond the Virginia State Convention adopted an ordinance of secession by the vote of 88 to 55, providing for a popular referendum on the issue May 23. The action of the convention, however, virtually put Virginia in the Confederacy. The convention also instructed the governor to call out as many volunteers as might be necessary to protect Virginia from Federal encroachment. While strong pro-Union sentiment still existed in Virginia, particularly in the western counties, the firing at Fort Sumter had clearly swung many Virginians and delegates to the convention to the side of secession.

At Montgomery President Davis invited applications for letters of marque, which permitted privateering on the high seas. In Washington President Lincoln conferred with Gen. Winfield Scott regarding Harper's Ferry, Va., the defenses of Washington, and the Gosport Navy Yard near Norfolk, Va. *Star of the West,* involved in the January incident at Fort Sumter, was taken near Indianola, Tex., by the Galveston Volunteers, a Confederate unit. More Federal troops landed at Fort Pickens, Fla., upon arrival of U.S.S. *Powhatan.*

Meetings of patriotic groups continued both North and South, but attention now was turning to volunteering and organizing of militia.

April 18, Thursday

Five companies of Pennsylvania troops reached Washington, the first to arrive. In New York the Sixth Massachusetts made a triumphal march, setting a pattern to be followed for some time to come. The U. S. Armory at Harper's Ferry, Va., at the confluence of the Potomac and the Shenandoah, was abandoned and burned by its garrison, although much of the machinery was left intact. At Pine Bluff, Ark., pro-secessionists seized the U. S. Army Subsistence Stores. In Richmond, Va., the U. S. Custom House and Post Office was taken over by state troops on order of the governor and two vessels seized in the James River. A pro-secession flag was raised on Federal Hill in Baltimore. At New York Maj. Robert Anderson and his men from Fort Sumter disembarked as heroes. Virginia was rapidly arming and organizing its state troops to defend its territory, even though not yet officially a part of the Confederacy. President Davis told Gov. Letcher that the Confederacy would furnish whatever aid it could.

President Lincoln received eyewitness reports of what had happened at Charleston, quartered a group known as the "Frontier Guards" composed of Kansas men under Jim Lane in the East Room of the White House, and reportedly had politician F. P. Blair, Sr., approach Col. Robert E. Lee regarding command of the Union Army, which he allegedly turned down. The Cabinet met to discuss such problems at Norfolk, Harper's Ferry, and the possibility of an attack on the Washington Navy Yard.

While both Northern and Southern shades of opinion were being expressed in the border and upper South states, there were some who were calling for neutrality or independence from either side. Various cities of the North were contributing money to aid volunteers enlisting in the Federal Army.

April 19, Friday

BALTIMORE RIOTS.

PRESIDENT LINCOLN DECLARES BLOCKADE OF CONFEDERATE STATES.

"Whereas an insurrection against the Government of the United States has broken out in the States of South Carolina, Georgia, Alabama, Florida, Mississippi, Louisiana, and Texas," therefore a blockade of the ports of those states was declared by President Lincoln in a proclamation. Later the blockade was extended to Virginia and North Carolina. While not immediately very effective, the blockade in time became a major instrument of war and for nearly four years was to make its impression upon the outcome of many events. Even at first, merely on paper, it did to some extent deter foreign shippers. Later, while blockade-runners continued to get through, the risks grew greater and greater. Historians have argued over the effectiveness of the Federal blockade, some claiming that at its best a few blockade-runners, at least, always got through, while others point out that the mere declaration of a blockade prevented many ships from sailing which otherwise would have taken advantage of the Southern need for both military and civilian supplies. The Federal Navy Department went to work rapidly to pull in its far-flung vessels and get them on blockading stations at major ports, meanwhile buying, building, and equipping new vessels for similar duty. On the other hand, both Southern and foreign vessels soon became adept at evading the naval blockaders. While events were sporadic in other fields of war, the blockade went on relentlessly, day after day, off the Atlantic and Gulf coasts, making its partly unsung contribution to the results of the conflict.

More dramatic in these early days of the Civil War was the clash of soldiers and civilians in Baltimore. In response to the call of President Lincoln, the Sixth Massachusetts had left home, moved through New York toward Washington. At Baltimore it had to detrain partially to transfer to the Washington depot. There had been talk of trouble from pro-secessionists in Baltimore for some days and the Federal government was faced not only with the defense of Washington, but with keeping touchy Maryland in the Union. In Washington politicians as well as military men were organizing companies, patrolling streets, and guarding Federal buildings. Harper's Ferry, evacuated by the Federals, had been taken during the morning by Virginia troops, and now a fracas in Baltimore. There were even fears of an attack on the capital. Baltimore was the major eastern rail center near Washington and with it cut off, Washington could well be in danger. Mayor George W. Brown of Baltimore said no notice of the coming of the troops was given him or the police. The crowd of bystanders grew as the rail cars were dragged between stations and four companies had to get out and push their way through. Some of the rioters carried Confederate flags, stones were thrown, the mob hooted and jeered. Then came shots by both crowd and soldiers. Casualty figures are not entirely clear but at least four soldiers and nine civilians were killed. Upon arrival in Washington the Sixth Massachusetts was quartered in the Senate Chamber at the Capitol. With the Baltimore riot, rumors flew thicker than ever. Washington was in effect cut off from the north via the railroad.

As the troops of Virginia moved into Harper's Ferry, aging Maj. Gen. Robert Patterson was assigned Federal command over Delaware, Pennsylvania, Maryland, and the District of Columbia. More Federal troops were leaving New York for Washington; merchants of New York pledged their loyalty to the Union. With Baltimore cut off, naval officers immediately began embarking troops at Philadelphia and the head of Chesapeake Bay to bring them to Annapolis by water and then to Washington by rail. Capt. David G. Farragut, a Southerner living in Norfolk, Va., left his home for New York City and eventual service with the Union.

April 20, Saturday

FEDERALS EVACUATE NORFOLK, VIRGINIA, NAVY YARD.

Several railroad bridges were burned to prevent passage of Union troops from Baltimore to Washington while rioting continued in the Maryland city. Gen. Benjamin F. Butler and the Eighth Massachusetts arrived at Annapolis, Md., heading for Washington, but bypassing Baltimore. The Fourth Massachusetts arrived at Fort Monroe to strengthen the garrison of that vital Federal enclave on Virginia soil. Many Southern merchants repudiated debts to the North until after the war. Pro-secessionists and state troops seized the U. S. Arsenal at Liberty, Mo. Col. Robert E. Lee formally resigned his commission in the U. S. Army. It is said by some that this step took much soul-searching, while other evidence seems to indicate that a decision to follow the fate of Virginia was never in doubt. In Washington President Lincoln conferred with Gen. Scott and others over the Baltimore situation. A large mass meeting favoring the Union was held in New York, while at Louisville, Ky., former Vice-President John C. Breckinridge denounced Lincoln's call for troops as illegal.

The night of April 20 the Federal Gosport Navy Yard near Norfolk, Va., was evacuated and partially burned by the garrison and several vessels scuttled. Commandant Charles S. McCauley had decided that the facility was threatened with capture. His decision was later censured by Federal authorities. Five vessels were burned to the water line. Four others, including U.S.S. *Merrimack,* later refloated as C.S.S. *Virginia,* were sunk after burning. The ancient frigate *United States* was abandoned. Three vessels got away intact. While many of the ships in the yard were old or in poor condition, others would have been of use in the blockade. Furthermore, the loss of Norfolk hampered Federal coastal operations and in turn gave the Confederates an important base. The South was able to make use of the dry dock, the industrial plant, and some of the vessels, and many of the thousand guns stored there furnished armament for Confederate defenses. At Annapolis the famed old U.S.S. *Constitution,* known as "Old Ironsides," was towed out into Chesapeake Bay to prevent seizure by the South.

April 21, Sunday

Washington was still isolated due to the riot in Baltimore; Harper's Ferry and Norfolk had been lost to the Confederates or Virginians. The

Federal situation in Washington looked particularly bleak at this time. But elsewhere in the North the parades, meetings, volunteering, and fund raising continued. President Lincoln conferred with Mayor Brown of Baltimore regarding the passage of troops. In western Virginia pro-Northern citizens of Monongahela County met to pass resolutions against secession. From pulpits North and South the clergy joined in the patriotic fervor of the day, pleading the justice of their causes. The illegal slave ship *Nightingale* with 961 slaves was captured by U.S.S. *Saratoga*.

April 22, Monday

Gov. H. M. Rector of Arkansas turned down the Federal requisition for troops, stating their purpose was "to subjugate the Southern States." State troops of North Carolina seized the U. S. Arsenal at Fayetteville. Florida ratified the Confederate Constitution, but had been part of the new nation since January.

President Davis told Gov. Letcher of Virginia that more troops were on the way and urged him to "Sustain Baltimore if practicable." President Lincoln was still sorely concerned over the Baltimore situation and told a peace-seeking committee from the Baltimore YMCA, "You express great horror of bloodshed, and yet would not lay a straw in the way of those who are organizing in Virginia and elsewhere to capture this city." He said he had no desire to invade the South but he must defend the capital, and added, "Keep your rowdies in Baltimore, and there will be no bloodshed." Troops now had to march across Maryland. The commandant of the Washington Navy Yard, Capt. Franklin Buchanan, resigned to go South and was succeeded by Com. John A. Dahlgren. The steamer *Boston* brought the Seventh New York to Annapolis. Gov. Hicks of Maryland urged the President to withdraw troops from Maryland and advocated cessation of hostilities with arbitrament by Lord Lyons, the British minister. Sec. of State Seward turned down these suggestions. Late at night Illinois troops arrived to garrison Cairo, Ill., which pointed like a sword at the heart of the South from its position at the junction of the Mississippi and Ohio rivers.

In Richmond Robert E. Lee was nominated by the governor and confirmed by the State Convention as commander of the forces of Virginia.

April 23, Tuesday

Arkansas state troops seized Fort Smith, an important frontier post. R. E. Lee, now a major general of Virginia, was formally assigned to command the forces of the state.

U.S.S. *Pawnee* arrived in Washington from Norfolk, strengthening the defenses of the Federal capital. In Montgomery President Davis wrote Gov. Claiborne Jackson of Missouri that he had received his envoys and that the Confederacy would aid the Missouri secessionists in attacking the St. Louis Arsenal. John Bell of Tennessee, lately Constitutional Union candidate for President, told a Nashville meeting he was opposed to the attempted subjugation of the South. Meanwhile, political meetings for various causes continued in both countries. Troops, both C.S.A. and U.S.A., were moving toward Virginia and Washington. Of the Federal forces, President Lincoln exclaimed, "Why don't they come! Why don't they come!" With the secession of Virginia accomplished, the focus of the struggle had shifted from Charleston northward. U.S. officers at San Antonio, Tex., were captured as prisoners of war.

April 24, Wednesday

"I don't believe there is any North. The Seventh Regiment is a myth. . . . *You* are the only Northern realities." So said Lincoln to troops in Washington. There was real fear now in the capital of attack from land, or possibly from the Potomac. The pressure on the Federal President was showing. To Maryland political leader Reverdy Johnson he wrote that the sole purpose of bringing troops to Washington was defensive and not to invade Virginia, except to repel attack: "I do not mean to let them invade us without striking back."

Gov. Beriah Magoffin of Kentucky called for the state to place herself in a state of defense and convened the legislature for May 5.

April 25, Thursday

U. S. Sen. Stephen A. Douglas addressed the Illinois legislature at Springfield, emotionally calling for support of the Union. The war was "in defense of those great rights of freedom of trade, commerce and intercourse from the center to the circumference of our great continent." Sadly he added, "I believe in my conscience that it is a duty we owe ourselves, and our children, and our God, to protect this Government and that flag from every assailant, be he who he may."

Meanwhile, more U.S. troops surrendered, this time at Saluria, Tex. In Washington President Lincoln reviewed the newly arrived Seventh New York, and wondered whether troops should not prevent the Maryland legislature from assembling to take action on secession. He concluded that he had no power to interfere. At St. Louis Capt. James H. Stokes of Chicago, told to get arms for Illinois troops from the St. Louis Arsenal, secretly took a steamer from Alton and late at night landed at the arsenal wharf. He and his men removed ten thousand muskets and other arms from under the noses of the pro-secessionist elements in St. Louis and returned safely to Alton, where they were unloaded Friday morning, April 26. U.S.S. *Constitution* left the Chesapeake for New York and Newport, R.I., under tow. The historic vessel would remain at Newport at the transferred U. S. Naval Academy. It was not considered safe to leave the Naval Academy at Annapolis, and the grounds had been turned into an army camp.

Brig. Gen. Edwin V. Sumner assumed command of the U. S. Army Department of the Pacific, relieving Albert Sidney Johnston.

April 26, Friday

Gov. Joseph Brown of Georgia issued an order for repudiation by citizens of all debts owed Northerners. Maj. Gen. Joseph E. Johnston of the Virginia Volunteers was assigned to command state forces in and around Richmond. Gov. John W. Ellis of North Carolina called a special session of the General Assembly and deprecated President Lincoln's call for troops. The Navy Department in Washington was rushing to implement the blockade, sending out what vessels it had and purchasing mercantile steamers.

The zeal of the people on both sides was unabated, with men and money pouring in. Women made shirts, blankets, even coats and pants for the new soldiers. Communities pledged to take care of the families of soldiers while they were gone, for most believed it could not be for long.

April 27, Saturday

The Federal blockade was extended to the coasts of Virginia and North Carolina by proclamation of President Lincoln. He also suspended the privilege of the writ of habeas corpus, for reasons of public safety, along a line from Philadelphia to Washington, upon the discretion of Gen. Scott. Several Federal command changes were made, with Maj. Gen. Patterson commanding the Department of Pennsylvania, Brig. Gen. B. F. Butler the Department of Annapolis, and Col. Joseph K. F. Mansfield the Department of Washington. On the Confederate side Col. Thomas Jonathan Jackson was officially assigned to command Virginia troops around Harper's Ferry. The Virginia Convention invited the Confederate government to make Richmond the nation's seat of government.

With the arrival of the Seventh New York, followed by other regiments, the pressure in Washington was slowly relieved and the city no longer felt isolated and besieged. Ever since the Baltimore riots the tension had been high, but now it subsided. A number of government employees were resigning and leaving for the South, as were military men from posts all over the country. Maryland seemed to be turning toward the Union, and the action of the special session of the state assembly was awaited with speculation.

April 28, Sunday

President Lincoln visited the Seventh New York, quartered in the House of Representatives Chamber in the Federal Capitol. The frigate *Constitution* arrived in New York en route to Newport, R.I.

April 29, Monday

"ALL WE ASK IS TO BE LET ALONE."

The Maryland house of delegates voted against secession 53 to 13, a heavy blow to the pro-Confederate element in the state.

The second session of the Provisional Congress of the Confederacy met at Montgomery and received a lengthy message from President Davis. He went over the history of the setting up of the Confederate government and termed Lincoln's proclamation of April 15 a declaration of war. Then followed a long explanation of the reasons for the secession of the South, along with a summary of efforts to treat with the Federals. He charged the United States with bad faith toward the Confederacy in the pre-Fort Sumter events. The President reported on the various departments and spoke of the manifested "patriotic devotion to our common cause." Mr. Davis concluded, "We feel that our cause is just and holy; we protest solemnly in the face of mankind that we desire peace at any sacrifice save that of honor and independence; we seek no conquest, no aggrandizement, no concession of any kind from the States with which we were lately confederated; all we ask is to be let alone; that those who never held power over us shall not now attempt our subjugation by arms."

April 30, Tuesday

Members of the New York Yacht Club proffered the services of their vessels to the Federal government. This was typical of the response of various groups, civic bodies, churches, schools, and other organizations who in their early-war fervor were jumping to the colors in whatever way they could. By the end of April there was still uncertainty, still some vague hope of peace, but at the same time the people were exhilarated by the war spirit, by the excitement, the anticipated thrill of the conflict—the grim awakening would come later.

Col. William H. Emory abandoned Fort Washita in the Indian Territory near the Texas border and marched his troops north toward Fort Leavenworth, Kas., following orders of the Federal government to evacuate garrisons in the Indian country. This left the Five Civilized Indian Tribes—Cherokees, Chickasaws, Choctaws, Creeks, and Seminoles—to the influence of the Confederates. A number of the Indians were slaveholders and already pro-secessionist or at least advocating neutrality.

MAY, 1861

Less than three weeks before, the firing began at Fort Sumter and war was under way. Most of the talk was over, and a few shells had flown instead. A form of unreal realism was crossing both the United and Confederate states. People were waking to what had happened and beginning to get ready to do more. They knew it was war now, but did they know what war was? Maybe, just possibly, it would all be patched up again; and if this war was real, could it possibly last very long? Could the North not see that the South had a right to their independence, to choose their own way of life? Could not the South see that it was bringing ruin to the Union? No one in truth could see anything very clearly but they had to peer around, gather their wits after a fashion, and do something.

The line-up was not quite complete—several other states were on the verge of leaving the old nation. Could any of the slave states be saved? The Confederate government at Montgomery, successful up to now in its effort at secession, must gird itself for a war—and with what? Patriotic manpower was not enough, and even that was limited. Of course major foreign powers would recognize the validity of the Confederacy—or would they? In Washington a new administration, a new President, and a new political party were in power and just what would and could they do with what was left of the country?

May 1, Wednesday

Under the authority of the governor of Virginia, Maj. Gen. R. E. Lee, commanding the state forces of Virginia, ordered out further volunteer troops, with a concentration at Harper's Ferry under Col. T. J. Jackson. The colonel was ordered to move all machinery from the rifle factory there to Winchester and Strasburg.

At Nashville the legislature of Tennessee approved a joint resolution authorizing the governor to appoint commissioners to enter into league with the Confederacy. The North Carolina legislature voted in favor of a state convention to consider secession. Throughout both nations meetings in support of their governments were being held amid general enthusiasm, speeches, and flag raisings. Wealthy citizens contributed money and as an example Samuel Colt was promoting a regiment and providing the soldiers with his new revolving breech-loading rifles. Gov. Samuel W. Black of Nebraska Territory called for a Union volunteer organization. Upon their arrival at Boston full military honors were accorded soldiers killed in the Baltimore riots. Rumors and even rumors of rumors were rife. Mr. Lincoln issued an invitation to Robert Anderson to visit the White House so the President could explain some points regarding "Fort Sumpter," and at the same time wrote Gustavus V. Fox that "You and I both anticipated that the cause of the country would be advanced by making the attempt to provision Fort-Sumpter, even if it should fail; . . ."

The U. S. Navy seized two Confederate vessels, adding to the several already taken. Texas militia occupied Fort Washita, Indian Terr., which became a Confederate staging area.

Troops continued to pour into Washington, including the New York Fire Zouaves of Col. Elmer E. Ellsworth. The Federal Navy placed the mouth of the James River and Hampton Roads, Va., under strict blockade. Judge John A. Campbell, Associate Justice of the Supreme Court, resigned, and eventually became Assistant Secretary of War of the Confederacy.

May 3, Friday

President Lincoln issued a call for 42,034 volunteers to serve for three years unless sooner discharged. The proclamation also called for eight regiments of infantry and one each of cavalry and artillery for the Regular Army, raising total strength of the regulars from 16,367 to 22,714. Enlistment of 18,000 seamen for not less than one year or more than three was asked as well. These calls would bring the total strength of the Army to 156,861 and the Navy to 25,000. To the south, Gov. Letcher called for volunteers to defend Virginia.

Orders were issued from Washington forming the Department of the Ohio, comprising Ohio, Indiana, and Illinois, and placing young George Brinton McClellan in charge. The general received his orders May 13.

In London Lord John Russell, British Foreign Minister, received the Confederate commissioners to Great Britain, William L. Yancey, A. Dudley Mann, and Pierre A. Rost. The British claimed this meeting was unofficial, but U.S. diplomats protested.

At home ferment was high in the border states. Both pro-Confederate and pro-Union meetings were being held in Maryland; fourteen Kentucky companies tendered their services to the Union; and pro-secessionist Gov. Claiborne Jackson of Missouri said that in calling out troops, President Lincoln threatened civil war and that the action tended toward despotism. He declared Missouri's sympathies were identical with those of the Southern states.

Gen. Scott told Gen. McClellan that the blockade could be relied on and that there should be a powerful movement down the Mississippi, clear to the mouth, with "a cordon of posts" set up. This would "envelop the insurgent States and bring them to terms with less bloodshed than by any other plan." The concept soon became known as the "Anaconda Plan."

May 4, Saturday

Meetings, meetings and more meetings—a pro-Union group met at Kingwood, Preston County, western Va., and another at Wheeling to declare against secession. Ladies of the South formed associations to make articles for hospital use. U.S. ordnance stores were seized at Kansas City, Mo. A Maryland legislative committee acknowledged the Federal right to transport troops through the state, but only after a protest to Lincoln. One of the first guns for the Confederate Navy was cast at Phoenix Iron Works at Gretna, La., and *Star of the West,* famed in the January Fort Sumter affair, became a receiving ship for the Confederates at New Orleans. Fort Arbuckle in the Indian Territory was evacuated by the Federals, the troops joining the march north to Kansas of Col. William H. Emory's command from Fort Washita.

May 5, Sunday

Alexandria, Va., across the Potomac from Washington, was temporarily abandoned by Virginia state troops. Gen. Benjamin F. Butler occupied Relay House on the Baltimore & Ohio Railroad between Baltimore, Annapolis, and Washington. In Raleigh, N.C., volunteers for the Confederate forces crowded into the city in answer to the governor's call. Southern forces occupied Fort Arbuckle in the Indian Territory.

May 6, Monday

ARKANSAS AND TENNESSEE LEGISLATURES PASS SECESSION ORDINANCES.
CONFEDERACY RECOGNIZES STATE OF WAR WITH UNITED STATES.

The ninth and tenth states left the Union and joined the Confederacy. In a solemn scene at the state Capitol in Little Rock, the legislature of Arkansas voted 69 to 1 to sever relations with the United States. As one description put it, "A weight seemed suddenly to have been lifted off the hearts of all present, . . ." The Tennessee legislature at Nashville passed an ordinance to "submit to the vote of the people a Declaration of Independence, and for other purposes." Election was set for June 8, but the action of the legislature was considered tantamount to secession. The vote was 20 to 4 in the senate and 46 to 21 in the house. In Montgomery President Davis approved a bill of the Confederate Congress passed May 3 declaring that the Confederacy recognized a state of war between the U.S.A. and the C.S.A. The measure also authorized issuing of letters of marque for privateers.

In Parliament Lord John Russell announced that the British had decided to recognize the Confederate States as belligerents, but this did not constitute recognition of them as a nation.

In St. Louis the police commissioners asked Capt. Nathaniel Lyon to remove troops from various buildings and the vehemently pro-Union officer, soon to be a general, refused. Pro-secessionist Missouri state militia gathered at a camp near St. Louis, posing a possible threat to unionists. President Lincoln told a Maryland legislative commission that military use or occupation of any soil of Maryland was contingent upon circumstances. Dorchester, Mass., voted $20,000 for war costs plus $20 a month for every married volunteer and $15 for every single volunteer.

May 7, Tuesday

Gov. Isham Harris of Tennessee told his legislature that he had agreed upon a military league between the state of Tennessee and the C.S.A. and submitted it for ratification or rejection by the legislature. The senate approved 14 to 6 with four not voting or absent and the house approved 42 to 15 with eighteen absent or not voting. To all intents and purposes Tennessee was now in the Confederacy, though the people had to approve secession in June.

President Lincoln ordered Col. Robert Anderson to recruit troops for the Union from Kentucky and western Virginia. The President also reviewed Elmer Ellsworth's flashy New York Fire Brigade of Zouaves, received a committee from a governors' convention, and told his secretaries that the question was "whether a full and representative government had the right and power to protect and maintain itself."

In Knoxville, Tenn., there was a serious riot between pro-Union and pro-secessionist elements, with several shots fired and one man mortally wounded.

Citizens of the North had already contributed $23,277,000 to the war effort, aside from usual taxes.

May 8, Wednesday

It appeared that Maryland was swinging toward the Union, with transportation by rail through the state restored, troops coming into Washington, and Union men being heard more and more. However, there were still pockets of intransigent pro-secessionists in the state. In the South the Richmond *Examiner* said, "We need a dictator" to win the war. At the same time the Southern press agreed not to publish news of military movements, a pledge that was soon to be violated by both sides.

May 9, Thursday

President Davis signed a bill, approved by the Confederate Congress May 7, which authorized the President to accept into volunteer service such forces as he might deem expedient for the duration of the war.

There was an exchange of shots between U.S.S. *Yankee* and Confederate shore batteries at Gloucester Point, Va., as the blockade in Virginia waters was being increased. In Washington the Lincolns held a reception and the President reviewed troops and watched gunnery practices. While Federal troops kept coming into Washington, pro-Confederate units left Maryland for Virginia. The Confederate Navy sent James D. Bulloch to Britain to purchase ships and arms, a mission ably carried out. U.S.S. *Constitution* and U.S. steamer *Baltic* arrived at Newport, R.I., to set up the Naval Academy dispossessed from Annapolis for the duration. Troops from abandoned Fort Cobb in the Indian Territory joined the column of Col. William Emory marching through the territory to Kansas.

May 10, Friday

ST. LOUIS CIVILIANS AND TROOPS RIOT.

St. Louis exploded into action. Troops marched, shots were fired, and people fell. The pro-Union elements in the city, including the vocal German group, were organized under Capt. Nathaniel Lyon, temporarily commanding the arsenal, and Francis Preston Blair, Jr., politician and member of the well-known Blair family. In addition to a few regulars, the unionists had organized some political marching clubs into Home Guards. The State Militia, on the other hand, was largely pro-secessionist or at least opposed to supporting the Union war effort. Gov. Claiborne Jackson had made this abundantly clear. On May 6 the militia had gathered at Camp Jackson in Lindell's Grove in the western part of the city under command of Gen. D. M. Frost, former army officer turned politician. The camp had definite Southern overtones, with streets unofficially reported to be named "Davis Avenue" and for Beauregard and other Confederates. Surplus arms from the arsenal had been sent into Illinois, but the unionists feared that the militia at Camp Jackson, named for the governor, would attack the arsenal; therefore the camp must be taken. The story is that on May 8 Lyon, dressed as an elderly woman, drove through the camp as a spy, but this is highly dubious, for all the information needed was readily available. Late on May 8 a boat had brought boxes marked "marble" to the city. They turned out to be loaded with mortars and guns for the secessionists. Frost's militia camp was set to disband May 11, and he denied any covert intentions. Lyon, urged on by Blair, decided to take the camp because of their "unscrupulous conduct, and their evident design. . . ."

Violent, sometimes almost wild in his patriotism, Lyon led possibly seven thousand men against the roughly seven hundred at Camp Jackson. Frost had neither attacked the arsenal nor retreated. Surrounded, he surrendered without a shot. During the march back to the arsenal the prisoners were guarded by the Germans and regulars. Excitement had been extreme in the city for days, with cries of "Hessians" against the Germans, and equally strong anti-Southern feelings expressed. A crowd of the curious and agitated viewed the march, including one William T. Sherman and his son, and of course it happened: someone pushed or shoved, a shot or two rang out, and then more and more with the unionists firing on the crowd. Accounts are many, facts few. When it was over some twenty-eight or twenty-nine people were dead or mortally wounded, including, reportedly, a child in arms. Mobs stormed through the streets of St. Louis that night; all saloons were closed. A strange sort of war: the "battle" of St. Louis.

Elsewhere, the Maryland legislature passed a resolution imploring President Lincoln to cease prosecuting the war against the South; authorities in Washington still almost hourly expected fighting in Maryland. The President himself continued to be involved with the business of appointments, both civil and military. Off Charleston U.S.S. *Niagara* began a blockade patrol. In Montgomery President Davis signed an act of Congress calling for purchase abroad of six warships, arms, and stores. Sec. of the Navy Mallory urged the building of ironclads because the obvious inequality of the Confederate Navy would have to be offset by quality, strength, and invulnerability. The Confederate government in Montgomery placed Virginia Maj. Gen. Robert E. Lee in command of Confederate troops in Virginia.

The Protestant Episcopal Diocese of Alabama announced its withdrawal from the Protestant Episcopal Church in the United States. A peculiar weapon known as the Winans steam gun was captured by Federals while being sent South from Baltimore.

May 11, Saturday

The rampant crowds in St. Louis continued to mill in the streets. At the northwest corner of Fifth and Walton, the Fifth Reserve Regiment tangled with the crowd and again firing broke out. Six or seven more persons died in the fray. William S. Harney arrived back in the city to resume his Federal command, much disturbed by Lyon's action. Slowly people became calmer, but the scars remained. Much discussion ensued; some felt St. Louis had been held for the Union, others felt the whole affair wrong. At any rate, with or without the Camp Jackson affair, St. Louis did remain Union and the secessionist voices gradually quieted.

At San Francisco business was suspended, flags waved, and people crowded the streets for a patriotic pro-Union demonstration complete with procession and speeches. But at the same time there were strong pockets of pro-secessionists in California, along with others who favored neutrality or even an independent Republic of the Pacific. Likewise a large Union meeting occurred at Wheeling, western Va.

May 12, Sunday

In St. Louis Gen. Harney, now back in Federal command, issued a proclamation saying the public peace must be preserved and the laws obeyed. There were reported attempts to damage railroads and bridges near Frederick and Baltimore, Md.

May 13, Monday

U.S. TROOPS OCCUPY BALTIMORE.

Without permission from Army Headquarters Brig. Gen. Benjamin F. Butler moved troops from Relay Station, Md., into Baltimore and took possession of Federal Hill. Butler claimed he had reports of a riot in the city. He added that he found several manufactories of arms, supplies, and munitions meant for the "rebels." Generally the move met with approval at the North, and probably did help keep down pro-Confederate activity, while at the same time rousing considerable resentment.

Queen Victoria officially issued a proclamation declaring Britain's determination to maintain a strict neutrality between contending parties in America, and to accord to both sides the rights of belligerents. British citizens were warned against assisting either side. U. S. Minister to Britain Charles Francis Adams arrived in London in the evening to learn the news. Adams had been instructed to try to prevent recognition of the South as a belligerent.

The Southern Baptist Convention meeting at Savannah tendered to the Confederacy their confidence and trust. The Virginia Union Convention assembled at Wheeling, western Va. Maj. Gen. George B. McClellan assumed command of the Department of the Ohio for the Federals.

May 14, Tuesday

In one of the strange anomalies of war, the Confederates had allowed the Baltimore & Ohio Railroad at Harper's Ferry to continue operating on the main line between Washington and the West. This was due to an unwillingness to alienate the people of Maryland. T. J. Jackson, however, determined to obtain some much needed rolling stock for the South. Therefore he ruled that the coal trains could not move at night and then, during the morning operations, bagged a large number of the trains, sending many of the locomotives to Winchester and Strasburg, Va.

In Baltimore Gen. Butler was extending his rule of the city, seizing suspected arms and persons, including Ross Winans, noted inventor of the steam gun. At Hampton Roads four blockade-runners were taken by Federal vessels. President Lincoln wrote Robert Anderson, now in Western command, that he should help pro-Union men in Kentucky receive arms from Cincinnati, despite the neutrality of Kentucky. Gen. Harney in St. Louis issued another proclamation maintaining that citizens should disregard the bill passed by the legislature raising pro-secessionist state troops. In Montgomery the Confederate Congress requested that President Davis declare a day of fasting and prayer. Gov. Thomas H. Hicks of Maryland called for four regiments to protect Maryland or the capital of the United States.

May 15, Wednesday

The Confederates named Brig. Gen. Joseph E. Johnston to command troops near Harper's Ferry now under T. J. Jackson. Off New Orleans the Confederate privateer *Calhoun* captured the bark *Ocean Eagle* from Rockland, Me. Nathaniel Lyon in St. Louis sent the Fifth Missouri Infantry out to Potosi, Mo., in Washington County to aid pro-Union citizens. Federal Brig. Gen. George Cadwalader was named to replace Brig. Gen. Butler in command of the Department of Annapolis, including Baltimore. Butler was sent to command Fort Monroe, the extremely vital Federal base in Virginia at Hampton Roads.

May 16, Thursday

Tennessee was officially admitted to the Confederacy by Congress at Montgomery. A Kentucky legislative committee on Federal relations proposed that the state remain neutral. Com. John Rodgers was ordered to set up Federal naval command on the rivers of the West under Gen. Frémont's command.

May 17, Friday

President Davis signed a bill authorizing a loan to the Confederacy of $50,000,000 and the issuance of treasury notes. The President also signed a bill admitting North Carolina to the Confederacy contingent upon approval of the ordinance of secession and ratification of the Constitution. John T. Pickett was named Special Agent of the Confederate States to Mexico. The California legislature pledged the state's support to the Federal government. Chief John Ross issued a proclamation of neutrality for the Cherokees in the Indian Territory.

May 18, Saturday

Arkansas was officially admitted to the Confederacy with her congressmen taking their seats at Montgomery. At Sewell's Point near Norfolk, Va., two Federal vessels briefly engaged a Confederate battery. President Lincoln wrote Missouri political leader Francis P. Blair, Jr., that Blair should withhold the discretionary order sent him the day before to remove Gen. Harney from St. Louis command. Harney had been relieved April 21 and restored May 8 and had gone back to St. Louis. Blair was watching Harney closely, feeling he was too tolerant of the pro-Confederate elements in St. Louis and Missouri. Delegations both pro- and anti-Harney had called on Lincoln.

The mouth of the Rappahannock River was blockaded, completing the increasingly effective blockade of Virginia.

May 19, Sunday

Confederate garrisons at Harper's Ferry were being reinforced by troops from the deep South as the position was strengthened. Captures by U.S. naval vessels of Confederate shipping slowly but steadily increased. Two Federal ships again dueled with the Confederate battery at Sewell's Point, Va., in Hampton Roads.

May 20, Monday

NORTH CAROLINA SECEDES.

CONFEDERATE CAPITAL TO MOVE.

In convention assembled at Raleigh, delegates voted unanimously for secession of North Carolina. At the same time the delegates ratified the Confederate Constitution, but defeated a move to submit the Constitution to popular vote. Thus the eleventh and last full state had left the Union; Kentucky and Missouri were to have both Confederate and Union governments. Gov. Beriah Magoffin of Kentucky issued a proclamation of neutrality. He forbade "any movement upon Kentucky soil" or occupation by either government and forbade citizens to make hostile demonstrations. The Provisional Congress of the Confederacy voted to move the capital of the nation from Montgomery, Ala., to Richmond, Va., a move calculated to ensure the support of Virginia.

In midafternoon U.S. marshals throughout the North descended upon telegraph offices and confiscated dispatches for the past year. The action was designed to uncover evidence against pro-secessionists and Confederate agents.

May 21, Tuesday

In Missouri Gen. Sterling Price, representing the state and the pro-secessionists, and Gen. Harney for the United States signed a proclamation in which they agreed that Price was to direct the power of the state officers to maintain order, and that Harney would not bring in the Federal Army if order were maintained. This was interpreted by Blair and Lyon as being a virtual surrender of the state.

In Washington President Lincoln sent a dispatch, signed and in part composed by Sec. of State Seward, to British minister Charles Francis Adams, instructing him to desist from contact with the British government as long as it continued intercourse with "the domestic enemies of this country."

On the last day of the second session of the Provisional Congress of the Confederacy President Davis announced that he had signed a bill to make the Provisional Constitution permanent. Meeting for the last time in Montgomery, Congress still debated moving the headquarters of the Confederacy. Some members favored other places or advocated Montgomery over Richmond. But the majority believed that military and psychological advantages gave the edge to the Virginia city. President Davis also signed one bill outlawing the payment by Southerners of money due Northern merchants, and approved another prohibiting cotton trade except through Confederate ports. The oldest active Federal warship, U.S.S. *Constellation,* veteran of the War of 1812, captured a slave ship off the mouth of the Congo.

May 22, Wednesday

Gen. Benjamin F. Butler arrived to take command at strategic Fort Monroe, Va. It was reported that the market in Europe for Confederate securities was weak.

May 23, Thursday

VIRGINIA CITIZENS APPROVE SECESSION.

The citizens of Virginia voted three to one in favor of secession. Many lukewarm secessionists felt they could not oppose the action of their state and, anyway, the referendum was after the fact. In western Virginia, however, the vote was overwhelmingly against secession, but that area was already breaking away from the Old Dominion. In the eastern and central parts of the state the vote was heavily in favor of secession. For the ordinance of secession, 96,750; against, 32,134.

Troops of Benjamin F. Butler moved out from Fort Monroe toward Hampton, Va., in a mild reconnaissance with little or no shooting. For almost a month, until June 17, Federal soldiers carried out scouting activities against Indians on the Mad and Eel rivers of California.

May 24, Friday

FEDERAL TROOPS ENTER VIRGINIA: TAKE ALEXANDRIA.

As stealthily as partially trained troops could move, the Federals advanced across the Potomac at Washington and occupied Alexandria, Va. A small Confederate detachment in the city quickly left as the three regiments, and other units, crossed by the Long Bridge or landed from steamers. The Virginia ends of the bridges were seized and by sunrise fortifications were going up. The Virginia troops retreated in good order; few shots were fired. The North had taken a primary step to defend its capital and set its foot upon the soil of Virginia.

Added to the strategy and the thrill of the first advance, was the tragic, dramatic death of youthful Elmer Ellsworth. Twenty-four, organizer of a famous Zouave drill team, Ellsworth led the First Fire Zouaves, or

Eleventh New York. Col. Ellsworth with a few companions rushing toward the center of Alexandria saw a secession flag flying from the Marshall House. Ellsworth and two others dashed in to haul down the enemy flag. Descending the stairs with the banner Ellsworth was confronted by the hotel keeper, James Jackson. Jackson blasted Ellsworth with his shotgun; Jackson was immediately fatally shot by Pvt. Francis E. Brownell.

Ellsworth's death plunged the North into a patriotic spasm of grief; the body lay in state in the White House. A friend of the President, Ellsworth became a martyr for the Federal cause. As the tears and cries of rage spread through the North, so, too, did Jackson become a martyr to the South. Poems, songs, graphic drawings circulated widely, dramatizing the incident. A beautiful and noble life ended, the Northern press proclaimed; "Jackson perished a'mid the pack of wolves," the South proclaimed. But as far as the war was concerned, the Federals had gained by force of arms a foothold on Virginia soil to add to that at Fort Monroe, maintained by wisely increased Federal garrisons.

Elsewhere, Gen. Benjamin Butler at Fort Monroe refused to give up three Negro slaves who came into his lines, holding them as "contraband" of war, thus raising the whole issue of treatment of slaves by the Federals. In Missouri the state troops of Gov. Jackson and Sterling Price refused to disband. A former U. S. Army captain, Ulysses S. Grant, offered his services to the Union but got no reply.

May 25, Saturday

Funeral services were held in the East Room of the White House for Col. Elmer Ellsworth. The President and Mrs. Lincoln were present. The President wrote the parents of young Ellsworth, "So much of promised usefulness to one's country, and of bright hopes for one's self and friends, have rarely been so suddenly dashed, as in his fall." Death in war was yet new—soon it would receive less attention.

President Davis wrote a committee of the Maryland legislature thanking them for their sympathies with the cause of vindicating "the right of Self-Government," and assuring them of the genuine desire for peace, but pointing out the failure of any peaceful relations with the United States.

May 26, Sunday

Maj. Gen. George B. McClellan, from Cincinnati, ordered three Federal columns into western Virginia to protect the Baltimore & Ohio Railroad and aid the pro-unionists of the area. The main drive was toward Grafton. Forces of Col. B. F. Kelley occupied Grafton on May 30, after a successful march across the Ohio.

Postmaster General Montgomery Blair of the United States ruled that postal ties with the Southern states would end May 31. Agitation continued both North and South over the Alexandria affair and the deaths of Ellsworth and Jackson, with hot words appearing editorially in many papers. Federal blockades were set up at Mobile by U.S.S. *Powhatan,* and at New Orleans by U.S.S. *Brooklyn.*

May 27, Monday

Troops of Gen. Butler from Fort Monroe were sent eight miles by boats to take Newport News, Va., the operation being completed without opposition by May 29. This gave the Federals at Fort Monroe a larger staging area for future operations.

Chief Justice William B. Taney ruled that the military arrest of John Merryman in Maryland had violated the privilege of the writ of habeas corpus and that the President did not have the authority to suspend this privilege. The case arose out of the arrest of Merryman for allegedly recruiting for a Confederate regiment and his imprisonment by Gen. Cadwalader in Baltimore. *Ex Parte Merryman* became a highly debated case. Cadwalader claimed that the President had authorized him to suspend the writ in such cases. President Lincoln later held he had the power of such suspension in certain cases and continued to execute it. His grounds were that the Constitution provided for suspension in cases of rebellion or invasion where public safety required it.

The President was concerned about events in Missouri and informed Gen. W. S. Harney that the reported mistreatment of citizens loyal to the Union should be stopped. Mr. Lincoln said that the professions of loyalty of the state authorities could not be relied upon.

May 28, Tuesday

Brig. Gen. Irvin McDowell assumed command of the Department of Northeastern Virginia, which included Federal troops in and around Alexandria. U.S.S. *Union* set up a blockade of the Confederate port of Savannah, Ga. In the British House of Commons debate opened on relations with both the United and Confederate States.

May 29, Wednesday

President Jefferson Davis arrived in the newly designated Confederate capital of Richmond, Va. A large assemblage led by Gov. John Letcher and military and civil dignitaries greeted him. The President had been ill on his trip from Montgomery, but had responded to the frequent stops when crowds called for "Jeff Davis." "The old Hero!" The trip was one continuous ovation.

In Washington the organization of nurses for the Army was well under way. Sec. of War Cameron had accepted the aid of Miss Dorothea Dix in establishing hospitals and caring for sick and wounded. For three days a trio of Federal vessels bombarded enemy batteries at Aquia Creek, Va.

May 30, Thursday

Federal troops under Col. B. F. Kelley occupied Grafton, western Va., in order to guard the Baltimore & Ohio Railroad and help protect pro-Union citizens in the western counties of Virginia. Appointment of officers and recruitment of troops continued both North and South and received most of the martial attention. Sec. of War Simon Cameron informed Gen. Butler at Fort Monroe that he should retain such fugitive slaves as came within his lines, employ them, and keep records of their services. The question of what to do about slaves within Federal lines had been raised by Butler and caused a great deal of correspondence and debate in Federal government circles, with Lincoln himself pondering the proper policy. Now the decision was that refugees should be cared for and given work in Federal military installations. At Norfolk, Va., the Confederates raised U.S.S. *Merrimack,* which had been burned when the Federals evacuated the navy yard.

May 31, Friday

The Federal Potomac Flotilla of three vessels shelled the Confederate batteries at Aquia Creek, Va., as part of the continuing small war going on along the Potomac River and Chesapeake Bay. The Confederates named Pierre Gustave Toutant Beauregard to command the Alexandria Line, which meant all the Southern troops in northern Virginia. He previously had commanded at Charleston. In a major Federal shift Brig. Gen. Nathaniel Lyon superseded William S. Harney in command of the Department of the West. Francis P. Blair and Lyon had finally exercised their authority, given them in mid-May, to relieve Harney when Blair thought necessary. The Harney-Price agreement to allow state authorities control, and the general's attempt to resolve things peaceably, had aroused great controversy. Harney felt the complaints of Union citizens in Missouri exaggerated, while Blair and Lyon were violently opposed to his pact with Price.

Federal troops arrived at Fort Leavenworth, Kas., from the Indian Territory after abandoning posts there. The course they followed became known as the Chisholm Trail, named for Jesse Chisholm, one of their guides.

JUNE, 1861

Prepare! Prepare! In the various states, they organized, gathered in the men, armed them after a fashion, paraded in gaudy uniforms if available, made speeches. More and more people realized that there was something called a war, but only a small part of the truth was dawning and that was the pretty part. Men came to the colors willingly, as state governments organized regiments, officered them in a somewhat haphazard manner, and sent them off to join the national banners. For the South there was not only an army to be organized, but a navy to be created. There would be considerable casting around to see how this could be done. What about the supplies, small arms, big guns, shot and shell, food, uniforms? Yes, it would be a problem, but there was tremendous hope this summer. Secession appeared to be succeeding every day, and the armies in the field and those gathering would cinch that success. At least many felt so. In the North there were still those who deplored the war and hoped for settlement, but they were fewer every day. Again there was the problem of men, guns, and supplies. Of course, there was more of everything than in the South, but it seemed quite a task at that. Patriotism was on the upsurge and speeches helped appear to make up for deficiencies. What few realized was that what had happened in the six weeks since the episode at Fort Sumter was hardly war—that would come later. All they knew was that the Federals were in Virginia around Alexandria and were moving into western Virginia—was that not action?

June 1, Saturday

Minor skirmishes occurred in northern Virginia at Arlington Mills and Fairfax Court House. Federal cavalry moved out to Fairfax, entered, and then pulled out. The insignificant affair attracted more attention than it deserved because serious fighting had not yet begun. Capt. John Q. Marr of the Confederacy was killed, one of the first Confederate battle deaths. Federal naval vessels continued to bombard enemy batteries in the Aquia Creek area of Virginia. At Cairo, Ill., junction of the Ohio and Mississippi rivers, the first thirty-two-pound ball was fired down the Mississippi as the big guns were planted in position.

In Richmond President Davis was serenaded and gave a patriotic address to the crowd, saying, "Upon us is devolved the high and holy responsibility of preserving the constitutional liberty of a free government." He claimed the North was "stripped of the liberty to which they were born" by "an ignorant usurper."

Great Britain, followed by other nations, proclaimed a policy of preventing belligerents from carrying prizes into any British ports or territorial waters.

June 2, Sunday

P. G. T. Beauregard took command of the Confederate forces in northern Virginia on the Alexandria Line. He succeeded Milledge L. Bonham. The force was known variously as the Department of Alexandria, the Potomac Department, and the Army of the Potomac. Federal forces moved out from Grafton, western Va., this night, heading southward in a heavy rain.

June 3, Monday

DEATH OF STEPHEN A. DOUGLAS.

PHILIPPI RACES, WESTERN VIRGINIA.

The "Little Giant" was dead. In Chicago the forty-eight-year-old senator from Illinois and former presidential candidate succumbed in the Tremont House of possible typhoid fever, following physical exhaustion. Personal financial difficulties, long campaigning, the war he sought to avoid, the rallying of strong support for the Union, and illness had finally downed one of the nation's prominent leaders. His last message to his two sons said, "Tell them to obey the laws and support the Constitution of the United States." In Washington President Lincoln denied himself to visitors in sorrow for the man who had beaten him for the U. S. Senate, and whom, in turn, he had beaten for the presidency. A Democrat, Douglas had long been the Northern leader of his party, the developer of popular sovereignty, and an advocate of western expansion. But Douglas had been all Union, as proved by the 1860 split in the Democratic party when he headed the ticket of the Northern wing against the South. Many disliked him politically but no one could deny his essential dedication to the country. The Union lost one of its strongest supporters and noblest soldiers with the death of the short, volatile, aggressive little man with the valiant spirit.

There were two main lines of attack through the mountains of western Virginia, and eventually the Federals utilized them both—one from Grafton, Philippi, and Beverly and the other from the Ohio River up the Great Kanawha Valley to Charleston. Brig. Gen. T. A. Morris of McClellan's command advanced from Grafton in two columns. Through the pitchy darkness and drenching rain over tortuous mountain roads the Federals filed. About daylight they struck at Philippi, completely surprising the sleeping Confederates. Col. G. A. Porterfield's command made no defense whatsoever, most of them fleeing, with the Federals in rapid pursuit. What few pickets there were failed. A joint report called the Confederate rout "disgraceful." A minor action, blown up in the press until it became known as the "Philippi Races," this skirmish did have some influence on the breaking away of western Virginia.

June 4, Tuesday

Southern papers suggested that slaves be employed on Confederate fortifications in place of the volunteer troops.

June 5, Wednesday

The Federal steamer *Harriet Lane* threw a few shells at the Pig Point batteries on the James River, Va., typical of the secondary actions of the period. At Manassas Gen. Beauregard issued a proclamation to the people of northern Virginia, saying, "A reckless and unprincipled tyrant has invaded your soil. Abraham Lincoln, regardless of all moral, legal, and constitutional restraints, has thrown his abolition hosts among you, who are murdering and imprisoning your citizens, confiscating and destroying your property, and committing other acts of violence and outrage too shocking and revolting to humanity to be enumerated." He added that the Federal "war cry is 'Beauty and booty,'" and called for citizens to rally to their state and country.

In Baltimore the U.S. marshal took possession of the gun factory of Merrill & Thomas. Federal authorities also seized powder from the Hazard Powder Co., Lower Canton, Conn., and from the Du Pont powder works in Delaware.

June 6, Thursday

Confederate Brig. Gen. Henry A. Wise, former governor of Virginia, was ordered to take command of troops in the Kanawha Valley of western Virginia. The Federal Cabinet decided that war expenses should be paid by the national government, except those of the states for mobilization prior to swearing in of the men.

June 7, Friday

Confederate troops carried out a minor reconnaissance from Yorktown to Newport News, Va. Federals blockaded Apalachicola, Fla. During funeral of Sen. Douglas, President Lincoln received no visitors. Government departments and many public schools in the North were closed, honoring the late senator from Illinois. The White House was draped in black.

June 8, Saturday

Tennessee voters approved secession by a large majority—104,913 for and 47,238 against. The eastern part of the state voted against secession two to one, but the rest was strongly pro-Confederate. The vote approved the previous action of the legislature, although Tennessee already was active in the Confederacy.

Brig. Gen. Robert S. Garnett was assigned to command Confederate troops in northwestern Virginia in an effort to stiffen defense after the failure of Porterfield at Philippi. Gov. John Letcher of Virginia officially transferred the forces of Virginia to the Confederate States. This put Gen. Robert E. Lee temporarily out of a regular job, as he had commanded the Virginia troops, but he still acted as adviser to President Davis. Mr. Lincoln and Sec. of War Cameron approved the setting up of the United States Sanitary Commission, which was to do so much to see to the health and comfort of the Federal soldiers.

June 9, Sunday

In the evening Federal troops moved out of Newport News and Fort Monroe against Confederate positions at Big Bethel or Bethel Church, Va. The night march for green troops ran into considerable trouble with Federals firing into their comrades by mistake.

June 10, Monday

ENGAGEMENT OF BIG BETHEL, VIRGINIA.

A strong Federal force of seven regiments from Fort Monroe had marched and blundered through the night to attack Confederate positions at Big or Great Bethel, also known as Bethel Church. The attack was hesitant and confused and after about an hour the Union troops had to retire. Among the Northern losses was Maj. Theodore Winthrop, a brilliant young author. Ebenezer W. Pierce was the Northern field commander under Benjamin F. Butler's direction. The Federals had something over 2500 men with 18 killed, 53 wounded, and 5 missing for 76. Confederates under the general command of Col. John Bankhead Magruder numbered about 1200 engaged with 1 killed and 7 wounded. This essentially small engagement gave encouragement to the South and caused some pain to the North. Trophies of the fight were displayed in Richmond store windows.

A Federal expedition under Col. Charles P. Stone began its march from the Washington area to Edwards' Ferry on the Potomac in what became known as the Rockville Expedition. During the period to July 7 there were several small skirmishes but the expedition did protect the Potomac line north and west of Washington.

Meanwhile, Federal captures of blockade-runners were increasing considerably, although a goodly amount of shipping still was getting through.

June 11, Tuesday

Delegates representing the pro-Union element in Virginia met at Wheeling to organize a pro-Union government that eventually became the state of West Virginia.

"This means war," said Gen. Nathaniel Lyon after he and Francis Preston Blair, Jr., met with pro-Confederate Gov. Claiborne Jackson and Gen. Sterling Price at the Planters' House in St. Louis to discuss a possible truce. Lyon declared that he would see the people of Missouri "under the sod" before he would allow the state to dictate Federal troop movements. Jackson and Price hurried back to Jefferson City and ordered the destruction of bridges over strategic rivers. Lyon began issuing troop movement orders.

In the far Southwest Col. Edward R. S. Canby took general charge of affairs in the Federal Department of New Mexico upon reports that Col. William W. Loring had abandoned his command to join the Confederacy.

June 12, Wednesday

Pro-Confederate Gov. Claiborne Jackson of Missouri called for fifty thousand state militia to protect citizens against what he termed Federal efforts to overthrow the state government. The steamer *City of Alton* moved down the Mississippi about five miles below Columbus, Ky., from Cairo, Ill., and seized a Confederate flag on shore despite the proclaimed "neutrality" of Kentucky.

June 13, Thursday

After a fatiguing march, some five hundred men of the Union command of Col. Lew Wallace entered Romney, western Virginia, after a brief fight. Following the raid, Wallace returned to Cumberland, Md. The intention had been to prevent alleged oppression of pro-Northern citizens by Confederates. At Harper's Ferry Gen. Joseph E. Johnston was pessimistic about holding that vital post because of lack of men. In the Confederacy a fast day was observed by proclamation of President Davis, to dramatize the needed war effort.

June 14, Friday

In what was called the Rockville Expedition the Federal troops of Col. Charles P. Stone fought a light skirmish near Seneca Mills, Md. Out in Missouri the pro-Confederates of Gov. Jackson evacuated the state capital at Jefferson City as Federal troops under Nathaniel Lyon drew near.

June 15, Saturday

Federal forces advanced in several areas. Confederates under Joseph E. Johnston evacuated Harper's Ferry, falling back in the Shenandoah Valley to Bunker Hill, north of Winchester. Johnston pulled out of the strategic point on the Potomac, burning the railroad bridge, due to the Federal raid on Romney and fear that troops of McClellan of western Virginia and Robert Patterson from the north might pinch off his small command. Patterson began to move forward cautiously upon the news of Johnston's withdrawal. On the Potomac Federals under C. P. Stone occupied Edwards' and Conrad's ferries. In Missouri Federals of Nathaniel Lyon entered Jefferson City. Pro-Confederate Gov. Jackson and his supporters moved westward to Boonville. Army engineers blasted a hundred-ton boulder which obstructed the Baltimore & Ohio track at Point of Rocks, Md. Confederates had pushed the rock down from the overhanging cliffs.

June 16, Sunday

The summer days of the early weeks of the war were active with enlistment, drilling after a fashion, equipping, shipment of troops, and all that goes into organizing for war. President Lincoln lent his moral support by often visiting camps along the Potomac, writing encouraging letters to governors, and carrying out the public relations aspects of his presidential post. There was of course confusion, waste, and ineptitude, but the job was being done on both sides.

June 17, Monday
ENGAGEMENT AT BOONVILLE, MISSOURI.

After capturing the state capital at Jefferson City on June 15 with no opposition and raising the Union flags to the strains of national airs, Nathaniel Lyon and his forces pressed on deeper into Missouri, following retreating Gov. Claiborne Jackson. Moving mainly by boat up the Missouri, Lyon landed about seventeen hundred men below Boonville, advanced on the town, and after a short fight occupied the place. Casualties were light on both sides, but it was in a sense a serious Confederate defeat. Not only were pro-Confederates in the area dispersed, but it helped the Union control the Missouri River and seriously hindered efforts to hold the pro-Southern part of Missouri north of the river. One Federal soldier wrote that in Missouri "We were both missionaries and musketeers. When we captured a man we talked him nearly to death; in other respects we treated him humanely. The Civil War was a battle of ideas interrupted by artillery." Following the loss of Boonville, pro-Southern Gov. Jackson, his small armed force, and his government "in transit" had to retire to the southwestern part of Missouri.

In Virginia there were several actions. Stone's Federals skirmished at Conrad's Ferry, Md., along the Potomac as part of the Rockville Expedition. There was also action near Vienna and New Creek, Va. At Vienna some Ohio troops were sent to repair and guard the Loudoun and Hampshire Railroad about fifteen miles from Alexandria when Confederates ambushed and captured the train. A brilliant little achievement by Col. Maxcy Gregg and his First South Carolina that meant little, but brought chagrin to the Federals.

At Washington balloonist Prof. Thaddeus S. C. Lowe and others ascended a short distance in the air to demonstrate the observation usefulness of balloons. Connected with the War Department by a telegraph wire, Prof. Lowe communicated with the President.

At Greeneville in east Tennessee a group of pro-unionists gathered to try to take action to keep their section of the state in the United States.

The government of Spain proclaimed its neutrality, but recognized the Confederacy as a belligerent, following the standard pattern of European powers.

June 18, Tuesday
Skirmishing continued along the Potomac, this time at Edwards' Ferry, Md. Occasional captures of blockade-runners still occurred—such as one

taken this day by U.S.S. *Union* off Charleston, S.C. At Boonville, Mo., Gen. Lyon issued another of his several proclamations warning Missourians against what he called "treason."

June 19, Wednesday

Francis H. Pierpoint was named provisional governor of Federal Virginia, or what was to become West Virginia, by a convention meeting in Wheeling. In Missouri pro-secessionists attacked pro-Union home guards, largely Germans, at Cole Camp. Accounts vary widely, but apparently the unionists were badly beaten with a minimum of fifteen killed and possibly many more. Chief John Ross of the Cherokees reminded his people in the Indian Territory of obligations to the United States under their treaties.

June 20, Thursday

The governor of Kansas issued a proclamation calling on citizens to organize military companies to repel attacks from pro-secessionists in Missouri.

June 21, Friday

There was criticism in Washington and elsewhere that the War Department had not prevented erection of Confederate batteries on the Potomac River. The convention of eastern Tennesseans meeting at Greeneville declared their preference for the Union and the Constitution.

June 23, Sunday

There was a mild skirmish at Righter, western Va. Prof. Lowe again went up in his balloon, this time as far as Falls Church, Va., where he observed Confederate troop positions. An artist was sent along to map the terrain. Gen. McClellan, in personal command in western Virginia, proclaimed that he would now prosecute the war vigorously. U.S.S. *Massachusetts* captured four vessels in the Gulf of Mexico.

June 24, Monday

Two U.S. gunboats shelled Confederate positions at Mathias Point, Va., on the Potomac, while on the Rappahannock there was a brief clash of gunboat and Confederates. There was a skirmish at Jackson, Mo. Major fighting for the moment was limited. President Lincoln showed his interest in military equipment by watching experiments with rifled cannon and the "Coffee Mill," an early rapid-firing weapon.

June 25, Tuesday

Many Northern cities, such as New York, were saying goodbye to their regiments as they left for Washington and other points. There was still a great spirit of celebration and exhilaration. The war remained almost a holiday to some.

June 26, Wednesday

Two minor skirmishes recorded—at Frankfort and on Patterson's Creek, in western Virginia.

June 27, Thursday

A Federal steamer tried to land troops on Mathias Point on the Potomac but Confederate troops rallied and drove them off. The chief of police of Baltimore, George P. Kane, was arrested on order of Maj. Gen. Nathaniel Banks. Kane was alleged to be pro-Confederate. At Dover, Del., a peace convention urged recognition of the Confederacy. In Washington representatives of the Army, Navy, and U. S. Coast Survey met to consider strategy on the Southern coasts. This board, in time, made a number of reports giving details of where and how landings could be made on the Atlantic and Gulf coasts. Many of their recommendations were carried out in combined operations that set up bases for both blockaders and land operations. It was one of the few key planning bodies in the total Federal strategy.

June 28, Friday

At Sacramento, Calif., the Central Pacific Railroad Company of California was incorporated for the purpose of aiding in completing a transcontinental railroad line. Midsummer brought minor but nasty hit-and-run incidents involving naval vessels and shore batteries in the lower Potomac and along the shores of Chesapeake Bay. On the night of June 28 a group of Confederates led by George N. Hollins boarded the side-wheeler *St. Nicholas,* a commercial vessel operating in Chesapeake Bay. Hollins, disguised as a woman, led his band in seizing the vessel. They then set out to search for U.S.S. *Pawnee,* but managed only to take three small commercial vessels on the twenty-ninth. Daring, dashing, adventurous, the incident meant little, but did sting the North's sensitivities.

June 29, Saturday

A special Federal Cabinet meeting with leading generals in attendance discussed future action, now being demanded by the public. Gen. Irvin McDowell outlined his plans for attacking the Confederates at Manassas and Gen. Scott explained his proposal for an expedition down the Mississippi River. Consensus seemed to be that the enemy in Virginia must be attended to first. There was fear that the public might lose enthusiasm. At the moment, though, the men were still streaming into Washington; the Eleventh Massachusetts Infantry had 25 baggage wagons for 950 men and on the White House grounds the Twelfth New York formed a hollow square during a flag raising by the President. In western Virginia there was a skirmish at Bowman's Place on Cheat River.

June 30, Sunday

Below New Orleans, C.S.S. *Sumter,* commanded by Raphael Semmes, ran the blockade and with three lusty cheers from the crew began a spectacular career as a commerce raider, causing consternation to Federal shipping. U.S.S. *Brooklyn* gave chase but soon lost her.

A brilliant comet crossed the skies. With a fiery head and a long streamer of light the dazzling comet cut across the midevening in a sudden, unexpected visit. Was it just an astronomical phenomenon or was it prophetic of something more? One paper said the scientists were astonished, the timid frightened, and that it had "taken the country by storm."

JULY, 1861

The war was young yet, and still it seemed a long time since mid-April. Event piled on event and certainly these unknown place names would last forever in history. But fortunately man cannot see far ahead, for if he had he would have known that the "great battles" of the early summer of 1861 were really not so very great, certainly in comparison with the struggles to come. But already it was clear there would have to be a big fight in Virginia, and that might well end the war before winter. The Federal advance in western Virginia seemed like a major invasion; citizens on both sides awaited news from Missouri. Out on the oceans the blockade was ponderously steaming into position but was yet a thin broken line rather easily evaded. On the other hand, the South could well use the cargoes from ships from foreign ports that never sailed, those that refused to attempt even the scanty blockade. And at home there was still intoxication; the war still had a bloom on it and was about to blossom again. The ideals for which it was being fought held glamour, courage, fascination. To the Confederate his new nation was a startling success, but then it was to be expected considering the people. To the Northerner there was some surprise things had gone as far as they had, but of course soon Northern power would crush this ridiculous secession. For that was still the main issue—could a handful of states simply pull out and set up for themselves?

July 1, Monday

The Federal War Department issued orders for raising U.S. troops in Kentucky and Tennessee as mobilization continued on both sides. Four members of the Baltimore Police Board were arrested by Federal authorities for alleged pro-Confederate activities in the city.

July 2, Tuesday

The Commanding General of the U. S. Army, Winfield Scott, was authorized by the President to suspend the writ of habeas corpus on or near any military line between the city of New York and Washington, presaging further suspension of the privilege.

Troops of Federal Brig. Gen. Robert Patterson crossed the Potomac at Williamsport, Md., into the Shenandoah Valley. Gen. Scott and Gen. Patterson, two aged warriors, argued over operations until finally on a bright midsummer day Patterson moved. It was part of the Federal plan to have Patterson march into the Shenandoah Valley to hold Confederate troops there while the main Union Army carried out a major attack toward Manassas. Meanwhile, the Confederates under Joseph E. Johnston had much the same idea—to hold Patterson in the valley and then shift their forces quickly to join Beauregard for offensive action toward Washington. Moving toward Martinsburg, western Va., the Federals pushed Confederate outposts before them, and there was a brisk skirmish at Falling Waters or Hoke's Run, western Va., a Union success.

In Washington President Lincoln reviewed troops and conferred with Maj. Gen. John Charles Frémont, who was slowly heading west to take command in Missouri, source of much worry to Federal authorities.

July 3, Wednesday

Federal troops of Gen. Robert Patterson advanced to Martinsburg, western Va., with Joseph E. Johnston's Confederate outposts falling back toward Winchester, Va. In New Mexico Territory Union forces abandoned Fort McLane. Galveston, Tex., was now blockaded as the Northern Navy extended its operations. President Lincoln conferred with his Cabinet on his message for Congress, due to convene the next day in special session.

July 4, Thursday

SPECIAL SESSION OF FEDERAL CONGRESS.

Independence Day. The great national holiday had come again and saw a country divided and at war. Patriotism was supreme as always, on both sides. In Washington the special session of the Thirty-seventh Congress gathered after being called by the President to deal with war measures. Many felt it should have been called sooner. Galusha A. Grow of Pennsylvania was elected Speaker of the House. In the message sent to Congress (dated July 4 but read to Congress July 5) the President outlined events since March 4, including the suspension of functions of the Federal government in areas of secession. Mr. Lincoln said he had exhausted all peaceful measures to solve the difficulties, and the Administration vowed to hold all public places and property. The President reviewed the Fort Sumter crisis and pointed out that to "abandon that position, under the circumstances, would be utterly ruinous . . . ." He denied that the South needed to assault Fort Sumter, as it was not an aggressive threat to them. He put the entire blame for opening the war upon the South. The issue "presents to the whole family of man, the question, whether a constitutional republic, or a democracy—a government of the people, by the same people—can, or cannot, maintain its territorial integrity, against its own domestic foes." And thus war came. The President then outlined the action instituted to mobilize and fight the war. He indicated that some measures taken were perhaps beyond the power of the President but since they were a public necessity he trusted that Congress would ratify them. Mr. Lincoln then recommended "that you give the legal means for making this contest a short, and a decisive one; that you place at the control of the government, for the work, at least four hundred thousand men, and four hundred millions of dollars." The President went on to make a strong case for the indivisibility of the Union and denied that secession was possible. "It was with the deepest regret that the Executive found the duty of employing the war-power, in defense of the government, forced upon him. He could but perform this duty, or surrender the existence of the government."

President Lincoln signed a temperance declaration (also signed by ten previous Presidents). There was a small skirmish at Harper's Ferry, Va., as part of the Federal advance into the Shenandoah, and another in Missouri at Farmington, south of St. Louis. Six blockade-runners were taken off Galveston, and two more on July 5.

July 5, Friday

ENGAGEMENT AT CARTHAGE, MISSOURI.

Gov. Claiborne Jackson, Confederate, in southwest Missouri with the itinerant government, was concerned about Nathaniel Lyon and the Federal troops in his rear. Now he discovered that Franz Sigel and his Germans were near Carthage in front of him. The governor's force, largely in civilian clothes, formed a line of battle and awaited Sigel's attack. The nondescript Missouri Southerners were hard pressed at first until their cavalry flanked both ends of Sigel's line. This forced the Federals judiciously to retreat, although the Northerners used their artillery to advantage. The Germans retired through Carthage and the Confederate pursuit ended at dark. The Federals had around 1100 men to some 4000 partly unarmed Confederates. Union losses were put at 13 killed and 31 wounded, and Confederates reported 40 to 50 killed and 120 wounded. At any rate, the Federal advance into southwest Missouri had received a setback. Sigel moved back to join Lyon at Springfield. Gov. Jackson marched southward to meet Sterling Price's army. In Virginia there was a small skirmish near Newport News.

Although officially dated July 4, the President's message was actually read to Congress on July 5. For the most part it met with enthusiastic approval of congressmen.

July 6, Saturday

The campaign in western Virginia became active again with skirmishing at Middle Fork Bridge east of Buckhannon. At a Cuban port C.S.S. *Sumter* deposited seven prizes taken in the first major commerce-raiding foray of the Confederates. They were later released by Cuba.

July 7, Sunday

There was skirmishing for several days at Bellington and Laurel Hill, western Va., and also one day of fighting at Glenville, where Federal troops were continuing their pressure on Confederate forces in the western counties of Virginia. There was a skirmish at Great Falls, Md. The pattern of frequent skirmishes and affairs was now becoming evident, nearly three months after war began. Clement L. Vallandigham, already known as favoring peace, visited Ohio regiments in Virginia and was greeted at one camp by a shower of stones, shouts, and anger which almost precipitated a riot.

July 8, Monday

Confederate Brig. Gen. Henry Hopkins Sibley was ordered to Texas to take command of Southern efforts to expel Union forces from New Mexico Territory. Since before secession irregular forces had been gathering under the guise of a "buffalo hunt," but really with the aim of conquering at least part of the Southwest for the South.

July 9, Tuesday

Slight action east and west—at Vienna, Va., and near Monroe Station, Mo.

July 10, Wednesday

After concentrating three brigades at Buckhannon and one at Philippi, western Va., McClellan was ready to move against Robert S. Garnett's much smaller Confederate force at Laurel Hill and Rich Mountain. With four regiments and cavalry Brig. Gen. William Starke Rosecrans, under McClellan, pressed forward with a skirmish at Rich Mountain July 10. At the same time Brig. Gen. T. A. Morris moved with a portion of the Federals from Philippi toward Laurel Hill. Meanwhile, Fort Breckinridge, N. Mex. Terr., was abandoned by Federals.

The Confederate government concluded a treaty with the Creek Indians, first of nine treaties arranged by agent Albert Pike. President Lincoln wrote Simon B. Buckner, inspector general of the Kentucky state guard, that he did not at present intend to send an armed force into neutral Kentucky. Buckner later was to join the Confederacy. The imperial Russian government instructed its ministry in Washington on its policy of neutrality.

July 11, Thursday

ENGAGEMENT OF RICH MOUNTAIN.

At Rich Mountain in western Virginia, about 2000 of McClellan's Federal troops, under the command of Rosecrans, attacked the position of Confederate Lieut. Col. John Pegram. Marching over rough terrain, Rosecrans surprised Pegram's left and, using an unguarded mountain path, got behind him, cutting off withdrawal to Beverly. Pegram was forced to surrender 555 Confederates on July 13. The victory opened the road for McClellan to Beverly. McClellan with the main Federal force was supposed to attack when Rosecrans made his move, but did not do so. McClellan received much credit for the victory, which, most historians agree, really belongs to Rosecrans, who originated the idea and performed the difficult part. To the north at Laurel Hill or Mountain, T. A. Morris' Federals demonstrated against the main Confederate force of Garnett. At Rich Mountain Pegram had about 1300 men, all told, and Garnett some 4000 at Laurel Hill. On the Federal side, Morris had about 4000 and McClellan and Rosecrans about 8000. Rosecrans lost 12 killed and 49 wounded, while Confederate reports of losses are unreliable. By midnight Garnett had evacuated his camp on Laurel Hill and, thinking falsely that he was unable to get to Beverly, turned off over Cheat Mountain into Cheat River Valley. To the west Jacob D. Cox began his movement toward Charleston, western Virginia, from the junction of the Ohio and Great Kanawha rivers.

The U. S. Senate expelled the senators from Virginia, North Carolina, Arkansas, and Texas, plus one from Tennessee. This was mere formality; they had already left.

July 12, Friday

Confederates under Garnett were retreating from Laurel Hill into the Cheat River Valley after the defeat on July 11. Part of Pegram's command from Rich Mountain escaped to Staunton, Va., although not far from half had to surrender July 13. McClellan occupied Beverly, western Va., about noon. To the north Morris and his Federals were pursuing Garnett.

Meanwhile, to the west and south another Federal column of about three thousand under Jacob Cox was moving up the Great Kanawha Valley against Brig. Gen. Henry A. Wise, former governor of Virginia. The movement began on July 11, by boat and on foot, from the mouth of the Kanawha where it joins the Ohio. On the twelfth they were well advanced up the winding river, moving into the craggy mountains.

Albert Pike signed treaties for the Confederates with the Choctaw and Chickasaw Indian nations in the Indian Territory.

July 13, Saturday

CONFEDERATES DEFEATED AT CORRICK'S FORD IN WESTERN VIRGINIA.

Attempting to save a part of his Confederate army, Brig. Gen. Robert S. Garnett crossed Cheat Mountain in his continuing retreat from Laurel Hill into Cheat River Valley. T. A. Morris with troops of McClellan's command had pursued Garnett in the rain. About noon the skirmishing began as the Confederates tried to protect their slowly moving wagons. Action increased at Corrick's Ford (a place of several spellings, often Carrick's). Garnett himself was killed a bit farther on while trying to withdraw his skirmishers. The Federal pursuit was now discontinued. McClellan's campaign plus the other operations in western Virginia gave the Union control of the mountain area, rivers, and other communication lines, and protected Northern east-west railroads. In addition, raiding parties from the area could constantly threaten Virginia itself. The fighting may not have been major compared to what was to come, but the significance of the western Virginia campaign has often been overlooked. At Corrick's Ford the Confederates suffered an estimated 20 killed and wounded and some 50 captured, with a total loss for the campaign of around 700, including the 555 men of Pegram who had surrendered at Beverly this day. Federals suffered only some 10 casualties, by one report. Other Federal troops fought an action at Red House near Barboursville, as part of the campaign along the Kanawha River in western Virginia.

President Lincoln signed a bill empowering him to collect customs at ports of delivery and to declare the existence of insurrection where the law could not be carried out.

July 14, Sunday

The blockade at Wilmington, N.C., was set up by U.S.S. *Daylight,* but soon required a large number of vessels. Brig. Gen. Henry Rootes Jackson at Monterey, Va., assumed command of Confederate forces that had escaped from the Rich Mountain-Laurel Hill-Corrick's Ford fighting. Pressure was mounting steadily in the North for an advance by McDowell's army into Virginia. From the beginning of hostilities there had been such a demand, but now it rose to a crescendo with Horace Greeley's "Forward to Richmond" on the masthead of the New York *Tribune,* and other such agitation. As a preliminary, Federal troops carried out a reconnaissance from Alexandria. News of the victories in western Virginia only increased the impatience for action at the North. Furthermore, Gen. Patterson in the Shenandoah seemed stalled south of Harper's Ferry, where he opposed J. E. Johnston's Confederates.

July 15, Monday

A small force of Confederate cavalry fought with front units of Gen. Patterson's Federals advancing from Martinsburg to Bunker Hill, north of Winchester in the Shenandoah Valley of Virginia. "Granny" Patterson, as some soldiers called him, said he would attack if occasion presented itself, but he seemed reluctant to find the occasion. In western Virginia there was a slight skirmish at Bowman's Place on Cheat River as the campaign in that area slowed down. As the news of victory in western Virginia spread over the North, the name of McClellan became a household word and he was the first real "hero general" of the war for the Federals. While the campaign was well planned by McClellan and well handled by his underlings, McClellan reaped a reputation that overran the events, in the opinion of many. Out in Missouri there was a minor skirmish at Mexico and another at Wentzville.

July 16, Tuesday

"Forward to Richmond! Forward to Richmond—The Rebel Congress must not be allowed to meet there on the 20th of July! BY THAT DATE THE PLACE MUST BE HELD BY THE NATIONAL ARMY!" For nearly a month now the New York *Tribune* and others had been so crying. And on this day the Federal army of Irvin McDowell moved out westward from the Potomac in the general direction of Centreville and Manassas, Va. At Manassas Brig. Gen. Beauregard had been in command since June 1; until now his Confederate force numbered some 22,000 men. McDowell's approximately 35,000 men paraded from the Washington area, making only six miles westward and slightly south the first day. As the jubilant Federals marched out "on the sacred soil of Old Virginia" they believed they were en route to Richmond, singing "John Brown's Body."

Beauregard had been expecting a Federal advance and there had been numerous rumors. Also he was planning on a quick switch of Joseph E. Johnston's troops from the Shenandoah to Manassas to enlarge his army. Out in western Virginia there was a slight skirmish at Barboursville. The Confederate prize crew of the schooner *S. J. Waring* was surprised and captured by the Yankee prisoners on the vessel led by William Tilghman, a Negro. The vessel got to New York on the twenty-second.

July 17, Wednesday

The morning papers of Washington carried the news—the Federal armies were advancing! Gen. Beauregard read it and, in fact, had heard it the night before by message sent from spy Mrs. Rose Greenhow in Washington. The Confederate commander wired President Davis that his outposts had been assailed and that he had "fallen back on the line of Bull Run near Manassas." Davis told Beauregard reinforcements were coming. Richmond ordered J. E. Johnston to move his force from the Shenandoah to Manassas "if practicable." Practicable it proved, because Gen. Patterson had pulled his Federals back to Charles Town rather than keeping pressure on the enemy by moving toward Winchester as ordered. Johnston was thus allowed to disengage and cross the mountains to aid Beauregard. On the Manassas front there was skirmishing at Fairfax Court House and Vienna as McDowell's Federals continued their march out from Washington. At Fairfax Court House they halted for the night, McDowell reporting his men too exhausted to go on. There they found large quantities of supplies and equipment left by the hastily departing Confederates.

Out in Fulton, Mo., there was a light skirmish. On the Great Kanawha where Jacob D. Cox was advancing into western Virginia toward Charleston the Federals were held up temporarily in the action at Scarey Creek where Confederates of Brig. Gen. Henry A. Wise blocked their advance up the river valley.

President Lincoln approved a loan passed by Congress for $250,000,000 in bonds and notes.

July 18, Thursday

ENGAGEMENT AT BLACKBURN'S FORD, VIRGINIA.

McDowell's Federal Army of Virginia moved slowly and with care from Fairfax Court House, Va., to Centreville, arriving about noon of a very warm day. Confederates under J. E. Johnston were moving rapidly by foot and rail from the Shenandoah Valley, heading toward Beauregard at Manassas. Patterson, with a superior Federal force, had failed to keep Johnston occupied. Beauregard at Manassas now had a line about eight miles long on Bull Run. Contemplating operations against the Confederate right, McDowell sent men of Brig. Gen. Daniel Tyler under Col. I. B. Richardson toward Blackburn's Ford in a reconnaissance that went farther than ordered. A fairly strong engagement followed, in which James Longstreet's men repulsed the Federals at Blackburn's Ford, and there also was skirmishing at Mitchell's Ford. Confederate losses were put at 15 killed and 53 wounded. Federal losses in the action that was unordered by McDowell were 19 killed, 38 wounded, and 26 missing. The fighting did reveal Beauregard's strength and caused McDowell to change his tactics. For the Confederates the action, which they later, confusingly, called the Battle of Bull Run, gave confidence to the men. Davis told Beauregard, "God be praised for your successful beginning."

Other action this day, outside Virginia, was at Martinsburg and Harrisonville, Mo.

July 19, Friday

McDowell's Federals brought forward supplies and prepared for further advance. The delay gave the Confederates time to strengthen their defenses along Bull Run, and, most important, Johnston's men from the Shenandoah were getting closer. In fact, the First Brigade of Thomas Jonathan Jackson arrived at Manassas Junction by 4 P.M. That evening at the Wilbur McLean House Gen. Beauregard and his generals were surprised when Gen. Jackson walked in and reported his arrival. Other troops of Johnston were behind him, some delayed by traffic problems on the single-line Manassas Gap railroad. A battle was clearly imminent near Manassas. There were a couple of minor affairs at the Back River Road and near New Market Bridge, Va.

Gen. McClellan issued an order congratulating his army for the victories in western Virginia and not too indirectly congratulating himself as well. In northern Missouri Brig. Gen. John Pope proclaimed that all who took up arms against the Union would be dealt with "without awaiting civil process."

July 20, Saturday

About sunrise more men of Joseph E. Johnston arrived to join Jackson's 2500 now at Manassas to reinforce Beauregard's threatened Confederates. To the new force 1400 more troops were added about noon, and Johnston himself arrived. There was a conference that night with Johnston, now the top commander, and Beauregard, to plan the Confederate attack. The strategy would be to swing with the Confederate right flank against the Federal left. Meanwhile, on the Federal side, McDowell had his plans too. They called also for a flanking movement, but by the Federal right against the Confederate left. Strangely, this could have resulted in both armies going in a circle. McDowell began his movement about 2:30 A.M. July 21, taking some 13,000 men from Centreville toward Sudley Ford on Bull Run, while other troops were to move against the Stone Bridge over Bull Run. Both plans were good; now it was a matter of execution by the newly gathered armies. A Federal soldier noted "the ominous stillness before a great struggle." The waiting would be over within a few hours.

President Lincoln received a report on McDowell's army from Sec. of War Simon Cameron, who had been out to Headquarters. In Richmond President Davis, anxious to go to the front, was doing all he could to aid Beauregard and Johnston. But the Confederate Congress convened today at the Capitol, with a sense of excitement at the "big battle" of the war impending to the north. In his message, read to Congress, President Davis told of the new states of Arkansas, North Carolina, Tennessee, and Virginia joining the Confederacy and of the shifting of the capital to Richmond. After discussing the background of secession, the President reported on the raising of armies, the abundant crops, the financial situation, and the eagerness of citizens to join the Army; "To speak of subjugating such a people, so united and determined, is to speak a language incomprehensive to them."

Brig. Gen. William W. Loring was assigned to command the Confederate Northwestern Army in western Virginia. Far to the west a Federal expedition operated from Springfield to Forsyth, Mo., until July 25.

July 21, Sunday

BATTLE OF FIRST BULL RUN OR MANASSAS, VIRGINIA.

"The stirring mass looked like a bristling monster lifting himself by a slow, wavy motion up the laborious ascent," an eyewitness reported. The Union army of Irvin McDowell was advancing to battle. The Federal commander, not knowing J. E. Johnston's men had arrived to swell the Confederate host, moved about 13,000 of his force of some 37,000 men during the bright moonlight night from Centreville around westward and south to turn the Confederate left and achieve surprise. About five-fifteen in the morning the Union artillery north of Bull Run opened fire. Then about eight-thirty the Confederates defending the Stone Bridge were told of the Federal column at Sudley Ford on the Southern left flank. McDowell's advance had been delayed by poor discipline, a night march, and inferior roads. Brig. Gen. N. G. Evans saw the threat and moved a portion of his small command to meet the Federals. The Confederate generals were informed of the surprise by E. P. Alexander and others.

J. E. Johnston and Beauregard, due to a mix-up in orders, had not been able to launch the Confederate drive against the Union left before learning of the well-planned Federal advance. Now the 35,000 Confederates would have to be on the defensive. The main battle began in midmorning as Evans opposed the Union column advancing from Sudley Ford upon the Southern left. He urgently called for help and it soon came, but of necessity by pieces, being brought in from the Confederate right and from encampments around Manassas Junction. Main help at first came from Barnard Bee, and the Confederates held until nearly noon when increased Federal troops moved into the attack. The Southern forces were compelled to retreat in some confusion, back over Young's Branch to the Henry House Hill. Here they made their stand with Bee, Francis Bartow, Evans, and Jackson. Here came the famous incident when Barnard Bee, who was soon to fall mortally wounded, shouted, "Look! There is Jackson standing like a stone wall! Rally behind the Virginians!" Here was won, in the midst of battle, Jackson's sobriquet, "Stonewall." Johnston and Beauregard arrived on the field as the Confederate line stiffened and even advanced. At approximately 2 P.M. McDowell's men ran forward two batteries to an exposed position near the Henry House. Confederates attacked the guns and seized them. Charges and countercharges ensued. Beauregard, directing the immediate fighting, advanced to clear the Henry House Hill area. Other Confederates, some of them fresh from the Shenandoah, moved up on the left and struck the Federal right in flank and rear. Coming shortly before 4 P.M., the Confederate drive ended the battle with a tremendous success. The Federal line fell back, at first in moderately good order. But as McDowell's men turned back over Bull Run, defeated, confusion mounted. A Confederate shell hit a wagon on Cub Run Bridge, jamming the main retreat route to Centreville. Panic took over some Federal troops. On the other hand, there were unblooded Northern units who did stand ground, and perhaps the extent of the Federal rout has been exaggerated. Soldiers mingled with congressmen and other sightseers who had come out to see the battle. As for the Confederates, no real follow-up was attempted or probably possible—for they had been in a terrific fight. There were heavy casualties on both sides, at least for that day, and the men were physically exhausted from their efforts, the heat, and the emotional strain of battle.

The dead and wounded gave witness to the severity of the first great battle of the war. Federals, 460 killed, 1124 wounded, and 1312 missing for 2896; Confederates, 387 killed, 1582 wounded, and 13 missing for 1982. A Confederate described it as "a square stand-up fight" in open terrain by novices at warfare. A Federal said, "This was war; compact, well-made and reasoning war. It was war, too, in all its panoply and glory, as well as in its strength."

At Washington that night the Cabinet met, Mr. Lincoln heard from civilian eyewitnesses to the reported stampede and spent the night calmly listening to the news. Mr. Davis, who had arrived at Manassas in time to witness the victory, was discussing the next move with Genls. Johnston and Beauregard. The argument continued for years over whether the Confederates could have gone on into or nearer to Washington that Sunday night or the next day, but the fact is they didn't. First Bull Run or First Manassas was over. Though there was dissatisfaction at the North, there also was a realization that this was a war and the people had better get busy and pull together. For the South it perhaps gave a bit of overconfidence—the Southern soldier had proved himself and the infant nation had taken a grown-up step forward.

Meanwhile, over in the Shenandoah, where most of Johnston's men had joined Beauregard, there was a brief skirmish at Charles Town. Gen. Scott in Washington ordered Maj. Gen. N. P. Banks to relieve Maj. Gen. Patterson in command of the Department of the Shenandoah, blaming Patterson for the failure to hold Johnston in the valley. Far to the west U.S. troops skirmished with Indians on the south fork of the Eel River in California.

July 22, Monday

Dismay over First Bull Run or Manassas spread in the North and elation spread in the South. The Confederate Congress in Richmond called for a day of thanksgiving. In Washington Maj. Gen. George B. McClellan, youthful victor in western Virginia, was ordered to come take command of the army which had suffered such a defeat under McDowell. Orders for reorganization were issued. Of course, McDowell had to be a scapegoat, although his strategy had been sound, and, while not a brilliant soldier, he had many capabilities.

While all attention was on Virginia, troops did skirmish at Etna and Forsyth, Mo., with the Federals capturing Forsyth.

In Washington the House of Representatives passed a resolution (the Crittenden Resolution) announcing that the war was being waged "To defend and maintain the supremacy of the Constitution and to preserve the Union," and not to interfere with slavery or subjugate the South. In Missouri the State Convention meeting at Jefferson City affirmed the loyalty of the state, declared the state offices vacant, and set up a new government July 31 with unionist Hamilton R. Gamble as governor. The capital was moved to St. Louis. Meanwhile, the pro-Confederate state government under Claiborne Jackson also claimed to represent the state.

July 23, Tuesday

While the reverberations of Bull Run or Manassas continued in both capitals and both nations, people did wonder what was coming next. It seemed that the battle in Virginia had ended one phase of the war or started another. Federal command changes continued, with Maj. Gen. John A. Dix taking over the Department of Maryland, and Brig. Gen. W. S. Rosecrans assuming command of the Department of the Ohio, which included western Virginia. In New Mexico Territory Federal troops were forced to abandon Fort Buchanan.

President Lincoln was busy indeed, but he did jot down a memorandum of military policy, a result of the Bull Run defeat. In this he suggested pushing the blockade, strengthening forces in the Shenandoah Valley, reorganizing the troops around Washington, bringing new men forward quickly, and in general firmly standing and preparing for increased war.

July 24, Wednesday

Confederate troops of Brig. Gen. Henry A. Wise at Tyler Mountain in western Virginia, near Charleston, retreated as the Federals of Jacob D. Cox, after a difficult march, began to attack the rear of the Confederate camp. During the night Wise pulled his entire force out of Charleston and vicinity and retired toward Gauley Bridge. There was slight skirmishing also at Back River, Va., and at Blue Mills, Mo., but fighting for the moment was limited.

July 25, Thursday

The United States Senate, following the course of the House, passed the Crittenden Resolution that the present war was being fought to maintain the Union and Constitution and not to interfere with established institutions such as slavery. Andrew Johnson of Tennessee moved adoption. The vote was 30 to 5.

Three new Federal commanders assumed important posts—Maj. Gen. Banks superseded Patterson in the Shenandoah, Maj. Gen. Dix took command in Baltimore, and Maj. Gen. John Charles Frémont assumed his post of command in the Western Department at St. Louis, soon to be a subject of much controversy.

There was skirmishing at Dug Springs in southwest Missouri, and indications were that more action would be seen in the general area of Springfield soon. There also was fighting at Harrisonville, Mo. In New Mexico Territory a force of Confederates moving up the Rio Grande were attacked at Mesilla by Maj. Isaac Lynde and his troops from nearby Fort Fillmore. The Confederates under Capt. John R. Baylor numbering about 250 had moved up from El Paso, Tex. They were part of the famous "buffalo hunt" organized by Baylor before action began—a group meant to attempt to take the Southwest out of Union control. Lynde made a desultory attack which was easily repulsed. In western Virginia Federals under Jacob Cox occupied Charleston on the Great Kanawha. Northern balloon observation operations began at Fort Monroe.

Robert Mercer Taliaferro Hunter, Virginia lawyer and political figure, was named Secretary of State of the Confederacy, succeeding Robert Toombs, who resigned to enter military service.

July 26, Friday

FEDERALS SURRENDER FORT FILLMORE, NEW MEXICO TERRITORY.

During the night and early on the twenty-seventh Major Isaac Lynde, Seventh U. S. Infantry, abandoned Fort Fillmore near Mesilla, N. Mex. Terr., in the face of Confederates under Capt. John R. Baylor. Although outnumbering the enemy 500 to 250, Lynde pulled out, heading for Fort Stanton.

At McCulla's Store, Mo., there was a small affair. Brig. Gen. Felix K. Zollicoffer was assigned Confederate command in east Tennessee.

July 27, Saturday

GENERAL MCCLELLAN ASSUMES COMMAND OF DIVISION OF THE POTOMAC.

Maj. Gen. George B. McClellan was officially put in command by

President Lincoln of the Federal Division of the Potomac, which included all troops in the vicinity of Washington. He had been called to the post the day after Bull Run and replaced defeated Maj. Gen. McDowell.

After giving up Fort Fillmore without a fight, Maj. Isaac Lynde surrendered his ten companies to Capt. John R. Baylor at San Augustine Springs, N. Mex. Terr., without firing a shot. The surrender left a large part of New Mexico open to Confederate invasion. Maj. Lynde was discharged from the Army in November, but after the war this was revoked and he was put on the retired list.

Mr. Lincoln added to his memo of July 23 regarding moves to be made following Bull Run. He wrote that Manassas Junction, Va., and Strasburg in the Shenandoah should be seized and that a joint movement be made from Cairo on Memphis and from Cincinnati on east Tennessee. The latter seems difficult in view of the "neutrality" of Kentucky. A congressional act was approved that called for indemnification of the states for expenses in defending the nation.

July 28, Sunday

Confederate troops occupied New Madrid, Mo., an important defensive point on the Mississippi just across from the Tennessee-Kentucky state line. Gen. R. E. Lee left his post as adviser in Richmond for an inspection in western Virginia, where the Confederates had suffered serious defeats. In the Confederacy a day of thanksgiving was observed for success of Southern arms in defending their homes.

July 29, Monday

Horace Greeley, who had called for "Forward to Richmond" in his New York *Tribune,* now wrote the President favoring negotiations for peace. Federal vessels of the Potomac flotilla dueled with a new Confederate battery and there was action against batteries at Marlborough Point, Va., also on the Potomac. There was a skirmish at Edwards' Ferry, Md., on the Potomac. Congress was rapidly approving the various measures already put into effect by the President. Today Mr. Lincoln approved a bill to call out the militia to suppress rebellion, which amended the old 1795 militia act. The Regular Army was enlarged by nine infantry regiments and one each of cavalry and artillery. Federal Brig. Gen. John Pope assumed command in northern Missouri.

July 30, Tuesday

The Federal troops of Jacob Cox had moved up the Great Kanawha Valley from Charleston and entered the area of Gauley Bridge. Gen. Benjamin F. Butler in command at Fort Monroe again wrote Sec. of War Cameron seeking clarification of policy on the continuing problems of "contraband," as he designated former slaves who came into Federal lines. He had some nine hundred Negroes in his care and asked "What shall be done with them?" He raised the question of whether or not they were property. The problem included their treatment under the fugitive slave law, but Butler had used the Negro men on fortifications and was anxious to make them an instrument of war by refusing to return them to the rebels.

July 31, Wednesday
The State Convention of Missouri formally elected Hamilton R. Gamble as pro-Union governor of the state, replacing pro-Confederate Claiborne Jackson. Gamble was inaugurated and made a patriotic speech. An act of the Federal Congress was approved which defined conspiracy against the United States and set up punishments for the crime of overthrowing or attempting to put down or destroy by force the government of the United States. Naval activity had been high during the latter part of July with Confederate privateers and C.S.S. *Sumter* active, while at the same time Federal blockaders were making their presence felt. President Lincoln nominated obscure Col. Ulysses S. Grant and others as Brigadier Generals of Volunteers.

AUGUST, 1861

That "big" battle was over and by August the true import of First Bull Run was discernible. Washington was still very much in Federal hands. The Confederates in Virginia showed no signs of invading the North. It was a time of stocktaking militarily, economically, politically, and spiritually, as it was obvious now that the war was going to last a few months at least. This was the legacy of First Bull Run or Manassas both North and South. Prepare, prepare, prepare, was the pattern of late summer. So far nothing of great excitement had broken loose in the uncertain West beyond the Alleghenies, but there were indications that out in Missouri a clash would be forthcoming. The Confederacy had not collapsed at one blow, and, taking a deep breath, they planted the feet of their new nation firmly. At the same time, the North, more united now, realized that there was no quick solution. The conflict was more serious than most people had been able to conceive.

August 1, Thursday
Gen. R. E. Lee, C.S.A. Army, and adviser to President Davis, arrived in western Virginia on an uncertain mission to coordinate and inspect the various Confederate forces there. However, the mission soon

developed into his taking command, replacing W. W. Loring, who had succeeded slain Gen. Garnett.

Way to the southwest in New Mexico Territory, John R. Baylor, with his "buffalo hunters" who were really Confederate soldiers, proclaimed in the name of the Confederacy the possession of all New Mexico and Arizona south of the 34th parallel. Pro-unionists of New Mexico, however, considered it more of a "Texas invasion." There was a slight skirmish at Endina, Mo. Brazil recognized the Confederate States of America as a belligerent.

President Davis wrote from Richmond to Gen. Joseph E. Johnston at Manassas on military matters and said, "We must be prompt to avail ourselves of the weakness resulting" from the moral effect produced by the Bull Run defeat of the Federals. The U. S. Senate debated a bill to suppress insurrection and sedition. The Onandaga County, N.Y., Cavalry, eighty strong, left for war with a young bride, Mrs. Cook, accompanying her husband as "daughter of the regiment." President Lincoln appointed Gustavus Vasa Fox Assistant Secretary of the Navy. Fox had been chief clerk of the department and already had a prominent role in the administration of things naval.

August 2, Friday

The Federal Congress passed the first national income tax measure, calling for 3 per cent on incomes of over $800. The bill also provided for new and stiffer tariffs.

Northern forces abandoned Fort Stanton, N. Mex. Terr., in the face of the Confederate invasion of the Southwest. At Dug Springs, Mo., not far from Springfield, a skirmish showed Federals that opposition forces of Missourians and Confederates were in the area. In southeastern Missouri there was a Federal reconnaissance from Ironton to Centreville.

While Gen. Nathaniel Lyon was expecting serious trouble in southwestern Missouri, the department commander, Gen. Frémont, was steaming down the Mississippi from St. Louis with eight boats and reinforcements, which were enthusiastically welcomed at Cairo, Ill.

At Fort Monroe, Va., Gen. Butler banned the sale of intoxicating liquors, but soldiers found ways of evading the order. Whisky was found in the gun barrels of pickets and in hair oil bottles.

August 3, Saturday

Fighting was still meager, with only a skirmish at McCulla's Store, Mo., and at Mesilla, N. Mex. Terr. But in Washington and Richmond activities were much more brisk. President Lincoln and his Cabinet conferred on a memorandum of Gen. McClellan regarding military affairs. Prince Napoleon of France visited the President at noon and found a notable lack of ceremony at the White House. In the evening the Lincolns gave a dinner for the prince.

Federal congressional acts approved included one for construction of one or more armored ships and floating batteries, and another for better organization of the Army. A number of military commissions were affirmed by the Senate. The Navy ordered certain Southern ports to be blockaded by sinking old vessels loaded with stone in the main channels, a method that proved ineffective.

In Baltimore military authorities seized a steamer after finding aboard contraband consisting of arms, ammunition, percussion caps, and quinine, all meant for the South. The ladies of upstate New York sent Lincoln thirteen hundred havelocks, a headdress supposed to keep dust and heat from the soldiers and made in great numbers with loving care, but given scant use by the men.

A balloon ascension was made at Hampton Roads from the deck of a Federal vessel. Scouting after Indians occupied Federal troops until the twelfth from Fort Crook to Round Valley, Calif.

August 4, Sunday

A quiet Sunday, and in New York a meeting was held to combat intemperance in the Federal Army. In Richmond President Davis wrote Beauregard at Manassas that as far as following up the Federal retreat at the late battle was concerned, "it would have been extremely hazardous to have done more than was performed."

August 5, Monday

The Federal Congress was winding up its thirty-four-day special session. Measures approved by Lincoln included an authorization for the President to enlist seamen for the entire length of the war; a tariff increase; issuance of new bonds; and a new, direct $20,000,000 real estate and income tax. After Jan. 1, 1862, the income tax of 3 per cent on incomes over $800 would go into effect. It was never enforced and was revised in 1862.

Fighting was confined to skirmishes at Athens, Mo., and opposite Point of Rocks, Md., in Virginia. The Confederate prize bark *Alvarado* was run ashore and burned by U.S.S. *Vincennes* near Fernandina, Fla. Off Galveston, Tex., a few shots were fired by blockaders, replied to by Confederate shore batteries. Federal troops under Gen. Nathaniel Lyon were falling back on Springfield, Mo., from Dug Springs upon reports that a large force of Confederate and Missouri state men were moving upon the major city of southwestern Missouri.

August 6, Tuesday

The Federal Congress adjourned after approving all acts, orders, and proclamations of the President concerning the Army and Navy issued after March 4, 1861. Mr. Lincoln was at the Capitol to sign bills, including one freeing slaves employed or used by Confederates in arms or labor against the United States, and another establishing increased pay for the private soldier. He hesitated, but signed the first act that confiscated property used for purposes of insurrection against the nation.

As a Kentucky congressman declared in the House that Kentucky was still firmly in the Union, near Lexington a pro-Union camp named Dick Robinson was established over the protest of pro-secessionists and neutralists.

August 7, Wednesday
The village of Hampton, Va., near Fort Monroe was burned by Confederate forces under Brig. Gen. John Bankhead Magruder in operations against Butler's Federal forces. Magruder said he had learned Butler had intended to use the town for what he called "runaway slaves" and what Butler called "contraband." Butler claimed the few residents remaining were given fifteen minutes to leave and that it was a "wanton act."

Federal authorities ordered construction of seven special ironclad gunboats of a new type from James B. Eads of St. Louis for operation on western waters. These, along with some converted steamers, were to become the backbone of the Union river flotilla.

Aug. 7–10 there was a small Federal expedition from Cape Girardeau, operating to Price's Landing, Commerce, Benton, and Hamburg, Mo.

August 8, Thursday
President Davis signed acts of the Confederate Provisional Congress to grant commissions to raise volunteers by persons of Kentucky, Missouri, Maryland, and Delaware; for deporting enemy aliens; and for public defense.

There was a brief skirmish at Lovettsville, Va. Indians attacked an emigrant train near Great Salt Lake, Ut. Terr. Newly named Brig. Gen. U. S. Grant assumed command of the District of Ironton, Mo. The office of the Concord, N.H., *Democratic Standard* was mobbed by soldiers of the First New Hampshire Volunteers because of an article reflecting on them. The Fifteenth Massachusetts left Worcester and were said to be "all tall, muscular, men, possessing the lightness of limb and full development of natural powers which denote the true specimen of a soldier."

Sec. of War Cameron wrote Gen. Butler in reply to his request for clarification of the policy on Negroes coming into Federal lines: while the fugitive slave laws must be respected in the states of the Union, in the states in insurrection the situation was different, and the problem varied in military areas. Of course, those slaves escaping from Confederate slaveholders could not now be returned.

August 9, Friday

Confederate and Missouri state troops were moving closer to Springfield, Mo. They were now ten miles to the southwest along an insignificant stream called Wilson's Creek. The evening of the ninth the Federal Army, commanded by Nathaniel Lyon, left Springfield to seek out the secessionists.

August 10, Saturday

BATTLE OF WILSON'S CREEK.

In the rolling hill country southwest of Springfield, Mo., amid the dense undergrowth of blackjack, hazel, and scraggly oaks, the major battle of the Civil War in Missouri was fought. Bitter, headstrong, but exceedingly capable Brig. Gen. Nathaniel Lyon led his outnumbered Federals into the attack. Separating his force of some 5400 men, Lyon allowed Brig. Gen. Franz Sigel to try to strike the Confederate rear, an unwise effort that failed miserably. Sigel, being dispersed, withdrew precipitately, and was heard of no more that day. Confederates under Gen. Benjamin McCulloch and Missouri state troops under Sterling Price, ill armed and supplied, were at first driven back by Lyon's main force but rallied and counterattacked. Two strong Confederate drives on Oak Hills or Bloody Ridge were repulsed by the Federals. Units were confused as to who was who in the smoking August heat. In midmorning a worried Lyon rallied his troops only to fall, killed at the head of his men. A third Confederate charge was halted, but the uncertain Federals, bereft of a commander, were withdrawn from the field by Maj. Samuel D. Sturgis. Many thought the Federals would have been victorious if they had remained on Bloody Ridge; others disagreed. As the army struggled back to Springfield the hard-used Confederates were unable to follow closely. But Springfield was not far enough; the Federal army withdrew clear back to Rolla, Mo., southwest of St. Louis, abandoning a huge section of the state to the Confederates and pro-secessionists. The loss of Lyon, the defeat of Sigel and his German troops, the retreat of the main Federal force, loss of a primary outpost in Missouri, all emphasized the Confederate victory. The second significant battle of the Civil War had been fought and won by the South, this time out beyond the Mississippi. But Wilson's Creek, Oak Hills, or Springfield was described by one soldier as being "a purty mean-faught fite." The figures prove it: Federal total for duty 5400, killed 258, wounded 873, missing 186 for total of 1317; Confederate effectives 11,000, killed 279, wounded 951 for total of 1230. Missouri was never to see its like again. An argument between McCulloch and Price over who was to command had been settled in favor of Ben McCulloch. Both leaders and their somewhat ragtag Southern forces had performed well in victory.

President Lincoln called on Lieut. Gen. Scott to try to ease friction between the General-in-Chief and youthful George B. McClellan.

August 11, Sunday

The disorganized and beaten Federals pulled away from Wilson's Creek, leaving the Springfield area to the Confederate and pro-Southern Missouri troops. Confederate sympathizers in Missouri and elsewhere took heart. There was a minor affair at Hamburg, Mo. In the Kanawha Valley of western Virginia, Brig. Gen. John B. Floyd, former member of President Buchanan's Cabinet, assumed command of Confederate forces. The appointment was a controversial one and led to trouble between Floyd and former governor Henry A. Wise, now Floyd's subordinate.

August 12, Monday

In Missouri Confederate Gen. Ben McCulloch proclaimed the victory at Wilson's Creek and said Missouri "must be allowed to choose her own destiny." He said Union people would be protected, but "you can no longer procrastinate. Missouri must now take her position, be it North or South." Home Guards were organized in California to cooperate with the Federal army there. President Lincoln designated the last Thursday in September "as a day of humiliation, prayer and fasting for all the people of the nation."

Three wooden gunboats—*Tyler, Lexington,* and *Conestoga,* converted from riverboats—arrived at Cairo. They were to bear the brunt of the river war for months, until the ironclads were ready.

A Confederate detachment rode into an ambush set by Chief Nicholas of the Mescalero Apaches in the Big Bend country south of Fort Davis, Tex. Fifteen Southerners were killed, only the Mexican guide escaping. Generally the Confederates took little offensive action against the Apaches, involved as they were with the invasion of the Southwest. Indian depredations rapidly increased.

August 13, Tuesday

There was a skirmish near Grafton, western Va. In Washington Lincoln conferred with Gen. McClellan and with now Brig. Gen. Robert Anderson when the hero of Fort Sumter dined with the President. In Richmond President Davis discharged from arrest Thomas A. R. Nelson of Tennessee, who had opposed his state's action, as the policy of the Confederacy was "not to enter into questions of differences of political opinion heretofore existing."

August 14, Wednesday

Maj. Gen. John Charles Frémont declared martial law in St. Louis city and county, which was followed by the suppression of two allegedly pro-Southern newspapers. Members of the Seventy-ninth New York Volunteers mutinied near Washington and refused to obey orders. Their desire for a furlough was one of the grievances. A number were arrested and the entire regiment put under guard.

President Davis proclaimed the banishing of enemy aliens who did not acknowledge the authority of the Confederate States of America. Brig. Gen. Paul O. Hébert, was assigned to command Confederate forces in Texas.

August 15, Thursday

Federal Brig. Gen. Robert Anderson of Fort Sumter fame was named commander of the Department of the Cumberland, consisting of Kentucky and Tennessee, with headquarters at Cincinnati. There was a brief Federal expedition from Ste. Genevieve, Mo. Meanwhile, unionists in Missouri feared that the Confederate forces of McCulloch and Price would further invade the state. Frémont called for reinforcements, and Lincoln saw to it the War Department requested the governors of western states to aid him. Sixty men of the Second Maine who had refused to obey orders were transferred to fatigue duty on Dry Tortugas off Key West, Fla. Federal troops operated until Aug. 22 against Indians from Fort Crook to the Pitt River, Calif.

August 16, Friday

President Lincoln proclaimed that the inhabitants of the Confederate States "are in a state of insurrection against the United States, and that all commercial intercourse," with certain exceptions, between loyal and rebellious states was unlawful. Charges of disloyalty for alleged pro-Southernism were brought against the New York *Journal of Commerce, Daily News, Day Book, Freeman's Journal,* and Brooklyn *Eagle* in U. S. Circuit Court. An alleged pro-secessionist or peace meeting was broken up at Saybrook, Conn. There were Federal operations around Fredericktown, Mo., and for four days around Kirksville, Mo.

August 17, Saturday

The Federal departments of Northeastern Virginia, of Washington, and of the Shenandoah were merged into the Department of the Potomac, from whence came the name of the main Northern army in Virginia, the Army of the Potomac. Lincoln appointed Henry Wager Halleck a major general in the Regular Army and also secretly provided for a commission as Brigadier General of Volunteers for Simon Bolivar Buckner of Kentucky. Buckner, however, declined and later joined the Confederate Army. Elderly but competent Maj. Gen. John E. Wool superseded Benjamin F. Butler in command of the Department of Virginia. Butler went on to head forces organizing to attack the Cape Hatteras area. There was minor fighting at Hunnewell, Palmyra, and Brunswick, Mo. Orders were issued providing for forty cents per day and one ration for nurses in the Northern Army.

August 18, Sunday

Another quiet Sunday with a skirmish of cavalry at Pohick Church, Va., and a minor Confederate attack near Sandy Hook, Md.

August 19, Monday

The Confederate Congress at Richmond agreed to an alliance with Missouri and virtually admitted the state into the Confederacy. Thus the state officially had two governments, one Union and one Confederate. Another act authorized a produce loan of $100,000,000 to be taken up by planters to help finance the war.

In Washington President Lincoln made several appointments. He named George H. Thomas of Virginia as Brigadier General and ordered Maj. Gen. Henry W. Halleck, then in California, to report to Washington. It was thought Halleck would be named to a top command. Newspapers at West Chester and Easton, Penn., were raided by unionists, and a publisher in Haverhill, Mass., was tarred and feathered by a mob for alleged pro-Southern sentiments.

There was a skirmish at Klapsford, Mo.; Federal forces from Bird's Point, opposite Cairo, railroaded to Charleston, Mo., and defeated a force of Missouri state troops.

August 20, Tuesday

Maj. Gen. George B. McClellan assumed command of the newly organized Department and the Army of the Potomac for the Union. A convention at Wheeling, western Va., provided for setting up a new pro-Union state to be called Kanawha. Skirmishing occurred at Hawk's Nest and Laurel Fork Creek, western Va.; and at Fish Lake, Mo. Confederates attacked a railroad train near Lookout Station, Mo.

President Davis wrote Gen. Joseph E. Johnston at Manassas about complaints in the Confederate Army of improper food and lack of care for the sick. Davis approved a bill increasing Confederate artillery and calling for other military measures. At Springfield, Mo., Gen. Sterling Price proclaimed the great Southern victory at Wilson's Creek and said Northern oppressors of Missouri had been defeated.

August 21, Wednesday

The Federal government ordered that copies of New York newspapers suppressed for allegedly aiding rebellion should not be carried by the mails, and papers were confiscated in Philadelphia. There was a skirmish at Jonesboro, Mo. Brig. Gen. Roswell S. Ripley was named to command the Confederate Department of South Carolina, and Brig. Gen. John B. Grayson the Department of Middle and East Florida. President Davis approved an act of the Confederate Congress to name two more commissioners to Europe, and another measure authorizing the President to cooperate and extend aid to Missouri.

August 22, Thursday

Two vessels, *W. B. Terry* and *Samuel Orr,* were seized by pro-Confederates at Paducah, Ky. Suppression of alleged pro-Southern Northern newspapers continued in New York, Canton, O., and Philadelphia.

August 23, Friday

As military build-up continued both North and South with regiments joining the armies, the military action increased slightly. There was engagement of two Federal steamers *Yankee* and *Release,* with Confederate batteries at the mouth of Potomac Creek, Va. Skirmishing broke out at Springfield, western Va.; Medoc, Mo.; and Fort Craig, N. Mex. Terr. Gov. Isham Harris of Tennessee appealed to mothers, wives, and daughters for clothing and blankets for the soldiers in the field.

August 24, Saturday

President Davis named commissioners to Europe: Pierre A. Rost to Spain, James M. Mason to Great Britain, and John Slidell to France. Their task was to attempt to obtain foreign recognition of the Confederacy and also to act as purchasing agents for guns, ammunition, and supplies. In Washington several persons were arrested, including Mrs. Philip Phillips and Mrs. Rose Greenhow, on charges of corresponding with the Confederates. Raids continued on "secessionist" newspapers in the North with several suppressions by the government. President Lincoln told Gov. Beriah Magoffin of Kentucky that he could not and would not remove the pro-Union forces being organized in Kentucky despite claims of the state to neutrality.

August 25, Sunday

Skirmishing occurred near Piggot's Mill, western Va., and near Fort Craig, N. Mex. Terr., while there was a Federal scout from Great Falls, Md., into Virginia. Aug. 25–Sept. 8 there were operations by Confederates against the Indians about Fort Stanton, N. Mex. Terr.

August 26, Monday

Moderately severe fighting broke out at Cross Lanes near Summerville, and there was skirmishing at Wayne Court House and at Blue's House, western Va. King Kamehameha IV of the Hawaiian Islands proclaimed the neutrality of his country in the war. Navy Capt. Andrew Foote was ordered to command of the Federal gunboat forces on Western rivers, replacing John Rodgers. Rodgers had done well, but there had been personality clashes. Federal combined operations against the Cape Hatteras area began as a naval squadron and army transports left Hampton Roads, Va.

August 27, Tuesday

ATTACK ON CAPE HATTERAS FORTS BEGINS.

On the wind-whipped beaches of the Outer Banks of North Carolina on Cape Hatteras the Confederates had erected two sand and wood fortifications to protect Hatteras Inlet, an important waterway for blockade-runners. On Aug. 26 a Federal naval and army expedition under Commodore Silas H. Stringham and Gen. B. F. Butler, numbering eight ships and nine hundred army men, headed for Cape Hatteras. Fort Clark was occupied with no opposition, the garrison having abandoned it. The Navy dueled with the batteries in Fort Hatteras on this day, though largely without effect. Some troops were landed with difficulty.

There was skirmishing at Antietam Iron Works in Maryland, north of the Potomac, and at Ball's Cross Roads, Va.

August 28, Wednesday

CAPTURE OF FORT HATTERAS.

Federal naval vessels opened fire upon Fort Hatteras, N.C., in the Union attempt to capture the Confederate defense positions in the Cape Hatteras area. After suffering severe damage, the fort surrendered, although casualties were very light on both sides. The fall of Forts Clark and Hatteras sealed off an important blockading route, and this successful invasion of North Carolina soil by the Federals had a propaganda effect out of proportion to its military value. Elsewhere there was a skirmish at Ball's Mills, Mo., and at Bailey's Cross Roads, Va. Gen. Nathaniel Lyon, killed at Wilson's Creek, received impressive funeral ceremonies in St. Louis.

August 29, Thursday

There was minor skirmishing at Lexington and Morse's Mills, Mo., while Federals were completing their cleanup operations at Hatteras Inlet, N.C. "Peace" meetings at Middletown, N.J., and Newton on Long Island failed to come off.

August 30, Friday

FRÉMONT'S EMANCIPATION PROCLAMATION.

In the early morning hours in his luxurious St. Louis headquarters, Maj. Gen. John Charles Frémont wrote and then issued his famous unauthorized emancipation proclamation and order of confiscation. Declaring martial law throughout Missouri, he further confiscated all property of "those who shall take up arms against the United States" and added that "their slaves, if any they have, are hereby declared free men." All persons found in the Union-controlled zone with guns in their hands would be shot if found guilty by military court-martial. The order also applied to all those who were "proven to have taken an active part with their enemies in the field." Frémont declared he did this because of the "disorganized condition, helplessness of civil authority and total insecurity of life" in Missouri. The cry against the order was immediate and largely unanimous, although there were a few then and later who supported it. But the consensus seems to agree with President Lincoln, who termed it "dictatorial."

August 31, Saturday
In Richmond the Confederate Congress adjourned and the government announced the appointment of five full generals in order of seniority: Samuel Cooper dating from May 16; Albert Sidney Johnston from May 28; Robert E. Lee from June 14; Joseph E. Johnston from July 4; and P. G. T. Beauregard from July 21. There was a skirmish at Munson's Hill or Little River Turnpike, Va.

SEPTEMBER, 1861

Peoples of the North and South began to wonder where the next military blow would fall, where the fighting would be, who would die. In the North, McClellan, awkward under the restraint of aging Gen. Scott, was building the Army of the Potomac and his own reputation. In the South the Confederates were building with what they had, and wondering how to stretch it far enough. Frémont's unauthorized "Missouri Emancipation" caused consternation in Washington, and in the Northern press, although here and there the abolitionists rejoiced. In the South it brought forth editorial comment that "we told you so"; the real purpose of the war was unmasked. Both sides asked how it would affect Kentucky. The neutral state was an immense barricade to military action from the Alleghenies to the Mississippi River. How and when would this unnatural barrier come down?

September 1, Sunday
Minor skirmishing occupied the day at Blue Creek, Boone Court House, and Burlington, western Va., as well as at Bennight's Mills and in Jefferson County, Mo., and near Fort Scott, Kas. Brig. Gen. U. S. Grant assumed command in southeastern Missouri at Cape Girardeau, a relatively unimportant event at the time. Almost daily there were actions on the waters framing the Confederacy. Captures, recaptures, failures were common on both sides.

September 2, Monday

President Lincoln requested Maj. Gen. Frémont to "modify" his proclamation of Aug. 30 which had ordained freedom for slaves of rebellious
owners, threatened the death penalty for certain secessionists and confiscated their property. Lincoln felt that the proclamation "will alarm our
Southern Union friends, and turn them against us—perhaps ruin our
rather fair prospect for Kentucky." Lincoln was gently attempting to
restore the prerogatives of the civilian government which had been pre-
empted by Frémont. Kentucky was foremost in Lincoln's mind these
days, and even though the new pro-Union legislature this day ordered
the Stars and Stripes raised above the State House at Frankfort, he
realized that the situation remained precarious.

Maj. Gen. Leonidas Polk, commanding Confederates along the Mississippi River and in Tennessee, was also given control over Arkansas and
Missouri.

The fighting picked up in western Virginia with skirmishing at Hawk's
Nest, Worthington, and Beller's Mill near Harper's Ferry. There was
action at Dry Wood Creek, toward Columbia and Iberia, and at
Dallas, Mo.

September 3, Tuesday

CONFEDERATE FORCES ENTER KENTUCKY.

Confederate forces under Gideon Pillow on orders of Gen. Leonidas
Polk entered Kentucky from Tennessee en route to Hickman and Columbus on the Mississippi River. This action ended the "neutrality" of Kentucky and created one continuous front from the Atlantic Ocean to Kansas
and the frontier. Polk feared that if he did not move, the Federals themselves would seize Columbus, as there had been light action in the
Belmont, Mo., area across the river and erroneous reports of a Federal
build-up. In fact, Frémont had indicated to Gen. Grant that he intended
to enter Kentucky. The Confederate action had many repercussions. At
first Polk was ordered by the Secretary of War to withdraw, but President Davis overruled the pullback. The move buttressed pro-Union feeling,
which had been increasing in many sections, and opened an all-out contest for military control of Kentucky. On the other hand, secessionists
in the state rejoiced that the issue was now clarified.

September 4, Wednesday

There was light shooting between Federal gunboats and shore batteries
at Hickman and Columbus, Ky., as the Confederates began strengthening
their strategically important position on the bluffs of the Mississippi at
Columbus. Gen. U. S. Grant arrived at Cairo, where he established his
headquarters and faced the problem of a fast-changing military situation.

There were skirmishes at Great Falls, Md., and Shelbina, Mo. Gen. Polk at Columbus, Ky., proclaimed that the Federal government had disregarded the neutrality of Kentucky by establishing camps and depots for armies, by organizing troops, and by an alleged build-up in Missouri "evidently intended to cover the landing of troops for the seizure" of Columbus.

September 5, Thursday

In Washington Mr. Lincoln met with Gen. Scott to discuss the military situation in the West and the future of Gen. Frémont. At Cairo Grant learned of the Confederate invasion of Kentucky. He immediately saw the importance of Paducah, located at the juncture of the Tennessee and Ohio rivers and near the mouth of the Cumberland. To counteract the Confederate occupation of Columbus, Grant prepared an expedition to leave that night for Paducah.

In addition there was a skirmish at Papinsville, Mo. The Charleston *Mercury* cried out against what it called the "masterly inactivity" of the Confederate army in Virginia, which it said had been stationary for six weeks with the capital at Washington nearly in sight. The paper called for an offensive to force the United States "to defend themselves."

September 6, Friday

FEDERAL CAPTURE OF PADUCAH.

In the morning a small squadron of two wooden gunboats and a few transports landed federal troops at Paducah, forestalling an obviously planned Confederate move from Columbus to the strategic Kentucky city at the mouth of the Tennessee. There were no fighting and no casualties. It was U. S. Grant's first major victory and it was bloodless. By seizing Paducah, and later nearby Smithland at the mouth of the Cumberland, Grant had prevented Confederate forces from claiming the entire state of Kentucky and planting their northern line on the Ohio River. The move also foreshadowed the river campaign of the coming year. Federal Brig. Gen. C. F. Smith was assigned to command in western Kentucky as Grant returned to Cairo. There were skirmishes at Rowell's Run, western Va., and Monticello Bridge, Mo.

September 7, Saturday

In the North Union meetings continued during these days in some cities, while in others peace and pro-secessionist elements mustered their forces. There were occasional arrests for alleged pro-rebellion activity, and suppression, or threat of suppression, of the press. The people were beginning to take sides more firmly and to evaluate their personal stands. In the South the issue of Kentucky had been decided, and here, too, people were declaring themselves. In the mountains of east Tennessee and Kentucky the pro-Union feeling was congealing. On this quiet day there were modest operations around Big Springs, Mo., and a skirmish involving Indians near Santa Ana Canyon, Calif.

September 8, Sunday

President Davis, concerned over the many areas of the military front that demanded attention, wrote Gen. Joseph E. Johnston at Manassas, "The cause of the Confederacy is staked upon your army. . . . I have felt, and feel, that time brings many advantages to the enemy, and wish we could strike him in his present condition; but it has seemed to me involved in too much probability of failure to render the movement proper with our present means. Had I the requisite arms, the argument would soon be changed."

In Missouri there were Federal operations against guerrillas and a reconnaissance from Cairo by the Federals with an engagement at Lucas Bend, Mo., Sept. 8–10. Four blockade-runners were taken off Cape Hatteras by Federals.

September 9, Monday

President Lincoln was troubled over the operations in the West and General Frémont, his commander there. The influential Blair family was urging the removal of Frémont. Lincoln sent Maj. Gen. David Hunter to advise and aid the general. There was a skirmish at Shepherdstown, western Va., as the threat of new major action loomed in that area. Federal forces under Rosecrans moved toward Confederates near Carnifix Ferry, Cox and other Federals were operating in the Kanawha Valley, while a third force dug in at Cheat Mountain to face Confederate operations under the general command of R. E. Lee.

September 10, Tuesday

ENGAGEMENT AT CARNIFIX FERRY.

Rosecrans' Federal command struck Confederates at Carnifix Ferry, western Va., but failed to break the Southern lines. However, outnumbered and in a bad position, Brig. Gen. John B. Floyd withdrew his Confederates during the night toward Dogwood Gap and Sewell Mountain. Casualties were light, but the Northern victory was useful in holding western Virginia for the Union. Meanwhile, to the north, Gen. R. E. Lee was planning his assault on Cheat Mountain. At Lewinsville, Va., there was a small skirmish. At Lucas Bend, Mo., Confederates fought the Federal gunboats *Lexington* and *Conestoga*.

Gen. Albert Sidney Johnston was appointed to the command of Tennessee, Missouri, Arkansas, and Kentucky for the Confederates and became, actually, commander of the Western armies of the South. Brig.

Gen. George H. Thomas, a Virginian who remained with the Union, was assigned to command Camp Dick Robinson in eastern Kentucky.

Late at night President Lincoln had a visitor—Mrs. John Charles Frémont, who had traveled from St. Louis to protest the treatment of her husband and to urge support of his emancipation and confiscation order. Although accounts vary, Mr. Lincoln is said to have received the demanding lady coolly.

September 11, Wednesday

CHEAT MOUNTAIN CAMPAIGN.

For five days Gen. R. E. Lee and his Confederates campaigned actively against the Federals, the heavy rains of the season, and the rugged mountains in western Virginia. Dividing his forces into five columns, Lee planned to attack the separated Union forces of J. J. Reynolds at Cheat Mountain Summit and Elkwater. There was light fighting at Conrad's Mill; on the twelfth one Confederate column under Col. Albert Rust failed to attack in what was to be the signal for a general assault. The element of surprise was now gone and the weather growing worse. By the thirteenth it was clear that Lee's plan had failed miserably, both because it required complicated movements and close cooperation, and because of the rough terrain and incessant rains. On the fifteenth the Confederates pulled back and the northern part of western Virginia was secured for the Union. Casualties were light on both sides, but, coupled with Carnifix Ferry, it was a considerable disaster to Confederate plans to regain western Virginia. Furthermore, the campaign brought forth severe criticism of Lee from newspapers, civilians, and soldiers, and dimmed his reputation for some months.

Near Washington there was a reconnaissance by Federals from Chain Bridge to Lewinsville, Va., and some action.

President Lincoln, after his interview with Mrs. Frémont of the night before, wrote the general that he would order that the clause in relation to confiscation of property and emancipation of slaves in his famous proclamation be modified to conform with the acts of Congress. The Kentucky legislature passed a resolution calling on the governor to order the Confederate troops in the state to depart. Another resolution calling for both Northern and Southern troops to leave was defeated. Unionists appeared to be in control of the political machinery of Kentucky.

September 12, Thursday

SIEGE OF LEXINGTON, MISSOURI, BEGINS.

In addition to the marching and fighting around Cheat Mountain and Elkwater, there was skirmishing at Petersburg and near Peytona, western Va., and in Missouri on the Blackwater. In the northwestern part of that state, on the Missouri River, Gen. Price and his Missouri troops converged on the commercial town of Lexington, where a Federal force under Col. James Mulligan was posted. Vastly outnumbering the Federals, Price's men pushed aside the pickets and began what became a nine-day siege of Lexington.

The Federal government ordered the arrest of allegedly disloyal members of the Maryland legislature scheduled to convene in Frederick Sept. 17. Numerous arrests were made between Sept. 12 and 17 and Maryland remained firmly loyal to the Union. President Lincoln wrote Mrs. Frémont that he protested "against being understood as acting in any hostility" toward the general. But he did send Joseph Holt to St. Louis to deliver to Frémont Lincoln's letter modifying the emancipation order. Despite Lincoln's instruction, Frémont freed at least two slaves of a Confederate officer.

At Russellville, Ky., Simon Bolivar Buckner called upon Kentuckians to defend their homes against the invasion of the North.

September 13, Friday

The siege of Lexington, Mo., was well under way as Confederate lines pressed in upon Union forces dug in around a small college. There was a minor action at Boonville, Mo., but no indication that Frémont and his commanders were doing much to relieve Mulligan at Lexington. The main action at Cheat Mountain, western Va., came to an end. President Davis wrote Gov. Letcher of Virginia protesting the governor's allegation of lack of security for the state.

September 14, Saturday

President Davis rejected a complaint by Gen. Joseph E. Johnston about the ranking of Confederate generals, one of the most galling incidents in a long series that led to the estrangement of the President and his general. There was a skirmish at Old Randolph, Mo., while at Pensacola Harbor, Fla., small boats from U.S.S. *Colorado* cut out the Confederate privateer *Judah* and destroyed her by fire.

September 15, Sunday

Mr. Lincoln and the Cabinet met again to discuss possible removal of Gen. Frémont, who was a sore problem to the Federal President at this time. The President also defended his government's action in arresting, without charges, allegedly disloyal citizens of Maryland. There was a light skirmish at Pritchard's Mill, Va., near Antietam Ford, Md. Gen. Albert Sidney Johnston assumed command of the Confederate armies in the West, superseding Maj. Gen. Polk. In Missouri the uproar against Gen. Frémont was heightened when he had colonel-politician Frank Blair arrested.

September 16, Monday

At Lexington, Mo., Maj. Gen. Price began his major push against the besieged Federal forces under Col. Mulligan. Confederates, on the other hand, evacuated Ship Island, Miss., not far from the mouth of the Mississippi and a few hours later it was occupied by Federal troops in small numbers. U.S.S. *Conestoga* took two prizes on the Cumberland River in Kentucky as river operations in the West heightened. There was skirmishing opposite Seneca Creek, Md., in Virginia; at Magruder's Ferry, Va.; and at Princeton, western Va.

September 17, Tuesday

The legislature of Maryland decided not to assemble at Frederick after the arrest of a number of its members. Federals completed the seizure of Ship Island, Miss., soon to be used as a base to prepare for further operations along the Gulf Coast. There was fighting at Blue Mills Landing, Mo. Ocracoke Inlet, N.C., was closed to blockade-runners by the destruction of Confederate fortifications by the Federal Navy. Skirmishing occurred near Harper's Ferry, western Va., and near Point of Rocks, Md.

September 18, Wednesday

Confederate forces occupied Bowling Green, Ky., with Brig. Gen. Simon Bolivar Buckner in command of the Central Division of Kentucky. Confederate Brig. Gen. Paul O. Hébert assumed command of the Department of Texas, and for the Federals Capt. S. F. Du Pont took over the South Atlantic Blockading Squadron. Mr. Lincoln's Cabinet met to hear reports of those who had investigated Frémont's Western command. Lincoln also informed Navy Sec. Welles that the contemplated expedition of the Army and Navy to the Southern coastline should be ready to move early in October. The Louisville, Ky., *Courier* was banned from the mails because of hostility to the Federal government.

September 19, Thursday

Fighting intensified at Lexington, Mo., and it became obvious that the Federals would soon have to surrender to Price's Missourians unless relieved. Confederate forces under Brig. Gen. Felix K. Zollicoffer advanced from east Tennessee and dispersed Kentucky Federal troops at Barboursville, Ky. This action completed the setting up of the three strong points of the Confederate western defense line: Columbus, Ky., Bowling Green, and the area around Cumberland Gap. The Union government also authorized the North Atlantic Blockading Squadron to operate to the southern boundary of North Carolina under the command of Capt. L. M. Goldsborough, while the South Atlantic Blockading Squadron operated south of it under S. F. Du Pont. The offices of the Louisville, Ky., *Courier* were seized and several arrests made by Federal authorities.

September 20, Friday

SURRENDER OF LEXINGTON, MISSOURI.

Col. James Mulligan, after a heartbreaking defense of his hilltop position at Lexington, surrendered his force of about 3600 Federal troops to Gen. Sterling Price's Missourians, numbering about 18,000. During the nine days of siege and fighting Price lost 25 killed and 72 wounded, while the Federals had 39 killed and 120 wounded. The later stages of the siege were made famous by the effective Confederate use of dampened hemp bales as breastworks, which they pushed ahead of them as they assaulted the Federal post. Mulligan had rightfully expected Frémont to send aid from St. Louis or from Pope at Jefferson City via the Missouri River; but none came, leading to new charges against Frémont of dereliction of duty. Barren of important strategic results, the siege of Lexington was a showy victory for the pro-secessionist Missourians, although they soon retreated and many of the soldiers dropped off at village and farm en route south toward Arkansas.

There was a brief skirmish in Virginia opposite Seneca Creek, Md. Confederate forces evacuated Mayfield, Ky.

The Maryland political prisoners were sent to Fort Lafayette in New York by Federal authorities. Brig. Gen. Robert Anderson, hero of Fort Sumter, in command at Cincinnati, was authorized to organize Union forces in Kentucky and establish headquarters at Louisville. Sept. 20–Oct. 7 there were operations by Federal troops against Indians from Camp Robledo, N. Mex. Terr.

September 21, Saturday

Gen. R. E. Lee was in immediate command of Confederate forces in the Kanawha Valley of western Virginia around Big Sewell Mountain, where he was preparing to oppose Rosecrans' main forces. Gen. Albert Sidney Johnston called upon Tennessee for thirty thousand men, and Maj. Gen. Polk was assigned to the Western Division of Johnston's department. For the Federals Brig. Gen. O. M. Mitchel assumed command of the Department of the Ohio.

September 22, Sunday

President Lincoln, writing to a friend, said Frémont's proclamation "as to confiscation of property, and the liberation of slaves, is *purely political,* and not within the range of *military* law, or necessity." The Confederate government called upon Arkansas and Mississippi for ten thousand men each for service in the West.

Federals carried out a reconnaissance from Cairo, Ill., toward Columbus,

Ky., with a skirmish at Mayfield Creek. Federal jayhawker James Henry Lane of Kansas and his men, who had been committing numerous depredations on the Kansas-Missouri border (as had their Confederate counterparts), raided, looted, and burned the town of Osceola, Mo. This was another incident in the cruel, irrational infighting in western Missouri and eastern Kansas, where no man knew where his neighbor stood and wasn't always sure about himself.

September 23, Monday

Federal troops descended upon Romney, western Va., Sept 23–25 with affairs at Mechanicsburg Gap and Hanging Rock Pass. There was also fighting at Cassville, western Va., and Albany, Ky. In St. Louis Frémont closed the *Evening News* and arrested the editor for criticizing the conduct of the Lexington siege. At the same time in Washington Lincoln was discussing with Sec. of State Seward the problem of Frémont himself.

September 24, Tuesday

President Lincoln, Gen. McClellan, other officers, department heads, foreign dignitaries, and others reviewed artillery and cavalry near Washington. There was a light skirmish at Point of Rocks, Md.

September 25, Wednesday

Smithland, Ky., at the mouth of the Cumberland River and not far from Paducah, was occupied by Federal troops. There was fighting near Lewinsville, Va.; Cañada Alamosa, N. Mex. Terr.; near Chapmansville, western Va.; and at Kanawha Gap as the forces of Lee and Rosecrans felt each other out in the Kanawha Valley. Two Federal ships dueled with a Confederate battery at Freestone Point, Va. Confederate Brig. Gen. Henry A. Wise was relieved from command in western Virginia after long, confusing, and acrimonious arguments with his superior, Gen. Floyd. Mr. Lincoln's secretary, John G. Nicolay, purchased a mahogany sofa for the executive offices for $24. President Davis continued to dispute with Gen. J. E. Johnston over reinforcements, supplies, strategy, and policy in general. By now the Confederate commerce raider *Sumter* was operating off South America's east coast. Until Oct. 5 a Federal expedition ranged from San Bernardino to Temecula Ranch and Oak Grove, Calif.

September 26, Thursday

It was a day of "humiliation, prayer and fasting" in the North. But the fighting went on anyway with skirmishing near Fort Thorn, N. Mex. Terr.; at Hunter's Farm near Belmont, Mo.; and at the mouth of the Muddy River in Kentucky. A Federal expedition went out Sept. 26–30 from Cumberland Ford, with light skirmishing, in Laurel County, Ky.

September 27, Friday

Gen. McClellan met with President Lincoln and the Cabinet and held a rather heated discussion over military policy as there were increasing cries for action by the Federal forces in Virginia. A skirmish near Norfolk, Mo., was the only fighting of even moderate note.

September 28, Saturday

Confederate forces evacuated Munson's Hill, Va., near Alexandria, after a brief affair near Vanderburgh's House today and on the twenty-ninth.

September 29, Sunday

Mr. Lincoln told a complaining Gov. Oliver P. Morton of Indiana, "As to Kentucky, you do not estimate that state as more important than I do; but I am compelled to watch all points." There was skirmishing at Albany and Hopkinsville, Ky.; Travisville, Tenn.; and Berlin, Md. Brig. Gen. Daniel H. Hill of the Confederate Army was ordered to North Carolina as it was feared there would be further Federal action there.

September 30, Monday

The month came to a quiet end, but it was clear that there was considerably more war to be fought on both sides. President Lincoln was concerned with Frémont in Missouri, stabilizing the situation in Kentucky, and the rising impatience over inaction in Virginia. In western Virginia rains and the rough country impeded operations in the struggle for control of the pro-Union area. The Confederacy was fighting to establish a strong front in Kentucky, was apprehensive over the ever increasing Federal army along the Potomac, and had to watch threatened spots on all its boundaries, including 3500 miles of seacoast.

OCTOBER, 1861

In the East there were rumblings both North and South for further action. Much was still expected of McClellan, but many wondered why the fine fall weather was being let slip by. McClellan himself was busy organizing what was fast becoming "his" army, and at the same time was having difficulties with General-in-Chief Scott, the Cabinet, and even Mr. Lincoln. In Richmond and the Confederacy, likewise, there was wonderment over why the victorious army of First Manassas was not being put to better use. In the West the issue of Kentucky had been settled for the time, but the end of "neutrality" brought new problems with it. The Confederates hastened work on their Western defense line; the Federals gave thought to future invasion of the South. In Missouri Frémont continued to be a touchy problem to the Lincoln administration and something would have to be done. East Tennessee and western Virginia still were in the limelight. At the Confederacy the question of hoped-for foreign recognition was paramount. The people of the two sections at war still were mainly optimistic, but questions of all kinds were being asked more and more frequently in the United and in the Confederate States.

October 1, Tuesday
President Davis, Genls. Joseph E. Johnston, Beauregard, and G. W. Smith held a conference on grand strategy at Centreville, Va., early in the month. The main topic was the future of the army in Virginia and what it should or should not do. Recognizing the cry of the populace for an offensive, it was finally decided that the Confederate Army could not be reinforced and supplied sufficiently to invade the North and would have to await Union attack and the distant spring. While the generals advised concentration in Virginia, it was recognized that politically, as well as militarily, the Confederacy had to defend numerous points on its vast frontier.

The transport and supply steamer *Fanny* was captured in Pamlico Sound, N.C., by three Confederate vessels. A considerable amount of stores and thirty-one Federals were taken. The Federal War Department created the Department of New England under command of Maj. Gen. Benjamin F. Butler, which was mainly a mechanism for recruiting troops to be used in future expeditions; in this case it turned out to be the New Orleans campaign force. President Lincoln wrote a memo, probably on this day, calling for a movement into east Tennessee and toward Cumberland Gap, with particular attention to the railroad connecting Virginia and Tennessee. He also asked for an expedition on the east coast which became the Port Royal operation of November. Meanwhile, the Federal Cabinet met with Gen. Scott and McClellan.

October 2, Wednesday
There was a brief skirmish at Springfield Station, Va.; in Missouri Federals from Bird's Point near Cairo, Ill., broke up a Confederate camp at Charleston. The Confederate government made a peace treaty with the Great Osage Indian tribe. Gov. A. B. Moore of Alabama issued a proclamation against tradesmen charging exorbitant prices for necessities of life.

October 3, Thursday

Federal troops from Cheat Mountain in western Virginia made a reconnaissance to the Greenbrier River and retired after an engagement. Other Federal troops occupied Pohick Church area, Va., and there was a skirmish at Springfield Station, Va. Gov. Thomas O. Moore of Louisiana issued a proclamation banning the sending of cotton to New Orleans "during the existence of the blockade." This was part of the plan to withhold cotton from Europe, to add weight to the cause for recognition of the Confederacy.

October 4, Friday

Confederates attacked an Indiana regiment at Chicamacomico, N.C., near Hatteras Inlet. There was also skirmishing near Edwards' Ferry, Md., and Buffalo Hill, Ky. Two Confederate blockade-runners with cargoes of arms were captured by U.S.S. *South Carolina* off Southwest Pass below New Orleans.

President Lincoln watched a balloon ascension, conferred with officials on Frémont's Department of the West, and approved a contract for iron-clad warships (one of which would be the *Monitor*) to be built by John Ericsson of New York. The Confederate government signed treaties with the Shawnee and Seneca Indians, and on Oct. 7 with the Cherokees.

October 5, Saturday.

Federal sailors burned a Confederate privateer at Chincoteague Inlet, Va. The London *Post* editorially backed British recognition of the Confederacy, while the London *Times* seemed to incline to the Union. Brig. Gen. Joseph K. F. Mansfield was assigned to the Federal command at Hatteras Inlet. Federal troops in California operating since Sept. 23 had carried out an expedition from San Bernardino to Oak Grove and Temecula Ranch against alleged pro-Confederates.

October 6, Sunday

Confederate blockade-runner *Alert* was captured by the Federal Navy off Charleston, S.C.

October 7, Monday

Federal gunboats *Lexington* and *Tyler*, operating on reconnaissance from Cairo, Ill., toward Lucas Bend, Mo., engaged Confederate shore batteries at Iron Bluffs on the Mississippi, not far from Columbus, Ky. Federal Gen. Frémont left St. Louis en route to Springfield, Mo., in his belated movement after Missourian Sterling Price, who was withdrawing from Lexington. Meanwhile, Sec. of War Cameron was sent west on an inspection trip, and Mr. Lincoln sent a letter with him to Brig. Gen. Samuel R. Curtis asking his judgment as to whether Frémont should be relieved. In Washington conferences and meetings were held by the Cabinet and others with the President in regard to Frémont and military problems. The Pony Express was officially discontinued after a brief but spectacular eighteen-month career.

October 8, Tuesday

Brig. Gen. William T. Sherman superseded Brig. Gen. Robert Anderson in command of the Union Department of the Cumberland with headquarters at Louisville. The veteran of Fort Sumter, a Kentuckian useful in this command, had been suffering for some time from nervous exhaustion, which now apparently took the form of a severe breakdown. Anderson never returned to active service. Sherman, aggressive in his command, was soon to make such demands for troops and to express so much concern for his position that he, too, was deemed, probably with some justification, on the verge of nervous collapse. There was a light skirmish at Hillsboro, Ky.

October 9, Wednesday

A band of a thousand Confederates under Gen. Richard Heron Anderson landed on Santa Rosa Island near Fort Pickens in Pensacola Bay, Fla., the night of Oct. 8–9 in order to break up Federal batteries. After routing one Federal camp the Confederates were forced to withdraw by Union reinforcements from the fort. President Lincoln continued his round of Cabinet meetings, hearing a report by Gen. McClellan on military operations.

October 10, Thursday

President Davis wrote Maj. Gen. G. W. Smith of his concern over controlling railroad transportation, the ranks of the generals, the organization of troops, the use of Negroes as laborers, the need for efficient staff officers, and threatened Federal operations. Federal Brig. Gen. O. M. Mitchel, former astronomer and popular lecturer, was ordered to organize an expedition into east Tennessee. There was a light attack by Confederates on Union pickets at Paducah, Ky.

October 11, Friday

Brig. Gen. William S. Rosecrans assumed command of the Federal Department of Western Virginia. There was a brief skirmish at Harper's Ferry, and a Confederate schooner was burned by Federals in Dumfries Creek on the Potomac. Oct. 11–16 Confederate troops carried out operations against Indians from Fort Inge, Tex.

October 12, Saturday

On a rainy, stormy night off Charleston, S.C., the steamer *Theodora* evaded the Federal blockaders and carried two gentlemen, whose names were soon to be on every tongue, to Cuba. John Slidell of Louisiana had been named Confederate Commissioner to France and James Mason of Virginia Commissioner to Britain. Their main object was to obtain recognition of the Confederacy by the powers of Europe and to purchase military supplies. Their escape was soon reported in the North, and Sec. of State Seward, thinking they were in C.S.S. *Nashville,* set about to have the commissioners captured.

The new Confederate ironclad ram *Manassas,* aided by two armed steamers, headed down the Mississippi to challenge the Federal squadron near Head of Passes at the mouth of the Mississippi River. U.S.S. *Richmond* was rammed by *Manassas* and went aground, as did *Vincennes,* but both finally were able to withdraw. For a brief spell the blockade was disrupted but not for long, although the incident was ignominious for the Federal Navy.

In other naval affairs the first ironclad of the U. S. Navy, the gunboat *St. Louis,* was launched at Carondelet, Mo. Federal Navy Sec. Welles wrote that Bull's Bay, St. Helena, Port Royal, S.C., and Fernandina, Fla., were being considered as fuel and supply depots on the Atlantic coast and that an expedition would soon be under way to seize one or more of them.

Skirmishing took place near Upton's Hill, Ky. Jeff Thompson's Southern raiders advanced from Stoddard County in the Ironton area of Missouri, the start of operations which lasted until Oct. 25. There were two days of skirmishes near Clintonville and the Pomme de Terre, Mo. A pro-Union meeting was held in Hyde County, N.C.

October 13, Sunday

At Wet Glaize, also known as Dutch or Monday Hollow, near Henrytown, Mo., sharp action resulted in dispersal of a Confederate party intent on raiding Federal communications between St. Louis and Springfield. Another skirmish occurred at Cotton Hill, western Va. Brig Gen. Thomas Williams superseded Brig. Gen. J. K. F. Mansfield in Federal command in North Carolina.

October 14, Monday

The citizens of Chincoteague Island, Accomack County, Va., took the oath of allegiance to the United States before Federal naval officers. "We are united as one man in our abhorrence of the secession heresies," the residents of the island off the Virginia mainland stated. Missouri State Guard pro-secessionist Jeff Thompson proclaimed in southeastern

Missouri that he had come to Washington, Jefferson, Ste. Genevieve, St. Francois, and Iron counties to help residents throw off the yoke of the North. He called on them to "drive the invaders from your soil or die among your native hills."

There was fighting at Linn Creek and at Underwood's Farm near Bird's Point, Mo. In command changes Col. James H. Carleton took over the Federal District of Southern California, and for the Confederates Maj. Gen. Braxton Bragg was given command of the Department of Alabama and West Florida.

In Washington President Lincoln authorized Gen. Scott to suspend the privilege of the writ of habeas corpus anywhere between Bangor, Me., and Washington if necessary, because of suspected subversion.

October 15, Tuesday

A band of Jeff Thompson's raiders captured a party of Federal soldiers and burned the Big River Bridge near Potosi, Mo., as a part of the increased activities of the Missourians. There was a skirmish on the Little River Turnpike in Virginia.

October 16, Wednesday

Union troops captured Lexington, Mo., from a small Confederate garrison. A party of Federals seized 21,000 bushels of wheat stored in a mill near Harper's Ferry, but on their return encountered a band of Confederates, and a sharp, brisk fight ensued before the Yankees were able to get back to Harper's Ferry. Near Linn Creek, Mo., there was yet another skirmish.

President Davis was having difficulties with state-conscious soldiers in the Army, and was trying to maintain the state regiments and at the same time create strong army corps. Furthermore, he had to refuse permission of one Kentucky group to leave the Army in the east and return to defend their state. Public interest prevented him from granting such requests.

October 17, Thursday

There was speculation North and South about where the Federal coastal invasion, obviously under way, would strike. Flag Officer Du Pont declared that Port Royal, S.C., was the most useful as a Federal naval and coaling base. There were skirmishes at Fredericktown, Mo., in which Federals were successful. During October the blockade was tightened, with numerous captures off the south Atlantic coast. President Lincoln asked jobs be given to two young men whose mother said "she has two sons who want to work." He added, "Wanting to work is so rare a merit, that it should be encouraged."

October 18, Friday

In Washington a Cabinet meeting discussed Gen. Winfield Scott's possible voluntary retirement. Mr. Lincoln was having problems between Genls. McClellan and Thomas W. Sherman regarding troops for the south coastal expedition. Sherman was asking for more and McClellan was refusing to furnish them from his army. In Virginia there was a Federal reconnaissance toward the Occoquan River, and another gunboat reconnaissance by Federals down the Mississippi. There was skirmishing near Rockcastle Hills, Ky., and at Warrensburg, Mo. Federal forces moved against Missourian Jeff Thompson from Cape Girardeau in the continuing operations in the Ironton area of Missouri. For the Confederates Maj. Gen. Mansfield Lovell superseded elderly Maj. Gen. David E. Twiggs in command in Louisiana and Texas.

October 19, Saturday

U.S.S. *Massachusetts* and C.S.S. *Florida* exchanged fire in an engagement near Ship Island in Mississippi Sound off the Mississippi shore. It was an inconclusive engagement. There was a limited action at Big Hurricane Creek, Mo., but the main interest militarily these fall days turned again to western Virginia. Oct. 19–Nov. 16 there were considerable operations in the Kanawha and New River areas, with a goodly amount of skirmishing, but nothing decisive. More important fronts would soon take the attention away from an area where earlier fighting had seemed important.

October 20, Sunday

Since the Battle of Bull Run or Manassas the area of the upper Potomac Valley from Washington to Harper's Ferry had been under Federal command of Maj. Gen. Nathaniel Banks. Pickets guarded the north bank of the Potomac to ward against possible invasion of Maryland. There had been scouting and brief clashes throughout the fall, but nothing of a major nature.

Among the important ferry points on the river were Edwards' Ferry and Conrad's Ferry near Leesburg, Va. Confederate Brig. Gen. Nathan G. "Shanks" Evans was stationed by Beauregard at Leesburg to watch the Federals. Nearly opposite Leesburg was Brig. Gen. Charles P. Stone. On Oct. 19 Gen. McClellan had ordered a major reconnaissance. Brig. Gen. George A. McCall on the nineteenth and this day occupied Dranesville, Va., south of the Potomac. Thereupon, today McClellan ordered Stone to keep a good lookout upon Leesburg and "Perhaps a slight demonstration on your part would have the effect to move them." Stone immediately crossed some troops in the Conrad's Ferry-Harrison Island-Ball's Bluff area but withdrew them in the evening. The stage was set unknowingly for one of the most controversial lesser events of the war. Included in the Virginia operations was a reconnaissance to Hunter's Mill and Thornton Station.

In the West Federal forces moved from Pilot Knob against guerrillas in the Ironton, Mo., area. Maj. Gen. E. V. Sumner relinquished command of the Federal Department of the Pacific, to be succeeded by Col. George Wright.

President Davis continued to have problems with Genls. Beauregard and Joseph E. Johnston over rank, distribution of regiments, and military planning. These areas of disagreements were slowly building up to a disrupting difficulty for the Confederacy. In a long letter to Beauregard Mr. Davis wrote, "My sole wish is to secure the independence, and peace of the Confederacy."

October 21, Monday

BATTLE OF BALL'S BLUFF OR LEESBURG, VIRGINIA.

On the edge of the south bank of the Potomac River at the precipitously steep, wooded Ball's Bluff was fought this day a battle or engagement whose repercussions far outweighed its relatively secondary strategic value. Brig. Gen. Charles P. Stone shuttled his Federal forces across the river in inadequate boats at Ball's Bluff and farther downstream at Edwards' Ferry. He also moved toward Leesburg as a continuation of his reconnaissance ordered from Washington. Col. Edward D. Baker, senator from Oregon and friend of Mr. Lincoln, had immediate command at Ball's Bluff while Stone directed operations from Edwards' Ferry. Baker kept bringing more and more troops over. After light fighting in the morning the Confederates began to drive the Federals back sharply in the afternoon at Ball's Bluff. The withdrawal became a disaster as Federals fell back to the crest of the bluff and then attempted to escape. About 4 P.M. Col. Baker fell dead, boats swamped in the river, men drowned, were shot, surrendered, or tried to get away along the riverbank. It was a dramatic, terrible, costly Federal defeat and a well-fought Confederate victory. Forces were about equal, 1700 on each side at Ball's Bluff, also known as Leesburg, Harrison's Island, or Conrad's Ferry. But in losses the Federals had 49 killed, 158 wounded, and 714 missing, many of whom drowned, for 921 casualties. Confederates lost 36 killed, 117 wounded, 2 missing for 155 casualties. Sen. Baker, despite his somewhat rash advance, was made a martyr, mourned by Lincoln and the nation. Gen. Stone, stolid defender of Washington earlier in the year, was accused in the press and elsewhere of friendliness with the enemy, ineptness in command, and downright treason. His imprisonment without being formally charged had definite political overtones, and although he later returned to service, his career was forever marred by a defeat for which historians have been more and more disinclined to blame him. McClellan, despite his indefinite and perhaps erroneous orders, escaped criticism. Investigation after investigation wrote reams into the official records, but that did not matter to those who stumbled down the tree- and brush-entangled slopes to their deaths. For the Confederates, Brig. Gen. Nathan G. "Shanks" Evans had, as at First Manassas, proved a quick-thinking soldier, but his alleged drinking was probably responsible for his never gaining the rank and reputation his obvious qualifications indicated. In the North—consternation, another defeat; in the South—jubilation, although it was clear the battle had meant little for Confederate independence.

This same day near Fredericktown, Mo., Federals under Col. J. B. Plummer pursued retreating Confederates and fought for three hours south of the town. Gradually the Confederates continued their withdrawal. Losses were moderate. There was action at Rockcastle Hills or Camp Wildcat, Ky., and at Young's Mill near Newport News, Va.

In Washington the grief-stricken President wrote Roman Catholic Archbishop John J. Hughes for names of those suitable to be appointed chaplains for hospitals.

October 22, Tuesday

The news of the tragedy at Ball's Bluff raced through the North by telegraph and newspapers. In the Confederacy an important command change was instituted: the Department of Virginia under Gen. Joseph E. Johnston was organized with Gen. Beauregard in command of the District of the Potomac, Brig. Gen. Theophilus Holmes the Aquia District, and Maj. Gen. Thomas J. "Stonewall" Jackson the Shenandoah Valley District. These were major decisions for the future. For the Federals Brig. Gen. Benjamin F. Kelley was assigned to the Department of Harper's Ferry and Cumberland. There was light fighting around Budd's Ferry, Md., on the Potomac. From the Federal Navy came the disquieting news that Confederate batteries commanded all major points on the Potomac below Alexandria. This problem, Frémont in the West, and, of course, Ball's Bluff occupied the Federal Cabinet. In Richmond there was concern over affairs in western Virginia, where it was feared the army would have to go into winter quarters, and with the reports of grumbling over the generalship of Robert E. Lee.

October 23, Wednesday

In the fighting along the Confederate line in Kentucky there was skirmishing at West Liberty and at Hodgenville, not far from President Lincoln's birthplace. Sherman continued to worry mightily over Confederate advance in Kentucky. For the South Zollicoffer in east Tennessee and Kentucky worried about Federal operations and pro-unionists in his area.

There was a skirmish at Gauley, western Va., as activity stepped up in the Kanawha Valley.

October 24, Thursday

TRANSCONTINENTAL TELEGRAPH COMPLETED.

Given impetus by the war, work on the first transcontinental telegraph was completed by Western Union. Though often to be broken by wind, weather, buffalo, and Indians, it represented a gigantic step forward in communications. The new segment of the line ran from Denver to Sacramento across the high mountains, linking earlier completed lines.

The people of western Virginia voted overwhelmingly in favor of forming a new state by ratifying the action of the Wheeling Convention. There was an attack by Confederates on Camp Joe Underwood, Ky.

President Lincoln wrote Brig. Gen. S. R. Curtis that he should deliver enclosed orders to Maj. Gen. Frémont and Gen. David Hunter in the West. The orders, culmination of a long problem, relieved Frémont from command of the Western Department and put Maj. Gen. Hunter temporarily in his place. However, Curtis was not to deliver the orders if Frémont had fought and won a battle or should "be in the immediate presence of the enemy, in expectation of a battle." This same day the President attended the funeral of Col. and Sen. Baker in Washington.

President Davis expressed his worries over the enemy's plans in northern Virginia, the force gathering for coastal invasion, a possible attack at Yorktown, Va., and a descent on North Carolina, adding, "Oh, that we had plenty of arms and a short time to raise the men to use them!"

The Knoxville, Tenn., *Whig* of pro-unionist Parson William Brownlow was forced by Confederates to suspend publication and Brownlow was charged with treason, one of the few instances of Southern press suppression.

October 25, Friday

With a cry of "Frémont and the Union" the cavalry of Frémont under Maj. Charles Zagonyi charged into Springfield, Mo., routing a small Confederate force. It was a relatively minor affair, but was blown up by Frémont partisans into a full-scale battle. Frémont now occupied Springfield, but was far from halting Price's retreat from Lexington or bringing him to battle. Frémont had intimations that his days were numbered and allegedly made arrangements to prevent anyone trying to relieve him from reaching his camp. A Federal force under Brig. Gen. Kelley left New Creek, western Va., in a drive on Romney.

But most important, and unheralded, at Greenpoint, Long Island, the keel of the ironclad U.S.S. *Monitor* was laid. President Davis continued to have difficulty with ambitious commanders, including Beauregard, who did not receive the commissions or commands they expected.

October 26, Saturday

Federal troops under Brig. Gen. Kelley took Romney, an important post in the northern part of western Virginia, with small losses. There was also action at South Branch Bridge and Springfield, western Va. The Federal converted gunboat U.S.S. *Conestoga* carried Union troops up the Cumberland River for a successful attack on Saratoga, Ky. Federal Col. George Wright formally assumed command of the Department of the Pacific, succeeding Edwin V. Sumner.

October 27, Sunday

There was a skirmish at Spring Hill, Mo. Gen. Frémont stated at Springfield, Mo., he was going to pursue and fight Confederate Gen. Price, who was believed to be advancing on Springfield from the southwest. Actually, Price was moving daily farther from the area and had no plans to attack Frémont at this time. Three Confederate vessels were burned by Federals at Chincoteague Inlet, Va.

October 28, Monday

Confederate Gen. Albert Sidney Johnston assumed immediate command of the Army of Central Kentucky at Bowling Green. There was a skirmish near Budd's Ferry, Md., on the Potomac; another at Laurel Bridge in Laurel County, Ky.; and a Federal scout to Fulton, Mo. A pro-secessionist was ridden out of Braintree, Mass., on a rail.

October 29, Tuesday

The huge combined land and sea expedition, under Brig. Gen. Thomas W. Sherman and Flag Officer Samuel F. Du Pont, left Hampton Roads, Va., for the Carolina coast and Port Royal, north of Savannah, Ga. There were seventy-seven vessels and about twelve thousand troops. The expedition, the largest ever assembled by the United States, soon encountered heavy gales off Cape Hatteras, suffering severely. There were skirmishes at and near Woodbury, Ky.

President Lincoln and Gen. McClellan again discussed military plans for the Army of the Potomac as they did so often during this fall of organization but offensive inactivity. In England pro-Union and pro-Confederate meetings were held, with considerable speechmaking by both sides. Lack of supplies and manpower were reported to be hurting both armies in western Va.

October 30, Wednesday

President Davis took Gen. Beauregard to task for permitting portions of his controversial report on the Battle of Manassas to be printed in the newspapers and saying that "it seemed to be an attempt to exalt yourself at my expense."

October 31, Thursday

A remnant of the Missouri legislature voted the state out of the Union and into the Confederacy at Neosho, which in effect created Missouri as a state in both nations. There was skirmishing at Greenbrier and Cotton Hill, western Va., and near Morgantown, Ky.

President Lincoln received a formal request from General-in-Chief Winfield Scott to retire from his post. The elderly Scott was unable to cope with the heavy duties of office and had been pressed by the young and ambitious McClellan, who believed his superior unfit to command.

NOVEMBER, 1861

The fall so far had seen no major military moves by either the Confederate or the United States, and some people of both nations were calling out loudly for offensive blows. It was thought that in both North and South there would soon be important command changes. In Virginia both armies appeared to be doing little except organizing; in western Virginia operations would soon be over for the year due to weather, and it appeared that the Union would hold most of the soon-to-be state. In Kentucky the new Confederate line was making a brave show from Cumberland Gap to Columbus; in Missouri guerrilla activities were mounting and Frémont and his army were in the Ozarks at Springfield supposedly seeking Price and his Confederates. On the south Atlantic coast it was known that a mighty Federal fleet had sailed from Fort Monroe. Where would they strike? Politically the South had an election set, but no one ran against President Davis. In the North two main forces were slowly developing as opposition to the Administration, one definitely for a peaceful settlement, the other for a war of conquest against the South and slavery.

November 1, Friday

MCCLELLAN SUPPLANTS WINFIELD SCOTT.

Youthful, self-contained, supposedly vigorous Maj. Gen. George Brinton McClellan succeeded aged, obese, ailing Lieut. Gen. Winfield Scott. The old man was stepping down voluntarily but under pressure after one of the most illustrious and lengthy careers in American military life. The Civil War was too new, too young, too immense. And furthermore, another man wanted the job. Scott realized he must go, but evidence shows he would have preferred another to the ardent thirty-four-year-old general who had been complaining about him publicly and privately for months. As Scott made his lonely trip to retirement at West Point, there was general approval that a younger man who promised so much would be at the helm as General-in-Chief. True, the fall was flitting past with little or no action, but the Army looked grand. Lincoln and his Cabinet paid a farewell visit to the fading commander.

The seventy-seven ships of the Port Royal expedition were swept by a violent storm off always dangerous Cape Hatteras on their way to South Carolina from Fort Monroe. Scattered, damaged, a transport sunk, the ships endeavored to reach their rendezvous after captains opened sealed orders prepared for such an emergency. U.S.S. *Sabine* went down the next day, but the Marine battalion on board escaped.

There was a skirmish with Indians on the Peosi River of Texas; three days of fighting near Gauley Bridge and Cotton Hill, western Va. From Rolla a Federal cavalry force operated against guerrillas in Missouri. Gen. Frémont at Springfield signed an agreement with commissioners from Confederate Gen. Price regarding exchange of prisoners and released those arrested "for mere expression of political opinions." This agreement was soon abrogated by Mr. Lincoln, as it went beyond local military authority.

November 2, Saturday

FRÉMONT REMOVED.

The career of flamboyant, effervescent, ineffective Maj. Gen. John C. Frémont in the Western Department came to an end when a messenger penetrated Frémont's guards at Springfield, Mo., and handed him the orders placing Maj. Gen. David Hunter temporarily in command of the department. Frémont complained he should not be relieved as he was about to fight the nearby enemy at the old field of Wilson's Creek. But Price and his Confederates were more than sixty miles away. An instant uproar rose from some of Frémont's notorious staff, the army, and a portion of the populace in St. Louis. There were rumors of actual revolt and supposedly there were those who desired Frémont to "set up for himself" his own nation in the West. This never got beyond the talking stage, however, and the disturbance caused by Frémont's removal soon died down.

Meanwhile, southeastern Missouri continued to be roiled from operations of Gen. Jeff Thompson's pro-Confederates. Federal troops Nov. 2–12 carried out operations against them from Bird's Point, Cape Girardeau, and Ironton, Mo. Confederate newspapers warned citizens of the impending invasion of the south Atlantic coast. Gov. Isham G. Harris of Tennessee called for citizens to furnish shotguns and other arms for troops now gathering.

November 3, Sunday

Maj. Gen. David Hunter took over active command of the Western Department from Frémont at Springfield, Mo. President Davis wrote Gen. J. E. Johnston of his concern over what he called the false reports that Davis prevented Gen. Beauregard from following the enemy after Manassas. He asked for Johnston's support.

November 4, Monday

Maj. Gen. Thomas J. "Stonewall" Jackson assumed command of his new Shenandoah Valley District, soon to be the scene of his greatest exploits. Davis, angered by his quarrel with Beauregard, wrote Genls. Cooper and Lee for information in regard to rumors that the President had rejected plans "for vigorous movements against the enemy." At Port Royal Sound north of Savannah a U. S. Coast Survey vessel prowled the area escorted by two naval vessels. They were fired on by small vessels of the Confederate naval squadron as the main Federal fleet assembled outside the sound.

November 5, Tuesday

Gen. Robert E. Lee was named commander of the new Department of South Carolina, Georgia, and East Florida by the Confederate government. Although his reputation was a bit tarnished by the fruitless campaigning in western Virginia, he still maintained an influence with the people of the South. Federal forces under Brig. Gen. William Nelson occupied Prestonburg, Ky. Four Federal naval vessels fought the small, weak Confederate flotilla in Port Royal Sound, S.C., forcing it up into the inland streams.

November 6, Wednesday

ELECTION OF JEFFERSON DAVIS.

Voters of the Confederate States of America went to the polls to select their President under their "permanent" government. Chosen without opposition for a six-year term was Jefferson Davis, who up to now had been Provisional President officially. Members to the first regular Congress were also selected. As yet there was only one political party—the Democratic—although within it there were various factions arising.

November 7, Thursday

BATTLE OF PORT ROYAL SOUND, SOUTH CAROLINA.

ENGAGEMENT AT BELMONT, MISSOURI.

Hundreds of miles apart, two noteworthy military events of the fall broke upon the citizens of the warring nations. At one an important base was won for the Federals; at the other a Northern general re-

ceived a course in offensive action. Flag Officer Du Pont led his powerful Federal naval squadron into Port Royal Sound, steaming straight in
between Forts Beauregard and Walker. The Confederate flotilla of four
small vessels could do little to oppose them. Circling slowly, the fleet
pounded the earthworks of Fort Walker on Hilton Head Island and
then of Fort Beauregard to the north. Outgunned Confederate defenders
were forced to flee the forts and withdraw inland to form a new line
of defense. Casualties were light with 11 Confederates killed, 48 wounded,
3 captured, and 4 missing. For the Federals, there were 8 killed, 6
seriously wounded, and 17 slightly wounded. No major damage was done
to the Federal vessels. Quickly landing parties went ashore and soon
Thomas W. Sherman's 12,000 men began their occupation of the Hilton
Head-Port Royal area. The Union now had a toe hold in Confederate
territory, between Savannah and Charleston. Although they did not exploit it sufficiently on land, it remained a threat throughout the war
and, most importantly, furnished a base for the coaling and supplying
of blockaders. Port Royal represented a valuable enclave carved in Confederate soil and its menace could never be forgotten by Confederate
commanders. Later it also became a center for Negro refugees.

Early the same morning far to the west, another naval flotilla carried
troops down the Mississippi from Cairo, Ill. Two wooden converted gunboats escorted other boats carrying a little over three thousand troops
under command of Brig. Gen. Ulysses S. Grant. Landing on the Missouri
shore north of the hamlet of Belmont opposite the bluffs of Columbus,
Ky., heavily defended by Confederate guns, Grant's men advanced swiftly
to Belmont, capturing it and driving the defenders to cover. Responding
with haste, reinforcements from Maj. Gen. Leonidas Polk's command
crossed the Mississippi, and soon forced Grant's men to retreat. Withdrawing hurriedly, they boarded their vessels and steamed northward
again. The "battle" was really a large raid or reconnaissance. A cooperating
demonstration, from Paducah toward Columbus, as a diversion had little
effect. Federal losses were put at 120 killed, 383 wounded, and 104 captured or missing for 607 out of some 3000. Confederate losses were 105
killed, 419 wounded, and 117 missing for 641 out of about 5000 men
put across the river. Aside from the casualties nothing of strategic value
to either side had been gained. Grant had tested Columbus although
he knew its strength anyway and had no intention of attacking it. But
there was the intangible result of a Union commander getting a schooling
in war in the field without being placed in a major battle before his
ripening; such was the legacy of Belmont to Grant and to the Federal
cause.

In Missouri Maj. Gen. Hunter repudiated the agreement of Frémont
and Price in regard to political prisoners.

November 8, Friday

SEIZURE OF MASON AND SLIDELL: THE *Trent* AFFAIR BEGINS.

On U.S.S. *San Jacinto,* cruising in the Old Bahama Channel, the word was "Beat to quarters" as smoke was seen on the horizon. The British mail packet *Trent* bound for Britain steamed into view. The ensuing events became a *cause célèbre* of international relations, threatened war between the United States and Britain, gave the Confederacy cause for outcries against Federal tyranny, and provided international law with a precedent forever after. James M. Mason of Virginia and John Slidell of Louisiana, named commissioners to Great Britain and France by the Confederate States of America, were en route to their new posts, having escaped the blockade at Charleston on Oct. 12. The Federal authorities had thought they were on a Confederate man-of-war and had made efforts to intercept them. *San Jacinto* under cantankerous, troublemaking, yet competent Capt. Charles Wilkes had called at Havana, Cuba, and found the commissioners there waiting passage on the *Trent. San Jacinto* in turn awaited *Trent's* departure from Cuba. Sailing in the early afternoon of this day, *Trent* was halted by threat of force, and after a spirited argument and some hot words, Mason and Slidell, with their secretaries, were taken under guard to *San Jacinto,* leaving behind outraged wives and children, and an irate and far from speechless British captain, officers, and crew. *San Jacinto,* proud of its accomplishment, headed for Hampton Roads and *Trent* drove on for Britain. For the remainder of the year the seizure on the high seas would hardly be out of the news.

In the Savannah, Ga., area Gen. Robert E. Lee, fresh from his depressing experience in western Virginia, took command of the Confederate Department of South Carolina, Georgia, and East Florida. With it he assumed the burden of a wide territory, difficult to defend, blockaded, inadequately manned and armed, and now seriously threatened by the Federal victory at Port Royal. Taking hold quickly, he prepared as best he could for further invasions of the Southern mainland. Meanwhile, Federals carried out a reconnaissance on Hilton Head Island and nearby territory around Beaufort, S.C.

In the mountains of east Tennessee, pro-unionists waited no longer for military help from the outside which apparently was not coming soon. In an ill-managed uprising the mountaineers burned railroad bridges and harassed Confederate outposts, forcing Brig. Gen. Felix Zollicoffer to call for reinforcements. In Virginia there was a skirmish at Dam No. 5 on the Chesapeake and Ohio Canal, while in Kentucky fighting broke out at Ivy Mountain and Piketon. The Federal gunboat *Rescue,* operating near Urbanna Creek up the Rappahannock in Virginia, captured a schooner, extracted her cargo, and burned her, in addition to dueling with shore batteries. In Missouri pro-Federal Gov. Hamilton R. Gamble made arrangements for the organization of a militia.

In Savannah large crowds filled the streets and collected near the telegraph offices for news of the invasion of the Confederate shore a few miles north. Many families packed for the upcountry. At Charleston the ever vocal *Mercury* cried, "Let the invaders come, 'tis the unanimous feeling of our people. Our Yankee enemies will, sooner or later, learn to their cost the difference between invaders for spoils and power, and defenders of their liberties, their native land."

November 9, Saturday

Federals from their new base at Port Royal captured the useful city of Beaufort. S.C., without a fight. Gen. Lee wrote Richmond that the Federal forces in the coastal area concerned him greatly, what with their control of the ocean and many inland streams.

The Union War Department made some important command changes that were to have immense influence on future events. The old Department of the West was discontinued and a new Department of Kansas under Maj. Gen. David Hunter created. The Department of New Mexico was to be under Col. E. R. S. Canby. But most vital was the new Department of the Missouri, including Missouri, Arkansas, Illinois, and Kentucky west of the Cumberland River. This command was to be entrusted to Maj. Gen. Henry Wager Halleck. Halleck was regarded as one of the most intelligent administrators in the Army, and it was to be his task to straighten out the considerable mess created by Frémont, and to direct operations along the Tennessee and Mississippi rivers. The new Department of the Ohio, which replaced those of Ohio and the Cumberland, consisted of Ohio, Indiana, Michigan and Tennessee, and Kentucky east of the Cumberland River. Command was given to Brig. Gen. Don Carlos Buell, who superseded W. T. Sherman. The job had proved too great a nervous strain for Sherman, who departed under a cloud with even his sanity questioned. Buell, like Halleck, was thought to be a stalwart, firm, and able soldier.

There was a skirmish at Ivy Mountain, Ky., and a small Federal expedition to Mathias Point, Va. The bridge burning in eastern Tennessee by pro-unionists continued for several days.

November 10, Sunday

President Davis wrote Gen. Joseph E. Johnston at Manassas that he was surprised the Army had shown so little increase since July, but that "we are restricted in our capacity to reinforce by want of arms." He hoped to augment the numbers, "but you must remember that our wants greatly exceed our resources." There was fighting at Gauley Bridge, Guyandotte, and Blake's Farm near Cotton Hill, western Va. Confederates began to withdraw troops eastward as fighting in much of western Virginia ended. Federals from Hilton Head at Port Royal Sound carried out an expedition to Braddock's Point, S.C., one of several such operations partially exploiting their landing on the South Carolina-Georgia coast. There was a skirmish near Bristol in east Tennessee.

November 11, Monday

Confederate Maj. Gen. George B. Crittenden was assigned to command the District of Cumberland Gap. At Columbus, Ky., one of the large 128-pound guns on the bluffs exploded accidentally, killing seven men and wounding Maj. Gen. Leonidas Polk. Fighting was confined to action at Little Blue River, Mo., between Kansas Jayhawkers and secessionists, and at New Market Bridge near Fort Monroe, Va. Professor Thaddeus Lowe sent up his Federal observation balloon from a special "Balloon-Boat" anchored in the Potomac River. Formal obsequies were held in New York for Col. Edward Baker, U.S. senator killed at Ball's Bluff. The body was sent to San Francisco. In Washington President Lincoln watched an impressive torchlight procession in honor of McClellan.

November 12, Tuesday

The Confederate government-owned blockade-runner *Fingal* (later C.S.S. *Atlanta*), bought in England, arrived in Savannah with military supplies. Federals made a reconnaissance to Pohick Church and Occoquan, Va., but were driven back. There was yet another skirmish near Cotton Hill, western Va., this time near Laurel Creek.

November 13, Wednesday

In the evening President Lincoln and his secretary John Hay visited Gen. McClellan at his home. The President waited some time before the general arrived, but McClellan immediately retired without speaking to Mr. Lincoln. This well-known incident is often cited to show the manner in which the youthful general treated his President. In northern western Virginia there was skirmishing near Romney; and in Missouri one Federal expedition operated from Greenville to Doniphan Nov. 13–15, and another moved through Texas and Wright counties Nov. 13–18.

November 14, Thursday

A small Federal force broke up a Confederate camp in Virginia, near Point of Rocks, Md., on the Potomac; a skirmish broke out on the road from Fayetteville to Raleigh, and another at McCoy's Mill, in western Va. Other secondary scouting and reconnaissance operations were carried on throughout the fall in northern Virginia by both warring parties.

November 15, Friday

U.S.S. *San Jacinto* under Capt. Charles Wilkes arrived at Fort Monroe, Va., with the captured Confederate commissioners to Britain and France, Mason and Slidell. In a few hours the news of their seizure from the British packet *Trent* resounded throughout the North. Cheers and rejoicing broke out as most Cabinet members and officials approved the course of the audacious naval officer. It was thought the United States had struck a blow against the Confederacy and foreign intervention on her behalf. The prisoners were ordered sent to Fort Warren in Boston Harbor. The Confederacy was at first aghast at such a treachery as taking diplomatic personnel off a non-belligerent vessel, but it soon realized that this incident might be what was needed to bring about the coveted foreign recognition. Within a few days in the North the bloom was off, as sober minds reconsidered and saw the danger of serious trouble with Britain and France, perhaps even war. The cheering for Wilkes's gallantry soon died away; lawyers and diplomats disputed and were concerned; fine points of international law were debated.

Brig. Gen. Don Carlos Buell assumed command of the new Department of the Ohio, operating from Louisville. It was hoped that a Federal drive into east Tennessee would at last be undertaken. Meanwhile, a camp of pro-unionist civilians was dispersed near Chattanooga, Tenn.

The Young Men's Christian Association organized the U. S. Christian Commission for service to Federal soldiers. Throughout the war they published tracts, furnished nurses, and aided the soldiers in countless ways.

The Confederate Navy Department called for offers for construction of ironclad men-of-war. The Louisville *Journal* published a suggestion of a Wisconsin volunteer challenging any fifer in the Confederate Army to compete with him on the fife for the sum of $500 a side. "Yankee Doodle" and "The Star-Spangled Banner" would be played, and "The trial match to come off when Buckner and his army have been taken prisoner."

November 16, Saturday

Federal foraging parties were captured by Confederates at Doolan's Farm, Va., and near Pleasant Hill in Cass County, Mo. Flour in Vicksburg, Miss., was reported to cost $20 a barrel. Sen. Charles Sumner of Mass. and Postmaster General Montgomery Blair protested the capture of Mason and Slidell and urged their surrender at once.

November 17, Sunday

Skirmishing occurred at Cypress Bridge, near Rumsey, McLean County,

Ky. A heavily laden British blockade-runner was seized by the gunboat *Connecticut* off Cape Canaveral, Fla. (now Cape Kennedy).

November 18, Monday

The fifth session of the Provisional Congress of the Confederate States of America met in Richmond. In Kentucky soldiers of the Confederate Army adopted an ordinance of secession in a convention at Russellville, creating a Confederate government for the state, which now, like Missouri, had governments representing both the United and Confederate States. Federal Com. David Dixon Porter was ordered to purchase vessels and organize a mortar flotilla for the forthcoming expedition to New Orleans.

There was fighting near Warrensburg and Palmyra, Mo., and Falls Church, Va. A group of pro-unionists was seized at Doe River, east Tenn.

In North Carolina a convention at Hatteras repudiated the secession of the state and reaffirmed loyalty to the Union, naming a provisional government. Jeff Thompson with his Missourians seized a Federal steamer at Price's Landing.

November 19, Tuesday

"Liberty is always won where there exists the unconquerable will to be free"—so Jefferson Davis informed the Confederate Congress in his presidential message read to the new session. In a generally optimistic report the President said in retrospect the year "is such as should fill the hearts of our people with gratitude to Providence." Crops were good, military operations were moderately satisfactory, an army was created in the midst of war, and the financial situation was hopeful. There were problems in coping with numerous Federal military operations, and a need for a more satisfactory transportation system and a husbanding of means and resources. The President inveighed against the "barbarous" hostilities of the North, citing several incidents.

Maj. Gen. Henry W. Halleck assumed command of the Department of the Missouri in St. Louis, taking over from temporary commander David Hunter, who in turn went to the Department of Kansas. A new regime had begun reorganization of the war in the West and in general its first steps were successful—a vast improvement over the rule of Frémont. Brig. Gen. George Wright was formally assigned to command the Federal Department of the Pacific although he was already in charge. For the Confederates, Lucius Q. C. Lamar was appointed a special agent to Russia. Gen. Albert Sidney Johnston called for all militia and volunteer forces in Tennessee to be armed if possible. There was fighting at Round Mountain, Indian Terr., where Creek Indians fleeing to Kansas held off pro-Southern Cherokees and Texans. The Confederate raider *Nashville* captured and burned the clipper ship *Harvey Birch* in the Atlantic, one of numerous seizures by Southern cruisers this fall.

November 20, Wednesday

Skirmishing occurred at Butler and Little Santa Fe, Mo., as well as at Brownsville, Ky. Maj. Gen. David Hunter assumed command of the Federal Department of Kansas. The Richmond *Dispatch* announced that the demand for "Yankee books" was still high in the South. In California Federal troops pursued and, on Nov. 29, captured a pro-Confederate band known as the Showalter Party. Daniel Showalter and seventeen others were taken near Warner's Ranch southeast of Los Angeles after a hard chase.

November 21, Thursday

Judah P. Benjamin was named by President Davis as Secretary of War for the Confederacy, succeeding LeRoy Pope Walker, who had not done too badly considering the pressures from all sides, including Davis. But it was a post which for a while would be subject to frequent change, and Benjamin was thought to be the man who could better handle the complex personnel problems involved. Walker had many critics. Thomas Bragg, brother of Gen. Braxton Bragg, succeeded Benjamin as Attorney General. Brig. Gen. Lloyd Tilghman was named to command Forts Henry and Donelson on the Tennessee and Cumberland rivers. The forts, just south of the Kentucky-Tennessee line, were begun in midsummer at spots not particularly suitable for forts but as far north as possible. The Confederates recognized that the two rivers would be as important routes for invasion as the Mississippi; all fall Federal vessels had been coming to poke around and investigate. Fearful for the safety of the post at Columbus, Ky., after the engagement of Belmont, the Confederates called for ten thousand volunteers from Mississippi. Confederates destroyed a supply of Federal stores at Warsaw, Mo.

November 22, Friday

Guns of Fort Pickens and U.S.S. *Niagara* and U.S.S. *Richmond* began two days of heavy bombardment against Confederates at Fort McRee, Fort Barrancas, and the Pensacola Navy Yard in the harbor of Pensacola, Fla. Both sides suffered some damage. The Confederate Department of the Indian Territory was established under Brig. Gen. Albert Pike.

November 23, Saturday

The bombardment of the Pensacola Confederate installations continued from Fort Pickens and two warships, but the results were negligible for both sides. In Kentucky Brig. Gen. George H. Thomas, under Buell's command, advanced with the Federal left wing from Danville in a demonstration toward east Tennessee.

November 24, Sunday

Forces of the United States landed on Tybee Island, Ga., on the Savannah River, controlling the entrance to the harbor and furnishing a foothold for an attack on Fort Pulaski, the brick fortification designed to defend the city of Savannah. There was skirmishing at Lancaster and Johnstown, Mo. A little-known Confederate cavalryman named Nathan Bedford Forrest undertook an expedition Nov. 24–Dec. 5 to Caseyville and Eddyville, Ky.

U.S.S. *San Jacinto* with its controversial, enforced passengers, Mason and Slidell, arrived at Boston, where the would-be diplomats were imprisoned at Fort Warren in Boston Harbor. In Washington Mr. Lincoln and his Cabinet conferred on what was now called the *"Trent* Affair" and its repercussions.

November 25, Monday

The Confederate Navy Department accepted a shipment of armor plate for the former U.S.S. *Merrimack,* now being converted at Norfolk into the ironclad C.S.S. *Virginia.* Meanwhile, another blockade-runner was taken near North Edisto, S.C., and at the same time a U.S. merchant brig was captured by C.S.S. *Sumter* off the Leeward Islands. In Washington Maj. Isaac Lynde was dismissed from the U. S. Army for abandoning Fort Fillmore, N. Mex. Terr., in July.

November 26, Tuesday

A convention at Wheeling in western Virginia adopted a constitution for a new state to be called West Virginia, created by secession from Virginia. Mr. Lincoln prepared the draft of a bill, never introduced into Congress, authorizing the Federal government to pay the state of Delaware $719,200 in bonds provided the state would abolish slavery through compensation to owners of slaves. In a skirmish near Vienna, Va., Federals were forced to retreat; there was also a two-day Federal expedition to Dranesville, Va., with skirmishing. Other skirmishing was at Independence, Mo. At Savannah Confederate vessels made a dash at the Federal blockaders attempting to draw them into the fire of Fort Pulaski, but failed. C.S.S. *Sumter* claimed another victim in the Atlantic. At Boston a banquet was given honoring Capt. Wilkes, who in *San Jacinto* had seized the Confederate commissioners to Europe.

November 27, Wednesday

News of the seizure of the Confederate commissioners from the British packet *Trent* had reached Great Britain. The word spread rapidly, igniting blazing indignation. "Outrage on the British Flag" placards announced. At Hampton Roads a second major Federal expedition got under way and headed south. This time it was bound for Ship Island, Miss., where a base was being established to operate against New Orleans and the Gulf Coast. There was a light skirmish near Fairfax Court House, Va.

November 28, Thursday
The Southern Congress officially admitted Missouri to the Confederate States of America. A day of thanksgiving was observed in the Northern states, with many prominent figures publicly proclaiming thanks that loyal men were fighting for their country. On the south Atlantic coast around Port Royal Sound Federal authorities were ordered to take possession of all crops in the area and to use Negro slaves to gather them and to work on the installations and defenses.

November 29, Friday
Flames were visible along much of the south Atlantic coast near Charleston and Savannah as Southern planters burned cotton to prevent it from falling into Federal hands. "Let the torch be applied whenever the invader pollutes our soil," the Charleston *Mercury* exclaimed. At Warner's Ranch, Calif., southeast of Los Angeles, Federal troops finally captured the Showalter Party, whom they had pursued since Nov. 20.

November 30, Saturday
British Foreign Secretary Lord John Russell wrote Lord Lyons, Minister to the United States, that the seizure of Confederate commissioners Mason and Slidell was aggression against Britain and that Her Majesty's Government trusted that the commissioners would be turned over to British protection with a suitable apology. If an answer was not forthcoming in seven days, Lyons was instructed to leave Washington with his legation and return to London. At the same time, Lord Russell directed the British Navy to take such measures as circumstances required, but to refrain from any act of hostility. In Washington high-level meetings on the *Trent* Affair continued.

There was skirmishing at Grand River, Mo., and near the mouth of Little Cacapon River, western Va. A "suspicious" lady passenger on a steamer at Baltimore was found to have gloves, stockings, and letters intended for the South, while a small boy on board carried a quantity of quinine. Both were allowed to pass after their cargo had been confiscated, just one of numerous such incidents.

DECEMBER, 1861

In the North excitement, tinged with anxiety and doubt, continued over the *Trent* Affair as acclamation for Wilkes's seizure of the Confederate commissioners began to sour. Congress would meet, and the President would comment on the state of the Union. Grumblings over the failure of the Army of the Potomac to act were rising; the first winter of the war was upon the people.

In the South indignation over the *Trent* Affair also shifted to a realization that it might be a blessing in disguise and that Mason and Slidell in Federal hands might be more useful than in posts in Britain and France. On the military front, there was concern over both men and arms, and, while not yet tight, the unceasingly present blockade cast forebodings for the future. Some bickering and discontent over both political and social affairs was bound to rise within a new nation and a new government fighting a war, but the people as a whole remained hopeful. In the coastal areas of the Carolinas and Georgia, planters continued to burn cotton crops to prevent seizure by Yankees and to create a cotton shortage abroad.

December 1, Sunday
President Lincoln in a memorandum to Gen. McClellan asked some pointed questions about a possible forward movement of the Army of the Potomac and "how *long* would it require to actually get in motion?"

There was skirmishing near Camp Goggin, and at Whippoorwill Creek, Ky.; Morristown, Tenn.; and Shanghai, Mo., with two weeks of minor operations around Mill Springs and Somerset, Ky. Federal gunboats demonstrated near Fort Holt, Ky. U.S. gunboat *Penguin* captured the blockade-runner *Albion* of Nassau off Charleston. Her rich cargo included arms, ammunition, salt, fruit, provisions, oils, tin, copper, saddles, bridles, and cavalry equipment valued at $100,000.

December 2, Monday
The second session of the Thirty-seventh Congress of the United States got under way in Washington against a background of exasperation over the military defeats at Ball's Bluff and First Bull Run, over the failure of the army in Virginia to take action during the fall, and over the *Trent* Affair. There were many expressions of discontent about the administration of the war and the nation in general. Slavery, too, was

more and more an issue. President Lincoln authorized Gen. Halleck in the Department of the Missouri to suspend the privilege of the writ of habeas corpus whenever he found it necessary. There was a small skirmish at Annandale, Va. Four Federal gunboats engaged Confederate steamer *Patrick Henry* near Newport News, Va. In the two-hour bombardment *Patrick Henry* was damaged.

December 3, Tuesday

"The Union must be preserved, and hence, all indispensable means must be employed. We should not be in haste to determine that radical and extreme measures, which may reach the loyal as well as the disloyal, are indispensable." So wrote President Lincoln in his annual State of the Union message to Congress. The President covered many fields, foreign and domestic, as well as reporting on the war effort. He claimed that "the insurrection is largely, if not exclusively, a war upon the first principle of popular government—the rights of the people." Then, turning to what he called popular institutions, he wrote, "Labor is prior to, and independent of, capital. Capital is only the fruit of Labor, and could never have existed if labor had not first existed. . . . Capital has its rights, which are as worthy of protection as any other rights." He concluded this long, moderate message with "The struggle of today, is not altogether for today —it is for a vast future also." In general he found the condition of the nation good, despite the war, and called again for colonization of free Negroes, a plan which was becoming more and more a part of Lincoln's policy.

Meanwhile, the war itself had pretty much reached a droning stage, although there was action at Salem, Mo., and Vienna, Va., and Federal forces reoccupied Ship Island, preparatory to moving against New Orleans or the Gulf Coast.

December 4, Wednesday

The Federal Senate, voting 36 to 0, expelled Sen. John C. Breckinridge of Kentucky. After the start of the war he had remained in his seat during the special summer session, seeking if possible to bring about peace, but in November he had entered the Confederate Army.

There was a skirmish near Burke's Station, Va. Confederate newspapers increased their clamor for strong military action in many areas of the South. Queen Victoria of Britain in a proclamation forbade export of gunpowder, firearms, and materials for manufacturing them. In St. Louis Gen. Halleck ordered the arrest of those giving aid to the secessionists.

December 5, Thursday

In the Federal Congress petitions and bills calling for the abolition of slavery, especially among slaveholders "in rebellion," were introduced.

There were 682,971 men in the Army and Navy according to the reports of the Secretaries of War and the Navy. Maj. Gen. William J. Hardee assumed command of the Confederate Central Army of Kentucky. Dec. 5–8 there was a Federal scout in the vicinity of Russellville, Ky., and from the fifth through ninth another expedition in the Current Hills of Missouri.

December 6, Friday
For two days Federals operated in the area around Port Royal Ferry and Beaufort, S.C., from their growing base on Hilton Head Island. Brig. Gen. George G. Meade led a foraging expedition to Gunnell's Farm, near Dranesville, Va.

December 7, Saturday
U.S.S. *Santiago de Cuba* under Com. Daniel B. Ridgely halted the British schooner *Eugenia Smith* near the mouth of the Rio Grande and seized J. W. Zacharie, New Orleans merchant, a Confederate purchasing agent. This incident added to the heat already created by the *Trent* Affair. There was a small skirmish near Glasgow, Mo.

December 8, Sunday
Three minor skirmishes broke the Sabbath near Romney and Dam No. 5 on the Chesapeake and Ohio Canal in western Va. and at Fishing Creek near Somerset, Ky. C.S.S. *Sumter* under Com. Semmes captured the Federal whaler *Eben Dodge* in mid-Atlantic. The American Bible Society announced it was distributing seven thousand copies a day of the Scriptures to Northern soldiers.

December 9, Monday
Following a lengthy discussion of military "disasters," the U. S. Senate approved 33 to 3 the setting up of what became the famous Joint Committee on the Conduct of the War, whose investigations caused great furor and criticism as well as considerable approval. In the course of their work they questioned many generals and other officers in regard to certain battles and campaigns. In some cases they seem to have applied liberal coats of whitewash, and in others they can be charged with being overly critical for political reasons. But their interrogations were revealing in many instances and provide excellent material for historical appraisal and research. Formation of the committee was urged mainly by the "radical" senators who desired an investigation of the Ball's Bluff fiasco.

Southern planters on the Georgia and South Carolina coasts continued burning cotton to prevent it from falling into Federal hands. The Charleston *Courier* said that this action deprived the Federals of "the extensive spoils with which they have feasted their imagination, and the obtainment of which was one of their chief objects."

There was skirmishing at Union Mills, Mo. In an engagement at Chusto-Talasah (Bird Creek or High Shoal), Indian Terr., not far from Tulsey Town (now Tulsa), Confederate forces, mainly Indians, defeated pro-Federal Creek Indians seeking to withdraw into Kansas. But the Southern forces were compelled temporarily to discontinue their drive against the Creeks under Opothleyahola, due to lack of supplies and the tenacious defense.

December 10, Tuesday

An act of the Confederate Congress in Richmond admitted the state of Kentucky to the Confederacy, thus completing the thirteen states, including Missouri and Kentucky, which were considered by the South members of the Confederate States of America. The Kentucky Confederate government was in exile or shifting continuously, as was that of Missouri, throughout the war. The U. S. House of Representatives approved the Senate resolution for the Joint Committee on the Conduct of the War, passed the day before. Soon the committee was in full operation.

December 11, Wednesday

A disastrous fire swept the business district of Charleston, S.C., east of King Street and near the Cooper River. Suffering as it was from the blockade and the threat of Federals at Hilton Head Island, this was a new blow to the spiritual center of the Confederacy. There was skirmishing near Bertrand, Mo., and at Dam No. 4 on the Chesapeake and Ohio Canal in Virginia. President Lincoln attended the Senate memorial services for Sen. Baker of Oregon, killed at Ball's Bluff. It was unusual at that time for the President to enter either House.

December 12, Thursday

Federal Marines and naval forces operated on the Ashepoo River in South Carolina, part of the continuing spread out from Port Royal Sound and investigation of nearby rivers, inlets, and communities. There was also skirmishing at Charleston, Mo.; Gradyville, Ky.; and on the Greenbrier River in western Virginia.

December 13, Friday

From the Cheat Mountain encampment of the Federal army in western Virginia, Brig. Gen. R. H. Milroy led Federal troops against the Confederates at Camp Alleghany or Buffalo Mountain. After rather severe fighting the Federals fell back with 137 casualties, the Confederates suffering 146. Both armies retreated, the Federals to Cheat Mountain and the Confederates to Staunton in the Shenandoah.

Arguing with Confederate congressmen over the command in Missouri, President Davis wrote, "I have, long since, learned to bear hasty censure in the hope that justice if tardy is sure, and in any event to find consolation in the assurance that all my ends have been my country's."

December 14, Saturday

His Royal Highness Prince Albert, deeply beloved consort of Queen Victoria, died. Two weeks before, ill though he was, he had drafted some of the important diplomatic correspondence of the British government in relation to the capture of the Confederate commissioners Mason and Slidell in the *Trent* Affair. From Windsor Castle Prince Albert had urged moderation but firmness toward the United States, without undue irritation. England and the entire British Empire was in mourning.

Brig. Gen. H. H. Sibley assumed command of the Confederate forces on the upper Rio Grande and in New Mexico and Arizona territories.

December 15, Sunday

Two Confederate blockade-runners were captured; one off Cape Fear and the other off Cape Hatteras, continuing the slow but steady tightening of the Federal blockade. There was a minor affair in Roane County and Dec. 15–21 activity around Meadow Bluff, western Va. For a couple of days there was patrolling on the lower Potomac in Virginia.

December 16, Monday

A resolution was introduced in the U. S. House of Representatives by Clement Vallandigham of Ohio, commending Capt. Charles Wilkes for capturing Confederate commissioners Mason and Slidell. It was referred to committee.

December 17, Tuesday

T. J. "Stonewall" Jackson continued his operations along the Potomac near Harper's Ferry, particularly against Dam No. 5 on the Chesapeake and Ohio Canal. There was a skirmish on Chisolm's Island, S.C., and Confederates evacuated Rockville, S.C., threatened by Federals from Hilton Head. There was action at Rowlett's Station near Woodsonville, Green River, Ky. Federals sank several old hulks loaded with stones in Savannah Harbor in an effort to halt shipping.

British newspapers began arriving in the United States. Their belligerent outcries over the apprehension of Mason and Slidell on the high seas caused consternation throughout the North and hope of recognition in the South.

December 18, Wednesday

The British minister in Washington, Lord Lyons, received his instructions from London, which included a firm demand for the release of the captive Confederate commissioners, Mason and Slidell. Mr. Lincoln and his Cabinet discussed the *Trent* Affair informally.

Union scouting and reconnaissance was carried out at Blackwater Creek, Shawnee Mound or Milford, Mo., and from Rolla toward Houston, Mo.; in Virginia toward Pohick Church; and from Somerset to Mill Springs, Ky.

In Washington Mr. Lincoln talked with McClellan at the general's home about future operations of the armies.

December 19, Thursday

Lord Lyons, British minister to the United States, conferred with Sec. of State Seward and acquainted him with the tenor and demands of the British government for the release of Southern commissioners Mason and Slidell. There were to be seven days in which to answer after the message was officially communicated.

There was a skirmish at Point of Rocks, Md., part of the nearly continuous action and probing along the Potomac.

December 20, Friday

From Britain two troop vessels sailed for Canada; bands played "Dixie" and "The British Grenadiers." Their purpose—to have soldiers available in case of need arising out of the *Trent* Affair. Sixteen old whaling vessels were sunk in the main ship channel off Charleston to impede blockade-runners. These methods, often applied, generally had little effect. There was a sharp fight at Dranesville, Va.

President Davis wrote Sterling Price, Missouri commander, that "the welfare of Missouri is as dear to me as that of other States of the Confederacy," in answer to charges that the Richmond government was neglecting the Trans-Mississippi, and Missouri in particular.

December 21, Saturday

Lord Lyons, representing Britain, conferred again with Sec. of State Seward over the demands for the release of Confederate commissioners Mason and Slidell. As a result of that interview Lyons wrote to Lord Russell, Foreign Minister, Dec. 23, "I am so convinced that unless we give our friends here a good lesson this time, we shall have the same trouble with them again very soon. . . . Surrender or war will have a very good effect on them." Southern papers were enthusiastically commenting on possibilities of war between the United States and the British Empire. For the Confederates, Brig. Gen. Henry A. Wise, after his difficulties in western Virginia, was assigned to duty in North Carolina, where it was thought a new threat would come.

December 22, Sunday

There was a light skirmish near New Market, Va., not far from Newport News. Federal Maj. Gen. H. W. Halleck cracked down on bridge burning and destruction of railroads and the telegraph in Missouri by ordering that anyone so caught would be immediately shot.

December 23, Monday

Lord Lyons conferred once again with Seward, presenting formally and officially the British note demanding surrender of Confederate commissioners Mason and Slidell. There was also a White House conference on the subject, with Sen. Charles Sumner of Mass. later urging the President to surrender the commissioners, now a cause of much embarrassment to the United States.

Small Federal forces advanced from Louisa, Ky., for a foray into eastern Kentucky, lasting until late January. There were similar minor operations around Lexington, Mo., and a skirmish at Dayton, Mo.

December 24, Tuesday

Christmas Eve—the first of the war—many hearts were torn, North and South, and many a soldier on a lonely, inactive post dreamed of home and fireside. In the U.S.A. and C.S.A. Christmas would not be the same this year. The Federal Congress passed a bill increasing duties on tea, coffee, sugar, and molasses. There was a skirmish at Wadesburg, Mo., and a scout by Federals toward Fairfax Court House, Va.

December 25, Wednesday

It was a busy Christmas Day in the White House. Mr. Lincoln and his Cabinet met for lengthy discussions about the British demands for release of Confederate commissioners Mason and Slidell. A decision was to be made the next day. The Lincolns at Christmas dinner entertained many guests.

The shooting did not stop for the holiday. There was skirmishing at Cherry, western Va., near Fort Frederick, Md.; a Union expedition operated near Danville, Mo. Off Cape Fear, N.C., a blockade-runner was taken.

December 26, Thursday

SURRENDER BY UNITED STATES OF MASON AND SLIDELL.

After another Cabinet meeting it was finally agreed that the seizure of Mason and Slidell while en route to Britain and France was illegal and that they would be released by the United States. The message was sent to Lord Lyons, British minister in Washington, and the crisis was ended. The U.S. government had swallowed its pride and concluded that the Confederate commissioners were a greater danger in their hands than if they were abroad. With the surrender of Mason and Slidell to the British went another hope of the Confederacy that their struggling nation would be recognized by major foreign powers.

Martial law was proclaimed in St. Louis and in and about all railroads operating in Missouri. There was an engagement at Chustenahlah, Indian Terr., scene of recent operations by Confederate Indians and Texans against pro-Union Creek Indians under Opothleyahola. After severe losses the Creeks fled, some of them reaching Kansas after awesome privations. Brig. Gen. Philip St. George Cocke, Confederate officer who had distinguished himself earlier in the year, committed suicide at his home in Powhatan County, Va. Over 150 horses died in a fire in the government stables near the Washington Observatory. At the mouth of the Savannah River a small Confederate flotilla of five ships attacked Federal blockaders and forced them to move away, but only temporarily.

December 27, Friday

Throughout the North and the South the press spread the word of the forthcoming release of Confederate commissioners Mason and Slidell. The *Trent* Affair, to everyone's relief, was over.

At Hallsville, Mo., a small skirmish broke out. Representative Alfred Ely of New York arrived in Washington from Richmond, Va., where he had been a prisoner of war since his capture in July while a civilian watcher at the Battle of Bull Run or Manassas. The Confederate and Union armies were settling in for winter building cabins and quarters.

December 28, Saturday

Federal forces occupied Beckley or Raleigh Court House, western Va.; there was fighting at Sacramento, Ky., and Mount Zion Church, Mo. There was a skirmish at Grider's Ferry on the Cumberland River in Kentucky.

December 29, Sunday

There were two days of skirmishing in Clay, Braxton, and Webster counties of western Virginia. Jeff Thompson's Confederates operated against Commerce, Mo., and unsuccessfully attacked the steamer *City of Alton*. Skirmishing continued in the Indian Territory in the wake of the exodus of the pro-Union Creeks, who were opposed by Choctaws, Chickasaws, and portions of the Seminoles and Cherokees.

December 30, Monday

The U.S. government and banks in some leading cities suspended specie payment. This suspension of redeeming paper money for metallic continued until 1879.

December 31, Tuesday

The last night of a climactic year; no one grieved its passing, but all wondered what 1862 would bring. A troubled President Lincoln, concerned over the lack of action by his Army, found that Maj. Gen. McClellan, General-in-Chief, was ill. In effect taking over, he wired Gen. Halleck in St. Louis, "Are General Buell and yourself in concert?" The President sought to goad someone into doing something. In Richmond the still young Confederate government had survived the year, but the new nation was in peril and not yet free of Federal bondage.

From Ship Island a Federal landing party captured Biloxi, Miss., destroyed a Confederate battery, but did not attempt to hold the town.

Eighteen sixty-one ended in sorrow, consternation, and doubt.

1862

The dawn of 1862 was dismal, uncertain, sobering, in both the North and the South. The past year had seen much: a new nation, an engulfing war, and agony of body and spirit. And yet at the same time there was a realization that the issues had been joined and there were jobs to be done. In the South their freedom had been proclaimed; it must now be solidified by the fire of war. In the North there was a disrupted Union to be rejoined in another concept of freedom.

How were these tasks to be completed? Would the coming year see them at an end? Some still hoped so; others were uneasy and disturbed.

JANUARY, 1862

It was a cold, bitter winter to those in camps from northern Virginia through the Kentucky line to Cairo and beyond. For those at home things were not yet too bad in the North, except when the casualty lists came or the regiments left for the South. To those at home in the South the stark verities of the battle for their rights were impregnating the whole Confederacy. There were still songs, still rallies, still a crusade; but the glitter was dimming.

In the White House at Washington a worried Mr. Lincoln virtually had to take command of the armies, for his top general was seriously ill. Besides, George Brinton McClellan, it appeared, had accomplished little of substance in five months. In the White House at Richmond an equally worried Mr. Davis watched his armies diminish in manpower, as many went home to fix things up so they could come back in the spring. The blockade was more than paper now, its impress growing with the days. There was not enough of *anything,* really, except valor.

January 1, Wednesday

At Provincetown, Mass., on Cape Cod four men boarded the British sloop of war *Rinaldo* en route to Halifax and Europe. The imprisoned Confederate commissioners Mason and Slidell and their secretaries had left Fort Warren in Boston Harbor after the Federal government had acceded to British demands for their release. The *Trent* Affair was finished, but it left a bad taste.

Presidents Lincoln and Davis opened the new year with traditional receptions. In Washington all the Cabinet members, diplomatic corps, justices, and army and navy officers attended, as well as the public. One guest, an Illinois politician, had his pocket picked of more than $50 in gold.

In Richmond bands played and thousands grasped Mr. Davis' hand at the door of his reception room.

Mr. Lincoln, though, had problems trying to get Gen. Halleck from St. Louis and Cairo and Gen. Buell from Louisville to cooperate "in concert" in drives on Nashville, Tenn., and Columbus, Ky. The General-in-Chief, George B. McClellan, remained ill.

In Pensacola, Fla., the new year was welcomed by a bombardment by Federals on shipping and on Fort Barrancas, and by Confederates on

Fort Pickens. There was a sharp engagement at Port Royal Ferry on the Coosaw River, S.C., part of the long-continuing operations by Federals enlarging their main enclave on the south Atlantic coast. Dayton, Mo., was virtually destroyed during a skirmish. Stonewall Jackson led a Confederate force toward Romney, western Va.

January 2, Thursday
The President learned Gen. McClellan was very much improved, but not yet back on duty leading the Federal land armies. In the South the Memphis *Argus,* like many Confederate papers, was beginning to ask why the soldiers were not used and to complain of taxes.

January 3, Friday
Stonewall Jackson was on the march despite winter weather. From Winchester, Va., he had moved north Jan. 1 on what is often called the Romney Campaign. There was a brief skirmish at Bath, western Va. Jackson's purpose was to break up the Baltimore & Ohio Railroad and destroy dams on the Chesapeake and Ohio Canal. In December he had struck at Dam No. 5 and now was aiming at more depredations. There was also action at Huntersville, western Va., and a Federal reconnaissance near Big Bethel, Va., as well as a skirmish at Hunnewell, Mo. President Davis, aware of Federal troops on Ship Island, Miss., realized the movement "no doubt is intended against Mobile or New Orleans," in writing the governor of Mississippi.

January 4, Saturday
As Jackson's Confederates entered and occupied Bath, western Va., there were other skirmishes in the soon-to-be-state at Slane's Cross Roads, Great Cacapon Bridge, Sir John's Run, and Alpine Depot. Mr. Lincoln as President and really temporary General-in-Chief, vice the ill McClellan, inquired of Gen. Buell in Kentucky as to the progress of his much desired movement toward and into east Tennessee. Buell somewhat doubted the wisdom of the move, and at times appeared to neglect it.

January 5, Sunday
Stonewall Jackson's Confederates, moving from Bath, western Va., to the Potomac opposite Hancock, Md., pursued the retiring Federals and bombarded the town for two days without receiving a surrender or making a crossing. For a week there were Federal operations in Johnson and La Fayette counties of Missouri with a skirmish at Columbus, Mo.

January 6, Monday
President Lincoln conferred with Gen. McClellan, recovering from what has been called typhoid fever; rejected a move of Radical senators to re-

move the general for lack of action; and wrote Gen. Buell in Kentucky of his distress over "our friends in East Tennessee," urging, without ordering, military advance in the area.

January 7, Tuesday

Jackson's forces, turning from Hancock, Md., moved toward Romney, western Va., away from the Potomac, with fighting at Hanging Rock Pass or Blue's Gap. In the eastern Kentucky operations, there was a skirmish near Paintsville and another at Jennie's Creek, as Federals moved slowly forward. The Federal Department of North Carolina was constituted and would be commanded by Brig. Gen. Ambrose E. Burnside.

January 8, Wednesday

Federals routed a Confederate camp at Roan's Tan-Yard on Silver Creek, Mo., while there was another skirmish at Charleston, Mo., and a minor affair on the Dry Fork of Cheat River, western Va. Near Somerset on Fishing Creek, Ky., there was a small skirmish, and as the armies were gathering in the area it presaged more to come. President Davis continued to correspond with the various governors, including Claiborne Jackson of Missouri, trying to persuade them that their states were not neglected and that the Confederacy needed manpower.

January 9, Thursday

President Lincoln informed Gen. McClellan that neither of the commanders in the West, Halleck or Buell, had met the President's request to name a day when they would be ready to move. At Cairo, Ill., however, Grant was preparing a reconnaissance in force into Kentucky toward Columbus. There was a brief skirmish near Columbus, and another near Pohick Run, Va. Orders went out in St. Louis to have a copy of each newspaper daily sent to the provost marshal general for inspection. That city's Chamber of Commerce was disrupted by withdrawal of pro-Union members. In the Congress of the United States petitions were continually being issued calling for an end to slavery, and members on the floor were suggesting emancipation, colonization of Negroes, and compensation to owners.

January 10, Friday

Grant's Federal troops in the cold and damp left the Cairo, Ill., area and moved toward Columbus, Ky. Meant largely as a diversionary action to take attention from Union operations toward east Tennessee, Grant led his men on a dreary, wearisome march with little fighting. By Jan. 21 they were back in Cairo, mission accomplished, and a lot learned about winter marching. Farther east in Kentucky, at Middle Creek, near Prestonburg, Federal forces under Brig. Gen. James A. Garfield advanced against

Confederates under Humphrey Marshall. Garfield was unable to penetrate the Confederate lines or force them back, but after the engagement both sides retreated, and both claimed victory. It was another event in the slow developing Federal drive toward east Tennessee.

In western Virginia Federals, without a fight, evacuated Romney in face of Stonewall Jackson's advance. Confederate troops entered the town and Jackson's command settled down a bit for the winter. For some time trouble had been a-making between Jackson and one of his commanders, Brig. Gen. W. W. Loring. Loring and his men contended that Jackson mistreated his army, and eventually Loring went over Jackson's head to Richmond with his complaint. This resulted in Jackson's submitting his resignation from the Confederate Army; this was refused and matters were patched up.

In a Confederate command change the Trans-Mississippi District of Department No. 2 was set up under command of Maj. Gen. Earl Van Dorn.

Mr. Lincoln, still anxious over his armies, wrote the Secretary of War that he was exceedingly discouraged over the failure to launch an offensive in the West. "As everywhere else, nothing can be done," he said. At the same time the President was considering the problem of Sec. of War Simon Cameron, who had appended a strong anti-slavery statement to his official report without permission. There were repeated charges of corruption in the War Department, and demands for Cameron's ouster. In the U. S. Senate Missouri senators Waldo P. Johnson and Trusten Polk, pro-Confederates, were unanimously expelled. The first auction of confiscated cotton from Port Royal, S.C., was held in New York.

January 11, Saturday

A fleet of about a hundred vessels carrying troops under Union Brig. Gen. Ambrose E. Burnside sailed from Hampton Roads, Va., for the coast of North Carolina. The navy squadron was under command of Commodore Louis M. Goldsborough. Forces numbered about fifteen thousand and posed a new threat to the already severely intruded Southern coast. Out west there was a brief clash of gunboats near Fort Jefferson north of Columbus, Ky., on the Mississippi.

In Washington President Lincoln accepted the public resignation of Sec. of War Simon Cameron and indicated that he would name him Minister to Russia. Cameron wrote the President that he had long wished to resign, and the President appeared relieved. But underneath the change were the charges of contract fraud, overactive politics, and incompetence in the management of the War Department. Cameron, while probably reasonably honest personally, was a Pennsylvania politician who could never forget his friends and associations. Few had been satisfied with War Department operations.

January 12, Sunday

From this day to the twenty-third the Thirty-seventh Ohio Infantry carried out an expedition to Logan Court House and the Guyandotte Valley of western Virginia, opposed by Confederate guerrillas.

In Washington, in addition to the shift of the Secretary of War, Lincoln had taken action regarding the stalled armies in Virginia. On Saturday, Jan. 11, a group of major officers had conferred about the possibility of a move. They met again this day with members of the Cabinet. McClellan, recovering from illness, surprisingly showed up at the White House, fearful that his command was being undermined.

January 13, Monday

The Federal sea-borne expedition under Brig. Gen. A. E. Burnside arrived at Hatteras Inlet, N.C., and the general assumed command of the Department of North Carolina, but lack of low-draft vessels and proper landing craft held up his intended invasion.

In Washington it was a busy day for Mr. Lincoln. The Cabinet met in the morning, and the President indicated he would name prominent Washington attorney and former Attorney General under Buchanan Edwin M. Stanton as Secretary of War. Stanton, a native of Ohio, was to supersede resigned Simon Cameron. At the same time the President sent to the Senate the nomination of Cameron as Minister to Russia replacing legendary Cassius Marcellus Clay. The council of generals, Cabinet members, Lincoln, and McClellan met once more in the afternoon to consider action by the armies. Gen. McClellan refused to divulge his plan of operations and apparently resented the interference by the generals and the President. Writing Genls. Buell and Halleck in the West, the President indicated his desire for action on all fronts against the enemy and pointed up the strategy of "menacing him with superior forces at *different* points, at the *same* time."

January 14, Tuesday

Three Federal gunboats moved down the Mississippi to near Columbus, Ky., throwing shells into Confederate encampments. Grant's reconnaissance into Kentucky operated near Blandville.

January 15, Wednesday

CONFIRMATION OF STANTON AS SECRETARY OF WAR.

The U. S. Senate confirmed the appointment of Edwin M. Stanton as Secretary of War. Stanton, an energetic, tireless worker, was known to have uttered statements derogatory to Mr. Lincoln. The new Secretary was also known to be a friend of Gen. McClellan, and soon he would become one of the most controversial figures of the war. There were, and still are, those who feel he was crafty, dishonest, arbitrary, and unfit for his position. There were, and still are, those who feel that, arbitrary though he was, he was a tower of strength for the Union and for Mr. Lincoln, and that Federal victory owes much to Stanton.

On the Tennessee River a Federal gunboat reconnaissance operated Jan. 15–25, going almost as far as Fort Henry just below the Kentucky-Tennessee line. The operation was in conjunction with Grant's overland operations from Cairo. In Missouri there were Federal expeditions to Benton, Bloomfield, and Dallas until the seventeenth.

January 16, Thursday

Federal naval forces descended on the harbor and village of Cedar Keys, Fla., and burned seven small blockade-runners and coastal vessels, a pier, and some railroad flatcars before withdrawing.

In Kentucky Confederate forces, encamped near Beech Grove with their backs to the Cumberland River to their south, heard reports of Federal advances under George H. Thomas, but did nothing about it. The Confederates under Brig. Gen. Felix K. Zollicoffer had been at Mill Springs, south of the Cumberland, but Zollicoffer had unwisely taken them north of the river. The new commander, Brig. Gen. George B. Crittenden, had ordered Zollicoffer to retire south of the river, but he had not done so.

In Washington Edwin M. Stanton took over the Federal War Department with a drive and efficiency that startled those used to the previous slipshod management. From the beginning Stanton was going to be a hard but generally just man to deal with.

January 17, Friday

Gunboats with troops under Brig. Gen. C. F. Smith demonstrated until the twenty-second against Fort Henry on the Tennessee River, as part of the two-prong major reconnaissance in Kentucky. The other prong consisted mainly of McClernand's troops of Grant's command from Cairo. Bad weather hampered the expeditions and a heavy ice gorge blocked the Mississippi twenty miles below St. Louis, halting shipping.

January 18, Saturday

Former President of the United States John Tyler, seventy-two, died in Richmond and was later buried with elaborate services in Hollywood Cemetery on the banks of the James. The Confederate Territory of Arizona was formed, consisting of the southern half of the Federal New Mexico Territory. In Kentucky, in the vicinity of Mill Springs and Somerset, Federal forces under Gen. George H. Thomas were converging on Confederates commanded by Brig. Gen. George B. Crittenden, who, thanks to his subordinate Brig. Gen. Felix Zollicoffer, was in a vulnerable position with his back to the Cumberland River.

January 19, Sunday
BATTLE OF MILL SPRINGS OR LOGAN'S CROSS ROADS, KENTUCKY.

On the north bank of the Cumberland River was fought one of the two principal battles of the war in Kentucky, variously known as Mill Springs, Logan's Cross Roads, Fishing Creek, Somerset, or Beech Grove. Confederate Brig. Gen. George B. Crittenden, realizing an attack was near, moved out in the darkness and heavy rain. Zollicoffer with his Southern brigade drove the Federals back temporarily. But Zollicoffer, wearing a white raincoat, was shot and killed when he became confused as to who was friend and who enemy. The Confederates later rallied, but more Federals under George H. Thomas came up, and eventually the Confederate left broke and the line collapsed. With difficulty the Southerners withdrew across the Cumberland during the night, leaving only the abandoned camps and supplies to the Federals the next day. Crittenden's troops were demoralized by the defeat, and the general himself was severely criticized for being in a position not of his own choosing. It was the first break in the Confederate Kentucky defense line, which ran from Cumberland Gap to Columbus on the Mississippi.

There were about 4000 Federals on the field, with 39 killed, 207 wounded, and 15 captured or missing for casualties of 261. The Confederates also had about 4000 effectives, with losses of 125 killed, 309 wounded, and 99 missing for a total of 533. A moderately small but strategically important battle, it presaged things to come in the West, showed the weakness of the Confederate line, and boosted the Federal cause among the people of Kentucky and eastern Tennessee.

January 20, Monday

As the Confederates completed their withdrawal across the Cumberland at Mill Springs, Ky., leaving the spoils of war to the Federals, down in Charleston Harbor a second group of hulks loaded with stone was sunk by the Yankees at the entrance of the shipping channel to halt blockade-runners. As usual, this operation was not long effective. Jan. 20–24 there were minor operations and skirmishing in and about Atchison, Kas. A blockade-runner, known as the British *Andracita* or Confederate *J. W. Wilder,* was run ashore by Federal vessels off the coast of Alabama. Federal small boats tried to take possession but were driven off by Confederate land troops.

January 21, Tuesday

The Federal reconnaissance of about five thousand from Grant's command in Cairo, Ill., returned from a difficult but satisfactory expedition into western Kentucky. There had been little or no fighting, yet a definite threat had been posed to the Confederate bastion at Columbus, Ky. In Richmond the news of the defeat at Mill Springs, the expedition from Cairo, the threat of Burnside's invasion of North Carolina, and the winter doldrums in the armies were having their effect.

January 22, Wednesday

The war went on with light shelling of Fort Henry on the Tennessee River by Federal gunboats; a skirmish at Knobnoster, Mo., and the occupation of Lebanon, Mo., by Federals. Richmond authorities named Brig. Gen. Henry A. Wise to the Confederate command at Roanoke Island, which was threatened seriously by Burnside's overwhelming force at Hatteras Inlet.

January 23, Thursday

In St. Louis Maj. Gen. Halleck put teeth into his martial law orders and seized the property of pro-secessionists who had failed to pay assessments for the aid of pro-Northern fugitives. Army officers were empowered to arrest anyone interfering with the execution of orders. A small Confederate force carried off the county records from Blandville, Ky.

January 24, Friday

Two blockade-runners were stopped off the mouth of the Mississippi; the Federal lightship off Cape Henry, Va., went ashore and its crew was captured; there was a week of small expeditions by Federals to the Little Sandy River and Piketon, Ky., part of the eastern Kentucky operations.

January 25, Saturday

At Hatteras Inlet the Burnside expedition was moving transports and naval war vessels with extreme difficulty over the shallow bar into Pamlico Sound. But the laborious operations were not menaced by the Confederates, undermanned on land and sea alike.

January 26, Sunday

There was a Federal naval reconnaissance Jan. 26–28 at Wilmington Narrows or Freeborn's Cut, Ga. The Confederate government ordered Gen. P. G. T. Beauregard from the Potomac District to the West, where he became second-in-command to Albert Sidney Johnston in that threatened area. This left Gen. Joseph E. Johnston in full command in Virginia.

January 27, Monday

FEDERAL ARMIES ORDERED TO ADVANCE.

President Lincoln took an unprecedented step by issuing the President's General War Order No. 1. Long disappointed and chagrined by the lack of action of the major Federal armies, the President "Ordered that the 22d of February 1862, be the day for a general movement of the Land and Naval forces of the United States against the insurgent forces." He called especially for advances from the army about Fort Monroe, the Army of the Potomac, the Army of Western Virginia, the army in Kentucky, the force at Cairo, and the naval force in the Gulf of Mexico. This remarkable order was intended to bring about aggressive military operations, and was issued only after constant urging by Mr. Lincoln for advances east and west.

Emperor Louis Napoleon of France told the French people that the American Civil War "has seriously compromised our commercial interests," but that France would confine herself to hoping for termination of the war as long as the rights of neutrals were respected.

January 28, Tuesday

There was skirmishing for several days near Greensburg, Ky., and Lebanon, Mo.

January 29, Wednesday

A small Federal force broke up a group of Confederate dancers at a party at Lee's House on the Occoquan in Virginia after a brief skirmish. Maj. Gen. Earl Van Dorn assumed command of the Trans-Mississippi District of the Confederacy. There were several days of mild skirmishing in and around Blue Springs, Mo.

January 30, Thursday

A large crowd gathered at Greenpoint, Long Island, N.Y., to witness the launching of U.S.S. *Monitor,* the revolutionary iron ship constructed by John Ericsson. The strange-appearing craft slid into the water with the cheers of the crowd and salutes from neighboring vessels. At Southampton, England, the two Confederate commissioners to Britain and France, Mason and Slidell, landed from a British vessel, completing their delayed voyage after having been captured by the Federals and held in prison.

January 31, Friday

To implement the President's General War Order No. 1, Mr. Lincoln issued the President's Special War Order No. 1, which pertained specifically to the Army of the Potomac. That army was ordered to form an expedition to seize and occupy "a point upon the Rail Road South Westward of what is known of [sic] Manassas Junction." This was to be done before or on Feb. 22, and was aimed at forcing Gen. McClellan to open offensive operations overland in Virginia. The Federal Congress authorized the President to take possession of telegraph and railroad lines whenever the public safety required it. In Britain Queen Victoria declared it was her purpose to observe neutrality in the American Civil War.

FEBRUARY, 1862

In the North the cries of the previous fall over the failure of Northern armies to advance had increased. Mr. Lincoln had ordered his forces forward, a move to be made on or before Washington's Birthday. In the Confederacy the wintering of the armies weakened them considerably, at least in Virginia, and already thin forces were spread even thinner. The South awaited another blow to its coastline from the Outer Banks of North Carolina, and a possible move from the Gulf toward New Orleans or Mobile. The Kentucky line was not much of a defense at all, as had been demonstrated at Mill Springs in January. There were signs that the Federals would soon be doing things on the rivers—the Mississippi, Tennessee, and Cumberland. Expectations were not too high and doubters were many, but most Confederates remained firm in their fight for freedom. During February the *Atlantic Monthly* printed a poem, as it often did, but this one would not be forgotten. Soon the words of Julia Ward Howe were transported into song and the "Battle Hymn of the Republic" inspired and reinspired Northern hearts. There was hope in the North that the "swift sword" would become truly swift and strike home.

February 1, Saturday
Although there was a skirmish near Bowling Green, Ky., and a meeting of Indian chiefs and Federal authorities at Leavenworth, Kas., the main events of the day were not immediately revealed. At Cairo, Ill., there was bustling activity as Grant prepared a campaign he had a few days before suggested opening immediately. On Jan. 28 he had stated to Gen. Halleck in St. Louis that he planned, with permission, to take Fort Henry on the Tennessee, and on the twenty-ninth he indicated he was aiming at a major offensive move from Fort Henry. Permission was granted Jan. 30 by Halleck, and Grant lost no time getting ready at Cairo.

February 2, Sunday
Only a small skirmish in Morgan County, Tenn., marked the day in fighting, but the expedition assembling on the Ohio at the mouth of the Tennessee was rapidly taking shape.

February 3, Monday

Troop transports were moving from Cairo to Paducah, Ky., and the gunboat fleet began heading up the Tennessee or south toward Fort Henry. In very quiet Virginia there was a Federal reconnaissance to Occoquan Village.

In Washington President Lincoln deftly declined the offer of war elephants from the King of Siam because the nation "does not reach a latitude so low as to favor the multiplication of the elephant." More importantly, he brought out in a letter to Gen. McClellan the conflict between their ideas of operations in Virginia. Mr. Lincoln urged him to go directly overland south, while McClellan favored landing on the coast and then moving on Richmond.

The Administration decided that crews of captured privateers were to be considered prisoners of war. In the U. S. Senate Zachariah Chandler of Michigan presented a resolution from the Michigan legislature which urged the putting down of insurrection, confiscation of property of Southerners, and abolition of slavery. This was similar to many petitions and pleas coming to Congress at this time, while in the other direction there were those who protested the trend toward making it a war against slavery.

February 4, Tuesday

Federal troops began landing in the rain on the soggy banks of the Tennessee north of Fort Henry, as gunboats carried out a reconnaissance to the fort on the east bank of the river just south of the Kentucky-Tennessee state line.

In Richmond the Virginia house of delegates discussed enrolling free Negroes in the Confederate Army; Sec. of War Judah P. Benjamin cracked down on speculators, particularly in sales of saltpeter needed for powder; and the Richmond *Examiner* felt "that the Southern people are not sufficiently alive to the necessity of exertion in the struggle they are involved in. Better to fight even at the risk of losing battles, than remain inactive to fill up inglorious graves." Meanwhile, Confederate generals appealed to troops whose terms were about to expire to reenlist.

February 5, Wednesday

Troops continued to file ashore north of Fort Henry on the Tennessee to cooperate with the gunboats in the coming Federal attack. They were to move on the fort early on the sixth. Gen. C. F. Smith's force was sent west of the river to take Fort Heiman, unfinished, on the bluffs above Fort Henry. It was found evacuated. Confederate Brig. Gen. Lloyd Tilghman, with somewhat over three thousand men in partly inundated Fort Henry, feared the worst but prepared for defense.

Indiana senator Jesse D. Bright was expelled from the U. S. Senate by a vote of 32 to 14 for alleged complicity with enemies of the United States. The East Room of the White House was filled that evening for a ball given by Mrs. Lincoln. The social press was full of praise. In Britain Queen Victoria lifted all prohibitions against shipping gunpowder, arms, ammunition, and military stores from the United Kingdom.

February 6, Thursday

SURRENDER OF FORT HENRY, TENNESSEE.

Threatened by land and water, Confederate Brig. Gen. Lloyd Tilghman decided to save the major part of his Fort Henry garrison, sending all but some artillerists and those on a hospital boat across country to stronger Fort Donelson on the Cumberland. Tilghman himself stayed behind to do what he could to defend the fort on the Tennessee River and delay pursuit. Due to the high water, rain, and bad roads, the Federal troops did not get under way until late morning. About 11 A.M. Flag Officer Andrew Foote with his four ironclads followed by three wooden gunboats moved upstream, firing rapidly into the almost open fort. The defenders gallantly replied, striking the flotilla with fifty-nine shots, a few of them causing damage. The boiler of *Essex* was pierced and scalded twenty-eight officers and men. *Cincinnati* was also struck. In the fort a shell exploded near the mouth of a thirty-two-pounder, wrecking the gun and crew. Another gun blew up. Shortly before 2 P.M. Tilghman lowered his flag and surrendered 12 officers, 66 men, and 16 patients on the hospital boat to Flag Officer Foote. The Confederates lost 5 killed, 6 wounded, 5 disabled, and 5 missing for a total of 21 casualties, but saved the main garrison. In Foote's Federal squadron 11 died, 31 were injured, and 5 were missing. Meanwhile, Grant's army of over 15,000, slogging through the mire, missed the fight.

With the fall of Fort Henry, a major impediment to Federal advancement south was removed; an important river highway, bypassing the Mississippi, was opened. But about ten miles away on the Cumberland a much more formidable fortification, Fort Donelson, still stood in the way. Foote immediately took his ironclads north for repairs and then planned to go around and ascend the Cumberland from the Ohio. The three wooden gunboats proceeded on a raid up the Tennessee to Florence, Ala. Over at Fort Donelson Brig. Gen. Bushrod R. Johnson succeeded Tilghman in command and called for reinforcements.

In South Carolina there was a Federal reconnaissance to Wright River. President Davis spent valuable time writing discontented officers over frictions in command.

February 7, Friday

Gen. Grant made a personal reconnaissance of Fort Donelson on the Cumberland near Dover, Tenn., and his force established itself near captured Fort Henry. The gunboats moved back down the Tennessee to the Ohio, preparatory to ascending the Cumberland to Fort Donelson. Confederate Gen. A. S. Johnston, realizing his Kentucky line had been wrecked, hurried troops into Donelson. Gen. Gideon Pillow from Clarksville, Tenn., and Gen. John B. Floyd from Russellville, Ky., were ordered to Donelson. At Bowling Green, Ky., Johnston, Beauregard, and William Joseph Hardee met to discuss the extremely serious situation. The populace North and South soon heard the news of the momentous, or tragic, breakthrough.

After laboriously moving vessels over the shallow bar at Hatteras Inlet on North Carolina's Outer Banks, Ambrose E. Burnside's Federal expedition headed toward Roanoke Island. Commodore Louis M. Goldsborough's squadron attacked and routed the few underarmed, makeshift Confederate naval defenders, while in the afternoon and evening Burnside landed his troops on the island. Meanwhile, to the north, Federals reoccupied Romney, western Va., as Confederates pulled back toward Winchester, Va. There was a small expedition and skirmish at Flint Hill and Hunter's Mill, Va. Federal batteries shelled Harper's Ferry briefly.

In the White House in Washington Willie Lincoln, youngest son of the President, lay critically ill.

February 8, Saturday

BATTLE OF ROANOKE ISLAND, NORTH CAROLINA.

Gen. Burnside with about 7500 Federals quickly moved inland on Roanoke Island against less than 2000 men of Confederate Gen. Henry A. Wise. Wise was ill and his force was temporarily under Col. H. M. Shaw in the field. Advancing rapidly to the center of the low-lying, sandy, tree-covered island, Burnside's troops attacked and overran the inferior Confederate entrenchments, pushing the enemy to the north end of the island. Col. Shaw had no recourse but to surrender something over 2000 men, including some reinforcements that came in too late for the fight and garrisons of batteries along the shore. Casualties were 23 killed and 62 wounded for the Confederates, and 37 killed, 214 wounded, and 13 missing for the Federals. There were also moderate casualties among the naval forces involved. Thirty guns fell into Federal hands. While a relatively small engagement from the standpoint of forces and casualties, Roanoke Island had considerable importance. Control of Pamlico Sound gave the Federals a first-rate base on the Atlantic coast for operations against North Carolina. At the Confederate capital the seriousness of the defeat was deeply felt; a back door to Richmond had been opened and a vital Southern state dangerously threatened. The Confederate government, newspapers, and citizenry saw Roanoke Island in a much truer light than later historians, who have dismissed it as a minor operation. Also, it came at a time when word of the fall of Fort Henry was spreading over the land

and as the obvious threat to Fort Donelson was developing. Depression in the Confederacy fed on constant bad news.

There was a skirmish at the mouth of the Blue Stone River, western Va.; a small affair at Bolivar, Mo.; and martial law was declared throughout Kansas.

Mr. Lincoln worried about his son, who was ill of typhoid. He asked McClellan if he had any further news from the West; what had happened to canal boats sent up to Harper's Ferry to bridge the Potomac? What about his contemplated movement?

February 9, Sunday

In the West at Fort Donelson, Tenn., on the Cumberland, Confederate Brig. Gen. Gideon J. Pillow assumed command of the increased forces, as delays upset Grant's original timetable for taking the fort. At Roanoke Island, N.C., there were cleanup operations by the victorious Federals. A light skirmish occurred at Marshfield, Mo.

In Washington the War Department ordered the imprisonment of Malcolm Ives, a correspondent of the New York *Herald,* on spying charges. Brig. Gen. Charles P. Stone was also arrested in Washington and sent to Fort Lafayette in New York Harbor without specific charges. He had been the Federal commander at the ill-fated Battle of Ball's Bluff in the fall of 1861, and allegedly had consorted with the enemy. Never brought to trial or actually charged, he was released Aug. 16, 1862. The Joint Committee on the Conduct of the War, Sec. of War Stanton, Gen. McClellan, and Mr. Lincoln have been blamed for what is now generally believed to have been an unjust act. The case was a *cause célèbre* in the press of the day.

February 10, Monday

To the north of Pamlico Sound the remainder of the Confederate "Mosquito" fleet was destroyed when Federals fought a successful engagement at Elizabeth City, N.C., the head of an important inland waterway to Virginia. Soon Burnside and his men had firm control of the coastal area and turned their attention to New Berne. On the coast in South Carolina there was a skirmish at Barnwell's Island. In the West the three Union wooden gunboats that had moved up the Tennessee to Florence, Ala., after Fort Henry's fall returned. Grant's build-up against Fort Donelson was nearing completion.

February 11, Tuesday

Gen. John A. McClernand's Federals led the advance from Fort Henry across toward Fort Donelson as Grant's army began its march. Foote's Federal gunboats were moving from the Tennessee to the Ohio at Paducah and thence up the Cumberland. For the Confederates, Brig. Gen. Simon Bolivar Buckner arrived at Fort Donelson as more troops came in. Confederates began evacuating Bowling Green, Ky., leaving only Columbus on the now useless Kentucky line. In South Carolina Edisto Island was occupied by Federals, and there were three days of activity at Aransas Pass, Tex.

February 12, Wednesday

By evening the lines had been firmly drawn at Fort Donelson, Tenn., on the Cumberland River. Grant's army was ranged in a semicircle upon hills near the fort and town of Dover, awaiting the help of the gunboat attack. Confederates could still bring in men from across the river to the east, but a mild form of siege had begun.

Federal naval forces captured Edenton, N.C., as they expanded their operations from Roanoke Island. There was skirmishing at Moorefield, western Va., and Springfield, Mo., where Confederates pulled farther southwest.

February 13, Thursday

FEDERAL ATTACK ON FORT DONELSON.

At Fort Donelson the fighting began. On the Federal left C. F. Smith launched an attack and on the right McClernand's front saw action. John B. Floyd arrived with more troops and took over Confederate command from Pillow. More troops came in for Grant. The gunboat *Carondelet* bombarded the fort in the morning. The fair and mild weather suddenly changed in the afternoon to sleety rain, with ten above zero that night. The siege was on.

Over at Fort Heiman on the Tennessee there was a brief skirmish. At Bowling Green, Ky., being evacuated by the Confederates, fire destroyed a number of buildings. Out in Missouri Springfield was once more occupied by Federal troops, and in North Carolina a Federal expedition left North River for the Albemarle Canal.

Meeting in Wheeling, the West Virginia Constitutional Convention adopted a provision that no slave or free person of color should come into the state for permanent residence.

February 14, Friday

GUNBOAT ATTACK AT FORT DONELSON.

Four ironclads and two wooden gunboats carried on the day's fighting against Fort Donelson on the Cumberland, while the land side was largely static. Grant's expectations that the Federal squadron would be able to repeat Fort Henry were dashed, for after heavy bombardment and fearsome damage, the gunboats were forced to withdraw downstream to the north. "Pandemonium itself would hardly have been more appalling," a Confederate exclaimed. Flag Officer Foote was wounded and his ironclads *St. Louis* and *Louisville* drifted away helpless, their steering mechanism shot away. Two others were badly struck and the wooden vessels could not face the well-posted fire of the Confederate fort on the bluff, which suffered little. The cold weather continued and two discouraged armies still faced each other at nightfall. A council of Confederate generals determined that a breakout by Pillow, followed by the rest of the command, would be made on the Federal right toward the south.

The rear guard of Gen. Hardee's remnants finally left the Kentucky town of Bowling Green and Federals soon marched in. Grant was assigned by the War Department to command the District of West Tennessee and William Tecumseh Sherman was given the District of Cairo. In other fighting there was skirmishing near Cumberland Gap, Ky.; at Crane Creek, Mo.; and at Bloomery, western Va.

In Washington and Richmond news from the West was anxiously awaited. Meanwhile, Lincoln granted amnesty to all political prisoners who would take an oath not to aid the rebellion.

February 15, Saturday

BATTLE AT FORT DONELSON.

At 5 A.M. of a cold morning the Confederate division of Gideon Pillow moved forward to assault the enclosing Federal lines at Fort Donelson. Pillow was aided by Buckner's division and after a morning's hot fighting the Federal line of McClernand on the right was broken and the way of escape to Nashville open. A victory had been won. But nothing was done. Floyd, after considerable argument, ordered his army to return to their fortifications. Vastly perturbed, Grant ordered his left under C. F. Smith forward, but his advance was checked. McClernand's division, aided by Lew Wallace's, reclosed the gap on the right. By evening the troops were in nearly their old positions. The day's fighting was for nought for the Confederates, while for the Federals it had been a near defeat. That night in an inn at Dover there was another momentous conference of Confederate generals. It was agreed they must surrender Fort Donelson, but who was to do it was the question. Floyd, allegedly fearing crimination against him for his Washington career, decided to flee, as did Pillow, next in command, leaving the surrender job to Gen. Buckner. In the battle lines that night "Mother" Mary Ann Bickerdyke administered to the wounded, self-appointed but with the blessings of all. Gen. Albert Sidney Johnston arrived personally in Nashville ahead of Hardee's forces.

From Cairo a Federal expedition moved down the Tennessee to Eastport, Miss., Feb. 15–22; there was a skirmish near Flat Creek, Mo.; and action at Venus Point, Ga. In St. Louis Brig. Gen. John M. Schofield assumed command of the District of St. Louis.

February 16, Sunday

SURRENDER OF FORT DONELSON, TENNESSEE.

At daybreak Southern boats pulled up at Fort Donelson bringing four hundred reinforcements—but too late. During the night, Nathan Bedford

Forrest and his cavalry fled to the southeast rather than surrender. Genls. Floyd and Pillow boated across the Cumberland and made their somewhat ignominious getaway. A few others here and there simply walked away. But the major Confederate force under Gen. Buckner stayed behind. Buckner asked for terms and Grant sent back his famous reply that made him a hero in the North: "No terms except unconditional and immediate surrender can be accepted. I propose to move immediately upon your works." It was take it or leave it, and Buckner took it. The siege of Fort Donelson was over, and with it a Confederate army surrendered. No one will ever know with accuracy how many surrendered that day—estimates run from 5000 to 15,000, but probably it was somewhere around 12,000. Confederate casualties are estimated at up to 1500. For the Federals, Grant had some 27,000 men plus the gunboats, and lost 500 killed, 2108 wounded, and 224 missing for 2832. The fall of Forts Henry and Donelson was a catastrophe for the South. The whole state of Tennessee was wide-open, Kentucky was lost, and two important rivers were in Federal hands. The victory received the acclaim it deserved in the North and the despair it deserved in the South. Winter was coming to a gloomy conclusion for the Confederacy; it was ending with signs of hope in the ever anxious North, at least in the West.

On the Cumberland, the gunboat *St. Louis* destroyed the Tennessee ironworks, and over in Arkansas there was short action at Pott's Hill on Sugar Creek. In Nashville, Tenn., Gov. Isham Harris packed up the state papers and left, as Hardee's retreating Confederate troops came in. The capital of the state was in terror at the thought of the approaching Yankees.

February 17, Monday

News of the fall of Fort Donelson was sensational, to both the U.S.A. and C.S.A. The North had a new hero in "Unconditional Surrender" Grant, while the South had wounds to lick and much to worry about. Genls. Floyd and Pillow, refugees from their command at Donelson, came into Nashville, followed the next day by Forrest and his cavalry. Attempts were made to bring order to the Tennessee capital, but the citizenry was alarmed, many leaving as best they could. Fighting continued at Sugar Creek, Ark.

In Washington Grant was promoted to Major General of Volunteers. In Richmond the Provisional Congress of the Confederate States adjourned.

February 18, Tuesday

In Richmond the First Congress of the Confederate States of America opened. Heretofore the old, unicameral secession convention had been the Provisional Congress, but the elections of the fall had established a formal two-house legislature. There was skirmishing at Independence, Mo.; Bentonville, Ark.; and Mount Vernon, Mo.; while a Federal expedition operated around Winton, N.C. President Lincoln proclaimed that the people should celebrate Washington's Birthday.

February 19, Wednesday

Federal forces of Gen. C. F. Smith from Grant's command occupied Clarksville, Tenn. While Grant was looking toward Nashville there was an interarmy squabble brewing. Grant's men were accused of entering the territory of Gen. Don Carlos Buell, who also was advancing slowly south toward Nashville from the Bowling Green, Ky., area. A skirmish at West Plains, Mo., marked the day. President Davis wrote Gen. Joseph E. Johnston that "Events have cast on our arms and our hopes the gloomiest shadows, and at such a time we must show redoubled energy and resolution." Meanwhile, the new Confederate Congress counted the electoral vote and ordered the release of two thousand Federal prisoners of war.

February 20, Thursday

In late afternoon at the White House William Wallace "Willie" Lincoln died, at the age of twelve, throwing personal tragedy upon the victories from the West. A weeping President tried to console his distraught wife. At the same time casualty lists from Fort Donelson were spread on bulletin boards North and South—more personal tragedy.

On the Mississippi the Confederate bastion of Columbus, Ky., was to be no more; the fall of the forts on the rivers had ordained its evacuation and orders were given from Richmond. Withdrawal into the middle South was a necessity for the Confederacy, and Kentucky was nearly devoid of organized Confederate troops. In North Carolina there was an expedition by Federals in Currituck Sound. Gov. Isham Harris announced the removal of Tennessee's capital from Nashville to Memphis. The Confederate Army, reassembling at Nashville, was pulling back to Murfreesboro, southeast of the city, at command of Gen. Albert Sidney Johnston.

February 21, Friday

ENGAGEMENT AT VALVERDE.

Up the valley of the Rio Grande in New Mexico Territory some 2600 Confederates of Brig. Gen. H. H. Sibley toiled toward Fort Craig, held by Federals under Col. E. R. S. Canby. The engagement of Valverde resulted from a contest over a ford by which the Confederates intended to cut off the fort on the west side of the Rio Grande. After brisk fighting the Federals withdrew to the fort, and the victorious Confederate column moved on north toward Santa Fe, bypassing Fort Craig. Canby's Federals had about 3810 men and lost 68 killed, 160 wounded, and 35 missing, while the Confederates lost 31 killed, 154 wounded, and 1 missing.

In Tangier, Morocco, U.S. consul James De Long seized two officers of the Confederate cruiser C.S.S. *Sumter*, John Smith and T. T. Tunstall.

After a long furor the pair were released. In New York City convicted slave trader Nathaniel Gordon was hanged.

February 22, Saturday

INAUGURATION OF PRESIDENT DAVIS.

"The tyranny of an unbridled majority, the most odious and least responsible form of despotism, has denied us both the right and the remedy. Therefore we are in arms to renew such sacrifices as our fathers made to the holy cause of constitutional liberty," spoke Jefferson Davis, newly inaugurated President of the Confederate States of America. In the pouring rain in the yard of the Confederate Capitol at Richmond, Davis took the oath of office as the regularly elected President and asked divine blessing on their cause. "Civil War there cannot be between States held together by their volition only," he said in going over the reasons for the present difficulty.

Meanwhile, there was a brief brush at Aransas Bay, Tex.; in Virginia a Federal expedition operated to Vienna and Flint Hill; there was a skirmish at Independence, Mo. In Kentucky Buell's Federals began moving in force from Bowling Green, Ky., toward Nashville.

At the Federal capital on this Washington's Birthday it was observed that the Army of the Potomac, ordered forth on or before this date by the President, had not moved, although operations aplenty had occurred in the West. Lincoln, sorrowing for the death of one son and concerned over the illness of another, Tad, did not attend the Washington's Birthday observances.

February 23, Sunday

Citizens and soldiers were evacuating Nashville, Tenn., more rapidly than ever, as Federal soldiers and gunboats began to draw nearer. President Lincoln named Andrew Johnson as military governor of Tennessee, to be confirmed March 4 by the Senate. In other command changes the Department of the Gulf was constituted under Maj. Gen. Benjamin F. Butler, and John Pope assumed command of the Army of the Mississippi at Commerce, Mo.

Federal troops occupied Fayetteville, Ark., in the northwestern part of the state, and there was fighting around Pea Ridge Prairie, Mo., to the north. Federals carried out reconnaissances of several days from Greenville to Little River, Mo., and on Bull River and Schooner Channel, S.C.

February 24, Monday

Northern troops under Gen. Don Carlos Buell reached the north bank of the Cumberland River at Nashville as troop transports began arriving. Forrest's cavalry formed the Confederate rear guard, retreating to the southeast. Other Federal troops under Gen. Nathaniel Banks occupied Harper's Ferry, western Va., strategically situated at the junction of the Potomac and Shenandoah rivers. There was fighting at Mingo Creek, near St. Francisville, at New Madrid, and in St. Clair and Henry counties, Mo.; as well as a small affair at Lewis Chapel, near Pohick Church, Va. Funeral services were held in Washington for Willie Lincoln, while his brother Tad showed improvement.

February 25, Tuesday

UNION OCCUPIES NASHVILLE.

Federal troops moved into Nashville in full force. The capital of Tennessee, C.S.A., was again capital of Tennessee, U.S.A., and a vital base for the Union, to be held throughout the remainder of the war. Its capture without bloodshed had been made possible by Grant's victory at Fort Donelson, although it was formally occupied by troops of Gen. Buell. Elsewhere there were minor operations in Loudoun County, Va., and at Keetsville in Barry County, Mo. Confederate Maj. Gen. E. Kirby Smith was assigned to command in east Tennessee.

The Federal War Department ordered control of all telegraph lines by the department to facilitate military moves. In Richmond President Davis sent a message to the Confederate Congress reviewing the war, calling for sterner measures, and stating, "we have been so exposed as recently to encounter serious disasters." Davis thought the financial system was adequate and the postal department was improving. He desired to establish a Supreme Court. Naval construction was proceeding despite limited resources, the need for more soldiers was being met, and strenuous efforts were being made to reinforce armies in the threatened West. It was not wholly a dark picture, although the military situation led to sobering thoughts.

February 26, Wednesday

There was a Confederate scout toward Nashville in a day of little or no fighting. Kentucky senator William E. Simms declared in the Confederate Congress that the Confederacy would defend her rights to the last extremity. In Washington Lincoln talked with Gen. McClellan, who was about to go to Harper's Ferry, supposedly to lead offensive operations into Virginia. Mr. Lincoln also signed the Loan and Treasury Bill creating a national currency of United States notes and providing for sale of stock to finance the currency.

February 27, Thursday

The Confederate Congress gave President Davis the power to suspend the privilege of habeas corpus, which was sparingly used. From New York

U.S.S. *Monitor* went to sea for trials and an unknown destination. President Davis ordered martial law for the threatened cities of Norfolk and Portsmouth, Va.

February 28, Friday

Federal forces under John Pope moved south along the west shore of the Mississippi from Commerce toward New Madrid, Mo., in another drive against the Confederate heartland in the West. Confederate batteries protected the Mississippi River at Island No. 10 north of New Madrid on both the Missouri and eastern sides. There was an affair at Osage Springs, Ark., near Fayetteville, where yet another Federal column was threatening.

In Washington President Lincoln talked with Gen. McClellan regarding the failure to institute operations at Harper's Ferry. He learned it was because the canal boats sent north to form a pontoon bridge over the Potomac were too large for the locks. Throughout the Confederacy it was a day of fasting and prayer, following a proclamation by President Davis. Davis wrote Gen. Joseph E. Johnston, who commanded the main Confederate army in northern Virginia. Davis was aware that the enemy appeared to be concentrating in Johnston's front, and that the general believed his position could be turned. Davis directed Johnston to make sure that the heavy guns could be removed, along with stores, and that lines of retreat be planned. "Recent disasters have depressed the weak, and are depriving us of the aid of the wavering. Traitors show the tendencies heretofore concealed, and the selfish grow clamorous for local, and personal, interests. At such an hour, the wisdom of the trained, and the steadiness of the brave, possess a double value."

MARCH, 1862

It was spring again, but a vastly different one from the year before. One crisis had been met—by war—but the war itself had brought many more. In the Confederacy the outlook was distinctly bleak. When the Southerner looked out from his beleaguered nation he saw Federal armies poised in northern Virginia near Washington and at Harper's Ferry; on the Peninsula at Fort Monroe, threatening Richmond and Norfolk; in North Carolina, again threatening Virginia; at Port Royal, S.C., aiming at Savannah and Charleston; on the Gulf Coast, menacing Mobile and New Orleans; in northwestern Arkansas; on the Mississippi; and on the Cumberland and Tennessee. Along with all this there was the blockade, no longer a nuisance, but a developed danger. The defeats of the late winter, Forts Henry and Donelson, the collapse of the line in Kentucky, the loss of Roanoke Island and a sizable portion of North Carolina, retreat in Missouri, all were leaving their mark. Increased and strenuous effort had to be made if the Confederacy was to live a second year.

Northerners, too, were far from optimistic. True, after long delays and much grumbling from the populace, the armies in the West were at last moving with effect, but in Virginia little that was constructive appeared to have been done. Dissatisfaction was especially high among those who desired peace above all, and among those who desired conquest and abolition of slavery. The Administration was gaining critics—civilian, political, and military—and it was becoming clear that the war would continue for quite a time.

March 1, Saturday

Maj. Gen. Henry W. Halleck, commanding Federals in the West, ordered Grant at Fort Donelson to proceed south up the Tennessee River to near Eastport, Miss., continuing the advance so well begun. Grant, hurrying from Donelson to Fort Henry, set the machinery in motion for another major movement of his army. Meanwhile, two wooden gunboats went up as far as Pittsburg Landing, Tenn., and silenced a Confederate field battery already sent there by Beauregard. In charge of Confederate troops along the Mississippi, Beauregard was concentrating his units from Columbus, Ky., and elsewhere at Island No. 10, Fort Pillow, and Corinth, Miss. A. S. Johnston with the remnants of his army from Bowling Green was beginning to move from Murfreesboro, Tenn., southeast of Nashville, across country toward Corinth. Already it was fairly clear that the next Western moves would be down the Mississippi and Tennessee by the Federals. In addition, there was a fight at Sikeston, Mo., this day.

President Davis proclaimed martial law in Richmond and Confederate authorities arrested Virginian John Minor Botts and other pro-Northern sympathizers accused of operating against the South.

March 2, Sunday

The final units of the Confederate garrison of the batteries of Columbus, Ky., under Gen. Polk, pulled out, leaving the town and bluffs on the Mississippi to the Federals. Most of the 140 guns (two were left behind) were taken south to Island No. 10 and nearby batteries, as that place and Fort Pillow were the new Mississippi River posts. With the end of Columbus the last fragment of the Confederate Kentucky line was gone and, while not again a line, new defense points were mainly in Tennessee and northern Mississippi. There was a light skirmish near New Madrid, Mo., as advance units of the Federals fought Confederates. In the far Southwest, H. H. Sibley's Confederates, marching north along the Rio Grande in their invasion of New Mexico Territory, forced the abandonment of Albuquerque by the Federals.

March 3, Monday

On the Mississippi Federals under Pope began the siege of New Madrid, Mo. Other Federals occupied evacuated Columbus, Ky., to the north. There was a skirmish at Martinsburg, western Va., as Federals occupied that town; Confederates evacuated Amelia Island, Fla.; Cubero, N. Mex. Terr., was taken by the Southerners; an action occurred at Comanche Pass, N. Mex. Terr., and there were several days of Federal operations around Berryville, Ark. In Richmond President Davis recalled Gen. Lee from Charleston and South Carolina to be a military adviser in Virginia.

In Washington President Lincoln approved a lengthy list of officers for appointment as major and brigadier generals. Gen. Halleck in St. Louis was authorized by Washington to place Brig. Gen. C. F. Smith in command of the expedition from Fort Henry up the Tennessee, after Halleck accused Grant of not reporting properly at the time of Fort Donelson and other misconduct.

March 4, Tuesday

Confederate forces in New Mexico Territory under H. H. Sibley entered Santa Fe after Federals retired to Fort Union to the northeast. The Confederate invasion of the Southwest had reached its crest. In Florida Amelia Island was occupied by Federals; for a week there was a Federal scout through Laclede, Wright, and Douglas counties of Missouri.

In command changes Grant was told to stay at Fort Henry, Tenn., as district commander while C. F. Smith was put in charge of the Federal advance up the Tennessee River, a direct slap at Grant by Gen. Halleck. The Senate of the United States confirmed Andrew Johnson as brigadier general and Military Governor of Tennessee. Maj. Gen. John C. Pemberton assumed command of the Confederate Department of South Carolina, Georgia, and East Florida in place of R. E. Lee. President Davis was having difficulties with Gen. J. E. Johnston over reenlistment of troops in Virginia, over furloughs, and with Confederate congressmen who wanted more guns for defense of the Mississippi, although the government was doing all it could to supply such guns.

March 5, Wednesday

Federal troops under Nathaniel Banks advanced up the Shenandoah Valley from Harper's Ferry toward Winchester, Va., and Jackson's command. There was a skirmish at Bunker Hill, north of Winchester, and over near Washington another skirmish at Pohick Church. In the West Beauregard at Jackson, Tenn., assumed command of the Confederate Army of the Mississippi, a sprawled-out army meant to defend the Mississippi Valley. Meanwhile, Albert Sidney Johnston's forces were moving west from Murfreesboro, Tenn., toward Corinth, Miss., to block the

Federal move up the Tennessee. The first of a large Federal force under C. F. Smith arrived at Savannah, Tenn., northeast of Corinth, soon followed by eighty troop transports and three gunboats. In northwest Arkansas Gen. Earl Van Dorn had joined Sterling Price in an effort to stop Federal Samuel Curtis, who, vastly superior, had pushed Price out of Missouri. Van Dorn decided to attack, and hurriedly concentrated his forces beyond Fayetteville and Elm Springs.

March 6, Thursday
ACTION BEGINS AT PEA RIDGE, ARK.

By late afternoon the four Federal divisions of Samuel R. Curtis' army in Arkansas were in position at Sugar Creek north of Fayetteville and well entrenched, looking south. However, Confederate Earl Van Dorn would not risk a frontal attack and decided late in the day, after some moderate fighting, to pass around the Federals by means of a night march, and attack from the north at Pea Ridge. Van Dorn had written, "I must have St. Louis and then Huza!" (sic).

Near New York the revolutionary new iron ship, U.S.S. *Monitor,* after very limited trials, left for Fort Monroe, Va., where the Federal squadron had been anticipating an attack from the Confederate ironclad *Merrimack* (or *Virginia*). *Virginia* was a heavy-draft ironclad, well armed and well protected, reconstructed from the former Federal frigate *Merrimack.* She was expected to control Hampton Roads and the harbor area, threatened by the Federals.

President Lincoln sent Congress a message calling for cooperation with any state that would adopt gradual abolition of slavery, and giving such states financial aid, to be used at their discretion. Lincoln had long urged and spoken for gradual, compensated emancipation as a war measure and an answer to the slavery problem, just as he had urged colonization of free Negroes in Central America and Africa. In Richmond the Confederate Congress passed a measure stipulating that military authorities should destroy cotton, tobacco, and other property if it could not be removed before it fell into the hands of the enemy. President Davis wrote Gen. Joseph E. Johnston in Virginia that he was aware of his problems and the possible need to retreat before McClellan's Army of the Potomac, expected to advance at any moment.

March 7, Friday
BATTLE OF PEA RIDGE OR ELKHORN TAVERN, ARKANSAS.

The weather was clear but cold after recent storms in northwest Arkansas as two Confederate columns passed around the Federal flank and Van Dorn's army attacked that of Curtis from the north at Pea Ridge or Elkhorn Tavern. The Federals, expecting a frontal attack from the south, discovered the move and quickly swung around. At first the

Confederates, aided by Indian forces, were successful. All day it was a swirling battle of gain and repulse. Van Dorn finally withdrew troops from his western wing to help his main attack. The death of Brig. Gen. Benjamin McCulloch on the Confederate right caused much confusion. Brig. Gen. James McIntosh likewise fell. Curtis concentrated his Federals by nightfall and determined to await renewal of the drive by Van Dorn the next day. The biggest battle west of the Mississippi during the Civil War was being fought. It was a frontier-type struggle, with much rough infighting and personal courage. A German-Yankee cried, "Boys, now strike that the chips fly." Both sides did just that. Charges of Confederate Indians scalping numbers of fallen Federals have been largely discounted.

From Washington McClellan's Federal Army of the Potomac, finally on the move, advanced ponderously southwestward toward Joseph E. Johnston's Confederates at Manassas, first step in the long-awaited Federal drive into Virginia. But, alerted, the much weaker Johnston began to pull out from Evansport, Dumfries, the Occoquan, and Manassas, heading south toward Fredericksburg. McClellan's army made a splendid sight as, after long, formal training and a winter's idleness, it paraded out to expected victory. At Winchester, Va., there was a skirmish between front units of Banks' advancing Federals and Jackson's small Confederate command. In Missouri lesser action occurred at Fox Creek, Point Pleasant, and Bob's Creek, with four days of operations in Saline County. And down in South Carolina Federals carried out reconnaissance up the Savannah River and to Elba Island.

March 8, Saturday

C.S.S. *Virginia* DESTROYS FEDERAL VESSELS.

BATTLE OF PEA RIDGE OR ELKHORN TAVERN, ARKANSAS, CONCLUDED.

In the wet early spring in northwest Arkansas, Federal troops of Gen. Curtis victoriously drove Confederates from Pea Ridge in what was really the third day of the battle near Elkhorn Tavern. Van Dorn's weakened Confederates retreated somewhat precipitately toward the Arkansas River, arriving at Huntsville on the ninth and then moving on to Van Buren, Ark. The battle meant, probably, the permanent loss of Missouri, and its adverse effects hampered Confederate plans to maintain the Mississippi River. It was the last major offensive of the South in the Trans-Mississippi until 1864. For Gen. Curtis it was his high point in the war. He and his outnumbered army had fought well. The Federals had about 11,000 troops, with 203 killed, 980 wounded, and 201 missing or captured, compared to Van Dorn's about 14,000, with probably 600 killed and wounded and 200 captured or missing. Curtis, contemplating the scene, wrote his brother, "The enemy is again far away in the Boston Mountains. The scene is silent and sad—the vulture and the wolf now have the dominion and the dead friends and foes sleep in the same lonely graves."

There was a different scene in Virginia. As McClellan's army stalked out after the disappearing Confederates in northern Virginia, a new type of battle broke out in Hampton Roads near Norfolk and Fort Monroe. The clumsy, ill-engined, but heavily armored C.S.S. *Virginia,* more generally called by its Yankee name, *Merrimack,* steamed slowly out of Norfolk Harbor under command of Flag Officer Franklin Buchanan. Opposed to the ironclad *Merrimack* was the old-type, traditional wooden fleet, including the forty-gun screw frigates *Roanoke* and *Minnesota,* the frigate *Congress,* fifty guns, and the sloop *Cumberland,* twenty-four guns. The sluggish *Merrimack* bore down firing, rammed *Cumberland* and forced badly damaged *Congress* aground. *Cumberland* went down fighting and *Congress* was burned after surrendering. Other Federal vessels went aground, including damaged *Minnesota.* Buchanan was wounded and succeeded by Lieut. Catesby ap Roger Jones. *Merrimack* returned to Norfolk confidently expecting to finish *Minnesota* on the morrow. Confederate losses were light and the vessel was still in reasonably good shape. Federal casualties were high, and higher still was the loss in prestige, occasioned by the destruction of two ships in unequal battle. "Pains, death, wounds, glory—that was the sum of it," according to a Southern officer. There was consternation in Washington and elsewhere. In the evening the new iron vessel, *Monitor,* after a harrowing trip south from New York, during which she was almost swamped, pulled into Hampton Roads and surveyed the damage. Confederate and Federal alike knew the Battle of Hampton Roads was not over.

In other fighting Federal forces occupied Leesburg, Va.; there were operations about Rolla, Mo.; Confederate cavalry under John Hunt Morgan raided suburbs of Nashville; and Chattanooga was occupied by Confederate forces. Meanwhile, W. T. Sherman's division embarked at Paducah, Ky., for its trip up the Tennessee. Confederate E. Kirby Smith reached Knoxville and assumed command of troops in east Tennessee.

In Washington President Lincoln conferred with McClellan over his planned move via Aquia Creek or the Peninsula southeast of Richmond, and also met with division commanders, who voted in favor of McClellan's plan. The President provided in General War Order No. 2 that sufficient forces be left to defend Washington while McClellan made his move to the Peninsula. It was clear that Mr. Lincoln intended to protect the spiritual and governmental center of the nation, although he would in most things let his commander have his own way.

March 9, Sunday

BATTLE OF THE *Monitor* AND *Merrimack.*

About nine o'clock in the morning the modern era of naval warfare began. The iron-constructed U.S.S. *Monitor,* with a single revolving turret housing two eleven-inch Dahlgren guns, battled the ironclad C.S.S. *Merrimack,* officially *Virginia.* The success of the wooden-hulled, iron-plated, floating battery of the South of the day before was forgotten. Now it was a duel of two revolutionary gladiators of the sea, circling, charging, ramming, and withdrawing. Shells bounced and slid over both vessels, neither one suffering serious damage. After more than two hours of fighting *Monitor* withdrew temporarily, due to the eye injury of Lieut. John L. Worden, but soon returned to the scene to find that *Merrimack,* also suffering some minor injuries, had withdrawn to Norfolk. By the end of the battle both vessels were commanded by their executive officers, Lieut. Samuel Dana Greene for *Monitor,* Lieut. Catesby ap Roger Jones for *Merrimack.* For the most part the strong Federal fleet and the small Confederate escort stood idly by—obsolete in such a fight. Tactically the struggle was a draw. Neither vessel had been seriously damaged; neither had given up. Strategically, however, the edge went to the Federals, though for weeks there was dread that *Merrimack* would sally forth to destroy the fleet or even appear off Washington or New York. But her poor engines and heavy draft imprisoned her in Hampton Roads. In Washington news of the battle brought a sigh of relief at the White House, and in Richmond a stronger realization that the time had come when Norfolk and the eastern end of the Peninsula, perhaps even Richmond, could be seriously threatened from the James. Both nations feared the new machines of war they could not understand. *Monitor's* chief engineer, Alban Stimers, wrote his father correctly that the fight "was the first of its kind that ever occurred in history."

Other things happened this day: skirmishing near Nashville on the Granny White Pike; at Big Creek and Mountain Grove, Mo.; and at Sangster's Station, Va. Federal troops of Grant's army, led by C. F. Smith, for several days probed toward Purdy, Tenn., in operations from Crump's Landing near Savannah on the Tennessee.

In northern Virginia there was no fighting, although an important move continued. Gen. Joseph E. Johnston's Confederates pulled out of Centreville, and the whole army was moving toward the Rappahannock River, reaching Rappahannock Station and a new line by the eleventh. The Federal army, substantially outnumbering its foe, was marching out, too, but not to battle—only to occupy the unoccupied Confederate camps for a brief time before returning to Alexandria. They found scant supplies, abandoned huts and fortifications, some of them still mounting fake wooden guns. McClellan's "victory" was hollow indeed. In New Orleans two precious Confederate powder mills blew up, with five killed.

March 10, Monday

After all the excitement of the last few days it was a quiet time on the battle fronts, though the press was full of Pea Ridge, Ark., the battle of *Monitor* and *Merrimack,* the advance and withdrawal in northern Virginia, and the build-up of Federals on the Tennessee River at Savannah and Pittsburg Landing. Citizens were studying maps, usually without such places yet on them. Only a brief skirmish in La Fayette County, Mo., is recorded for the day. In Richmond President Davis tried to reassure Gen. Joseph E. Johnston, falling back in Virginia: "you shall be promptly and adequately reinforced." In Washington Mr. Lincoln wrote that "General McClellan is after him," but, of course, all the Army of the Potomac was doing was getting exercise. Lincoln and Washington remained keyed up over the *Monitor-Merrimack* fight and the President paid a visit to Lieut. Worden, commander of *Monitor*, who suffered an eye injury in the melee. Congress discussed various aspects of slavery.

March 11, Tuesday

MAJOR CHANGES IN FEDERAL COMMAND.

President Lincoln in his War Order No. 3 officially relieved Maj. Gen. George B. McClellan from his post as General-in-Chief of the Federal Armies, but retained him in command of the Department and Army of the Potomac. In the West the departments were consolidated when Maj. Gen. Henry W. Halleck was given command of not only the Department of Missouri, but that of Kansas and part of the Department of the Ohio. These became the Department of the Mississippi. A new department in the mountains of Virginia and western Virginia to be termed the Mountain Department was created under command of Maj. Gen. Frémont, still in the Army despite the controversies over his Missouri reign. All generals were to report directly to the Secretary of War. There was to be no General-in-Chief, at least for a while. In Washington most Cabinet members and many other officials applauded Lincoln's command changes, although some were bitter over the downgrading of McClellan.

At Manassas, Va., the Federal Army of the Potomac found burning remains of supplies, wrecked railroad tracks and installations, but only a small amount of usable matériel, reminders of the retreating Confederate army.

There was a skirmish near Paris, Tenn. In the Shenandoah at Stephenson's Depot north of Winchester, Va., there was another brief fight. However, the main action in that important area was the withdrawal of Stonewall Jackson and his 4600 men from Winchester. The Confederates fell back rapidly up the valley, southward, followed by Federals from Banks' larger command.

In Richmond President Davis refused to accept the reports of Brig. Genls. Floyd and Pillow, who had fled Fort Donelson before the surrender. Both officers were relieved from command.

March 12, Wednesday

Federal soldiers marched into Winchester, Va., close on the heels of Stonewall Jackson's Confederates, who were moving southward up the

Shenandoah Valley. It was all a part of the general spring advance of the Northern armies. Elsewhere, Federal naval forces under Lieut. T. H. Stevens temporarily occupied Jacksonville, Fla.; and there was a skirmish near Aubrey, Kas. A combined Federal army-navy expedition sailed from Roanoke Island, N.C., to near the mouth of the Neuse River below New Berne.

President Davis wrote Gen. Albert Sidney Johnston, "We have suffered great anxiety because of recent events in Kentucky and Tennessee." The President was concerned about the adverse public reaction and blame that was being heaped on Johnston. However, Davis added, "I suppose the Tenn. or Mississippi river will be the object of the enemy's next campaign, and I trust you will be able to concentrate a force which will defeat either attempt."

March 13, Thursday

Gen. McClellan and his newly named corps commanders held a consequential conference at Fairfax Court House, Va. McClellan pressed his plan to shift the Army of the Potomac by boat to the York and James rivers and head for Richmond from the Peninsula, rather than from Urbanna near the mouth of the Rappahannock. The generals agreed, particularly as Joseph E. Johnston's Confederates were now on the line of the Rappahannock. Mr. Lincoln once more emphasized to McClellan, through the Secretary of War, that Manassas Junction and Washington must be left secure, although he agreed that the army could move via the Peninsula. The letter ended, "at all events, move such remainder of the army at once in pursuit of the enemy by some route." In St. Louis Gen. Halleck assumed command of the new Department of the Mississippi. Federal forces of John Pope severely bombarded Confederate works at New Madrid, Mo., on the Mississippi. There was fighting at Spring River, Ark., and Beach Creek Bridge, Tenn.

Under cover of the Navy, Federal troops under Burnside landed on the west bank of the Neuse River south of New Berne, N.C., and advanced at once.

In Richmond Gen. Lee was charged by President Davis with the conduct of military operations in the armies of the Confederacy, which seemed to be a sort of advisory post, never clearly defined.

March 14, Friday

FEDERALS CAPTURE NEW MADRID, MISSOURI, AND NEW BERNE, NORTH CAROLINA.

After the Federal capture of Roanoke Island, Burnside, with some 11,000 men, moved on the important old community of New Berne, N.C. He captured it after some fighting, driving back the Confederate force of about 4000 under L. O'B. Branch. The attack began on the thirteenth and worked its way up the right, or west, bank of the Neuse River through rain and over muddy roads. Casualties were 471 for the Federals, including 90 killed, to nearly 600 for the Confederates, most of them captured or missing, with 64 killed. Another serviceable base had been established for Federal inland expeditions and a new vantage point gained for cultivating the considerable pro-Union elements of North Carolina.

On the Mississippi after severe Union cannonading on the thirteenth, it was found that Confederates had evacuated the works at New Madrid, Mo., fleeing to Island No. 10 or across the river. Gen. John Pope had not yet conquered this bastion on the Mississippi, but he had made a good start. Federals now occupied the New Madrid earthworks, had secured considerable supplies and guns, and began to concentrate on the island itself and the fortifications east of the river in Tennessee. Elsewhere in Tennessee there was fighting at Big Creek Gap and Jacksborough; on the Tennessee River W. T. Sherman, who had taken his command toward Eastport, Miss., returned toward Pittsburg Landing, Tenn., south of Savannah; at Pittsburg Landing some explorations or reconnaissances were being carried out.

In a change of boundaries of departments, Maj. Gen. John C. Pemberton was assigned to the Confederate Department of South Carolina and Georgia. President Davis proclaimed martial law in threatened areas of southeastern Virginia. In Washington Mr. Lincoln tried to explain that compensated emancipation of the slaves "would not be half as onerous, as would be an equal sum, raised *now*, for the indefinite prossecution [sic] of the war."

March 15, Saturday

As the divisions of W. T. Sherman and Stephen Hurlbut came into Pittsburg Landing on the Tennessee, Maj. Gen. Buell was ordered by Halleck to head from Nashville toward Savannah, Tenn. Buell was to aid Grant's advancing army, but he was seriously delayed by lack of bridges over the Duck River. For four days John Hunt Morgan carried out Confederate operations about Gallatin, Tenn.; and there was a skirmish near Marshall, Mo. The Federal Department of Florida was merged into the Department of the South with Maj. Gen. David Hunter commanding and headquarters at Hilton Head, S.C. President Davis told Gen. Joseph E. Johnston that there was no immediate necessity for throwing troops into Richmond and that the general should decide on his new position.

President Lincoln approved an act of Congress authorizing a joint commission of the United States, France, and Great Britain to consider means of preserving Atlantic fisheries. Gen. Halleck in St. Louis exonerated Gen. Grant of the rather superficial charges arising out of Fort Donelson and restored him to field command of the forces in Tennessee. Grant replaced C. F. Smith, incapacitated by a leg injury.

March 16, Sunday

There was light skirmishing in the Pittsburg Landing area of Tennessee as Confederates tried to find out what the Federals were about. Other action was at Pound Gap, Ky., and near Marshall, Mo. Martial law was instituted by the United States in San Francisco, Calif., as city defenses were increased in view of rumors of possible attack.

March 17, Monday

At Alexandria, Va., Gen. McClellan began embarking the huge Army of the Potomac, en route to the James and York rivers and what became the Peninsula Campaign. Supposedly he was to leave sufficient troops in the immediate vicinity of Washington to guard the capital from the Confederate army on the Rappahannock and in the Shenandoah. In Tennessee Maj. Gen. Grant regained his active command and as two more divisions arrived, set up his headquarters in a mansion at Savannah, north of the army concentration point at Pittsburg Landing on the Tennessee River. There was a skirmish at Riddle's Point, Mo., as well.

March 18, Tuesday

A major Confederate Cabinet change: Judah P. Benjamin, often criticized for his management of the War Department, was named Secretary of State by President Davis to succeed resigned R. M. T. Hunter, who went to the Senate. George W. Randolph of Virginia was appointed Secretary of War. Att. Gen. Thomas Bragg stepped down for Thomas H. Watts of Alabama. The shifts represented internal politics of the Confederate government and its lifelong search for a really able War Secretary.

In Mississippi first units of Albert Sidney Johnston's men from Murfreesboro began coming into Corinth, but the move was not completed until March 24. There was a skirmish at Middletown, Va., and fighting at Point Pleasant, Mo., part of Pope's Federal drive on Island No. 10. Till the end of the month in Missouri there was Union activity and skirmishing in Johnson, St. Clair, and Henry counties.

March 19, Wednesday

Action of the day was confined to skirmishing at Elk Mountain, western Va., and Strasburg, Va. In the latter, Federal troops under James Shields had advanced against Jackson's retreating Confederates in the Shenandoah. Meanwhile, most of the remainder of Banks' command in the valley had been ordered east toward Washington, to help protect the capital. There was a reconnaissance of several days' duration by Federals on May River, S.C.

March 20, Thursday

Federal troops, threatened by Stonewall Jackson, moved back from Strasburg, Va., toward Winchester in the Shenandoah as Banks' command was weakened by diversion of a major portion of his army toward Washington. Jackson followed close on the heels of the withdrawing Federals. There was a skirmish at Philippi, western Va., a Union reconnaissance to Gainesville and another to Dumfries, Va. Burnside's Federals from New Berne, N.C., moved toward Washington, N.C., capturing the town on the twenty-first. In South Carolina there were operations near Bluffton and brief fights at Buckingham and Hunting Island until the twenty-fourth, part of the Federal operations from Hilton Head. After a long sea voyage Maj. Gen. Benjamin F. Butler assumed command of the Department of the Gulf at Ship Island, Miss., continuing the build-up of Northern forces looking toward an attack on New Orleans.

March 21, Friday

Nothing of moment occurred this day, which was unusual in this spring of violent action. There was a slight affair at McKay's Farm, Mo.; a reconnaissance and skirmish at Cumberland Gap, Tenn. A Norfolk, Va., paper, the *Day-Book,* complained about increased drinking, particularly among Confederate officers, who were said to imbibe "in quantities which would astonish the nerves of a cast-iron lamp-post, and a quality which would destroy the digestive organs of the ostrich."

March 22, Saturday

Skirmishing occurred at Kernstown as Shields' retreating Federals clashed with front elements of Stonewall Jackson's command in what was the prelude to a battle on the morrow. Other fighting was on the Post Oak Creek and at Little Santa Fe, Mo. The ostensibly British ship *Oreto,* destined to become C.S.S. *Florida,* sailed from Britain for Nassau in the Bahamas. The Federal government created the Middle Military Department with headquarters at Baltimore and commanded by Maj. Gen. John A. Dix.

March 23, Sunday

FIRST BATTLE OF KERNSTOWN, VIRGINIA.

At the village of Kernstown, Va., a few miles south of Winchester in the Shenandoah Valley, T. J. Stonewall Jackson's Confederates drove in on the Federal forces of James Shields. Confederate cavalry under Turner Ashby, having fought a skirmish the day before, had reported only a rear guard left in Winchester. Jackson struck hard with his 3500, but found Shields strongly placed with 9000. Despite this disparity, Jackson's men fought well and won deserved honors before gathering in their wounded and retreating southward up the Shenandoah. Jackson suffered 80 killed, 375 wounded, and 263 missing, total 718; the Federals had 118 killed, 450 wounded, and 22 missing for 590.

Kernstown marked the opening of what would become the famous Shenandoah Valley Campaign. Furthermore, it had its effect: Gen. J. E. Johnston had directed Jackson to divert Federal attention from his main army and keep troops from the gathering Army of the Potomac. Jackson did so by attacking. Washington, fearing a threat on Harper's Ferry and Washington, ordered Banks and his Federal troops to return to the valley and others that had been heading for the Peninsula were withdrawn from McClellan's command. The threat also influenced Lincoln to keep Irvin McDowell's large corps south of Washington, instead of sending it by sea to the Peninsula, for Lincoln had soon discovered that McClellan had not fully honored his agreement to protect Washington properly. Thus, what became the First Battle of Kernstown was a small battle large in results. For the remainder of March, Jackson withdrew up the Shenandoah, protected by Ashby's cavalry, while Banks and his Federals slowly pursued as far as Strasburg.

Elsewhere there was an affair at Smyrna, Fla., and a Federal expedition from Point Pleasant, near New Madrid, Mo., to Little River.

Fort Macon was a brick fort on a long, narrow, sandy island near the town of Beaufort, N.C., which had been garrisoned by a small command of Confederates. Burnside, as part of his attempted Federal conquest of North Carolina, ordered Brig. Gen. John G. Parke to move against the old-style fortification. On March 23 Parke and his command arrived at the fort and demanded surrender, which was refused. The Federals then instituted siege operations.

March 24, Monday

The Federal Congress was still discussing the possibility of compensated emancipation. Abolitionist Wendell Phillips, attempting to lecture in Cincinnati, was hissed and pelted with eggs and rocks. Finally the meeting broke up in a wild fist fight, with Phillips taken away by friends. Lincoln, in a letter to Horace Greeley regarding his proposed gradual compensated emancipation, said, "we should urge it persuasively, and not menacingly, upon the South." There was a skirmish at Camp Jackson, Tenn. At Corinth, Miss., Albert Sidney Johnston's army was completing its movement from Murfreesboro, Tenn., preparing to oppose Grant, who was some twenty miles away at Pittsburg Landing.

March 25, Tuesday

It was a day of Federal expeditions, with a three-day reconnaissance from Murfreesboro to Shelbyville, Tullahoma, Manchester, and McMinn-

ville, Tenn.; a four-day expedition in Moniteau County, Mo.; a reconnaissance to Agnew's Ferry, Tenn.; and a skirmish at Mount Jackson, Va.

March 26, Wednesday

ENGAGEMENT AT APACHE CANYON, NEW MEXICO TERRITORY.

The Confederate campaign in New Mexico was building to its climax.
From Santa Fe a Confederate column marched out on the Santa Fe Trail
southeast, where it unexpectedly met a Federal column of Colorado volunteers advancing from Fort Union to oppose the Southern offensive. At
Apache Canyon near Johnson's Ranch, portions of the two forces converged. After fairly severe fighting in the valley, the Federals, although
victorious, fell back to Pigeon's Ranch near Glorieta. Maj. John M.
Chivington had made his first mark in the war. But it was clear that
the campaign was not over. Elsewhere, farther east, there was action
at Humansville, on the Post Oak Creek at the mouth of the Brier, and
near Gouge's Mill, Mo.

President Davis wrote Gen. Albert Sidney Johnston at Corinth, Miss.,
"You have done wonderfully well, and now I breathe easier in the
assurance that you will be able to make a junction of your two armies."
By this the Confederate President meant Beauregard's and Johnston's meeting so they could face the Federals moving on the Tennessee River
before more Yankees arrived from Nashville. A major clash was unavoidable in the West.

March 27, Thursday

In Richmond Gen. Joseph E. Johnston was ordered to reinforce the
Confederates on the Peninsula under John Bankhead Magruder, now
about to be seriously threatened by McClellan's Army of the Potomac
moving from Fort Monroe, Va. There were minor operations in the
vicinity of Middleburg and White Plains, Va., and a reconnaissance
on Santa Rosa Island, Fla.

March 28, Friday

ENGAGEMENT OF GLORIETA OR PIGEON'S RANCH.

A major fight of the Civil War in the Far West. At Pigeon's Ranch
in La Glorieta Pass, not far from Santa Fe, N. Mex. Terr., the Federal
command of Col. John P. Slough met a portion of H. H. Sibley's
Confederates under Col. W. R. Scurry. Brisk fighting ensued and the
Federals, both Colorado volunteers and regulars, slowly fell back, outnumbered and on the defensive. Meanwhile, about 400 men commanded
by Maj. J. M. Chivington scrambled over the mountains and descended
upon the parked Confederate wagons and supplies at Johnson's Ranch
in the rear of the fighting column. After Col. Scurry heard of the
disaster he was forced to retreat to Santa Fe, and the Southern invasion

was nearly at an end. The Confederates had about 1100 men in the fight, with 36 killed, 60 wounded, and 25 missing; the Federals, 1342 men in all, 31 killed, over 50 wounded, and 30 missing. It soon would be necessary for Sibley to pull his thinning forces out of the territorial capital at Santa Fe and retreat southward along the Rio Grande.

Elsewhere there was a Confederate expedition in Scott and Morgan counties, Tenn.; and there were several days of skirmishes on the Orange and Alexandria Railroad in Virginia. Brig. Gen. George W. Morgan was assigned to command the Seventh Division of the Federal Army of the Ohio with an important object in mind: he was to capture Cumberland Gap, vital mountain pass at the junction of Kentucky, Tennessee, and Virginia.

March 29, Saturday

At Corinth, Miss., the Confederate armies of Kentucky and the Mississippi were consolidated under Gen. Albert Sidney Johnston. P. G. T. Beauregard was second-in-command, with corps under Leonidas Polk, Braxton Bragg, William J. Hardee, and George Bibb Crittenden. For the Federals Maj. Gen. John Charles Frémont took command of the Mountain Department in western Virginia from William S. Rosecrans. There was an affair on Edisto Island, S.C., and a skirmish on the Blackwater near Warrensburg, Mo.

March 30, Sunday

Federals descended upon Union City, Tenn.; there was skirmishing near Clinton, Mo.; and a couple of days of fighting on Wilmington and Whitemarsh Island, Ga.

March 31, Monday

The month ended with no major warfare, but armies were poised east and west. Action included the Federal capture of Union City, Tenn.; skirmishes at Deep Gully, N.C.; on the Purdy Road near Adamsville, Tenn.; and at Pink Hill, Mo. At Island No. 10 and New Madrid Bend on the Mississippi, Confederate Brig. Gen. William W. Mackall superseded Maj. Gen. John Porter McCown in command. In the Federal Department of the South at Hilton Head, S.C., Maj. Gen. David Hunter assumed command.

President Lincoln, fearing for the safety of Washington and pressured by those accusing Gen. McCellan of deserting the capital, ordered back a large division under Louis Blenker to join Frémont in the Mountain Department. He told McClellan he did so "with great pain, understanding that you would wish it otherwise." The picture of McClellan being denied troops was building up to engender the endless discussion that plagued the leaders of the Civil War and is with us today.

APRIL, 1862

The month opened on notes of anticipation and fear. The character of the war seemed much the same as it had been when March began. For the North, the people could see their armies advancing almost everywhere; at last offensives were under way that might capture Richmond, split the Confederacy in the West, and wound it severely elsewhere. For the South, the people could see clearly the many-pronged threat and knew something had to be done, and done quickly, to defend their nation.

In Virginia Gen. McClellan was moving a vast army to the Peninsula, nearer Richmond. Federal soldiers stood guard at Washington, in the Shenandoah Valley and in western Virginia. In North Carolina Fort Macon was besieged and Burnside's expedition had chewed a big gap in Confederate territory. From Port Royal, S.C., the threat against Savannah, Ga., was growing daily. It was hoped the forts in the delta of the Mississippi could protect New Orleans. In the far Southwest the Confederate advance had not only been stopped, but defeated. In Arkansas, too, the Southerners were falling back. On the Mississippi, Island No. 10 was under siege, and a growing Federal army deep in southern Tennessee was threatening the state of Mississippi. A bit to the east, Union activities indicated a move on Alabama and perhaps Chattanooga.

April 1, Tuesday

The transfer of the huge Northern Army of the Potomac from near Alexandria, Va., to Fort Monroe via the Potomac and Chesapeake Bay continued. The headquarters of the army also shifted, as Gen. George B. McClellan prepared his assault upon the weak line across the Peninsula near Yorktown, held by less than fifteen thousand men under Maj. Gen. John Bankhead Magruder. In the Shenandoah Banks' Federals, now considerably strengthened, pushed from Strasburg to Woodstock and Edenburg while Stonewall Jackson, guarded by his cavalry, fell back up the valley southward. Fighting consisted of skirmishes at Salem, Va.; on the Little Sni and at Doniphan, Mo.; and there was a Federal expedition by gunboats from Pittsburg Landing, Tenn., to Eastport, Miss., and Chickasaw, Ala., on the Tennessee River. On the Mississippi at Island No. 10 soldiers landed stealthily from small boats, quickly brushed aside the Confederate guards, spiked six guns, and returned safely.

The congregation of the Second Baptist Church of Richmond, having contributed their bell to be cast into cannon, also agreed to purchase enough metal to provide what would be called the Second Baptist Church Battery.

April 2, Wednesday

Gen. Albert Sidney Johnston, in command of the newly organized Confederate army at Corinth, Miss., issued orders for the movement and attack against Grant's Federals at Pittsburg Landing, Tenn. The Confederates were to move early on April 3. At Pittsburg Landing, not far from Shiloh Church or Meeting House, there was a brief skirmish. Elsewhere in the West there was a skirmish near Walkersville, and a Federal reconnaissance from Cape Girardeau to Jackson, Whitewater, and Dallas, all in Missouri. In the Shenandoah a skirmish occurred at Stony Creek, Va., near Edenburg.

Severe tornadoes hit Cairo, Ill., and New Madrid, Mo. The notorious Mrs. Rose Greenhow, Confederate spy in Washington, and two other persons were ordered sent into Virginia beyond the Union lines. The U. S. Senate passed a House resolution proposed by Lincoln whereby the United States would give states financial aid if they adopted gradual, compensated emancipation. None of the Northern states ever took action on this proposal, so strongly urged by Mr. Lincoln.

April 3, Thursday

The Confederate army under Albert Sidney Johnston set out toward the Tennessee River for its attack on Grant's army near Pittsburg Landing and Shiloh Church, Tenn. But, as often happened, delays piled on delays and the march from Corinth, Miss., slowed down so badly that there was no chance to launch the attack on April 4 as planned. Meanwhile, Federal gunboats carried out reconnaissance from Savannah, Tenn., to Eastport, Miss., and Chickasaw, Ala., and there was a small skirmish near Monterey, Tenn., between Corinth and Pittsburg Landing. However, despite occasional light action, Grant's encamped force was generally unaware of the approaching Confederates. There was a skirmish at Moorefield, western Virginia, and a two-day Federal expedition from Ship Island to Biloxi and Pass Christian, Miss. Federal seamen accepted the surrender of Apalachicola, Fla.

President Lincoln, discovering that fewer than twenty thousand troops had been left by Gen. McClellan to defend Washington, despite his directions to the contrary, instructed Sec. of War Stanton to retain one corps which was under orders to go to McClellan on the Peninsula. McDowell's corps was kept back and immediately McClellan protested that he had been shortchanged, albeit he soon had 100,000 troops on the Peninsula. Furthermore, Lincoln ordered that "Gen. McClellan commence his forward movement from his new base at once." The U. S. Senate voted to abolish slavery in the District of Columbia, 29 to 14.

April 4, Friday

Action was increasing. Two major movements, one Union, one Confederate, were under way. In Tennessee Albert Sidney Johnston's army marching out of Corinth, Miss., toward Pittsburg Landing suffered further delays; heavy rain this night prevented the army from being deployed for attack on the fifth. By now it was believed that any chance of surprise must be gone. Yet the skirmishing around Grant's army continued to increase extensively.

On the Peninsula southeast of Richmond, Va., McClellan moved slowly toward Yorktown, his massive army confronted by about fifteen thousand Confederates and a frail line of fortifications along the Warwick River. Despite his numbers, McClellan failed to make a decided effort to cross the river or to drive the Confederates away from Yorktown. In the meantime, Joseph E. Johnston with the principal Confederate army in Virginia was shifting southward from the line of the Rappahannock to bolster Magruder on the Peninsula. There was a skirmish near Howard's Mills at Cockletown, Va. Pressure was being lightly applied to Johnston's Rappahannock line by small Federal units. In command changes, Banks' Fifth Army Corps was put into the Federal Department of the Shenandoah and the First Army Corps of McDowell was put into the Department of the Rappahannock.

On the Mississippi at Island No. 10 a canal had been laboriously cut through the tangled swamps near New Madrid so that Federals could move small vessels southward around the forts of the island. This was one of the few times that such a canal really worked. Under cover of night the Federal gunboat *Carondelet* ran the Confederate batteries of the island during a heavy thunderstorm, the scene made unholy by the flashes of lightning, the din of thunder vying with the blast and roar of the guns. But *Carondelet* got down and became an immediate threat to the Confederates, as it could help cover landing of Federals on the Tennessee shore below the important island. Other fighting occurred at Lawrenceburg, Tenn.

April 5, Saturday

SIEGE OF YORKTOWN BEGINS.

McClellan in front of Yorktown, Va., began establishing his siege lines instead of directly attacking the fifteen thousand Confederate defenders. Joseph E. Johnston was rapidly bringing in reinforcements from the Rappahannock to the Peninsula, though the Confederates never numbered much more than half the Federal Army of the Potomac. The other Johnston, Albert Sidney, with his Confederate army near Shiloh Church and Pittsburg Landing in Tennessee, failed to attack this day and only managed to get ready by late in the afternoon. Although the Confederates could hardly understand it, evidently the Federals of Grant were not yet aware of the enemy army nearly in their midst. Jefferson Davis wrote Johnston, "I anticipate victory." In South Carolina Union forces occupied Edisto Island, and there was a small affair at San Louis Pass, Tex. In Nashville Federal military governor of Tennessee Andrew Johnson suspended the mayor, aldermen, and councilmen of Nashville for refusing to take an oath to the Union.

April 6, Sunday

BATTLE OF SHILOH OR PITTSBURG LANDING, TENNESSEE.

Over the rolling countryside with blossoming peach trees and bursting spring came the Confederate army of Albert Sidney Johnston—moving through the woods and occasional open fields upon what was, to their amazement, the largely unsuspecting Federal army of General Grant. There had been skirmishing for several days and many rumors, and in the early morning the firing in front of Shiloh Church mounted drastically. Nevertheless, the Yankees, for the most part, were unprepared for the charge that burst upon them. Although none of the Federals were caught in bed, as commonly reported, there was far too much surprise for an alert army. Gen. Grant himself was at his headquarters at Savannah, Tenn., several miles north or down the Tennessee River. The first units of Buell's army from Nashville under Brig. Gen. William "Bull" Nelson had arrived at Savannah the night before after a forced march, while most of Buell's troops were much farther behind. Gen. Buell himself was nearby. Hearing the heavy gunfire from Pittsburg Landing, Grant boated rapidly to the scene, pausing at Crump's Landing north of the battle to order Lew Wallace's division to the field.

All day long the battle reeled toward the Tennessee River, the Federals falling back before the furious but disjointed charge of the Confederates. At the so-called Sunken Road, at the Hornets' Nest, around Shiloh Church, at the Bloody Pond, and in the Peach Orchard, heroes were made on both sides and a few cowards were revealed. Federal Brig. Gen. Benjamin M. Prentiss held the Hornets' Nest gallantly, only to surrender in late afternoon. Although bent back and sorely pounded, with stragglers hiding under the riverbanks, the Federals did not break in large numbers. By evening a line of artillery, stiffening of some units, and reinforcements of Gen. Nelson set up a new line nearer the river. Grant had been surprised, had been at least partially beaten, but he was not yet defeated. For the Confederates, an ill-advised attack formation had caused costly mix-ups of units, coordination had been lacking, casualties high, and victory not completely gained. About two-thirty in the afternoon Gen. Albert Sidney Johnston had fallen, wounded in the leg, to die shortly afterward, perhaps unnecessarily, from loss of blood. Gen. Beauregard, second-in-command, tried to pull his army together for a final assault, but was compelled to wait till the morrow. On the Northern side Brig. Gen. W. H. L.

Wallace was mortally wounded. The rain of the night could not wash away the marks of the great battle on the Tennessee. A Rebel soldier said later, "Oh God forever keep me out of such another fight. I was not scared I was just in danger."

Over on the Mississippi John Pope was preparing his assault on Island No. 10 and on the Confederate troops guarding the river on the Tennessee side near Tiptonville. In the mountains a Federal expedition operated April 6–11 from Greeneville, Tenn., into Laurel Valley of North Carolina.

Washington expectantly awaited word from McClellan on the Peninsula that the Confederate line had been broken and the enemy brushed aside at Yorktown. Not hearing such, Mr. Lincoln wired Gen. McClellan, "I think you better break the enemies' line from York-town to Warwick River, at once. They will probably use *time,* as advantageously as you can." And the President was correct; Magruder was desperately holding his weak line while Joseph E. Johnston hurried his army from the Rappahannock.

April 7, Monday

CONCLUSION OF BATTLE OF SHILOH OR PITTSBURG LANDING.

FALL OF ISLAND NO. 10.

During the stormy night of April 6–7 on the western bank of the Tennessee River at Pittsburg Landing more Federal troops of Don Carlos Buell joined those of Grant's battered but stubborn army, as did the division of Lew Wallace, delayed the day before. Thus freshened with new life Grant's forces faced the second day of Shiloh or Pittsburg Landing in better shape than their fatigued, somewhat disorganized, and equally blooded opponents. At first the Federals managed to retake most of the ground lost April 6, but near the Peach Orchard, the Confederates rallied and heavy fighting swirled back and forth. Beauregard, replacing the fallen Johnston, awaited word of reinforcements from Earl Van Dorn of the Trans-Mississippi. Word came, but it was that Van Dorn was unable to make it from Arkansas. Faced now with a greatly superior enemy, Beauregard broke off the battle and, pulling together his shattered legions, drew back slowly toward Corinth. Grant was content to reoccupy his old camps and repair the human and physical damage of battle. Then too, there was the problem of whether Grant had had the authority to order Buell's largely unfought army forward or not. As with all the great conflicts of the war, the conflict of words long outlasted the echoes of the gunfire, but strategically Grant held the field and the Confederates went back from whence they came. For the South, which had much to gain from victory, it must be considered a defeat in its effects. For the North, a victory only in that it held what had been taken earlier, but gained little. The statistics: Federal, Grant's Army of the Tennessee effectives put at around 42,000 plus three divisions of Buell's Army of the Ohio totaling about 20,000; losses 1754 killed, 8408 wounded, and 2885 missing for a total of 13,047. Confederate effectives about 40,000, with 1723 killed, 8012 wounded, and 959 missing, total of 10,694. Among the dead for the South, Gen. Albert Sidney Johnston, of whom much had been expected. A Northern soldier wrote, "Gentle winds of Springtime seem a sighing over a thousand new made graves."

For more than a month Gen. John Pope, his army, and the Federal gunboats had been battling not only Confederate opponents but geography in the campaign at Island No. 10 or New Madrid Bend, where the swamps were worth divisions to the South. With the passage of *Carondelet* below the island April 4, and followed by *Pittsburg* on April 7, Pope now had floating artillery and transportation below the strongly placed island and could launch his attack on Confederates in the Tiptonville area on the soggy mainland of Tennessee. Pounding the batteries on the Tennessee shore the gunboats forced evacuation. Pope's troops had landed behind the Confederate defenders and blocked the only escape road. The garrison surrendered both on the mainland and at Island No. 10, with the formal ceremonies April 8. Perhaps seven thousand men, including Brig. Gen. W. W. Mackall, twenty-five field guns, the artillery in the batteries, small arms, and considerable ammunition and other supplies were captured. Confederate defense had not been outstanding, but the Federal victory, considering the obstacles of nature, was ably achieved. Pope, his men, the Navy, all had done well and, briefly, the North had a new hero from the West. Unfortunately the focus of the nation was on Shiloh and Virginia, and Pope's record soon would be marred by defeat. But the Federal victory at Island No. 10 was another serious break in the Confederate defense of the Mississippi, opening the river, with only Fort Pillow in the way, to undefended Memphis and beyond. Gunboats and combined operations had again recorded an achievement that deserves rank with the major events of the Civil War.

Much lesser action continued these days. In Virginia McClellan was preparing his siege lines around Yorktown to the consternation of Washington and the Administration. There was an affair at St. Andrew's Bay, Fla.; a skirmish at Foy's Plantation, N.C.; and a small Federal expedition near Newport, N.C. In the Federal Congress a House committee on emancipation and colonization of Negroes was appointed. The United States signed a treaty with Great Britain for more efficient suppression of the illegal slave trade.

April 8, Tuesday

As the news of Shiloh or Pittsburg Landing swept the nations, the formal surrender of the Confederates at New Madrid Bend or Island No. 10 added to the excitement. Two more heavy blows had fallen on the Confederacy. As the Confederate army, now under Beauregard, withdrew painfully from Shiloh to Corinth, Miss., only a brief Federal reconnaissance annoyed their passage. At Albuquerque, N. Mex. Terr., there was light skirmish as H. H. Sibley's Confederates, having left Santa Fe, continued their retreat southward along the Rio Grande in the face of a superior Federal column. Other fighting occurred near Warrensburg, at Warsaw, on Medicine Creek, Mo. There was scouting in southwestern Missouri, including skirmishes, and increased guerrilla activity in western Virginia. President Davis proclaimed martial law in eastern Tennessee, threatened by Federal troops and pro-Union civilians.

April 9, Wednesday

The Confederate Senate at Richmond passed a bill calling for conscription of troops. Many Confederates opposed the move bitterly, believing it an infringement of liberties, while others recognized that, with its limited manpower, the South must raise armies somehow.

Federal units evacuated Jacksonville, Fla. There was skirmishing at Jackson, Mo., and fighting for several days involving three minor scouting expeditions in Missouri.

In Washington President Lincoln and his Cabinet members discussed McClellan's activity or lack of it at Yorktown on the Peninsula. Mr. Lincoln tried to explain to his general that he had held back troops because he discovered that insufficient men had been left in and around Washington: "My explicit order that Washington should, by the judgment of *all* the commanders of Army corps, be left entirely secure, had been neglected." The President wondered at the discrepancy between McClellan's reports of the size of his army and that of the Sec. of War. Several times urging him to strike, Mr. Lincoln concluded, *"But you must act."*

As victory bells for Shiloh and Island No. 10 rang in many parts of the North, relief organizations rushed money, boats, food, and hospital supplies to the army at Pittsburg Landing, Tenn.

April 10, Thursday

President Lincoln approved the joint resolution of Congress calling for gradual emancipation of the slaves by the states.

For several weeks Brig. Gen. Quincy Adams Gillmore had been preparing the Federal attack on Fort Pulaski on Cockspur Island near the entrance to the harbor of Savannah, Ga. Gillmore's men had erected heavy batteries on Tybee Island, across the Savannah River facing the fort. The sturdily built work was garrisoned by 385 men under Col. Charles H. Olmstead and held 48 guns. It was feared that ordinary smoothbore shot and shell could never penetrate the brick walls from the distance they had to be placed, and so for the first time against such fortifications rifled guns with long range and penetrating shells were brought into play. On the clear, cool morning of April 10 the Federal bombardment from Tybee Island began. Fire from both sides increased rapidly, with many scars appearing on the outer walls of the fort. In the afternoon the bombardment slackened, but several guns in the fort had been dismounted and the walls badly dented.

Elsewhere there was a skirmish near Fernandina, another episode in the "small war" that plagued Florida. For the Federals, Maj. Gen. Samuel R. Curtis assumed command of the District of Kansas. President Davis wired governors of Confederate states, "Genl. Beauregard must have reinforcements to meet the vast accumulation of the enemy before him." Police broke up a counterfeiting ring in St. Louis. Federal Brig. Gen. W. H. L. Wallace of Illinois died of wounds received at Shiloh.

April 11, Friday

FALL OF FORT PULASKI, GEORGIA.

Federal guns from Tybee Island roared forth again in the morning against wounded Fort Pulaski on the Savannah River near the major Confederate port of Savannah, Ga. Soon Pulaski's fire slackened as the rifled guns and heavy artillery of the Federals, well protected, silenced more of the fort's guns and blasted two visible holes through the brick walls. Youthful Confederate commander Col. Charles H. Olmstead made his decision and in midafternoon surrendered. Over five thousand shot and shell had been fired against the fort, with only one Federal killed. For the Confederates, the fort was a wreck, but only one man died, although others were wounded. The fall of Fort Pulaski successfully blocked the main channel to Savannah and greatly strengthened the effectiveness of the never-ceasing Federal blockade. Once more, as it had so often this spring, the Confederacy reeled from another blow.

And there was yet more. Troops of Brig. Gen. Ormsby Mitchel occupied Huntsville, Ala., on the Memphis and Charleston Railroad, not far from Chattanooga, albeit his forces were small in number. Still they were threatening. There was a skirmish at Wartrace, Tenn., and at another Shiloh, this time in Missouri. At the siege of Yorktown on the Peninsula there was further light skirmishing. At Pittsburg Landing, Tenn., Maj. Gen. Henry W. Halleck, Federal commander in the West, arrived to take over active field command, a move which relegated Grant to second spot behind him. Meanwhile, orders were out to concentrate the Federal Army. Already Grant and Buell were there, and Pope soon would be. From the build-up it was clear the Federals intended to move against Corinth and the deep South. Confederate governors were trying to respond to Davis' call for troops for defense of Mississippi.

Once more the redoubtable *Merrimack* was out. From Norfolk, Va., the Confederate ironclad steamed forth into Hampton Roads with accompanying gunboats. There was uproar and consternation among the Federal transports, supply vessels, and fleet, with "tugs whistling and screaming about." Northern ships scurried out of harm's way. Nearby, *Monitor*, steam up, awaited the attack. The Confederates managed to capture three merchant vessels, but there was no fight. The Southern commander indicated he awaited combat with *Monitor,* but she did not come forth.

The Federal House of Representatives by a vote of 93 to 39 passed a measure abolishing slavery in the District of Columbia.

April 12, Saturday

GREAT LOCOMOTIVE CHASE.

It was breakfast time at Big Shanty, Ga.; the Atlanta to Chattanooga passenger train of the Western & Atlantic had pulled in. At Marietta some twenty-two men had gotten on board, but they did not go in for breakfast at Big Shanty. They were a party of Union volunteers under James J. Andrews, bent on breaking the vital rail line to Chattanooga. Detaching the locomotive and three freight cars from the passenger train, the raiders headed north. The mightily surprised train crew, their meal unfinished, took out after their locomotive, the *General.* The chase lasted most of the day, with excitement enough for everyone. Soon the Federals in the *General* were pursued by Confederates in the locomotive *Texas.* North of Ringgold, Ga., out of fuel and being closely followed, the Yankees abandoned the engine and took to the woods, only to be captured. Andrews and seven others were later executed, eight eventually escaped, and six were finally paroled. As a military operation it meant little; as an adventure story it ranks high.

Slowly the defenders of Yorktown on the Peninsula were being reinforced from Joseph E. Johnston's army on the Rappahannock and elsewhere. Magruder now had more than 30,000 men to face McClellan's more than 100,000, but the siege continued. The authority of Gen. Johnston was extended over the Departments of Norfolk and the Peninsula. In the Southwest Confederates began evacuation of Albuquerque, N. Mex. Terr. There was a two-day Federal expedition to Bear Creek, Ala.

The commander of the Federal Department of the South, David Hunter, ordered that all slaves in and around Fort Pulaski, Ga., be confiscated and declared free. This was one of several such orders by Hunter which were later rescinded by President Lincoln, who felt it was beyond the province of military leaders to free slaves.

April 13, Sunday

For nearly the remainder of April Federal troops pursued the retreating Confederates in New Mexico Territory, until the Southerners reached the El Paso area. Meanwhile, a Federal expedition left southern California this day, under James H. Carleton, moving through Arizona to New Mexico and northwestern Texas, ending Sept. 20. On the Tennessee Federals carried out reconnaissance on the Corinth, Miss., and Purdy, Tenn., roads. In North Carolina there was a skirmish at Gillett's Farm on Pebbly

Run. Federal forces under Gen. Ormsby Mitchel occupied Decatur, Ala., on the Tennessee River.

April 14, Monday

Federal mortar boats bombarded Fort Pillow, Tenn., on the Mississippi River. The U.S. naval flotilla on Chesapeake Bay carried out reconnaissance on the Rappahannock. There were skirmishes at Montevallo, Diamond Grove, and near the Santa Fe Road, Mo. In South Carolina there was a reconnaissance on Seabrook Island by Federals.

April 15, Tuesday

Skirmishes marked the day at Peralta, N. Mex. Terr., and Lost Creek, Mo. At Picacho Pass, Ariz., a small Federal victory threatened the Confederates in Tucson.

April 16, Wednesday

President Davis approved an act of the Confederate Congress calling for conscription of every white male between eighteen and thirty-five years of age for three years' service. The measure provided for administration of enrollment and draft by state officials, assignment to units from their own states, election of company, battalion, and regimental officers, and for substitutions. There were no specific exemptions; those provided by the act of April 21 exempted government officials, ferrymen, pilots, employees in iron mines and foundries, telegraph operators, ministers, printers, educators, hospital employees, and druggists, among others. There were a number of later revisions in exemptions.

In military operations there occurred an engagement at Lee's Mill, also known as Burnt Chimneys and Dam No. 1, Va. On the Peninsula near Yorktown there was some minor fighting; skirmishing at Whitemarsh Island, Ga.; and near Blackwater Creek, Mo. Federal troops kept on the move in Alabama, occupying Tuscumbia.

President Lincoln signed a bill ending slavery in the District of Columbia.

April 17, Thursday

The activities of the day were light, but the Confederates had a mounting worry on their minds. It had been clear for some time that Federals were about to move against New Orleans, thus culminating their drive on the Mississippi River from both north and south. The build-up of Federal troops on Ship Island, Miss., had been observed, and now in the passes and river below Forts Jackson and St. Philip there was the large fleet of Flag Officer David Glasgow Farragut, plus the mortar fleet of David Dixon Porter, and transports with troops of Benjamin F. Butler. The Confederates were putting their faith in the two major forts and the barrier of old hulks and chains in the Mississippi itself. New Orleans, up the river, was virtually indefensible otherwise. Furthermore, the Confederacy was rushing work on huge ironclad gunboats, for its existing river fleet was comparatively weak. President Davis wrote Gov. Thomas O. Moore of Louisiana of his concern over attack from both directions: "The wooden vessels are below, the iron gun boats are above; the forts should destroy the former if they attempt to ascend. The Louisiana may be indispensable to check the descent of the iron boats. The purpose is to defend the city and valley; the only question is as to the best mode of effecting the object."

There was skirmishing at Warsaw, Mo.; near Monterey, between Pittsburg Landing, Tenn., and Corinth, Miss.; and near Woodson's Gap, Tenn., where a group of Union refugees were captured. In the Shenandoah Banks' Federals were still moving forward, occupying New Market, Va., as Stonewall Jackson retired slowly before them. A Federal expedition from Summerville to Addison, western Va., operated until the twenty-first.

April 18, Friday
BOMBARDMENT OF FORTS BELOW NEW ORLEANS BEGINS.

The squat, short, wide-mouthed mortars rumbled forth, lobbing their shot into and around Forts Jackson and St. Philip on the Mississippi below New Orleans as the Federal fleet began its bombardment of the defenders of the vital river. Farragut had little belief in David Dixon Porter's mortars, but had allowed them to try to reduce the forts. General consensus would be that after six days of action no crippling damage had been done the forts. But at least the softening-up process was being tried preparatory to an actual effort at passage up the river.

In Virginia Gen. Irvin McDowell, marching overland toward McClellan from Washington, occupied Falmouth near Fredericksburg. But he still was between Washington and the Confederate army, despite McClellan's entreaties that McDowell be sent to the Peninsula, where the huge Federal army was doing little to win the siege of Yorktown. In the Shenandoah Jackson left Harrisonburg for Elk Run Valley and Conrad's Store, where the Confederate forces remained until near the end of April, leaving the valley mainly to Banks' Federals.

April 19, Saturday
While the mortars boomed in the waterways of the Mississippi below New Orleans, Federals ponderously put pressure on Yorktown, Va. Halleck was enlarging and reorganizing his army at Pittsburg Landing. There was less important fighting elsewhere. Edisto Island, S.C., saw another skirmish, as did Talbot's Ferry, Ark.; South Mills in Camden County, and the Trent Road, N.C.

April 20, Sunday
During the night, parties from U.S.S. *Itasca* and *Pinola* tackled the troublesome river obstructions near Forts Jackson and St. Philip on the

Mississippi in a daring operation. Although explosives failed to work, the Federals did manage to weaken and force a break in the barricade of old hulks and chains that blockaded the Mississippi.

Gen. McDowell met President Lincoln at Aquia Creek near Fredericksburg and accompanied the President and Secretaries Stanton and Chase back to Washington.

April 21, Monday

The regular Confederate Congress adjourned after declaring certain classes of persons exempt from military conscription. President Davis was concerned over the two-pronged attack of McClellan and McDowell toward Richmond. The only new fighting recorded was a skirmish at Pocahontas, Ark., although the mortars continued firing in the Mississippi below New Orleans, the siege continued at Fort Macon in North Carolina, and in general there was no improvement in the deteriorating Confederate military picture.

April 22, Tuesday

Additional Federal reinforcements swelled McClellan's already mighty ranks near Yorktown as the siege against Joseph E. Johnston's Confederates continued. In Aransas Bay, Tex., daring Confederate raiders captured several Union launches.

April 23, Wednesday

Farragut, his fleet below the forts on the Mississippi, reached a decision. The bombardment of the mortars had not yet reduced the forts, land operations were inadvisable due to the low-lying, swampy, waterway-cut nature of the geography. Therefore Farragut would attempt to pass his wooden, deep-sea vessels past Forts Jackson and St. Philip the following morning and head for New Orleans itself. In another Federal naval operation, the Chesapeake and Albemarle Canal in North Carolina was successfully blocked, shutting off an important small-boat waterway. There was a skirmish at Bridgeport, Ala.

April 24, Thursday

FARRAGUT'S FEDERAL FLEET PASSES FORTS BELOW NEW ORLEANS.

At 2 A.M. two red lanterns rose to the mizzen peak of U.S.S. *Hartford* on the Mississippi River below New Orleans. Farragut's large fleet of wooden frigates and gunboats was about to attempt to run past the Confederate forts, crash through the remainder of the barricade, and head for New Orleans. About 3 A.M. of a dark and chilly night the fleet was under way. The first division of eight vessels got through the barricade without discovery. But at three-forty, as the moon rose, Forts Jackson and St. Philip opened fire. The second group of nine ships, including Farragut's

Hartford, followed, slowly coming under heavy fire. Porter's Federal mortars from below added to the din and fury of the fight. Darkness, smoke, flashes of guns, screams of shells, Confederate fire rafts, and some confusion among the Federals, but they got through—all but three smaller vessels, which were badly disabled. The forts had been proficiently manned but they were no match for the moving targets on the river. An important lesson was being learned—that ships could generally, although at a cost, get past fixed fortifications.

Once upstream, Farragut's fleet faced more fighting against Confederate gunboats, including the ram *Manassas.* The ram, battling gallantly, struck both *Mississippi* and *Brooklyn* but to no avail. A few of the Confederate squadron fought capably, while others of the makeshift fleet fled before the Federals. Although considerably cut up, the North had lost only *Varuna* and 37 men killed, 149 wounded. The forts suffered light casualties, but the Confederate squadron had at least 61 killed and 43 wounded. Altogether 8 Confederate vessels were lost, only 2 escaping. Moving rapidly forward, leaving the forts to die on the vine, Farragut advanced on New Orleans, anchoring April 25 at the panic-stricken, undefended city. Confederate Mansfield Lovell had been unable to defend his area. By courage and daring the Federals had climaxed with victory a campaign that resulted in the capture of the South's largest city and most vital port. Soon the North had a new base for operations against the heartland of the Confederacy. The Battle of New Orleans was one of the more decisive in the West, and a new hero had been found, this time a naval man. "Like Grant, Farragut always went ahead," wrote young officer George Dewey, years later to "go ahead" himself at Manila Bay.

Other fighting of the day was pale in comparison, but there was skirmishing at Tuscumbia, Ala.; at Lick Creek and on the Shelbyville Road, Tenn.; and on the Corinth Road, Miss., all part of the Federal probing into northern Alabama and Mississippi.

April 25, Friday

FEDERAL FLEET ARRIVES AT NEW ORLEANS.

SURRENDER OF FORT MACON, NORTH CAROLINA.

With eleven vessels Farragut moved up the Mississippi from his scene of victory at the forts. After a brief, successful duel with Confederate guns near English Turn, the Federal fleet anchored off the blazing waterfront of New Orleans, set afire by the populace. Floating down the river came the flaming hulk of the unfinished Confederate gunboat *Mississippi.* A rude, noisy, and vindictive throng met Farragut's officers as they went ashore to confer with Mayor John Monroe, who claimed he had no authority to surrender the city. Military commander Gen. Mansfield Lovell also refused to surrender, but indicated he and his forces were retiring from the city. A teen-age New Orleans girl told her diary: "We are conquered but not subdued."

On the coast of North Carolina near Beaufort the more than month-long siege of Fort Macon reached its culmination. Federal troops of John G. Parke opened a heavy fire on the fort, dismounting over half the guns. Gunboats went into action from the water side. Late in the afternoon the white flag rose and firing ceased as Col. Moses J. White had no recourse but to surrender. Casualties were light, but yet another bastion of the South was gone.

Elsewhere on the active fronts there was skirmishing at Tuscumbia, Ala.; an affair at Socorro, N. Mex. Terr.; and a skirmish on the Osage, near Monagan Springs, Mo. At Savannah, Tenn., Maj. Gen. C. F. Smith died of a seemingly minor leg injury. An experienced soldier, Smith had been a most valuable subordinate to Grant at Fort Donelson and in other operations.

April 26, Saturday

Formal surrender ceremonies were held at Fort Macon, N.C., where the Confederate garrison of four hundred became prisoners of the Federals. Skirmishing occurred at Neosho and Turnback Creek, Mo., as well as at Atkins' Mill, Tenn. There were several days of operations on Forked Deer River, Tenn. In the Shenandoah Valley Federals under Banks were concentrating at Harrisonburg and New Market. President Lincoln visited the French man-of-war *Gassendi* at the Washington Navy Yard, to the crew's shouts of "Vive le Président." At New Orleans negotiations continued between Farragut and the mayor. One William Mumford removed the U.S. flag from the mint as mobs still thronged the streets.

April 27, Sunday

Four small forts—Livingston, Quitman, Pike, and Wood—protecting New Orleans surrendered to Federal forces. Elsewhere there was fighting at Pea Ridge, Tenn., near Pittsburg Landing; at Bridgeport, Ala.; and at Haughton's Mill near Pollocksville, N.C. Mutiny broke out at Fort Jackson below New Orleans with half the stranded garrison departing.

April 28, Monday

Surrounded and cut off from any hope of relief, Forts Jackson and St. Philip surrendered to Federals, completing the opening of the Mississippi to New Orleans. At the city Farragut threatened to bombard the place unless the Federal flag was respected. In northern Mississippi it became evident that Gen. Halleck's huge Federal army was about to advance on Beauregard at Corinth. There was a skirmish at Monterey, Tenn.; at Bolivar and Paint Rock Bridge, Ala.; and at Warsaw, Mo. At Nassau in the Bahamas the British *Oreto* arrived to be outfitted officially as a Confederate raider, C.S.S. *Florida*.

April 29, Tuesday

The massive army of Gen. Halleck was completing its preliminary preparations for marching from Pittsburg Landing, Tenn., toward the Confederates at Corinth, Miss. By now Halleck had over 100,000 men; Beauregard had about two thirds as many. Grant was relegated to second-in-command under Halleck, and was much upset by what he considered a demotion. In early operations Federals occupied Purdy, and there was skirmishing near Monterey, Tenn. In addition, other fighting occurred at West Bridge, near Bridgeport, Ala.; on the Mobile and Ohio Railroad near Bethel Station, Tenn.; at Pineberry Battery, Willstown, and White Point, S.C.; Cumberland Gap, Ky.; and Batchelder's Creek, N.C. Federal officers raised the U.S. flag at the New Orleans Customs House and the city hall over the opposition of the frustrated populace and city authorities.

April 30, Wednesday

As the most active month of the war to date (and most disastrous to the Confederacy so far) ended, Stonewall Jackson left Elk Run near Swift Run Gap in Virginia's Blue Ridge and headed for Staunton and what would become the major part of the famed Shenandoah Valley Campaign.

MAY, 1862

Federal armies and the Navy were still on the march, and the Confederacy was still on the defensive. The picture was growing dimmer for the struggling Southern nation as spring rolled into summer. At many points the offensives of the North were pressing home. The threat in Virginia came from the north, in the Shenandoah, and, mainly, from the Peninsula. In the West there was danger on the Mississippi from above Memphis and from the New Orleans enclave. Near northern Mississippi and in northern Alabama powerful forces were operating against the South. In North Carolina, in South Carolina, in the mountains of Tennessee, and elsewhere the pressure was felt. Would the war end this summer? No one said much about defeat at the South, but the sickening possibility was there. Those in the North who had long agitated for action were getting it, though they were not yet satisfied that the various movments would be consummated in victory. Mr. Lincoln must get McClellan to move energetically; Halleck must do something more. Otherwise there might be a slowing down of the momentum gained by the spring victories.

May 1, Thursday

Steadily increasing Federal pressure was soon to force decisive action by besieged Confederates at Yorktown, Va. The siege guns of the Federals under McClellan were being mounted. And when Yorktown went, so would Norfolk, the naval yard, and other important points along the James River. Maj. Gen. Benjamin F. Butler, with his troops, officially took over in New Orleans, beginning a reign of efficiency in sanitary and other conditions, corruption in administration, and suppression of the people. Citizens of New Orleans were never to forget or forgive Butler for what were termed "bestial acts." Others, mostly Northerners, then and later, mitigated the charges. Controversy still surrounds Butler's rule. Elsewhere, Federal Brig. Gen. James G. Blunt assumed command of the Department of Kansas. Skirmishing was considerable at Rapidan Station, Va.; Clark's Hollow and Camp Creek in Stone River Valley, western Va.; and near Pulaski, Tenn. In northern Alabama there were two days of operations around Athens, Mooresville, Limestone Bridge, and Elk River.

President Davis wrote Gen. Joseph E. Johnston at Yorktown, "accepting your conclusion that you must soon retire, arrangements are commenced for the abandonment of Navy Yard and removal of public property both from Norfolk and Peninsula." But the plan to withdraw so soon did take Davis by surprise. At the same time President Lincoln wired McClellan on the Peninsula that the general's call for heavy guns "alarms me— chiefly because it argues indefinite procrastination. Is anything to be done?"

May 2, Friday

Gen. Beauregard called on the soldiers of the Confederacy to defend Corinth, Miss., from the invading "despoilers of our homes," as the Federal army under Halleck began to move toward the Southern concentration point. There was skirmishing at Trevilian's Depot and Louisa Court House, Va.; at Litchfield, Ark.; and near Deep Gully on the Trenton Road, N.C. Edward Stanly was appointed Federal military governor of North Carolina.

May 3, Saturday

EVACUATION OF YORKTOWN, VIRGINIA.

Faced by overwhelming numbers, giant siege guns and a threat from more Federals to the north on the Rappahannock, Gen. Joseph E. Johnston withdrew his Confederate army from Yorktown on the Virginia Peninsula before McClellan could mount his major bombardment. The Confederates pulled back through Williamsburg toward Richmond. They had defied the Army of the Potomac for over a month; their strength finally reached about fifty-five thousand, compared to nearly twice that many for McClellan.

Still, the Federal commander believed that Washington had deprived him of manpower and that the Confederates seriously outnumbered his host.

In other military action, bridges were destroyed on Lookout Creek near Lookout Mountain and there was skirmishing at Watkins Ferry, Ga.; and at Farmington near Corinth; and on the Memphis and Charleston Railroad in Mississippi. Near Batesville, Ark., there was yet another skirmish, and in southwest Virginia the Confederates proclaimed martial law. Gen. Halleck told Washington he was personally leaving Pittsburg Landing and that his army would be in front of Corinth by the night of May 4.

May 4, Sunday

The Army of the Potomac entered Yorktown, Va., following Confederate evacuation. The month-long siege had been successful in part, but Johnston's Confederate army had not been attacked. McClellan declared, "The success is brilliant." Brief skirmishes broke out near Williamsburg as forward units of the Federals battled with retiring Confederates. There was more skirmishing at Farmington Heights, Miss., as Halleck's army closed in toward Corinth, and there was a raid on the Mobile and Ohio Railroad near Bethel and a skirmish near Purdy, Tenn. W. T. Sherman's division was within six miles of Corinth's defenses. There was a skirmish at Pulaski, Tenn., south of Nashville. In view of Col. Carleton's "California Column" moving east from California, Confederates evacuated Tucson, N. Mex. Terr.

May 5, Monday

BATTLE OF WILLIAMSBURG, VIRGINIA.

A sharp engagement broke out just east of the old capital of Williamsburg, Va., as advancing units of McClellan's Army of the Potomac under Joseph Hooker and Phil Kearny clashed with rearguard divisions of James Longstreet and then D. H. Hill. There was heavy fighting for a line of defensive redoubts built earlier by Magruder. The Federals were unsuccessful at first, but eventually, as more troops came in, they managed to occupy a part of the line, Winfield S. Hancock's division outflanking the Confederates. In the evening the last of the Southerners pulled out as Johnston's army continued its retreat west toward Richmond. Federals had about 40,000 engaged, to some 31,000 Confederates. Rather uncertain figures show Federal losses ran 456 killed, 1410 wounded, and 373 missing for 2239; Confederate killed and wounded 1570 and 133 missing, total 1703—heavy casualties for what was essentially a delaying and a probing action.

Other fighting this day was at Lebanon, Tenn.; Princeton and Franklin, western Va.; and Columbia Bridge, Va. In the evening President Lincoln, with Cabinet members Stanton and Chase, left by ship for Fort Monroe to take a personal look at the advance into Virginia.

May 6, Tuesday

Union forces occupied Williamsburg, Va., close behind the retiring enemy on the Peninsula. Stonewall Jackson's Confederates had arrived at Staunton in the Shenandoah after their stay at Conrad's Store. They confused the Federals under Banks at Harrisonburg, who fell back toward New Market and went on to Strasburg by May 13. It was the beginning of the main portion of Jackson's famous Valley Campaign. Jackson and his reinforced command marched westward toward McDowell, aiming at Federal forces in that area. There was a brief skirmish near Harrisonburg; and in western Va. at Camp McDonald and Arnoldsburg; as well as a skirmish on the White River out in Arkansas. Near Corinth, Miss., Halleck's advance from Pittsburg Landing, Tenn., decelerated, and soon became more of a siege than an offensive.

In the late evening President Lincoln and his party disembarked at Fort Monroe.

May 7, Wednesday

On the Pamunkey River near the mouth of the York on the Virginia Peninsula, William B. Franklin's division of Federals advancing toward Richmond was attacked at Eltham's Landing by Confederates under G. W. Smith, who were protecting the wagon trains withdrawing from Williamsburg and Yorktown. It was a sharp engagement, known as West Point, Barhamsville, or Eltham's Landing. Elsewhere there was a skirmish at Horse Creek, Mo.; another at Purdy, Tenn.; as well as a two-day reconnaissance to Mulberry Point on the James River in Virginia; and a two-day Federal expedition from Roanoke Island toward Gatesville, N.C. Still more light fighting occurred near Wardensville, western Va., and Somerville Heights, Va.

President Lincoln visited U.S.S. *Monitor* near Fort Monroe and conferred with naval and army officers. He was taking an active part in attempting to push the drive on Richmond.

May 8, Thursday

BATTLE OF MCDOWELL, VIRGINIA.

Stonewall Jackson fought Federal troops at the Battle of McDowell or Bull Pasture Mountain, Va. Jackson's roughly 10,000 troops were attacked by around 6000 under Robert Schenck from Frémont's command. The Confederates repulsed the Federals, who were forced to withdraw toward Franklin, western Va. Jackson attempted a pursuit but halted after reaching Franklin May 12. He then returned to the Shenandoah and proceeded north. Federal casualties at McDowell were 26 killed, 227 wounded, 3 missing for 256; Confederate casualties were 75 killed, 423 wounded for 498. It was Jackson's first battle victory of his campaign, and already his forces were feared in the Shenandoah Valley and surrounding mountain country. Rapid movement on foot was becoming his trademark.

In Mississippi Halleck's Federal army, within a few miles of Corinth, sent out a reconnaissance toward the Confederate-held rail center. There was a skirmish at Glendale, Miss. In Hampton Roads, Va., Federal gunboats carried out a demonstration against Sewell's Point and its batteries. Other fighting occurred at Athens, Ala.

May 9, Friday
EVACUATION OF NORFOLK.

Confederate forces evacuated Norfolk, Va., and its valuable naval and army supply depot in face of Federal occupation of the Peninsula across Hampton Roads and the threat of invasion. The loss of this major base was a severe blow to Confederate control of southside Virginia and northern North Carolina. Supplies and machinery were destroyed, but enough was left to give the Federals a fine haul when they marched in the following day. Most important, C.S.S. *Merrimack* (or *Virginia*) was left without a port from which to operate and it, too, would have to be disposed of.

In northeastern Mississippi there was severe fighting between forward units of Halleck's forces advancing on Corinth, Miss., and Confederates at Farmington and another skirmish nearer Corinth as well.

Near McDowell, Va., Jackson's forces followed retreating Federals toward Franklin, western Va. Other fighting was on Elk River near Bethel, Tenn., and at Slatersville, Va. Confederate forces began evacuating the Pensacola, Fla., area after holding out in the city against Fort Pickens and the naval squadron since the start of the war. By May 12 Union forces had occupied the town and nearby region.

Maj. Gen. David Hunter at Hilton Head Island, S.C., ordered emancipation of slaves in Florida, Georgia, and South Carolina, and authorized the arming of all able-bodied Negroes in those states. This order, without approval of Congress or President Lincoln, caused a lively ferment at the North and was disavowed May 19 by Lincoln. But it did indicate support for emancipation among some army officers, at least as a war measure.

Mr. Lincoln remained at Hampton Roads, Va., and toured the area by boat, looking for a place for Federal soldiers to land near Norfolk. He also told Gen. McClellan, slowly moving up the Peninsula toward Richmond, that he did not want the corps structure of the Army broken up. He urged greater cooperation between McClellan and his corps commanders.

May 10, Saturday
BATTLE OF PLUM RUN BEND, TENNESSEE.

Federal mortar boats appeared on the Mississippi just north of Fort

Pillow, Tenn. The ill-disciplined, makeshift Confederate River Defense Fleet, puny in firepower and protection, attacked the mortars and the strong Federal ironclad flotilla of seven boats under Capt. Charles H. Davis. Capt. James E. Montgomery boldly commanded the Confederates. The unarmored Southern flotilla drove at the ironclads, although it was almost suicidal. Fighting valiantly, the Confederates managed to ram and sink ironclads *Cincinnati* and *Mound City,* in shoal water. Later they were raised. Four of the eight Confederate boats were badly disabled and rendered helpless by the superior firepower of the Federals. Montgomery had to withdraw his remnants to Fort Pillow and then to Memphis. The Battle of Plum Run Bend or Plum Point is nearly forgotten in history, but it was one of the few "fleet actions" of the war, and on a river at that.

Federal troops were occupying Norfolk and Portsmouth in Virginia, watched by President Lincoln. They also took over Pensacola in Florida, climaxing a day of defeat for the South. In the fighting near Corinth there was another skirmish near Farmington and a reconnaissance on the Alabama Road and toward Sharp's Mill, Miss. Other action was at Bloomfield, Mo.; Lamb's Ferry, Ala.; and Giles Court House, western Va. Jackson continued his advance toward Franklin, western Va.

In New Orleans Gen. Butler furthered his popularity by seizing $800,000 in gold from the Netherlands consulate.

President Davis wrote Gen. Johnston on the Peninsula, "I have been much relieved by the successes which you have gained, and I hope for you the brilliant result which the drooping cause of our country now so imperatively claims. . . ." But he was also concerned about the enemy advance on the Fredericksburg route.

May 11, Sunday
 LOSS OF C.S.S. *Merrimack*.

Merrimack was no more. Scuttled off captured Norfolk, Va., by the Confederates, the noble antagonist of *Monitor* went down. There was no place she could be taken for safety, so destruction was a galling necessity forced by land warfare. President Lincoln returned from Fort Monroe to Washington and heard the news on the way. The President wired Gen. Halleck, "Norfolk in our possession, Merrimac blown up, & Monitor & other boats going up James River to Richmond. Be very sure to sustain no reverse in your Department." Halleck was being quite sure as his advance upon Corinth had slowed so drastically that it was hardly distinguishable from a siege. Other fighting broke out at Pulaski, Tenn.; Cave City, Ky.; Princeton, western Va.; and on the Bowling Green Road near Fredericksburg, Va.

May 12, Monday

Farragut's Federal flotilla from New Orleans briefly occupied Natchez, Miss., receiving the surrender of the city from the mayor. To the northeast there was more skirmishing near Farmington, Miss., between men of Halleck's and Beauregard's armies not far from Corinth, Miss. Other skirmishing occurred at Lewisburg, western Va., and at Monterey, Va. Jackson's army left the Franklin, western Va., area for the Shenandoah Valley and Banks' Federals. There was a convention of pro-unionists at Nashville, Tenn., as the military government was taking hold. President Lincoln proclaimed the opening to commerce of the ports of Beaufort, N.C., Port Royal, S.C., and New Orleans.

May 13, Tuesday

In the Shenandoah Jackson was on his way back from Franklin and McDowell toward the main valley to face Banks' reduced force at Strasburg. Gen. Frémont, meanwhile, reached Franklin with his Union troops. There was a skirmish at Baltimore Crossroads near New Kent Court House, and an affair on the Rappahannock River, Va. Near Corinth, Miss., Federal troops raided the Memphis and Charleston Railroad, and in Alabama Union forces under Gen. Mitchel occupied Rogersville and skirmished at Lamb's Ferry.

President Davis wrote to his wife, who had been sent out of threatened Richmond, "If the withdrawal from the Peninsula and Norfolk had been done with due preparation and a desirable deliberation, I should be more sanguine of a successful defense of this city. . . . I know not what to expect when so many failures are to be remembered, yet will try to make a successful resistance. . . ." Martial law was declared in Charleston, S.C. In Charleston Harbor a crew of Negroes took over the steamer *Planter* and surrendered it to the blockaders.

May 14, Wednesday

Skirmishing continued near Corinth, Miss., on the Memphis and Charleston Railroad, and on the Mobile and Ohio as well. McClellan's army skirmished at Gaines' Cross Roads, Va., as it marched nearer Richmond. Other skirmishes were at Cotton Plant, Ark., and Fayetteville, Tenn.

May 15, Thursday

BATTLE OF DREWRY'S BLUFF, VIRGINIA.

Five Federal naval vessels, including *Monitor,* moved up the James toward Richmond now that the menace of *Merrimack* had been eliminated. The alarm echoed in Richmond, but at Drewry's Bluff, on the south side of the river about eight miles below the Confederate capital, Southern batteries met the Federal invasion. For four hours the guns of Fort Darling and the Federal gunboats dueled with heavy fire. Union vessels were not able to elevate their guns sufficiently to attack the land batteries directly, and *Monitor* drew too much water in the narrow, shallow river to get fully into action. *Galena* was struck eighteen times and suffered grievous damage. The well-posted Confederate guns proved that a water approach alone to Richmond was impracticable, as they forced the Federals to withdraw.

Meanwhile, Joseph E. Johnston's army pulled back across the Chickahominy and at some points was within three miles of Richmond. There was more fighting at Gaines' Cross Roads and Linden, Va. Jackson's Confederates reached the Shenandoah Valley once more after their excursion to McDowell and Franklin. There was fighting in western Va. at Ravenswood, Wolf Creek, and Princeton.

Farther west there was action again along the Memphis and Charleston Railroad near Corinth, Miss., and a Federal naval demonstration upon Galveston, Tex. In Missouri there was Federal scouting on the Little Blue with a skirmish near Independence. Other action this day occurred near Trenton Bridge at Young's Cross Roads and near Pollocksville, N.C. At Liverpool, England, a vessel known only as 290 was launched at the Laird shipyards. It was not a well-kept secret, however, that the ship was destined to become a Confederate raider—the famed C.S.S. *Alabama*.

In Washington Lincoln approved congressional establishment of the Department of Agriculture as a branch of the Federal government, although its secretary did not obtain Cabinet status until 1889.

The most sensational news of the day was an order issued in New Orleans by the commander of the occupying forces, Maj. Gen. Benjamin F. Butler. "As the officers and soldiers of the United States have been subject to repeated insults from the women (calling themselves ladies) of New Orleans in return for the most scrupulous non-interference and courtesy on our part, it is ordered that hereafter when any female shall by word, gesture, or movement insult or show contempt for any officer or soldier of the United States she shall be regarded and held liable to be treated as a woman of the town plying her avocation." Nothing in Butler's already unpopular, dictatorial reign over New Orleans incited Confederates as did the notorious Order No. 28. Throughout the South the "beast" was an object of venom, although some later historians mitigate the tyranny of the order.

May 16, Friday

Maj. Gen. Butler added to his stringent measures in New Orleans by suspending publication of the New Orleans *Bee,* and the *Delta* was taken over by Federal authorities. Meanwhile, in Virginia, Gen. McClellan established his personal headquarters at White House, formerly a Lee family property, on the Pamunkey River.

President Davis wrote his wife of the defeat of the Federal squadron at Drewry's Bluff, adding, "The panic here has subsided and with increasing confidence there has arisen a desire to see the city destroyed rather than surrendered." He further said, "The great temporal object is to secure our independence and they who engage in strife for personal or party aggandisement, deserve contemptuous forgetfulness."

May 17, Saturday

Gen. McDowell on the Rappahannock was ordered to march upon Richmond in cooperation with McClellan's Army of the Potomac. Meanwhile, there was a small Federal expedition up the Pamunkey as McClellan's army settled in before Richmond. Near Corinth, Miss., there was more skirmishing as Halleck's Federal army also sat in front of a major Confederate center. Today's action was at Russell's House. In Arkansas there was a skirmish at Little Red River.

As Mr. Lincoln conferred with his Secretary of War regarding McClellan's oft-repeated calls for reinforcements, President Davis wrote Gen. Johnston giving various suggestions but, like Lincoln, declined to direct military operations.

May 18, Sunday

The Shenandoah Valley was coming into its own as a scene of battle and marching. Jackson's Confederates were northward bound from Mount Solon, as Federals fell back in the western valley along the north fork of the Shenandoah. Union Gen. Banks was not sure what Jackson was going to do, but he wanted to be ready. There was a skirmish at Woodstock, Va., in the valley.

On the Mississippi Farragut's fleet arrived at Vicksburg to demand surrender of the city, but Confederate Brig. Gen. M. L. Smith refused.

May 19, Monday

Still the skirmishing continued on the fringes of the two main Federal offensives, east and west. In Virginia there was fighting at Gaines' Mill and at City Point, in the West action at Farmington, Miss., near Corinth. Other skirmishing was at Searcy Landing, Ark. On the Mississippi a Federal expedition operated to Fort Pillow May 19–23.

A worried President Davis wrote Mrs. Davis of the threat to Richmond, "We are uncertain of everything except that a battle must be near at hand." An equally concerned President Lincoln disavowed the emancipation proclamation of Maj. Gen. David Hunter issued in the Department of the South, and reserved for the President the power, if it became necessary in order to maintain the government, to issue such a proclamation. Mr. Lincoln again appealed for adoption by the states of his policy of gradual, compensated emancipation.

May 20, Tuesday

FEDERAL HOMESTEAD LAW SIGNED.

President Lincoln signed into law the Homestead Act, which granted a free plot of 160 acres to actual settlers on land in the public domain who would occupy and improve it for five years. President Davis was disturbed by the impression of governors and others in Arkansas and elsewhere in the Trans-Mississippi that their cause was being neglected.

Stonewall Jackson moved rapidly in the Shenandoah. Reaching New Market, he suddenly halted his northward march and crossed Massanutten Mountain to Luray in the eastern or Luray Valley of the Shenandoah. He then turned northward again, along the south fork of the Shenandoah River. He was joined by Richard Ewell and his troops, giving Jackson sixteen thousand men and forty-eight guns. The intent was to get around Banks' Federals and perhaps trap them in the main or western portion of the Shenandoah Valley. Along the Chickahominy there were minor operations near Bottom's Bridge as McClellan's Federals and Johnston's Confederates waited. There was raiding on the Virginia Central Railroad at Jackson's River Depot, Va. On the coast Cole's Island, S.C., was bombarded by Federals and there was an affair on Crooked River, Fla. In Tennessee skirmishing broke out on Elk River. Tucson, N. Mex. Terr., was occupied by Union troops after a small body of Confederates had retreated.

May 21, Wednesday

The "foot cavalry" of Jackson were on the march north in the Luray Valley of Virginia, heading toward Front Royal, where a brief Federal reconnaissance went out but found little. Banks in the other branch of the Shenandoah Valley beyond Massanutten was confused by Jackson's moves, but he, too, was pulling his Federals north. Over on the Chickahominy there was a Federal advance across Bottom's Bridge in lowlands just east of Richmond. In the West skirmishing continued near Corinth, Miss., today at Widow Serratt's and Phillips' Creek. Elsewhere there was fighting at Village Creek, Ark.; Battery Island, S.C.; and at Parajé, N. Mex. Terr.

President Lincoln replied to Gen. McClellan's request for help from McDowell's corps, which was moving overland to Richmond, saying, "You will have just such control of Gen. McDowell and his force as you therein indicate. McDowell can reach you by land sooner than he could get aboard of boats if the boats were ready at Frederick'sburg,—unless his march shall be resisted, in which case, the force resisting him, will certainly not be confronting you at Richmond."

May 22, Thursday

As Jackson moved toward Front Royal in the Luray Valley and McClellan moved into position along the Chickahominy in Virginia, skirmishing continued around Corinth, Miss., between Halleck's forces and Beauregard's defenders. Action was at Farmington, primarily. Elsewhere the fighting was at Winchester, Tenn.; John's Island, S.C.; and at the Trenton and Pollocksville Crossroads, N.C. Federals carried out a two-day reconnaissance to Burnsville and Iuka, Miss. President Lincoln journeyed to Fredericksburg, Va., to consult with Gen. McDowell.

May 23, Friday

ENGAGEMENT AT FRONT ROYAL, VIRGINIA.

Jackson entered Front Royal in the Shenandoah Valley, easily defeating the Federal forces of about eight hundred men under Col. John R. Kenly and capturing many of them. As a battle or engagement it was not a major one, but the seizure of Front Royal meant that Jackson, with his sixteen thousand troops, had a splendid opportunity to cut off Banks' main Federal force, which was pulling north on the valley pike to the northwest of Front Royal. The task was to prevent Banks from reaching Winchester and if possible to destroy him. Jackson's rapid movement and victory at Front Royal caused fear in Washington of a major northward move by the Confederates, possibly even toward the capital. This distracting diversion took attention from McClellan's efforts on the Peninsula near Richmond. In that area there were Federal reconnaissances from Bottom's Bridge to Turkey Island Creek Bridge and toward Richmond, as well as skirmishing at Mechanicsville, Hogan's, and Buckton Station. Elsewhere the fighting was at Lewisburg, western Va., and near Fort Craig, N. Mex. Terr. President Lincoln talked with Gen. McDowell at Aquia Creek, Va., and in the Fredericksburg area before returning to Washington.

May 24, Saturday

There was significant skirmishing at Berryville, Strasburg, Middletown, and elsewhere in the Shenandoah. Stonewall Jackson, after his victory at Front Royal, attempted to cut off Banks' retreat route to Winchester on the valley pike. It was a very near thing for the Federals, but most of them got away just in time. Failing to trap the enemy, Jackson moved on Winchester itself. Meanwhile, in Winchester Banks ordered his wagon trains north toward Williamsport on the Potomac. After months of defeat and withdrawal, or at best stalemate, the tide seemed to be bringing Confederate victories.

In Washington, early in the morning, Mr. Lincoln conferred with Stanton and others and issued new orders. Frémont in western Virginia was instructed to head for the Shenandoah to cut off Jackson from retreat. To McDowell near Fredericksburg the President sent orders to lay aside the movement on Richmond and send twenty thousand men toward the Shenandoah: "Your object will be to capture the forces of Jackson & Ewell." In two messages to McClellan, Lincoln explained that the defeat in the valley was due to thinning the line to get troops for elsewhere. And later the President reluctantly wrote, "In consequence of Gen. Banks' critical position I have been compelled to suspend Gen. McDowell's movement to join you. . . ." Diversion of McDowell gave McClellan another excuse to blame the Administration for his delays and failures on the Peninsula, and to say he was undermanned, despite his more than 100,000 troops.

At New Bridge, Seven Pines, Mechanicsville, and Hanover Court House, Va., there was fighting as a part of the main campaign against Richmond. To the west the skirmishing was closer to Corinth, Miss., and there was action near Spring Hill, Mo., and Winchester, Tenn.

May 25, Sunday

BATTLE OF WINCHESTER, VIRGINIA.

Despite religious scruples, Jackson fought on Sunday, attacking Banks' retreating Federals at Winchester in the Shenandoah. For a time Federals held off Jackson on the right and Ewell on the left, but eventually they broke and then pulled back in hasty confusion toward Harper's Ferry. Jackson's pursuit was feeble. The confederate total: 16,000 men and 400 casualties—68 killed, 329 wounded, 3 missing. Banks lost 2019 of his 8000 Federal troops—62 killed, 243 wounded, 1714 missing or captured. A Federal soldier described the battle as "hell—or at least about as good an imitation as is often produced in the 'upper world.'" Substantial amounts of supplies, munitions, and a number of wagons fell into Jackson's hands. The name of "Stonewall" was becoming legendary. The Confederates now had cleared all but a small portion of the Shenandoah Valley, to the consternation of Washington and the North. But Frémont from the west and McDowell from the east were moving toward the area south of Winchester to get in Jackson's rear and cut off his retreat.

Down near Richmond there was a Union expedition from Bottom's Bridge on the Chickahominy to James River; in South Carolina an affair between James and Dixon's islands; and there were several days of operations about Miami and Waverly, Mo., until May 28.

At Washington President Lincoln wired McClellan, "I think the time is near when you must either attack Richmond or give up the job and come to the defence of Washington." He also told his general of the troubles in the Shenandoah, and that the government was sending "such regiments and dribs" as could be found. The Administration called for all troops available anywhere and declared that all railroads were to be used when needed for transport of troops and munitions. Sec. of War Stanton called upon the states for help in furnishing men.

May 26, Monday

As Jackson occupied Winchester and prepared to continue north toward Harper's Ferry, Banks kept pulling back with what little he had left after the Shenandoah Valley campaigning. Frémont and McDowell marched to intercept Jackson's line of retreat. McClellan still failed to take action along the Chickahominy near Richmond. There was a skirmish near Franklin, western Va.; at Calico Rock, Ark.; at Crow's Station near Licking, Mo.; and at Grand Gulf, Miss. The Confederates extended their Trans-Mississippi Department to include Arkansas, the Indian Territory, Missouri, west Louisiana, and Texas.

Mr. Lincoln told McClellan that Banks was apparently safe at Williamsport on the Potomac and asked, "What impression have you, as to intrenchments—works—for you to contend with in front of Richmond? Can you get near enough to throw shells into the city?"

May 27, Tuesday

As Banks crossed the Potomac at Williamsport, Jackson began to push northward again, toward Harper's Ferry. He skirmished at Loudoun Heights. Near Richmond there was fighting at Slash Church, White Oaks, and Hanover Court House. Near Corinth, Miss., minor fighting continued, with skirmishing on Bridge Creek. In Missouri there was a skirmish at Monagan Springs near Osceola, and in Arkansas at Big Indian Creek in White County. An expedition operated from Searcy Landing to West Point, Searcy, and Bayou des Arc, Ark. Excitement continued high in the North, particularly in New York, over Jackson's successes in the Shenandoah.

May 28, Wednesday

Skirmishing occurred in front of Corinth, Miss., and at Charles Town, western Va., as a part of Jackson's campaign. Confederate supplies at Ashland, Va., were destroyed, as was a bridge on the Virginia Central Railroad on the South Anna. Meanwhile all eyes looked toward Corinth and to the Shenandoah and Richmond for more news.

President Davis wrote his wife, "We are steadily developing for a great battle, and under God's favor I trust for a decisive victory." He was disappointed that a planned offensive by Joseph E. Johnston's army had not been launched against McClellan.

President Lincoln told Gen. McDowell that his move toward the Shenandoah to hit Jackson was "for you a question of legs. Put in all the speed you can."

May 29, Thursday

Jackson's men demonstrated near Harper's Ferry. Behind Jackson, the Federals mustered Frémont's 15,000, McDowell's 20,000, and, to the north,

Banks' remnant of about 5000. Other Federals gathered around Harper's Ferry. On the Chickahominy there was skirmishing near Seven Pines, and farther north some operations along the South Anna. In western Va. there was a skirmish near Wardensville; in South Carolina at Pocotaligo; in Arkansas at Kickapoo Bottom and Whitesburg; and in Mississippi near Booneville.

During the night Beauregard, finally seeing there was no hope against Halleck's huge Federal army near Corinth, Miss., gave orders to pull out toward Tupelo. To give the impression of reinforcements, however, he had trains and troops make loud noises in an effort to fool the waiting Federals.

President Davis was carrying on a lengthy mail discussion with Georgia governor Joseph E. Brown over matters of States' rights and Confederate government rights. President Lincoln still held in close rein the direction of operations against Jackson in the northern Shenandoah.

May 30, Friday
CONFEDERATES EVACUATE CORINTH, MISSISSIPPI.

Commencing the night of May 29 Beauregard, with great skill and efficiency, pulled his Confederate army out of besieged Corinth, Miss., and headed south toward Tupelo. The immense Federal army under Halleck sat a few miles outside the town to the north, oblivious to the strategy going on so short a distance away, though there were those who were aware that the Confederates planned a move. On this day Halleck's troops cautiously moved into the important rail and road center after more than a month's campaigning. The Federals had been successful but the evacuation by Beauregard, the slowness of the campaign, and the general lack of battle or results tarnished Halleck's victory. Nearby Booneville, Miss., was captured by Federals and the Cypress Creek Bridge, Tenn., and Tuscumbia Bridge, Miss., destroyed.

In the Shenandoah McDowell's forces under James Shields reached Front Royal, where there was a skirmish as Jackson began to fall back from near Harper's Ferry to avoid the trap being set by Frémont's and McDowell's converging forces. Other fighting in Virginia was at Fair Oaks and Zuni; in North Carolina at Tranter's Creek; in western Virginia at Lewisburg and Shaver's River. Heavy rains fell on the Virginia Peninsula, inundating bottom lands.

President Lincoln continued to urge his commanders in the Shenandoah— Banks, Frémont, and McDowell—to press on to capture or destroy Jackson.

May 31, Saturday
BATTLE OF SEVEN PINES OR FAIR OAKS, VIRGINIA.

Gen. McClellan on the Chickahominy had split his large Federal army, putting three corps on the northeast side of the river, reportedly to enable him to hook up with McDowell, expected from the north. Only two corps were on the south side of the Chickahominy. Realizing this disposition, Joseph E. Johnston attacked the corps of Erasmus Keyes and S. P. Heintzelman at Fair Oaks or Seven Pines, east of Richmond. In a series of failures to move at appointed times, the Confederates did not get their attack going until about 1 P.M., and then the fighting was done by separate units, with others failing to get into action. Nevertheless, the South made some inroads on the defenders. President Davis himself toured the battle area. McClellan, hearing the firing, ordered Edwin V. Sumner's corps to cross the Chickahominy to aid his compatriots. Sumner had not waited for orders but moved quickly over the shaky bridges and swampy bottom lands. The reinforcements blunted the Confederate drive and, as the day ended, the impetus was gone from the Southern assault. Gen. Joseph E. Johnston was severely wounded, and was succeeded for a few hours by G. W. Smith, and shortly after by R. E. Lee on June 1. For the first time, Lee took over a major army, an army that soon would be heralded as the Army of Northern Virginia. At the end of the day little had been decided except that Johnston had failed to rout or destroy the two isolated corps. During the night Federal positions were considerably strengthened.

In the Shenandoah Jackson hurried south of Winchester through heavy rain with about fifteen thousand men, squeezing between converging Frémont and McDowell. There was some skirmishing near Front Royal, but the Federals were too late to halt the Confederates or destroy them as Lincoln wished.

In Missouri there was skirmishing on Salt River near Florida, near Neosho and Waynesville; while in Mississippi there was skirmishing at Tuscumbia Creek. For the Confederates Maj. Gen. T. C. Hindman assumed command of the Trans-Mississippi District.

In Washington Lincoln anxiously awaited news from Richmond and the valley, hopeful for the best. It had been a month of some fighting and much movement.

JUNE, 1862

Summer, and the high days of military campaigning were upon the armies and the people. In the long, hot days men would be marching and fighting even more, and dying in larger numbers. The South still reeled from the blows of the spring. The Union military advances were slowing just a little at the moment. Jackson had been victorious in the Shenandoah. However, Richmond was still in danger, with a battle nearly in the outskirts. Corinth, Miss., was occupied by an immense Federal host, New Orleans had fallen, and the whole Mississippi River Valley was threatened. But the armies of the Confederacy was still intact, and it could be that the summer would bring better fortune.

In the North apprehension increased once more. Halleck had been slow to occupy Corinth, McClellan continually cried for more men and did little toward capturing the capital of the Confederacy. And Jackson was giving everyone quite a scare.

June 1, Sunday

BATTLE OF SEVEN PINES OR FAIR OAKS CONCLUDED.

Although the battle near the Chickahominy just east of Richmond continued with a Confederate attack by James Longstreet, it was anticlimactic. The second day of Seven Pines or Fair Oaks was a faltering attempt by the Confederates which was repulsed by the reinforced Federals. Joseph E. Johnston had been wounded, and there was a new Southern commander—Robert E. Lee. But Lee was the Lee of failure in western Virginia, no real success in South Carolina, and a brief term as adviser to President Davis. Yet, as a Virginian of gentlemanly and soldierly reputation, who had the confidence of the government, his name engendered a degree of optimism. At least there was no despair over the change.

In midafternoon Lee ordered a withdrawal to the original positions. The cost: for the Confederates, 980 killed, 4749 wounded, and 405 missing for a total of 6134 casualties out of about 42,000 effectives; for the Federals, 790 killed, 3594 wounded, and 647 missing or captured for 5031, also out of about 42,000 engaged, although many additional Federals never got into action. Very little, if anything, had been decided. McClellan was still near Richmond, with forces vastly outnumbering Confederates, although he would not admit it, or did not really know it. For the Confederates the long-called-for attack had failed and the danger remained just as great.

In Washington Lincoln awaited the news from the battlefield and wired McClellan three times, including: "Hold all your ground, or yield any only, inch by inch and in good order."

On June 2 President Davis was to write of the two-day battle near the Chickahominy: "On Saturday we had a severe battle and suffered severely in attacking the enemy's entrenchments of which our Generals were poorly informed. . . . Unaccountable delays in bringing some of our troops into action prevented us from gaining a decisive victory on Saturday. The opportunity being lost we must try to find another."

In the Shenandoah the mercurial Stonewall Jackson was at Strasburg with Frémont coming at him from Warrensville. Shields of McDowell's command was at Front Royal. But as he moved south up the valley pike between the two foes who meant to cut him off, Jackson, outnumbered, was adding to his reputation. He was becoming a glamorous figure to the

North as well as the South. In a day or two by desperate marching he would be safe, moving swiftly up the valley toward Harrisonburg. There was some skirmishing, mostly cavalry, at Mount Carmel, near Strasburg, but that was all.

In Oregon County of Missouri there were several days of operations with a skirmish at Eleven Points. For the Federals the Department of Virginia was extended and included in McClellan's command. Maj. Gen. John Wool was assigned to the Middle Department, and Maj. Gen. John A. Dix would command Fort Monroe.

June 2, Monday

As Jackson escaped from the Federal pincers in the Shenandoah there was skirmishing at Strasburg and Woodstock. Near Corinth, Miss., Federal troops under John Pope, following Beauregard's withdrawing Confederates, fought briefly near Rienzi, Miss. Other fighting was at Galloway's Farm near Jacksonport, Ark.; on the Little Blue in Jackson County, Mo.; and at Tranter's Creek, N.C. Near Richmond both the Army of the Potomac and the Army of Northern Virginia were resting from the two days of battles at Seven Pines or Fair Oaks. (Though officially the Army of Northern Virginia since April, it only popularly became known as such after Lee took over.)

Confederates at Memphis held a mass meeting to rally their people to the defense of the city, but more than mass meetings were needed. Lincoln telegraphed Genls. McClellan and McDowell, checking carefully on weather and events.

June 3, Tuesday

EVACUATION OF FORT PILLOW, TENNESSEE, JUNE 3-5.

The fall of Corinth, Miss., to the Federals broke the Memphis and Charleston Railroad, a vital Confederate east-west link. More than that, it rendered the northern outposts of the South on the Mississippi useless and practically doomed the city of Memphis, Tenn. Beginning on this day the Confederates at Fort Pillow, threatened by the navy flotilla north of them, had no recourse but to take all the guns they could and pull out. The earthworks on the bluff above the river were vacated completely by the night of June 4. Only a weak Confederate naval flotilla remained between the Federals and Memphis.

Along the Chickahominy, McClellan sent out a reconnaissance to the James to make contact with the Union river boats. There was a skirmish on James Island, S.C., not far from Charleston, as Federals began their drive to take or render impotent the city where the war had its inception. In Mississippi there was skirmishing at Blackland and a reconnaissance toward Baldwyn and Carrollsville south of Corinth; Halleck studied the Confederate dispositions at Tupelo. In the Shenandoah Valley, Jackson continued his withdrawal southward, safe now, although there was skirmishing at Mount Jackson and Tom's Brook.

To Mrs. Davis the heavyhearted President of the Confederacy wrote on his fifty-fourth birthday, "It is hard to see incompetence losing opportunity and wasting hard-gotten means, but harder still to bear, is the knowledge that there is no available remedy."

June 4, Wednesday

Southern troops regretfully completed their evacuation of Fort Pillow on the Mississippi. Elsewhere there was skirmishing at Huntsville, Ala., where O. M. Mitchel's Federals still posed a threat to Chattanooga; at Osborn's and Wolf's creeks, Miss.; at Sweden's Cove near Jasper, Tenn.; at Woodville, Ala.; and at Big Bend, western Va. There was activity for several days around Miami, Cambridge, Frankfort, Waverly, and Pink Hill, Mo. The Federal push was still on, with Pope of Halleck's army probing Beauregard south of Corinth, the gunboats ready to move on the Mississippi, Mitchel in Alabama, operations on the islands near Charleston, Jackson withdrawing in the Shenandoah, and McClellan perched on the Chickahominy within sound of Richmond. Frightened Southern planters were burning immense amounts of cotton on the Yazoo and the Mississippi to prevent its capture. In Richmond Jefferson Davis had to deal with calls for troops in many places, but if he weakened one to support another he might be in worse trouble.

June 5, Thursday

Northern troops found Fort Pillow, Tenn., deserted. The navy gunboats pushed rapidly down the Mississippi toward Memphis. Scattered skirmishing occurred at Little Red River, Ark.; near Sedalia, Mo.; Round Grove, Indian Terr.; Tranter's Creek, N.C.; and New Bridge, Va. President Lincoln signed a bill granting him authorization to appoint diplomatic representatives to Haiti and Liberia, first Negro nations to be recognized by the United States. Heavy rains hindered Federal actions on the Chickahominy and added to McClellan's already lengthy delays near Richmond.

June 6, Friday

BATTLE OF MEMPHIS, TENNESSEE.

Throngs of people lined the bluffs of the Mississippi at Memphis early in the morning to witness what proved to be the last so-called "fleet action" of the war on the rivers. Commodore Charles Davis, with five Federal ironclads and four rams, mounting a total of sixty-eight guns, had passed Fort Pillow and headed for the major city of Tennessee. Opposed to this force were eight inferior Confederate makeshifts, mounting twenty-eight guns, under Capt. James E. Montgomery. The battle became a melee with ramming by both sides and close-quarter fighting. After notable action by *Queen of the West* and other Federal rams, the gunboats took up the fray and blasted the weakly protected Confederates. Only one Southern gunboat, *Van Dorn*, escaped. Three were totally destroyed and four others fell into Union hands. The Confederates also lost five large transports and other vessels which were in the process of being built. The Federals suffered some damage to the *Queen* and *Carondelet*. The two-hour fight was over about seven-thirty and the crowds on the bluffs went home, many of them in tears. By 11 A.M., after the mayor surrendered his city, Federal troops accompanying the flotilla took possession. The North had a new and useful base and a concentration point for its campaigning into the heart of the South. The Mississippi was now open to the Federals except in the state of Mississippi. Vicksburg was the next prime target on the river.

In the Shenandoah, near Harrisonburg, Jackson continued his retreat toward Port Republic. In a rearguard action with the Federals, Jackson's colorful, popular cavalry chief, Turner Ashby, was killed in the fields just south of Harrisonburg. By this time, with Frémont coming south in one branch of the Shenandoah and men of Shields' command in the other, another trap could possibly be set for Stonewall. In the West, south of Corinth, the fighting and reconnaissance continued with action from Booneville toward Baldwyn, Miss. Elsewhere there was skirmishing near Tompkinsville, Ky.; Grand River, Indian Terr.; and at Port Royal Ferry, S.C.

June 7, Saturday

Gen. Benjamin F. Butler, considered by some to be a tyrant, and by others to be a just ruler at New Orleans, added to his fame or censure this day by having William B. Mumford hanged for tearing down and destroying the United States flag over the New Orleans Mint. Even many favorable to Butler were critical of the punishment. The event raised bitter recriminations in Richmond and throughout the Confederacy.

From north of the Tennessee River, Federal troops under Ormsby Mitchel shelled and launched an attack upon Chattanooga which was beaten off. But it convinced the Confederates that they must fortify and garrison more effectively this extremely important point. In the Shenandoah there was more skirmishing near Harrisonburg between retiring Confederate cavalry and advancing Federals. There also was a skirmish at Big Bend, western Va. Near Richmond there was a reconnaissance by Federals on the Chickahominy. In the Charleston Harbor area of South Carolina skirmishing continued on James Island.

Farther west Federal troops took Jackson, Tenn., a fairly important rail and road center. There was skirmishing at Readyville, Tenn., and at Fairview and Little Red River, Ark. Federal troops also carried out a three-day expedition from Baton Rouge, La.

June 8, Sunday
BATTLE OF CROSS KEYS, VIRGINIA.

Stonewall Jackson at Port Republic, Va., faced two Federal columns coming south up the Shenandoah, one to the west commanded by Frémont and one to the north commanded by James Shields. Jackson was attacked by Frémont on the west side of the South Fork of the Shenandoah at Cross Keys. At the same time he was almost captured by a small Federal party from the north at nearby Port Republic, but they were beaten off. The main Confederate fighting at Cross Keys was commanded by R. S. Ewell, who successfully defended his position and forced Frémont partially to withdraw. Ewell had about 6500 men, to 10,500 for Frémont. The Federals lost 114 killed, 443 wounded, and 127 missing, a total of 684, while Confederates had 41 killed, 232 wounded, and 15 missing, a total of 288. Meanwhile, Jackson watched for Shields' column from the north under Brig. Gen. Erastus B. Tyler, who was expected to attack soon.

There was skirmishing near Fair Oaks and on the New Market Road near the Chickahominy, and once more McDowell's Federals, having failed to defeat Jackson, were ordered to operate in the direction of Richmond. There was a skirmish at Muddy Creek, western Va., as well. At Charleston, S.C., there were affairs and skirmishes for two days as Federals tried to enlarge their holdings on the key islands near Charleston Harbor.

June 9, Monday
BATTLE OF PORT REPUBLIC, VIRGINIA.

Stonewall Jackson left an enlarged brigade west of the south fork of the Shenandoah River. They were to watch Frémont while Ewell's men were brought across the stream to Port Republic. Jackson's command opposed Shields' main Federal force under E. B. Tyler north of the village. At first the attacking Confederates were driven back, but the arrival of Ewell allowed them to envelop a portion of the Federal line. By late morning Tyler's men retired and the Confederates followed briefly. Frémont, meanwhile, had pushed cautiously ahead but had not crossed the river. Federals had no more than 3000 engaged to 5900 for Jackson. The Union had 67 killed, 393 wounded, and 558 missing or captured for 1018, to total losses for the Confederates of 804.

Cross Keys and Port Republic were the last battles in Jackson's brilliant Shenandoah Valley Campaign. In thirty-eight days, Apr. 29–June 5, he had marched about 400 miles, and kept many thousands of Federals guessing. By other figures, counting from March 22 to June 25, Jackson in forty-eight *marching* days covered 676 miles and fought five battles. Despite the fact that they outnumbered him, at no time could the Union armies bring him to bay. Not only did he keep reinforcements from McClellan, but Jackson's name became a symbolic byword, caused frustration and trepidation in the North, and led the South out of the doldrums of almost continuous defeat. A Confederate wrote, "I had rather be a private in such an Army than a Field Officer in any other Army."

After Port Republic Shields' division was ordered back with the rest of McDowell's corps toward Fredericksburg. President Lincoln ordered Frémont to halt at Harrisonburg and pursue Jackson no farther.

At the Confederate-held batteries of Grand Gulf on the Mississippi there was a brief engagement between the guns onshore and the Federal vessels *Wissahickon* and *Itasca*. In Mississippi, south of Corinth, Federal reconnaissance continued to Baldwyn and Guntown.

June 10, Tuesday

There was little or no action on the main front in Virginia along the Chickahominy. Elsewhere skirmishing continued on James Island, S.C., near Charleston; at Winchester, Rogers' Gap, and Wilson's Gap, Tenn.; at the mouth of West Fork, western Va.; and on the White River in Arkansas. At Corinth Gen. Halleck reassigned U. S. Grant, D. C. Buell, and John Pope to their separate army corps. Grant, after being second-in-command in the Corinth campaign, was thus again actually leading troops.

June 11, Wednesday

Gen. Frémont pulled back from the Port Republic area to Mount Jackson in the Shenandoah under orders from Washington. Meanwhile, there was speculation about what Stonewall Jackson would do—renew his valley fighting, or go to Richmond to aid Lee? Fighting was confined to skirmishing near Booneville, Miss., not far from Corinth; Monterey, Ky.; Cassville, Deep Water, and Pink Hill, Mo. In the mountains of Tennessee there was skirmishing at Big Creek Gap as a small Federal expedition carried out operations.

Jefferson Davis wrote to his wife of his worry over the "prejudice in our Army against Labor." As for the enemy, he stated, "If we succeed in rendering his works useless to him and compel him to meet us on the field, I have much confidence in our ability to give him a complete defeat, and then it may be possible to teach him the pains of invasion and to feed our Army on his territory."

June 12, Thursday

JEB STUART BEGINS RIDE AROUND MCCLELLAN.

"Gentlemen, in ten minutes every man must be in his saddle!" Thus spoke Brig. Gen. James Ewell Brown Stuart at 2 A.M. as he prepared to lead his twelve hundred cavalrymen and some artillery on an expedition that developed into a famous ride around the entire Federal army on the Peninsula. This spectacular four-day reconnaissance in force covered some twenty-two miles from Richmond the first day, and encamped for the evening near the South Anna at Winston Farm.

The Confederates under Lee meanwhile sent reinforcements to Jackson in the valley to give the impression that a major thrust would be made northward in that area. Jackson's men were encamped near Weyer's Cave while Federal troops left Harrisonburg and occupied Mount Jackson. President Lincoln told Gen. Frémont of reports that "Jackson is largely reinforced, and is turning upon you. Stand well on your guard. . . ."

In Arkansas there was skirmishing at Waddell's Farm near Village Creek, and near Jacksonport. In South Carolina there was activity on Hutchinson's Island.

June 13, Friday

Turning southeast from the South Anna north of Richmond, Stuart's troopers moved around the right flank of McClellan's army, through Hanover Court House, Va. At Haw's Shop there was a brief skirmish, with another at Old Church a few miles farther on. Now was the time for the decision to go back or continue on around the Army of the Potomac. Stuart made what for him was the obvious choice: he would go ahead. At Tunstall's Station a Federal train escaped the raiders, but Stuart rode on into the night and by morning attempted to cross the Forge Bridge over the Chickahominy. Elsewhere there was fighting near Hilton Head, S.C., and at New Market in the Shenandoah.

June 14, Saturday

Working desperately, Jeb Stuart's Confederates rebuilt the destroyed bridge on the Chickahominy at Forge Site, fearful that the overwhelming Federal forces around them on Virginia's Peninsula would cut them off. After three hours the band of troopers proceeded. Stuart was only thirty-five miles from Richmond and he had to go around the left flank of the enemy this time. Stuart himself hurried on to report and left the command in the hands of Fitzhugh Lee. The main column moved via Charles City Court House and Malvern Hill to Richmond, arriving on June 16. Near Baldwyn, Miss., there was a skirmish at Clear Creek; and in Florida a two-day Federal expedition was undertaken from Pensacola to Milton.

June 15, Sunday

A triumphant Jeb Stuart arrived in Richmond to report personally to Gen. Lee on his successful ride around McClellan. Meanwhile his troopers were drawing near the Confederate capital. Daring, startling, a great morale-booster to the South, a draught of chagrin to the North, it is certain that Stuart furnished Lee with valuable information on terrain, Federal dispositions, and the condition of the country. On the other hand, it may well have alerted McClellan to the danger on his flanks and made him better prepared to resist the attack that came later in the month. At any rate, it was an exploit that brought Stuart and his cavalrymen the plaudits of fame as dashing cavaliers of Dixie. Meanwhile, there was a skirmish near Seven Pines and a Federal reconnaissance near New Market, Va. In Florida, Federal naval forces descended upon St. Mark's; there was fighting at Big Creek Gap in the Cumberland Mountains of Tennessee. President Lincoln wrote Frémont in the Shenandoah that Jackson "is much more likely to go to Richmond than Richmond is to come to him." The President divined that Confederate moves were to make it appear that they were reinforcing the valley when their intention was to move Jackson from the valley to Lee.

June 16, Monday
ENGAGEMENT OF SECESSIONVILLE, SOUTH CAROLINA.

Federal troops of Brig. Gen. H. W. Benham from James Island near Charleston assaulted Confederate works at Secessionville, S.C., a hamlet on the low-lying island, defended by men under N. G. Evans. Benham's assaults failed completely, and he disobeyed orders and advice in making the drive. Eventually he was relieved of his command. The outcome of the engagement seriously retarded Federal operations aimed at controlling Charleston Harbor. In this nearly forgotten struggle the Union force of some 6600 suffered 107 killed, 487 wounded, and 89 missing for 683 casualties. For the Confederates losses were 52 killed, 144 wounded, and 8 missing for 204 out of about 2500 engaged.

Elsewhere there was skirmishing in the Shenandoah at Mount Jackson; and at Winchester, Tenn.; plus some scouting from Batesville to Fairview and other communities in Arkansas.

June 17, Tuesday

Stonewall Jackson was leaving the valley of the Shenandoah. After attempts to fool the Federals by sending reinforcements, the Confederates began shipping Jackson's men rapidly east toward Richmond and a hoped-for offensive on the Peninsula of Virginia against McClellan. Other fighting was minor: skirmishes at Eminence, and near Warrensburg, Mo.; near Smithville, Ark., and Pass Manchac, La.

In command changes Maj. Gen. John Charles Frémont resigned his post when ordered to serve under Maj. Gen. John Pope. Pope was being brought east from the Mississippi Valley to command a new Army of Virginia which would consist primarily of Frémont's and Banks' Federal commands. Franz Sigel was given Frémont's position.

There was an even more important change for the Confederates. Gen. Braxton Bragg was named commander of the Western Department of the Confederate Army, now mainly in and around Tupelo, Miss. He succeeded the ailing and disgruntled Gen. Beauregard. With the rise of Bragg to

major command, Beauregard's most active days were over for a considerable time. Bragg, never a popular commander, was given an opportunity to see what he could do with the precarious military situation
in the West.

June 18, Wednesday

Northern troops under Brig. Gen. George W. Morgan occupied Cumberland Gap, an important trail through the rugged mountains where Kentucky, Tennessee, and Virginia join. The Confederates withdrew because
of the Federal threats, but only after destroying stores. The occupation
had a stimulating influence on the alleged pro-Union sentiments of many
of the residents of the area. At the same time there was skirmishing
at nearby Wilson's Gap.

Below Vicksburg on the Mississippi, Farragut was assembling his
Federal flotilla, including the mortar fleet, preparatory to a move northward past the batteries. In Vicksburg the Confederates were hastily building extensive fortifications, long neglected, and were preparing themselves
for eventual attack. There was a skirmish at Hambright's Station, Mo.
In Virginia another skirmish occurred at Fair Oaks east of Richmond,
and there was light skirmishing near Winchester this day and June 19.

President Lincoln asked McClellan when he could attack Richmond.
The President also reportedly discussed drafts of his proposed Emancipation Proclamation with Vice-President Hannibal Hamlin.

June 19, Thursday

SLAVERY IN TERRITORIES PROHIBITED.

In Washington the President signed into law a measure prohibiting
slavery in the territories of the United States. Near Richmond there was
a skirmish on the Charles City Road, while other fighting took place at
Knight's Cove, Ark. In Richmond President Davis wrote Gov. John J.
Pettus of Mississippi, "My efforts to provide for the military wants of
your section have been sadly frustrated."

June 20, Friday

From Baton Rouge, La., a Federal expedition was under way toward
Vicksburg. By boat some three thousand men under Brig. Gen. Thomas
Williams traveled north. The objects of this movement, aided by Farragut's gunboats, were to establish a base at Swampy Toe on the
west side of the Mississippi opposite Vicksburg and to attempt to dig
a canal by which small vessels could bypass the ever increasing batteries
on the east side. Maj. Gen. Earl Van Dorn assumed command of the
Confederate Department of Southern Mississippi and East Louisiana,
charged with the defense of the Mississippi. There was a skirmish at

Bayou des Allemands, La.; and in Virginia near New Bridge and at Gill's Bluff on the James; while there were several days of guerrilla activities in Owen County, Ky.

June 21, Saturday

Skirmishing was slight along the battle lines on the Chickahominy near Richmond but there was another fight near Fair Oaks Station. Elsewhere there were skirmishes at Simmons' Bluff, S.C., and at Battle Creek and Rankin's Ferry, near Jasper, Tenn. Federals carried out an expedition to Hernando, Miss., with skirmishing at Coldwater Station.

"We are preparing and taking position for the struggle which must be near at hand. The stake is too high to permit the pulse to keep its even beat. . . . A total defeat of McClellan will relieve the Confederacy of its embarrassments in the East, and then we must make a desperate effort to regain what Beauregard has abandoned in the West." So wrote a tense President Davis to his wife. At Washington Lincoln asked by telegram that McClellan give him his views as to military affairs throughout the whole country.

June 22, Sunday

A quiet day, but it was apparent that in Virginia major action would occur soon. McClellan must move, and the Confederates must attack. The stalemate at Richmond had lasted long enough. Near White Oak Swamp there was a reconnaissance, and scattered action in the Shenandoah around Strasburg. Thirty Sisters of Charity arrived at Fort Monroe to administer to the sick and wounded of the Army of the Potomac.

June 23, Monday

Still the lesser fighting continued, at Pineville, and near Raytown, Mo.; Augusta, Ark.; and New Kent Court House, Va. There were several days of operations about Sibley and Pink Hill, Mo. President Lincoln left Washington late in the afternoon for New York and West Point, where he was to confer with Gen. Winfield Scott.

A conference took place at the Dabbs' House north of Richmond. Lee gathered his principal generals, including Stonewall Jackson, who had traveled rapidly ahead of his army coming from the Shenandoah. Although Lee had already decided to take the offensive, many details had to be worked out. Richmond could not withstand a siege; an offensive now was imperative. This counterattack must attempt to turn McClellan's line. Stating his case, Lee withdrew, allowing the other officers to work out the plans which were approved. The drive was to begin June 26. With the decision, Jackson headed west again to hurry forward his indispensable three divisions.

June 24, Tuesday

Skirmishing increased at Mechanicsville, Va., just north of Richmond, as Confederates probed the Federal lines. In North Carolina there was a reconnaissance from Washington to Tranter's Creek; and near Grand Gulf, Miss., there was skirmishing at Hamilton's Plantation. President Davis told Gen. Van Dorn at Vicksburg, "The people will sustain you in your heroic determination, and may God bless you with success."

June 25, Wednesday

THE SEVEN DAYS BEGIN.

What became known as the Seven Days' Campaign before Richmond began mildly enough, with the secondary engagement known as Oak Grove, King's School-House, French's Field, or the Orchard. Gen. George B. McClellan ordered forward advance units on his left which he said were preparatory to a general forward movement. However, the main attack by men of Samuel Heintzelman's corps was well met by Confederates of Benjamin Huger. By evening there was little change in the lines a few miles east of Richmond. Federals lost at least 51 killed, 401 wounded, and 64 missing for 516, compared to 40 killed, 263 wounded, and 13 missing for 316 for the Confederates. There also was skirmishing near Ashland, Va. In the Confederate ranks the mild Union advance did not upset the plans for the attack scheduled for June 26, a result of the conference of war on June 23. Jackson's forces approached from the west and north, and it was hoped all would be ready for a coordinated attack on McClellan's right.

In other sectors there was a skirmish at Yellville, Ark.; another at Mungo Flats, western Va.; and an affair near La Fayette Station, Tenn. On the Mississippi Thomas Williams and his three thousand Federals, escorted by Farragut's squadron, arrived opposite Vicksburg, where they were to make rather ineffective attempts to isolate the city by digging a canal across Swampy Toe.

President Lincoln left West Point in the morning after his conference with Gen. Scott and reached Washington in early evening. At Pekin, Ill., a group known as the Union League was organized. A patriotic and political group, it was to have considerable influence in postwar years. Its wartime purpose was to bolster Northern morale and faith.

June 26, Thursday

BATTLE OF MECHANICSVILLE, BEAVER DAM CREEK OR ELLERSON'S MILL.

Three Confederate divisions were ready to strike at McClellan's army east of Richmond. Jackson's force was not yet up, but Lee's plan was clear. A. P. Hill was to cross the Chickahominy at Meadow Bridge, push the Federals out of Mechanicsville, and clear the way for D. H.

Hill and Longstreet. Jackson was to come in on the left and all were to sweep backward Fitz John Porter's large Federal corps. The rest of the Federal army was out of reach, on the southwest side of the Chickahominy. But where was Jackson? At 3 P.M. A. P. Hill attacked without him. The Confederates pushed through Mechanicsville as planned and Porter fell back to Beaver Dam Creek and Ellerson's Mill to a strong, prepared position. Hill did not stop, but threw his men forward in frontal assault. The charge was a failure. Jackson did not get into things, first of several delays charged to Jackson during the Seven Days. Lee's control seemed very loose. The cost for the Confederates was 1484 to 361 for the Federals. The effective forces engaged were around 14,000 Southerners and over 15,000 Federals. During the night, Porter, threatened by the bulk of the Confederate army, withdrew to another prepared position near Gaines' Mill, behind Boatswain Swamp. His base at White House on the Pamunkey severely threatened by the Confederate move, McClellan ordered his supplies sent to the James River, where a new base would be set up at Harrison's Landing. Other fighting in Virginia this day included skirmishes at Hundley's Corner, Hanover Court House, and Atlee's Station. Also in Virginia there was fighting at Point of Rocks on the Appomattox River.

On the Mississippi the mortar boats bombarded the Confederate gun positions at Vicksburg from the south, preparing the way for Farragut's fleet to pass to the north and hook up with the gunboats above Vicksburg. In Missouri there was a skirmish at Cherry Grove in Schuyler County.

A primary command change was announced in Washington. Maj. Gen. John Pope was formally assigned command of the newly created Army of Virginia, which included the old Mountain Department, the Department of the Rappahannock, and the Department of the Shenandoah. The main task of the new command was to protect Washington and, more importantly, to consolidate all land forces in Virginia, not including the Army of the Potomac, so that they could move overland to aid McClellan and take the pressure off his army near Richmond. At the same time Lincoln continued to tell McClellan that he was sending the general all the men he could. The constant complaints of McClellan pained Mr. Lincoln.

June 27, Friday

BATTLE OF GAINES' MILL, FIRST COLD HARBOR, OR THE CHICKAHOMINY.

Lee had to strike again. Most of his army had moved away from Richmond and there was little between the capital of the Confederacy and the main Federal Army of the Potomac. But McClellan, too, was in trouble. The enemy was on his right flank and rear. Fitz John Porter north of the Chickahominy, was ordered to hold Gaines' Mill at any cost so as to enable McClellan to prepare a change of base to the James River. Confederates attacked in midafternoon across ravines, fields, and swamps against the strong semicircle defense positions. Again there was poor coordination by Southern commanders, and again the Federals exacted great toll. Again Jackson was delayed. At dark, John Bell Hood's Texas Brigade and troops of George E. Pickett broke through Porter's line. But the disorganized Confederates could not fully exploit the success, despite confusion among the Federals. Porter withdrew the remains of his gallant corps across the Chickahominy and rejoined the main Army of the Potomac.

South of the river there had been only minor fighting at Fair Oaks and elsewhere as John Bankhead Magruder skillfully demonstrated with his inferior force against the bulk of the Union army. Porter had perhaps 36,000 for duty with 894 killed, 3107 wounded, and a huge 2836 missing or captured—a total of 6837 casualties. Confederate effectives numbered about 57,000, with casualties around 8750. The attackers, weaker in total armies, were suffering more, but the Seven Days would continue. McClellan must withdraw now and retreat to the James in the face of the Southern drive. Some called it a strategic withdrawal, not a defeat. Others named it a "great skedaddle." For the Confederacy, it looked as if the pressure on Richmond was to be relieved. A Confederate private spoke of "the din and the roar, and the pulse of artillery, and the cheers, and cries of Forward! Forward! and the grey smoke mixed with it all."

At Vicksburg a mortar bombardment from the south continued and Federal troops began the active phase of their canal digging on the Louisiana side, across from the threatened fortress. Lost in the news of the day was a skirmish at Stewart's Plantation, Ark.

In northern Virginia John Pope assumed command of his new Army of Virginia. For the Confederacy, Gen. Bragg assumed permanent command of the Department of the West. Down in Louisiana there were three days of Federal reconnaissance to the Amite River, with skirmishing. In Washington Mr. Lincoln accepted Gen. Frémont's resignation, offered June 17. It was the end of the military trail for the controversial explorer, soldier, and politician.

June 28, Saturday

PASSAGE OF VICKSBURG.

At 2 A.M. Farragut's fleet was under way from south of Vicksburg, steaming up the Mississippi in its attempt to force a passage past the batteries of the city. In two columns the fleet proceeded and by 4 A.M. the battle was joined. By 6 A.M. all but three vessels had made it. Fifteen men were killed and thirty wounded in the Federal fleet. Confederate casualties were negligible. The action proved two points: first, a fleet could pass powerful land batteries without excessive damage or danger, and second, it was clear that a fleet alone could not take Vicksburg. A campaign that was to last more than a year had begun. However, the last major bastion held by the Confederacy on the Mississippi was threatened.

On the quietest of the Seven Days in Virginia, McClellan, his army, its herd of cattle and immense wagon trains began to withdraw south from near Richmond toward the James River. Lee reorganized his command for another offensive blow, for by evening he knew the Army of the Potomac was headed toward the river. White House on the Pamunkey was evacuated and burned. There was fighting at Garnett's and Golding's Farms, and at Dispatch Station on the Richmond and York River Railroad. Meanwhile, the navy moved up the James from Fort Monroe to open communications with McClellan's army expected at Harrison's Landing. Federal cavalry finished destruction of abandoned Union supplies at White House Landing.

President Lincoln received an angry telegram from distraught McClellan. "I have lost this battle because my force was too small," he wrote, blaming the President and the Administration bitterly and disclaiming responsibility for the defeat at Gaines' Mill despite the fact that he had not used a major part of his army. Two sentences of this message were deleted by War Department staff as unfit for Mr. Lincoln to see. They read, "If I save this army now, I tell you plainly that I owe no thanks to you or to any other persons in Washington./ You have done your best to sacrifice this army." Lincoln, however, in replying to what he did see of the message, stated, "Save your Army at all events. . . . If you have had a drawn battle, or a repulse, it is the price we pay for the enemy not being in Washington."

Sparta, Tenn., saw a skirmish this day, as did Blackland, Miss. In Charleston Harbor, Federals pulled off James Island and momentarily gave up the attempt to get at Charleston and its harbor forts from the low-lying islands.

June 29, Sunday

BATTLE OF SAVAGE'S STATION.

Confederate forces north of the Chickahominy crossed the stream and followed the retreating McClellan; Confederates south of the river also gave pursuit. But McClellan's rear guard withstood another disorganized drive that never fully materialized. Jackson again was accused of being tardy, though critics vary in their views. Again the Federals safely withdrew, but were forced to leave 2500 sick and wounded at Savage's Station on the Richmond and York River Railroad east of Richmond. Farther south skirmishing occurred on the James River Road near Willis' Church, and other fighting at Peach Orchard or Allen's Farm near Fair Oaks.

On another front there was an affair at Moorefield, western Va. In the Shenandoah Valley there was a Federal reconnaissance from Front Royal to Luray.

June 30, Monday

BATTLE OF FRAYSER'S FARM OR WHITE OAK SWAMP.

Again the armies near Richmond fought a confused major battle. This one has as many as eight names: White Oak Swamp, Frayser's Farm, Glendale, Nelson's Crossroads, Charles City Crossroads, New Market Road, Willis' Church, and Turkey Bridge. On this sixth day of the campaign, Lee's Army of Northern Virginia was trying to attack McClellan from the north, across the desolate mire of White Oak Swamp, and from the west. McClellan realized the plan and effectively halted it, aided by the same lack of coordination which had plagued the Confederate offensive. Jackson again was accused of not carrying out his role, long a debated point. Longstreet could not break the Union lines. By night McClellan drew his lines in tightly upon Malvern Hill just north of the James. In perhaps the decisive day of the week-long campaign, Lee lost his last chance to cut McClellan's army in two and prevent it from reaching its haven. It was clear that Richmond had been saved and a Southern victory of major proportions won, although the Federal army was still greater in size by far than that of the Confederacy. A Northern officer felt the army had been left to take care of itself "and was saved by its own brave fighting."

Other action was comparatively insignificant. There was minor fighting at Henderson, Ky., and Rising Sun and Powell River, Tenn.

In Washington President Lincoln wrote of his anxiety over McClellan's position to his Secretary of State: "The loss of enemies does not compensate for the loss of friends."

JULY, 1862

The war had changed sharply within a month. The string of Northern victories had ended. While the South was still in a sense at bay, there was more cause for hope. Jackson had been victorious in the Shenandoah Valley, and had built a legend. Lee had attacked on the Virginia Peninsula, nearly in the shadow of the Confederate capital, and was still pushing McClellan's huge invading force back from Richmond, with the issue undecided. The guns still echoed clear to the city. In the West Farragut had not captured Vicksburg with his fleet; Halleck had not moved far from Corinth; Chattanooga had not fallen. All had seemed likely possibilities in June. Charleston, S.C., appeared safe for the moment. McClellan was quarreling almost openly with Washington and the President; discontent among the citizens was not still. For the South there was a great deal to worry about yet, but also something to cheer about. However, the summer was fresh—a lot of fighting days lay ahead.

July 1, Tuesday

BATTLE OF MALVERN HILL.

FEDERAL INCOME TAX AND RAILROAD ACTS APPROVED.

The Seven Days Campaign east of Richmond came to an end on Malvern Hill north of the James River. McClellan's retreating Army of the Potomac took its stand at a strong defensive position, readily adaptable for well-placed artillery and infantry alike. Lee, hoping to destroy the Federals, decided to attack. Delay after delay and incoherent organization prevented any thrust until late in the afternoon. Confederate artillery proved no match for the expertly handled Union guns. The several attacks, when they did come, were disjointed and uncoordinated; a large portion of the Southerners never saw action. By nightfall the Confederates were spent and the battered Federals continued their withdrawal down the James to Berkeley Plantation or Harrison's Landing, ancestral home of the Harrison family. A correspondent wrote, "The vast aerial auditorium seemed convulsed with the commotion of frightful sounds."

McClellan had failed to take Richmond despite his greatly superior numbers. He had been forced to withdraw, but at Malvern Hill his men defended courageously. Lee, after successfully driving the Federals from his capital, failed to destroy or seriously cripple McClellan and was criticized both for making the costly assaults at Malvern Hill and for the clearly faulty management of the battle, known also as Crew's or Poindexter's Farm. Violent opinions were plentiful on both sides. For the battles of June 29–July 1 (Savage's Station, White Oak Swamp, and Malvern Hill) Federal casualties were 724 killed, 4245 wounded, 3067 missing for a total of 8036 out of some 83,000 engaged in an army of more than 115,000. Confederate losses were 8602 killed and wounded and 875 missing for 9477 of a total of perhaps 86,500 engaged out of an effective 88,000 plus. For the whole of the Seven Days the losses were appalling in this still "young" war—Confederates over 20,000 casualties, including 3286 killed, 15,909 wounded, and 946 missing. Federals nearly 16,000, including 1734 killed, 8062 wounded, and 6053 missing. The guns fell silent on Virginia's Peninsula but the Federal army was still there, and not too far from Richmond at that.

In Mississippi Federal Col. Philip H. Sheridan defeated Confederate troops in an action near Booneville, Miss., south of Corinth in the northeastern portion of the state. Skirmishes occurred at Fort Furnace at

Powell's Big Fort Valley, Va.; Cherry Grove in Schuyler County, Mo.; and Holly Springs, Miss. Farragut's fleet from New Orleans, now north of Vicksburg, joined Flag Officer Charles Davis' western flotilla on the Mississippi.

President Lincoln approved two significant acts of the Federal Congress. The Federal Income Tax was revised with 3 per cent on income between $600 and $10,000, and 5 per cent above $10,000. This measure became operative where the 1861 measure did not. Another measure approved a Union Pacific-Central Pacific railroad across the west. Government aid was provided and rights secured for postal, military, and other purposes. The President announced to the Northern governors that he was calling for 300,000 more men "to bring this unnecessary and injurious civil war to a speedy and satisfactory conclusion."

July 2, Wednesday

EDUCATIONAL LAND GRANT APPROVED.

Heavy rain fell on the Peninsula of Virginia as McClellan pulled his army away from Malvern Hill and continued his retreat to Harrison's Landing on the James River. Lee's army was in no condition for a real follow-up, but there was action between Confederate cavalry and Federal infantrymen. Charges and countercharges on both sides began at once over the management of the campaign. Other fighting was at Huntsville, Ala.; and there was a reconnaissance up Powell's Big Fort Valley, Va. The Confederates created the Military District of Mississippi under command of Maj. Gen. Earl Van Dorn.

President Lincoln received news from Virginia and also signed several acts, including one banning polygamy in the territories. Another law called for a loyalty oath by every elected or appointed government officer. Most important, Mr. Lincoln signed the Morrill Act, introduced in the Senate by Justin S. Morrill of Vermont, which provided for the states to receive thirty thousand acres of land for each senator and representative as an endowment for proposed agricultural and mechanical schools. The measure made possible land grant agricultural colleges in every state.

July 3, Thursday

The news of the retreat of the Union army from before Richmond spread. In the North, especially, the disappointment and chagrin was vehemently expressed. McClellan and his army were the subject of agitated controversy.

There was bombardment at Vicksburg; there were skirmishes at Locust Grove, Indian Terr.; near Russellville, Ala.; near Herring Creek close to Harrison's Landing, Va.; and a reconnaissance from Harrison's Landing by Federals. Confederate Maj. Gen. Sterling Price assumed command of the Army of the West.

July 4, Friday

Independence Day was greeted by the North with even more than usual enthusiasm notwithstanding the discouraging news from Virginia. Speeches, proclamations, and general orders ruled the day. But the fighting also continued with a Federal reconnaissance from Harrison's Landing, Va.; a skirmish at Westover, Va.; an affair at Port Royal Ferry, S.C.; and a Confederate attack on U.S. vessels near Velasco, Tex. Confederate John Hunt Morgan embarked on his first Kentucky raid, which lasted until July 28 and included fights at Tompkinsville on July 9, Lebanon on the twelfth, and Cynthiana on the seventeenth. Confederate gunboat *Teaser* was captured by Federals as it attempted to go down the James and launch an observation balloon made of old silk frocks. At Vicksburg the bombardment continued, as Federals puzzled over how best to reduce the fortress on the Mississippi bluffs.

July 5, Saturday

Jefferson Davis agreed with Lee that Confederate armies were not numerous enough and were so "battle thinned" that an attack on McClellan on the James would be impossible at this time. Skirmishes at Battle Creek, Tenn.; on the Hatchie River, Miss.; and an affair at Walden's Ridge, Tenn. Confederates carried out minor operations against Federal shipping on the James this day and July 6. A Federal expedition operated from Ponchatoula, La., July 5–8, to flush out Confederate guerrillas.

July 6, Sunday

From North Carolina, Federal Maj. Gen. A. E. Burnside sailed with reinforcements for the Army of the Potomac on the James. Skirmishes were fought at Bayou Cache, Ark., and Salem, Mo. There was a Federal scout from Waynesville to the Big Piney, Mo.; and another Federal expedition toward Blackwater and Chapel Hill, Mo.

July 7, Monday

Military action on the James was relatively light as both North and South rested and repaired their weary ranks. But the crescendo of controversy between McClellan and the Lincoln administration increased. McClellan attempted to enlarge the scope of his influence by advising the President on political as well as military policy, and he tried to limit the war to opposing armies and political organizations. Military operations should not interfere with slavery, he wrote the President in what came to be known as the "Harrison's Bar letter."

There were skirmishes at Inman Hollow and Newark, Mo. Other operations included a Federal reconnaissance from Yorktown, Va., July

7–9; operations around Cumberland Gap, Tenn., July 7–11; and in Aransas Bay, Tex., July 7–17.

July 8, Tuesday

President Lincoln arrived at Fort Monroe and Harrison's Landing for conferences with Gen. McClellan and reviews of the Army of the Potomac. Skirmishes were at Orient Ferry or Black Run, Ark., and Pleasant Hill, Mo.

July 9, Wednesday

Confederate cavalry under raider John Hunt Morgan routed Federals and captured Tompkinsville, Ky. Union forces captured Hamilton, N.C. There was a skirmish at Lotspeich Farm, near Wadesburg, Mo.; a Federal reconnaissance on the Long Branch Road, Va.; and a Southern expedition to Fenwick's Island, S.C. On this day and the tenth Northern troops demonstrated against Pocotaligo, S.C. Public meetings were held in England asking the government to use its influence to bring about a reconciliation in America.

July 10, Thursday

Federals in Virginia carried out a reconnaissance from Harrison's Landing on the James toward White Oak Swamp, and fought a skirmish. On this day and the eleventh there was a Federal expedition under a flag of truce to Guntown, Miss., where Southern and Northern officers exchanged dispatches and newspapers and discussed in a friendly manner topics of the day. Confederate John Hunt Morgan called for citizens of Kentucky to "rise and arm, and drive the Hessian invaders from their soil." Ninety Confederate guerrillas drilling in a field between Gallatin and Hartsville, Tenn., were captured by Union forces.

Gen. John Pope issued controversial orders which ruled that in the Shenandoah Valley and throughout the area of operations of his Army of Virginia the people would be held responsible for injury to railroads, attacks upon trains or straggling soldiers. In case of guerrilla damage, citizens would be responsible financially, and if a Federal soldier were fired upon from any house, it should be razed. People detected in acts against the army would be shot without civil process.

July 11, Friday

Maj. Gen. Henry W. Halleck was named General-in-Chief of all U.S. land forces by President Lincoln. Halleck had been commander in the West during the successful campaigns of Grant, and had been field commander at the capture of Corinth, Miss. He was considered a top-grade administrator with a sound military mind.

There was quiet in Virginia on the Peninsula except for another Federal reconnaissance from Harrison's Landing beyond Charles City Court House. Missouri state militia fought Confederate guerrillas at Sears' House and Big Creek Bluffs near Pleasant Hill, Mo. The Federal congressional act to carry into effect the treaty with Great Britain for suppression of African slave trade was approved by the President.

July 12, Saturday

Morgan and his Confederate raiders captured Lebanon, Ky. There was excitement in Cincinnati, O., and in Frankfort, Lexington, and Louisville, Ky., over reports that Morgan's men were coming. President Lincoln appealed to border-state congressmen at the White House to support compensated emancipation of slaves. Gen. Samuel Curtis' Federal army arrived at Helena on the Mississippi River after marching across Arkansas. It was reported that the city of New Orleans, while suffering under the virtual dictatorship of Benjamin Butler and Federal occupation forces, was cleaner than ever "in the memory of the oldest inhabitant" and was "never more healthy at this season of the year."

Federal troops carried out an expedition July 12–16 from Decatur, Ala., to lend support to unionists of north Alabama. Federal troops under John Pope made a reconnaissance to Culpeper, Orange, and Madison Court Houses, Va., July 12–17.

July 13, Sunday

Action increased. Nathan Bedford Forrest and his Confederates captured Murfreesboro, Tenn., southeast of Federal-held Nashville, including the Union garrison. Stonewall Jackson's force advanced from Hanover Court House upon Gordonsville, Va. A portion of Lee's army began to move away from the defenses of Richmond as a prelude to new campaigning. Union forces destroyed the railroad bridge over the Rapidan River at Rapidan Station, Va., during a skirmish. Another skirmish was fought near Wolf River, Tenn. Lincoln and McClellan continued their correspondence over how many men McClellan had and whether or not he could take Richmond. Lincoln was beginning to have increasing doubts about his evasive commander on the Peninsula.

July 14, Monday

Federal Gen. John Pope moved his newly created Army of Virginia between the Confederates and Washington in order to draw the pressure from McClellan on the Peninsula. Now he issued a bombastic address to his troops calling for offensive action and an advance against the enemy: "I have come to you from the West, where we have always seen the backs of our enemies."

John Hunt Morgan carried his Confederate raiding activities to the area of Cynthiana, Ky. There were skirmishes near Batesville and Helena, Ark. A Federal reconnaissance operated July 14–17 from Grand River to Fort Gibson, Tahlequah, and Park Hill, Indian Terr.

Confederate Adj. Gen. Samuel Cooper put the conscription law into stricter operation. President Lincoln, in a message to Congress, asked for an act to compensate "any State which may abolish slavery within it's [sic] limits." He thus continued his attempt to deal with the slavery issue while still favoring compensated emancipation on a state-control basis. An act setting up a system of pensions for men disabled in service since the start of the war and for next of kin in case of death was signed into law. Twenty border-state representatives and senators replied that they opposed Mr. Lincoln's plan of compensated emancipation presented to them July 12. On July 15 seven congressmen replied in support of the appeal. The U. S. Senate passed a bill granting secession of western Virginia from Virginia and creating the new state.

July 15, Tuesday
c.s.s. *Arkansas* ATTACKS.

In the morning Federal naval vessels in the Yazoo north of Vicksburg met the newly completed Confederate ironclad *Arkansas,* under Com. Isaac Brown, coming downriver. *Arkansas* fought three Union vessels, passed with guns firing through other units of the fleet on the Mississippi, and anchored under the Vicksburg bluffs. Farragut with his fleet north of the city now decided to attack *Arkansas* by running past Vicksburg. In the evening Farragut's fleet passed below the city, dueling with the land batteries and *Arkansas,* but failing to destroy the newly built Confederate ironclad. Three Union vessels were badly damaged and *Arkansas* suffered considerably in the day's fighting. Federals had 18 killed, 50 wounded, and 10 missing to 10 killed and 15 badly wounded on *Arkansas.* In one spectacular dash a Confederate gunboat had changed the complexion of warfare on the Mississippi.

Federal cavalry defeated Confederates in an action near Fayetteville, Ark. There were skirmishes at Orange Court House and Middletown, Va.; Wallace's Cross Roads, Tenn.; and Apache Pass, N. Mex. Terr., where Union troops from California fought the Apaches.

July 16, Wednesday

Napoleon III of France received Confederate commissioner John Slidell, who requested recognition of the Confederacy and aid from warships in breaking the blockade in exchange for cotton. Confederate Maj. Gen. Theophilus H. Holmes was assigned to command the Trans-Mississippi Department. There was a reconnaissance by Federals from Westover, Va., on the Richmond Road near the James. The Federal District of

West Tennessee was extended to embrace the Army of the Mississippi, all to be commanded by U. S. Grant. Gen. Halleck relinquished command of the Department of the Mississippi to assume his new role as general of all U.S. armies.

Measures of the U. S. Congress approved by the President included creating the grade of rear admiral to be conferred on all flag officers; increasing temporary protective tariffs on sugar, tobacco, and liquor; and forbidding all financial interest in public contracts to members of Congress, officers, and agents of the government. William H. Aspinwall of New York presented the Federal War Department with a check for $25,290.60 as his share of profits on an arms contract.

July 17, Thursday
CONFISCATION ACT APPROVED.

President Lincoln signed the Second Confiscation Act after lengthy and acrimonious congressional debate and after weighing a possible veto. Supported by the Radicals and the ultra-abolitionist forces, it could readily be interpreted as a virtual act of emancipation. The measure provided that slaves of all those who supported or aided the rebellion would be free when they came within Union control. It called for confiscation of other forms of property, gave the President power to "employ" Negroes for suppression of the rebellion, and authorized the President to provide for colonization "in some tropical country beyond the limits of the United States, of such persons of the African race, made free by the provisions of this act, as may be willing to emigrate." The bill also authorized the President to tender pardon and amnesty to those he saw fit. Mr. Lincoln opposed some provisions and wording, but last-minute changes took care of most of the objections. The measure later gave rise to a political struggle between the President and Congress over who was to handle the slavery and reconstruction measures. Many provisions of this confiscation act were never enforced.

Another measure signed by the President upon the adjournment of the Congress authorized calling up men between the ages of eighteen and forty-five for nine months' militia service. This was later interpreted as a draft though never put into effect. Another bill provided for the use of postage stamps as money, due to the shortage of metal coins.

Maj. Gen. U. S. Grant assumed command of all troops in the Army of the Tennessee and Army of the Mississippi, and in the District of the Mississippi and Cairo. Confederate Gen. D. H. Hill was assigned to command the Department of North Carolina. Morgan's Confederate raiders took Cynthiana, Ky., while Pope's Federals captured Gordonsville, Va., a Southern supply base. There was a skirmish in the vicinity of Mount Pleasant and Columbia, Tennessee.

July 18, Friday

Federal Maj. Gen. Pope announced that his Army of Virginia would "subsist upon the country in which their operations are carried out," and that the citizens of the area through which his army operated would be held responsible for damage done to railroads, bridges, and telegraph lines by guerrillas. Furthermore, the people would be compelled to repair the damage and be assessed for such depredations.

Confederate troops crossed the Ohio River and raided the town of Newburg, Ind., near Evansville. There was a skirmish near Memphis, Mo. A motion in the British House of Commons to mediate between the Federal and Confederate governments was discussed and withdrawn.

July 19, Saturday

Lincoln named John S. Phelps of Missouri as military governor of Arkansas. Confederates raided Brownsville, Tenn., and there was a skirmish near Paris, Ky., between Federal troops and men of John Hunt Morgan's command. Meetings to stimulate enlistments were held in various Northern cities. A Federal expedition destroyed military stores and the railroad at Beaver Dam Station, Va., July 19–20. July 19–23 a Union scout was carried out in Polk and Dallas counties, Mo.

July 20, Sunday

Minor fighting continued, with skirmishes at Greenville and Taberville, Mo., and Gaines' Landing, Ark. There was an affair at Hatchie Bottom, Miss.

July 21, Monday

Confederate troops captured Federal pickets five miles from Nashville and burned bridges on the Chattanooga road. The Confederate Army of the Mississippi was ordered to Chattanooga, and Maj. Gen. Price assumed command of the Confederate District of the Tennessee. Luray, Va., was occupied by Federal troops operating in the Shenandoah Valley. Lincoln and his Cabinet discussed the possible use of Negroes as soldiers.

July 22, Tuesday

PRESIDENT LINCOLN PRESENTS EMANCIPATION PROCLAMATION TO CABINET.

At a Cabinet meeting in Washington Mr. Lincoln surprised most of his advisers by reading the first draft of the Emancipation Proclamation. It included warnings of the consequences of the Confiscation Act, renewed his offer of compensation to loyal states for gradual emancipation, and proposed that as of Jan. 1, 1863, slaves in all states then in rebellion should be free. After long thought, the President had, independent of consultation, decided upon this course. After a discussion Mr. Lincoln followed Sec. of

State Seward's suggestion that announcement of the emancipation phases of the proclamation be delayed until the armies achieved a military success. The Federal War Department issued an order authorizing military and naval commanders within states in rebellion to seize and use for military purposes any real or personal property and to employ Negroes as laborers.

In Virginia there was reconnaissance by Federals from Luray to Columbia Bridge and White House Ford, plus a skirmish at Verdon, and an affair near Westover. Other activities included a reconnaissance July 22–24 by Federals to James City and Madison Court House, and a scout in King William, King and Queen, and Gloucester counties, Va. Maj. Gen. A. E. Burnside took command of the Ninth Army Corps of the Union Army.

John Hunt Morgan's command arrived at Livingston, Tenn., after its raid into Kentucky. At Vicksburg two Federal vessels were unsuccessful in an attack on the Confederate ram *Arkansas*. The canal that was to afford passage for Federal vessels around Vicksburg was completed but the current and the low water apparently would make it useless.

It was found that a Confederate telegraph operator under Morgan had been intercepting most of the Federal dispatches for the past twelve days, thus giving the Confederates warning of Northern operations.

July 23, Wednesday

Maj. Gen. Henry Wager Halleck assumed command of the Armies of the United States. Federal cavalry from Fredericksburg carried out a raid on Southern cavalry and supplies near Carmel Church, Va. There were skirmishes at Boles' Farm, Mo., and on the Blackwater, near Columbus, Mo. A Federal expedition was carried out July 23–25 from Helena, Ark., to Coldwater; and a skirmish was fought at White Oak Bayou, Miss. Gen. Pope in northern Virginia added to his already highly restrictive orders to the people. This time any male who refused to take an oath to the Union would be sent South, and if found again would be considered a spy. Any person violating the oath would be shot and his property confiscated.

The major portion of Braxton Bragg's Confederate force was moving from Tupelo, Miss., south to Mobile and then to Montgomery, Ala., and Atlanta, en route to Chattanooga. The 776-mile trip over six railroads was admirably carried out and in record time.

July 24, Thursday

Former President Martin Van Buren, seventy-nine, died at Lindenwald, N.Y. Adm. Farragut pointed his Union fleet toward New Orleans, leaving five gunboats to guard the river between Vicksburg and Baton Rouge. Skirmishing broke out on the Amite River, La.; Santa Fe and Moore's

Mill near Fulton, Mo.; and White Oak Bayou, Miss. There was action July 24–26 in Wyoming County, western Va.; from Fredericksburg toward Orange Court House, Va.; from Helena to Marianna, Ark.; and from New Berne to Trenton and Pollocksville, N.C., July 24–28.

July 25, Friday

Mr. Lincoln promulgated the Confiscation Act of Congress, calling for suppression of the insurrection. In a proclamation he besought persons in the rebellion to cease participating in or abetting it, and "to return to their proper allegiance to the United States, on pain of the forfeitures and seizures. . . ."

There were skirmishes at Summerville, western Va.; Courtland and Trinity, Ala.; and Clinton Ferry, Tenn. Other operations were July 25–26 near Mountain Store, Mo.; July 25–Aug. 2 around Lake Ponchartrain, Pass Manchac, and up the Pearl River, La.; July 25–Aug. 1 from Holly Springs, Miss., to Bolivar and Jackson, Tenn.

July 26, Saturday

Fighting this day was near Orange Court House, Va.; Mill Creek near Pollocksville, N.C.; Spangler's Mill near Jonesborough, Ala.; and Taze-well, Tenn. July 26–29 there were operations in southeastern Missouri with skirmishes July 28 at Bollinger's Mill; and from Newport to Young's Cross Roads, N.C.

July 27, Sunday

Minor fighting continued at Bayou Bernard near Fort Gibson, Indian Terr.; Madisonville and Covington, La.; Brown's Spring, Mo.; Flat Top Mountain, western Va.; and near Toone's Station or Lower Post Ferry, Tenn. July 27–29 there were operations from Rienzi to Ripley, Miss.; July 27–30 from Woodville to Guntersville, Ala., with several skirmishes; and in Carroll, Ray, and Livingston counties, Mo.

July 28, Monday

The governors of Texas, Missouri, Arkansas, and Louisiana wrote to Jefferson Davis requesting a commanding general, money, arms, ammuni-tion, for "without them we cannot use our strength, nor fully develop the mighty power of resistance that is in our midst."

Fighting was at Cross Timbers and Fulton, Mo.; Stevenson, Ala.; Humboldt, Tenn.; Culpeper to Raccoon Ford, Va.; and July 28–31 in Pettis County, Mo.; and from Helena to Old Town and Trenton, Ark.

The office of the St. Croix *Herald* in St. Stephens, New Brunswick, Canada, a pro-Union paper, was attacked by a mob and the equipment wrecked.

July 29, Tuesday

The Confederate cruiser *Alabama* (known in Britain as *Enrica*) left Liverpool, unarmed, ostensibly on a trial run. Actually on the thirty-first she proceeded from the Irish Sea into the Atlantic for a rendezvous to receive her arms and ammunition before commencing her attacks on Federal shipping. Federal authorities in Britain had attempted for weeks to prevent the sailing.

Northern Maj. Gen. John Pope left Washington to make his head-quarters in the field with his Army of Virginia. There was fighting or reconnaissance at Arrow Rock, Bloomfield, and Saline County, Mo.; Orange Court House, Va.; Harrison's Landing to St. Mary's Church, Va.; Russellville, Ky.; Hatchie Bottom, near Denmark, Tenn.; and Federal naval forces attacked Fort McAllister on the Ogeechee River near Savannah, Ga.

"A woman named Belle Boyd" was captured near Warrenton, Va., by Federals. She was accused of being a Confederate spy and mail courier and was sent to the Old Capitol Prison at Washington. Released Aug. 28 for lack of evidence, she continued in her role as the most famous of Confederate women spies.

July 30, Wednesday

Halleck ordered Gen. McClellan to remove his sick and wounded from Harrison's Landing. The intention was to eventually move the whole army from the James toward Washington and northern Virginia. Confederate Maj. Gen. Theophilis Holmes assumed command of the Trans-Mississippi Department. There were military operations at Clark's Mill in Chariton County, Mo., and a reconnaissance from Harrison's Landing to Jones' Ford, Chickahominy River, Va.

In Boston, bells which had been contributed by Southern churches and individuals to be cast into cannon were sold at auction. Gen. Butler had confiscated them at New Orleans.

July 31, Thursday

President Davis wrote to Gen. Lee that on July 22 a cartel for exchange of prisoners had been signed, but that shortly afterward the Federal authorities "commenced a practice changing the character of the war, from such as becomes civilized nations into a campaign of indiscriminate robbery and murder." He referred to the orders of seizure of private property without compensation, the threats that citizens would be shot as spies if found in or near Pope's lines, and the seizure of citizens as hostages. Therefore Mr. Davis issued orders that any commissioned officers captured from Pope's army be treated as felons rather than prisoners of war, for, he said, they had put themselves in the position "of robbers and murderers."

He regretted having to threaten retaliation on the officers, but laid the blame upon the United States.

Confederates attacked Union camps and shipping between Shirley and Harrison's Landing, Va.

AUGUST, 1862

A midsummer breathing spell after the Seven Days before Richmond would come to an end soon. McClellan with his massive Army of the Potomac crouched at Harrison's Landing on the James. Would he strike? A question asked North and South. In northern Virginia the Federal Army of Virginia under John Pope was obviously readying an offensive. How could Gen. Lee oppose two great armies? To the west the new commander for the North, U. S. Grant was planning for widely scattered forces, mainly in northern Mississippi. Could the sparse ranks of the Confederacy in the West defend the Mississippi? The makeshift ironclad *Arkansas* was bravely defending Vicksburg. The Federal squadrons north and south of Vicksburg had not been successful. Buell with his Federals was not making much progress marching from Corinth, Miss., toward Chattanooga. At Chattanooga Bragg was preparing an advance into Tennessee and Kentucky. But whether Bragg's Confederate army could permanently retake Southern lands was questionable. Talk of emancipation as a part of the war effort was rising in the North, while at the same time there was increased opposition to making it a war against slavery. Confederates awaited the outcome of their efforts to achieve recognition by France.

August 1, Friday

Fighting on the first day of the month consisted of skirmishes at Ozark, Grand River, and Carrollton, Mo., and at Barnett's Ford, Va. Jefferson Davis wrote Gen. Lee protesting against alleged atrocities to civilians and soldiers and the arming of slaves by Federal authorities. A Federal official in South Carolina announced the issuance of papers indicating their freedom to Negro soldiers, not yet legally enlisted.

August 2, Saturday

Elements of the Army of Virginia under John Pope advanced on Orange Court House and skirmished with Confederates. Other skirmishing was on Clear Creek, near Taberville, Mo.; Jonesborough, Ark.; near Totten's Plantation, Coahoma County, and at Austin, Tunica County, Miss. Aug. 2–8. Federal forces from Harrison's Landing reoccupied Malvern Hill, Va.

Other operations were Aug. 2–5 from Meadow Bluff to the Greenbrier River, western Va.; Cumberland Gap and near Tazewell, Tenn., Aug. 2–6; and about Wyoming Court House, western Va., Aug. 2–8. Federal Sec. of State Seward instructed Minister to Great Britain Charles Francis Adams to neither receive nor discuss any offers of mediation of the war by Great Britain.

August 3, Sunday

Gen. Halleck ordered Gen. McClellan to move his Federal Army of the Potomac from the Peninsula north to Aquia Landing near Fredericksburg and to Alexandria. McClellan was to aid in the defense of Washington and in opposing the Confederate offensive against Pope's Army of Virginia. McClellan protested vehemently against this order, maintaining that he should remain on the Peninsula.

Skirmishing increased, with action at Chariton Bridge, Mo.; L'Anguille Ferry, Jackson, and Scatterville, Ark.; Greenbrier River, western Va.; Morganfield, Ky.; Nonconah Creek, Tenn.; on the south side of the James River and at Sycamore Church, Va. The British vessel *Columbia,* carrying twelve pieces of artillery, several thousand Enfield rifles, and other munitions, was captured after a seven-hour chase off the Bahamas by the Federal steamer *Santiago de Cuba.* Another blockade-runner was taken off Charleston as the effectiveness of the Federal blockade steadily developed.

August 4, Monday

President Lincoln ordered a draft of 300,000 militia to serve for nine months, unless discharged sooner. This draft was never put into effect. The President also ordered the military to get rid of incompetent persons holding commissions, and to promote worthy officers. Burnside's Federal corps from North Carolina arrived at Aquia Creek to assist Pope in defending against Lee's advance into northern Virginia. In New Orleans Gen. Benjamin F. Butler, commanding the Federal occupation forces, issued an order assessing "secessionists" a total of $341,916 to provide for the poor of the city.

There was skirmishing at Gayoso and on White River, near Forsyth, Mo. Other operations included a Federal reconnaissance from Coggins' Point beyond Sycamore Church, Va., Aug. 4–5; attack by Confederates on Union pickets near Woodville, and a Union reconnaissance from Woodville to Guntersville, Ala., Aug. 4–7; expedition of Confederate Gen. J. E. B. Stuart from Hanover Court House to near Fredericksburg, Va., Aug. 4–8; a Union scout on Sinking Creek, Mo., Aug. 4–11; a Federal expedition from Helena to Clarendon, Ark., Aug. 4–17.

Lincoln told a delegation of "Western gentlemen" who offered two Negro regiments from Indiana that he was not prepared to enlist Negroes as soldiers, although he suggested employing them as laborers.

August 5, Tuesday
ENGAGEMENT AT BATON ROUGE, LOUISIANA.

Confederate forces once more controlled the Mississippi north and south of Vicksburg from Helena, Ark., to Baton Rouge, La. Moving southward toward Baton Rouge, Maj. Gen. John C. Breckinridge and about 2600 men attacked 2500 Federals under Brig. Gen. Thomas Williams. Through a dense fog the Confederates charged in. It was largely an open fight with the original Southern attack blunted. The Federals then counterattacked to end the battle in midmorning, aided by heavy Federal gunboats in the Mississippi. Gen. Williams was killed the moment the Northern offensive began. Losses for the Federals were 84 killed, 266 wounded, and 33 missing for 383; Confederates also 84 killed, 315 wounded, and 57 captured or missing for 456. Breckinridge pulled back a few miles north and began seriously to fortify Port Hudson on the bluffs. The Confederate ram *Arkansas,* ordered down from Vicksburg, arrived too late to be of help due to continual breakdown of her faulty engines.

There was a light engagement at Malvern Hill and a skirmish at White Oak Swamp Bridge on Virginia's Peninsula, as well as one at Thornburg or Massaponax Church, Va. Elsewhere the fighting was at Montevallo and near Cravensville, Mo.; Wyoming Court House, western Va.; Sparta, Tenn.; and New Market, Ala. There was a Federal expedition Aug. 5–8 from Fredericksburg to Frederick's Hall Station, Va., and another at the same time by Union troops from Helena to the mouth of White River, Ark. Recruiting for old and new regiments proceeded briskly at the North after Lincoln's call for 300,000 more men. Confederate President Jefferson Davis wrote of some of the problems of his administration, stating, "Revolutions develop the high qualities of the good and great, but they cannot change the nature of the vicious and the selfish."

August 6, Wednesday
LOSS OF C.S.S. *Arkansas.*

The Federal ironclad *Essex* and four other vessels attacked *Arkansas* at Baton Rouge; as had happened the day before, *Arkansas*'s engines failed, making her an easy target. Badly damaged, *Arkansas* fought back despite a raging fire on board. The crew was ordered to abandon and she was blown up. The Confederates did not again attempt to put formidable warships on the Mississippi. In twenty-three days C.S.S. *Arkansas* had carved a career that became legend in the river war.

There was more skirmishing at Malvern Hill and around Thornburg, Va.; Beech Creek, Pack's Ferry on New River, western Va.; and Kirksville, Mo. War meetings were held in many Northern cities to stimulate enlistments. Brig. Gen. Robert L. McCook, of the famous McCook clan of Ohio, died from wounds after being attacked by a party of Confederate guerrillas while he was riding ill in an ambulance from Athens, Ala., to Decherd, Tenn.

August 7, Thursday

In New Mexico Territory near Fort Fillmore Federals under E. R. S. Canby defeated the Confederate forces retreating from Santa Fe. There was other fighting at Rocky Bluff in Platte County and near Montevallo, Mo.; Wolftown, Va.; Decatur, Ala.; and at Wood Springs near Dyersburg, Tenn. Aug. 7–9 there was a Union Scout from Ozark to Forsyth, Mo., and from the seventh to tenth a Federal reconnaissance from Pensacola to Bagdad and Milton, Fla. Federal forces on the Peninsula of Virginia withdrew once more from Malvern Hill. At Blackburn, England, a public meeting advocated the recognition of the Confederate States of America because "it was impossible for the North to vanquish the South."

August 8, Friday

Skirmishing continued from Missouri to Virginia with fighting on Panther Creek, near Newtonia, and near Stockton in Macon County, Mo.; Slaughter's House and near Madison Court House, Va. The Federal War Department issued orders to prevent evasion of military duty and for suppression of disloyal activities. At Baltimore arrests were made to prevent those seeking to evade the draft from leaving the area. At Huntsville, Ala., after a series of firings into trains by Confederate guerrillas, the Federal authorities ordered that ministers and leading churchmen who had been active secessionists be arrested and one each day be placed on board the trains.

British Prime Minister Lord Palmerston stated at a banquet that Britain would continue to preserve "a strict and rigid neutrality."

August 9, Saturday

BATTLE OF CEDAR MOUNTAIN OR SLAUGHTER MOUNTAIN, VIRGINIA.

The Federal Army of Virginia under John Pope advanced from the general area of Culpeper, Va., south toward Orange Court House and Gordonsville. Stonewall Jackson's large corps was posted south of Culpeper, north of the Rapidan, intending to attack separate Union corps. But Nathaniel Banks got in the first blow at Cedar Mountain, also known as Slaughter Mountain, Cedar Run, Cedar Run Mountain, or Southwest Mountain. Banks' corps of Pope's army drove in sharply and successfully against two of Jackson's divisions until the third, under A. P. Hill, came up to stem the tide and counterattack. Banks pulled back, but the battle, ill fought on both sides, told the Confederates again that Pope was moving south in a major offensive. Furthermore, news reached Richmond that McClellan had been ordered north from his position on the James. Federal casualties were 314 killed, 1445 wounded, and 622 missing for 2381 of the 8000 engaged. The Confederates had about 16,800 men and suffered 1341 casualties.

In Missouri there were skirmishes at Walnut Creek, Sears' Ford on the Chariton River, and at Salem; in Louisiana at Donaldsonville. Recruiting in the North continued at a rapid pace although there were reports of individuals mutilating themselves to avoid the proposed militia draft and others attempting to flee to Canada.

August 10, Sunday

Skirmishing continued at Cedar Run, Va., on a quiet Sunday. The Confederate steamer *General Lee* was captured near Fort Pulaski, Savannah, Ga. Other fighting was at Switzler's Mill and Linn Creek, Mo.; Nueces River near Fort Clark, Tex.; Bayou Sara and Donaldsonville, La. On this day and the eleventh there was a Federal reconnaissance from Brownsville, Tenn., toward the mouth of the Hatchie River.

August 11, Monday

Confederate guerrillas captured Independence, Mo., in a daring raid. Stonewall Jackson's corps withdrew briefly from north of the Rapidan River to the vicinity of Gordonsville, Va. There was more skirmishing in Missouri at Compton's Ferry or Little Compton, Grand River, and Taberville. Other fighting was near Helena, Ark.; Brown's Plantation, Miss.; Velasco, Tex.; and Saulsbury, Kinderhook, and Williamsport, Tenn. Gen. Grant from Corinth, Miss., ordered that fugitive slaves coming into his lines be employed in various departments.

August 12, Tuesday

John Hunt Morgan was active again, capturing Gallatin, Tenn., and a Union garrison. To the west there was skirmishing between Stockton in Cedar County and Humansville, and at Van Buren, Mo.; a Federal expedition from this day to the fourteenth from Fort Leavenworth, Kas., to Independence, Mo.; and between this day and the eighteenth from Camp Gamble, Mo., a Federal expedition went searching for guerrillas. U.S.S. *Arthur* captured the Southern vessel *Breaker* at Aransas Pass, and *Elma* and *Hannah* were burned to avoid capture by Federals off Corpus Christi, Tex.

August 13, Wednesday

Preliminary orders were issued for the movement of the remainder of Lee's Army of Northern Virginia from the Peninsula toward Gordonsville, Va., as what was to become the Second Manassas Campaign got under way. The steamers *George Peabody* and *West Point* collided in the Potomac River, with the loss of seventy-three lives, many of them convalescent soldiers of Burnside's corps.

In Virginia there were reconnaissances and skirmishes toward Orange

Court House. Skirmishes also occurred on Yellow Creek or Muscle Fork, Chariton River, Mo.; at Huntsville and Medon, Tenn.; and on Black River, S.C. On this day and the fourteenth there were skirmishes at Blue Stone, western Va.

August 14, Thursday

President Lincoln received a deputation of free Negroes at the White House to which he said, "But for your race among us there could not be war. . . . It is better for us both, therefore, to be separated." He advocated colonization in Central America and promised them help in carrying out the project.

Two army corps of McClellan's Army of the Potomac, the Third and Fifth, moved from Harrison's Landing, Va., to Aquia Creek, Aug. 14–15. There was a reconnaissance from Newport to Swansborough, N.C.; Aug. 14–17 a Federal expedition from Ozark to Forsyth, Mo.; and Aug. 14–19 Union cavalry covered the rear of the Army of the Potomac from Harrison's Landing to Williamsburg, Va. Skirmishes were at Barry, Mo., and Mount Pleasant, Tenn.

August 15, Friday

There was a skirmish at Clarendon, Ark., and a Federal expedition from Fredericksburg to Port Royal, Va.

August 16, Saturday

The Federal Army of the Potomac under McClellan completed the evacuation of Harrison's Landing as its troops moved north to Aquia Creek and Alexandria, Va., to aid Pope against Lee's Army of Northern Virginia, which advanced from Gordonsville. The Confederate Army of Kentucky under Maj. Gen. Edmund Kirby Smith crossed the Cumberland Mountains into Kentucky, from Tennessee. Aug. 16–22 there were operations about Cumberland Gap, Tenn., including several skirmishes.

Federal troops were defeated in an action near Lone Jack, Mo., but Confederate raiders were driven off by Northern reinforcements. From Aug. 16–25 a Union gunboat expedition on the Mississippi, with some troops, left Helena, Ark., captured a Confederate steamer at Millikin's Bend, and caused other destruction. In western Va. there was a skirmish at Wire Bridge; and others at Meriwether's Ferry, Obion River, Tenn.; and Horn Lake Creek, Miss. Other operations included a Union reconnaissance Aug. 16–17 toward Louisa Court House, Va., and the Aug. 16–18 bombardment of Corpus Christi, Tex., by Federal naval vessels.

August 17, Sunday

SIOUX UPRISING BEGINS.

Maj. Gen. James E. B. Stuart was assigned to command all the cavalry of the Confederate Army of Northern Virginia. There was a reconnaissance toward Forge Bridge, Va.; a skirmish near Mammoth Cave, Ky.; and Aug. 17–27 a Federal expedition from Fort Leavenworth, Kas., to Hickory Grove, Mo.

In southwestern Minnesota on this day the tragic Sioux uprising began and lasted until Sept. 23. The Sioux, allegedly facing semistarvation on their reservations, revolted. After murdering settlers near Acton, Minn., on this day, vicious depredations continued and Federal soldiers were ambushed on the eighteenth at Redwood Ferry. More troops under former Minnesota governor Henry Hastings Sibley moved in and successfully defended New Ulm and Fort Ridgely and defeated the Indians at Wood Lake Sept. 23. More than 1000 Indians were captured and on Dec. 26 38 Sioux were executed at Mankato, Minn. The uprising took possibly 450 to 600 lives; exact figures are unknown.

August 18, Monday

Gen. Pope's Army of Virginia, pressed by Lee's advancing Confederates, pulled back to the north bank of the Rappahannock and awaited reinforcements from McClellan's Army of the Potomac.

The second session of the Confederate Congress met in Richmond. President Davis sent a message reviewing the progress of the war and of the Confederate nation. He said the prospects "give assurance to the friends of constitutional liberty of our final triumph in the pending struggle against despotic usurpation." He inveighed against the alleged atrocities of the Yankees, naming especially Benjamin F. Butler. He called for increasing the army and did not minimize the difficulties facing the Confederacy. "We have never-ceasing cause to be grateful for the favor with which God has protected our infant Confederacy," he concluded.

There were skirmishes and operations at White Oak Ridge, Mo.; Milliken's Bend, La.; Rapidan Station and Clark's Mountain, Va.; Huttonsville, western Va.; in Tennessee at Dyersburg and on the Tennessee River near Waggoner's. Col. R. Mason of the Seventy-first Ohio surrendered the important city of Clarksville, Tenn., to Confederate forces without a fight. Col. Mason was later dismissed from service "for repeated acts of cowardice in the face of the enemy." At Redwood Ferry, Minn., nineteen soldiers of forty-six survived a Sioux ambush. Around Fort Ridgely houses were in flames, victims were mutilated, and the settlers fled to the fort.

August 19, Tuesday

Federal troops carried out an extensive raid on the Louisville and Nashville Railroad Aug. 19–21, with skirmishes at Pilot Knob, Drake's Creek, and Manscoe Creek, near Edgefield Junction, and on the Hartsville Road near Gallatin, Tenn. Another Union expedition operated from Rienzi to Marietta and Bay Springs, Miss., on the same days, and there was a scout Aug. 19–20 from Woodville to Guntersville, Ala. A Federal expedition against the Snake Indians in Idaho lasted from this day to Oct. 11. There was a skirmish on Clear Creek, Ark.

In the valley of the Minnesota the Sioux uprising was in full cry. The Indians moved past Fort Ridgely toward New Ulm, desolating the countryside with murder and arson as they went.

The Federal Department of the Ohio was created, made up of Ohio, Michigan, Indiana, Illinois, Wisconsin, and Kentucky east of the Tennessee River and including Cumberland Gap. Maj. Gen. H. G. Wright was named to the command.

Horace Greeley of the New York *Tribune* in a letter dated the nineteenth and printed in his paper on the twentieth, and labeled "The Prayer of Twenty Millions," questioned the President's policy on slavery. "We complain that the Union cause has suffered . . . from mistaken deference to Rebel slavery. . . . All attempts to put down the Rebellion and at the same time uphold its inciting cause are preposterous and futile."

August 20, Wednesday

The Federal Army of the Potomac under McClellan was still on the move from the Peninsula toward Aquia Creek and Alexandria, Va., in support of Pope's threatened Army of Virginia. Along the Rappahannock Pope's men skirmished with the advancing forces of Lee at Raccoon Ford, Stevensburg, Brandy Station, Rappahannock Station, and near Kelly's Ford. There was action at Baton Rouge, La., and Pilot Knob and Edgefield, Tenn. The Sioux uprising continued in Minnesota with Indians unsuccessfully attacking Fort Ridgely. In Missouri Aug. 20–27 there was a Union scout in Wayne, Stoddard, and Dunklin counties. The Confederate Department of the Trans-Mississippi was set up to include Missouri, Arkansas, the Indian Territory, Louisiana west of the Mississippi, and Texas. Maj. Gen. Richard Taylor, C.S.A., was assigned to command of the District of West Louisiana.

August 21, Thursday

Events moved toward another climax in Virginia as McClellan's army continued to proceed north toward Washington and Pope's men skirmished with Lee's along the Rappahannock again, at Kelly's, Beverly, and Freeman's fords. Federal troops evacuated Baton Rouge, La.; there was an affair on Pinckney Island, S.C.; and a skirmish at Neosho, Mo. In the North the issuing of postage stamps for small currency began. In Tennessee Braxton Bragg crossed the Tennessee River above Chattanooga preparatory to the start of a new campaign. President Davis proclaimed that Federal Maj. Gen. David Hunter and Brig. Gen. John W. Phelps should be treated as outlaws and if captured should be held as felons because they were organizing slaves for the Union Army.

Phelps himself this day resigned from the Union Army because Washington disavowed his policy.

August 22, Friday

President Lincoln replied to Horace Greeley's "The Prayer of Twenty Millions," by writing the New York editor, ". . . I would save the Union. I would save it the shortest way under the Constitution. The sooner the national authority can be restored; the nearer the Union will be 'the Union as it was.' . . . If I could save the Union without freeing *any* slave I would do it, and if I could save it by freeing *all* the slaves I would do it; and if I could save it by freeing some and leaving others alone I would also do that. . . ."

Skirmishing between Lee's and Pope's armies continued along the Rappahannock and there was a raid on Catlett's Station, wherein Jeb Stuart captured Pope's baggage train, papers and all. There was a skirmish at Trinity, Ala., and more fighting at Fort Ridgely, Minn., in the Indian uprising, where the Sioux were repulsed again. There was a lengthy expedition into western Virginia and Ohio by Confederates, ending Sept. 19. Meanwhile, McClellan's army continued to pour into Aquia Creek and Alexandria, Va. Gen. Butler in New Orleans authorized enlisting free Negroes as Federal soldiers.

August 23, Saturday

Extensive small fighting increased along the entire war front. In Missouri it occurred at Four Mile, Hickory Grove, and near Wayman's Mill or Spring Creek; in Louisiana at Bayou Sara; in Kentucky at Big Hill; in Mississippi at Greenville; in Alabama at Trinity; in Tennessee near Fort Donelson; in western Virginia at Moorefield; and in Virginia at Rappahannock Station, Beverly Ford, Fant's Ford, Smithfield, Sulphur or Warrenton Springs. A train was captured between Harper's Ferry and Winchester by Confederates. Federal Maj. Gen. Horatio G. Wright assumed command of the Department of the Ohio. U.S. sloop of war *Adirondack* was wrecked on a coral reef near Little Abaco, West Indies, but the crew was saved.

August 24, Sunday

c.s.s. *Alabama* COMMISSIONED.

Near the Azores in the Atlantic, C.S.S. *Alabama* was commissioned as a cruiser of the Confederate Navy and received its armament and supplies. In Missouri skirmishing continued on Coon Creek near Lamar, on Crooked Creek near Dallas, and there was also action near Bloomfield. There was a Federal scout which continued until the twenty-eighth from Salem to Current River, Mo. In Virginia there were actions on this day and the twenty-fifth at Waterloo Bridge.

August 25, Monday

Sec. of War Edwin M. Stanton authorized the commander of the Southern Department to "receive into the service of the United States" Negro soldiers up to five thousand in number and to train them as guards for plantations and settlements.

In Kentucky skirmishes were at Red Bird Creek and Madisonville; in Tennessee at Fort Donelson; and in Mississippi at Bolivar. Fighting in Virginia was at Sulphur Springs. After two days of fighting the Sioux Indians were driven off and the garrison and civilian population of New Ulm, Minn., evacuated the town, fearing further attack.

Stonewall Jackson was on the march again, heading north from below the Rappahannock, followed by Longstreet's corps. Lee's offensive had begun in earnest.

August 26, Tuesday

SECOND BULL RUN OR MANASSAS CAMPAIGN BEGINS.

The Second Manassas Campaign might be said to have opened this day. Confederate cavalry under Fitzhugh Lee entered Manassas Junction and captured the rail point. Jackson's troops hurried their march, begun Aug. 25, from below the Rappahannock to the area of the Battle of First Bull Run or Manassas of a year before. There were skirmishes at Bristoe Station, Bull Run Bridge, Gainesville, Haymarket, Manassas Junction, and Sulphur Springs. By evening Jackson's main force, which had pushed through Thoroughfare Gap in the Bull Run mountains, was at Bristoe Station. At Manassas the Confederates captured a few hundred prisoners and large amounts of quartermaster and commissary supplies. Meanwhile, Pope's Federal Army of Virginia rested, not comprehending Jackson's movement. McClellan's Federal Second Army Corps of the Army of the Potomac left Fort Monroe for the north, continuing evacuation of the James position. There was skirmishing at Cumberland Iron Works and Cumberland Gap, Tenn., and near Rienzi, Miss.

August 27, Wednesday

JACKSON AT MANASSAS JUNCTION.

In the morning Pope abandoned his now outflanked Federal lines on the Rappahannock and sent troops north toward Manassas and other points. For Pope, a time of confusion had begun. Most of Jackson's force was now destroying stores and facilities at Manassas. Lee, with Longstreet's corps, which had also left the Rappahannock, was marching to support Jackson. Federals attempted to halt Confederate operations in various skirmishes but were badly outnumbered. There was action at Bull Run Bridge, Kettle Run near Bristoe Station, Buckland Bridge or Broad Run, Salem, and Waterford. Lincoln, cut off the day before from communication with

Pope, wired Gen. Burnside at Falmouth for news of Pope. Nearly half of the Confederate army was now between Pope and Washington, where strong forces under McClellan were disembarking and regrouping after coming north from the James. Other portions of McClellan's army which had landed at Aquia Creek were moving to aid Pope.

In Alabama there was a skirmish at Bridgeport on the Tennessee River. In Tennessee fighting was at Fort McCook or Battle Creek, Reynolds' Station, Richland Creek near Pulaski, near Murfreesboro, at Round Mountain near Woodbury, and near Cumberland Gap. In Mississippi there was a skirmish near Kossuth. Most of the fighting in Tennessee was the result of the Confederate Army under Gen. Braxton Bragg undertaking preliminary dispositions for what was to be his fall invasion of Tennessee and Kentucky. E. Kirby Smith, cooperating with Bragg, had moved from northeastern Tennessee toward central Kentucky.

August 28, Thursday

GROVETON OR BRAWNER'S FARM, VIRGINIA.

BRAGG BEGINS CONFEDERATE CAMPAIGN INTO TENNESSEE AND KENTUCKY.

On the night of Aug. 27–28 Stonewall Jackson did not wait to be attacked at Manassas but withdrew, taking position along the Warrenton Turnpike west of the old Bull Run battlefield. John Pope and some of his Federals, hurrying north from the Rappahannock, reached Manassas about noon to find Jackson gone. Receiving conflicting reports as to the Confederates' whereabouts, Pope finally ordered his scattered troops to concentrate on Centreville, erroneously thinking the enemy to be there. The division of Rufus King moved along the Warrenton Turnpike and late in the afternoon was fired on by Jackson near Groveton or Brawner's Farm. The fierce fight resulted in heavy casualties. Pope now believed Jackson was retreating and gave orders to reconcentrate his forces against the Confederate corps. In midafternoon, Lee and Longstreet arrived at Thoroughfare Gap, to the west of Jackson, and after a brief engagement bypassed the enemy. There were also skirmishes at Centreville, Lewis' Ford, and Haymarket. The board was being set for a major battle on the morrow.

From just north of Chattanooga Gen. Braxton Bragg led his Confederate Army of Tennessee (though not yet officially given that name) northward into central Tennessee over Walden's Ridge. Bragg intended to recover eastern Tennessee and Kentucky as well as draw back Buell's threat to Chattanooga.

In Minnesota H. H. Sibley and his men relieved Fort Ridgely in their efforts to put down the Sioux uprising. In Missouri there was skirmishing at Ashley and in Howard County. Another skirmish occurred near Corinth, Miss.; and from this day to Sept. 3 there was a Federal expedition from Helena to Eunice, Ark. Notorious Confederate spy

Belle Boyd was released from Old Capitol Prison in Washington for lack of evidence.

August 29, Friday

SECOND BATTLE OF MANASSAS OR BULL RUN, VIRGINIA.

A portion of Pope's command attacked Jackson's Confederates near Groveton, Va., in order to prevent their escape, though of course the Confederates had no desire to escape. Pope's Federals were dispersed over northern Virginia and worn from constant marching. He attempted to concentrate his army against Jackson, posted in a railroad cut near Sudley Springs north of Groveton and the Warrenton Turnpike. The drive against Jackson was piecemeal and failed, but Second Bull Run or Manassas had begun. Maj. Gen. Fitz John Porter was ordered to strike Jackson, but failed to do so. Later Pope and others accused him of disobeying orders and of dragging his feet. Porter said it was because Longstreet had come up and outnumbered him. The argument has not been stilled to this day. Longstreet did come up around noon. Pope handled his army badly, and at nightfall the Confederates of Lee were strongly posted on their original line of battle. Meanwhile, Halleck, in Washington, urged McClellan to send the bulk of his forces from Alexandria. McClellan claimed he did all possible to comply, but many felt that his opposition to Pope was such that his effort was at best only halfhearted. This day's action, that of the following day, and the entire campaign of Second Manassas were to bring discredit to many Federal leaders, including Halleck, McClellan, Pope, Porter, and McDowell. On the Confederate side it was one of Jackson's brightest hours and one of Lee's greatest achievements. In Washington, three times this day, Mr. Lincoln telegraphed his generals, "What news?"

Forgotten out in Missouri were skirmishes at Bloomfield and Iberia; another near St. Charles Court House, La.; as well as an engagement between the Confederate batteries at Port Hudson, La., and U.S.S. *Anglo-American*. In Confederate command changes Beauregard was assigned to the Department of South Carolina and Georgia, relieving John C. Pemberton. For the North, Brig. Gen. Frederick Steele assumed command of the Army of the Southwest.

In Kentucky Confederate E. Kirby Smith invaded and his advance units fought with a Federal brigade south of Richmond in the afternoon. The Confederates were driven back briefly and the Federals took a position defending Richmond.

August 30, Saturday

SECOND BATTLE OF MANASSAS OR BULL RUN, VIRGINIA, CONCLUDED.
BATTLE OF RICHMOND, KENTUCKY.

Federal Gen. Pope, believing the Confederates had retreated, attacked

Jackson's corps on the Southern left, but Longstreet on the right pushed ahead, taking Bald Hill and attacking Henry House Hill, scene of bitter fighting in '61. Jackson repulsed Porter's attack and then drove back the Federal line. At nightfall the primary action of the Battle of Second Manassas or Bull Run was over, with the whipped Federals stubbornly holding Henry House Hill and lines of retreat to Centreville. Pope's army was beaten but not routed. Lee's army was victorious but had failed to destroy Pope. In Alexandria McClellan's feeble efforts to send support to Pope had also failed. There was nothing left for Pope but withdrawal and humiliation. Immediately the charges and countercharges began. For the South Lee had relieved Richmond and taken the offensive.

For the entire campaign Aug. 27–Sept. 2, Federals lost 1724 killed, 8372 wounded, 5958 missing for a total of 16,054 casualties. Total engaged is put at 75,000. The Confederates lost 1481 killed, 7627 wounded, and 89 missing for a total of 9197 casualties of 48,500 engaged. Once more Confederate armies stood near Washington and the victories in the West did not look so bright.

In Kentucky, south of Lexington and below the small city of Richmond, Confederate Gen. E. Kirby Smith decided to attack. After attack and counterattack, the Federal right and left began to give way. Federals, unable to disengage, withdrew in considerable confusion, formed a new defense line, were driven from that, and retreated toward Louisville. William "Bull" Nelson arrived to command Federals late in the battle. The figures: 206 Federals were killed and 844 wounded. Captured or missing are put officially at 4144 for total losses of 5194, which is probably high considering the 6500 engaged. For the Confederates, of 6800 engaged, 78 were killed, 372 wounded, and 1 missing for a total of 451. The invasion of Kentucky was well under way with a small but impressive Confederate victory. Skirmishes this day were near Plymouth, N.C.; Altamont, Tenn.; and near Marietta, Miss. In Washington President Lincoln anxiously awaited news from both Virginia and Kentucky.

August 31, Sunday

Gen. Pope gathered his defeated Army of Virginia on the Washington side of Bull Run at the heights of Centreville. Finally two fresh Federal corps of the Army of the Potomac reported to Pope, but too late to retrieve the victory. Stuart's cavalry reviewed the Federal scene and reported to Lee, who planned to turn the Union right. In the afternoon Jackson moved to just west of Chantilly with Longstreet following the next day. There was small skirmishing at various points of the lines.

Fighting also occurred at Little River Bridge, Mo.; Stevenson, Ala.; on the Kentucky River, Ky.; at Rogers' Gap, Tenn.; and Franklin, Va.

Fredericksburg, Va., was evacuated by the Federals with considerable loss of supplies. On the Tennessee River Federal transport *W. B. Terry*, with a few troops, passengers, and a load of coal, grounded on the Duck River Sucks and was attacked by Confederates. After a brief defense the vessel was forced to surrender. Thus the month came to an end with victories for the South and defeats for the North. In the North there was consternation and alarm and preparations for receiving the wounded they knew would come, particularly from Virginia. The Surgeon General of the Army called for women and children to scrape lint for bandages.

SEPTEMBER, 1862

Although Mr. Lincoln was anxious for news, the results of recent action were not clearly discernible. Both the President and the public wondered what was really happening in northern Virginia. How close to Washington was R. E. Lee? If Pope's Army of Virginia had been beaten, how disastrous was it? In Richmond there was some feeling of relief, for McClellan was gone from the Peninsula and Lee was on the move. But many asked whether the Army of Northern Virginia could carry the war north of the Potomac. The Northern threat to Vicksburg appeared far less ominous now that the Yankee gunboats had moved north to Helena and south to Baton Rouge. But *Arkansas* had been lost. How long the Confederates could continue to defend the Mississippi with such limited river power was a matter for speculation.

While Grant still threatened northern Mississippi and Alabama, and Federals occupied New Orleans, Braxton Bragg and E. Kirby Smith were moving into Tennessee and Kentucky with Smith actually not far from Lexington, Ky. This would undoubtedly bring Buell's Federal command back from northern Alabama. Anxiety began to rise at Louisville among pro-unionists and hope reappeared among others who would welcome the return of the Confederates to the mid-South. In Iowa, Wisconsin, and Minnesota, especially, lurid reports of the Sioux uprising in Minnesota brought fear that the trouble would spread into a general Indian revolt. Overall there did appear to be less pressure at the moment on the Confederacy, although probably few believed the tide had fully changed. At the North the word "Copperhead," popular or unpopular depending upon how one looked at peace advocates, indicated a simmering anti-war feeling in some circles. On the other hand, the cries of the abolitionists increasingly called for action against slavery.

September 1, Monday

CHANTILLY OR OX HILL, VIRGINIA

The last scene of fighting in the Second Battle of Bull Run or Manassas was at Chantilly or Ox Hill, Va. Lee, maintaining his offensive, sent Jackson's corps north around the Union right. He was met by Federals under I. I. Stevens and Philip Kearny. After severe fighting in heavy rain that lasted until evening, the Federals withdrew. Stevens and Kearny, two of the most promising Union officers, were killed. The death of the beloved and admired Kearny particularly was mourned both North and South. Pope's troops had held off the Confederate advance and during the night withdrew closer to Washington from Centreville, Germantown, and Fairfax Court House. Lee kept the pressure on the distraught Federals, but Washington itself was well protected.

There was skirmishing at Putnam, Neosho, and Spring River, Mo. Maj. Gen. Ormsby M. Mitchel, famed astronomer and lecturer who had fought well in Tennessee, was assigned to command the Union Department of the South. For the Confederates Maj. Gen. J. P. McCown assumed command of the Department of East Tennessee. Excitement in the North continued to rise; in the east over Second Bull Run, and in the west, particularly at Louisville and Cincinnati, over the nearness of Kirby Smith and his Confederates. The Federal Navy stopped the "spirit ration" of the sailors.

President Davis was having difficulty with South Carolina authorities over the enforcement of conscription. President Lincoln, McClellan, and Halleck conferred about the military situation in Virginia.

September 2, Tuesday

MCCLELLAN RESTORED TO FULL COMMAND IN VIRGINIA.

Pope ordered his beaten but not routed Federal Army of Virginia to pull back into the Washington area entrenchments. There were skirmishes near Fairfax Court House, Falls Church, Vienna, Flint Hill, and Leesburg. Mr. Lincoln restored McClellan to full command in Virginia and around Washington, a move opposed by Secretaries Stanton and Chase. Lincoln had doubts about McClellan, but suppressed them. Pope was left without a command. The victorious Confederates gathered their forces near Chantilly for new adventures. Union forces evacuated Winchester in the Shenandoah Valley.

In Minnesota Sioux Indians besieged a Federal detachment at Birch Coulee. H. H. Sibley's men relieved the siege Sept. 3. There was a skirmish near Nashville, Tenn., and Confederates under E. Kirby Smith occupied Lexington, Ky. Bragg's army continued to march north from Chattanooga. There was a skirmish near Memphis, Tenn., and a Federal expedition from Suffolk, Va., Sept. 2–3. Federal Flag Officer Louis M. Goldsborough was relieved of command of the North Atlantic Blockading Squadron.

About this time Mr. Lincoln penned a "Meditation on the Divine Will," in which he stated, "In great contests each party claims to act in accordance with the will of God. Both *may* be, but one *must* be wrong. God can not be *for,* and *against* the same thing at the same time." Business was suspended and citizens began drilling in Cincinnati, O., Covington and Newport, Ky., after learning that Confederate forces were nearby. Martial law was declared.

September 3, Wednesday

Lee's Army of Northern Virginia, realizing the futility of attacking Washington, edged toward Leesburg and the crossings of the Potomac. Confederates occupied Winchester and there were skirmishes at Falls Church, Bunker Hill, Edwards' Ferry, and other points in northern Virginia. There were operations around Harper's Ferry, Ravenswood, Weston, Charles Town, and Martinsburg, western Virginia, and Lovettsville, Va.

Gen. Pope conferred with President Lincoln, and then delivered a written report to Halleck charging Gen. Porter with disobeying orders and McClellan with failing to support him. Second Manassas or Bull Run was to be refought many times in words.

In Dakota Territory there was action with the Indians at Fort Abercrombie. Joseph Holt of Kentucky was appointed Judge Advocate General of the United States. A skirmish occurred at Geiger's Lake, Ky. In the North Lee's operations in Virginia kept the citizens in suspense, while Kentucky was aroused over E. Kirby Smith's invasion. Troops of Smith's command had occupied the state capital of Frankfort.

September 4, Thursday

Lee's army began its principal crossings of the Potomac by fords in the Leesburg area, an operation which continued until the seventh. The Confederates were on their way to Maryland. There was skirmishing at Point of Rocks, Berlin, Poolesville, Monocacy Aqueduct, Md. McClellan was reorganizing the Army of the Potomac amid Cabinet discussions in Washington. Federals were evacuating Frederick, Md.

In Minnesota skirmishing with the Indians continued at Hutchinson. There were actions in Callaway County and at Prairie Chapel, Mo.; Shelbyville, Ky.; Boutte Station and Bayou des Allemands, La. John Hunt Morgan and his men joined E. Kirby Smith at Lexington, Ky. Confederate Brig. Gen. A. G. Jenkins culminated his raiding in western Virginia by crossing the Ohio River in the Point Pleasant area for a brief excursion into the North.

September 5, Friday

In response to a query from Federal Gen. John Pope about his command, General-in-Chief Halleck replied that the Army of Virginia was being consolidated with the Army of the Potomac under McClellan and that Pope should report for orders. The orders soon came, assigning Pope to a secondary post as head of the Department of the Northwest, where the Sioux depredations were continuing. His uneven career in the main war sector was largely at an end; he remained a partially broken man, though loudly articulate. McClellan, back in full power, gathered together the forces around Washington. Lee continued his move toward Frederick, Md., news of which was unsettling to the entire east.

In the West Sept. 5–10 there was a Union expedition from Fort Donelson to Clarksville, Tenn., with several skirmishes. Other action included a skirmish at Neosho, Mo.; near Madisonville, Ky.; Burnt Bridge, near Humboldt, Tenn.; and a scout toward Holly Springs, Miss., Sept. 5–6. Gov. Morton of Indiana called upon citizens to form military companies in areas along the Ohio River, believed to be threatened by E. Kirby Smith and Braxton Bragg. At Sparta, Tenn., Bragg proclaimed that Alabama "is redeemed. Tennesseans! your capital and State are almost restored without firing a gun. You return conquerors. Kentuckians! the first great blow has been struck for your freedom." Meanwhile, Buell had already pulled out of northern Alabama, withdrawing to Murfreesboro, southeast of Nashville.

September 6, Saturday

Stonewall Jackson's men occupied Frederick, Md., as the Confederate Army of Northern Virginia established their base of operations north of the Potomac. Federal cavalry kept in contact with the enemy in Maryland; fighting occurred every day from the sixth to the fifteenth. The Confederates had expected to pick up recruits in Maryland, but as they entered Frederick, all stores were shut, no flags flew, and an observer wrote, "everything partook of a churchyard appearance." The Southerners treated Frederick courteously as a rule, with little or no pillaging or looting.

Back in Virginia the Union evacuated Aquia Creek, near Fredericksburg, leaving much property destroyed at the important rail and port facility. John Pope formally was assigned to the Department of the Northwest, newly created out of Wisconsin, Iowa, Minnesota, and Nebraska and Dakota territories. His main job was to cope with the Sioux uprising. On this day the Indians unsuccessfully assailed Fort Abercrombie, Dakota Terr., for the second time. Other fighting was near Roanoke, Mo.; Washington, N.C.; on the Gallatin Road, Tenn.; and there were operations in the Kanawha Valley of western Virginia.

September 7, Sunday

The Federal Army of the Potomac under Gen. McClellan moved slowly northward from Washington, protecting the capital and Baltimore, not knowing the enemy's whereabouts or plans. Much of the Confederate Army of Northern Virginia was concentrating now at Frederick, Md. Union garrisons at Harper's Ferry and Martinsburg were virtually cut off from Washington. Harrisburg, Pa., Hagerstown, Md., Baltimore, and other cities were scenes of "tremendous excitement." Streets were thronged, rumors rampant, citizens armed; some fled the reported coming of Southern troops. President Lincoln, concerned over two fronts, east and west, asked "Where is Gen. Bragg?" and "What about Harper's Ferry?"

Bragg in Tennessee moved steadily north toward Kentucky, bypassing the main Federal force under Buell at Murfreesboro and Nashville. Skirmishing occurred at Murfreesboro and Pine Mountain Gap, Tenn., and Shepherdsville, Ky. Clarksville, Tenn., was retaken by Federal forces after its ignominious fall. On the Mississippi U.S.S. *Essex* dueled the Port Hudson batteries. Other action was at Lancaster, Mo., and St. Charles Court House, La.

President Davis wrote his advancing generals, Lee, Bragg, and E. Kirby Smith, that they should make clear to the people "That the Confederate Government is waging this war solely for self-defence, that it has no design of conquest or any other purpose than to secure peace and the abandonment by the United States of its pretensions to govern a people who have never been their subjects and who prefer self-government to a Union with them."

September 8, Monday

Apprehension became more intense in Maryland and Pennsylvania under the threat of Lee's invasion. To the inhabitants of Maryland Lee proclaimed, "The people of the Confederate States have long watched with the deepest sympathy the wrongs and outrages that have been inflicted upon the citizens. . . . We know no enemies among you, and will protect all, of every opinion. It is for you to decide your destiny freely and without constraint. This army will respect your choice, whatever it may be." In Washington President Lincoln asked McClellan at Rockville, Md., "How does it look now?"

There was fighting at Poolesville, Md., and elsewhere on the fringes of the two armies in Virginia. Maj. Gen. N. P. Banks assumed command of the defenses of Washington, and the West India Squadron under Commodore Charles Wilkes was formed for protection of commerce. In Kentucky there was a skirmish at Barboursville and an affair known as Kentucky Line. In Tennessee a skirmish occurred at Pine Mountain. From this day to the thirteenth there was a Union expedition to the Coldwater

River and Hernando, Miss.; and Sept. 8–13 from Fort Leavenworth, Kas., through Jackson, Cass, Johnson, and La Fayette counties, Mo.

September 9, Tuesday

At Frederick, Md., Gen. Lee issued field orders for future operations. Special Orders No. 191 called for Jackson to march on Harper's Ferry; other troops were to be sent to Crampton's Gap. Much of Longstreet's corps was to go to Boonsborough, Md., and a rear guard was provided for as well. There were skirmishes at Monocacy Church and Barnesville, Md. On the Peninsula a small-scale Confederate attack failed at Williamsburg.

Federal Maj. Gen. Samuel P. Heintzelman was put in command of the defenses of Washington south of the Potomac. Other action was at Big Creek, Mo.; on the Franklin and Scottsville roads, Ky.; Columbia, Tenn.; and Cockrum Cross Roads and Rienzi, Miss.

September 10, Wednesday

Cavalry reports informed McClellan that Lee had fallen back across the Monocacy away from Frederick, and he speeded up his hitherto extremely cautious pursuit of the Confederates. There were skirmishes near Boonsborough, Frederick, and Sugarloaf Mountain, Md.

Other action included an engagement at Fayetteville, western Va., a Federal defeat; on the Kilkenny River, S.C.; Rogers' and Big Creek gaps and Columbia, Tenn.; Fort Mitchel near Covington, Woodburn, and Log Church, Ky.

Tension rode high in Maryland, Pennsylvania, and along the Ohio. A thousand "squirrel hunters" from the Ohio Valley volunteered their services in Cincinnati as home guards. No one was quite sure how far the Confederate invasions east or west would go.

September 11, Thursday

Confederate forces entered Hagerstown, Md., and the turmoil at the North increased. There were more skirmishes between the two armies as the Federals moved north from Washington. Gov. Andrew G. Curtin of Pennsylvania called for fifty thousand men. Militia were gathering.

Other action was from Clarendon to Lawrenceville and St. Charles, Ark.; at St. John's Bluff, Fla.; Bloomfield, Mo.; Smith's, Ky.; and in western Virginia's Kanawha Valley at Gauley. Maysville, Ky., was occupied by forces under E. Kirby Smith. Confederate units pushed to within about seven miles of Cincinnati with considerable skirmishing.

September 12, Friday

The Army of the Potomac, marching northward, groping for the Confederate army, began to move into Frederick, Md., as the Confederates were dispersing to their assigned tasks. Jackson was converging on Harper's

Ferry. There was skirmishing at Frederick, Md., and at Hurricane Bridge, western Va. Near Leesburg in Loudoun County, Va., there was scattered fighting Sept. 12–17.

In Kentucky Confederates occupied Glasgow and there was skirmishing at Brandenburg and near Woodburn. A mild fight broke out at Coldwater Railroad Bridge, Miss.

The First, Second, and Third Corps of the Army of Virginia were designated the Eleventh, Twelfth, and First Army Corps of the Army of the Potomac. The Federal Army of Virginia was no more.

In the North the archives, bonds, and treasure of the state of Pennsylvania at Harrisburg and Philadelphia were sent to New York. The mayor of Philadelphia was given full power to defend the city. The Confederate Congress debated the propriety of the invasion of the North. A worried Mr. Lincoln wired McClellan, "How does it look now?" and was told by the general that he was concerned that Lee would recross the Potomac before he could get to him. Turning to the threat in Kentucky, Lincoln asked military authorities in Louisville, "Where is the enemy which you dread in Louisville? How near to you?" E. Kirby Smith's main body was less than fifty miles away, while Bragg's command was about a hundred miles to the south. President Jefferson Davis wrote to the governors of Texas, Missouri, Louisiana, and Arkansas, attempting to reassure them that he was not neglecting the Trans-Mississippi area.

September 13, Saturday
"LOST ORDER" FOUND BY FEDERALS.

In the morning at Frederick, Md., two lounging Union soldiers picked up a paper wrapped around a few cigars. It was a lost copy of Lee's orders for the Maryland campaign. The "Lost Order of Antietam" was rushed to McClellan and he began to move accordingly and a little more rapidly, though not entirely trusting his fortuitous intelligence. How the order was lost has never been fully explained. By evening McClellan was pushing west toward the mountains beyond Frederick. Lee had Stuart and his cavalry at South Mountain and other troops nearby. Longstreet was near Hagerstown, Jackson near Harper's Ferry. That night Stuart learned of the lost order and informed Lee that it was in McClellan's possession. Battle was looming. Already there had been skirmishes at Catoctin Mountain, Middletown, Jefferson, and South Mountain.

Down in western Virginia Federals evacuated Charleston, after some fighting, in the face of the Confederate offensive under W. W. Loring in the Kanawha Valley. In Missouri skirmishing broke out anew at Newtonia, at Bragg's Farm near Whaley's Mill, and at Strother Fork of Black River in Iron County. Other fighting was at Iuka, Miss.; and there were operations at Flour Bluffs, Tex.; and a Union expedition to Pass Manchac and Ponchatoula, La.

In New Orleans Gen. Butler ordered all foreigners to register with his occupation authorities.

September 14, Sunday

BATTLE OF SOUTH MOUNTAIN.

BATTLE OF CRAMPTON'S GAP.

The left wing of McClellan's army under Maj. Gen. William B. Franklin moved toward Crampton's Gap in an effort to relieve the Harper's Ferry garrison and to cut off Confederates advancing on that stronghold. Franklin carried the pass against Lafayette McLaws, but, believing he was outnumbered, Franklin entrenched and did not push on from Pleasant Valley toward Harper's Ferry. At South Mountain, at Fox's and Turner's gaps, Federal cavalry under Pleasonton fought with D. H. Hill's Confederates until the two Federal corps of Reno and Hooker of the right wing under Burnside came up. After severe battling the Confederates withdrew late in the evening, both flanks enveloped. Federal Maj. Gen. Jesse L. Reno was killed. Federal casualties for the day are put at 443 killed, 1807 wounded, and 75 missing, a total of 2325 of more than 28,000. An estimated 325 Confederates were killed, 1560 wounded, 800 missing for a total of 2685 of about 18,000 engaged, but casualties may have been higher. These battles are known as South Mountain, Boonsborough, Boonsborough Gap, Turner's Gap, and Crampton's Gap or Crampton's Pass. There also was a skirmish near Petersville, Md. Meanwhile, Jackson and McLaws besieged the Federal garrison at Harper's Ferry.

In the West Bragg's Confederate forces moved on Munfordville, Ky., and advance units were repulsed. There was fighting at Henderson, Ky., as Federal Gen. Don Carlos Buell, marching rapidly north from Tennessee to head off Bragg, reached Bowling Green, Ky. To the south in Mississippi the third prong of the Confederate offensive was in operation, with Sterling Price occupying Iuka, Miss., near Corinth.

September 15, Monday

CONFEDERATES CAPTURE HARPER'S FERRY.

Harper's Ferry fell to Stonewall Jackson's command after short resistance. The Confederates captured about twelve thousand prisoners. The Federal defense, led by Dixon S. Miles, who was mortally wounded, was generally considered inadequate and there was great argument over whether the strategic point should have been held at all. Confederates at South Mountain, faced by McClellan's army, fell back to Sharpsburg, Md. Lee was concentrating his scattered force at the small village preparatory to withdrawing across the Potomac. But hearing Harper's Ferry had fallen, he reversed his plan and established a line to the west of Antietam Creek. Lafayette McLaws withdrew his division from Maryland Heights, crossed the Potomac, and joined Jackson at Harper's Ferry. Meanwhile, the

Union Army of the Potomac pushed through South Mountain Passes to Keedysville, with a small skirmish ensuing, and another at Boonsborough.

In the West E. Kirby Smith appeared before Covington, Ky., on the Ohio across from Cincinnati, but retired rapidly. Bragg was besieging Munfordville, Ky., to the south. Sept. 15–20 there was a Union scout in Ralls County, Mo.

September 16, Tuesday

Along the quiet Antietam Creek Lee gathered his forces and formed his lines. A hard night march had brought Jackson from Harper's Ferry and McLaws was on his way. A division under A. P. Hill remained at the Ferry to complete surrender arrangements. Union forces moved cautiously forward from Keedysville; there was some desultory firing, but no major attack by McClellan and his Army of the Potomac. Many said later that a great opportunity was lost by the Federals. Down in Virginia there was a Federal reconnaissance toward Thoroughfare Gap and Aldie, and from this day to the nineteenth a Union reconnaissance from Upton's Hill to Leesburg.

In Kentucky some four thousand Federals were surrounded at Munfordville by Bragg. There was skirmishing near Oakland Station, Ky.; another fight in Monroe County, Mo.; and there were minor operations around Iuka, Miss. Kirby Smith's Confederates continued their withdrawal from the Ohio River near Cincinnati back toward Lexington.

The still-worried President Lincoln wired Gov. Andrew Curtin of Pennsylvania, "What do you hear from Gen. McClellan's army?" Later in the day he heard from his general.

September 17, Wednesday

BATTLE OF ANTIETAM OR SHARPSBURG.

MUNFORDVILLE, KENTUCKY, SURRENDERS.

This September day along Antietam Creek was one of the bloodiest of the Civil War. Badly outnumbered, Lee made his stand in Maryland and McClellan attacked, throwing in his corps piecemeal and failing to use his very strong reserve. At first the fight raged on the Confederate left against Jackson in the woods, the cornfield, the Bloody Lane, and the Dunkard Church. Federal gains were small and costly. The roar of battle moved south, with uncoordinated Northern attacks on the center. Then Burnside with the Federal left finally drove in against the Confederate right at what became known as Burnside Bridge, crossed the Antietam, and headed for the town. At the critical moment A. P. Hill's "Light Division" arrived at Antietam after a hurried march from Harper's Ferry and the Federal advance was halted. Thus ended a savage day of five main Federal drives with dreadful losses. Federal casualties were put at 2010 killed, 9416 wounded, and 1043 missing for a total of 12,469 out of over 75,000 estimated effectives. Confederate casualties were estimated at 2700 killed, 9024 wounded, and about 2000 missing for a total of 13,724 out of around 40,000 engaged, although the exact figures are uncertain. Nightfall found the Confederate army holding its position in the face of an overpowering enemy.

A Pennsylvania soldier walked over the battlefield after the battle. "No tongue can tell, no mind conceive, no pen portray the horrible sights I witnessed this morning. God grant these things may soon end and peace be restored. Of this war I am heartily sick and tired." A Wisconsin man called the fearful battle "a great tumbling together of all heaven and earth."

The Federal garrison of slightly over four thousand men under Col. John T. Wilder at Munfordville, Ky., surrendered to Bragg's Confederates. Also in Kentucky there was skirmishing near Falmouth and on Bowling Green Road and at Merry Oaks. There was an engagement at St. John's Bluff, Fla., and operations around Shiloh, N.C.

Maj. Gen. Ormsby M. Mitchel, U. S. Army, assumed command of the Department of the South stationed along the southeast coast.

Pro-unionists in the Tennessee mountains suffered a setback when Brig. Gen. George W. Morgan was forced to evacuate Cumberland Gap due to Confederate invasion of Kentucky.

September 18, Thursday

Confederate officers advised Lee to withdraw across the Potomac on the night of the seventeenth but he remained at Sharpsburg, finally pulling out of Maryland the night of Sept. 18–19 at Boteler's or Blackford's Ford. McClellan, despite arrival of 12,000 men plus some 24,000 others who had seen little or no action, allowed the day to pass without attack. Even with his greatly superior numbers, McClellan feared the consequences of defeat. Lee's Maryland Campaign was over, but the aftermaths were many.

Elsewhere across the active battle fronts, there was fighting at Glasgow, Florence, Owensborough, and Cave City, Ky.; a skirmish at Rienzi, Miss.; and operations about Forts Henry and Donelson, Tenn., which continued until the twenty-third. In a Federal command change Brig. Gen. James H. Carleton took over for Brig. Gen. E. R. S. Canby in command of the Department of New Mexico.

Out in the Atlantic the Confederate cruiser *Alabama* was marauding—capturing and burning the New Bedford, Mass., whaler *Elisha Dunbar*. At Glasgow, Ky., Bragg proclaimed that his Confederate army had come to Kentucky to free the people from tyranny and not as conquerors and despoilers.

September 19, Friday

BATTLE OF IUKA, MISSISSIPPI.

The scene of action swung quickly southwestward from Maryland to Mississippi, where Confederates had been attempting to prevent the Federals under Grant from reinforcing Buell, who was opposing Bragg in Kentucky. Sterling Price had moved his Southern force to Iuka Sept. 14 from Tupelo, Miss., and was awaiting the arrival of Earl Van Dorn's men. Grant, with William S. Rosecrans leading the main advance, drove at Iuka from Corinth. Rosecrans, after a hard fight, bested Price, who, knowing that Grant with a column under E. O. C. Ord was nearby, pulled out southward during the night. Federal casualties were 141 killed, 613 wounded, and 36 missing for a total of 790 out of about 17,000 in the area; Confederates lost 263 killed, 692 wounded, 561 captured for 1516 out of a total of 14,000. However, indications are that about 4500 Federals opposed about 3200 Confederates in the actual fighting. Elsewhere in Mississippi there was fighting at Barnett's Corners, Peyton's Mill, and Prentiss, and there was an attack on the Federal gunboat *Queen of the West* near Bolivar.

In Missouri there was skirmishing at Hickory Grove and an affair at Mount Vernon; in Kentucky skirmishing was at Horse Cave, Southerland's Farm, and Bear Wallow. There was action near Helena, Ark., and Brentwood, Tenn. The Federal Department of the Missouri was reestablished and the Department of Kansas discontinued.

Along the Potomac McClellan's cavalry pursued the retreating Confederates but were halted by Southern batteries. Fitz John Porter also pushed forward and by evening had crossed the Potomac to gain a foothold on the southern shore. There was skirmishing at Sharpsburg, Shepherdstown, and near Williamsport, Md.

September 20, Saturday

McClellan sent two divisions across the Potomac in a mild pursuit of Lee. Opposed by A. P. Hill, the Federals fell back and Lee's army withdrew to the valley of Opequon Creek. The active part of the campaign had ended with fighting near Shepherdstown, Hagerstown, Williamsport, and Ashby's Gap.

In the West there was skirmishing on Fulton Road south of Iuka, Miss.; at Munfordville, Ky.; and Shirley's Ford on Spring River near Carthage, Mo. From this day to the twenty-second there was a Union expedition from Bolivar to Grand Junction and La Grange, Tenn.

In the White House Lincoln prepared the preliminary Emancipation Proclamation, long discussed by Cabinet and President.

September 21, Sunday

In Kentucky Bragg's Confederate army marched to Bardstown in order to make connection with Kirby Smith's command, but the move left the road open for Buell to beat the Confederates to Louisville. Federal troops reoccupied Munfordville, Ky.

There was skirmishing at Cassville, Mo.; Van Buren, Tenn.; and a Union expedition from Carrollton to Donaldsonville, La., which lasted until the twenty-fifth.

Citizens of San Francisco contributed $100,000 for relief of Federal sick and wounded.

September 22, Monday

PRELIMINARY EMANCIPATION PROCLAMATION ANNOUNCED.

"That on the first day of January in the year of our Lord, one thousand eight hundred and sixty-three, all persons held as slaves, within any state, or designated part of a state, the people whereof shall then be in rebellion against the United States shall be then, thenceforward, and forever free." Thus wrote Mr. Lincoln in the Preliminary Emancipation Proclamation presented to the Cabinet. After long contemplation the President had awaited a military victory and now, after Antietam, came the public announcement of the proclamation. He also called for restoration of the Union and congressional approval of compensated emancipation. The door was at least partially opened for the final constitutional moves to end slavery.

Federal troops reoccupied Harper's Ferry, which had been evacuated by the Confederates. There was also a skirmish at Ashby's Gap, Va.

September 23, Tuesday

Indian troubles broke out again at Fort Abercrombie, Dakota Terr. At Wood Lake, near Yellow Medicine, Minn., H. H. Sibley won an important victory over the Sioux. There were skirmishes at McGuire's Ferry, Ark.; Wolf Creek Bridge, near Memphis, Tenn.; and a Federal expedition to Eureka, Boone County, Mo. On the Ohio River Confederate guerrillas plundered the steamer *Emma* at Foster's Landing. On the Mississippi *Eugene* was attacked near Randolph, Tenn., but she got away. Federal troops took revenge by burning the town of Randolph. Word of the Preliminary Emancipation Proclamation was spreading over the North and soon would penetrate the South as well.

September 24, Wednesday

President Lincoln issued a new proclamation suspending the privilege of the writ of habeas corpus and providing for military trial of "all Rebels and Insurgents, their aiders and abettors within the United States, and all persons discouraging volunteer enlistments, resisting militia drafts, or guilty of any disloyal practice, affording comfort to Rebels against the authority of the United States." Of the Preliminary Emancipation Proclamation Lincoln told a crowd, "I can only trust in God I have made no mistake." Fourteen Northern governors met at Altoona, Pa., and approved emancipation, although the conference had been called earlier by those deploring the Administration's policy on slavery and the unsatisfactory progress of the war. The Secretary of War created the office of Provost Marshal General.

Fighting was on Skull Creek, S.C.; at Granby, Mo.; and Sabine Pass, Texas. Confederate Gen. P. G. T. Beauregard superseded Maj. Gen. John C. Pemberton in command of the Department of South Carolina and Georgia. Maj. Gen. Samuel R. Curtis assumed command of the Federal Department of Missouri. The Confederate Senate adopted a seal for the Confederacy.

September 25, Thursday

Buell's Federal army arrived at Louisville, beating Bragg's advancing Confederates to the vital city on the Ohio. There was fighting at Snow's Pond and Ashbysburg, Ky., and at Davis' Bridge on the Hatchie River, Tenn. In the east there was a Federal reconnaissance from Shepherdstown, western Va., and a Federal expedition from Centreville to Bristoe Station and Warrenton, Va.

September 26, Friday

A quiet day on the major fronts. In Arkansas there were Federal expeditions from Helena to La Grange and Helena to Jeffersonville and Marianna, Tenn.; also a skirmish at Catlett's Station, Va.; a Federal expedition from Point Pleasant to Buffalo, western Va.; and a skirmish at Fort Abercrombie, Dakota Terr. Mr. Lincoln and his Cabinet conferred on colonization of the Negroes.

September 27, Saturday

The Second Conscription Act of the Confederate Congress authorized President Davis to call out men between thirty-five and forty-five. Federal troops carried out reconnaissance from Harper's Ferry toward Charles Town, western Va. There was fighting at Taylor's Bayou, Tex.; and Augusta and Brookville, Ky.; along with a skirmish near Iuka, Miss.

President Lincoln interrogated Maj. John J. Key and ordered his dismissal from military service for allegedly saying that the object of the Battle of Antietam was "that neither army shall get much advantage of the other; that both shall be kept in the field till they are exhausted, when we will make a compromise and save slavery." Such views had been reportedly rife in McClellan's army. Mr. Lincoln was much perturbed over McClellan's lack of aggressive action since Antietam.

The first regiment of free Negroes was mustered in at New Orleans as the First Regiment Louisiana Native Guards. The regiment called themselves "Chasseurs d'Afrique." Gen. Butler had authorized enlistment of free Negroes Aug. 22.

September 28, Sunday

Minor fighting was near Lebanon Junction, Ky.; Friar's Point, Miss.; Standing Stone, western Va.; and from this day to Oct. 5 there was a Federal expedition from Columbus, Ky., to Covington, Durhamville, and Fort Randolph, Tenn. President Davis wrote Gen. Lee of his concern over enrollment of conscripts "to fill up the thinned ranks of your regiments."

September 29, Monday

Federal Brig. Gen. Jefferson Columbus Davis shot and mortally wounded Brig. Gen. William "Bull" Nelson during a quarrel in a hotel in Louisville. Skirmishing broke out on the Elizabethtown Road, and near New Haven, Ky. There was a Federal expedition from Centreville to Warrenton and Buckland Mills, Va. Maj. Gen. John F. Reynolds assumed command of the First Army Corps. The Confederate Army of West Tennessee, 22,000 strong under Van Dorn, marched out of Ripley, Miss., heading toward Corinth, Miss.

September 30, Tuesday

The month ended with a number of lesser actions: at Russellville, Glasgow, and near Louisville, Ky.; at Newtonia, Mo.; Goodlettsville, Tenn.; Glenville, western Va.; a Federal reconnaissance from Rienzi, Miss., to the Hatchie River. Sept. 30–Oct. 3 there were Union reconnaissances on the Savannah River, Ga.; and Sept. 30–Oct. 13 a Federal sea-land expedition, from Hilton Head, S.C., to Saint John's Bluff, Fla.

OCTOBER, 1862

The people had experienced much in September of 1862. President Lincoln had opened the door to freedom for the slaves by issuing the Preliminary Emancipation Proclamation. Although for the moment it would not apply directly to a single slave, for it referred only to those held in territory deemed in rebellion, a momentous policy for the future had been laid down. Debate was extensive. Northern abolitionists felt it was too little; other unionists believed the war had wrongly changed course—from saving the Union to ending slavery. In the view of many Confederates, the Proclamation exposed the North's real purpose. The news quickly filtered through to the Negroes of the South and the message was clear, though often confused in detail. Negro troops began to be recruited by the North.

On the military fronts the South had advanced considerably in September, into Maryland, into Tennessee and Kentucky. But the three main offensives seemed blunted as fall began. Lee was back in Virginia, his excursion north only a partial success. Bragg and E. Kirby Smith were still in central Kentucky, but powerful Union forces protected the Ohio River cities from serious threat. In northern Mississippi, Van Dorn and Price had not made spectacular headway. The Mississippi around Vicksburg remained reasonably secure for the Confederacy, but for how long? McClellan continued to frustrate the Federal administration. To many, Antietam seemed a halfhearted effort by McClellan.

October 1, Wednesday

As the month opened, Bragg's Confederate campaign was reaching a climax in Kentucky. The Ohio River cities had apparently been successfully defended by Buell's Federals, but there was fighting on the Bardstown Pike near Mount Washington and on Fern Creek along the Louisville and Frankfort Road.

There was considerable skirmishing between Confederate and Federal cavalry along the Potomac near Sharpsburg, Md., Shepherdstown, and Martinsburg, western Va., and a Federal reconnaissance from Harper's Ferry to Leesburg, Va. Other fighting was at Ruckersville, Miss., and at Davis' Bridge and near Nashville, Tenn.

Maj. Gen. John C. Pemberton was given command of the new Confederate Department of Mississippi and East Louisiana, replacing Van Dorn. His main duty was the defense of Vicksburg on the Mississippi, obviously the aim of Federal operations.

Disturbed ever since Antietam about operations of the Army of the Potomac, or the lack of them, Mr. Lincoln, with a party of advisers, journeyed from Washington to Harper's Ferry to confer with McClellan and other officers. In an important administrative move the Federal gunboat flotilla on western waters was transferred from the War to the Navy Department. David Dixon Porter was named commander of the new Mississippi Squadron, replacing Charles Davis. The Richmond *Whig* said of the Emancipation Proclamation: "It is a dash of the pen to destroy four thousand millions of our property, and is as much a bid for the slaves to rise in insurrection, with the assurance of aid from the whole military and naval power of the United States."

October 2, Thursday

President Lincoln shifted from Harper's Ferry to the Headquarters of the Army of the Potomac, occupying a tent next to Gen. McClellan's. The President made a memo of total troops in the Army of the Potomac, arriving at a figure of 88,095.

Scattered fighting broke out on the Shepherdsville Road, Ky.; near Columbia, Mo.; Beaumont, Tex.; and at Baldwyn and near Ramer's Crossing, Miss. Confederate troops were moving in on Corinth, Miss. There were operations Oct. 2–4 at Blue's Gap or Hanging Rock, Little Cacapon Bridge, and Paw Paw Tunnel, western Va. Federal troops of Buell were pressing slowly toward Bardstown, Ky., from the Louisville area.

October 3, Friday

BATTLE OF CORINTH, MISSISSIPPI.

In midmorning Confederates under Earl Van Dorn and Sterling Price drove in against Rosecrans' Federals from northwest of Corinth, Miss. After severe fighting and piecemeal assaults, the Federals were driven into strong defensive redoubts closer to the city. By night the issue was still in doubt. Grant, at Jackson, Tenn., in over-all command of the area, had not been sure where the combined Confederate attack would be made. Van Dorn was gambling that victory at Corinth would force the Federals in west Tennessee to draw back to Kentucky and the Ohio River.

Reviews and conferences continued at McClellan's Headquarters in Maryland between the President and his general. Lincoln commented, on looking over the camps, "This is General McClellan's bodyguard."

Fighting was confined, outside of Corinth, to skirmishes on the Blackwater and near Zuni, Va.; at La Fayette Landing, Tenn.; Cedar Church, near Shepherdsville, Ky.; and Jollification, Mo. A Federal naval expedition attacked the defenses of Galveston, Tex.

The Confederate cruiser *Alabama* took three more prizes. Cries of anguish from Yankee shippers were soon to sound louder than ever. A battered force of Federals who had evacuated Cumberland Gap arrived at Greenupsburg, Ky., after a sixteen days' march under harsh conditions and with much skirmishing.

October 4, Saturday

BATTLE OF CORINTH, MISSISSIPPI, SECOND DAY.

At Corinth, Miss., the Confederates of Gen. Van Dorn renewed their heavy attacks against the well-posted Federals of Rosecrans. Both the assaults and Union counterattacks were costly, particularly at Battery Robinette, with little decided. Eventually repulsed, the Confederates withdrew in early afternoon to Chewalla, ten miles northwest from Corinth. More Federals came in after the battle ended, but there was no pursuit until Oct. 5. The figures: Union, 355 killed, 1841 wounded, and 324 missing for 2520 out of about 23,000 effectives; Confederates, 473 killed, 1997 wounded, and 1763 missing for total of 4233 out of probably 22,000 total troops. The Southerners succeeded in taking the pressure off Bragg in Kentucky by preventing reinforcements to Buell, but they failed to capture the important rail and road center of Corinth, or to wreck Rosecrans' force and thus make Grant pull back toward the Ohio.

At the Kentucky state capital of Frankfort, Richard Hawes was inaugurated Confederate governor in ceremonies attended by Bragg and other officers. Meanwhile, there was skirmishing elsewhere in the state near Bardstown, Clay Village, and on the Bardstown Pike. Other fighting took place at Newtonia, Granby, and in Monroe County, Mo.; near Middleton, Tenn.; Donaldsonville, La.; and at Conrad's Ferry, Va. There was a Federal reconnaissance from Loudoun Heights to Hillsborough in Virginia Oct. 4–6.

Mr. Lincoln remained with Gen. McClellan visiting camps, hospitals, and battlefields, leaving in the afternoon for Washington.

October 5, Sunday

Rosecrans' Federals ineffectively pursued Van Dorn, who was withdrawing from Corinth, Miss. However, Federal forces under E. O. C. Ord from Bolivar, Tenn., did intercept the retreating Confederates at the Hatchie River in Tennessee near Pocahontas, where there was brief but severe fighting in the afternoon. While the Federals regrouped, the battered Confederates managed to extricate themselves and continue to Holly Springs, Miss., thus ending the Corinth campaign. In addition there was minor action around Corinth, Miss., Chewalla, and Big Hill, Tenn.

Other fighting was at Cole Camp and Sims' Cove on Cedar Creek, Mo.; Neely's Bend on the Cumberland River and at Fort Riley, near Nashville, Tenn. Federal naval forces captured Galveston, Tex., with no resistance, and occupied the city briefly with a small force. Bragg's Confederate army was slowly pulling back from Bardstown, Ky., Buell following. Kirby Smith's army was still in the Frankfort, Ky., area.

October 6, Monday

President Lincoln, disturbed by McClellan's delays, sent instructions to the general in Maryland through Halleck: "The President directs that you cross the Potomac and give battle to the enemy or drive him south. Your army must move now while the roads are good." In Kentucky Bragg's main Confederate force was moving back toward Harrodsburg as Buell moved after him, occupying Bardstown. There were skirmishes at Fair

Grounds, Springfield, Burnt Cross Roads, Beach Fork, and Grassy Mound, Ky.

In western Virginia there was a Federal reconnaissance from Bolivar Heights toward Charles Town, and a skirmish at Big Birch; and in Missouri there were skirmishes at Sibley and Liberty.

October 7, Tuesday

Don Carlos Buell's Federal army, on the move in Kentucky against Bragg, neared the village of Perryville, while the Confederates were divided, partly at Frankfort and partly near Perryville. There were skirmishes at Brown Hill and near Perryville.

Other fighting was in Mississippi on the Hatchie near Box Ford, at Ruckersville and near Ripley; in Missouri at Newtonia, and near New Franklin. Federals were victorious in a small fight near Le Vergne, Tenn.

There were several command changes. Maj. Gen. Gordon Granger assumed command of the Federal Army of Kentucky and Brig. Gen. E. A. Carr, the Army of the Southwest. For the Confederates, middle and east Florida were embraced in Beauregard's southeast coast command.

In Britain, Chancellor of the Exchequer W. E. Gladstone proclaimed that Davis and the Confederate leaders "have made a nation," and he anticipated the success of their fight for separation. Gladstone's remarks were highly criticized in Britain and the United States, as well as by later historians.

October 8, Wednesday

BATTLE OF PERRYVILLE OR CHAPLIN HILLS, KENTUCKY.

Along the Chaplin Hills above Doctor's Creek near Perryville was fought the major battle of the war on Kentucky soil. A strange engagement, in which parts of Buell's Federal army battled portions of Bragg's. Both sides obtained advantages at times and a strong Confederate attack was fought off by men under a relatively new commander named Philip H. Sheridan. Due to an atmospheric phenomenon by which battle noise was not heard back of the lines, Buell did not realize until late in the day that a major fight was in progress and failed to get his full force into battle. Likewise, parts of Bragg's army were still in the Frankfort area. By day's end Buell had won at least a partial victory and Bragg pulled off to the southeast, ending the Confederate invasion of Kentucky. Thus two major Southern thrusts north had been halted and pushed back this fall of 1862. The cost at Perryville or Chaplin Hills: Federals, 845 killed, 2851 wounded, 515 missing for a total of 4211 out of 37,000 estimated effectives, although many of those did not see active fighting; Confederates, 519 killed, 2635 wounded, and 251 missing for a total of 3405, nearly a fourth of the possibly 16,000 effectives.

There was skirmishing at Lawrenceburg, Ky., and a Federal reconnaissance from Fairfax Court House to Aldie, Va.

Mr. Lincoln congratulated Grant on the recent victories in Mississippi.

October 9, Thursday

A little skirmishing on the Mackville Pike and Bardstown Road in Kentucky was an anticlimax to the fighting of the day before at Perryville. There was also action at Dry Ridge, Dog Walk or Chesser's Store near Salt River, Ky., and an affair near Humboldt, Tenn. A Federal expedition that lasted until Nov. 25 moved from Fort Union to the Canadian River and Utah Creek, N. Mex. Terr.

In the east Confederate J. E. B. Stuart, following Lee's suggestion, aggravated raw Federal wounds by eluding garrisons, crossing the Potomac on the tenth near Black Creek, and, with about eighteen hundred men, moving on to Chambersburg. After gathering horses and destroying public stores on the tenth and eleventh, Stuart moved east to Cashtown, thence down the Monocacy Valley, and recrossed the Potomac near Poolesville, coming back into Virginia on the twelfth. Federal cavalry tried to halt this new ride around McClellan's inert army, but to no avail. At great risk, and with only one man wounded, Stuart performed another sensational though not militarily vital foray against the North.

The Confederate Congress organized military courts for the armies in the field and defined their powers.

October 10, Friday

There was fighting at Harrodsburg and Danville Cross Roads, Ky., as Bragg's Confederates began their retreat east and southward. In Virginia Jeb Stuart crossed the Potomac on his raid, which began the day before, and by evening entered Chambersburg, Pa. In Tennessee there was a skirmish at Medon Station; on the upper Missouri River below Fort Berthold, Dakota Terr., a party of Sioux fought with a boatload of miners. Indiana home guards drove a group of rebel guerrillas from Hawesville, Ind.

President Davis asked Virginia for a draft of 4500 Negroes to work on completion of the fortifications of Richmond, and Maj. Gen. John B. Magruder, Confederate hero of the siege of Yorktown, was assigned to command the District of Texas.

October 11, Saturday

Jeb Stuart at Chambersburg reported that all officials had fled on the approach of the Confederates. His men cut telegraph wires, seized horses, and destroyed what military equipment they could not bring away. Railroad machine shops, depots, and several trains were also wrecked. In the afternoon Stuart moved eastward and then south through Emmitsburg, Md., en route to the Potomac.

There was sharp skirmishing near Helena, Ark., and operations in Lewis, Clarke, Scotland, and Schuyler counties of Missouri. In Kentucky there was skirmishing at Lawrenceburg and Danville. The Confederate cruiser *Alabama* captured and sank the grain ship *Manchester*. An act of the Confederate Congress, approved by President Davis, amended the draft exemption law, enlarging the number of those exempted by reason of occupation. Most controversial was the exemption of an owner or overseer of more than twenty slaves. Richmond papers began to speak of a possible early peace as a result of Confederate successes.

October 12, Sunday

Stuart's Confederate cavalry, after brief skirmishing near the mouth of the Monocacy in Maryland, crossed the Potomac back into Virginia near Poolesville, completing another ride around McClellan. There was skirmishing near Arrow Rock, Mo., and at Dick's Ford, Ky. Confederate Maj. Gen. Earl Van Dorn assumed command of all troops in Mississippi. Mr. Lincoln, worried by Buell's follow-up in Kentucky, continued to inquire for reports from the West. A Federal expedition that would last until the nineteenth started from Ozark, Mo., toward Yellville, Ark.

October 13, Monday

The second session of the First Congress of the Confederate States of America adjourned at Richmond after renewal of the law authorizing suspension of the privilege of the writ of habeas corpus until Feb. 12, 1863. However, it was required that investigation be made of persons arrested. In a lengthy letter to Gen. McClellan, President Lincoln urged renewed activity and asked, "Are you not over-cautious when you assume that you can not do what the enemy is constantly doing?" Mr. Lincoln advised a drive against Lee and Richmond.

Federal troops carried out a reconnaissance with some action about Paris, Snickersville, and Middleburg, Va. Other fighting was at New Franklin, Mo.; Lancaster and on Crab Orchard Road, Ky.; and on the Lebanon Road, near Nashville, Tenn. Maj. Gen. Jacob D. Cox assumed command of the Federal District of Western Virginia.

Bragg's Confederates, pulling back from Perryville, Ky., took up the march for Cumberland Gap.

October 14, Tuesday

Congressional elections in Iowa, Ohio, Indiana, and Pennsylvania resulted in gains by the Democrats, except in Iowa, where the Republicans carried the state. President Lincoln ordered the removal of army bakeries from the basement of the Capitol building.

Confederate Lieut. Gen. John C. Pemberton assumed command of the Department of Mississippi and Eastern Louisiana. There was fighting at Hazel Bottom, Mo.; Trenton, Ark.; and continuing action in Kentucky at Manchester, Lancaster, and Crab Orchard Road.

October 15, Wednesday

Skirmishing continued on widely scattered fronts: Fort Gibson, Indian Terr.; Neely's Bend on the Cumberland River, Tenn.; Crab Orchard and Barren Mound, Ky.; and near Carrsville, Va. There were operations from this day to the twentieth against Confederate guerrillas in Henry, Owen, and Gallatin counties, Ky. Federal Adm. Farragut reported from Pensacola Bay that Galveston, Corpus Christi, and Sabine City, Tex., were in Union possession. A small-boat naval expedition cut out and captured a Confederate blockade-runner up the Apalachicola River in Florida, despite shore opposition. Gov. Zebulon Vance of North Carolina called upon the people of the state to furnish blankets, carpets, and clothing for the Confederate Army.

October 16, Thursday

Gen. McClellan launched two major Federal reconnaissances from Sharpsburg, Md., to Smithfield, western Va., and from Harper's Ferry to Charles Town, western Va., with some skirmishing ensuing. Lee's army remained in the northern portion of the Shenandoah Valley. In Kentucky Bragg moved slowly toward Cumberland Gap without major interference. There was skirmishing at Mountain Gap and Mount Vernon, Ky. In Missouri there was action at Auxvasse Creek in Callaway County and at Portland; in Arkansas at Shell's Mill and Elkhorn Tavern. The draft began in Pennsylvania and other portions of the North. The Federal Department of the Tennessee was constituted under command of Maj. Gen. Ulysses S. Grant.

October 17, Friday

Resistance to the ineffective Federal militia draft was developing in some states, particularly several counties of Pennsylvania. At Berkley in Luzerne County troops had to put down opposition. Skirmishes were at Lexington, Mo.; Mountain Home and Sugar Creek, Ark.; Valley Woods and Rock Hill, Ky.; and Island No. 10, Tenn. There was an expedition on this day and the eighteenth by Federals to Thoroughfare Gap, Va. President Lincoln asked Att. Gen. Bates to make out a commission for David Davis of Illinois as Associate Justice of the Supreme Court.

October 18, Saturday

John Hunt Morgan and his Confederate raiders defeated Federal cavalry near Lexington, Ky., entered the city, captured the garrison, and moved off toward Versailles. There was other fighting this day at Kirk's Bluff, S.C.; Bloomfield, Big Hill, Little Rockcastle River, and Mountain Side, Ky.; Uniontown and California House, Mo.; and Cross Hollow and Helena, Ark.

October 19, Sunday

Bragg's retiring Army of Tennessee arrived in the area of Cumberland Gap, Ky., where they took until the twenty-fourth to get through completely, taking with them large amounts of grain and supplies appropriated in Kentucky. Federal opposition was fairly light. It was a quiet wartime Sunday, although there was the usual skirmishing, this time at Bardstown and Wild Cat, Ky.; between Catlett's Station and Warrenton Junction, Va.; and at Bonnet Carré in St. John the Baptist Parish, La.

October 20, Monday

President Lincoln ordered Maj. Gen. John A. McClernand, Illinois politician, to proceed to Indiana, Illinois, and Iowa to organize troops for an expedition against Vicksburg under McClernand's command. This conflicted with Gen. Grant's new command and was to result in many charges and countercharges and much friction between Grant and McClernand. Lincoln also penned memorandums, one showing the Army of the Potomac had a total of 231,997 men of which 144,662 were fit for duty, the other establishing a provisional court in Louisiana. Fighting included Federal repulse of a force under N. B. Forrest on the Gallatin Pike near Nashville, Tenn.; and skirmishes near Helena, Ark.; Marshfield, Mo.; Hermitage Ford, Tenn.; Wild Cat, Ky.; and Hedgesville, western Va.

October 21, Tuesday

Confederate President Davis wrote Maj. Gen. T. H. Holmes in Missouri of tentative plans to have Southern armies join together to drive the Federals from Tennessee and Arkansas and recapture Helena, Memphis, and Nashville. Mr. Lincoln meanwhile called upon military and civil authorities in Tennessee to support elections for a state government, legislature, and members of Congress. There was a reconnaissance from Loudoun Heights to Lovettsville, Va., by Federals; a skirmish at Woodville, Tenn.; and another at Pitman's Cross Roads, Ky.

October 22, Wednesday

It appeared, after two weeks of skirmishing and less than vigorous pursuit, that Bragg's Confederate army was making good its escape from Buell in Kentucky, following the Battle of Perryville. Cotton speculation caused Mr. Lincoln to say that individuals purchasing cotton should not impose terms not included in the Federal rules. Fighting occurred at two points in Arkansas, Helena and Huntsville; at Van Buren, Mo.; Snickersville, Va.; and Confederate cavalry under Gen. Joseph Wheeler took London, Ky. A Union attack on Pocotaglico or Yemassee, S.C., was repulsed after several skirmishes Oct. 22–23. A Federal expedition from Fort Donelson to Waverly, Tenn., fought several times Oct. 22–25. There was a skirmish at Fort Wayne, Ind. Terr., near the Arkansas border.

October 23, Thursday

Bragg's Confederate army passed into Tennessee through Cumberland Gap on their retreat from Kentucky. President Davis wrote of his worries over the pro-Union sentiments of east Tennessee. C.S.S. *Alabama* continued to prowl the seas and raid Federal shipping, adding frequently to its list of captures. There was a skirmish at Clarkton, Mo.; and Waverly and Richland Creek, Tenn.; the Goose Creek Salt Works near Manchester, Ky., were destroyed by Federals.

October 24, Friday

ROSECRANS REPLACES BUELL.

Don Carlos Buell was removed from Federal command in Kentucky and Tennessee largely due to the escape of Bragg's Confederates. Maj. Gen. William S. Rosecrans was assigned to command these troops and the new Department of the Cumberland, following his victories in Mississippi. Fighting was confined to a skirmish near Fayetteville, Ark.; an affair on St. Helena Island, S.C.; skirmishes at Manassas Junction and near Bristoe Station, Va.; and at White Oak Springs, Tenn. A Federal expedition Oct. 24–26 chased guerrillas from Independence to Greenton, Chapel Hill, and Hopewell, Mo. Oct. 24–Nov. 6 there were military operations in the La Fourche District, La.

October 25, Saturday

President Lincoln, piqued at McClellan's delays after Antietam, wired the commander of the Army of the Potomac, "I have just read your despatch about sore tongued and fatiegued [sic] horses. Will you pardon me for asking what the horses of your army have done since the battle of Antietam that fatigue anything?" McClellan, of course, defended his cavalry and operations, pointing out various reconnaissances and raids. Meanwhile, Maj. Gen. Grant assumed command of the Thirteenth Army Corps and the Department of the Tennessee. There was skirmishing near Zuni, Va.; Lawrenceburg, Ky.; Donaldsonville, La.; Helena, Ark.; and near Pike Creek and Eleven Points, Mo.

October 26, Sunday

The Army of the Potomac, nearly idle since the Battle of Antietam in mid-September, began crossing the Potomac into Virginia. Confederate Gen. Bragg completed the evacuation of Kentucky, retiring into Tennessee toward Knoxville and Chattanooga. Samuel Heintzelman succeeded Banks in command of the defenses of Washington. There were operations Oct. 26–Nov. 10 in Loudoun, Fauquier, and Rappahannock counties of Virginia. Indianola, Tex., fell to Union gunboats.

In Washington President Lincoln wrote McClellan that he "rejoiced" that the army had begun to cross the Potomac. In an interview with the English Quaker leader Mrs. Eliza P. Gurney, Mr. Lincoln is reported to have said, "If I had my way, this war would never have been commenced; If I had been allowed my way this war would have been ended before this, but we find it still continues."

October 27, Monday

Along the coasts the blockade continued its vigilance, with two blockade-runners reported captured as the pressure on Confederate commerce increased. There was fighting at Fayetteville, Ark., and at Georgia Landing, La., as well.

October 28, Tuesday

The Federal Army of the Potomac under McClellan continued its movement southward into Virginia from Maryland. The march was east of the Blue Ridge in the general direction of Warrenton. Lee, in the Shenandoah, began shifting troops southward to avoid being flanked by McClellan. Confederate Maj. Gen. John C. Breckinridge assumed command of the Army of Middle Tennessee. There was action at Oxford Bend on the White River near Fayetteville, and at McGuire's, Ark.

October 29, Wednesday

President Lincoln told Gen. McClellan, "I am much pleased with the movement of the Army. When you get entirely across the river let me know. What do you know of the enemy?" President Davis, plagued by trying to defend many areas, wrote the governor of Alabama, "Our only alternatives are to abandon important points or to use our limited resources as effectively as the circumstances will permit." There was skirmishing at Island Mount, Mo.; Sabine Pass, Tex.; on the Blackwater in Virginia; opposite Williamsport, Md., on the Potomac; and near Petersburg, western Va.

October 30, Thursday

Maj. Gen. Rosecrans assumed command of the Department of the Cumberland, replacing Maj. Gen. Buell. Emperor Napoleon III of France proposed to Russia and Great Britain that they should unite in making overtures of mediation in the American Civil War. Maj. Gen. Ormsby MacKnight Mitchel, astronomer, lecturer, and prominent Union officer, died of yellow fever at Beaufort, S.C.

October 31, Friday
There was a skirmish at Franklin, Va., and another near the falls of the Kanawha, western Va. A Union scout was undertaken in Monroe county, Mo.; and on this day and Nov. 1, Federal forces bombarded Lavaca, Tex. Other Union contingents advanced from Bolivar, Tenn., and Corinth, Miss., upon Grand Junction, Tenn., in preliminaries of Grant's move upon Vicksburg.

NOVEMBER, 1862

Little but memory was left of the three Confederate thrusts of late summer and early fall. Lee was back in Virginia and McClellan's Army of the Potomac had begun to move again, though slowly and with numerous delays. Bragg was gone from Kentucky, his Army of Tennessee not much injured. The new Federal commander, Rosecrans, still had a formidable enemy to contend with. In northern Mississippi Van Dorn had failed to do much against the Corinth area except to sustain losses, and Grant was preparing an overland campaign down the north-south railroad, aimed at Vicksburg. News of the successful Confederate sea raider *Alabama* was seeping in, but the blockade was still there, and continually tightening. For the South, the faint hope of foreign recognition seemed further away than ever. In the North there was scattered resistance to the draft. The Preliminary Emancipation Proclamation was still a subject of controversy. But at least the immediate threats of Confederate invasion were gone. At the moment, in fact, the war seemed to be dragging.

November 1, Saturday
November opened with McClellan finally back on Virginia soil but hardly in active pursuit of Lee's army, which was still licking its own wounds after Antietam. In Kentucky the new Federal commander, William S. Rosecrans, was prepared to resume operations against Confederate Braxton Bragg, who had escaped nearly intact from his drive toward the Ohio River. On the Mississippi, Grant, although aware of political intrigue behind his back involving John A. McClernand, prepared an overland campaign against Vicksburg. Confederate operations of the fall had been partially successful, but in a defensive-offensive sense had bought little but time.

Gen. Butler in New Orleans issued orders tightening pass requirements and authorizing discharge from confinement of all "slaves not known to be the slaves of loyal owners." President Davis continued to worry about the relations of the Confederate states to the central government, the raising of troops, and the danger of Federal invasion of the coasts.

Nov. 1–12 a Federal expedition from New Berne fought several skirmishes at Little Creek and Rawle's Mill, N.C. Operations early in the month were in Boone and Jackson counties, Mo., and Berwick Bay, La. Other fighting this day was at La Grange, Ark., and in Henderson County, Ky.

November 2, Sunday

There was minor fighting in Virginia at Philomont and Snicker's Gap in the Blue Ridge. The latter was occupied by McClellan's army. Mrs. Lincoln was visiting New York City.

November 3, Monday

There was a skirmish near Harrisonville, Mo., and an expedition by Federals along the coasts of Georgia and east Florida lasting until the tenth. Among the regiments used in this latter operation was the First South Carolina Volunteers (African Descent) under Col. Thomas Wentworth Higginson. This Negro regiment, still incomplete and somewhat unofficial, was not to be mustered in until the first of the year, but it had been slowly growing out of the earlier abortive attempts to form Negro regiments on the southeastern coast. Longstreet's Confederate corps arrived at Culpeper Court House, Va., thus getting in front of McClellan, who was in the Warrenton area. Jackson's corps of Lee's army remained in the Shenandoah Valley.

November 4, Tuesday

DEMOCRATS GAIN IN FEDERAL ELECTIONS.

Democrats made sizable gains in Northern state and congressional elections especially in New York, where Democrat Horatio Seymour was chosen governor. Strong Democratic gains were made also in New Jersey, Illinois, and Wisconsin, adding to those of the October elections. The Republicans kept control of the House of Representatives, however, with victories in New England, the border slave states, California, and Michigan. Undoubtedly war weariness accounted for many of the Democratic victories.

Gen. Grant's forces occupied La Grange and Grand Junction, Tenn., important rail and road keys to northern Mississippi, as plans for a drive on Vicksburg progressed.

November 5, Wednesday

LINCOLN ORDERS MCCLELLAN REPLACED BY BURNSIDE.

"By direction of the President, it is ordered that Major General McClellan be relieved from the command of the Army of the Potomac; and that

Major General Burnside take the command of that Army." It had come, after months of pressure from all sides. Mr. Lincoln had finally reached the end of his ample patience with the dilatory McClellan. The failure to complete a partial victory at Antietam, the snail-like advance in the weeks that followed brought to an end the controversial military career of "Little Mac." Repercussions would be strenuous. Two days later the general was informed. At the same time Fitz John Porter was relieved from his corps command. Porter, a pro-McClellan corps commander charged with willful disobedience at Second Manassas, was replaced by Joseph Hooker.

There was a Federal reconnaissance from La Grange toward Somerset, Tenn.; action near Nashville; an affair near Piketon, Ky.; a skirmish at Jumpertown, Miss.; and action at Lamar, Mo.; as well as operations lasting several days from Helena to Moro, Ark.; in Augusta, Bath, and Highland counties, Va.; and Pendleton and Pocahontas counties, western Va.

November 6, Thursday

Changes were also being made in the Confederate Army of Northern Virginia. Among the promotions were James Longstreet and Thomas Jonathan Jackson, who were promoted from major general to lieutenant general and to command of the First and Second Army Corps, respectively, moves of great importance in battles to come.

There was skirmishing at Martinsburg, western Va.; Garrettsburg, Ky.; Old Lamar, Miss.; and a Federal reconnaissance from La Grange, Tenn., toward Lamar, with further skirmishing. Federal expeditions from Fort Scott, Kas., operated Nov. 6–11.

November 7, Friday

MCCLELLAN RELIEVED.

At 11:30 P.M. an officer from Washington appeared at McClellan's Rectortown, Va., headquarters with the orders of Nov. 5 removing him from command and turning the Army of the Potomac over to Ambrose E. Burnside. McClellan, surprised, stunned, hurt, wrote, "I am sure that not the slightest expression of feeling was visible on my face." He added, "Poor Burnside feels dreadfully, almost crazy—I am sorry for him." The military career of the most controversial general of the Civil War was ended. He was replaced by a competent, rather stodgy, and definitely uncertain officer who professed no desire for the command and who tried to turn it down.

Lincoln placed the ram fleet on the Mississippi under navy control despite War Department objections. For the Confederates, Gen. Bragg, resuming command of the Army of the Mississippi after a brief absence, put one army corps under former bishop Leonidas Polk and the other under William Hardee. Meanwhile, Rosecrans was moving the Federal Army of the Cumberland to Nashville from Kentucky.

There was increased fighting in Tennessee at Gallatin, Tyree Springs, and White Range; as well as at Boonesborough, Rhea's Mills, and Marianna, Ark.; Clark's Mill in Douglas County, Mo.; and at Spaulding's or Sapello River in Georgia.

November 8, Saturday

The Federal Army of the Potomac, concentrated in the area of Warrenton, Va., was rocked by the news of McClellan's dismissal. In Tennessee Grant continued reconnaissance from La Grange, with some skirmishing extending to Hudsonville, Miss. There was also action on the Cumberland River near Gallatin, Tenn.; Burkesville, Ky.; Marianna, La Grange, and Cove Creek, Ark.; and Cato, Kas. Confederate cavalry carried out an expedition Nov. 8–14 from Hardy into Tucker County, western Va.

In another command change, Maj. Gen. Nathaniel P. Banks was named to command the Union Department of the Gulf, replacing Maj. Gen. Ben Butler, whose dictatorial rule of New Orleans had brought charges and countercharges of cruelty, speculation, and dishonesty. In receiving his orders it was made clear to Banks that "The President regards the opening of the Mississippi River as the first and most important of our military and naval operations." The same day Gen. Butler closed up all the breweries and distilleries within the department.

November 9, Sunday

Maj. Gen. Burnside assumed full command of the Army of the Potomac at Warrenton, Va. Federal cavalry under Ulric Dahlgren made a sensational dash into Fredericksburg, Va. There was skirmishing on the south fork of the Potomac in western Va. and a Union expedition into Greenbrier County, as well as a Federal reconnaissance from Bolivar Heights. Other action was at Huntsville and Dry Wood, Mo.; between Fayetteville and Cane Hill at Boston Mountains, Ark.; and at Silver Springs and Lebanon, Tenn.

November 10, Monday

Maj. Gen. McClellan took an emotional, spectacular farewell of the Army of the Potomac, so long considered "his" army. A soldier wrote, "The men were wild with excitement. They threw their hats into the air and cheered their old commander as long as his escort was in sight." The idolization of Little Mac continued despite his defeats and failures in battle; although some officers and men had come to recognize his shortcomings. The feelings of the army presented a problem to its new commander, Burnside. Maj. Gen. Hooker took over for Fitz John Porter in command of the Fifth Corps.

There was skirmishing at Charles Town, western Va., and operations along the Orange and Alexandria Railroad in Virginia. Mr. Lincoln asked for the record on the conviction of 303 Indians condemned to death for the Sioux uprising in Minnesota.

November 11, Tuesday
A day of lessened activity except for a Confederate demonstration at New Berne, N.C., and a skirmish at Jefferson, Va.

November 12, Wednesday
There was some action along Stone's River in Tenn., and operations Nov. 12–14 about Suffolk, Va., including skirmishes at Providence Church and Blackwater Bridge.

November 13, Thursday
Federal troops took possession of the valuable rail center of Holly Springs, Miss., after a brief skirmish. Other skirmishes were near Nashville, Tenn.; and Sulphur Springs, Va.; as well as an expedition on the Georgia coast lasting until Nov. 18. Bragg began moving the main body of the Army of Tennessee north from Chattanooga toward Murfreesboro to join Breckinridge.

Mr. Lincoln charged Att. Gen. Edward Bates with enforcement of the Federal Confiscation Act.

November 14, Friday
Mr. Lincoln approved Burnside's moves for driving on Richmond as the new commander of the Army of the Potomac reorganized his force into grand divisions: the Right Grand Division under Maj. Gen. Edwin V. Sumner, the Center Grand Division under Maj. Gen. Joseph Hooker, and the Left Grand Division under Maj. Gen. William B. Franklin. There was fighting at Waterloo, Zuni, and Jefferson, Va. In Tennessee Bragg was concentrating his army around Tullahoma, southeast of Nashville. In New Orleans a proclamation called for election of members of the U. S. Congress from portions of the state held by Federals.

November 15, Saturday
The Army of the Potomac began moving from Warrenton, Va., toward Fredericksburg, first action under Burnside. There was an action near Warrenton at Sulphur Springs; another on the Guyandotte River in western Va.; and at Yocum Creek, Mo. Nov. 15–20 Federals carried out a reconnaissance from Edgefield Junction toward Clarksville, Tenn.

President Davis quickly accepted the resignation of his Secretary of War, George W. Randolph, which came without prior notice. Mr. Davis' Secretaries of War had trouble over many things, but especially with their chief's virtual operation of their department. Mr. Lincoln called for "orderly observance of the Sabbath" by officers and men of the Army and Navy.

November 16, Sunday

Burnside moved his headquarters from Warrenton to Catlett's Station as his army shifted toward Fredericksburg, closely watched and followed by part of Lee's army. The movement involved a small fight at U. S. Ford on the Rappahannock. Other fighting was at Gloucester Point on Virginia's Peninsula; and Nov. 16–21 there was a Federal expedition from Helena against Arkansas Post, Ark.

November 17, Monday

Sumner's Right Grand Division of the Army of the Potomac arrived at Falmouth on the bluffs across the Rappahannock from Fredericksburg, Va., with light skirmishing. There was another fight near Carrsville, Va.; operations about Cassville and Keetsville, Mo.; and a Federal expedition from Sparta, Tenn., into Kentucky. President Davis, without a Secretary of War after the hasty resignation of George W. Randolph, named Maj. Gen. G. W. Smith temporary Secretary of War of the Confederacy.

November 18, Tuesday

As the Federal and Confederate armies in the east marched toward Fredericksburg and in the west were concentrating at Nashville and Tullahoma, there was minor fighting at Franklin, Va.; Doboy River, Ga.; Double Bridge and Rural Hill, Tenn.; and Core Creek, N.C.

November 19, Wednesday

Confederate forces of Longstreet's corps took position on the heights above Fredericksburg after marching from the main base at Culpeper. Federal Gen. Burnside arrived the same day, making his headquarters near Falmouth. There was fighting at Philomont, Va.; Tunnel Hill and Tomkinsville, Ky.; and Pineville, Mo. Nov. 19–20 there was a Union expedition from Grand Junction, Tenn., to Ripley, Miss., as Grant continued to probe the Confederate defenders of Vicksburg.

November 20, Thursday

Gen. R. E. Lee arrived at Fredericksburg, Va., as the build-up of Union and Confederate troops continued on the Rappahannock. Jackson's Confederate corps was still at Winchester, about to move toward Fredericksburg. The Confederate Army of Tennessee was officially constituted under Bragg, and consisted of corps under E. Kirby Smith, Polk, and Hardee. There was an affair near Matagorda, Tex., and a Federal reconnaissance until the twenty-third toward Van Buren and Fort Smith, Ark.

November 21, Friday

SEDDON NAMED CONFEDERATE SECRETARY OF WAR.

President Davis appointed James A. Seddon, prominent Richmond lawyer, former U.S. and Confederate congressman, as Secretary of War. Seddon, who appeared to be anything but warlike, was to prove the most able of the Confederate War Secretaries, though subject to abuse and criticism. In the West Bragg sent Forrest to cut communications of Grant's army in western Tennessee. On the Rappahannock Gen. Burnside called upon Fredericksburg, Va., to surrender but was refused. The mayor was threatened with bombardment of the town and sixteen hours were allowed for removal of sick, wounded, women, children, the aged and infirm. The mayor requested more time. Jackson was now marching from Winchester toward Fredericksburg. There was skirmishing at Bayou Bonfouca, La.

Mr. Lincoln told Union Kentuckians that he "would rather die than take back a word of the Proclamation of Freedom," and again urged support of his gradual slavery-abolishment plan.

November 22, Saturday

Federal Sec. of War Stanton discharged nearly all political prisoners held by the military. At Winchester, Va., Federals skirmished with Confederates while Southerners attacked Halltown, western Va., but were driven back. There was a reconnaissance from Williamsburg, Va., by Confederates. Twelve Southern salt works were destroyed, along with a number of vessels, in Matthews County, Va., on Chesapeake Bay. In Louisiana there was an affair at Petite Anse Island.

Federal Gen. E. V. Sumner agreed not to bombard Fredericksburg, despite the ultimatum of the day before, "so long as no hostile demonstration is made from the town."

November 23, Sunday

Federal Naval Lieut. William Cushing with the steamer *Ellis* went up New River, N.C., and at Jacksonville captured two schooners. However, while returning, he ran onto a shoal and lost his own vessel, but escaped in one of the captured schooners.

November 24, Monday

Confederate Gen. Joseph E. Johnston was assigned to the major command in the West, embracing western North Carolina, Tennessee, northern Georgia, Alabama, Mississippi, and eastern Louisiana. Johnston's main task would be to supervise Bragg in Tennessee and Pemberton at Vicksburg. Bragg was now moving his three corps to Murfreesboro southeast of Nashville. Stonewall Jackson's corps was well en route from Winchester to Fredericksburg, Va. There was skirmishing at Newtown, Va., and Beaver Creek, Mo. An expedition Nov. 24–25 by the Federals from Sharpsburg, Md., to Shepherdstown, western Va., fought several skirmishes. In western Virginia Nov. 24–30 there was an expedition from Summerville to Cold Knob Mountain by the Federals.

Mr. Lincoln wrote politician Carl Schurz, "I certainly know that if the war fails, the administration fails, and that I *will* be blamed for it, whether I deserve it or not."

November 25, Tuesday

Confederate cavalry crossed the Potomac at Poolesville, Md., and seized the government telegraph office briefly. Other fighting was at Pitman's Ferry and Cane Hill, Ark.; Henderson's Station and Clarksville, Tenn.; Calhoun, Ky. There was a Federal expedition Nov. 25–29 to Yellville, Ark. Confederate Maj. Gen. Samuel Jones was assigned to command the Trans-Allegheny or Western Department of Virginia.

November 26, Wednesday

President Lincoln went down the Potomac to Belle Plain for a conference with Burnside. President Davis wrote the governors of the Confederate states appealing for aid in enrolling conscripts and forwarding them to rendezvous, in restoring to the Army all absent without leave, and in securing more supplies for army use. He also called for use of slave labor on defense works.

There was a skirmish near Somerville, Tenn.; a Federal reconnaissance from Bolivar Heights to Charles Town, western Va.; an affair in Jackson and La Fayette counties, Mo.; and in Tennessee these last days of the month there were operations about Springfield, a Union reconnaissance at La Vergne, and a Federal expedition from Edgefield to Clarksville.

November 27, Thursday

Mr. Lincoln spent the morning at Aquia Creek, Va., conferring with Gen. Burnside. The general favored a direct assault on Lee at Fredericksburg, while Lincoln proposed building up a force south of the Rappahannock and another on the Pamunkey for a three-pronged attack. Burnside turned down the President's plan. There was a skirmish at Mill Creek, Tenn.; and another at Carthage, Mo.; while a Federal expedition that lasted until Dec. 6 probed near Grenada, Miss.

November 28, Friday

Federal forces won an engagement at Cane Hill or Boston Mountains, Ark., when Northerners under James Blunt attacked Confederates under John S. Marmaduke and drove them back with considerable loss, giving the Federals a momentary edge in the Trans-Mississippi fighting. There were skirmishes for two days at Holly Springs, Miss., where the Federals were beginning a build-up of supplies for their advance on Vicksburg. There was also a skirmish in Mississippi at the junction of the Coldwater and Tallahatchie; skirmishes on the Carthage Road, near Hartsville and

Rome, Tenn.; near Hartwood Church, Va.; and a three-day Federal reconnaissance from Chantilly, Va., to Berryville.

November 29, Saturday
Maj. Gen. John B. Magruder, C.S.A., assumed command of the District of Texas, New Mexico, and Arizona. There were skirmishes at Lumpkin's Mill and Waterford, Miss.; and at Stewart's Ferry and Baird's Mills, Tenn., near Stone's River.

November 30, Sunday
A quiet end to a month of lesser fighting, command changes, and preparations for things to come. There were skirmishes, however, at Chulahoma, Miss., and on the Tallahatchie; and a Federal expedition operated from Rolla to the Ozarks in Missouri until Dec. 6.

DECEMBER, 1862

The last month of the first full year of the Civil War showed a military picture quite different from that of the summer and early fall. While Confederate arms had been victorious on the Peninsula, at Second Manassas, Antietam, and for a time in Kentucky, the long-term outlook was anything but bright for the new nation. Everywhere they were even more on the defensive. In mid-Virginia Burnside's Army of the Potomac was obviously preparing for direct action against Lee at Fredericksburg, in mid-Tennessee Bragg at Murfreesboro was confronted by a readying Rosecrans at Nashville, and on the Mississippi Grant was building up for a drive by land or by river against Vicksburg. In Arkansas, from New Orleans, and along the Carolina, Georgia, and Texas coasts lesser forces were plaguing the Confederacy. Offshore there was always the blockade, not to be upset by the spectacular roaming of C.S.S. *Alabama*.

President Lincoln faced negative reactions to his Emancipation Proclamation. Democratic victories in the fall elections, resistance to the draft, and sensitive military commanders presented additional problems. At the South President Davis was trying to direct all the operations of the Confederate government, obtain men and supplies from the governors, and protect the many vulnerable points of his nation. He well saw the threat of the poised Northern armies and attempted to gather his widely spread forces together despite lack of men and matériel.

December 1, Monday

"WE CANNOT ESCAPE HISTORY"—LINCOLN.

The third session of the Thirty-seventh Congress of the United States convened and received the State of the Union message from the President. Mr. Lincoln reported that foreign relations were satisfactory, commerce was generally in good shape, Federal receipts were exceeding expenditures. Most importantly, he recommended three constitutional amendments: first, every state which abolished slavery before 1900 would receive compensation; second, all slaves who had gained freedom during the war would remain free, and loyal owners compensated; third, Congress would provide for colonization outside the country of free colored persons with their consent. He concluded, "As our case is new, so we must think anew, and act anew. We must disenthrall ourselves, and then we shall save our country. Fellow-citizens, *we* cannot escape history. . . . In *giving* freedom to the *slave,* we *assure* freedom to the free—honorable alike in what we give, and what we preserve. We shall nobly save, or meanly lose, the last best, hope of earth."

Early in December there were skirmishes near Oxford, Hudsonville, and on the Yocknapatalfa River near Mitchell's Cross Roads in Mississippi, as Grant continued to move southward. In Virginia there was fighting at Beaver Dam Church, Grove Church near Hartwood, a Federal expedition to Westmoreland County. In western Virginia there was a skirmish at Romney and a ten-day Federal expedition toward Logan Court House. On the Rosecrans-Bragg front in Tennessee there was a skirmish at Nolensville. After their march from the Shenandoah Valley troops of Jackson's corps were moving into position to form the right of Lee's army at Fredericksburg.

December 2, Tuesday

Along the Rappahannock at Leeds' Ferry there was a skirmish as Burnside and Lee faced each other. Other fighting in Virginia was on the Blackwater near Franklin, near Dumfries, and Dec. 2–6 a Federal reconnaissance operated from Bolivar Heights to Winchester. In the Indian Territory there was a skirmish at Saline.

December 3, Wednesday

There was an attack on a Federal forage train on the Hardin Pike near Nashville, Tenn., and a skirmish at Moorefield, western Va. In Mississippi Grant continued to press Confederates along the Yocknapatalfa River, and there was action at Prophet, Spring Dale, and Free Bridges and Oakland. Three blockade-runners were taken off the North Carolina coast.

December 4, Thursday

Confederate Gen. Joseph E. Johnston assumed over-all command in the West. Sporadic fighting continued on the major fronts. There was an engagement on the Rappahannock River near Port Royal, not far from Fredericksburg, Va.; and skirmishing on the Franklin Pike and near Stewart's Ferry on Stone's River, Tenn. In Mississippi the action was near Oxford and Water Valley. There were operations about Cane Hill and Reed's Mountain, Ark., and in Cherokee Country, Indian Terr. Citizens attacked Indian prisoners at Mankato, Minn. At Prestonburg, Ky., Confederates captured some supply boats with arms, ammunition, and uniforms. There also was a skirmish in Floyd County, Ky.

December 5, Friday

Grant's cavalry received a setback in an engagement on the Mississippi Central Railroad at Coffeeville, Miss.

December 6, Saturday

Lincoln ordered the execution by hanging of 39 Indians of the 303 convicted of participating in the Sioux uprising in Minnesota. The date was set for Dec. 19. There was skirmishing near Kimbrough's Mill, Mill Creek, Tenn., and at Parkesville, Mo.

December 7, Sunday

BATTLE OF PRAIRIE GROVE, ARKANSAS.

In a confusing battle at Prairie Grove, about twelve miles southwest of Fayetteville, Ark., on Illinois Creek, Confederates under Thomas C. Hindman attacked Federal forces under James Blunt and Francis J. Herron. Herron had been ordered to Blunt's support. Hindman, advancing from Van Buren, Ark., attempted to defeat the two Federal units separately, but they managed to join after a hard march by Herron's men from Wilson's Creek, Mo. Confederates held their position but bitter winter weather forced them to withdraw during the night. Federals maintained control of northwest Arkansas. The figures are put at 175 Federals killed, 813 wounded, and 263 missing for a total of 1251 casualties out of an estimated 10,000 troops. For the Confederates 164 were killed, 817 wounded, and 336 missing for a total of 1317 casualties, also out of about 10,000 men. President Davis, worried about Vicksburg, wired Pemberton at Grenada, Miss., "Are you in communication with Genl. J. E. Johnston? Hope you will be re-inforced in time." The Confederate Department of Mississippi and East Louisiana was organized with Maj. Genls. Van Dorn and Price commanding the First and Second Corps. There was an affair at Padre Island, Tex. John Hunt Morgan, with about 1400 men, surprised and captured a Federal garrison at Hartsville, Tenn. Col. A. B. Moore lost 2096 men, about 1800 of whom were taken prisoner.

December 8, Monday

President Davis, concerned over the several threats to the Confederacy, wrote Lee at Fredericksburg, "In Tennessee and Mississippi the disparity between our armies and those of the enemy is so great as to fill me with apprehension." He announced his intention to go west immediately. As to Lee's desire to concentrate forces to defend Richmond, Davis regretted he could do so little to help him as to manpower. There was a Federal reconnaissance from Suffolk to the Blackwater and skirmishes at and about Zuni, Va., Dec. 8–12.

December 9, Tuesday

In the West there was a skirmish at Dobbins' Ferry, near La Vergne, Tenn., and a Federal reconnaissance toward Franklin with a skirmish near Brentwood. There was also a skirmish at Mudtown, Ark. For several days there were Federal expeditions from Ozark, Mo., into Marion County, Ark.; and from Corinth, Miss., toward Tuscumbia, Ala., with considerable skirmishing during the latter reconnaissance.

December 10, Wednesday

Burnside increased his activities at Falmouth, indicating an attack on Fredericksburg was imminent. Confederate forces seized Plymouth, N.C., defeating a Federal garrison. The United States House of Representatives passed a bill creating the state of West Virginia. The measure granting secession of western Virginia from Virginia and creating a state had previously passed the Senate July 14. There was a skirmish at Desert Station, La.

December 11, Thursday

FEDERALS OCCUPY FREDERICKSBURG, VIRGINIA.

On a foggy December morning, Burnside's Federals began constructing five pontoon bridges across the Rappahannock to Fredericksburg. Sharpshooters from a Confederate brigade under William Barksdale drove the builders away time after time. In midmorning Federal guns on the east side of the river opened on the city, but the sharpshooters remained. By noon two bridges were laid. A four-regiment Federal force crossed in boats, drove out the Confederates, and the other three bridges were laid. On the Federal left troops under William B. Franklin began crossing in the afternoon, and a division of E. V. Sumner's corps occupied Fredericksburg by nightfall. Jackson was a few miles back at Guiney's Station with his divisions at Yerby's and on the lower crossings of the Rappahannock. He was ready to move wherever needed to aid Longstreet's defending corps. The main question was just where Burnside would strike.

There was a skirmish at La Vergne and near Nashville, Tenn.; and at Darkesville, western Va.; as well as a two-day Federal reconnaissance toward Franklin, Tenn. Federals began a ten-day expedition from New Berne to Goldsborough, N.C.; and a five-day reconnaissance from Yorktown to Gloucester, Matthews, King and Queen, and Middlesex counties of Virginia. Nathan Bedford Forrest, with about 2500 Confederates, left Columbia, Tenn., for a raid against Grant's communications.

December 12, Friday

Both the Federal Right and Left Grand Divisions continued crossing the Rappahannock to Fredericksburg and the flat ground to the southeast. Plans were made for the main attack by the Federal left under Franklin. Jackson ordered Early and D. H. Hill to join him on the Confederate right flank along the extension of the ridge which ran back of the city. Longstreet's men held the left. As night came, it was obvious Burnside would make his major assault the next day.

Elsewhere there were operations on the Yazoo River in Mississippi, and on the Neuse River in North Carolina. On the Yazoo River north of Vicksburg the Federal ironclad *Cairo* struck a mine, or torpedo as they were called, and sank. The crew escaped. The vessel remained there a century before being raised. In the Shenandoah there was a Federal reconnaissance from North Mountain to Bunker Hill and a skirmish between Harper's Ferry and Leesburg. There was a skirmish at Dumfries, Va., and Dec. 12–20 operations in Loudoun County, Va. Confederates raided Poolesville, Md., on Dec. 14. The Union expedition to Goldsborough, N.C., soon ran into trouble and was repulsed by the eighteenth.

President Lincoln wrote Mayor Fernando Wood of New York that if the Southern states would cease resistance to national authority "the war would cease on the part of the United States." This was in response to recurring rumors and reports of peace overtures.

December 13, Saturday

BATTLE OF FREDERICKSBURG, VIRGINIA.

As the fog rose in midmorning from the plain southeast of Fredericksburg, Federal troops drove toward the hills defended by Jackson's Confederates. The Battle of Fredericksburg had opened. Spirited assaults by troops of George G. Meade and John Gibbon dented Jackson's lines for a short time, but William B. Franklin's Left Grand Division was repulsed and thrown back to the low ground from whence it started. From the city itself, Edwin V. Sumner's Right Grand Division, backed by Joseph Hooker's Center Grand Division, debouched against Longstreet's corps. Longstreet's men were posted on and at the foot of Marye's Heights, a ridge behind the city. Confederate and Union artillery added to the crescendo of battle as time after time the Federals approached the stone wall along a narrow road at the foot of Marye's Heights, only to meet murderous fire. They fought for feet and yards until late afternoon. A futile, wild, fantastic, direct slam by Federals against the exceedingly well entrenched Confederates of Lee failed miserably. Burnside's action counteracted McClellan's slothfulness, but at the cost of defeat, blood, and carnage. This winter day at Fredericksburg tested men and officers alike to the utmost. The heroism was there, but not the strategy.

Gen. Lee remarked, "I wish these people would go away and let us alone." A Federal said, "It was a great slaughter pen . . . they might as well have tried to take Hell."

The cost—1284 Federals were killed, 9600 wounded, and 1769 missing, a total of 12,653 casualties for the proud Army of the Potomac. An estimated 114,000 men were engaged. For the Confederates, 595 were killed, 4061 wounded, and 653 missing for 5309 casualties of about 72,500 engaged. The result—Federals remained in the city, Confederates on the hills.

There was fighting elsewhere: at Leesburg, Va.; on Southwest Creek, N.C.; and a Federal raid Dec. 13–19 on the Mobile and Ohio Railroad from Corinth to Tupelo, Miss.

At Murfreesboro, Tenn., President Davis, on his Western inspection tour, reviewed Bragg's army and conferred with his generals.

December 14, Sunday

The aftermath of battle caused consternation in the North, but little rejoicing in the South. Burnside, driven to rashness by his failure, ordered the attack renewed at Fredericksburg, but was persuaded by his officers not to attempt it. Lee was criticized, probably unjustly, because he did not counterattack. Although the huge Federal army lay beaten in his front, it was still a mighty host and protected by massive batteries on the heights across the river. Finally, during the night, the Army of the Potomac began to withdraw across the Rappahannock. In Washington the President called upon his generals and advisers for conferences.

In the West there was an affair near Helena, Ark.; an attack on a Federal forage train on the Franklin Pike near Nashville; and a four-day Federal expedition against the Mobile and Ohio Railroad in Mississippi. A skirmish was fought at Waterford, Va.; and the Federal expedition under Maj. Gen. John G. Foster from New Berne succeeded in taking Kinston, N.C.

December 15, Monday

The humiliated Army of the Potomac sullenly completed its withdrawal across the Rappahannock as officers bickered, grumbled, and quarreled, and everyone questioned Burnside's decisions. Lee and the Army of Northern Virginia stood triumphant in defense.

Nathan Bedford Forrest, who had left Columbia, Tenn., Dec. 11 to harass Grant's lines of communications, crossed the Tennessee at Clifton with about 2500 men. Something had to be done to aid Pemberton at Vicksburg.

There was an affair at White Hall Bridge, N.C., in John G. Foster's Federal move toward Goldsborough; and a skirmish at Neosho, Mo. At New Orleans Maj. Gen. Benjamin Butler bade farewell to his command and to the people of New Orleans, most of whom were jubilant over his departure.

December 16, Tuesday

The Army of the Potomac crouched on Stafford Heights overlooking the Rappahannock, still disheartened after Fredericksburg. At New Orleans Maj. Gen. Nathaniel P. Banks assumed command of the Federal Department of the Gulf, replacing the departed Butler.

In the West Confederate Forrest continued his march in Tennessee. The Union Goldsborough expedition in North Carolina neared its goal with an engagement at White Hall and fighting at Mount Olive Station and Goshen Swamp. In western Virginia there was a skirmish at Wardensville.

President Lincoln postponed the execution of the Sioux Indians from Dec. 19 to Dec. 26.

December 17, Wednesday

Gen. Grant from his headquarters at Holly Springs issued his controversial General Order No. 11: "The Jews, as a class violating every regulation of trade established by the Treasury Department and also department orders, are hereby expelled from the department within twenty-four hours from the receipt of this order." It would appear that Grant was trying to eliminate the tremendous amount of illegal speculation along the Mississippi. Perhaps Grant equated Jews with the peddlers and speculators that plagued his camps. On the other hand, it could be charged as an indictment of a religious group. At any rate, the order had political and social ramifications for years. It mattered little that Halleck and Lincoln rescinded it Jan. 4, 1863; the damage to Grant had been done. It also resulted in discomfort to a number of Jews, though never put entirely into effect.

As a result of continual political disputes with Sec. of the Treasury Salmon P. Chase, the Union Secretary of State, William H. Seward, and his son and assistant, Frederick W. Seward, resigned. However, the resignations were not accepted.

Near Goldsborough, N.C., the Federal expedition fired an important bridge, fought a stubborn engagement, and withdrew by Dec. 20 to New Berne. There was Federal reconnaissance on Virginia's Peninsula to Diascund Bridge and Burnt Ordinary; and from this day to the twenty-first there was a Federal expedition from New Madrid to Clarkton, Mo.

December 18, Thursday

Confederate Forrest defeated Union cavalry at Lexington, Tenn., in his campaign against Grant's supply lines. Meanwhile, Grant's army was formally organized with the Fifteenth Corps under William T. Sherman, the Sixteenth Corps under Stephen A. Hurlbut, the Seventeenth under James B. McPherson, and the Thirteenth under John A. McClernand. The latter appointment practically ended the machinations of McClernand, aided by Lincoln, to form a completely separate army to operate against Vicksburg. Meanwhile, there was a skirmish near Water Valley, Miss.

President Lincoln received a committee of nine Republican senators and discussed reconstruction of the Federal Cabinet and the submitted resignation of Seward as Secretary of State.

President Davis, visiting Chattanooga, Tenn., wrote Sec. of War Seddon that the troops at Murfreesboro were in good condition and fine spirits. He added that cavalry expeditions under Forrest and Morgan were expected to break up Federal communications to both Buell and Grant. Mr. Davis was anxious over sentiment in east Tennessee and north Alabama as "There is some hostility and much want of confidence in our strength." South Carolina passed a law providing for the organization of Negro labor to work on defenses.

December 19, Friday

The Cabinet crisis in Washington took most of Mr. Lincoln's day. In the evening there was a joint meeting of the Cabinet, except Seward, and the Senate Republican caucus committee. Postmaster General Montgomery Blair also offered to resign. Lincoln advised Burnside to come to Washington if it were safe to do so.

Forrest struck the railroads near Jackson, Tenn., in his drive against Grant's supply lines, with a skirmish nearby. Other skirmishes were at Spring Creek, Tenn., and on the Occoquan in Virginia.

December 20, Saturday

HOLLY SPRINGS, MISSISSIPPI, RAID.

FEDERAL CABINET CRISIS ENDED.

Earl Van Dorn's Confederates, moving rapidly from Grenada, Miss., pounced on Grant's huge advance supply depot at Holly Springs, Miss., capturing at least fifteen hundred Federals and destroying upwards of a million and a half dollars' worth of military supplies. Van Dorn also hit other lesser posts. To the north, Forrest further ruptured the railroads and fought skirmishes at Trenton and Humboldt. As a result, Grant was forced to relinquish his plans for an overland campaign and he withdrew from Oxford, Miss., to La Grange, Tenn. The Confederate successes also disrupted Grant's plan to cooperate with Sherman's move down the Mississippi toward Chickasaw Bayou north of Vicksburg. Sherman's force was leaving the same day from Memphis in about a hundred transports. Fighting included Forked Deer River, Tenn.; and Coldwater, Miss.; as well as skirmishes at Kelly's Ford and Occoquan, Va., and Halltown, western Va.; and Cane Hill, Ark.

In Washington, Sec. of the Treasury Chase handed Mr. Lincoln his resignation, adding it to Seward's. Cabinet members called and the President finally ended the dispute by refusing to accept any of the resignations and asking the Secretaries of State and the Treasury to resume their duties. They did so, but the crisis left its mark.

December 21, Sunday

Raiding and minor fighting seemed to be the order of the early winter. Confederate John Hunt Morgan left Alexandria, near Carthage, Tenn., on a Christmas raid into Kentucky against Federal supply lines. Fighting occurred at Davis' Mill, Miss.; Rutherford's Station, Union City, and on the Wilson Creek Pike, Tenn.; at Van Buren, Ark.; and Strasburg, Va. There were two-day reconnaissances from Stafford Court House to Kellysville and from Potomac Creek Bridge toward Warrenton, and another to Catlett's Station and Brentsville, all by Federals in Virginia. There also was a Union expedition Dec. 21–23 from Fayetteville to Huntsville, Ark.

President Davis, at Vicksburg, wrote to Gen. T. H. Holmes that it seemed "clearly developed that the enemy has two principal objects in view, one to get control of the Missi. River, and the other to capture the capital of the Confederate States." However, Davis thought that the defeat at Fredericksburg had probably halted any move toward Richmond for the winter. He added that to prevent the Federals from controlling the Mississippi and "dismembering the Confederacy, we must mainly depend upon maintaining the points already occupied by defensive works: to-wit, Vicksburg and Port Hudson."

December 22, Monday

President Lincoln conferred in Washington with Gen. Burnside as disputes raged over responsibility for the Fredericksburg debacle and the actions of various generals before and after the battle. Mr. Lincoln issued an order congratulating the army for its bravery at Fredericksburg and called the defeat an "accident."

Morgan's Confederates crossed the Cumberland River on their Kentucky raid. There were skirmishes near Windsor and at Joyner's Ferry on the Blackwater in Virginia.

December 23, Tuesday

President Davis issued a proclamation calling the former Federal commander of New Orleans and the Gulf, Maj. Gen. Benjamin F. Butler, a felon, an outlaw, a common enemy of mankind; if captured he should not be considered a military prisoner but should be hanged immediately. This was a result of Butler's alleged tyrannical rule in New Orleans. Mr. Davis, from Jackson, Miss., wired his Secretary of War, "There is immediate and urgent necessity for heavy guns and long range field pieces at Vicksburg." Maj. Gen. Simon Bolivar Buckner assumed command of the Confederate District of the Gulf, and Lieut. Gen. E. Kirby Smith resumed command of the Department of East Tennessee.

There was a skirmish near Nashville, Tenn.; and another on the St. Francis Road, near Helena, Ark. Operations in the Sugar Creek Hills of Missouri lasted until the end of the month.

December 24, Wednesday

Union army forces occupied Galveston, Tex., already partially in control of the Navy. In Kentucky John Hunt Morgan occupied Glasgow, after a skirmish. There was fighting near Nashville, Bolivar, and Middleburg, Tenn. Sherman's expedition from Memphis drew closer to Vicksburg.

December 25, Thursday

Christmas Day brought no cessation of lesser action throughout the warring nations. Sherman's expedition operated near Milliken's Bend north of Vicksburg. Morgan's men in Kentucky fought at Green's Chapel and Bear Wallow. There was a skirmish near Warrenton, Va.; and a Federal reconnaissance from Martinsburg to Charles Town, western Va. Fighting occurred on the Wilson Creek Pike near Brentwood and at Prim's Blacksmith Shop on the Edmondson Pike, Tenn., as well as at Ripley, Miss. President and Mrs. Lincoln visited wounded soldiers in Washington hospitals.

December 26, Friday

Gen. Sherman's expedition down the Mississippi from Memphis landed on the Yazoo near Steele's Bayou. He advanced toward the line of bluffs known as Walnut Hills and Haynes' Bluff, protecting Vicksburg on the north. Federal forces under Rosecrans moved out from Nashville toward Bragg's army at Murfreesboro, Tenn., with action at La Vergne, Franklin, Nolensville, and Knob Gap.

In raiding, Morgan fought at Bacon Creek and Nolin, Ky., and operated against Rosecrans' railroad lines. Forrest was withdrawing from

Grant's lines in Tennessee after considerable destruction. For the Federals, S. P. Carter's small force of cavalry left Manchester, Ky., for the upper Tennessee Valley, destroying railroad bridges and fighting skirmishes, in particular one at Perkins' Mill or Elk Fort, Dec. 28. The raid lasted until Jan. 5. Federals attacked a guerrilla camp in Powell County, Ky. At Mankato, Minn., 38 Indians were hanged for participating in the Sioux uprising that altogether cost 450 or more lives. Another was pardoned at the last minute.

December 27, Saturday

Sherman's troops picked their way across the swamps and bayous north of Vicksburg toward the bluffs. They engaged in minor fighting at Snyder's Mill against Confederate pickets as Pemberton rushed in troops to defend Vicksburg. Rosecrans' army continued its march toward Bragg at Murfreesboro, Tenn.; there was some skirmishing on the Jefferson Pike at Stewart's Creek Bridge, Triune, Franklin, and on the Murfreesboro Pike at another Stewart's Creek Bridge. Morgan's Confederates captured a Union garrison at Elizabethtown, Ky. There was a skirmish at Elizabeth City, N.C., and another at Dumfries, Va.

December 28, Sunday

Light fighting continued as Sherman approached the Vicksburg bluffs near the Yazoo and as Rosecrans proceeded toward Murfreesboro. Morgan destroyed a bridge at Muldraugh's Hill in Kentucky near Lincoln's birthplace, and also fought at Bacon Creek before escaping into Tennessee by Jan. 1. There was skirmishing near Suffolk and at Providence Church, Va. Federals evacuated New Madrid, Mo. The Federal Army of the Frontier under James Blunt fought the Confederates at Dripping Springs, Ark., and drove them in and through Van Buren, capturing about forty wagons, four steamers, and other equipment.

December 29, Monday

BATTLE OF CHICKASAW BAYOU, MISSISSIPPI.

Sherman's forces advanced despite destructive fire toward the foot of the bluffs north of Vicksburg near Chickasaw Bayou. However, the advance was to no avail. A relatively small portion of Pemberton's army easily held off the more numerous Federals. Although there was follow-up action in the next few days, a second attempt on Vicksburg had been foiled. Sherman, admitting his failure, lost 208 killed, 1005 wounded, and 563 missing for a total of 1776 out of about 31,000 effectives. The Confederates lost only 63 killed, 134 wounded, and 10 missing for 207 out of about 14,000 engaged. The position was simply too strong to storm—it was reminiscent of Fredericksburg.

On the roads to Murfreesboro from Nashville there was skirmishing at

Lizzard between Triune and Murfreesboro and at Wilkerson's Cross Road. Morgan was still skirmishing near Johnson's Ferry or Hamilton's Ford on Rolling Fork, and he captured a stockade at Boston, Ky. Federal S. P. Carter in his east Tennessee expedition passed Moccasin Gap and captured a small group of Confederates on the Blountsville Road. There also was an affair near Plaquemine, La.

December 30, Tuesday

Sherman remained in his frustrating Chickasaw Bayou position in front of the bluffs at Vicksburg. Rosecrans slowly approached the main Confederate force outside Murfreesboro with fighting at Jefferson, La Vergne, Rock Spring, and Nolensville, Tenn. Morgan fought again at Springfield and at New Haven, Ky., as he withdrew. Carter in his Federal raid captured Union and Carter's Depot, Tenn., and destroyed bridges across the Holston and the Watauga. There also was a skirmish at La Grange, Ark., and a two-day Union expedition in Virginia from Falmouth to Warrenton and another from Potomac Creek to Richards' and Ellis' Fords.

In Washington Mr. Lincoln produced for his Cabinet a preliminary draft of the final Emancipation Proclamation, to be issued the first of the year, with a request for suggestions. Concerned over dejection and dissension in the Army of the Potomac, Lincoln wired Burnside at Fredericksburg, "I have good reason for saying you must not make a general movement of the army without letting me know."

Shortly after midnight U.S.S. *Monitor* foundered off Cape Hatteras in heavy seas with the loss of sixteen officers and men. *Monitor* sent a distress signal at 11 P.M. Her escort, *Rhode Island,* rescued forty-seven officers and men. The hero of the battle with *Merrimack,* never very seaworthy, was being towed to the Carolina coast.

December 31, Wednesday

BATTLE OF MURFREESBORO OR STONE'S RIVER, TENNESSEE.

ACT ADMITTING WEST VIRGINIA APPROVED.

The Confederates at Murfreesboro, Tenn., had awaited assault from Rosecrans' advancing Federal army, but it had not come on the thirtieth. Now both generals resolved to attack on the last day of the year. Bragg was to swing with his left to crush the Federal right flank; Rosecrans was to swing in much the same way. But Bragg got the initiative and immediately after dawn Hardee's reinforced Southern corps opened strongly on the Federal right. From the beginning the Federals were on the defensive. The Confederate divisions wheeled into line and the Federals wheeled with them, holding for a time until, after several assaults on the Northern flank, the Federals were forced back to the Murfreesboro-Nashville Pike and pinned with their backs against Stone's River. Rosecrans' offensive was called off and by noon he had a strong defensive line along the turnpike. Assaults continued until late afternoon, but the Federals did not break. Casualties of the assaulting Confederates had been heavy but success was theirs. After the day-long fight the armies remained on the field within range of each other; the Confederates entrenching, the Federals conferring. They could withdraw toward Nashville, for the road was still open; they could stay along the road with their backs to the river. Rosecrans, supported by George H. Thomas, decided to stay. Confederate cavalry under Joseph Wheeler had been active all day, riding completely around the Federal army, seizing wagons and supplies and fighting skirmishes. The armies rested as the early December evening fell upon the battlefield.

Sherman continued to explore various plans for assaulting the bluffs at Vicksburg from Chickasaw Bayou. There was an affair at Muldraugh's Hill in Kentucky and a skirmish at Overall's Creek, Tenn.; as well as an affair at Plaquemine, La., that lasted until Jan. 3. At Parker's Store or Cross Roads, Tenn., near Lexington, Forrest, attempting to escape Federal pursuers after his successful raid on Grant's lines, found his way blocked. He managed to push forward, but then was hit also from behind. Forrest was beaten, losing three hundred prisoners, guns, horses, and matériel of war he had captured. But his command managed to escape. Confederate John S. Marmaduke began a month-long raid from Arkansas into Missouri.

In Washington Mr. Lincoln met with his Cabinet to make final adjustments in the Emancipation Proclamation. Burnside, called for court-martial testimony, met with the President. Mr. Lincoln approved an act admitting West Virginia into the Union as the thirty-fifth state, and also signed an agreement with a promoter for a colony of free Negroes on Île à Vache, Haiti.

Mr. Davis wired his Secretary of War from Mobile, "Guns and ammunition most effective against iron clads needed at Vicksburg and Port Hudson. Very much depends upon prompt supply."

1863

As the new year opened, people both North and South wondered what Lincoln's Emancipation Proclamation would really mean. All knew full well the year would see more names on casualty lists, more sorrow, more suffering, and more loss. Many in the Army felt the dread of perhaps not seeing another New Year. They could not foresee the events, but they could possibly foresee some of the results.

What had the year 1862 brought? Since the day in April of 1861 at Fort Sumter some two thousand fights had brought bleeding and death to the American soil. A whole new way of life had evolved from the war. It was evident in political changes, economic changes, social changes, and spiritual changes.

JANUARY, 1863

The new year opened with the sound of artillery and small arms in Tennessee, where the battle at Murfreesboro or Stone's River remained to be decided. In the east the Confederacy could pause a little as Burnside's Federal army was held on the hills beyond Fredericksburg, and Lee's taut host lay between him and the southland. But elsewhere the Confederacy still saw the prongs of possible eventual defeat striking for its vitals. Threats continued on the Mississippi, where more assaults against Vicksburg would come soon, along the coastline, from New Orleans, and from Tennessee. For the North the defeat at Fredericksburg rankled, and there was criticism of the Army, of generals, of Washington. Lincoln had already announced emancipation. For the abolitionists it was not enough; for others it was far too much.

January 1, Thursday
EMANCIPATION PROCLAMATION.
"I do order and declare that all persons held as slaves within said designated States, and parts of States, are, and henceforward shall be free." Thus read the final Emancipation Proclamation of Jan. 1, putting into effect President Lincoln's preliminary proclamation of Sept. 22. Even that very morning discussions had continued, but shortly after noon the President signed the document that opened the door to the end of slavery in the United States. No slaves were freed specifically at that moment, for the Proclamation pertained only to areas "the people whereof shall then be in rebellion against the United States." These areas were indicated. However, as Federal armies advanced into these areas, the slaves were to be free. Further, this final Proclamation provided that former slaves would be officially received into the armed services of the nation. In Tremont Temple, Boston, people met in celebration; at Norfolk, Va., the Negro populace marched through the town, Union flag at their head, cheering; at Beaufort, S.C., the freedmen heard speeches, sang an "Ode for Emancipation Day," and enjoyed five roasted oxen.

In Tennessee at Murfreesboro the armies of Bragg and Rosecrans were poised, awaiting renewal of the struggle along Stone's River. Some troops were shifted and Bragg made a slight indication of attack; there was skirmishing at La Vergne, Stewart's Creek, and Clifton, Tenn. Before dawn on the lowlands around Galveston, Tex., Confederate John B. Magruder, with troops and improvised gunboats, attacked the Union-held city and its flotilla. After about four hours the city surrendered. *Harriet Lane,* her top officers killed, was captured, and *Westfield* was blown up by its crew. Other Federal ships escaped, the blockade temporarily disrupted. One small Northern enclave in Southern land had been erased. Sherman was about to abandon his efforts at Chickasaw Bayou north of Vicksburg; there was an affair near Helena, Ark.; and a skirmish at Bath Springs, Miss.

In Washington the after effects of Fredericksburg came to a head. Burnside consulted with Lincoln on the general's plans to launch another assault across the Rappahannock. Burnside then wrote a frank, open, modest letter stating that officers and men lacked faith in Sec. of War Stanton, in Halleck, and in himself. Burnside pointed out that not a single grand division commander agreed with his plan and that in view of this he believed he should retire to private life, to "promote the public good." Lincoln goaded Halleck into deciding on the military plan and this provoked a resignation from the General-in-Chief. The windup—both Halleck and Burnside stayed. Lincoln's tiring day included the usual New Year's Day reception at the White House.

At Charleston, S.C., one Robert Yeadon offered $10,000 reward for the capture and delivery of Ben Butler, dead or alive.

January 2, Friday

BATTLE OF MURFREESBORO OR STONE'S RIVER, SECOND DAY.

The main fighting at Murfreesboro was on the northeast side of Stone's River. John C. Breckinridge's Confederates succeeded in taking a small hill, only to be driven off with great loss by Federal guns and a countercharge. Again the armies of Bragg and Rosecrans paused on the battlefield, each expecting or hoping the other would withdraw.

Losses for the entire battle are put at 1677 Federals killed, 7543 wounded, and 3686 missing for 12,906 out of 41,400 estimated effectives; 1294 Confederates killed, 7945 wounded, about 2500 missing for a total of 11,739 out of estimated effectives of 35,000.

A Confederate in the ranks wrote of the battle: "I am sick and tired of this war, and, I can see no prospects of having peace for a long time to come, I don't think it ever will be stopped by fighting, the Yankees cant whip us and we can never whip them, and I see no prospect of peace unless the Yankees themselves rebell and throw down their arms, and refuse to fight any longer."

North of Vicksburg on the Yazoo, Sherman gave up his hopeless drive against the bluffs and withdrew to the Mississippi, where his forces came under orders of McClernand. Both Morgan and Forrest completed their campaigns; Morgan recrossed the Cumberland River, while Forrest recrossed the Tennessee at Clifton, Tenn. Another Confederate raider, John

S. Marmaduke, skirmished with Federals at White Springs and Boston Mountains in Arkansas in his advance on Missouri which started from Lewisburg, Ark., Dec. 31. Other fighting included a skirmish near Fort Donelson, Tenn.; a skirmish at Jonesville in Lee County, Va.; an expedition to Moorefield and Petersburg, W. Va., by Federals; and the reoccupation of New Madrid, Mo., by Union troops.

Salutes, celebrations, and meetings followed the Emancipation Proclamation in many Northern cities. In Richmond, belt tightening and high prices were among the new year's gifts to the Confederate people.

January 3, Saturday

Federals pushed two brigades forward at Murfreesboro in a mild attack on Southern lines near Stone's River. During the night, Bragg's Confederate Army of Tennessee, despite apparent victory in the first stages of the battle, withdrew from Murfreesboro toward Tullahoma, Tenn.

Confederates failed in an attack on Moorefield, W. Va.; and there was skirmishing at Burnsville, Miss.; Somerville, and Insane Asylum, Cox's Hill, or Blood's, Tenn.

January 4, Sunday

On the Mississippi Maj. Gen. A. McClernand, with the Federal Army of the Mississippi, including Sherman's corps, began an unauthorized move up the Arkansas River with thirty thousand troops and fifty transports and gunboats toward Arkansas Post or Fort Hindman. There was skirmishing at Murfreesboro and on the Manchester Pike as Bragg continued to withdraw. There was other fighting at Monterey, Tenn., and a scout Jan. 4–6 by Federals from Ozark, Mo., to Dubuque, Ark. Beginning in January and continuing until May, there were continuous operations against Indians in New Mexico Territory by forces of the United States.

In Washington Gen. Halleck, ordered by the President, instructed Grant to revoke General Order No. 11, the controversial document expelling Jews from his department. Grant complied on Jan. 7. A blockade-runner with important dispatches aboard was captured off Charleston by U.S.S. *Quaker City.*

January 5, Monday

Federal troops entered Murfreesboro, although fighting on a minor scale continued at Lytle's Creek, on the Manchester Pike, and on the Shelbyville Pike, Tenn. Confederates raided near Moorefield, W. Va., and there was a skirmish at Cub Run, Va.

Mr. Lincoln tendered the thanks of the country to Rosecrans for his Tennessee victory. In Richmond President Davis, being welcomed home from his trip west, told a serenading crowd that the Confederacy was the last hope "for the perpetuation of that system of government which our forefathers founded—the asylum of the oppressed and the home of true representative liberty." He went on, saying, "Every crime which could characterize the course of demons has marked the course of the invader."

Burnside, pinned down at Fredericksburg, wrote President Lincoln that despite the opinion of his subordinate officers he still thought a crossing of the Rappahannock should be attempted. Again he formally tendered his resignation, "to relieve you from all embarrassment in my case."

January 6, Tuesday

A day of light fighting along Linn Creek in Missouri, and at Fort Lawrence, Beaver Station, Mo., part of the raid by Confederate John S. Marmaduke. A British steamer was seized off Mobile by the blockaders, one of the numerous captures by the day-in, day-out blockade of the Confederate coast. Southern troops captured a Northern riverboat, *Jacob Musselman*, near Memphis.

January 7, Wednesday

Marmaduke's Confederates captured Ozark, Mo., and moved on Springfield. There was a scout from Big Spring Creek to Rock Ford, Miss. Jan. 7–9 a Federal army-navy expedition operated from Yorktown to West Point and White House, Va.

A group of 450 women and children left Washington for Richmond, Va., and the South with permission of the Federal government. The Richmond *Enquirer* called the Emancipation Proclamation "the most startling political crime, the most stupid political blunder, yet known in American history. . . . Southern people have now only to choose between victory and death."

Gen. Halleck wrote Burnside a letter, endorsed by Lincoln, emphasizing that "our first object was, not Richmond, but the defeat or scattering of Lee's army." He also strongly backed Burnside's plan to attack across the Rappahannock. President Davis wrote Lee asking him to call upon the commander of U.S. forces and "prevent the savage atrocities which are threatened." If this met a rebuff, Lee should tell the Federals that "measures will be taken by retaliation to repress the indulgence of such brutal passions."

January 8, Thursday

The Federal garrison of Springfield, Mo., successfully defended the important Ozark area city from Marmaduke's Confederates. Other fighting included a skirmish at Knob Creek near Ripley, Tenn.; an expedition by Federals from Suffolk toward the Blackwater River in Virginia; a Federal reconnaissance to Catlett's and Rappahannock stations, Va.; and a Federal scout from Elkhorn to Berryville, Ark., all three lasting until the tenth.

Confederate Joseph Wheeler carried out a raid Jan. 8–14, which included affairs at Mill Creek, Harpeth Shoals, and Ashland, Tenn.

The U. S. Senate confirmed the nomination of John P. Usher of Indiana as Secretary of the Interior. Usher replaced Caleb Smith, who resigned due to ill health. Mr. Lincoln wrote troubled Gen. Burnside, "I do not yet see how I could profit by changing the command of the A. P. & if I did, I should not wish to do it by accepting the resignation of your commission." Lincoln, defending his Emancipation Proclamation, wrote to Gen. McClernand, saying, "it must stand. . . . As to the States not included in it, of course they can have their rights in the Union as of old."

Mr. Davis wrote his commander in the West, Joseph E. Johnston, "To *hold* the *Mississippi* is *vital.*"

January 9, Friday

The Federal Army of the Cumberland under Rosecrans was reorganized into three corps, the Fourteenth under George H. Thomas, the Twentieth under Alexander McD. McCook, and the Twenty-first under Thomas L. Crittenden. There was skirmishing at Fairfax Court House, Va. The Federal garrison at Hartville, Mo., surrendered to Marmaduke; Holly Springs, Miss., was evacuated by Union forces. In Arkansas there was an expedition from Huntsville to Buffalo River. Salt works near St. Joseph's, Fla., were destroyed by boat crews from U.S.S. *Ethan Allen.*

January 10, Saturday

Federal forces under McClernand had arrived the night of the ninth near Arkansas Post, or Fort Hindman, about fifty miles up the Arkansas River from its junction with the Mississippi. Late in the morning McClernand started his envelopment of the Confederate fort and drove in upon the outer earthworks. Naval bombardment stopped Confederate artillery. Land units were poised to attack the besieged Confederates under Brig. Gen. T. J. Churchill.

There was skirmishing at Carrollton, Ark., and Clifton, Tenn. Federal warships bombarded Galveston, Tex. Mr. Lincoln wrote to Maj. Gen. Curtis in St. Louis of his concern with the slave problem in Missouri. Maj. Gen. Fitz John Porter was sentenced by court-martial to be cashiered from the Army for his alleged failure to obey orders at Second Manassas.

January 11, Sunday

CAPTURE OF ARKANSAS POST OR FORT HINDMAN.

Gunboats under David Dixon Porter battered Confederate guns at Fort Hindman, Ark., and land forces of McClernand began their attack, which continued for three and a half hours. Porter received white flags at the fort and the vastly outnumbered Confederates in the outerworks surrendered. Federal losses were 134 killed, 898 wounded, and 29 missing for a total of

1061 out of 29,000 effectives and 13 gunboats; Confederates lost 28 killed, 81 wounded for a total of 109, with missing (mainly captured) put at 4791, out of close to 5000. While the operation was successful, it failed to help the Vicksburg campaign materially. Grant ordered McClernand to return from this unauthorized expedition and to join his Vicksburg forces.

In one of the rare ship-to-ship duels of the Civil War, C.S.S. *Alabama* under Raphael Semmes sank U.S.S. *Hatteras* off Galveston, Tex. *Hatteras,* on blockade, had investigated a strange ship, only to be attacked and beaten by the superior guns of *Alabama.*

There was fighting at Lowry's Ferry, Tenn.; Wood Creek, Mo.; and an engagement at Hartville, Mo., where Marmaduke's Confederates retreated. Above Memphis on the Mississippi a small group of Confederates surprised, captured, and burned U.S.S. *Grampus No. 2.*

January 12, Monday

The third session of the First Confederate Congress gathered at Richmond and received a message on the state of the Confederacy from President Davis. He optimistically reviewed the military situation, pointing out the halting of Federals in Virginia, at Vicksburg, and in Tennessee. He then went into a long review of foreign relations and the hopes for recognition of the Confederacy. Speaking of the Emancipation Proclamation, Davis said it meant the extermination of the Negro race and encouraged mass assassination of their masters. He called it proof of the "true nature of the designs" of the Republican party. Davis asked for financial legislation, revision of the draft-exemption laws, and relief to citizens suffering war damage.

There was a skirmish at Lick Creek near Helena, Ark. Maj. Gen. John E. Wool assumed command of the Federal Department of the East.

January 13, Tuesday

A Federal expedition from Helena operated up the White River until the nineteenth, capturing St. Charles, Clarendon, Devall's Bluff, and Des Arc, Ark. At the same time there was a Union reconnaissance from Nashville to the Harpeth River and Cumberland River Shoals, and another from Murfreesboro to Nolensville and Versailles, Tenn. There was a skirmish at Carthage, Mo., and a Union expedition from Yorktown to West Point, Va. At the Harpeth Shoals on the Cumberland in Tennessee, U.S. gunboat *Sidell* surrendered to Confederate troops under Joseph Wheeler. Three transports with wounded troops were also seized. The wounded were put on board one vessel and allowed to go on, while the other boats were burned.

Federal officials formally authorized the raising of Negro troops for the South Carolina Volunteer Infantry to be commanded by Col. Thomas Wentworth Higginson. U.S.S. *Columbia* ran aground off North Carolina.

Efforts to float her failed, and the vessel was captured and burned by Confederates.

January 14, Wednesday
   At Bayou Teche, La., three Federal gunboats and troops attacked the Confederate gunboat *Cotton* and land fortifications. After a sharp assault' the gunboat was burned by Confederates the following morning. Confederate Gen. E. Kirby Smith was assigned to command the Army of the, Southwest.

January 15, Thursday
   Federal troops and sailors burned Mound City, Ark., a center of guerrilla activities. The Confederate raider *Florida* sailed from Mobile the night of Jan. 15–16 in a foray against Federal shipping. President Davis suggested' to Gen. Bragg, who had retreated from Murfreesboro to Tullahoma, Tenn., "For the present all which seems practicable is to select a strong position and fortifying it to wait for attack." Lincoln asked if a concentrated horse food should be tested, and ordered a test of some gunpowder, showing his interest in inventions and scientific developments.

January 16, Friday
   There was a Federal expedition from Fort Henry to Waverly, Tenn. Federal gunboat *Baron De Kalb* seized guns and munitions at Devall's Bluff, Ark.

January 17, Saturday
   President Lincoln signed a resolution of Congress providing for the immediate payment of the armed forces, and asked for currency reforms to halt the additional issue of notes that increased the cost of living through inflation. McClernand's Army of the Mississippi began its move downriver to Milliken's Bend near Vicksburg. There was a skirmish near Newtown, Va. From this day to the twenty-first there was a reconnaissance by Federals from New Berne to Pollocksville, Trenton, Young's Cross Roads, and Onslow, N.C., with skirmishes on the nineteenth at White Oak Creek and on the twentieth near Jacksonville.

January 18, Sunday
   There was a skirmish in the Cherokee Country of the Indian Territory, and there was fighting as the Federal expedition proceeded up the White River in Arkansas.

January 19, Monday
   The Confederate Congress debated the Emancipation Proclamation. There was a Federal scout from Williamsburg and a skirmish at Burnt Ordinary, Va. In Tennessee there was a skirmish near Woodbury.

On the Rappahannock Burnside's Federal army began to move in his long-contemplated second attempt to cross the river. Shortly after noon the troops started for U. S. Ford, about ten miles above Fredericksburg. By night the grand divisions of Hooker and Franklin were near the ford. Weather had been mostly excellent since the December battle of Fredericksburg.

Mr. Lincoln, in answer to an address from Manchester, England, workingmen, said he knew and deplored the sufferings among mill hands in Manchester and Europe caused by the cotton shortage, but it was the fault of "our disloyal citizens."

January 20, Tuesday

Burnside, northwest of Fredericksburg, spent the day changing his plans for crossing the Rappahannock, and by evening rain began. The Union general said, "From that moment we felt that the winter campaign had ended." During the night guns and pontoons were dragged into position through the mud and along "shocking" roads. A midwinter storm swept the East, and it snowed in Washington.

Confederate Marmaduke took Patterson, Mo., in his continuing raiding. Maj. Gen. David Hunter, U. S. Army, resumed command of the Department of the South.

January 21, Wednesday

The winter rains continued to be Burnside's worst enemy along the Rappahannock. His advance bogged down in the mud and slime, failing to progress to any appreciable extent. At Sabine Pass, Tex., two Federal blockaders were seized by Confederate steamers. There was a skirmish near Columbia, Mo. A Federal forage train was taken near Murfreesboro, Tenn., while other Union troops carried out a reconnaissance from that city.

Mr. Davis in Richmond ordered Joseph E. Johnston to go to Bragg's army and investigate the retreat from Murfreesboro and criticisms of Bragg's conduct. Davis stated that there was a lack of confidence in their commander among Bragg's officers, and that it was vital that the situation be cleared up. The governor of North Carolina warned the legislature of the Federal invasion. In Ashton, England, the president of the British Board of Trade urged continuation of the policy of neutrality.

At Washington Mr. Lincoln endorsed a letter from Halleck to Grant explaining the revocation of Grant's Order No. 11. It stated that the President did not object to expelling "traitors and Jew peddlers," but "as it in terms proscribed an entire religious class, some of whom are fighting in our ranks, the President deemed it necessary to revoke it." Lincoln formally ordered that Maj. Gen. Fitz John Porter be cashiered and dismissed from the service of the nation and forever disqualified from holding any office of trust or profit in the government. This came after an investigation of the proceedings against Porter for his part in Second Manassas. In 1879 a review of Porter's case resulted in a decision in his favor, but it was not until 1886 that he was reappointed to the rank of colonel.

January 22, Thursday
FAILURE OF BURNSIDE'S "MUD MARCH."

The Federal winter campaign to cross the Rappahannock had failed again, this time due to weather; the Army of the Potomac was literally stalled in the mud. Ammunition trains and supply wagons were mired, horses and mules dropping dead, the whole army dispirited, wet, and hungry. No longer was it a question of how to go on, but of how to get back to the camps opposite Fredericksburg. Ironically Mr. Davis wrote to Lee of his concern over Burnside's movement and pointed out the hazards of retreat if the Federals crossed the Rappahannock.

In the West Grant assumed command of all the Union troops in Arkansas within reach of his orders, reducing McClernand from expedition chief to corps commander. Lincoln let McClernand down gently, writing him, "for my sake, & for the country's sake, you give your whole attention to the better work."

Meanwhile, Grant renewed his attempt to cut a canal across "Swampy Toe" opposite Vicksburg in an effort to move boats and men around the fortress city. There was little fighting except a skirmish in Pocahontas County, W. Va.

January 23, Friday

Another severe winter storm continued to buffet Virginia as Burnside's Federal army pulled back to Fredericksburg, the famed "mud march" a miserable failure. Burnside, stung by defeat and dissension in his army, issued orders to be approved by the President that Hooker, William B. Franklin, W. F. Smith, and others be removed from command. Hooker was to be dismissed from the service entirely. The proposed orders accompanied a request to see the President. They were never carried out.

There was skirmishing at Carthage, and on Bradyville Pike near Murfreesboro, Tenn.; and a scout by Federals Jan. 23-27 from Fayetteville to Van Buren, Ark. Meanwhile, a Union expedition moved until Feb. 1 from Beaufort, S.C., up the St. Mary's River, in Georgia and Florida.

Mr. Lincoln began to draw up orders returning Gen. Butler to New Orleans in place of Gen. Banks. They were never completed, and the action never taken.

January 24, Saturday

The soggy Army of the Potomac settled back into its winter quarters across from Fredericksburg while the arguing, bickering, and quarreling increased. There was a skirmish at Woodbury, Tenn., and a scout in

Fauquier County, Va. Lincoln conferred with Halleck on the military situation and awaited the arrival of Burnside.

January 25, Sunday

HOOKER REPLACES BURNSIDE.

President Lincoln conferred early in the day with Gen. Burnside, who pressed for removal of Hooker, Franklin, and others from command. If this were not done, Burnside would resign as head of the Army of the Potomac. Later in the morning Lincoln told Halleck and Sec. of War Stanton that he was relieving Burnside and naming Joseph Hooker to command the Army of the Potomac. In addition, Lincoln relieved E. V. Sumner and W. B. Franklin from duty with the army. For not quite three months Burnside, who had been reluctant to accept the job in the first place, had commanded the Federal army in Virginia. He had been defeated by Confederates and by mud, and had proved inept, if earnest. Now a new commander was chosen—Hooker, a man who allegedly wanted the job and who was known as a fighter. The news was not unexpected by the army.

In military action Marmaduke's raiding Confederates reached Batesville, Ark.; there was a skirmish near Mill Creek, Tenn., a Union reconnaissance from Murfreesboro to Auburn, Tenn.; and a Yankee scout between Bolivar, Tenn., and Ripley, Miss.

The organization of the first regiment of Union Negro South Carolina soldiers was completed on the Carolina coast.

January 26, Monday

Maj. Gen. Joseph Hooker proudly took command of the Federal Army of the Potomac at Fredericksburg. But Lincoln, in one of his most famous letters, had advice for the new commander: "there are some things in regard to which, I am not quite satisfied with you. I believe you to be a brave and skilful soldier, which, of course, I like. I also believe you do not mix politics with your profession, in which you are right. You have confidence in yourself, which is a valuable, if not an indispensable quality. You are ambitious, which, within reasonable bounds, does good rather than harm. But I think that during Gen. Burnside's command of the Army, you have taken counsel of your ambition, and thwarted him as much as you could, in which you did a great wrong to the country, and to a most meritorious and honorable brother officer. I have heard, in such way as to believe it, of your recently saying that both the Army and the Government needed a Dictator. Of course it was not *for* this, but in spite of it, that I have given you the command. Only those generals who gain successes, can set up dictators. What I now ask of you is military success, and I will risk the dictatorship."

Skirmishing occurred at Township, Fla.; Mulberry Springs, Ark.; Grove Church near Morrisville, Va., and near Fairfax Court House and Middleburg, Va. On the high seas C.S.S. *Alabama* seized another vessel off San Domingo.

January 27, Tuesday

Federal naval forces, led by the monitor U.S.S. *Montauk,* attacked Fort McAllister, a huge earthwork on the Ogeechee River south of Savannah, Ga. After several hours' bombardment, the squadron withdrew. There were affairs at Bloomfield, Mo.; near Germantown, Tenn.; a Federal reconnaissance on the Neuse, Dover, and Trent roads, N.C.; and a skirmish at Deserted House near Suffolk, Va.

The proprietor of the Philadelphia *Journal,* A. D. Boileau, was arrested and taken to Washington for printing anti-Northern material.

President Davis complimented Gov. Brown of Georgia for cutting back cotton cultivation and urging produce cultivation, adding, "The possibility of a short supply of provisions presents the greatest danger to a successful prosecution of the war."

January 28, Wednesday

Mr. Davis wrote Maj. Gen. T. H. Holmes in the Trans-Mississippi that "The loss of either of the two positions,—Vicksburg and Port Hudson, —would destroy communication with the Trans-Mississippi Department and inflict upon the Confederacy an injury which I am sure you have not failed to appreciate."

There were skirmishes at Indian Village, La.; Nashville, Yorkville, and Collierville, Tenn.; and a Federal scout from La Grange, Tenn., toward Ripley, Miss.

In St. Louis a mass meeting ratified the Emancipation Proclamation. Still another heavy snowstorm hit Virginia and the armies on the Rappahannock.

January 29, Thursday

Federal troops defeated the Bannock tribe of Indians in an engagement at Bear River or Battle Creek in Utah Terr. There was skirmishing near Richmond, La.; a Confederate expedition to Daufuskie Island, S.C.; and Federal ships again bombarded defenses of Galveston.

The Confederate Congress authorized the borrowing of $15,000,000 through the French financier Émile Erlanger. Mr. Davis, still apprehensive over Vicksburg, wired Pemberton, "Has anything or can anything be done to obstruct the navigation from Yazoo Pass down?"

January 30, Friday

Gen. Grant assumed immediate command of the entire expedition against Vicksburg and proceeded with various plans to isolate the city. Federal gunboat *Isaac Smith,* reconnoitering in the Stono River near

Charleston, was fired upon by Confederate batteries, went aground, and was captured. There was an engagement at Deserted House or Kelly's Store, near Suffolk, Va., in which Confederates withdrew. A skirmish also occurred at Turner's Mills, Va.

January 31, Saturday
SOUTHERN GUNBOATS ATTACK AT CHARLESTON, SOUTH CAROLINA.

Confederate gunboats *Chicora* and *Palmetto State* moved out of Charleston Harbor, obscured in the haze, and raided the Federal blockaders. *Mercedita* was so severely damaged by ramming and shellfire that she surrendered, but later was able to get under way and escape. *Keystone State* was set afire, her boilers struck with ten or more shell. Other vessels were less seriously damaged. As usual, scalding steam caused most of the casualties, with four killed and three wounded on *Mercedita* and twenty killed and twenty wounded on *Keystone State*. The Confederate ironclads withdrew unhurt. The Confederates took the victory to mean a lifting of the blockade and so declared to foreign powers. But the blockade was not really broken, despite the temporary interruption.

There was an affair on Bull Island, S.C. Jan. 31–Feb. 13. A Federal expedition from Murfreesboro to Franklin included skirmishing at Unionville, Middleton, and Dover, Tenn.

In Morgan County, Ind., the arrest of alleged deserters was resisted and Federal cavalry sent out. After brief shooting, the civilian rioters were dispersed or captured, and the deserters taken into custody.

FEBRUARY, 1863

Thus far it had been a busy winter on the military fronts, but the heavy storms of late January and the usual reluctance to mount major offensives in winter meant a quiet time. There were the usual skirmishes, reconnaissances, the blockade, and similar actions; but the big battles would wait for spring. Nevertheless, the threats present at the first of the year were still apparent to the Confederacy—on the Mississippi at Vicksburg, in Tennessee below Murfreesboro, on the coastline, and of course in Virginia. A new commander for the North, Hooker, was shaping the Army of the Potomac to his taste across from Fredericksburg, while Lee tried to strengthen his Army of Northern Virginia and gather its energy for events to come.

February 1, Sunday

Federal naval forces made their second attack on Fort McAllister south of Savannah, Ga., and again were unsuccessful. Federals occupied Franklin,

Tenn., during a reconnaissance. Feb. 1–10 there was another Federal expedition from New Berne to Plymouth, N.C.

February 2, Monday

Union ram *Queen of the West* ran past the Vicksburg batteries in broad daylight. She was struck twelve times, but not seriously. Her commander, Col. Charles R. Ellet, had been instructed to pass the city, attempt to ram Confederate *City of Vicksburg,* and disrupt Confederate shipping clear down to the Red River. Federals destroyed some salt works at Wale's Head, Currituck Beach, N.C. There were scouts and skirmishes at Vine Prairie on White Oak River and near the mouth of Mulberry River, Ark., and in and about Mingo Swamp, Mo. In Virginia Federals explored the Rappahannock River fords and engaged in a skirmish at Rappahannock Station. Feb. 2–5 there was a Federal reconnaissance near Saulsbury, Tenn.

February 3, Tuesday

Queen of the West under Ellet took three Confederate vessels below Vicksburg. Pork, hogs, salt, molasses, sugar, flour, and cotton were destroyed and a number of prisoners taken, including several ladies. A Confederate attack by Forrest's men on Fort Donelson in Tennessee was repulsed by the Federal garrison and gunboats. In Tennessee also there was a skirmish at the Cumberland Iron Works, and Feb. 3–5 an expedition from Murfreesboro to Auburn, Liberty, and Alexandria, by the North.

In Washington the French minister, M. Mercier, talked with Sec. of State Seward, offering French mediation of the war, but the suggestion was turned down. The levee at Yazoo Pass, far north of Vicksburg, Miss., was opened in an attempt to reach the city via the Yazoo River.

February 4, Wednesday

Federal troops drove Marmaduke's men out of Batesville, Ark.; and there was a skirmish near Murfreesboro, Tenn. Maj. Gen. John Sedgwick succeeded W. F. Smith in command of the Sixth Corps of the Army of the Potomac. Mr. Davis wrote Lee of the worry of authorities over the Federal threats on the South Carolina and Georgia coasts.

February 5, Thursday

Queen Victoria's address to the British Parliament stated that Britain had abstained from attempting to "induce a cessation of the conflict between the contending parties in the North American States, because it has not yet seemed to Her Majesty that any such overtures could be attended with a probability of success."

In Virginia Hooker eliminated the grand divisions of the Army of the Potomac and corps commands were given to J. F. Reynolds, Darius

N. Couch, Daniel E. Sickles, George G. Meade, John Sedgwick, Wm. F. Smith, Franz Sigel, and H. W. Slocum. George Stoneman was assigned to command the cavalry. Operations at Rappahannock Bridge and Grove Church, Va., continued for three days. There was also a skirmish near Olive Branch Church, Va.; a four-day Union scout from Camp Piatt into Wyoming County, W. Va.; a skirmish in Pope County, Ark.; and another on Bear Creek, Johnson County, Mo. Feb. 5–12 Federal scouts operated from Fayetteville to the Arkansas River, with skirmishes at Threlkeld's Ferry and near Van Buren, Ark.

February 6, Friday

Minor fighting occurred at Dranesville, Millwood, at Wiggenton's Mill on Aquia Creek, Va.; there was a Federal scout in the vicinity of Fort Pillow, Tenn. Sec. of State Seward informed the French government that Napoleon III's offer of mediation had been refused by the North.

The Federal Ninth Army Corps under W. F. Smith was transferred from the Army of the Potomac to Newport News, Va., to increase the threat to Richmond from the east.

February 7, Saturday

Three blockade-runners successfully broke through the Federal cordon and arrived at Charleston, S.C. Skirmishing broke out at Olive Branch Church, Va.; Edenton, N.C.; and near Murfreesboro, Tenn. Maj. Gen. S. P. Heintzelman assumed command of the re-created Federal Department of Washington.

February 8, Sunday

The circulation of the Chicago *Times* was suspended by military order for allegedly disloyal statements, only one of numerous such incidents in the North. The order later was rescinded. There was a skirmish near Independence, Mo., and an affair near Camp Sheldon, Miss.

February 9, Monday

There was an affair near Moscow, Tenn., and a skirmish near Somerville, Va. The Confederate Southwestern Army was extended to embrace the entire Trans-Mississippi Department.

February 10, Tuesday

Federal *Queen of the West,* below Vicksburg, steamed down the Mississippi for the Red River in response to orders from David D. Porter. There was skirmishing at Old River, La.; Batchelder's Creek, N.C.; Sarcoxie Prairie, Mo.; and Chantilly, Va. In addition there was an affair near Camp Sheldon, Miss.; a three-day Federal expedition from

Beverly into Pocahontas County, W. Va.; and, until the sixteenth, operations in Westmoreland and Richmond counties, Va.

February 11, Wednesday

The Confederate commissioner to Great Britain James M. Mason addressed a Lord Mayor's banquet in London in his continuing drive for British recognition of the Confederacy.

February 12, Thursday

Action remained limited except for skirmishes near Smithfield and Charles Town, W. Va.; three-day Federal expeditions from Belle Plain to Mattox Creek, Currioman and Nomini bays, Va., and from Pratt's Landing to Heathsville, Va. There also was a two-day Union expedition from Batchelder's Creek and a skirmish on the fourteenth at Sandy Ridge, N.C. On the Red River *Queen of the West* destroyed a train of twelve army wagons, plus seventy barrels of beef and ammunition and stores from another wagon train. U.S.S. *Conestoga* captured two steamers on the White River, Ark. C.S.S. *Florida* captured and later destroyed the clipper ship *Jacob Bell* in the West Indies. Cargo was valued at over $2,000,000.

February 13, Friday

U.S.S. gunboat *Indianola* under George Brown passed Vicksburg batteries at night with two barges, without being struck, despite efforts of the Confederates. There was a skirmish near Washington, N.C.; and a two-day Federal expedition from La Grange, Tenn., to Mount Pleasant and Lamar, Miss.; as well as a skirmish at Dranesville, Va.

At the White House in Washington, Mrs. Lincoln entertained the famous midget Gen. Tom Thumb and his diminutive bride.

February 14, Saturday

On the Red River *Queen of the West* captured the Confederate *New Era No. 5*. A few hours later, while engaging Confederate batteries, the *Queen* went aground. The steam pipe was severed and the vessel had to be abandoned. The men escaped mainly by floating to the U. S. army steamer *De Soto* on cotton bales. The commander, Charles Ellet, put his crew on the captured *New Era No. 5* and burned *De Soto*. Ellet blamed the loss of the *Queen* on a disloyal pilot. On the morning of the fifteenth below Natchez on the Mississippi he met *Indianola*. There were affairs in Virginia near Union Mills, and on the Hillsborough Road, and a scout to Leesburg. From this day to the twenty-sixth there was a Federal expedition to Greenville, Miss., and Cypress Bend, Ark., with several skirmishes.

February 15, Sunday

A day of skirmishing at Arkadelphia, Ark.; and in Tennessee at Auburn, Cainsville, and Nolensville. In Washington Mr. Lincoln was worried about the expedition being planned to attack Charleston.

February 16, Monday

The U. S. Senate passed the Conscription Act. Skirmishing broke out at Bradyville, Tenn.; Yazoo Pass, Miss.; and near Romney, W. Va. At Yazoo Pass the action was part of the delaying operations of Confederates opposing Grant's plan to move gunboats and men down the Yazoo and to the rear of Vicksburg by the back door.

February 17, Tuesday

Indianola posted itself at the mouth of the Red River on the Mississippi below Vicksburg in its operations against Confederate riverboats. Confederate guerrillas attacked the Federal boat *Hercules,* and Federals burned Hopefield, Ark., near Memphis, in retaliation. Two Federal expeditions operated for four days, one from Murfreesboro to Liberty, Tenn., another from Memphis against guerrillas harassing the rear of the advancing Federals. Still another five-day Federal expedition operated from Lexington to Clifton, Tenn.

In Chicago the order restricting circulation of the Chicago *Times* for its allegedly Copperhead sentiments was rescinded by Grant.

Mr. Lincoln, concerned over the raiding in the rear of Federal armies and against their communications, suggested to Gen. Rosecrans that counterraids be made.

Again Virginia and the armies along the Rappahannock were plagued by heavy snow.

February 18, Wednesday

Gen. Beauregard, in command at Charleston, warned Confederates against anticipated attacks on either Charleston or Savannah and cried, "To arms, fellow citizens!" Two divisions of Longstreet's corps from the Army of Northern Virginia were ordered to move from Fredericksburg to east of Richmond to protect the capital from Federal threats via the Peninsula or south of the James. There was an affair near Moscow, Tenn., and until March 5 operations in central Kentucky with several skirmishes. A Democratic convention at Frankfort, Ky., was broken up by Federal authorities, as members were said to be pro-Confederate.

February 19, Thursday

Skirmishing broke out as Grant's army continued reconnaissance and scouts north of Vicksburg. Main fighting was near the Coldwater and

Yazoo rivers. There was a skirmish at Leesburg, Va.; a four-day Federal scout in Barton and Jasper counties, Mo.; a skirmish near Rover, Tenn.; and a Union expedition from Indian Village to Rosedale, La.

At Liverpool and Carlisle in Britain two mass meetings supported Lincoln's Emancipation Proclamation.

President Davis wrote Gen. J. E. Johnston that he regretted "the confidence of the superior officers in Genl. Bragg's fitness for command has been so much impaired. It is scarcely possible in that state of the case for him to possess the requisite confidence of the troops." But he was reluctant to remove Bragg. Davis also continued to be anxious about the Vicksburg situation.

February 20, Friday

There was skirmishing near Fort Halleck, Dakota Terr., between Federal troops and Indians; and in Tennessee on the Shelbyville Pike. The Confederate Congress act providing for issuance of bonds for funding treasury notes was approved. Currency and coins in small denominations being very scarce in the North, merchants were issuing personal notes of one, two, and three cents' value.

February 21, Saturday

Two Federal gunboats attacked Confederate batteries at Ware's Point on the Rappahannock in Virginia; there was a Federal reconnaissance from Franklin on the Lewisburg, Columbia, and Carter Creek roads, Tenn. A public reception was held at the White House in Washington, where the social life had been increasing of late.

February 22, Sunday

On this anniversary of the birth of George Washington, ground was broken at Sacramento, Calif., for the Central Pacific Railroad. There was fighting at Tuscumbia, Ala., and on the Manchester Pike, Tenn.

February 23, Monday

President Lincoln received the resignation of Simon Cameron, former Secretary of War, as minister to Russia. There was an engagement at Fort Caswell, N.C., and an affair at Athens, Ky. Union meetings were held at Cincinnati, Russellville, Ky., and Nashville, Tenn.

February 24, Tuesday

On the Mississippi the Federal gunboat *Indianola* was attacked in the evening by four Confederate vessels including *Queen of the West*, captured and repaired by the Confederates. Rammed repeatedly, *Indianola* fought at close quarters. After seven blows in all, Lieut. Com. George

Brown surrendered *Indianola,* "a partially sunken vessel." The action was a serious blow to Union river operations below Vicksburg.

The Yazoo Pass expedition, intended to move through the Yazoo, Coldwater, and Tallahatchie rivers to the rear of Vicksburg, was well under way. There was a skirmish near Strasburg, Va.

Arizona Territory was organized by the United States as separate from New Mexico Territory.

February 25, Wednesday

The Federal Congress completed passage of the Conscription Act. Mr. Lincoln signed an act setting up a national bank system and national currency, and a Currency Bureau of the Treasury was established with a Comptroller of the Currency. In addition, an act to prevent correspondence with the "present pretended rebel government" was approved.

Off St. Thomas in the West Indies U.S.S. *Vanderbilt* seized the British merchantman *Peterhoff* as a blockade-runner. The capture had been ordered by Acting Rear Admiral Charles Wilkes, "star" of the Trent Affair, from his West India Squadron flagship *Wachusett. Peterhoff* was bound for Matamoros, Mex., and the British claimed the United States had no right to stop such trade, albeit some of the shipments into Mexican ports found their way into the Confederacy. While a major international crisis was averted, the incident focused attention on the considerable trade from Mexico into the South. Eventually courts ruled that the United States could not halt shipping into a neutral port no matter what its ultimate destination.

Skirmishing occurred at Hartwood Church and near Winchester, Strasburg, Woodstock, and Chantilly, Va. Maj. Gen. D. H. Hill assumed command of Confederate troops in North Carolina. In Charleston, S.C., the price of bread per half-pound loaf went to twenty-five cents and flour sold at sixty-five dollars a barrel.

February 26, Thursday

The Cherokee Indian National Council repealed its ordinance of secession, abolished slavery, and vigorously proclaimed for the Union. There was an affair near Germantown, Va. Gen. Longstreet assumed command of the Confederate Department of Virginia and North Carolina. Mr. Davis wrote Gen. T. H. Holmes in the Trans-Mississippi of his concern for that area and the need for full crops and military success to preserve that section for the Confederacy.

Near Woodburn, Tenn., Confederate guerrillas halted, captured, and burned a Federal freight train with merchandise, government stores, and 240 mules.

On the Mississippi during the night a huge, dark hulk moved down from the Federal fleet and silently passed Vicksburg. The now Confederate *Queen of the West* spotted the monster and warned *Indianola*, also now in possession of the Confederates. The Confederate cavalry on board quickly blew up the vessel and fled; "With the exception of the wine and liquor stores of *Indianola*, nothing was saved." But the awesome enemy was nothing more than an old coal barge fitted up by Federals to resemble an ironclad and sent down the river as a joke.

February 27, Friday

President Davis called for a day of fasting and prayer on March 27. Confederate Maj. Gen. Sterling Price was ordered to the Trans-Mississippi Department.

There was a skirmish near Bloomington on the Hatchie River in Tennessee; a Federal expedition from Fort Pillow, Tenn.; and a two-day scout from Centreville to Falmouth, Va.

February 28, Saturday

The Federal monitor *Montauk*, under command of J. L. Worden of *Monitor* fame, moved up the Ogeechee River south of Savannah, aided by other vessels, and destroyed C.S.S. *Nashville* near Fort McAllister. *Nashville*, now the Southern privateer *Rattlesnake*, had been aground near the fort. She was struck numerous times and set afire.

In the Indian Territory a skirmish occurred near Fort Gibson. President Lincoln convened the U. S. Senate for March 4 in a special session to act on a backlog of appointments and promotions. Gen. Lee announced to his army the various achievements of the winter by detachments of the Army of Northern Virginia.

MARCH, 1863

The first glimmerings of spring after a winter of bitter weather brought with them increased worries in the South and hope mingled with discontent in the North. In Virginia Hooker continued to prepare to move against Lee. In Tennessee Rosecrans and Bragg were doing little; grumbling swelled on both sides. Northern citizens were critical even of Grant, who was apparently spasmodically trying one thing after another on the Mississippi in futile attempts to take Vicksburg. The Confederate government saw the signs that Vicksburg would soon be attacked in earnest, and extensive, though futile, efforts were being made to save it.

March 1, Sunday

Sunday was broken by skirmish at Bradyville and Woodbury, Tenn., with other action March 1–2 near Bloomfield, Mo. A Federal expedition

March 1–6 from New Berne to Swan Quarter, N.C., was marked by several skirmishes. The Federal Congress was preparing to end its session. Mr. Lincoln conferred with Sec. of War Stanton and other officers about military appointments.

March 2, Monday

Skirmishing occurred at Eagleville and Petersburg, Tenn.; Neosho, Mo.; and Aldie, Va. There was a two-day Federal scout from La Grange, Tenn., to Hudsonville and Salem, Miss., and Saulsbury, Tenn. Federals began an expedition from New Orleans to the mouth of the Rio Grande that lasted until the twentieth.

The Federal Congress confirmed the appointment of four major and nine brigadier generals for the Regular Army, as well as forty major and two hundred brigadier generals of volunteers. Thirty-three U. S. Army officers, found guilty by court-martial of various charges, were dismissed from the service.

March 3, Tuesday

FEDERAL DRAFT ACT APPROVED.

President Lincoln signed "An Act for enrolling and calling out the National Forces, and for other purposes." This, the first effective Federal draft, imposed liability on all male citizens between twenty and forty-five with the exception of the physically or mentally unfit, men with certain types of dependents, those convicted of a felony, and various high Federal and state officials. Draft quotas for each district would be set by the President on the basis of population and the number of men already in the service from each district. A drafted man could hire another as a substitute or purchase his way out for $300. Despite its many defects, the measure increased volunteering. For the entire war only 162,535 men, or about 6 per cent, were raised by the draft. Of these 46,347 were held to personal service and 116,188 furnished substitutes. An additional 86,724 paid commutation.

Other acts approved by the President as Congress neared the end of a session were: an act to prevent and punish frauds on revenue; an act to turn over to the Treasury in trust all captured and abandoned cotton, sugar, rice, and tobacco in states in insurrection; a loan to the government authorizing $300,000,000 for 1863, and $600,000,000 for 1864; an act fixing the number of Supreme Court justices at ten; authorization for the President to suspend the privilege of writ of habeas corpus in any necessary case during the war; issuance of not more than $50,000,000 in fractional currency to replace postage stamp currency; a measure making Idaho a territory; and one naming Jay Cooke as government agent to direct the campaign to popularize the sale of U.S. bonds.

Still another Federal naval attack on Fort McAllister below Savannah,

Ga., failed despite eight hours of bombardment. Confederates raided Granby, Mo., and there was skirmishing near Bear Creek, Tenn. Federal expeditions operated for six days each from Murfreesboro to Woodbury, Tenn., and from Belle Plain to Coan River and Machodoc Creek, Va. Still another Union expedition, of four days, was from Concord Church to Chapel Hill, Tenn.

March 4, Wednesday

The Federal Congress adjourned. There was fighting at Unionville, Tenn., and at Independent Hill in Prince William County, Va. Federal forces from Franklin moved toward Thompson's Station or Spring Hill, Tenn. Surrounded by Van Dorn and Forrest, the Federal cavalry escaped, but the Union infantry was forced to surrender on March 5 after a heavy engagement. The same day a ten-day Federal expedition from Murfreesboro began operating in the same area, with several skirmishes.

March 5, Thursday

Federals continued digging a canal opposite Vicksburg despite occasional shells thrown in that direction by the Confederate batteries in the city. Federal soldiers acting on their own badly damaged the offices of the allegedly pro-Southern Columbus, Ohio, *Crisis.*

There was a skirmish opposite Fort Smith, Ark. March 5–12 a Federal expedition operated from Helena up the St. Francis and Little rivers with a skirmish at Madison, Ark. Another Federal operation was carried out March 5–13 in Newton and Jasper counties, Mo.

March 6, Friday

A skirmish on the White River, Ark., and three expeditions featured a quiet day. March 6–8 there were forays by Federals from New Berne to Trenton and Swansborough, N.C., and also demonstrations on Kinston, N.C. March 6–10 troops operated from Helena to Big and Lick creeks, Ark.

March 7, Saturday

On the Mississippi Gen. Banks' Federal force moved north from New Orleans to Baton Rouge and toward Port Hudson in its operations to cooperate with Grant's activities against Vicksburg to the north. For the Confederacy, Lieut. Gen. E. Kirby Smith assumed command of all forces west of the Mississippi River. There was a skirmish at Green Spring Run, W. Va. Expeditions, scouts, reconnaissances continued at accelerated pace. March 7–9 there was a Federal reconnaissance from Suffolk to near Windsor, Va.; March 7–10 from Newport Barracks to Cedar Point, N.C.; and March 7–14 an expedition from New Berne to Mattamuskeet Lake, N.C.

In Baltimore the Federal army forbade the sale of "secession music" and confiscated all such song sheets.

March 8, Sunday

It was a quiet night at Fairfax County Court House, Va., where Brig. Gen. E. H. Stoughton and his garrison lay in bed. Twenty-nine men under Capt. John S. Mosby stealthily entered the town, reached the general's headquarters and his bedroom. The startled general, himself looking for the "rebel guerrilla" Mosby, was captured ignominiously in bed. The loot of the daring raid included Gen. Stoughton, two captains, thirty other prisoners, fifty-eight horses of high quality, and arms and equipment. Mosby's band and his captures evaded numerous Federal outposts and camps on their departure from Fairfax County Court House. A chagrined North and a jubilant South saw this adventure of war in different lights.

Two four-day Federal expeditions operated from La Grange to near Covington, and from Collierville, Tenn. March 8–16 Confederate forces operated against New Berne, N.C., with several skirmishes, but were driven off.

March 9, Monday

In Charleston, S.C., James Louis Petigru died at seventy-four. Admired and known throughout the country as a jurist, a loyal unionist in the midst of secession, Petigru was the outstanding pro-Northern advocate in the Confederacy. Full of pithy and sarcastic statements, Petigru nevertheless maintained the respect and friendship of Charlestonians despite his political views.

At Vicksburg a second "Quaker" or fake ironclad made of logs with pork barrels for funnels drifted down past the city and was subjected to fire from the Confederate batteries. There was a skirmish at Hazle Green, Ky.; a skirmish near St. Augustine, Fla.; an affair at Fairfax Court House, Va.; and skirmishes on the Comite River at Montesano Bridge near Port Hudson, La. A Federal expedition operated March 9–15 from Bloomfield, Mo., to Chalk Bluff, Ark., and to Gum Slough, Kennett, Hornersville, Mo.; while in Tennessee from this day to the fourteenth a Union reconnaissance operated from Salem to Versailles.

March 10, Tuesday

Federal troops, mainly Negro, reoccupied Jacksonville, Fla., without difficulty. There was a skirmish near Murfreesboro, Tenn.; and three days of fighting near Plymouth, N.C.; as well as, March 10–16, a Federal scout to La Fayette and Moscow, Tenn.

President Lincoln issued a proclamation of amnesty to soldiers absent without leave if they reported before April 1; otherwise they would be arrested as deserters. President Davis questioned Gen. Pemberton at Vicksburg over Federal progress.

March 11, Wednesday

FORT PEMBERTON BLOCKS YANKEES.

Federal gunboats and troops moved through the tangle of bayous and overgrown waterways from Yazoo Pass off the Mississippi to the Yalobusha River, ninety miles from Vicksburg. But Pemberton had sent Maj. Gen. W. W. Loring to construct Fort Pemberton near Greenwood. The fort, built rapidly of earth and cotton bales on flooded ground, successfully repelled the first of several attacks by Union gunboats seeking passage. By March 16 the Federals were forced to withdraw. Another of Grant's efforts against Vicksburg had come to an end, foiled by geography and the Confederates.

There was a mild affair near Paris, Ky. In Baltimore a Federal commander prohibited the sale of pictures of Confederate generals and statesmen.

March 12, Thursday

The Federal force under Gordon Granger that had been operating to the Duck River in Tennessee returned to Franklin, after several skirmishes. March 12–16 Northern troops scouted from Camp Piatt through Boone, Wyoming, and Logan counties of West Va.; and March 12–20 there was a Federal expedition from Columbus, Ky., to Perryville, Tenn.

March 13, Friday

Federal gunboats and troops renewed their fruitless bombardment at Fort Pemberton on the Yalobusha near Greenwood, Miss. After a hard day of fighting, the fort still stood between them and Vicksburg.

There was a skirmish at Rover and an affair near Charlotte, Tenn. An explosion at the Confederate Ordnance Laboratory in Richmond killed or injured sixty-nine, including sixty-two women. A friction primer accidentally ignited.

March 14, Saturday

PASSAGE OF PORT HUDSON.

During the night, Adm. Farragut in his flagship *Hartford* led his Union squadron up the Mississippi past the batteries of Port Hudson, La. *Hartford* and *Albatross* succeeded in getting through, but *Monongahela* and *Richmond* were damaged and had to drop back. *Mississippi* ran aground and was under severe fire. She was set ablaze and abandoned, soon exploding in the river. Confederate batteries were deadly accurate and for a time threatened to destroy the entire flotilla. Meanwhile, Gen. Banks' troops carried out demonstrations on the land side of Port Hudson. There was a skirmish at Davis' Mill, Tenn.

March 15, Sunday

There were skirmishes at Hernando, Miss.; Rover, Tenn.; an affair near Dumfries, and a Federal scout from Harper's Ferry to Leesburg, Va. In San Francisco authorities seized the schooner *J. M. Chapman,* about to depart with twenty alleged secessionists and six Dahlgren guns. The British *Britannia* successfully ran the blockade into Wilmington, N.C., but all along the coasts this spring interception of blockade-runners had been increasing.

March 16, Monday

While the Yazoo Pass expedition was ending at Fort Pemberton on the Yalobusha north of Vicksburg, Grant and Porter launched another effort against the city via Steele's Bayou. The plan was to move through some two hundred miles of tortuous, twisting bayous from the Yazoo River to Steele's Bayou and thence behind the fortress. Eleven vessels were supported by Sherman's infantry. Confederates, ready for such an effort, had obstructed the narrow waterways even more than nature already had, making progress laborious and slow.

There was also a Federal expedition from Jackson to Trenton, Tenn.

March 17, Tuesday

BATTLE OF KELLY'S FORD.

Federal cavalry under William Woods Averell, ordered to operate against Confederates around Culpeper, crossed the Rappahannock at Kelly's Ford, Va., and were strongly engaged by Confederates who rushed up to halt the Federal troops. In the brush-covered country and on the Wheatley Farm a small but hard-fought contest resulted in Averell's withdrawal late in the afternoon. Casualties were 78 for the Federals and 133 for the Confederates. Young John Pelham, "the gallant Pelham," was killed, although he was merely a Southern observer at the fight. Mourned by the South, Pelham had been heroic at Fredericksburg and was marked as a rising soldier.

There were skirmishes at Bealeton Station, Herndon Station, and near Franklin, Va. On the Mississippi Farragut was off Natchez with U.S.S. *Hartford* and *Albatross.*

Lincoln answered a complaining telegram from Gen. Rosecrans, ". . . you wrong both yourself and us, when you even suspect there is not the best disposition on the part of us all here to oblige you."

March 18, Wednesday

Mr. Lincoln wrote Congressman Henry Winter Davis in regard to the House of Representatives, "Let the friends of the government first save the government, and then administer it to their own liking." In Paris the house of Erlanger opened a loan of three million pounds to the

Confederacy based on 7 per cent bonds for twenty years. Lieut. Gen. Theophilus H. Holmes assumed command of the Confederate District of Arkansas.

March 19, Thursday

Farragut's *Hartford* and *Albatross* ran past the Grand Gulf, Miss., batteries just below Vicksburg. Skirmishing increased on the various fronts with action near Winchester, Va.; at Frog Bayou, Ark.; Mount Sterling and Hazle Green, Ky.; and Richland Station, Spring Hill, Liberty, and College Grove, Tenn. In Missouri from this day to the twenty-third there was a Federal scout toward Doniphan. Two divisions of the Federal Ninth Army Corps embarked at Newport News headed for the Department of the Ohio.

March 20, Friday

President Lincoln, concerned over Vicksburg, asked Maj. Gen. Stephen A. Hurlbut at Memphis, "What news have you? What from Vicksburg? What from Yazoo Pass? What from Lake Providence? What generally?" Hurlbut told him of the various unsuccessful efforts to reach Vicksburg.

There was a small engagement at Vaught's Hill near Milton, Tenn., and an affair in St. Andrew's Bay, Fla.

March 21, Saturday

On Steele's Bayou the gunboats, backed up by Sherman's troops, were harassed by sharpshooting Confederates along the banks. A skirmish was fought on Deer Creek, Miss. Other fighting was in Tennessee: skirmishing at Salem and Triune, a Confederate guerrilla attack on a railroad train between Bolivar and Grand Junction, and a two-day Union scout from La Grange to Saulsbury. For the last part of the month, there were two Federal expeditions operating, one from New Orleans to Ponchatoula, La., and another from Bonnet Carré to the Jackson Railroad and Amite River, La. Farragut's gunboats anchored just below Vicksburg on the Mississippi.

Federal Maj. Gen. Edwin Vose Sumner, an aged yet sturdy fighter, who had done well in the Peninsula and at Antietam, died at Syracuse, N.Y.

March 22, Sunday

Confederates under Basil Duke of Morgan's cavalry began a new campaign with the capture of a Federal garrison at Mount Sterling, Ky. Other Confederates under John Pegram operated in Kentucky until April 1.

There was a skirmish at Blue Springs near Independence, Mo.; another near the head of White River, Ark.; yet another near Murfreesboro, Tenn. Affairs occurred at Seleeman's Ford and Mrs. Violett's near Occoquan, Va.

March 23, Monday

Federal troops carried out operations near Jacksonville, Fla. The Federal *Hartford* and *Albatross* attacked the Confederate batteries at Warrenton on the Mississippi below Vicksburg. Other fighting was at Winfield, N.C.; Thompson's Station, Tenn.; and Little River Turnpike near Chantilly, Va.

A Confederate act provided for the funding of treasury notes issued previous to Dec. 1, 1862, and for further issuance of treasury notes for not less than $5 nor more than $50 each.

Mr. Lincoln wrote Gov. Horatio Seymour of New York, sometime opponent of the Administration, "there can not be a difference of *purpose* between you and me. If we should differ as to the *means,* it is important that such difference should be as small as possible—that it should not be enhanced by unjust suspicions on one side or the other."

The treaty between the United States and Liberia was promulgated.

March 24, Tuesday

In the watery web of Steele's Bayou north of Vicksburg there was another skirmish, this time on Black Bayou, as the Federal expedition struggled to make its way through the swamps and lowlands. The action signified the end of the Steele's Bayou effort as the gunboats slowly withdrew, Sherman's troops with them. While annoying to the Confederates, the expedition proved little except the impracticability of using the inland waterways to reach Vicksburg. It was the last of a number of unsuccessful efforts to find entrance to Vicksburg, the last before the slowly mounting major effort under Grant.

Basil Duke with part of Morgan's Confederate cavalry fought at Danville, Ky. There was skirmishing at Rocky Hock Creek, N.C.; on Davis' Mill Road near La Grange, Tenn.; and an affair in Ocklockonnee Bay, Fla. Federal scouts operated from Fayetteville, Ark., during the last week of the month.

March 25, Wednesday

There was more fighting on Black Bayou as the Federal expedition on Steele's Bayou continued to bog down. Two Federal rams attempted to run the Vicksburg batteries from north to south. *Lancaster,* struck some thirty times, sank with most of the crew escaping. *Switzerland,* badly disabled, floated down out of firing range. Confederate Forrest raided Brentwood and Franklin, Tenn. There was skirmishing at Jacksonville, Va.; an affair at Norfolk, Va.; skirmishing near Louisa, Ky.; and a Federal expedition from Belle Plain into Westmoreland County, Va.

Gen. Burnside, former commander of the Army of the Potomac, superseded Maj. Gen. Horatio G. Wright in command of the Department of the Ohio. Federal monitors were reported leaving Hilton Head for Charleston Harbor.

March 26, Thursday

The voters of West Virginia approved gradual emancipation of slaves. A Confederate congressional act authorized the impressment of forage or other property, including slaves, when necessary for the army in the field.

There was a Federal reconnaissance from Murfreesboro to Bradyville, Tenn. Mr. Lincoln wrote to Gov. Andrew Johnson of Tennessee, "The colored population is the great *available* and yet *unavailed* of, force for restoring the Union. The bare sight of fifty thousand armed, and drilled black soldiers on the banks of the Mississippi, would end the rebellion at once."

March 27, Friday

There was a skirmish at Palatka, Fla., and another on the Woodbury Pike, Tenn. President Lincoln addressed representatives of a number of Indian tribes, saying, "I can see no way in which your race is to become as numerous and prosperous as the white race except by living as they do, by the cultivation of the earth."

March 28, Saturday

There was an engagement at Pattersonville, La., between Confederate land forces and Union gunboats. U.S.S. *Diana* was captured. In addition to a skirmish at Hurricane Bridge, W. Va., a Federal expedition operated from La Grange to Moscow and Macon, Tenn., until April 3.

March 29, Sunday

Gen. Grant ordered McClernand to march south from Milliken's Bend on the west side of the Mississippi to New Carthage, below Vicksburg. Sherman and McPherson were to follow. At this time Sherman's men were digging another canal to the west of Vicksburg. Known as the Duckport Canal, it was another failure. There was skirmishing at Jacksonville, Fla.; Kelly's Ford and Williamsburg, Va.; an affair at Moscow, Tenn.; and another at Dumfries, Va.

March 30, Monday

It was a day of extensive skirmishing: Basil Duke of Morgan's cavalry at Dutton's Hill, Ky.; Zoar Church, Va.; Point Pleasant, W. Va.; Cross Hollow, Ark.; Tahlequah, Indian Terr.; "The Island" in Vernon County, Mo. In North Carolina Confederates laid siege to the city of Washington, with skirmishing at Rodman's Point on the Pamlico River and near Deep Gully.

President Lincoln set aside April 30 as a national fast and prayer day.

March 31, Tuesday

Grant's operations from Milliken's Bend to New Carthage were well under way as he began still another attempt to capture Vicksburg. Jacksonville, Fla., was evacuated by Federals. On the Mississippi Adm. Farragut successfully took *Hartford, Switzerland,* and *Albatross* past the Grand Gulf batteries, moving below them after engaging. There was fighting at Eagleville and Franklin, Tenn.; Clapper's Saw Mill on Crooked Creek; and at Cross Hollow, Ark. Federals carried out a four-day scout from Lexington, Tenn., to the mouth of the Duck River.

In Washington a careworn Lincoln attended a Union meeting and also authorized restricted commercial intercourse with states in insurrection under the regulations prescribed by the Secretary of the Treasury.

APRIL, 1863

Spring had come and major battles would soon follow. Both Federal and Confederate detachments moved along the fronts, penetrating here and there, constantly looking for the strategical advantage. Vital events would soon occur along the Rappahannock near Fredericksburg, and out on the Mississippi at Vicksburg. Meanwhile, the public watched the movements of Grierson and Streight, Wheeler, Forrest, and others.

The new commander of the Army of the Potomac was expected to do something. The long series of futile adventures on the Mississippi around Vicksburg brought queries from the North. At the South discontent increased in isolated places, though spirits remained high. Confederate forces had not had too bad a winter, and had confidence in Lee and Jackson.

April 1, Wednesday

April, 1863, began with minor skirmishes at Chalk Bluff and Clarendon, Ark.; White River and Carroll County, Mo.; Columbia Pike, Tenn.; and near the mouth of Broad Run in Loudoun County, Va. An engagement occurred at Rodman's Point, N.C. April 1–5 Federals scouted from Linden to White River, Mo. Federal expeditions in Tennessee from Murfreesboro to Lebanon, Carthage, and Liberty, and from Jackson to the Hatchie River lasted until April 8.

Longstreet's command was reorganized by the Confederates to create the Department of North Carolina under Maj. Gen. D. H. Hill, the Department of Richmond under Maj. Gen. Arnold Elzey, and the Department of Southern Virginia under Maj. Gen. S. G. French.

Maj. Gen. Francis J. Herron superseded Brig. Gen. John M. Schofield in command of the Federal Army of the Frontier.

April 2, Thursday
RICHMOND "BREAD RIOT."

A mob crowded around a wagon in Richmond, demanding bread. What followed was the so-called "bread riot" of the Confederate capital. Exact causes are still obscure, but there was genuine want in Richmond and elsewhere in the beleaguered South. The unruly mob and allegedly disreputable citizens who gathered plundered other than bread as they broke into shops and purloined what met their fancy. President Davis addressed the throng from a wagon near the Capitol building, and threw them the money he had in his pocket. Careful action by militia and police dispersed the crowd and arrests were made without bloodshed. Although a minor incident, it gave pause to the Confederate government and was unsettling throughout the Confederacy.

Fighting included an engagement at Hill's Point on Pamlico River in North Carolina. Skirmishing occurred on the Little Rock Road, Ark.; on the Carter Creek Pike, and at Woodbury and Snow Hill, Tenn.; and an affair occurred in Jackson County, Mo. April 2–6 there was a Union scout in Beaver Creek Swamp, Tenn., and a reconnaissance by Federals from near Murfreesboro. A Federal expedition operated until the fourteenth to Greenville, Black Bayou, and Deer Creek, Miss.

Maj. Gen. O. O. Howard superseded Maj. Gen. Carl Schurz in command of the Eleventh Corps of the Army of the Potomac.

President Lincoln revoked exceptions to his August, 1861, proclamation banning commercial intercourse with insurgent states. Experience had shown, he said, that the proclamation as it was could not be enforced. Trading was restricted to that permitted by the Secretary of the Treasury.

President Davis, in response to criticism of Northern-born Gen. Pemberton, wrote, "by his judicious disposition of his forces and skilful selection of the best points of defence he has repulsed the enemy at Vicksburg, Port Hudson, on the Tallahatchie and at Deer Creek, and has thus far foiled his every attempt to get possession of the Mississippi river and the vast section of country which it controls."

April 3, Friday
President Davis wrote to Gov. Harris Flanagin of Arkansas regarding the Mississippi Valley, "if we lost control of the Eastern side, the Western must almost inevitably fall into the power of the enemy. The defense of the fortified places on the Eastern bank is therefore regarded as the defense of Arkansas quite as much as that of Tennessee, Mississippi, and Louisiana." Gov. Milledge L. Bonham of South Carolina asked the legislature

for measures to halt increasing speculation and hoarding of flour, corn, bacon, and other goods.

President Lincoln told Gen. Hooker that he planned to visit the Army of the Potomac that weekend. At Reading, Pa., there was an uproar over the arrest of four men alleged to be members of the pro-Southern Knights of the Golden Circle.

Operations were confined to a four-day expedition through Logan and Cabell counties, W. Va., and a five-day scout from Carrollton to Yellville, Ark., both by Federals. Union sailors and marines carried out operations in the Bayport, Fla., area until April 9. Federal riverboat crews destroyed Palmyra, Tenn., in retaliation for an attack on a Union convoy April 2.

April 4, Saturday

Federal forces failed to capture a strong Confederate battery in an engagement at Rodman's Point, not far from Washington, N.C. Skirmishes occurred at Woodbury, on the Lewisburg Pike, and on Nonconnah Creek near Memphis, Tenn., and at Richmond, La. The latter involved forces of Grant's command, who were moving from Milliken's Bend toward New Carthage, La., on the west side of the Mississippi.

Lincoln and his party left Washington by boat for Fredericksburg.

April 5, Sunday

Mr. Lincoln conferred with Gen. Hooker. There were skirmishes at Davis' Mill, Tenn., and near New Carthage, La. Two-day Federal scouts operated from La Grange, Tenn., to Early Grove and Mount Pleasant, Miss., and from Grand Junction to Saulsbury, Tenn.

April 6, Monday

Mr. Lincoln, at Hooker's headquarters, about this date expressed his opinion of military strategy in Virginia. In a memorandum he wrote, "our prime object is the enemies' army in front of us, and is not with, or about, Richmond. . . ."

At Liverpool the British government seized the Confederate vessel *Alexandria* which was fitting out in the British harbor. Near New Carthage, La., on the Mississippi, skirmishing continued, and fighting broke out at Town Creek, Ala.; Nixonton, N.C.; and Burlington, Purgitsville, and Goings' Ford, W. Va. Near Green Hill, Tenn., a Federal dash captured a few Confederates and destroyed a stillhouse with forty casks of liquor.

April 7, Tuesday

NAVAL ATTACK ON CHARLESTON.

Nine Federal ironclads under Flag Officer Samuel Du Pont steamed into Charleston Harbor and attacked Fort Sumter in the afternoon. Both Sumter and Fort Moultrie returned the fire. *Weehawken* was struck 53 times in 40 minutes, *Passaic* 35 times, *Montauk* 47 times, *Nantucket* 51 times, *Patapsco* 47 times. Other vessels were similarly hit and damaged. Confederates threw 2209 shells compared with 154 from the ironclads. Battered by the forts and endangered by obstructions and torpedoes or mines, the Federal fleet withdrew, five vessels disabled. At darkness Du Pont decided that Charleston could not be taken by naval force alone. Fort Sumter suffered severe damage to its walls and casemates, which nonetheless were readily repaired. U.S.S. *Keokuk,* hit ninety times, sank the next morning. Casualties were light on both sides.

Confederate Joseph Wheeler raided the Louisville and Nashville and the Nashville and Chattanooga railroads in Tennessee, April 7–11. Other fighting included skirmishes at Liberty, Tenn., and at Dunbar's Plantation near Bayou Vidal, La. Federals operated from Gloucester Point to Gloucester Court House, Va. On the Amite River in Louisiana the Federal steamer *Barataria* was attacked and captured while making a reconnaissance.

April 8, Wednesday

McClernand's men continued operations below Milliken's Bend around New Carthage on the Mississippi. In addition to preparing roads and bringing in supplies, skirmishing was frequent, including a brief fight at James' Plantation. Skirmishing occurred on the Millwood Road near Winchester, Va., and at St. Francis County, Ark.

President Lincoln reviewed portions of Hooker's army at Falmouth, across the Rappahannock from Fredericksburg.

April 9, Thursday

A day of small operations with skirmishes at Sedalia, Mo.; White River, Ark.; Franklin, and near the Obion River, Tenn.; Berwick Bay, La.; Gloucester Point, Va.; and Blount's Mills, N.C.

April 10, Friday

"Let fields be devoted exclusively to the production of corn, oats, beans, peas, potatoes, and other food for man and beast; let corn be sown broadcast for fodder . . . and let all your efforts be directed to the prompt supply of these articles in the districts where our armies are operating;" wrote President Davis, concurring with congressional opposition to planting of cotton and tobacco. In a proclamation, the Confederate President said, "Alone, unaided, we have met and overthrown the most formidable combination of naval and military armaments that the lust of conquest ever gathered together for the subjugation of a free people. . . . We must not forget, however, that the war is not yet ended, and that we are still confronted by powerful armies and threatened by numerous fleets; and that the Government which controls these fleets and armies is driven to the most desperate efforts to effect the unholy purposes in which it has thus far been defeated." Meanwhile, Lincoln reviewed more troops at Falmouth, Va., and left Aquia Creek for Washington in the afternoon.

Confederates under Earl Van Dorn attacked Federals at Franklin, Tenn., in a sharp engagement, but a counterattack forced the Confederates to withdraw. Skirmishing on Folly Island, S.C.; an expedition from Humboldt to Cottonwood, Kas.; and a two-day Federal scout from La Grange, Tenn., into Mississippi, completed the day's activities.

April 11, Saturday

Longstreet's Confederate corps from the Army of Northern Virginia advanced upon Suffolk, south of the James, beginning a siege of nearly a month. Scouts and skirmishes filled the day with action at Williamsburg, and on the South Quay Road near the Blackwater in Virginia; near Pattersonville, La.; La Grange to Saulsbury, Tenn.; Courtney's Plantation, Miss.; Webber's Falls, Indian Terr.; and near Squirrel Creek Crossing, Colo. Terr. In West Virginia from this day to the eighteenth Federals scouted from Beverly to Franklin. In Utah Territory there was an expedition by Federals against the Indians, April 11–20 from Camp Douglas to the Spanish Fork Cañón. A half-dozen Federal blockaders managed to force the blockade-runner *Stonewall Jackson* ashore off Charleston, S.C.

Out from Nashville Col. A. D. Streight moved with a force of seventeen hundred Federal cavalry on a raid to operate deep into Georgia.

Mr. Lincoln, just returned from the camps of Hooker's Army of the Potomac, conferred with Cabinet members and Gen. Halleck on military problems.

April 12, Sunday

President Lincoln received a letter from Gen. Hooker proposing to outflank Lee's army, opposing Hooker on the Rappahannock. Hooker would move across the river, turn the Confederate left, and use cavalry to sever connections with Richmond.

In Louisiana there was an affair on the Amite River. Skirmishing and reconnaissances occurred at Stewartsborough, Tenn.; from Gloucester Point to the vicinity of Hickory Forks, Va.; Edenton, Providence Church, and Somerton Roads, Va., and from Winchester up the Cedar Creek Valley of Virginia. In the Far West a Federal expedition operated against marauding Indians to the twenty-fourth from Camp Babbitt to Keysville, Calif.

April 13, Monday

Mr. Lincoln ordered Adm. Du Pont to hold his position inside the Charleston Harbor bar. The President had expressed anxiety over the failure of the Federal ironclads in their operations against the South

Carolina port. In the Department of the Ohio, Gen. Burnside ordered the death penalty for anyone guilty of aiding the Confederates and also ordered deportation of Southern sympathizers to Confederate lines.

Fighting flared in widely separated areas: at Porter's and McWilliams' plantations at Indian Bend, La.; Chapel Hill, Tenn.; Elk Run and Snicker's Ferry, Va. Banks' Federals assaulted Fort Bisland on Bayou Teche, La., in a heavy engagement. The Confederates withdrew during the night. Federals carried out expeditions to the twenty-first from New Berne to Swift Creek Village, N.C.

April 14, Tuesday

Federal troops marched into evacuated Fort Bisland, La., on Bayou Teche. The Confederates burned two of their own gunboats and the former Federal gunboat *Queen of the West,* veteran of so many engagements, was destroyed by Federal naval fire.

Also in Louisiana there was an engagement at Irish Bend, and a skirmish at Jeanerette. In Virginia, not far from Suffolk, an engagement was fought at the mouth of West Branch near the Norfleet House on the Nansemond River. In the vicinity of Rappahannock Bridge, and at Kelly's, Welford's, and Beverly fords, Va., cavalry of Hooker's army carried out operations. Again Lincoln impressed upon his officers the need for remaining before Charleston.

April 15, Wednesday

Grant's forces continued to move from Milliken's Bend on the Mississippi to below Vicksburg, skirmishing near Dunbar's Plantation on Bayou Vidal, La. Confederate troops withdrew from their siege of Washington, N.C., begun March 30, on the approach of a Federal relieving force. For the second day troops engaged near the Norfleet House, Va., not far from Suffolk. A skirmish occurred at Piketon, Ky.; and an expedition operated from La Grange to Saulsbury, Tenn. Banks' Federals occupied Franklin, La. From this day to May 2, Federals carried out an expedition from Corinth, Miss., to Courtland, Ala. C.S.S. *Alabama* took two U.S. whalers off the island of Fernando de Noronha, Brazil.

Lincoln expressed concern to Gen. Hooker over the slowness of Gen. Stoneman's cavalry operations on the Rappahannock.

April 16, Thursday

PASSAGE OF VICKSBURG.

Flares and tar barrels burst into flames along the Vicksburg bluffs as, a little before midnight, Acting Rear Admiral David D. Porter's fleet of twelve vessels attempted to run past the city. They came downriver to aid Grant's crossing. Although often hit by the Confederate batteries, all but one of the vessels got through safely and concentrated near Hard

Times on the west side of the Mississippi. The dramatic passage of the flotilla was one more step in the build-up for the forthcoming land campaign.

Other fighting included a skirmish at Newtown, La.; an affair on the Pamunkey River near West Point, Va.; and skirmishes at Eagleville, Tenn., and Paris, Ky. Action continued in the New Berne area of North Carolina, with affairs at Hill's and Rodman's Points and a Federal expedition from New Berne toward Kinston, April 16–21.

President Davis approved acts of the Confederate Congress to allow minors to hold army commissions and to prevent absence of soldiers and officers without leave.

April 17, Friday

GRIERSON'S AND MARMADUKE'S RAIDS.

From La Grange, Tenn., Col. Benjamin H. Grierson of Illinois headed south with seventeen hundred cavalry on a startling raid into Mississippi. The intent was to draw attention from Grant's offensive against Vicksburg. To the east, Col. Abel D. Streight's raiders moved south from Nashville into Alabama. Dashing, handsome Brig. Gen. John Sappington Marmaduke led his Confederate raiders out of Arkansas into Missouri. Both Grierson and Marmaduke completed their operations on May 2. Other Union expeditions operated April 17–19 from New Berne to Washington, N.C., assisting in raising the siege of Washington; from Winchester to Sump's Tannery, Va., April 17–18; and April 17–21 from St. Martinsville to Breaux Bridge and Opelousas, La.

There was general skirmishing on the lines around Suffolk, Va.; fighting on the Amite River and at Bayou Vermillion, La.; at Core Creek, N.C.; on White River, Mo.; and at Lundy's Lane, Cherokee Station, Great Bear Creek and Barton's Station, Ala.

April 18, Saturday

Grierson's raiders met their first minor opposition between Ripley and New Albany, Miss., as skirmishing broke out on the line of march. A Confederate attack on Fayetteville, Ark., was repulsed by the Union garrison. Other fighting included an affair at Sabine Pass, Tex.; a skirmish at Hartsville, Tenn.; and an affair near Johnstown, Harrison County, W. Va. Federals destroyed Confederate salt works near New Iberia, La. Federals scouted through Shannon County, Mo., and for four days from Salem to Sinking Creek, Current River, and Big Creek, Mo. The Confederate Congress authorized a volunteer navy whereby qualified persons could procure and fit out vessels for cruising against the enemy, the main compensation to be prize money. The idea never went into operation, however.

April 19, Sunday

President Lincoln, Gen. Halleck, and Sec. of War Stanton took a quick one-day trip to Aquia Creek on army matters; the venture was carried out almost secretly.

As Grierson's men moved deeper into Mississippi, skirmishing continued, this time at Pontotoc. Other skirmishing occurred at Big Swift Creek, N.C.; at Battery Huger, Hill's Point, near Suffolk, Va.; Celina and Creelsborough, Ky.; Dickson Station, Ala.; and Trenton, Tenn. April 19–20 there was a Federal scout near Neosho, Mo.

April 20, Monday

A proclamation by President Lincoln declared that the state of West Virginia, having the approval of Congress, would officially join the union on June 20.

In Louisiana Federal forces occupied Opelousas and Washington and the Union navy squadron captured Butte-à-la-Rose. Marmaduke's Confederate raiders fought a skirmish at Patterson, Mo., and an affair occurred at Bloomfield, Mo. In North Carolina, skirmishing was at Sandy Ridge; and in Virginia a Federal reconnaissance operated from Winchester toward Wardensville and Strasburg. In West Virginia Confederate cavalry under John D. Imboden operated until May 14, with several skirmishes. A strong Federal expedition patrolled from Murfreesboro to McMinnville, Tenn., April 20–30. In the Suffolk, Va., area Federal troops and the Navy captured a strong position at Hill's Point on the Nansemond River.

April 21, Tuesday

Confederates under Brig. Gen. William E. Jones began a raid on the Baltimore & Ohio Railroad in West Virginia, which lasted until May 21, resulting in considerable minor fighting. A Federal expedition operated April 21–May 2 from Lake Spring, Mo., to Chalk Bluff, Ark. A skirmish occurred at Palo Alto, Miss., and a Federal expedition moved from Opelousas to Barre's Landing, La.

April 22, Wednesday

In front of Vicksburg a Federal flotilla of six transports and twelve barges attempted to pass the batteries. One transport and six barges were sunk, but the remainder carried their precious supplies to Grant's men below the city.

Marmaduke and his Confederates fought a skirmish at Fredericktown, Mo. Other fighting included skirmishing at the Bayou Boeuf Road near Washington, La.; Hartsville, Tenn.; Rock Cut near Tuscumbia, Ala.; Point

Pleasant, W. Va.; and Fisher's Hill, Va. A three-day Federal expedition operated from Belle Plain to Port Conway and Port Royal in Virginia.

President Davis, concerned about Vicksburg, advised Pemberton to float fire rafts down the Mississippi when the Federals tried to pass, or to anchor them in the river on dark nights.

April 23, Thursday

Minor skirmishes occurred at Independence, Mo.; Chuckatuck near Suffolk, Va.; on the Shelbyville Pike, Tenn.; and at Dickson Station, Tuscumbia, Florence, and Leighton, Ala.

Reportedly, a medium conducted a séance at the White House. After Mr. Lincoln left, the "spirits" are said to have pinched Sec. of War Stanton's nose and tweaked the beard of Sec. of the Navy Welles.

Lincoln informed a sensitive Gen. Rosecrans at Murfreesboro that he had not heard any complaints about the general. Four vessels evaded the blockade and reached Wilmington, N.C., with valuable cargoes.

April 24, Friday

The Congress of the Confederate States levied a comprehensive "tax in kind" of one tenth of all produce of the land for the year 1863.

Federal raiders under Gen. Grenville Dodge captured Tuscumbia, Ala.; Grierson, deep in Mississippi, skirmished at Garlandville and Birmingham; and Marmaduke's Confederates fought at Mill or Middle Creek Bridges, Mo. There was a skirmish on Edenton Road near Suffolk, Va.; a Federal expedition to Lake Saint Joseph, La.; and a skirmish in Gilmer County, W. Va. April 24–May 27 Union forces carried out operations against the Indians in Owen's River and adjacent valleys of California. In the Gulf of Mexico U.S.S. *De Soto* captured four blockade-runners.

April 25, Saturday

Skirmishing occurred near Hard Times Landing as Grant's forces continued to push south after bypassing Vicksburg.

Skirmishes broke out near Fort Bowie, Ariz. Terr.; Greenland Gap, W. Va.; and at Webber's Falls, Indian Terr. Maj. Gen. Dabney H. Maury assumed command of the Confederate Department of East Tennessee, a difficult assignment in view of the prevailing pro-Union sentiment.

The British Parliament loudly debated the seizure of British vessels by American cruisers on blockade duty.

April 26, Sunday

The increased springtime fighting continued. Marmaduke's busy Confederates unsuccessfully attacked Cape Girardeau, Mo., and also skirmished near Jackson, Mo. Grierson's men rode on in central Mississippi. Streight launched the main part of his Federal raid from Tuscumbia, Ala., and headed toward Rome, Ga. Confederate raiders under W. E. "Grumble" Jones fought at Altamont, Oakland, Cranberry Summit, Md., and Rowlesburg, W. Va. Fighting also broke out at Burlington and Portland, W. Va.; Oak Grove, Va.; College Grove, Tenn.; and near Independence, Mo. April 23–29 saw a Federal expedition from Opelousas toward Niblett's Bluff, La., and an expedition to Celina, Ky. April 26–May 12 there were operations in southeastern Kentucky and around Monticello.

April 27, Monday

In Virginia the Northern Army of the Potomac began to move. Hooker's forces marched from Falmouth up the Rappahannock toward the fords over the river. Preparations were over. Lincoln, anxious as always, particularly about Hooker, wrote, "How does it look now?" But it was too early to tell.

Marmaduke and his Southerners continued their fighting at Jackson and near White Water Bridge, Mo. In Tennessee fighting flared on Carter Creek Pike; and in Kentucky at Barboursville and at Negro Head Cut near Woodburn. In Virginia a Union expedition continued from Yorktown beyond Hickory Forks; other action occurred in Alabama at Town Creek; in West Virginia at Morgantown and Independence; and in South Carolina at Murray's Inlet. In North Carolina April 27–May 1 a Federal expedition operated from New Berne toward Kinston with a skirmish at Wise's Crossroads.

In the Confederate Department of East Tennessee Maj. Gen. Dabney H. Maury was relieved by Maj. Gen. Simon Bolivar Buckner. Maury took command of the District of the Gulf. The Confederate Congress provided for the issue of 8 per cent bonds or stock to discharge certain agreements prior to Dec. 1, 1862.

April 28, Tuesday

Hooker's Army of the Potomac began crossing the Rappahannock in the Wilderness area, upstream from Fredericksburg. Meanwhile, a large force still confronted the Confederates across from the city. A flank attack by the Federals was obviously planned. At Fredericksburg early in the morning the bell in the Episcopal church rang out the alarm.

In Mississippi Grierson's troops skirmished at Union Church. In Kentucky a series of skirmishes near Monticello lasted several days. Town Creek, Ala., was another site of action.

Lincoln commuted the death sentence of Sergeant John A. Chase, convicted of striking and threatening an officer, but ordered him imprisoned at hard labor "with ball and chain attached to his leg" for the remainder of the war.

April 29, Wednesday

The Northern push was on in earnest—east and west. In Virginia the major part of Hooker's army crossed the Rappahannock at Kelly's and U.S. fords, plunging into the Wilderness, clear of the left flank of Lee's Army of Northern Virginia. Stoneman, with the Federal cavalry, operated against Lee's communications. Other actions in the area broke out at Franklin's Crossing or Deep Run just below Fredericksburg, and at Pollock's Mill Creek, known also as White Oak Run or Fitzhugh's Crossing. Federals from Falmouth tried to divert the Confederates from the major effort above the city. Other skirmishing in Virginia was at Crook's Run and Germanna Ford, near Kellysville, Brandy Station, and Stevensburg. In West Virginia Confederate Grumble Jones fought a skirmish at Fairmont.

In the West Federal gunboats pounded enemy gun emplacements at Grand Gulf on the Mississippi and attempted to clear the way for Grant's army to cross. But six hours of firing failed, so during the night Grant's leading force marched southward from Grand Gulf along the Louisiana shore to a new landing opposite Bruinsburg. Under darkness the fleet followed the army down and prepared to take it across. North of Vicksburg Sherman's men demonstrated against Haynes' and Drumgould's bluffs near Snyder's Mill to draw attention from the main attack. A Federal scouting party moved out from La Grange, Tenn., into northern Mississippi for two or three days.

Farther south, Grierson's tiring troops skirmished at Brookhaven, Miss. In Tennessee there were reconnaissances from Murfreesboro on the Manchester Pike and on the Chapel Hill Pike; while in Missouri Marmaduke fought Federals at Castor River. A two-day Federal expedition operated from Opelousas to Chicotville and Bayou Boeuf, La.

April 30, Thursday

In Virginia's Wilderness Joseph Hooker and his Army of the Potomac set up camp around the Chancellor family house, known as Chancellorsville. Brief skirmishing erupted in the area and near Spotsylvania Court House. Stoneman's cavalry fought at Raccoon Ford. A confident Hooker told his army that "the operations of the last three days have determined that our enemy must ingloriously fly, or come out from behind their defences and give us battle on our ground, where certain destruction awaits him." "Splendid successes," he added. In Fredericksburg Lee probed and planned.

By noon Grant's first forces were across the Mississippi south of Vicksburg and preparing to move inland. Grant felt relief: "All the campaigns, labors, hardships, and exposures, from the month of December previous to this time, that had been made and endured, were for the

343

accomplishment of this one object." Aided by Sherman's demonstration north of Vicksburg and Grierson's sensational ride, Grant was ready to move against the fortress itself. President Davis told Gen. J. E. Johnston, who was trying to aid the defender, Pemberton, "General Pemberton telegraphs that unless he has more cavalry, the approaches to North Mississippi are almost unprotected and that he can not prevent cavalry raids."

Still another Federal raider was active, this time in Alabama. Streight's men fought actions at Day's Gap or Sand Mountain, Crooked Creek, and Hog Mountain. Confederate raiders were active as well. W. E. "Grumble" Jones in West Virginia fought at Bridgeport and Marmaduke skirmished at Bloomfield, Mo. Skirmishing broke out at Fort Gibson, Indian Terr., where Union forces were holding on tenuously.

MAY, 1863

On two of the three major fronts, Northern armies moved in new offensives. The vast Army of the Potomac under mercurial Joseph Hooker was positioned at Chancellorsville in the Wilderness of Virginia, ready to move swiftly between Lee and Richmond. At Fredericksburg a portion of Hooker's army under Sedgwick threatened the Confederates from that direction.

On the Mississippi Union attempts to capture or lay siege to the fortress of Vicksburg had long been frustrated. Now Grant was below the city and on Mississippi soil. To Confederates the threat was real, desperately crucial. It took no genius to see the tragedy that would result if Vicksburg and the Mississippi Valley fell. Pemberton kept a vigilant eye on Sherman's demonstration north of Vicksburg. Johnston gathered strength, hoping to relieve Pemberton in an attempt to save both the city and the Confederate army. Only in east-central Tennessee, where Rosecrans and Bragg were largely inactive, was there no sense of immediate crisis. Smaller operations, such as Grierson's in Mississippi and Streight's in Georgia, also stung the South.

May 1, Friday

BATTLE OF CHANCELLORSVILLE BEGINS.

BATTLE OF PORT GIBSON, MISSISSIPPI.

An alert Army of Northern Virginia, under Lee, grasped the threat in Hooker's movement of 70,000 men across the Rappahannock, and hurriedly moved out of Fredericksburg to block the Army of the Potomac's exits from the Wilderness. Jubal Early remained in Fredericksburg with ten thousand men to oppose Sedgwick's forty thousand. In late morning Hooker moved his main force forward and skirmished briefly with the advancing Confederates.

In the afternoon, Hooker amazed his own officers and the Confederates by ordering his main units to withdraw from the advance and concentrate in a five-mile area near Chancellorsville. With few shots and little fighting, Hooker surrendered the initiative and returned to the defensive. Lee, surprised by the lack of opposition and concerned over his dangerously split army, cautiously moved forward. With Longstreet at Suffolk, southeast of Richmond, and Early defending Fredericksburg, Lee was reduced to about 47,000 men.

That night in the woods of the Wilderness Lee and Jackson talked. Out of that cracker-barrel conference came one of the most daring decisions of military history. Lee would split his army once more, disobeying the laws of strategy and tactics. Jackson would take about 26,000 men through the scraggly brushlands to attack the vulnerable right flank of Hooker's immobile army. Meanwhile, Lee would demonstrate with the remainder of his army at Chancellorsville. The stage was set for full battle.

Hundreds of miles away on the Mississippi, Grant's army continued to move across the river at Bruinsburg, south of Vicksburg. McClernand's corps headed rapidly inland toward Port Gibson, about thirty miles south of Vicksburg. A small Confederate force at Grand Gulf, outflanked, hurried toward Port Gibson to intercept McClernand. Throughout the day McClernand's men fought with those under Maj. Gen. John S. Bowen in a land of steep, sharp ridges and gullies covered with thick vines and snaring undergrowth. Pushed slowly backward by the overwhelming Union force, Bowen retired to Port Gibson and then evacuated the town. Grant's bridgehead on the east side of the Mississippi was now secure and his army had room to move toward Jackson and Vicksburg. At Wall's Bridge, near the Mississippi-Louisiana state line north of Baton Rouge, Grierson's Federal raiders fought one of their major skirmishes of the expedition which had begun in Tennessee April 17. Riding rapidly to avoid converging Confederate columns, Grierson's men crossed the Amite River at Williams' Bridge and headed for Baton Rouge.

Streight's Federal raiders fought skirmishes throughout the day at Blountsville and on the east branch of the Big Warrior River, Ala. Other fighting broke out near Washington, La.; South Quay Bridge near Suffolk, Va.; La Grange, Ark.; and between Murfreesboro and Lizzard, Tenn. In Arkansas Marmaduke's Confederate raid into Missouri ended with skirmishes May 1-2 at Chalk Bluff on the St. Francis River.

Before adjourning, the third session of the First Confederate Congress created a Provisional Navy in addition to the Regular Navy; authorized the President to contract for construction of vessels in Europe; provided for election of delegates to Congress from some Indian nations; created the office of Commissioner of Taxes; tightened some of the exemptions in the draft law; and adopted a new national flag known as the Stainless Banner. A resolution stated that captured white officers of Northern Negro troops should be put to death or otherwise punished at the discretion of a court-martial for inciting insurrection.

May 2, Saturday

BATTLE OF CHANCELLORSVILLE CONTINUES.

Early in the morning Stonewall Jackson's Confederate flanking force moved past Catherine Furnace deeper into the Wilderness. He did not move completely undisturbed or even unseen, but Federals failed to recognize his motives and thought the Southern army was withdrawing. By late afternoon Jackson's main columns were on the Orange Turnpike within striking distance of the quietly encamped Eleventh Corps of the Army of the Potomac under O. O. Howard. Jackson's watch showed 6 P.M. when he gave the orders to go in. Scurrying wildlife alerted the Federals, but Union outposts fled back upon the main position and Jackson's attack rolled forward. A few Federal units fought well, but the mass rushed back toward Chancellorsville in various stages of disorder. On the Union left flank Lee opened fire, striking Meade's corps strongly to draw attention from Jackson.

In the gloomy scrub timber Confederates often fired upon their own men. Jackson, trying to cut Hooker off from U. S. Ford on the Rappahannock, rode forward with a small party. In the darkness he was mistaken for Federal; a Confederate soldier fired, wounding the beloved chieftain in the arm. A. P. Hill, wounded a short time later, was unable to take over, and the command of Jackson's force fell to cavalryman Jeb Stuart. Jackson's condition was critical and his arm had to be removed during the night. One of the greatest battles of the war had been fought here in the darkening woods. Lee had triumphed over numbers and inept Federal reconnaissance and had made Chancellorsville a battle that would be studied the world over.

During the day, on the fringes of the major battle, fighting also broke out at Ely's Ford and near Louisa Court House. Lee's other brilliant corps leader, Longstreet, at Suffolk, skirmished for two days near Hill's Point and Reed's Ferry on the Nansemond River and at Chuckatuck, Va.

Grant's force near Vicksburg moved speedily inland from Bruinsburg and Port Gibson, fanning out into Mississippi with a skirmish on the south fork of Bayou Pierre. Fearing to halt or rest, Grierson's remaining nine hundred Union riders pushed on from Williams' Bridge to Baton Rouge, his pursuers steadily gaining. A quick skirmish at Roberts' Ford on the Comite River and then a parade of tattered, saddle-weary horsemen rode into Baton Rouge in midafternoon, the road lined with cheering spectators and waving banners. Col. Grierson reported that in 16 days about 100 Confederates had been killed, 500 prisoners taken, 50 or 60 miles of railroad and telegraph destroyed, 3000 arms captured or destroyed, and other stores, including 1000 horses and mules, taken. Losses were 3 killed, 7 wounded, 5 left behind sick, and 9 missing. Grierson's men had traveled 600 miles in 16 days, 76 miles in the last 28 hours, and fought 4 engagements. It was a dramatic ride which confused the Confederates during a critical period of the defense of Vicksburg. Meanwhile, Streight's Federal cavalry raid ran into trouble, with fighting at Black Creek near Gadsden, Blount's Plantation, and near Centre, Ala. Forgotten on this day of headline events was a skirmish near Thompson's Station, Tenn., and another near Lewisburg, W. Va. For a week Union gunboats fought Confederates in and around Greenville, Miss.

May 3, Sunday

BATTLE OF CHANCELLORSVILLE; SECOND FREDERICKSBURG; SALEM CHURCH.

Lincoln asked the Army of the Potomac: "Where is Gen. Hooker? Where is Sedgwick? Where is Stoneman?" Both Hooker and Sedgwick were busy indeed. At daybreak Stuart, with Jackson's corps, seized a low hill known as Hazel Grove, from which artillery fired on Chancellorsville itself. The rest of the Confederate line attacked the ever constricting Federal semicircle. A shell struck a column of the Chancellor House and a falling brick or column temporarily disabled Hooker. Gen. Darius Couch, though not in full command, withdrew the beaten army toward U. S. Ford, reluctantly following Hooker's orders. A firm, short position with the right on the Rapidan and the left on the Rappahannock prevented further disaster.

Lee's army occupied Chancellorsville about 10 A.M. and was preparing a new assault which never came. On the night of May 2, Hooker had ordered Sedgwick to drive Early's defenders from Fredericksburg and to attack Lee from the rear. Sedgwick assaulted Marye's Heights and failed twice. Other moves were equally unsuccessful in this battle, often referred to as Second Fredericksburg. Eventually, however, the weakened Confederate line gave way and Sedgwick's men surged forward. The way to Chancellorsville lay open as Early retired south. Lee turned a portion of his line around to confront Sedgwick at Salem Church. A sharp battle broke out in the late afternoon, and lasted until dark. Lee successfully halted Sedgwick's advance. Stoneman and his Federal cavalry skirmished at South Anna Bridge, north of Richmond.

Confederates evacuated Grand Gulf on the Mississippi. Though it had stanch batteries, Grant's inland movement made it a useless position. Skirmishing occurred along the edges of Grant's advance on the north fork of Bayou Pierre, at Willow Springs, Ingraham's Heights, Jones' Cross

Roads, Forty Hills, and Hankinson's Ferry on the Big Black River. Grant marched steadily toward Jackson, Miss.

At Cedar Bluff, Ala., a tired, discouraged band under Col. A. D. Streight surrendered to Nathan Bedford Forrest after a skirmish. Forrest thereby partly avenged Grierson's success and thwarted Streight's main purpose, which was to destroy Southern railroads.

Longstreet abandoned his siege of Suffolk, Va., on being recalled to Lee's Army of Northern Virginia. There was skirmishing at Warrenton Junction, Va.; a Federal scout in Cass and Bates counties, and a Union expedition on the Sante Fe Road, Mo. A Yankee scout moved from Triune to Eagleville, Tenn.

The Roman Catholic Bishop of Iowa warned Church members that they had two weeks to leave the pro-Southern Knights of the Golden Circle or face excommunication.

May 4, Monday

BATTLE OF CHANCELLORSVILLE; SALEM CHURCH.

Hooker's battered Army of the Potomac failed to take the initiative near Chancellorsville and Lee was able to reinforce troops opposing Sedgwick's advance near Salem Church. Early, defeated the day before and driven off Marye's Heights at Fredericksburg, moved against Sedgwick's rear. Sedgwick, threatened on three sides, was forced to go on the defensive. In late afternoon the Confederates attacked, but failed to cut Sedgwick off from Banks' Ford over the Rappahannock. Sedgwick fell back to the ford and crossed the river by pontoons during the night. This ended the major action of the Chancellorsville campaign, and for a second time Federals failed in the Fredericksburg area. The Federals had at least 133,868 men at Chancellorsville and Fredericksburg; 1606 were killed, 9762 wounded, and 5919 missing for a total of 17,287 casualties between April 27 and May 11. Confederate effectives are estimated at 60,000, with 1665 killed, 9081 wounded, and 2018 missing for a total of 12,764, a higher casualty percentage by far than the Federals suffered. One of those wounded and soon to die was T. J. "Stonewall" Jackson.

At a late-night conference, Hooker decided to withdraw the Army of the Potomac back across the Rappahannock. From Richmond President Davis wired Lee his thanks in the name of the people "reverently united with you in giving praise to God for the success with which He has crowned your arms." He added his regrets for "the good and the brave who are numbered among the killed and the wounded." Lincoln, in suspense in Washington, asked Hooker if it was true that the enemy had reoccupied heights above Fredericksburg.

Meanwhile, Grant's army, some of it still crossing the Mississippi, spread out south of Vicksburg, with another skirmish at Hankinson's Ferry on the Big Black River. Farther south three gunboats attacked Fort De Russy on the Red River in Louisiana, but after severe damage to *Albatross,* the Federals were forced to retire.

Stoneman's Federal cavalry initiated skirmishes at Flemmings' or Shannon's Crossroads, Tunstall's Station, and Ashland Church, Va. A brief skirmish flared at Leesville, Va., as the Suffolk campaign concluded. Other action included fighting at Hungary Station, Hanovertown Ferry, Ayletts, Va.; a six-day Union scout from Winchester, Va., into Hampshire County, W. Va.; an affair at Murray's Inlet, S.C.; another affair near Nashville, Tenn.; and operations about Lexington, Mo. Also an expedition began against Indians to the Snake Indian Country of Idaho Territory, and lasted until Oct. 26.

May 5, Tuesday

Lee's Army of Northern Virginia spent the day preparing to attack Hooker's failing forces near Chancellorsville. But during the day and night the Army of the Potomac began to recross the Rappahannock in defeat. In Washington the Administration began to realize it faced another failure. Stoneman's cavalry skirmished at Thompson's Crossroads, Va.

Other action included skirmishing at Big Sandy Creek, and action at King's Creek, near Tupelo, Miss. Skirmishes also occurred at Peletier's Mill, N.C.; Rover, Tenn., and Obion Plank Road Crossing, Tenn. In the West Federals scouted from Fort Scott, Kas., to Sherwood, Mo., with skirmishes, until May 9; and Federals launched an expedition against Indians from Camp Douglas, Ut. Terr., to Soda Springs on the Bear River, Id. Terr., which lasted until May 30.

A reinforced Federal flotilla under Porter moved up to Fort De Russy on the Red River to cooperate with Gen. Banks' advance on Louisiana from New Orleans. Porter found that the Confederates had abandoned the works and removed all but one gun.

The leader of the Peace Democrats or Copperheads of the Northwest, former congressman Clement L. Vallandigham, was arrested in Dayton, Ohio. Tried by a military commission in Cincinnati the following day, he was convicted by a military commission of expressing treasonable sympathies. In speeches at Columbus and Mount Vernon, Vallandigham had called the war "wicked and cruel" and declared that it was an attempt to destroy slavery in order to establish a Republican dictatorship. He had long been a thorn to the Administration, but now his arrest presented real problems to Washington.

May 6, Wednesday

Lee's victorious Confederates cautiously advanced in the Wilderness, only to find Hooker had withdrawn during the night before and in the morning. Hooker informed Washington of his movements and Lincoln gained further knowledge by reading Richmond newspapers. In the morning he wired

Hooker, "God bless you, and all with you. I know you will do your best." Late in the afternoon President Lincoln and Halleck left to meet Hooker. On the Confederate side, A. P. Hill was assigned to command the Second Corps of the Army of Northern Virginia, replacing the critically wounded Jackson, who now lay in a small house at Guiney's Station.

On the Red River in Louisiana Porter's Federal flotilla occupied Alexandria, La., which the Confederates had just evacuated. There were skirmishes at Warrenton, Va., and West Union, W. Va. A Federal expedition operated from Bowling Green, Ky., to the Tennessee state line. Federals scouted between the White and St. Francis rivers in Arkansas until the fifteenth; and until the nineteenth from Creek Agency, Indian Terr., to Jasper County, Mo. During the latter scout skirmishes broke out at Martin's House, Centre Creek, and near Sherwood, which was destroyed.

From Nashville a group of allegedly disloyal citizens were sent into Confederate lines.

May 7, Thursday

Two worried Presidents spent the day trying to strengthen their military positions. Lincoln and Gen. Halleck, after meeting with Hooker at his Army of the Potomac Headquarters, returned to Washington in the evening. The President wrote Hooker, saying, "If possible I would be very glad of another movement early enough to give us some benefit from the fact of the enemies communications being broken, but neither for this reason or any other, do I wish anything done in desperation or rashness." But Lincoln was concerned over the effect on morale of the Chancellorsville defeat. Stoneman's cavalry expedition against communication lines between Fredericksburg and Richmond still operated, but with negligible results.

Confederate President Davis wired Pemberton, commanding in Mississippi: "Am anxiously expecting further information of your active operations. . . . To hold both Vicksburg and Port Hudson is necessary to our connection with Trans-Mississippi. You may expect whatever it is in my power to do for your aid."

Meanwhile, Federal troops occupied West Point, Va., on the Peninsula; there were affairs at Cairo Station and Harrisville, W. Va.

On the Mississippi, Grant, joined by Sherman's corps from Milliken's Bend, began to move from the Grand Gulf area toward Jackson and the railroad between Vicksburg and Jackson. Grant began to depend less on his supply lines and live off the country, although he did carry some necessities with him. At the village of Spring Hill, Tenn., Confederate Maj. Gen. Earl Van Dorn was assassinated by Dr. Peters. It was alleged that the general and Mrs. Peters had a "liaison," although some denied it.

May 8, Friday

Only a skirmish near Grove Church, Va., marked the day militarily. Lincoln issued a proclamation that being an alien would not exempt anyone from military service if he had declared his intention to become a citizen. Records are replete with names of those who claimed to be aliens to escape the draft.

Mr. Davis wrote leading citizens of Columbus, Miss., "It would be needless to explain to you how far my ability falls short of my earnest desire, or to recount the causes which so often prevent me from affording the full protection to various portions of our common country which is called for by every consideration that can animate manly and patriotic breasts or excite a public officer to greatest exertion."

May 9, Saturday

Confederate Gen. Joseph E. Johnston was ordered to take command of all Southern troops in imperiled Mississippi. Grant's advancing army fought skirmishes on this day and the tenth near Utica, Miss. Other skirmishes occurred near Big Sandy Creek, Miss., and at Bayou Tensas near Lake Providence, La. Operations May 9–18 along the Amite River and Jackson Railroad involved several skirmishes in Louisiana. Fighting also broke out in Stone County, Mo.; and near Caney Fort, Tenn. Federal oil works at Oiltown, W. Va., were destroyed.

May 10, Sunday

DEATH OF STONEWALL JACKSON.

In a small house near Guiney's Station, south of Fredericksburg, Va., Stonewall Jackson died. Pneumonia had set in after the amputation of his arm. Lee, sorely grieved, knew not how to replace him. Flags dipped in mourning throughout the South and solemn honor guards escorted the body back to Lexington, Va. "The Gallant Stonewall was no more," went the words of a song. Indeed, the South had lost one of its greatest captains and had gained a timeless legend.

But the fighting continued: skirmishes at Caledonia and Pin Hook or Bayou Macon, La.; action at Horseshoe Bottom on the Cumberland River; skirmishes at Phillips Ford on Red Bird Creek, Ky. On the Ouachita River, four Federal gunboats shelled the Confederates at Fort Beauregard, La.

May 11, Monday

Lincoln's Secretary of the Treasury, Salmon P. Chase, again created a problem for the President. In an argument over an appointment, Chase tendered his resignation. Lincoln turned it down, but, coming as it did after the Cabinet crisis of the preceding December, it foretold more trouble in the official family.

Federal cavalry raided the New Orleans and Jackson Railroad near Crystal Springs, Miss. There was skirmishing at Warrenton, Va.; La Fayette, Tenn.; and Mount Vernon and Taylor's Creek or Crowley's Ridge,

Ark. Other Federal cavalry operated until May 15 from La Grange, Tenn., to Panola, Miss., as a part of the campaign against Vicksburg.

May 12, Tuesday
ENGAGEMENT OF RAYMOND, MISSISSIPPI.

Grant, who had been moving steadily northeastward toward a position between Jackson and Vicksburg, Miss., had a division at the village of Raymond, about fifteen miles from the state capital. Here this division under Maj. Gen. John A. Logan of McPherson's corps was struck by a Confederate brigade commanded by Brig. Gen. John Gregg. An engagement lasted for several hours, until the outnumbered Confederates were driven back toward Jackson. Each side suffered about 500 casualties. Meanwhile, McClernand and Sherman found Confederate skirmishers along Fourteen-Mile Creek. All this caused Grant to decide to deal with Jackson before striking directly at Vicksburg. Besides, intelligence had correctly placed Pemberton's main forces at Edwards' Station and along the Big Black River between Jackson and Vicksburg. Joseph E. Johnston endeavored to aid Pemberton at Jackson. Davis wired Pemberton of his confidence in him, adding that reinforcements should now be arriving, and urged cordial relations with the people. But there was an undertone of uneasiness in the message.

Skirmishing occurred at Greenville, Miss.; Linden, Tenn.; and Bloomfield, Mo. Confederate Maj. Gen. S. B. Buckner assumed command of the Department of East Tennessee. Other operations included, May 12–14, those about Buck's and Front Royal fords, and from Snicker's Ferry to Upperville, Va. May 12–26 there were operations on the Seaboard and Roanoke Railroad with several skirmishes near Carrsville, Va. In Tennessee Federals carried out a reconnaissance from Murfreesboro toward Liberty and Lebanon.

May 13, Wednesday
Two corps of Grant's army moved toward Jackson under McPherson and Sherman, while McClernand headed north to Clinton. At Jackson, Johnston could muster only about twelve thousand men and knew full well that Grant's army stood between him and Pemberton. There were skirmishes at Mississippi Springs and at Baldwin's and Hall's ferries, Miss. Other fighting broke out near Woodburn and South Union, Tenn.; and May 13–18 a Federal scout operated from Newtonia to French Point and Centre Creek, Mo.

Lincoln asked General Hooker to come to Washington if he were not too busy. Davis, concerned over Vicksburg, learned of further trouble from Gov. Z. B. Vance of North Carolina. The governor expressed his anxiety over desertion in the Confederate Army and reported the steps he had taken to reduce it. He put the cause to homesickness, fatigue, hard fare, lack of furloughs, and inability to enter regiments of their choice.

May 14, Thursday

ENGAGEMENT OF JACKSON, MISSISSIPPI.

By midmorning McPherson's and Sherman's corps of Grant's army neared Jackson, Miss., in a driving rainstorm. Johnston, knowing it was futile to oppose Grant with twelve thousand men, began to evacuate vital supplies and withdrew to the north. He left two brigades to delay the Federals. The Yankees easily overcame the two Confederate brigades and by midafternoon occupied the capital. McClernand, meanwhile, was in part solidly on the rail line from Jackson to Vicksburg, between Johnston and Pemberton. Grant's task was now to turn west from Jackson and move against Pemberton near Edwards' Station.

South of Vicksburg, Gen. Nathaniel Banks left Alexandria, La., for operations against Port Hudson, above Baton Rouge. Port Hudson was the only other major Confederate bastion on the Mississippi. In the area of Boyce's Bridge on Cotile Bayou and near Merritt's Plantation on the Clinton Road there was brief fighting. Skirmishes occurred at Fort Gibson, Indian Terr., and in Virginia near Warrenton Junction.

Hooker had written Lincoln of his problems with the Army of the Potomac, which had delayed further operations since the Battle of Chancellorsville. Lincoln, in turn, wrote the general that he would not complain if he kept the enemy at bay but would not restrain him from renewing the attack. He warned Hooker that he had intimations that "some of your corps and Division Commanders are not giving you their entire confidence."

May 15, Friday

Using several roads, Grant's forces converged on Edwards' Station, east of Vicksburg. Sherman and two divisions remained in Jackson to destroy Confederate supplies and installations. Pemberton's main force was near Edwards' Station and a strong garrison was at Vicksburg. Portions of the two armies were only four miles apart at nightfall. Pemberton had decided it was impossible to join Johnston and so planned to seek out Grant's nearly non-existent communications.

Skirmishes occurred at Fort Smith, Ark., and at Big Creek, near Pleasant Hill, Mo. A Federal expedition operated from West Point to King and Queen County, Va. There was a scout May 15-22 from Parkersburg into Calhoun County, W. Va. From this day to the twenty-eighth operations on the Norfolk and Petersburg Railroad southeast of Richmond included several skirmishes.

May 16, Saturday

BATTLE OF CHAMPION'S HILL, MISSISSIPPI.

Grant's army advanced from Jackson toward Vicksburg, threatening to cut the feeble communications between Pemberton, near Edwards' Station, and Johnston to the north. Pemberton, after refusing to attempt to join

Johnston the day before, responded now to a second order and marched out to make the junction in order that together they might fight Grant. The Confederates were blocked, however, by Federal forces at Champion's Hill. A division of McClernand's Union corps attacked a bit before noon, driving the Confederates back on the left. Confederates counterattacked successfully. Grant reinforced his right with McPherson's men and in midafternoon the hill changed hands a third time. Pemberton failed to rally and began to withdraw toward Vicksburg and the Big Black River. Federal effectives for the battle of Champion's Hill or Baker's Creek numbered about 29,000, with 410 killed, 1844 wounded, and 187 missing for 2441 casualties. Confederate effectives are estimated at under 20,000, with 381 killed, about 1800 wounded, and 1670 missing for a total of 3851 casualties. Pemberton had no choice but to fall back toward Vicksburg. Grant's campaign was rising to its climax.

Fighting elsewhere included skirmishes near Carthage, Mo.; at Elizabeth Court House and Ravenswood, W. Va.; Tickfaw Bridge, La.; Berry's Ferry and Piedmont Station, Va.; and Charles Town, W. Va.

Democrats protested the conviction of Vallandigham.

May 17, Sunday
ENGAGEMENT OF BIG BLACK RIVER BRIDGE, MISSISSIPPI.

Confederate Gen. Pemberton, with his back to the Big Black River between Vicksburg and Jackson, awaited a missing division. The division was cut off from Pemberton and forced to join Johnston. The Union army opened fire on the entrenched Confederates, who, in danger of being cut off from crossing the river, retired in disorder and burned the bridges. Grant's army was temporarily halted. Pemberton continued to pull back to the defenses of Vicksburg while the Federals hastened to bridge the swampy lowlands and the Big Black. Federal losses were 39 killed, 237 wounded, and 3 missing for 279. Some 1700 Confederates were captured.

Meanwhile, Banks' Federals moved into position with operations on the west side of the Mississippi across from Port Hudson. There was skirmishing near Bridgeport, Miss.; Dumfries, Va.; and on the Bradyville Pike, Tenn. A Federal scout operated from La Grange, Tenn.

May 18, Monday
SIEGE OF VICKSBURG BEGINS.

One of the great campaigns of military history came to an end as Grant's triumphant Federal army moved across the Big Black River, took Haynes' Bluff, and began to invest Vicksburg. Confederate Pemberton, ordered by Johnston to evacuate the city, considered the problems—how to get out, and the effect of losing such a position—and, advised by his under-officers, decided to stay. The siege had begun.

Minor fighting elsewhere included affairs at Hog Island, Bates County,

Mo., and near Cheneyville, La. Skirmishes broke out near Island No. 82 above Greenville, Miss., and on Horn Lake Creek, Tenn. Operations lasting a day or two occurred around Fayetteville, W. Va., and near Merritt's Plantation and on the Bayou Sara Road, La.

President Davis called for civilians and militia to join Gen. J. E. Johnston in Mississippi. He urged Johnston to link up with Pemberton and attack the enemy.

In Britain's House of Lords, debate on decisions of the American prize courts brought demands that Britain actively defend the rights of her shipowners. Lord Russell said that the Crown found no objections to the prize courts' proceedings and that Britain had no wish to interfere in the American Civil War.

May 19, Tuesday
FIRST ASSAULT ON VICKSBURG.

Grant, anxious to cap his campaign with the surrender of Vicksburg, completed investing the city. Sherman stood on the north or right, McPherson in the center, and McClernand on the left. Skirmishing broke out as the Federals approached the well-prepared fortifications. Grant hoped a sudden assault would prevent Pemberton from completing his arrangements. In midafternoon Sherman attacked, despite heavy fire on the Union right, and made some advance at Stockade Redan. However, he failed to penetrate the works and was driven back. McPherson and McClernand had even less success. About a thousand Federal casualties attested to the strong Confederate position. Federal mortars began pounding Vicksburg from the Yazoo.

Federal scouts operated from La Grange, Tenn., and there was a skirmish near Richfield, Clay County, Mo. In Virginia a Federal force operated from Gloucester Point into Matthews County.

Sec. of War Stanton, on orders of President Lincoln, directed that former Ohio congressman Clement L. Vallandigham, convicted of aiding the Confederates, be sent beyond the military lines of the United States and not be permitted to return, under threat of arrest.

May 20, Wednesday

Grant considered the problems of a direct attack on Vicksburg. President Davis had been ill for several weeks but was improving. Two blockade-runners arrived safely at Charleston, S.C., from Nassau with valuable cargoes. But two others were captured, one off the Neuse River, N.C., the other near Nassau. Confederates fought with Federals near Fort Gibson, Indian Terr. Skirmishing occurred at Salem and Collierville, Tenn., and near Cheneyville, La. Troops began to gather for Banks' major Federal push toward Port Hudson on the Mississippi. May 20–23 there were demonstrations at Kinston, N.C., and skirmishes at Gum Swamp and

Batchelder's Creek, N.C. A Federal scout operated May 20–22 from Clarksville, Tenn.; and Union troops moved to Yazoo City, Miss., at the same time. In Virginia minor operations in the Northern Neck and in Middlesex County lasted until the twenty-sixth.

May 21, Thursday
SIEGE OF PORT HUDSON BEGINS.

A portion of Banks' Federals moved out of Baton Rouge on the Clinton Road toward Port Hudson. The main army, coming from Alexandria, approached Bayou Sara on the west side of the Mississippi. Minor action occurred at Plains Store near Port Hudson. Although Federal operations were not complete, the siege of Port Hudson can be said to have begun. At Vicksburg, Grant issued orders for a general assault on Pemberton's lines for the twenty-second. A Federal flotilla went up the Yazoo to Yazoo City, Miss. Before the flotilla arrived Confederates destroyed their shops and the navy yard, including two steamboats and an unfinished gunboat.

Federal guerrillas operated on the Santa Fe Road near Kansas City, Mo. May 21–22 a Federal expedition moved from Murfreesboro to Middleton, Tenn., and fought a skirmish; May 21–26 another Federal expedition probed from La Grange, Tenn., to Senatobia, Miss. Operations on the Teche Road between Barre's Landing and Berwick, La., took place May 21–26. A Federal scout from Cassville through northwestern Arkansas, into Newton and Jasper counties, Mo., lasted until May 30 and included several skirmishes.

May 22, Friday
SECOND ASSAULT ON VICKSBURG.

Grant attacked a three-mile section of the crescent-shaped defenses of Vicksburg with all the power he could muster. At 10 A.M. the Federals surged forward against the Confederate lines extending from Stockade Redan on the north to Fort Garrott on the south. The charge over deep, narrow ravines that added to the man-made defenses of the city was against six strong points and a line of high breastworks protected by dirt and logs. Sherman's troops reached the top of the wall but failed to hold it. McClernand's men likewise managed to gain the barricades here and there, but to no avail. One breakthrough at Railroad Redoubt was briefly successful, but counterattacks closed the breach. Strong Confederates defenses beat back continued charges. Federal gunboats and mortars bombarded. Later, Grant regretted making the suicidal attack. Losses were heavy. It created further antagonism between Grant and McClernand. Of 45,000 Federals, 502 were killed, 2550 wounded, and 147 missing for 3199 casualties. Confederate losses were under 500. Grant never again tried to assault Vicksburg. Instead the Federals began the siege in earnest, digging approach trenches and building artillery positions. Union and Confederate soldiers alike soon knew the tedium as well as the dangers of a siege.

In Washington Lincoln had just heard of Grant's successful campaign in approaching Vicksburg. In Richmond Davis wired Gen. Braxton Bragg at Tullahoma, Tenn., "The vital issue of holding the Missi. at Vicksburg is dependent on the success of Genl. Johnston in an attack on the investing force. The intelligence from there is discouraging. Can you aid him? . . ."

Skirmishes occurred at Fort Gibson, Indian Terr.; on Yellow Creek, Tenn.; near Barre's Landing, Bayou Teche, and at Bayou Courtableau, La. Banks' army neared Port Hudson.

Lincoln greeted a group at the White House known as the "One-Legged Brigade." He told the convalescent veterans that there was no need for a speech "as the men upon their crutches were orators; their very appearance spoke louder than tongues." The War Department of the United States established a bureau in the Adjutant General's Office to organize Negro troops. Brig. Gen. Alfred Pleasonton assumed command of the Cavalry Corps of Hooker's Army of the Potomac, replacing Stoneman. The British and Foreign Anti-Slavery Society held an anniversary meeting in London, and expressed strong support for the Union.

May 23, Saturday

Near Bayou Sara Banks' main Federal force crossed the Mississippi at night and in a heavy storm headed for Port Hudson. In front of Port Hudson there was skirmishing on the Springfield and Plains Store roads. At Vicksburg Grant's army began to set up supply lines and to receive reinforcements. There was a brief skirmish at Haynes' Bluff.

Other fighting broke out at Hartville, Mo.; Warrenton, Va.; and West Creek, W. Va. Two Federal expeditions, lasting several days, operated from Helena to near Napoleon, Ark., and from Memphis to Hernando, Miss. Federals countered guerrilla activities and Confederate raids in Union-occupied Southern territory with almost continuous expeditions, scouts, and reconnaissances.

Lincoln conferred with military and naval officials about the unsuccessful attack on Charleston, S.C. Davis wired Gen. J. E. Johnston, who was outside Vicksburg and unable to aid Pemberton, that he was "hopeful of junction of your forces and defeat of the enemy." To Pemberton, Davis wired, "Sympathizing with you for the reverse sustained."

In Ohio petitions circulated protesting the "arbitrary arrest, illegal trial, and inhuman imprisonment of Hon. C. L. Vallandigham."

May 24, Sunday

After a month of major military activity, the war entered a period of comparative quiet. The lesser actions continued, as always, but on principal fronts the armies rested and waited. In Virginia Hoker faced Lee at

Fredericksburg; in Tennessee Rosecrans' Federals regrouped at Murfreesboro while their opponent, Bragg, remained near Tullahoma, Sparta, and Wartrace. And of course at Vicksburg the siege was only beginning. At Port Hudson various units of Banks' army joined for another siege.

Skirmishing occurred at Woodbury, Tenn.; Mill Springs, Ky.; Mechanicsburg, Miss.; and at Mound Plantation near Lake Providence, La. A Federal expedition operated May 24–31 up the Yazoo and Big Sunflower rivers of Mississippi. Federal marines burned Austin, Miss., in reprisal for Confederate firing on their boat.

Maj. Gen. John A. Schofield was ordered to supersede Samuel R. Curtis in command of the Federal Department of Missouri. President Lincoln spent the day visiting hospitals in and near Washington.

President Davis wired Johnston that he knew Pemberton would hang on tenaciously at Vicksburg, "but the disparity of numbers renders prolonged defence dangerous. I hope you will soon be able to break the investment, make a junction and carry in munitions."

May 25, Monday

Confederates failed to evacuate Port Hudson and Federal efforts to surround the post got fully under way. There was a skirmish at Thompson's Creek near Port Hudson and Federals captured the Confederate steamers *Starlight* and *Red Chief* on the Mississippi.

Other fighting was at Polk's Plantation near Helena, Ark.; Centreville, La.; and Woodbury, Tenn. C.S.S. *Alabama* took two prizes in raids off Bahia, Brazil.

Federal military authorities in Tennessee turned over former Ohio congressman Clement L. Vallandigham to the Confederates. His prison sentence had been changed by Lincoln to banishment from the U.S. after his conviction of expressing alleged pro-Confederate sentiments.

May 26, Tuesday

Federal troops under Gen. Banks completed setting up siege operations at Port Hudson below Vicksburg on the Mississippi. A Federal expedition from Haynes' Bluff to Mechanicsburg, Miss., May 26–June 4 included skirmishing. Other Federal expeditions moved from Corinth, Miss., to Florence, Ala., May 26–31 and from Bolivar to Wesley Camp, Somerville, and Antioch Church, Tenn., May 26–29. Both involved skirmishing. A Federal scout from Fort Heiman, Ky., lasted until June 2. In Missouri fighting erupted at Mountain Store and Bush Creek; and a Federal expedition moved from Memphis, Tenn., toward Hernando, Miss.

In Alder Gulch, in what became Montana, gold had been discovered and, despite the war, a wild boom followed. Alder Gulch, renamed Virginia City, became the epitome of a frontier mining town. The spectacular strike relieved Federal authorities, who had feared a threat to the California gold mines.

Mr. Davis, discussing army problems and command changes with Lee, also wrote him that "Pemberton is stoutly defending the entrenchments at Vicksburg, and Johnston has an army outside, which I suppose will be able to raise the siege, and combined with Pemberton's forces may win a victory."

May 27, Wednesday
FIRST ASSAULT ON PORT HUDSON.

In the rolling, ravine-cut, heavy-timbered country near Port Hudson, La., Gen. Banks' Federal army of about 13,000 effectives, made its first assault on the estimated 4500 Confederates under Maj. Gen. Franklin Gardner within the beleaguered post. In a somewhat disorganized attack, the Federals, including some Negro troops, got close to the Confederate parapets. But the disjointed movements failed along the entire lines, with heavy losses. Federal casualties were 293 killed, 1545 wounded, and 157 missing for a total of 1995. Confederate killed and wounded together were about 235. Assaults on fortified Confederate areas had again proved costly.

In the Vicksburg theater Confederates attacked Union gunboats near Greenwood, Miss., and skirmished near Lake Providence, La. On the Mississippi itself Gen. Sherman decided to attempt to reduce a Confederate strong point, Fort Hill, with the aid of the gunboats. *Cincinnati,* with added logs and bales of hay as protection, engaged the heavy Confederate batteries. The high position of the Confederates enabled them to shell the gunboat. *Cincinnati* sank, her colors still flying from the stump of her mast, with forty casualties.

A Federal scout moved from Memphis toward Hernando, Miss., and May 27–28 a Federal reconnaissance operated from Murfreesboro on the Manchester Pike in Tennessee. In Virginia Federals scouted May 27–28 from Snicker's Ferry to Aldie, Fairfax Court House, and Leesburg.

An anxious President Lincoln wired Hooker at the Rappahannock, "what news?" and to Rosecrans at Murfreesboro, "Have you any thing from Grant? Where is Forrest's Head-Quarters?"

C.S.S. *Chattahoochee* blew up accidentally on the Chattahoochee River, Ga.; eighteen men died.

May 28, Thursday
From Boston the Fifty-fourth Massachusetts Volunteers left for Hilton Head, S.C. It was the first Negro regiment sent from the North. There was a skirmish near Fort Gibson, Indian Terr., and another near Austin, Miss.

May 29, Friday
Maj. Gen. Burnside, in command at Cincinnati, offered his resignation to Lincoln as a result of the arrest, conviction and banishment of Vallandigham. Lincoln, however, refused the resignation. Gov. Oliver P. Morton of

Indiana and others had also protested the arrest on grounds that it increased opposition to the war effort in the states on the Ohio.

A skirmish broke out near Mill Springs, Ky., scene of a major battle early in 1862.

May 30, Saturday

Lee's Confederate Army of Northern Virginia was reorganized into three corps under Lieut. Gen. R. S. Ewell, Lieut. Gen. A. P. Hill, and Lieut. Gen. James Longstreet. Skirmishes occurred at Jordan's Store, Tenn.; near Greenwich, Va.; and at Port Isabel, Tex. At Newark, N.J., a large meeting of Democrats protested the earlier arrest and conviction of Vallandigham.

May 31, Sunday

A turbulent month drew quietly to a close. Chancellorsville had been fought in Virginia but the armies of Lee and Hooker remained on the Rappahannock. In the West Rosecrans faced Bragg north of Tullahoma, and on the Mississippi the sieges continued at Vicksburg and Port Hudson. There was a small affair on James Island, S.C., and a skirmish at Warrenton, Va. West Point, Va., on the Peninsula, was evacuated by the Union May 31–June 1. President Davis discussed army appointments and dispositions of units with Lee and at the same time stated that "Genl. Johnston did not, as you thought advisable, attack Grant promptly, and I fear the result is that which you anticipated if time was given." He was less and less hopeful over affairs at Vicksburg.

JUNE, 1863

As the month began, the war-weary eyes of both nations were turned toward the town on the bluffs of the Mississippi. Pemberton's Confederate forces and the citizens of Vicksburg were beginning to tighten belts and endure the siege guns of Grant's army encamped outside. At the same time the only other strong point held by Confederates on the Mississippi, Port Hudson, also lay under siege. At Murfreesboro and Tullahoma, Tenn., Union and Confederate armies were relatively inactive, but action of some sort was expected and urged. In Virginia it was obvious there would be a new campaign in the near future, but where and by whom was the question. Problems of the home front plagued both North and South as the war entered its third summer.

June 1, Monday

Gen. Burnside, now in command of the Department of the Ohio, issued a general order: "On account of the repeated expression of disloyal and incendiary sentiments, the publication of the newspaper known as the Chicago Times is hereby suppressed." Suppression of the anti-Administration paper aroused immediate excitement in Chicago and elsewhere. A group of Chicago's leading citizens, including Mayor F. C. Sherman, asked the President to rescind the order. Lincoln conferred with Stanton on the problem of shutting down various newspapers. In Philadelphia a meeting protested the treatment of C. L. Vallandigham.

Heavy bombardment continued at Vicksburg and Port Hudson, while fighting elsewhere was limited to skirmishes near Rocheport, Doniphan, and Waverly, Mo.; Snicker's Gap, Va.; and Berwick, La.

June 2, Tuesday
President Lincoln, uncertain about Hooker's ability to command the Federal Army of the Potomac properly, is said to have conferred with Maj. Gen. John F. Reynolds regarding that command and possibly even offered it to Reynolds. Equally concerned with events in the West, Lincoln wired Grant, "Are you in communication with Gen. Banks? Is he coming toward you, or going further off?" Washington had urged the two forces to join up. However, Banks wisely continued his siege of Port Hudson and Grant was fully occupied at Vicksburg.

President Davis ordered C. L. Vallandigham sent to Wilmington, N.C., and put under guard as an "alien enemy."

Federals raided Confederate property and stores on the Combahee River, S.C. Skirmishing occurred at Upperville and Strasburg, Va., and at Jamestown, Ky. A Federal expedition operated from Haynes' Bluff to Satartia and Mechanicsburg, Miss., June 2–8.

June 3, Wednesday
Gen. Robert E. Lee's Army of Northern Virginia was on the move. First elements of the Confederate army of about 75,000 men left the Fredericksburg area in a westerly direction. McLaws' division of Longstreet's corps was in the van. Other units prepared to follow. The decision to invade the North a second time had been made. The Gettysburg Campaign, which would last nearly two months, was under way. One of the first actions was a minor skirmish near Fayetteville, Va.

The Ninth Army Corps from Kentucky was ordered to Vicksburg to augment Grant's army. There were operations during the week in northern Louisiana and a Federal expedition to Clinton, La., as part of the Port Hudson campaign. In Tennessee action included a small Federal expedition from Jackson and skirmishing at Murfreesboro; fighting also occurred near Simsport, La.

Democrats, led by Mayor Fernando Wood, met at the Cooper Institute in New York to urge peace. At Sheffield, England, a meeting honored Confederate Gen. Stonewall Jackson. The Fifty-fourth Massachusetts, a Negro regiment under Col. Robert Gould Shaw, arrived at Port Royal, S.C.

June 4, Thursday

Lee, moving out from Fredericksburg toward Culpeper Court House, sent Ewell's corps to follow Longstreet's, leaving only A. P. Hill at Fredericksburg. Hooker, on the Falmouth side of the Rappahannock, was not sure whether it was a major movement or just a change of camps.

In Tennessee Confederates operated on the Shelbyville Pike near Murfreesboro. Fighting broke out at Snow Hill and Franklin, and Federals scouted around Smithville. In Virginia a two-day Federal expedition moved from Yorktown to Walkerton and Aylett's. Skirmishes occurred on Lawyer's Road near Fairfax Court House and at Frying Pan. Other action included a Federal expedition from Fort Pulaski, Ga., to Bluffton, S.C.; skirmishing at Fayetteville, Ark.; at Atchafalaya and at Lake Saint Joseph, La.

Lincoln suggested to Sec. of War Stanton that the order suspending publication of the Chicago *Times* be revoked and the Secretary so ordered.

Siege life was entering the droning stage at Vicksburg.

June 5, Friday

Federals from Hooker's Army of the Potomac made a reconnaissance at Franklin's Crossing, above Fredericksburg, and found Confederates in position. Hooker, at Falmouth, and Lincoln and Halleck exchanged telegrams on how to counter the apparent shifting of at least part of Lee's army. Washington indicated Hooker should try to attack the moving Confederates rather than cross the Rappahannock and engage those still at Fredericksburg. Skirmishing between Sedgwick's Federals and A. P. Hill's Confederates continued at Franklin's Crossing or Deep Run for several days. But there was no real opposition to Lee's progress.

In North Carolina a Federal reconnaissance moved through Gates County and down the Chowan River.

June 6, Saturday

As Lee's army marched from Fredericksburg toward Culpeper Court House, Hooker's Federals sought to determine their destination. Meanwhile, at Brandy Station eight thousand sabers flashed and horses pranced as Jeb Stuart's cavalry spread in review along the railroad track, displaying their colorful movements to the assembled dignitaries and their ladies in carriages and in "cars" on the railroad.

But the real fighting went on, with skirmishing at Berryville, Va.; near Richmond, La.; on the Shelbyville Pike, Tenn.; at Waitsborough, Ky.; and in Kansas at Shawneetown. From this day to the twentieth there was skirmishing about Fort Gibson, Indian Terr.

Mr. Lincoln wondered how the investment of Vicksburg was succeeding as reports were delayed for several days.

June 7, Sunday

Confederate forces attacked the Federal garrison at Milliken's Bend, La., near Vicksburg, pushing through the works and forcing the Federals, which included the African Brigade, to the Mississippi riverbank. The tide was turned by Union gunboats *Lexington* and *Choctaw,* and the Confederates fell back. Federals suffered 652 casualties and the Confederates 185. Below Vicksburg, Federals burned and sacked the Brierfield Plantation of Jefferson Davis and his brother Joseph. Other action included a skirmish near Edmonton, Ky., and an expedition from Gainesville, Va., June 7–8.

June 8, Monday

Lee, with Longstreet's and Ewell's corps, arrived in the area of Culpeper Court House, the first stopping point in their new invasion route. Again Stuart held a review of his cavalry, this time for Gen. Lee, other officers and dignitaries, and Gen. John Bell Hood and "his people." The latter turned out to be his whole division and there was some high jocularity between the infantry and cavalry.

Fighting included an affair near Brunswick, Ga.; skirmishes at Camp Cole, Mo.; Fort Scott, Kas.; Triune, Tenn.; and a Federal scout from Suffolk, Va., to South Mills, N.C. In the West Federal expeditions operated from Glasgow, Ky., to Burkesville, and from Pocahontas, Tenn., to Ripley, Miss.

Mr. Lincoln wrote Gen. John A. Dix that all was going well at Vicksburg and that there was nothing new from Port Hudson. A resident of Vicksburg wrote of the bombardment: "Twenty-four hours of each day these preachers of the Union made their touching remarks to the town. All night long their deadly hail of iron dropped through roofs and tore up the deserted and denuded streets." Some residents stayed in their homes; others lived at least part of the time in hillside caves.

June 9, Tuesday

BATTLE OF BRANDY STATION, VIRGINIA.

The Confederate cavalry under Stuart quietly watched the Rappahannock near Brandy Station. Behind them stood the bulk of Lee's army at Culpeper. Hooker knew a movement was on, and sent Alfred Pleasonton's cavalry, supported by some infantry, to find what he could. Pleasonton moved across the Rappahannock in two columns, one at Beverly Ford and the other downstream at Kelly's Ford. For ten to twelve hours horsemen charged horsemen at Brandy Station, also known as Fleetwood Hill or Beverly Ford, in the greatest cavalry battle on American soil. A surprised Stuart barely managed to stave off defeat at Fleetwood Hill and at Stevensburg near Kelly's Ford. At day's end the Confederates held the field, but Hooker had some information, and the underrated Federal cavalry had redeemed itself. For the first time Southern cavalry had met a match. Casualties are uncertain, but records indicate 81 Federals killed, 403 wounded, and 382 missing for a total of 866. Confederate casualties are put at 523. Each side had approximately 10,000 men engaged. No longer could the infantry jibe—"Whoever saw a dead cavalryman."

Twenty Federals were killed and fourteen injured when a powder magazine exploded near Alexandria, Va. The Federals hanged two Southern soldiers as spies at Franklin, Tenn. Skirmishes occurred at Triune, Tenn.; Monticello and Rocky Gap, Ky.; Macon Ford on Big Black River, Miss.; and near Lake Providence, La.

June 10, Wednesday

Ewell's Confederate corps left Culpeper and headed northwest. Lee continued to advance. Hooker wrote Lincoln that now was the time to march to Richmond. Lincoln replied, "I think *Lee's* Army, and not *Richmond,* is your true objective point. . . . Fight him when opportunity offers. If he stays where he is, fret him, and fret him." Citizens north of the Potomac were already alarmed, though no Confederate army was yet on their soil. Maj. Gen. Darius N. Couch assumed command of the Department of the Susquehanna. The governor of Maryland called for the people to rally in defense against invasion.

Federals scouted on the Middleton and Eagleville pikes, Tenn. Skirmishing occurred at Edwards' Station, Miss., and near Suffolk and at Diascund Bridge, Va. Off Cape Henry, Va., the steamer *Maple Leaf,* en route from Fort Monroe to Fort Delaware with rebel prisoners, was run ashore by the prisoners, who then escaped. Confederate Gen. Braxton Bragg was confirmed in the Episcopal faith at Chattanooga as a wave of religious fervor moved through Southern ranks in the West.

June 11, Thursday

As the armies marched in Virginia and sullenly faced each other at Vicksburg, there were lesser happenings elsewhere. Confederate outposts were captured at Port Hudson, La. Forrest caused trouble to Federals at Triune, Tenn. Skirmishing occurred at Smith's Bridge near Corinth, Miss.; at Scottsville, Ky.; Jacksonport, Ark.; and Darien, Ga. June 11–13 there were operations on Little Folly Island, S.C., and at the same time Federals patrolled the Potomac looking for Confederate outriders.

In Ohio C. L. Vallandigham was nominated for governor by the Peace Democrats, although absent from the state. Although sent to the Confederacy by order of Lincoln, Vallandigham had been equally unwelcome in the South and was transshipped to Canada.

June 12, Friday

The head of Lee's army under Ewell crossed the Blue Ridge into the Shenandoah Valley toward Winchester, and engaged in skirmishes at Newtown, Cedarville, and Middletown, Va. Federals scouted on the Salem Pike, Tenn. A Federal expedition operated from Pocahontas, Tenn., to New Albany and Ripley, Miss., June 12–14, and included skirmishing; from this day to the eighteenth another Federal expedition moved from Suffolk to the Blackwater, Va. Federal Brig. Gen. Quincy Adams Gillmore superseded Maj. Gen. David Hunter in command of the Department of the South.

Vice-President Alexander Stephens of the Confederacy offered to President Davis to take part in a mission to effect "a correct understanding and agreement between the two Governments." Of course, no adjustment could be made that did not admit the right of each state "to determine its own destiny." In Washington Lincoln visited the War Department, concerned over Lee's movements. In answer to a complaint about arbitrary arrests, Lincoln stated that while he regretted such, "Still, I must continue to do so much as may seem to be required by the public safety."

Off Cape Hatteras Lieut. Charles Read, daring commander of C.S.S. *Clarence*, captured the Union bark *Tacony*. He destroyed *Clarence*, which had taken six prizes in a week, transferred his crew to *Tacony*, and continued raiding exploits into the north Atlantic.

June 13, Saturday

The advance corps of the Confederate Army of Northern Virginia under Ewell drove in the Federal outposts at Winchester in the Shenandoah and occupied Berryville. Hooker, with the Federal Army of the Potomac, started to move northward toward the Potomac during the night, leaving the position held for nearly seven months on the Rappahannock. Around Winchester fighting broke out at Opequon Creek, Bunker Hill, and White Post.

Other action occurred at Howard's Mills, Ky., and near Mud Lick Springs in Bath County, Ky. June 13–22 there were operations in northeastern Mississippi; meanwhile, Federals probed Johnston's forces outside Vicksburg. From this day to the twenty-third there was action in eastern Kentucky.

President Davis, concerned over reinforcements going to Grant at Vicksburg, asked Bragg at Tullahoma if he could either advance his own army or detach troops.

June 14, Sunday

BATTLE OF SECOND WINCHESTER, VIRGINIA.

ASSAULT ON PORT HUDSON, LOUISIANA.

A nervous Washington had ordered or at least suggested strongly that Federal forces under Maj. Gen. R. H. Milroy at Winchester retreat to Harper's Ferry. Milroy disagreed, not believing that Lee's army could evade Hooker on the Rappahannock. Waiting too long, Milroy's garrison of about

6900 effectives was attacked late in the day from the west and threatened from the south and east by two divisions of Ewell's Confederate corps.

Early's division succeeded in taking one of the earthworks and severely menaced the main forts. Fearing that Milroy would attempt to escape during the night, Ewell moved Edward Johnson's division to the north and blocked the road toward Harper's Ferry. Following an evening conference, Milroy decided to withdraw after destroying his wagons and guns. Losses were small in the first day's fighting. Meanwhile, Confederates under Robert E. Rodes of Ewell's corps moved from Berryville to capture Martinsburg, along with seven hundred prisoners, five guns, and stores. At Fredericksburg A. P. Hill's corps moved out unopposed to join Lee. Skirmishing occurred at Nine-Mile Ordinary, Va.

At Port Hudson, above Baton Rouge, Banks called on the Confederates to surrender. When they refused, Banks ordered an assault at dawn. Two main spearheads advanced, gained some ground, but failed to break the lines. About 6000 Federals took part in the assault against about 3750 Confederates. For the Federals 203 were killed, 1401 wounded, and 188 missing for a total of 1792 casualties; 22 Confederates were killed and 25 wounded for a total of 47. The siege continued both at Port Hudson and at Vicksburg.

A skirmish broke out at Green Hill, Tenn. Raiding in the eastern part of that state lasted 14–24. U.S.S. *Marmora* was fired into by Confederate guerrillas near Eunice, Ark. In retaliation Federals burned much of the town and then destroyed Gaines' Landing on the fifteenth.

Both Hooker and the Administration in Washington were uncertain as to the whereabouts and strength of Lee's army. Late in the afternoon Lincoln wired Hooker, "If the head of Lee's army is at Martinsburg and the tail of it on the Plank road between Fredericksburg and Chancellorsville, the animal must be very slim somewhere. Could you not break him?"

June 15, Monday

BATTLE OF WINCHESTER: STEPHENSON'S DEPOT.

About 1 A.M. Milroy began to withdraw his Federal garrison from Winchester. But his route had been effectively stopped by Edward Johnson's division of Ewell's corps at Stephenson's Depot, about four miles north of Winchester. After a sharp fight some Federal units managed to escape toward Harper's Ferry, but the loss was high; 4000 men were reported captured or missing. Federal dead totaled 95, and 348 were wounded. The Confederates also seized 23 guns, 300 loaded wagons, over 300 horses, and large quantities of commissary and quartermasters' stores. Ewell suffered 47 killed, 219 wounded, and 3 missing for 269. Gen. Rodes of Ewell's corps crossed the Potomac with three brigades near Williamsport, engaged in minor skirmishing, and sent the cavalry forward toward Chambersburg. Longstreet began moving his corps north and west from Culpeper Court House via Ashby's and Snicker's gaps, with Stuart's cavalry in front. Excitement mounted in Baltimore and elsewhere in Maryland and Pennsylvania as the threat of invasion developed. Hooker told Lincoln, "it is not in my power to prevent" invasion.

Other fighting included an affair near Trenton, Tenn.; action near Richmond, La.; a two-day Federal expedition near Lebanon, Tenn.; and operations by both sides in northwestern Mississippi which lasted for nearly the rest of the month.

The British House of Lords debated seizures of British ships by U.S. naval vessels. A Federal enrolling officer in Boone County, Ind., was seized by a group of men who held him while women pelted him with eggs. At Pittsburgh business was suspended and bars and saloons closed, in alarm over Lee's invasion.

In Washington Lincoln reacted to the new threat by calling for 100,000 militia from Pennsylvania, Ohio, Maryland, and West Virginia. The Navy Department dispatched a considerable force to seek out C.S.S. *Tacony*, commanded by Charles Read, whose raiding along the Atlantic seaboard was causing damage to Union shipping.

June 16, Tuesday

As the Confederates began to cross the Potomac, their army strung out over a large part of Virginia, Hooker moved most of his Army of the Potomac to Fairfax Court House. He now became involved in argument with Halleck in Washington. Hooker wanted to move north of Washington to confront Lee. Halleck wanted Hooker to follow Lee and possibly to relieve Harper's Ferry, now severely menaced. Hooker wired Lincoln that he did not have the confidence of Halleck. Lincoln replied, "You do not lack his confidence in any degree to do you any harm." Hooker had been reporting direct to Lincoln, bypassing Halleck. Now, late in the day, Lincoln told Hooker he was in strict military relation to Halleck and that Halleck would give the orders.

At Harrisburg, Pa., a reporter described the scene as "perfect panic." "Every woman in the place seemed anxious to leave," and people loaded down with luggage crowded the trains. At the state Capitol books, papers, paintings, and valuables were packed for evacuation.

In Kentucky skirmishes occurred at Maysville, Mount Carmel, Fox Springs, and Triplett's Bridge. Other action included a demonstration on Waterloo in west Louisiana; a skirmish in the Jornada del Muerto desert area in New Mexico; a Confederate raid on Union lines at Port Hudson, La.; a skirmish at Quinn's Mills on the Coldwater in Mississippi; a Federal scout from Memphis to the Hatchie River; and two days of skirmishes near Holly Springs, Miss. A Federal expedition against the Sioux Indians in the Dakotas lasted until Sept. 13. Opposition to the draft and the war in general caused trouble in Holmes County, O., and a Federal expedition from La Grange, Tenn., to Panola, Miss., operated until June 24.

June 17, Wednesday

In early morning at the mouth of the Wilmington River in Wassaw ·
Sound, Ga., the Confederate ironclad *Atlanta,* or *Fingal,* fought Federal
Weehawken and *Nahant.* In a short engagement *Atlanta* was struck five
times and surrendered to Capt. John Rodgers of *Weehawken.* Casualties
were light but the ship-starved Confederate Navy suffered a severe blow.

As Lee's movement in Virginia and into Maryland continued, there were
skirmishes at Catoctin Creek and Point of Rocks, Md. Cavalry units skirmished at Middleburg, Thoroughfare Gap, and Aldie, Va.

In the Vicksburg area the siege continued. Federals were constantly
annoyed by attacks on transports and other vessels on the Mississippi, such
as one this day near Commerce, Miss. In Missouri fighting erupted near
Westport and Wellington; in Tennessee at Wartburg near Montgomery.
In North Carolina Yankees scouted from Rocky Run to Dover and Core
Creek. For five days a Federal expedition operated from Pocahontas,
Tenn., toward Pontotoc, Miss.

June 18, Thursday

At Vicksburg Gen. Grant relieved Maj. Gen. John A. McClernand
from command of the Thirteenth Army Corps. For a long time McClernand
had posed a difficult problem for Grant. He had originally been given
permission by Washington to organize and probably command the Vicksburg expedition. Grant thought him insubordinate, self-seeking, and incompetent. The final break came when McClernand issued a congratulatory
order to his troops after the assault on Vicksburg, praising his men and
casting aspersions on other segments of the army. McClernand could never
forget he was a politician. Maj. Gen. E. O. C. Ord was appointed to
command the corps, creating more peace and cooperation in Grant's official
family. Other action in Mississippi involved skirmishing at Coldwater
Bridge and Belmont, and an affair at Birdsong Ferry on the Big Black
River.

In Virginia Lee reported that his three corps were continuing their
northward advance and that Stuart's cavalry held the approaches to the
Blue Ridge. There was skirmishing near Aldie.

Federals scouted on the Peninsula of Virginia. Skirmishes broke out
on Edisto Island, S.C.; near Rocheport, Mo.; and at Plaquemine, La.
A two-day Union scout operated on the Big and Little Coal rivers of West
Virginia.

June 19, Friday

In the east Ewell moved north of the Potomac toward Pennsylvania
while A. P. Hill and Longstreet followed from Virginia. Federal probes

toward the passes of the Blue Ridge, including one at Middleburg, Va., were beaten off.

Otherwise events fell into the usual pattern of siege at Vicksburg. Nearby, fighting erupted on the Coldwater near Hernando, Miss., and at Panola, Miss. There was Confederate raiding on Bayou Goula, La.; an affair at Lenoir's Station and skirmishing near Knoxville and at Triune, Tenn., also marked the day.

On the Vicksburg siege lines most evenings the sharpshooters ceased firing at dusk. Truces were made, "Johnny Reb and Jonathan Fed had many a set-to to see who could say the funniest things, or who could outwit the other in a trade, which generally ended by a warning cry, 'going to shoot, Johnny.'"

June 20, Saturday

West Virginia officially took its place in the Union as the thirty-fifth state by virtue of a presidential proclamation.

A skirmish occurred at Middletown, Md.; another at Diascund Bridge, Va.; and one involved Indians near Government Springs, Ut. Terr. Federal scouts probed for three days from Waynesville, Mo. At La Fourche Crossing, La., Federals repulsed Confederate attacks in two days of spirited fighting. There was an especially heavy six-hour Union bombardment by both army and navy guns at Vicksburg.

In Baltimore breastworks were being erected north and west of the city as a precaution against Confederate raids. At Shippensburg, Penn., the owner of the Union Hotel blurred his sign with brown paint.

June 21, Sunday

Relatively heavy skirmishing continued along the fringes of Lee's advance northward, with action at Upperville, near Gainesville, at Haymarket Thoroughfare Gap, Va., and at Frederick, Md.

In Mississippi fighting erupted at Hudsonville and on Helena Road; in Louisiana at Brashear City; in Tennessee at Powder Springs Gap; and in South Carolina on Dixon's Island.

At Vicksburg a Confederate major said, "One day is like another in a besieged city—all you can hear is the rattle of the Enemy's guns, with the sharp crack of the rifles of their sharp-shooters going from early dawn to dark and then at night the roaring of the terrible mortars is kept up sometimes all this time."

June 22, Monday

In another day of lesser fighting, Confederates continued to move north in Maryland and Virginia, with skirmishes near Aldie and Dover, Va., and Greencastle, Pa. Around Vicksburg troops fought again on the Big

Black River, at Jones' Plantation near Birdsong Ferry, and at Hill's Plantation near Bear Creek. A skirmish occurred at Powell Valley, Tenn. Confederate raider Charles Read in *Tacony* captured five fishing schooners off New England, adding to his mounting record.

June 23, Tuesday

TULLAHOMA, TENNESSEE, CAMPAIGN BEGINS.

From Murfreesboro, Tenn., Federal Maj. Gen. William S. Rosecrans, after much urging, finally moved toward Gen. Braxton Bragg's Confederates at Tullahoma. Exhorted to take the pressure off Grant at Vicksburg by preventing Confederate reinforcements, Rosecrans conducted the Tullahoma or Middle Tennessee Campaign brilliantly. Rosecrans outflanked Bragg and finally forced him to fall back behind the Tennessee River by the end of the month. The campaign ended in early July. No major fighting marked the campaign, but a number of skirmishes occurred, including two this day at Rover and Unionville, Tenn. Now all three major fronts of the war—Virginia, the Mississippi, and middle Tennessee—were active.

Lee believed the Federals were preparing to cross the Potomac in Virginia, and he was right. Hooker was considering such a move as he groped after the Confederates.

At Brashear City, La., about a thousand Federals surrendered after a Confederate attack. Other fighting included action at Sibley and Papinsville, Mo.; Pawnee Agency, Neb. Terr.; a three-day Union raid on Brookhaven and a skirmish at Rock Creek, near Ellisville, Miss.; and an affair with Indians at Cañon Station, Nev. Terr. June 23–28 a Federal expedition operated from Yorktown, Va., to the South Anna Bridge, and involved skirmishing.

June 24, Wednesday

Longstreet's and A. P. Hill's corps of the Army of Northern Virginia began crossing the Potomac in order to join Ewell in Maryland and then invade Pennsylvania. A skirmish broke out at Sharpsburg, Md.

Rosecrans, moving forward in middle Tennessee, fought Bragg's men at Middleton, near Bradyville, Big Springs Ranch, and Christiana. June 24–26 saw skirmishes at Hoover's Gap, and June 24–27 at Liberty Gap, Tenn.

On the third front, the situation inside Vicksburg grew more and more serious; Federal shelling continued and the people suffered from lack of food and other supplies. With reinforcements, the Federal grip became even stronger.

Skirmishes flared at Mound Plantation and near Lake Providence, La., and at Bayou Boeuf Crossing and Chacahoula Station in western Louisiana.

Gen. Hooker, at Headquarters of the Army of the Potomac, wrote Washington that he would send a corps or two across the Potomac, make Washington secure, and then strike on Lee's probable line of retreat.

He asked for orders, since, he said, except in relation to his own army, "I don't know whether I am standing on my head or feet."

June 25, Thursday

At 1 A.M. Jeb Stuart left from Salem Depot, Va., receiving permission from Gen. Lee to join the Confederate army north of the Potomac after passing between the Federal army and Washington. It was the beginning of a ride which took his cavalry away from much of the Gettysburg operations and over which controversies rage still. Ewell's men and Federals skirmished near McConnellsburg, Pa.

President Davis, deeply disturbed, wrote Bragg at Shelbyville, Tenn., and Beauregard at Charleston for reinforcements for Mississippi: unless Johnston was substantially and promptly reinforced, "the Missi. will be lost." Johnston still tried to operate in the rear of Grant's line to relieve Vicksburg. There was a skirmish at Milliken's Bend, La., near Vicksburg, and a Federal expedition June 25–July 1 from Snyder's Bluff to Greenville, Miss.

In middle Tennessee skirmishing erupted at Guy's Gap and Fosterville, and in Arkansas at Madison.

June 26, Friday

Confederate Gen. Early and a portion of his command entered Gettysburg, Pa., in their advance north of the Potomac. The next day they marched toward York. Federal militia fled after a brief skirmish near Gettysburg and a number were captured. Federal Gen. Hooker reported himself on the way to Frederick, Md., and said he wanted to evacuate Maryland Heights at Harper's Ferry. Washington appeared to doubt Hooker's ability to act against the Confederate invasion. Gov. Andrew G. Curtin of Pennsylvania called for sixty thousand men to serve three months to repel the invasion.

In the Tullahoma Campaign troops skirmished at Beech Grove, Tenn.; and in West Virginia a skirmish broke out on Loup Creek; at besieged Port Hudson, Confederates captured some Union outposts.

Rear Admiral Andrew H. Foote, hero of much fighting on Western waters, died in New York City.

Excitement raged on the coast of Maine. Rumors of Confederate raiders off eastern shores had been rife. In late afternoon the Confederate schooner *Archer* sailed into Portland and that night seized the Federal revenue cutter *Caleb Cushing*. But the Confederates under Lieut. Charles W. "Savez" Read were unable to get away when attacked by two steamers and three tugboats. The cutter was blown up and the Confederates surrendered. The U. S. Navy had deployed forty-seven vessels to look for Read, who had captured twenty-one ships in nineteen days. Read had done much of his raiding in *Tacony* but transferred to a prize, *Archer,* near the end of his adventures.

June 27, Saturday

HOOKER REPLACED BY MEADE.

In Washington President Lincoln decided to relieve Maj. Gen. Hooker and name Maj. Gen. George Gordon Meade commander of the Army of the Potomac. Meanwhile, the Confederates in Pennsylvania had nearly a free hand. The main forces of Lee, Hill and Longstreet's corps, arrived at Chambersburg. Gen. Early accepted the surrender of undefended York, Pa., from local officials near the city, as Confederates moved near Harrisburg, the state capital. By this time Hooker was well across the Potomac at Frederick with three corps at Middletown, one at Knoxville, two at Frederick, and the remaining corps near there. Hooker had advised evacuation of Harper's Ferry, and if this advice were not taken, he asked to be removed from the command of the Army of the Potomac.

General-in-Chief Halleck sent a message to Gen. Meade putting him in command of the Army of the Potomac. He was expected to deal with Lee. Hooker's argument over Harper's Ferry appeared to be only the last straw of the case. His removal for failure to win at Chancellorsville and again to stop Lee's invasion had been urged repeatedly for some time.

In Tennessee there was action at Shelbyville, and skirmishes broke out at Fosterville, Guy's Gap, and Fairfield. Federals occupied Manchester, as part of Rosecrans' campaign against Bragg. Stuart's cavalry skirmished near Fairfax Court House, Va. Minor action occurred at Carthage, Mo.

June 28, Sunday

At 7 A.M. at Frederick, Md., Maj. Gen. George Gordon Meade received Halleck's orders placing him in command of the Army of the Potomac. Meade wrote that it was unexpected and that he was in ignorance of the "exact condition of the troops and the position of the enemy," but he would move toward the Susquehanna, cover Washington and Baltimore, and give battle. Washington concurred. The Federals had over 100,000 men in and around Frederick. Scattered fighting erupted between Offutt's Cross Roads and Seneca, and near Rockville, Md.; and at Fountain Dale and Wrightsville, Pa. Lee, planning a drive on Harrisburg, learned the Federals were north of the Potomac. Lee then changed his plans and ordered Longstreet, Hill, and Ewell to march toward Gettysburg and Cashtown. Early entered York, Pa., requisitioned shoes, other clothing, rations, and $100,000. He got some of the supplies and $28,600. Meanwhile, part of Early's men fought with militia near Wrightsville and Columbia.

In the Middle Tennessee or Tullahoma Campaign there was skirmishing at Rover, Tenn. Other fighting broke out at Russellville, Ky., and near Nichol's Mills, N.C. Confederates attacked Donaldsonville, La., and were repulsed with the aid of gunboats. On the Mississippi at Vicksburg and at Port Hudson the sieges ground on.

June 29, Monday

Meade's new command moved rapidly forward in Maryland and by evening the Federals had their left at Emmitsburg and their right at New Windsor. John Buford's cavalry had his advance at Gettysburg. Judson Kilpatrick's cavalry had contacted Stuart's Confederates on the right flank of the Federals. Stuart, now well north of the Potomac, was ranging far and wide. Both armies were heading in the general direction of Gettysburg, Pa. Skirmishing broke out at McConnellsburg, Pa., and Westminster and Muddy Branch, Md.

Meanwhile, there was considerable fighting near Tullahoma, Hillsborough, Decherd, and Lexington, Tenn., as part of Rosecrans' Tullahoma Campaign. Skirmishes flared at Mound Plantation, La.; Columbia and Creelsborough, Ky.; Messinger's Ferry on the Big Black in Mississippi; and around Beverly, W. Va.

June 30, Tuesday

Both Federals and Confederates wondered how long the siege at Vicksburg could continue. In mid-Tennessee Confederates evacuated Tullahoma and began to withdraw to and across the Tennessee River.

From Chambersburg, Pa., and elsewhere Confederates converged on the Gettysburg area. Ewell's corps left York for Gettysburg. Gen. Meade ordered the Federal troops of Gen. Reynolds to occupy Gettysburg.

Fighting broke out at Hanover, Fairfield, and at Sporting Hill near Harrisburg, Pa.; and Westminster, Md. Skirmishing occurred near Hudson's Ford, Neosho River, in Missouri, and at Goodrich's Landing, La. In the House of Commons Gladstone said that reunion of the North and South was not obtainable.

Mr. Lincoln was resisting clamor to put McClellan back in command of the Army of the Potomac.

JULY, 1863

By the end of June it was clear that events were rising to a climax. Lee was in Pennsylvania; that state and Maryland were anxious and uncertain. The Federal Army under a new commander was moving north to meet the Confederate invasion. Across the Alleghenies, Rosecrans was at last on the march, shifting Bragg's Confederates out of Tennessee and making Chattanooga a new key position. Farther west, it was doubtful that the six-week-old siege of Vicksburg could last much longer. Confederate efforts to relieve the garrison were ineffective. On the Atlantic coast the North, damaged by the gunboat attack on Charleston in April, appeared determined to try again, this time from land.

In the North discontent was mounting over the draft, over the pace of the war, over Administration policies, and over emancipation. Such unrest came from those who believed in a settled peace and also from those who believed in a war of conquest and domination. There seemed to be little doubt that the United States could achieve victory; but how and in what form were the questions. In the South worry increased over how long defense could last. Discontent prevailed too with the Davis administration in Richmond, with officers in the field, and with economic hardship.

July 1, Wednesday

BATTLE OF GETTYSBURG, FIRST DAY.

At daybreak Confederates of A. P. Hill's corps moved forward along the Chambersburg–Gettysburg Pike, searching for Union forces near Gettysburg. About four miles west of the town, Southerners collided with John Buford's Federal cavalry pickets. The field had been chosen by underlings; the tempo steadily mounted. At 8 A.M. two Confederate brigades deployed across the Chambersburg Road, at first opposed by Buford's dismounted cavalry, and in midmorning by John F. Reynolds' infantry corps. Along Willoughby Run, McPherson's Ridge, Herr Ridge, they fought. The Federals held, but in midmorning Maj. Gen. Reynolds, one of the ablest Federal generals, was killed at the edge of McPherson's Woods. By afternoon both armies flooded toward Gettysburg, and Confederates of Ewell's corps came in from the north. The Federal First Corps, now under Abner Doubleday, was hard pressed from west and north.

Two divisions of the Eleventh Federal Corps under O. O. Howard came through town and moved out north toward Oak Ridge. Early's men of Ewell's corps struck hard against Howard. The Federals withdrew in some confusion, through the town to Cemetery Hill, southeast of the village. The Federals west of Gettysburg, on Oak Ridge and McPherson's Ridge, in danger of being flanked, also pulled back toward Cemetery Hill and Cemetery Ridge. Losses were heavy on both sides, but the Federals suffered more and victory on the first day went to the South. Confederates held the town when Lee himself arrived. Despite the commander's wish, Cemetery Hill was not attacked and an opportunity was lost. More Federals came in during the evening and night as the lines developed. The Federals stretched from Spangler's Spring and Culp's Hill on the north, along Cemetery Ridge, to the Little Round Top on the south. The Confederates established a long line from the town south along Seminary Ridge facing the Union army. Federal Gen. Meade arrived from Taneytown around midnight.

Indications at Vicksburg were that the siege could not endure much longer. For Pemberton's imprisoned army surrender was the only alternative to starvation. Johnston's force lurking around the edges in Mississippi was unable to cope with constantly enlarging Federal besiegers under Grant. There was skirmishing near Edwards' Station on the edge of the Vicksburg encirclement. At Port Hudson, too, there appeared only one course.

In middle Tennessee the main part of Rosecrans' Tullahoma Campaign was ending; Federals occupied Tullahoma and Confederates under Bragg continued to withdraw toward Chattanooga. Skirmishing broke out near Bethpage Bridge, Elk River, and near Bobo's Cross Roads, not far from Tullahoma.

On the Peninsula secondary Federal movements from White House to the South Anna and Bottom's Bridge with a skirmish at Baltimore Cross Roads caused some apprehension in Richmond. Other fighting occurred in Christiansburg, Ky., and Cabin Creek, Indian Terr.

The Missouri State Convention (Union) adopted an ordinance declaring that slavery should cease in the state as of July 4, 1870. The Federal government signed a convention with Great Britain regarding war claims.

July 2, Thursday

BATTLE OF GETTYSBURG, SECOND DAY.

By late morning the lines had been drawn south of Gettysburg. The Federal army extended on Cemetery Ridge from beyond Culp's Hill down to Little Round Top; the Confederate army massed on the somewhat lower Seminary Ridge. The battleground lay between. It was a day of struggle, of death, then years of controversy. Lee ordered Longstreet's corps to attack the Federal left while Ewell's corps was to drive on Cemetery and Culp's hills. But there were delays. Longstreet opposed the plan; the Confederate troops were reshuffled. For the Federals Maj. Gen. Daniel E. Sickles, commanding the Third Corps, believed the Confederate line threatened his flank, so he moved forward without permission to the Peach Orchard, the Devil's Den, and along the Emmitsburg Road, forming an exposed salient. But an observant Federal officer, Maj. Gen. G. K. Warren, chief engineer for Meade, found the rocky crest of Little Round Top unoccupied by Federals and realized that if that eminence were gained by the enemy, the whole line might collapse.

Warren gathered brigades and hurried to Little Round Top. The Confederates' attempted end run against Little Round Top and in the vale between it and Big Round Top almost succeeded. But after a bitter, heavy fight, the situation at the Round Tops stabilized and Federals held the position. Then Longstreet's entire line went into action against the Wheatfield and the Peach Orchard, along the Emmitsburg Road. Sickles' exposed corps responded nobly but futilely, and after several hours' severe fighting the corps fell back to Cemetery Ridge. Sickles suffered a serious leg wound, and the Confederates held the field at Devil's Den, Peach Orchard, and the lower slopes of the Round Tops. Yet the Federal line remained intact and unflanked.

To the north, on the Confederate left, Early's men of Ewell's corps charged gallantly at East Cemetery Hill in the dusk of evening. Early received no help and Federal reinforcements finally forced him off the hill about 10 P.M. On Culp's Hill a Confederate attack by Maj. Gen. Edward Johnson's division gained and held some of the lower works. The day was over and neither army had made any appreciable gain. The poorly coordinated Confederate attack had failed; the Federals had held despite Sickles' costly move. The years would echo with the charges that Longstreet had been slow, that Sickles had erred in his advance, that Lee had not properly coordinated his attacks, that Federals had failed to see the danger at Little Round Top. The Devil's Den, the Wheatfield, the Peach Orchard, Cemetery Hill, Culp's Hill, and the Round Tops bore testimony to the day's violence. On the edges of the battle there was skirmishing near Chambersburg and Hunterstown, Pa.

In the West the Vicksburg siege continued. To the south, at Port Hudson, there was an affair at Springfield Landing, La. In the campaign of movement in middle Tennessee between Rosecrans' Federals and Bragg's Confederates there was skirmishing at Morris's Ford, Elk River, Rock Creek Ford, Estill Springs, Pelham, and Elk River Bridge, Tenn. Other action included an engagement at Beverly, W. Va., and skirmishing at Baltimore or Crump's Cross Roads and Baltimore Store, Va., during a Federal expedition from White House.

In Kentucky John Hunt Morgan and about 2500 cavalry crossed the Cumberland River near Burkesville and headed north. They avoided Federal forces, although skirmishing broke out briefly at Marrowbone, Ky. Also in Kentucky troops skirmished at the mouth of Coal Run, in Pike County.

In Washington a deeply concerned President Lincoln spent long hours at the War Department. In Richmond President Davis authorized Vice-President Alexander Stephens to "proceed as a military commissioner under flag of truce to Washington," primarily to negotiate prisoner exchange, but ready to discuss an end to the war. Mr. Davis wrote President Lincoln in regard to the same matter. But the whole plan, originally suggested by Stephens, came to nought with Lincoln's reply: "The request is inadmissible." Meanwhile, Davis continued to urge that forces in the Trans-Mississippi attempt to relieve Vicksburg.

July 3, Friday

BATTLE OF GETTYSBURG ENDS WITH PICKETT'S CHARGE.

SURRENDER CONFERENCE AT VICKSBURG.

In the little white cottage on Cemetery Ridge, Gen. George G. Meade met with his corps commanders shortly after midnight to discuss the future of the army. It was decided to stay at Gettysburg and await Confederate attack. Meade began to dig fortifications on Cemetery Ridge and brought troops there from Culp's Hill and elsewhere. Guns were moved up. There was a dawn artillery duel at Culp's Hill and Spangler's Spring. Union forces attacked the Confederates at Spangler's Spring heavily and often, and eventually the Southerners retreated.

Now it was up to Lee and the remainder of the Army of Northern Virginia. Both flanks of the Federals had been tried; perhaps a powerful attack at Meade's center would do the job and crack the enemy line. Once more Longstreet opposed the plan. The possibly 15,000 attacking infantry (other estimates give 10,500) would be the divisions of George E. Pickett, Henry Heth (commanded by James J. Pettigrew), and Dorsey Pender (commanded by Isaac Trimble).

About 1 P.M. a most thunderous artillery duel opened. Confederates began, and were answered by eighty Federal guns. For two hours the shelling continued. Then the Federals slackened off. Believing the Union line to be weakening, the Confederates prepared to attack. Messages were sent, Longstreet gave a reluctant nod to Pickett, and Pickett's three brigades moved toward the Emmitsburg Road. Pettigrew and Trimble also marched forward. Near the Emmitsburg Road, the Southerners realigned ranks. Union batteries opened fire, cutting gaps in the solid gray ranks.

An eyewitness wrote, "Men fire into each other's faces, not five feet apart. There are bayonet-thrusts, sabre-strokes, pistol-shots; . . . men going down on their hands and knees, spinning round like tops, throwing out their arms, gulping up blood, falling; legless, armless, headless. There are ghastly heaps of dead men. . . ."

The Confederates moved smartly ahead through the artillery fire; musketry opened, and the infantry charged the dug-in Federals. General officers fell—Armistead reached the stone fence, crossed it, and shouting "Follow me!" he fell. Artillery and Federal infantry closed in mercilessly. Units were broken, battle flags falling with the men. The Confederates retreated across the trampled fields to a sorrowing commander. All Lee could say was, "All this has been my fault." The Battle of Gettysburg was over.

Meanwhile, a "side show" was going on east of Gettysburg. Stuart's Confederate horse had finally arrived on July 2 after encircling Meade's army, and now Lee sent them to the rear of the Federals to cut off a possible retreat. In the afternoon Stuart's cavalry, three miles east of town, fought with Union cavalry. Stuart was forced to retire after three hours of assault and repulse.

The casualty figures for the three-day battle are staggering. For the Federals, out of a total engaged of over 85,000 men, 3155 died, 14,529 were wounded, and 5365 missing for a total of 23,049. For the Confederates, whose strength was near 65,000, official losses were 2592 killed, 12,709 wounded, and 5150 missing for 20,451.

Hundreds of miles away, on the Mississippi, white flags of truce flew on Confederate earthworks as Genls. Pemberton and Grant conferred under an oak tree for the surrender of the fortress of Vicksburg. For over a year the Federals had operated against the city. It had resisted all attempts by land and water, but now six weeks of siege had done the job. Pemberton had no choice. No chance remained that Joseph E. Johnston's Confederate force could defeat Grant or relieve the city. Food, while not exhausted, was very scarce, and it would only have lasted a few days more. (Mule meat was declared quite palatable by some.) After some discussion the terms were settled upon, including paroling of prisoners. The formal surrender would take place July 4.

In middle Tennessee there was a skirmish at Boiling Fork near Winchester, as the successful Federal Tullahoma Campaign concluded with Rosecrans forcing Bragg's Confederates out of most of Tennessee and eventually to Chattanooga. It was a period of Federal victories that were defensive as well as offensive.

Morgan continued his foray in Kentucky with a skirmish at Columbia, Ky. Elsewhere there was a Federal scout from Memphis, Tenn.; in Virginia Federals evacuated Suffolk and pulled back toward Norfolk; in Georgia Union forces undertook an expedition to Ossabaw Island; in North Carolina Federals raided the Wilmington and Weldon Railroad; and for a week another Federal expedition operated from Beaver Creek, Ky., into southwestern Virginia, with skirmishing at Pond Creek, Ky., and Gladesville, Va.

In Washington Lincoln was at the War Department reading dispatches from Gettysburg. In Richmond Jefferson Davis, too, awaited news of the Confederate invasion of the North, but he had no direct communications with Lee's army. In New Orleans public gatherings, except church services, were forbidden without written permission; no more than three persons were allowed to congregate at one place on the streets; a 9 P.M. curfew and other restrictions were imposed by the occupying Federal forces.

July 4, Saturday

VICKSBURG SURRENDERS.

LEE RETREATS FROM GETTYSBURG.

On this Independence Day Vicksburg, Miss., was surrendered formally by Confederates under Pemberton to Federals under Grant. About 29,000

Southern soldiers laid down their arms and marched out of the sorely tried city. A quiet Union army observed their departure. Gen. Grant himself entered Vicksburg and watched the Stars and Stripes replace the Confederate flag on the courthouse. In the river the naval vessels shrilled their whistles. The Mississippi River was nearly open now, except for Port Hudson, still strongly besieged. But it was clear that the news of Vicksburg's fall would undoubtedly cause the end at Port Hudson also.

"All will sing 'Hallelujah!' 'The heroic city has fallen!' 'Vicksburg *is* ours!'" proclaimed a Federal captain. A resident of the city who had spent weeks living in a hillside cave said of the surrender: "I wept incessantly, meeting first one group of soldiers and then another many of them with tears streaming down their faces." The "hateful tunes" of the Yankee bands sounded bitterly in the ears of the heroic defenders, soldiers and civilians alike.

From Seminary Ridge at Gettysburg, a long wagon train of wounded and supplies began to head toward the Potomac and Virginia in late afternoon. Soon Confederate infantry and artillery followed, pelted by the heavy rains that washed some evidence of the great battle from the soil of Pennsylvania. Meade with his weary Federal army did not immediately pursue, despite urging from Washington.

After the early July days of 1863, military hopes of the Confederacy appeared bleak indeed. War weariness in the North, intervention from overseas, a miracle, were nearly all the hopes that seemed left for the Confederate States of America.

Confederates attacked Helena, Ark., in a vain and much too late effort to aid Vicksburg. It failed from want of strength and coordination. Cavalry skirmished at Monterey Gap and Fairfield Gap, Pa., and near Emmitsburg, Md., on the fringes of the Gettysburg area. There was another skirmish at University Depot, Tenn., part of the Tullahoma Campaign. John Hunt Morgan suffered a repulse on the Green River at Tebb's Bend in his invasion of Kentucky, a momentary setback. As an aftermath of Vicksburg there was a brief skirmish at Messinger's Ferry on the Big Black River in Mississippi. Still more fighting occurred at Huttonsville and Fayetteville, W. Va.; near Fort Craig, N. Mex. Terr.; at Cassville and in the Black Ford Hills, Mo.; and at the South Anna Bridge on the Richmond and Fredericksburg Railroad, north of Richmond.

Meanwhile, to the people went the news of Gettysburg, and, more slowly, that of Vicksburg. President Lincoln announced to the country "a great success to the cause of the Union," for the Army of the Potomac.

The Confederate gunboat *Torpedo* carried Vice-President Alexander Stephens down the James River to Hampton Roads. But upon Mr. Lincoln's instructions, Stephens was refused permission to negotiate with the Federal authorities on prisoner exchange or, as he desired, on possible terms to end the war. (There is some question whether this message was sent on July 4 or 6.)

July 5, Sunday

The beaten Army of Northern Virginia moved toward Hagerstown, Md., while Lee's wagon trains went by way of Chambersburg. Meade's main force did not follow, although there was skirmishing, mainly by cavalry, at Smithsburg, Md., and near Green Oak, Mercersburg, Fairfield, Greencastle, Cunningham's Cross Roads, and Stevens' Furnace or Caledonia Iron Works, Pa. The North continued to rejoice and yet hoped for a fast pursuit, and even destruction, of the Confederate army.

In Mississippi, following Vicksburg's surrender, there was an engagement at Birdsong Ferry and Bolton as Federal troops under Sherman once more turned toward the capital at Jackson and Johnston's army. In Kentucky Morgan's raiders gained speed, taking Lebanon and Bardstown after light skirmishing. Other fighting took place at Woodburn, Ky.; Franklin and Yellow Creek, Tenn.; Warsaw and Kenansville, N.C. At Vicksburg Grant began the work of paroling Pemberton's surrendered forces.

July 6, Monday

Still more light fighting occurred as Lee's army withdrew from Gettysburg toward the Potomac: at Boonsborough, Hagerstown, and Williamsport, Md. Still no major Federal pursuit was in sight. In Mississippi, however, Sherman, with a sizable portion of Grant's army, continued to press toward Jackson, Miss., seeking out Joseph E. Johnston's elusive Confederates. Fighting at Jones' and Messinger's ferries marked the day's campaigning. Elsewhere, fighting was at Free Bridge near Trenton, N.C., and Federals raided the Wilmington and Weldon Railroad nearby. John Hunt Morgan's raiders occupied Garnettsville as they moved rapidly northward now in Kentucky, heading for the Ohio River.

At Huntington, Ind., the Knights of the Golden Circle, a Copperhead group, forced their way into the depot and seized guns and ammunition.

A new commander of the Federal South Atlantic Blockading Squadron was named. Rear Admiral John A. Dahlgren formally relieved Rear Admiral Samuel F. Du Pont. The transfer came after considerable friction between Du Pont and Sec. of the Navy Welles over responsibility for failure of the attack on Charleston. It was the end of a career for the brilliant Du Pont.

July 7, Tuesday

Gen. Braxton Bragg's Confederate Army of Tennessee was now encamped around Chattanooga, Tenn., after losing most of the state to Rosecrans' Army of the Cumberland.

Federal forces reoccupied Maryland Heights, on the north bank of the Potomac at Harper's Ferry. Skirmishing broke out at Downsville and Funkstown, Md., as well as at Harper's Ferry, W. Va. It was all a part of the aftermath of Gettysburg. In Mississippi skirmishing increased with fighting at Queen's Hill and near Baker's Creek, as well as farther north of the Vicksburg area at Ripley and Iuka. In Kentucky Morgan's men fought at Shepherdsville and at Cummings' Ferry, as he prepared to cross the Ohio River. Further skirmishing occurred at Dry Wood, Mo., and Grand Pass, Id. Terr. Col. "Kit" Carson began his Federal expeditions against Indians in Arizona Terr., which lasted until Aug. 19.

Meanwhile, the Union Conscription Act took effect. Rumblings of discontent arose, especially in New York City and the western states.

From Hagerstown, Md., Gen. Lee wrote President Davis of his decision to withdraw farther southward.

Mr. Lincoln, considerably concerned over Meade's failure to strike Lee during the retreat, received the good news of Vicksburg's surrender. The President wrote Halleck, "Now, if General Meade can complete his work, so gloriously prosecuted thus far, by the literal or substantial destruction of Lee's army, the rebellion will be over."

July 8, Wednesday

SURRENDER OF PORT HUDSON, LOUISIANA.

MORGAN'S RAIDERS CROSS THE OHIO.

News of the surrender of Vicksburg slowly spread south to Port Hudson, La., and the last Confederate garrison on the Mississippi. Seeing that there was no hope, Gen. Franklin Gardner asked Federal Gen. Banks for terms, and surrendered unconditionally. After six weeks of siege, it was doubtful if Gardner could have held out much longer. About 7000 prisoners were taken by Banks' 33,000, although figures are contradictory. Soon Union steamers were moving the whole length of the Mississippi, although subjected to considerable danger from guerrilla attacks. To the north, in Mississippi, as part of Sherman's campaign against Jackson, there was skirmishing near Bolton Depot and Clinton.

Raider John Hunt Morgan and his men reached the Ohio River at Cummings' Ferry and Brandenburg, Ky., west of Louisville, after some brief skirmishing and crossed into Indiana. Only militia and a small gunboat opposed their passage. The news caused consternation along the Ohio and many feared that the Copperheads would rise and support this invasion. Morgan's force was only a raiding party—but the propaganda effect was electric.

In the final stages of the Gettysburg campaign fighting broke out at Boonsborough and near Williamsport, Md. In Tennessee Federals scouted from Germantown. The draft began in Massachusetts.

Gen. Lee, from Hagerstown, Md., told President Davis that the condition of his army was good and that due to the rising Potomac he might have to accept battle if the enemy attacked. He told the President he was "not in the least discouraged."

July 9, Thursday

The drums beat again for a surrender ceremony; this time at Port Hudson on the eastern shore of the Mississippi in Louisiana, and the Confederate forces of Gen. Gardner formally surrendered to Federal Nathaniel Banks, after capitulating July 8. Federals occupied the fortifications, and the final fortress on the great river was in Northern hands. Anticlimactic to the surrender of Vicksburg, perhaps, but in some ways Port Hudson was a better position to block the river if strongly enough fortified and garrisoned. Now all that remained were extensive mopping-up operations in the Mississippi Valley and the protection of the river. But it did not prove quite that simple for the Federals. Sherman was operating against Joseph E. Johnston near Jackson, Miss., and there was frequent harassment by guerrillas along the river before war's end. Skirmishes broke out near Clinton and Jackson, Miss., as Sherman drew near the state capital.

Just north of Brandenburg, Ky., Morgan and his band, safely across the Ohio River, headed into Indiana and skirmished briefly with home guard forces along the way to Corydon, onetime capital of the state. A small fight flared at Corydon itself, but the Confederates had time for plundering homes and businesses.

The retreat from Gettysburg continued with a skirmish at Benevola or Beaver Creek, Md. At Charleston the mayor warned the people of South Carolina that the Federals were preparing to attack once more, this time at Morris Island.

To Gen. Johnston, President Davis expressed his hopes that Confederates could attack the enemy and that they "may yet be crushed and the late disaster be repaired by a concentration of all forces." But it was too late now, if it had ever been possible.

July 10, Friday

SIEGE OF BATTERY WAGNER, CHARLESTON HARBOR, BEGINS.

As anticipated for some time, Federal troops landed on the south end of Morris Island near Charleston, S.C. Their object was Fort or Battery Wagner, one of the main defenses of Charleston Harbor. It marked the first action in a siege that was to last until September. The Federals prepared for an assault on Wagner, hoping that a decisive victory there could be combined with naval operations that would secure Charleston itself. Naval support had been extensive, with *Catskill* hit sixty times. There was also an engagement at Willstown Bluff, Pon Pon River, S.C.

As Lee gathered his retreating forces at the Potomac in the area of Williamsport, action increased. Meade followed somewhat more energetically, for the Potomac was running high. Skirmishing took place near

Hagerstown, Jones' Cross Roads near Williamsport, Funkstown, Old Antietam Forge, near Leitersburg, and near Clear Spring, Md. Heavier action occurred at Falling Waters, Md. Many wondered how long Lee could remain north of the Potomac without being attacked.

In the West Morgan's raiders skirmished at Salem, Ind., before turning eastward toward Ohio. Sherman invested Jackson, Miss., held by Joseph E. Johnston. Other fighting was at Florence, Mo., and Martin Creek, Bolivar, and Union City, Tenn. In New Mexico Territory Federals fought Indians at Cook's Cañon.

President Davis, distressed over Gettysburg, middle Tennessee, Vicksburg, Port Hudson, and Jackson, Miss., now was perturbed over Charleston as well. He wrote Gov. M. L. Bonham of South Carolina to send local defense troops immediately to the attacked city and harbor.

July 11, Saturday

FIRST ASSAULT ON BATTERY WAGNER.

Federal troops of Brig. Gen. Quincy A. Gillmore made a futile assault on Fort or Battery Wagner on Morris Island in Charleston Harbor. Federals gained the parapet of the strong fortifications but were forced to withdraw under heavy fire. The Yankees then settled down to prepare an even more energetic assault.

Lee continued to fortify his defensive position north of the Potomac and await the falling of the water. Meade slowly began mounting what might be a general attack upon the Army of Northern Virginia. In the West Jackson, Miss., was under partial siege. In middle Tennessee things remained quiet, with Bragg at Chattanooga and Rosecrans to the north, both consolidating after the Tullahoma Campaign. Morgan skirmished at Pekin, Ind., and other fighting broke out at Stockton, Mo., and in the Ashby's Gap area of Virginia.

A worried President Davis wrote Johnston that Beauregard at Charleston and Bragg at Chattanooga were both threatened and "The importance of your position is apparent, and you will not fail to employ all available means to ensure success."

President Lincoln, on the other hand, appeared more satisfied with the operations of Meade and the Army of the Potomac against Lee. He still hoped his general would attack.

July 12, Sunday

Just north of the Potomac in the Williamsport area, the last act of the Gettysburg Campaign was about to open. Meade's army was preparing to attack Lee's Army of Northern Virginia, which as at Antietam, was again defending its position with its back to the river. Lincoln learned of Meade's attack plans but feared it was too late to destroy or cripple Lee. Lee wrote

Davis that if the river continued to subside he could cross the Potomac the next day.

Elsewhere, Sherman's men fought a skirmish near Canton, Miss., in the Jackson campaign, and there was also skirmishing near Switzler's Mill, Chariton County, Mo. Morgan and his men were now at Vernon, Ind., on an eastward course toward Ohio, but they were beset by straggling and the adverse pressure of an aroused Hoosierdom. As part of the cleanup in the Mississippi Valley, Federal troops began a two-week expedition from Vicksburg to Yazoo City, Miss., and there was a two-day engagement on the La Fourche near Donaldsonville, La.

July 13, Monday

DRAFT RIOTS IN NEW YORK CITY AND ELSEWHERE.

LEE RETREATS TO VIRGINIA.

On Saturday, July 11, the first names of the new Federal draft had been drawn in New York City, and they appeared in the papers on Sunday. Seething unrest had long existed in the city over the draft, particularly its provision for substitution and the purchase of exemption. Aggravating the situation were certain politicians who, if not Peace Democrats, were not wholeheartedly in support of the war. On this Monday morning the draft situation came to a head. As the drawing of lots began again, a mob consisting of a high percentage of foreign laborers gathered. Soon a full-scale riot developed. The draft headquarters were stormed, residences raided, and business establishments looted. Authorities (including police, firemen, and the Army) were overpowered as crowds tore through the streets spreading destruction and death.

Fires broke out in various parts of the city, a Negro church and orphanage were burned, and casualties mounted. Negroes became the primary victims, along with Federal officials, of the rampaging mob, now composed mainly of Irish working people. Only the return of troops from Gettysburg, and firm army control, brought it to an end on July 16. The draft had to be postponed until Aug. 19. Figures are uncertain, but one estimate is that a thousand people were killed and wounded, with property losses placed at $1,500,000. The New York draft riot was one of the darkest periods of the Northern homefront during the war.

Considerably less destructive riots occurred at Boston, Portsmouth, N.H., Rutland, Vt., Wooster, O., and Troy, N.Y. Eventually the North became acclimated to the draft; but as long as the war continued there was grumbling and resistance.

In Maryland R. E. Lee pulled out of his defensive positions north of the Potomac and, during the night, crossed the river to safety in Virginia. Lee's Army of Northern Virginia had been resting on a bend of the river and covered Williamsport and Falling Waters. Now with pontoon trains and a fordable river, Lee made good his escape ten days after the conclusion of the Battle of Gettysburg. Meade's Army of the Potomac had moved up cautiously and now was in front of Lee, reconnoitering for an opening and planning an attack or demonstration on the fourteenth. But the next morning, instead of an opponent, Meade found abandoned entrenchments. Lee's last invasion of the North was over. The war returned to where it had started in the east: in northern Virginia.

Meanwhile, John Hunt Morgan, after exploiting southeastern Indiana, crossed into Ohio at Harrison and headed for the Hamilton or Cincinnati area. Federal authorities declared martial law in Cincinnati.

Aided by the gunboats, Federal troops took Yazoo City, Miss., and occupied Natchez without fighting. In Tennessee skirmishing occurred on Forked Deer River and at Jackson; in Louisiana at Donaldsonville. Federals carried out expeditions lasting several days each: one from Rosecrans' army to Huntsville, Ala.; another from Newport Barracks to Cedar Point and White Oak River, N.C.; and a third from Fayetteville, W. Va., to Wytheville, Va.

To add to President Davis' troubles, Gov. F. R. Lubbock of Texas requested more arms to defend Texas. In Washington President Lincoln wrote to Gen. Grant, "I do not remember that you and I ever met personally. I write this now as a grateful acknowledgment for the almost inestimable service you have done the country. . . . I thought you should go down the river and join Gen. Banks; and when you turned Northward East of the Big Black, I feared it was a mistake. I now wish to make the personal acknowledgment that you were right, and I was wrong." The President was also upset by the arrest of William McKee, editor of the *Missouri Democrat* in St. Louis, for publishing a letter of Lincoln's. The President wrote Gen. Schofield, in command in St. Louis, "I fear this loses you the middle position I desired you to occupy."

July 14, Tuesday

The draft riots raged on in New York as the mobs continued to loot and destroy. Lee's Confederate army was south of the Potomac now and Meade's crestfallen troops trudged through the empty Confederate defenses. In a letter he did not sign or send, Lincoln wrote to Meade, ". . . I am very-*very*-grateful to you for the magnificent success you gave the cause of the country at Gettysburg; and I am sorry now to be the author of the slightest pain to you. But I was in such deep distress myself that I could not restrain some expression of it. . . . Your golden opportunity is gone, and I am distressed immeasureably [sic] because of it."

Minor skirmishing occurred at Falling Waters and Harper's Ferry, W. Va.; Williamsport, Md.; Elk River Bridge in middle Tennessee; and Iuka, Miss. Morgan's raiders fought a skirmish at Camp Dennison, O., near

Cincinnati. For the Confederates, Maj. Gen. W. H. C. Whiting was named to command the Department of North Carolina. Farther down the coast Confederates carried out a sortie from Battery Wagner on Morris Island near Charleston, S.C. Federal naval forces took Fort Powhatan on the James River. The Union now controlled the James up to Chaffin's and Drewry's bluffs, Va.

President Davis, struck with numerous defeats, wrote to Sen. R. W. Johnson, "In proportion as our difficulties increase, so must we all cling together, judge charitably of each other, and strive to bear and forbear, however great may be the sacrifice and bitter the trial. . . ."

July 15, Wednesday

The violent action of the past two weeks was dissipating now. The draft riots, in their third day at New York, were becoming less virulent. Skirmishing broke out at Halltown and Shepherdstown, W. Va., as Lee's army slowly moved south up the Shenandoah Valley, where it remained most of the rest of the month. Other skirmishing occurred near Jackson, on Forked Deer River, and at Pulaski, Tenn.; and Federals occupied Hickman, Ky. Sherman pressed Joseph E. Johnston at Jackson, Miss. The pursuit of Morgan increased in strength as the raider moved east from the area of Cincinnati toward the Ohio River. President Davis wrote Lt. Gen. T. H. Holmes in the Trans-Mississippi, "The clouds are truly dark over us." Davis also wrote a long letter to Joseph E. Johnston, with whom he had been bickering over military command and decisions. President Lincoln issued a proclamation of thanksgiving for the recent victories and set aside Aug. 6 as a day of praise and prayer.

July 16, Thursday

Thousands of miles from the fighting fronts occurred one of the strangest battles of the Civil War period. U.S.S. *Wyoming* under David Stockton McDougal was one of several vessels searching for the Confederate raider *Alabama*. Putting in at Yokohama, McDougal found the foreign colony huddled about the dock and terrified by a recent order of the Japanese lords to expel all foreigners and cut off the oft-used passage known as the Straits of Shimonoseki. McDougal moved into the straits and took on the Japanese fleet and shore batteries. Junks and steamers swarmed around him, but he managed to sink some and destroy a few of the batteries. The engagement was fierce but short, and McDougal was victorious. *Wyoming* suffered some damage and had five dead and six wounded. Later an international squadron forced the revocation of the oppressive measures. However, the United States had won its first naval battle with Japan.

Back home Joseph E. Johnston, outnumbered and outmaneuvered, abandoned Jackson, Miss., to Sherman's Federals. As part of the campaigning, skirmishing occurred at Clinton, at Grant's Ferry on Pearl River, and at Bolton Depot, Miss. In the aftermath of Gettysburg there was also skirmishing at Shepherdstown and Shanghai, W. Va. Morgan continued to roam in Ohio, but the pursuers were closing in. On James Island, S.C., Union troops and war vessels beat off a Confederate assault in an engagement near Grimball's Landing. In Tennessee Federals scouted for a couple of days from Germantown.

From Bunker Hill, north of Winchester, Va., Gen. Lee wrote President Davis that "The men are in good health and spirits, but want shoes and clothing badly. . . . As soon as these necessary articles are obtained, we shall be prepared to resume operations."

The steamer *Imperial* tied up at New Orleans, La., having come down the Mississippi from St. Louis. It was the first boat to travel between the two great river ports in more than two years. In New York City the draft riots had run their bloody course.

July 17, Friday

A day of lesser engagements included a cavalry fight at Wytheville, Va., in the southwest; skirmishes near North Mountain Station, W. Va., and at Snicker's Gap, Va.; skirmishing on Stone's River, Tenn.; and at Bear Creek, near Canton, Miss. At Elk Creek near Honey Springs in Indian Territory Union Gen. James G. Blunt attacked Brig. Gen. Douglas H. Cooper's command. In this, the largest engagement in the territory, the Confederates were forced to retire for lack of ammunition. Included in the combatants were Federal Negro soldiers opposed to Confederate Indians. Federals operated for four days from New Berne to Swift Creek Village, N.C. In Ohio Morgan ran into more resistance and faced serious trouble as his raiders fought near Hamden and Berlin.

July 18, Saturday

SECOND ASSAULT ON BATTERY WAGNER, SOUTH CAROLINA.

Shot and shell arched in fiery chorus at Battery Wagner on Morris Island in Charleston Harbor. After pounding the Confederate earthworks with mortars, ironclads, and some thirty-six guns, Brig. Gen. Truman Seymour's six thousand Federals made a frontal charge that failed. One small angle of the earthwork fort was seized momentarily, but the attack was repulsed in the dusk of evening. At the head of the Federal dash was the Fifty-fourth Massachusetts Colored Infantry, which suffered frightful losses, including the death of its colonel and organizer, Robert Gould Shaw. For the Federals, 246 died, 880 were wounded, and 389 were missing for a total of 1515, more than 25 per cent, compared to 36 killed, 133 wounded, and 5 missing for 174 Confederate casualties out of a garrison of about 1785 men.

The failure against a stubborn and courageous defense caused the Federals (under the over-all command of Quincy Adams Gillmore) to change their whole concept of taking Charleston. A siege must be undertaken. Meanwhile, the Confederates transferred guns from Fort Sumter to other points in the harbor. For nearly a month the preparations continued, with Gillmore's artillery setting up heavy batteries on Morris Island, including the huge "Swamp Angel" which fired a two-hundred-pound shot.

In Ohio John Hunt Morgan was in serious trouble; pursuers closed in on his weary column. Morgan passed through Pomeroy and Chester, O., and then headed for Buffington on the Ohio, intending to recross into Kentucky. But a Federal redoubt barred their crossing and Morgan had to await daylight. Skirmishing increased as the adventure became a nightmare.

In Sherman's campaign against Jackson, Miss., skirmishing broke out at Brookhaven. Other fighting occurred near Germantown and Memphis, Tenn., and Des Allemands, La. Federals skirmished with Indians on the Rio Hondo, N. Mex. Terr. There was skirmishing at and near Hedgesville and Martinsburg, W. Va.

Federal Maj. Gen. John G. Foster assumed command of the Department of Virginia and North Carolina, and Maj. Gen. John A. Dix took over the Department of the East. Federal scouts and expeditions lasting for several days moved from Cassville, Mo., to Huntsville, Ark.; and from New Berne to Tarborough and Rocky Mount, N.C. Federal forces entered Wytheville, Va., in the southwestern part of the state. At New Albany, Ind., George W. L. Bickley, one of the leaders of the Knights of the Golden Circle, was arrested. President Lincoln commuted a number of sentences of soldiers found guilty of various crimes. President Davis called for enrollment in the Confederate Army of those coming under jurisdiction of the Conscription Act.

July *19, Sunday*

Meade's Army of the Potomac completed crossing the Potomac in pursuit of Lee at Harper's Ferry and Berlin (now Brunswick), Md. Moving rapidly, the Federal army headed south into Virginia and toward the passes in the Blue Ridge, beyond which lay the Army of Northern Virginia.

In an engagement at Buffington Island on the Ohio, John Hunt Morgan was foiled by Federal troops, militia, and gunboats in another attempt to cross the river to safety in Kentucky. Morgan suffered about 820 casualties, including 700 captured. Federal casualties were light. The Confederate remnant of about 300 turned north and headed along the Ohio toward Pennsylvania.

Elsewhere there was action at Brandon, Miss., a part of Sherman's Jackson Campaign. Indians and Federals skirmished on the Rio de las Animas, N. Mex. Terr. Federals scouted from Danville, Miss.; and operations in the vicinity of Trenton, Tenn., lasted several days. D. H. Hill replaced William Hardee in command of the Second Corps in Bragg's Confederate army.

Despite his disappointments over the Gettysburg follow-up, Lincoln was in such good humor that he wrote a little doggerel for secretary John Hay.

July 20, Monday

In Virginia skirmishing flared near Berry's Ferry and at Ashby's Gap in the Blue Ridge as Meade's Federal Army of the Potomac moved southward from the Potomac and began to send troops to cover the passes of the Blue Ridge. Meanwhile, Lee's Army of Northern Virginia began to move southward in the Shenandoah from the area around Bunker Hill north of Winchester.

On the Ohio River the bedraggled remainder of John Hunt Morgan's Confederate raiders fought a skirmish near Hockingport, O., and at Coal Hill near Cheshire before turning northward away from the river.

Other action included fighting at Cabin Creek, Indian Terr., and Tarborough and Sparta, N.C. Federals bombarded Legare's Point on James Island, S.C. U.S.S. *Shawsheen* captured five schooners on the Neuse near Cedar Island, N.C. Federals scouted from Memphis, Tenn., July 20–21; and Federal troops carried out operations against Indians July 20–26 in Round Valley, Calif. The Cincinnati Chamber of Commerce expelled thirty-three members for refusing to take the oath of allegiance. New York merchants met to take measures for relief of Negro victims of the draft riots.

July 21, Tuesday

Through the twenty-third cavalry and infantry fought at Manassas Gap, Chester Gap, Wapping Heights, Snicker's Gap, and Gaines' Cross Roads in the Blue Ridge of Virginia as Federal advance units attempted to gain control of the passes into the Shenandoah in order to determine Lee's movements. Lee, for his part, had to worry about Meade's army east of the Blue Ridge interposing itself between the Confederates and Richmond.

The Confederates named Brig. Gen. John D. Imboden to command the Valley District. Skirmishing erupted at Street's Ferry, N.C., as a Federal expedition moved from New Berne to Tarborough and Rocky Mount.

In a letter to Gen. O. O. Howard, President Lincoln expressed his confidence in Gen. Meade "as a brave and skillful officer, and a true man." In addition, the President directed Sec. of War Stanton to renew vigorous efforts to raise Negro troops along the Mississippi River. President Davis wrote Lee of his concern over losses resulting from Gettysburg and the problems of reorganization of the units and commands. He also told Lee of the threat to Charleston Harbor.

July 22, Wednesday

As action increased at Manassas and Chester gaps in the Blue Ridge, Meade ordered the Federal Third Corps, under Maj. Gen. William H. French, to move forward and attack Confederates in Manassas Gap on the twenty-third, so as to push through into the Shenandoah and pierce Lee's long column moving southward. Some of French's men did occupy the gap during the night. Behind French were two other Federal corps. It was a bold, forthright plan that might well have worked.

In Ohio Morgan's remnant skirmished at Eagleport as they fled northward. Federal forces reoccupied Brashear City, La.; and there was skirmishing at Scupperton, N.C. A five-day Federal expedition operated from Clinton, Ky., in pursuit of Confederate cavalry in the area. The New York Chamber of Commerce estimated that Confederate raiders had taken 150 Union merchant vessels valued at over $12,000,000.

July 23, Thursday

FEDERAL FAILURE AT MANASSAS GAP.

Federal troops of French's Third Corps pushed into and through Manassas Gap in the Blue Ridge and then, facing a brigade of Confederates, were delayed for hours. During those hours Longstreet's and Hill's corps of Lee's army moved swiftly southward through the Luray Valley of the Shenandoah to safety. Two divisions of Ewell's corps came up and established lines of defense. One Federal brigade attacked at Wapping Heights, but French's delays meant that Meade had failed to isolate even one corps of the Confederates or to strike a major blow at the enemy. During the night Ewell, too, pulled off, leaving only a light rear guard near Front Royal. The Confederates continued unmolested to Culpeper Court House, below the Rappahannock. Skirmishing also broke out in the Blue Ridge at Snicker's Gap, Chester Gap, and Gaines' Cross Roads.

Morgan's fast-fading force fought again at Rockville, O. A Federal expedition operated from Memphis to Raleigh, Tenn.

July 24, Friday

Longstreet's Confederate corps arrived at Culpeper Court House south of the Rappahannock and south of Meade's advancing Federals. Troops of the Federal Third Corps moved into the Shenandoah Valley to Front Royal and found the Confederates gone. Meade now began concentrating at Warrenton. The only skirmishing occurred at Battle Mountain, near Newby's Cross Roads, Va.

Again Morgan's men were forced to skirmish, this time at Washington and Athens, O. Other skirmishes took place in Dade County, Mo., and between Federals and Indians at Cook's Cañon, N. Mex. Terr.

Gen. Lee wrote President Davis that after returning to Virginia he had intended to march east of the Blue Ridge, but high water and other obstacles prevented him from doing so before the Federals also crossed the Potomac into Loudoun County. He told Mr. Davis of his plans to recuperate the army.

Union ironclads and gunboats bombarded Battery Wagner in Charleston Harbor. The Federal army continued to advance its siege lines.

July 25, Saturday

Moving farther north in Ohio, John Hunt Morgan's men fought skirmishes near Steubenville and Springfield. In Virginia there was fighting at Barbee's Cross Roads, and a Federal expedition to Gloucester Court House. In the West skirmishing occurred at Brownsville, Ark., and at Williamsburg and near New Hope Station, Ky. The Confederate Department of East Tennessee was merged in the Department of Tennessee under Bragg's command. Various Federal expeditions operated from Portsmouth, Va., toward Jackson, N.C.; from New Berne to Winton, N.C.; and along Goose Creek, Va. Confederates moved into eastern Kentucky.

July 26, Sunday

CAPTURE OF JOHN HUNT MORGAN.

One last skirmish remained for John Hunt Morgan. At Salineville, O., not far from the Ohio-Pennsylvania line, Morgan and his 364 exhausted men surrendered. Morgan and his main officers were sent to the Ohio State Penitentiary in Columbus. The raid had been spectacular and had caused some consternation in the North, but it accomplished little and generally was considered a foolhardy waste of precious Southern soldiers.

Two prominent Americans died. Sam Houston, Texas patriot, soldier, and statesman, long a towering figure in American politics and Western life, died in retirement at his home at Huntsville, Tex. He had opposed secession, but knew that as long as people had turned to it they could not go back. Likewise, John J. Crittenden, who tried so futilely to bring about compromise before the resort to arms, died in Frankfort, Ky. After a long career in Congress and efforts to keep Kentucky in the Union, Crittenden opposed many Federal political moves, including emancipation. One son had joined the Confederacy and another the Union, and both rose to high rank.

In Virginia military action was slight as the Federals moved in and around Warrenton and the Confederates toward Culpeper. In eastern Kentucky Confederate raiders skirmished at London; and in Dakota Territory Federal troops fought Sioux at Dead Buffalo Lake. Elsewhere, a Federal expedition moved from Plymouth to Foster's Mills, N.C.; and Union operations from Natchez, Miss., lasted several days.

July 27, Monday

Minor affairs took place near Cassville, Mo.; Rogersville, Ky.; at the mouth of Bayou Teche, La.; and near Bridgeport, Ala. In Kansas Federals operated from Baxter Springs to Grand River. Confederate "fire-eater" William Lowndes Yancey died in Montgomery, Ala.

July 28, Tuesday

Skirmishing marked the day at Marshall and High Grove, Mo.; Stony Lake, Dak. Terr.; Richmond, Ky.; and Fayetteville, W. Va. John S. Mosby was active until Aug. 3 around Fairfax Court House and Aldie, Va., behind Meade's Army of the Potomac. Mosby's raiders would strike quickly and then virtually disappear. In Missouri a two-day Federal scout operated from Newtonia to Oliver's Prairie. Four Federal vessels shelled New Smyrna, Fla., after which troops landed and burned some buildings.

President Davis wrote Gen. Lee at Culpeper that efforts were being made to send him convalescents and absentees, and that the Administration was trying to eradicate such problems as lack of horseshoes. Noting the difficulties on other fronts, Davis stated, "I have felt more than ever before the want of your advice during the recent period of disaster." He spoke of the many complaints against him and added, "If a victim would secure the success of our cause I would freely offer myself."

July 29, Wednesday

The major military moves of midsummer tapered off, although heavy skirmishing continued. There was a fight near Bridgeport, Ala., occupied by Federals. Skirmishes occurred near Fort Donelson, Tenn.; and at Paris and near Winchester, Ky., brought on by Confederate raids in occupied territory. Federals fought with Indians at Conchas Springs, N. Mex. Terr., and at the Missouri River, Dak. Terr.

Queen Victoria told the British Parliament that she saw "no reason to depart from the strict neutrality which Her Majesty has observed from the beginning of the contest."

President Lincoln wrote Gen. Halleck that he did not demand that Meade engage Lee immediately. He opposed "pressing" Meade into offensive action.

July 30, Thursday

President Lincoln issued orders that the government of the United States would "give the same protection to all its soldiers, and if the enemy shall sell or enslave anyone because of his color, the offense shall be punished by retaliation upon the enemy's prisoners in our possession."

Skirmishing took place near Elm Springs, Ark.; near Lexington and Marshall, Mo.; at Irvine, Ky.; Grand Junction, Tenn.; and Barnwell's Island, S.C.

July 31, Friday

A momentous month which had seen the fall of Vicksburg and Port Hudson and the Battle of Gettysburg came to a close with skirmishing at Lancaster, Stanford, and Paint Lick Bridge, Ky.; St. Catherine's Creek near Natchez, Miss.; and Morris' Mills, W. Va. In Virginia Federal forces pushed across the Rappahannock with fighting at Kelly's Ford.

AUGUST, 1863

After the crisis of July, a time for assessment and realignment was welcome. The North was more optimistic and confident now that the Mississippi Valley was clear and Lee back deep in Virginia. However, no one forgot that Charleston was untaken and Lee was far from beaten. In the Confederacy, a growing depression had to be conquered and the people called upon once more for renewed effort. If many suspected that such effort would be futile, as yet they seldom said so openly.

Both sides wondered whether their army could mount an offensive in Virginia after Gettysburg, and, if so, where. Confederates hoped they could hold against men and ironclads in Charleston Harbor. What would be done with Grant's army in the West? Could Bragg keep Rosecrans out of Chattanooga and the deep South? Could the blockade be eased? The Confederacy had survived a series of monumental defeats a year before. Could it again?

August 1, Saturday

A cavalry action in the oft-fought-over area of Brandy Station, south of the Rappahannock, marked the conclusion of the Gettysburg Campaign. Federal cavalry felt out the enemy and attempted to determine Lee's plans. A week-long Federal expedition moved from Warrenton Junction into the country between Bull Run and the Blue Ridge Mountains.

In Kentucky there was a small expedition by the North from Columbus to Hickman and a skirmish at Smith's Shoals on the Cumberland River. Skirmishes broke out on the Little Blue River at Taylor's Farm and at Round Ponds near the Castor River, Mo. Union forces began to advance on Little Rock, with cavalry operating for several days from Witteburg to Clarendon, Ark. In the Charleston Harbor area Federals began the build-up for an attack on Battery Wagner and Fort Sumter. The Federal War Department disbanded the Fourth and Seventh Army Corps. Rear Admiral David D. Porter assumed naval command on the Mississippi River, where the major problems were now Confederate raids and firings upon Federals. Porter encouraged legal river trade.

President Davis declared that all soldiers absent without leave and those who had not reported for service would be granted pardon and amnesty if they reported within twenty days. He called for greater exertion by the people of the Confederacy, saying, "no alternative is left you but victory, or subjugation, slavery and utter ruin of yourselves, your families and your country." Prominent Confederate spy Belle Boyd was in prison in Washington for a second time after her arrest in Martinsburg, W. Va.

August 2, Sunday

As reconnaissance by both sides continued on the line of the Rappahannock in Virginia there was skirmishing at Newtown, Va.; Stumptown, Mo.; and a Confederate scout from Pocahontas, Ark., to Patterson, Mo. At Cummings Point, on Morris Island in Charleston Harbor, Federals attacked the Confederate steamer *Chesterfield*. President Davis wrote Gen. Lee of the problems of returning stragglers to the Army and said, "It is painful to contemplate our weakness when you ask for reinforcements."

August 3, Monday

As events began to quiet down along the Rappahannock in Virginia, there was only minor action elsewhere, including skirmishing at Ripley, Miss., and Jackson, La. A Federal scout from Fort Pillow, Tenn., skirmished near Denmark. The Federal Ninth Army Corps left the Vicksburg area for service in Kentucky and eventually east Tennessee. Gov. Horatio Seymour of New York asked President Lincoln to suspend the draft in his state.

August 4, Tuesday

Minor fighting continued in Virginia: there was yet another skirmish at Brandy Station, plus action near Amissville and Fairfax Court House. On the James River a reconnaissance by Federal army and navy units lasted four days. Elsewhere action included at the mouth of Vincent's Creek, S.C.; at Burlington, W. Va.; as well as a Federal reconnaissance near Rock Island Ferry, Tenn. For four days Federal naval guns had bombarded Battery Wagner in Charleston Harbor as Yankees prepared the famous Swamp Angel, a mammoth gun, for future operations.

August 5, Wednesday

For the rest of the month Federal cavalry carried out an expedition under William Woods Averell from Winchester, Va., into West Virginia, with a skirmish this day at Cold Spring Gap, W. Va. Other areas of fighting were Little Washington and Muddy Run, Va., and Mount Pleasant, Miss.; while a week-long Union expedition operated from Kempsville, Va., into Currituck and Camden counties, N.C. Maj. Gen. Frederick Steele assumed command of Federal forces at Helena, Ark. In Charleston Harbor Confederates strengthened their defenses at Fort Sumter and Battery Wagner, realizing the Federals would soon launch an all-out attack. Near Dutch Gap, Va., an electric torpedo severely damaged U.S.S. *Commodore Barney*.

President Lincoln, writing Gen. Banks regarding affairs in Louisiana, stated that he was "an anti-slavery man" and "For my own part I think I shall not, in any event, retract the emancipation proclamation; nor, as executive, ever return to slavery any person who is free by the terms of that proclamation, or by any of the acts of Congress."

August 6, Thursday

Following Lincoln's proclamation, the North observed a day of thanksgiving for recent victories, with church services and suspension of business. Skirmishes took place at Cacapon Mountain and at Moorefield, W. Va.; while Mosby's Southern guerrillas captured a wagon train near Fairfax Court House, Va. In addition, Federal expeditions and scouts operated for several days in Missouri and in Kansas on the Missouri border. Three Federal vessels were heavily bombarded by shore batteries while on a James River reconnaissance. Cheering crowds watched C.S.S. *Alabama* capture the bark *Sea Bride* near the shore of Table Bay, Cape of Good Hope.

From Richmond President Davis wrote Gov. M. L. Bonham of South Carolina that he would do all possible for the safety and relief of Charleston, "which we pray will never be polluted by the footsteps of a lustful, relentless, inhuman foe."

August 7, Friday

Fighting broke out at Burke's Station, Va., and near New Madrid, Mo. In Washington Lincoln told Gov. Seymour of New York that he would not suspend the draft in New York and added, "My purpose is to be, in my action, just and constitutional; and yet practical, in performing the important duty, with which I am charged, of maintaining the unity, and the free principles of our common country."

August 8, Saturday

Gen. Robert E. Lee offered to resign as commander of the Army of Northern Virginia. He wrote President Davis that he realized there had been discontent as a result of the failure of the Gettysburg Campaign and "I, therefore, in all sincerity, request your excellency to take measures to supply my place." His health and general depression influenced his request, which Davis rejected.

On Morris Island in Charleston Harbor Federals continued to construct approaches to Battery Wagner, illuminating the island at night with calcium lights. Fighting flared at Waterford, Va.; Rienzi, Miss.; and on Clear Creek, near Ball Town, Mo. U.S.S. *Sagamore* took four prizes off Indian River and Gilbert's Bar, Fla.

August 9, Sunday

President Lincoln wrote Gen. Grant that he believed that Negro troops were "a resource which, if vigorously applied now, will soon close the contest." Meantime the usual skirmishes erupted at Brandy Station and Welford's Ford, Va.; Sparta, Tenn.; and Garden Hollow, near Pineville, Mo. Operations of several days' duration took place from Cape Girardeau to Poplar Bluff, Mo.

August 10, Monday

Federal troops under Gen. Frederick Steele began to march from Helena, Ark., toward the capital at Little Rock. Elsewhere there was skirmishing at Dayton, Mo.; Bayou Tensas, La.; and the start of a thirteen-day expedition by Federals from Big Black River, Miss., to Memphis, with considerable skirmishing. Meanwhile, Grant's huge army at Vicksburg was slowly being broken up; the Thirteenth Army Corps was sent to Carrollton, La. Discontent over rations and lack of furloughs appeared to be the reason for a mutiny of several Confederate regiments at Galveston, Tex., but order was soon restored.

President Lincoln assured Gen. Rosecrans, in command north of Chattanooga, that "I have not abated in my kind feeling for and confidence in you." He added, "Since Grant has been entirely relieved by the fall of Vicksburg, by which Johnston is also relieved, it has seemed to me that your chance for a stroke, has been considerably diminished. . . ."

August 11, Tuesday

Confederate guns at Battery Wagner, Fort Sumter, and on James Island opened furiously on Federal trenches on Morris Island, halting the Northern working parties. Meanwhile, Beauregard, in command of the Charleston area, ordered the defense lines on James Island shortened. In Virginia Confederates captured a Union wagon train near Annandale. A Federal expedition from Portsmouth, Va., operated toward Edenton, N.C., for over a week. At Washington, N.C., a large pro-Union meeting supported the Federal war effort.

Replying to Gen. Lee's offer to resign, President Davis refused to consider it: "our country could not bear to lose you." President Lincoln, in a letter to Gov. Seymour of New York, once more defended his policy regarding the draft.

August 12, Wednesday

Heavy Parrott rifles opened from the low-lying sand batteries of Morris Island, firing against Fort Sumter and Battery Wagner. Although just a practice to establish the range, the firing in effect marked the opening of a new Federal offensive in Charleston Harbor. Even in practice the breeching batteries caused considerable destruction to the brick walls of Fort Sumter.

In Mississippi a skirmish occurred at Big Black River Bridge; and a ten-day Union expedition started from Memphis, Tenn., to Grenada, Miss. The First Division of the Federal Ninth Army Corps from Vicksburg arrived at Covington, Ky., en route to east Tennessee. President Lincoln refused to give Maj. Gen. John A. McClernand a new command. McClernand had been relieved of corps command at Vicksburg by Grant.

August 13, Thursday

On Morris Island Federal guns continued practice firing against Fort Sumter, now from both land batteries and naval guns. Other action was limited to skirmishes at Pineville, Mo.; Jacinto, Miss.; and a four-day Federal expedition up the White and Little Red rivers in Ark. Federal troops began a month-long expedition against the Indians in Dakota Territory.

A Confederate army chaplain wrote to Davis and expressed the feeling of many in and out of the Western armies "that every disaster that has befallen us in the West has grown out of the fact that weak and inefficient men have been kept in power," and "I beseech of you to relieve us of these drones and pigmies." He included Pemberton and Holmes.

August 14, Friday

At Charleston Federal guns continued their practice firing. Most of the action was in Missouri at Sherwood, Wellington, and near Jack's Fork; as well as at West Point, Ark. Skirmishes broke out at Washington, N.C., and there was a Federal scout in the Bull Run Mountains of Virginia. There was also a Federal scout to Winchester, Va. Gen. Meade, in Washington, related details of the Gettysburg Campaign to the President and Cabinet and discussed future operations.

August 15, Saturday

As the month wore on there was skirmishing at Beverly Ford and Hartwood Church along the Rappahannock line in Virginia, and at Bentonville, Ark. A Federal scout from Centreville to Aldie, Va., operated against partisan rangers for five days.

August 16, Sunday

At last Federal troops were moving in Tennessee. After urging from Washington, Rosecrans and the Army of the Cumberland started toward the Tennessee River and Chattanooga from the area south of Tullahoma. Rosecrans had delayed, he said, because of ripening crops to be harvested, repair of railroads, and need of support on both flanks. Gen. Burnside left

Camp Nelson, Ky., near Lexington, and headed for east Tennessee, reaching the Tennessee River Aug. 20. What was to become the Chickamauga Campaign had begun. Meanwhile, Gen. Bragg, with the Army of Tennessee, called for more troops. Plans were laid quickly to supply him with whatever units could be spared from elsewhere. Rosecrans planned to cross the Tennessee south and west of Chattanooga while feinting at the Tennessee north of Chattanooga; thus he hoped to trap Bragg between his army and Burnside's.

In Charleston Harbor Federal guns on Morris Island continued practice firing. For the past several weeks crews of laborers at Fort Sumter had been filling in damaged masonry with sand, strengthening the faces near Morris Island and removing many of the guns, leaving only thirty-eight with a garrison of five hundred.

Action was limited to skirmishes at Falls Church, Va., and near Corinth, Miss. Maj. Gen. G. K. Warren assumed command of the Federal Second Army Corps, superseding Brig. Gen. William Hays. A five-day Union expedition operated from Memphis, Tenn., to Hernando, Miss.

President Lincoln again wrote Gov. Seymour of New York regarding problems of the draft, concluding, "My purpose is to be just and fair; and yet to not lose time."

August 17, Monday
FIRST GREAT BOMBARDMENT OF FORT SUMTER.

With reverberating roars accelerating in frequency, the eleven guns of the Federal breeching batteries on Morris Island, aided by naval armament, fired a total of 938 shots in the first major bombardment of Fort Sumter. Batteries Wagner and Gregg were also fired upon. Sumter's brick walls crumbled under the blows of the Parrotts, including the two-hundred-pounder Swamp Angel. But the rubble and sand formed an even more impregnable bulwark against Federal fire.

Far to the west in Arkansas a Federal expedition to Little Rock skirmished at Grand Prairie. In initial action of the Federal campaign toward Chattanooga, a skirmish broke out at Calfkiller Creek, near Sparta, Tenn. To the twenty-sixth Federal expeditions operated from Cape Girardeau and Pilot Knob, Mo., to Pocahontas, Ark.

August 18, Tuesday

The second day of heavy bombardment at Charleston against Fort Sumter and Battery Wagner showed that the Federals were tenacious in their attempts to reduce the Confederate forts. Although severely damaged, they held on despite the pounding fire.

Inland skirmishes flared at Bristoe Station, Va.; near Pasquotank, N.C.; and near Crab Orchard and Albany, Ky. In New Mexico Territory Federal troops skirmished with Indians at Pueblo Colorado. President Lincoln tested the new Spencer rifle in Washington by firing a few shots in Treasury Park.

August 19, Wednesday

Northern authorities resumed the draft in New York City with no difficulties, although troops protected the draft headquarters against a repetition of the disastrous riots of July. In Charleston Harbor the guns boomed for a third day against Fort Sumter and Battery Wagner. In West Virginia Averell's Federal raiders destroyed a saltpeter works near Franklin. A Confederate signal station was captured at St. John's Mill, Fla., and a skirmish occurred at Weems' Springs, Tenn.

August 20, Thursday

The bombardment of Fort Sumter and Battery Wagner continued in Charleston Harbor. Rosecrans' advancing Army of the Cumberland neared the Tennessee River west of Chattanooga, and more Federal troops arrived at Covington, Ky., for the offensive into east Tennessee. In Kansas guerrilla forces under William Clarke Quantrill approached the unsuspecting town of Lawrence. In an expedition lasting until Aug. 28, Federals operated from Vicksburg, Miss., to Monroe, La.

In the Far West Col. Christopher "Kit" Carson had been commanding expeditions against the Navajo Indians in Ariz. Terr. lasting July 7–19. This day Carson's command left Pueblo Colorado, operating until Dec. 16 to the area of Cañon de Chelly, in reprisal against Indian depredations. The plan was for the government to move them to a reservation at Bosque Redondo on the Pecos near Fort Sumner, N. Mex. Terr.

August 21, Friday

SACKING OF LAWRENCE, KANSAS.

About 150 men and boys died and a million and a half dollars' worth of property was destroyed in the massacre at Lawrence, Kas. Storming into the town at dawn, some 450 Confederate and Missouri guerrillas or bushwhackers under William Clarke Quantrill sacked, burned, and murdered. Only women and smaller children were spared, although some men did escape. The raid grew out of festering bitterness created by the so-called Kansas War, by the Federal raid on Osceola, Mo., and by Quantrill's personal grudge against Lawrence. One eyewitness said, "The town is a complete ruin. The whole of the business part, and all good private residences are burned down. Everything of value was taken along by the fiends. . . . I cannot describe the horrors." Other forces skirmished near Brooklyn and Paola, Kas.

Gen. Q. A. Gillmore demanded the surrender of Fort Sumter and immediate evacuation of Morris Island, threatening to bombard Charleston if his terms were not met. When the Confederates refused, the bombardment of the forts continued for the fifth day. Casualties remained low. About 1 A.M. a Confederate steam torpedo boat moved speedily out of Charleston Harbor to attack *New Ironsides*. However, the torpedo's detonating device failed, and the Confederate vessel retreated under heavy fire.

Federal troops threw a few shells into Chattanooga. Skirmishing occurred at Maysville, Ala., and Shellmound, Tenn., as Rosecrans drew nearer the strategic city. In West Virginia there was a skirmish near Glenville.

August 22, Saturday

Fort Sumter was feeling the impact of the sustained bombardment, now in its sixth day. Only four guns remained serviceable in the fort. Five Federal monitors made a night attack Aug. 22–23, and only two guns returned fire. Nevertheless, there was no indication of surrender. Other Union guns opened fire on Charleston itself. The Federals suffered a severe blow, however, when the famed Swamp Angel exploded while firing its thirty-sixth round.

As Quantrill's men withdrew from smoldering Lawrence, Kas., there was a skirmish on Big Creek, near Pleasant Hill. Elsewhere, fighting broke out at San Pedro Crossing, Ariz. Terr.; Huntersville, W. Va.; and Stafford Court House, Va. As part of the Federal advance toward Chattanooga, troops operated around Tracy City, Tenn., to the Tennessee River. Meanwhile, President Davis sought reinforcements for Bragg's threatened army in Tennessee.

August 23, Sunday

The first period of the bombardment of Fort Sumter came to an end but only after 5009 rounds had been fired by Federals and only one gun left in good condition in the fort, now a mass of rubble and wreckage. There was a skirmish at Fayetteville, Ark., and Federals scouted on Bennett's Bayou, Mo. Confederates captured two small Federal gunboats, *Satellite* and *Reliance,* at the mouth of the Rappahannock in Virginia. Lieut. L. Taylor Wood accomplished the feat in four small boats with sixty men and thirty army sharpshooters. It was a galling experience for the North.

August 24, Monday

For the rest of August, John Singleton Mosby and his Confederate raiders were especially active in Virginia north of Meade's Rappahannock line. Other action included a Federal scout at Barbee's Cross Roads and skirmishing at Coyle's Tavern near Fairfax Court House, near King George Court House, and near Warm Springs, Va. In Charleston Harbor the bombardment of Fort Sumter and Battery Wagner was considerably lighter. In Alabama skirmishing occurred at Gunter's Landing near Port Deposit.

August 25, Tuesday

Extensive skirmishing flared in Missouri near Waynesville, near Independence, and at Hopewell. Federals scouted from the Sedalia area. Union forces moving toward Little Rock skirmished at Brownsville, Ark. On Morris Island, S.C., Federal troops failed to capture Confederate rifle pits in front of Battery Wagner. Along the Rappahannock there was a skirmish at Hartwood Church and along the Chickahominy near Lamb's Ferry. At the mouth of the Rappahannock a Confederate vessel seized three Union schooners. In West Virginia Federals destroyed Confederate saltpeter works on Jackson's River.

Guerrilla warfare in Missouri and Kansas had reached a climax in the Lawrence, Kas., massacre four days before. Now Federal Brig. Gen. Thomas Ewing, in command at Kansas City, issued General Orders No. 11. All persons in Jackson, Cass, and Bates counties, Mo., plus parts of Vernon County, were to leave their homes. Those who could prove their loyalty would be permitted to stay at military posts. All others had to get out of the area. An estimated twenty thousand people lost their homes around Kansas City. Barns, houses, and crops were burned. This anti-guerrilla move had little effect on the raiders, but it caused deep animosities that lasted for years.

August 26, Wednesday

In a second effort, Federals captured the Confederate rifle pits in front of Battery Wagner on Morris Island. In West Virginia Averell's Federal expedition fought a heavy engagement at Rock Gap, near White Sulphur Springs. Other fighting took place near Moorefield and Sutton. In Virginia a four-day Federal expedition operated from Williamsburg to Bottom's Bridge. In the West skirmishing broke out at Bayou Meto, Ark., and at Perryville, Indian Terr. Former U. S. Secretary of War and Confederate general John B. Floyd died at Abingdon, Va.

President Davis confirmed by telegram Gen. Beauregard's decision to hold Fort Sumter. President Lincoln, in a letter to "Unconditional Union Men" in Springfield, Ill., said, "I do not believe any compromise, embracing the maintenance of the Union, is now possible." He added, "Peace does not appear so distant as it did."

August 27, Thursday

At least nine skirmishes marked the day: at Bayou Meto or Reed's Bridge, Ark.; Mount Pleasant and near Vicksburg, Miss.; Carter County and Clark's Neck, Ky.; Elk River, Glenville, and Ball's Mill, W. Va.; Edwards' Ferry, Md.; Little Washington and Weaverville, Va. Firing was all but suspended in Charleston Harbor. President Davis was deeply concerned, wiring Beauregard regarding his strength and possible reinforcements. Increased pressure at Chattanooga and in east Tennessee also demanded Davis' attention.

August 28, Friday
Only three skirmishes and two expeditions are recorded. Fighting was at Hartwood Church, Va.; the Narrows near Shellmound, Tenn.; and Jacksborough, Tenn. The expeditions, both by Federals, operated from Stevenson, Ala., to Trenton, Ga.; and from Lexington into La Fayette, Johnson, Cass, and Henry counties, Mo.

August 29, Saturday
Operations against the Navajo in New Mexico Territory intensified. Skirmishing occurred at Texas Prairie, Mo. Activity mounted along the Tennessee River west of Chattanooga with a skirmish at Caperton's Ferry, Ala. Rosecrans' army slowly but methodically moved south below Chattanooga, actually flanking the Confederate-held city. In Charleston Harbor the Southern submarine *H. L. Hunley* sank with five men lost.

August 30, Sunday
The breeching batteries once more inflicted heavy damage on Fort Sumter. Meanwhile, the Confederates continued to dig out guns from the rubble and move them to the city. A small transport steamer with troops on board was fired upon from Fort Moultrie by mistake and sank. There was further skirmishing in Arkansas as a part of the Little Rock Campaign at Washington and at Shallow Ford on Bayou Meto. The last two days of the month Federals carried out a reconnaissance from Shellmound toward Chattanooga, Tenn. A Federal expedition operated in the vicinity of Leesburg, Va.

August 31, Monday
Minor fighting marked the end of August, with action on the Marais des Cygnes, Kas.; at Winter's Gap, Tenn.; and Will's Valley, Ala.

SEPTEMBER, 1863

Although Virginia and the Mississippi Valley remained quiet, there were other sectors to watch. The results of Federal bombardment of Battery Wagner and Fort Sumter remained undetermined. Rosecrans and his Federal Army of the Cumberland were moving into Alabama and toward Chattanooga; how would Bragg and his Army of Tennessee respond?

What about the thrust to Knoxville and east Tennessee? Farther west, a Northern offensive against Little Rock was under way, and there were indications of forthcoming operations on the Texas and Louisiana coasts. On the homefronts discontent seemed somewhat less rampant than it had earlier in the summer. However, many Northerners realized that despite Gettysburg and Vicksburg the war was not near an end. Southerners took comfort in the fact that despite defeats in Pennsylvania and on the Mississippi, the Confederacy was still afloat and fighting.

September 1, Tuesday

Fort Smith, on the western border of Arkansas, fell to Union forces, while in the eastern part of the state operations proceeded against Little Rock. Fighting also broke out at Jenny Lind and Devil's Backbone or Backbone Mountain, Ark.

In Charleston Harbor mortar fire smote Battery Wagner on Morris Island, and heavy Parrott rifles and ironclads hammered Fort Sumter once more. Firing of 627 shot ended the second phase of the first major bombardment. Once more Fort Sumter crumbled, and its magazine was threatened, but the garrison continued to shore up the ruins and remained defiant.

Rosecrans' Federal Army of the Cumberland was crossing the Tennessee River, preparatory to moving on Chattanooga and Bragg's Confederate Army of Tennessee. The crossing, which lasted several days, was largely unopposed. Skirmishing did occur at Will's Creek, Davis' Gap, and Neal's Gap, Ala.

Virginia saw only cavalry operations and skirmishing at Corbin's Cross Roads, Lamb's Creek Church near Port Conway, Leesburg, and Barbee's Cross Roads. The "small war" in northern Virginia continued unabated. A week of Federal operations from Natchez to Harrisonburg, La., included some skirmishing; and Federals carried out ten days of expeditions into Tennessee from Paducah, Ky., and Union City, Tenn.

President Davis told Gov. Isham G. Harris of Tennessee that reinforcements and arms were being sent to Chattanooga and Bragg's threatened army.

September 2, Wednesday

Federal troops under Gen. A. E. Burnside entered Knoxville, Tenn. The fall of Knoxville effectively cut the fairly direct railroad link between Chattanooga and Virginia and forced Confederates to use a roundabout route from Virginia down the Atlantic coast, thence to Atlanta and Tennessee. Burnside's move was destined to aid Rosecrans' major effort against Chattanooga and Bragg.

At Charleston artillery fire died to desultory proportions, but Federals entrenched within eighty yards of Battery Wagner's earthworks on Morris Island. Skirmishing took place near Oak Shade and Rixey's Ford, Va., while Federal cavalry wrecked two Confederate (formerly Federal) gunboats, *Satellite* and *Reliance,* at Port Conway on the Rappahannock. In Arkansas a skirmish broke out near Shallow Ford. Near Mier, Mex., Confederate troops routed banditti under Zapata, who had been raiding both Mexican and Confederate territory. During most of the month Federal expeditions operated from Martinsburg, and involved some skirmishing at Smithfield, W. Va., and Strasburg, Va. The U. S. Navy destroyed buildings and four small boats in a raid on Peace Creek, Fla.

The people of Nevada rejected the proposed state constitution. President Lincoln told Sec. of the Treasury Chase that he could not include parts of Virginia and Louisiana in the Emancipation Proclamation because there was no military necessity to do so and "The original proclamation has no constitutional or legal justification except as a military measure."

A joint committee of the Alabama legislature approved use of slaves in Confederate armies and the Alabama house adopted the resolution after modifying it somewhat.

September 3, Thursday

Some of Rosecrans' forces skirmished near Alpine, Ga. In the West, soldiers and Indians fought in the Hoopa Valley, Calif., and near White Stone Hill, Dak. Terr. For the rest of the year there were military operations in the Humboldt Military District of California. During the night Battery Wagner at Charleston received and returned fire, as other guns blazed in the harbor area.

September 4, Friday

The Federal Army of the Cumberland under Rosecrans completed its crossing of the Tennessee River in the Bridgeport, Ala., area and at Shellmound, Tenn. Bragg's Confederate army in Chattanooga was threatened from the south and west, his situation growing more serious by the hour. From New Orleans Federal transports and four shallow-draft but weak gunboats headed toward the Texas-Louisiana coast at Sabine Pass. It was the first of several moves by Banks' Federal command to occupy important points in Texas, both as an offensive against Confederates and as a display of force to the French occupying Mexico. Fighting was confined to an affair at Quincy, Mo., and skirmishing at Moorefield and Petersburg Gap, W. Va. Federals scouted from Cold Water Grove, Mo.; and from Fort Lyon, Colo., toward Fort Larned, Kas. In northwest Arkansas skirmishing flared at Bentonville, Flint Creek, Hog Eye, and Round Prairie.

In Mobile, Ala., indignant women marched on supply stores with signs reading "Bread or Blood" and "Bread and Peace" and took food, clothing, and other goods. In New Orleans Gen. Grant was severely injured when his horse shied and fell on him; there is some evidence that Grant had been drinking during this visit, partly social and partly to confer with Gen. Banks. He was partially incapacitated for weeks.

September 5, Saturday

"LAIRD RAMS" DETAINED.

For some time Federal authorities in Britain and Washington had been apprehensive over official British "eye-winking" at the construction of Confederate vessels in yards at Liverpool and elsewhere. With two ironclads known as the "Laird Rams" nearing completion, Minister Charles Francis Adams told British Lord Russell that if the rams were released "it would be superfluous for me to point out to your Lordship that this is war." But even before Adams' communiqué, Lord Russell directed (Sept. 3) that the rams at Birkenhead should be detained. They were never turned over to the South. Thus ended the last major crisis in Federal-British foreign relations during the war.

Amid firing in Charleston Harbor against Battery Wagner, Federals drew near the ditch in front of the earthwork. An assault was expected momentarily. Small-boat attacks on Battery Gregg and the north end of Cummings Point on Morris Island failed.

In Alabama Federal forces of Rosecrans moved into the mountains of northwestern Georgia south of Chattanooga, skirmishing at Lebanon and Rawlingsville, Ala., and Alpine, Ga. In the East Tennessee Campaign, a skirmish occurred at Tazewell, Tenn., as Federals moved in on Cumberland Gap from Knoxville. A skirmish broke out near Maysville, Ark.; and in Dakota Territory Federals skirmished with Indians near White Stone Hill.

President Davis urgently asked General Bragg, "What is your proposed plan of operation? Can you ascertain intention of enemy? . . . can you not cut his line of communication and compel him to retreat for want of supplies?" The Confederate government was increasingly concerned over the threats to Chattanooga and Bragg, as well as the Federal movement to Knoxville and east Tennessee. The Charleston *Mercury* attacked President Davis: "He has lost the confidence of both the army and the people."

September 6, Sunday

CONFEDERATES EVACUATE BATTERY WAGNER AND MORRIS ISLAND, SOUTH CAROLINA.

Siege guns and seven monitors and ironclads bombarded Battery Wagner on Charleston's Morris Island as the garrison crouched, virtually unhurt, in the bombproofs. However, Beauregard, in over-all command, realized that the earthwork's usefulness was at an end, and that a Federal infantry assault the next day would probably succeed. During the night of Sept. 6–7 the Confederate garrisons of Battery Wagner and Battery Gregg, besieged since early July, were evacuated. Fort Sumter, a mass of rubble and broken masonry, still held out, as did Charleston.

In the campaign below Chattanooga there was skirmishing at Stevens' Gap, Ga., and in the East Tennessee Campaign fighting near Sweet Water. Elsewhere, battling occurred at Carter's Run, Va.; Petersburg, W. Va.; between Fort Scott, Kas., and Carthage, Mo.; and in the Hutton Valley of Missouri.

September 7, Monday

Federal troops moved in to find Battery Wagner and Battery Gregg evacuated. Federal Adm. Dahlgren demanded the surrender of Fort Sumter and the monitors engaged Fort Moultrie. *Weehawken* ran aground between Fort Sumter and Cummings Point but was extricated.

Below Chattanooga Federal forces still advanced, with skirmishing at Stevenson, Ala., reconnaissance toward Chattanooga, and fighting in Lookout Valley, Tenn. At Cumberland Gap Federal troops moved into the vital link between Virginia and Tennessee. On the Gulf Coast the Federal expedition under Gen. William B. Franklin had arrived off Sabine Pass on the Texas-Louisiana border. Elsewhere fighting broke out at Bear Skin Lake, Mo.; Ashley's Mills or Ferry Landing, Ark.; Morgan's Ferry, on the Atchafalaya, La.; Holly Springs and Jacinto or Glendale, Miss.; and Bath, W. Va. Federal expeditions operated several days from Springfield, Mo., into Arkansas and the Indian Territory and to Big Lake in Mississippi County, Ark.

September 8, Tuesday

CONFEDERATES VICTORIOUS AT SABINE PASS, TEXAS.

Four Federal gunboats and transports moved into Sabine Pass on the Texas-Louisiana border, intending to gain a foothold for a drive on Beaumont and Houston. Ashore, some forty Confederates, under Lieut. Dick Dowling, manned a partly finished earthwork with a few guns. A few other troops and two ineffective cotton-clads gunboats, all that Gen. John Bankhead Magruder could afford, comprised the rest of the extremely weak defense force. The Union gunboats opened up on the fort and Dowling replied. Both lead gunboats were struck, grounded, and forced to surrender, with considerable loss. The other two withdrew, along with the troop transports, only after difficulty. It was a humiliating Federal failure and a tremendous morale booster to Western Confederates. Magruder was sure there would be more attempts; Nathanial Banks was mortified at the failure of Gen. W. B. Franklin and his combined force. However, the legend which grew up about the conflict outweighed its military significance.

Federal naval vessels bombarded the forts in Charleston Harbor as Adm. Dahlgren's men prepared for a small-boat operation by night against Fort Sumter. At the same time, apparently independently, infantry commander Quincy Adams Gillmore was preparing a similar expedition. Other fighting occurred at Winston's Gap, Ala., and Alpine, Ga., in what became the

Chickamauga Campaign, and in east Tennessee at Limestone Station and Telford's Station. Skirmishing broke out at Brandy Station, Va., once more; at Beech Fork in Calhoun County and at Sutton, W. Va.; on the Atchafalaya, La.; and in the Chiricahua Mountains, Ariz. Terr.

President Davis told Lee of the increasing threats to Bragg and that he had considered sending Lee west, but feared the effect of Lee's absence from Virginia. Confederate Att. Gen. Thomas H. Watts resigned, having been elected governor of Alabama in August. He was succeeded ad interim by Wade Keyes.

September 9, Wednesday

FEDERALS ENTER CHATTANOOGA.

Gen. Braxton Bragg and the Confederate Army of Tennessee had left Chattanooga. Realizing that Rosecrans' Army of the Cumberland was cutting in behind him, Bragg reluctantly abandoned the city and withdrew into Georgia. Troops of Rosecrans' army entered, while others marched ahead seeking to push Bragg farther south. The Federals were in a vulnerable position, being spread out over forty miles of mountains south of Chattanooga, and they soon learned that Bragg was at La Fayette, Ga., much closer than suspected. But the Union army did hold the rail and river center of Chattanooga. A skirmish broke out at nearby Lookout Mountain, Ga.

After conferences in Richmond early in September, Davis and his generals had decided to detach Longstreet's corps of the Army of Northern Virginia to aid Bragg. Therefore, Longstreet left the Rapidan line and headed toward Richmond. Due to recent Federal occupation of east Tennessee which culminated this day in the surrender of Cumberland Gap to the Federals, Longstreet had to go by way of North Carolina and Atlanta to get to Bragg. He moved rapidly, especially considering the condition of Southern railroads, but it was to be about ten days before the movement was completed. Even then not all the troops and guns were up in time for battle.

At 1 A.M. two columns of small boats with landing parties from the Federal fleet moved toward Fort Sumter, where they were greeted by heavy and disastrous small-arms fire. The Federals suffered 125 casualties. A similar infantry expedition, not coordinated with the navy effort, never got under way.

Elsewhere there was a skirmish at Webber's Falls, Indian Terr.

September 10, Thursday

FALL OF LITTLE ROCK, ARKANSAS.

Still another important Confederate center fell, as Southerners evacuated Little Rock, capital of Arkansas. Sterling Price's Confederates withdrew to Rockport and Arkadelphia. Federal occupation severely threatened Kirby

Smith's entire Confederate Trans-Mississippi area, already under attack from Frederick Steele's expedition which had moved across Arkansas from Helena. There was an engagement at Bayou Fourche, Ark.

Meanwhile, in Georgia, Federals operated from Alpine toward Rome, La Fayette, and Summerville, probing Confederate positions south of Chattanooga. Bragg had ordered an attack on isolated Federal forces in Mc-Lemore's Cove, but it failed to materialize. Skirmishing occurred at Summerville, Pea Vine Creek, and near Graysville. In the East Tennessee Campaign, fighting broke out at Brimstone Creek, Ky., and Athens, Tenn. Fort Sumter enjoyed the first of eighteen days of respite from bombardment. In Virginia the main action was Longstreet's move to Richmond en route to Bragg in Georgia. At Raleigh, N.C., Confederate soldiers pillaged the offices of the *Standard,* owned by W. W. Holden, pro-Union editor and politician who advocated peace.

September 11, Friday

Considerable reconnaissance and skirmishing continued in northwest Georgia with operations toward Rome and skirmishes near Blue Bird Gap, Davis' Cross Roads, Rossville, Ringgold, and around Lee and Gordon's Mills. The Federal advance was gradually building toward a climax. Bragg again ordered an attack on detached Yankees but again it was not made. Elsewhere, fighting flared near Greenville, Ky.; at Waldron, Ark.; Baldwin's Ferry on the Big Black, Miss.; and Moorefield, W. Va. A brief mutiny in Terrell's Texas Cavalry in Texas was soon put down. Federal expeditions of several days' duration operated from La Grange to Toone's Station, Tenn.; from Corinth, Miss., into Tennessee; and from Camp Piatt near Fayetteville, W. Va.

President Lincoln turned down Gen. Burnside's resignation, asked Gov. Andrew Johnson of Tennessee to inaugurate a state government at once, and conferred with Stanton, Halleck, and others about the Charleston situation.

September 12, Saturday

The probing, skirmishing, and reconnaissance continued on the long front south of Chattanooga, with fighting at Alpine, Dirt Town, Leet's Tanyard, and on the La Fayette Road near the Chattooga River, Ga. In the east Tennessee operations a skirmish took place at Rheatown. Minor fighting occurred at South Mills, N.C.; White Plains and Bristoe Station, Va.; Roane County, W. Va.; Houston in Texas County, Mo.; Brownsville, Ark; and Stirling's Plantation near Morganza, La. Federals scouted from Harper's Ferry, W. Va.

September 13, Sunday

The fairly quiet Virginia front became less so as Meade's Army of the Potomac occupied Culpeper Court House. The Union move from the

Rappahannock to the Rapidan was brought about by a Confederate withdrawal by Lee, weakened from the loss of Longstreet's corps. Fighting broke out in the area of Brandy Station, Muddy Run, Culpeper Court House, Pony Mountain, and Stevensburg, a much fought-over section. Washington ordered Gen. Grant to send all available from the Army of the Tennessee toward Chattanooga to aid Rosecrans. Near Chattanooga operations and skirmishes centered around Lee and Gordon's Mills, toward La Fayette and near Summerville, Ga. A reconnaissance probed from Henderson's Gap to La Fayette, Ga. Bragg ordered Polk to attack Thomas L. Crittenden's divided corps at Lee and Gordon's Mills. Polk did not attack. Elsewhere there was a skirmish near Salem, Mo. Scouts and expeditions lasting several days included one by Federals from Fort Larned to Booth's Ranch on the Arkansas River, Kas., and another by Confederates near Lake Ponchartrain, La. In South Carolina Confederates captured a Union telegraph party near Lowndes' Mill on the Combahee River. Southern cavalry seized twenty crewmen of U.S.S. *Rattler* while they attended church at Rodney, Miss.

September 14, Monday

Still the skirmishing continued between the Rappahannock and Rapidan as Federal forces pushed toward the Rapidan against Lee. Fighting was at Somerville, Raccoon, and Robertson's fords and Rapidan Station. On the Chattanooga front there was a skirmish near La Fayette, Ga. Other action was a Federal reconnaissance on the Blackwater River, N.C.; a Confederate attack on Vidalia, La.; at Smyth County, Va.; and Cheat Mountain Pass, W. Va.

September 15, Tuesday

As a result of the existing "state of rebellion" Lincoln suspended the privilege of the writ of habeas corpus through the nation in cases where military or civil authorities of the United States held persons under their command or in custody. Lincoln also wrote Gen. Halleck that Gen. Meade should attack Lee at once. Meanwhile, Meade's advance to the Rapidan had been largely completed.

In Georgia below Chattanooga both Bragg and Rosecrans were concentrating their forces: Rosecrans drawing in his scattered corps; Bragg gathering in all he could preparatory to taking action against Rosecrans. Skirmishing occurred at Trion Factory and Summerville, Ga., as well as at Catlett's Gap on Pigeon Mountain. Other action was near Kempsville, Va., and in Jackson County and at Enterprise, Mo. Union expeditions in Missouri, New Mexico, and one from Great Bridge, Va., to Indiantown, N.C., all lasted several days. On James Island near Charleston, S.C., a magazine at Confederate Battery Cheves exploded, killing six men.

September 16, Wednesday

Rosecrans was concentrating his Army of the Cumberland in the area of Lee and Gordon's Mills on Chickamauga Creek, Ga., about twelve miles south of Chattanooga, and there were several days of skirmishing in the vicinity. The Reserve Corps Rosecrans held near Chattanooga, Crittenden was at the Mill, Thomas to the south, and Alexander McDowell McCook far to the south near Alpine. Otherwise fighting was limited to affairs at Brownsville, Ark., and Smithfield, W. Va.

President Davis wrote Gen. Lee of his concern over the withdrawal from Chattanooga and the "inexplicable" loss of Cumberland Gap. He hoped Bragg would soon recover the lost ground.

September 17, Thursday

Action increased as the armies below Chattanooga drew closer together. By nightfall Rosecrans' three corps were within supporting distance of each other. Bragg had failed to prevent such concentration or to mount an attack against isolated Federal elements on at least three occasions. He blamed his officers and they blamed him. Bragg now planned to turn the Union left north of Lee and Gordon's Mills, force Rosecrans back into the mountains, and get between him and Chattanooga. Part of Longstreet's corps was arriving from Virginia and plans were ready. However, Rosecrans understood Bragg's moves and hurried to protect the roads to Chattanooga.

In Virginia there was yet another skirmish at Raccoon Ford on the Rapidan. In Missouri troops skirmished on Horse Creek.

September 18, Friday

CHICKAMAUGA CAMPAIGN BEGINS.

Braxton Bragg moved all but three divisions of his Army of Tennessee from the Ringgold area across West Chickamauga Creek, aided by a portion of Longstreet's corps which arrived in the morning from Virginia. Heavy skirmishing with Federal cavalry broke out at Pea Vine Ridge, Alexander's and Reeds' bridges, Dyer's Ford, Spring Creek, and near Stevens' Gap, Ga. For his part, Rosecrans moved Thomas' corps of the Army of the Cumberland in a hard march northeast so that Bragg would not outflank the Federals toward Chattanooga. A major battle was in sight. In the East Tennessee Campaign skirmishing flared at Calhoun, Cleveland, Kingsport, and Bristol, Tenn. Other action was at Crooked Run, Va., and near Fort Donelson, Tenn.

President Lincoln himself honorably discharged William "Duff" Armstrong from army service. As an attorney Lincoln had defended Armstrong in a famous murder case in 1858.

September 19, Saturday

BATTLE OF CHICKAMAUGA, FIRST DAY.

Neither the Federal Army of the Cumberland under Rosecrans nor the Army of Tennessee under Bragg was quite sure of the exact position of the other as they moved into roughly parallel lines west of West Chickamauga Creek, southeast of Chattanooga. The section was densely wooded and underbrushed. Gen. George H. Thomas, on the Federal left or north flank, sent part of his corps forward to investigate the enemy. This body ran into dismounted cavalry of Nathan Bedford Forrest, and actually opened the battle. Fighting in this section grew more severe as other units joined in, and by afternoon the greater portions of both armies were engaged along a ragged three-mile line. McCook's Union Corps came from the south. Bragg was unable to penetrate between Chattanooga and the Federals, who held the roads to the city. Losses in the sporadic but heavy fire were high but results were negligible. At night Rosecrans tightened his line; breastworks were built. For the Confederates, Longstreet himself and more of his men arrived from the east. Bragg put Gen. Leonidas Polk in command of the right wing and Gen. Longstreet the left wing.

Elsewhere, cavalry fought at Culpeper, Va. Skirmishes broke out at Raccoon Ford, Va.; Como, Tenn.; and Greenwell Springs Road near Baton Rouge, La.; and a Federal expedition from Fort Pillow to Jackson, Tenn., lasted six days. John Y. Beall and fellow Southerners captured a schooner in Chesapeake Bay, the first of several daring operations against Yankee shipping.

President Lincoln wrote Gen. Halleck, "I have constantly desired the Army of the Potomac, to make Lee's army, and not Richmond it's [sic] objective point."

September 20, Sunday

BATTLE OF CHICKAMAUGA, SECOND DAY.

Daybreak on this fall Sunday in the Georgia woods was supposed to see the Confederate drive renewed from the right, commanded by Polk. Then other divisions were to join in. There was no attack until about nine-thirty, when Breckinridge's division moved forward. The Union left under Thomas fell back, but held at the breastworks. Neither side gained or lost much from the heavy Confederate attacks until shortly before noon. Longstreet came in opposite the Federal center, to find that by a blunder of orders Thomas J. Wood's Union division had been pulled out and left a gap in the Northern line. Longstreet hit, driving two divisions away, thus cutting the Federal line and causing a major portion of it to flee in considerable disorder. Rosecrans, McCook, and Crittenden were caught up in the retreat toward Chattanooga. Only Thomas' corps, aided by a few other units, remained.

Thomas managed to form a new line on a rounded eminence known as Snodgrass Hill. Here the Federals held through the afternoon, repelling assault after assault. Thomas' men, and fragments of other units joined later by Gordon Granger's reserve, fought a great defensive battle which earned for Thomas his famous nickname "Rock of Chickamauga." For a while it seemed as if Confederates would take the hill, so furious and desperate were the charges. However, there were not enough Confederate reinforcements. They fought until night, when, obeying orders, Thomas withdrew toward Rossville and the mountain gaps that led to Chattanooga. Splendid as the Union defensive was, the battle was a great Confederate tactical victory.

The estimated figures are 58,000 Federal effectives, with 1657 killed, 9756 wounded, and 4757 missing for 16,170 casualties; 66,000 Confederates, with 2312 killed, 14,674 wounded, 1468 missing for 18,454. The casualty rate for both sides was about 28 per cent. A dispatch from Gen. Rosecrans increased President Lincoln's anxiety for further details.

Other fighting included skirmishes at Hornersville, Mo.; and Carter's Depot and Zollicoffer in eastern Tenn.; an affair on Shaver Mountain, W. Va.; and a ten-day Federal expedition from Paducah, Ky., to McLemoresville, Tenn.

September 21, Monday

At Rossville Gen. Thomas, with the remnant of the defeated Army of the Cumberland, stood his ground all day. However, due to the danger of being flanked, Thomas retired to Chattanooga. By morning of Sept. 22 the Federal army occupied a good defensive position in and around Chattanooga. Gen. Bragg ordered a pursuit and then canceled it, giving up possible greater fruits of victory. Bragg, aided by geography, was in an excellent position to besiege the city. Fighting was listed as skirmishing at Rossville, Lookout Church, and Dry Valley, Ga.

President Lincoln, who thought the Chickamauga defeat extremely serious, wired Burnside in east Tennessee: "Go to Rosecrans with your force, without a moments delay." To Rosecrans he wired, "Be of good cheer. We have unabated confidence in you, and in your soldiers and officers . . . save your army, by taking strong positions. . . ."

Other action flared at Jonesborough, Tenn., and at Moorefield, W. Va. A Federal scout until Sept. 26 from Harper's Ferry into Loudoun Valley, Va., included sporadic fighting. In Virginia a Federal reconnaissance crossed the Rapidan, skirmishing at White's Ford and Madison Court House. Operations about Princess Anne Court House lasted five days.

September 22, Tuesday

Black plume on hat, Joseph O. "Jo" Shelby led his band of Confederate light-horse troops on a fast-paced raid through Arkansas and Missouri which lasted until late October. The command set out from Arkadelphia, Ark., headquarters of Confederate activity since the fall of Little Rock.

In the windup of the Chickamauga Campaign, skirmishing occurred at Missionary Ridge and Shallow Ford Gap near Chattanooga. Although Federal troops were in a strong position at Chattanooga, they were hemmed in by the mountains, the Tennessee River, and the Confederates who held Missionary Ridge and Lookout Mountain overlooking the city. Washington had long realized that Rosecrans needed reinforcements; they now became imperative. Three divisions of the Fifteenth Corps of Grant's army left Vicksburg for Chattanooga. The advisability of an even more massive concentration was discussed in Washington.

In the East Tennessee Campaign skirmishing broke out at Carter's Depot, and Blountsville, Tenn., and Marrow Bone Creek, Ky. Burnside was hard put to control the rugged, mountainous area from his Knoxville headquarters. In Virginia skirmishing continued between Centreville and Warrenton, and at Rockville, Md., Confederates raided far behind the lines of the Army of the Potomac. On the main lines there was fighting at Orange Court House and Raccoon Ford. At Darien, Ga., Federals destroyed the Confederate salt works. A four-day Union scout in La Fayette County, Mo., involved skirmishes.

In Washington President Lincoln, distraught over Rosecrans' situation, also mourned the death of his Confederate brother-in-law Brig. Gen. Ben Hardin Helm, a victim of Chickamauga.

September 23, Wednesday

President Lincoln, Sec. of War Stanton, and other Cabinet and military officers met in the evening to discuss relieving Rosecrans at Chattanooga. After considerable debate, they agreed to send the Eleventh and Twelfth Corps of the Army of the Potomac, under Hooker's command, west to Rosecrans. Some thought this would take a month or more; Stanton and others believed it could be done in an incredible seven days. Immediately telegrams were dispatched to railroads and to the Army, rail lines were commandeered, red tape broken, and it was done. Troops were moving by Sept. 25 and by Oct. 2 the last of the Eleventh Corps arrived in Alabama, shut off from Chattanooga by the mountains. The Twelfth Corps was passing through Nashville. Gen. Hooker commanded the troops, but Stanton, the War Department, and the railroads made it possible. The brilliant logistical operation still stands as a superlative feat of ground transportation of troops. Meanwhile, at Chattanooga skirmishing at Summertown and Lookout Mountain lasted several days. In the East Tennessee Campaign skirmishing flared at Federal-held Cumberland Gap.

On the Rapidan in Virginia skirmishing occurred at Liberty Mills and Robertson's Ford. Maj. Gen. George E. Pickett, who had taken one division of Longstreet's corps with him, was assigned to command the Confederate Department of North Carolina. Other fighting broke out near Bayou Meto Bridge, Ark., and opposite Donaldsonville, La.

Two vessels of the Imperial Russian Navy's Atlantic Fleet arrived in New York. Four other ships followed shortly, and on Oct. 12 six vessels entered San Francisco Bay. The Russians received an extremely friendly welcome. Parades, dinners, a visit to the Washington area early in December, and special programs marked their seven months in American waters. The main purpose of their presence was to avoid being tied up for the winter in Baltic ice; Russia feared a European war after her brutal suppression of a Polish revolt.

September 24, Thursday

The great rail transfer of the two Federal corps from the Army of the Potomac got under way with the organization of rolling stock. Skirmishes occurred at Zollicoffer, Tenn.; Bristoe Station, Va.; and Greenbrier Bridge, W. Va. There were six days of Union expeditions from Carrollton and Baton Rouge to the New and Amite rivers, La.

The Confederate government appointed A. Dudley Mann as special agent to the Holy See in Rome. President Lincoln wrote his wife, visiting in New York, of Chickamauga and said, "the result is that we are worsted." To Rosecrans he wrote that forty to sixty thousand men were on the way.

September 25, Friday

Military action declined as the Federal government concentrated on relieving Rosecrans. The Confederate government focused on how best to exploit the victory of Chickamauga. In east Tennessee there were skirmishes at Athens, Calhoun, and Charleston. An annoyed Lincoln wrote, but did not send, a letter to Burnside saying that he had been "struggling . . . to get you to go assist Gen. Rosecrans in an extremity, and you have repeatedly declared you would do it, and yet you steadily move the contrary way." Other fighting occurred in the vicinity of Baton Rouge, La., and Seneca Trace Crossing on the Cheat River, W. Va.

September 26, Saturday

As Rosecrans remained entrenched in Chattanooga and troops hurried to his aid, lesser action flared at Richards' Ford, Va.; Winchester and

Calhoun, Tenn.; Hunt's Mill near Larkinsville, Ala.; and Cassville, Mo. Confederate Maj. Gen. W. H. C. Whiting was assigned to the separate commands of the District of Cape Fear and Defenses of Wilmington, N.C. President Lincoln and the Administration were distressed that the New York *Post* revealed the movement of troops west to Rosecrans. In the Trans-Mississippi Confederate commander E. Kirby Smith tried to arouse the citizenry by proclaiming, "Your homes are in peril. Vigorous efforts on your part can alone save portions of your State from invasion. You should contest the advance of the enemy, thicket, gully, and stream; harass his rear and cut off his supplies."

September 27, Sunday

Jo Shelby's Confederate raiders were active at Moffat's Station in Franklin County, Ark. Skirmishing took place at Newtonia, Mo.; Locke's Mill near Moscow, Tenn.; and in east Tennessee at Athens and near Philadelphia. Two Federal expeditions operated until October on the Big Black to Yazoo City, Miss.; and from Corinth, Miss., into west Tennessee. Federals scouted in Bates County, Mo., and on Hazel River, Va. President Lincoln wrote Gen. Burnside in east Tennessee, "My order to you meant simply that you should save Rosecrans from being crushed out, believing if he lost his position, you could not hold East Tennessee in any event." Burnside denied any delay.

September 28, Monday

President Davis told Gen. Bragg of the reported Federal movement of two corps and other troops to reinforce Rosecrans. Maj. Gen. Alexander McDowell McCook and T. L. Crittenden were relieved of their corps commands and ordered to Indianapolis for a court of inquiry into the conduct of the Battle of Chickamauga. A minor bombardment of Fort Sumter, with about a hundred Federal shots fired, lasted for six days, until Oct. 3. Skirmishing developed at Buell's Ford and Jonesborough, Tenn.

September 29, Tuesday

Military action was limited to an expedition lasting for a month from Pilot Knob to Oregon County, Mo.; and action at Stirling's Plantation, La.; and Leesburg, Tenn. President Lincoln told the Sons of Temperance, "I think that the reasonable men of the world have long since agreed that intemperance is one of the greatest, if not the very greatest of all evils amongst mankind."

September 30, Wednesday

From this day to Oct. 17 Confederate cavalry under Maj. Gen. Joseph Wheeler raided communications of Rosecrans' Army of the Cumberland.

The raid opened with a skirmish at Cotton Port Ford, Tenn. Skirmishing at Neersville and Woodville and destruction of Confederate salt works at Back Bay, Va., also marked the day. Mild bombardment of Fort Sumter continued in Charleston Harbor.

OCTOBER, 1863

As the third autumn of the war arrived, the South was still besieged, but breathed a bit easier than during the disastrous midsummer. Confederates had been successful at halting the drives on Charleston and Texas, and had won at Chickamauga. On the other hand, the North was in Chattanooga and troops were rallying to their relief; east Tennessee had fallen to the Federals, as had Little Rock, Ark. The Union advance may have been dulled momentarily, but was not reversed. In Virginia, now that both Lee and Meade had sent troops to the West, there were questions about what would happen next. Bragg was harassed by the continuous bickering among his generals that blighted his entire career. Nothing had been done to date to garner the victory fruit from Chickamauga.

October 1, Thursday

In Virginia investigations and skirmishing occurred near Culpeper Court House, Auburn, and Lewisville. Elsewhere, fighting broke out at Elizabethtown, Ark., and near Harper's Ferry, W. Va. In cavalry operations around Chattanooga, Wheeler's Confederate forces fought at Mountain Gap near Smith's Cross Roads, and also captured a large Federal wagon train. From Nashville President Lincoln was informed that all the Eleventh Corps and part of the Twelfth Corps en route to the Chattanooga area had passed through the Tennessee capital. The President advised Gen. John M. Schofield, in command in Missouri: "Your immediate duty, in regard to Missouri, now is to advance the efficiency of that establishment, and to so use it, as far as practicable, to compel the excited people there to leave one another alone."

October 2, Friday

As Federal troops arrived at Bridgeport, Ala., from the Army of the Potomac, a skirmish flared near besieged Chattanooga. Fighting also erupted at Pitt's Cross Roads in the Sequatchie Valley, Anderson's Cross Roads, Valley Road near Jasper, and near Dunlap, Tenn., all part of Wheeler's annoying Confederate cavalry raid. Within a few days about 20,000 men and 3000 horses and mules under Hooker had arrived at Bridgeport, having traveled 1159 miles in seven to nine days. Nevertheless, the pressure increased as Rosecrans' food supplies dwindled. Confederates controlled the Tennessee River to the city, all roads on the south side, and the important road to Bridgeport north of the river. The only open road was a mountainous trail over Walden's Ridge and through Sequatchie Valley.

Elsewhere, fighting was limited to skirmishes at Carthage, Mo.; Greeneville, Tenn.; and Vance's Store in Arkansas.

The Augusta, Ga., *Constitutionalist* defined a major problem of the Confederate citizen of Mississippi and elsewhere: "If he takes refuge further East, he is censured for leaving home; and if he remains home to raise another crop in the Confederate lines, as soon as the Union enemy again presses forward, his supplies will once more be taken by the Confederate cavalry, and his cotton committed to the flames again!"

October 3, Saturday

On the Gulf Coast near New Orleans, Gen. Banks attempted once more to gain a foothold in Texas following the failure at Sabine Pass. This time Maj. Gen. William B. Franklin's troops moved westward from Berwick Bay and New Iberia, La., in what was known as the Bayou Teche Campaign. The campaign lasted well into November but failed to reach the Sabine.

The six-day secondary bombardment of Fort Sumter from Morris Island ended after 560 shot. Confederate batteries on James and Sullivan's islands responded irregularly to the Federal fire. Wheeler's Confederate cavalry fought Federals in the Chattanooga area at McMinnville, and at Hill's Gap near Beersheba, Tenn. Elsewhere, fighting took place at Bear Creek, Tenn.; Forked Deer Creek, Miss.; and Lewinsville, Va. Federal operations in Bates and Vernon counties, Mo., lasted four days. The Federal War Department ordered enlistment of Negro troops in the slave states of Maryland, Missouri, and Tennessee.

President Lincoln issued a proclamation of thanksgiving, calling for observance on the last Thursday of November in gratitude for the blessings of the past year and "in humble penitence for our national perverseness and disobedience. . . ." President Davis, writing Gen. Bragg, tried to smooth over the acrimonious controversy that had risen once more between Bragg and Gen. Polk over Polk's actions at Chickamauga. Davis told Bragg, "The opposition to you both in the army and out of it has been a public calamity in so far that it impairs your capacity for usefulness. . . ."

October 4, Sunday

The Confederate cavalry invasion of Missouri, led by Jo Shelby, pressed northward from the southwestern part of the state. There was action at Neosho and skirmishing at Widow Wheeler's, Oregon or Bowers' Mill, Mo. Wheeler's Confederate cavalry, having taken McMinnville, Tenn., skirmished nearby. In the Federal Bayou Teche operations an affair occurred at Nelson's Bridge near New Iberia, La. In Virginia a six-day Federal expedition moved from Yorktown into Matthews County; in west Tennessee and northern Mississippi Confederate cavalry under J. R. Chalmers operated until Oct. 17. President Lincoln told Gen. Rosecrans at Chattanooga, "If we can hold Chattanooga and East Tennessee, I think the rebellion must dwindle and die. I think you and Burnside can do this. . . ." He further suggested harassing or attacking Bragg's besieging Confederate army.

October 5, Monday

TORPEDO BOAT ATTACK ON *New Ironsides.*

At ten o'clock on a hazy night, a cigar-shaped, steam-driven vessel, barely visible above the waterline, moved out of Charleston Harbor toward the formidable Federal fleet. Approaching the mighty ironclad *New Ironsides,* the torpedo boat *David,* under Confederate Com. W. T. Glassell, thrust her torpedo at the side of the Federal warship. A tremendous blast and a fountain of water caused surprise and consternation aboard *New Ironsides.* The four-man Confederate crew of *David* fought for life in their nearly swamped vessel. *New Ironsides* suffered severely, although not critically, from the torpedo. Federal authorities recognized a new force in naval warfare. Glassell and one crewman were captured, but the other two managed to rekindle the fires in *David* and bring her back to Charleston.

Citizens and soldiers of Federally occupied Nashville were alarmed. Confederate cavalry under Joe Wheeler skirmished near Readyville, Tenn., and then destroyed an important railroad bridge over Stone's River near Murfreesboro, temporarily breaking the vital supply line to troops near Chattanooga. Other Confederate raiders under Jo Shelby fought Federals at Stockton and Greenfield, Mo. Still a third raider, James Ronald Chalmers, was active for the South in fighting at New Albany, Miss. Additional skirmishing took place at Syracuse, Mo.; Greenwell Springs Road, La.; and Blue Springs in east Tennessee. More troops moved from Memphis toward Chattanooga to help Rosecrans' beleaguered army. President Lincoln told a group of Missouri dissidents that he would not fire Gen. Schofield from command in St. Louis and added that "I hold whoever commands in Missouri, or elsewhere, responsible to me, and not to either radicals or conservatives."

October 6, Tuesday

Wheeler's Confederate cavalry continued to cause trouble in Tennessee, this time with skirmishing at Christiana, Readyville, Wartrace, and Garrison's Creek near Fosterville. Chalmer's Confederate cavalry fought at Lockhart's Mill on the Coldwater River, Miss. Shelby's men were engaged at Humansville, Mo. Additional fighting broke out in the East Tennessee Campaign at Glasgow, Ky., and Morgan County, Tenn. Other action occurred in Arkansas at Waldron; in Kansas at Baxter Springs; and near Catlett's Station, Va.

President Davis left Richmond on a trip to South Carolina, including threatened Charleston, to north Georgia, and to Bragg's army besieging Chattanooga. Davis hoped "to be serviceable in harmonizing some of the difficulties" in Bragg's command.

October 7, Wednesday

Federal signalmen observed unusual movement in the Confederate army along the Rapidan; something was about to happen. Skirmishing flared at Hazel River, and at Utz's and Mitchell's fords, Va. Still the Confederate raiders were active in the West, Wheeler at Farmington, Blue Springs, and Sim's Farm near Shelbyville, Tenn.; Shelby near Warsaw, Mo. Other action was seen at Evening Shade and Ferry's Ford, Ark.; in the Choctaw Nation, Indian Terr.; and at Charles Town and Summit Point, W. Va. Federals scouted in the Spring River country of Arkansas until the tenth. A Union expedition from Sedalia to Marshall, Mo., lasted until the seventeenth. U. S. Navy men burned two steamers on the Red River. President Lincoln asked Gov. Andrew Johnson of Tennessee, "What news have you from Rosecrans' Army . . . ?"

October 8, Thursday

A quiet day, but fighting broke out near James City and along Robertson's River, Va., and near Chattanooga. In the East Tennessee Campaign there was a Federal reconnaissance to Olympian Springs, Ky.

October 9, Friday

BRISTOE, VIRGINIA, CAMPAIGN TO OCTOBER 22.

Lee's Army of Northern Virginia was on the move. After crossing the Rapidan, the Confederate troops moved west and northward once more, attempting to turn Meade's right flank and head toward Washington. Meade's army had suspected a major move for several days and now it was under way. Lee was trying both to take advantage of the Federal reduction in force caused by sending troops west, and to prevent any more such movement. However, the Army of the Potomac still greatly outnumbered the Confederates. Action in Virginia included a skirmish near James City and a five-day Federal expedition to Chesnessex Creek. Down in the Teche country of Louisiana troops fought at Vermillion Bayou; in Missouri

Shelby's raiders skirmished near Cole Camp; in the East Tennessee Campaign fighting broke out at Cleveland, and skirmishing at Elk River, near Cowan, and at Sugar Creek. Wheeler's Confederate raiders concluded their operations against Federal communications between Nashville and Chattanooga by recrossing the Tennessee River at Muscle Shoals, Ala.

President Davis had arrived in Atlanta Oct. 8 and this day proceeded northward through Marietta toward Bragg's army. At Atlanta and Marietta Davis praised Georgia's war effort, eulogizing the patriotism of the troops. He was greeted by cheers.

October 10, Saturday

Extensive skirmishing broke out in the Rapidan area of Virginia as Federals probed to find the meaning of Lee's advance northward. Fighting took place at Russell's Ford on Robertson's River, Bethesda Church, James City, and Raccoon, Germanna, and Morton's fords. Once more President Lincoln wired his commander Meade the familiar words, "How is it now?" Meade thought Lee would move into the Shenandoah. Then, on the morning of the eleventh, Meade told Lincoln he was falling back to the Rappahannock: "The enemy are either moving to my right and rear or moving down on my flank." Actually they were moving by the Federal right flank, seeking to get behind the Army of the Potomac.

Shelby's Confederates were active again in Missouri, with fighting at Tipton, Syracuse, and La Mine Bridge. Elsewhere action occurred at Tulip, Ark.; Ingraham's Plantation near Port Gibson, Miss.; and, in the East Tennessee Campaign, at Blue Springs and Sweet Water, Tenn., and Salyersville, Ky. Three Federal expeditions operated for several days: from New Berne to Elizabeth City and Edenton, N.C.; from Memphis to Hernando, Miss.; and from Gallatin to Carthage, Tenn.

President Davis, with Bragg's army in north Georgia, surveyed the military scene and tried to establish harmony among the dissident generals.

October 11, Sunday

Heavy skirmishing continued between the Rapidan and Rappahannock in Virginia as Lee's army gained momentum in its newest move northward. Fighting erupted near Culpeper Court House, Griffinsburg, Brandy Station, Morton's Ford, Stevensburg, near Kelly's Ford, and near Warrenton or Sulphur Springs.

In the West Shelby's Confederates captured Boonville, Mo., on the Missouri River. Other action included fighting near Fayetteville, Ark., and at Brazil Creek, Choctaw Nation, Indian Terr. In Tennessee Chalmers' Confederate cavalry fought at Collierville, and in east Tennessee skirmishes broke out at Henderson's Mill and Rheatown.

October 12, Monday

President Lincoln, for the third time, asked Gen. Meade, "What news this morning?" Reports of the Confederate offensive in Virginia circulated widely. Lee's Army of Northern Virginia was indeed moving west and north of Meade in the general direction of Manassas and Washington. Skirmishing flared at Jeffersonton and Gaines' Cross Roads, Brandy Station or Fleetwood, Hartwood Church, and near Warrenton Springs in Meade's rear.

Raids continued in the West: Wheeler fought at Buckhorn Tavern near New Market, Ala.; Shelby at Merrill's Crossing and Dug Ford near Jonesborough, Mo.; and Chalmers near Byhalia, Quinn, and Jackson's Mill, Miss. Skirmishes took place at West Liberty, Ky., part of the east Tennessee campaigning; at Webber's Falls, Indian Terr.; and at Tulip, Ark. Troops operated against outlaws from Fort Garland, Colo. Terr., for several days.

President Lincoln wrote Gen. Rosecrans at Chattanooga that he and Burnside in east Tennessee now had the enemy "by the throat."

October 13, Tuesday

UNION CANDIDATES SUCCESSFUL.

The Confederate Army of Northern Virginia under R. E. Lee, with A. P. Hill's corps in the lead, closed in toward Manassas and Washington, following once more a pattern similar to that used at Second Manassas in 1862. There was skirmishing near the important road center of Warrenton and at Fox's Ford and Auburn. Meade, no longer in severe danger of being cut off from Washington, although his skillful withdrawal continued, headed toward Manassas and Centreville.

Confederate raider Shelby suffered defeat at the hands of the Federals near Arrow Rock, and also fought at Marshall, Mo. Joe Wheeler skirmished at Maysville, Ala., and Fayetteville, Tenn.; Chalmers at Wyatt, Miss. In West Virginia fighting broke out at Bulltown and Burlington; and Federals scouted from Great Bridge, Va., to Indiantown, N.C.

Ohio voters decisively defeated Clement L. Vallandigham, Democratic candidate for governor, in favor of War Democrat John Brough, who ran on the Republican or Union ticket. Vallandigham, who compaigned by mail from Canada, polled a surprisingly large vote despite his exile and condemnation as a Copperhead. Gov. Andrew Curtin, a stanch Union supporter, was reelected in Pennsylvania. Union candidates also won in Indiana and Iowa. Mr. Lincoln was particularly interested in Curtin being renamed.

In northern Georgia, President Davis, after touring Chickamauga and conferring with Bragg and other officers, authorized Bragg to relieve Lt. Gen. D. H. Hill from command. Hill and Bragg had long been at odds.

October 14, Wednesday

ENGAGEMENT AT BRISTOE STATION, VIRGINIA.

A. P. Hill's leading corps of the Army of Northern Virginia struck the retreating rear units of Meade's Army of the Potomac near Bristoe Station, Va. But Hill's force was not sufficient to defeat the strongly posted Federals and the Confederates also failed to strike the center of the long Union column as it retreated. The rearguard action gave Meade time to prepare his lines in and around Centreville, Va., not far from Manassas and the two previous battlegrounds. While there was skirmishing over the old fighting area there was no Third Battle of Manassas or Bull Run. Lee had no chance to disrupt the Federal army, although he succeeded in forcing them back near the Potomac. On the other hand, Meade held a good defensive position but was unable to find an opening for attack. It was a campaign of maneuver, with several lost opportunities on both sides. Other fighting in the same area broke out at Catlett's Station, Gainesville, McLean's Ford on Bull Run, St. Stephen's Church, Grove Church, and near Centreville and Brentsville.

Elsewhere, action included fighting near Man's Creek, Shannon County, Mo.; a skirmish with Shelby's cavalry at Scott's Ford, Mo.; skirmishing at Creek Agency, Indian Terr.; Carrion Crow Bayou, La.; Blountsville and Loudoun, Tenn.; and Salt Lick Bridge, W. Va. Maj. Gen. Christopher C. Augur superseded Maj. Gen. Samuel P. Heintzelman in command of the Federal Department of Washington, D.C. Union expeditions of several days operated from Messinger's Ferry on the Big Black toward Canton, Miss.; and from Natchez and Fort Adams, Miss., to the Red River in Louisiana, seeking Confederate guerrillas.

President Davis in a message to the Army of Tennessee said, "Though you have done much, very much yet remains to be done. Behind you is a people providing for your support and depending on you for protection. Before you is a country devastated by your ruthless invader. . . ."

October 15, Thursday

The Army of Northern Virginia and the Army of the Potomac, facing each other in the area along Bull Run, skirmished at McLean's, Blackburn's, and Mitchell's fords and at Manassas and Oak Hill. Each army tried to ascertain the other's strength and intentions. Federal troops operated toward Canton, Miss., skirmishing at Brownsville. Shelby's cavalry continued its scrapping at Cross Timbers, Mo. There was also an affair near Hedgesville, W. Va. In Charleston Harbor the Confederate submarine *H. L. Hunley* sank for a second time during a practice dive. Hunley, the inventor, and seven men died. The vessel was raised again. A skirmish occurred at Creek Agency, Indian Terr. In the east Tennessee fighting skirmishes were at Bristol and Philadelphia.

October 16, Friday

GRANT TO COMMAND NEW DIVISION OF THE MISSISSIPPI.

Orders from Washington created the Military Division of the Mississippi, combining the Departments of the Ohio, the Cumberland, and the Tennessee with Gen. U. S. Grant in command. Grant had been ordered from Vicksburg to Cairo, Ill. Sec. of War Stanton himself was on his way west to see Grant.

Although things were quiet in Virginia, skirmishes erupted at Grand Coteau, La.; Fort Brooke, Fla.; near Island No. 10 in Tennessee; at Treadwell's near Clinton and Vernon Cross Roads, Miss.; and at Pungo Landing, N.C. Shelby's cavalry in Missouri fought at Johnstown, Deer Creek, and near and at Humansville.

President Lincoln wrote Gen. Halleck, "If Gen. Meade can now attack him [Lee] on a field no worse than equal for us, and will do so with all the skill and courage, which he, his officers and men possess, the honor will be his if he succeeds, and the blame may be mine if he fails." Meade replied when shown Lincoln's message that he intended to attack if he could find the proper opportunity. He did not find it in the Bristoe Campaign.

October 17, Saturday

Gen. Grant, at Cairo, Ill., was ordered to proceed to Louisville to receive instructions. En route, at Indianapolis, Grant accidentally arrived at the same time as Sec. of War Stanton, also heading for Louisville to see the general. Proceeding together, Stanton handed Grant his orders creating the Military Division of the Mississippi under Grant's command. There were two versions. One left department commanders much as they were; the other relieved Gen. Rosecrans from command of the Department of the Cumberland and the army at Chattanooga. Grant accepted the one relieving Rosecrans and placing Maj. Gen. George H. Thomas in command. Gen. Sherman was to lead the Department of the Tennessee, and Burnside to continue in command of the Department of the Ohio. Rosecrans, badly beaten at Chickamauga, had been criticized for slowness, for the defeat, and now for being surrounded at Chattanooga. It was believed a more stable commander operating under Grant directly would be more effective.

In Washington President Lincoln issued a proclamation calling for 300,000 more volunteers for Federal armies.

Meanwhile, Lee began to pull back from Bull Run toward the Rappahannock, skirmishing near Chantilly, at Manassas Junction, Frying Pan Church, near Pohick Church, and at Groveton, Va. The Confederates were not prepared to await an attack by Meade. Also in Virginia there was a skirmish at Berryville and an affair at Accotink. Skirmishes in North

Carolina near Camden Court House, and in Missouri in Cedar County, courtesy of Jo Shelby. In Mississippi the Federal expedition fought near Satartia, Bogue Chitto Creek, and at Robinson's Mills near Livingston.

October 18, Sunday

Gen. Grant assumed command of the Military Division of the Mississippi, which gave him control over Federal military operations from the Mississippi east to the mountains. This came after rumors from Chattanooga that Rosecrans might retreat. Thomas, now in command and told he must hold Chattanooga at all hazards, replied, "We will hold the town till we starve."

In Virginia the Army of Northern Virginia under Lee neared its old line, the Rappahannock, as it withdrew from the Bull Run-Manassas area. A skirmish at Bristoe Station occurred during the withdrawal. Other fighting broke out near Annandale and Berryville, Va.; at Charleston, W. Va.; Carrion Crow Bayou, La.; Carthage, Mo.; and near Clinton, Miss.

President Davis, having left north Georgia and Bragg's army, proceeded west through Selma, Ala.

October 19, Monday

Jeb Stuart and his "Southern Horse" routed Gen. Kilpatrick and the Federal cavalry at Buckland Mills in Virginia, better known as the "Buckland Races." It marked the last fighting of any significance in the Bristoe Campaign, although skirmishing took place at Gainesville, New Baltimore, Catlett's Station, and Haymarket. In east Tennessee the fighting was at Zollicoffer and Spurgeon's Mill; in Mississippi at Smith's Bridge; in South Carolina at Murrell's Inlet; and in Missouri at Honey Creek.

October 20, Tuesday

The Confederate cavalry retired across the Rappahannock as the campaign toward Bristoe and Manassas ended, resulting in little change of territory and few losses. Confederate losses for Oct. 10–21 were 205 killed, 1176 wounded, a total of 1381 casualties. Federal casualties are put at 136 killed, 733 wounded, and 1423 missing or captured for a total of 2292.

Gen. Grant, after conferring with Sec. of War Stanton, left Louisville for Chattanooga. From Nashville he wired instructions to Burnside in east Tennessee and to other officers. Near beleaguered Chattanooga a Federal reconnaissance operated from Bridgeport toward Trenton, Ala. Other action included skirmishing at Barton's and Dickson stations and Cane Creek, Ala.; Treadwell's Plantation, Miss.; Warm Springs, N.C.; and Philadelphia, Tenn.

October 21, Wednesday

Gen. Grant conferred with displaced commander Rosecrans at Stevenson, Ala., and then went on to Bridgeport. From Bridgeport to Chattanooga he faced almost impassable, muddy, washed-out mountain roads and was further handicapped by being on crutches since his fall from a horse in New Orleans.

In the Bayou Teche operations, Federal forces under Gen. Franklin occupied Opelousas, La., after fighting there and at Barre's Landing. Other action took place at Cherokee Station, Ala.; Sulphur Springs, Tenn.; and Greenton Valley near Hopewell, Mo. Federals scouted from Charleston to Boone County Court House, W. Va.

October 22, Thursday

Gen. Grant toiled over the atrocious roads en route to Chattanooga, where Gen. George H. Thomas doggedly resisted the Confederate siege. Fighting broke out near Volney, Ky.; New Madrid Bend, Tenn.; Brownsville, Miss.; Bloomfield, Mo.; Annandale, Va.; and on the Rappahannock at Rappahannock Bridge and near Bealeton, Va.

October 23, Friday

In a major command change President Davis relieved Gen. Leonidas Polk from command of a corps in the Army of Tennessee. Polk was assigned to organizational work in Mississippi, replacing Gen. Hardee. Davis issued his orders from Meridian, Miss., another stop in his Western tour.

About dark Gen. Grant and his party arrived at Chattanooga and stopped at Gen. Thomas' headquarters. Soon Grant learned the details of the threatened situation of the besieged Army of the Cumberland.

Yet another skirmish broke out near Rappahannock Station, Va., as the armies in Virginia again probed each other. A skirmish was also fought at Warm Springs, N.C.

October 24, Saturday

At Chattanooga Gen. Grant made a personal inspection and ordered a supply line, known as the "cracker line," to be opened at Brown's Ferry on the Tennessee River. This would enable the bases in Alabama to supply the city more directly than by the extremely long, rugged, and difficult mountain trail north of the Tennessee. Farther west, Maj. Gen. Willam T. Sherman formally assumed command of the Army of the Tennessee, replacing Grant.

Skirmishing in Virginia was at Liberty and Bealeton; in Louisiana at Washington; and in Alabama at Tuscumbia. Shelby's raiders skirmished near Harrisonville, Mo., and Buffalo Mountains, Ark. At last Shelby was apparently leaving Missouri.

President Lincoln instructed Gen. Halleck that "with all possible expedition the Army of the Potomac get ready to attack Lee. . . ." Meade replied that he would "make every preparation with the utmost expedition to advance. . . ."

October 25, Sunday

Confederate John S. Marmaduke attacked Pine Bluff, Ark., after his demand for its surrender was refused. Eventually he withdrew after partial occupation. In Virginia there were skirmishes at and near Bealeton; and in Tennessee fighting broke out at Philadelphia.

October 26, Monday

Grant's operations to reopen the Tennessee River route into Chattanooga got under way. Joseph Hooker's force from Virginia crossed the Tennessee at Bridgeport and moved eastward toward Chattanooga. The guns roared again at Charleston as the second great bombardment opened from land and sea. Guns and mortars fired on into the night.

Shelby fought in Johnson County, Ark., after his lengthy Missouri raid, and a fight broke out at King's House near Waynesville, Mo. Confederates attacked a wagon train near New Baltimore, Va. Other action flared at Ravenswood, W. Va.; Warm Springs, N.C.; Jones' Hill and Sweet Water, Tenn.; Vincent's Cross Roads near Bay Springs, Miss.; and near Cane Creek and Barton's Station, Ala. Until Nov. 15 Federal troops operated from Cape Girardeau to Doniphan, Mo., and Pocahontas, Ark.

October 27, Tuesday

CHATTANOOGA RELIEVED: CHARLESTON BOMBARDMENT RENEWED.

The second major bombardment of Fort Sumter got into high gear with 625 Federal shot fired. A pontoon bridge was thrown across the Tennessee River below Chattanooga at Brown's Ferry in a daring operation. In addition, Hooker advanced from the west to the Wauhatchie Valley at the western foot of Lookout Mountain. This opening of the cracker line from Lookout Valley to Bridgeport relieved Chattanooga and within a few days full supplies were getting through; Bragg's siege was being loosened.

The usual fighting occurred elsewhere: Tulip, Ark.; near Bealeton and Rappahannock stations, Va.; Cherokee County, N.C.; on Sandy River near Elizabeth, W. Va.; Clinch Mountain, Tenn.; and Little Bear Creek, Ala. Federals scouted from Columbia toward Pulaski, Tenn. From New Orleans Gen. Banks got his expedition under way toward the Rio Grande and the coast of Texas. He still hoped to establish a foothold in Texas, despite failure at Sabine Pass and on the Teche.

October 28, Wednesday

During the night of Oct. 28–29 Confederates under Longstreet, concerned over the attempts to relieve Chattanooga, attacked Brig. Gen. John W. Geary's troops of Hooker's force at Wauhatchie in Lookout Valley. Despite an intense drive with larger numbers, the Confederates failed and by 4 A.M. the confused engagement ended. The cracker line to Chattanooga was safe for the rest of the campaign. Wauhatchie was one of the few fairly important night engagements of the war. Northern losses were 78 killed, 327 wounded, and 15 missing for 420 casualties. Confederates lost an estimated 34 killed, 305 wounded, and 69 missing for 408.

In Arkansas Federal cavalry occupied Arkadelphia south of Little Rock. Skirmishing erupted at Clarksville and Leiper's Ferry, Tenn. At Charleston 679 shot were fired against the almost wrecked Fort Sumter, but the garrison held on. The fort was more a symbol now than a valuable military objective.

Lincoln, still upset over the political situation in Missouri, wrote Gen. John M. Schofield in St. Louis about the evils of allegedly arming disloyal citizens and disarming the loyal in Missouri, admonishing, "Prevent violence from whatever quarter; and see that the soldiers themselves, do no wrong."

October 29, Thursday

For the last three days of October, Fort Sumter received the heaviest fire of the prolonged and bitter experience. Some 2961 rounds pounded the rubble and there were 33 casualties. But at month's end the flag, often replaced, still flew.

Fighting was confined to Warsaw and Ozark, Mo.; Cherokee Station, Ala.; and a Federal scout Oct. 29–Nov. 2 from Winchester to Fayetteville, Tenn. President Davis approved a request of Brig. Gen. N. B. Forrest to be detached from service with Bragg's army to go into north Mississippi and west Tennessee. Davis himself was in Atlanta, Ga., and busy writing various generals regarding the many controversies that had arisen in the West. His calls for "harmonious co-operation" did not seem too effective.

October 30, Friday

The shuddering thunder of guns echoed over Charleston Harbor as the Federal artillery blasted Fort Sumter. Elsewhere, skirmishing occurred at Fourteen Mile Creek, Indian Terr.; near Opelousas, La.; at Ford's Mill near New Berne, N.C.; Catlett's Station, Va.; Salyersville, Ky.; and Leiper's Ferry on the Holston River, Tenn. Unconditional unionists of Arkansas met at Fort Smith, naming a representative to Congress.

October 31, Saturday
As the third day of tremendous fire made service in Fort Sumter a nightmare, three skirmishes broke out on other fronts: at Washington, La.; Barton's Station, Ala., and Yazoo City, Miss.

NOVEMBER, 1863

Attention had turned from the midsummer fronts on the Mississippi and, in Virginia and Pennsylvania to new theaters. Lee's presence along Virginia's Rappahannock and Rapidan rivers created a potentially explosive situation, but at the moment the focus was on Chattanooga and Charleston. How Bragg would respond to Grant's opening of a supply line to the threatened garrison and what countermeasures Grant would take were questions of intense interest North and South. At Charleston the guns had roared out once more against Fort Sumter during the last days of October. How much more could the pulverized fort stand? If Charleston fell, what would it mean for each side? The blockade was becoming more of a strangling burden than ever, with frequent captures of blockade-runners. Politically the North seemed more stable, although there were dissident cries, and 1864 was a presidential election year. The Federal government now controlled, or partially controlled, large chunks of Southern soil, but the Confederate States of America still existed.

November 1, Sunday
Seven hundred and eighty-six rounds of artillery fire were thrown against Fort Sumter in the graceful arc of the mortars and the flatter, rapid trajectory of the rifled breaching batteries. One man was wounded. The garrison stood stanchly in the bombproofs, while the wreckage piled up outside.
Near Chattanooga Grant's new supply line began to function and the siege was no longer a true siege. Federal cavalry under William Woods Averell left Beverly, W. Va., while another column left Charleston Nov. 3 for an expedition toward Lewisburg, W. Va. In Virginia another skirmish broke out at Catlett's Station. Other action included fighting at Eastport and Fayetteville, Tenn.; Quinn and Jackson's Mill, Miss.; and a Federal scout from Bovina Station to Baldwin's Ferry, Miss. On the Gulf Coast Federal forces of Gen. Franklin retired from Opelousas to New Iberia, La., ending for a time the operation in the Bayou Teche area.
Jefferson Davis was returning to Richmond from his trip west. From

Savannah Davis wrote Bragg of his disappointment that Grant had opened the Chattanooga supply line.

November 2, Monday

President Lincoln received an invitation to make a "few appropriate remarks" at the dedication of the new National Cemetery at Gettysburg, Pa. Although the time was short (Nov. 19) and the invitation obviously somewhat of an afterthought, the President accepted.

Lincoln expressed concern over the possibility of violence at the November elections in some states, including Maryland. In a letter about newspaper comments, the President wrote, "I have endured a great deal of ridicule without much malice; and have received a great deal of kindness, not quite free from ridicule. I am used to it." Distinguished citizens, military units, and the general public welcomed President Davis to Charleston, while from the harbor came the sound of 793 Federal shells exploding about Fort Sumter. While Charleston "was now singled out as a particular point of hatred to the Yankees," Davis said he "did not believe Charleston would ever be taken." If it should be, he urged that the "whole be left one mass of rubbish."

On the Rio Grande Gen. Banks' Federal expeditionary force occupied Brazos Island in its effort to gain a toehold in Texas. Skirmishes occurred in Louisiana at Bayou Bourbeau in the Teche operations; in Arkansas in Bates Township; in Mississippi once more at Corinth; and in Tennessee at Centreville and Piney Factory. Brig. Gen. John McNeil assumed command of the Federal District of the Frontier.

November 3, Tuesday

Still the sound of guns crashed over Charleston Harbor as 661 rounds added to the tremendous total of artillery fire already expended on Fort Sumter. In the lowlands of the Gulf Coast of Louisiana a fierce engagement was fought at Bayou Bourbeau on Grand Coteau, and a skirmish at Carrion Crow Bayou nearby. In the Louisiana engagement Confederates drove back Federal troops but reinforcements regained the position. Federal losses were put at 604, of which 536 were captured or missing; total Confederate casualties were set at 181.

Confederate cavalry operated Nov. 3–5 against the important Memphis and Charleston Railroad. Skirmishing developed at Collierville and Lawrenceburg, Tenn.; Quinn and Jackson's Mill on the Coldwater, Miss.; and Confederates scouted about Catlett's Station, Va. Federal troops under Alfred N. Duffie left Charleston, W. Va., to join Averell's Beverly expedition.

President Lincoln wrote Sec. Seward in Auburn, N.Y., that dispatches "from Chattanooga show all quiet and doing well."

November 4, Wednesday

Gen. Braxton Bragg had arrived at a bold decision: he sent Gen. James Longstreet and his corps from the Chattanooga area against the Federals under Burnside in east Tennessee. It was a desperate gambit by the Confederates, for the force under Bragg would be gravely weakened, but a blow must be struck to try to retrieve the Knoxville area and re-establish communications with Virginia. For Grant and the Federal government it was an ominous move. Sherman was on his way from Vicksburg, but until he arrived, Grant believed he could not act at Chattanooga. Meanwhile, Burnside would have to hold on as best he could.

The usual skirmishing continued near Neosho and Lexington, Mo; Falmouth, Va.; Rocky Run, N.C.; Cackleytown, W. Va.; Maysville, Ala.; Motley's Ford on the Little Tennessee River, Tenn.; and in the Pinal Mountains on the Gila River, Ariz. Terr. Federal expeditions and scouts operated from Houston to Jack's Fork and in Reynolds, Shannon, and Oregon counties of Missouri; and up the Chowan River, N.C.

President Davis visited James Island and forts and batteries around Charleston.

November 5, Thursday

Federals reduced the bombardment of Fort Sumter to slow, occasional firing. Grant, at Chattanooga, hoped Sherman would arrive in time to allow the Federals to strike Bragg before Longstreet could attack Burnside. Mosby, the irrepressible Confederate raider, was active most of November in northern Virginia. Also in Virginia, near the main armies, a skirmish broke out at Hartwood Church. Other fighting was at Neosho, Mo.; at Vermillionville, La.; Mill Point, W. Va.; Loudon County, Moscow, and La Fayette, Tenn.; and Holly Springs, Miss. Two Yankee vessels seized three blockade-runners off the mouth of the Rio Grande, an example of the increasing effectiveness of the blockade. Three other runners were taken off Florida and South Carolina.

President Lincoln wrote Gen. Banks, commanding in Louisiana and Texas, of his disappointment that a constitutional government had not yet been set up in Louisiana and urged Banks to "lose no more time." He emphasized that such a government must "be *for* and not *against*" the slaves "on the question of their permanent freedom."

November 6, Friday

ENGAGEMENT AT DROOP MOUNTAIN, WEST VIRGINIA.

Moving over the mountains of West Virginia from Beverly, heading for Lewisburg, Federal forces under Brig. Gen. William W. Averell encountered Confederates blocking the road at Droop Mountain. Averell divided his force, sending a major portion of his men on a lengthy detour to the rear of the Confederates under Brig. Gen. John Echols. In midafternoon the two Federal forces attacked and the Confederates were forced to pull away down the pike or scatter into the woods. The engagement enabled the Federals to proceed toward Lewisburg, W. Va., to effect part of Averell's over-all plan to clean out the remnants of Southern opposition and destroy important railroad links between Virginia and the Southwest. At the same time a skirmish took place at Little Sewell Mountain, W. Va. Banks' Federals extended their holdings near the Mexican border around Point Isabel and Brownsville, Tex. Other fighting broke out near Rogersville, Tenn., and Falmouth, Va.

President Davis, en route to Richmond, stopped at Wilmington, N.C., where he said he recognized the importance of the harbor, the only one really open for trade, even though it was strongly blockaded. In an inspector's report from the Trans-Mississippi, Davis was told, "The morale of the army is good and the feelings [sic] of the people is better than it was" in Arkansas, now separated from the remainder of the Confederacy.

November 7, Saturday
ENGAGEMENTS ON THE RAPPAHANNOCK.

Once more the Virginia front sprang to life as the Army of the Potomac under Meade pushed across the Rappahannock at Rappahannock Station and Kelly's Ford, with severe engagements at both places. Lee began withdrawing to the line of the Rapidan. It was not a major Federal offensive, but essentially restored the same positions that existed before the Bristoe Campaign. In addition to the main fighting on the Rappahannock, some Union pickets were captured near Warrenton. In West Virginia a skirmish flared near Muddy Creek. Averell's Federal expedition made contact with other Northern troops under A. N. Duffie and captured Lewisburg, W. Va. In Arkansas Nov. 7–13 there was an expedition by Federals from Fayetteville to Frog Bayou which involved some skirmishing.

November 8, Sunday

The Union advance across the Rappahannock in Virginia continued with fighting at Warrenton, Jeffersonton, Rixeyville, Muddy Creek near Culpeper Court House, Brandy Station, and Stevensburg. None of the fighting in this familiar territory was heavy but it did indicate that Meade and Lee were not entirely idle, but were maneuvering and awaiting a proper opportunity.

In West Virginia the Federal expedition from Beverly fought at Second Creek, on the road to Union. In the Louisiana Teche country there was a skirmish at Vermillionville and fighting at Bayou Tunica or Tunica Bend.

In an important command change, Maj. Gen. John C. Breckinridge superseded Lieut. Gen. D. H. Hill in command of the Second Corps in Bragg's Army of Tennessee—another attempt to alleviate the ill-feeling between Bragg and his generals.

November 9, Monday

The brief furor of activity decreased for the moment, although skirmishing took place in the Choctaw Nation, Indian Terr.; near Bayou Sara and Indian Bayou, La.; and near Weldon, N.C., and Covington, Va. A Federal expedition moved from Williamsburg toward New Kent Court House, Va., east of Richmond. A fairly heavy early snowstorm fell in Virginia as President Davis returned to Richmond from his southern trip.

President Lincoln attended the theater and saw John Wilkes Booth in *The Marble Heart.* The President, pleased by the Union advances in West Virginia and Virginia, wired Meade, "Well done."

November 10, Tuesday

Since Nov. 7 Fort Sumter had received 1753 rounds in the Federal bombardment in Charleston Harbor. Confederate casualties were limited to a few wounded. For a week expeditions operated from Benton to Mount Ida, Ark., and from Springfield, Mo., to Huntsville, Carrollton, and Berryville, Ark. Both were part of extensive Federal attempts to clear up Confederate guerrilla activities and raids in Missouri and Arkansas. In Mississippi Federal operations from Skipwith's Landing to Tallulah Court House lasted four days.

November 11, Wednesday

Maj. Gen. Benjamin F. Butler returned to active Federal command, superseding Maj. Gen. John G. Foster in the Department of Virginia and North Carolina. The ill-famed former commander at New Orleans ordered the arrest of anyone annoying loyal persons by "opprobrious and threatening language." To the North Confederates raided Suffolk, Va., with modest results. Skirmishing flared in the Fouché-le-Faix Mountains of Arkansas; Greenleaf Prairie, Indian Terr.; near Natchez, Miss.; and again at Carrion Crow and Vermillion bayous in the Teche country of Louisiana. President Davis suggested to Gen. Bragg that he "not allow the enemy to get up all his reinforcements before striking him, if it can be avoided. . . ." The President was deeply concerned about the situation in Chattanooga and Charleston.

November 12, Thursday

A new bombardment which would last four days opened against Fort Sumter. Skirmishing broke out near Cumberland Gap, Tenn.; at Corinth,

Miss.; Roseville, Ark.; Greenleaf Prairie, Indian Terr.; and there were more operations about St. Martinsville, La., in the Bayou Teche country. At Little Rock, Ark., unionists conferred on means of restoring the state to the Union.

The daughter of Federal Sec. of the Treasury Salmon P. Chase was married in Washington. President Lincoln attended the wedding of Kate Chase and Rhode Island senator William Sprague.

November 13, Friday

As the Federal guns still thundered in Charleston Harbor, Federal cavalry reached Charleston, W. Va., in the expedition from Beverly. Other action occurred at Mount Ida, Ark.; near Winchester, Va.; Blythe's Ferry on the Tennessee River; and at Palmyra, Tenn. A Federal reconnaissance operated around the entrances of the Cape Fear River, N.C. In California Union troops skirmished with Indians near the Big Bar, on the south fork of the Trinity River.

November 14, Saturday

All was quiet on the major fronts in Virginia and at Chattanooga, but the bombardment continued at Charleston. Cavalry fought at Huff's Ferry, Tenn., and in east Tennessee at Maryville, Little River, and Rockford. In Virginia fighting broke out at Tyson's Cross Roads, and small affairs occurred on the eastern shore. Other action included a five-day Federal scout from Martinsburg, W. Va.; a Federal expedition from Helena, Ark.; skirmishing at Danville, Miss.; and Union operations from Maysville to Whitesburg and Decatur, Ala. In an important Confederate command change, Brig. Gen. N. B. Forrest was assigned to Federally controlled west Tennessee. The Confederate government said force and confiscation should be used if necessary to collect the tax in kind from reluctant farmers in North Carolina.

November 15, Sunday

Four divisions of Gen. Sherman were at Bridgeport on the Tennessee, while the general himself went into Chattanooga to confer with Grant and look over the ground before moving his troops closer to the city. The bombardment of Fort Sumter slowed, with 2328 rounds fired since Nov. 12. Only two men were killed and five wounded. Skirmishing occurred in Newton County, Ark.; Pillowville, near Loudon, and at Lenoir's Station, Tenn.; and on John's Island, S.C., near Charleston. Federal cavalry operated for four days from Charles Town, W. Va., to Woodstock, New Market, Edenburg, and Mount Jackson, Va.

Federal authorities in west Tennessee and north Mississippi tightened prohibitions against trading with the enemy or war profiteers, and consorting with guerrilla bands. Federal occupation of the area had become a difficult problem, with much winking at rules and regulations.

November 16, Monday

Confederates under Gen. James Longstreet moving north from Chattanooga were nearing Knoxville, Tenn. In an engagement at Campbell's Station Longstreet failed to cut off Burnside's retreat line. Burnside withdrew to Knoxville. The city was now besieged for all practical purposes. Other fighting was about Kingston, east Tenn. Federal troops of Gen. Banks' command entered Corpus Christi, Tex., in their continuing campaign to gain a base on the Texas coast. At Charleston 602 rounds were fired. Federal monitors engaged the batteries on Sullivan's Island, with U.S.S. *Lehigh* aground under fire and badly damaged before getting off. In Louisiana a Union expedition operated from Vidalia to Trinity; in West Virginia a skirmish broke out near Burlington; in Virginia an affair occurred at Germantown.

President Lincoln sent his familiar query: "What is the news?", this time to Burnside in Knoxville, Tenn., who replied that Longstreet had crossed the Tennessee and that the Federals had slowly retired to Knoxville.

November 17, Tuesday

The siege of Knoxville, Tenn., was under way, the partial siege of Chattanooga continued, and bombardment at Charleston roared on. Near Corpus Christi, Tex., Federals captured a Confederate battery at Aransas Pass. There were skirmishes at Bay Saint Louis, Miss., and near Willow Creek on the Trinity River, Calif. Averell's Federal cavalry reached New Creek, W. Va.; and Union scouts probed around Houston, Mo., for ten days.

In Washington Mr. Lincoln had apparently composed a portion of the remarks he was to give at the dedication of the new military cemetery at Gettysburg, Pa., on the nineteenth.

November 18, Wednesday

A special train of four cars left Washington for Gettysburg. Although depressed because Tad was ill and Mrs. Lincoln very upset, the President related a few stories en route. Upon arrival at Gettysburg Lincoln spoke briefly to a crowd outside the Wills House, where he was staying, and retired to work on his remarks. Just what Mr. Lincoln wrote that night or exactly what version he used the next day remain subjects of debate by scholars.

Military operations included skirmishing near Germanna Ford, Va.; at Trenton, Ga.; Carrion Crow Bayou, La.; and on Shoal and Turkey creeks, Jasper County, Mo. For several days Confederates operated against

U.S. gunboats and transports near Hog Point, Miss., and there were lengthy explorations by Federals from Vienna toward the Blue Ridge in Virginia and from Skipwith's Landing to Roebuck Lake, Miss.

November 19, Thursday

LINCOLN'S GETTYSBURG ADDRESS.

On horseback the President of the United States rode in a procession to the military cemetery newly established for those who fell in the Battle of Gettysburg. After a detailed, colorful, two-hour address by the orator of the day, Edward Everett, the President rose and in a few words commented on the task at hand—that of officially dedicating the cemetery. Some of the audience appeared moved, others just respectful. Some newspapers commented favorably; others gave it normal or passing coverage. Mr. Lincoln himself felt that perhaps the brief talk had fallen flat. Stories that the President's words were ignored are not substantiated, but it seemed to excite few at first. Somewhat ill, the President returned that night to Washington, his task complete; but the message was never to be forgotten.

As Mr. Lincoln spoke, the guns echoed at Dr. Green's Farm near Lawrenceville, Ark., and near Grove Church, Va. Federals scouted from Memphis, Tenn., to Hernando, Miss. In Tennessee the action was at Meriwether's Ferry near Union City, at Mulberry Gap, and at Colwell's Ford. In Charleston Harbor one man was wounded as 694 shells were fired; 200 Federals in small boats attempted to assault Fort Sumter, but withdrew after being discovered. President Davis wrote officials in the Trans-Mississippi of his distress over the loss of a large part of Arkansas, and suggested what might be done.

November 20, Friday

Firing intensified at Charleston, with 1344 rounds. Three men died, and eleven were wounded. Light skirmishing occurred at Camp Pratt, La., and Sparta, Tenn. President Davis asked Gen. J. E. Johnston for more help for Gen. Bragg at Chattanooga. Mr. Lincoln received a note from orator Edward Everett commenting on how near the President had come "to the central idea of the occasion" the day before at Gettysburg. In reply Mr. Lincoln said, "I am pleased to know that, in your judgment, the little I did say was not entirely a failure."

November 21, Saturday

At Chattanooga Grant prepared for action. Sherman was moving up to cross the Tennessee at Brown's Ferry and march to the right flank of the Confederates before recrossing the Tennessee and striking them at the north end of Missionary Ridge. Thomas was also to attack Missionary Ridge in the center. Hooker was to move from Lookout Valley to Chattanooga Valley and hit the Confederate left. Rains were delaying the movement, however.

Other action included an affair at Jacksonport, Ark.; another at Liberty, Va.; a Federal scout near Fort Pillow, Tenn.; a Federal expedition from Island No. 10 to Tiptonville, Tenn.; and a Union expedition from Bealeton toward Thoroughfare Gap, Va.

At the White House President Lincoln was ill with varioloid, a mild form of smallpox.

November 22, Sunday

On Missionary Ridge the unsuspecting Confederates under Bragg detached Buckner's command, sending him to reinforce Longstreet, who was besieging Knoxville, Tenn. Grant changed his plans again, ordered Gen. Thomas to demonstrate next day on his front facing Missionary Ridge. The battle for Chattanooga was about to begin.

On the Texas coast Banks moved against Fort Esperanza and Matagorda Island; by the end of the month he would control the fort, the island, and the nearby area. Skirmishing broke out at Winchester, Tenn.; Fayette and Camp Davies, Miss.; near Houston, Mo.; and on Lake Borgne, La.

November 23, Monday

BATTLE OF CHATTANOOGA THROUGH NOVEMBER 25.

Gen. George H. Thomas' Army of the Cumberland moved forward, with two divisions from Fort Wood, toward Orchard Knob, a Confederate-held eminence about a mile in front of the main enemy position on Missionary Ridge. It marked the first attempt by Grant to break the siege of Chattanooga completely and hit Bragg's Army of Tennessee. The divisions of Maj. Gen. Philip H. Sheridan and Brig. Gen. T. J. Wood drove out Confederates and captured Orchard Knob with few casualties. Grant now lined up his units for the primary thrust. During the night of Nov. 23–24, Sherman, north of the Tennessee, sent a brigade across the river near South Chickamauga Creek to make a foothold and prepare a bridge.

At Knoxville both Federal and Confederate troops tried limited assaults on the siege and besieged lines. The Federals were only partially successful against an enemy parallel and the Confederates drove in Union pickets. Far to the south, skirmishes erupted at Cedar Bayou in the Rio Grande operations, Tex.; and at Bayou Portage on Grand Lake in the lengthy Louisiana Teche operations. Until Dec. 18 Federal expeditions moved from Springfield to Howell, Wright, and Morgan counties, Mo.

In Washington an ailing Lincoln wondered whether or not Burnside could hold Knoxville.

November 24, Tuesday

BATTLE OF LOOKOUT MOUNTAIN, TENNESSEE.

Three Federal divisions under Joseph Hooker crossed Lookout Creek in the morning and began the difficult climb up Lookout Mountain, hoping to drive the sparse Confederate defenders from the heights. The Confederates offered major resistance at Cravens' Farm, a bench of fairly level land on the mountainside. Heavy fog enshrouded the crest from view of the Federals in Chattanooga. By the end of the day the Federals held Lookout Mountain and the Confederates had withdrawn to Missionary Ridge. Although there was no fighting on the mountaintop, the engagement became known as the "Battle Above the Clouds," a misnomer caused by the fog banks. Losses were small and fighting relatively light, but the drive did clear the way for the primary effort against Missionary Ridge. At the foot of Missionary Ridge near the Tennessee, Sherman seized what he thought was the north end of the ridge, only to find that a wide ravine separated him from the main part of Missionary Ridge and Tunnel Hill, site of an important railroad tunnel. But the attack did reveal to the Confederates one direction of the Northern drive.

Action at Kingston, Tenn., marked the Knoxville Campaign. Elsewhere, action occurred at and near Sparta, Tenn.; Woodville and Little Boston, Va.; Cunningham's Bluff, S.C.; and Clarksville, Ark. Until the twenty-seventh troops fought during a Union raid on the East Tennessee and Georgia Railroad with skirmishing at Charleston and Cleveland, Tenn. In Missouri there were four days of Union scouts from Salem to Bushy and Pigeon creeks, Gladen Valley, and Dry Fork. Some 270 rounds fired against Fort Sumter at Charleston left 3 killed and 2 wounded.

Gov. Zebulon Vance of North Carolina told his legislature, "We know, at last, precisely what we would get by submission, and therein has our enemy done us good service—abolition of slavery, confiscation of property, and territorial vassalage." The Richmond *Examiner* proclaimed, "Our sole policy and cunningest diplomacy is fighting; our most insinuating negotiator is the Confederate army in line of battle."

November 25, Wednesday

BATTLE OF MISSIONARY RIDGE.

Gen. U. S. Grant ordered Sherman to move against Tunnel Hill and the north end of Missionary Ridge. Hooker was to move from Lookout Mountain to try to cut off a Confederate retreat into Georgia or to follow the enemy. Thomas was to move in the center when Sherman reached the ridge. On the ridge itself the Confederates were strongly dug in but weakened by the loss of Longstreet and other troops. Soon after sunrise Sherman attacked, but without success, as Gen. Patrick Cleburne's men stubbornly resisted. Heavy fighting continued until midafternoon with Sherman making little or no progress. The Confederates still held Missionary Ridge. Hooker, too, ran into difficulties because the bridge over Chattanooga Creek was burned and it was late afternoon before his men ascended the southern end of Missionary Ridge. That left only Thomas in the center.

In the afternoon Grant ordered Thomas to move toward the lower Confederate breastworks near the foot of steep, ravine-broken Missionary Ridge. Four Federal divisions overwhelmed the emplacements on the lower slopes and charged on up the two hundred to four hundred feet of rock- and bush-incrusted incline. Confederates on top could not fire readily for fear of hitting their own retreating men. There is argument even yet whether it was a spontaneous advance after taking the first position or simply the result of somewhat confusing orders. At any rate, it was done. With the Confederate line on Missionary Ridge cut in several places, Bragg's beaten army staggered back toward Chickamauga Creek. Sheridan's division pursued, but Confederate Gen. Hardee held firmly before withdrawing in the darkness. Cleburne's division also covered the retreat. The Confederate army crossed Chickamauga Creek during the night. Though badly defeated, Bragg had rescued most of his army. Grant issued orders for the follow-up. Chattanooga and the surrounding area were now entirely in Union hands. Yankees screamed, "Chickamauga! Chickamauga!" as they won their revenge.

Despite the sometimes desperate fighting on Missionary Ridge, casualties were relatively low for a major battle: Federal engaged are put at more than 56,000 (and others available), with 753 killed, 4722 wounded, and 349 missing for a total of 5824; Confederate engaged around 46,000, with 361 killed, 2160 wounded, and 4146 missing for a total of 6667, many of these prisoners. The road into Georgia was at least partially opened for the Federals.

There remained the siege lines at Knoxville, where Burnside was daily becoming more hard pressed. On this day and the twenty-sixth, 517 rounds were thrown against Sumter at Charleston. Skirmishes broke out in Crawford County, Ark.; near Houston on the Big Piney and near Waynesville and Farmington, Mo.; at Camp Pratt and near Vermillion Bayou, La.; Sangster's Station, Va.; Greenville, N.C.; and Yankeetown, Tenn. From Britain the unfinished C.S.S. *Rappahannock* sailed to France to avoid probable detention by the British.

November 26, Thursday

MINE RUN, VIRGINIA, CAMPAIGN BEGINS.

The major fight for Chattanooga was over, but Sherman and Thomas pursued Bragg through Chickamauga Station toward Graysville and Ringgold. The Federals ran into Cleburne's rear guard near Ringgold, and engaged in fairly severe fighting at Chickamauga Station, Pea Vine Valley, and Pigeon Hill, Tenn., and Graysville, Ga. Then the Federals halted and Bragg pulled together his wounded army. At Knoxville Longstreet was preparing an assault.

The front on the Rapidan in Virginia was coming to life. Gen. George Gordon Meade and the Army of the Potomac crossed the Rapidan, attempting to turn Lee's right flank and carry out the oft-repeated urgings from Washington to take offensive action. Skirmishing flared at and near Raccoon Ford and Morton's Ford, as Lee's outposts carried the word to the Army of Northern Virginia. Meade had hoped to maneuver Lee out of his position and to force him to fall back toward Richmond. Again it was a campaign of marching and maneuver. Meade had some 85,000 troops to Lee's 48,500.

In other action there was skirmishing near Woodson, Mo.; Brentsville, Va.; Plymouth and Warm Springs, N.C.; as well as a Union scout from Columbia, Ky., to the south side of the Cumberland River.

President Lincoln was still confined to his room with varioloid.

November 27, Friday

South of the Rapidan, Lee moved quickly eastward to block Meade's new offensive. There was skirmishing at Payne's Farm, Robertson's Tavern or Locust Grove, action near New Hope Church, and near Wilderness Church. Meade headed toward the small valley of Mine Run, and Lee strongly posted the Army of Northern Virginia. Meade blamed Maj. Gen. William Henry French for delaying attack this day and later termed it a major factor in the failure of the campaign. French's corps took the wrong road and ran into Early. Fighting also occurred at Catlett's Station, Va.

In the West fighting at Ringgold Gap and Taylor's Ridge, Ga., wound up the Chattanooga Campaign. Kentucky saw skirmishing at Monticello and La Fayette. Some 280 rounds were fired at Fort Sumter in Charleston Harbor. At Columbus, O., Gen. John Hunt Morgan and several of his officers escaped from the Ohio State Penitentiary and managed to reach Confederate territory. Presumably they tunneled their way from the cell-block and then got over a wall, but for years there have been rumors that the tunnel was a blind and that money actually changed hands. Grant ordered two divisions under Gordon Granger to rush to the relief of Burnside, besieged by Longstreet in Knoxville.

President Davis, greatly perturbed over Tennessee, advised Bragg to concentrate rapidly, an almost impossible thing to do under the new circumstances.

November 28, Saturday

In Virginia Meade probed the strong Confederate positions along Mine Run, with considerable skirmishing. There were more delays because the

Federals could not find a spot for a major assault. It was already becoming clear that Lee had halted the Union offensive before it really started.

In the West Sherman and more troops were ordered, along with Granger, to hurry to Burnside at Knoxville. Gen. Bragg telegraphed Richmond from Dalton, Ga., "I deem it due to the cause and to myself to ask for relief from command and investigation into the causes of the defeat."

A skirmish took place near Molino, Miss. Operations against the Memphis and Charleston Railroad in west Tennessee by Forrest's men lasted until Dec. 10.

Between Nov. 28 and Dec. 4 a total of 1307 shot and shell were fired at Sumter and surrounding batteries around Charleston. Still there was no sign of surrender or evacuation.

November 29, Sunday

CONFEDERATE ASSAULT ON FORT SANDERS, TENNESSEE.

In the early dawn Confederates of Gen. Longstreet's command drove at Fort Sanders or Fort Loudon near Knoxville, attempting to break Burnside's defense lines and take the city before Federal reinforcements could arrive. Against the earthworks the Confederates hurled themselves over the frozen and sleet-covered ground. For a time the Southrons had their flag on the parapet of the fort, but eventually they were forced to withdraw. It was Longstreet's last major attempt to penetrate Knoxville. Knowing that Grant was sending reinforcements after the defeat of Bragg, there was little to do but retreat toward Virginia, which he did early in December. Longstreet has often been criticized both for the assault and for the manner in which it was conducted.

In the Mine Run Campaign of Virginia action broke out at Parker's Store and New Hope Church as Meade, preparing an assault, sought fruitlessly for a weak spot in Lee's defensive line. Skirmishing occurred also at Brentsville and near Jonesville, Va., and at Bloomfield, Mo.

President Lincoln was reported much better following his bout with a mile form of smallpox.

November 30, Monday

BRAGG'S RESIGNATION ACCEPTED.

Although it would be another day before Meade gave up along Mine Run in Virginia and retired across the Rapidan, it was becoming clear that his offensive never would get under way. Corps commander Warren called off an attack because of Lee's position. Skirmishing continued along the Mine Run lines and at Raccoon Ford, as well as at Licking Run Bridge, Va.

Elsewhere, action included affairs at Charleston and Yankeetown, Tenn.; and skirmishes at Salyersville, Ky.; and Port Hudson and Vermillion

Bayou, La. Federal troops moved into Fort Esperanza in Matagorda Bay, Tex. Confederates had evacuated the night before, after skirmishing and siege operations.

In northwest Georgia Bragg gathered together his defeated army and Grant solidified his position around Chattanooga while sending many of his men toward beleaguered Knoxville, Tenn. From Richmond Gen. Samuel Cooper wired Bragg at Dalton, Ga., ". . . Your request to be relieved has been submitted to the President, who, upon your representation, directs me to notify you that you are relieved from command, which you will transfer to Lieutenant-General Hardee. . . ."

DECEMBER, 1863

As the principal fighting of the fall ended, the military and political leaders and the citizens of both sides could take a quieter look at things as they were and were likely to be. On the military fronts the balance tipped toward the Federal side. In Virginia Meade's Mine Run Campaign had failed but he still threatened Lee. At Charleston the fantastic bombardment of Fort Sumter had not achieved its purpose but it still continued. At Knoxville Federals were holding against Longstreet and it was clear that Confederates would soon have to give up their siege. At Chattanooga Grant began building a base for future operations into Georgia in the face of an embittered and tangled Confederate command setup that offered little hope for anything more than continued defense. In the West operations were on a much smaller scale, with Confederates mounting only guerrilla and hit-and-run operations. Many asked whether the South could hold out long enough to exhaust the North or win the daydream of foreign recognition. Politics came to the fore in the North; 1864 was a presidential election year. The people of both sides looked back over the bloody events of 1863 and forward to an uncertain 1864.

December 1, Tuesday

In Virginia Meade gave up trying to penetrate Lee's Confederate line along Mine Run and the Army of the Potomac began retiring across the Rapidan before going into winter quarters.

A major command change was evolving in the Confederate army at Dalton, Ga., south of Chattanooga. After Davis accepted Gen. Braxton Bragg's resignation, Bragg told Richmond he would relinquish his command on the second. He then wrote Davis of the criticism against him by his generals and said, "The disaster admits of no palliation, and is justly disparaging to me as a commander. . . . I fear we both erred in the conclusion for me to retain command here after the clamor raised against me." Bragg had at times proved himself an able soldier, but unable to work with his subordinates. For years to come the quarrels, charges, and countercharges would echo.

December opened with considerable, if not major, fighting. Fort Sumter was surviving another bombardment which began Nov. 28. At Maynardville, Tenn., another fight marked the Knoxville Campaign; Longstreet still besieged Burnside's Federals, but knew Federal reinforcements were on the way. In Arkansas skirmishing took place near Benton and Devall's Bluff; in North Carolina at Cedar Point; in Virginia near Jonesville and at Jenning's Farm near Ely's Ford; in Kentucky at Salyersville, Mount Sterling, and Jackson; and in Mississippi at Ripley. Federals scouted around Pulaski, Tenn., and operated about Natchez, Miss., for ten days.

Suffering from typhoid, Belle Boyd, Confederate spy, was released from prison in Washington, sent to Richmond, and told to stay out of Union lines.

December 2, Wednesday

The Army of the Potomac was completing its withdrawal to north of the Rapidan in Virginia, abandoning the abortive Mine Run Campaign. Longstreet was now being threatened from the rear by fast-approaching Federal troops intent on breaking the siege of Knoxville. Still the guns bellowed in Charleston Harbor against Fort Sumter. Elsewhere, fighting broke out at Walker's Ford on the Clinch River, and there was a Confederate descent on Saulsbury and a skirmish at Philadelphia, Tenn. In Arkansas Federals scouted through the seventh from Waldron to Mount Ida, Caddo Gap, and Dallas.

Gen. Braxton Bragg turned over the command of the Army of Tennessee to Lieut. Gen. William Hardee at Dalton, Ga. Hardee, however, would be only temporarily in charge of the army that had been beaten back from Chattanooga. Bragg reminded the army of his two-year association with it and called for support of the new commander. He advised President Davis that the army should assume the offensive. Many of Bragg's chief officers were glad to see him go. Although the Confederates were losing a fine disciplinarian and a dedicated soldier, he was also a man under whom few could operate successfully.

December 3, Thursday

From Knoxville, Tenn., Longstreet began moving his army east and north toward Greeneville, where he later took up winter quarters at a position enabling him to move either to Virginia and Lee's army, or to take offensive action in the West. The withdrawal marked the end of the fall campaign in Tennessee, a full-scale Federal victory. In east Tennessee a skirmish occurred at Log Mountain; and elsewhere fighting broke out at Saint Martinsville, La.; Ellis' Ford, Va.; Greenville, Ky.; and Wolf River Bridge near Moscow, Tenn.

December 4, Friday

As Longstreet pulled out of Knoxville, under pressure from Federal reinforcements, and retreated eastward in Tennessee, skirmishing flared near Kingston and Loudon. Skirmishing also occurred at Niobrara, Neb. Terr.; Meadow Bluff, W. Va.; La Fayette, Tenn.; and Ripley, Miss. At Charleston seven days of bombardment ended after 1307 rounds fired by the Union.

December 5, Saturday

Fighting took place at Walker's Ford on Clinch River, Tenn., as Longstreet continued toward Greeneville. Other action occurred at Murrell's Inlet, S.C.; Raccoon Ford, Va.; and Crab Gap, Tenn. A Union scout operated from New Berne toward Kinston, N.C., and a reconnaissance by Federals from Rossville to Ringgold, Ga. In other operations there was Federal reconnaissance Dec. 5–13 from Little Rock to Princeton, Ark.; Dec. 5–25 from Norfolk, Va., to South Mills and Camden Court House, N.C.; and scouts Dec. 5–10 from Columbia, Ky. Only sixty-one shells were fired in Charleston Harbor after the second great bombardment ended the day before. A Federal small-boat expedition to Murrell's Inlet, S.C., failed.

December 6, Sunday

Gen. William T. Sherman and his staff entered Knoxville, Tenn., formally ending the siege of Burnside's Federal troops. His troops were not far behind. Meanwhile, Longstreet's Confederates were moving toward Greeneville, Tenn. Fighting broke out near Fayetteville and Clinch Mountain, Tenn. Elsewhere a skirmish took place on the Cheat River, W. Va. In Charleston Harbor the monitor *Weehawken* sank at her anchorage near Morris Island because of imperfect design.

President Davis considered sending Lee to Dalton, Ga., to help reorganize the Army of Tennessee.

December 7, Monday

CONGRESS MEETS—AT WASHINGTON AND RICHMOND.

In Washington the first session of the Thirty-eighth Congress convened, and in Richmond the fourth session of the First Congress. President Davis in his message to Congress wrote of the "grave reverses" of the past summer, but stated the progress of the enemy "has been checked." There had been no improvement in foreign relations; finances demanded attention; no effort must be spared to augment the Army; it was regrettable that the enemy had refused to exchange prisoners of war; the

Trans-Mississippi, virtually cut off from the rest of the Confederacy, had special problems. Davis concluded by condemning the "savage ferocity" of the Federals, and added, "Nor has less unrelenting warfare been waged by these pretended friends of human rights and liberties against the unfortunate negroes. . . . The hope last year entertained of an early termination of the war has not been realized, . . . [but] The patriotism of the people has proved equal to every sacrifice demanded by their country's need."

Fighting was confined to Rutledge and Eagleville, Tenn., and Independence, Miss. A four-day Federal scout operated in Hampshire, Hardy, Frederick, and Shenandoah counties of West Virginia.

December 8, Tuesday

LINCOLN PROCLAIMS AMNESTY AND RECONSTRUCTION; MESSAGE TO CONGRESS.

President Lincoln issued his Proclamation of Amnesty and Reconstruction, pardoning those who "directly or by implication, participated in the existing rebellion" if they took an oath to the Union. Exceptions included high-ranking military officers, members of the Confederate government, all who resigned commissions in the U. S. Army and Navy to join the Confederacy, and those who treated Negroes or whites "otherwise than lawfully as prisoners of war." If at least one tenth of the citizens who voted in the election of 1860 so wished, a state government would be recognized in any seceded state. Of course, said citizens must take an oath to support the United States, and slavery would be barred. Thus Lincoln made a significant step toward reconstruction, and indicated his future course of moderation.

Lincoln also issued his annual message to Congress, read to both Houses on Dec. 9. He reported that for the most part foreign relations were peaceful and friendly; the territories were in satisfactory condition except for some Indian difficulties; the Treasury balance as of July 1 was over $5,329,000; the blockade had been increasingly efficient.

A year before, the President said, public opinion at home and abroad had not been satisfactory. "The crisis which threatened to divide the friends of the Union is past," he declared optimistically. The enemy had been pushed back, the Mississippi opened, and emancipation was having a favorable effect. Praising those fighting for the Union, Lincoln concluded that to them "the world must stand indebted for the home of freedom disenthralled, regenerated, enlarged, and perpetuated." The President also wrote a note of gratitude to Maj. Gen. Grant for the victory at Chattanooga and Knoxville.

In Richmond President Davis, apprehensive over the military situation, asked Gen. Lee to visit him. In the Confederate Congress Representative

Henry S. Foote, of Mississippi, bitterly criticized the President's military and civil policy.

Federal cavalry under Averell operated until the twenty-first from New Creek, W. Va., raiding railroads in southwestern Virginia. There were also demonstrations up the Shenandoah Valley of Virginia and from the Kanawha Valley, W. Va.

John C. Braine, leading a group of Confederate sympathizers, seized the Northern merchant steamer *Chesapeake* off Cape Cod. Federal naval vessels pursued and *Chesapeake* was captured Dec. 17 in Sambro Harbor, Nova Scotia.

December 9, Wednesday

As the Federal Congress heard President Lincoln's annual message read by the clerks, Maj. Gen. John G. Foster superseded Maj. Gen. A. E. Burnside in command of the Department of the Ohio. Burnside, criticized for his handling of the Copperhead movement and for not supporting Rosecrans at Chickamauga, had for some time wanted to leave his departmental command.

A mutiny of Negro troops at Fort Jackson, La., below New Orleans was put down by Federal white officers. It arose over alleged mistreatment by one officer of his soldiers. Skirmishes broke out at Okolona, Miss.; near Lewinsville, Va.; and there was an affair at Cumberland Mountain on the road to Crossville, Tenn. Scouting and skirmishing also occurred for several days around Bean's Station, Tenn., part of the waning Knoxville Campaign. Federals scouted from Waldron down Dutch Creek, Ark., and from Houston, Mo. As if to emphasize Lincoln's message to Congress, a blockade-runner, the English *Minna,* was taken off Charleston, just one of many captures during these months.

December 10, Thursday

Fighting flared in east Tennessee as Longstreet tried to gather his command in the Greeneville area. Skirmishing at Gatlinburg, Long Ford, Morristown, and Russellville marked the day. From Harper's Ferry Federal cavalry operated on what was called the West Virginia, Virginia, and Tennessee Railroad raid. In North Carolina a skirmish occurred at Hertford, and Federal naval and army forces destroyed Confederate salt works in Choctawatchie Bay, Fla. President Davis expressed concern over the disposition of troops for the Confederate armies. President Lincoln, increasingly active, appeared much improved in health.

December 11, Friday

A relatively light bombardment of 220 rounds at Fort Sumter in Charleston Harbor exploded a magazine, killing 11 and wounding 41.

The last bombardment of the year against Fort Sumter, it brought no sign of surrender.

The Federal West Virginia raid on railroads involved skirmishing at Big Sewell and Meadow Bluff. In Virginia skirmishing was at Marling's Bottom Bridge. Federal scouts operated for three days from Waldron to Dallas, Ark., and for a week from Pulaski, Tenn., to Florence, Ala.

Confederate Sec. of War Seddon's annual report admitted serious defeats, especially in Mississippi, and reduced military effectiveness because of desertion, straggling, and absenteeism. He recommended repeal of the substitute and exemption provisions of the draft law.

December 12, Saturday

Federals successfully attacked Gatewood's, Lewisburg, and Greenbrier River, W. Va., in the continuing cavalry raids on Confederate railroads. On the front southeast of Chattanooga there was a skirmish at La Fayette, Ga., and in the Knoxville Campaign fighting at Cheek's Cross Roads and Russellville. Action in Virginia flared at and near Strasburg and from Williamsburg to Charles City Court House.

December 13, Sunday

Skirmishing increased with action at Hurricane Bridge, W. Va.; Powell's River near Stickleyville, Strasburg, and Germantown, Va.; and in east Tennessee at Farley's Mill and Dandridge's Mill. Other fighting occurred at Ringgold, Ga., and at Meriwether's Ferry, Bayou Boeuf, Ark. Emily Todd Helm, Mrs. Lincoln's half sister and widow of slain Confederate Gen. Helm, was visiting the White House.

December 14, Monday

Gen. Longstreet attacked Federal troops at Bean's Station, Tenn. In a sharp engagement, Federals under Brig. Gen. James M. Shackelford were driven back, then made a stand, only to withdraw on Dec. 15. Other fighting in the area included the capture of a Union wagon train near Clinch Mountain Gap, and skirmishing at Granger's Mill and near Morristown. In Georgia a Federal reconnaissance moved from Rossville to La Fayette. In Arkansas skirmishing broke out at Caddo Mill; in West Virginia on Blue Sulphur Road near Meadow Bluff; and in Virginia near Catlett's Station. For most of the rest of December there were miscellaneous cavalry affairs in Virginia.

President Lincoln announced that his wife's half sister, Mrs. Ben Hardin Helm, had been granted amnesty after taking the oath to the Union, as provided by the presidential proclamation of Dec. 8.

December 15, Tuesday

Action was near Pulaski and Livingston, Tenn., and at Sangster's Station,

Va. Confederate Maj. Gen. Jubal A. Early was assigned to the Shenandoah Valley District.

December 16, Wednesday

J. E. JOHNSTON TO COMMAND ARMY OF TENNESSEE.

The Confederates announced major command changes. Gen. Joseph E. Johnston was named to command the Department and Army of Tennessee, succeeding Lieut. Gen. Hardee, who had temporarily taken over from Bragg. Gen. Polk was left with the Army of Mississippi, to which he was assigned formally on Dec. 22. Johnston had serious differences with President Davis, but Davis had little choice, and Confederates for the most part approved the decision. Johnston, at Brandon, Miss., was ordered to his new post at Dalton, Ga., leaving his old forces in Polk's charge.

Fighting included a skirmish at Salem, Va.—part of the railroad raiding; a demonstration on Fort Gibson, Indian Terr.; skirmishes near Springfield, Mo.; Free Bridge, N.C.; fighting at Upperville, Va.; and at Rutledge, Tenn. For the remainder of the month Federals operated from Fayetteville with fighting at Stroud's Store and on the Buffalo River, Ark. Brig. Gen. John Buford was named Federal major general a few hours before his death in Washington. Buford, who succumbed to typhoid, had had a brilliant career, particularly at Gettysburg. A million-dollar fire destroyed a regimental hospital, an arsenal, and a bakery at Yorktown, Va.

December 17, Thursday

President Lincoln forwarded to Congress a plan by the Freedmen's Aid Society to set up a Federal Bureau of Emancipation to assist freed Negroes; nothing came of it until the Freedmen's Bureau was established in March, 1865. Skirmishing was confined to Sangster's Station, Va., and Rodney, Miss. A Federal expedition operated from Washington to Chicoa Creek, N.C.

December 18, Friday

For some time Lincoln had been disturbed over relations between the Missouri state government and the military under Gen. Schofield. In a letter to Sec. of War Stanton the President said he believed Schofield must be relieved from command of the Department of the Missouri, but promoted to major general at the same time. He suggested Rosecrans for the command post.

Minor fighting continued with action at Bean's Station and Rutledge, Tenn.; Indiantown or Sandy Swamp, N.C.; near Culpeper, Va.; and at Sheldon's Place near Barren Fort, Indian Terr. For the rest of the month there were scattered operations in northern Mississippi and western Tennessee, and for three days Federal scouts operated against guerrillas from Vienna to Middleburg, Va. The Richmond *Dispatch* called for postponement of minor differences and criticisms of the Confederate government in view of "this decisive crisis in the national affairs." Chaplains of Lee's army met at Orange Court House, where reports indicated a "high state of religious feeling throughout the army."

December 19, Saturday

Several skirmishes in Virginia and West Virginia resulted from the long-continuing Federal raids on railroads connecting southwest Virginia and West Virginia with the seaboard area. In east Tennessee there was a skirmish at Stone's Mill. President Davis wrote Gen. Johnston, new commander of the Department of Tennessee: "The difficulties of your new position are realized and the Government will make every possible effort to aid you. . . ." In Washington the Lincolns held a reception for congressmen, other officials, and the officers of Russian warships visiting the United States. Yankee naval forces continued destruction at St. Andrew's Bay, Fla., including 290 salt works and 268 buildings in ten days.

December 20, Sunday

President Lincoln told an official of the Massachusetts Anti-Slavery Society: "I shall not attempt to retract or modify the emancipation proclamation. . . ." Federal troops scouted from Lexington, Mo.

December 21, Monday

Skirmishing was confined to Hunter's Mill, Va., and McMinnville and Clinch River, Tenn. Federal scouts operated from Rossville to La Fayette, Ga.; from Rocky Run toward Trenton, N.C.; and from Bealeton to Luray, Va.

December 22, Tuesday

Desultory fighting occurred at Cleveland, Tenn., and Fayette, Miss.; and Union scouts probed in east Tennessee.

December 23, Wednesday

Fighting broke out at Jacksonport, Ark.; Culpeper Court House, Va.; Corinth, Miss.; and Mulberry Village and Powder Springs Gap, Tenn. Action around Centreville, Mo., lasted three days. President Davis wrote Gen. Johnston, new commander of the Department of Tennessee, that he hoped the general would "soon be able to commence active operations against the enemy."

December 24, Thursday

While the major fronts in Virginia and Georgia near Chattanooga remained quiet, skirmishing flared near Germantown and in Lee County,

Va.; Rodney, Miss.; at Estenaula, Jack's Creek, Peck's House near New Market, Mossy Creek Station, and at Hays' Ferry near Dandridge, Tenn. President Lincoln wrote Maj. Gen. Banks, in command of the Department of the Gulf, "I have all the while intended you to be *master*, as well in regard to re-organizing a State government for Louisiana, as in regard to the military matters of the Department. . . ." He reassured the general that the new state government was to help, not thwart, the military authorities.

December 25, Friday

On the third Christmas Day of the war Federal gunboats operated in the Stono River, S.C., and Confederate field and siege guns sorely damaged U.S.S. *Marblehead*. There was fighting at Fort Brooke, Fla., and Federals destroyed Confederate salt works on Bear Inlet, N.C. Union cavalry under Averell reached Beverly, W. Va. In addition, Federals skirmished with Indians near Fort Gaston, Calif., and scouted from Vienna to Leesburg, Va., for three days. Shore batteries and U.S.S. *Pawnee* dueled at John's Island near Charleston.

December 26, Saturday

Despite the winter season the skirmishing went on: near Fort Gibson, Indian Terr.; at Sand Mountain, Ala.; Port Gibson, Miss.; near Fort Gaston, Calif.; and at Somerville, New Castle, and Mossy Creek, Tenn. Federals scouted for three days from Salem, Mo., and for eight days from Forsyth, Mo., to Batesville, Ark. C.S.S. *Alabama* took two prizes near the Straits of Malacca.

December 27, Sunday

President Lincoln and Sec. of War Stanton visited Confederate prisoners at Point Lookout, Md. Gen. Joseph E. Johnston assumed command of the Department of Tennessee at Dalton, Ga. Skirmishing occurred at Huntington, Collierville, Grisson's Bridge, Moscow, and Talbott's Station, all in Tennessee. In North Carolina a Federal expedition operated from Newport Barracks to Young's Cross Roads, Swansborough, and Jackson.

December 28, Monday

Confederate congressional acts abolished substitution for military service and authorized changes in the tax in kind. Other methods of increasing manpower for the Army were under consideration. Skirmishing broke out at Charleston and Calhoun, Tenn.; John's Island, S.C.; Moorefield, W. Va.; and Mount Pleasant, Miss. Federal troops operated for a number of days from Vienna to Hopewell Gap, Va., and from Nashville, Tenn., to Creelsborough, Ky., in efforts to keep down activities of Confederate guerrillas.

December 29, Tuesday
Skirmishing increased, with fighting at Waldron, Ark.; on Matagorda Peninsula, Tex.; at Coldwater, Miss.; and in Tennessee at Mossy Creek, Talbott's Station, Cleveland, and La Vergne.

December 30, Wednesday
There were skirmishes near St. Augustine, Fla., and Greenville, N.C. Gov. Z. B. Vance of North Carolina wrote President Davis of the discontent in his state: "I have concluded that it will be perhaps impossible to remove it, except by making some effort at negotiation with the enemy."

December 31, Thursday
For the last day of 1863 a skirmish in Searcy County, Ark., was the only recorded fighting. The Richmond *Examiner* reflected the opinion of many Confederates when it said, "To-day closes the gloomiest year of our struggle." Spring had seen Confederate successes in Virginia, but the Battle of Gettysburg, the loss of the Mississippi Valley, the Federal occupation of Chattanooga had disillusioned many. President Davis nominated Confederate Sen. George Davis of North Carolina as attorney general, succeeding Wade Keyes, ad interim appointee.

1864

By the third winter of the war the character of the conflict had altered and the future was more definite. As hope lessened in the South it increased somewhat in the North. The Federal war objective was clear, made so by policy and action, implemented by manpower and material supremacy. Emancipation was an irrevocable commitment. Military conquest of the Confederacy was being pursued relentlessly. The Lincoln administration faced an election, but would that really make a difference?

In the South, they felt pressed back toward their inner bastion, and the dreams of Northern collapse, foreign intervention, lifting the blockade, and dramatic military victories became more and more nebulous. No military campaigns or great battles appeared immediate, but the threat was there and many believed it was only a matter of time until disaster. The armies in Virginia, near Chattanooga and elsewhere, were quiet, but guerrilla activities and small skirmishes were almost continuous. It was a time of regrouping, reassignment of commanders, and soul-searching.

JANUARY, 1864

Since November there had been no major military action and none was in immediate prospect. In areas of the Confederacy controlled by the North reconstruction efforts began. The Federal Congress was becoming more conscious of the forthcoming elections. Routine fighting continued in many areas. The Confederacy had command problems, particularly in the West, and discontent with policies of the Davis administration increased in Richmond and throughout the remaining sections of the C.S.A.

January 1, Friday

Extreme cold swept across much of the North and South and temperatures below zero as far south as Memphis, Tenn., and Cairo, Ill., caused much suffering among the soldiers. The usual New Year's Day ceremonies took place at both White Houses.

Despite the cold skirmishing broke out at Dandridge, Tenn., and Bunker Hill, W. Va. For most of January there was only desultory firing against Fort Sumter in Charleston Harbor, S.C. Until Jan. 5 Federal cavalry saw action in Hampshire and Hardy counties, W. Va., and a four-day expedition operated against Confederate guerrillas from Bealeton to Front Royal, Va. Throughout January minor operations occurred in northeastern Arkansas with skirmishing at Lunenburg, Sylamore, and Sylamore Creek. Union action against Indians in the Humboldt District of California also continued for much of January. In Tennessee small-scale fighting between pro-Confederate elements and various Federal outposts and garrisons flared on several occasions. The Union Department of Kansas was reestablished as separate from that of Missouri.

January 2, Saturday

The Confederate Senate confirmed Sen. George Davis of North Carolina as Attorney General, succeeding Wade Keyes, who had served ad interim since September. Davis, formerly a pro-Union Whig, had eventually supported secession. In the New York market the price of gold rose steadily. There was a light skirmish at LaGrange, Tenn. Off Los Angeles, Calif., Federal troops occupied Santa Catalina Island, driving out squatters and possible smugglers.

January 3, Sunday

Union cavalry entered Jonesville, in southwestern Virginia, driving out Confederates. However, on the fifth the Confederates returned and after a severe fight the Federals surrendered over two hundred men. Farther north Federals carried out a reconnaissance from Charles Town, W. Va., to Winchester, Va. Another Northern scout operated from Memphis toward Hernando, Miss. Maj. Gen. Francis J. Herron assumed command of Union forces on the Rio Grande.

January 4, Monday

President Davis, endeavoring to obtain food supplies for the Army of Northern Virginia, said to Gen. Lee, "The emergency justifies impressment. . . ." A minor affair occurred at Lockwood's Folly Inlet, N.C. For about ten days Federals operated around Sparta, Tenn.

January 5, Tuesday

President Lincoln suggested to Congress that bounties to volunteers be continued for at least a month and that the subject be reconsidered despite a resolution of Congress prohibiting the payment of the $300. The fighting continued to be of little significance, with skirmishes at Lawrence's Mill, Tenn., and on the Pecos River near Fort Sumner, N. Mex. Terr.

January 6, Wednesday

Confederate guerrillas attacked the steamer *Delta* on the Mississippi, one of numerous such incidents occurring on the Western rivers. Skirmishes took place at Flint Hill, Va., and at Dalton, Ga., both areas where the major armies remained at rest. Until near the end of the month Federal troops under Kit Carson operated against the Navajo Indians from Fort Canby, N. Mex. Terr., to the Cañon de Chelly area. Many Navajos were sent to a reservation at Bosque Redondo in a sad condition.

January 7, Thursday

On Waccamaw Neck, S.C., near Charleston, a lieutenant and a private of the Twenty-first Georgia Cavalry captured twenty-five Federals. Other fighting occurred at Martin's Creek, Ark., and Warrenton, Va. The Confederacy named William Preston as envoy to Mexico. Federal Judge Caleb Blood Smith, Secretary of the Interior in Lincoln's Cabinet until December, 1862, died in Indianapolis, Ind.

President Lincoln commuted the death sentence in the case of another deserter "because I am trying to evade the butchering business lately." The day before, President Davis had suspended execution of a Virginia private.

January 8, Friday

In New Orleans pro-Union elements convened to consider reconstruction of Louisiana. David O. Dodd, convicted as a Confederate spy, was executed in Little Rock, Ark., in a case which aroused considerable agitation. In Richmond a reception honored John Hunt Morgan, the Western raider. President Davis wrote Gov. Zebulon B. Vance of North Carolina regarding discontent in the state, "I cannot see how the mere material obstacles are to be surmounted" in order to bring about a cessation of hostilities. Repeating his desire for peace with independence, Davis added, "this struggle must continue until the enemy is beaten out of his vain confidence in our sub-jugation. Then and not until then will it be possible to treat of peace."

Action occurred at Moorefield Junction, W. Va. Federals bombarded Confederate works at the mouth of Caney Bayou, Tex., Jan. 8–9.

January 9, Saturday

President Davis warned his commanders in Alabama, Georgia, and Mississippi of reports that Adm. Farragut was preparing to attack Mobile and attempt to pass the forts as he had at New Orleans. A skirmish at Terman's Ferry, Ky., was the only recorded military operation.

January 10, Sunday

Federal cavalry under William Sooy Smith operated from Memphis to Meridian, Miss., until Jan. 25, when they were finally driven back by Forrest and his men. Other action included a skirmish at Mossy Creek and a two-day Federal scout from near Dandridge to Clark's Ferry, Tenn.; a skirmish at Loudoun Heights and a Federal scout to Sperryville, Va.; plus skirmishing at Petersburg, W. Va.; and King's River, Ark.

Off the south Atlantic coast the blockade was tighter than ever, with numerous blockade-runners captured by the Federals. But blockader U.S.S. *Iron Age* was lost off Lockwood's Folly Inlet, S.C., after it went aground and was bombarded from land.

January 11, Monday

Sen. John B. Henderson of Missouri proposed a joint resolution in the U. S. Senate abolishing slavery throughout the United States by amendment (the Thirteenth) to the Constitution. Two blockade-runners were captured off Florida and two others forced ashore and burned off Lockwood's Folly Inlet, N.C. Federals scouted near Lexington, and a two-day Union expedition operated from Maryville up the Little Tennessee River, Tenn.

January 12, Tuesday

Skirmishing increased toward mid-January but still there was no large-scale fighting. Action took place near Mossy Creek, Tenn.; Marshall, Ky.;

Accotink, Ellis' Ford and a Federal raid operated on Northern Neck, Va. A two-day affair occurred at Matamoros, Mexico, where two Mexican factions were warring and Federal troops were sent in to protect and remove the U. S. Consul, L. Pierce.

January 13, Wednesday

President Davis told Gen. Joseph E. Johnston at Dalton, Ga., that for the army to fall back would be so detrimental, both militarily and politically, that "I trust you will not deem it necessary to adopt such a measure." President Lincoln told Gen. Banks at New Orleans to "proceed with all possible despatch" in constructing a free state government for Louisiana; he also urged Maj. Gen. Quincy A. Gillmore to cooperate in reconstructing a loyal government for Florida.

Skirmishes erupted at Ragland Mills, Bath County, Ky.; near Collierville, Tenn.; near Ely's Ford, Va.; at Sevierville and Shultz' Mill, Cosby Creek, Tenn., Jan. 13–14. A two-day Federal scout probed from Pine Bluff to Monticello, Ark.

January 14, Thursday

Watching affairs in the West, President Davis told Gen. Johnston that, if necessary, troops should be sent to Mobile or north Mississippi. Johnston was to advise Davis as to the proper course. Fighting occurred at Dandridge and Middleton, Tenn.; Shoal Creek, Ala.; and Bollinger County of Missouri. Union scouts operated from Collierville, Tenn., and to Baldwin's Ferry, Big Black River, Miss.

January 15, Friday

Southern newspapers in January tried to build up Confederate spirits and gird the people for the struggle sure to come. Mr. Lincoln paid more and more attention to reconstruction in individual states. Fighting was confined to a skirmish near Petersburg, W. Va. There was Federal scouting in Jackson County, Mo.

January 16, Saturday

A fairly severe two-day engagement between cavalry units was fought at and near Dandridge, Tenn., with considerable casualties. Eventually the Federals withdrew toward Strawberry Plains. Other fighting occurred in White County, Tenn.; Oak Ridge, Miss.; and near Turkey Creek, Va. Until the middle of February sporadic operations took place in northwestern Arkansas. Federal Maj. Gen. Samuel R. Curtis assumed command of the reestablished Department of Kansas.

January 17, Sunday

Federals scouted from Brownsville, and skirmishing occurred at Lewisburg, Ark., and at Ellis' and Ely's fords, Va. A fire killed two officers in their quarters at Camp Butler, Springfield, Ill., and destroyed quantities of quartermaster's supplies.

January 18, Monday

Substantial opposition to the Confederate conscription law continued to develop in western North Carolina, and protest meetings were held throughout the winter. Federals skirmished with Confederate guerrillas at Grand Gulf, Miss. Union pickets drove off Confederates in an affair at Flint Hill, Va.

January 19, Tuesday

The Arkansas pro-Union Constitutional Convention at Little Rock adopted an anti-slavery measure. The new constitution was ratified by popular vote March 14. Skirmishes took place at Branchville, Ark., and at Big Springs near Tazewell in east Tennessee. Federal scouts from Williamsburg, Va., lasted several days. In Washington the Administration continued to be concerned over the problem of cotton trading with people in Confederate territory.

January 20, Wednesday

Federal naval vessels made a reconnaissance of Forts Morgan and Gaines at the mouth of Mobile Bay. For some time Grant and others had urged an attack on Mobile, and Confederates feared such an effort. Skirmishing broke out at Tracy City, Tenn., and Island No. 76 on the Mississippi. For ten days there were minor operations in the District of North Carolina.

President Lincoln suspended five scheduled army executions. The President also told Gen. Frederick Steele, commanding in Arkansas, that in view of the proposed anti-slavery state constitution, an election should be ordered at once.

January 21, Thursday

Indicative of the trend in many areas of the occupied Confederacy, pro-Northern citizens of Tennessee met at Nashville and proposed a constitutional convention and abolition of slavery. Limited military action included skirmishing at Strawberry Plains and Armstrong's Ferry, Tenn., Jan. 21–22; a scout from Chattanooga by Federals to Harrison and Ooltewah, Tenn.; other Union scouting from Rossville toward Dalton, Ga., and the Confederate lines, Jan. 21–23; five days of reconnaissance by Federals on the Matagorda Peninsula, Tex.; and five days of Yankee scouting in Arkansas from Waldron to Baker's Springs. Distillation of whisky was forbidden in the Federal Department of the Ohio, due to the scarcity of grain.

January 22, Friday

In an important shake-up Maj. Gen. Rosecrans was named commander of the Federal Department of the Missouri, replacing Maj. Gen. J. M. Schofield. Schofield, replaced because of the political uproar between moderate and radical Union men, soon took over the Department of the Ohio.

Isaac Murphy was inaugurated provisional governor of Arkansas in the restored pro-Union government, pending elections in the spring. He had been chosen by the State Convention. President Lincoln told an Arkansas delegation to Washington that he would not appoint a separate military governor but would leave administration to Gen. Steele, now in command of the state, until the new state government could be set up.

In military operations some Federal forage wagons were captured near Wilsonville, Tenn. Fighting occurred at Germantown and Ellis' Ford, Va.; Subligna, Ga.; and at Clear Creek and Tomahawk in operations in northwest Arkansas.

January 23, Saturday

President Lincoln approved a policy whereby plantation owners would recognize the freedom of their former slaves and hire them by fair contracts in order "to re-commence the cultivation of their plantations." He urged the military authorities to support such a free-labor system. The Treasury Department annulled most restrictions upon trade in Kentucky and Missouri. Minor fighting increased somewhat, with a skirmish near Newport, Tenn.; an affair near Woodville, Ala.; a Union scout from La Grange, Tenn., to Ripley, Miss.; an affair at Cowskin Bottom, Indian Terr.; a four-day Federal scout from Patterson, Mo., to Cherokee Bay, Ark.; an affair at Bailey's on Crooked Creek, with skirmishing on Rolling Prairie in northwest Ark.; and a Union scout from Charles Town, W. Va., to Woodstock, Va., until the twenty-fifth.

January 24, Sunday

While the principal fronts remained quiet, small fights and guerrilla depredations continued. Operations took place near Natchez, Miss.; Confederates captured some Union pickets at Love's Hill near Knoxville, Tenn.; and a skirmish flared at Tazewell, Tenn. Federals undertook a two-day expedition up the James River in Virginia.

January 25, Monday

Union forces evacuated Corinth, Miss., in a move to consolidate their occupation points in the West. Skirmishing occurred at La Grange, Tenn.; Mount Pleasant, Miss.; Bainbridge Ferry and near the Sweet Water, northern Alabama; on the Little Missouri River and at Sulphur Springs, Ark.

To Feb. 5 a Federal expedition operated from Scottsborough, Ala., toward Rome, Ga. In Florida an affair took place at Bayou Grand.

In Charleston, as the intermittent firing on Fort Sumter continued, the *Courier* said, "The whizzing of shells overhead has become a matter of so little interest as to excite scarcely any attention from passers-by." Fire destroyed Confederate hospital buildings at Camp Winder near Richmond.

January 26, Tuesday
President Lincoln officially approved new trade regulations for dealing with former Confederate territory and for so-called "trading with the enemy." Mr. Lincoln ordered suspension of execution in nine cases. In Tennessee skirmishing erupted near Knoxville and at Sevierville; in northern Alabama at Athens; and in Arkansas at Caddo Gap. An affair occurred in the San Andres Mountains, N. Mex. Terr.

January 27, Wednesday
President Davis asked Gen. Braxton Bragg to come to Richmond from Montgomery, Ala., if his health permitted. President Lincoln told Gen. Steele in Arkansas that Steele and the civilian authorities could handle details of the new Arkansas government so long as the free state constitution provisions were retained.

Fighting included action at Fair Gardens or Kelly's Ford, and near Knoxville, Tenn.; on the Cumberland River, Ky.; near Thoroughfare Mountain, Va.; and forays until Feb. 7 in Hampshire and Hardy counties, W. Va.

January 28, Thursday
There were operations around New Berne, N.C., to Feb. 10; a skirmish at Dallas, Ark.; an affair at Lee's House on Cornersville Pike, Tenn.; and skirmishes near Jonesville, Va.

January 29, Friday
Cavalry skirmished at Medley, W. Va. Confederates attacked the steamer *Sir William Wallace* on the Mississippi, an example of their continuous harassment of Union shipping. Skirmishes flared near Cobb's Mill, northern Alabama, and near Benn's Church and Smithfield, Va. An affair occurred near Gloucester Court House, Va. Jan. 29–Feb. 23 a Federal cleanup expedition operated from Vicksburg to Waterproof, La. Bombardment at Charleston intensified Jan. 29–31 with 583 rounds fired. The Confederates added a new ironclad, *Charleston*, to their defenses.

January 30, Saturday
Maj. Gen. William S. Rosecrans superseded Maj. Gen. John M. Schofield in command of the Federal Department of the Missouri and Maj. Gen.

Frederick Steele assumed full command of the Department of Arkansas. Action included skirmishing at Chickamauga Creek, Ga.; Windsor, N.C.; Medley, W. Va.; and a Union scout from Culpeper to Madison Court House, Va. In Arkansas Federals scouted for five days from Batesville to near Searcy Landing.

January 31, Sunday

President Lincoln told Gen. Banks in New Orleans that he was "at liberty to adopt any rule which shall admit to vote any unquestionably loyal free state men and none others. And yet I do wish they would all take the oath." Troops fought an engagement at Smithfield, where Federals threatened Virginia from south of the James. A Union reconnaissance probed near Madison Court House; another from Maryville, Tenn., to Quallatown, N.C., lasted until Feb. 7.

FEBRUARY, 1864

Despite a seeming stalemate, a nasty war was developing further. This was the increase of small patrols, guerrilla activities, desperate forays, and sniping at river vessels. The blockade squeezed its garrote relentlessly around the Southern coastline. Politically, in the North, as the conventions and election drew nearer, the mutterings of various groups from peace advocates to Radical Republicans increased. Lincoln's government was trying to think clearly of reconstruction, one of the imperatives of the apparent forthcoming victory and the present occupation of Confederate territory. Davis' government concentrated on fathering enough strength to defend its shrinking core of territory, to hold its people, and somehow to rouse languishing hopes. Events would pick up a little in the weeks to come, but it would be spring before the armies once more marched en masse. In the meantime the occasional ennui of nations at war had temporarily taken control of both peoples.

February 1, Monday

President Lincoln, acting under the congressional conscription act, ordered that 500,000 men be drafted on March 10 to serve for three years or for the duration of the war. Further, the President ordered Sec. of War Stanton to send a transport to Île à Vache on the coast of San Domingo to bring back Negro colonists who desired to return. The decision reflected further frustration in Lincoln's plans for colonization of Negroes. The U. S. House passed a measure reviving the rank of lieutenant general, after some debate. Congress obviously had Gen. Grant in mind for the promotion.

Confederate troops under Pickett moved from Kinston toward New Berne, N.C., in an effort to recapture the important Federal base. Fighting along Batchelder's Creek marked the beginning of the attack. Brig. Gen. I. N. Palmer withdrew portions of his command to the inner defenses, which the Confederates did not assault. About midnight Pickett began to withdraw.

Throughout most of February Federals fired sporadically on Fort Sumter. In Virginia a skirmish flared at Bristoe Station, and an army gunboat sank near Smithfield during an abortive Federal expedition. Another skirmish broke out at Waldron, Ark. A number of Union scouts and reconnaissances got under way. These included four days of operations around Madisonville to Franklinton, La.; month-long expeditions in the Indian Territory; a week of reconnoitering in New Mexico and Arizona territories; scouts from Rolla, Mo.; reconnaissance from Maryville toward Sevierville, Tenn.; a week of scouting in White and Putnam counties, Tenn.; and an expedition from Knoxville to Flat Creek, Tenn.; all were by Union forces. Until June 30 Federal troops operated against Indians in the Humboldt Military District of California.

February 2, Tuesday

Confederate navy men in small boats captured the U.S. gunboat *Underwriter* in the Neuse River near New Berne, N.C., but were forced to set fire to her and flee. Near Beaufort, N.C., fighting occurred at Gale's Creek, Bogue Sound Blockhouse, and Newport Barracks, as Federals drew in their defenses. No further attack was made by Confederates either at New Berne or Beaufort.

Skirmishes took place in Tennessee near La Grange, scene of much small action; in Alabama at Whitesburg; in Virginia at Strasburg; and in Missouri on Halcolm Island. Brig. Gen. George A. Custer's Federal cavalry remained active, primarily in Albemarle County, Va. Off Charleston the Federal fleet destroyed a British blockade-runner. In Chattanooga 129 Confederate deserters took the oath of allegiance to the United States.

February 3, Wednesday

SHERMAN'S MERIDIAN, MISSISSIPPI, CAMPAIGN BEGINS.

With over 26,000 men, Maj. Gen. W. T. Sherman left Vicksburg, Miss., on an expedition to destroy Confederate-held railroads in the state and to damage the enemy in and about Meridian. Cooperating with Sherman were some 7600 cavalry from Memphis under William Sooy Smith, who was delayed in starting. Confederates in Mississippi, under Gen. Leonidas Polk, were scattered and numbered roughly 20,000. In a light action at Liverpool Heights on the Yazoo River, Federal gunboats silenced enemy batteries. In Louisiana a Union expedition operated from Brashear City

Feb. 3–6; and on the Kanawha River of West Virginia, Confederates captured the steamer *Levi*.

President Davis called the attention of the Confederate Congress to the fact that "discontent, disaffection, and disloyalty" were often manifested among those who "have enjoyed quiet and safety at home." He recommended suspension of the privilege of the writ of habeas corpus as a "sharp remedy" but one necessary to combat the evils of spying, desertion, associating with the enemy, and disloyal gatherings and activities.

February 4, Thursday

Skirmishing became heavier as Sherman's men advanced from Vicksburg through the old battlefields of 1863. As Polk's Confederates fell back before the invaders fighting broke out at Liverpool Heights, Champion's Hill, Edwards' Ferry, and near Bolton Depot in what became the Meridian Campaign. Elsewhere, action occurred at Moorefield, W. Va.; Columbia, La.; and Hot Springs, Mountain Fork, and Rolling Prairie, Ark. A five-day Federal expedition moved from Helena up the White River in Arkansas.

February 5, Friday

After what was described as a continued skirmish for eighteen miles, Sherman's Federals marched into Jackson, Miss., en route to Meridian. Opposed mainly by cavalry, they fought on Baker's Creek, at Clinton, and at Jackson. In Virginia there was a skirmish near Aldie and another affair at Winchester. In Missouri action included a skirmish near Cape Girardeau and a thirteen-day Federal scout from Houston into Arkansas. Also in Arkansas a skirmish occurred on Crooked Creek. Federal Brig. Gen. Truman Seymour, ordered to move from Hilton Head, S.C., to Jacksonville, Fla., and proceed inland, immediately got the expedition under way.

February 6, Saturday

Federal troops under Sherman left Jackson, Miss., and headed for Meridian; the cooperating column under William Sooy Smith departed Memphis. Union foragers fought a skirmish at Bolivar, Tenn.; and a skirmish also broke out at Hillsborough, Miss. On the Rapidan in Virginia Federal forces crossed the river at Morton's Ford and ran into trouble. Pinned down by Confederate fire, they withdrew north of the river at night. In North Carolina a skirmish took place near Newport Barracks, not far from New Berne. On the Virginia Peninsula a three-day Federal expedition from Yorktown toward Richmond involved skirmishes at Bottom's Bridge and near Baltimore Store. The raid, ordered by Gen. Butler, was intended to release prisoners in Richmond. In Missouri Federals scouted for five days in the Sni Hills. In the Charleston Harbor area Federals sent an expedition to John's and James islands.

Acts which the Confederate Congress approved included a ban on the importation of luxuries and the circulation of U.S. paper money. No cotton, tobacco, naval stores, sugar, molasses, or rice could leave ports unless the government received half the total tonnage.

February 7, Sunday

Two Federal expeditions were making progress. Troops under Brig. Gen. Truman Seymour, and under the over-all command of Maj. Gen. Q. A. Gillmore, occupied Jacksonville, Fla. Meeting little opposition, the Union troops prepared to advance inland. In Mississippi Sherman's men moved toward Meridian, with skirmishing at Brandon, Morton, and Satartia. Polk's Confederates fell back slowly, offering only moderate opposition. Other action included an affair at Waccomo Neck, N.C.; at the mouth of Caney Bayou, Tex.; and a skirmish at Vidalia, La.

President Davis told Lee that Federals were "in force" at Bottom's Bridge on the Chickahominy, that Gen. Pickett had just returned from an unsuccessful foray to New Berne, N.C., and that two of Pickett's brigades would come to Richmond. The city's home guards were called out in response to considerable apprehension over the reported approach of Federals. It soon proved an unnecessary alarm.

February 8, Monday

Federals and Confederates skirmished at Ten-Mile Run, near Camp Finegan, as the Florida expedition advanced from Jacksonville. Sherman's men skirmished at Coldwater Ferry, near Morton, and near Senatobia in Mississippi as part of the Meridian campaigning. Fighting also occurred at Barboursville, Ky.; Ringgold, Ga.; near Maryville, Tenn.; and at Donaldsonville, La.

February 9, Tuesday

Laboriously tunneling their way out of Libby Prison in Richmond, 109 Federal officers, including raider A. D. Streight, made their escape. Eventually 59 reached the Federal lines, 48 were recaptured, and two drowned. The largest and most sensational escape of the war, it was engineered and led by Col. Thomas E. Rose of Pennsylvania.

Union troops moving westward from Jacksonville skirmished near Point Washington. Another Federal expedition proceeded from Fernandina up the Nassau River, Fla. In the Meridian Campaign, Federals occupied Yazoo City, Miss.

Union troops carried out a reconnaissance in force on John's Island near Charleston, but were forced to withdraw hastily on Feb. 11. Elsewhere, action included a Union reconnaissance toward Swansborough, N.C.; skirmishing in Hardin County, Tenn.; at New River, La.; and at Morgan's Mill on Spring River, at Tomahawk Gap, and in White County, Ark.

Maj. Gen. John M. Schofield, former commander in Missouri, superseded Maj. Gen. John G. Foster in command of the Federal Department of the Ohio.

Before attending one of the largest White House levees of the season, President Lincoln had several photographs taken, including the one eventually used on the $5 bill.

February 10, Wednesday

Six horses and ponies died in a fire in the White House stables in Washington. The President tried to get the animals out, but to no avail.

The Florida expedition captured Confederate war matériel as it advanced from Jacksonville toward Lake City. On the south fork of the St. Mary's River a skirmish was fought at Barber's Ford, and Federals captured Camp Cooper. Sherman's Meridian campaigners skirmished at Hillsborough and Morton, Miss. Other fighting occurred at Pocahontas and Lake Village, Ark. Confederate raider *Florida* came out of Brest, France, after being laid up since August, and evaded the watching U.S.S. *Kearsarge*. Two blockade-runners were destroyed by U.S.S. *Florida* off Masonborough Inlet, N.C.

February 11, Thursday

President Davis told Gen. Joseph E. Johnston that the Federal advance in Mississippi "should be met before he reaches the Gulf and establishes a base to which supplies and reinforcements may be sent by sea." Though the plans called for nothing so ambitious, Sherman was moving upon Meridian, Miss., and Gen. W. Sooy Smith's column from Memphis was moving beyond Collierville, Tenn. An affair occurred at Raiford's Plantation, near Byhalia, Miss. The other Federal expedition, in Florida, fought a skirmish at Lake City. Fighting also broke out near Madisonville, La., and there was a Union descent on Lamar, Tex. Confederate raiders under Maj. H. W. Gilmor attacked the Baltimore & Ohio Railroad near Kearneysville, W. Va., throwing a train off the tracks and robbing the crew and passengers.

February 12, Friday

In the Meridian Campaign there was an affair at Wall Hill and a skirmish at Holly Springs as the two Federal columns, one under Sherman and the other under William Sooy Smith, continued to advance into Mississippi. In Missouri fighting occurred near California House and at Macon; and in Arkansas at Caddo Gap. A nine-day Union expedition operated from Batesville, Ark.

February 13, Saturday

Troops of the Florida expedition who set out to destroy Confederate supply bases skirmished for two days at Pease Creek. In the Meridian

Campaign fighting flared between Chunky Creek and Meridian and at Wyatt, as Sherman's men neared the important Mississippi point. Other action included fighting in Fentress County, Tenn., a Federal scout near Knoxville, and a two-day Federal expedition from Helena up the Saint Francis River of Arkansas.

February 14, Sunday
FEDERALS CAPTURE MERIDIAN, MISSISSIPPI.

Troops of Sherman's command entered Meridian, Miss., after a march from Vicksburg, and Gen. Polk's Confederates continued to fall back. Union troops stayed in Meridian until Feb. 20, destroying railroads and supplies in the area. As Sherman put it, "For five days 10,000 men worked hard and with a will in that work of destruction. . . . Meridian, with its depots, store-houses, arsenals, hospitals, offices, hotels and cantonments no longer exists." About 115 miles of railroad, 61 bridges, and 20 locomotives were destroyed in the course of the expedition. The enterprise had encountered little Confederate opposition, except for cavalry harassment around the Union perimeter. Confederates worried that the Federals were headed for Mobile, Ala.

In Florida an offshoot of the main Northern expedition captured Gainesville and fought a skirmish. Elsewhere the action erupted near Larkinsville, Ala.; Brentsville, Va.; and Ross' Landing and Scott's Farm, Ark. In Washington Lincoln, unwell, conferred with cavalry Gen. Judson Kilpatrick.

February 15, Monday
President Davis now wondered if Sherman's column, which he thought was headed for Mobile, was instead marching toward Montgomery, Ala. In fact, Sherman had not gone beyond Meridian, Miss. Some of his troops skirmished at Marion Station. From Vicksburg a small expedition to Grand Gulf ranged until March 6. Skirmishes broke out in West Virginia at Laurel Creek in Wayne County and in Arkansas at Saline River. In Missouri an affair took place near Charleston. Until Feb. 23 another Federal expedition in Florida made its way from Fernandina to Woodstock and King's Ferry Mills.

February 16, Tuesday
President Davis, still concerned over supplies of food and other matériel to the armies solicited suggestions to remedy defects in the logistical arrangements.

In the Meridian Campaign there was fighting at Lauderdale Springs, Miss.; and elsewhere there was an affair at Fairfield, N.C.; a skirmish at Indian Bay and Caddo Gap, Ark. Some minor Federal probings and ship and shore operations, including bombardment of Fort Powell, took place until late March around Mobile, aggravating the Confederate fear of an attack. In Washington Territory Federal troops campaigned against Indians from Fort Walla Walla to the Snake River, Feb. 16–23. Two blockade-runners were halted near Wilmington, N.C. *Pet* was captured by the block-aders and *Spunky* chased ashore and destroyed.

February 17, Wednesday

CONFEDERATE SUBMARINE SINKS U.S.S. *Housatonic* OFF CHARLESTON, SOUTH CAROLINA.

About 8:45 P.M. an officer of the sloop U.S.S. *Housatonic,* on duty off Charleston, spotted "something in the water" speeding toward the ship. The torpedo struck near the magazine; an explosion flashed, and the *Housatonic* sank rapidly, stern first. All but five of the crew clambered into the rigging and were saved. The attacker, C.S.S. *H. L. Hunley,* was an experimental cigar-shaped "semi-submersible," with a torpedo, or mine, at the end of a long spar in the prow. Before the successful attack, at least thirty-three men had died testing *Hunley.* This time, too, Lieut. George E. Dixon and his six-man crew perished, and *Hunley* was not heard from again. Although the daring attack sent consternation through the blockading fleet, the perils of such pioneer submarines made them still ineffective instruments of warfare.

In the Meridian, Miss., Campaign skirmishing erupted near Pontotoc, and in the Houlka Swamp near Houston. In Arkansas there were skirmishes at Black's Mill and Horse Head Creek. A two-day Federal scout from Warrenton, Va., involved skirmishing near Piedmont. A Union expedition moved from Motley's Ford, Tenn., to Murphy, N.C.

An act of the Confederate Congress suspended the privilege of the writ of habeas corpus until Aug. 2 to meet resistance to the conscription law and other disloyal activities. Suspension was restricted to arrests made under authority of the President and the Secretary of War. President Davis arranged to send reinforcements from J. E. Johnston's army in north Georgia to Polk, believed to be threatened in Mississippi by a Federal move to the Gulf.

The First Confederate Congress adjourned its fourth session amid overt discontent with the Davis administration and the progress of the war.

February 18, Thursday

Sherman's force at Meridian, Miss., still disrupted Confederate railroads and supply depots. Fighting broke out, with a skirmish at Aberdeen, near Okolona, in the northern part of Mississippi, in conjunction with the Federal column cooperating with Sherman from Memphis. Other action was recorded at Mifflin, Maryville, and Sevierville, Tenn.; Ringgold, Ga.; and near the headwaters of the Piney in Missouri. A two-day Federal scout operated from Ooltewah, Tenn., to Burke's and Ellidge's mills, Ga.

President Lincoln wrote Gov. John A. Andrew of Massachusetts that if "it be really true that Massachusetts wishes to afford a permanent home within her borders, for all, or even a large number of colored persons who will come to her, I shall be only too glad to know it. . . ." The President also issued a proclamation lifting the blockade of Brownsville, Tex., thereby allowing normal trade, but of course no commerce in military articles.

February 19, Friday

Fighting occurred about Brown's Ferry, Ala.; near Houston, at Egypt Station, and near Meridian, Miss.; Grossetete, La.; near Independence, Mo.; and at Waugh's Farm near Batesville, Ark. President Davis asked Adm. Franklin Buchanan what plans he had for defeating a reported naval demonstration on Mobile.

February 20, Saturday

BATTLE OF OLUSTEE OR OCEAN POND, FLORIDA.

Brig. Gen. Truman Seymour and some 5500 Federal troops were near Olustee or Ocean Pond on a march from Barber's Plantation toward Lake City, Fla. Seymour's force advanced against Confederates under Brig. Gen. Joseph Finegan. Two Union regiments, the Seventh New Hampshire and the Eighth U. S. Colored Troops, gave way in confusion at the opening of the battle. The approximately 5000 Confederates renewed the attack from strong fieldworks and fought vigorously until dark, when Seymour withdrew. The cavalry ineffectively pursued the retreating Federals. While the Northerners fell back to Jacksonville, Confederates rapidly repaired the damaged railroads. Casualties for the Federals were heavy, with 203 killed, 1152 wounded, and 506 missing for a total of 1861. The Confederates suffered 93 killed and 841 wounded for 934 casualties, in what was the major battle of the war in Florida.

Sherman, at Meridian, Miss., while anxious about W. Sooy Smith's operations to the north, withdrew in leisurely fashion toward Vicksburg with no fighting. The march had totaled between 360 and 450 miles, with 21 killed, 68 wounded, 81 missing for a total of 170. Confederates immediately went to work repairing the railroads and other damage.

Elsewhere, fighting broke out on the Sevierville Road near Knoxville, at Flat Creek, and Strawberry Plains, Tenn.; West Point, Miss.; Upperville and Front Royal, Va.; near Hurricane Bridge, W. Va.; and Pease Creek, Fla. For a week a Union expedition operated from Helena up the White River of Arkansas.

February 21, Sunday

The northern part of the Meridian Campaign was not as successful for the Federals as Sherman's in Mississippi. After fighting at Union, Ellis' Bridge, West Point, Prairie Station, and near Okolona, William Sooy Smith retreated toward Memphis, bested by Forrest's Confederate cavalry. Casualties were light on both sides. Smith had destroyed considerable railroad facilities, cotton, and corn. Hundreds of Negroes flocked to the Northern column. Smith did not feel that he could get through to join Sherman.

Elsewhere, fighting was light, with skirmishes near Circleville and Dranesville, Va., and a Union scout from New Creek to Moorefield, W. Va.

President Davis was worried about the pressure on the inner bastion of the Confederacy: in Mississippi; against Johnston in north Georgia; at Charleston, S.C.; and against Longstreet in east Tennessee; and, of course, the front in Virginia.

February 22, Monday
FEDERALS DEFEATED BY FORREST AT OKOLONA, MISSISSIPPI.

Sec. of the Treasury Salmon P. Chase, again enmeshed in political intrigue, once more offered to resign. (Eventually Lincoln refused this resignation.) The crisis arose from the so-called "Pomeroy Circular," a document indicative of the machinations of a few Radical Republicans and violent abolitionists opposed to Lincoln's reelection. Signed by Sen. Samuel C. Pomeroy of Kansas, the paper advocated Chase for President. Chase, in a letter to the President, denied knowledge of the circular, but admitted consultation with those urging him to run. Other evidence suggests that Chase was cognizant of and approved the publication.

Meanwhile, qualified voters in the restored Union government of Louisiana elected Michael Hahn governor of the army-occupied state.

Early in the morning, Forrest's Southern cavalry mounted a furious charge against Federal positions near Okolona, Miss. W. Sooy Smith's force was retiring toward Memphis after its frustrated attempt to join with Sherman's Meridian Campaign. Under the attack, a Tennessee Union regiment gave way and a five-mile running fight developed. Smith's men took a stand as Forrest charged again. Federals counterattacked to cover the retreat to Memphis. During the often hand-to-hand combat, Jeffrey Forrest, brother of the general, was killed. The engagement of Okolona, also known as Ivey's Farm or Ivey Hills, was one of Forrest's greatest victories and an ignominious loss for Smith. During the whole campaign Smith lost 54 killed, 179 wounded, and 155 missing for 388 out of over 6000. Forrest claimed he had 2500 men at Okolona, losing 25 killed, 75 wounded, and 8 or 10 captured.

Union troops of Thomas' Army of the Cumberland moved out to investigate J. E. Johnston's Confederate positions around Dalton, Ga. Confederate cavalry was pushed in and Federals moved toward Dalton and Tunnel Hill and along Rocky Face Ridge in demonstrations lasting until Feb. 25.

Skirmishes erupted at Luna Landing, Ark.; Lexington and Warrensburg, Mo.; Indianola, Tex.; Whitemarsh Island, Ga.; Gibson's and Wyerman's mills on Indian Creek, Va.; and Powell's Bridge and Calfkiller Creek, Tenn. Confederates raided Mayfield, Ky.

February 23, Tuesday

Federal troops of Thomas' Army of the Cumberland under Maj. Gen. J. M. Palmer drove toward Johnston's Confederate position near Dalton, with fighting at Catoosa Station and Tunnel Hill in what is often called the Demonstration on Dalton, Ga. President Davis, trying to reinforce Johnston in Georgia and Polk in Mississippi, queried Johnston as to whether "the demonstration in your front is probably a mask."

A skirmish occurred near New Albany, Miss. Feb. 23–March 9 Federals scouted from Springfield, Mo., into northern Arkansas, and fought several skirmishes.

President Lincoln wrote Sec. Chase that he would comment more fully later about the Pomeroy Circular, in which Chase was advocated as a Republican presidential candidate to replace Lincoln. The Cabinet met without Chase in attendance.

Richmond saw a buyer's panic, with food and whisky jumping rapidly in price.

February 24, Wednesday

Gen. Braxton Bragg was charged with the conduct of military operations in the Armies of the Confederacy, thus becoming in effect chief of staff. Bragg, still very controversial, enjoyed Davis' trust, but his reputation had suffered from his defeat at Missionary Ridge and the constant conflicts with his generals.

The U. S. Senate passed a measure to revive the rank of lieutenant general, with Grant clearly in mind. President Lincoln approved an act of Congress to compensate every Union master whose slaves enlisted in the Army, the sum not to exceed $300; the volunteer was to become free. The act also increased bounties for volunteers, redefined quota credits, increased penalties for draft resistance, subjected Negroes to the draft, provided that those who opposed bearing arms for religious reasons should be assigned non-combatant tasks with freedmen or in hospitals, and gave the President authority to call for such men as required. Debate began on recognizing the restored state government of Louisiana.

In northern Georgia, fighting continued at Tunnel Hill, Buzzard Roost, and Rocky Face Ridge or Crow's Valley during the Federal Demonstration on Dalton. Elsewhere, skirmishing took place at Tippah River and near Canton, Miss.; and until Feb. 29 there was a Federal scout from Camp Mibres, N. Mex. Terr.

February 25, Thursday

Federals under Maj. Gen. J. M. Palmer made their main effort at

Buzzard Roost in the Demonstration on Dalton, Ga. Johnston's Confederate positions proved too strong for the limited probing attack, and Palmer withdrew his forces to the main lines of the Army of the Cumberland on Feb. 26.

An affair occurred near Hudsonville, Miss.; and a Union scout from Whiteside's, Tenn., to Stevens' and Frick's gaps, Ga., lasted two days.

Maj. Gen. John C. Breckinridge was assigned to command the Confederate Trans-Allegheny Department or Western Department of Virginia, relieving Maj. Gen. Samuel Jones.

February 26, Friday

Sherman's troops skirmished near Canton, Miss., as their withdrawal after the successful Meridian Campaign neared completion. To the north, W. Sooy Smith's wing of the expedition straggled into Memphis after severe harassment by Forrest. Other fighting flared at Washington and Sulphur Springs, Tenn. A Confederate navy picket boat off Fort Sumter captured a small Union boat in Charleston Harbor.

A memorandum from President Lincoln confirmed his confidence in Gen. Benjamin Butler and asked that the controversial general be sustained in his efforts. Lincoln also ordered that the death sentence of all deserters be commuted to imprisonment during the war, thus continuing his policy of leniency. The U. S. Senate completed passage of the bill reviving the rank of lieutenant general.

February 27, Saturday

Near Americus, Ga., Federal prisoners of war began arriving at an unfinished prison camp, officially Camp Sumter, but known to history as Andersonville. Insufficient food, shelter, clothing, and accommodation soon made the prison notorious.

The Demonstration by Federals on Dalton, Ga., ended with a skirmish at the Stone Church near Catoosa Platform or Station. Skirmishing took place in the Sequatchie Valley, Tenn.; at Madisonville and Sharon, Miss.; near Poplar Bluff, Mo.; and at Pinos Altos, Ariz. Terr. Federals destroyed a large Confederate salt works on Goose Creek near St. Marks, Fla.

February 28, Sunday

After preliminary planning in Washington a cavalry force of about 3500 men under Judson Kilpatrick left the Rapidan, intent on penetrating weakly held Richmond and releasing Federal prisoners there. With Kilpatrick was Col. Ulric Dahlgren, a name soon known to fame. A minor affair at Ely's Ford marked the beginning of the expedition. As a diversionary support, Brig. Gen. Custer began a raid into Albemarle County, Va., which lasted until March 1.

Other skirmishing occurred at Dukedom, Tenn.; on Pearl River and near Yazoo City, Miss.; and Federals scouted in Gloucester County, Va.

President Lincoln ordered Adj. Gen. Lorenzo Thomas to proceed west to resolve the pressing predicament of contraband along the Mississippi. The plight of the Negroes, the need to restore plantations to usefulness, the problems of cotton and other trading were becoming increasingly urgent and troublesome.

February 29, Monday

Lincoln approved the congressional act reviving the grade of lieutenant general. It was clear that Congress and the President had Maj. Gen. Ulysses S. Grant in mind for this promotion, highest rank in the Army since Washington. Retired Gen. Winfield Scott was lieutenant general by brevet only.

Kilpatrick's cavalry pushed south from the Rapidan, skirmishing at Beaver Dam Station near Taylorsville. Kilpatrick split his command, sending a detachment of five hundred men toward Goochland C.H. under Col. Ulric Dahlgren, while he kept the main force with him. By evening the Confederates at Richmond were aware of an impending raid and were taking steps to resist.

Elsewhere, fighting broke out on Redwood Creek, Calif.; near Canton, Miss.; and at Ballahock on Bear Quarter Road and at Deep Creek, Va. In West Virginia Federal troops operated until March 5 against Petersburg and destroyed saltpeter works near Franklin. Cavalry under Custer fought skirmishes at Stanardsville and Charlottesville on their raid into Albemarle County, Va. In Missouri a two-week Federal expedition moved from Rolla to Batesville, Ark. In a prelude to the Red River expedition, a Union naval reconnaissance operated until March 5 on the Black and Ouachita rivers of Louisiana.

MARCH, 1864

As spring approached in many of the battle areas, major military movements were still postponed. In Virginia Lee and Meade marked time, although Richmond was agitated by Kilpatrick's approaching cavalry raid. Now that the U. S. Congress had created the rank of lieutenant general, the people awaited Grant's ascendancy to over-all command. Confederates in north Georgia knew a Union drive southeastward was certain, but did not know when or exactly how it would be launched. In the Confederacy the grim perseverance showed some signs of weakening. In the North there was awareness of the approaching presidential election and there were sanguine hopes for a victorious summer. Yet there was dissension in some quarters, and a queasy uncertainty as to the meaning of the war.

March 1, Tuesday

RAID ON RICHMOND FAILS.

Both branches of the Federal cavalry raid on Richmond were within a few miles of the Confederate capital. Wounded, veterans, office and factory workers, and home guards rallied to defend their city. There was consternation aplenty. Judson Kilpatrick approached with the larger Union force but decided against assault as the outer fortifications were too well manned. Kilpatrick turned east toward the Chickahominy and the Peninsula. Col. Ulric Dahlgren and his five hundred men coming in from the west approached to within a little over two miles of Richmond by nightfall. Faced with considerable resistance from a force under Custis Lee, Dahlgren, his own troops divided, realized Kilpatrick had failed. Dahlgren himself withdrew in the dark, wet night. The cavalry raid sputtered out, despite an audacious start, through lack of surprise, lack of force, and, finally, lack of drive to see it through.

In Florida skirmishing flared at Cedar and McGirt's creeks.

As expected, President Lincoln nominated Maj. Gen. Ulysses S. Grant for the newly created rank of lieutenant general.

March 2, Wednesday

The U. S. Senate confirmed the nomination of U. S. Grant as lieutenant general.

As Kilpatrick's discomfited raiders rode toward a junction with Butler's Federals near New Kent Court House, Col. Ulric Dahlgren and his detachment also moved north and east of Richmond, opposed by Confederate cavalry from Hanovertown on. Confederates of Fitzhugh Lee's cavalry division under Capt. E. C. Fox and Lieut. James Pollard got ahead of Dahlgren's men and prepared an ambush at Mantapike Hill between King and Queen Court House and King William Court House. During the night Dahlgren fell into the trap and was killed. Over a hundred of his men were captured. In the aftermath, papers were said to be found on Dahlgren which indicated a plot to assassinate President Davis. Historians then and now have been uncertain of their authenticity. However, the threat to Richmond ended dramatically and conclusively.

There was a skirmish recorded for Canton, Miss., and a two-day Federal expedition from Larkin's Landing to Gourd Neck and Guntersville, Ala. Having acted as a decoy for Kilpatrick's raid, George A. Custer returned to Union lines from his own fairly successful raid in the Albemarle area of Virginia.

March 3, Thursday

In a day of minor fighting, skirmishes occurred at Liverpool and Browns-ville, Miss.; Petersburg, W. Va.; at Jackson and near Baton Rouge, La. The Federal Treasury was authorized by Congress to issue $200,000,000 in ten-year bonds. Maj. Gen. U. S. Grant was ordered to Washington to receive his commission as lieutenant general.

March 4, Friday

The U. S. Senate confirmed Andrew Johnson as Federal Military Gover-nor of Tennessee. In New Orleans the new pro-Union Louisiana govern-ment of Gov. Michael Hahn took office.

The bulk of Gen. Sherman's forces returned to Vicksburg after the campaign to Meridian, Miss. Confederates demonstrated against Ports-mouth, Va.; a skirmish broke out near Murfreesboro, Tenn.; and another at Rodney, Miss. Minor operations continued until May in Florida.

Adm. John A. Dahlgren called on President Lincoln to learn the fate of his son, Col. Ulric Dahlgren, whose death near Richmond was not yet known in Washington.

March 5, Saturday

The Confederate government ordered every vessel to give one half of its freight capacity to government shipments. This was an effort to cut down on private profit from blockade-running and to aid the government in obtaining badly needed supplies. Maj. Gen. John C. Breckinridge assumed command of the Confederate Department of Western Virginia.

Fighting centered at Leet's Tanyard, Ga.; Panther Springs, Tenn.; and Yazoo City, Miss. A telegraph station and two small Federal steamers were seized in a daring raid by Confederates under Com. John Taylor Wood at Cherrystone Point, Va.

March 6, Sunday

Federal forces, after being attacked the preceding day, pulled out of Yazoo City, Miss. Confederate torpedo boats failed in an attack on U.S.S. *Memphis* in North Edisto River, S.C. Confederate raiders attacked Union pickets at Columbus, Ky., and there was an affair near Island No. 10 on the Mississippi. Skirmishing occurred at Flint Creek, Ark., and Snickersville, Va.

March 7, Monday

Anxious over the military situation in the West, President Davis wrote Gen. Longstreet, at Greeneville in east Tennessee, "It is needless to point out to you the value of a successful movement into Tennessee and Kentucky, and the importance—I may say necessity—of our taking the initiative."

President Lincoln wrote to Representative John A. J. Creswell of Maryland that while he had preferred gradual emancipation in Maryland, he would have no objection to immediate emancipation. The President issued an order designating the starting point of the Union Pacific Railroad on the western boundary of Iowa.

Fighting was limited to skirmishes at Decatur, Ala., and Brownsville, Miss. Richmond newspapers reported the first arrival of Negro prisoners of war in the Confederate capital.

March 8, Tuesday

The White House in Washington echoed with cheers and handclaps as a rather squat man in a disheveled major general's uniform stood on a sofa in the East Room. U. S. Grant, Lieutenant General and soon to be General-in-Chief of the U. S. Armies, met President Lincoln for the first time. Both men appeared somewhat embarrassed, and little was said, but a working partnership was unobtrusively being forged.

Fighting occurred near Baton Rouge and at Cypress Creek, La.; and at Courtland and Moulton, Ala.

March 9, Wednesday

GENERAL GRANT COMMISSIONED LIEUTENANT GENERAL.

The President of the United States, in the presence of his Cabinet, officially handed Ulysses S. Grant his commission as lieutenant general. In the brief White House ceremony both President and general uttered rather perfunctory remarks. Grant, already busy with plans, talked privately with the President about future operations.

Spasmodic skirmishing continued near Nickajack Gap, Ga., and near Greenwich and Suffolk, Va. Expeditions lasting several days were carried out by Federals in King and Queen County and to Piankatank River, Va.

March 10, Thursday

Gen. Grant was given the official authority to take command of the Armies of the United States, but the general himself was not in Washington to receive the order. He was in Virginia visiting the Army of the Potomac, still commanded by George Gordon Meade. The generals discussed the position, condition, and future of the army, and worked out their relationship to each other, for Grant expected to be in the field with his army commander. In another command change the controversial Maj. Gen. Franz Sigel superseded Brig. Gen. Benjamin F. Kelley in command of the Federal Department of West Virginia.

Confederate raiders hit Clinton and Mayfield, Ky.; and skirmishing flared near Charles Town and at Kabletown, W. Va. A three-day Federal expedition operated from Batesville to Wild Haws and Strawberry Creek, Ark. In the Southwest the first detachment of what was to become the Federal expedition up the Red River in Louisiana left Vicksburg. For some time Gen. Nathaniel Banks, in the New Orleans area, had been readying a massive effort aimed at the heartland of the Confederate Trans-Mississippi domain. Ships, troops, transports were heading for concentration points before starting into Louisiana. Plans also called for Union troops to the north to strike south through Arkansas and join Banks.

March 11, Friday

Grant returned to Washington from Virginia, and in the evening left for Nashville, Tenn., to confer with Sherman, now to be commander in the West.

For the rest of the month there were operations about Sparta, Tenn., with a few skirmishes. President Davis told Gen. Pemberton that he thought his defense of Vicksburg had been the correct action and that if it had not been attempted, "few if any would have defended your course."

March 12, Saturday

RED RIVER CAMPAIGN UNDER WAY.

The official order setting up the new top command of the United States Armies was announced, albeit somewhat after the event. Maj. Gen. Halleck was relieved, at his own request, as General-in-Chief and named chief of staff; Grant, of course, was assigned to command all the armies; Maj. Gen. W. T. Sherman was assigned to the Military Division of the Mississippi commanding the Departments of the Ohio, the Cumberland, the Tennessee, and the Arkansas; Maj. Gen. J. B. McPherson replaced Sherman in command of the Department and Army of the Tennessee. In the general orders the President also expressed his approbation and thanks to Halleck for "able and zealous" service.

On the Mississippi Gen. Banks, his army, and the gunboats started up the Red River into the heart of Louisiana.

A skirmish near Union City, Tenn., and a Federal scout to Nola Chucky Bend near Morristown, Tenn., were recorded actions.

President Davis suspended the execution of a deserter. The Lincolns entertained a number of top-ranking military men but Gen. Grant was not there—he was heading west to confer with Sherman. Mr. Lincoln wrote Gen. Butler that two ladies, seeking to visit Maryland, could not do so unless they took the oath of allegiance.

March 13, Sunday

President Lincoln "barely" suggested to the recently elected free-state governor of Louisiana, Michael Hahn, that some of the "very intelligent" Negroes be seated in a convention which would define the elective franchise.

As to the skirmishing, it happened at Cheek's Cross Roads and Spring Hill, Tenn.; Carrollton, Ark.; and Los Patricios, Tex. For nearly the rest of March Federals scouted from Yellville to the Buffalo River, Ark.

March 14, Monday

The advance of Banks' Red River expedition captured Fort De Russy near Simsport, La. Brig. Gen. Andrew Jackson Smith with his troops from Sherman's old command did the job with little difficulty. Meanwhile, another force of Federals moved from Franklin, La., toward Alexandria. The Union Red River operation looked promising. Otherwise skirmishing erupted at Bent Creek, Tenn.; Claysville, Ala.; Jones County, Miss.; and Hopefield, Ark. Fort Sumter was hit by another bombardment, with 143 rounds fired.

President Lincoln issued a draft order for 200,000 men for the Navy and to provide "an adequate reserve force for all contingencies" in the entire military service.

March 15, Tuesday

Gov. Michael Hahn of Louisiana was invested with powers previously held by the military governor of Louisiana as President Lincoln acted to reconstruct occupied areas of the South. The President also said that the United States should not "take charge of any church as such" in New Orleans.

Federal gunboats on the Red River arrived at Alexandria, La., as the expedition of men and vessels proceeded up the important Confederate-held stream. A skirmish at Marksville Prairie was part of the campaign. Skirmishing also occurred at Bull's Gap and Flat Creek Valley, Tenn., and at Clarendon, Ark. A Federal scout in Arkansas from Batesville to West Point, Grand Glaize, and Searcy Landing lasted for seven days.

March 16, Wednesday

Federal troops occupied Alexandria, La., a salient Red River town. For the Confederates, Nathan Bedford Forrest began an expedition into west Tennessee and Kentucky that lasted until April 14. In Virginia fighting broke out at Annandale and Bristoe Station and there was a Federal reconnaissance toward Snicker's Gap. In Tennessee Confederates raided the Nashville and Chattanooga Railroad near Tullahoma. Federals scouted in Cabell and Wayne counties, W. Va. Skirmishing occurred near Palatka, Fla., and at Santa Rosa, Tex. In Missouri a ten-day scout by Federals operated from Pilot Knob to the Arkansas line. Maj. Gen. Sterling Price took command of the Confederate District of Arkansas, succeeding Lieut. Gen. Theophilus Holmes.

March 17, Thursday

Lincoln, pushing for emancipation in the Union state of Maryland, wrote to Representative John A. J. Creswell, "It needs not to be a secret, that I wish success to emancipation in Maryland. It would aid much to end the rebellion."

At Nashville, Tenn., where he was conferring with Gen. Sherman, Lieut. Gen. Grant formally assumed command of the armies of the United States and announced that "Headquarters will be in the field, and, until further orders, will be with the Army of the Potomac."

Fighting was confined to skirmishes at Manchester, Tenn.; on Red Mountain near Blue Rock Station, Calif.; and at Corpus Christi, Tex. Union operations included a reconnaissance March 17–18 to Sperryville, Va.; an expedition from Yorktown into Mathews and Middlesex counties, Va., March 17–21; and a scout March 17 to April 1 from Lebanon, Mo., into northern Arkansas.

March 18, Friday

Arkansas voters ratified a pro-Union constitution which ended slavery in the state. Maj. Gen. William T. Sherman officially assumed command of the Military Division of the Mississippi. At the closing of the Sanitary Commission Fair in Washington, President Lincoln said, "if all that has been said by orators and poets since the creation of the world in praise of woman applied to the women of America, it would not do them justice for their conduct during this war."

Fighting occurred at Monticello and Spring Creek, Ark.; and Federals scouted from Island No. 10, Tenn., to New Madrid, Mo.

March 19, Saturday

The Georgia legislature expressed its confidence in President Davis and resolved that the Confederate government should, after each victory, make an offer of peace to the North based on independence of the South and self-determination by the border states.

Minor fighting continued, with action at the Eel River, Calif.; Beersheba Springs, Tenn.; on the Cumberland River, Ky.; at Laredo, Tex.; and Black Bay, Ark. Federals scouted for four days from Lexington, Mo.; and a Union expedition from Rolling Prairie to Batesville, Ark., lasted until April 4.

March 20, Sunday

Skirmishing flared at Arkadelphia and Roseville Creek, Ark.; while on the Red River of Louisiana fighting was at Bayou Rapides. The last ten days of the month saw Federal scouting in Jackson and La Fayette counties,

Mo., with skirmishing against guerrillas. Famed raider C.S.S. *Alabama* arrived at Capetown, South Africa.

March 21, Monday

Lincoln approved an act of the Federal Congress enabling the territories of Nevada and Colorado to become states, despite their relatively small populations.

Still the skirmishing continued, now at Reynoldsville, Tenn.; Moulton, Ala.; and Velasco, Tex. There was a small affair at Henderson's Hill, La., on the Red River.

President Lincoln told the New York Workingmen's Democratic Republican Association, "Property is the fruit of labor—property is desirable— is a positive good in the world. That some should be rich, shows that others may become rich, and hence is just encouragement to industry and enterprize. Let not him who is houseless pull down the house of another. . . ."

March 22, Tuesday

"I never knew a man who wished to be himself a slave. Consider if you know any *good* thing, that no man desires for himself," Lincoln wrote, apparently for an autograph album for a Sanitary Fair. Heavy snow fell in Richmond, Va. Federal Maj. Gen. Lewis Wallace superseded Brig. Gen. Henry H. Lockwood in command of the Middle Department with headquarters in Baltimore.

Fighting erupted at Bald Spring Cañon on Eel River, Calif.; Langley's Plantation in Issaquena County, Miss.; Fancy Farms, Ky.; Corpus Christi, Tex.; and Winchester, Va.

March 23, Wednesday

From Little Rock, Ark., Federal columns moved south under the command of Frederick Steele to join Banks' expedition coming up the Red River. If successful, the two-pronged advance would go far toward breaking up the Confederacy west of the Mississippi. Even at first Steele's men had to fight a bit—on the Benton Road toward Camden, Ark.

Gen. Grant returned to Washington from his conferences with Sherman and others in the West, preparatory to a general advance of Union armies. Meanwhile, in the Army of the Potomac, Maj. Gen. G. K. Warren superseded Maj. Gen. George Sykes in command of the Fifth Army Corps, an important shift. In Washington a number of "radical" members of Congress pressed for removal of Gen. Meade as commander of the Army of the Potomac.

March 24, Thursday

Nathan Bedford Forrest was on the move again, this time into west

Tennessee, where his command captured Union City. Other fighting took place near Goodrich's Landing, La., and at Oil Trough Bottom, Ark. Until the end of the month Federals operated from Batesville to Coon Creek and Devil's Fork of the Red River in Arkansas. In the far northwest a Federal expedition against Indians moved from Camp Lincoln near Canyon City to Harney Valley, Ore., March 24–Apr. 16. In the evening President Lincoln and his new General-in-Chief conferred at the White House.

March 25, Friday

Confederates were on the Ohio River. Federal outposts at Paducah, Ky., were driven in sharply as Southern cavalry attacked the important Ohio River city. Although they occupied part of Paducah, two attacks by Forrest's men were repulsed at Fort Anderson. Unable to destroy or capture the Federal garrison, the Confederates withdrew on the morning of March 26. The raid failed, but not before it had alarmed the Ohio Valley.

In other fighting the guns spoke at Rockport, Dover, White River, and in Van Buren County, Ark.; in South Carolina at McClellansville. Two Federal scouts operated to the twenty-sixth—from Batesville to Fairview, Ark., and from Beaufort to Bogue and Bear inlets, N.C.

Federal cavalry in Virginia had a temporary new commander when Brig. Gen. David McM. Gregg superseded Maj. Gen. Alfred Pleasonton, who was sent to Missouri.

March 26, Saturday

Lieut. Gen. Grant was in Virginia again; he established his permanent headquarters with the Army of the Potomac at Culpeper Court House. Maj. Gen. James B. McPherson assumed command of the Army of the Tennessee, under Sherman. Skirmishes took place near Black Jack Church, N.C., Quitman, Ark., and for several days at Long View and Mount Elba, Ark.

President Lincoln, in a new proclamation, explained his previous statements on amnesty by saying that it did not apply to prisoners of war but only to those free and at large who voluntarily came forward and took the oath of allegiance. President Davis was still arguing with governors of North and South Carolina over enforcement of policies of the Confederacy regarding trade and troop procurement and allocation.

March 27, Sunday

A few more routine affairs added to the mounting record: at Livingston, Miss.; Louisville, Tenn.; Columbus, Ky.; on the Ohio River, where Forrest's men were operating; at Deepwater Township, Mo.; on the Eel River, Calif.; and in the Federal movement into southern Arkansas, now known as the Camden Expedition, at Branchville and Brooks' Mill.

March 28, Monday

"This afternoon a dreadful affair took place in our town," said a Charleston, Ill., newspaper. About a hundred Copperheads vented long-pent-up feelings by attacking Federal soldiers on furlough at Charleston. By the time the fighting was ended by troop reinforcements, five men were dead and more than twenty wounded. It was one of the more severe anti-war outbreaks in the North.

The real war went on, with: an engagement on the Eel River, Calif.; an affair at New Hope, Ky.; a skirmish at Obey's River, Tenn.; an affair at Bloomery Gap, W. Va.; and skirmishes at Danvillle and Mount Elba, Ark. Federal scouts were carried out to Caperton's Ferry, Ala.; in Gloucester County, and to Aldie and Middleburg, Va. Federal troops moved northwestward from Alexandria, La., as Banks' Red River Campaign entered a new phase, and Confederates under Gen. Richard Taylor gathered to resist the invasion of the Trans-Mississippi.

March 29, Tuesday

Fighting increased as March became more springlike. Scenes of battle were at Caperton's Ferry, Ala.; about Monett's Ferry and Cloutierville, La., on the Red River; Bolivar, Tenn., in Forrest's raid; and Roseville, Long View, and Arkadelphia, Ark. Union scouts moved from Lookout Valley to Deer Head Cove, Ga.; and from Bellefonte to Burrowsville, Ark.

President Lincoln, in his usual skillful way, dissuaded Gen. Meade from formally requesting a court of inquiry in regard to Gettysburg. Criticisms of Meade's command had been appearing in the press, possibly written by other officers in the battle.

March 30, Wednesday

Fighting included an affair at Greenton, Mo.; action at Mount Elba and Big Creek, Ark.; capture of a Confederate outpost at Cherry Grove, Va.; and a Federal reconnaissance from Lookout Valley, Tenn., to McLemore's Cove, Ga. Federals scouted around Woodville and Athens, Ala., and from Columbus to Clinton and Moscow, Ky. Confederates attacked Snyder's Bluff, Miss.

March 31, Thursday

Skirmishing at Natchitoches, La., marked the Red River Campaign. Other action included skirmishes near Arkadelphia, Ark.; at Palatka, Fla.; at Forks of Beaver in east Kentucky; and an affair at Spring Island, S.C. Federals scouted from Bridgeport, Ala., to Caperton's Ferry.

APRIL, 1864

Not since the fall of 1863 had there been a major confrontation between North and South. Nevertheless, the war still bore heavily on the people. It was unavoidable. Gen. Banks' Union army on the Red River was running into trouble from Gen. Taylor's opposition, low water in the rivers, and geography. In Arkansas the cooperating Federal column was stumbling, too. At Charleston the Federal guns still fired occasionally, still making further rubble of Fort Sumter. Elsewhere, raids, sniping, patrols, reconnaissances, and guerrilla activities continued. But eyes turned anxiously toward Virginia—when would it again become the focal point of the struggle? Grant was with Meade's Army of the Potomac, but in front of him was Lee and the now legendary Army of Northern Virginia. At the South dissatisfaction with Davis and his administration increased as the territory of the Confederacy dwindled.

April 1, Friday

April wafted in with the monotonous small war in far-off, strange places. Federals and Confederates fought a skirmish at Arkadelphia, Ark., as the Northerners of Frederick Steele headed south to join Banks on the Red River. There was also action at Fitzhugh's Woods near Augusta, Ark.; and skirmishes broke out near Plymouth, N.C., and Bloomfield, Mo. U.S. transport *Maple Leaf* sank after hitting a torpedo or mine in St. John's River, Fla. A Federal expedition operated from Palatka to Fort Gates, Fla.; another expedition patrolled for ten days along the Pearl River in Louisiana. Fort Sumter received only irregular fire during April.

April 2, Saturday

The list of skirmishes lengthened once more: Cleveland, Tenn.; Grosse-tete Bayou, La.: Crump's Hill, La.; Okolona, Antoine or Terre Noir Creek, and Wolf Creek, Ark.; Cedar Creek and Cow Ford Creek near Pensacola, Fla. Cape Lookout Light, N.C., was destroyed by Confederates.

April 3, Sunday

Skirmishing on the Red River occurred at Grand Ecore, La. Eight gunboats and three other vessels brought reinforcements to the Union expedition. Forrest and his men fought near Raleigh in their West Tennessee Campaign. Other skirmishes were at Cypress Swamp, Tenn.; Ducktown Road, Ga.; Clinton, Miss.; and Fort Gibson, Indian Terr. In addition there was an engagement at Elkin's Ferry on the Little Missouri River, Mo., and an affair at Clarksville, Ark. There were four nights of brisk mortar shelling of Fort Sumter.

April 4, Monday

The Army of the Potomac had still another cavalry commander— Maj. Gen. Philip Sheridan from the West—and to many it meant the continual improvement of the Federal horse. He succeeded D. McM. Gregg, who had temporarily supplanted Pleasonton. The U. S. House of Representatives passed a joint resolution saying that the nation would not permit the establishment of a monarchy in Mexico. This was intended to thwart the plans of Napoleon III of France to place Maximilian of Hapsburg on the throne of Mexico. Several changes in Federal corps commanders helped set the stage for renewed operations. Skirmishing occurred at Charlestown and Roseville, Ark., and at Campti, La., on the Red River. The New York Sanitary Commission Fair opened with eventual receipts of $1,200,000 used for needs of the soldiers.

President Lincoln put in writing some thoughts upon slavery that he had framed orally a few days before: "I am naturally anti-slavery. If slavery is not wrong, nothing is wrong. . . . And yet I have never understood that the Presidency conferred upon me an unrestricted right to act officially upon this judgment and feeling."

April 5, Tuesday

Up the Red River Gen. Banks' Federal expedition slowed down. The low river was hindering their advance and Confederate forces, refusing to be engaged in quantity, fell away before the Yankees. Banks' main force fought a slight skirmish at Natchitoches, La. Elsewhere, skirmishing occurred at Marks' Mills and Whiteley's Mills, Ark.; Quicksand Creek, Ky.; and in the swamps of the Little River near New Madrid, Mo., April 5–9. There also was an affair at Blount's Creek, N.C.

April 6, Wednesday

The Constitutional Convention of Louisiana met at New Orleans and adopted a new state constitution, abolishing slavery. The Federal Department of the Monongahela was merged into the Department of the Susquehanna. Affairs took place at Prairie du Rocher, Ill.; at Piney Mt., on the Little Missouri, and on the Arkansas River near Prairie Grove, Ark.

April 7, Thursday

The Confederacy ordered Longstreet's corps, which had spent the winter and spring in east Tennessee, to return to Lee's Army of Northern

Virginia. Longstreet had been detached since early September, 1863, before the Battle of Chickamauga.

On the Red River Banks had advanced to near Mansfield as Taylor drew his Confederates back. The two forces skirmished at Wilson's Plantation near Pleasant Hill, La. Other skirmishing was at Woodall's Bridge, Ala.; Brushy Creek and Rhea's Mills, Ark.; near Port Hudson, La.; and at the foot of the Sierra Bonito, N. Mex. Terr.

April 8, Friday

BATTLE OF SABINE CROSSROADS OR MANSFIELD, LOUISIANA.

Confederates of Gen. Richard Taylor had formed a defensive line at Sabine Crossroads, near Mansfield, La. Here was the place, Taylor decided, to halt Banks' advance upon Shreveport. The Federal expedition, moving on a road too far inland from the Red River, was strung out in a long file, and had injudiciously placed wagon trains in the line of march. Low water made the Union gunboats at Grand Ecore useless to Banks. Banks stopped and ordered his forces consolidated. Small units had already been engaged, and late in the afternoon Taylor struck in a disjointed attack. A full-scale shooting match was on, known as Sabine Crossroads, Mansfield, or Pleasant Grove. Banks' men were forced back sharply and lost several guns. Outflanked on both sides, the Federals gave way, with panic and confusion in many cases. The road of retreat was blocked by a wagon train, adding to the difficulties. Finally, at Pleasant Grove the troops of William H. Emory stood hard and the Southern attack died out. During the night Banks withdrew to Pleasant Hill and formed yet another defense line. One Yankee called it "our skedaddle from the rebs." Losses for the Federals are put at 113 killed, 581 wounded, and 1541 missing and captured for 2235—high casualties for an engaged force of about 12,000. Confederate losses are uncertain; estimates are 1000 killed and wounded out of some 8800.

Other fighting included skirmishes at Paint Rock Bridge, Ala.; Winchester, Va.; Bayou De Paul or Carroll's Mill near Pleasant Hill, La.; and on James Island, S.C.

The U. S. Senate passed a joint resolution 38 to 6 abolishing slavery and approving the Thirteenth Amendment. The resolution reflected the change in the attitude of Congress since the beginning of the war, and there was little real opposition to it.

April 9, Saturday

ENGAGEMENT OF PLEASANT HILL, LOUISIANA.

Gen. Banks' Federals, beaten at Sabine Crossroads on the eighth, drew up in line of battle near Pleasant Hill, La., expecting another attack from Confederates under Gen. Taylor. At first the skirmishing was light, but late in the afternoon the Confederates made their main drive, gaining some ground and pushing the Federals back on their reserve. A counter-charge worked and the Federals in turn drove the Confederates back, ending the engagement, tactically a Northern victory. The Union, out of about 12,000 engaged, had 150 killed, 844 wounded, and 375 missing for a total of 1369. For the Confederates around 12,500 were engaged with killed and wounded put at 1200 and 426 missing. The Confederate Trans-Mississippi commander, Gen. E. Kirby Smith, arrived late at night.

To the north the Federals under Gen. Steele, stalled in their advance through Arkansas, skirmished until the twelfth on Prairie D'Ane, a part of the Camden Expedition. Forrest, still operating dangerously close to the Federal communications in western Tennessee, skirmished near Raleigh.

Gen. U. S. Grant issued campaign orders: Meade and the Army of the Potomac would make Lee's army the objective; "Wherever Lee goes, there you will go also." Banks was to move on Mobile, Ala.; Sherman was to head into Georgia against Joe Johnston; Sigel was to march south in the Shenandoah; Benjamin Butler was to move against Richmond from the south side of the James River. The armies of the Union would be on the march in one grand, over-all operation designed to put simultaneous pressure on all major armies of the Confederacy.

Confederate torpedo boat *Squib* damaged U.S.S. *Minnesota* off Newport News, Va., by exploding a torpedo and escaping. Heavy spring rains fell on northern Virginia, washing out or damaging a number of bridges.

April 10, Sunday

Banks pulled back his force on the Red River toward Grand Ecore, La., and in Arkansas Steele's Union expedition headed back toward Little Rock, with a skirmish at Prairie D'Ane. E. Kirby Smith ordered Taylor to take his Southern force back from Pleasant Hill to Mansfield. The only other action was a Federal scout to Dedmon's Trace, Ga., and a skirmish at Cypress Swamp, Tenn.

April 11, Monday

Banks' Red River army was back at Grand Ecore after its failure at Mansfield and Pleasant Hill, La. Porter's gunboats, a bit farther up at Loggy Bayou and Springfield Landing, encountered steadily lowering water and there was concern that they would be caught in the shallow river. They pulled back, bedeviled by shore batteries and small-arms fire. Forrest and his Confederate cavalry were at Columbus, Ky., on the Mississippi and there was a skirmish nearby. Affairs were recorded at Greenwich, Va.; near Kelly's Plantation on Sulphur Springs Road, Ala.; and in Chariton County, Mo. A skirmish broke out at Richland, Ark. Federal scouts and reconnaissance operated from Stevenson to Caperton's Ferry, Ala.; and from Rossville to La Fayette, Ga.

At Little Rock, Ark., a pro-Union state government was inaugurated, with Dr. Isaac Murphy as governor. Thus two seceded states—Arkansas and Louisiana—were back in the fold, at least in part. Pro-Union Virginians voted to accept a constitution for the "Restored State of Virginia" which included abolishing slavery. A convention had deliberated in February in Alexandria, drawing up the constitution. The government headed by F. H. Pierpoint represented only a few northern and coastal areas of Virginia firmly held by the Union army.

April 12, Tuesday

CONFEDERATES CAPTURE FORT PILLOW, TENNESSEE.

Nathan Bedford Forrest's Confederate cavalry struck at Fort Pillow in an assault whose repercussions are still heard. Opinion varied then and now as to whether it was simply a successful attack on a military objective or a massacre of Negro and white soldiers after the surrender. Fort Pillow, on the Mississippi, was held by 557 Federal troops, including 262 Negro soldiers. Gen. Forrest, on his active raid against important Federal communications and posts in west Kentucky and Tennessee, sent 1500 men against Fort Pillow. Forrest demanded surrender of the fort but Maj. William F. Bradford refused and Forrest's Confederates attacked. With little difficulty they poured into the large earthwork on the bluff. According to Forrest and other Southern sources, the Federal casualties of about 231 killed, 100 wounded, and 226 captured or missing resulted from fighting before surrender. According to extensive testimony taken afterward by the Federals, the Union troops surrendered almost at once and the soldiers were shot down afterward in what amounted to a "massacre," especially of the Negroes. Confederate losses were put at 14 killed and 86 wounded. Later the Joint Committee on the Conduct of the War heard purported evidence of numerous atrocities including the killing of many of the garrison after the surrender. Confederate military and civil authorities hotly denied these charges and called them hysterical propaganda. Perhaps a reasonable conclusion is that much confusion existed during the attack and that there were some unnecessary acts of violence by the Confederates, but that the majority of the casualties were the result of legitimate, though hardly humane, warfare. Nevertheless, "Fort Pillow" echoed infamously throughout the war and long remained an emotional issue with reliable evidence hard to come by.

The Fort Pillow affair dwarfed all the other fighting: an engagement at Blair's Landing, La., on the Red River; skirmishes at Florence, Ala.; Pleasant Hill Landing, Tenn.; Van Buren, Ark.; Fort Bisland, La.; and Fremont's Orchard, Colo. Terr. Expeditions by Federals moved up Matagorda Bay, Tex., and from Point Lookout, Md. A Federal reconnaissance probed for a couple of days from Bridgeport down the

Tennessee River to Triana, Ala. Maj. Gen. Simon Bolivar Buckner assumed command of the Confederate Department of East Tennessee.

Gen. Robert E. Lee told his President, "I cannot see how we can operate with our present supplies. Any derangement in their arrival, or disaster to the R.R. would render it impossible for me to keep the army together. . . ."

April 13, Wednesday

Adm. Porter, with his Federal gunboats, reached Grand Ecore on the Red River despite the rapidly falling water level and enemy harassment. Banks' Federal retreat continued with no hope of renewal of the campaign.

In Arkansas skirmishing broke out at and near Richland Creek, and on Spring River near Smithville. Action also occurred at Moscow, as the Federal cooperating column intending to join Banks on the Red River further bogged down. Elsewhere, Forrest's men skirmished again at Columbus, Ky., and there was skirmishing at Mink Springs, near Cleveland, Tenn.; near Decatur, Ala.; Paintsville, east Kentucky; and an affair at Nokesville, Va. In Virginia, also, expeditions by Federals of varying durations went out from Portsmouth to the Blackwater and from Norfolk to Isle of Wight County.

April 14, Thursday

Forrest's Confederate cavalry, still active up toward the Ohio, skirmished again at Paducah, Ky. Small Union gunboats helped repulse the Southerners. In Arkansas the skirmishing was at Bayou Saline, Dutch Mills, and White Oak Creek; in Georgia at Taylor's Ridge; and in eastern Kentucky at Half Mountain on Licking River and near Booneville. At Charleston Fort Moultrie fired during the night on the U.S. tug *Geranium*. A five-day Union expedition operated from Camp Sanborn, Colo. Terr., to Beaver Creek, Kas.

President Lincoln reviewed sixty-seven court-martial cases, and issued several pardons.

April 15, Friday

Small affairs continued as spring weather improved, with considerable action in the Trans-Mississippi near Camden and Roseville, Ark.; in the Indian Territory; and at Spencer's Ranch near Presidio del Norte, N. Mex. Terr. Other fighting flared near Baton Rouge, La.; Greeneville, Tenn.; and Bristoe Station and Milford, Va. Federals demonstrated on Battery Island in Charleston Harbor, S.C. On the Red River ironclad U.S.S. *Eastport* struck a torpedo or mine and was severely damaged. She was refloated and tried to escape April 21, only to go aground numerous times. The crew finally destroyed her on April 26.

At Knoxville, Tenn., Gov. Andrew Johnson vociferously supported emancipation at a large pro-Union meeting. The Richmond *Examiner* expressed concern over the forthcoming campaign in Virginia: "So far, we feel sure of the issue. All else is mystery and uncertainty. Where the first blow will fall, when the two armies of Northern Virginia will meet each other face to face; how Grant will try to hold his own against the master spirit of Lee, we cannot even surmise."

April 16, Saturday

A skirmish at Grand Ecore, La., marked the Red River Campaign. In the allied Camden, Ark., Expedition fighting broke out about Camden and at Liberty Post Office, and an affair occurred on the Osage Branch of King's River. Skirmishing erupted at Rheatown, Tenn.; Salyersville, Ky.; and an affair took place at Catlett's Station, Va. U.S. transport *General Hunter* was destroyed by a torpedo in St. John's River, Fla.

A report on U.S. prisoners since the beginning of the war showed that the Federals had captured 146,634 Confederates.

April 17, Sunday

Gen. Grant ordered no further exchange of prisoners until the Confederates balanced Federal releases. Also, he pronounced "no distinction whatever will be made in the exchange between white and colored prisoners." The move injured the South, with its shortage of manpower, far more than the North, but it brought Grant caustic criticism from both sides.

Confederate land forces, soon to be joined by the newly finished ram *Albemarle,* began an attack on Plymouth, N.C. The Confederates were under Brig. Gen. Robert Frederick Hoke. Skirmishes flared at Beaver Creek, N.C.; Ellis' Ford, Va.; Holly Springs, Miss.; Limestone Valley and Red Mount, Ark. Confederate women defied local troops in a demonstration demanding bread at Savannah, Ga.

April 18, Monday

Confederate attacks continued at Plymouth, N.C. Other action included skirmishing near Decatur, Ala.; at Citrus Point, Va.; an affair at Hunnewell, Mo.; and a Federal expedition from Burkesville, Ky., to Obey's River, Tenn. In the Trans-Mississippi at Poison Springs, Ark., Sterling Price's Confederates under direct command of John S. Marmaduke hit the Federals and a foraging train. After a heavy engagement the Federals withdrew, abandoning 198 wagons. This was another bitter blow to the Federal attempt to join Banks' Red River expedition.

In an important Confederate command change, Gen. P. G. T. Beauregard was assigned to lead the Department of North Carolina and Southern Virginia. Leaving Charleston, he was to be in charge of defending Richmond, the southern part of Virginia, and the northern portion of North Carolina against threatened Federal invasion by Benjamin F. Butler from the coast.

In an address to the Baltimore, Md., Sanitary Fair, Mr. Lincoln said, "We all declare for liberty; but in using the same *word* we do not all mean the same *thing*."

April 19, Tuesday

C.S.S. *Albemarle* joined in the Confederate attack on Plymouth, N.C., sinking by ramming U.S.S. *Smithfield*, damaging another wooden gunboat, and driving off still others. Confederate troops had surrounded the town and surrender was believed near. In other fighting there were affairs at Leesburg, Va.; Marling's Bottom, W. Va.; plus skirmishes at King's River, Ark.; Charleston, Mo.; and Waterhouse's Mill and Boiling Springs, Tenn. To the twenty-third a Union expedition moved up the Yazoo River, Miss., with skirmishing and loss by capture of U.S. gunboat *Petrel* on April 22. Confederate troops carried out operations against pro-unionists in Marion County, Ala.

An enabling act to permit Nebraska Territory to join the Union was approved after passage by the U. S. Congress.

April 20, Wednesday

Confederate troops under Brig. Gen. R. F. Hoke, aided by C.S.S. *Albemarle*, captured Plymouth, N.C., and Federals lost about 2800 men plus a large quantity of supplies. The capture marked the first major Confederate victory in the area for a long time and brought hope to the defenders of the Atlantic coast.

On the Red River there were skirmishes about Natchitoches, La.; and in Arkansas more skirmishing occurred around Camden. Elsewhere, Confederates attacked Jacksonport, Ark., and Waterproof, La. Until late October Federal troops moved against Indians in expeditions from Fort Dalles, Ore., and Fort Walla Walla, Wash. Terr., to southeastern Oregon.

Maj. Gen. Samuel Jones succeeded Gen. P. G. T. Beauregard in command of the Confederate Department of South Carolina, Georgia, and Florida. Beauregard moved to the heavily threatened post of southern Virginia and northern North Carolina. President Lincoln ordered death sentences exacted by court-martial to be commuted to imprisonment on Dry Tortugas off Key West, Fla. The President also conferred with Gen. Grant, who was completing plans for a spring offensive in Virginia.

April 21, Thursday

Gen. Banks' harassed Federals were withdrawing from Grand Ecore, La., to Alexandria, which they reached April 25, as the Red River expedition drew to a rather ignominious conclusion. Confederate units pursued Banks with hit-and-run attacks, but mounted no offensive. Affairs took place at Tunica Bend, La.; Cotton Plant, Ark.; and Harrison's Gap, Ala. A skirmish erupted at Red Bone, Miss. Confederate salt works were destroyed at Masonborough Inlet, N.C., and at Cane Patch near Murrell's Inlet, S.C.

President Lincoln conferred with governors from Ohio, Indiana, Illinois, and Iowa, and also reviewed seventy-two court-martial cases.

April 22, Friday

Confederate harassment on the Red River in Louisiana continued with attacks on transports, and skirmishes at and near Cloutierville, La. Other fighting included a skirmish on Duck River, Tenn.; an affair near Cotton Plant, Ark.; and a three-day Union expedition with skirmishing from Jacksonport to Augusta, Ark.

The motto "In God We Trust" was first stamped upon coins under an act of the Federal Congress. Pres. Davis wrote Lieut. Gen. Polk in Alabama, "If the negro soldiers [captured] are escaped slaves, they should be held safely for recovery by their owners. If otherwise, inform me."

April 23, Saturday

Confederates pressured the Federal column in Arkansas, plaguing the Camden Expedition at Camden and Swan Lake. In the Red River Campaign a heavy engagement occurred at Monett's Ferry or Cane River Crossing, La. Elsewhere, fighting included an affair near Hunter's Mill, Va.; a skirmish at Independence, Mo.; and a Confederate attack at Nickajack Trace, Ga.

April 24, Sunday

The "small war" continued with still more skirmishing near Camden, Ark.; an affair near Decatur, Ala.; near Middletown, Va.; Pineville, La.; and a Federal scout from Ringgold to La Fayette, Ga.

April 25, Monday

In Arkansas the fighting went on, with action at Marks' Mills and in Moro Bottom. Troops skirmished at Cotile Landing, La., on the Red River, as Federals began arriving at Alexandria in their retreat. Most of the gunboats were already near Alexandria. Otherwise there was a skirmish near Natchez, Miss., and a Federal expedition of three days from Bull's Gap to Watauga River, Tenn. Confederate Maj. Gen. Robert Ransom was assigned to command the Department of Richmond, Va.

April 26, Tuesday

Federal troops in North Carolina began to evacuate Washington, following the fall of Plymouth. The move was completed by April 30. Skirmishing about Alexandria, La., lasted almost a month as Federal troops from the Red River expedition continued to arrive. Meanwhile, the rapidly falling water in the Red River trapped the Union gunboat fleet above the rapids. Those vessels still above Alexandria suffered considerable damage in a running engagement with onshore Confederates. There was an engagement of two days at the junction of the Cane and Red rivers, part of the campaign. Skirmishes also flared at Bayou Rapides Bridge near McNutt's Hill, and at Deloach's Bluff, La. Frederick Steele's Federal column in Arkansas began its retreat from Camden after failing to join up with Banks on the Red River.

Elsewhere, there was an affair at Winchester, Va.; skirmishing in Wayne County, Mo.; at Berwick, La.; and near Little Rock, Ark. A Federal expedition operated until May 6 from Jacksonville to Lake Monroe, Fla.

April 27, Wednesday

President Davis instructed Jacob Thompson to proceed at once to Canada as a special commissioner and a few days later asked C. C. Clay, Jr., to join him. While not officially spelled out, the mission was apparently to see what help could be obtained and to communicate with certain parties in the United States as to possible peace or truce.

In the fighting there was a skirmish near Decatur, Ala.; a Confederate attack on Taylor's Ridge near Ringgold, Ga.; skirmishing at Troublesome Creek, Ky.; an affair at Masonborough Inlet, N.C.; skirmishing at Dayton, Mo.; and an expedition until the twenty-ninth by Federals from Williamsburg, Va.

The Maryland Constitutional Convention met at Annapolis; sessions lasted until Sept. 6.

April 28, Thursday

A minor bombardment of Fort Sumter lasted seven days, during which 510 rounds were fired by Federals. The fighting was listed as skirmishing at Princeton, Ark.; in Johnson County, Mo.; and Big Bend of Eel River, Calif.; a Federal reconnaissance to Madison Court House, Va.; and a Union scout from Vienna toward Upperville, Va.

President Davis told Gen. E. Kirby Smith, commanding the Trans-Mississippi Department, "As far as the constitution permits, full authority has been given to you to administer to the wants of your Dept., civil as well as military."

April 29, Friday

On the Red River yet another skirmish broke out at Grand Ecore, La. In Arkansas the Federal retreat from Camden involved skirmishing on the Ouachita River and near Saline Bottom.

Elsewhere, action included skirmishes in the Sni Hills, Mo.; and in

Berry County, Tenn.; a Federal reconnaissance from Ringgold toward Tunnel Hill, Ga.; and a Union expedition from Newport Barracks to Swansborough, N.C.

The U. S. Congress by a joint resolution raised all duties 50 per cent for sixty days, later the rate was extended until July 1.

April 30, Saturday

President Jefferson Davis again wrote Gen. Polk that "Captured slaves should be returned to their masters on proof and payment of charges." Then personal tragedy struck—five-year-old Joe Davis died after falling off the high veranda of the Confederate White House in Richmond. Thus while in the service of their countries, both Presidents lost sons.

Others died on the battlefield: at Whitmore's Mill and Jenkin's Ferry, part of the ill-fated Federal Camden, Ark., Expedition; at Decatur, Ala.; and in an expedition by Federals from Memphis, Tenn., to Ripley, Miss., that lasted until May 9. Three blockade-runners escaped from Galveston, Tex., under cover of night and rain.

President Lincoln wrote Gen. Grant to express his "entire satisfaction with what you have done up to this time, so far as I understand it."

MAY, 1864

An attack in Virginia by the Army of the Potomac was certain; exactly how, where, or when Grant would strike was the question. Lee's Army of Northern Virginia was as ready as its depleted numbers and inferior equipment and sustenance could make it. The South also expected action by Sherman in Georgia; a new drive by Butler from the James in Virginia; campaigning in the Shenandoah; perhaps a long-anticipated attack on Mobile. Tension increased. Was there any real hope left for the Confederacy? Criticism of Davis, of some generals, even of the armies grew louder, though dreams of recognized independence, courage, and faith remained. In the North Lincoln was more and more concerned with the problems of emancipation in the seceded and border slave states, restoring pro-Union governments in conquered land, and the presidential election in the fall.

May 1, Sunday

The first day of May saw action primarily west of the Mississippi. As the Red River Campaign drew to a close with the Federal withdrawal to Alexandria, La., Confederates captured U.S. transport *Emma* at David's Ferry and there were four days of skirmishing at Gov. Moore's plantation. Elsewhere in Louisiana skirmishing broke out at Clinton and Ashton, and an affair took place at Berwick. In Arkansas skirmishes occurred at Pine Bluff and Lee's Creek. Far off in California an affair at Booth's Run marked the Humboldt River Indian operations. At Stone Church, Ga., near Chattanooga, a skirmish presaged the increase in scouting, which culminated in Sherman's move against J. E. Johnston. Brig. Gen. John P. Hatch assumed command of the Federal Department of the South, relieving Maj. Gen. Q. A. Gillmore.

May 2, Monday

Skirmishing continued along the Red River as Confederates harassed Federals at Wells' Plantation, Wilson's Landing, and Bayou Pierre, La. In California there was a skirmish at Kneeland's Prairie; in Tennessee a skirmish at Bolivar and a ten-day Union scout in Hickman and Maury counties; in Missouri an affair on Bee Creek. To the nineteenth Federal expeditions operated against the Virginia and Tennessee Railroad in southwestern Virginia, a land of resources for the Confederates now being invaded by the foe. In Georgia, near Tunnel Hill and Ringgold Gap, outposts of Johnston and Sherman skirmished.

In Richmond the first session of the Second Confederate Congress gathered. President Davis in his message again condemned the "barbarism" of the Federals in their "Plunder and devastation of the property of noncombatants, destruction of private dwellings, and even of edifices devoted to the worship of God; expeditions organized for the sole purpose of sacking cities, consigning them to the flames, killing the unarmed inhabitants, and inflicting horrible outrages on women and children." He saw no immediate hope for foreign recognition, but about military and other matters he was optimistic.

May 3, Tuesday

The orders went out from Gen. U. S. Grant through Maj. Gen. George G. Meade that the Army of the Potomac was to move across the Rapidan next morning, march around the right flank of Lee's Army of Northern Virginia, and head toward Richmond once more.

There was a minor Federal raid on Bulltown, W. Va. In the West the defeated Federal column of Frederick Steele arrived back at Little Rock from the Camden Expedition. Also in Arkansas skirmishing broke out near the mouth of Richland Creek. Skirmishes occurred between Bayous Redwood and Olive Branch near Baton Rouge, La., and between Federals and Indians at Cedar Bluffs, Colo. Terr. Along Chickamauga Creek, at Catoosa Springs and at Red Clay the Georgia Campaign became more lively as skirmishing increased.

The Federal Cabinet and President Lincoln discussed the alleged atrocities committed by Confederates during the attack on Fort Pillow, Tenn.

May 4, Wednesday

ARMY OF THE POTOMAC CROSSES THE RAPIDAN.

"Soon after midnight, May 3d–4th the Army of the Potomac moved out from its position north of the Rapidan, to start upon that memorable campaign." So wrote Gen. Grant. It was the beginning of the big Federal push in Virginia that culminated in the siege of Petersburg and finally Appomattox. From now on the pressure would not be relaxed. By late in the day Grant had 122,000 men present for duty. He positioned the Second Corps of Hancock, the Fifth Corps of Warren, and the Sixth Corps of Sedgwick across the river via Germanna and Culpeper Mine fords, and Burnside's Ninth Corps was coming up. Grant moved quickly around Lee's right, and the Army of Northern Virginia, some 66,000 present for duty, rushed up from the Orange Court House-Gordonsville area to meet him. Ewell led the Confederates, followed by A. P. Hill and Longstreet. However, only a brief skirmish near burned-out Chancellorsville showed the battling to come.

Other Federal advances marked the day. Following Grant's many-pronged strategy to weaken the thin Confederate defense, Ben Butler's Army of the James assembled in transports in Hampton Roads. The army would move up the James River to operate against Richmond from the south side. At first almost nothing barred his way.

Farther south, along Albemarle Sound, N.C., skirmishing flared on the Trent Road and south of the Trent River, and Federals lost an outpost at Croatan to attacking Confederates. C.S.S. *Albemarle,* the powerful iron-clad ram built on the Roanoke River, presented a real menace to the Federal position in North Carolina and a challenge was expected soon. May 4–21 a Federal expedition from Vicksburg to Yazoo City included skirmishing.

On a fourth front Gen. Sherman prepared to move his 98,000 men from the Chattanooga area toward Atlanta. Light skirmishing continued in Georgia with a fight at Varnell's Station. On Louisiana's Red River Confederates destroyed a U.S. steamer and captured two others May 4–5 during an engagement at David's Ferry, and a skirmish took place at Ashwood Landing. There was skirmishing also at Doubtful Canyon, N. Mex. Terr., and an affair at Callaghan's Station, Va. The Federal House passed the controversial and radical Wade-Davis Reconstruction Bill 73 to 59.

May 5, Thursday

BATTLE OF THE WILDERNESS BEGINS.

"It is a beautiful spring day on which all this bloody work is being done," wrote a Confederate private of the Army of Northern Virginia. In Virginia's Wilderness Gouverneur K. Warren's Fifth Corps faced

Richard Ewell's Second Corps on the Orange Turnpike. The first great battle of 1864 was joined. Warren advanced, supported by some of Sedgwick's force, but was driven back by Ewell, who also moved ahead. By late morning the two corps were in the throes of full-scale combat. In a separate afternoon engagement Hancock fought A. P. Hill, who came in for the Confederates from the Orange Plank Road. Desperate but indecisive fighting proved to the Federals that the enemy opposed them in force and to the Confederates that they had to attack Grant's full army. Both armies entrenched east of the Germanna Plank Road during the night and anxiously awaited the morrow.

Southward, along the James, Gen. Butler landed some thirty thousand Federals at City Point and Bermuda Hundred on the south side of the river, aiming at Richmond via Petersburg. Butler's proposed night march on Fort Darling on the James was turned down by his officers. May 5–11 Federal cavalry raided toward Petersburg and the Weldon Railroad with several skirmishes.

In North Carolina Confederate attempts to retake New Berne were defeated and the ironclad ram C.S.S. *Albemarle* engaged the Union squadron in Roanoke River. Federals remained in possession of Albemarle Sound, N.C.; *Albemarle* retired up the Roanoke at night but not until a severe ship-to-ship bombardment disabled U.S.S. *Sassacus*. Federals captured C.S.S. (former U.S.S.) *Bombshell*.

Federal cavalry under William W. Averell set out from Logan Court House, W. Va., on another expedition against the Virginia and Tennessee Railroad. Confederate troops raided the Baltimore & Ohio between Bloomington and Piedmont, W. Va. Federal scouts in Craighead and Lawrence counties, Mo., lasted five days. On the Red River skirmishing at Graham's Plantation and at Natchitoches, La., marked the slow Federal withdrawal after the campaign. At Dunn's Bayou two Federal wooden gunboats and a transport were lost in a duel with Confederate shore batteries. In Georgia skirmishing at and near Tunnel Hill lasted three days; in Kentucky Federals scouted in Meade and Breckinridge counties.

President Davis informed Gen. Lee of Butler's landings on the James and it appeared in Richmond that two major drives were heading toward the capital.

May 6, Friday

BATTLE OF THE WILDERNESS, CONTINUED.

The entrenched armies of Grant and Lee awaited each other in the dawn of the Wilderness.

On the Federal right along the Orange Turnpike, Sedgwick and Warren drove westward early in the morning. To the south, on the Federal left, Hancock's men inched ahead on the Orange Plank Road. Sedgwick and Warren made little or no progress against Ewell, and Hancock was in trouble in his fight against A. P. Hill. At first Hancock made some advance, but troops of Longstreet and another division of Hill's came up. For most of the morning the firing rolled on with no great advantage won by either side. Toward noon part of Longstreet's corps struck the Federal line on its left flank and rear. Hancock's men reeled back and more Confederates drove in, but Longstreet was severely wounded.

In late afternoon another Confederate attack by Longstreet's men was halted at the Union breastworks. Horsemen fought this day also, with Sheridan's troops opposing Stuart's near Todd's Tavern. Toward sunset Gen. John B. Gordon's brigade swept the Federal right flank, proceeding rapidly and successfully until darkness, but without real support, despite Gordon's pleas to Ewell for full attack. However, "the great fight of the Wilderness" was over. At headquarters, Gen. Grant coolly smoked a cigar and whittled. Gen. Lee rode among his men and was shouted to the rear by his protective troops. No one supposed it was over—somewhere soon it would start up again, unless of course the Federals pulled back over the river as they had done in the months gone by.

The casualties were staggering. Of over 100,000 Federals engaged, 2246 were killed, 12,037 wounded, and 3383 missing for a total of 17,666; Confederates numbered something over 60,000; losses are uncertain but probably totaled more than 7500.

On the James, Butler's men saw the steeples of Petersburg seven miles to the southwest. Richmond lay about fifteen miles to the north. There were fewer than 10,000 Confederates in a fifty-mile area around Richmond and Petersburg to oppose the Army of the James, numbering nearly 39,000. Butler ordered troops of his two corps, commanded by W. F. Smith and Quincy A. Gillmore, to break the Richmond and Petersburg Railroad. Smith sent one brigade, Gillmore none. Gen. Pickett, no longer with Lee, gathered what men he could. After modest skirmishing, the Federals returned to camp; the first of numerous half-hearted attempts at Petersburg, Richmond, and the lines of communication in between had failed.

Far from the Wilderness, guns sputtered as always. On the Red River there were skirmishes at Bayou Lamourie and at Boyce's and Wells' plantations, La. Skirmishing at Princeton, W. Va., marked the Virginia and Tennessee Railroad expedition. Other skirmishes broke out on the Blackwater River in Virginia; at Tampa, Fla. (temporarily occupied by Federals); near Boynton's Prairie, Calif.; and Morganfield, Ky. Federals scouted from Bloomfield and Patterson, Mo. Five days of Confederate operations in Calcasieu Pass, La., included capture of U.S.S. *Granite City* May 6. Confederates staged a raid on Napoleonville, La. In Georgia skirmishing continued at Tunnel Hill. U.S.S. *Commodore Jones* was sunk by a torpedo in the James River, Va.

Conscious of the double threat to Richmond from the north and from the southeast, President Davis wired Gen. Beauregard, commanding south of the capital, "I hope you will be able at Petersburg to direct operations both before and behind you, so as to meet necessities."

May 7, Saturday

SHERMAN BEGINS MARCH ON ATLANTA.

In Virginia the great armies paused in the Wilderness. Grant had long since decided to continue toward Richmond and Lee, anxious not to face superior numbers of Federals out in the open, preferred to fight in the scraggling woods. By midevening Grant's troops were on their way toward Spotsylvania Court House to the southeast. Lee, aware of his opponent's move, ordered Maj. Gen. Richard Heron Anderson, commanding in place of the wounded Longstreet, to march by night for the same place. Spotsylvania Court House was important only because roads went through it to Chancellorsville, Wilderness Tavern, and Fredericksburg. Confederate cavalry slowed the Federal advance by cutting down trees and harassing the columns.

Gen. Grant had instructed Sherman to move against Johnston and head into the interior of Georgia. There is controversy over just whose idea it was, but nevertheless, the task was now begun. At Dalton Johnston was soundly entrenched along a high ridge with only a few gaps. Toward Atlanta were more barriers, the roads were poor, the country rough. Sherman's force of nearly 100,000 men was divided into the Army of the Cumberland under Thomas near Ringgold; the Army of the Tennessee under McPherson at Lee and Gordon's Mills on the Chickamauga field; and the Army of the Ohio under Schofield north of Dalton. To oppose the Federals, nearly 60,000 Confederates held a fine defensive position.

Sherman found the main position too strong to assault and so he determined to turn Johnston's left flank. McPherson, with cavalry in front, headed toward Snake Creek Gap; Thomas' army demonstrated against Tunnel Hill and Rocky Face Ridge, Johnston's main position. There was skirmishing at Varnell's Station and near Nickajack Gap, Ga.

Once more Butler's men moved forward south of the James. Some 8000 Federals seized the Richmond and Petersburg Railroad, held a section briefly, and retired again. The opposition force numbered less than 2700. Soldiers began to call the campaign a "stationary advance."

Meanwhile, on the James U.S. gunboat *Shawsheen* was taken at Turkey Island. Skirmishing occurred at Stony Creek Station, Va.; near Florence, Ala.; and on the Red River at Bayou Boeuf. Ironclad ram C.S.S. *Raleigh* went aground and had to be destroyed, but not until she had engaged two blockaders on the sixth and four Federal vessels off the mouth of the Cape Fear River, N.C., on this day.

At a marine band concert in Washington the President declined to make a speech but proposed three cheers for Grant "and all the armies under his command."

May 8, Sunday

SPOTSYLVANIA COURT HOUSE, MAY 8–21.

Through the night men had marched in Virginia's Wilderness and when Warren's Union column neared Spotsylvania Court House in what they thought was a move around Lee's right flank, there they found that flank—Anderson's corps had beaten the Federals to the Court House area. Fighting revealed the new line. Other troops came in on both sides and in late afternoon Federals of Warren and Sedgwick assaulted the entrenched Confederates of R. H. Anderson and Ewell. The attack failed and during the night both sides established new lines. Grant ordered Sheridan with the cavalry to move around Lee, hit railroads and supply lines, and then join Butler on the James. A prime object would be to divert Stuart's Confederate cavalry from Grant. The various fights of the day went by the names of Todd's Tavern, Corbin's Bridge, Alsop's Farm, and Laurel Hill. Maj. Gen. Jubal Early took temporary command of A. P. Hill's corps, as Hill was sick. Thus, with Longstreet and Hill gone, two of Lee's three corps had new commanders in the midst of battle. On the south side of the James, Federal cavalry skirmished at Jarratt's Station and White's Bridge.

Sherman's army in Georgia continued its movement with demonstrations against Rocky Face Ridge and fighting at Buzzard Roost or Mill Creek Gap and Dug Gap. McPherson was penetrating into Snake Creek Gap on the right in his attempt to swing past Johnston's occupied army.

Sporadic action elsewhere included an affair at Halltown near Harper's Ferry and a skirmish at Jeffersonville, W. Va., on the Virginia and Tennessee Railroad; skirmishing near Decatur, Ala.; near Maysville, Ark.; and at Bayou Robert on the Red River.

A disturbed Lincoln awaited the news in Washington.

May 9, Monday

UNION FAILURE AT SNAKE CREEK GAP, GEORGIA.

The crescendo of action continued across the various fronts. There was no heavy fighting at Spotsylvania but plenty of skirmishing, sharpshooting, and the establishing of lines. In the morning the Union lost a brave, modest, and very capable corps commander when Maj. Gen. John Sedgwick was killed. Brig. Gen. Horatio G. Wright assumed command of the Sixth Corps. Burnside's Ninth Corps, attached to the Army of the Potomac, moved up nearer the battle lines and there was constant readjustment on both sides. Lee was firmly entrenched in the Wilderness in an irregular position somewhat resembling a horseshoe. Late at night orders were issued for a Federal advance the next day. Meanwhile, Sheridan's cavalry, drawing Stuart with them for a while, began a sixteen-day ride and raid toward Richmond. Fights at Davenport, Beaver Dam Station, North Anna, and Davenport Ford marked the first day.

Federal troops in Georgia under Thomas and Schofield pressed hard against Johnston's hill positions near Dalton at Buzzard Roost and Rocky Face Gap, testing the Confederate defenses. At times the intended skirmishes took on the aspects of a major assault against the rocky stronghold. By midafternoon McPherson, coming through Snake Creek Gap, a moderately wide valley in the mountain wall, pushed toward Resaca to get in Johnston's rear. However, McPherson decided the defenses were too strong to assault and he pulled back to the lower mouth of Snake Creek Gap and reported to Sherman. Sherman was disappointed in McPherson's failure to cut in behind Johnston and it has been a source of dispute ever since. Considerable cavalry skirmishing flared around the edges of the armies, with a serious combat at Varnell's Station. Other skirmishes broke out at Boyd's Trail, Snake Creek Gap, and Sugar Valley.

Farther west, Federal engineers and soldiers under Lieut. Col. Joseph Bailey were building dams on the Red River near Alexandria in order to raise the water level so that Union gunboats could retire downriver. In the Far West May 9–June 22 a Federal expedition operated against Indians from Fort Crittenden, Ut. Terr., to Fort Mojave, Ariz. Terr. May 9–10 Federals scouted from Indian Ranch to Cedar Bluffs, Colo. Terr. May 9–June 3 the Gila, Ariz. Terr., expedition operated against Indians. Federal troops on a railroad-destroying raid in Virginia fought Confederates at Cloyd's Mountain, successfully assaulting a strong position. Casualties were considerable on both sides. In Kentucky a skirmish took place near Pound Gap and a five-day Federal expedition moved from Louisa, Ky., to Rock House Creek, W. Va. In St. John's River, Fla., Confederates destroyed the U.S. transport *Harriet A. Weed*. In Arkansas there was a skirmish at Eudora Church. Maj. Gen. Stephen D. Lee assumed command of the Confederate Department of Alabama, Mississippi, and East Louisiana, as Polk and many of his troops had gone to join Johnston in Georgia.

Butler ordered his whole army out against the Richmond-Petersburg lines of communications south of the James. Gillmore's men started to destroy the railroad. The rest of the advance moved slowly despite little opposition. The fighting was recorded as being at Fort Clifton, Ware Bottom Church, Brandon or Brander's Bridge, Swift Creek or Arrowfield Church. Confusion set in. Butler ordered the army back to its original lines the next morning. Everyone seemed to be at fault.

President Davis wrote embattled Gen. Lee, "Your dispatches have cheered us in the anxiety of a critical position. . . ." President Lincoln told another serenading group, "Our commanders are following up their victories resolutely and successfully. . . . I will volunteer to say that I am very glad at what has happened; but there is a great deal still to be done."

May 10, Tuesday

GENERAL ATTACK AT SPOTSYLVANIA.

Hancock, Warren, and Wright's corps of the Army of the Potomac attacked Anderson's Confederate corps northwest of Spotsylvania in the late afternoon and early evening. Assaulting the entrenched Confederates twice, the Federals were thrown back, though some reached the parapets. At the salient or "Mule Shoe" in the center of the Confederate line, Emory Upton's division of Wright's corps struck at 6 P.M. and breached Ewell's lines, but Gordon's Confederates came up to plug the gap partially. Finally Upton had to withdraw in the darkness. On the far Federal left Burnside's corps moved close to Spotsylvania Court House itself and entrenched in front of Early's corps. The first major day of the Spotsylvania battle ended in repulse of Union assaults after dents in the Confederate lines.

Sheridan's raiders still fought skirmishes with Stuart's cavalry along the North Anna and near Beaver Dam Station. By nightfall Sheridan was south of the South Anna, less than twenty miles from Richmond. Stuart's cavalry took position between Sheridan and Richmond. Custer's brigade destroyed railroad tracks and running equipment between the North and South Anna rivers on the Virginia Central.

South of the James action erupted at Chester Station, and a Confederate torpedo station on the James was destroyed. Other lesser fighting included skirmishing at Lost River Gap, W. Va., and Dardanelle, Ark. A two-week Union scout moved from Pilot Knob, Mo., to Gainesville, Ark.; guerrilla fighting occurred at Winchester, Tenn.; and in the Virginia railroad raiding engagements took place at Cove Mountain or Grassy Lick, near Wytheville, and there was a skirmish at New River Bridge. Off Charleston, Rear Admiral Dahlgren's ship commanders voted against attacking Fort Sumter directly.

In Georgia Joe Johnston learned of McPherson's efforts to turn his left at Resaca and Snake Creek Gap. Demonstrations and skirmishes continued. Polk's corps from Mississippi was on the way to reinforce Johnston. Sherman, now that McPherson had partially failed, decided to swing his entire army by the right flank through Snake Creek Gap.

May 11, Wednesday

BATTLE OF YELLOW TAVERN, VIRGINIA; JEB STUART MORTALLY WOUNDED.

Some six miles north of Richmond at a place called Yellow Tavern, Jeb Stuart and his cavalry faced the Federal raiders of Philip Sheridan. In a sharp, helter-skelter encounter Stuart fell from his horse, mortally wounded. Sheridan's men drove back Stuart's troops but the engagement gave the Confederates time to strengthen the defenses of Richmond and Sheridan had to return toward the James. Other fighting broke out at nearby Ground Squirrel Church or Bridge, Glen Allen Station, and Ashland. Once more victory was mixed with sorrow—the capital of the Confederacy was saved from raiders but the "Cavalier of Dixie" died May 12.

To the north there was a breathing spell along the entrenched lines around Spotsylvania, with only a reconnaissance on Grant's left flank by men of Burnside's corps. However, Grant, learning about the bulge in the Confederate center, determined to attack it.

In Georgia Sherman ordered a general movement toward Resaca from Snake Creek Gap on the twelfth. A Confederate reconnaissance in Sugar Valley resulted in rather extensive casualties.

In the seldom considered but strategically important Union raids on Confederate railroads deep in southwest Virginia there was a skirmish at Blacksburg. A Federal expedition May 11–14 moved from Point Lookout, Md., to the Rappahannock in Virginia. Maj. Gen. E. R. S. Canby assumed command of the Union Military Division of West Mississippi. Three Federal ironclads escaped from Alexandria, La., after dams raised the water level. Other naval vessels got over the rapids on the thirteenth.

At the Louisiana Constitutional Convention in New Orleans the reconstructed Federal state government adopted an ordinance of emancipation without compensation. It was ratified by the people July 22. President Davis wrote Lee that he was trying to send more troops, but "we have been sorely pressed by enemy on south side. Are now threatened by the cavalry. . . ."

May 12, Thursday

BATTLE OF SPOTSYLVANIA RENEWED.

JOHNSTON EVACUATES DALTON, GEORGIA.

A fierce day of fighting at Spotsylvania opened at 4:30 A.M. Straight at the salient of the Confederate lines charged Hancock's Federals. Possibly four thousand prisoners, including two generals, artillery, small arms, and stands of colors were taken from Ewell's corps. Bayonets bristled in the charge. Through the brush and small trees the Federals pushed Ewell's overwhelmed but hard-fighting defenders back to a second line of defense. Masses of Federal troops were opposed mainly by infantry, due to an unfortunate withdrawal of Ewell's artillery. But the Confederate lines were stiffening and holding now. To the right of Hancock's drive Wright's corps moved in to help; until past midnight raged the ferocious struggle known as the "Bloody Angle of Spotsylvania." All told, twenty-four Federal brigades attacked only a few hundred yards of entrenchments. For the most part the main Confederate line held, but eventually they were withdrawn to a new line as their salient was eliminated. Even farther to the right Warren's corps drove in against Anderson but was repulsed. Meade and Grant believed Warren had been slow. On the Federal left Burnside also attacked Early and part of Ewell's force but gained little except to keep Confederate reinforcements from the main battle line.

It was one of the murderous days of the war: Federal killed, wounded, and missing are put at about 6800; Confederates lost perhaps 5000 killed and wounded alone. Two great armies had fought, and only rather unimportant bits of ground changed hands. Yet attrition was more serious for the Confederates. Where were the replacements to come from?

One Yankee exclaimed, "This has been the most terrible day I have ever lived." Again his soldiers shouted "Lee to the rear" when they thought him in danger. One Southern man wrote of Grant, "We have met a man this time, who either does not know when he is whipped, or who cares not if he loses his whole Army." Northerners, too, accused Grant of butchery.

Sheridan, riding east of Richmond along the Chickahominy, tried to get to Butler's camps on the James. Confederates fought Sheridan's cavalry at Meadow Bridge, Mechanicsville, Strawberry Hill, Brook Church, and along the Richmond defenses. Other fighting during Sheridan's operations near Richmond included, until May 24, action at Mattapony Church, Jones' Bridge, Haxall's, White House Landing, and Hanover Court House.

South of the James, Butler's troops from City Point and Bermuda Hundred were supposedly threatening both Petersburg and Richmond. So far the Federals had bungled the campaign. Beauregard, who had succeeded Pickett, was gathering in what few troops he could find for defense. There had already been considerable skirmishing and forays by Federal cavalry. Butler advanced upon Drewry's Bluff and Confederate Fort Darling on the south side of the James. Meanwhile, Federal cavalry under Brig. Gen. A. V. Kautz raided the Richmond and Danville Railroad. The Confederate capital was thus threatened from the north and from the southeast and pestered by cavalry raids as well.

Down in Georgia, Sherman's army, except for one corps, had passed through Snake Creek Gap and was near Resaca by day's end. Johnston learned of the threat to his rear and during the night evacuated Dalton and positioned his army at Resaca in front of Sherman's army. It was the first major step in a campaign by two masters of maneuver.

Fighting elsewhere was minor by comparison, but an affair occurred at Strasburg, Va.; and skirmishes at Jackson's Ferry, Ala.; Smith's Station, Neb. Terr.; Bayou Lamourie on the Red River, La.; and in southwest Virginia at Newport, Brown's Ferry, Salt Ponds, and Gap Mountain.

May 13, Friday

Around Resaca, Ga., Joseph E. Johnston had taken up new positions, joined by Polk's reinforcements, and faced the advance of Sherman's full army. Fighting broke out at Tilton, Resaca, and near Dalton during the course of the realignment.

Late in the day, Warren's corps in Virginia shifted around to the left as Grant, having failed to break Lee's line at Spotsylvania, continued his move to the south and east. Sheridan's cavalry left the Richmond area and headed for the James at Haxall's Landing.

At Drewry's Bluff Butler's Federals were laboriously getting into position to attack, thus giving Beauregard's Confederates time to arrange their thin line of defenders.

On the Red River the Federal gunboats and Banks' infantry column continued their retreat. Meanwhile, to the north, Steele's Federal column had returned to Little Rock. The Federals' entire spring operation across the Mississippi had been a failure.

May 13–16 Federal guns struck Fort Sumter again at Charleston, firing 1140 rounds in four days. Skirmishes flared at Pulaski, Tenn.; Spavinaw, Ark.; and Cuba, Mo. Jo Shelby's Confederate cavalry began a new campaign north of the Arkansas River, with skirmishing at Cypress Creek in Perry County. Shelby's operations lasted the rest of the month.

President Davis, beset with many threats and concerns, wrote Gen. Lee, "If possible will sustain you in your unequal struggle so long and nobly maintained."

May 14, Saturday
BATTLE FOR RESACA, GEORGIA.

Sherman's Federals still intended to assault Johnston's lines at Resaca, Ga., but delays and extensive deployments held down the attack. Although there was some fighting on both flanks, with moderate Union success, the real struggle for Resaca would have to wait. It still was primarily a campaign of movement and probing operations.

In Virginia Grant continued to shift his troops to the left, Wright following Warren, as both armies sought to recover from the pounding each had received around Spotsylvania. The hard march and heavy rain caused a Federal attack to be called off. Other skirmishing was at Wilson's Landing on the Red River in Louisiana.

There were prospects of renewed action in Virginia's Shenandoah Valley. Franz Sigel had moved south with some 6500 Union men, facing only cavalry opposition by Confederate John D. Imboden. But now Gen. Breckinridge was bringing in about five thousand Confederate defenders and a skirmish at Rude's Hill gave indication that things would be different.

Mr. Davis wrote Gen. Lee from Richmond, "Affairs here are critical . . ." meaning Butler's operations against Drewry's Bluff and Petersburg.

May 15, Sunday
BATTLE OF NEW MARKET, VIRGINIA.
BATTLE OF RESACA, GEORGIA, CONTINUES.

Every spring at the Virginia Military Institute at Lexington, Va., an impressive, solemn review is held in honor of the cadets who fell in the

Battle of New Market. Threatened in the Shenandoah Valley from the north by Franz Sigel's Federal advance, Maj. Gen. Breckinridge had gathered in everyone he could find, including 247 students from VMI. The Federal line lay across the Valley Pike and toward the north fork of the Shenandoah. Breckinridge attacked, and by late morning Sigel was falling back. After trying futilely to hold, Sigel retreated to Strasburg. From about 5500 troops, Federals suffered 93 killed, 482 wounded, and 256 missing for 831 casualties; Confederates had 42 killed, 522 wounded, and 13 missing for 577 from about 5000, though as usual figures are in dispute. Of the VMI contingent 10 were killed and 47 wounded. The sharp defeat proved somewhat humiliating for the Federals; the pressure eased momentarily in the Shenandoah Valley. The courage of the cadets has made New Market a legend, though they were a small part of the victorious Southern force.

In front of Resaca, Ga., Hood's reinforced Confederate corps advanced; Hooker's Federal corps advanced. They met in battle and Hood's men were driven back. Fighting raged all along the line and at Lay's Ferry on the Oostenaula River south of Resaca. Sherman sent out cavalry and an infantry division, planning to make a flanking movement south of the Oostenaula. Johnston's Resaca position was too strong for direct attack. However, realizing the danger of being flanked with the river at his back, the Confederate general withdrew from Resaca during the night. His troops burned the railroad bridge over the Oostenaula and headed toward Calhoun and Adairsville. There was also skirmishing near Rome and at Armuchee Creek, Ga.

In the Spotsylvania area the only fighting was a skirmish at Piney Branch Church. However, the Federals were changing their positions and reestablishing their main lines. The whole battle front moved more to the east and south of Spotsylvania; tactical maneuver temporarily replaced the fighting. Sheridan's cavalry, frustrated in its efforts to reach Butler's troops, recuperated at Haxall's Landing on the James. At Drewry's Bluff Butler planned an attack but was occupied with arranging his defensive lines. Telegraph wire was strung on stumps, one of the first uses of wire entanglements in Virginia, although it had been previously at Knoxville.

Shelby's Confederates skirmished near Dardanelle, Ark.; in West Virginia Federals scouted from Beverly into Pocahontas, Webster, and Braxton counties. Confederates attacked Mount Pleasant Landing, La.; and skirmishes occurred at Centre Star, Ala.; and Avoyelles or Marksville Prairie, on the Red River, in Louisiana.

President Davis called to Virginia all troops he could from South Carolina, Georgia, and part of Florida. The President was particularly concerned by the threat to Drewry's Bluff. He warned Gen. Lee not to expose himself to the enemy for "The country could not bear the loss of you. . . ." In Washington President Lincoln seemed confident after hearing news from the fronts.

May 16, Monday

DREWRY'S BLUFF OR FORT DARLING, VIRGINIA.

At Drewry's Bluff and the Fort Darling area on the James, Beauregard's ten Confederate brigades attacked in the dense fog of early morning. The Federal right under W. F. Smith was badly hurt, but Union troops held in the center. Heavy fighting on the Federal left under Q. A. Gillmore was indecisive, but Smith and Butler thought they had to withdraw the Union forces due to the danger on the right. Some of Beauregard's hastily gathered army did not get under way in time to press the Federals. Furthermore, the Southern force expected to come up in the Federal rear from Petersburg never arrived. Butler pulled back in the rain toward Bermuda Hundred, beaten in his attempt to take Petersburg and possibly Richmond. Ineptness in top Union command was never more evident than in this campaign. Drewry's Bluff or Fort Darling could have been disastrous to the entire state of Virginia and possibly Lee's army as well. Over 16,000 Federals faced some 18,000 Confederates. There were 390 Union soldiers dead, 2380 wounded, and 1390 missing for 4160 total; 355 Confederates were killed, 1941 wounded, and 210 missing for 2506.

Elsewhere there was more action than usual—an action at Big Bushes near Smoky Hill, Kas.; skirmishing at Dry Wood Creek, Mo.; and an Indian affair at Spirit Lake, Minn.; an engagement at Mansura, Belle Prairie or Smith's Plantation, La., on the Red River; a skirmish on the Ashepoo River, S.C.; and a skirmish at Pond Creek in Pike County, Ky. In addition, Federal expeditions operated from Patterson to Bloomfield and Pilot Knob, Mo.; and from Fort Craig, N. Mex. Terr., to Fort Goodwin, Ariz. Terr., against Indians. Union naval vessels dueled with enemy shore batteries on the Mississippi near Ratliff's Landing, Miss., part of the continuing small war on the river.

May 17, Tuesday

Pulling back southeastward toward Atlanta from Calhoun, Johnston set up his lines briefly at Adairsville, Ga., followed up by Sherman. The Federal Army of the Cumberland under Thomas was in Johnston's front and Schofield and McPherson were moving around both flanks. Again Johnston ordered a withdrawal during the night; two corps went to Cassville and one toward Kingston. Skirmishing broke out at Adairsville with action also at Rome, Ga. An affair occurred at Madison Station, Ala.

The Spotsylvania front in Virginia remained relatively quiet except for some shifting of positions. To the south Butler's Army of the James withdrew completely from the Drewry's Bluff area, pushed by Beauregard. By this day the Army of the James was around Bermuda Hundred, again prevented from threatening Petersburg by geography, by Beauregard's army, and by its own ineffectiveness. Butler was pinned between the James on the north, the Appomattox on the south, and the Confederates in front. Some likened his position to "being corked in a bottle." A dangerous threat to Richmond had been stopped.

In Arkansas Shelby's Confederate raiders captured Dardanelle and in Louisiana skirmishing flared at Yellow Bayou and an action took place at Moreauville. In Virginia Sheridan's cavalry had left Haxall's Landing on the James and headed north again, endeavoring to get back to Grant's army.

The Federal Congress passed measures setting up what became the postal money order system.

May 18, Wednesday

SPOTSYLVANIA AGAIN.

Sherman's armies in Georgia, still on the march, followed Johnston's withdrawing forces through Adairsville and toward Kingston. By evening, Schofield, Thomas, and McPherson converged on the Confederates in the Cassville-Kingston area and fighting broke out near Cassville, near Kingston, and at Pine Log Creek.

The several days of comparative quiet around Spotsylvania Court House, Va., ended. The corps of Hancock and Wright led a dawn assault on Lee's left, mainly against Ewell's troops fighting from behind stanch new entrenchments. The Federals charged several times without success. Gen. Meade ordered the futile drive abandoned. Farther to the Federal left, Burnside also attacked and failed. During the night further shifts went on in the Federal lines. Grant, deciding the enemy was too strong to be defeated in his present position, once more started sidling toward his own left to attempt to get around Lee's right flank.

Farther south Beauregard was completing his investment of Butler's Army of the James at Bermuda Hundred. Fighting occurred at Foster's Plantation and near City Point. Sheridan's cavalry made its way back toward the Army of the Potomac from its resting places on the north side of the James.

In Alabama skirmishing broke out at Fletcher's Ferry and in Kentucky in Pike County and along the Wolf River. In the Red River country an engagement occurred at Yellow Bayou, also known as Bayou De Glaize, Norwood's Plantation, or Old Oaks, La. Other fighting included a skirmish at Clarksville and an affair near Searcy, Ark. For several days Federals scouted near Neosho and Carthage in Missouri.

President Davis expressed his disappointment to Gen. Johnston over the withdrawal in Georgia. The New York *World* and the *Journal of Commerce* published a spurious proclamation from Lincoln calling for 300,000 more troops. The President believed it wicked and traitorous and ordered the arrest of the editors, proprietors, and publishers and the occupation of the offices by troops. However, the newsmen were released soon and the papers resumed publication; the editors claimed a fraud had been perpetrated upon them by a stock manipulator.

May 19, Thursday

LAST ENGAGEMENT OF SPOTSYLVANIA.

News of war and politics was temporarily eclipsed—Nathaniel Hawthorne died in his sleep at Plymouth, N.H., the night of May 18–19. One of the great New England school of writers, the sixty-year-old Hawthorne was recognized and honored as a classic American author.

Gen. Lee ordered Ewell's corps, on the left of his line at Spotsylvania, Va., to make a demonstration to determine whether Grant was once more moving to the Confederate right. Fairly severe fighting resulted, and action continued until late evening, when Ewell pulled back. But Lee was right; Grant was swinging to the east and south again, heading now for the Po River.

For the series of battles known as Spotsylvania, the Federal casualties are put at around 17,500 out of about 110,000 men engaged. The Confederates had probably over 50,000 engaged, but total losses are not reliably recorded. For the combined campaign of Wilderness and Spotsylvania, Federal losses had come to over 33,000 men, a frightful toll even though progress was being made. But they could be replaced by the North. Confederate losses, much lower, could not be as readily rectified, as their total numbers were so many fewer. Maneuvers in the area continued for two more days but the Battle of Spotsylvania Court House was over.

From his position near Cassville, Ga., Gen. Johnston ordered an attack on the separated units of Sherman's army. Hood was to make the main effort, but instead of attacking he fell back on the defensive after apparently erroneous rumors of Federals on his flank and rear. Johnston had to take up a defensive position south and east of Cassville. Sherman pushed nearer; artillery opened fire. In the evening two of Johnston's three corps commanders, Hood and Polk, felt the position could not be held, while Hardee was opposed to falling back. Johnston reluctantly yielded to retreat. The Confederates retired through Cartersville to the Etowah River and crossed on the twentieth. Dissension was again causing trouble among the generals of Johnston's forces in the West. Sherman, on the other hand, wanted to fight before Johnston crossed the Etowah. Also in Georgia, skirmishing took place at Mill Springs Gap.

The tag end of the Red River Campaign occurred as the Federal army crossed the Atchafalaya on their retreat from Alexandria. Fayetteville, Ark., saw a skirmish; Shelby's Confederate cavalry operated near Norristown, Ark. In Florida, May 19–27, there were small fights and other operations by both sides on the St. John's River. Union forces reached Meadow Bluff, W. Va., in their raid on the railroads of far southwestern Virginia. There was a skirmish at Dandridge, Tenn. At Fort Sumter the guns fired on Federal small boats off the southwestern angle.

President Davis told Lee of Beauregard's success in driving back Butler's forces and told Lee to use his own discretion about the future.

May 20, Friday

It was a day of movement in Georgia and in Virginia. Gen. Joseph E. Johnston left Cassville and pulled back through Cartersville, Ga., across the Etowah River to a strong position at Allatoona Pass. Sherman must now revise his future maneuvers. Federal troops of Schofield's army moved into Cartersville after a skirmish at the Etowah. Other fighting occurred around Cartersville and at Allatoona Mills.

In Virginia Grant issued orders for Meade's Army of the Potomac to move by its left and then cross the Mattapony. During the night of May 20–21, Hancock's corps led the way, going to Guiney's Station. Lee with the Army of Northern Virginia was not blinded by the large movements and prepared to pull his army out to the south to block Grant once more. To the south side of the James a skirmish flared at Ware Bottom Church, not far from Bermuda Hundred, where Beauregard was effectively blocking Butler's Federals.

Other action occurred at Lamar, Mo.; Greenbrier River, W. Va.; Mayfield, Ky.; Greenville, Miss.; and Stony Point, Ark.

President Lincoln ordered that no person engaged in trade in accordance with the treasury regulations should be hindered or delayed by the Army or Navy. It was part of the continuing difficulties regarding trade in occupied territory or with the enemy.

President Davis wrote Lee in detail about other fronts, but left movements in Virginia up to Lee.

May 21, Saturday

Grant's army in Virginia was shifting en masse to the east and south toward and around Guiney's Station following Hancock's advance. Lee made some preliminary shifts to counter whatever Grant might be doing. Lee planned to withdraw to the North Anna River and so ordered late in the day. Combats broke out at Guiney's Station and at Stanard's Mill. South of the James a skirmish took place at Fort Powhatan but things quieted down on the front near Petersburg. Maj. Gen. David Hunter took over for Maj. Gen. Franz Sigel in the Union Department of West Virginia, following Sigel's failure in recent Shenandoah Valley actions.

Elsewhere, a detachment from the Army of the Tennessee that had been on Banks' Red River Campaign headed back to Vicksburg. There were three days of demonstrations on James Island near Charleston; an affair on the Blue River in Missouri; skirmishing at Pine Bluff in Arkansas; and a skirmish at Newtown, Va. Sheridan and his cavalry, coming north from the James, arrived at White House en route back to Grant.

Sherman regrouped, repairing bridges and getting a brief breathing spell in the Cassville-Kingston-Cartersville area. Johnston was in position around Allatoona Pass.

President Lincoln urged Western state governers to continue sending forward hundred-day troops to "sustain Gen. Sherman's lengthening lines. . . ."

May 22, Sunday

There was a race on in Virginia—Grant versus Lee. Grant was moving south from Guiney's Station toward the North Anna River. Lee was moving south a few miles to the west. In the morning two corps of his troops came into Hanover Junction, beating Grant into position and staying in front of him, but much nearer to Richmond. Grant ordered the Federal army to press on the next day.

Sherman was ready to move again and in the evening cavalry engaged at Cassville. Orders were issued to the bulk of the Federal army to head toward Dallas, Ga., thus going around Johnston's left flank, posted in the Allatoona area near the vital Chattanooga-Atlanta railroad.

Otherwise it was a quiet day with an affair near Devall's Bluff, Ark.; a skirmish at Front Royal, Va.; and another near Mount Pleasant, Miss. U.S.S. *Stingaree* was taken by Confederates off Brazos, Tex., and then recaptured.

May 23, Monday

BATTLE OF THE NORTH ANNA, VIRGINIA, TO MAY 26.

General Lee was ready, south of the North Anna between Hanover Junction and the stream. His army formed a line with an apex, a strong position, and ahead of Grant. But Grant moved, too. Late in the afternoon Warren's Fifth Corps crossed the North Anna. A. P. Hill hit Warren near Jericho Mills about 6 P.M., gaining some, but finally being stopped by the Federals. Wright's Sixth Corps began crossing the North Anna to Warren's aid, arriving the morning of the twenty-fourth. Farther east Hancock's Second Corps pushed Confederates out of positions near Old Chesterfield on the north side of the North Anna. Lee now had an opportunity to attack a divided Federal Army of the Potomac, but due to his own illness and other factors, he was unable to take advantage of it.

In Georgia Sherman's entire army headed toward Dallas from the Cassville area, once again trying to turn Johnston's left flank, and crossed the Etowah River. Johnston tried to determine Sherman's action from his contracted lines around Allatoona Pass.

Minor action in Georgia was recorded at Stilesborough. Elsewhere, fighting was limited to a skirmish at Grouse Creek, Calif., in the Humboldt River operations against Indians; and a three-day Federal scout from Warrensburg, Mo. In Florida Confederates captured U.S.S. *Columbine.*

May 24, Tuesday

Grant continued to move across the North Anna River. Wright's Sixth Corps moved in on the right to aid Warren's Fifth Corps, while farther east

Hancock's Second Corps crossed at the Chesterfield Bridge. One of Burnside's Ninth Corps divisions crossed. The Army of the Potomac, however, was in effect divided into three parts due to the bend in the river and Lee's apex-shaped line. Wright and Warren were on the right, Hancock on the left, and Lee in between. Most of Burnside's men were north of the river. However, the long-absent cavalry force of Sheridan, after its raid to the James, rejoined Grant. A brief fight broke out at Ox Ford, but Lee held his strong position.

Sherman pressed on from the Etowah toward Dallas. Skirmishing took place at Cass Station, Cassville, Burnt Hickory or Huntsville, and near Dallas, Ga. Much of the action involved Wheeler's Confederate cavalry against Federal wagons in Sherman's rear. Johnston, at Allatoona, realized Sherman's intent and ordered his army toward Dallas by way of New Hope Church, to attempt to get in front of Sherman once more. But the New Hope-Dallas area was closer than ever to Atlanta, albeit Sherman was now quite a ways from his vital railroad supply line, and Johnston's lines of communication were ever contracting.

Lesser action increased, with skirmishing near Nashville, Tenn.; at Holly Springs, Miss.; near Little Rock, Ark.; near Morganza, La.; at Wilson's Wharf, Va.; and near Charles Town and Lewisburg, W. Va. Confederate raiders under Col. Colton Greene operated on the west bank of the Mississippi River until June 4, engaging Federal steamers, harassing river shipping, and capturing two Northern vessels.

May 25, Wednesday

CAMPAIGN OF NEW HOPE CHURCH, GEORGIA, TO JUNE 4.

The Federal right south of the North Anna moved forward only slightly, for Grant realized that Lee's position was too strong for further offensive action. The operations on the North Anna were a frustrated Federal advance, ably held off by the Confederates despite Lee's illness. Total Union losses were 425; Confederate casualties are not clear.

Around New Hope Church, Ga., a little over twenty-five miles northeast of Atlanta, Johnston had his army in position, Hardee on the left, Polk in the center, and Hood on the right. Sherman still advanced, with Schofield on the left, Thomas in the center, and McPherson on the right. Hooker's corps found Hood's men along Pumpkin Vine Creek. Hooker drove toward New Hope Church but Confederates repulsed several attacks in a fierce thunderstorm. Casualties were high. Sherman's forward side-slide ground to a halt.

Raiders were active: Colton Greene's Confederates from the shore engaged U.S.S. *Curlew* on the Mississippi and captured U.S.S. *Lebanon*. Shelby's men skirmished with Federals at Buck Horn, Ark. Elsewhere, fighting occurred at Cripple Creek, Woodbury Pike, Tenn.; Camp Finegan, and Jackson's Bridge near Pensacola, Fla. The crew of a small boat failed to destroy C.S.S. *Albemarle* near Plymouth, N.C. A joint Federal army-navy expedition up the Ashepoo and South Edisto rivers, S.C., did not succeed in breaking the Charleston-Savannah Railroad.

May 25–July 12 a Federal expedition operated from Fort Wingate, N. Mex. Terr., to the Gila and San Carlos rivers, Ariz. Terr.

May 26, Thursday

END OF BATTLE OF NORTH ANNA, VIRGINIA.

As darkness fell, Grant and Meade began withdrawing the Army of the Potomac across the North Anna. The army would then cross the Pamunkey River and head toward Hanovertown, far around Lee's right. Sheridan's cavalry preceded the infantry. Hanovertown was about eighteen miles southeast of Lee's apex. Once more Lee had halted Grant, but Grant continued the strategic offensive.

Farther west, in the Shenandoah Valley, the new Federal commander, David Hunter, headed from Strasburg and Cedar Creek toward Staunton, Va. Hunter had about 16,000 men and was opposed by W. E. "Grumble" Jones (who had replaced Breckinridge) with about 8500 men.

McPherson, on the right of Sherman's Georgia advance, moved forward and reached Dallas early in the day. Schofield also moved up to the general area of New Hope Church-Dallas. As Sherman's entire army pushed slowly forward, skirmishing was quite heavy. By evening the two armies were very close to each other and entrenched. The character of the Atlanta Campaign now changed from mainly a campaign of movement and occasional fighting, to a war of entrenchments on both sides. The actions were known as "about Dallas" and Burned Church, Ga.

Cavalry engagements occurred at Decatur and Moulton, Ala. In the Mississippi Valley an affair took place on Lane's Prairie, Maries County, Mo. In South Carolina on the Ashepoo, U.S. transport *Boston* was destroyed by her crew at Chapman's Fort, after being grounded and under Confederate fire. Maj. Gen. John G. Foster assumed command of the Federal Department of the South. Montana Territory was formally created largely from Dakota Territory in the continued development of the Federal West.

May 27, Friday

Sheridan's Federal cavalry occupied Hanovertown, Va., south of the Pamunkey River, with little opposition. Meanwhile, the infantry corps continued their march from the North Anna to the Pamunkey. Fighting, mainly by cavalry, erupted at Hanover Junction, Sexton's Station, Mount Carmel Church, Dabney's Ferry, Hanovertown, Little River, Pole Cat Creek, and Salem Church. Learning of Grant's advance, Lee also began moving back on his shorter lines from his position near Hanover Junction, heading south and then eastward.

On the New Hope Church-Dallas line in Georgia there was some shifting of positions and rather heavy fighting, especially near Mount Zion Church. Howard's corps attacked at Pickett's Mills northeast of New Hope Church and was repulsed with fairly heavy losses in the difficult and heavily wooded country.

Other fighting broke out at Pond Springs, Ala.; Greenville, Miss.; Cassville, Ga.; Shanghai, Mo.; and at Thomas' House on the Trinity River, Calif. Confederate Gen. Shelby assumed command of Southern troops north of the Arkansas River.

May 28, Saturday

Lee and the Army of Northern Virginia, hurrying from the North Anna, arrived north of the Chickahominy and Mechanicsville. Then moving southeast toward Cold Harbor, Lee again got in front of Grant's army, which was crossing the Pamunkey near Hanovertown. Fighting, mainly between cavalry forces, occurred at Aenon Church, Jones' Farm, Crump's Creek, and Haw's Shop, as well as along the Totopotomoy River. Although Lee was in front of Grant, both he and President Davis had cause for concern. Davis told Lee that Beauregard, south of Richmond, was strengthening his defenses but was outnumbered at least two to one.

In Georgia Johnston, hoping to disrupt Federal plans for a shift to the left, ordered Hardee to make a reconnaissance in force against McPherson near Dallas. In a sharp contest, the Confederates suffered heavily and pulled back.

In Missouri Confederates sacked Lamar and skirmishes broke out at Warrensburg and Pleasant Hill. Action flared near Little Rock and at Washington, Ark., and at Pest House opposite Port Hudson, La. A skirmish took place near Jacksonville, Fla., and fighting continued at Big Flat, Calif., during the Humboldt operations.

Far from the scene of the American Civil War, Maximilian of Hapsburg landed at Vera Cruz to take the throne of Mexico, backed by Napoleon III of France and opposed by Mexican leader Benito Juárez.

May 29, Sunday

The Army of the Potomac marched toward Richmond south of the Pamunkey, meeting little opposition. But Lee, a bit farther on, was preparing his lines. In Georgia there was mostly shifting of positions and more sharp skirmishing. At night Johnston opened up his artillery and outposts were pushed near McPherson's works. The lines were close everywhere and irregular fire commonplace these days in the Georgia woodlands; commonplace, too, were the mounting casualties, not part of a big battle, but the inevitable attrition of a big campaign.

Elsewhere on the war fronts there were skirmishes on Bayou Fordoche Road, La.; at Hamlin, W. Va.; Middleburg and Newtown, Va.; Moulton,

Ala.; Yazoo River, Miss.; and guerrilla depredations at Winchester, Tenn. Confederates captured a Federal wagon train at Salem, Ark.

May 30, Monday

In Virginia fighting broke out at Matadequin Creek, Old Church, Shady Grove, Armstrong's Farm, and Ashland. Grant's main force arrived along the Totopotomoy River and faced Lee's line north of the Chickahominy. At White House on the Pamunkey W. F. Smith brought two corps of reinforcements to Grant. Grant was now nearly as close to Richmond as McClellan had been in 1862 but again the Confederates barred the way. Fighting was heavy as the Federals felt the Confederate line, determining where it lay.

In Georgia the lines still held around New Hope Church and Dallas and the skirmishing and sharpshooting continued with action near Allatoona and at Burned Church, Ga. In Charleston Harbor a minor bombardment of Fort Sumter was opened by the Federals lasting until June 5, and consisting of 319 rounds.

John Hunt Morgan was on his way again—this time into Kentucky to take pressure off Johnston in Georgia by attacking Sherman's more distant communications. Then too, there were skirmishes on Mill and Honey creeks in Missouri; a Federal expedition until June 5 from Morganza to the Atchafalaya, La.; and a skirmish at Greeneville, Tenn. Federals under Brig. Gen. George Crook started from Meadow Bluff, W. Va., toward Lynchburg, Va., part of the Federal move by Hunter against Lynchburg.

May 31, Tuesday

A hectic month came to an end with many changes since May began. Grant shifted part of his lines toward Cold Harbor, still moving to get around Lee's right. Lee and his Confederates shifted, too, and were there in front of him, setting the scene for the horrible days known as Cold Harbor. Fighting occurred at Mechump's Creek, Shallow Creek, Turner's Farm, and Bethesda Church, Va. When May began Grant had been north of the Rapidan; now he was knocking on the still locked door of Richmond.

In Georgia Sherman had moved many miles toward Atlanta from far northwest Georgia, but he, too, confronted a determined and skillful foe. Federals and Confederates had each lost about nine thousand men during the May campaign. A bright spot for the Confederates was that John Hunt Morgan was raiding into Kentucky again, and Richmond and Atlanta still held. Nevertheless, the spring had been a rough one for the South.

Already the November presidential election attracted a lot of attention in the North. Lincoln had been hearing from the politicos. At Cleveland a dissident group of Radical Republicans, unhappy over Lincoln's emancipa-

tion policies and his lack of vindictiveness, met to nominate Gen. John
Charles Frémont for President and Brig. Gen. John Cochrane of New York
for Vice-President. A splinter group of no great strength or outstanding
leaders, it nevertheless caused the President some distress.

JUNE, 1864

Crisis loomed on two fronts: Federals had plunged deeper than ever into
Georgia and moved some miles nearer Richmond. Just what could President
Davis and his government do to aid the armies under Genls. Lee and
Johnston? With shrinking territory, supplying even its main armies became
increasingly problematical for the Confederacy. Possible threats from the
Mississippi Valley and along the coasts, morale on the homefront, and
criticism of the Davis administration presented further difficulties.

The roll calls of the casualties from the Wilderness and Spotsylvania
began to reach the homes of the North. But Grant moved on. Had a new
means of crushing the South really been found? Was Sherman about to
take Atlanta, perhaps even without a major battle? Would the replacements
for the Federal armies still come?

The Union party, a combination of Republicans and War Democrats,
was about to meet at Baltimore and obviously to nominate Lincoln. Already, late in May, John C. Frémont had been nominated by a group of
Radical Republicans urging an extremely harsh war policy. On the other
end of the spectrum Peace Democrats and others attacked the President
with increasing violence and urged negotiation or some other non-belligerent
method of ending the war.

June 1, Wednesday

BATTLE OF COLD HARBOR, VIRGINIA, TO JUNE 3.

As Federal infantry converged on the Cold Harbor area of Virginia near
the 1862 Seven Days' battlefields, they found the Confederates had already
arrived and were making dispositions. Confederate infantry of R. H.
Anderson's corps attacked Sheridan's Federal cavalry near Old Cold Harbor
in the morning, and two Southern charges were defeated. Wright's Federal
Sixth Corps passed by the rear of the rest of the Federal army and
arrived on the left, relieving Sheridan in midmorning. Meanwhile, W. F.
Smith and the Eighteenth Corps of the Army of the James were delayed as
they came from White House. Lee's army saw the arrival of Wright's
corps and shifted to the right accordingly. Not until 6 P.M. were Wright
and Smith ready to assault. At first the Federals made some gains, but
Confederate resistance stiffened. Both Union corps entrenched in their ad-

vanced position. To the north, moderate Confederate attacks on the Federal right were repulsed. During the afternoon Hancock's Second Corps was ordered to shift to the Union left or south end of the line. Farther off, beyond the Federal right, Yankee and Confederate cavalry clashed at Ashland, with the Union troops falling back toward Hanover Court House. During the night both lines continued to entrench; the Federals planned to renew the offensive in the morning.

In Georgia, where the main armies of Johnston and Sherman faced each other in the New Hope Church-Dallas area, Federal cavalry under George Stoneman captured Allatoona Pass, through which ran the all-important railroad to Chattanooga. With the seizure of this indispensable pass Sherman could advance his railhead closer to the fighting lines. He sidled northward toward the railroad, moving away from the New Hope Church area. Skirmishing occurred near Marietta and Kingston, Ga.

Still another Federal offensive opened as Federal Brig. Gen. S. D. Sturgis and about eight thousand men moved out from Memphis to find and destroy the elusive Forrest. Sturgis headed toward Ripley, Miss. Forrest was now in the vicinity of Tupelo reorganizing after his raid north. Sherman determined to eliminate Forrest's continual threat to his long supply lines. John Hunt Morgan also had to be considered; on his raid into Kentucky he fought a skirmish near Pound Gap. A skirmish broke out near Arnoldsville and Federals raided near New Market, Mo. Col. Colton Greene's Confederate raiders, operating along the west bank of the Mississippi River near Columbia, Ark., fought an affair with U.S.S. *Exchange*.

President Davis ordered Maj. Gen. Robert Ransom, commanding at Richmond, to summon all local forces possible to the Chickahominy to meet the threat to the capital. Gen. Lee urged Beauregard, who commanded south of the James facing Federal Gen. Butler, to move part of his command north of the James if possible. Beauregard would thereby cover the area from the James north to the Chickahominy in front of Richmond.

June 2, Thursday

BATTLE OF COLD HARBOR CONTINUES.

Grant's planned attack upon Lee at Cold Harbor was set for early morning but troop movements, ammunition problems, and fatigue necessitated postponement until five in the afternoon. Sharp skirmishes erupted during the morning of a very hot day that ended with rain in the evening. Once more the attack was put off—until the morning of the third. Preparations continued. Many of the privates fashioned crude "dog tags." Lee, who since Spotsylvania had received some reinforcements from the Shenandoah and southern Virginia, also made readjustments in his well-entrenched lines. On the Confederate left Early had made an abortive attack. The stage was set on the flat lowlands along the Chickahominy for one of the bloodiest battles of history.

Sherman, with Allatoona Pass firmly in his hands, slowly shifted his three armies northeastward by the left flank from New Hope Church toward Allatoona and the Chattanooga-Atlanta railroad. Action flared at Acworth and Raccoon Bottom, Ga. Colton Green, still waging his private war with Union shipping on the Mississippi, engaged U.S.S. *Adams* and U.S.S. *Monarch* near Columbia, Ark. U.S.S. *Louisville* was also severely damaged in the same encounter.

Federal troops under David Hunter fought at Covington, Va., in what would become known as the Lynchburg Campaign. Some sixteen thousand Federals opposed about half that number under W. E. "Grumble" Jones. The Federals were aiming toward Staunton.

June 3, Friday

CHARGE AT COLD HARBOR.

The rain ceased and dawn approached. A sudden crash of cheers and the drumming of musket fire signaled the attack by Grant, Meade, and the Army of the Potomac. With Richmond scarcely beyond the horizon, Grant hoped a surprise shift in tactics would split, possibly crush, Lee's army. The Army of Northern Virginia was lined up behind strong fortifications from the Chickahominy on the south to the swamps along the Totopotomoy on the north. Disposition of units was mixed, but basically A. P. Hill's corps was on the right, Anderson's in the center, and Early's on the left. Grant planned to use the three corps of Hancock, Wright, and Smith, on the left and center, for the main assault. Warren and Burnside to the north would join in later.

At 4:30 A.M. the blow came. For both sides it was a crisis, but for the Confederates it was crucial; a serious breakthrough by Grant might end the war in Virginia. Listing units and their movements is of little import. For this was a smashing, headlong attempt to ram through regardless of cost. Immediately the cost was great. As the three Federal corps made some early gains, Confederate guns and infantry enfiladed various units; the issue was determined in an incredibly short time. Just how long that ferocious storm lasted is disputed, as is the number of fallen assailants. But it failed, and Grant later regretted that it was ever made. It was a great victory for Lee—if the stemming of a tide by a human wall can be called victory—and was his last major triumph in all out battle. Nevertheless, Richmond and his army were still in danger.

Federal killed and wounded for the June 3 assault may be put at around 7000 in well under an hour, with perhaps 5000 more for June 1–2. Confederate losses June 3 were probably under 1500. The North utilized perhaps 50,000 out of around 117,000 present for duty; the South about half of the less than 60,000 available. Around noon Grant called off his entire attack; the day was spent strengthening lines and caring for the casualties of the futile assault of Cold Harbor, though countless wounded went unsuccored.

To the north, on the fringes of the main battle, Federal cavalry were beaten off at Haw's Shop and near Via's House.

Charles Francis Adams, Jr., while he had great faith in Grant, wrote that the army "has literally marched in blood and agony from the Rapidan to the James." Eight miles away in Richmond the people listened to the sounds of the struggle.

Federal cavalry entered Acworth, Ga., pushing out a few Confederate vedettes. Johnston realized that with Sherman's main force moving off north of New Hope Church, the Confederates could no longer hold their position in the New Hope area and must once more respond to a Federal move.

Federal Brig. Gen. W. W. Averell's cavalry set out from Bunger's Mills in Greenbrier County, W. Va., to aid Hunter's main effort in the Shenandoah aimed at Lynchburg. Skirmishes occurred at Searcy, Ark., and Neosho, Mo. A three-day Union scout moved from Sedalia to the Blackwater Creek, Mo. Confederates captured the Federal gunboat *Water Witch* in Ossabaw Sound, Ga.

Lincoln approved an act of Congress calling for a national currency secured by pledges of government bonds and establishing a Bureau of Currency with an office of Comptroller of the Treasury. This act replaced a similar act of Feb. 25, 1863. Mr. Lincoln wrote a New York political gathering, "My previous high estimate of Gen. Grant has been maintained and heightened by what has occurred in the remarkable campaign he is now conducting. . . ."

June 4, Saturday

In a rainstorm Joseph E. Johnston shifted his Confederate Army of Tennessee during the night from the New Hope Church area outside Atlanta northward to an already prepared position along Lost, Pine, and Brush mountains. Once again he got in front of Sherman before the Federals could complete their move and once more he was in an immensely strong defensive position. Fighting broke out near Big Shanty and Acworth, Ga., during the day.

At Cold Harbor the armies of Grant and Lee lay entrenched, often only yards apart, and each appeared so strong that no further assault seemed possible. The dead and some wounded still lay between the lines. As Hunter's Federals advanced in the Shenandoah there was fighting at Port Republic and Harrisonburg, Va., and a skirmish took place at Panther Gap, W. Va. Elsewhere, the guns were heard at Ossabaw Sound, Ga.; Hudson's Crossing on the Neosho in Indian Territory; and near Vicksburg, Miss. Federal scouts operated from Huntersville and Clinton, Ark. Gen. John Hunt Morgan and his raiders, in Kentucky for what proved to be the last time, headed toward Lexington. Meanwhile, the Federal column of S. D. Sturgis from Memphis marched slowly into northern Mississippi toward Forrest's Confederates.

June 5, Sunday

Confederates under W. E. "Grumble" Jones moved to stop Hunter's destructive raid in the Shenandoah. With about 5600 men in all, Jones met Hunter's main force of around 8500 at Piedmont, about seven miles southwest of Port Republic. Charges and countercharges lasted until midafternoon, when Federal infantry and cavalry routed the Southern troops. Jones was killed in the engagement. Hunter moved on into Staunton to continue his raids on civilian property, which made his name anathema to the people of the Shenandoah Valley. Federals lost around 780 men and Confederates about 1600, of which around 1000 were captured. One of the secondary prongs of Grant's over-all offensive appeared to be working at last.

In Georgia Sherman was shifting more rapidly northeast toward the Atlanta-Chattanooga rail line and Johnston's new position on the mountains in front of Marietta. Skirmishing broke out at Pine Mountain and Acworth. On the quietly entrenched lines around Cold Harbor, Grant proposed to Lee an arrangement for tending to the wounded and burying the dead. On the seventh a truce was agreed. In the Trans-Mississippi a skirmish flared at Worthington's Landing, Ark., and Federals scouted in Missouri. At Charleston a minor bombardment against Fort Sumter by Federal guns ended with 319 rounds fired and only four casualties.

At Washington and other political discussion centers the question was what Lincoln would do about a vice-presidential candidate. Many held that Hannibal Hamlin would be dropped in favor of a war-minded Democrat to create the atmosphere of a united political ticket.

June 6, Monday

Sherman continued shifting position in Georgia to face Johnston's entrenchments, although there was action at Big Shanty and Raccoon Creek. Grant and Lee were largely quiet about Cold Harbor except for an abortive movement by Early toward Burnside on the Federal right. Federal troops under Hunter occupied Staunton, an important operational center in the Shenandoah. A skirmish occurred near Moorefield, W. Va.; and out in Arkansas fighting broke out at Lake Chicot or Old River Lake, and at Bealer's Ferry on the Little Red River. For most of the rest of June there was desultory firing by Federal guns against Fort Sumter in Charleston Harbor.

June 7, Tuesday

Delegates to the National Union Convention, representing most Republicans and some War Democrats, gathered in Baltimore to nominate a candidate for President of the United States. Their support for Lincoln was almost unanimous. Open to possible question was the vice-presidential nomination. The day was devoted to the usual preliminaries, with the nominations set for June 8. Lincoln had told John Hay and others that he wanted to keep hands off the vice-presidency and the platform. The Radical Republicans conceded the nomination of Lincoln but hoped for a drastic hard-war platform. Plans to postpone the convention had dissipated.

Federal troops under S. D. Sturgis skirmished with Confederates at Ripley, Miss., as the Union expedition headed into Mississippi in search of Forrest. In Missouri there was action at Sikeston and New Frankfort, and in Arkansas a skirmish at Sunnyside Landing.

Grant and Lee remained poised in the Cold Harbor area, but clearly Grant would have to cross the James. For diversion, prior to this momentous shift, Sheridan and two divisions of his cavalry were to join Hunter at Charlottesville, Va., and operate against the railroads. Sheridan moved west between the North Anna and the Mattapony on what became known as the Trevilian Raid.

President Davis, in a letter to a citizen of Canton, La., spoke of his desire "to prevent the oppression and redress the wrongs of citizens, but I cannot hope to have effected all I desired."

June 8, Wednesday

LINCOLN NOMINATED FOR SECOND TERM.

In Georgia Sherman's troops sloshed through mud and rain to the Western & Atlantic Railroad, preparing to face Johnston once more in front of Marietta. Francis P. Blair came up with a reinforcing corps, although Sherman had his force depleted by the necessity of garrisoning the railroad back to Chattanooga. There was action near Acworth and a skirmish at Lost Mountain. In Virginia troops of Crook and Averell augmented Hunter's Federal force aiming at Lynchburg, bringing his total to eighteen thousand.

Morgan, on what proved to be his last raid, captured Mount Sterling, Ky., and its Federal garrison. Some of Morgan's unruly men robbed the local bank of $18,000. Morgan's share of the blame has never been determined. Some speculated that the money was to go to Canada to help the Northwest Conspiracy or that Morgan's command was so tenuous that he could not prevent the looting. Morgan blocked investigation and never explained.

Elsewhere, action included an engagement at Simsport, La., and an affair at Indian Bayou, Miss. Until Aug. 9 Federal troops operated from Fort Churchill to the Humboldt River in Nevada Territory.

Politics diverted attention even from the military operations in Georgia and Virginia. At Baltimore, on the second day of the National Union party convention, Lincoln was nominated for President as expected. Andrew

Johnson, military governor of Tennessee, became the vice-presidential candidate in place of the incumbent Hannibal Hamlin. The party platform called for the integrity of the Union, quelling of the rebellion, no compromise with the rebels, and a constitutional amendment ending slavery. The vote for President was 484 for Lincoln, 22 for Grant. Then Missouri changed its vote to make it unanimous. Upon the nomination, "the long pent up enthusiasms burst forth in a scene of wildest confusion." "Hail, Columbia" from the band increased the racket. For Vice-President, Democrat Johnson received 200 votes; Hamlin 150; and Democrat Daniel S. Dickinson of New York 108. Most delegates changed to Johnson and then it was made unanimous. The President's role in dropping Hamlin and selecting Johnson has never been entirely clear. On the surface Mr. Lincoln indicated he wanted an open choice. That evening a Union League council differed from the convention and favored, as did the Cleveland Radical convention, confiscation of rebel property.

June 9, Thursday

Crowds of delegates from the Baltimore convention rushed to the White House to congratulate the President on his nomination. Convention president William Dennison formally notified Lincoln. The President expressed his gratitude and approved the call for a constitutional amendment prohibiting slavery: "such (an) amendment of the Constitution as (is) now proposed became a fitting, and necessary conclusion to the final success of the Union cause." He pointed out that those in revolt had been given the opportunity to desist without "the overthrow of their institution" but had failed to do so. In the evening Mr. Lincoln was serenaded by a brass band.

Federals drove Morgan's men out of Mount Sterling, Ky., and they retreated toward Winchester. A smaller fight took place near Pleasureville, Ky.

Sherman was just about ready for the next act of the Atlanta Campaign against Johnston at the Lost, Pine, and Brush mountains position. Skirmishing broke out near Big Shanty and near Stilesborough, Ga.

Gen. Benjamin Butler sent an expedition out to capture Petersburg but it was poorly managed and Beauregard halted it successfully. An affair occurred near Breckinridge, Mo. For five days Federals scouted from Cassville, Mo., to Cross Hollow, Ark. At La Fayette, Tenn., there was yet another skirmish. Near Cold Harbor orders went out to build fortifications to cover the proposed Federal march to the James River.

President Davis warned Lee that "The indications are that Grant despairing of a direct attack is now seeking to embarrass you by flank movements." He also worried about the threats at Petersburg and was concerned that Johnston had not yet struck the enemy in Georgia.

June 10, Friday

BATTLE OF BRICE'S CROSSROADS, GUNTOWN, OR TISHOMINGO CREEK, MISSIS-
SIPPI.

Gen. Samuel D. Sturgis' Federals from Memphis found Forrest near Brice's Crossroads, south of Corinth, Miss. Forrest abandoned his plan to move on Sherman's communications and concentrated near Guntown not far from Brice's Crossroads. The Confederates vigorously attacked the Federals, exhausted by a rapid march and the hot weather. The Union lines fell back from the crossroads and withdrew over Tishomingo Creek. The bridge was blocked, creating panic. The retreat much of the way to Memphis was a near rout. Forrest garnered most of the enemy artillery, 176 wagons, and supplies, plus over 1500 prisoners. It was one of the cavalry master's greatest moments and a classic of its kind. Sturgis had about 8000 men and lost 223 killed, 394 wounded, and 1623 missing or captured for a total of 2240. Forrest lost 96 killed and 396 wounded for 492, and he had only about 3500 men.

Morgan's somewhat riotous raiders entered Lexington, Ky., after a "slight engagement" and burned the Federal depot and stables, taking about seven thousand horses. At once Morgan moved on to Georgetown, Ky., and a smaller band headed toward Frankfort, Ky., carrying out a demonstration.

In Georgia Sherman's three armies moved forward cautiously toward Johnston's mountainous positions northwest of Marietta. Action occurred at Acworth, Pine Mountain, Roswell, Lost Mountain, and Calhoun. Muddy roads and swollen streams still hampered operations.

Hunter and his combined force moved toward Lexington and Lynchburg in the Valley of Virginia. Confederates under Breckinridge again gathered to oppose him, with action at Middlebrook, Brownsburg, and Waynesborough. Grant at Cold Harbor refined his plans for the movement of the Army of the Potomac to the James River. Fighting erupted at Old Church and Newport, Va., and Kabletown, W. Va. In the West the day was marked with an affair near St. James, Mo.; another at Lewisburg, Ark.; and considerable scouting in Missouri.

The Confederate Congress in Richmond authorized military service for men between seventeen and eighteen years of age and between forty-five and fifty.

June 11, Saturday

COMBAT OF TREVILIAN STATION, VIRGINIA.

The beaten Federals, struggling back toward Memphis from Brice's Crossroads, fought rearguard actions at Ripley and Salem, Miss. Morgan's raiders entered Cynthiana, Ky., after action at nearby Keller's Bridge.

The principal fighting was in Virginia, where Sheridan's cavalry attempted to join Hunter at Charlottesville. Wade Hampton and Fitzhugh Lee went to block his way. In the confused, twisted engagement at Trevilian Station, Federal horse under Custer had some success getting in the Confederate rear, but Hampton recovered. Fitzhugh Lee had less luck and was driven back. By nightfall Hampton was entrenching across Sheridan's route. The battle was a Federal victory so far, but the achievement was not encouraging. Sheridan said he decided that night to give up trying to meet Hunter. Farther west and north, in the Valley of Virginia, Hunter's men skirmished at Lexington, as the Federals entered the historic college town and burned the Virginia Military Institute. Hunter also raided Arrington's Depot. Hunter's name was fast becoming a hated one in Virginia. To combat him Lee detached Jubal Early from the battle lines. Down on the Peninsula preparations neared completion for the grand movement of the Army of the Potomac, to begin on the morrow.

As Sherman's men pressed forward in Georgia toward Johnston's positions fighting broke out at McAffee's Crossroads and skirmishing near Lost and Pine mountains lasted several days. Other minor actions were reported at Ridgeley, Mo., and Midway, Va. An expedition by Federals from Point Lookout, Md., to Pope's Creek, Va., lasted until the twenty-first. Famed raider C.S.S. *Alabama* arrived at Cherbourg, France, in bad need of a refit.

June 12, Sunday

ARMY OF THE POTOMAC BEGINS MOVE ACROSS JAMES RIVER.

With secrecy, efficiency and rapidity the Army of the Potomac, over 100,000 strong, began one of the great army movements in military history. Pulling out of the positions near Cold Harbor, Grant and Meade directed four corps toward the James River. W. F. Smith's corps was to go by water down the Pamunkey and York and up the James. Light skirmishing did occur at Long Bridge and White House Landing. The movement had begun at dark. Warren's corps was left behind to cover the passage of the rest of the army, taking position near Long Bridge. This move, intended to deceive Lee and the Army of Northern Virginia, did so for some days.

At Trevilian Station the battle begun the day before continued. Sheridan and his cavalry unsuccessfully attacked the entrenched Confederates under Wade Hampton. The frustrated assault forced Sheridan to give up his planned route of retreat and confirmed his decision not to try to join Hunter in the Valley. He gradually pulled back the way he had come and eventually joined Grant on the James late in June. Sheridan had about 8000 men and lost 102 killed, 470 wounded, and 435 missing for 1007. The Confederates had possibly 5000 men; partial reports of losses are 612, but they undoubtedly were larger.

In Kentucky Morgan, who had captured about three hundred Federals at Cynthiana the day before, was attacked by Yankees and severely beaten.

He retreated to Abingdon, Va., in the far southwestern part of the state, arriving June 20.

Meanwhile, in Mississippi the shambles of Sturgis' command continued their post-Brice's Crossroads retreat with Forrest following. Skirmishing took place at Davis' Mill, Miss. In Missouri fighting broke out at Montevallo, Calhoun, and Kingsville. In Georgia skirmishing erupted near Acworth once more, as Sherman's Federals carefully inched forward against Johnston. Meanwhile, supplies for the Union Army were being brought in from Chattanooga and the communication lines strengthened.

June 13, Monday

What was to become the final campaign for Richmond got under way. The bulk of the Army of the Potomac moved rapidly from Cold Harbor toward the James. Lee learned that the Federals had left Cold Harbor and had reports they were aiming at Richmond from the Long Bridge area of the Chickahominy. So the Army of Northern Virginia shifted southward, taking position from Malvern Hill to White Oak Swamp, blocking the road to Richmond, a road Grant did not intend to take. Grant repeated his order to Butler to obstruct navigation in the James by sinking old hulks in the river. By late afternoon Hancock's Second Corps reached the James at Wilcox's Landing. A lengthy pontoon bridge was still under construction and vessels had been assembled to carry part of the army across the wide river. There was skirmishing at White Oak Swamp and Riddell's Shop. Lee, unaware of the magnitude of Grant's move and impressed with the threat in the Valley of Virginia, moved Early's corps toward the Valley to halt Hunter's Federals. In the Valley action included a skirmish near Buchanan and Union scouting from Lexington to around Lynchburg. Lieut. Gen. Richard S. Ewell, who had been ailing, was assigned to command the Confederate Department of Richmond. He replaced Maj. Gen. Robert Ransom, Jr., who went to the Department of Western Virginia.

In Georgia the pressure against Johnston by Sherman mounted and there was a skirmish at Burnt Hickory. Sturgis' ill-fated Union expedition returned to Tennessee and fought a skirmish near Collierville. Federal troops from Morristown, Tenn., operated for a month into North Carolina. And farther west a four-day Federal scout moved from Fort Leavenworth, Kas. to Weston, Mo.

President Davis, replying to complaints of neglect from the Trans-Mississippi commander E. Kirby Smith, said, "my ability to sustain you will be the measure of the assistance rendered to you." More than ever, Mr. Davis could only equivocate when called upon for help.

June 14, Tuesday

GRANT'S ARMY BEGINS CROSSING OF THE JAMES.

POLK KILLED AT PINE MOUNTAIN, GEORGIA.

The Second Corps of the Army of the Potomac under Gen. Hancock began crossing the James River in boats from Wilcox's Landing to Windmill Point. By morning of the fifteenth all the infantry and four batteries of artillery had crossed to the south bank. Meanwhile, W. F. Smith's Eighteenth Corps had traveled by water from the Peninsula, reported to Butler at Bermuda Hundred, and received orders to move to Petersburg on the fifteenth. Confederate and Federal cavalry skirmished near Harrison's Landing. Thus the Union army continued to give Lee false evidence that they planned to attack north of the James. In the Valley of Virginia an affair took place at New Glasgow.

In Georgia Sherman, aided by a lessening of the heavy rain, sent skirmish lines forward toward the well-positioned Confederate works. The Confederate high command, Johnston, Hardee, and Polk, observed the movement from atop Pine Mountain. Noticing Federal artillery aimed in their direction, the generals began to break up their conference when a Federal shell struck Lieut. Gen. Leonidas Polk, bishop of the Protestant Episcopal Church and Confederate corps commander, and killed him instantly. Historians generally do not rate Polk as a great military leader. However, Polk exerted great personal influence among Confederate ranks in the West, so his death was a serious loss to Johnston.

U.S.S. *Kearsarge* arrived off Cherbourg, France, to blockade C.S.S. *Alabama.* In Tennessee fighting broke out near Bean's Station and in Lincoln County, while in Missouri the action was near Lexington and Melville.

In Richmond, again feeling the threat from east and south, the Confederate Congress adjourned after imposing new taxes on property and income.

June 15, Wednesday

ATTACK ON PETERSBURG, VIRGINIA, FAILS.

On this day Petersburg, the back door to Richmond, might well have fallen. W. F. Smith from Bermuda Hundred had Grant's orders through Butler to move very early to attack Petersburg. Hancock's Second Corps, which had just crossed the James as the vanguard of the Federal Army of the Potomac, had farther to go but could have cooperated well. Beauregard's some three thousand troops, all he had for most of the day, could never have stopped the sixteen thousand Federals. But an unholy mix-up of orders, lack of rations, poor maps, missed opportunities, and delays by commanders, combined with courageous Southern defense, saved Petersburg and undoubtedly lengthened the war by many months. Grant spent the day on the James supervising the crossing of other troops at the pontoon bridge. Smith was overly cautious in front of the thin Confederate defenses. Late in the day Smith's corps did take Battery Five and a mile or more of the outer lines. Hancock, adding considerably to the sixteen thousand, could not get up until 7 P.M. and despite a moonlight night no attack in force was made. Beauregard told Richmond and Lee that the attack would be at Petersburg and asked for troops. Lee still believed Grant's main army was north of the James, thus forcing him to protect Richmond. The Federal commander had at least partially deceived him, but had not been able to capitalize on his advantage. North of the James troops skirmished at Malvern Hill and near Smith's Store.

George H. Thomas moved his army forward beyond Pine Mountain toward Kennesaw on the Georgia front, with some severe skirmishing. McPherson and Schofield also pressed ahead against Confederate trenches. Fighting occurred near Allatoona, at Noonday Creek, Brush Mountain, and Gilgal or Golgotha Church.

On the other far-flung fronts of the war Confederates attacked Union gunboats at Ratliff's, Como, and Magnolia landings, La., and fighting occurred at Newport Crossroads June 15–17. Skirmishes flared near Moscow, Tenn.; near White Hare, Mo.; at San Bois Creek, Indian Terr.; and Federals evacuated Pass Cavallo, Tex. U.S.S. *Lexington* captured three riverboats at Beulah Landing, Miss.

Clement L. Vallandigham returned to Dayton, O., from Canada to add to the election turmoil. The Federal House voted 95 for to 66 against a joint resolution abolishing slavery, but a two-thirds majority was needed as this was really a vote on the Thirteenth Amendment.

At this time Lincoln in Washington was greatly interested in the army on the James; he wired Grant, ". . . I begin to see it. You will succeed. God bless you all."

June 16, Thursday

ASSAULT ON PETERSBURG.

Beauregard stripped his Bermuda Hundred defense line facing Butler to a mere thousand and pulled in all the troops he could to the Petersburg line, which even then numbered only fourteen thousand. More Federal troops came up after crossing the James. Burnside's Ninth Corps arrived at 10 A.M. and by midnight Warren's Fifth Corps came in; only the Sixth Corps of Wright had yet to arrive. Federal attackers captured a redan in the morning and about 6 P.M. assaulted heavily and, despite severe losses, captured three redans and some trenches. Confederates failed to recover the works, and had to take up temporary entrenchments farther back. On the Bermuda Hundred front Federals hit the weakened Confederate lines and took them. Lee, still not convinced that Grant was in force south of the James, felt compelled to send two divisions to reoccupy the Bermuda Hundred positions. Pickett's division drove the Federals out about 6 P.M.

Farther west in the Valley of Virginia Federals under Hunter invested Lynchburg and the Confederates under Breckinridge, but Early came up rapidly. Skirmishes flared near Lynchburg on Otter Creek, near Liberty, and at New London, Va.

Gen. Joseph E. Johnston's left had been weakened by Federal advances and he made readjustments around Gilgal Church, retiring to a new line near Mud Creek.

Union forces were being organized at Morganza, La., preparatory to striking against Mobile. Other action included a skirmish at West Point, Ark.; an affair near Preston, Mo.; and a foray by Federals from Fort Leavenworth, Kas. In West Virginia there was a scrap at Spencer. The Confederate War Department authorized Lieut. Bennett H. Young to organize raiders in Canada to dash into New England. A small army-navy expedition by Federals took five small enemy schooners near the mouth of Pamlico River, N.C.

President Lincoln traveled to Philadelphia for the Great Central Fair. The President made several speeches and in the main address at the Sanitary Fair he said, "War, at the best, is terrible, and this war of ours, in its magnitude and in its duration, is one of the most terrible. . . . We accepted this war for an object, a worthy object, and the war will end when that object is attained."

June 17, Friday

PETERSBURG ASSAULTS CONTINUE.

Federal troops of the Ninth Corps made a surprise attack at the Shand House on the Petersburg lines, but with only limited results. In fact, Beauregard's Confederates launched a successful counterattack late in the day. After midnight the Southerners pulled back to a shorter, more defensible prepared position. Beauregard was still trying to convince Lee that the bulk of the Army of the Potomac had moved south of the James. Lee, finally convinced, ordered A. P. Hill's and R. H. Anderson's corps to Petersburg. Meade ordered an assault readied for the next day. David B. Birney took over the Second Corps because of the reopening of Hancock's war wound.

In the Valley of Virginia Early's Confederates joined Breckinridge in the defense of Lynchburg against Hunter's Federals. There was a skirmish at Diamond Hill nearby.

Sherman's right wing troops vigorously attacked the new Confederate lines along Mud Creek in front of Marietta, Ga., and made some progress against Hardee's corps of Johnston's army. Elsewhere, skirmishes erupted near Columbia, Mo., and on the Monticello Road near Pine Bluff, Ark.

President Lincoln returned to Washington in the morning from his Philadelphia trip. At 8:30 A.M. a blast, followed by fire, rocked the cartridge-making building of the Washington Arsenal; eighteen were killed or fatally injured and fifteen to twenty injured.

June 18, Saturday

PETERSBURG ASSAULTS FAIL—SIEGE BEGINS.

Gen. Grant arrived at a decision—Petersburg could not be carried by assault; it would have to be invested and the railroads cut off. The decision came after Meade's Army of the Potomac moved in against the new Confederate lines. However, with the arrival of Lee and his main army, the defense stiffened. Morning and afternoon attacks failed to gain the works. Losses were heavy in gaining positions near the basically intact Confederate lines. But at least the Northerners were entrenched and the siege of Petersburg was under way. The Federals held two of the five railroads into the city and several roads. The four days at Petersburg cost about 8150 Federal killed and wounded. Confederate losses are uncertain. More than six weeks of movement and battle from the Rapidan to Petersburg were over and a new style of warfare undertaken. There would be approximately 50,000 Confederates against over 110,000 Federals.

In the Valley of Virginia Hunter made light attacks against Early at Lynchburg. He then began to withdraw northward, knowing he could not take Lynchburg in the face of the reinforced Confederates. Cavalry fought at King and Queen Court House, Va.; Confederate raiders descended on Laclede, Mo.; and Federals scouted from Kansas City.

On the Georgia front Joseph E. Johnston moved his Army of Tennessee back again to still another line of defense—this time closer to Marietta in a semicircle. His men skirmished at Acworth and Allatoona. The new line ran mainly along Big and Little Kennesaw mountains. It was a strong position, perhaps impregnable to direct assault.

June 19, Sunday
U.S.S. *Kearsarge* SINKS C.S.S. *Alabama* OFF CHERBOURG, FRANCE.

For many months the Federal Navy had sought the elusive, strikingly successful Confederate raider *Alabama*. At last they cornered her in Cherbourg, France. Raphael Semmes, whose commands had taken eighty-two Federal merchantmen, sixty-five with *Alabama,* had been forced to take his worn-out ship into the French harbor for a refit. Having arrived June 11, *Alabama* was awaiting permission for overhaul when off the coast came U.S.S. *Kearsarge* under Capt. John A. Winslow. Knowing he faced combat, Semmes readied his 8-gun ship with its 360-pound total projectile weight. In midmorning Semmes sailed out of Cherbourg Harbor in fine weather. *Kearsarge,* with 7 guns, having a projectile weight of 430 pounds, lay off the three-mile limit. The English yacht *Deerhound* watched the action, and onshore throngs of people lined the cliffs. Shortly before 11 A.M. *Alabama* opened fire, and then *Kearsarge* took the offensive. Circling rapidly, the vessels exchanged broadsides, gradually drawing closer. Soon the sides of *Alabama* were wrecked by shells, and casualties mounted. By noon *Alabama* ceased firing and withdrew toward shore, filling rapidly. Semmes was forced to strike his colors. (There were charges later that *Kearsarge* fired on a white flag.) *Deerhound* took off some survivors of the fight, including Semmes. This also sparked dissension. Semmes reported

9 killed and 21 wounded for a total of 30 on *Alabama,* while there were only 3 wounded on *Kearsarge.* Superior gunnery is generally credited for the Federal victory. In the greatest ship-to-ship combat of the war in open seas, the most famous commerce raider of its time went down, far from the Confederacy it represented.

On land the two major Federal offensives seemed stalled, facing defiant Confederate defenders. Grant's army got its breath on the Petersburg lines, while Lee's army dug in. In Georgia Sherman's Federals discovered Johnston had moved into a new line and, despite continuing rains and mud, went forward to test their opponents. Skirmishing broke out at Noonday Creek and Noyes' Creek. Lesser fighting occurred at Bayou Grossetete, La.; Eagle Pass, Tex.; Hahn's Farm near Waldron, Ark.; and Iron Bridge, Indian Terr. A six-day Federal scout began from Mount Vernon, Mo.

From the Valley of Virginia Hunter's Federals continued their withdrawal, Early's Confederates in pursuit. By heading into the Kanawha Valley of West Virginia, Hunter left the Shenandoah open to the Confederates, but he felt he could not retire that way. A skirmish took place at Liberty, Va.

June 20, Monday

Sherman's forces in Georgia continued to press toward Johnston's new Kennesaw defenses. Often the Confederates countered and skirmishing broke out in many places, with action at Cassville, Noonday Church, Noyes' Creek, Powder Springs, Lattimer's Mills, and Noonday Creek.

In Virginia Petersburg remained quiet as two mighty armies stared at each other across growing entrenchments. To the north, Sheridan's cavalry skirmished at White House and at King and Queen Court House. In the Valley of Virginia retreating Federals fought at Buford's Gap. Under brisk Federal fire the Confederate flagstaff on Fort Sumter was replaced, one of several such incidents. Scouts by Federals occurred around Lewisburg, Ark., and Cassville, Mo.; there were Union operations on the White River, Ark.; a skirmish at White's Station, Tenn.; and a Federal expedition from Batchelder's Creek, N.C.

President Lincoln left to visit Grant's army on the James. Before he left he wrote the governor of Ohio to watch Copperhead Vallandigham closely, and if he should see any danger to the military, "arrest all implicated."

June 21, Tuesday

Grant and Meade got a cavalry operation under way against the railroads into Petersburg. Orders were also issued to the Second and Sixth Corps to extend the siege lines to the left toward the Appomattox River west of Petersburg. The goal was to form a semicircle south around Petersburg from the Appomattox on the east to the Appomattox on the west. Farther north fighting broke out near White House and at Black

Creek or Tunstall's Station, part of the remainder of Sheridan's Trevilian Raid. A Confederate flotilla bombarded the Union squadron on the James at Trent's and Varina reaches. To the west, pursuing Confederates and retreating Federals from the Valley of Virginia engaged at and near Salem and at Catawba Mountains. Johnston, in Georgia, faced heavy pressure on his left from Sherman, and shifted the corps under Hood from his right to the left of the defensive lines. Action was mainly at Noonday Creek. The only other fighting recorded was in Decatur County, Tenn.

Gen. Grant and other officers visited President Lincoln aboard his steamer at City Point, Va. Later Lincoln and Grant toured the Petersburg lines on horseback. President Davis reluctantly accepted the resignation of Christopher G. Memminger as Secretary of the Treasury. He told Memminger, "I knew the extreme difficulty of conducting the Treasury Department during the pending struggle." Memminger had long been aware of the severe criticisms of his operation of the Confederate Treasury, criticisms on matters that in most cases were undoubtedly unavoidable.

June 22, Wednesday

ENGAGEMENT AT PETERSBURG: ATTEMPT AGAINST WELDON RAILROAD.

General Lee was cognizant of the move planned by Grant to extend the siege lines to the south and west of Petersburg. A. P. Hill's corps moved out and struck the Federal Second Corps, which was heading for its new position. (The Second Corps was now under David B. Birney, as Hancock's war wound had forced him to take sick leave.) The Second Corps was driven back, losing seventeen hundred prisoners in an engagement on the Jerusalem Plank Road. Grant's drive against the Weldon and Petersburg Railroad had been halted. The plan to extend lines to the west was given up for a while. Meanwhile, James Harrison Wilson and two Union cavalry divisions started toward Burkeville to break the South Side Railroad. A skirmish at Reams' Station marked the raid, which ended at Light House Point July 2. The raid did destroy considerable railroad, quickly repaired by the Confederates. Wilson's men fought a number of skirmishes, losing severely and several times barely escaping annihilation. W. H. F. Lee's Confederate cavalry was diligent and effective in pursuit.

At White House north of the James, Sheridan, pressed by Hampton's cavalry, broke up the supply depot and then headed toward the James with nine hundred wagons. In North Carolina a brief Federal scout probed from Piney Green to Snead's Ferry and Swansborough. Brig. Gen. John Hunt Morgan, his raiding about over, assumed command of the Confederate Department of Western Virginia and Eastern Tennessee.

On the James President Lincoln, Grant, and others steamed upriver to visit the navy squadron and talk with Gen. Butler. In the afternoon the President left for Washington.

In Georgia Hood's corps, now on the Confederate left, made a strong attack near Zion Church and Culp's Farm. But the Federals, prepared for the move, repulsed the Southern drive.

June 23, Thursday

In the Valley of Virginia Jubal Early's command was advancing from Lynchburg toward the Shenandoah as Hunter's Federals had withdrawn into West Virginia. The last fights with Hunter occurred at New Castle, Va., and Sweet Sulphur Springs and Cove Gap, W. Va. Sheridan, with the immense wagon train, was en route to the Army of the Potomac from White House. As he crossed Jones' Bridge over the Chickahominy there was skirmishing. Wilson's cavalry, raiding against the South Side Railroad near Petersburg, fought near Nottoway Court House. The Federal Second and Sixth Corps recovered some of the ground lost the day before and took position west of the Jerusalem Plank Road at Petersburg. However, they did not control the Weldon Railroad. A Confederate attack drove off Union cavalry that briefly held a section of the railroad.

In Georgia the weather improved and roads began to dry out. Sherman planned an attack against Johnston's strong position. For several days Sherman readjusted lines preparatory to the attack. There was considerable skirmishing, such as that at Allatoona. On other fronts fighting took place at Okolona, Miss., and Collierville, Tenn.

Late in the afternoon a weary Lincoln arrived at Washington after his visit to the army in southern Virginia.

June 24, Friday

At St. Mary's Church, Va., Confederate cavalry attacked Sheridan and the wagon train heading from White House to the James. Federal cavalry fell back in considerable confusion. On the Georgia front a skirmish occurred at La Fayette, where Sherman was protecting his supply lines. Once more the shot-torn flag on Fort Sumter was replaced under fire by Confederates. In Arkansas an affair took place near Fayetteville. On the White River Jo Shelby's Confederates on land fought three U.S. steamers, and attacked, captured, and destroyed U.S.S. *Queen City*.

The Constitutional Convention of Maryland voted to abolish slavery.

June 25, Saturday

At Petersburg Federal engineers began digging a tunnel toward the Confederate lines for the purpose of blowing apart the Southern earthworks.

Skirmishing flared again at Allatoona and Spring Place, Ga. There were skirmishes at Roanoke Station, Va.; Morganfield, Ky.; Ashwood, Miss.; Point Pleasant, La.; Rancho Las Rinas, Tex.; and operations on the Yellow River, Fla. The main fronts were relatively quiet.

June 26, Sunday

Sheridan's cavalry and wagon trains completed the crossing of the James by ferry at Couthard's Landing, and moved to join the main army. Fighting broke out at Olley's Creek, Ga., and yet again the flag of Fort Sumter was replaced under fire. In Arkansas, in operations on the White River, Federals pursued Confederates near Clarendon to Bayou De View. Other fighting took place at Wire Bridge, Springfield, and Smithfield, W. Va., and on the Sedalia and Marshall Road, Mo. Early reached Staunton, Va., with about fourteen thousand men after a hard march.

June 27, Monday

BATTLE OF KENNESAW MOUNTAIN, GEORGIA.

The armies of the Cumberland and of the Tennessee moved forward against Big and Little Kennesaw near Marietta, Ga. The Army of the Ohio threatened the left of the Confederate army. It was a day of tragedy for the Federals as they rushed head on against Johnston's well-entrenched positions. In the biggest battle of the campaign thus far Northern losses totaled 1999 killed and wounded and 52 missing for over 2000. The Confederates suffered possibly 270 killed and wounded and 172 missing for 442, though the total may have been over 500. Federals rushing pell-mell up the slopes seized outpost positions but could not break the main lines. Some did manage to dig in and hold some of the territory gained. Retreat would have been even more disastrous in the face of Johnston's carefully planned lines, which took every advantage of the rocky terrain. Sherman, often criticized for the assault, undoubtedly had Missionary Ridge in mind, but this time he faced a veteran force under an able commander. Three major drives made on very narrow fronts and the subsidiary movements by the Federals got nowhere. It was a serious defeat for Sherman but could not affect his ultimate goals of Atlanta and Johnston's army. For the Confederates it was a victory indeed, but another defensive one.

The day was pretty quiet at Petersburg. Yet another flag was replaced at Fort Sumter. There were affairs at Crittenden, Ky.; Big Cove Valley, Ala.; near Dunksburg, Mo., and Federals scouted around Brownsville, Ark.

President Lincoln formally accepted the nomination for President.

June 28, Tuesday

Large-scale fighting seemed over for a time. Only skirmishes at Tunnel Hill, Ga., and Howlett's Bluff, Va., broke the quiet. Early and his Confederates left Staunton for the Shenandoah Valley, arousing concern in Washington. In the capital President Lincoln signed a bill repealing the fugitive slave acts. In Georgia Johnston, who seemed to be ready for all eventualities, prepared new defensive positions along the Chattahoochee, back of the Kennesaw line.

June 29, Wednesday

President Davis told Gov. Brown of Georgia that he had sent Johnston "all available reinforcements, detaching troops even from points that remain exposed to the enemy." He did not see how he could do more. Skirmishes marked the day at Charles Town and Duffield's Station, W. Va.; La Fayette, Tenn.; Davis' Bend, La.; and Meffleton Lodge, Ark.

June 30, Thursday

CHASE LEAVES CABINET.

Sec. of the Treasury Salmon P. Chase, who obviously had dreams of the presidency and was backed by some Radical Republicans, resigned once more. This time President Lincoln accepted. "You and I have reached a point of mutual embarrassment in our official relation which it seems can not be overcome, or longer sustained, consistently with the public service," Lincoln wrote. Asst. Sec. George Harrington assumed the duties temporarily. Former Gov. David Tod of Ohio was nominated for the post but declined because of poor health. The ostensible cause of Chase's resignation was dispute over an appointment, but it had been brewing for some time. Chase appeared surprised at the acceptance, for several times before his resignation had been refused; this time Lincoln had had enough. The President also signed several acts increasing duties, providing for more revenue, and broadening the base of the income tax.

Gen. Early and his advancing Confederates in the Shenandoah arrived at New Market. Skirmishes occurred in Georgia at La Fayette, Allatoona, and Acworth. Actions also took place at Four-Mile Creek and Deep Bottom, Va.

JULY, 1864

Union armies were besieging Petersburg only a few miles south of the Confederate capital at Richmond. In Georgia Union armies were forcing their way nearer and nearer to Atlanta. Elsewhere there were no major operations immediately pending but Jubal Early was moving north in the Shenandoah Valley; perhaps he could be of more than nuisance value in threatening Washington and the Yankee nation, but it was at best a diversion.

Northern eyes looked to Washington and the election. There was still considerable shock over Grant's manpower expenditure, which some termed needless. Congress was beginning to press the President for strong, even vindictive, reconstruction policies.

In the Confederacy, too, grumbling continued to increase. Casualties there were also great and a huge chunk of Georgia had been lost. Was Davis wise in sticking with "Retreating Joe" Johnston? Grant's army pounded Petersburg. (At the same time many Southerners viewed Grant's campaign as a failure since he had not taken Richmond or conquered Lee.) Confederate citizens had no protection in vast undefended areas of the West. The loss of C.S.S. *Alabama* on the high seas had been bitter, but C.S.S. *Tallahassee* and *Florida* operated effectively against Federal shipping. Still, the blockade left few ports for the evaders to reach.

July 1, Friday

Lincoln appointed William Pitt Fessenden, long-time senator from Maine, Secretary of the Treasury in place of Chase. The appointment was immediately confirmed. Fessenden had extensive experience on the Finance Committee, opposed inflation, and believed in heavier taxation. Although he took the job reluctantly and considered it temporary, Fessenden in less than a year in office operated the wartime Treasury efficiently and soundly.

Sporadic fighting occurred on the Georgia front at Howell's Ferry, Allatoona, and Lost Mountain. The Petersburg lines remained quiet, for the most part. There was a skirmish near Fayette, Mo. For the entire month scouts and relatively minor actions took place in Arkansas and along the west coast of Florida. Federal troops operated against Indians in Minnesota. Maj. Gen. Irvin McDowell assumed command of the Department of the Pacific, a post far from the war for the Federal commander at First Bull Run. The U. S. Senate passed the House-approved Wade-Davis reconstruction bill 26 to 3, with 20 absent.

July 2, Saturday

Joseph E. Johnston evacuated his entrenchments on Kennesaw Mountain in Georgia during the night and pulled back the entire front to still another prepared line below Marietta. Johnston moved in response to Sherman's shifting armies, recognizing that otherwise his flanks would be turned. At Charleston Harbor Federal troops landed on James Island and were checked at first, but the Confederate defenders fell back. Other action occurred near Secessionville, S.C.

In Virginia Early's Confederate column, heading north toward the Potomac, reached Winchester with little opposition. At Bolivar Heights, W. Va., Early's outposts were active in driving in Federals. In Mississippi skirmishing occurred on the Byhalia Road near the state line south of

Collierville, Tenn. Farther south in Mississippi a Federal expedition moved from Vicksburg to the Pearl River and engaged in several skirmishes en route; the affair ended July 10.

The Federal Congress granted public land in the Pacific Northwest for railroad and telegraph lines to Puget Sound, and also chartered the Northern Pacific Railroad. Mr. Lincoln signed this bill, which also opened land for settlement from Lake Superior to the Pacific. He also discussed the Treasury with Sec. Fessenden and the congressional proposal to confiscate Confederate estates with Representative George W. Julian of Indiana.

July 3, Sunday

Confederates moved into the Harper's Ferry area once again. Early's men, marching northward from Winchester, drove Sigel's Federals before them, with skirmishing at Leetown, Darkesville, Martinsburg, North Mountain, North River Mills, W. Va., and Buckton, Va. The small Union force escaped across the Potomac into Maryland at Shepherdstown. Citizens north of the Potomac were in an uproar and even Washington was apprehensive. Was it only a raid or a serious invasion?

In the Charleston Harbor area Federals renewed their efforts against the city and forts. Landing in barges, a Federal assault force failed in a dawn attack on Fort Johnson from Morris Island, and lost 140 as prisoners. James Island was also invaded by a strong column of 5000 but driven back to the Stono by July 5, where they were covered by the Federal Navy.

Sherman's armies moved forward, past Kennesaw Mountain and through Marietta, toward Johnston's new Confederate line along Nickajack Creek. Skirmishes erupted at Kingston, Ruff's Mills, Big Shanty, and Sweetwater Bridge as cavalry operated in the rear of Federal lines. Other fighting occurred in Platte County, Mo.; and for the rest of July Federals operated around Baton Rouge and along the Amite River, La.

Sec. of the Treasury Fessenden tried to decline his new Cabinet post but President Lincoln refused.

July 4, Monday

RECONSTRUCTION CONTROVERSY.

The first session of the Thirty-Eighth Congress of the United States adjourned amid new tensions over what would be the policy of reconstruction of the seceded states and who would control it—Congress or the President. Mr. Lincoln signed many bills, including one setting up the office of Commissioner of Immigration, and one repealing certain exemption clauses of the Enrollment Act. But he did not sign the controversial Wade-Davis reconstruction bill, to the chagrin of ultraradical members of Congress. Frantic pressure was applied even at this late hour, but the President pocket-vetoed the bill backed by Sen. Benjamin Wade of Ohio and Representative Henry Winter Davis of Maryland. The bill called for reorganization of a seceded state only after a majority of the enrolled white male citizens had taken an oath of allegiance and adopted a constitution acceptable to Congress and the President. No one who had held any Confederate state or national office or who had voluntarily borne arms for the South would be able to vote on or serve as a delegate to the convention whether he took the oath or not. The measure also called for complete emancipation of slaves through congressional action rather than a constitutional amendment, plus further restrictions on officeholding and voting, as well as repudiation of all Confederate debts. In effect it called for Congress rather than the President to control reconstruction. Provisions of the bill as to voting would obviously make it extremely difficult to reconstruct a state and would lead to control by the Radicals of Congress. The President had already instituted much more lenient reconstruction in Louisiana and Arkansas, where 10 per cent of the previous voters could restore a state, and the oath called merely for future support of the Union.

General Early's Confederates operated near Harper's Ferry, W. Va., preparatory to crossing the Potomac, and fighting broke out at South Branch Bridge, Patterson's Creek Bridge, and Frankford, W. Va. Sporadic action continued on James Island in Charleston Harbor. Federal lines continued to move forward toward Johnston in Georgia. Sherman's right flank, under McPherson, was now closer to Atlanta than Johnston, actually touching the Chattahoochee. So yet again the Confederates pulled back during the night to new prepared fortifications on the Chattahoochee. Action was at Burnt Hickory, Rottenwood Creek, Campbellton. Ruff's Mills, Neal Dow Station, and Mitchell's Crossroads. An especially heavy engagement took place at Vining's Station as Federals pressed ahead. Other action of the day occurred in Clay County, Mo.; Cross Bayou, La.; and in Searcy County, Ark. For most of July a Federal expedition operated from Memphis to Grand Gulf, Miss., with several skirmishes.

July 5, Tuesday

Early began crossing the Potomac into Maryland at Shepherdstown after finding Harper's Ferry too strong to take. As a result Confederates and Federals fought at Keedysville, Noland's Ferry, Point of Rocks, and Solomon's Gap, Md. Meanwhile, the call went out for 24,000 militia from New York and Pennsylvania to help defend Maryland and the North. Washington and nearby areas were seriously alarmed now.

Sherman's Federals pressed Johnston's line on the Chattahoochee, seeking a soft spot and investigating possible openings on the flanks. Skirmishes flared at Pace's Ferry, Howell's Ferry, Turner's Ferry, and Isham's Ford, Ga.

Federal cavalry moved out of La Grange, Tenn., and headed for northern Mississippi. Yankees, now under A. J. Smith, were hunting Forrest again, attempting to bring him to bay and halt any planned depredations against Sherman's lengthening supply line. Otherwise there were operations in western Missouri, a six-day Union expedition from New Madrid to Caruthersville, and Federal scouts along the Big Piney, Mo.

President Lincoln suspended the privilege of the writ of habeas corpus in Kentucky and proclaimed martial law. The President stated that many Kentucky citizens had joined or helped the "forces of the insurgents." New York *Tribune* editor Horace Greeley, long discontented with the Administration, received a letter from Canada alleging that two emissaries of the Confederacy with powers to negotiate peace were in the country. Greeley urged the President to investigate the emissaries' offer of a meeting.

July 6, Wednesday

Early's Confederates in Maryland captured Hagerstown, skirmished at Sir John's Run and Big Cacapon Bridge, W. Va., and at Antietam, Md. Early himself and the rest of the Confederate force completed crossing the Potomac at Shepherdstown. John McCausland, commanding Confederates at Hagerstown, levied $20,000 on the population in retribution for Hunter's depredations in the Shenandoah. In Washington Federal authorities conferred on reinforcing the defenses of the capital.

Cavalry operations and reconnaissances continued on the Atlanta front, with skirmishing at Sandtown and Nickajack Creek. The Petersburg lines were sluggish, but some forces skirmished at Mount Zion Church near Aldie, Va. Other action included a skirmish near Benton, Ark.; operations the rest of the month in western Missouri; Federal scouting in southeastern Arizona Terr.; and a skirmish on the Little Blue, Jackson County, Mo.

July 7, Thursday

Federal troops and militia hurried toward Washington and Maryland to protect the North and its capital from Early's "invading army." The Third Division of the Sixth Army Corps arrived at Baltimore from the Army of the Potomac at Petersburg. Fighting occurred at Middletown, Brownsville, and Hager's or Catoctin Mountain, Md.

In Charleston Harbor Confederates attacked Federal entrenchments on James Island and carried them by the ninth. The Northern troops fell back, withdrawing from the islands and from the Stono. Federal losses in the ten days' fighting, 330; Confederate, 163. A third major bombardment of sadly battered Fort Sumter began. Federal guns threw 784 rounds at the mound of rubble that was the fort; four times the flag was shot away and four times restored.

At Ripley, Miss., Union troops heading out from Memphis after Forrest again skirmished with Confederates. In east Tennessee a series of Federal scouts lasted several days each. Across the Mississippi, fighting broke out at Parkville, Mo., and Van Buren, Ark. Sherman's troops near Atlanta, but with the Chattahoochee between them and their goal, continued investigating crossing places. Reconnaissance and raids on their lines of communications brought fighting at Adairsville, Dark Corners, Vining's Station, and Summerville, Ga. July 7–12 there were small sealand raids by the Union at Brookville and Bayport, Fla.

The fallback of Joseph E. Johnston to the Chattahoochee rendered President Davis "more apprehensive for the future." He wrote his general that he was fearful of Johnston having the river in back of him but felt to cross it would give the enemy too much opportunity. Davis added that he could send him no further reinforcements.

July 8, Friday
RECONSTRUCTION PROCLAMATION.

President Lincoln proclaimed his backing of a constitutional amendment abolishing slavery, but declared that he was not prepared to support the idea that Congress had the authority to eradicate the institution. The proclamation was a statement of his pocket veto July 4 of the Wade-Davis reconstruction bill. He said he could not be inflexible on any one plan of reconstruction or to set aside the new Federal governments in Arkansas and Louisiana, but if people of a state wished to choose the system of restoration in the bill, that would be proper.

One division of the Federal Sixth Corps had reached Baltimore from the Petersburg lines, and was preparing to move out against Early's invading Confederates. Early's men fought at Antietam Bridge, Frederick, and Sandy Hook, Md. Near Frederick miscellaneous Federal units gathered under Lew Wallace in an effort to halt what looked like a move on Washington.

Schofield's army, on the left of Sherman's forces in Georgia, crossed the Chattahoochee near the mouth of Soap Creek, against little opposition. McPherson on the Union right feinted at Turner's Ferry. This surprise move around Johnston's right flank made the Confederate position on the northwest side of the Chattahoochee untenable and Johnston was obviously going to be forced to pull back across the river, closer to Atlanta. Skirmishes were recorded at Cove Springs and Isham's Ford. Elsewhere, troops fought at Vienna, Ala.; near Richmond, Mo.; and near Kelly's Mill, Miss.

July 9, Saturday
BATTLE OF THE MONOCACY, MARYLAND.

Some 6000 men of the Federal Army, gathered from various sources, stood directly in the way of Jubal Early's Confederate advance upon Washington from Frederick, Md. Early's 10,000 infantry moved forward to the

Monocacy River southeast of Frederick. Many of the Federals were inexperienced, untrained, and short-term men. After a stubborn fight, Lew Wallace's pickup force was routed and the march onward was clear for Early. The Confederates suffered around 700 casualties and the Federals nearly 2000, over 1200 of whom were missing. While not a major battle, it did delay the progress toward Washington at least a day and provided a little more time for defensive measures in Northern cities. At Frederick the Confederates imposed a levy of $200,000 on city officials. Early moved on with his total force, which probably did not exceed 18,000. The dry heat of the past few weeks was telling upon the armies throughout Virginia and Maryland and upon civilians, too. Near-panic held sway in Baltimore as home defenders of various kinds hurried to the fortifications. In Washington there was apprehension, too, and preparations were being rushed. Two divisions of the Federal Sixth Army Corps left City Point, Va., bound for the capital.

At Petersburg Gen. Meade ordered the Army of the Potomac to start regular siege approach lines to increase pressure on Lee's army. On John's Island in Charleston Harbor there was action on Burden's Causeway. Federals also operated around Wellington, Mo.

During the night Joseph E. Johnston took his Army of Tennessee across the Chattahoochee, retreating once more—this time to the gates of Atlanta. The Confederates carefully destroyed all bridges as they retired into previously prepared fortifications. Severe skirmishing had occurred during the day along the river and at Vining's Station and Nickajack Creek. Sherman, with Schofield's whole force already across the Chattahoochee to the north, built up supplies and prepared for a full press forward. President Davis instructed Gen. Bragg to go to Georgia and consult with Gen. Johnston about Johnston's plans. C.S.S. *Florida* took four prizes only thirty-five miles off the eastern shore of Maryland.

In Washington the President told Horace Greeley that if anyone had a peace proposition in writing that included the restoration of the Union and the ending of slavery, he should come to Lincoln.

July 10, Sunday

Early's Confederates moved on, a bit more slowly now, fighting at Rockville and Gunpowder Bridge, very near the capital. In Mississippi A. J. Smith's Federal expedition skirmished at Cherry Creek and Plentytude. Also in Mississippi a skirmish took place in Issaquena County, and a week-long Federal expedition moved from Vicksburg to Grand Gulf with some skirmishing against roving bands of Confederates.

Sherman was laying his plans to invest Atlanta and keep after Johnston's army. Lovell Harrison Rousseau, Federal cavalry commander, led some 2500 men from Decatur, Ala., northeast of Atlanta to operate against the railroad line between Columbus, Ga., and Montgomery, Ala. By July 22 he was back in Marietta after wrecking a considerable amount of Southern rail line. Fighting in Georgia took place at Alpharetta and Campbellton. In the West skirmishes erupted at Little Rock and near Petit Jean, Ark., and at Platte City, Mo. Federals unsuccessfully attacked Fort Johnson and Battery Simkins in Charleston Harbor.

President Lincoln and his family came back to the White House due to possible danger at their summer residence at the Soldiers' Home. Lincoln told a Baltimore group that he believed Early was moving on Washington and that "They can not fly to either place. Let us be vigilant but keep cool. I hope neither Baltimore or Washington will be sacked." Mr. Lincoln told Grant that Halleck believed they could defend Washington with invalids and hundred-day men.

July 11, Monday

CONFEDERATES INVADE WASHINGTON SUBURBS.

Confederate soldiers were in the environs of Washington. At Silver Spring, Md., Jubal Early's men burned the home of the Blair family as Early tried to determine what sort of defensive troops were in the Federal capital. After a reconnaissance he ordered an assault for the next morning. Skirmishing broke out at Frederick, Md., and Fort Stevens near Washington, and Confederates captured Federal trains near Magnolia, Md. The militia of the District of Columbia was called up, invalids organized, office personnel put under arms; units of the Nineteenth Corps from New Orleans, now under Maj. Gen. Q. A. Gillmore, readied for the Southern attack. Two divisions of Maj. Gen. Horatio Wright's Sixth Corps from City Point arrived about noon. Over twenty thousand men, many of them raw troops, now opposed Early, and the Confederate general was becoming apprehensive of being able to do more than throw Washington and Baltimore into consternation.

Skirmishing increased in northern Mississippi, with action at and near Pontotoc. Federals scouted from Gunter's Landing to Warrenton, Ala. The U. S. Navy destroyed salt works near Tampa, Fla.

In the financial world the Federal dollar was worth only thirty-nine cents, lowest price for the dollar during the war. President Lincoln and Mrs. Lincoln visited threatened Fort Stevens, where they witnessed an attack. Soldiers ordered him away from the dangerous parapets. While concerned, Lincoln appeared more curious than worried.

July 12, Tuesday

CONFEDERATES WITHDRAW FROM WASHINGTON.

Seeing Federal troops moving into the fortifications of the capital, Early gave up his plans for assault and settled for extensive skirmishing in the northern outskirts, particularly at Fort Stevens. At night they headed for the Potomac at Leesburg. Once more President Lincoln rode out to see the action at Fort Stevens. Again he came under fire and youthful officer Oliver Wendell Holmes, Jr., shouted, "Get down, you fool." Prompt reinforcement saved Washington from a major attack and, possibly, occupation. The raid had failed to be anything but a period of excitement. It did not relieve Federal pressure on Petersburg or materially change the Confederate military picture.

Elsewhere, Federals scouted in Lincoln County, Tenn. Skirmishes flared at Campbellton, Ga., and at Warwick Swamp and Turkey Creek, north of the James in Virginia.

Greatly disturbed over Georgia, President Davis wrote Gen. Lee, *"Genl. Johnston* has *failed* and there are strong indications that he will *abandon Atlanta. . . .* It seems necessary to *relieve him* at once. Who should *succeed* him? What think you of Hood for the position?"

July 13, Wednesday

Jubal Early's frustrated Confederate veterans hurried toward the Potomac at Leesburg. Grant ordered Maj. Gen. Horatio Wright and the Sixth and Nineteenth Corps to pursue. By evening about fifteen thousand Federals were on the way. A slight affair at Rockville, Md., marked the retreat and follow-up.

In Georgia Sherman prepared to advance his whole force across the Chattahoochee and then around the north side of Atlanta toward Decatur on the east. Federal cavalry operated against bridges and railroads, but generally failed to wreck the railroads close to Atlanta.

Union cavalry moved into Tupelo, Miss., and fighting erupted at Camargo Cross Roads. A. J. Smith's Federals were getting nearer Forrest's Confederate cavalry. The Confederates moved to the attack, and there were harassing Southern forays during the day. Smith's force of some fourteen thousand arrived at Harrisburg, a mile or so from Tupelo, late in the day, and took up a strong position on a low, open ridge.

Elsewhere, action occurred at Camden Point and Versailles, Mo. Skirmishing took place near Brownsville, Ark. A Union reconnaissance probed from Pine Bluff, Ark., and a four-day Federal expedition moved from Helena, Ark., to Buck Island in the Mississippi. In Kentucky a skirmish broke out at Bell Mines and a Union scout operated from Munfordville to Big Spring.

President Davis told Gen. Lee that Gen. Bragg had arrived in Atlanta to investigate what Davis believed to be Joseph E. Johnston's failure to stop Sherman. "It is a sad alternative, but the case seems hopeless in present hands," he wrote. "The means are surely adequate if properly employed, especially the cavalry is ample."

July 14, Thursday,
BATTLE OF TUPELO OR HARRISBURG, MISSISSIPPI.

The Federals of A. J. Smith were ready at Harrisburg, Miss., well posted to defend against the coming Confederates. On the other hand, the object of Smith's expedition was to defeat Forrest. Stephen D. Lee, commanding Southern forces in Alabama, Mississippi, and east Louisiana, gave a large part of the field command to Forrest. But the Confederate right moved ahead of Forrest's left wing and headed east against the Federal line. Wave after wave of Confederates attacked but were forced back. The disjointed battle was largely over by noon. Smith held his position but Lee and Forrest were not destroyed. It was a Federal victory on the field but meaningless for them strategically. Smith's 14,000 suffered 77 killed, 559 wounded, and 38 missing for 674, while the Confederates, with nearly 9500 in all, had a total loss of 1347. Evidence of the real results of the battle came the next day when Smith's Union force began its pullback to Memphis, and Forrest was free again to roam.

The Confederates of Jubal Early crossed the Potomac at White's Ford and were safely in Virginia at Leesburg. Rear guards fought a skirmish with advancing Federals at Poolesville, Md. Northern commander Wright told Washington that Early had crossed before the Yankees could get there and did not advise pursuing into Virginia.

In Virginia a slight action occurred at Malvern Hill. In Missouri skirmishing broke out near Fredericksburg and Bloomfield; and there was action at Bayou des Arc, Ark. Skirmishing in Webster and Union counties of Kentucky lasted four days.

President Lincoln moved back to the Soldiers' Home after the Confederate invasion scare. Personality differences among Cabinet members concerned him and he wrote a memo that as President he would be the judge of how long an official remained in his Cabinet.

July 15, Friday

In the Harrisburg-Tupelo area of Mississippi the Federal army of A. J. Smith stood its ground until afternoon, when it began a slow retreat toward Memphis. The announced reason was short supplies. Forrest followed up but failed to bring on another major battle. Among the several skirmishes was one at Old Town Creek. The withdrawing Federals did manage to keep Forrest occupied and thus protected the Nashville to Chattanooga lines of Sherman's Georgia forces. In the east Early's Confederates remained just south of the Potomac at Leesburg. The Federals under Wright were just north of the Potomac. Light skirmishing broke out near Hillsborough. Va. The Petersburg lines were quiescent except for sniper fire and fortifying operations. The roll of action elsewhere included an affair at Accotink,

Va.; an affair at Lindley in Grundy County, and action at Huntsville, Mo.; and a five-day Federal expedition from Jacksonville, Fla.

In Washington President Lincoln was unhappy that Early's Confederates had got away freely from Washington.

July 16, Saturday

Gen. Early left Leesburg, Va., near the Potomac, and headed back toward the Shenandoah Valley, unimpeded except for action near Purcellville and at Wood Grove, Va. Elsewhere in Virginia there was fighting at Four-Mile Creek and Malvern Hill. A. J. Smith's and Forrest's men skirmished at Ellistown, Miss., as Federals continued their retreat from Tupelo. In Missouri skirmishing erupted on Clear Fork near Warrensburg and on the Fayette Road near Huntsville; and in South Carolina on James Island near Charleston.

Sherman's major move across the Chattahoochee and out around the north side of Atlanta toward Decatur on the east got under way, though not without delays. Johnston and the Confederates planned to attack as Sherman moved around the city, when the wings of his army might be separated from the center. Meanwhile, Johnston continued work on fortifications extending from near the Chattahoochee south of Peachtree Creek around to the Atlanta and Decatur Railroad. During the various movements there was skirmishing at Turner's Ferry.

President Davis sent a firm wire to Gen. Johnston in Georgia: ". . . I wish to hear from you as to present situation and your plan of operations so specifically as will enable me to anticipate events." Johnston replied somewhat ambiguously, "As the enemy has double our number, we must be on the defensive. My plan of operations must therefore, depend upon that of the enemy. It is mainly to watch for an opportunity to fight to advantage. We are trying to put Atlanta in condition to be held for a day or two by the Georgia militia, that army movements may be freer and wider."

Mr. Lincoln, still cautiously interested in possible contacts by Confederate representatives looking to peace, sent Sec. John Hay to New York to consult with those involved.

July 17, Sunday

HOOD REPLACES JOHNSTON IN GEORGIA.

" . . . as you failed to arrest the advance of the enemy to the vicinity of Atlanta, far in the interior of Georgia, and express no confidence that you can defeat or repel him, you are hereby relieved from the command of the Army and Department of Tennessee, which you will immediately turn over to General Hood." So read the message received by Gen. Joseph E. Johnston at Nelson's House on the Marietta road three miles from Atlanta. Johnston and Davis had misunderstood each other since the war began.

Richmond could not ignore the loss of so much territory, whereas Johnston believed he had adopted the only strategy possible in view of Federal numbers and he *had* preserved the Army of Tennessee, not only intact but in excellent condition.

John Bell Hood, impetuous and a fighter, would now take over in place of the cautious, careful Johnston. Many in the Confederate Army protested the move, but others cheered. Historians have disputed the wisdom of the change ever since. Most Federal officers, believing they could trounce the Confederates in the expected fight, also cheered.

Early's Confederates took post near Berryville in the Shenandoah. At Snicker's Ferry or Parker's Ford they engaged Federals of Hunter and Crook who had moved in from the north and west. Federal units scattered throughout West Virginia and the Valley were at last joining together.

The Federal armies in Georgia continued to build pontoon bridges across the Chattahoochee and partially to invest Atlanta. Skirmishing occurred at Vining's Station, Ga., and at Herring Creek, Va. Other action took place at Fredericksburg in Ray County, Mo., and at Davison's Ford near Clinton, La. Federals scouted from Columbus to Hickman, Ky., and on the South Platte River in Colorado Territory.

President Lincoln, apparently disturbed over the uproar attending Federal casualties in the Virginia Campaign, wrote Grant that he was glad to hear he planned to make a desperate effort to get a position at Petersburg but hoped "you may find a way that the effort shall not be desparate [sic] in the sense of great loss of life."

July 18, Monday

President Lincoln issued a call for 500,000 volunteers, thus emphasizing the need to refill army ranks after the severe fighting in Virginia. Editor Horace Greeley traveled to Niagara Falls to speak with those said to represent Confederate peace feelers. The effort came to nothing, since the Confederacy still demanded independence. In Washington this was emphasized when J. R. Gilmore, who had talked with President Davis, told Mr. Lincoln that any terms must be based on recognition of the Confederacy. On the other hand, Mr. Lincoln had given a document to Greeley which said that any proposition must include restoration of the Union and abandonment of slavery. This, for all intents and purposes, ended the flurry of peace overtures.

In Georgia Joseph E. Johnston moved into semiretirement and John B. Hood took over. Near Peachtree Creek, north of Atlanta, skirmishing at Buckhead presaged more severe action to come. Other skirmishing broke out at Campbellton and along the Chattahoochee.

Otherwise things were fairly quiet, with an affair at Kabletown, W. Va., near the Shenandoah; Union scouting from Falls Church, Va.; Federal scouting in Shannon County and southwest and southeast Missouri. In

Arizona Territory a Yankee expedition to the Pinal Mountains against Indians was under way.

At Richmond President Davis named George A. Trenholm, a wealthy Charleston merchant, Secretary of the Treasury, replacing Christopher Memminger. Trenholm reluctantly accepted—the job was certainly not one anyone would wish on himself.

July 19, Tuesday

Northern troops seeking Early located him near Berryville and engaged in a series of skirmishes at Ashby's Gap and Berry's Ford, Va., and Darkesville, Charles Town, and Kabletown, W. Va. The engagement at Berry's Ford on the Shenandoah was particularly sharp; Early threw a major portion of his force against the advancing Federals. At night Early retreated from Berryville toward Winchester in the Shenandoah.

Sherman's men, mainly the Army of the Cumberland under George H. Thomas, pushed forward along Peachtree Creek, north of Atlanta. John M. Schofield's Army of the Ohio, farther east, also moved toward the city. East of Atlanta, James B. McPherson's Army of the Tennessee was in the Decatur area where there was skirmishing. Hood prepared to attack, particularly along Peachtree Creek. He hoped to mass superior force against the Army of the Cumberland while it was separated from the Army of the Ohio and the Army of the Tennessee. (It is uncertain whether this was Johnston's plan or Hood's.)

Additional events included a skirmish on the Benton Road near Little Rock, Ark.; a Confederate attack on Webster, Washington County, Missouri; a Federal scout to Taos, Mo.; a week of Confederate guerrilla operations along the White River, Ark.; and a skirmish at Iron Bridge, Ind. Terr.

July 20, Wednesday

BATTLE OF PEACHTREE CREEK, GEORGIA.

The Federal Army of the Cumberland under George H. Thomas crossed Peachtree Creek, heading toward the fortifications of Atlanta from the north. Hood decided to attack, but there were delays of over three hours, for which Hood blamed Gen. Hardee, perhaps unjustly. After some success the fierce Southern assaults failed. Gen. Thomas and his men again steadfastly held off the frantic Confederates, who charged for about two hours. Something over 20,000 Federals were engaged, with about 1779 killed, wounded, and missing. Nearly the same number of Confederates were in the charges with losses totaling 4796. Hood, who was not present, had failed in his first big test in command. Unlike Johnston, Hood opened battle, but little had been accomplished. Sherman's Federals controlled almost half the perimeter of Atlanta and the only open routes were to the south and southwest. Hood tried to make Hardee a scapegoat both for the delays and because, he alleged, Hardee's men did not attack vigorously enough. The Battle of Peachtree Creek showed that the fight for Atlanta would continue and that the only hope for the Confederates probably lay in further efforts to make their lesser numbers effective aganist a portion of the Federals. Also in the Atlanta area, there was an engagement at Bald or Leggett's Hill, skirmishing near Decatur and at Flint Hill Church, and an action around Howard House.

Federals pressed harder against Early's Confederate force in the Shenandoah. The two forces skirmished at Newtown and near Berryville, and fought a heavy engagement at Stephenson's Depot, just north of Winchester. Federal infantry and Averell's cavalry defeated a Confederate division under Stephen D. Ramseur in a milling fight around the little red brick depot. A Confederate brigade broke, and over 250 Confederates were captured. The main body of Early's troops continued to withdraw southward toward Strasburg.

Other action for the day was at Philomont, Va.; in Blount County, Tenn.; in La Fayette and Johnson counties and at Arrow Rock, Mo. A long Federal expedition from Fort Boise to Boonville in Idaho Territory began, and lasted until Aug. 17. At Fort Sumter the current major bombardment continued. Commandant J. C. Mitchel was mortally wounded. During 14 days the Federals had thrown 4890 rounds at the fort and once more battered the already nearly wrecked work.

July 21, Thursday

Gen. Hood sent Hardee's reinforced corps out of Atlanta on a fifteen-mile night march to the south and then east, to attack the flank and rear of McPherson's Army of the Tennessee between Atlanta and Decatur. Hood drew the Peachtree Creek line defenders into the breastworks. McPherson had meantime turned from Decatur and come west toward Atlanta and the entrenchments. In fact, from the north and east all three of Sherman's armies were closing in on the city. Federal forces, under Maj. Gen. Francis Preston Blair, Jr., of McPherson's army, assaulted enemy positions on Bald or Leggett's Hill (so named later for Federal Brig. Gen. M. D. Leggett, who led a division). After furious fighting, Federals took the position, despite a valiant defense by Patrick Cleburne and his men, and intense heat. From the hill the Northerners had a full view of Atlanta.

Otherwise the record includes a skirmish at Atchafalaya, La.; a Confederate attack on Plattsburg, Mo.; and a five-day expedition by Federals from Barrancas, Fla., with several skirmishes.

July 22, Friday

BATTLE OF ATLANTA.

After their tiring, hot, night march, the Confederates of William Hardee hit the flank of McPherson's Federals between Decatur and Atlanta. Hood was making his second effort to defeat a portion of Sherman's force and so restore the balance of numbers. Hardee was to get in flank and rear and crumple McPherson, while Cheatham's corps, facing east, was to continue the action as Hardee attacked. By partial coincidence two Federal divisions of Grenville Dodge's corps had been sent out to extend McPherson's left flank during the night, thus filling the space for which Hardee was driving. Once more Hood said Hardee failed to move out far enough and get in the Federal rear and that he was late. But Hardee's men fought extremely hard, as did Cheatham's. Confederate Maj. Gen. W. H. T. Walker died, and then Federal Maj. Gen. James B. McPherson also fell. At nightfall the Confederates retired to their entrenchments. Hood, again not present on the field, had failed a second time; his policy of hard fighting at whatever cost was not paying off. For the Federals casualties included 430 killed, 1559 wounded, and 1733 missing for a total of 3722 out of more than 30,000 engaged. For the Confederates, of nearly 40,000 engaged, estimates of casualties run from 7000 to as high as 10,000.

Sherman and the Federal armies mourned at the loss of McPherson. Maj. Gen. John A. Logan, the "Blackjack" Logan whose action that day was ferocious and able, took over on the field as commander of the Army of the Tennessee. On the fringes of the gigantic battle, fighting occurred near Decatur, at Beachtown, and along the Chattahoochee. Kenner Garrard and Federal cavalry spent three days on a raid to Covington, Ga. But in the main the Confederates still held Atlanta and the Federals still ringed it with unrelenting force. The siege of Atlanta may be said to have begun.

Elsewhere, skirmishes broke out near Pine Bluff, Ark.; in Wright County, near Camden Point and Union Mills, Mo.; at Coldwater River, Miss.; Clifton, Tenn.; and Vidalia and Condordia, La. In the Shenandoah the Federal pursuers and Early's men skirmished at Newtown and near Berryville, Va. Federal forces at Winchester were building up. Early had fallen back with his main force to the Strasburg area but covered the Winchester roads. Meanwhile, Grant and Washington tried to decide just how to deal with Early. Wright and the Federal Sixth Corps returned to Washington, leaving the defense of the Valley to Hunter.

July 23, Saturday

President Lincoln wired Gen. David Hunter at Harper's Ferry, "Are you able to take care of the enemy when he turns back upon you, as he probably will on finding that Wright has left?" Mr. Lincoln was correct. Early had turned and, from Strasburg, marched north on the Valley Turnpike toward Kernstown, just south of Winchester. The Federals deployed to meet him and sharp skirmishing ensued. At Atlanta both armies rested and repaired damage, caring for the dying and wounded after the battle of the twenty-second, although a skirmish did occur near Sweetwater, Ga. In western Missouri there was a skirmish at Liberty, and for six days a Federal column operated from Jacksonville toward Baldwin, Fla. Action took place in Randolph County, Mo.; until Oct. 10 Federal troops carried out desultory operations in southwest New Mexico Territory against the Indians. Gen. A. J. Smith and his beaten Federals returned to Memphis after their failure against Forrest and S. D. Lee near Tupelo.

The Louisiana Constitutional Convention adopted a constitution which included an end to slavery, one of the several steps in restoring Louisiana to the Union. It was ratified by the unionists on Sept. 5, at least by those taking the loyalty oath.

July 24, Sunday
SECOND BATTLE OF KERNSTOWN, VIRGINIA.

Marching north on the Valley Pike, Jubal Early's entire army headed toward Kernstown, south of Winchester, where George Crook's Federal force was in position on the same ground Jackson had struck in 1862 at the First Battle of Kernstown. Ramseur's Confederates went to the left, or west, to get around the Union right. Breckinridge, on Early's right, hit the Federal left, throwing it into considerable confusion. With further pressure from Early's center and left the Federal line broke. The pike filled with troops, trains, and equipment; and back through Winchester they went. By evening the Yankees reached Bunker Hill, W. Va., on the way toward Harper's Ferry. The total Federal loss numbered about twelve hundred and the Confederate casualties were light. Early's men followed northward once more. Skirmishes broke out at Falling Waters, W. Va.; Whitesville, Fla.; Collierville, Tenn.; and Cartersville, Ga., on Sherman's communication line.

July 25, Monday
Early's Confederates in the northern Shenandoah followed Crook's retreating Federals in a heavy rain to Bunker Hill, north of Winchester, Va. Fighting erupted at Bunker Hill, Martinsburg, W. Va., and Williamsport, Md. The Federals encamped on the Potomac. There were Federal cavalry operations from Decatur to Courtland, Ala.; a skirmish near Benton's Ferry on the Amite River, La.; a skirmish at Pleasant Hill, Mo.; and an affair at Benton, Ark. In Dakota Territory Federal soldiers carried out an expedition against the Sioux until Oct. 8. Grant decided to send the Second Corps and two cavalry divisions to the north bank of the James to press toward Richmond and to destroy railroads. By this method he hoped to reduce Lee's grip on Petersburg. Meanwhile, mining operations by Federals and some countertunneling by Confederates were in full swing at Petersburg.

President Lincoln wrote Abram Wakeman that the coming election "will almost certainly be no other than a contest between a Union and Disunion candidate, disunion certainly following the success of the latter."

July 26, Tuesday
Federal cavalry under Gen. George Stoneman left on a raid from the Atlanta area toward Macon, Ga. Skirmishing also flared near Decatur on

the Atlanta front. Early's pursuing Confederates fought withdrawing Federals at Falling Waters, W. Va., and Muddy Branch, Md., as Crook and his command crossed into Maryland. Early began breaking up the Baltimore & Ohio near Martinsburg, W. Va. Further fighting occurred at Rapidan Station, Va., and White's Station, Tenn. Confederates attacked Shelbina, Mo. A three-day Union scout operated to Searcy and West Point, Ark.; and a Federal scout in Johnson County, Mo., lasted six days. Action took place at Wallace's Ferry, Big Creek, Ark., and a skirmish broke out near Haddix's Ferry, Ky. Maj. Gen. Dabney H. Maury was assigned to command the Confederate Department of Alabama, Mississippi, and East Louisiana.

President Lincoln wrote Gen. Sherman his "profoundest thanks to you and your whole Army for the present campaign so far."

July 27, Wednesday

Having decided to lay at least partial siege to Atlanta, Sherman sent out several cavalry expeditions to cut the railroads south of Atlanta and otherwise harass the Confederates. McCook raided the Atlanta and West Point and Macon and Western railroads until the end of the month and engaged in several skirmishes. Garrard was raiding to the South River, also with skirmishing. Stoneman raided toward Macon, again with considerable fighting, and not much success. Maj. Gen. Oliver Otis Howard assumed command of the Federal Army of the Tennessee, succeeding Maj. Gen. John A. Logan, who had earlier succeeded the slain McPherson. Maj. Gen. Hooker, as a result of Howard's promotion, resigned his command of the Twentieth Corps, feeling he ranked Howard. Many supporters of Logan, both a politician and a general, felt Sherman had been unfair. Thomas reportedly had opposed Logan as a permanent commander.

Early carried out various rail-wrecking operations in the northern Shenandoah and prepared once more to cross the Potomac. There was a skirmish at Back Creek Bridge, W. Va. Maj. Gen. Halleck took command of the departments around Washington concerned with the defense of the area.

The Second Corps of Gen. Hancock and two cavalry divisions under Sheridan moved across the James from Grant's army preparatory to brief diversionary operations toward Richmond from north of the river. Advancing by the New Market and other roads, the Federals fought several brief skirmishes. The main fighting, until the twenty-ninth, was at Deep Bottom, also known as Darbytown, Strawberry Plains, and New Market Road. The Federals, not intending to assault but mainly to bring pressure on Lee, faced heavy opposition.

Elsewhere, action occurred at Whiteside on Black Creek in Florida and at Massard Prairie near Fort Smith, Ark. Severe bombardment continued against Fort Sumter in Charleston Harbor. A skirmish flared at Snapfinger Creek, Ga., and a Federal expedition operated from Norfolk, Va., into North Carolina. Skirmishing also broke out on the Blackwater Creek and on

Big Creek, and Federals scouted in Chariton County, Mo. Throughout the last part of July the Union Navy carried out reconnaissances in the Mobile Bay area as Adm. Farragut developed his plans for attack.

July 28, Thursday

BATTLE OF EZRA CHURCH, GEORGIA.

With several cavalry raids under way near Atlanta, Sherman also sought to extend his own siege lines by sending infantry down the western borders of the city toward the important railroad outlets on the south. Howard, with the Army of the Tennessee, had shifted from the eastern to the western side of the city and was moving south toward the railroads. Gen. Hood sent Gen. Stephen D. Lee and A. P. Stewart to halt Howard. The forces met at Ezra Church, where Confederate attacks for the third time failed to overcome a segment of the Federals placed in a good defensive position. From early afternoon to dark they fought, and then the Confederates withdrew into the fortifications of Atlanta. The Federals lost a little under six hundred and the Confederate losses were estimated as high as five thousand. Hood's policy of attack proved even less successful than Johnston's policy of withdrawal and preservation of his army.

Other fighting in Georgia was at Flat Rock Bridge, Lithonia, and near Campbellton. Along the Potomac Federals made some command changes in order better to oppose Early's new threat. North of the James River, Hancock and Sheridan found that the Confederates had reinforced their positions. After some reconnaissance and minor fighting along Four-Mile Creek, the Federal expedition virtually ended. Other action included a skirmish at Long's Mills near Mulberry Gap, Tenn.; a four-day Federal expedition from New Berne to Manning's Neck, N.C.; a two-day Federal scout around Cedar Bluff, Ala.; a skirmish on the Morgan's Ferry Road near Morganza, La.; and an action against Sioux Indians at Tahkahokuty Mountain in Dakota Territory.

July 29, Friday

Cavalry of Jubal Early under John McCausland crossed the Potomac west of Williamsport near Cave Spring, entering Maryland and Pennsylvania. Other Confederate cavalry demonstrated against Harper's Ferry. Another unit at Williamsport went north to skirmish at Hagerstown, Md. Skirmishing also flared at Clear Spring, Md., and Mercersburg, Pa. Once more panic erupted among Northerners in the east. Union cavalry and other units responded to the new threat of Early's men. On the Richmond-Petersburg front Hancock and Sheridan withdrew from north of the James to the Petersburg line to take part in the impending assault. The Federal expedition forced a shift of some Confederate units away from Petersburg. The mining operations at Petersburg neared completion, and the explosion was planned for July 30. Troops of Burnside and other units moved into position.

On the Atlanta front Federal cavalry fought Confederates at Lovejoy's Station and Smith's Crossroads in their efforts to wreck the vital Southern railroads. Otherwise there was an affair at Highland Stockade near Baton Rouge and other action near Napoleonville, La. In Missouri Federals carried out a five-day expedition from Warrensburg to Chapel Hill.

July 30, Saturday

PETERSBURG MINE EXPLOSION AND ASSAULT.

CAPTURE OF CHAMBERSBURG, PENNSYLVANIA.

"A fort and several hundred yards of earth work with men and cannon was literally hurled a hundred feet in the air," wrote a Southern soldier on witnessing "probably the most terrific explosion ever known in this country." For more than a month the Forty-eighth Pennsylvania, composed in large part of coal miners, had been digging a 586-foot-long tunnel under the 400 feet between the Federal and Confederate lines at Elliott's Salient on the eastern side of the siege lines at Petersburg. At four forty-five in the morning the blast went off. Possibly 278 Confederates were killed in the blast, which dug a hole 170 feet long, 60 to 80 feet wide, and 30 feet deep. Union Ninth Corps troops advanced. Shocked Confederates rallied and concentrated back of the crater, firing rapidly into the Federals. By eight-thirty about 15,000 troops, including many Negro elements, were in the crater area. Rapid volleys and counterattacks by Confederates under Maj. Gen. William Mahone halted the Federal advance. By early afternoon the Federals were ordered back. The North had lost 4000 killed and wounded to 1500 Confederates. The second major frontal assault on Petersburg had failed. In the aftermath, many charges, including ineffectiveness and drunkenness, were bandied about. At any rate, the successful mining operations ended in the failure of the assault, due to Confederate resistance and some Federal ineptitude.

Confederates entered Pennsylvania once more. In the morning cavalry of Early's command rode into Chambersburg under McCausland. He threatened to burn the town unless $500,000 in currency or $100,000 in gold be paid to him, in reparation for Hunter's depredations in the Shenandoah. The people could not raise such a sum so the town was fired. With Chambersburg in flames, McCausland moved west to McConnellsburg. Averell's Federals soon pursued the Confederates. Other places in Early's path saw skirmishing, including Emmitsburg, Monocacy Junction, and near Shepherdstown, W. Va.

In Georgia Sherman's cavalry raiders fought near Clear Creek, near Newman, at Macon and Clinton, and along the Chattahoochee River. Elsewhere, fighting erupted at Paint Rock Station, Ala.; Clifton, Tenn.; Bayou Tensas, La.; Hay Station No. 3 near Brownsville and at Pine Bluff,

Ark.; and a scout by Federals in Phelps and Maries counties, Mo. Confederate forces reoccupied Brownsville, Tex., after some skirmishing nearby.

President Lincoln left Washington for Fort Monroe to confer with Gen. Grant.

July 31, Sunday

Confederate cavalry, after burning Chambersburg, Pa., was now fully occupied with Averell's pursuing Federals. At Hancock, Md., on the Potomac, Averell attacked McCausland's Southerners, who pulled out to the northwest at Cumberland, Md. Otherwise the month ended quietly, with an affair at Orange Grove near Donaldsonville, La., and action near Fort Smith, Ark. President Lincoln held a five-hour conference with Gen. Grant and then headed back toward Washington. Meanwhile, at Petersburg, the lines were being reestablished in the area of the huge crater.

AUGUST, 1864

Many aspects of the war had changed immensely since May. In Virginia the entire outlook was vitally different. With Petersburg under severe partial siege, Richmond and the Confederate government were seriously threatened as well. The defense lines looked solid but Lee's Army of Northern Virginia was sadly outnumbered. In the Shenandoah Early could expect concentrated opposition. In Georgia, Atlanta, too, was under a form of siege and Hood appeared no more successful against Sherman than Joseph E. Johnston had been. Dissension increased in political circles.

For the North the victories of midsummer had been encouraging, but there, too, dissension was rife. Radicals on one side and peace elements on the other badgered the Lincoln administration. The cost in manpower of Grant's campaign was both a political issue and a true concern. Since Grant had not taken Petersburg and Richmond and ended the war, many faced with dread the prospect of another fall and winter of conflict.

August 1, Monday

From their base of operations in the Shenandoah Valley the Confederate forces under Early still threatened the Federals. McCausland's cavalry, successful in its expedition against Chambersburg, Pa., engaged the Federal garrison at Cumberland, Md. McCausland was now in trouble, with more Federals closing in. There was also an affair at Flintstone Creek near Cumberland. Meanwhile, Early faced a new adversary. The Federals named Maj. Gen. Philip H. Sheridan commander of the Army of the Shenandoah with the special task of ridding the Valley of Early and all Confederates.

In the Richmond-Petersburg area the siege went on with a skirmish at Deep Bottom, Va., amid indications that soon Grant would try to cut the railroads still bringing supplies to the Confederate capital.

Otherwise there was a series of scouts and expeditions, largely by Union forces. Operations in southwest Missouri, which lasted for most of August, included a skirmish at Diamond Grove Prairie. Also in Missouri skirmishes occurred at Rolla and near Independence, and Federals scouted out toward Gunter's Mills. A Union scout probed against Indians near Smoky Hill Fork, Kas. Federals operating in eastern Arkansas skirmished at Lamb's Plantation. After a skirmish at Athens, Tenn., Federals pursued the Confederates into North Carolina. For six days a Federal scout operated from Strawberry Plains to Greeneville, Tenn. For most of the month a Union expedition marched from La Grange, Tenn., to Oxford, Miss.; and there were considerable operations in eastern Kentucky with a skirmish near Bardstown, Ky. Sherman's guns shelled Atlanta.

August 2, Tuesday

Early's cavalry under McCausland fought again at Hancock, Md., as they sought to recross the Potomac after their Chambersburg raid, with skirmishing at Old Town, Md., and Green Spring Run, W. Va. At Mobile the obvious build-up of Federal naval forces continued. Of the two remaining major Confederate ports, Mobile, Ala., and Wilmington, N.C., Mobile would be easier to attack. But it did have two well-placed forts at the mouth of the bay and a fairly powerful Confederate naval armament. A Federal reconnaissance moved from Berwick to Pattersonville, La., and nine days of operations took place near Holden, Mo. Confederate naval officials decided it was impossible to get C.S.S. *Rappahannock,* laid up at Calais, out to sea as a raider. The French would allow her only a thirty-five-man crew.

August 3, Wednesday

Federal land forces landed on Dauphin Island and invested Fort Gaines at the entrance to Mobile Bay. However, the fort remained in Confederate hands, guarding the entrance from the west, along with Fort Morgan on the east. McCausland had made good his escape from Maryland to West Virginia with part of Early's command. In Georgia Federal troops increased their pressure on Atlanta by crossing Utoy Creek, fighting at Sunshine Church, Frogtown, Jug Tavern, and Mulberry Creek. Meanwhile, the cavalry units sent out by Sherman ran into opposition. On the southern Virginia front action erupted near Wilcox's Landing. Elsewhere, action involved skirmishes at Triune, Tenn.; a four-day Federal scout from Cumberland Gap, Tenn., into Lee County, Va., and to Tazewell, Tenn.; operations about Woodville, Tenn.; a skirmish near Fayette, Mo.; and a series of Union scouts until November from Fort Sumner, N. Mex. Terr.

Lincoln, annoyed by the inaction of officers in the Shenandoah, told Grant that his idea of following the enemy "to the death" "will neither be done nor attempted unless you watch it every day, and hour, and force it." As a result of the message Grant came to Washington Aug. 4 to see what could be done. Gen. Sheridan reached Washington to take over in the Shenandoah.

August 4, Thursday

Early's men still skirmished at Antietam Ford, Md., with action at New Creek, W. Va., as the Confederate force remained a bane of the Federals in Virginia. Action occurred near Harrison's Landing, Va., and a skirmish broke out at Tracy City, Tenn. There were ten days of operations in and around Brazos Santiago, Tex., and a three-day Federal expedition from Natchez, Miss., to Gillespie's Plantation, La. Firing on Fort Sumter by Federals continued until Aug. 23 but slackened. Federals continued crossing Utoy Creek on the west side of Atlanta in their slow extension of the siege line toward the south side of the city. Gen. Grant left City Point for Washington and Frederick, Md., to straighten out plans to thwart Early.

August 5, Friday

BATTLE OF MOBILE BAY.

"I am going into Mobile Bay in the morning if 'God is my leader' as I hope he is . . ." wrote Adm. Farragut to his wife Aug. 4. In the morning his Union fleet of eighteen ships including four monitors entered Mobile Bay, passing between the fearsome forts guarding the three-mile channel. Adm. Farragut had desired to launch the long-delayed attack since resuming command of his squadron in January. In addition to the stanchly armed Forts Gaines and Morgan were three small gunboats and the formidable C.S.S. *Tennessee,* said to be the most powerful ironclad afloat. Furthermore, only a narrow passage in the harbor channel remained unblocked by obstructions and torpedoes or mines. Farragut had his four ironclad monitors in the starboard column led by *Tecumseh* and fourteen wooden ships in the port column, with *Brooklyn* in the lead and *Hartford* as flag. At 5:30 A.M. the fleet moved in, and Fort Morgan opened on *Brooklyn* shortly after 7 A.M. Action became general between the Yankee navy and Fort Morgan (Gordon Granger had invested Fort Gaines on Aug. 3).

The Confederate fleet joined in. U.S.S. *Tecumseh* headed for C.S.S. *Tennessee.* Then one or more torpedoes exploded under her. In seconds *Tecumseh* went down prow first, two hundred yards from the enemy. Shortly after this Adm. Farragut, in the port rigging of *Hartford,* is said to have shouted, "Damn the torpedoes, full speed ahead." Regardless of just what he said, that is what the fleet did. There were anxious moments as *Hartford* took the van. However, the rest of the fleet passed the forts with minor loss. Three Federals rammed the sluggish *Tennessee* by midmorning. The Union monitors opened and *Tennessee,* rather vulnerable despite her armor, went out of control. Confederate Adm. Franklin Buchanan suffered a broken leg. At 10 A.M., after heavy pounding, *Tennessee* surrendered. The Federals suffered 145 killed, including 93 drowned on *Tecumseh,* 170 wounded, and four captured. Confederate losses were 12 killed, 20 wounded, and 270 captured. U.S.S. *Philippi* was destroyed, C.S.S. *Selma* was forced to surrender, and C.S.S. *Gaines* was sunk.

Adm. Farragut had again proven that ships could handle forts. Closing Mobile as a Confederate port set the stage for land operations against the city.

On the front along the Potomac, northwest of Washington, skirmishing broke out at Keedysville, Williamsport, and Hagerstown as Confederates once more entered Maryland in a brief foray. A skirmish at Huttonsville, W. Va., also marked the minor fighting between Early's men and the pursuing Federals. Sharp fighting along Utoy Creek near Atlanta further thwarted Schofield in his attempt to edge south of Atlanta along the western fringe. At Petersburg a Confederate mine exploded in front of the Federal Eighteenth Corps. Other skirmishing occurred at Cabin Point, Va.; near Remount Camp, Ark.; at Olive Branch, Doyal's Plantation, and Concordia Bayou, La.

The Radical Republican elements in Congress opened their campaign against President Lincoln. Representative Henry Winter Davis of Maryland and Sen. Benjamin Wade of Ohio issued, in the New York *Tribune,* what became known as the Wade-Davis Manifesto. In answer to Lincoln's proclamation on his pocket veto of the Radical reconstruction plan, the authors said, "it is their right and duty to check the encroachments of the Executive on the authority of Congress. . . ." They accused Lincoln of personal ambition in refusing to sign the Wade-Davis bill. Also charging the President with attempting to make, not execute, the laws, they claimed "the authority of Congress is paramount and must be respected."

August 6, Saturday

With the Federal fleet in Mobile Bay and troops near Fort Gaines, the Confederate Fort Powell, guarding a secondary bay entry, was evacuated the night of Aug. 5–6 after being bombarded by U.S.S. *Chickasaw.* *Chickasaw* then bombarded Fort Gaines on the sixth. Confederate cruiser *Tallahassee* left Wilmington, N.C., for a three-week cruise, during which she would take more than thirty prizes. The fighting at Utoy Creek southwest of Atlanta continued as Sherman, with Schofield's army in the lead, attempted to cut the Confederate railroads south of Atlanta. The Confederates had firmly entrenched, aided by tangled undergrowth and felled trees. Federals finally outflanked the Confederate line and forced it to fall back to a new position. Elsewhere, the fighting was at Indian Village and Plaquemine, La. Federals scouted in Saline County, Mo., and an expedition by Federals from Little Rock to Little Red River, Ark., lasted until the sixteenth. Early pulled back south of the Potomac again, due to threats to his rear.

August 7, Sunday

Fort Gaines in Mobile Bay surrendered to the Federal army on Dauphin Island, but Fort Morgan remained in Confederate hands. Col. Charles D. Anderson of Fort Gaines was censured by his superiors for raising the white flag. They believed he should have continued fighting and overruled his surrender. Skirmishes erupted at the Tallahatchie River in Mississippi; at Enterprise and near Huntsville, Mo.; at Oldfields near Moorefield, W. Va. There were affairs near Fort Lyon, Colo. Terr., and at Grand Bayou, Fla. A two-day Federal scout from Independence into La Fayette County, Mo., operated against guerrillas. Confederates raided into Union County, Tenn.

Maj. Gen. Philip H. Sheridan was assigned command of the new Middle Military Division, which included the Middle Department and those of Washington, the Susquehanna, and West Virginia. His army became known as the Army of the Shenandoah. The main object was to coordinate operations against Early's Confederate force. In Washington Grant, Halleck, and Stanton conferred with the President. President Davis was concerned over the personality conflicts between Gen. Hood and Gen. Hardee at Atlanta.

August 8, Monday

After considerable confusion among Confederate authorities, Fort Gaines finally surrendered to Federal forces on Dauphin Island in Mobile Bay. Skirmishing occurred at Fairfax Station, Va.; Salem, Ky.; and La Fayette, Tenn. Federal scouts against Indians operated from Salina to Mulberry Creek, Kas.; on the Little Missouri in Dakota Territory; and from Camp Anderson to Bald Mountain, Calif.

August 9, Tuesday

In Virginia the siege lines at Petersburg were quiet. Sheridan prepared to move from Halltown and Harper's Ferry, W. Va., toward Winchester, Va., and Early's Confederates. At Atlanta Sherman's Federals regrouped and rested for new moves against Hood and the city. In the Mobile Bay area Federal troops began building up their siege lines around Fort Morgan, completely cut off from the Confederate-held city. John S. Mosby was becoming more active in his raiding of Federal-held sections of Virginia. During mid-August minor but extensive operations in central Arkansas included some skirmishing. A Federal expedition from La Grange, Tenn., to Oxford, Miss., skirmished at Hurricane Creek and Oxford.

A tremendous explosion rocked City Point, Va., killing 43, injuring 126, and causing vast property damage. Two Confederate agents smuggled a small box on board a Union transport. The explosive went off just before noon. Gen. Grant, sitting in front of his tent, was showered with debris but was uninjured.

President Lincoln wrote Gen. Banks that he was anxious for the people of Louisiana to ratify the new state constitution. Mr. Lincoln also wrote Horace Greeley that most of the correspondence regarding negotiations by Greeley and others with Confederates could be published except for a few portions he did not think it wise to reveal.

August 10, Wednesday

Confederate cavalry under Joseph Wheeler began a raid lasting until Sept. 9 on Federal rail lines and other communications in north Georgia and east Tennessee. Jubal Early moved his Confederate forces southward in the Shenandoah from Bunker Hill, W. Va., to near Winchester, Va. Sheridan's forces were marching south from the Halltown-Harper's Ferry area. Near Atlanta action flared at Lovejoy's Station, Ga. Other fighting was at Baldwin, Fla.; Tallahatchie River, Miss.; and near Stone Chapel, Va. Union scouts operated from Morganza, La. President Davis wrote to Lee about obtaining an adequate supply of soap for the army in front of Petersburg. Three small Federal vessels suffered severely during a two-day duel with Southern artillery at Gaines' Landing, Ark., on the Mississippi. C.S.S. *Tallahassee* took seven prizes off Sandy Hook., N.J.

August 11, Thursday

Faced with Sheridan's advancing Federals, Jubal Early pulled his Confederates out of Winchester and headed south up the Shenandoah toward Cedar Creek. Fighting broke out near Winchester, Newtown, and at Toll-Gate, near White Post. As news of the Federal victory at Mobile Bay spread, the main active front remained the turbulent campaign in the Shenandoah, a plaguing thorn in the Federal flanks.

Meanwhile, other operations continued at a steady pace—a Union expedition from Rome, Ga., to Jacksonville, Ala.; skirmishing in Arkansas on White Oak Creek and in Crawford County; a skirmish at Hartville, Mo.; an expedition of U.S. Negro troops to Kent's Landing, Ark.; and Federal operations in Johnson County, Mo. Federal troops operated against Indians in Nebraska Territory until late October. The Yankees skirmished with Indians near Sand Creek in Colorado Territory.

President Davis told Lee at Petersburg, "It is thought idle to attack your entrenchments but feasible to starve you out."

August 12, Friday

Sheridan moved toward Early in the Shenandoah as the Confederates entrenched along Cedar Creek, south of Winchester. A brief skirmish along Cedar Creek initiated the feeling-out process. Elsewhere, there were operations in Madison County, Ala.; in Ray and Carroll counties of Missouri; skirmishing near Van Buren, Ark.; and operations against Indians in the San Andres Mountains of New Mexico and near Fort Garland, Colo. Terr. Confederate cruiser *Tallahassee* gathered in six more Yankee ships off New York. Alarm spread along the mid-Atlantic and New England coasts.

In Washington some politicians, among them Thurlow Weed, told Lincoln he was in danger of being defeated in the election. There was even some talk, completely unsubstantiated, that Gen. Grant would be a candidate.

August 13, Saturday

For a full week there were serious demonstrations by Federals on the north bank of the James River east of Richmond at Four-Mile and Dutch creeks, Deep Bottom, Fussell's Mill, Gravel Hill, Bailey's Creek, White's Tavern, Charles City Road, and New Market Road. The Federals hoped to divert attention from Petersburg and to probe or take Confederate defenses. Lee was attentive but not too concerned. In the Shenandoah Valley fighting broke out at Berryville and near Strasburg as Sheridan's Federals met stiffening resistance from Early's force at Cedar Creek.

Illinois saw some minor operations by pro-Confederates in the Shawnee-town area on the Ohio River. Federals operating against Forrest skirmished at Hurricane Creek, Miss. Other fighting occurred at Palatka and near Fort Barrancas, Fla. Federal operations in La Fayette, Saline, and Howard counties of Missouri lasted ten days.

August 14, Sunday

Skirmishing flared near Strasburg in the Shenandoah as Sheridan withdrew from Early's front toward Berryville. Skirmishing at Lamar, Miss., marked the long, frustrating Federal drive to halt Forrest. The only action on the Atlanta front consisted of skirmishes near Dalton, at Pine Log Church, and near Fairmount, Ga.

August 15, Monday

In the Shenandoah there was more skirmishing at Cedar Creek, at Strasburg, Va., and near Charles Town, W. Va. Sheridan at night began his withdrawal from Cedar Creek toward Winchester, believing he could not hold the line and could not properly supply his army. North of the James, east of Richmond, the Federal expedition to Chaffin's Bluff and the capital's defenses encountered delays and frustration at the hands of Confederate defenders. In Georgia Sherman's men moved slowly toward Utoy Creek, southwest of Atlanta, fighting on Peachtree Road, at Buchanan, Sandtown, and Fairburn. Confederate cavalry raided the

Nashville and Northwestern Railroad in Tennessee. Federals raided the Florida Railroad near Gainesville, Fla., Aug. 15–19. A Federal scout in Alabama probed from Triana to Valhermoso Springs. Across the Mississippi fighting took place at Dripping Spring, Mo. Minor operations in southwest Missouri and northwest Arkansas lasted ten days. Federals captured the English-built Confederate cruiser *Georgia* outside of Lisbon. However, the never too successful *Georgia* had been sold by the Confederates to an English shipowner and had been disarmed. C.S.S. *Tallahassee* captured six schooners off New England. Lieut. Gen. Richard Taylor was assigned to command the Confederate Department of Alabama, Mississippi, and East Louisiana.

August 16, Tuesday

Cavalry skirmished at Allatoona, and Kilpatrick's Federals raided from Fairburn around Atlanta. Sheridan pulled back successfully toward Winchester with little knowledge of the withdrawal reaching Early at Cedar Creek, although there was an engagement at Front Royal or Guard Hill. Federal troops north of the James unsuccessfully attacked Confederate fortifications near Fussell's Mill. Northerners under Gen. Hancock had erroneous information as to enemy works and the whole expedition finally withdrew to Petersburg and Bermuda Hundred on Aug. 20. Federals undertook operations from Mount Vernon, Ind., into Kentucky until Aug. 22. Other action was at Columbia, Mo., and near Smoky Hill Crossing, Kas. C.S.S. *Tallahassee* took four schooners and a bark off New England.

August 17, Wednesday

Jubal Early's Confederates pushed northward from Cedar Creek after Sheridan's withdrawing army. Sheridan had moved on to the Berryville area, leaving a rear guard at Winchester. In a sharp fight near Winchester Federal cavalry held well, protecting the main column. Skirmishes broke out in Georgia at South Newport, and in Mississippi in Issaquena County. On the Arkansas River near Pine Bluff, Ark., Confederates captured the Federal steamer *Miller*.

President Lincoln told Grant, ". . . Hold on with a bull-dog gripe [sic], and chew & choke, as much as possible." Grant had indicated his desire to continue the siege of Petersburg without weakening his army.

August 18, Thursday

BATTLE OF THE WELDON RAILROAD, VIRGINIA, BEGINS.

The Federal Fifth Corps under G. K. Warren from the Petersburg lines moved out to the west or left of the Federal siege positions and occupied over a mile of the vital Weldon Railroad running south from Petersburg. After taking the area around Globe Tavern, Yellow House, and Blick's Station, Warren turned northward toward Petersburg. Terrain and Henry Heth's men halted them in the woods south of the city for the night. Despite the heat and heavy rain the Federals had made the first important move since the crater to penetrate toward Petersburg or extend the lines significantly. It cost 544 killed and wounded, plus 292 missing. In the Shenandoah Sheridan pulled out of Berryville, Va., and headed toward Charles Town, W. Va. Early, learning this, headed toward Bunker Hill, north of Winchester. Skirmishing was along Opequon Creek.

In Georgia Judson Kilpatrick's Federal cavalry began its raid to Lovejoy's Station which lasted until Aug. 22. Their efforts to destroy the Macon and Western Railroad were largely frustrated. Meanwhile, Schofield's Army of the Ohio pushed forward along Utoy Creek. This point southwest of Atlanta was to provide the pivot for Sherman to swing east in his efforts to cut off the south side of the city. There was combat at Camp Creek in addition. In Arkansas fighting broke out at Benton and near Pine Bluff; and in Tennessee a skirmish took place at Charleston.

For the second time Gen. Grant refused to exchange Confederate prisoners of war; he had expressed a belief that such exchange would prolong the war. The Confederates urged exchange for humanitarian reasons and because they could use their men now in Federal hands, and were sorely strained to feed, house, clothe, and guard Federals in their control.

August 19, Friday

BATTLE OF THE WELDON RAILROAD CONTINUED.

During the afternoon troops of A. P. Hill's Confederate corps hit Warren's Federal infantry in the dense woods south of Petersburg, Va. The Union forces suffered severely and Warren had to pull back toward Globe Tavern, seized the day before in his operations against the Weldon Railroad. But the Northerners still held the important railroad. Warren lost 382 killed and wounded, but 2518 were missing, many of whom were captured from S. W. Crawford's broken division. Confederate casualties are uncertain.

In the Shenandoah Early attempted to move north from Winchester to Bunker Hill, W. Va. His men skirmished near Opequon Creek on the Berryville and Winchester Pike and at Franklin, West Va. In Georgia Federal reconnaissances continued toward East Point and the Confederate defenses south of Atlanta. There was combat at Red Oak, Flint River, and Jonesborough, Ga., and the usual cavalry action. A five-day Federal Indian scout began on the Republican River in Kansas; and a skirmish erupted on Hurricane Creek, Miss.

President Lincoln was quoted in an interview as saying, "I cannot but feel that the weal or woe of this great nation will be decided in the approaching canvas."

August 20, Saturday

Despite some skirmishing along the Weldon Railroad near Globe Tavern south of Petersburg, the Confederates suspended temporarily their efforts to dislodge the Federals. Hancock's forces, unsuccessful in their ill-planned diversion north of the James, pulled back to Petersburg and Bermuda Hundred. In the Valley the sparring and skirmishing between Early and Sheridan continued, with action at Berryville, Opequon Creek, Va., and Bulltown, W. Va.

Combat at Lovejoy's Station on the Macon and Western Railroad in Georgia marked the Federal cavalry operations; Federals burned Legareville, S.C. Skirmishes occurred at Pine Bluff, Tenn., and near Rocheport, Mo.

President Davis expressed his distress at the presence of Federal troops on the Weldon Railroad.

August 21, Sunday

Confederates occupied Memphis. In a daring early morning raid, some two thousand men of Nathan Bedford Forrest entered the Tennessee city, held it for part of the day, nearly captured Federal Maj. Genls. S. A. Hurlbut and C. C. Washburn, and left with few losses. The raid frustrated, demoralized, and embarrassed the North. As a result, A. J. Smith's Federal column pulled back, leaving Forrest free to operate against Sherman's supply lines. Many lives, months of time, and large amounts of matériel had been spent in Federal efforts to bring Forrest to bay and still they were unsuccessful.

A. P. Hill once more assaulted Warren's Federals south of Petersburg to try to recover the Weldon Railroad. On another hot, rainy day of battle the Confederate attack failed, although Warren lost 301 more killed, wounded, and missing. The new Federal lines held and Lee had to accept the loss of the northern section of the Weldon Railroad, an invaluable supply line for Richmond and Petersburg. Aug. 18–21 Union losses for the Battle of the Weldon Railroad or Globe Tavern totaled 198 killed, 1105 wounded, and 3152 missing for 4455 out of something over 20,000 engaged. Southern losses are estimated at 1600 out of about 14,000 engaged.

In the Shenandoah, Early and R. H. Anderson planned to hit Sheridan in a two-pronged attack. The drive failed for lack of coordination after fighting near Berryville, Va., Charles Town, Middleway, and Summit Point, W. Va. Late at night Sheridan pulled back from Charles Town to Halltown near Harper's Ferry and the Potomac River, into a virtually impregnable position. Once more the Valley was largely free of Federals, but the area had been too much fought over to be of great value. Otherwise there was action in Loudoun County, Va.; at Grubb's Crossroads, Ky.; and Diamond Grove, Mo.

August 22, Monday

Early demonstrated toward Harper's Ferry, with a skirmish at Charles Town, W. Va. Globe Tavern and the Weldon Railroad were quiet. Sputtering cavalry skirmishes broke out at Jonesborough and Caton, Ga. Other fighting took place at Canton and Roaring Spring, Ky.; in Yell County, Ark.; and Cove Point, Md. Federals scouted from Helena to Mount Vernon, Ark. President Lincoln told the 169th Ohio, "The nation is worth fighting for, to secure such an inestimable jewel" as opportunity under a free government.

August 23, Tuesday

After fierce bombardment on Aug. 22 by land batteries, three monitors, and other Union naval vessels, Fort Morgan, the last major Confederate post at the entrance to Mobile Bay, fell to the Federals. Since Aug. 17 it had been besieged by troops in the rear and completely shut off from Mobile. The fall of Fort Morgan gave Federals control of the port, although the Confederates still held the city itself. With the surrender of Fort Morgan, Wilmington, N.C., remained the only significant port partially open to Confederate blockade-runners.

Early continued to demonstrate against Sheridan at Halltown in the northern end of the Shenandoah Valley. At Petersburg Hancock's Federal corps destroyed portions of the Weldon Railroad on the left of the Union siege lines. Brief action flared on the Dinwiddie Road near Reams' Station during this work of destruction, and there were indications that the Confederates would attempt to halt this breakup of the railroad. President Davis expressed his apprehension over loss of the Weldon Railroad and other supply lines.

Other action included a skirmish at Abbeville, Miss.; an affair at Webster, Mo.; and a skirmish at Kearneysville, W. Va. Union scouts operated Aug. 23–26 from Ozark, Mo., to Dubuque Crossing and Sugar Loaf Prairie; Aug. 23–29 from Clinton, La., to the Comite River; and Aug. 23–28 from Cassville, Mo., to Fayetteville, Ark.

At a Cabinet meeting President Lincoln asked members to sign, without reading, a memo: "This morning, as for some days past, it seems exceedingly probable that this Administration will not be re-elected. Then it will be my duty to so co-operate with the President elect, as to save the Union between the election and the inauguration; as he will have secured his election on such ground that he can not possibly save it afterwards." A pessimism over possible defeat in the election and a feeling that a new President, supposedly Gen. McClellan, would not carry out the war aims apparently weighed upon Mr. Lincoln.

August 24, Wednesday

On the Petersburg front Federals realized that Confederate infantry was building up near the Union troops who were destroying large sections of the Weldon Railroad. In fact, skirmishing broke out near Reams' Station and on the Vaughan Road nearby. Elsewhere, skirmishing flared at Annandale, Va., Huttonsville, and Sutton, W. Va., while at Halltown, W. Va., Early's Confederates continued demonstrating against Sheridan's forces on the Potomac. Skirmishes took place at Claiborne, Ga.; on Gunter's Prairie, Indian Terr.; and there were actions at Ashley's and Jones' stations near Devall's Bluff, Ark.

President Lincoln wrote politician and editor Henry J. Raymond that Raymond might seek a conference with Jefferson Davis to discuss peace, and to tell him hostilities would cease "upon the restoration of the Union and the national authority."

August 25, Thursday

BATTLE OF REAMS' STATION, VIRGINIA.

Striking sharply against Federal infantry destroying the Weldon Railroad south of Petersburg, A. P. Hill's beefed-up Confederate corps defeated Hancock's Second Corps in a surprise attack. Federal losses totaled 2372 and Confederate casualties are put at 720. Over 2000 of the Northern losses were captured or missing. Hancock's men withdrew somewhat and Hill's men returned to the Petersburg defense line. The Southern victory did not deter destruction or the build-up of the new westward extension of the Union siege lines around Petersburg.

With Sheridan in an unassailable position near the Potomac, Early sent part of his force to Williamsport, Md., on the Potomac, left another at Halltown, W. Va., to face Sheridan, and personally moved with a third unit to Shepherdstown, W. Va. Thus he threatened a new invasion of Maryland and Pennsylvania. Fighting did occur near Kearneysville, W. Va., Shepherdstown, and at Halltown, but the fords of the Potomac were well guarded by Federals and nothing came of the whole move. C.S.S. *Tallahassee* ran the blockade into Wilmington, N.C., after a successful three-week cruise in which she captured thirty-one Northern ships.

In Georgia Sherman began his principal movement to cut off Atlanta completely. Troops marched toward the south side of the Atlanta area, in the general direction of Jonesborough. Otherwise there were skirmishes at Morgan's Ferry and on the Atchafalaya River, La., and scouting in Jackson, Platte, and Cass counties of Missouri.

August 26, Friday

Threatening East Point, Ga., south of Atlanta, Schofield's Federals massed and demonstrated as other units of Sherman's army came into position, endangering Hood's last entry lines into and out of Atlanta. Skirmishes took place along the Chattahoochee and at Pace's and Turner's ferries, Ga. At Halltown, W. Va., near Harper's Ferry, the Confederates found it impossible to attack Sheridan and decided to move back to west of the Opequon toward Bunker Hill and Stephenson's Depot, Va. Skirmishing took place at Halltown, and near Charles Town, W. Va., and at Williamsport, Md. In Louisiana there was skirmishing near Bayou Tensas.

August 27, Saturday

Sherman's army was ready. Much of it was in position southwest of Atlanta on the Sandtown Road, ready to push farther south and swing east toward Jonesborough to cut Hood's last railroads into the city. Hood and the Confederates had not been able to interfere with the preparations to any extent. Fighting broke out at Farmer's Ferry and Fairburn, Ga.

Early, back at Bunker Hill, W. Va., with one division at Stephenson's Depot, Va., had given up attacking Sheridan's strong positions around Harper's Ferry. Fighting occurred at Nutter's Hill and Duffield's Station, W. Va. For much of the fall Union troops carried out an expedition against Indians from Fort Boise to Salmon Falls, Id. Terr., with several skirmishes. There was action at Backbone, Ind. Terr., fighting at Owensborough, Ky.; and Federals carried out an expedition from Little Rock and Devall's Bluff to Searcy, Fairview, and Augusta, Ark., until Sept. 6. Adm. Farragut asked for leave due to poor health.

August 28, Sunday

Sherman was advancing now. Thomas and the Army of the Cumberland reached Red Oak on the Montgomery and Atlanta or West Point Railroad while Howard and his Army of the Tennessee were near Fairburn on the railroad. Schofield with the Army of the Ohio was near Mount Gilead Church. Meanwhile, the Twentieth Corps under Maj. Gen. Henry W. Slocum held the Union lines around Atlanta. During the advance fighting broke out at Red Oak and Sandtown.

Sheridan advanced to Charles Town, W. Va., in the Shenandoah with no opposition, although light skirmishes took place at Leetown and Smithfield, W. Va. In Charleston Harbor Union Army plans to "shake" the remaining walls of Fort Sumter to pieces by exploding a raft loaded with powder came to nought when the blast went off harmlessly with little or no damage to the fort. Other action included skirmishing near Rocheport and in Polk County, Mo.; at Fayetteville, Ark.; and an affair near Holly Springs, Miss.

August 29, Monday

Confederates were on the move again in the Trans-Mississippi. Maj. Gen. Sterling Price assumed command of a new expeditionary force at Princeton, Ark. Price hoped to recover Missouri for the South. The expedition lasted until Dec. 2 and involved extensive fighting.

Sherman's army in Georgia continued its preliminary operations for the major move toward Jonesborough. Skirmishing at Red Oak Station and near Sandtown marked Confederate probing operations. In the Shenandoah Sheridan moved forward and Federal troops won an engagement at Smithfield Crossing of the Opequon. Skirmishing broke out at Charles Town, W. Va. Federal operations near Greeneville, Tenn., against John Hunt Morgan's troops lasted several days. In addition, fights are recorded as being near Ghent, Ky., and Milton, Fla. Confederates attacked the steamer *White Cloud* on the Mississippi near Port Hudson, La. A four-day Federal expedition moved up the White River from Helena, Ark. Five sailors were killed and nine injured when a torpedo exploded at Mobile Bay during operations by the Union Navy to remove obstructions.

The Democratic National Convention gathered in Chicago determined to nominate a candidate who could defeat Lincoln and settle the war issues. August Belmont told the convention that "Four years of misrule by a sectional, fanatical and corrupt party, have brought our country to the verge of ruin." Committees were formed and work began. Maj. Gen. George B. McClellan's was the most prominent name being discussed as presidential candidate.

August 30, Tuesday

Sherman severed one of the last two railroads into Atlanta and marched rapidly toward the Macon line. Atlanta was in dire danger. Hood countered late in the day by sending his own old corps under Cleburne and S. D. Lee's corps to attack the Federal flank at Jonesborough. Sherman had his three armies separated considerably and they were more than Hood could cover. Fighting broke out near East Point, Flint River Bridge, and Jonesborough.

In the Shenandoah Valley Sheridan shifted more of his troops toward Berryville with the clear intention of threatening Winchester once more. A skirmish erupted near Smithfield, W. Va. Maj. Gen. George Crook replaced the ineffective Maj. Gen. David Hunter in command of the Federal Department of West Virginia. A skirmish took place near Dardanelle, Ark. A four-day Federal expedition operated to Natchez Bayou, La.

The Democrats meeting in Chicago adopted a platform and placed names in nomination for President. Maj. Gen. George B. McClellan and Thomas H. Seymour, former governor of Connecticut, were named. Sen.

CANADA
WASHINGTON TERR.
MONTANA TERR. 1864
DAKOTA TERR.
MINNESOTA
WISCONSIN
MICH.
NEW YORK
VT.
N.H.
ME.
MASS.
CONN.
R.I.
N.J.
PENNSYLVANIA
DEL.
MD.
OREGON
IDAHO TERR. 1864
DAKOTA
NEBRASKA TERR. TO 1864
NEBRASKA TERR.
IOWA
ILLINOIS
IND.
OHIO
W. VA.
VIRGINIA
KENTUCKY
N. C.
S. C.
TENN.
GEORGIA
ALA.
MISS.
LA.
FLORIDA
ARKANSAS
MISSOURI
KANSAS
PUBLIC LAND STRIP
INDIAN TERRITORY
TEXAS
NEVADA TERR. 1861
NEVADA STATE 1864
UTAH TERR.
COLO. TERR.
CALIFORNIA
ARIZONA TERR. 1863
NEW MEXICO TERR.
MEXICO
Pacific Ocean
Atlantic Ocean
Gulf of Mexico
Lake Superior
Lake Michigan
Lake Huron
L. Ontario
L. Erie
MISSOURI R.
PLATTE R.
COLORADO R.
ARKANSAS R.
RED R.
RIO GRANDE
MISS. R.
TENN. R.
CUMBERLAND R.
BEAR R.
Portland
Salem
FT. VANCOUVER
Canyon City
FT. BOISE
Last Chance Gulch
Alder Gulch
Virginia City
Sacramento
San Francisco
Virginia City
Carson City
Salt Lake City
FT. BRIDGER
FT. LARAMIE
Julesburg
Denver
SAND CREEK
FT. LYON
FT. KEARNY
FT. LEAVENWORTH
FT. LARNED
Topeka
Lawrence
Omaha
FT. ABERCROMBIE
St. Paul
Birch Couley
Wood Lake
FT. RIDGELY
New Ulm
Mankato
Spirit Lake
Des Moines
Madison
Rock Island
Chicago
Springfield
Indianapolis
Detroit
Johnson's Is.
Salineville
Steubenville
Columbus
Louisville
St. Louis
Springfield
Cairo
Buffalo
Albany
St. Albans
Augusta
Portland
Boston
New York
Philadelphia
Pittsburgh
Harrisburg
Gettysburg
Baltimore
Washington
Richmond
Knoxville
Nashville
Memphis
Raleigh
Wilmington
Columbia
Charleston
Savannah
Atlanta
Montgomery
Jackson
Vicksburg
Mobile
Pensacola
New Orleans
Jacksonville
St. Augustine
New Smyrna
Cape Canaveral
Tampa
Key West
FT. JEFFERSON
Dry Tortugas
Little Rock
FT. SMITH
FT. GIBSON
FT. ARBUCKLE
FT. WASHITA
Dallas
Austin
Galveston
Matagorda Bay
Aransas Pass
Corpus Christi
PALMITO RANCH
Brownsville
Matamoros
Laredo
FT. CLARK
FT. INGE
FT. UNION
Santa Fe
Glorieta
Apache Canyon
Albuquerque
FT. CRAIG
Valverde
FT. FILLMORE
FT. BLISS (EL PASO)
Los Angeles
San Diego
FT. YUMA
Picacho Pass
Tucson
Apache Pass
0 100 200 300
Miles
barbara long

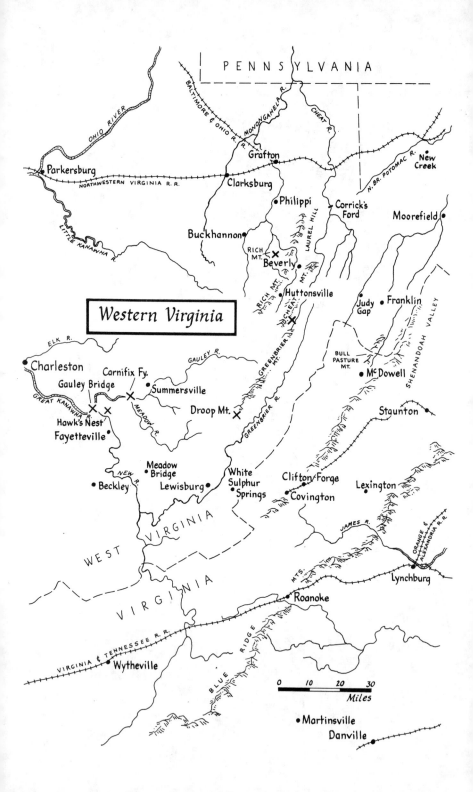

Virginia

PENNSYLVANIA

• Chambersburg • York

• Cashtown
Gettysburg • • Hanover
• Emmitsburg

MARYLAND

Cumberland
POTOMAC R.
Hagerstown
Williamsport
BALTIMORE & OHIO R.R.

Antietam ✕ Boonsborough
Martinsburg Sharpsburg
Shepherdstown Harper's Frederick
Charles Ferry ✕ Monocacy
Town BALTIMORE & OHIO R.R.
Romney Stephenson's
Depot Opequon
Winchester ✕ Cr. Ball's
Bluff ✕
Cedar Cr. ✕ Kernstown Leesburg • Edwards' Fy.
Fisher's Hill ✕ ✕ Middletown Dranesville •
New Market Strasburg Chantilly Washington
SHENANDOAH VALLEY Front ✕ Centreville
Royal Bull Run
Groveton ✕ • Centreville
Warrenton Manassas Jct. Alexandria
Harrisonburg • Bristoe Sta.
Cross Keys ✕ Brandy
Sta.
Culpeper C.H. Rappahannock Sta. Port Tobacco
Kelly's Fd.
Port Cedar Mt. ✕ Aquia Cr.
Republic Chancellorsville
Orange C.H. ✕ ✕ Fredericksburg
Staunton Gordonsville Wilderness ✕ Salem Port Royal
Church
Spotsylvania
C.H. Guiney's
Waynesborough Trevilian Sta. Sta.
Charlottesville Louisa C.H.
Beaver Dam Sta. Hanover Jct.
Goochland C.H. Hanover C.H.
Urbanna
West Point
Richmond White
Lynchburg Appomattox C.H. House
Harrison's Ldg. Williamsburg
Farmville Amelia C.H. City Point Yorktown
Appomattox Sta. Jetersville Petersburg Big Bethel ✕
Prince Edward Burke's Sta. Five Forks ✕ Ft. Monroe
C.H. Nottoway C.H. Dinwiddie C.H. Globe Norfolk
Tavern Portsmouth
Reams' Sta. Suffolk

Clarksville
ROANOKE R.

NORTH
CAROLINA
Weldon

0 5 10 15 20 25
Miles

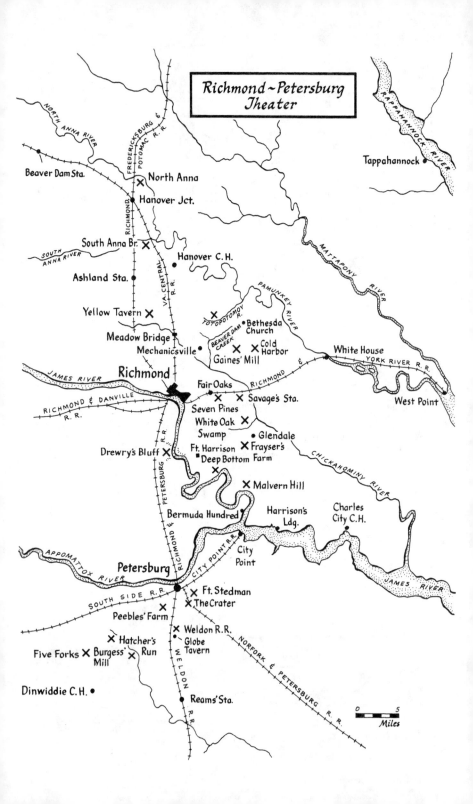

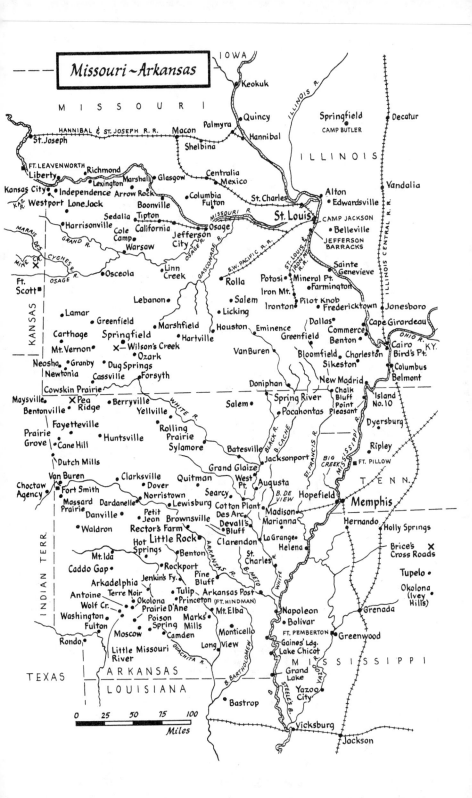

Kentucky ~ Tennessee

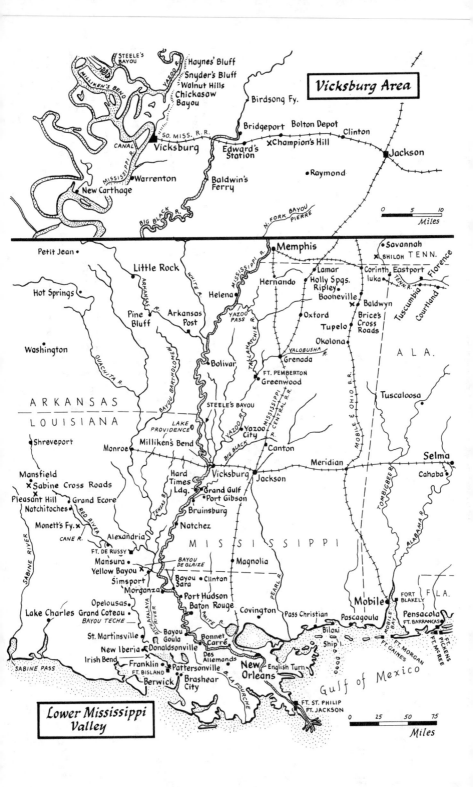

Vicksburg Area

STEELE'S BAYOU
Haynes' Bluff
Snyder's Bluff
Walnut Hills
Chickasaw Bayou
MILLIKEN'S BEND
YAZOO
Birdsong Fy.
SO. MISS. R.R.
Bridgeport
Bolton Depot
Clinton
Jackson
CANAL
Vicksburg
Edward's Station
Champion's Hill
MISSISSIPPI
Warrenton
Baldwin's Ferry
Raymond
New Carthage
BIG BLACK R.
N. FORK BAYOU PIERRE

0   5   10
Miles

Petit Jean
Memphis
Savannah
SHILOH
TENN.
Little Rock
WHITE R.
MISSISSIPPI R.
Hernando
Lamar
Holly Spgs.
Ripley
Corinth
Iuka
Eastport
Florence
Hot Springs
ARKANSAS R.
Helena
Booneville
Baldwyn
Tuscumbia
Courtland
Pine Bluff
Arkansas Post
YAZOO PASS
Oxford
Brice's Cross Roads
TENN. R.
Tupelo
Washington
OUACHITA R.
TALLAHATCHIE R.
Okolona
A L A.
Bolivar
YALOBUSHA R.
Grenada
BAYOU BARTHOLOMEW
FT. PEMBERTON
Greenwood
Tuscaloosa
A R K A N S A S
STEELE'S BAYOU
MISSISSIPPI CENTRAL R.R.
L O U I S I A N A
LAKE PROVIDENCE
Yazoo City
MOBILE & OHIO R.R.
Shreveport
Monroe
Milliken's Bend
YAZOO R.
BIG BLACK R.
Canton
Meridian
Selma
Mansfield
Sabine Cross Roads
Hard Times Ldg.
Vicksburg
Jackson
Cahaba
Pleasant Hill
Grand Ecore
Grand Gulf
Port Gibson
TOMBIGBEE R.
Natchitoches
RED RIVER
TENSAS R.
Bruinsburg
Monett's Fy.
CANE R.
Natchez
M I S S I S S I P P I
ALABAMA R.
Alexandria
FT. DE RUSSY
BAYOU DE GLAIZE
Magnolia
Mansura
Yellow Bayou
Bayou Sara
Simsport
Morganza
Clinton
PEARL R.
SABINE RIVER
Opelousas
Grand Coteau
ATCHAFALAYA RIVER
Port Hudson
Baton Rouge
Covington
Pass Christian
Mobile
FORT BLAKELY
F L A.
Lake Charles
BAYOU TECHE
WHITE R.
Pascagoula
Pensacola
FT. BARRANCAS
St. Martinsville
Bayou Goula
Clinton
Biloxi
MOBILE BAY
FT. GAINES
FT. PICKENS
FT. MORGAN
FT. McREE
New Iberia
Donaldsonville
Bonnet Carré
Des Allemands
Ship I.
Irish Bend
Franklin
FT. BISLAND
Pattersonville
Brashear City
BAYOU LAFOURCHE
New Orleans
English Turn
Gulf of Mexico
SABINE PASS
Berwick
FT. ST. PHILIP
FT. JACKSON

0   25   50   75
Miles

Lower Mississippi Valley

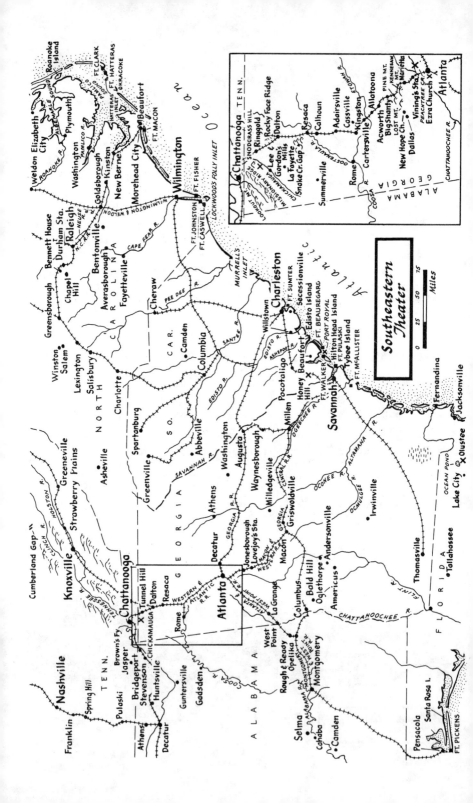

Southeastern Theater

L. W. Powell of Kentucky and former President Franklin Pierce withdrew their nominations. The aggressive platform called for fidelity to the Union under the Constitution and complained that the Administration had failed to restore the Union "by the experiment of war," had disregarded the Constitution, and trodden down public liberty and private rights. It proclaimed that "justice, humanity, liberty and the public welfare demand that immediate efforts be made for a cessation of hostilities, with a view to an ultimate convention of the States, or other peaceable means, to the end that at the earliest practicable moment peace may be restored on the basis of the Federal Union of the States." Thus the Democrats made a strong bid for peace. They also deplored the alleged interference of the military in state elections and announced "That the aim and object of the Democratic party is to preserve the Federal Union and the rights of the States unimpaired." They charged "administrative usurpation of extraordinary and dangerous powers not granted by the constitution," arbitrary arrests, subversion of civil by military law, test oaths, and interference with the right of people to bear arms in their defense. The convention thus adopted, for the most part, the program of the Peace Democrats and Copperheads, a platform diametrically opposed to that of Lincoln and the Administration, let alone the Radical Republicans.

August 31, Wednesday

GENERAL MCCLELLAN NOMINATED FOR PRESIDENT.

BATTLE OF JONESBOROUGH, GEORGIA.

The Democrats balloted in Chicago for the presidential nomination, with Maj. Gen. George B. McClellan receiving 174 votes on the first ballot to 38 for Thomas H. Seymour, 12 for Horatio Seymour, and a few others scattered. Revised, as states changed notes, McClellan swept the field with 202½ to 28½ for Thomas H. Seymour. Clement L. Vallandigham, the notorious Ohio Copperhead back from exile in the South and Canada, and who had much to do with the platform, moved McClellan's nomination be unanimous. George H. Pendleton of Ohio received the vice-presidential nomination on the second ballot.

Hardee with two corps of Hood's Confederate army attacked the entrenched positions of O. O. Howard's Army of the Tennessee near Jonesborough, south of Atlanta. The strong midafternoon drive nevertheless lacked the effectiveness of previous attacks and was seriously repulsed. Federal losses are put at 170 killed and wounded out of an estimated 15,000 or more. Southern losses are put at possibly 1725 out of 25,000 present for duty. To the north, at Rough and Ready Station Schofield's Army of the Ohio cut the Macon and Western Railroad between Jonesborough and Atlanta, after some fighting. Hood got the disturbing news by courier. Sherman that night ordered Slocum to enter Atlanta if possible. Further activity against the Macon Railroad was ordered. It appeared that Sherman was more interested in securing Atlanta than in cutting off Hood's retreat.

There was still another skirmish in the Shenandoah, this time at Martinsburg, W. Va. Fighting also occurred at Clifton, Tenn., and Steelville, Mo.

SEPTEMBER, 1864

It was increasingly apparent that Atlanta, second in importance only to Richmond, would soon have to yield to Sherman and his huge army. The siege at Petersburg, near the Confederate capital, was tightening but not yet critical. To the north Sheridan and Early sparred back and forth. To the west the war consisted mostly of raids and sporadic operations, although Forrest remained active and Price was on his way back to Missouri. Nevertheless, both nations now looked mainly to the southeast.

On the homefronts the fall harvests continued. So did political talk in the North. Three candidates for President were in the field: incumbent Lincoln, aspiring Gen. George B. McClellan, and Radical dissident John Charles Frémont. The President and his followers showed signs of nervous jitters. Voices of opposition from War Democrats, Peace Democrats, Copperheads and others were coupled with loud, though perhaps not numerous, Radicals and ultra-Radicals some of whom dreamed of dictating to every Southerner his future way of life. Election day was but two months away.

September 1, Thursday

CONFEDERATES EVACUATE ATLANTA, GEORGIA.

BATTLE OF JONESBOROUGH, GEORGIA, CONTINUES.

Explosions and fires broke out at night around Atlanta's railroad depot and yards. The enemy had fled the city. Hood, beset by Sherman's encircling force to the south at Jonesborough and fearing a direct attack on the city, evacuated, beginning in the late afternoon. Time did not remain to remove the extensive munitions and other supplies, so they went up in flames along with a great deal of railroad equipment. Like his predecessor, Johnston, Hood now was intent on saving his army for a better day. However, without question, Hood had failed in his major task, to fight and hold Atlanta.

At Jonesborough Hood had moved S. D. Lee's corps back toward Atlanta but it was halted at Rough and Ready. Howard's army and units of Thomas and Schofield opposed Hardee's corps. Shortly after noon the

Battle of Jonesborough reopened. After furious fighting Federals all but eliminated two Confederate brigades, although other forces held on. At nightfall Hardee pulled back to join Hood at Lovejoy's Station, where the Army of Tennessee was reassembling after the retreat. Losses in the two days at Jonesborough numbered at least 1450 for the Federals and are unrecorded for the Confederates. Forces engaged varied, but Confederates outnumbered Federals Aug. 31, and the balance was reversed Sept. 1.

Sheridan's Union army regrouped and began to threaten Winchester, Va., once more. One of many skirmishes flared along Opequon Creek north of Winchester. Another Northern powder raft exploded without effect at Fort Sumter. Skirmishes broke out at Tipton, Mo., and Fort Smith and Beatty's Mill, Ark. Scouts and cavalry operated in Johnson County, Mo. During most of the month Federals scouted from Camp Grant to the North Fork of the Eel River, Calif. Federal operations against Indians in the Trinity River Valley, Calif., continued through the fall.

September 2, Friday

FEDERAL ARMY IN ATLANTA.

"Fairly won" were the words Sherman used to inform Washington that his army had taken Atlanta. On the other side Hood had fought and lost and was gathering together his army around Lovejoy's Station, southeast of Atlanta, northwest of Macon, Ga. Slocum's corps actually entered the battered city in the morning and Slocum hastened the word of the city's capitulation to Sherman, who was moving toward Lovejoy's Station and Hood. There was action for several days around Lovejoy's but Sherman pulled back to Atlanta to reorganize, breathe, and plan. Likewise, Hood had to reorganize his shattered elements, rest the strong ones, and plan. Back on the Union supply lines there was skirmishing at Glass Bridge and Big Shanty, Ga., and a considerable amount of scouting as usual.

Although fighting was light at Darkesville and Bunker Hill, W. Va., it would soon be different—Sheridan obviously planned an offensive toward the Shenandoah. Lee pressed Early to return troops loaned to him, as Lee felt their absence at Petersburg. On that front, Federals operated beyond Yellow Tavern on the Weldon Railroad south of Petersburg (not the same Yellow Tavern where Stuart fell).

Secondary action also increased, with skirmishing at The Tannery near Little Rock and near Quitman, Ark.; at Mount Vernon, Mo.; and near Union City, Tenn. Federal expeditions operated on the Blackwater and on the Little Blue in Jackson County, Mo. Guerrillas raided Owensborough, Ky.

President Lincoln talked with various observers and political leaders to get the "feel" of the nation in respect to the coming election. At the

Headquarters of the Army of Northern Virginia, Gen. Lee was perturbed over the "importance of immediate and vigorous means to increase the strength of our armies. . . ." He wrote Davis that Negroes should be substituted for whites "in every place in the army or connected with it when the former can be used." He urged tightening rules for enlistments and exemptions all along the line, for "Our ranks are constantly diminishing by battle and disease, and few recruits are received; the consequences are inevitable. . . ."

September 3, Saturday

The shooting had nearly ended for the moment in Georgia, with Sherman centering his army in Atlanta and beginning his personal rule over the Confederate citizenry. Hood's Army of Tennessee licked its wounds at Lovejoy's Station. Sheridan, in the Shenandoah, started his enlarged army toward Berryville and Early's shrinking Confederate force. R. H. Anderson's corps left Winchester for Richmond. As Anderson's men approached Berryville they stumbled upon a corps of Sheridan. After a sharp engagement that was a complete surprise to both sides, it was evident a new crisis had arisen in the Valley. In Charleston Harbor the armies exchanged captive surgeons and chaplains. Skirmishing occurred in Shelby County, Ky.; near Rocheport, Mo.; and near Sycamore Church, Va.

President Lincoln declared Sept. 5 a day of celebration for the victories at Atlanta and Mobile. He also called home from New Hampshire Postmaster General Montgomery Blair. Sen. Chandler of Michigan and others had been advising that Blair be dropped from the Cabinet for his support of the Democrats. President Davis, meanwhile, tried to gather troops in Georgia to aid Hood.

September 4, Sunday

JOHN HUNT MORGAN KILLED.

Famed Confederate raider and cavalry leader John Hunt Morgan was dead. For many months his reputation had been somewhat beclouded but he was in Greeneville, Tenn., preparing an attack on east Tennessee. A Federal raiding party, duplicating Morgan's own methods, slipped into town early in the morning and Morgan was shot trying to join his own men. The legends of Morgan and his "terrible men" would live long in the annals of poem, song, and story as well as in military records of honor.

At Atlanta Sherman was preparing to pull in his armies for a month's regrouping and resting and was arguing with the civilian authorities of the city. Hood was likewise gathering in his tattered ranks near Lovejoy's Station. At Charleston the third great bombardment of Fort Sumter ended after 60 days, with 81 casualties and 14,666 rounds fired. After a skirmish at Berryville, Early pulled his entire army back from the Opequon in the face of Sheridan's advance. Elsewhere, fighting broke out at Brownsville, Ark., and Donaldsonville, La. Confederates attacked the steamers *Celeste* and *Commercial* at Gregory's Landing on the White River, Ark.

In answer to a letter from Eliza P. Gurney of the Society of Friends, President Lincoln wrote, "The purposes of the Almighty are perfect, and must prevail, though we erring mortals may fail to accurately perceive them in advance."

September 5, Monday

Along the Opequon in the Shenandoah, portions of Sheridan's and Early's forces skirmished near Stephenson's Depot, north of Winchester. Both sides continued to probe, to try to catch the other off balance. Elsewhere in Virginia there was a Federal reconnaissance to Sycamore Church. Voters of Louisiana who had taken the oath ratified the new state constitution, which included the abolition of slavery.

September 6, Tuesday

The major battle fronts in Virginia, the Shenandoah, and Georgia were quiet. Maryland's convention adopted a new constitution abolishing slavery. Secondary action took place at Readyville, Tenn.; Eight Mile Post on the Natchez and Liberty Road, Miss.; Richland and Searcy, Ark.; Brunswick, Mo.; and on the Brazos Santiago, Tex. Federals scouted in Arkansas and Missouri, and a Union expedition moved from Morganza to Bayou Sara, La. The eighth minor bombardment began at Charleston and lasted nine days; the Confederates suffered casualties and 573 rounds were thrown against Fort Sumter. Lieut. Gen. Richard Taylor assumed command of the Confederate Department of Alabama, Mississippi, and East Louisiana.

September 7, Wednesday

EVACUATION OF ATLANTA ORDERED.

"I have deemed it to the interest of the United States that the citizens now residing in Atlanta should remove, those who prefer it to go South and the rest North." So wrote Gen. Sherman to Gen. Hood. Between Sept. 11 and 20 they left: some 446 families totaling about 1600 people. Not only forced to abandon their homes, most of them had to leave behind nearly all their possessions. Outrage, indignation, and protests were to no avail. Sherman felt he had trouble enough in feeding his own army, and he had written, "If the people raise a howl against my barbarity and cruelty, I will answer that war is war and not popularity-seeking." Hood was furious and there was a lengthy, heated correspondence with Sherman.

In the Shenandoah small units of Early and Sheridan skirmished again near Brucetown and Winchester. An affair occurred at Centralia, Mo., and an expedition by Federals in Louisiana to Lake Natchez lasted five days.

September 8, Thursday

In Orange, N.J., Maj. Gen. George B. McClellan formally accepted the Democratic nomination for President by a letter to the official notification committee. McClellan disavowed the so-called "peace plank" in the Democratic platform. "The Union is the one condition of peace," he said, and he emphasized that cessation of hostilities should hinge on the re-establishment of the Union. The platform demanded that "immediate efforts be made for a cessation of hostilities," looking toward a convention or other means of restoring the Union.

Only two light skirmishes near Hornersville and Gayoso, Mo., were recorded for the day. A Federal army-navy expedition destroyed fifty-five furnaces at Salt House Point on Mobile Bay.

September 9, Friday

The Federal President and his Cabinet, still concerned over the serious problems connected with cotton trading with the Confederates, leaned increasingly toward open trading. Northern scouting expeditions in the West expanded their efforts to control guerrilla activities. Expeditions operated from Mobile Bay to Bonsecours, Ala.; from Pine Bluff toward Monticello, Ark.; from Fort Pike, La., to the Pearl River; from Lewisburg to Norristown, and from Helena to Alligator Bayou, Ark. Fighting broke out on the Warrensburg Road near Warrensburg, Mo.; Confederates attacked the steamer *J. D. Perry* at Clarendon, Ark.; and a skirmish erupted at Currituck Bridge, Va.

September 10, Saturday

Although the primary fronts were largely quiet, the virtually unknown small wars continued with an affair at Campbellton, Ga.; a skirmish at Woodbury, Tenn.; fighting near Roanoke, Pisgah, and Dover, Mo.; Darkesville, W. Va.; and an assault on Confederate works at the Chimneys, Va. Until early October Federals carried out expeditions in east Tennessee with some skirmishing.

September 11, Sunday

For most of the month there were various operations in the Cherokee Nation, Indian Terr., with some fighting, including affairs between Indian units of both sides. The never ceasing Union scouts continued in Monroe, Ralls, Moniteau, and Morgan counties, Mo. Skirmishes occurred near Hodge's Plantation, La., and Fort Smith, Ark. Sept. 11–30 Federal troops undertook an expedition from Fort Rice, Dak. Terr., to relieve an emigrant train.

September 12, Monday

Both Grant and Lincoln were disturbed over what the President called "a dead lock" in the Shenandoah. Neither Sheridan nor Early seemed to be making any progress around Winchester. To the fighting list were added a skirmish near Memphis, Tenn.; one at Caledonia, Mo.; and a Federal scout from Fayetteville to Huntsville, Ark.

September 13, Tuesday

Skirmishing increased in the Shenandoah with action at Bunker Hill, near Berryville, and at Locke's and Gilberts' fords on Opequon Creek. Skirmishes also broke out near Searcy, Ark. and Longwood, Mo. A five-day Federal expedition moved from Morganza to Fausse River, La. In Washington the President responded at a political serenade, but made no policy statement.

September 14, Wednesday

For the second time R. H. Anderson's corps started from the Shenandoah to join Lee at Petersburg, where the men were badly needed to face Grant's spreading siege lines. The return of Anderson to Lee seriously depleted Early's force opposing Sheridan. Grant had ordered Sheridan's defensive measures but there was great pressure on the Federal Army to break Early's hold on the Shenandoah Valley and threat to the Baltimore & Ohio Railroad and the Chesapeake and Ohio Canal. The day's struggles included skirmishes near Centerville, W. Va.; near Weston, Ky.; at Bullitt's Bayou, La.; and at Thomasville, Mo.

September 15, Thursday

Grant headed north from the fairly quiet Petersburg siege lines to discuss future action in the Shenandoah with Sheridan. A Federal reconnaissance toward Dinwiddie Court House involved a skirmish. In Georgia skirmishes broke out at Snake Creek Gap on Sherman's supply line and in Lumpkin County. For five days Federals operated in Randolph, Howard, and Boone counties, Mo.

September 16, Friday

With about 4500 men, Forrest, so greatly feared at the North, began operating against Sherman's communications in northern Alabama and middle Tennessee. His expedition left from Verona, Miss., and would continue until mid-October.

Grant and Sheridan conferred at Charles Town, W. Va. Sheridan had learned that Kershaw's division and other units of Anderson's corps had been sent to Petersburg, thus weakening Early's force. Grant approved Sheridan's proposal to cut Early's supply and retreat lines south of Winchester. Meanwhile, there was a skirmish at Snicker's Gap, Va., and and about ten days of Union operations near Morganza, La.

South of the James Wade Hampton's Confederate cavalry and Federal soldier-herders skirmished at little-known Coggins' Point, Va., and around Sycamore Church. Hampton (who started his raid Sept. 11) succeeded in bagging some 2400 cattle, plus 300 prisoners, at the cost of 61 casualties to the Confederates. More fighting ensued on the seventeenth, but Hampton and his "cowboys" brought the desperately needed animals back to Petersburg.

September 17, Saturday

FRÉMONT WITHDRAWS FROM ELECTION CONTEST.

John C. Frémont informed a committee of the Radical Republicans of his "intention to stand aside from the Presidential canvass." He pledged support to the "radical Democracy." Frémont said later he withdrew to prevent the election of McClellan, as election of a Democrat would mean either "separation or re-establishment with slavery." He still considered Lincoln a failure, but he urged a united Republican party to save emancipation. Sen. Chandler and other politicians had also urged a bargain with Frémont in order to help the Lincoln cause. Part of the arrangement was reported to be the retirement of Montgomery Blair from the Lincoln Cabinet, possible removal of Stanton, and an active command for Frémont. Frémont apparently refused these inducements.

Instead of placing his numerically weakened army in a better defensive position with adequate lines of retreat against Sheridan, Early began an advance against the Baltimore & Ohio Railroad from Stephenson's Depot north of Winchester toward Martinsburg, some twenty-two miles north of Winchester. At this time Early had about twelve thousand men to Sheridan's total field force of more than forty thousand troops. For the rest of the month, minor operations occurred around Buckhannon, W. Va. An affair took place at Limestone Ridge, Va.

September 18, Sunday

Early moved a portion of his force in the Shenandoah from Bunker Hill north to Martinsburg. He drove away Federal cavalry but by evening had pulled back toward Bunker Hill. Nevertheless, his four small divisions were perilously spread out. Sheridan, learning of this, changed his plans and moved directly upon Winchester, hoping to hit Early's divisions separately. Elsewhere, there was a skirmish near Lexington, Mo. Federals scouted until Oct. 5 on the Cimarron River in northeastern New Mexico Territory, and a Federal expedition operated from Barrancas to Marianna, Fla., until Oct. 4.

President Davis, still somewhat optimistic, at least in writing, told a Confederate congressman that he thought Atlanta could be recovered and that "Sherman's army can be driven out of Georgia, perhaps be utterly destroyed."

September 19, Monday

THIRD BATTLE OF WINCHESTER OR OPEQUON CREEK, VIRGINIA.

North and east of Winchester Sheridan's superior Union army of about forty thousand hit Early's separated force of about twelve thousand. Federal cavalry crossed the Opequon north of the city and headed west toward the Martinsburg Pike and Stephenson's Depot. Meanwhile, the main force of infantry came in along the Berryville Pike and headed west to strike the highway running north out of Winchester. Maj. Gen. S. D. Ramseur's Confederate division was forced to retire along the Berryville Pike and Early called in his three other divisions from the north. The Confederates hit a gap in the Union line. Southern Gen. Robert E. Rodes was mortally wounded. The Federals held and slowly drove the Confederates back. Breckinridge's Southern division withdrew from north of town in face of Northern cavalry and then formed the left of a new Confederate line east and still north of Winchester. Late in the afternoon the Federals advanced again and Early was forced to order a general retreat up the Valley Pike. The losses were heavy: Federal, 697 killed, 2983 wounded, and 338 missing for 4018; Confederate, estimated at 276 killed, 1827 wounded, and 1818 missing or captured for 3921. A mix-up in movement may have cost Sheridan an even more successful battle, but Early was badly beaten.

Far off to the west, a rather desperate column under Sterling Price entered Missouri in the last significant Trans-Mississippi invasion by the Confederates. An affair at Doniphan, Mo., marked the beginning. Brig. Genls. Stand Watie and Richard M. Gano successfully attacked a Union wagon train at Cabin Creek, in northeastern Indian Territory. Federals reported losses of 202 wagons, 5 ambulances, 40 horses, and 1253 mules, valued at $1,500,000. Later in the same day action occurred at Pryor's Creek not far from Cabin Creek.

Off Charleston desultory firing on Fort Sumter by the Federals lasted the rest of the month and totaled 494 rounds. On the Mississippi Union expeditions from Natchez lasted several days. A skirmish is recorded for Culpeper, Va.

In a daring, somewhat farfetched adventure, Confederate agents under John Yates Beall captured the steamer *Philo Parsons* on Lake Erie and then captured and burned *Island Queen*. Beall was to sail near Johnson's Island, where U.S.S. *Michigan* guarded Confederate prisoners. Meanwhile, Capt. Charles H. Cole, C.S.A., was to capture *Michigan*. The two vessels would then release the prisoners and carry out operations on the lake.

However, near Sandusky the commander of *Michigan* had discovered the plot and arrested Cole, a passenger. Beall was forced to burn *Philo Parsons* at Sandwich, Canada.

President Lincoln urged Sherman to allow Indiana soldiers to go home as long as they could not vote in the field. Indiana was a pivotal state to the Republicans and Lincoln in the coming election.

President Davis wrote the governors of South Carolina, North Carolina, Alabama, Georgia, Virginia, and Florida that "harmony of action between the States and Confederate authorities is essential to the public welfare." He was referring to state proclamations requiring aliens to serve in the military or leave the South. He pointed out that such a policy deprived the Confederacy of needed skilled workmen and asked that such aliens be encouraged to serve in non-military capacities.

September 20, Tuesday

Sheridan's men followed rapidly on the heels of Early's retiring Confederates, with fighting at Middletown, Strasburg, and Cedarville in the Shenandoah. By evening the Federals were fortifying on the high land north of Strasburg. The Confederates were south of the town on Fisher's Hill. Early had escaped disaster; he later said that Sheridan should have crushed him at Winchester.

In Georgia Sherman was suffering some at Atlanta from Confederate cavalry in his rear. A skirmish at Cartersville threatened the vital railroad to Chattanooga. In northern Alabama Forrest, at work again, headed north toward Tennessee.

In Missouri Price and twelve thousand (eight thousand armed) men were on the move. There was action at Ponder's Mill on the Little Black River, and Keytesville, Mo., surrendered to Price. Until Oct. 17 Federals raided from Kentucky and east Tennessee into far southwestern Virginia.

President Davis left Richmond for Georgia to see what could be done to retrieve Confederate fortunes.

September 21, Wednesday

Philip H. Sheridan was assigned to permanent command of the Middle Military District, including the Shenandoah Valley. At Strasburg Sheridan positioned his large army preparatory to attack on the Confederates under Early at Fisher's Hill. There was a skirmish in the town, another near Fisher's Hill, and a third at Front Royal, where Confederates tried to prevent Federal cavalry from occupying the Luray Valley.

Forrest was moving in northern Alabama across the Tennessee River and was about to threaten Athens, Tenn. Sept. 21–26 there were Federal expeditions north from Vicksburg to Deer Creek and Rolling Fork.

President Lincoln continued his interest in the political campaign, obtaining information from various sources and using members of the Administration to feel the pulse of the politicos and the people.

September 22, Thursday

BATTLE OF FISHER'S HILL, VIRGINIA.

Skillfully using his large force, Sheridan held the heights at Strasburg and threatened Early's Confederates posted on Fisher's Hill and along Tumbling Run. Meanwhile, George Crook, with one of Sheridan's three corps, moved during the night of Sept. 21–22 and the morning of the twenty-second to the right and beyond the Confederate left. With a wild shout, Crook advanced late in the afternoon and seized the Confederate entrenchments in rear and flank. As Crook advanced, the two other Federal corps attacked in front into the Tumbling Run ravine and up Fisher's Hill. Confederate "Sandie" Pendleton, who had served so nobly under Jackson, was mortally wounded trying to stem the advance. For four miles the pursuit continued before Early could rally. Crook lost only 8 killed, 153 wounded, and 1 missing, while the whole Union army suffered 528 casualties. Early put his losses at 1235, including almost 1000 men missing, plus 12 guns and numerous small arms.

Price's Confederates moved deeper into Missouri with skirmishing at Patterson and Sikeston. Fighting also broke out at Carthage and near Longwood, Mo. A seven-day Yankee scout probed from Helena to Alligator Bayou, Ark.

President Lincoln was still involved in lining up support for reelection. Victories at Atlanta and in the Shenandoah helped his cause.

Quite unexpectedly President Davis arrived in Macon, Ga., by train. To a refugee relief meeting, the President said, "Friends are drawn together in adversity." He added, "Our cause is not lost. Sherman cannot keep up his long line of communication, and retreat, sooner or later, he must." Mr. Davis said he would confer with Gen. Hood about recovering Georgia. He called for army absentees to return, and concluded, "Let no one despond."

September 23, Friday

Early's battered forces were moving back to New Market and beyond in the Shenandoah. Nevertheless, his cavalry fought at Front Royal, Woodstock, near Edenburg, and at Mount Jackson. Sheridan did not push his pursuit. Victories at Winchester and Fisher's Hill seemed enough. Meanwhile, a Federal expedition operated for the rest of the month in the Kanawha Valley of West Virginia.

To the west Forrest's troops in northern Alabama skirmished at Athens, and Price's Confederates fought near Rocheport, Mo. For the Federals, Maj. Gen. S. A. Hurlbut assumed command of the Department of the Gulf.

President Lincoln asked Postmaster General Montgomery Blair to resign and Blair formally tendered his resignation. Blair had offered to step out when Mr. Lincoln thought best and now the President said, "the time has come." Blair had long been unpopular with the Radical Republicans, many of whom had demanded his ouster as the price of supporting Lincoln's reelection.

September 24, Saturday

Two major Confederate raiding expeditions were pressing now. Forrest captured Athens, Ala., after a fight, and in Missouri Price's troops attacked Fayette and skirmished at Jackson and Farmington. Magnolia, Fla., also experienced a skirmish. In the Shenandoah Valley fighting occurred at Mount Jackson, New Market, Luray, Forest Hill or Timberville. Mainly, however, the defeated forces of Early—badly needing reorganization, rest, and, most of all, reinforcements—were retiring further. Sheridan's infantry and cavalry began burning barns, crops, and other property in response to Grant's orders that the Valley cease to be a granary and sanctuary for the enemy. A Union naval force destroyed four small Confederate vessels, captured five others, and leveled a fishery at Milford Haven, Va., in the Rappahannock River area.

President Lincoln named former Ohio governor William Dennison Postmaster General. A leading Republican and businessman, Dennison would, it was hoped, be less controversial than Blair, who had resigned at the President's request. Mr. Lincoln also approved congressional authorization for the Union purchase of products from states "declared in insurrection."

September 25, Sunday

Sheridan's large Federal army moved forward slowly toward Staunton and Waynesborough, Virginia, destroying railroads and other property and eventually forcing Early back to Brown's Pass in the Blue Ridge. In the West Forrest continued raiding railroads, taking Sulphur Branch Trestle in Alabama. Price fought at Farmington and Huntsville in Missouri. Skirmishes erupted near Henderson, Ky.; near Johnsonville, Tenn.; and at Walnut Creek, Kas. Federals operated an expedition from Little Rock to Fort Smith, Ark., until Oct. 13.

President Davis visited Gen. Hood's headquarters at Palmetto, Ga., to confer on the military situation. Hood had been asking the removal of Gen. Hardee from his army.

September 26, Monday

Sheridan's cavalry clashed with Early's horse and infantry around Port Republic, Weyer's Cave, and Brown's Gap, Va., before the Federals pulled out and left Early to restore his chaotic army. Meanwhile, in Richmond and elsewhere, news of Early's defeat gave rise to severe criticism. Minor fighting broke out near Roswell, Ga.; at Vache Grass, Ark.; and Osage Mission,

Kas. Expeditions by Federals moved from Natchez to Waterproof, La., and from Napoleonville to Grand River, La. Forrest skirmished with the Union garrison at Richland Creek near Pulaski, Tenn. Price and his Confederates fought in Arcadia Valley, Shut-in-Gap, and Ironton, Mo., as the Army of Missouri also headed north toward St. Louis.

September 27, Tuesday

While action in Virginia continued against Early at Port Republic and Weyer's Cave, Forrest fought in the Pulaski, Tenn., area. The invasion of Missouri by Sterling Price was developing rapidly with skirmishing at Arcadia, Ironton, and Mineral Point. At Fort Davidson at Pilot Knob some twelve hundred Federals held off a full charge. During the night Brig. Gen. Thomas Ewing, Jr., evacuated the fort secretly. St. Louis was becoming concerned. A thirty-man Confederate guerrilla force of Bloody Bill Anderson, including George Todd and the James boys, looted and burned Centralia, Mo. Twenty-four unarmed soldiers were killed. Federal troops came to the rescue and were ambushed near Centralia, with 116 killed. In addition there were isolated skirmishes at Lobelville and Beardstown, Tenn.

September 28, Wednesday

The lull continued on the principal fronts at Petersburg and Atlanta. A skirmish was fought near Decatur, Ga. Sheridan fell back briefly toward Harrisonburg in the Shenandoah after more secondary action against Early's outposts at Port Republic and Rockfish Gap. Price skirmished in Polk County, Mo., and at Caledonia while continuing his advance into Missouri despite the repulse at Pilot Knob. Fighting also occurred at Brownsville, Miss.; Wells Hill, Tenn.; and near Rheatown, Tenn.

From West Point, Ga., President Davis wired Hood to relieve Lieut. Gen. Hardee from the Army of Tennessee and send him to command the Department of South Carolina, Georgia, and Florida. Hardee and Hood had long had their difficulties and such a move seemed necessary if the President was to support Hood. Writing of their talks, Davis raised the possibility of putting Beauregard in charge of an over-all Western Department. The whole trip was an effort by the President to prop up the dangerously penetrated western portion of the Confederacy.

September 29, Thursday

BATTLE OF PEEBLES' FARM, VIRGINIA, TO OCT. 2.

BATTLE OF FORT HARRISON OR CHAFFIN'S FARM, VIRGINIA.

The Petersburg-Richmond front exploded with a two-pronged Federal drive—one north of the James against the Richmond defenses and one west of Petersburg seeking to extend the lines and penetrate to the South Side Railroad and the Appomattox River.

Worried about possible Confederate reinforcements to Early, Grant dispatched the Tenth and Eighteenth Corps under David Birney and E. O. C. Ord north of the James to attack the outer Richmond defenses. Advancing rapidly, George Stannard's division stormed Fort Harrison, capturing a major Confederate bastion and nearby works. To the north, however, the Tenth Corps' attack against Fort Gilmer on the New Market Road failed. The Federals promptly rebuilt Fort Harrison as a Union bastion. Fort Harrison was considered so important that both Lee and Grant personally directed operations in the battle.

To the west of Petersburg, about sixteen thousand men of the Army of the Potomac under Meade pressed to increase the encirclement of Petersburg west of the Weldon Railroad and take the vital South Side Railroad. Near Peebles' Farm the fighting began and continued for four days. These engagements included combats at Wyatt's, Peebles', and Pegram's farms, the Chappell House, Poplar Spring Church, and Vaughan Road. Fighting was mainly by the vanguard.

This day saw action on all fronts. Men of Early and Sheridan fought at Waynesborough, Va.; Price's raiders clashed with Federals at Leasburg or Harrison, and at Cuba, Mo. Forrest was carrying out his raid, with action near Lynchburg, Tenn. In addition, skirmishes occurred at Centreville and Moore's Bluff, Tenn. An expedition by Federals moved from Vicksburg to beyond Port Gibson, Miss. Operations also took place in northwestern Tennessee around Jonesborough and the Watuga River; at Scuppernong River, N.C.; and Plum Creek, Neb. Terr.

September 30, Friday

BATTLES OF FORT HARRISON AND PEEBLES' FARM, VIRGINIA, CONTINUED.

After losing Fort Harrison north of the James on the previous day, Lee directed vigorous counterattacks. But the Federals, having virtually turned the earthwork around, beat off the Southern assaults. This ended major Federal attempts against Richmond from north of the James. The Confederates constructed new outer works between the Fort Harrison line and Richmond, while the Federals built up and manned siege lines east of the Confederate capital. The North lost 383 killed, 2299 wounded, and 645 missing for 3327 out of about 20,000. Losses for the more than 10,000 Southerners are uncertain.

At Peebles' Farm, southwest of Petersburg, Warren's Fifth Corps moved out toward Poplar Spring Church, followed by John G. Parke's Ninth Corps. Warren was successful at first, but Confederates under A. P. Hill counterattacked strongly and a division of Parke's corps was forced back when the enemy drove in between the two corps. The Federal troops formed a new line and entrenched on Squirrel Level Road and near Peebles' Farm, with the Fifth and Ninth Corps merging, in effect, to extend the siege lines and thus oblige the Confederate defenders to spread out. The two-pronged Federal attack north and south of the James had strained the Confederates to the utmost, and forced rapid shifting of troops from one threatened front to the other.

While most of the fighting was in Virginia, skirmishing did break out at Waynesville, Mo.; Camp Creek, Ga.; and Carter's Station, Tenn.

OCTOBER, 1864

The significance of the capture of Atlanta was obvious to both North and South. To the North it was helpful to Mr. Lincoln's campaign for reelection, offsetting the stalemate at Petersburg and the continual threat of Early in the Shenandoah. To the South it was an intolerable incursion that must be eradicated, if possible. By the end of September Hood, after conferring with Jefferson Davis, moved out to try to sever Sherman's lengthy supply line from Chattanooga to Atlanta. Hood hoped to force Sherman to pull his army back to Tennessee. Meanwhile, Forrest, operating in north Alabama and Tennessee against railroads, also attempted to force the withdrawal of some of Sherman's troops. In Missouri Price began seriously to alarm unionists in and around St. Louis. At Petersburg Grant had extended lines but failed to break through anywhere. Sheridan believed the Valley Campaign over and Early beaten, but the small and gallant Confederate force in the Shenandoah was reorganizing, receiving some reinforcements, and looking for a new advance. In short, the uncertainty on both sides indicated that the fall would see new military moves. In the South new doubts and additional disaffections resulted from the unnerving loss of Confederate territory.

October 1, Saturday

Forrest's Confederates, fully active now, skirmished with Union garrisons at Athens and Huntsville, Ala., and captured blockhouses at Carter's Creek Station, Tenn. In Missouri the other major Southern raiders under Price also skirmished with Union forces at Union, Franklin, and Lake Springs. In southwest Virginia and Tennessee Federal raiders skirmished at Clinch Mountain and Laurel Creek Gap, Tenn. In Georgia, where Hood was moving around south of Atlanta toward Sherman's railroad supply line, a skirmish occurred at Salt Springs. The Shenandoah was quiet as Sheridan prepared to pull back north toward Cedar Creek from Harrisonburg. At Petersburg the siege ground on, punctuated by fighting in the rain around Peebles' Farm. A lengthy expedition by Federals went out from Fort Craig, N. Mex. Terr., to Fort Goodwin, Ariz. Territory.

The British blockade-runner *Condor*, being pursued by U.S.S. *Niphon*, went aground off New Inlet, near Fort Fisher, N.C. Fearing capture because of dispatches and $2000 in gold she was carrying, the famed Confederate spy Mrs. Rose O'Neal Greenhow left *Condor* in a small boat. The surf overturned the boat, the gold weighed her down, and she drowned.

October 2, Sunday

Troops of the Army of Tennessee reached Sherman's supply line. Skirmishing ensued at Big Shanty and Kennesaw Water Tank, Ga., where Hood's men broke the Western & Atlantic Railroad and interrupted the Federal link between Atlanta and Chattanooga. Other action in the area occurred near Fairburn and Sand Mountain, and at the Sweet Water and Noyes' creeks near Powder Springs, Ga.

Four days of action around Peebles' Farm, southwest of Petersburg, ended when advancing Federals encountered only limited opposition. The main Confederate force of infantry and cavalry had withdrawn to their entrenched lines. Meade's men had managed from Sept. 30 through Oct. 2 to advance the left flank of the Union siege lines about three miles west. The cost for Sept. 30 alone was put at 187 killed, 900 wounded, and 1802 missing or captured for 2889. Southern figures are uncertain.

A Federal expedition aimed at the salt-mining operations in southwest Virginia was repulsed at Saltville, Va. In the Shenandoah skirmishing erupted at Mount Crawford and Bridgewater, Va. Farther west, Forrest's raiders fought Federals near Columbia, Tenn. Price's Confederate expedition occupied Washington, Mo., on the Missouri River, some fifty miles west of St. Louis. Other minor actions occurred at Marianna, Fla.; and there were ten days of Federal movements in southwest Mississippi and east Louisiana, along with expeditions to the Amite River, New River, and Bayou Manchac, La.

At Augusta, Ga., President Davis told Beauregard to assume command of the two western departments now under Genls. Hood and Richard Taylor. Beauregard would have the top command, but he was not to interfere with field operations except when personally present. Davis thereby hoped to coordinate the deteriorating defenses of the Confederacy in Georgia, Alabama, and Mississippi, and to resume the offensive.

October 3, Monday

Hood's Army of Tennessee was squarely on the Chattanooga-Atlanta railroad in Sherman's rear and seized Big Shanty, Kennesaw Water Tank, and the nearby area, breaking the track even more. Sherman, forced to take notice of Hood's operations, began sending troops back from Atlanta to cope with what had become far more than nuisance raids. George H. Thomas arrived in Nashville, sent by Sherman to command defensive forces against any possible invasion by Hood.

Confederate troops under Price still operated to the west of St. Louis along the Missouri River at Hermann and Miller's Station, Mo. There was

Union action from Morganza to Bayou Sara, La., and a skirmish near Mount Elba, Ark. In the Shenandoah fighting broke out at Mount Jackson and North River, Va., as Confederates harassed Sheridan's troops in the Harrisonburg area.

En route to Richmond, President Davis arrived at Columbia, capital of South Carolina, to an enthusiastic welcome. He offered encouragement to the people and said of Hood, "His eye is now fixed upon a point far beyond that where he was assailed by the enemy. . . . And if but a half, nay, one-fourth, of the men to whom the service has a right, will give him their strength, I see no chance for Sherman to escape from a defeat or a disgraceful retreat."

October 4, Tuesday

Hood's troops increased their grip on the Chattanooga-Atlanta railroad and engaged in skirmishes at Acworth, Moon's Station, and near Lost Mountain. Sherman, however, leaving one corps in Atlanta, was on the way to rescue his various beleaguered garrisons along the railroad. He set up his headquarters at Kennesaw Mountain.

Out in Missouri a skirmish took place near Richwoods as Price began to shy away from St. Louis, unable actually to threaten the city. Other skirmishes occurred near Memphis, Tenn., and near Bayou Sara, La.

In Washington the newly appointed Postmaster General William Dennison joined the Cabinet.

October 5, Wednesday

ENGAGEMENT OF ALLATOONA, GEORGIA.

From his perch on Kennesaw Mountain, Sherman saw the smoke along the railroad to the north toward Chattanooga, indicating the destruction wreaked by Hood's army during the last few days. About eighteen miles away Sherman could barely espy a combat of major proportions at Allatoona, the site of a railroad pass garrisoned now by Federals under Brig. Gen. John M. Corse. During the night of the fourth, Maj. Gen. S. G. French's Confederate division had got slowly into position. After a cannonade at dawn, French demanded surrender; Corse refused. The Confederates assaulted, gained some ground and positions, but did not take Allatoona. Overlooked in the dramatic heroics of the day were the high figures: the Federals had nearly 2000 men, and lost 142 killed, 352 wounded, and 212 missing for 706; Confederates lost 122 killed, 443 wounded, 234 missing for 799 out of a little over 2000 men. French received reports that Gen. Jacob D. Cox and a huge Federal force was on its way to cut him off. Out pulled French. Cox was not on his way despite Sherman's message sent to Allatoona the day before: "General Sherman says hold fast. We are coming." Corse held brilliantly. From it all an inspired evangelist, P. P. Bliss, wrote the hymn "Hold the Fort, For We Are

Coming," which echoed in camp meetings long after Allatoona was forgotten. Also, in the area, skirmishing flared near New Hope Church.

There was considerable secondary action in Louisiana, with skirmishing
at Thompson's Creek near Jackson, Alexander's Creek near St. Francisville, Atchafalaya, and Saint Charles. In addition Federal expeditions of
several days each operated from Tunica Landing to Fort Adams, and from
Natchez to Homochitto River, Miss.; from Baton Rouge to Clinton and
Camp Moore, La. To the north Price's Confederate Missouri expedition
skirmished with Federals along the Osage River.

President Lincoln conferred with navy officials in regard to naval prisoners. His secretary, John Nicolay, went west to plumb the sympathies of pro-
Union men in Missouri in regard to the election.

Surrounded by Beauregard, Hardee, and other generals, President Davis
told a cheering crowd at Augusta, Ga., "Never before was I so confident
that energy, harmony and determination would rid the country of its enemy
and give to the women of the land that peace their good deeds have so well
deserved." He proclaimed that the Confederacy was a "free and independent people." Georgia had been invaded but "We must beat Sherman,
we must march into Tennessee . . . we must push the enemy back to
the banks of the Ohio."

In Indiana military authorities arrested Copperhead Lambdin P. Milligan for conspiring against the United States, giving aid and comfort to the
rebels, and inciting to insurrection. In December, 1864, he was convicted
by a military commission and, on June 2, 1865, sentenced to be hanged.
President Johnson issued a reprieve and in December, 1866, the Supreme
Court freed Milligan, ruling in the case (ex parte Milligan) that military
authorities had no power to try a civilian on such charges outside the
actual theater of war.

October 6, Thursday

Confederate cavalry under Thomas L. Rosser attacked two regiments
of George A. Custer's cavalry at Brock's Gap, Va., near Fisher's Hill in the
Shenandoah Valley. Custer repulsed the attack but it showed that the
Southerners were still active in the Valley. Federal raiders in the southwest
Virginia area skirmished just over the line at Kingsport, Tenn. Other
action occurred near Florence, Ala., where Federals and Forrest's cavalry
fought; and in Cole County, Mo. The Richmond *Enquirer* printed an
article favoring enlistment of Negro soldiers in the Confederacy, a view
that was receiving increasing support.

October 7, Friday
CAPTURE OF C.S.S. *Florida.*

In an attempt to push Federal troops back from their threatening position
near Richmond north of the James, Confederate troops attacked on the

Darbytown and New Market roads with combats at Johnston's Farm and Four-Mile Creek. After some initial success, the Confederates were repulsed. Elsewhere in Virginia, fighting erupted on Back Road near Strasburg, and near Columbia Furnace.

Price's men in Missouri skirmished near Jefferson City, the state capital, and fighting also took place at Moreau Creek and at Tyler's Mills on Big River. Farther west, Federals and Indians skirmished on Elk Creek in Nebraska Territory.

In Georgia fighting continued at Dallas as Hood's army moved toward Alabama. There also was a skirmish at Kingston, Tenn.

March, 1862, the ship that became C.S.S. *Florida* left Liverpool and began her spasmodic career as a Confederate raider, taking thirty-seven prizes. Oct. 5, 1864, she had arrived at Bahia, Brazil, where she found U.S.S. *Wachusett.* Com. Napoleon Collins of the Federal sloop determined that *Florida* should not leave. *Wachusett* rammed *Florida* but failed to disable her. After a few shots, *Florida* surrendered; her commander and many of her crew were ashore at the time. The Brazilians protested and even fired at *Wachusett,* but to no avail. *Wachusett* steamed out northward with her prize. Although the citizenry approved *Wachusett's* action, Sec. of State Seward condemned it as unauthorized and unlawful. (On Nov. 28 *Florida* sank, following a Nov. 19 collision with an army transport.)

October 8, Saturday

The last major Confederate cruiser, *Sea King* or *Shenandoah,* left London, soon to meet her supply ship near Funchal, Madeira, where she was commissioned as a commerce destroyer by Capt. James I. Waddell Oct. 19.

In the Shenandoah Valley cavalry fought in the Luray Valley and at Tom's Brook. Near Petersburg, Va., a Federal reconnaissance probed on the Vaughan and Squirrel Level roads. In the scattered fighting in the mountains of Tennessee and Virginia there was a skirmish at Rogersville, Tenn. Price's Confederate forces battled Federals again near Jefferson City, Mo., and fighting also broke out in Barry County.

October 9, Sunday

ENGAGEMENT AT TOM'S BROOK, VIRGINIA.

After considerable harassment in the Shenandoah by Confederates, Sheridan had A. T. A. Torbert turn on the enemy. At Tom's Brook or Round Top Mountain near Fisher's Hill the cavalry divisions of George A. Custer and Wesley Merritt hit Confederate cavalry under Thomas L. Rosser and L. L. Lomax. The Confederates were heavily charged and pursued many miles down the Shenandoah. Federals captured over 300 prisoners and lost 9 killed and 48 wounded.

Price's Confederates in Missouri moved past Jefferson City and fought skirmishes at Boonville, Russellville, and California. Other action was recorded near Piedmont, Fauquier County, Va.; Bayou Sara, La.; Van Wert, Ga.; and a Federal scout in St. Francois County, Mo.

October 10, Monday

Federal forces under Sheridan moved north across Cedar Creek in the Shenandoah and took a strong position on both sides of the Valley Pike. The Sixth Corps moved toward Washington via Front Royal. Fighting was limited to skirmishes near Rectortown, Va.; Thorn Hill near Bean's Station, east Tenn.; South Tunnel, near Gallatin, Tenn.; in Colorado Territory near Valley Station; and in Pemiscot County, Mo. Hood's men skirmished with Sherman's supply line guards near Rome, Ga. Federal troops, carried upstream by boats, attempted to attack Forrest at Eastport, Miss., on the Tennessee River. Confederate gunfire damaged the gunboat *Undine* and disabled two transports. The transports pulled away, leaving most of the troops, who later escaped.

President Lincoln wrote Maryland political leader Henry W. Hoffman that he favored the new state constitution which called for an end to slavery: "I wish all men to be free. I wish the material prosperity of the already free which I feel sure the extinction of slavery would bring. I wish to see, in process of disappearing, that only thing which ever could bring this nation to civil war."

October 11, Tuesday

Elections in Pennsylvania, Ohio, and Indiana showed the Republicans and Lincoln supporters stronger than had been supposed. Oliver P. Morton was reelected governor of Indiana and the Republicans made sizable gains in congressional contests. An anxious Lincoln stayed at the War Department telegraph office until after midnight to get the election returns.

Price's Confederate invaders along the Missouri River fought skirmishes near Boonville and at Brunswick. On the White River near Clarendon, Ark., bushwhackers attacked the steamer *Resolute*. In the east action occurred near White Plains and there was a Federal scout around Stony Creek Station, Va., and at Petersburg, W. Va. A three-day Federal scout probed from Camp Palmer to Gum Swamp, N.C. Federal troops moved out for five days from Atlanta to Flat Creek, Ga., fighting several skirmishes. Confederate cavalry attacked a Federal Negro recruiting detachment near Fort Donelson, Tenn., but were driven off. Sherman's forces began to concentrate at Rome, Ga., upon hearing that Hood was just below the city.

October 12, Wednesday

Chief Justice of the United States Roger Brooke Taney died in Washington. Although criticized for many of his decisions, and particularly in the

Dred Scott case, Taney nevertheless remains one of the major figures in American jurisprudence.

Elements of Hood's and Sherman's forces skirmished at Resaca, La Fayette, and on the Coosaville Road near Rome, Ga. Fighting also occurred at Greeneville, Tenn., and a small cavalry action occurred at Strasburg, Va., in the Shenandoah. Rear Admiral David Dixon Porter assumed command of the North Atlantic Blockading Squadron, with the idea of reducing Fort Fisher near Wilmington, N.C. He relieved Acting Rear Admiral S. P. Lee. Farragut was to have had the post but his health did not permit.

October 13, Thursday

Maryland voters adopted a new state constitution which included abolition of slavery. The vote was very close: 30,174 for and 29,799 opposed, a majority of only 375.

Sherman's Federal defenders in north Georgia held Resaca Oct. 12 and this day, but Hood's troops seized the important railroad north to Tunnel Hill, including Dalton and Tilton, Ga. There was considerable isolated skirmishing involved. In Virginia Early's Confederates were back on their old line at Fisher's Hill while Sheridan was at nearby Cedar Creek. A skirmish along Cedar Creek resulted from Confederate probing. In the West action near Mullahla's Station, Neb.; on Elm Creek, Tex.; and a week of scouting in the Sacramento Mountains, N. Mex. Terr., pitted Federals against Indians. Federal troops operated until the eighteenth from Pine Bluff to Arkansas Post, Ark.

Ranger Mosby and his men took up a section of the Baltimore & Ohio tracks near Kearneysville, west of Harper's Ferry. They wrecked a passenger train, seized $173,000, largely from two army paymasters, and then burned the train.

President Lincoln, still worried about the election despite the recent victories, made an estimate of the electoral vote, giving the "Supposed Copperhead Vote" 114 electoral votes, the "Union Vote" 120. He also was trying to see that as many soldiers as possible got home to vote, figuring he had strong support in the Army.

October 14, Friday

Action increased in the Shenandoah, where two armies faced each other a few miles apart. Skirmishing took place at Strasburg near Hupp's Hill, Va., and at Duffield's Station, W. Va. Price continued to move through Missouri with a skirmish near Glasgow. Price made a public plea for the people to join with him to "redeem" Missouri. Confederates attacked Danville, Mo. Other skirmishing was near Fort Smith, Ark.; Boca Chica Pass, Tex.; and Adamstown, Md.

October 15, Saturday

The usual fighting included action at Hernando, Miss.; Snake Creek Gap, Ga.; Mossy Creek, east Tenn.; Bayou Liddell, La.; and a three-day Federal expedition from Bernard's Mills to Murfree's Station, Va. Jo Shelby's men of Price's command attacked Sedalia, Mo., where citizens and home guards stampeded and the Federal troops put up a losing fight before surrendering. There also was action in Missouri at Glasgow, and Confederates occupied Paris.

In Washington funeral services were held for Chief Justice Taney with the President in attendance. Back in Richmond after his long trip south, President Davis detached Gen. Bragg from service at the capital and sent him to take immediate command of Wilmington and its approaches.

October 16, Sunday

Minor fighting in north Georgia between Hood and Sherman continued, this time at Ship's Gap. The secondary war in the mountains saw a skirmish near Bull's Gap, east Tenn. Federal troops from City Point, Va., moved out for a few days' reconnaissance into Surry County. Price's expedition in Missouri seized Ridgely, while Federal troops operated from Devall's Bluff toward Clarendon, Ark. Skirmishing erupted near Morganza, La.

October 17, Monday

The Army of Tennessee under Hood had practically given up harassing Sherman's Chattanooga-Atlanta rail line and moved toward Gadsden, Ala. Gen. P. G. T. Beauregard assumed command of the Confederate Military Division of the West, comprising all the operations east of the Mississippi in the Western region. There was an affair at Cedar Run Church, Va., a skirmish at Eddyville, Ky. In Missouri Price approached Lexington, in the northwestern part of the state. Fighting increased with Federal troops both in front and behind him. Carrollton, Mo., surrendered and Smithville was burned. Confederate Lieut. Gen. James Longstreet received orders to resume command of his corps, having recovered from wounds received at the Wilderness.

October 18, Tuesday

Confederate generals clambered around the edges of Massanutten Mountain in the Shenandoah overlooking Federal positions at Cedar Creek, and plotted a full-scale attack on Sheridan's position by Early's small but willing force. Otherwise, fighting involved a skirmish near Milton, Fla.; Confederate raids on the Nashville and Northwestern Railroad; skirmishes near Summerville, Ga.; Huntsville, Ala.; Clinch Mountain, east Tenn.; and in Barry County, Mo.

Pro-Southern ladies of Britain held a benefit for Confederate soldiers at St. George's Hall in Liverpool.

October 19, Wednesday

BATTLE OF CEDAR CREEK OR BELLE GROVE, VIRGINIA.

CONFEDERATE RAID ON ST. ALBANS, VERMONT.

Working their way carefully around the base of Three-top Mountain by a concealed pathway, and hidden by early morning fog, the three main forces of Gen. Jubal Early struck the Federal encampment at Cedar Creek or Belle Grove. The Northern positions crumpled and some still-sleeping soldiers were rudely awakened. As the sun rose and the fog lifted, the Confederates of Joseph B. Kershaw and John Brown Gordon had full possession of the camps and earthworks of the Eighth and Nineteenth Corps of Sheridan's army and had taken many prisoners, considerable artillery, camp equipment, and trains. Next Early attacked the Federal Sixth Corps, which had just returned to the army. Sixth Corps commander Horatio Wright was in charge of the entire army due to Sheridan's absence. Sheridan had been in Washington part of Oct. 17 and hurried back toward the Valley by special train the same night. On Oct. 18 he went from Martinsburg, W. Va., to Winchester, arriving in midafternoon. Instead of leaving directly for Cedar Creek, Sheridan paused to survey the defenses of the town.

The Sixth Corps did manage to make brief stands against Early's thrusts, withdrawing to a post north and west of Middletown, supported by the other slowly rallying Federals. Some of the Confederates looted the Cedar Creek camps as Early halted the drive. About ten-thirty in the morning Sheridan arrived from Winchester, helped inspire the Federals, strengthened the lines, and about 4 P.M. attacked. He drove Early back to Fisher's Hill with heavy losses in men and matériel. The Confederates were badly beaten but they had made a gallant showing. Sheridan's return became the theme of the famous poem of T. Buchanan Read, "Sheridan's Ride," which perhaps exaggerated the Federal commander's role. Out of more than 30,000 engaged, the North lost 644 killed, 3430 wounded, and 1591 missing for 5665 casualties. Confederate figures are disputed, with estimates of numbers engaged ranging from 8800 infantry to 18,000. Losses were possibly 320 killed, 1540 wounded, and 1050 missing for 2910. Confederate Maj. Gen. Stephen D. Ramseur was mortally wounded. Cedar Creek marked the last major battle of the war in the Shenandoah. Early's remnant continued to be a nuisance, but Federals controlled the Valley until the end.

War came to Vermont. Confederate Lieut. Bennett H. Young and about twenty-five Confederate soldiers descended upon St. Albans, Vt., some fifteen miles from the Canadian border. Young, operating from Canada, planned to burn and loot several towns. The Southerners robbed three banks of over $200,000 at St. Albans. The citizens began to resist; one was mortally wounded and others hurt. In half an hour the Confederates were gone, pursued over the border, where Young and twelve others were arrested. About $75,000 was recovered.

Gen. Forrest led his cavalry force out of Corinth, Miss., toward Jackson, Tenn., on a new raid designed to cooperate with Hood's move toward Alabama and Tennessee. Meanwhile, the skirmishing continued in Georgia at Turner's and Howell's ferries and Ruff's Station. Action in Missouri increased as Price's men pushed James G. Blunt's Federals at Lexington back to the Little Blue River. There also were skirmishes near Montevallo, Mo.; and in Crawford County, Ark.; and a five-day Federal reconnaissance from Little Rock to Princeton, Ark., with skirmishing at Hurricane Creek on Oct. 23. C.S.S. *Shenandoah* was officially received into the Confederate Navy after fitting out in the Madeira Islands.

Marylanders in Washington serenaded the President, who responded, "I am struggling to maintain government, not to overthrow it. I am struggling especially to prevent others from overthrowing it." He was referring to charges and rumors that the Democrats reportedly would seize the government immediately if their nominee were elected.

October 20, Thursday

Although Price was at Lexington, far up in the state of Missouri, his invasion was far from a total success. He had not picked up the expected recruits and skirmishing became heavier and more frequent. In fact, the invader was nearly penned in, with the Missouri River on his right, Alfred Pleasonton's heavy cavalry force behind him, a strong infantry corps under A. J. Smith moving up on the left, and in front of him the Army of the Border under Maj. Gen. Samuel R. Curtis. The expedition had caused disruption of some Federal supply lines, diversion of Smith's force from going to Nashville, and a great deal of local uproar, but it did not seem of any material advantage to the Confederacy.

In Virginia brief fighting broke out near Fisher's Hill as Early's men fell back after their defeat at Cedar Creek. Firing was also heard at Blue Pond and Little River, Ala.; near Memphis, Tenn.; at Waterloo, La.; and Benton County, Ark. Indians attacked settlements in the Platte Valley near Alkali Station, Neb. Terr.

President Lincoln issued a proclamation setting aside the last Thursday in November "as a day of Thanksgiving and Praise to Almighty God the beneficent Creator and Ruler of the Universe."

October 21, Friday

Price's Confederates, moving out from Lexington, Mo., fought a successful action on the Little Blue against the Union defenders as the Federals evacuated Independence. More desperate battling obviously lay ahead as the invasion force faced ever mounting Federal opposition. Fighting elsewhere was limited to skirmishes at Bryant's Plantation, Fla.; Harrodsburg, Ky.; Leesburg, Ala.; Sneedville, east Tenn.; and another fight with Indians at Alkali Station, Neb. Terr. Sherman had halted at Gaylesville, Ala., in his pursuit of Hood's Army of Tennessee and soon would head back for Atlanta. Meanwhile, Thomas at Nashville built up his forces against Hood's expected invasion. In celebration of the victory at Cedar Creek there was a serenade at the White House. Lincoln proposed three cheers for Sheridan, Grant, and "all our noble commanders and the soldiers and sailors. . . ."

October 22, Saturday

As fighting broke out near Independence, at Mockabee Farm, on the Big Blue at Byram's Ford, and at State Line, Confederate Price, now at Westport (today part of Kansas City), prepared to turn on the Federals closing in on him in northwest Missouri. He intended to send his train south and have Jo Shelby and James F. Fagan attack Curtis' Federal Army of the Border under Maj. Gen. James G. Blunt in front. Meanwhile, John S. Marmaduke would protect the rear from Pleasonton. It was a desperate gamble, given his inferior numbers, but Price viewed the plan as his only chance to get out of the developing Federal trap.

To the south Confederate guerrillas attacked a Union transport on the White River near St. Charles, Ark.; Federals carried out a three-day expedition from Brashear City to Belle River, La.; and Indians and Federals skirmished near Midway Station, Neb. Terr.

Confederates of Hood's army marched from Gadsden to Guntersville, Ala., intending to head toward Tennessee. At Guntersville Hood found the Tennessee River high, supplies short, and Forrest at Jackson, Tenn. So the Army of Tennessee continued west across northern Alabama.

Captures of blockade-runners off Charleston and Wilmington were increasing with the Federal Navy becoming more proficient at stopping the illicit trade, while at the same time the trade became ever more lucrative.

October 23, Sunday

BATTLE OF WESTPORT, MISSOURI.

Along Brush Creek at Westport, Mo., just south of Kansas City, the gunfire of the numerically largest battle in Missouri broke out as Jo Shelby's Confederates opened the day. "Pap" Price attacked, intending to defeat Curtis' Federals under Blunt in front of him and then turn on Pleasonton's troops coming up behind. Shelby's men charged effectively at first but then met a counatercharge of the Federals. After two hours of fighting, Confederates pushed the Northern troops back across Brush Creek. Curtis ordered the Federals to cross Brush Creek again. For two hours more the fighting raged on the plateau. The Federals meanwhile found a small ravine and were able to turn the Confederate left. To the east, at Byram's Ford on the Big Blue, Pleasonton launched his attack in mid-morning. Two brigades crossed the ford, charged across an open field, and pushed back Marmaduke's defending rear guard. Spreading out, Pleasonton's men pressed on after Marmaduke's fleeing Confederates. Pleasonton came up to the flank and rear of Shelby's already frantically occupied fighters. By early afternoon Price was obliged to withdraw his entire army southward down the Missouri-Kansas state line. The last Confederate effort in Missouri of any moment was over, as was all major fighting west of the Mississippi. The two Federal commands probably numbered 20,000, to about 8000 Confederates. Killed and wounded are estimated at 1500 for each side.

Westport has sometimes been lost in the light of more spectacular battles farther east, but it was, like all the fighting in Missouri, rugged and desperate. Skirmishes also broke out at King's Hill, Ala., and Dry Run, Va.

October 24, Monday

Federal discussion delayed the pursuit of Price's retreating Confederates in Missouri. Price himself seemed in no great hurry as he moved south along the Kansas state line, protecting his long and valuable wagon train, which included much plunder. However, although slow in starting, Curtis pushed the pursuit under Blunt and Pleasonton. Otherwise, the fall day was marked by a skirmish near Magnolia, Fla., and another near South River, Ga. Federal operations from Pine Bluff toward Mount Elba, Ark., lasted several days; and those in Issaquena and Washington counties, Miss., continued for most of the rest of the month.

President Lincoln told the 189th New York volunteers, "While others differ with the Administration, and, perhaps, honestly, the soldiers generally have sustained it; they have not only fought right, but, so far as could be judged from their actions, they have voted right. . . ."

October 25, Tuesday

Pursuing Federals caught up with Price's retreating Confederates south of Westport, Mo. Pleasonton attacked in a heavy engagement at the Marais des Cygnes and Mine Creek, Kas. Two Confederate divisions broke, and the wagon train was damaged. Shelby's men, some miles away, came up to aid the other Confederates, forming near the Little Osage River. They held for a while before falling back to protect the remaining wagons, with more fighting near the Marmiton River. Price was forced to burn about a third of his train and hurry on south with the remnant of his command.

Meanwhile, in Alabama, fighting erupted near Round Mountain, at Turkeytown, and on the Gadsden Road between outposts of Hood's army and defending Federals. A Union expedition operated for four days up Blackwater Bay, Fla. There was a minor skirmish near Memphis, Tenn.

Skirmishing occurred at Milford, Va., and near Halfway House between Little Rock and Pine Bluff, Ark.

October 26, Wednesday

The Army of Tennessee at Decatur, Ala., demonstrated against the Federals holding the position, and they proceeded westward, giving up any idea of crossing the Tennessee River at Decatur. Skirmishing near Glasgow and Albany, Mo., marked Price's continuing retreat. By now Pleasonton believed the pursuit had gone far enough and took his two brigades to Fort Scott, Kas. A squabble over command seriously hindered the follow-up. But Curtis continued marching against Price. Confederate guerrilla Bloody Bill Anderson was killed in an ambush near Richmond, Mo.

Small affairs took place in Scott County, Va., and at Winfield, W. Va. Federal expeditions operated from Vidalia to the York Plantation, La.; from Little Rock to Irving's Plantation, Ark.; and from Brownsville to Cotton Plant, Ark.

October 27, Thursday

ENGAGEMENT OF BURGESS' MILL OR BOYDTON PLANK ROAD, VIRGINIA.

SINKING OF C.S.S. *Albemarle,* PLYMOUTH, NORTH CAROLINA.

The fighting front at Petersburg had been quiet for several weeks except for sniper fire by both sides. Now the Federals moved once more to the left, toward Boydton Plank Road and Hatcher's Run to near Burgess' Mill, about twelve miles west and south of Petersburg, aiming toward the South Side Railroad. Some seventeen thousand Federal troops were in the advance. At Burgess' Mill (the engagement also known as Boydton Plank Road or Hatcher's Run) the advance was halted by Confederate opposition, including Hampton's cavalry and infantry under Heth and Mahone. Lack of cooperation between the Second and Fifth Union Corps under Hancock and Warren played a role as well. The Federal encircling force retired, and the Boydton Plank Road and the South Side Railroad remained in Confederate hands for the winter. Union losses were 166 killed, 1028 wounded, and 564 missing for 1758. Confederate losses are uncertain.

At the same time, north of the James, the Federal Army of the James carried out a diversion with fighting at Fair Oaks and Darbytown Road. Skirmishing on the Petersburg front occurred at Fort Morton and Fort Sedgwick. Until February of 1865, the sieges of Petersburg and Richmond consisted mainly of building fortifications, occasional sniping, picketing, and patrolling. Some thirty-five miles of Confederate lines extended from the Williamsburg Road east of Richmond to Hatcher's Run, well to the southwest of Petersburg. For most of the time Grant outnumbered Lee nearly two to one.

During the night, a steam launch with a torpedo on the end of a pole moved silently up the Roanoke River to Plymouth, N.C., where lay the Confederate ironclad *Albemarle*. Union Naval Lieutenant William B. Cushing had planned the operation for some time. As the launch headed for the enemy the alarm sounded and firing commenced. The launch struck the log boom protecting *Albemarle*, smashed through, and exploded the torpedo against her hull. The crew of the launch plunged into the water; *Albemarle* sank. The twenty-one-year-old Cushing had pulled off one of the most daring adventures of the entire Civil War. He escaped injury or capture as did one other of the fifteen-man crew.

In other action Confederate guerrillas attacked the steamer *Belle Saint Louis* at Fort Randolph, Tenn.; and skirmishes erupted at Mossy Creek and Panther Springs, east Tenn.

October 28, Friday

Gen. Curtis caught up with the retreating and enfeebled column of Price south of Newtonia, Mo. Blunt, with the two leading brigades, attacked Shelby. The Confederates held the upper hand until Federal reinforcements forced Shelby to withdraw. Curtis now felt he was in a position to decimate Price. However, on the morning of Oct. 29, the troops of Curtis' command belonging to Rosecrans' Department of Missouri were ordered back to their stations. This left Curtis with only three small brigades. He protested to Halleck in Washington and received word that Grant wanted Price to be pursued. Curtis tried to reassemble his depleted troops, but intraservice wrangling caused delay until further effort to follow Price was out of the question.

Action in Alabama increased as Hood moved westward across the state, with skirmishing at Ladiga and Goshen. In East Tennessee there was action at Morristown and skirmishing at Russellville; in Virginia a skirmish at Newtown, and action around Snicker's Gap. Indians engaged in depredations near Midway Station, Neb. Terr. Gen. Forrest moved north from Jackson, Tenn., and set up a trap for Federal shipping on the Tennessee River.

Sherman, at Gaylesville, Ala., learned that Hood had left Gadsden for Decatur, and decided to return to Atlanta where he could march toward the coast. Thomas at Nashville would have to handle Hood. Two major armies were now marching in opposite directions when it seemed that normally their aims should have been to destroy each other.

October 29, Saturday

Hood's Army of Tennessee continued toward Courtland from Decatur, Ala. A skirmish at Upshaw's Farm, Barry County, Mo., brought to an end the pursuit of Price. Other fighting occurred at Johnson's Farm, Va.; Beverly, W. Va.; Warrenton, Mo.; Nonconnah Creek, Tenn.; and Confederates attacked Vanceburg, Ky.

October 30, Sunday

Advance elements of the Army of Tennessee reached Tuscumbia, Ala. Confederates also occupied Florence, north of the Tennessee River. Skirmishing flared at nearby Muscle Shoals or Raccoon Ford. Meanwhile, Federals gathered in Tennessee to oppose Hood; the Fourth Corps headed from Chattanooga toward Pulaski, Tenn., where it was concentrated by Nov. 3.

Hood expected Forrest's command to join him, but that inspiring warrior had moved north from Jackson, Tenn., to the Tennessee River near Fort Heiman and Fort Henry. Arriving on the twenty-eighth, Forrest mounted artillery and on Oct. 29 captured the boat *Mazeppa* with a load which included nine thousand pairs of shoes. On this day they badly damaged the gunboat *Undine* and captured it and two transports.

C.S.S. *Olustee*, formerly the raider *Tallahassee*, ran the Wilmington blockade and took six prizes during the first week of November.

October 31, Monday

Hood personally arrived at Tuscumbia, Ala., and reinforced his troops across the Tennessee at Florence. There was minor skirmishing near Shoal Creek, Ala. Hood now felt he had a base for the invasion of Tennessee and still hoped Sherman would follow him. On the Tennessee River to the north Forrest himself arrived near Fort Heiman, where his men had disrupted Federal river traffic. Forrest decided to organize a makeshift Confederate "navy" on the Tennessee using the vessels he had captured. Union commander William H. Macomb with seven vessels took Plymouth, N.C., on the Roanoke River, after a heavy duel with shore batteries.

Nevada entered the Union as the thirty-sixth state by proclamation of the President.

NOVEMBER, 1864

The election, rather than the war, commanded the most attention in the North. For the first time in history the armies of a major nation would vote during a war. Rampant electioneering involved not only politicians but army officers as well. President Lincoln was still anxious about the outcome, but the October state elections had given him more confidence. Gen. McClellan remained popular among those discontented with the progress of the war, but the victories at Atlanta, in the Shenandoah, on the coast, and in Missouri had undoubtedly quieted some opposition.

Southerners, of course, also followed the election campaign with interest.

Some favored McClellan, as he might bring peace. Others favored Lincoln because at least they knew exactly where he stood. After all, McClellan *might* try to restore the Union. Many Southerners still did not want any part of the old nation.

November 1, Tuesday

Nathan Bedford Forrest headed south up the Tennessee River with his "navy" of two captured vessels. The boats, with the artillery dragging its guns through the mud on the banks alongside, moved toward Johnsonville, Tenn. In Missouri action occurred at Rolla, on the Big Piney near Waynesville, near Lebanon, and at Greenton. Otherwise skirmishes are recorded for Green Spring Run, W. Va., and Union Station, Tenn. A six-day Federal scout moved from Bermuda Hundred into Charles City County, Va. Throughout the month Federals operated against guerrillas in central Arkansas. Meanwhile, two divisions of the Sixteenth Army Corps under A. J. Smith, detained in Missouri to help expel Price, finally headed toward Nashville to join Thomas' command.

November 2, Wednesday

Venus, of Forrest's makeshift naval-cavalry command operating along the Tennessee River, was driven ashore by two Federal gunboats six miles below Johnsonville, Tenn. C.S.S. *Undine* was damaged but escaped. An affair took place at Hazen's Farm near Devall's Bluff, Ark. Sec. of State William H. Seward told the mayor of New York of rumors from Canada that Confederate agents planned to set fire to the city on Election Day.

November 3, Thursday

The Confederate gunboat *Undine,* captured by Forrest's men, challenged three Federal gunboats at Johnsonville, Tenn., on the Tennessee River, but the three would not fight. Otherwise the day was unusually quiet with only a skirmish at Vera Cruz, Mo. The Federal Fourth Corps arrived at Pulaski, Tenn., south of Nashville, to defend against a possible thrust by Hood. Other troops were on the way.

November 4, Friday

ENGAGEMENT AT JOHNSONVILLE, TENNESSEE.

". . . that devil Forrest was down about Johnsonville and was making havoc among the gun-boats and transports," wrote Gen. Sherman when he heard of Forrest on the Tennessee River. Placing batteries on the west bank, Forrest shelled the Federal gunboats, transports, barges, bulging warehouses, open storage, two wagon trains, and the Union soldiers at the supply base of Johnsonville. Confederates estimated the damage at $6,700,-000. The Southerners did have to abandon their captured gunboat *Undine,* but they disrupted Thomas' supply line and diverted forces he needed at

Nashville. Union officers at Johnsonville were censured for negligence. On Nov. 5 Forrest pulled away, unscathed, and headed south toward Hood by way of Corinth, Miss.

Maj. Gen. John C. Breckinridge led a "miscellaneous force" from southwest Virginia into east Tennessee until Nov. 17. He drove the Federals back to Strawberry Plains, Tenn., before he withdrew.

November 5, Saturday

Minor skirmishes broke out in front of Forts Haskell and Morton, Va.; Bloomfield and Big Pigeon River, Ky.; Shoal Creek, Ala.; and Charleston, Mo. A Union expedition from Rolla to Licking in Texas County, Mo., lasted until the ninth; and operations against Indians in Colorada Territory continued until the eleventh. Federals on an expedition from Springfield, Mo., to Fort Smith, Ark., fought several skirmishes before the expedition ended Nov. 16. Nov. 5–23 a Federal expedition moved from Lewisburg to Fort Smith, Ark. A week of Confederate operations in the Kanawha Valley, W. Va., included the capture of two U.S. steamers on the Big Sandy River.

November 6, Sunday

Federals fought Price's men at Cane Hill, Ark. Yankees skirmished with Indians at Sand Hills Stage Station, Neb. Terr. Small affairs broke out at Fort Lyon, Colo. Terr. Other action included a three-day Federal expedition from Vicksburg to Bayou Macon, La.; Union scouting in Callaway County, Mo.; a skirmish on the McDonough Road near Atlanta, Ga.; and a three-day Federal expedition from New Creek to Moorefield, W. Va. In Chicago the Confederate ringleaders of a plot to take over the city and free Camp Douglas prisoners were arrested.

November 7, Monday

The Congress of the Confederate States of America gathered in Richmond for the second session of the Second Congress, a meeting destined to be its last. President Davis sent his message, and it was surprisingly optimistic. He played down the capture of Atlanta: "There are no vital points on the preservation of which the continued existence of the Confederacy depends." Supplies would be found and even the financial outlook was "far from discouraging." The President called for a general militia law and an end to most exemptions from service. Touching on a controversial issue, Mr. Davis recommended that the government purchase slaves for work in the Army, then free them on discharge. Such a plan would replace the impressment system. He did not advocate use of Negroes as soldiers, although he left the door open in case the situation later required such employment. He concluded by saying the Confederacy favored a negotiated peace, but only with independence, not "our unconditional submission and degradation."

By telegram President Davis urged Gen. Hood to attempt to beat Sherman in detail "and subsequently without serious obstruction or danger to the country in your rear advance to the Ohio River." On the fighting fronts there was a skirmish near Edenburg, Va., and a Federal reconnaissance toward Stony Creek, Va. In the United States it was election eve.

November 8, Tuesday

LINCOLN REELECTED.

Abraham Lincoln was reelected President of the United States with Andrew Johnson of Tennessee as Vice-President. Lincoln, the Republican or Union candidate, received 2,330,552 popular votes to Democrat Maj. Gen. George B. McClellan's 1,835,985, giving Lincoln a plurality of 494,567 and over 55 per cent of the total vote. In the electoral vote Lincoln and Johnson received 212, while McClellan and George H. Pendleton of Ohio got 21, carrying only Delaware, Kentucky, and New Jersey. New York had been close. In the military vote Lincoln really triumphed, with 116,887 to 33,748 for McClellan, although these ballots did not change any state result. Gen. McClellan wrote a day or two later that he was resigning from the Army and, as to the election, "For my country's sake I deplore the result. . . ." He disclaimed personal disappointment. Some Confederates said the election simply proved that the Federal policy of subjugation was popular in the North.

McClellan may once have been a popular general, but that and discontent with the war had not been sufficient to overcome the basic strength of the incumbent, nor the disapproval among many Democrats of their own platform. The Republicans and unionists increased their strong majority in the House to over two thirds and retained a heavy plurality in the Senate.

President Lincoln spent the evening at the War Office getting telegraphic election returns. Early in the morning he responded to a serenade and said that the election result "will be to the lasting advantage, if not to the very salvation, of the country."

November 9, Wednesday

The Federal Twenty-third Corps was going through Nashville on its way to reinforce the Fourth Corps at Pulaski, in expectation of a move into Tennessee by Hood. Meanwhile, on the Tennessee River in Alabama, Hood's men skirmished at Shoal Creek and near Florence. Otherwise Federals scouted around Devall's Bluff to Searcy, Ark., and sent an expedition from Memphis to Moscow, Tenn. Forrest continued toward Corinth, Miss.

While election returns were still coming in, assessment of the results began, with the usual afterthoughts and speculations.

Gen. Sherman at Kingston, Ga., issued portentous orders. He organized his army into a right wing consisting of the Fifteenth and Seventeenth Corps under O. O. Howard and a left wing with the Fourteenth and Twentieth Corps under Maj. Gen. H. W. Slocum. There would be no general train and only a bare minimum of wagons. "The army will forage liberally on the country during the march." If they met resistance from inhabitants, army commanders "should order and enforce a devastation more or less relentless. . . ." and, furthermore, horses, mules, wagons might be appropriated freely. Sherman was about to plunge deeper into Georgia, toward the sea. He had long been urging such an expedition with another force to come in from the coast to meet him. Hood was in northern Alabama, and Sherman thought he had provided Thomas with sufficient force to halt Hood's expected invasion of Tennessee.

November 10, Thursday
Jubal Early, still trying to make a show of opposition in the Shenandoah Valley, moved north from New Market toward Sheridan. However, his force was far too small to have any impact. Sherman in Georgia continued preparing to move back toward Atlanta, destroy the railroad and other bases, and set out on his own. Forrest, back at Corinth, Miss., from his successful west Tennessee foray to Johnsonville, was about ready to join Hood. A Federal scout probed near Memphis and a skirmish broke out at Neosho, Mo.

In response to another election victory serenade, Lincoln said, "It has long been a grave question whether any government, not *too* strong for the liberties of its people, can be strong *enough* to maintain its own existence, in great emergencies. . . . We cannot have free government without elections; and if the rebellion could force us to forego, or postpone a national election, it might fairly claim to have already conquered and ruined us." He pointed out that the election in the midst of Civil War showed "how *sound,* and how *strong* we still are." Now he called for unity in "a common effort, to save our common country."

November 11, Friday
Federals at Rome, Ga., destroyed bridges, foundries, mills, shops, warehouses, and other property of use to the enemy, and started off for Kingston and Atlanta. The railroad in and about Atlanta and between the Etowah and the Chattahoochee was ordered destroyed. Garrisons from Kingston were sent to take up the rails from Resaca back toward Chattanooga. Action included skirmishes at Shoal Creek, Ala.; at Russellville, east Tenn.; at Manassas Junction and near Kernstown, Va.; and a two-day Federal scout from Springfield, Mo., to Huntsville and Yellville, Ark.

At a Washington Cabinet meeting the sealed document disclosing Lincoln's doubts about the election and pledging Cabinet members to support the President-elect after the election was opened. This had been signed, unread, by the Secretaries Aug. 23.

November 12, Saturday

Sherman's army now "stood detached and cut off from all communication with the rear." Four corps totaling 60,000 infantry, plus about 5500 artillery, were ready for one of the great military adventures. Sherman sent his last message to Gen. Thomas and began to concentrate his force toward Atlanta. In that city the Federals were at work destroying the city, except for houses and churches. Far to the north, in the Shenandoah Valley, action picked up briefly as Early's and Sheridan's men fought at Newton or Middletown, and at Cedar Creek and Nineveh, Va. Out in Missouri troops skirmished near Centreville.

November 13, Sunday

Confederates in the Shenandoah moved back to New Market and a good portion of Early's force was detached to strengthen the siege lines at Richmond and Petersburg. Since June Early marched some 1670 miles and fought 75 engagements of one kind or another. The 1864 Valley Campaign was to suffer by comparison with Jackson's in 1862, but, considering the condition and size of the Confederate force and the strength of Sheridan's opposition, it had been a memorable attempt to bring the war closer to the North. As happened so often these days, conflict with Indians flared, this time at Ash Creek near Fort Larned, Kas. In Missouri Federals carried out a four-day scout against guerrillas in Pemiscot County.

November 14, Monday

Sherman's sixty thousand men were in and around Atlanta, preparing to depart for the coast. The cavalry of Judson Kilpatrick had already started toward Jonesborough and McDonough. Slocum took the Twentieth Corps out to Decatur and Stone Mountain, burning bridges and tearing up railroads as other units went to work in Atlanta itself. Sherman wanted to make sure that Atlanta's military, manufacturing, and communications facilities could not be immediately reactivated by the Confederates.

Meanwhile, Thomas was getting his troops in Tennessee into position, with John M. Schofield commanding two corps at Pulaski, south of Nashville. Near Florence, Ala., Hood prepared for his northward march and waited for Forrest to come in from Corinth, Miss. A skirmish near Russellville, Tenn., marked John C. Breckinridge's operations in southwest Virginia and east Tennessee. Otherwise there was a minor brush on Cow Creek, Kas.

President Lincoln accepted the resignation of Maj. Gen. George B. McClellan and named Sheridan to the rank of Major General in the Regular Army. Lincoln wrote Maj. Gen. Stephen A. Hurlbut in Louisiana that there appeared to be "bitter military opposition to the new State Government of Louisiana." He called for cooperation by Federal officers with the new civil government. On Nov. 29 Hurlbut replied that Lincoln was misinformed and added that the new government had done nothing "to protect and prepare the emancipated bondsmen for their new status & condition."

November 15, Tuesday

As most of Sherman's men moved out from Atlanta on their March to the Sea, others finished laying waste to the city, creating desolation and a scar that has never been fully erased from the hearts of the people of Georgia. Light skirmishing between militia and cavalry broke out near Atlanta at Jonesborough, East Point, near Rough and Ready, and at Stockbridge. Otherwise the action was near Collierville, Tenn., and at Clinton, La.

November 16, Wednesday

SHERMAN LEAVES ATLANTA ON MARCH TO THE SEA.

Gen. William T. Sherman, riding with the Fourteenth Corps, left Atlanta, signaling the real start of the new campaign in Georgia. Behind him was a smoking city, its economy in ruins, what people remained desolate and bitter. Since Sherman had cut communication with the rear, the North would hear little of him for weeks to come. Sherman's force encountered only light opposition from militia and a few cavalry units. Skirmishing, heavier at first than later in the campaign, occurred at Lovejoy's Station, Bear Creek Station, and Cotton River Bridge. "My first object was, of course, to place my army in the very heart of Georgia," Sherman wrote.

On the Tennessee River front in northern Alabama skirmishes occurred along Shoal Creek. Forrest brought his cavalry in from Corinth, Miss., to join Hood at Tuscumbia and Florence. In east Tennessee Breckinridge's Confederates skirmished at Strawberry Plains before pulling back into southwest Virginia. There was a skirmish near Lee's Mill, Va.; plus several Federal expeditions: Nov. 16–17 from Barrancas to Pine Barren Ridge, Fla.; Nov. 16–23 from Brookfield to Salisbury, Mo.; and Nov. 16–25 from Cape Girardeau to Patterson in Wayne County, Mo. The expeditions were designed to counter guerrilla activities, for Federals could not occupy in force the vast territory they had cleared of major Confederate armies. Nov. 16–18 Federals scouted from Devall's Bluff to West Point, Ark.

November 17, Thursday

Sherman's troops headed east and south toward the Georgia coast, taking four routes to confuse the enemy. However, there was not much in the way of an enemy to confuse. A small affair did occur at Towaliga Bridge, Ga. Meanwhile, skirmishing increased in northern Alabama, with fighting near Maysville and New Market. Breckinridge's Confederates skirmished at Flat Creek, east Tenn. Federal expeditions operated from Brashear City to Bayou Portage, La., and from Little Rock to Fagan's Ford on the Saline, Ark.

President Lincoln told a Maryland committee, according to a Washington paper, that he was gratified at the election results and that it confirmed "the policy he had pursued would be the best and the only one that could save the country."

President Davis wrote to a group of Georgia state senators expressing strong objection to any suggested possibility of separate state action for peace negotiations.

November 18, Friday

Sherman's army marched generally between the Ocmulgee and Oconee rivers in Georgia. Sherman himself was with the left wing. Heavy storms and other still unexplained factors had delayed Hood's advance into Tennessee, but he was now about to begin. Skirmishing flared at Fayette, Mo., and Kabletown, W. Va.

President Davis told Gen. Howell Cobb at Macon to "get out every man who can render any service even for a short period" to oppose Sherman and to employ Negroes in obstructing roads.

November 19, Saturday

Gov. Joe Brown of Georgia called for men between the ages of sixteen and fifty-five to oppose Sherman, but to no significant avail. President Lincoln ordered the blockade lifted at Norfolk, Va., Fernandina and Pensacola, Fla. Federals fought Indians near Plum Creek Station, Neb. Terr., and a skirmish took place at Duckett's Plantation near Paint Rock River, Ala. A Union expedition moved from Terre Bonne to Bayou Grand Caillou, La.

November 20, Sunday

Sherman's advancing army skirmished with cavalry, militia, and "pickup" troops at Clinton, Walnut Creek, East Macon, and Griswoldville, Ga. Federals skirmished with Indians near Fort Zarah, Kas.

November 21, Monday

CONFEDERATES ADVANCE TOWARD TENNESSEE.

John Bell Hood moved his Army of Tennessee out from Florence, Ala., and headed for Tennessee. His object was to get between the Federals at Pulaski and Nashville. Benjamin F. Cheatham's corps led, going to Rawhide, Ala. Stephen D. Lee and A. P. Stewart followed, accompanied by Forrest's cavalry. The Confederates numbered some thirty thousand infantry plus eight thousand cavalry. On the other major front, Sherman's forces defeated Georgia state troops at Griswoldville, and skirmishing broke out near Macon, at Gordon, near Eatonton and Clinton, Ga. None of these actions significantly hampered Sherman's advance.

Abraham Lincoln wrote a letter to be known the world over, although the original manuscript has disappeared.

To Mrs. Lydia Bixby he wrote that he had learned she was the mother "of five sons who have died gloriously on the field of battle.

"I feel how weak and fruitless must be any words of mine which should attempt to beguile you from the grief of a loss so overwhelming. But I cannot refrain from tendering to you the consolation that may be found in the thanks of the Republic they died to save.

"I pray that our Heavenly Father may assuage the anguish of your bereavement, and leave you only the cherished memory of the loved and lost, and the solemn pride that must be yours, to have laid so costly a sacrifice upon the altar of Freedom." The President's eloquence was misplaced, for only two sons had been killed, two were said to have deserted, and the fifth was honorably discharged.

November 22, Tuesday

Gen. Slocum's wing of Sherman's army occupied the Georgia state capital at Milledgeville. Howard and Kilpatrick were in or near Gordon. The Georgia legislature passed a levy en masse for troops and fled. The first stage of Sherman's campaign had been more than successful. Georgia was in ferment, nearly powerless to oppose the Federals. Yankee "bummers" and foragers operated far and wide along the paths of the various corps, taking what they needed and a lot they did not need, occasionally burning and looting, particularly if residents had departed. The unenviable reputation that would endure permanently was being made. Another fight broke out at Griswoldville.

In the Confederate advance toward Nashville there was action at Lawrenceburg, Tenn. Schofield pulled back north from Pulaski toward Columbia since the Confederates at Lawrenceburg were in a position to flank him and get in his rear. Minor action flared at Front Royal and Rude's Hill, Va., and Federals scouted from Devall's Bluff to Augusta, Ark.

President Davis wired officers in Georgia "that every effort will be made by destroying bridges, felling trees, planting sub-terra shells and otherwise, to obstruct the advance of the enemy." Supplies in danger were to be destroyed. Bragg was told to go to Georgia from Wilmington to join Hardee, Beauregard, and others.

November 23, Wednesday

Schofield's Union force in Tennessee moved northward from Pulaski toward Columbia. A few miles to the west, Hood's Confederates advanced toward the same place. There was skirmishing at Henryville, Fouche Springs, and Mount Pleasant, Tenn.

In Georgia much of Sherman's army was grouped in and around Milledgeville, where there was yet another skirmish. Other skirmishes occurred at Ball's Ferry and the Georgia Central Railroad Bridge on the Oconee River. Gen. William J. Hardee took command of troops opposing Sherman, a difficult assignment, since he did not know Sherman's intended route and had too few troops to block even one road.

Elsewhere, the action included skirmishes at Morganza, La.; an expedition by Federals lasting until Dec. 10 from Fort Wingate against Indians in New Mexico Territory; and a Federal expedition from Vicksburg to Yazoo City, Miss., which lasted until Dec. 4. Gen. Grant and other officers conferred with the President, Sec. Stanton, and Gen. Halleck in Washington.

November 24, Thursday

Moving before daylight, Schofield's Union force marched northward on the road from Pulaski, Tenn., toward Columbia. Jacob D. Cox got to Columbia first; he found a skirmish going on between Federals and Forrest's cavalry and drove the Confederates away. Schofield followed with the rest of his force to Columbia, beating Hood's Army of Tennessee to the important river crossing on the main road to Nashville. The Federals took a strong position south of the Duck River. Action at Campbellsville and at Lynnville, Tenn., also marked the campaign.

Skirmishes took place at St. Charles, Ark., and near Prince George Court House, Va. Federal Att. Gen. Edward Bates, who had gradually found himself out of place in the Cabinet, resigned.

In Georgia Sherman continued on from Milledgeville. Referring to Sherman, President Davis told Gen. W. J. Hardee, "When the purpose of the enemy shall be developed, every effort must be made to obstruct the route on which he is moving, and all other available means must be employed to delay his march, as well to enable our forces to be concentrated as to reduce him to want of the necessary supplies."

November 25, Friday

CONFEDERATE ATTEMPT TO BURN NEW YORK FAILS.

The public was not aware just what Sherman was doing in Georgia; at least he had departed Atlanta for the sea. They were uncertain, too, just what was up in Tennessee south of Nashville. But they did learn the details of a flamboyant, somewhat harebrained scheme to set fire to New York City.

Confederate agents, arranged for in Canada, set fires in ten or more New York hotels and in Barnum's Museum. None of the hotel fires was at all successful and the blaze at Barnum's caused little more than excitement. Help from the Copperheads in New York was not forthcoming, and there were even rumors that the chemist who compounded the combustibles purposely made them defective. Southern agent R. C. Kennedy was later captured and hanged for setting the fire at Barnum's.

Sherman's troops moved toward Sandersville, Ga., where Slocum's men skirmished with Wheeler's cavalry before entering the town on Nov. 26. At Columbia, Tenn., Schofield was entrenching both south and north of the Duck River, while Hood was delayed in getting his force to Columbia. Fighting occurred against Indians at Plum Creek Station, Neb. Terr., and Adobe Fort on the Canadian River, N. Mex. Terr. There was also an affair at Raccourci, near Williamsport, La.

November 26, Saturday

Major units of Hood's Army of Tennessee arrived in front of Federal positions south of the Duck River at Columbia, Tenn. Sherman's troops continued skirmishing with Confederate cavalry at Sandersville, Ga. In the West action included an affair near Plum Creek Station and a skirmish at Spring Creek, Neb. Terr.; a skirmish at Osage, Mo.; and a Union expedition until Dec. 2 from Lewisburg to Strahan's Landing, Ark. In northern Virginia troops skirmished at Fairfax Station, Va. President Lincoln offered the post of Attorney General to Joseph Holt but he refused.

November 27, Sunday

By evening the Army of Tennessee ranged in front of Columbia, Tenn., just south of the Duck River. The Federal commander, Schofield, expected Hood to attempt to turn his position, so he moved his entire command north of the river to prepared positions during the night of Nov. 27–28, partly destroying the railroad and pontoon bridges. Schofield was getting erroneous reports from his cavalry commander, James H. Wilson, that Forrest had crossed the Duck to the east above Columbia.

In the Georgia Campaign, Wheeler's Confederate cavalry halted Kilpatrick in two days of action at Waynesborough. Otherwise there was skirmishing at Moorefield, W. Va.; and the usual scouts, one by Federals from Little Rock to Benton, Ark.; and another lasting until Dec. 13, from Baton Rouge, La., against the Mobile and Ohio Railroad. Gen. Butler's headquarters, the steamer *Greyhound,* was destroyed, apparently by saboteurs, on the James River, Va.

November 28, Monday

Cavalry of Gen. Forrest crossed the Duck River above Columbia the evening of Nov. 28 with most of the rest of Hood's army ready to follow. Other troops of the Army of Tennessee occupied Columbia itself. Cavalry units of both armies skirmished at the crossings of the Duck River and at Shelbyville, Tenn. Fighting increased in Georgia, with action at Buckhead Church and Buckhead Creek or Reynolds' Plantation. Cavalry fought again near Davisborough and Waynesborough. Thomas L. Rosser led his Confederate cavalry from the Shenandoah Valley to New Creek west of Cumberland, Md., and the Baltimore & Ohio, capturing prisoners and extensive supplies. After knocking out the railroad bridge they pulled out, but they showed that Confederate raiders were not through in the East. Skirmishes occurred at Goresville, Va.; Cow Creek, Kas.; and several lesser scouts and expeditions operated.

November 29, Tuesday
AFFAIR AT SPRING HILL, TENNESSEE.

SAND CREEK MASSACRE, COLORADO TERRITORY.

Early in the morning two of the three corps of Hood's Army of Tennessee, plus another division, crossed the Duck River above Columbia. They hoped to flank Schofield's Federals north of the Duck and cut him off at Spring Hill from the route to Franklin and Nashville. Forrest's cavalry skirmished at Spring Hill about midday, and in midafternoon Confederate infantry came in under Pat Cleburne. Meanwhile, there was firing along the Duck between the main body of Schofield and Confederates under S. D. Lee. Confederates at Spring Hill were thwarted by darkness and a few defenders. The Federals under David S. Stanley had worked nobly to keep the turnpike to Franklin open. Schofield finally pulled all his troops away from the Duck. Somehow or other he managed to pass his entire army northward up the pike under the nose of Hood's army without suffering attack. Participants and historians were never able to determine what did or did not happen—charges and countercharges were many. At any rate, the entire Federal force, wagon train and all, got away clear to Franklin and took up a new position south of town. Hood had been told the Federals were passing and apparently did order some troops out, but nothing came of it except some ineffectual skirmishing. The "Spring Hill Affair" became one of the most controversial non-fighting events of the entire war.

Sand Creek, Colo. Terr., will remain forever a blot on American history in the opinion of most historians. The citizens of the Denver area felt the need to put down the Indians who had been taking advantage of the lack of Federal troops and had committed numerous depredations. With some nine hundred volunteers, Col. J. M. Chivington moved out to the Indian camp on Sand Creek, some forty miles south of Fort Lyon, where there were over five hundred Arapahoes and Cheyennes. The Indians had insisted they were peaceable and contended they had not taken part in recent raids. Chivington's force attacked the village without warning and massacred warriors, women, and children. Chivington reported, "It may perhaps be unnecessary for me to state that I captured no prisoners." Chivington claimed between five hundred and six hundred killed, although that boast may be high. Among the dead was Black Kettle, a major chief. Some westerners approved, but easterners as a whole were aghast. Eventually the government condemned the massacre and paid indemnity to the survivors.

Sherman's men continued what was becoming their destructive romp through Georgia with a skirmish near Louisville. There was also fighting near Boyd's Landing, S.C.; Charles Town, W. Va.; Doyal's Plantation, La. Confederate guerrillas attacked the steamer *Alamo* on the Arkansas River, near Dardanelle, Ark.

November 30, Wednesday
BATTLE OF FRANKLIN, TENNESSEE.

Leading units of the retreating Federals of Schofield's force under Jacob Cox arrived at Franklin, Tenn., about dawn. They formed a defensive line south of the town and the Harpeth River. Schofield wished to hold Franklin until he could repair the bridges and get his trains across. Stung by the lost opportunity at Spring Hill, Hood moved rapidly toward Franklin on the main pike. A skirmish at Thompson's Station south of the town and other Federal delaying moves slowed the Confederate advance. About 4 P.M. Hood debouched from the Winstead Hills in a massive frontal attack against the well-posted Federals on the southern edge of Franklin. Gallantly the Confederates pressed ahead, carrying forward works of the enemy, though suffering heavily. After a near break, the Federals rallied on the interior lines. Some of the bloodiest and most tragic fighting of the war occurred in front of the Carter House and up and down the lines at Franklin, but to no avail for Hood. The battle lasted well into the night.

For the Confederates the toll included six generals: the famous and capable Pat Cleburne, S. R. Gist, H. B. Granbury, John Adams, O. F. Strahl, all killed outright, and John C. Carter, mortally wounded. The Confederates had between 20,000 and 27,000 men in action, and lost 1750 killed, 3800 wounded, and 702 missing for 6252. Schofield's Federals numbered between 22,000 and 27,000 engaged and they suffered many fewer casualties: 189 killed, 1033 wounded, and 1104 missing for 2326. For Schofield's valiant defenders, Gen. Jacob D. Cox, commanding the Twenty-third Corps and really in command of the field, deserves much credit.

During the night, Schofield pulled his battered units north across the Harpeth and headed toward Nashville. The Confederates had failed to break the Union lines and suffered ghastly casualties they could not afford, but they did proceed on to Nashville.

Sherman marched on, with a skirmish at Louisville, Ga. There was also action near Dalton, Ga.; Kabletown, W. Va.; and Snicker's Gap, Va. At Honey Hill or Grahamville, near the South Carolina coast, Federal troops from Hilton Head moved out to attack. Their purpose was to enlarge Union holdings and outposts in the area and to cut the Charleston and Savannah Railroad. But the Georgia militia threw back the Federals, who then withdrew. There was no real attempt to aid Sherman by marching in from the seacoast, though this had been discussed.

In a message to Beauregard, President Davis said he believed Sherman "may move directly for the Coast." The Confederates must concentrate and his army must be reduced and rendered ineffective. Davis thought Hood would not have an effect on Federal strategy until the Confederates reached Union territory.

DECEMBER, 1864

Winter did not slow down military operations. The public knew Sherman was deep in Georgia, probably headed toward Savannah, but even Washington did not know just where he was or how he was faring. Everyone knew that Hood and the Confederate Army of Tennessee were in front of Nashville, where George H. Thomas had effectively deployed his Federal defenders. The Petersburg-Richmond area looked relatively quiet.

In Washington Congress was about to assemble to face the problems of constitutional abolition of slavery and the even more thorny question of reconstruction. Radical Republicans claimed the seceded states were in fact out of the Union and must be readmitted on the Radicals' own terms. President Lincoln believed the Union could not be severed and favored a more lenient plan which he had tried to put into operation in Louisiana and Arkansas. Calls for negotiations with the Confederate government could still be heard. In Richmond Congress and many others showed discontent, but what was to be done, and how, remained unanswerable.

December 1, Thursday

The Federal troops of John M. Schofield had successfully withdrawn from Franklin, Tenn., and were now taking their places in the Nashville defense lines of Gen. George H. Thomas. The Federals formed a rough semicircle south of the Tennessee capital, with both flanks resting on the Cumberland River. John Bell Hood's weary Army of Tennessee moved upon Nashville with little pause to take care of the casualties or to reorganize after the woeful toll exacted at Franklin on Nov. 30. Already he was too late, for the Union had stanchly entrenched on the hills of the city. Hood faced two alternatives: to lie in front of the city in partial siege and await attack, or to bypass Nashville, which would leave Thomas in his rear. Some minor scraps included one at Owen's Cross Roads.

Sherman's invaders, more than halfway from Atlanta to Savannah, proceeded with little difficulty as they approached Millen, Ga., site of a prison camp for Northern soldiers. Federals were reported heading toward notorious Andersonville, far to the south, to free the prisoners there. There was a skirmish at Shady Grove, of little consequence. Skirmishing also occurred at Stony Creek Station, Va. In the West several Federal expeditions operated against guerrillas. Other action included a fight near Cypress Creek in Perry County, Ark., and operations near Waynesville, Mo.

James Speed of Kentucky was told he was appointed Attorney General by the President, succeeding resigned Edward Bates.

December 2, Friday

Advance units of Hood's Army of Tennessee approached the Federal lines at Nashville, establishing their own positions this day and on Dec. 3. Cavalry carried out operations against blockhouses and outer positions of Thomas' Federal defenders, with some skirmishing. Washington ordered Thomas to attack Hood soon. Maj. Gen. Grenville M. Dodge was named to replace Gen. Rosecrans as commander of the Department of Missouri. Rosecrans long had experienced difficulty with the various divided political forces in Missouri and had proved inept in the administration of his difficult command, one which had defeated several generals.

December 3, Saturday

With both sides dug in at Nashville, that front appeared to be at a standstill for a while, although Federal authorities in Washington and Gen. Grant in Virginia were urging Thomas to attack. Sherman was at Millen, Ga., with the Seventeenth Corps. The other corps in Georgia were the Fifteenth, south of the Ogeechee, the Twentieth, on the Augusta railroad about four miles north of Millen, and the Fourteenth, near Lumpkin's Station on the Augusta railroad. All units began to march toward Savannah, and from now on the opposition was even lighter than it had been. As they neared the coast, the country grew more sandy and then tended to marshes and creeks. The soldiers lived off the country and their reckless destruction of property continued. There was a mild skirmish at Thomas' Station. Elsewhere, skirmishes took place in Perry County, Ark.; and near New Madrid, Mo.; and a Federal naval expedition operated against salt works at Rocky Point, Tampa Bay, Fla. President Lincoln worked on his annual message to Congress and conferred about the possibility of naming Salmon P. Chase Chief Justice.

December 4, Sunday

Late on Dec. 3, Wheeler's Confederate cavalry attacked troops guarding railroad wreckers at Waynesborough, Ga. A heavy engagement, largely involving cavalry, continued throughout the day. Kilpatrick advanced his Federals to charge Wheeler's Confederates, who, in turn, countercharged. Eventually the dismounted Federal troops drove the Confederates from several positions. There also was skirmishing in Georgia near Statesborough,

Station No. 5 on the Georgia Central, at the Little Ogeechee River, and near Lumpkin's Station. In Tennessee Thomas realized he must attack Hood's Confederates. Thomas prepared energetically and awaited further reinforcements. Skirmishing developed at White's Station and Bell's Mills, Tenn. Otherwise, action occurred on the New Texas Road near Morganza, La.; with Indians on Cow Creek near Fort Zarah, Kas.; and near Davenport Church, Va.

December 5, Monday

The Congress of the United States gathered for the second session of the Thirty-eighth Congress.

At Nashville Hood sent Forrest's cavalry and a division of infantry toward Murfreesboro. They carried out three days of demonstrations during which there was some fighting, but the Confederates were unable to take the town and the infantry withdrew. Sherman's men fought a brief skirmish at the Little Ogeechee River in Georgia. There was also a minor skirmish to the north, at Dalton, Ga.

December 6, Tuesday

SALMON P. CHASE NAMED CHIEF JUSTICE OF THE UNITED STATES.
LINCOLN'S MESSAGE TO CONGRESS.

Former Sec. of the Treasury Salmon P. Chase was named Chief Justice, succeeding the deceased Roger B. Taney. Although Lincoln had had difficulties with him during his Cabinet years, the President had considered Chase at the head of the list for the Supreme Court since Taney's death. Perhaps Lincoln thought of eliminating Chase as a perennial presidential candidate, perhaps he recognized that Chase's abilities were well suited to the post.

Following the custom of the day, President Lincoln sent his annual message to Congress, where it was read to the highly interested members, for all were aware of the momentous questions of war and reconstruction facing the Union. Opening the message without emphasis on the war, Mr. Lincoln noted that the state of foreign affairs was reasonably satisfactory. He mentioned some previously closed ports now open and hoped foreign merchants would trade there rather than resort to blockade-running. "I regard our emigrants as one of the principal replenishing streams which are appointed by Providence to repair the ravages of internal war, and its wastes of national strength and health," he wrote. Financial conditions were satisfactory and, despite the war, the Treasury showed a balance for the year ending July 1, 1863. The War and Navy departments had spent $776,525,135.74 out of expenditures of $865,234,087.86. He did call for increased taxation. The public debt was $1,740,690,489.49. Westward expansion was continuing, the new Agricultural Department was developing. Still, "The war continues." However, the armies had steadily advanced. He reported favorably on the reconstruction efforts in Louisiana, Maryland, and elsewhere. The President asked for reconsideration of the Thirteenth Amendment abolishing slavery, which he said the people approved in their election decision. The people are united on "the distinct issue of Union or no Union," for "The public purpose to re-establish and maintain the national authority is unchanged, and, as we believe, unchangeable." As to peace, the insurgents "cannot voluntarily reaccept the Union; we cannot voluntarily yield it." The issue can only be decided by war. But if the insurgent government cannot accept peace and re-union, the people can, and some desire it. The President admitted re-admission of members of Congress was not in presidential hands. "I mean simply to say that the war will cease on the part of the government, whenever it shall have ceased on the part of those who began it."

Gen Grant issued new orders to Gen. Thomas at Nashville: "Attack Hood at once and wait no longer for remount of your cavalry. There is great danger of delay resulting in a campaign back to the Ohio River." Thomas obediently said he would attack at once, although it would be hazardous without cavalry. A Union naval flotilla on the Cumberland engaged Southern batteries near Bell's Mills, Tenn. Federal troops on the south Atlantic coast demonstrated against the Charleston and Savannah Railroad, but did not break it. Other action included a skirmish at Lewisburg, Ark.; Federal expeditions in Arkansas and Virginia; and a Confederate raid from Paris, Tenn., to Hopkinsville, Ky.

December 7, Wednesday

Federal military authorities were in ferment over Thomas' failure to attack Hood at Nashville. Grant told Stanton if Thomas did not attack promptly he should be removed. Fighting was fairly severe at Murfreesboro, where Confederates under Forrest demonstrated against the Union outpost. Sherman's marauding army, getting closer to Savannah daily, skirmished at Jenks' Bridge on the Ogeechee River, at Buck Creek and Cypress Swamp near Sister's Ferry, Ga. At Fort Monroe, Va., ships, men, and supplies were being gathered for the forthcoming expedition to Fort Fisher, N.C., aimed at cutting off the last major Confederate port open to blockade-runners. Fighting broke out at Moselle Bridge near Franklin, Mo., and near Paint Rock Bridge, Ala. Federal expeditions continued around Devall's Bluff and elsewhere in Arkansas and in Virginia.

December 8, Thursday

Sherman's marching army could almost smell the sea; the changing terrain and vegetation indicated that they were fast approaching their goal. Skirmishing flared at Ebenezer Creek and near Bryan Court House, Ga.

Gen. Grant told Halleck in Washington, "If Thomas has not struck yet, he ought to be ordered to hand over his command to Schofield." Grant admitted he feared Hood would get to the Ohio River. Halleck demurred, saying the decision to remove Thomas was up to Grant. Grant again urged Thomas directly to attack, but Thomas wired that his cavalry would not be ready before Dec. 11. There was skirmishing on the Petersburg front at Hatcher's Run. Va. Out in Missouri an affair took place at Tuscumbia.

December 9, Friday

Activity increased at Petersburg; a two-day Federal reconnaissance to Hatcher's Run involved several skirmishes. Down in Georgia Sherman's men moved close to Savannah, particularly to the immediate south of the city. Skirmishing broke out at the Ogeechee Canal between Eden and Pooler stations, at Cuyler's Plantation and Monteith Swamp. Gen. Grant issued an order replacing Thomas at Nashville with Gen. Schofield. He suspended the order when Thomas told him he had planned to attack on the tenth, but a heavy storm of freezing rain had set in, making advance impossible. Thomas blamed his delay on necessary concentration of men, horses, and supplies. U.S.S. *Otsego* and a tug were sunk by torpedoes in the Roanoke River near Jamesville, N.C.

December 10, Saturday

SHERMAN'S ARMY ARRIVES BEFORE SAVANNAH, GEORGIA.

The marching part of Sherman's Georgia Campaign was over. He had arrived in front of Savannah! The Federal army was almost in sight of the ocean, but Hardee's defenders were strongly entrenched and had flooded the rice fields, leaving only five narrow causeways as approaches to the city. Sherman determined not to assault but to invest the city. The Federal army had not made contact with the supply vessels and the Federal navy offshore, although stores were not too short, at least for men. Horses, however, soon began to suffer. Immense amounts of forage were needed daily, and with the army stationary, all nearby feed was soon used up. Cavalry was ordered to investigate Fort McAllister guarding the Ogeechee, obvious path of contact between Sherman and the fleet. In the defense Hardee had something under eighteen thousand men. Richmond had been suggesting withdrawal and concentration of all available Confederate forces in South Carolina, assuming Sherman would turn northward. There was a skirmish at Springfield, Ga.; and a Confederate steamer, *Ida,* was captured and burned on the Savannah River.

Bad weather continued at Nashville, making any movements hazardous. On other fronts there was skirmishing at Petersburg in front of Fort Holly; Federal scouting from Core Creek to Southwest Creek, N.C.; a Union expedition until Dec. 21 against Indians in central Arizona Territory. Federal troops under George Stoneman moved from Knoxville toward east Tennessee and southwestern Virginia, aiming at the Confederate salt works and supply depots. President Lincoln named Maj. Gen. William F. Smith and Henry Stanbery as special commissioners to investigate civil and military affairs on and west of the Mississippi.

December 11, Sunday

Sherman's Federals were busy investing Savannah, although the route north to Charleston was not yet cut off and, in fact, never would be. The lengthy King's Bridge over the Ogeechee, direct route to Fort McAllister, had to be rebuilt. It had been destroyed by Confederates. In Virginia there were minor operations about Broadwater Ferry and the Chowan River. Grant again urged Thomas to attack Hood and Thomas replied that he would as soon as the weather improved at all.

December 12, Monday

The Federal army at Savannah was getting its lines set for enveloping the city and was preparing to attack Fort McAllister, the last barrier to contact with the Northern fleet. The Federals captured another Rebel vessel, C.S.S. *Resolute,* on the Savannah River. A skirmish erupted on the Amite River, La. Stoneman's cavalry plus other troops pushed ahead from Knoxville and east Tennessee toward southwest Virginia, with a skirmish at Big Creek near Rogersville, Tenn. Gen. Thomas at Nashville informed Halleck in Washington that he had his troops ready to attack Hood as soon as the sleet had melted, for it was now almost impossible to move on the ice-covered ground.

President Lincoln explained to Gen. Edward R. S. Canby, in command in the Gulf area, the government policy in Louisiana, such as getting cotton away from the Confederates, and said "it is a worthy object to again get Louisiana into proper practical relations with the nation. . . ." President Davis was still casting about for troops to oppose Sherman, without weakening Lee.

December 13, Tuesday

FALL OF FORT MCALLISTER, GEORGIA.

Gen. Sherman reached the sea. The Federal commander made contact with the Union fleet after the capture of Fort McAllister on the Ogeechee River below Savannah. About 5 P.M. Federal troops of W. B. Hazen's division of the Fifteenth Corps charged the earth fort from the land side, despite mines and other obstructions. Sherman watched the courageous assault from a rice mill across the Ogeechee. The Confederate garrison under Maj. G. W. Anderson numbered 230 men and suffered 35 casualties, while Hazen had 24 killed and 110 wounded. The fall of the fort opened river communication with the Union fleet. Savannah was doomed. Signals flew between Sherman and the vessels coming up the Ogeechee; soon the general personally visited his naval compatriots and on Dec. 14 he conferred on the river with Gen. John G. Foster and later with Adm. Dahlgren. Supplies could reach Sherman's army now, and contact with the North, although still slow, was reestablished.

Stoneman's Union raiders in east Tennessee reached Kingsport, pushed across the Holston, and defeated remnants of John Hunt Morgan's old command. Federal expeditions were active from Barrancas, Fla., to Pollard, Ala.; from Morganza to Morgan's Ferry, La.; and up the White River from Devall's Bluff, Ark. Confederates attacked a railroad train near Murfreesboro. On the Nashville front both Hood and Thomas waited out the sleet storm. Thomas still promised to move when the weather abated, but Grant now ordered Maj. Gen. John A. Logan to proceed to Nashville to supersede Thomas. Logan was not to take over if Thomas had moved. Grant then headed for Washington, intending to go on to Nashville himself.

December 14, Wednesday

Gen. Thomas told Washington that the ice had melted and he would attack Hood south of Nashville the next day. Field orders for the advance were issued. In Georgia Federal naval units for a week bombarded Forts Rosedew and Beaulieu on the Vernon River. In the Stoneman expedition toward southwest Virginia there was an affair at Bristol, Tenn. Skirmishes occurred on the Germantown Road near Memphis, Tenn., and in the Cypress Swamp near Cape Girardeau, Mo. Until Jan. 5 Federals operated in the vicinity of Hermitage Plantation near Morganza, La. President Davis deferred to Lee's judgment as to whether troops could be spared from Petersburg to operate against Sherman.

December 15, Thursday

BATTLE OF NASHVILLE.

Somewhat ponderous, but massively effective, George H. Thomas' Army of the Cumberland came out from the works of Nashville in the heavy fog and struck John Bell Hood's Army of Tennessee a devastating blow. A holding demonstration was made by Thomas' left against the Confederate right while the main Federal force, totaling 35,000, attacked the thin Confederate left. They carried redoubts and then successfully assaulted Montgomery Hill and drove the enemy from the main defensive line to a position about a mile to the rear along the Brentwood Hills. Hood had been beaten back but still held the main road to Franklin and remained an effective force. He claimed his lines had been overextended and that the new positions were taken to shorten the line. Both sides made troop readjustments during the night. There was some thought among Federals that Hood would withdraw, but it was soon clear that the new Southern line was solidly posted. Thomas had skillfully handled his troops and had moved surely. When the message of the day's outcome reached Washington before midnight, Grant canceled his plans to go farther than Washington. Logan, who had been sent to supersede Thomas, had not yet arrived in Nashville. On the morning of the sixteenth the President wired his congratulations and urged Thomas to continue. On the Confederate right flank another train was captured near Murfreesboro.

In the east Tennessee-southwestern Virginia Federal expedition skirmishes broke out near Abingdon and Glade Springs, Va. Federals carried out an expedition from Fort Monroe to Pagan Creek, Va.

December 16, Friday
BATTLE OF NASHVILLE CONTINUES.

At 6 A.M. in rain and snow, Union troops on the left pressed back the Confederate right on the Franklin Pike to the main entrenchments, but S. D. Lee's corps held. Federals completed aligning for battle south of Nashville and the movement against the enemy's left continued along the Granny White Pike. On Hood's left the Union cavalry had gained his rear and the whole flank was threatened and encircled. Then, late in the afternoon, came the main assault, after a punishing artillery bombardment. Up the hills they went in the face of rigorous fire. The Federals were successful everywhere, capturing many prisoners and much artillery. The Southern left at Shy's Hill gave way and then the center fell back, leaving the right to cover the withdrawal. The Confederates were, as Thomas said, "Hopelessly broken," and they "fled in confusion." Federals pursued for several miles until after dark, but Hood's rear guard fended them off. Hood said his Army of Tennessee resisted all assaults until midafternoon, when part of the line to the left of center gave way and "In a few moments our entire line was broken. . . ."

Thomas had some 50,000 to 55,000 Federals on the field and suffered 387 killed, 2562 wounded, and 112 missing for 3061. Confederate figures are far less certain; Hood probably had well under 30,000 men, of which about 4500 were captured. Killed and wounded were possibly 1500. For a two-day battle of such magnitude, the casualties were remarkably low. The Army of Tennessee was decimated, its effectiveness ended; yet, despite some accounts, it was not "destroyed." A hard core remained capable of defensive fight, but there was not to be the material to build the army up again after Nashville. The fighting around the Tennessee capital was the last major battle in the West. Washington and Grant appear to have been overanxious in ordering Thomas' replacement. The Army of the Cumberland under Thomas had won an impressive victory in eliminating the major western Confederate army as an aggressive force, and halting forever the dream of a Southern advance into the North.

Sherman's army was at work getting resupplied from sea, completing its lines and occupation of the area near Savannah. There was a skirmish at Hinesville, Ga. In the Southwest Virginia Campaign, Stoneman's Federal cavalry saw action at Marion, and the Union forces captured Wytheville. In Louisiana there was an expedition from Morganza to the Atchafalaya River. In Arkansas a skirmish took place near Dudley Lake.

December 17, Saturday

The cavalry of James H. Wilson and some infantry led the Federal pursuit of Hood from Nashville. Hood managed to concentrate toward Columbia, encamping at Spring Hill. Skirmishing broke out between the Federals and Hood's rear guard at Hollow Tree Gap, West Harpeth River, and Franklin. The firm Confederate stand enabled the rest of the army to withdraw through Franklin. Federal troops in southwest Virginia captured and destroyed several lead mines and fought skirmishes near Mount Airy and Marion. President Davis told Hardee at Savannah, Ga., that Lee was unable to detach troops from Virginia and that Hardee should make dispositions "needful for the preservation of your Army." However, Gen. Sherman now demanded surrender from Hardee.

December 18, Sunday

Union cavalry in Tennessee pursued Hood as far as Rutherford Creek, north of Columbia, which was found impassable. There was skirmishing at Spring Hill, Tenn. The only other recorded fight was on Little River in New Madrid County, Mo. Both North and South, hearing the news of Nashville, realized that it was a serious blow to Confederate hopes. At Savannah Gen. Hardee refused Sherman's surrender demand of Dec. 17, but it was clear that the city must be evacuated before the escape route to the north was closed. Beauregard was with Hardee at the moment and urged evacuation at once, but Hardee seemed reluctant to leave. To the north, an immense Federal fleet sailed from Fort Monroe for Wilmington and Fort Fisher.

The Congress of the United States and the President engaged in continuing discussions concerning reconstruction of the seceded states. The schism between the Radicals and Mr. Lincoln seemed to be increasing. President Davis wrote Sec. of War Seddon that he opposed the plan to abolish conscription and substitute a rigid military organization. The Confederacy, he said, did not have time to experiment.

December 19, Monday

More skirmishing broke out at Rutherford and Curtis' creeks, Tenn. Federals tried unsuccessfully to cross the flooded Rutherford Creek north of Columbia. Hood hoped to be able to halt his retreat at Columbia, on the line of the Duck River. In the Shenandoah Valley both Early and Sheridan had sent troops to the Richmond-Petersburg front. Following Grant's wishes, Sheridan now detached A. T. A. Torbert with eight thousand cavalry toward the Virginia Central Railroad and Gordonsville, an expedition which lasted until Dec. 23 with several skirmishes: at Madison Court House, Liberty Mills, and Gordonsville. Confederate defenders managed to hold off the Federals, who withdrew on the twenty-third. In the other direction in Virginia an expedition moved from Kernstown to Lacey's Springs until Dec. 22. In Arkansas there was a skirmish at Rector's Farm.

At Washington the President issued a call for 300,000 more volunteers to replace casualties.

December 20, Tuesday
CONFEDERATES EVACUATE SAVANNAH.

The Federal left at Savannah, Ga., moved slowly to cut off Hardee's escape route across the Savannah River into South Carolina, but they did not succeed. Hardee, urged by Beauregard and others to pull out, finally did. Without opposition, he headed northward toward concentration with other Confederate units. Hardee left behind some 250 heavy guns and large amounts of cotton, but, with an ingenious pontoon bridge of 30 rice flats, he managed to evacuate all his 10,000 troops. Nevertheless, the loss of the important port city was a severe blow to the Confederates psychologically. The only fighting was a skirmish near Pocotaligo Road, S.C.

Thomas' troops, following up Hood's retreat in Tennessee, constructed a floating bridge over Rutherford Creek and pushed on for Columbia. There they found the bridges destroyed and the enemy across the Duck River. Some skirmishing occurred near Columbia. Federals of Stoneman's command captured and destroyed salt works in and around Saltville, Va. In addition, there was an engagement at Poplar Point, N.C. A Federal expedition from Cape Girardeau and Dallas, Mo., to Cherokee Bay, Ark., and the St. Francis River lasted until Jan. 4. Small boats from the Union Navy tried to clear out torpedoes or mines at Rainbow Bluff, N.C., and often engaged in skirmishing.

President Davis expressed considerable concern to Beauregard, noting that the enemy was concentrating against Wilmington. He had left the decisions to evacuate Savannah and Charleston to Beauregard.

December 21, Wednesday
Federal troops, finding no opposition, occupied Savannah, Ga., with John W. Geary's division of the Twentieth Corps leading the march. Hardee's escape was a great disappointment to Sherman but he covered it

up well in his writings. Historians later criticized Sherman for leaving an escape route open, but, on the other hand, Hardee had been watching carefully and would have evacuated whenever the safety valve was in danger of being closed. Hood's suffering Army of Tennessee continued its march southward from Columbia toward Pulaski, Tenn., leaving a rear guard behind. Thomas' following force was plagued by weariness and swollen streams. The Union forces under Stoneman at Saltville, Va., began to retire after their successful raid. A Federal expedition moved out from Memphis to attack the Mobile and Ohio Railroad; there also was a skirmish at Franklin Creek, Miss. The Congress of the United States set up the new grade of Vice-Admiral with Rear Admiral Farragut in mind for the promotion.

December 22, Thursday

At Savannah Gen. Sherman sent his famous message to President Lincoln: "I beg to present you, as a Christmas gift, the city of Savannah, with 150 heavy guns and plenty of ammunition, and also about 25,000 bales of cotton." Sherman himself had just arrived at Savannah. He had been at Port Royal, S.C., on military business when Savannah was evacuated. The Federal troops went to work on the defenses, replenishing their supplies and reorganizing their army. Meanwhile, Hardee's retreating Confederates headed northward in South Carolina. Hood's rear guard and Thomas' pursuing force skirmished on the Duck River near Columbia, Tenn. Another skirmish erupted on Franklin Creek, Miss.

December 23, Friday

The Federal fleet from Fort Monroe, intending to attack Fort Fisher near Wilmington, N.C., had encountered very heavy seas and storms off Cape Hatteras and had been badly scattered. By now the battered vessels had arrived at the Beaufort rendezvous. Gen. Benjamin F. Butler was in personal command of the two army divisions, numbering some 6500 men. David D. Porter commanded the fleet. Butler had planned to explode an old hulk loaded with 215 tons of powder near the fort, predicting that it would destroy it and the garrison. The powder boat was set off right enough, but it caused no damage to friend or foe. This was the first fiasco of an expedition which had been plagued by mistakes, storms, dissensions, and Gen. Butler from the start. Elsewhere, a skirmish at Warfield's near Columbia, Tenn., marked the continuing operations of Hood's rear guard and Thomas' pursuing forces. A two-day Federal expedition operated from Baton Rouge to Clinton, La.

December 24, Saturday

BOMBARDMENT OF FORT FISHER BEGINS.

The formidable Federal naval fleet under David D. Porter opened fire upon Fort Fisher, N.C., after the failure of the powder ship the night before. With *New Ironsides* leading, the fleet fired a tremendous bombardment at the earth and sand fort, defended by about five hundred men under Col. William Lamb. Fort Fisher had long been effective in helping vessels run the blockade off Wilmington, the last major port even partially open. The fort itself did not respond significantly to the Federal fire and several explosions inside set buildings on fire. There were modest casualties on both sides, but, despite the navy's expectations, very little damage was done to either fort or garrison. The transports were now ready to attempt a landing above the fort.

On the Tennessee front skirmishing occurred at Lynnville and Richland Creek, but the primary operations following the Battle of Nashville were over. In Arkansas Federals scouted from Pine Bluff to Richland and a skirmish broke out near Fort Smith. President Davis wrote Gen. E. Kirby Smith, commanding the Trans-Mississippi Department, that he greatly regretted troops had not been sent east to aid in Tennessee and he again asked for such men.

December 25, Sunday

FEDERAL LANDINGS AT FORT FISHER FAIL.

Nearly sixty warships continued the Federal bombardment of Fort Fisher, easily hitting the parapets and traverses of the sand-built fort. Meanwhile, the Federal troops landed two miles north, captured a battery, and pushed close to the fort itself. However, as darkness came on, Confederate troops closed in from the north. Furthermore, assault was deemed too expensive in lives, so the troops were taken off (the last on Dec. 27) and the whole fleet returned to Hampton Roads, devoid of success but with light casualties. Fort Fisher still stood active at the entrance to the Cape Fear River. The Confederates realized this would not be the last attempt, but at the moment they had been victorious. For the Federals it was an ignominious failure, resulting in violent charges and counter-charges between Butler and Porter, Butler and army officers, Butler and nearly everyone else.

Hood's Army of Tennessee reached Bainbridge on the Tennessee River. There were skirmishes at Richland Creek, and King's or Anthony's Hill or Devil's Gap, and White's Station, Tenn. Other action included an engagement at Verona, Miss., and a skirmish at Rocky Creek Church, Ga. Price's Confederate command, still retreating from Missouri, reached Laynesport, Ark.

December 26, Monday

Hood and the Army of Tennessee began crossing the Tennessee River at Bainbridge, Tenn. This virtually ended the campaign, although there was a skirmish at Sugar Creek, Tenn. Otherwise activity was confined to scouting by Federals in northern Virginia, and an expedition until Jan. 1 against Indians in central Arizona Territory. President Lincoln told Sherman at Savannah that he had been *"anxious, if not fearful"* when Sherman left Atlanta. He went on to congratulate Sherman for his victorious campaigns, including the vanquishing of Hood by Thomas at Nashville.

December 27, Tuesday

The Army of Tennessee completed crossing the Tennessee River at Bainbridge, Tenn., and headed toward Tupelo, Miss. Skirmishes broke out at Decatur, Ala.; and Okolona, Miss.; while scouting continued around Pine Bluff, Ark.

December 28, Wednesday

Skirmishing near Decatur, Ala., and a fight at Egypt, Miss., marked the winter day. In Washington President Lincoln asked Grant "what you now understand of the Wilmington expedition, present & prospective." Grant replied that "The Wilmington expedition has proven a gross and culpable failure. . . . Who is to blame I hope will be known."

December 29, Thursday

In the fading Franklin-Nashville Campaign light skirmishing occurred at Hillsborough and Pond Springs, Ala.

December 30, Friday

The Wilmington fiasco was causing repercussions in Washington; at the Cabinet meeting Mr. Lincoln indicated Butler would be removed from command of the Army of the James. Francis Preston Blair, Sr., powerful Maryland political figure, wrote President Davis that he wished to visit Richmond "to explain the views I entertain in reference to the state of the affairs of our Country." Although his visit would be unofficial he indicated that he wanted to explore the possibilities of peace. There was skirmishing near Caruthersville, Mo., and Leighton, Ala.

December 31, Saturday

The year came uneventfully to an end with skirmishing at Sharpsburg, Ky., and affairs at Paint Rock Bridge and Russellville, Ala. However, as usual, people everywhere were wondering about the future.

1865

Peace was in the air. Reality could not be escaped, though wishful thinking remained. Whispers of negotiations were commonplace, but no one knew quite how, when, where, or by whom they would be carried out. Militarily things were quiet, with Sherman at Savannah, Grant at Petersburg, Thomas in Tennessee, all with massive armies. It was clear that Sherman would turn north into the Carolinas, where there was little Confederate armed might to face him. Perhaps he would try to join Grant and together they would crush Lee. To the west, the Confederate Army of Tennessee existed, but was only capable of small operations and some defense. The Shenandoah Valley was firmly in Union hands, and, along the Gulf Coast, Mobile undoubtedly would soon be attacked. Attempts certainly would again be made to take Fort Fisher and Wilmington.

The Lincoln administration had received its mandate. The leading question as the North now looked ahead was how the states would rejoin the United States. Were they "erring sisters" to be welcomed back on equal footing, or vanquished lands begging admittance to a nation they had deserted? The Thirteenth Amendment which would constitutionally abolish slavery was to come up again after earlier defeat. And in the South—was there really any chance of an honorable settlement? Dreams and talk of victory remained, but reality was something else.

JANUARY, 1865

The attention and thoughts of both nations for the moment were more on civil than military affairs, except, of course, on the now somewhat stationary fronts. Both Congresses were in session. In Richmond Congress expressed increasing dissatisfaction with the Davis administration and talked of restoring Joseph E. Johnston to command, of making Lee General-in-Chief, rehashing whether to use slaves as soldiers, and discussing the possibility of peace overtures. In the North constitutional abolition of slavery and reconstruction were paramount subjects. Political victors in the election again bombarded Washington for the spoils. Gen. Butler's failure at Fort Fisher was a subject of controversy. The more willing peace factions were taking negotiations, and several parties were endeavoring unofficially to get something started with Richmond. Generally the Northern economy was in good shape and thoughts turned to post-war Western expansion and business opportunities.

January 1, Sunday
The year opened quietly, with only a skirmish at Bentonville, Ark. Throughout most of the month Federals operated against guerrillas in Arkansas. On the James River Gen. Butler had ordered a canal cut to bypass a large bend in the river at Dutch Gap, Va. On the first day of the year the project was to culminate with a powder blast for the final excavation. The explosion came; the dirt and gravel fell back into the ditch. The project was dropped. In the cold trenches of Petersburg, on the streets of Savannah, in central Tennessee, the Union troops remained largely inactive. Confederates attempted to consolidate, to somehow put together a major fighting force. Their only remaining sizable fighting army was that of Northern Virginia, pinned down at Petersburg and Richmond.

January 2, Monday
Union troops operating against the Mobile and Ohio Railroad fought Confederates at Franklin and Lexington, Miss. There was scouting for bushwhackers by Federals in Shannon County, Mo., as well as a Federal scout from Benvard's Mills to South Quay, Va.
A group of Kentuckians applied to have Butler assigned to their state and the President said, "You howled when Butler went to New-

Orleans. Others howled when he was removed from that command. Somebody has been howling ever since at his assignment to military command. How long will it be before you, who are howling for his assignment to rule Kentucky, will be howling to me to remove him?" The regular New Year's reception was held at the Washington White House for the diplomatic corps, Cabinet officers, judges, and military officers attending. There were complaints that congressmen were not invited. President Davis told Beauregard that if it became necessary he should remove Hood as commander of the Army of Tennessee and name Richard Taylor to command.

January 3, Tuesday

A Federal expedition was readying for another attempt on Fort Fisher and Wilmington. Preparations were under way at Bermuda Hundred and at Fort Monroe for the combined army-navy operations. In Georgia Sherman, planning for the move northward into South Carolina, began transferring part of Howard's Army of the Tennessee from Savannah to Beaufort, S.C. A skirmish broke out near Hardeeville, S.C. To the west, Federals operating along the Mobile and Ohio Railroad fought a skirmish near Mechanicsburg, Miss.

January 4, Wednesday

Federal troops embarked at Bermuda Hundred for the new expedition against Fort Fisher, N.C. This time they were under command of Maj. Gen. Alfred H. Terry, a sound soldier. Most of the men had taken part in the abortive Butler expedition of December. The huge fleet was again under Adm. Porter. At Thorn Hill, Ala., there was a brief skirmish, part of the aftermath of the December Franklin-Nashville Campaign. On the Mobile and Ohio a skirmish flared at The Ponds, Miss. A Union expedition from Bloomfield to Poplar Bluff, Mo., lasted until Jan. 16. Until Jan. 27 Federals operated from Brownsville to Augusta, Ark.

January 5, Thursday

President Davis continued to be concerned and frustrated by the increasing dissension, controversy over the draft, manpower problems, and the war itself. In Washington Lincoln, bothered by job seekers after election rewards, tried to concentrate on trade in recovered areas and domestic affairs. The President issued a pass to go through the lines to James W. Singleton, one of the several unofficial and self-named envoys seeking a possible settlement of the war. Sec. of War Stanton headed for Savannah to consult with Sherman; Lincoln wrote Stanton that *"time,* now that the enemy is wavering, is more important than ever before. Being on the down-hill, & some what confused, keeping [keep] him going. . . ."

January 6, Friday

In the United States House of Representatives, Republican J. M. Ashley of Ohio again brought up the proposed Thirteenth Amendment to abolish slavery. The amendment had passed the Senate, where Republicans and unionists had the requisite two thirds, but had failed in the House. Mr. Lincoln, the Administration, and of course the Radicals, as well as some non-Radical Republicans, were putting pressure on certain Democrats to change their votes. Republicans undoubtedly would be able to pass the measure in the Thirty-ninth Congress, but that did not meet until December, and many, including the President, were anxious to see the amendment in effect as soon as possible. For the rest of the month the debate took up much of the time of the House. Ashley said, "Mr. Speaker, if slavery is wrong and criminal, as the great body of enlightened Christian men admit, it is certainly our duty to abolish it, if we have the power." James Brooks of New York replied, "Is the abolition of slavery the only object for which this war is hereafter to be prosecuted, or is now prosecuted? I do not believe it."

Gen. Grant at Petersburg wired President Lincoln asking that Gen. Butler be removed from command of the Army of the James. Grant felt there was a lack of confidence in his military ability, "making him an unsafe commander for a large army." By rank Butler would have commanded in Grant's absence. There was probably no more controversial figure in the North than Butler and since the Fort Fisher fiasco agitation for his removal had increased.

Military action was confined to a skirmish at Huntsville, Ark. President Davis wrote a lengthy and contentious letter to Vice-President Alexander H. Stephens, who had long been extremely critical of Davis. He objected mainly to Stephens' alleging that Davis had preferred Lincoln over McClellan in the Union election: "I am aware that I was unfortunate enough to incur your disapproval of my policy. . . . I assure you that it would be to me a source of the sincerest pleasure to see you devoting your great and admitted ability *exclusively* to upholding the confidence and animating the spirit of the people to unconquerable resistance against their foes." Meanwhile, Davis was trying still to find troops to defend the Carolinas.

January 7, Saturday

The active military career of Maj. Gen. Benjamin F. Butler came to an end. Orders were issued by the Secretary of War removing Butler from command of the Department of Virginia and North Carolina. His replacement was Maj. Gen. E. O. C. Ord. For a long time Butler had held high military posts, possibly because Lincoln felt he was less a thorn in the side that way; but there had to be an end. The mess of

Fort Fisher had brought matters to a head, and now Butler had to go regardless of political implications. More Federal troops were pulled out of the Shenandoah Valley, now static, and sent elsewhere. Military action remained light, with skirmishing in Johnson County, Ark., and with Indians at Valley Station and Julesburg, Colo. Terr. Union scouts operated from Pine Bluff, Ark., and from Fort Ellsworth, Kas. Danish ironclad *Sphinx* left Copenhagen for Quiberon Bay, France. She had been secretly purchased by the Confederates and would become C.S.S. *Stonewall.*

January 8, Sunday

The huge naval fleet under Rear Admiral David D. Porter, plus the transport fleet containing Terry's expeditionary force, arrived at rendezvous off Beaufort, N.C., before again attempting to take Fort Fisher. Maj. Gen. E. O. C. Ord took command of the Department of Virginia and North Carolina, as well as the Army of the James, in place of the relieved Butler. Maj. Gen. John A. Logan resumed command of the Union Fifteenth Corps, relieving Maj. Gen. Peter J. Osterhaus. Skirmishing occurred only near Ivey's Ford, Ark., and at Dove Creek, Concho River, Tex.

January 9, Monday

The Constitutional Convention of Tennessee adopted an amendment abolishing slavery in the state and putting it to the vote of the people, who ratified it Feb. 22. John Bell Hood moved his discouraged and greatly diminished Army of Tennessee to Tupelo, Miss. There would have to be an effort to pick up the pieces of the Confederate army in the West, for it was desperately needed in the Carolinas. Fighting broke out in Texas County of Missouri, and near Disputanta Station, Va. Federals carried out a reconnaissance from Eastport to Iuka, Miss.

In the U. S. House, Democrat Moses Odell of New York indicated his change of position regarding abolition of slavery: "The South by rebellion has absolved the Democratic party at the North from all obligation to stand up longer for the defense of its 'cornerstone.'" Odell later received an important political job from Lincoln and was one of the Democrats who made it possible to pass the Thirteenth Amendment. In opposition, Robert Mallory of Kentucky said, "the Constitution does not authorize an amendment to be made by which any State or citizen shall be divested of acquired rights of property or of established political franchises."

January 10, Tuesday

The debate in the U. S. House of Representatives over slavery continued heatedly. John A. Kasson of Iowa: "you will never, never, have reliable peace in this country while that institution exists, the perpetual occasion of moral, intellectual, and physical warfare." Fernando Wood of

New York: "The Almighty has fixed the distinction of the races; the Almighty has made the black man inferior, and, sir, by no legislation, by no partisan success, by no revolution, by no military power, can you wipe out this distinction. You may make the black man free, but when you have done that what have you done?"

A skirmish near Glasgow, Mo., was the only fighting. The one major operation now under way, the second expedition to Fort Fisher, was being held up by raging seas and stormy weather off Beaufort, N.C.

January 11, Wednesday

The Constitutional Convention of Missouri, meeting in St. Louis, adopted an ordinance abolishing slavery.

Thomas Lafayette Rosser, with a small band of about 300 Confederates, was raiding in West Virginia. This time he fell on Beverly in bad weather, capturing 580 Federals and causing some 28 casualties, and seizing considerable rations. Union investigators called it a disaster due to Federal carelessness and lack of discipline. There was a skirmish near Lexington, Mo.; a Union expedition from Helena, Ark., to Harbert's Plantation, Miss.; and a Federal scout until Jan. 21 from Fort Wingate to Sierra del Datil and vicinity, N. Mex. Terr.

In Richmond President Davis was still trying to build up an army to face Sherman in South Carolina. He planned to bring the Army of Tennessee, or most of what was left, to the east coast, and to gather all available reserves, militia and recruits.

January 12, Thursday

In the early evening the immense Federal war fleet of about sixty vessels and a large number of troop transports bearing eight thousand army men arrived off Fort Fisher. The seas were calmer now and Adm. Porter's fleet and Gen. Terry's expeditionary force were anxious to erase the stain of the first failure to take the vital fort that had kept Wilmington partially open to blockade-runners. Landings, however, had to be put off until the thirteenth. Onshore Col. William Lamb at Fort Fisher learned of the expedition's arrival and notified Gen. Bragg, who commanded the Wilmington area.

Elsewhere, an affair took place near Sugar Loaf Prairie, Ark. Union operations included a four-day expedition from Morganza, La., with skirmishes; a four-day scout from Camp Grover to Texas Prairie, Mo.; and a six-day scout from Warrensburg to Miami, Mo.

Francis Preston Blair, Sr., aging Democratic political leader, conferred with President Davis in Richmond on possible peace. Blair, unofficially but with apparent sanction of President Lincoln, presented suggestions to Davis. The Confederate President gave Blair a letter to be shown Lincoln which indicated Davis was willing to enter into peace negotiations and that he would appoint an agent "to enter into conference, with a view to secure peace to the two countries." That was the rub—Davis was not willing to give up independence for the South and the North's entire policy was that "of one common country." But at least there had been talk between the two contending sides.

The abolition debate continued in the U. S. House as Democrat Samuel S. Cox of Ohio said, "Whatever it may be termed, I am opposed to compounding powers in the Federal Government." Republican James A. Garfield of Ohio said, "Mr. Speaker, we shall never know why slavery dies so hard in this Republic and in this Hall, till we know why sin outlives disaster, and Satan is immortal. . . ." Thaddeus Stevens, Radical leader from Pennsylvania, stated that slavery was "the worst institution upon earth, one which is a disgrace to man and would be an annoyance to the infernal spirits."

President Davis wrote Lieut. Gen. Richard Taylor, son of President Zachary Taylor, "Sherman's campaign has produced bad effect on our people, success against his future operations is needful to reanimate public confidence. Hardee requires more aid than Lee can give him, and Hood's army is the only source to which we can now look." Davis said some troops should be kept by Taylor in the West to hold Thomas in check, but the main part of what was left of the Army of Tennessee should be sent "to look after Sherman."

January 13, Friday

ATTACK ON FORT FISHER, NORTH CAROLINA BEGINS.

GENERAL HOOD RESIGNS.

The extremely powerful Federal naval fleet of Adm. Porter, packing the greatest firepower in naval history, 627 guns in 59 vessels, began bombarding Fort Fisher, N.C., at the mouth of the Cape Fear River. The firing in three days totaled around 20,000 projectiles and appeared to be much more effective than the December attack. Accuracy was high and Confederate guns and defensive works were battered. Meanwhile, with small boats from the navy, some eight thousand Union troops under Gen. Alfred Terry were put ashore on the narrow north-south peninsula above Fort Fisher. There was no opposition to the landing from Gen. Bragg's some 6000 men between Wilmington and the fort. The fort was relatively powerless, and the naval vessels suffered little damage during the fight. The army dug in, constructing a defense line facing north to hold off Bragg, and then prepared to move southward to assault the fort after its softening by the fleet. Meanwhile, Col. William Lamb, in command of Fort Fisher, called upon Bragg to attack the Federal landing party and crush it.

John Bell Hood resigned as commander of the Army of Tennessee, ending the flamboyant career of a gallant, hard-fighting, but often losing general. Lieut. Gen. Richard Taylor was to be named to succeed him under the supervision of P. G. T. Beauregard.

January 14, Saturday

BOMBARDMENT OF FORT FISHER CONTINUES.

Gen. Terry's expeditionary force secured its position on the sandy peninsula north of Fort Fisher, N.C., and completed its defensive, or north, line to hold off Bragg's Confederates. Terry also carried out reconnaissance and other preparations for assaulting Fort Fisher, now isolated except by boat on the Cape Fear River side. The fire of the Union fleet, monitors and wooden ships alike, was termed "magnificent" for its power and accuracy. In Fort Fisher the Confederates had no chance to repair damage to the fortification. Their commander, Col. William Lamb, increased his calls to Bragg for help, as did Maj. Gen. W. H. C. Whiting, who was with Lamb in the fort. Already both were bitter in their denunciation of Bragg for his alleged failure to attack the Federal defensive lines.

To the south some of Sherman's forces moved out to a new position from Beaufort to Pocotaligo, S.C., with skirmishing. For the rest of January Federal troops operated against Indian depredations on the Overland Stage Road between Julesburg and Denver, Colo. Terr., with intermittent fighting.

Beauregard temporarily took command of the Army of Tennessee at Tupelo, Miss., but it was to be under Richard Taylor from Jan. 23.

January 15, Sunday

ASSAULT AND CAPTURE OF FORT FISHER, NORTH CAROLINA, BY FEDERALS.

After a continuing heavy naval bombardment, the Federal forces attempted a two-pronged assault of Fort Fisher, N.C. A naval and marine brigade of about 2000 moved forward on the ocean, or east, side of the narrow peninsula. However, they met the full force of the defenders' infantry and three remaining movable guns, and fell back in panic and defeat. On the Cape Fear River, or west side, the enlarged division of Adelbert Ames of Gen. Terry's command, totaling 3300 men, also rushed forward and was much more successful. After being held up for a time by the strong traverses constructed by the Confederates, they got through. By late evening they had taken the entire fort and its garrison of about 1900 men, many of whom, including the two top officers, Col. Lamb and Gen. Whiting, were injured. Confederate casualties were about 500, while Federal army and navy losses were 266 killed, 1018 wounded, and 57 missing for 1341 casualties. To the north, the remainder of the Federal army, 4700 strong, manned the defensive works against R. F. Hoke's men of Bragg's command, 6000 strong, but were never seriously attacked. The Southern officers at the fort violently assailed Bragg for failing to relieve the pressure. Bragg claimed the defensive line was too strong. The result, though belated, was significant: Wilmington was cut off as a blockade-running port and it had been the last major access point for the South. While Wilmington itself remained in Confederate hands, it was now of little importance.

Federal monitors at Charleston, S.C., had been demonstrating nightly near the forts at the entrance of the harbor. The Confederates therefore placed torpedoes somewhat farther out. U.S.S. monitor *Patapsco,* dragging for torpedoes, struck one herself. In some fifteen seconds the ironclad went down with the loss of sixty-two men. A number on deck did escape. Meanwhile, at Clifton, Tenn., Schofield's Twenty-third Army Corps left for the east and would eventually take Wilmington and move inland. There was a skirmish in Madison County, Ark. Federal expeditions of several days each moved from New Orleans to Mandeville, La., and from Pine Bluff, Ark. Jan. 15–21 a Union scout operated from Fort Larned to Pawnee Fork, Walnut Creek, and Smoky Hill River, Kas.

Edward Everett, clergyman, teacher, congressman, writer, and famous orator who spoke at Gettysburg with President Lincoln, and who had been the 1860 vice-presidential candidate of the Constitutional Union party, died at seventy-one in Boston.

President Lincoln wrote Maj. Gen. Grenville M. Dodge in St. Louis of his concern over "so much irregular violence in Northern Missouri as to be driving away the people and almost depopulating it." The President told Dodge to appeal to the people to "let one another alone."

In Richmond President Davis wrote Gen. Hardee in South Carolina, "I hope you will be able to check the advance of the enemy," and added that he was seeking all possible reinforcements to oppose Sherman. He wrote the intransigent Gov. Joseph E. Brown of Georgia asking for troops.

January 16, Monday

Francis Preston Blair, Sr., reported to President Lincoln on his Jan. 12 talk with President Davis in Richmond. Blair showed Mr. Lincoln the Confederate leader's letter in which Davis spoke of negotiations between the two nations. The elderly politician told Lincoln in detail of his conversation with Davis and submitted a lengthy report in which he outlined the plan for peace, coupled with the conquest of Mexico. In a few days President Lincoln was in effect to turn down such a plan as it did not involve "one common country." Blair returned to Richmond, but nothing more came of his effort.

At Fort Fisher, N.C., in the wake of the successful conquest by the Federals, the main magazine accidentally exploded, perhaps caused by intoxicated soldiers, sailors, and marines discharging firearms and looting the fort. Some 25 were killed, 66 wounded, and 13 missing for 104 casualties. Meanwhile, Fort Caswell, N.C., and defensive positions at Smithville and Reeves' Point were blown up and abandoned by Confederates. Elsewhere, there were operations until Jan. 22 about Waynesville, Mo.; a Union expedition from Brashear City to Whisky Bayou, La.; and Federal scouting until mid-February about Franklin, Tenn.

President Davis, informed of the fall of Fort Fisher, urged Gen. Bragg at Wilmington to retake it if possible. By a vote of 14 to 2 the Confederate Senate passed a resolution that it was the judgment of Congress that Gen. Robert E. Lee should be assigned General-in-Chief of the Armies of the Confederacy and that Beauregard should command the army in South Carolina, Georgia, and Florida, and J. E. Johnston the Army of Tennessee. Many had long favored the move.

January 17, Tuesday

Sherman's army was about ready to move northward from the Savannah area, although rain and high water in the rivers delayed their actual start. News of the Union victory at Fort Fisher spread throughout the nations. At Richmond and Petersburg the siege went on. Confederates desperately tried to find enough troops to defend all the major threatened points, but it was impossible. The Federals slowly but steadily increased the pressure.

President Davis told South Carolina Gov. A. G. Magrath at Charleston, "I am fully alive to the importance of successful resistance to Sherman's advance, and have called on the Governor of Georgia to give all the aid he can furnish."

January 18, Wednesday

Gen. Sherman transferred command of Savannah and area to Maj. Gen. Foster and the Department of the South. Action included a small affair near Lovettsville, Va.; a skirmish at Clarksville, Ark.; a two-day Union expedition from Napoleonville to Grand River, La.; and a five-day Federal scout from Warrensburg to the Snibar Hills, Mo.

Once more President Lincoln talked with Francis P. Blair, Sr., on his mission to Richmond and gave him a letter saying Blair might tell Mr. Davis "that I have constantly been, am now, and shall continue, ready to receive any agent whom he, or any other influential person now resisting the national authority, may informally send to me, with the view of securing peace to the people of our one common country." Thus the difference—for Lincoln "one common country" and for Davis two separate countries. In Richmond President Davis was still beating the bushes for troops to oppose Sherman and again urged Gen. Lee to extend his command to include that of all the armies of the Confederacy, plus the immediate command of the Army of Northern Virginia.

January 19, Thursday

SHERMAN ORDERS MARCH FROM SAVANNAH THROUGH SOUTH CAROLINA.

Gen. Sherman issued orders for his army to get under way in its new march from the area of Savannah, Ga., northward into South Carolina. The troops did not start off simultaneously, but on this day movement of some segments began. Their goal was Goldsborough, N.C., by about March 15. The attitude of the army marching into South Carolina was changed. The men felt much more vindictive toward South Carolina than they had toward Georgia. To the army, South Carolina had been the birthplace of the rebellion. President Davis, Genls. Hardee, Beauregard, and others continued their desperate struggle to recruit men to oppose Sherman, but without success. The bottom of the barrel had been scraped, and there were still too few men to stop Sherman's two-pronged drive toward Columbia, S.C.

A skirmish occurred at Corinth, Miss.; and there was a Federal reconnaissance around Myrtle Sound, N.C.; Federal scouting from Donaldsonville, La.; and a four-day Union expedition from Memphis, Tenn., to Marion, Ark.

President Lincoln inquired of Gen. Grant as a friend whether there was a place in Grant's military family for his son Robert. The young man was soon appointed captain and assistant adjutant general on Grant's staff.

Gen. Lee rather reluctantly told President Davis he would "undertake any service to which you think proper to assign me," but he felt, if named General-in-Chief, "I must state that with the addition of the immediate command of this army I do not think I could accomplish any good." He added, "If I had the ability I would not have the time." However, pressure continued on Davis to appoint Lee.

January 20, Friday

As the four Federal corps under Sherman, plus Kilpatrick's cavalry, got under way or prepared to move into South Carolina against very light opposition, there was a reconnaissance from Pocotaligo to the Salkehatchie River, S.C. Slocum's left wing was held up by heavy rain at Savannah. All troops would not be in motion until Feb. 1, Sherman later reported, but preliminary movements were now well advanced. In Kansas, at Point of Rocks or Nine Mile Bridge near Fort Larned, there was a skirmish.

Sec. of War Stanton reported to President Lincoln on his visit to Savannah and Fort Fisher.

January 21, Saturday

Federal troops carried out a two-day expedition from Brashear City to Bayou Sorrel, La. Gen. Sherman embarked with his entire headquarters from Savannah for Beaufort, S.C., pausing at Hilton Head. Sherman had tried to give out that his army was heading for Charleston or Augusta rather than Columbia. For the rest of the month Sherman reconnoitered in person and visited various units.

January 22, Sunday

Fighting again tapered off, with a skirmish on the Benton Road, near Little Rock, Ark., and a Federal expedition from Little Rock to Mount

Elba, Ark., until Feb. 4. Gen. Sherman and his staff were en route from Savannah to Beaufort, S.C.

January 23, Monday

President Davis signed an act providing for appointment of a General-in-Chief of Confederate Armies. Congress obviously had Lee in mind. Confederate Lieut. Gen. Richard Taylor assumed command of the Army of Tennessee (now reduced to about 17,700 men) after the resignation of John Bell Hood, so disastrously beaten at Nashville. However, Taylor would soon have little to command except a large area, as a main force of the Army of Tennessee was sent east to the Carolinas to try to halt Sherman. Even so, due to dissipation, desertion, and other causes, only about five thousand reached Johnston, according to that general. On the James River there was action at Fort Brady as eleven Confederate vessels tried to pass obstructions and head downriver below Richmond to attack the weakened Union squadron. Four warships went aground and the move came to nought. A Federal scout operated until Jan. 27 from Cumberland Gap, Tenn. A skirmish broke out at Thompson's Plantation, La.

January 24, Tuesday

The Congress of the Confederate States offered again to exchange prisoners with the Federals. This time Gen. Grant accepted. His previous refusal to exchange prisoners had been intended to cut down further on Southern manpower. Nathan Bedford Forrest assumed command of the Confederate District of Mississippi, East Louisiana, and West Tennessee. There were skirmishes at Fayetteville, Ark.; Bayou Goula, La.; and a Federal expedition from Cape Girardeau, Mo., to Eleven Points River, Ark. President Lincoln wired Vice-President-elect Andrew Johnson at Nashville that he should be in Washington for inauguration March 4.

January 25, Wednesday

Confederate cruiser *Shenandoah* reached Melbourne, Australia, and later left for the northern Pacific to plague Federal fishing and whaling fleets. There was a reconnaissance by Sherman's men from Pocotaligo to the Salkehatchie River, S.C., "to amuse the enemy," as Sherman put it. Skirmishing flared near Powhatan, Va., and near Simpsonville, Shelby County, Ky. A Union expedition moved from Irish Bottom to Evans' Island, Tenn.

January 26, Thursday

Scouting increased by Federals—until the thirty-first from Pine Bluff toward Camden and Monticello, Ark.; until Feb. 4 from Plaquemine to The Park, La.; and from Memphis into southeast Arkansas and northeastern Louisiana until Feb. 11. Skirmishing occurred near Pocotaligo, S.C., and Paint Rock, Ala. Sherman continued to threaten Charleston although he did not have any intention of attacking it, but it was a useful means of diverting the enemy.

January 27, Friday

Minor military activities continued at Ennis' Cross Roads, S.C. Elsewhere, skirmishing erupted at Eldrod's Tanyard in DeKalb County, Ala., and a Union expedition operated from Fort Pinney to Kimball's Plantation, Ark. Gen. Lee pointed out again to Richmond the "alarming frequency of desertion from this army." He also said the "ration is too small for men who have to undergo so much exposure and labor as ours." He believed the Commissary Department could do a better job.

January 28, Saturday

President Jefferson Davis named three commissioners to hold informal talks with Federal authorities. This came about as a result of the visits of Francis Preston Blair, Sr., to Richmond and the other efforts looking toward a possible peace. The Southern commissioners were Vice-President Alexander Stephens, R. M. T. Hunter of Virginia, and former U. S. Supreme Court justice John A. Campbell. Sec. of War Seddon recommended to Davis that Gen. Lee be appointed General-in-Chief of all Confederate armies under the act of Congress approved Jan. 23.

In South Carolina a skirmish took place on the Combahee River on Sherman's front. Operations against Indians were carried out by Federals until Feb. 9 on the upper Arkansas River, Kas.; Union scouts probed from Bayou Goula to Grand River, La., until Feb. 7; and an expedition until the thirty-first moved from Strawberry Plains to Clinch Mountain, Tenn.

January 29, Sunday

Skirmishes at Robertsville, S.C.; and near Harrodsburg, Ky., marked the day. There was an affair at Danville, Ky. There was considerable interest in just where and how Sherman would move when he got rolling in South Carolina, and whether there really was any hope for the proposed conference between Federal and Confederate officials.

January 30, Monday

President Lincoln issued a pass for the three Confederate commissioners to go through U.S. military lines to Fort Monroe. Skirmishing broke out in La Fayette County, Mo.; near Lawtonville, S.C.; and at Chaplintown, Ky. There was a scout to Long Bridge and Bottom's Bridge, north of the James in Virginia; as well as an expedition from Thibodeaux to Lake Verrett and Bayou Planton, La., both Union. Maj. Gen. John Pope was assigned to command of the new Military Division of the Missouri, consisting of the combined Missouri and Kansas areas.

January 31, Tuesday

U. S. HOUSE PASSES ABOLITION OF SLAVERY AMENDMENT.

LEE NAMED GENERAL-IN-CHIEF OF CONFEDERATE ARMIES.

With an outburst of enthusiasm from the gallery and the floor, the U. S. House of Representatives passed by two thirds the Thirteenth Amendment to the Constitution, abolishing slavery. There were 119 in favor, 56 opposed, and 8 not voting to send the amendment, long since approved by the Senate, to the states for ratification. On Feb. 1 Illinois ratified the amendment, but it was not until Dec. 18, 1865, that two thirds of the states had given their approval, and it became a part of the Constitution. Mr. Lincoln had vigorously backed the measure and had gone to great efforts to see it past the House, where it had failed previously. There were reports of political deals involving Democrats who had been opposed to the amendment in 1864. The debate had been furious and lengthy. Radicals such as Thad Stevens of Pennsylvania had declared that states could not "return" to the Union, but had to be admitted as new states, a view opposed by the Administration. But at least on the abolition of slavery Mr. Lincoln and the Radicals temporarily agreed. The vote confirmed what had been evident for a long time: one result of the war would be the end of slavery. Also, it put on a constitutional level the Emancipation Proclamation of the President, which he maintained was strictly a war measure.

President Davis recommended to the Confederate Senate, and it promptly approved, the appointment of Gen. Robert E. Lee as General-in-Chief of the Confederate Armies. Often urged, the measure came too late to have any real effect. Lee continued primarily as commander of the Army of Northern Virginia.

In Washington President Lincoln issued instructions for Sec. of State Seward to go to Fort Monroe to confer with the Confederate commissioners "on the basis of my letter to F. P. Blair, Esq., on Jan. 18, 1865." This meant that the President was willing to confer on restoration of the national authority throughout all states, but would not recede from his position on slavery, and there could be no cessation of hostilities short of an end of the war and disbandment of hostile forces. Of course, he would only treat the problem as that of one nation, whereas President Davis would carry on discussions as between two nations.

The last day of January had been important politically and socially, but on the military front there was only a Union expedition from Morganza to New Roads, La., and a two-day Federal expedition from Fort Pike to Bayou Bonfouca, La.

President Davis told Lee of his attempt to bring Confederate troops east from the Trans-Mississippi to defend against Sherman. Davis pointed out that Congress had not adopted his manpower measures, and asked Lee for suggestions "in this, our hour of necessity. . . ."

FEBRUARY, 1865

The fighting fronts had been relatively quiet for over a month, except for the fall of Fort Fisher. The abolition of slavery had been confirmed as a major mission of the North in prosecuting the war now that Congress had passed the Thirteenth Amendment. It was quite probable that the amendment ending slavery would find fairly quick approval in most of the states. While abolition had been in the war aims for some time, it had moved out of military policy and more into domestic principles. A few at the North complained, but the climate had been prepared for the amendment. In some areas of the South the amendment's passage possibly strengthened resistance, but at the same time the futility of that resistance became more and more evident.

Hopes of peace were sweeping across both lands and many yearned for the forthcoming negotiations, or something like them, to yield results. If that did not work, then the Northern might would roll ahead, with Grant increasing pressure at Richmond and Petersburg, Sherman heading out from Savannah and Hilton Head into South Carolina, and the blockade much more effective now that primary ports were virtually sealed. In the West Thomas or the Federal cavalry could clean out what weak resistance remained without much effort. Lee commanded all the Southern armies now, but there was not very much to command outside of Virginia.

February 1, Wednesday

CAROLINA CAMPAIGN IN FULL OPERATION.

After about two weeks of preliminary movements and extensive preparations, William T. Sherman today actively began his march into South Carolina from Savannah, Ga., and Beaufort, S.C. The troops of the Seventeenth and Fifteenth Corps moved ahead despite felled trees and burned bridges. The Federal Pioneer battalions were well trained and quickly cleared the way. As Gen. O. O. Howard's right wing advanced, Gen. Henry Slocum's left wing struggled with the flooded Savannah River at Sister's Ferry, but soon got across. Sherman was attempting still to confound the enemy as to his aim—Charleston, S.C., or possibly Augusta, Ga. Actually, the first goal was Columbia, S.C., capital of the state. In front of them Hardee had his battered troops from Savannah, units of militia, and various others. Efforts of course were being made to send the Army of Tennessee, and calls were made in every direction. Few troops responded. Confederate cavalry harassed the edges of the advance, which in no wise hindered the Federal march. There were skirmishes at Hickory Hill and Whippy Swamp Creek, S.C.

For most of February Union soldiers operated against Indians about Fort Boise, Id. Terr. A minor skirmish occurred in McLemore's Cove, Ga., and a Federal scout probed from Warrensburg to Wagon Knob, Tabo Creek, and other spots in Missouri. The Union Navy made what turned out to be a final foray against Southern salt works at St. Andrews Bay, Fla.

Illinois became the first state to ratify the Thirteenth Amendment, abolishing slavery. President Lincoln signed a resolution submitting the amendment to the states even though his signature was not required. Later he responded to a serenade, "The occasion was one of congratulation to the country and to the whole world." Now the task was to get the amendment approved. The President announced the Illinois legislature's approval and thought "this measure was a very fitting if not an indispensable adjunct to the winding up of the great difficulty . . . this amendment is a King's cure for all the evils (Applause.) It winds the whole thing up."

Early in the day a cipher to Gen. Grant at City Point, Va., from Lincoln read, "Let nothing which is transpiring, change, hinder, or delay your Military movements, or plans." By this the President meant that the forthcoming conference with Confederate leaders or other possible peace overtures should not interfere with the military phase of the war.

President Davis, with considerable reluctance, accepted the resignation of Sec. of War James A. Seddon, long the subject of much criticism and controversy. A Virginia delegation in the Confederate Congress had even called for relieving all the Cabinet. Davis defended the right of the President to choose his own advisers.

February 2, Thursday

Sherman's right wing was on the Salkehatchie River. The rivers and swamps were as much obstacles to the Federal advance into South Carolina as the Confederate cavalry and other troops trying vainly to block the way. Severe skirmishing took place at Lawtonville, Barker's Mill on Whippy Swamp, Duck Branch near Loper's Cross Roads, and Rivers' and Broxton's bridges on the Salkehatchie. There was a skirmish on St. John's River, Fla. Operations against the Indians lasted until Feb. 18 on the North Platte River in Colorado and Nebraska territories, after Indians attacked the Overland Stage Station at Julesburg, Colo. Terr.

Rhode Island and Michigan joined Illinois in ratifying the constitutional amendment abolishing slavery.

President Lincoln left Washington for Hampton Roads, Va., where the three Confederate commissioners were already gathered. They were Vice-President Alexander Stephens, Asst. Sec. of War and former U.S. justice John A. Campbell, and Sen. and former Confederate secretary of state R. M. T. Hunter. In the evening the President arrived at Fort Monroe and boarded *River Queen,* where Sec. of State William H. Seward already had his headquarters. The Confederate commissioners had hoped to go to Washington, but they had been halted at Fort Monroe.

February 3, Friday

HAMPTON ROADS CONFERENCE.

Five men sat in the salon of *River Queen* in Hampton Roads off Fort Monroe, Va., discussing the fate of the United States and the Confederate States of America. On one side President Lincoln and Sec. of State William H. Seward; for the other Alexander H. Stephens, John A. Campbell, and R. M. T. Hunter. After some pleasantries and reminiscences, Mr. Lincoln gave firm understanding that the national authority of the United States must be recognized within the rebellious states before anything else could be considered. There was talk again of a movement by the states of the two nations against Mexico and French intervention in North America. Mr. Lincoln said this could not be entertained as no treaty with the Confederate States was possible, for they were not a country in the eyes of the North.

Armistice was suggested but the President said this was impossible before reestablishment of the United States. The Confederates asked what manner of reconstruction would be effected if the Union were restored. The President said that troops must be disbanded and national authorities would resume functions. Lincoln and Seward did say courts would determine rights of property and that Congress would no doubt be liberal. As to slavery, Congress had passed the Thirteenth Amendment and it was being ratified by the states. In summation, the Confederate commission said that the terms seemed to be unconditional submission. Mr. Seward said the word had not been used or implied and President Lincoln said that if the matter was left in his own hands he would be liberal in his policies but he could not answer for Congress. Mr. Lincoln told a few stories, everyone was reasonably friendly, but nothing came of it or could come of it, considering the Federal demand for unconditional restoration of the Union and the Confederate demand for terms between two independent nations. The Confederate commissioners reported to President Davis, and thus ended the last and only real effort at peace before surrender.

Maryland, New York, and West Virginia ratified the Thirteenth Amendment. On the war fronts, Sherman's right wing, with the Seventeenth Corps, forced its way across three miles of swamp, sometimes shoulder-deep, along the Salkehatchie River, S.C. After crossing the river the troops cleared the Confederate defenders in an action at Rivers' Bridge with other skirmishing at Dillingham's Cross Roads or Duck Branch. From the Salkehatchie Sherman's troops pressed on quite rapidly in an almost straight northerly direction into South Carolina toward Columbia. Over in Hog Jaw Valley, Ala., a skirmish occurred at Ladd's House, and an affair broke out at Harper's Ferry, W. Va. Union scouts operated Feb. 3–8 in La Fayette County, Mo., and Feb. 3–8 from Fort Larned to the south fork of Pawnee Creek and Buckner's Branch, Kas.

February 4, Saturday

President Lincoln returned home from the unsuccessful Hampton Roads conference and reported to the Cabinet. Lincoln again told Grant through Stanton that "nothing transpired, or transpiring with the three gentlemen from Richmond, is to cause any change hindrance or delay, of your military plans or operations."

Skirmishing at Angley's Post Office and Buford's Bridge, S.C., marked the now full advance of Sherman's four corps. Slocum and the left wing had had considerable difficulty crossing the swollen Savannah River but now were completing the operation. Federal troops made a three-day expedition from Winchester, Va., to Moorefield, W. Va. There was slight action at Mud Springs, Neb. Terr. Maj. Gen. John Pope assumed command of the Military Division of the Missouri.

Discouraged by Federal advances in South Carolina, President Davis wrote Gen. Beauregard at Augusta, Ga., that things were worse than he expected, and that Beauregard should take over-all command in Georgia and concentrate all the troops possible.

February 5, Sunday

BATTLE OF HATCHER'S RUN, VIRGINIA, UNTIL FEBRUARY 7.

Grant was active again after the months of siege at Petersburg. The Federal Second and Fifth Corps plus cavalry again headed toward the Boydton Plank Road and Hatcher's Run. Despite inclement weather they reached the Boydton Plank Road with little difficulty. The movement was in line with the obvious strategy of Grant to extend the Federal lines south and west of Petersburg to weaken the already strained defensive positions of Lee. The Confederates did move out troops but were unable to do much against the Federal cavalry and infantry. The Battle of Hatcher's Run was also known as Dabney's Mill and included Armstrong's Mill, Rowanty Creek, and Vaughan Road.

In South Carolina there was skirmishing at Duncanville and Combahee Ferry, as Sherman's four corps continued crossing the various streams and swamps of the southern part of the state. In addition, fighting occurred at Charles Town, W. Va.; Braddock's Farm near Welaka, Fla.; and near McMinnville, Tenn.

President Lincoln had not given up his plan for compensated emancipation. He read to the Cabinet a proposal to pay $400,000,000 to the slave states if they abandoned resistance to the national authority before April 1. One half would be paid upon the ending of hostilities and the remainder upon approval of the constitutional amendment abolishing slavery. But the

Cabinet unanimously disapproved the measure which would never have passed Congress.

February 6, Monday

JOHN C. BRECKINRIDGE NAMED CONFEDERATE SECRETARY OF WAR.
LEE ASSUMES COMMAND OF CONFEDERATE ARMIES.

President Jefferson Davis named capable Maj. Gen. John C. Breckinridge as Confederate Secretary of War, replacing James A. Seddon. A Kentuckian, Breckinridge had served in the U. S. House, the Senate, and as Vice-President, and as a prominent Confederate general. The Senate approved the appointment the same day. Gen. Robert E. Lee received orders to assume the duties of General-in-Chief of the Armies of the Confederate States, following the act of the Confederate Congress approved by President Davis Jan. 23. While important posts, these two appointments came too late in the war to have much bearing on the outcome.

President Davis also submitted to Congress the report of the Confederate commissioners at Hampton Roads, and told Sen. Benjamin H. Hill that "Nothing less would be accepted than unconditional submission to the government and laws of the United States. . . ." To Congress he told of the amendment to the U. S. Constitution abolishing slavery, and added, "the enemy refused to enter into negotiations with the Confederate States, or with any one of them separately, or to give our people any other terms or guaranties than those which the conqueror may grant. . . ."

On the Petersburg front, fighting at Dabney's Mill or Hatcher's Run increased. Southern Brig. Gen. John Pegram, commanding a division, was killed trying to halt the Union advance to Hatcher's Run. Federal troops held the Boydton Plank Road without much difficulty, and pushed on to Hatcher's Run, thus extending their lines substantially. However, Warren's Fifth Corps was forced back in some confusion when Confederate reinforcements came in.

Sherman's troops fought with Confederates trying to delay the Federal advance at Fishburn's Plantation near Lane's Bridge on the Little Salkehatchie, and at Cowpen Ford, and near Barnwell, S.C. There were three days of Union operations in Ozark County, Mo.; a Northern scout from Fairfax Court House to Brentsville, Va.; and an affair at Corn's Farm, Franklin County, Tenn.

February 7, Tuesday

Maine and Kansas got on the bandwagon of states hurriedly approving the Thirteenth Amendment; in Delaware the amendment failed to receive the necessary votes.

The fighting at Hatcher's Run ended with Federals abandoning the Boydton Plank Road but fortifying their new lines to Hatcher's Run at the Vaughan Road Crossing, some three miles below Burgess' Mill. The Confederate army of around 46,000 now had to defend some 37 miles of Richmond-Petersburg lines. This was the last principal Federal move to extend its lines prior to the final push in late March and early April. About 35,000 Federals were at least partly engaged Feb. 5–7, with 170 killed, 1160 wounded, and 182 missing for 1512; there were about 14,000 Confederates involved and casualties are not clear.

Sherman's four corps, plus Kilpatrick's cavalry, continued their march in South Carolina against very light Confederate resistance. They encountered more difficulty with geographical obstacles such as swamps and rivers. Skirmishing took place at Blackville, the Edisto River Bridge, and there was a Federal reconnaissance to Cannon's Bridge on the South Edisto River. There were four days of Union scouting from Morganza to Fausee River and Grossetete Bayou, La.; and a Federal scout on the Hernando Road, Tenn.

February 8, Wednesday

The Federal House of Representatives passed a joint resolution declaring that the states of Virginia, North Carolina, South Carolina, Georgia, Florida, Alabama, Mississippi, Louisiana, Texas, Arkansas, and Tennessee were not entitled to representation in the electoral college. Mr. Lincoln signed the resolution but disclaimed he had thus expressed any opinion as he also disclaimed any right to interfere in the counting of votes.

In the South Carolina Campaign, skirmishing erupted at Williston, White Pond or Walker's or Valley Bridge on the Edisto, and at Cannon's Bridge on the South Edisto. In Kentucky action occurred at New Market and Bradfordsville. In Arkansas there were two days of Federal operations on the Arkansas River near Little Rock, and a six-day Union scout from Helena to Madison. Fighting against Indians on the North Platte River near Rush Creek, Neb. Terr., lasted for a couple of days. Massachusetts and Pennsylvania ratified the Thirteenth Amendment.

February 9, Thursday

The daily, relatively light skirmishing along the edges of Sherman's advance into South Carolina continued, with action at Binnaker's Bridge on the South Edisto and at Holman's Bridge, S.C. In addition action included skirmishing near Memphis, Tenn., and a Yankee scout until Feb. 19 from Pine Bluff to Devall's Bluff, Ark. In Union command changes, Maj. Gen. Quincy A. Gillmore took over the Department of the South, replacing Maj. Gen. John G. Foster, and John M. Schofield assumed command of the Department of North Carolina. The advance of Schofield's Twenty-third Corps arrived at Fort Fisher preparatory to attacking Wilmington and eventually pushing inland to join Sherman in North Carolina.

Robert E. Lee took his duties as Confederate General-in-Chief, saying he would rely on the field commanders and that manpower was a paramount necessity. He proposed a pardon to deserters who reported within thirty days. President Davis approved this measure. Virginia unionists ratified the Thirteenth Amendment.

February 10, Friday

Action around Charleston Harbor included skirmishing on James Island and at Johnson's Station, S.C., as Confederates guarded against attack both from Sherman's invading column and from the sea. A skirmish broke out at Kittredge's Sugar House near Napoleonville, La.; a Federal scout from Friar's Point, Miss., also involved a skirmish. Union expeditions operated from Brashear City to Lake Verret, La., for two days, and from Thibodeaux to Lake Verret, La., for four days. An affair occurred near Triune, Tenn., and there was a skirmish in Johnson's Crook, Ga. All Federal troops in the Departments of Kentucky and the Cumberland were declared subject to the orders of Maj. Gen. Thomas except for posts protecting the Mississippi River.

President Lincoln, like Mr. Davis, reported to his Congress on the Hampton Roads conference. Capt. Raphael Semmes was named Rear Admiral, C.S.A., and put in command of the James River Squadron. Ohio and Missouri ratified the Thirteenth Amendment.

February 11, Saturday

Sherman's men, now on the railroad from Midway to Johnson's Station, S.C., divided the Confederates who were in Branchville and Charleston on the east and near Aiken and in Georgia near Augusta on the west. There were actions at Aiken, Johnson's Station, near Sugar Loaf, and on Battery Simkins, as well as about Orangeburg, S.C. In Arkansas minor skirmishes occurred at Clear Creek and near Pine Bluff. In Virginia there was an affair at Williamsburg and Federals carried out a five-day expedition from Bermuda Hundred to Smithfield. President Davis wrote Hardee that if the army had concentrated sufficiently, Davis was hopeful Sherman could be defeated at Charleston. On the other hand, Beauregard urged evacuation, for the Confederates could not afford to lose an army. Of course, Sherman did not intend to attack Charleston but to bypass and cut it off.

February 12, Sunday

The electoral vote was taken and Lincoln was officially elected with 212 votes to 21 for McClellan. Lincoln was still concerned by reports that Missouri provost marshals were selling confiscated property.

Sherman's troops swept enemy opposition from the Orangeburg Bridge on the North Edisto as the march continued in South Carolina. Other skirmishing was recorded near Columbia and Macon, Mo.; Lewisburg, Ark.; and Waterloo, Ala. Union operations until Feb. 20 took place about Forts Riley and Larned, Kas.

February 13, Monday

For the Confederates in South Carolina prospects were dark. Beauregard had only remnants of troops to defend Augusta, Ga., and Hardee waited for the possible time when he must abandon Charleston and Fort Sumter. Wade Hampton had been sent from the Virginia front to his home state to command cavalry, but he had not been able to do anything significant. Minor fighting continued at Station Four, Fla., and in Mississippi County, Mo. A Federal expedition against raiders operated until Feb. 17 from Camp Russell near Winchester to Edenburg and Little Fort Valley, Va.

A west Tennessee group objected to military interference in civil affairs. President Lincoln told officers in the area that "the object of the war being to restore and maintain the blessings of peace and good government, I desire you to help, and not hinder, every advance in that direction."

In Richmond and elsewhere there was increasing clamor for Joseph E. Johnston to be put in over-all command in the Carolinas, but Gen. Lee wrote Vice-President Stephens that Beauregard should be retained at present and that continual command change was unwise, although he held a high opinion of Johnston.

In London Lord Russell protested to Federal commissioners against the St. Albans raid of Oct. 19, 1864, its aftermath in Canada, and activity on the Great Lakes.

February 14, Tuesday

Troops of Sherman in South Carolina pushed across the Congaree River and the whole army turned more toward Columbia "without wasting time or labor on Branchville or Charleston," as Sherman reported. Skirmishing flared at Wolf's Plantation and Gunter's Bridge on the North Edisto. President Davis again advised Hardee to hold Charleston as long as prudent before evacuation, but said it was up to Beauregard and Hardee to decide military strategy. Until Feb. 18 Federal expeditions moved from Donaldsonville to Grand Bayou and Bayou Goula, La.

February 15, Wednesday

Fairly heavy skirmishing at Congaree Creek, Savannah Creek, Bates' Ferry on the Congaree River, Red Bank Creek, and Two League Cross Roads near Lexington, S.C., marked the Federal march toward Columbia. They made rapid progress despite harassing opposition, still difficult swamps, mud, rivers, burned bridges, and blocked roads. Scouting from Nashville, Tenn., on the Nolensville Pike and from Fairfax Court House to Aldie and Middleburg, Va., are the only other recorded Union operations.

February 16, Thursday

Federal soldiers sighted the capital of South Carolina. Sherman's men arrived on the south bank of the Congaree River opposite Columbia. People, including a few Confederate cavalry, could be seen running about the streets in confusion. Some Union shells were fired into the city, allegedly at the enemy cavalry and the railroad depot. Some skirmishing occurred about the city as the various Federal units practically surrounded Columbia. Beauregard left the city by late afternoon after wiring Lee that he could not prevent its capture. At Charleston Hardee hurriedly sent out what war matériel he could preparatory to evacuation. Sherman's army had marched and waded its way to the first objective of the campaign and left even more destruction than in Georgia.

Virginia was quiet again as the siege continued. Widely scattered actions took place at Bennett's Bayou and Tolbert's Mill, Ark.; Gurley's Tank, Ala.; and Cedar Keys, Fla. Confederates attacked the garrisons of Athens and Sweet Water, Tenn. Federal scouting until the twentieth was carried out in Ozark County, Mo.; Marion County, Ark.; and, until the twenty-first, from Fort Larned, Kas. Indiana, Nevada, and Louisiana ratified the Thirteenth Amendment.

February 17, Friday

FEDERALS CAPTURE COLUMBIA, SOUTH CAROLINA—CITY IN FLAMES.
CHARLESTON, SOUTH CAROLINA, EVACUATED BY CONFEDERATES.

The mayor of Columbia, S.C., and a delegation of officials rode out in carriages to meet the Federal invader and to surrender the city. As Sherman's troops entered the capital as an army of occupation, remnants of Confederate cavalry fled. Some burning cotton bales were found, supposedly set afire by Wade Hampton's men. The blue-clad troops were met by jubilant released Federal prisoners and Negroes. Soon liquor supplies were found, with resulting depredations put down by the provost guard set up by Sherman. In the new state Capitol building roisterous Northern soldiers held a mock session of the "state legislature."

Sherman and his officers took up headquarters in some of the elegant mansions of this tree-shaded, quiet rural capital. And then it happened. That night much of Columbia burned. And ever since the argument has raged almost as violently as the flames as to who burned Columbia. Sherman was quick to blame Wade Hampton's cavalry, who had allegedly set fire to the cotton bales, these blazes said to have been fanned by the high winds that blew all day. Others believed the culprits were drunken Negroes, soldiers, and released prisoners, for the fires sprang up at many places both in the center and in outlying neighborhoods. Confederates charged that Sherman deliberately burned the city as part of his destructive policy, or that at the very least it was his uncontrolled looters. A Southern minister wrote, "Hell was empty, and all its devils were in this devoted city, learning new deviltry from Yankee teachers. A perfect reign of terror existed." The home of Wade Hampton, a fine house with a great library, and other plantation residences nearby met with flames. Southerners called it barbaric, but Sherman at least left some cattle and other subsistence when he moved north. The burning of Columbia soon became to the South the symbol of the Federal invasion, the epic depredation of the war.

At the same time, Charleston was evacuated. Proud birthplace of secession, spiritual capital, in a sense, of the whole South, Charleston with its Fort Sumter battered to rubble had stood defiant and unconquerable for nearly four years. But now, its defenders in danger of being penned up, Hardee reluctantly and belatedly pulled out. He took with him movable guns and much matériel but sacrificed heavy guns and other supplies, plus the irreplaceable symbol that was Charleston. With its fall something of the heart of the Confederacy departed. Columbia in flames and Charleston deserted—this was indeed a tragic day in the Southland.

Fighting took second place this day to fire and defeat. Action included a skirmish in Washington County, Ark.; Union scouting from Pine Bluff, Ark., to the Arkansas River; a Federal expedition until Feb. 22 from Plaquemine to The Park, La.; and skirmishing near Smithville, N.C. Yankee expeditions moved from Eastport to Iuka, Miss., and from Whitesburg to Fearn's Ferry, Ala.

The United States Senate voted to repudiate all debts by Confederate governments.

February 18, Saturday

The holocaust at Columbia, S.C., was burning itself out, but Sherman added to its toll by destroying railroad depots, supply houses, and other public buildings he deemed of military significance. Meanwhile, the citizens probed the wreckage of their homes, cursed the Federals, and began again to take up their disrupted lives. At Charleston the evacuation continued until early morning. About nine o'clock Northern troops of Brig. Gen. Alexander Schimmelfennig entered the city and it was surrendered by the mayor. Some cotton and other supplies were fired; a Northern reporter called it "A city of ruins,—silent, mournful, in deepest humiliation. . . . The band was playing 'Hail, Columbia,' and the strains floated through the desolate city, awakening wild enthusiasm in the hearts of the colored people. . . ."

Federal naval units bombarded Fort Anderson on the Cape Fear River as the combined land and sea forces began their campaign for Wilmington itself. There also was land action at Fort Anderson and Orton Pond, N.C., as Federals probed the land defenses below Wilmington. Confederate raiders attacked Fort Jones near Colesburg, Ky. There was a Union scout in Prince William County, Va., and a two-day Federal expedition from Camp Averell near Winchester into Loudoun County, Va. C.S.S. *Shenandoah* left Melbourne, Australia, after a refit.

Vote on recognition and admission of the restored state of Louisiana to Congress was postponed in the U. S. Senate. The move was blocked by the Radicals, who opposed the President's Louisiana reconstruction plan.

February 19, Sunday

Federal troops under Jacob D. Cox were on their way to outflank Fort Anderson and the Confederate defense line on the west side of the Cape Fear River in the Union drive toward Wilmington, N.C. By evening the Federals had marched about fifteen miles in a detour around the enemy works and fought several skirmishes, including one at Town Creek. In front of Fort Anderson the infantry had demonstrated and the fleet had cannonaded. During the night the Confederates pulled out toward Wilmington and they also fell back on the east side of the Cape Fear River.

At Columbia, S.C., Sherman's men continued to destroy the arsenal, railroad installations, machine shops, foundries, and railroad lines. Meanwhile, the march north toward North Carolina began. There were, in addition, Federal expeditions from Barrancas to Milton, Fla., and, until the twenty-second, from Helena, Ark., to Friar's Point, Miss. For several days Confederate and Federal troops in Mississippi and Alabama engaged in considerable operations from Eastport, Miss., to Russellville and Tuscumbia, Ala. Federals were obviously aiming toward Selma, Ala.

February 20, Monday

Federal troops marched rapidly toward Wilmington, N.C. They had outflanked the defenders on the west bank of the Cape Fear River, but still faced opposition on the east bank. Action occurred at Fort Myers, Fla., and Centre Creek, Mo. Federals carried out expeditions from Nashville to Pine Wood, and to Greeneville and Warrensburg, Tenn.

President Lincoln wrote Gov. Thomas C. Fletcher of Missouri that, while there was no organized military force of the enemy in the state, "destruction of property and life is rampant every where." He called for citizens to control the situation. The Confederate House of Representatives authorized use of slaves as soldiers, after long debate.

February 21, Tuesday

The Union forces in North Carolina were close to Wilmington, with shaky resistance in front of them. Columns of smoke rose in the city as the Confederates began destroying their stores. Braxton Bragg arrived and ordered evacuation in order not to jeopardize what forces he had left. Skirmishing broke out at Eagle Island and Fort Strong, N.C. To the south Sherman's men were moving into northern South Carolina; Slocum's corps reached Winnsborough. Confederates raided Cumberland, Md. Operations around St. Marks, Fla., lasted until March 7, and a Federal scout moved from Pine Bluff to Douglas' Plantation, Ark.

A dispirited Jefferson Davis in Richmond wrote Mobile editor John Forsyth, "It is now becoming daily more evident to all reflecting persons that we are reduced to choosing whether the negroes shall fight for us or against us. . . ." The Confederate Senate postponed debate on the House bill authorizing use of slaves as soldiers. Gen. Lee wrote Sec. of War John C. Breckinridge of his plan to abandon the army's position on the James River if necessary. Lee hoped to unite the army about Burkeville, Va., and maintain communications south and west with other Confederate forces. He asked that Gen. Joseph E. Johnston be ordered to report for duty, as he was not certain of the health of Gen. Beauregard, now commanding in the Carolinas. To his wife, Lee sounded more discouraged. He expected Grant "to move against us soon," and Sherman in South Carolina and Schofield in North Carolina "are both advancing & seem to have everything their own way. . . ." Nevertheless, he vowed "to fight to the last."

February 22, Wednesday

FALL OF WILMINGTON, NORTH CAROLINA.

JOSEPH E. JOHNSTON RESTORED TO COMMAND.

The last major port of the South was now lost. The Federals entered Wilmington without opposition. Gen. Bragg had withdrawn the last of his troops before daylight. With cooperation from the Weldon and Wilmington Railroad the Confederates got off their most important stores; much of the rest was destroyed. The two-pronged Union attack, a force operating on each side of the Cape Fear River, had been successful under over-all command of Maj. Gen. John M. Schofield. Union losses from Feb. 11 to the fall of the city had been about 200 total casualties, and they captured some 66 pieces of light and heavy artillery.

Official orders from Gen. Lee assigned Gen. Joseph E. Johnston to the Department of South Carolina, Georgia, and Florida and the Department of Tennessee and Georgia. He was ordered to concentrate available forces, including those slowly coming in from the West. Beauregard was ordered to report to Johnston for assignment. This was one of the principal acts of Lee's command of the Confederate armies, for Johnston had long been a subject of contention. It was well known that Davis disapproved of many of his previous actions, but the President was fully aware now that no talents could be neglected. Beauregard had been in ill health, but he felt aggrieved at being displaced, although he did cooperate fully with Johnston. The Confederates now had a formidable group of generals in the Carolinas: Johnston, Beauregard, Hardee, Hampton, Bragg. What they lacked were men.

Skirmishing near Camden and on the Wateree River marked Sherman's advance north of Columbia, S.C. Railroad destruction and desolation of much of the country continued as the Twentieth Corps reached Rocky Mount, S.C., on the Catawba River. Also, there were skirmishes at Smith's Creek and Northeast Ferry, N.C. It appeared that Sherman was moving on Charlotte, N.C., but actually that was a feint; the main drive aimed generally toward Goldsborough farther east. The usual Union scouts and expeditions continued, with one Feb. 22–24 from Pine Bluff to Bayou Meto, Ark., and another Feb. 22–25 from Barrancas to Milton, Fla. Fighting broke out at Douglas Landing near Pine Bluff, Ark.

Tennessee voters approved the new state constitution which included the abolition of slavery and abrogation of all Confederate debts. Meanwhile, Kentucky rejected the Thirteenth Amendment abolishing slavery.

Gen. Lee, worried over the disintegrating prospects of the Confederacy, wrote Gen. Longstreet of possible military strategy in view of Grant's expected movements. If forced to retreat through Amelia Court House to Burkeville, the Army of Northern Virginia could perhaps strike Grant or Sherman before they could unite.

February 23, Thursday

Union troops at Wilmington consolidated their gains, while Sherman's Twentieth Corps crossed the Catawba River in South Carolina, getting closer to the North Carolina line. There was a skirmish near Camden. But heavy rains now set in, causing delays until the twenty-sixth, although some movement continued. Federal troops carried out a small expedition from Yorktown to West Point, Va.; and other Union scouts moved until March 2 from Salem and Licking, Mo., to Spring River Mills, Ark.

Gen. Lee told President Davis that, unfortunately, troops in South Carolina were scattered "but by diligence & boldness they can be united." He informed Davis that he had put Johnston in command in the Carolinas and expressed confidence in him. He again mentioned the possibility of having to abandon the line of the James. Minnesota ratified the Thirteenth Amendment.

February 24, Friday

The heavy rain holding up Sherman's advance also hindered Confederate concentration, but there was a skirmish at Camden, S.C. In the Trans-Mississippi action included an affair at Switzler's Mill, Mo., and a Northern scout from Helena to Clarke's Store, Ark. Lee once more wrote the War Department concerned over the "alarming number of desertions that are now occurring in the army."

February 25, Saturday

Gen. Joseph E. Johnston assumed command of the Army of Tennessee, now in the Carolinas, and all troops in the Department of South Carolina,

Georgia, and Florida. Meanwhile, there was a skirmish at West's Cross Roads, and Federal troops occupied Camden on the Wateree River, S.C. Cavalry and other detached units were operating over a wide expanse of South Carolina. Gen. Johnston, at Charlotte, N.C., pointed out to Lee the difficulties of concentrating his Confederates and stressed that, including cavalry, militia, and units not recently heard from, he had between 20,000 and 25,000 men to oppose Sherman. "In my opinion, these troops form an army far too weak to cope with Sherman." He urged that his force join Bragg in North Carolina. In Kentucky a skirmish broke out at Piketon.

February 26, Sunday

Sherman's Twentieth Corps reached Hanging Rock, S.C., but other movements were slowed by the incessant rain. Skirmishing occurred at Lynch's Creek and near Stroud's Mill, S.C. A Federal expedition from Pine Bluff to McMilley's Farm, Ark., lasted three days.

February 27, Monday

The Shenandoah Valley was coming alive again. Sheridan's force of some ten thousand cavalry under immediate command of Wesley Merritt left Winchester, Va., heading south. Sheridan had orders from Grant to destroy the Virginia Central Railroad and James River Canal, take Lynchburg, and then either join Sherman or return to Winchester. Early, in front of him, had only two weakened brigades and a few pieces of artillery, his other troops being employed elsewhere. In the Carolina Campaign, minor skirmishing flared near Mount Elon and Cloud's House, S.C. The only other actions were near Sturgeon, Mo., and Spring Place, Ga.

February 28, Tuesday

Near Rocky Mount and Cheraw, S.C., skirmishes marked the inexorable march of Sherman. Meanwhile, Johnston tried to gather some sort of an army to oppose the Federals. On the whole, the Confederate military position by the end of February looked precarious indeed.

MARCH, 1865

The end was coming. It could not be otherwise; the only question was exactly how and when. Gen. Lee saw the inevitable in planning possible strategy if and when the line of the James at Petersburg and Richmond had to be abandoned. Even if Grant could be held off, there were insufficient troops to counter Sherman in the Carolinas. And now there was a threat from the coast at Wilmington, N.C. To the west, it was clear there soon would be action at Mobile and that Thomas' men would move against Forrest and Taylor in northern Alabama. In the Trans-Mississippi Kirby Smith still held some territory, by now of scant significance.

At the North attention turned increasingly to the political ramifications of any peace settlement. Abraham Lincoln would be inaugurated President for four more years on March 4. The split over reconstruction policy widened almost daily. Peace with new activities, new opportunities, westward expansion, business, farming, and all the enticements of a non-war world began to attract, with real possibility of being soon achieved. At least it was so in the North, while for the South there was growing dismay. Slavery was dead. What now would happen to the Negroes? Was there still any use of grasping at some vague straw whereby victory, or at least a settlement without submission, might be seized upon? Assuredly this would be a different spring.

March 1, Wednesday

The cavalry of Philip Sheridan, moving rapidly south in the Shenandoah Valley in pursuit of remnants of Jubal Early's force, skirmished near Mount Crawford, Va. Sherman pushed slowly but firmly ahead in South Carolina, with skirmishing at Wilson's Store. Federal troops moved out from Baton Rouge until March 12 to Jackson and Clinton, La.; another expedition operated from Gravelly Springs to Florence, Ala., until March 6. A skirmish occurred near Philadelphia, Tenn.

The Thirteenth Amendment was still a prime subject in the North. Wisconsin ratified the amendment, but New Jersey rejected the measure to abolish slavery constitutionally.

March 2, Thursday

ENGAGEMENT AT WAYNESBOROUGH, VIRGINIA.

The remains of Jubal Early's once powerful Confederate army were dispersed by Federal cavalry at Waynesborough, Va. George Armstrong Custer, of Sheridan's army, led the assault with nearly five thousand men. Confederate troops on the left gave way and could not be rallied. Custer defeated two Confederate infantry brigades and a small cavalry force of between one and two thousand. Early and some of his officers escaped but the Federals seized some two hundred wagons, seventeen flags, and well over a thousand men. Early told of "the mortification of seeing the greater part of my command being carried off as prisoners." Although not a major battle, Waynesborough was the last of that long line of names which made the war in the Shenandoah a legend spun by Jackson, Early, Sheridan, and others. Sheridan's cavalry now turned toward Charlottesville, Va., across the Blue Ridge. Early and his pitifully few followers found their way to Richmond.

Sherman's Twentieth Corps entered Chesterfield, S.C., after skirmishing nearby and at Thompson's Creek. Three days of minor operations took place about Athens, Tenn.

Gen. Lee wrote to Gen. Grant, proposing a meeting to try to arrive "at a satisfactory adjustment of the present unhappy difficulties by means of a military convention. . . ." Grant replied March 4 that he had no authority to hold such a conference, and that there had been some misunderstanding.

President Lincoln asked Grant about news from Sherman and the general answered that there was every indication he and his army were safe.

March 3, Friday

The Thirty-eighth Congress of the United States held its last regular session, finally adjourning about 8 A.M. March 4. President Lincoln and Cabinet members went to the Capitol in the evening to consider a flurry of last-minute bills. Most important was an act establishing a Bureau for the Relief of Freedmen and Refugees. The Freedmen's Bureau would supervise and manage all abandoned lands and have "control of all subjects relating to refugees and freedmen from rebel States." It would provide temporary subsistence, clothing, and fuel and also would assign land. Another act set up the Freedmen's Savings and Trust Company. Other measures dealt with Indian tribes, freedom for wives and children of Negro soldiers, railroad expansion, appropriations, and soldiers' affairs.

Federal troops entered Cheraw, S.C., after skirmishes at Thompson's Creek and Big Black Creek, as well as near Hornsborough and Blakeny's, S.C. The Confederates pulled back across the Pee Dee River and burned the bridges. Large amounts of ammunition and supplies were taken at Cheraw. Otherwise there was skirmishing near Tunnel Hill, Ga., and at Decatur, Ala. A Union reconnaissance March 3–5 probed from Cumberland Gap toward Jonesville, Va. Federal expeditions operated from Memphis into northern Mississippi until March 11, and until March 7 from Bloomfield into Dunklin County, Mo. Union operations against raiders about Warrenton, Bealeton Station, Sulphur Springs, Salem, and Centreville, Va., lasted until March 8. The Northern escort convoying prisoners from Waynesborough northward in the Shenandoah Valley was attacked several times until March 7. Meanwhile, Sheridan's unopposed troops occupied Charlottesville, Va., as they headed in the general direction of Petersburg.

President Davis wrote a Confederate congressman, "In spite of the timidity and faithlessness of many who should give tone to the popular feeling and hope to the popular heart, I am satisfied that it is in the power of the good man and true patriots of the country to reanimate the wearied spirit of our people. . . . I expect the hour of deliverance."

Lincoln wrote a message, signed by Stanton, directing Grant "to have no conference with General Lee unless it be for the capitulation of Gen. Lee's army . . . you are not to decide, discuss, or confer upon any political question. Such questions the President holds in his own hands; and will submit them to no military conferences or conventions. Meantime you are to press to the utmost, your military advantages." This signal order laid the policy for the generals in the surrenders to come, although the message was sent only to Grant and not to Sherman.

March 4, Saturday

WITH MALICE TOWARD NONE—SECOND INAUGURATION OF PRESIDENT LINCOLN.

"With malice toward none; with charity for all; with firmness in the right, as God gives us to see the right, let us strive on to finish the work we are in; to bind up the nation's wounds; to care for him who shall have borne the battle, and for his widow, and his orphan—to do all which may achieve and cherish a just, and a lasting peace, among ourselves, and with all nations." So President Abraham Lincoln concluded his brief, eloquent second inaugural Address in Washington. There was no discussion of policy or review of the past—just words of inspiration, hope, and understanding. "Neither party expected for the war, the magnitude, or the duration, which it has already attained. Neither anticipated that the *cause* of the conflict might cease with, or even before, the conflict itself should cease. Each looked for an easier triumph, and a result less fundamental and astounding. Both read the same Bible, and pray to the same God; and each invokes His aid against the other. . . . The prayers of both could not be answered; that of neither has been answered fully. . . . Fondly do we hope—fervently do we pray—that this mighty scourge of war may speedily pass away. . . ."

Before the inauguration, Vice-President Andrew Johnson of Tennessee took the oath succeeding Hannibal Hamlin. Ill, and having taken too much whisky as a medicine (as most historians now agree), the new Vice-President made a rambling, incoherent address which shocked many and was an inauspicious beginning to the day soon to be made great by the President's words of conciliation, which were to echo far beyond that hour. The Senate met in special session to consider appointments and other business. In the evening there was a public reception at which it was estimated the President shook hands with some six thousand persons. William G. Brownlow was elected governor of Tennessee by acclamation of unionists replacing now Vice-President Johnson.

In Richmond the Confederate Congress approved a revision of the design of the official Confederate national flag.

The fighting went on, with Federal troops of Sherman moving on an expedition until March 6 from Cheraw, S.C., to Florence. There was a skirmish at Phillips' Cross Roads, N.C., and one at East River Bridge, Fla. U.S. transport *Thorn* was destroyed by a torpedo in the Cape Fear River below Fort Anderson, N.C. The Navy was busy trying to clear coastal waters of torpedoes or mines.

March 5, Sunday

Sherman's victorious Federal army was in and around Cheraw, S.C., with only a minor skirmish nearby in the way of fighting. They were preparing now to enter North Carolina in the direction of Fayetteville. Federal troops operated from Fort Monroe to Fredericksburg, Va., until March 8; and Federals scouted from Waynesville to Rolla and Lebanon, Mo., until the twelfth. A skirmish broke out at Newport Bridge, Fla.

President Lincoln asked Hugh McCulloch, Comptroller of the Currency, to be Secretary of the Treasury. William Fessenden had resigned after being reelected to the Senate from Maine.

March 6, Monday

Gen. Joseph E. Johnston assumed command of all troops in the Department of North Carolina in addition to his other tasks. He now led all Confederate troops in the Carolinas and south of Petersburg, Va. Sherman's forces meanwhile crossed the Pee Dee and all the army was en route to Fayetteville, N.C. The only listed action occurred at Natural Bridge, Fla.

Lincoln appointed Hugh McCulloch of Indiana as Secretary of the Treasury in place of Fessenden. In the evening the gala inaugural ball was held at the Patent Office, capped by a sumptuous midnight supper.

March 7, Tuesday

In North Carolina it was found, after the capture of Wilmington, that New Berne was even a better supply base, and a large force under Jacob D. Cox was established there. Organization completed, troops had moved out some sixteen miles early in March in order to expedite railroad repair toward Goldsborough. It was learned that Confederates had reached Kinston on the Neuse River. The area of the Federal advance, located between the Neuse and the Trent, was known as the Dover Swamp in one section and Gum Swamp in another. To the west and south Sherman's army, plagued by miserable weather, entered North Carolina with skirmishing at Rockingham and Southwest Creek, southwest of Fayetteville. For most of the month there were operations about Licking, Mo., and March 7–15 a Yankee scout operated from Glasgow to the Perche Hills in the same state. Federals skirmished with Indians eighty miles west of Fort Larned, Kas. Fighting occurred at Elyton, Ala., and near Flint Hill, Va. A Union expedition moved until the twelfth from Jacksonville into Marion County, Fla.

President Lincoln was issuing a large number of orders these days permitting private persons owning or controlling products in "the insurrectionary states" to bring such products into national military lines and sell them to agents authorized by the Treasury.

March 8, Wednesday

BATTLE OF KINSTON, NORTH CAROLINA, THROUGH MARCH 10.

Joseph E. Johnston had been sending troops to Bragg in North Carolina as they came in from the West, most of them from the Army of Tennessee.

These troops were to confront the Federals moving out from New Berne. The Confederates under Bragg attacked men of Jacob D. Cox in the morning and a green Federal brigade broke. However, other units stiffened and repulsed further attacks in what was called the Battle of Kinston or Wise's Forks, N.C., which lasted through March 10. Actually it was intended to be a major move against the Federal invasion from the coast, but Confederate numbers were insufficient to sustain more than momentary drives.

Meanwhile, farther south, there was skirmishing at Love's or Blue's Bridge, S.C., as Sherman's army continued toward Fayetteville, N.C. Otherwise skirmishes flared in Jackson County, Tenn.; at Duguidsville, Va., in Sheridan's move to Petersburg; and on Poison Creek, Id. Terr., with Indians.

Sec. of the Interior John P. Usher submitted his resignation to President Lincoln.

The Confederate Senate, 9 to 8, approved use of Negroes as soldiers. Gen. E. Kirby Smith, Confederate commander in the Trans-Mississippi, wrote President Davis that he was aware of newspaper attacks on him and that, if the President desired, this letter might be regarded as an application to be relieved. Davis refused this, although he had long tried to obtain closer cooperation from Smith and troops across the Mississippi. On the other hand, Smith had his own problems, both military and administrative.

March 9, Thursday

Heavy skirmishing continued at Kinston or Wise's Forks, N.C., between Confederates of Bragg and Federals of Jacob Cox, under over-all command of Gen. Schofield. In Virginia Sheridan's cavalry occupied Columbia on its march from Winchester to Petersburg. Other action included a skirmish at Howard's Mills, Ky.; a Union scout from Fort Larned to Crooked Creek, Kas.; and a Union scout until March 15 from Cape Girardeau into Bollinger, Wayne, and Stoddard counties, Mo. Confederate cavalry under Wade Hampton and Joe Wheeler moved in to attack and completely surprised Federal cavalry encamped near Solemn Grove and Monroe's Cross Roads, S.C. Gen. Judson Kilpatrick was nearly captured in his bed, but managed to escape and rally his men, although he allegedly fled without his trousers. The Federals overcame the Southern advantage with their own attack and defeated Hampton. Kilpatrick was a very unpopular commander both with his own men, whom he pushed to extremes, and with the Confederates, due to his relentless destruction of their property. Later the affair was dubbed "the Battle of Kilpatrick's Pants," but was more officially known as Monroe's Cross Roads, S.C.

Without comment, President Lincoln accepted the resignation of Sec. of the Interior John P. Usher to take effect May 15. Asst. Sec. William Otto handled the department until Harlan assumed the post.

Gen. Lee, in a letter to Sec. of War Breckinridge, stated frankly that the military condition of the Confederacy "is full of peril and requires prompt action." Supplies were a very pressing problem and "Unless the men and animals can be subsisted, the army cannot be kept together, and our present lines must be abandoned." However, if the Army could be maintained in efficient condition, "I do not regard the abandonment of our present position as necessarily fatal to our success." He was not sanguine of the prospects from Johnston's scattered force in the Carolinas, but he concluded that everything depended on the disposition and feeling of the people, and things were no worse than the Confederates had been justified in expecting from the beginning. Vermont ratified the Thirteenth Amendment.

March 10, Friday

Sherman's army was nearing Fayetteville, N.C., with some difficulty from the wet weather, and after minor skirmishing with Confederate cavalry. Meanwhile, Johnston tried to gather his army together into one more potent force. The fighting at Kinston or Wise's Forks, N.C., ended after several serious Confederate attacks on Cox's defenders. At night Bragg retreated to Kinston and then to Goldsborough to join Johnston. At Monroe's Cross Roads, S.C., Kilpatrick's Federal cavalry rallied against Hampton and Wheeler, the leaders of the surprise attack of the night before. In Alabama there was a skirmish near Boyd's Station. In Virginia a two-day Union expedition moved from Suffolk to Murfree's Depot, N.C.; and in Arkansas there was a four-day Yankee scout, until the thirteenth, from Little Rock to Clear Lake.

Gen. Lee wrote President Davis that he advised putting the proposed law authorizing use of Negro troops into operation as soon as practicable, provided the President had approved it, and said, "I attach great importance to the result of the first experiment with these troops. . . ." But the Confederate Congress was still debating.

March 11, Saturday

FEDERAL TROOPS OCCUPY FAYETTEVILLE, NORTH CAROLINA.

The second step of Sherman's Carolina Campaign came to an end with the occupation of Fayetteville, N.C. The whole army pulled up to and around the important center in the southern part of North Carolina after some light skirmishing. Sherman reported, "Up to this period I had perfectly succeeded in interposing my superior army between the scattered parts of my enemy." But now he realized that Johnston would soon be in front of him. Sherman had sent messengers to Wilmington to make contact with Schofield, in order to report his presence and to arrange for cooperation with the force coming in from the sea, so as to form a two-pronged attack against Johnston.

In Virginia Sheridan's cavalry was at Goochland Court House after a skirmish while en route from the Shenandoah to Petersburg. From Fort Monroe Federal troops moved out on an expedition into Westmoreland County, Va., that lasted until March 13. In the West there was an affair near the Little Blue River, Mo., and a skirmish at Washington, Ark.

All those who had deserted from the military or naval forces of the United States and who returned within sixty days would be pardoned, President Lincoln proclaimed. If they did not return, they would forfeit their rights of citizenship. The Senate adjourned after a brief special session to deal primarily with appointments. Presidential secretary John Nicolay was confirmed as U.S. consul in Paris.

March 12, Sunday

Sherman's army remained at Fayetteville, N.C., until March 14. They undertook the usual destruction of machinery, buildings, and property they deemed of use to the enemy, including the former U. S. Arsenal and the machinery brought from the old Harper's Ferry Arsenal in 1861. In the morning a tug came up the Cape Fear River from Wilmington giving Sherman knowledge of the "outer world." Naval units later joined in. Sherman told the Federals at Wilmington and New Berne that he would move on March 15 for Goldsborough, after a feint toward Raleigh. Sherman ordered the coastal troops to march straight for Goldsborough.

Elsewhere, there were skirmishes near Peach Grove, Va., and at Morganza Bend, La.; and an affair near Lone Jack, Mo. Federal operations included an expedition from Fort Churchill to Pyramid and Walker's lakes, Nev.; a scout in Loudoun County, Va., until the fourteenth; a scout until March 23 from Lewisburg into Yell and Searcy counties, Ark.; and a three-day expedition from Vicksburg, Miss., to Grand Gulf and vicinity.

March 13, Monday

CONFEDERACY APPROVES NEGRO SOLDIERS.

The Confederate Congress, after much delay and debate, finally sent to the President a measure calling for putting Negroes in the Army and President Davis immediately signed it. The President was authorized to call upon owners to volunteer their slaves, and it was generally understood, although not specifically stated, that any slaves who fought for the Confederacy would be made free by action of the states. The law was too late to be of much value, but a few troops were raised and training began. Late in March Negro soldiers were seen in Richmond.

President Davis also sent a message to Congress which brought instant and stern opposition. He had requested Congress to stay in session as there was a need for "further and more energetic legislation." He pointed up the perils facing the Confederacy but maintained that triumph was still possible through prompt decisions, including those of Congress. Davis accused Congress of retarding action. He suggested means of obtaining men and supplies, changes in the impressment law, stronger revenue acts, implementing recruiting laws—such as abolishing all class exemptions, a general militia law, and suspension of the writ of habeas corpus. As an indictment of Congress the message may well have been necessary, but it only alienated many members of both Houses.

There was a mild skirmish down at Fayetteville, N.C., where Sherman's army was recuperating from its march. Skirmishing also erupted at Beaver Dam Station, Va., involving Sheridan's cavalry; near Charles Town, W. Va.; and near Dalton, Ga. Union naval forces and troops were mopping up along the Rappahannock in Virginia.

March 14, Tuesday

The Federal troops of Gen. Cox occupied Kinston, N.C., in their advance inland from the sea toward Goldsborough and a junction with the northward-moving Sherman. At Fayetteville Sherman's men carried out reconnaissance to the Black River and Silver Run Creek, N.C. In Virginia Sheridan's cavalry fought a skirmish at the South Anna Bridge as they moved steadily on toward junction with Grant. In the Shenandoah there was a skirmish at Woodstock as Confederates harassed Federal outposts. In West Virginia Federals scouted against enemy pockets of resistance until the sixteenth from Philippi to Corrick's Ford and until the seventeenth from New Creek to Moorefield. There was, in addition, a small skirmish near Dalton, Ga.

Gen. Lee told his President that Johnston was uniting his army at Raleigh and although it was inferior in numbers and lacking "tone," the plan was to "strike the enemy in detail." Lee added, "The greatest calamity that can befall us is the destruction of our armies. If they can be maintained, we may recover from our reverses, but if lost we have no resource."

March 15, Wednesday

Sherman was on the move again. From Fayetteville, N.C., and the Cape Fear River the Federal troops moved out en masse with Kilpatrick's cavalry in front of Slocum's left wing. The cavalry skirmished heavily with rear guards of the enemy near Smith's Mills on the Black River and at South River, evidence of stiffening resistance. Sheridan meanwhile moved on in Virginia and was now at Hanover Court House and near Ashland. Skirmishing broke out at Boyd's Station and Stevenson's Gap, Ala., and a Federal scout operated against Indians from Fort Sumner, N. Mex. Terr., until March 21.

March 16, Thursday

BATTLE OF AVERASBOROUGH, NORTH CAROLINA.

Four miles south of Averasborough, N.C., the advancing columns of

Sherman's left, under Slocum, attacked Hardee's force blocking the route toward Goldsborough. Slocum turned Hardee's right and the Confederates pulled back, throwing off other attacks. In late afternoon Hardee was told of Federals crossing the Black River below to turn his left further. During the stormy night Hardee gave up the position and marched toward Smithfield. There were 95 Federals killed and 533 wounded, with 54 missing, for 682. Total Confederate losses are put at 865. While hardly a major battle, Averasborough, or Taylor's Hole, showed that the Confederates were once more actively opposing the Union invasion, albeit their army was small and far from ready.

In the Shenandoah Federals scouted from near Winchester to Front Royal, Va., and from Summit Point through Kabletown and Myerstown to Shenandoah Ferry, W. Va. Until the eighteenth a Union naval expedition operated up the Rappahannock and destroyed a supply base at Montrose, Va.

The Confederate Congress, piqued at Davis' recent message, put out a statement denying his charge of insufficient congressional action. "Nothing is more desirable than concord and cordial cooperation between all departments of Government. Hence your committee regret that the Executive deemed it necessary to transmit to Congress a message so well calculated to excite discord and dissension. . . ."

March 17, Friday

As an aftermath to Averasborough there was skirmishing in the area and at Falling Creek, N.C. A new theater of operations was about to open. Federal Maj. Gen. E. R. S. Canby began maneuvering his some 32,000 men against Mobile, Ala. One Federal force moved from Pensacola and another from the area of Mobile Point up the east side of Mobile Bay. About 2800 Confederates under Brig. Gen. R. L. Gibson defended the city. Union scouting continued in the Shenandoah Valley from Winchester to Edenburg, Va. There was also a Northern expedition until March 20 from Pine Bluff to Bass' Plantation, Ark.

Concerned over increasing sales of arms and munitions to Indians, President Lincoln directed that all persons detected in this commerce should be arrested and tried by military court-martial. In a speech to the 140th Indiana Regiment, Lincoln said, "Whenever [I] hear any one, arguing for slavery I feel a strong impulse to see it tried on him personally."

March 18, Saturday

CONFEDERATE CONGRESS ADJOURNS.

The Confederate Congress ended its session, which proved to be its last, in a fit of contention with President Davis. Many essential war measures were left unpassed, and for the last few days its main business had been to argue with the President over whether he or Congress had delayed action and was responsible for some of the difficulties facing the Confederacy. It was probably symptomatic of the need to blame someone for the fast-approaching and now nearly obvious disaster.

Johnston was attempting to concentrate against the Federals advancing toward Goldsborough, N.C. In the morning the left wing of two Northern corps under H. W. Slocum stood just south of Bentonville. Hampton's Confederate cavalry kept Johnston posted. Howard's right wing of Sherman's army was to the south and east. The Confederates had about 20,000 troops, to 30,000 for Slocum and Kilpatrick. Overburdened with generals, Johnston's army was makeshift in organization. However, he had to try to strike one column of the Federals at a time. He did not stand a chance against Sherman's full army, which together with troops marching in from Wilmington totaled about 100,000. The Battle of Bentonville really opened when Hampton's cavalry skirmished along Mingo Creek, at Bushy Swamp, and near Benton's Cross Roads, holding off the Union advance units of Slocum. During the night Johnston and Hampton conferred on the attack for the next day.

Elsewhere, skirmishes occurred at Livingston, Tenn.; near Dranesville, Va.; and on the Amite River, La. A Union expedition from Fort Gibson to Little River and Hillabee, Indian Terr., operated for the rest of March. At Mobile Bay some seventeen hundred Federal troops advanced from Dauphin Island on the west side of the bay to deceive the enemy as to which side would be attacked. The main effort was to be on the east. (The Yankees on the west side withdrew on March 20, their mission of deception accomplished.)

March 19, Sunday

BATTLE OF BENTONVILLE, NORTH CAROLINA.

Gen. Sherman did not expect an attack and departed Slocum's left wing during the morning to go to Howard on the right. But the Federals had only just resumed their march when they ran into the waiting Confederates south of Bentonville, S.C. At first they did not seem to be a serious obstacle to Slocum, but by afternoon he was being pressed. However, some mix-up occurred delaying the Confederates. When the drive was made the Union troops were solidly entrenched. Hardee, A. P. Stewart, and D. H. Hill led their men. At first the Confederates crashed through the Federal breastworks, partially demoralizing one section of the Northern force and routing the left. Troops of Jefferson C. Davis, however, withstood the continuing Southern attack, and other Federal units came in to stem the advance. The battle lasted until after dark. Three main Confederate assaults were beaten off. In the evening the Confederates pulled back to their starting points and both sides spent the night preparing positions.

Meanwhile, some twenty miles to the east, Howard's Union right wing hurried toward Bentonville. Over on the Neuse, Schofield's advancing forces skirmished at the Neuse River Bridge near Goldsborough and near Cox's Bridge.

The cavalry of Phil Sheridan reached White House on the Pamunkey after wrecking the Virginia Central Railroad and the James River Canal in its successful march from Winchester to join Grant's army near Petersburg. Skirmishing at Celina, Tenn., and Welaka and Saunders, Fla., completed the day.

March 20, Monday

Federal reinforcements from Howard's right wing arrived by daybreak at Bentonville, N.C., to relieve Slocum's left wing. Wheeler's Southern cavalry resisted the new advance. Some shifting of Confederate positions south of Bentonville was necessary and by late afternoon Sherman's entire army was united in front and on both flanks of Johnston's position. There was no heavy fighting but considerable skirmishing occurred.

George Stoneman and some four thousand cavalry from Thomas' army in Tennessee left Jonesborough, Tenn., to support Sherman in the Carolinas by carrying out wrecking operations. The Federal column cooperating with the main attack on Mobile moved toward that city from Pensacola, Fla. There were skirmishes in North Carolina near Falling Creek; in Georgia at Ringgold; in Arkansas at Talbot's Ferry. Federal activities included a three-day expedition from Brashear City to Bayou Pigeon, La.; a scout from Lexington, Mo.; scouting to Kabletown, Myerstown, and Myers' Ford, W. Va.; a two-day scout from Winchester to Edenburg, Va.; and yet another, lasting until the twenty-fifth, from Harper's Ferry into Loudoun County, Va.

March 21, Tuesday

BATTLE OF BENTONVILLE CONCLUDED.

Sherman's troops kept up the pressure on Johnston at Bentonville, N.C. The men of Maj. Gen. J. A. Mower moved from the far Union right around the Confederate left late in the afternoon and threatened the Mill Creek Bridge on Johnston's retreat line. Counterattacks arrested the menace after considerable fighting. This ended the Battle of Bentonville, the last significant Confederate effort to halt Sherman's advance. During the night Johnston ordered evacuation after reports that Schofield had taken Goldsborough. Casualties for the North totaled over 1500 and for the Confederates over 2600, many of whom were captured. Even if Slocum had been beaten, the Carolina Campaign could scarcely have had any other outcome. In truth, with nearly 100,000 Federals in North Carolina, at Goldsborough and in Sherman's main army, there was little his opponent could have done. Otherwise the day saw only the start of a three-day Federal scout from Pine Bluff to Monticello, Ark.

President Davis wrote Gen. Lee, concurring with him that Mobile should be held and "all the recent indications are that the purpose of the enemy is to cut off all communication with Richmond. . . ."

March 22, Wednesday

Yet another Federal offensive began, adding to those in North Carolina, at Mobile, and the continuing siege at Petersburg. The Union forces of James Harrison Wilson struck from the Tennessee River toward Selma, Ala., one of the few centers left to the South. The raid was to be in conjunction with the Federal attack on Mobile to the south of Selma. In North Carolina skirmishing flared at Mill Creek, Hannah's Creek, and Black Creek. Fighting also occurred near Patterson's Creek Station, W. Va.; at Celina, Tenn.; and Stephenson's Mills, Mo. At Bentonville Sherman checked his brief follow-up of the retreating Confederates of Johnston. He now issued orders to concentrate about Goldsborough.

March 23, Thursday

Sherman and Schofield joined at Goldsborough, practically on the schedule set by Sherman. The Federal force of some 90,000 to 100,000 men now dominated North Carolina. Immediately work began to reequip the army after its long marches. The Carolina Campaign was all but over—a triumphant journey. It was true there had been no opposition of any size until the last few days. Johnston placed what force he had on the two roads he thought Sherman would take toward Virginia, through Raleigh or through Weldon. This position would also make junction with the Army of Northern Virginia practicable should Lee retire from Petersburg. The Confederates now had a desperately needed breathing spell to recuperate. There was another skirmish at Cox's Bridge on the Neuse River, N.C. On other fronts skirmishing broke out near Dannelly's Mills, Ala., and a Union scout probed for two days from Donaldsonville to Bayou Goula, La.

President Lincoln left Washington for City Point, Va., and Grant's headquarters, accompanied by Mrs. Lincoln and Tad. It was to be a combination vacation and conference with Grant concerning what all could see would be a determined and concentrated effort to end the war.

March 24, Friday

For the Confederates it was a day and night of preparation. John B. Gordon had been assigned to lead an attack the next day at Fort Stedman on the Federal right at Petersburg. If the siege line could be broken here the indispensable supply line to City Point might be cut. Then perhaps Grant would shorten his lines and Lee could assist Johnston. At least a successful assault would help Lee in his possible retreat from Richmond.

Near Moccasin Creek, N.C., there was a skirmish; near Dannelly's Mills and near Evergreen, Ala., affairs; near Rolla, Mo., an affair; and a Union scout from Bayou Boeuf to Bayou Chemise, La.

The vessel containing President Lincoln and his party arrived at Fort Monroe. Confederate ironclad raider *Stonewall* put out from Ferrol, Spain. Two Union wooden frigates refused to engage *Stonewall*.

March 25, Saturday

CONFEDERATES ATTACK FORT STEDMAN AT PETERSBURG, VIRGINIA.
SIEGE OF MOBILE, ALABAMA, BEGINS.

Southerners who said they were deserters showed up about 3 A.M. at the Union lines near Fort Stedman on the east side of the Petersburg, Va., siege fortifications. In fact, they were advance men aiming at sabotage when, an hour later, Maj. Gen. John B. Gordon launched his massive attack at Fort Stedman and surrounding entrenchments. The Confederates quickly overwhelmed the opposition and rushed into the fort, completely surprising the Federal garrison. Several batteries and other trenches were taken until about three fourths of a mile of Union position was in Southern hands. Small columns pressed on toward City Point and the Federal supply railroad, one of the first specially built military railroads in history. But, like so many Confederate attacks late in the war, it lost momentum and there was not the strength to exploit and maintain the momentary advantage. Union troops rallied, changed position, and forced the attackers back to Fort Stedman. About seven-thirty a Federal division assaulted the fort and Gordon withdrew, although not all the Confederates could get back to their own lines. By seven forty-five the Federal line was restored and the entire attack defeated. It had never been more than a forlorn hope, and now little remained except disheartening withdrawal from Petersburg and Richmond. Gen. Lee rode back from the field, careworn and dejected. Against less than 1500 Federal casualties, Lee lost some 4000, many of them prisoners.

After a trying march due to drenching rains, the Federal troops neared Spanish Fort and the fortifications of Mobile, Ala., on the east side of the bay. By March 27 the investment would be complete. Confederate Brig. Gen. R. L. Gibson tried to organize his 2800 men to oppose Canby's 32,000. Despite strong earthworks around the city it was manifestly impossible for the South to hold out long without help.

Otherwise there was the usual roll of skirmishes—on the Deer Park Road, Ala.; at Cotton Creek, Mitchell's or Canoe Creek, and Escambia River, Fla.; Brawley Forks, Tenn.; Glasgow, Ky.; Watkins House and Fort Fisher, Va. Two Federal expeditions operated from Brashear City, one to Indian Bend, La., and the other to Oyster Bayou, La.

President Lincoln visited Gen. Grant at City Point, Va. Lincoln then took the military railroad to the Petersburg lines, where he rode horseback over part of the Fort Stedman battlefield.

March 26, Sunday

The cavalry command of Phil Sheridan crossed the James River and headed toward a junction with Grant at Petersburg, Va. This would give Grant an even larger force with which to extend the lines and thus further thin out Lee's already numerically inadequate defenders. Lee wrote Davis of the failure at Fort Stedman the day before: "I fear now it will be impossible to prevent a junction between Grant and Sherman, nor do I deem it prudent that this army should maintain its position until the latter shall approach too near." Lee was preparing now to give up Petersburg and Richmond and pull back westward to attempt to join Johnston in North Carolina.

On the Mobile, Ala., front skirmishing erupted as Union troops pushed in nearer Spanish Fort. Other skirmishing occurred at Muddy Creek, Ala., and Federals entered Pollard. In Kentucky there was a skirmish in Bath County and a four-day Union expedition in Louisiana from Bonnet Carré to the Amite River.

Mr. Lincoln reviewed troops and watched Sheridan's men cross the James while on his junket to the main fighting front at Petersburg. Grant conferred with Sheridan and prepared instructions for the start of the coming campaign.

March 27, Monday

LINCOLN, GRANT, AND SHERMAN MEET.

Aboard *River Queen* at City Point, Va., President Lincoln conferred with Genls. Grant and Sherman and Adm. Porter. Sherman had come up from Goldsborough, N.C., where his army was concentrated. The first day's talk, largely social, included an account of Sherman's campaign. A three-day Union scout moved from Winchester to Woodstock, Va. In the Mobile Campaign one Federal column reached Canoe Station, Ala.

March 28, Tuesday

Shifting of troops by the Federals at Petersburg marked preparations for the move to begin March 29. Meanwhile, a small expedition operated until April 11 from Deep Bottom, Va., to Weldon, N.C. Skirmishing took place near Snow Hill, N.C.; at Boone, N.C., involving Stoneman's Union cavalry column moving in from the west; near Elyton, Ala., with Wilson's cavalry moving into the northern part of the state; and at Germantown, Tenn. Until March 30 a Federal expedition operated from Fort Pike, La., to Bay St. Louis, Miss.

Genls. Grant and Sherman, along with Adm. Porter, continued their conversations with President Lincoln on *River Queen* off City Point, Va. The generals detailed their plans and pointed out that one more major campaign would be needed. Sherman later said the President told them he was ready, once the Rebels laid down their weapons and resumed civil pursuits, to grant them all their rights as citizens of the United States. Just how specifically Lincoln revealed his reconstruction plans is hard to say. Sherman, however, claimed these talks were the basis for his later terms with Gen. Johnston, which were turned down by the Federal government and President Johnson.

In a letter to his daughter, Gen. Lee said, "Genl Grant is evidently preparing for something & is marshalling & preparing his troops for some movement, which is not yet disclosed. . . ."

March 29, Wednesday

APPOMATTOX CAMPAIGN BEGINS.

The Northern Army of the Potomac and the Army of the James, together numbering about 125,000, were on the move against Lee at Petersburg and Richmond. On the lengthy, extended line from north of the James to well west of Petersburg, Lee could muster less than half the Yankee manpower. Lee had been collecting matériel and food and waiting for passable roads before pulling out in early April to join Johnston. Now the Federals threatened him on his weakly held right flank and might well cut off his retreat route westward. Lee sent George E. Pickett and Fitzhugh Lee to the right, near the Five Forks area, where he expected the Federal flanking movement. There was an engagement at Lewis' Farm near Gravelly Run, and skirmishing at the junction of the Quaker and Boydton roads and on the Vaughan Road near Hatcher's Run. Rain in the evening slowed the Union advance. Sheridan's cavalry rode out westward toward Dinwiddie Court House south of Five Forks while two supporting Federal infantry corps, the Fifth under G. K. Warren and the Second under A. A. Humphreys, marched to aid Sheridan. The intent was to force Lee out of his entrenched lines. The sharpest fighting occurred near the junction of the Boydton and Quaker roads, where Warren's men forced the enemy back. The day's movements plainly indicated Grant's strategy and the danger to the Confederates in the siege lines.

Stoneman's Federal cavalry fought a skirmish at Wilkesborough, N.C., in their move from east Tennessee. The Yankees continued to converge on Mobile defense lines. U.S.S. *Osage* was sunk by a torpedo in the Blakely River, Ala. There was skirmishing in southwest Missouri and a Union scout until April 2 from Waynesville, Mo. Other skirmishing occurred at Blackwater River, Ky., and Mosely Hall, N.C. A Federal scout operated from Stephenson's Depot, Va., to Smithfield, W. Va.

Sherman had gone back to Goldsborough, N.C. Lincoln continued on at City Point, inquiring of Grant and others how things looked as to the new movement. Gen. Lee kept Richmond posted on the enemy's movements at Petersburg.

March 30, Thursday

Pelting rains bogged down most of the Federal advance on the Petersburg front, where Sheridan, at Dinwiddie Court House, was ready to move with infantry assistance against the Confederate right flank. There was skirmishing, however, on the line of Hatcher's Run and Gravelly Run, and near Five Forks. Humphreys did continue the advance of his Second Corps, pressing up close to the enemy entrenchments along Hatcher's Run, while Warren's Fifth Corps moved ahead to occupy a line toward Gravelly Run. Meanwhile, the Confederates of Pickett and Fitzhugh Lee consolidated near Five Forks, where Fitzhugh Lee repulsed Merritt of Sheridan's cavalry. The Confederate moves, of course, sorely weakened Lee on other parts of his line. Reconnaissance near Petersburg by Federals ascertained it was practicable for the Federals to assault.

Union cavalry of James Harrison Wilson in northern Alabama skirmished at Montevallo with troops under Forrest's general command. There also was an affair near Patterson's Creek, W. Va., and a four-day Federal expedition from Baton Rouge, La., to Clinton and the Comite River.

President Lincoln at City Point said he should be back in Washington "and yet I dislike to leave without seeing nearer to the end of General Grant's present movement." In Richmond President Davis wrote a friend that "Faction has done much to cloud our prospects and impair my power to serve the country."

March 31, Friday

WHITE OAK ROAD AND DINWIDDIE COURT HOUSE, VIRGINIA.

The heavy rain ended in the morning and the action began. Somewhat over ten thousand Confederates were arrayed against more than fifty thousand Federals on the western part of the Petersburg line. Sheridan pressed forward from Dinwiddie Court House with a portion of his troops. Confederates drove them back toward the main body at the Court House, a tactical defeat for the Union. However, during the night Pickett realized Sheridan and Warren's Fifth Corps were too strong, so he pulled back toward Five Forks. Warren's Fifth Corps also had its difficulties on the White Oak Road and there was fighting at Hatcher's Run or Boydton Road, and Crow's House. Warren's task was to aid Sheridan against Pickett; Humphreys' Second Corps was also ordered in support. Warren's men, however, were able to repulse and turn back the enemy. It was the beginning of the operations that were to end only with the surrender of Lee, and later became the subject of many acrimonious controversies among Union generals and historians. The comparatively small actions of March 31 laid the scene for the first day of April.

In Alabama the Northern cavalry of James Harrison Wilson wrecked iron furnaces and collieries around Montevallo, Ala. Skirmishing occurred nearby and at Six Mile Creek. Confederate opposition was too weak to prevent widespread destruction. At Mobile Federals were occupying nearby towns and drawing in their siege lines. Skirmishes broke out at Magnolia, Tenn., and at Gulley's and Hookertown, N.C. About Agua Fria, N. Mex. Terr., there were two days of minor operations.

APRIL, 1865

It was full spring now of the new year. While it was a time for growth and planting, it was also a time for more bloodshed on the battlefields. The Confederacy had little left except spirit, and even that was fading rapidly. Nearly 1,000,000 men of the North were in arms against possibly 100,000 effective men in the South. The land of the Confederacy had shrunk to isolated sections; its industrial and commercial potential was in a shambles. Victory for the Union was accomplished in all but the final acts. War was no longer the main preoccupation of those in power or of thoughtful citizens. How would the pieces of society fit back together? Of course, the reelected President of the United States had four years to serve and he favored what were considered by some to be moderate policies, yet he had demanded at the same time what amounted to unconditional surrender. The questions were many as Gen. Grant's combined armies struck the enfeebled Army of Northern Virginia, as Sherman towered over Johnston in North Carolina, and as final mop-up operations went on in northern Alabama and at Mobile.

April 1, Saturday
BATTLE OF FIVE FORKS, VIRGINIA.
"Hold Five Forks at all hazards," Gen. Lee told George E. Pickett in the morning. If the far right flank of the Confederate line at Petersburg should fall, the entire retreat route of the Army of Northern Virginia from Petersburg and Richmond would be threatened. As it was, Lee had necessarily attenuated his defenses to the ultimate danger point to send something over ten thousand to the right. Grant's strategy was obvious: continue to move to the left and westward, forcing the Confederates to weaken their positions. With Sheridan and an infantry corps freed from the siege lines, he had more than sufficient manpower to do so. Pickett's men dug in, singing "Annie Laurie" and "Dixie." Late in the afternoon Sheridan's cavalry and Warren's Fifth Corps infantry attacked at Five Forks. Since the preceding day many conflicting messages had passed among Federal com-

manders, with charges of delay laid to Warren. Likewise, on the Confederate side, there were reports that leading generals were having a fish fry (often termed a shad bake) just before the battle, causing their absence from close control. As the dismounted cavalry of Sheridan attacked in front, Warren's corps got on the left flank of the enemy and both forces successfully crushed the Confederate defenders. During the height of the battle, Sheridan, with permission from Grant, removed Gen. Warren as commander of the Fifth Corps. Sheridan said Warren had been slow, had disobeyed orders, and had not cooperated properly in the attack. Warren eventually was cleared of most of the charges against him, but the stigma of removal from command ruined his future. Five Forks split the remnant of Pickett from the main Confederate army.

The Federals had not only crumpled Lee's right and seized the Five Forks area, but they almost encircled Petersburg south of the Appomattox River. Now Grant was close to the vital South Side Railroad, an important Confederate supply and retreat route. Before he had news of the battle, Lee advised Davis of the seriousness of the Federal threat and observed that they should be prepared to evacuate their position in front of Richmond and Petersburg to save the army. The figures are disputed, but it appears that Federals suffered about 1000 casualties and captured not fewer than 4500 Confederates of the entire Southern force of a bit over 10,000. The Federals had some 53,000 men available, but Sheridan's 10,000 cavalry and Warren's 17,000 foot soldiers did most of the fighting. Humphreys' large Second Corps was involved in skirmishing on White Oak Road.

In North Carolina, while Sherman reorganized his army, a skirmish occurred at Snow Hill. In northern Alabama James H. Wilson's Federals continued their successful advance toward Selma against Forrest, with skirmishes near Randolph, Maplesville, Plantersville, Ebenezer Church, Centerville, and Trion. Forrest had to pull back his scattered units and attempt to concentrate at Selma. Elsewhere, action included a skirmish at White Oak Creek, Tenn.; a Union expedition from Dalton to Spring Place and the Coosawattee River, Ga.; scouts during most of April from Licking, Mo.; operations by Federals against Indians west of Fort Laramie, Dak. Terr., until May 27; and a Northern scout until April 4 from Pine Bluff to Bayou Bartholomew, Ark. On the Mobile front skirmishing flared near Blakely, Ala.

A distraught President Davis wrote Gen. Lee that he had "been laboring without much progress to advance the raising of negro troops," and he admitted, "The distrust is increasing and embarrasses in many ways." At City Point President Lincoln was serving mainly as an observer and was forwarding messages to Washington on the progress of the Petersburg fighting. C.S.S. *Shenandoah* put in to Lea Harbor, Ascension Island (now

Ponape Island, Eastern Carolines), in the Pacific and captured four Northern whalers. Union tinclad *Rodolph* was sunk by a torpedo in the Blakely River, Ala.

April 2, Sunday

CONFEDERATE GOVERNMENT EVACUATES RICHMOND.

FEDERALS CAPTURE PETERSBURG LINES.

SELMA, ALABAMA, TAKEN BY FEDERALS.

"I think it is absolutely necessary that we should abandon our position tonight . . ." telegraphed Gen. Lee at Petersburg to President Davis in Richmond. The Confederate capital of Richmond was doomed, and with it the whole Petersburg-Richmond front. At four-forty in the morning, Federals advanced under a heavy fog along the Petersburg lines. By 7 A.M. the drive was fully under way and was everywhere successful. Horatio Wright's Sixth Corps dashed through the defenses to the South Side Railroad. Along Hatcher's Run the Confederate lines vanished. West of Boydton Plank Road, while attempting to rally his men, Lieut. Gen. A. P. Hill was killed. Only two forts, Gregg and Baldwin, held out at noon on the western part of the Petersburg lines, and retreat was possible only by crossing the Appomattox River.

Lee determined to hold inner fortifications until night enabled him to withdraw. The delaying action at Forts Gregg and Baldwin did buy enough time for new lines to be formed. In a few places the Confederates stiffened in the afternoon but it was obvious they had to pull out. Orders were issued in midafternoon to evacuate Petersburg and for the defenders north of the James River to retreat through Richmond and join the remainder of the Army of Northern Virginia. The retreat soon began, with Amelia Court House, some forty miles west, the concentration point. Federals may have numbered over 63,000 engaged with 625 killed, 3189 wounded, and 326 missing for 4140 total. Possibly 18,500 Confederates were engaged; losses are unknown. During the day Lee told an officer, "This is a sad business, colonel. It has happened as I told them in Richmond it would happen. The line has been stretched until it is broken."

For the Federals it had been a well-organized attack to reap the reward of Five Forks and the long months of siege and extending of the lines. Some called the Union charge the deathblow to Lee's army, and a reporter wrote, "With that Sunday's sun the hope of the Rebels set, never to rise again."

Also in the Petersburg area there was an engagement at Sutherland's Station on the South Side Railroad, skirmishing at Gravelly Ford on Hatcher's Run and action at Scott's Cross Roads.

In Richmond a messenger had entered St. Paul's Church as the minister gave the prayer for the President of the Confederate States. Mr. Davis left quietly and went to his office to learn of the disaster to Lee's army.

Mrs. Davis and the children had already left the capital. By 11 P.M. Davis and most of the Cabinet departed on a special train for Danville, Va. Scenes in Richmond were heart-rending as the news spread. Many wept openly and then prepared either to stay and face the enemy or to attempt evacuation. Rail stations were jammed and the streets filled with many of the local citizens and refugees crowding the city. Soon the unruly began looting. Inmates broke from the state prison and the Local Defense Brigade was unable to keep order. Government records were either sent away or burned. Cotton, tobacco, and military stores were set afire, and the fires soon raged out of control; others were set by looters. Shells from the arsenals roared upward as the main section of Richmond became a great inferno. Many business houses, hotels, and residences, as well as factories and warehouses, were destroyed. In the James Confederate gunboats exploded, shaking the city anew. After four years and many threats, Richmond at last was falling. On the train going into the night toward Danville, "Silence reigned over the fugitives." But the Confederate government still existed in transit; the war was not quite over.

At Selma, Ala., some 12,000 Federal troops of James Harrison Wilson had reached near the city after besting Forrest's men in various small engagements for several days. Forrest attempted to bring his about 7000 to 8000 men into Selma, but the investment by Wilson prevented it. Department commander Richard Taylor barely escaped as he left to gather men for Forrest. Near evening Wilson's men attacked the thinly held works of Selma. The charge was completely successful and confusion reigned. Forrest and a few of his officers and men escaped. The Federals captured 2700 prisoners, about 40 guns, large stores of supplies, plus the important manufacturing center of Selma. The Union victors, with light casualties, now turned toward Montgomery, Ala. At last Forrest, the invincible, had been beaten, but assuredly his force was no longer what it had been in numbers or in spirit.

On the Mobile front, the siege of Fort Blakely began, while that of Spanish Fort continued. It was only a question of time before overwhelming Federal numbers would force the capitulation of Mobile itself. But by now it was too late for the campaign to be of much strategic importance.

Elsewhere, skirmishing broke out near Goldsborough, N.C., and Van Buren and Hickory Station, Ark. Two Union expeditions in Louisiana lasted several days, one from Thibodeaux, Bayou City, and Brashear City to Lake Verret and The Park, and the other from The Hermitage to French Settlement.

President Lincoln went to the front at Petersburg and saw some of the fighting from a distance, meanwhile keeping Washington informed as to the progress of Grant's armies. At eight-fifteen in the evening he telegraphed Grant, "Allow me to tender to you, and all with you, the nations grateful thanks for this additional, and magnificent success."

April 3, Monday

UNION TROOPS OCCUPY RICHMOND AND PETERSBURG, VIRGINIA.

"I saw them unfurl a tiny flag, and I sank on my knees, and the bitter, bitter tears came in a torrent." So wrote Mrs. Mary A. Fontaine of Richmond as Federal cavalry dashed into the city in the morning. The first flag, a small guidon, was raised by Maj. Atherton H. Stevens, Jr., of Massachusetts over the State House, erstwhile Capitol of the Confederacy. As the people, many of them jubilant Negroes, swarmed into the streets, much of the city still in flames, more Federals arrived. "Then the Cavalry thundered at a furious gallop. . . . Then the infantry came playing 'The Girl I left Behind me,' that dear old air that we heard our brave men so often play; then the negro troops playing 'Dixie'." An eyewitness wrote that the former slaves in Richmond were "completely crazed, they danced and shouted, men hugged each other, and women kissed." Looting continued, with one old woman seen rolling a huge sofa in the street. Dozens of bands competed with each other. "Oh! it was too awful to remember, if it were possible to be erased, but that can not be." A reporter wrote, "This town is the Rebellion; it is all we have directly striven for." Now this was suddenly changed. Maj. Gen. Godfrey Weitzel, with troops from the Army of the James, commanded the occupation. At eight-fifteen, in the City Hall, he received the surrender. Union troops immediately set about to restore order and subdue the fires. By midafternoon progress had been made as Richmond slowly quieted down.

Petersburg, too, was occupied by Federal troops, but destruction there was largely averted. At a private home President Lincoln and Gen. Grant conferred. Mr. Lincoln reviewed the troops passing through the city, which had undergone more than nine months of siege.

Meanwhile, Lee's army struggled westward by various roads in the general direction of Amelia Court House. Grant pursued—not in the rear, but on a somewhat parallel route heading toward Burkeville to intercept Lee and keep him from junction with Johnston in North Carolina. Sheridan's troops had pressed the retiring Confederates on the Namozine Church Road and fought a skirmish.

The train from Richmond to Danville moved slowly the night of April 2–3 due to roadbed difficulties. But by midafternoon the cars bearing President Davis, most of the Cabinet, and many records arrived in Danville, Va., where citizens had hurriedly prepared to receive their guests. Headquarters for the President were established in the home of Maj. W. T. Sutherlin. Davis declared that he was not abandoning the cause.

At Northport, near Tuscaloosa, Ala., an action broke out between the cavalry of Wilson and Forrest. In addition, there were skirmishes at Mount Pleasant, Tenn.; Hillsville, Va.; and a two-day Federal scout from Huntsville to near Vienna, Ala. Federals pursued bushwhackers near Farmington, Mo.; and until April 11 there was a Union expedition to Asheville, N.C.

April 4, Tuesday

PRESIDENT LINCOLN IN RICHMOND, VIRGINIA.

President Lincoln traveled up the James on *River Queen,* transferred to U.S.S. *Malvern,* and then had to take a smaller vessel, a gig rowed by twelve sailors. The party landed in Richmond not far from Libby Prison. Adm. D. D. Porter, three other officers, and ten sailors armed with carbines served as the meager escort for the President as he walked to the White House of the Confederacy. Crowds surrounded the President, mostly cheering and grateful Negroes, although many rowdies were still abroad in the city. He toured the home President Davis had lately vacated and conferred with Maj. Gen. Godfrey Weitzel. In the afternoon the President, well escorted this time, drove through the city. Before leaving Richmond, Mr. Lincoln also talked with John A. Campbell, former U. S. Supreme Court justice and former Assistant Secretary of War for the Confederacy. Judge Campbell admitted the war was over and urged Lincoln to consult with public men of Virginia as to restoration of peace and order. The President returned to *Malvern* for the night.

The retreating Army of Northern Virginia skirmished with Federals at Tabernacle Church or Beaver Pond Creek, and at Amelia Court House. By the fifth Lee's entire army was at the Court House. But the expected supplies were not there and Lee's army had to scrounge the neighborhood for sustenance. This lack of supplies, available at Lynchburg and Richmond, brought intense postwar discussion, with the apparently unfounded charge that they had been delayed because President Davis was using the necessary railroad equipment. It was probably caused by confusion and disrupted communications. Sheridan arrived at Jetersville on the Danville Railroad southwest of Amelia Court House and thus blocked Lee's further use of that route toward North Carolina.

In Alabama Federal cavalry of James H. Wilson entered Tuscaloosa.

At the new capital of the Confederacy in Danville, Va., President Davis issued a proclamation to the remaining people of the crumbling nation. "It would be unwise, even if it were possible, to conceal the great moral, as well as material injury to our cause that must result from the occupation of Richmond by the enemy. It is equally unwise and unworthy of us, as patriots engaged in a most sacred cause, to allow our energies to falter, our spirits to grow faint, or our efforts to become relaxed, under reverses however calamitous." He admitted there was now a new phase of the conflict, but he vowed to maintain the struggle.

April 5, Wednesday

Gen. Lee was confounded by the lack of supplies at Amelia Court

House, Va., and later observed, "This delay was fatal and could not be retrieved." With Sheridan and infantry in front of him near Jetersville, he could no longer use the Danville Railroad and turned toward Farmville, where supplies were ordered from Lynchburg by railroad. Sheridan wanted to attack but Meade refrained until more troops could arrive. There was skirmishing at Paine's Cross Roads and an engagement at Amelia Springs.

At Danville President Davis wrote his wife that he was out of touch with Lee but that he was fitting up an executive office. "I am unwilling to leave Virginia," he stated. In Richmond President Lincoln came ashore again from *Malvern*. For a second time he conferred with John A. Campbell and then read a statement. It said peace was possible only through restoration of the national authority throughout all the states, that there must be no receding on the abolition of slavery, and that hostilities would not cease short of an end to the war and disbanding of all hostile forces. Campbell said the President stated he was contemplating calling the Virginia legislature together to vote restoration of the state to the Union. The exact words and meaning of this proposal became a subject for much controversy, and still are not clear. The President then returned to City Point. At six o'clock he received news that Sec. of State Seward had been critically injured in a carriage accident in Washington that afternoon.

Two Federal expeditions started out in South Carolina: one until April 15 from Charleston to the Santee River, and another until April 25 from Georgetown to Camden. Confederates burned two Federal steamers near Maple Cypress and Cowpen Landing, N.C. There also was an expedition against Indians on the west coast from Camp Bidwell to Antelope Creek, Calif.; and for three days Federals operated a scout from Huntsville to New Market and Maysville, Ala.

April 6, Thursday
ENGAGEMENT OF SAYLER'S CREEK.

The last major engagement occurred between the Army of Northern Virginia and the Army of the Potomac. Lee's army was nearing the Farmville and High Bridge crossings of the Appomattox River. Crossing the stream was imperative for safety. The army attempted to keep together, but it was impossible. In the bottom land of Sayler's Creek, the retreating column split and the Federals moved in. Lee, Longstreet, and William Mahone continued on, unaware of the gap between them and the forces of Ewell and R. H. Anderson. The wagons were ordered on a detour to cross the river. John B. Gordon's troops followed the wagons by mistake. Anderson and Ewell were quickly pressed back, but mounted a countercharge which failed in face of strong artillery fire. Federal flanks closed in toward the middle and Ewell was forced to surrender. Farther north, down Sayler's Creek, Gordon's Southerners were heavily engaged. Only a few of his men cut their way out. Some 8000 Confederates surrendered; Federals suffered about 1180 casualties. Sheridan's cavalry and Horatio Wright's Sixth Corps did most of the work against Ewell while the Second Corps of A. A. Humphreys confronted Gordon. It is estimated that the loss represented about a third of the men Lee had when he left Amelia Court House—a huge number in view of the already decimated Confederate ranks. Longstreet meanwhile retired toward Farmville and halted briefly at Rice Station. E. O. C. Ord's Federal column made some contact with Longstreet. There was considerable skirmishing along much of the route of Lee's retiring army.

In southwest Virginia there was action at Wytheville and also an affair near Charles Town, W. Va. In Alabama Wilson's cavalry and Forrest's remaining men fought skirmishes near Lanier's Mills, Sipsey Creek, and King's Store.

At City Point President Lincoln wrote Gen. Weitzel in Richmond, "It has been intimated to me that the gentlemen who have acted as the Legislature of Virginia, in support of the rebellion, may now now [sic] desire to assemble at Richmond, and take measures to withdraw the Virginia troops, and other support from resistance to the General government. If they attempt it, give them permission and protection. . . ."

April 7, Friday

Grant opened correspondence with Lee: "The result of the last week must convince you of the hopelessness of further resistance on the part of the Army of Northern Virginia in this struggle. I feel that it is so, and regard it as my duty to shift from myself the responsibility of any further effusion of blood, by asking of you the surrender of that portion of the C.S. Army known as the Army of Northern Virginia." Lee's reply, received by Grant at Farmville on April 8, said that although he did not entertain "the opinion you express of the hopelessness of further resistance on the part of the Army of Northern Virginia, I reciprocate your desire to avoid useless effusion of blood, and therefore, before considering your proposition, ask the terms you will offer on condition of its surrender."

Meanwhile, the battered Confederates were receiving more punishment, but did repulse the Federals in an engagement near Farmville and crossed the Appomattox River to continue their retreat on the north side. Longstreet crossed the Appomattox River at Farmville and other troops crossed at High Bridge, where William Mahone's men guarded the crossing of the wagon train on the wagon bridge near the railroad span. The Confederates attempted in vain to burn the bridges. At Farmville Lee's men had received rations. The Yankees eventually crossed in force at High Bridge and engaged the enemy north of the Appomattox before being repulsed. Nevertheless Lee's retreat had been delayed for several irreplaceable hours and Sheridan with infantry behind him was able to move west and then north to block Lee at Appomattox Station and Court House. Thus Lee was about to be squeezed between overwhelming Federal force on the east and west.

Wilson's and Forrest's men skirmished at Fike's Ferry on the Cahawba River, Ala.; and there was a Federal scout near Mobile from Blakely toward Stockton, Ala., as the siege went on.

Tennessee ratified the Thirteenth Amendment, and an avowed abolitionist and unionist, W. G. "Parson" Brownlow, was inaugurated as governor. The U. S. State Department and Britain opened correspondence over the claims arising from the depredations of the Confederate raider *Alabama*.

At City Point President Lincoln wired Grant that "Gen. Sheridan says 'If the thing is pressed I think that Lee will surrender.' Let the *thing* be pressed." Meanwhile, at Danville President Davis and his Cabinet were trying to do what they could, but their efforts would have little effect.

April 8, Saturday

The road to Lynchburg, next goal of Lee's badly harried army, passed through hamlets and villages and Appomattox Station near Appomattox Court House. Behind what was left of the Army of Northern Virginia was Meade with the Second and Sixth Corps of Grant under Humphreys and Wright. To the south, Sheridan's cavalry, Warren's old Fifth Corps now under Charles Griffin, and some of Ord's men of the Army of the James were by evening in front of Lee and blocking the route to Lynchburg. Skirmishing occurred throughout the day, but Meade was unable to bring on a general engagement. Sheridan's cavalry seized Confederate supply trains at Appomattox Station.

Grant, at Farmville, had received Lee's note of April 7 asking what terms the Union offered. Grant replied, "Peace being my great desire, there is but one condition I would insist upon, namely that the men and officers surrendered shall be disqualified from taking up arms again against the Government of the United States until properly exchanged." He offered to meet with Lee to receive a surrender. Later in the day, Lee replied, "I did not intend to propose the surrender of the Army of Northern Virginia, but to ask the terms of your proposition." He did not think "the emergency has arisen to call for the surrender of this army. . . ." But still Lee wanted to talk with Grant.

In the morning Lee was informed that a number of officers had conferred the evening before and agreed the army could not get through to join Johnston and that he ought to open negotiations. Lee refused the suggestion, made to spare him from taking the lead in surrender. Other officers disagreed also. That night, near Appomattox, Lee held his final council of war. What could they do? If there was infantry as well as cavalry in front of them it would be impossible to break through, but it had to be tried.

At Danville President Davis got information from Sec. of War Breckinridge and messenger John S. Wise that the situation was critical. Neverthe-less, a certain amount of routine business continued. President Lincoln again visited Petersburg and late in the evening left City Point by boat for Washington.

Heavy Union bombardment began late in the afternoon at Spanish Fort outside Mobile, Ala. At a weak point in the thinly held Confederate line the Federal troops charged, failing at first and then succeeding in taking a portion of the lines. Using a narrow escape passage the Southern defenders evacuated Spanish Fort during the night. In North Carolina there was action at Martinsville. Federals pursued guerrillas in northeast Missouri, and carried out scouts from Vienna and Fairfax Court House into Loudoun County, Va.

April 9, Sunday

SURRENDER OF THE ARMY OF NORTHERN VIRGINIA AT APPOMATTOX COURT HOUSE.

On Palm Sunday a clear spring sun rose in Virginia. But when the sun went down, with it went "the hopes of a people who, with prayers, and tears, and blood, had striven to uphold that fallen flag." Confederate sol-dier Edward M. Boykin told of men who came "to their officers with tears streaming from their eyes, and asked what it all meant, and would, at that moment, I know, have rather died the night before than see the sun rise on such a day as this." Robert E. Lee had surrendered the Army of Northern Virginia to Ulysses S. Grant.

At dawn, near Appomattox Station, the Confederates had attacked with the hope of forcing a passage through the Federals in front of them. At first the infantry of Gordon and Fitzhugh Lee's cavalry were successful, but there was more than just enemy cavalry in front of them. The route was blocked by infantry. The Union forces drove in, and on the east other Federals under Meade attacked the Confederate rear guard. Escape was impossible. After hearing the news, Gen. Lee said, "It would be useless and therefore cruel to provoke the further effusion of blood, and I have arranged to meet with General Grant with a view to surrender. . . ." Early in the day, Grant had written Lee that he had "no authority to treat on the subject of peace." Only surrender was possible. Lee could but reply and request an interview: "I ask a suspension of hostilities pending the adjustment of the terms of the surrender of this army. . . ."

There was some confusion on various parts of the field—truce flags, some small-arms fire, Federal Brig. Gen. Custer demanding the surrender of Confederates. But the drama centered on the neat, comfortable home of Wilmer McLean at Appomattox Court House. There, in the early after-noon, Gen. Lee and one aide met Gen. Grant, his staff, and several of the major commanders—Sheridan, Ord, and others, although Meade was not present. After pleasantries, Lee called attention to the matter at hand.

There was a brief discussion of terms, which Grant said were the same as in his message: officers and men surrendered were to be paroled and disqualified from taking up arms until properly exchanged; arms, ammunition, and supplies were to be turned over as captured property. This was in line with Lincoln's direct instructions to Grant of March 3. The army was not to arrange a peace—just take care of surrender.

Grant wrote out his proposal, went over it with his staff, and presented it to Lee. The terms did not include surrender of side arms of officers or of their private horses or baggage, and allowed each officer and man to go home and not be disturbed as long as parole was observed. Lee then brought up the fact that cavalrymen and artillerists owned their own horses, which would be needed for the spring planting. After a short conference Grant agreed to let those who claimed horses have them. Arrangements also were made to feed Lee's army from Federal supplies. Thus it was completed—a document from Grant to Lee giving terms of surrender of the Army of Northern Virginia, and one from Lee to Grant accepting those terms. Legend to the contrary, Lee did not surrender his sword to Grant.

Lee returned to his waiting, anxious army. As the men crowded around him, he spoke softly, "I have done for you all that it was in my power to do. You have done all your duty. Leave the result to God. Go to your homes and resume your occupations. Obey the laws and become as good citizens as you were soldiers." Hats off, the men stood with "swimming eyes." Lee rode bareheaded, his eyes to neither left nor right.

Of course, the war was not over; there were armies in the field and a government about to take flight from Danville. But never again would the grand, proud Armies of the Potomac and Northern Virginia clash. It was only after a gentle reminder somewhat later in the afternoon that Gen. Grant remembered to inform Washington of what had transpired.

President Lincoln arrived back in Washington in early evening as the news was spreading throughout the land. Bonfires sprang up as crowds jammed streets. In Chicago one hundred cannon awakened sleepers, and bells rang. It was the same throughout the North. In the Army of the Potomac, flags waved, bands played, cannon boomed, and the air was filled with knapsacks, canteens, tin cups, and roaring cheers. That, too, soon ended; the noise receded, a silence of respect to the fallen dead and the vanquished foe fell over Appomattox. Four years of war in Virginia had ended.

At Mobile, things were also concluding. The combined Federal army of E. R. S. Canby attacked Fort Blakely now that Spanish Fort had fallen. The assault was successful without heavy loss and only Forts Huger and Tracy remained in action against the Federals. The city was virtually open for occupation. At Danville President Davis was mainly concerned with building entrenchments for defense.

April 10, Monday

As joyous citizens thronged the streets of Northern cities, villages, and hamlets, the armies at Appomattox began the business of parole, feeding the Confederates, and making various arrangements before Lee's men could go home. News of the surrender arrived at Danville late in the afternoon. By evening what was left of the Confederate government took to the railroad again and headed for Greensborough, N.C., fearful that the cavalry of Stoneman in the area might overtake them.

President Lincoln was serenaded several times during the day by relieved and happy crowds in Washington. He promised to make a more formal utterance the following evening. The President asked the band of one group to play "Dixie," as it was "one of the best tunes I have ever heard."

At Mobile Forts Huger and Tracy kept up their bombardment; but it was clear that with less than five thousand Confederates at hand, Maj. Gen. D. H. Maury would be forced to evacuate the city. Wilson's cavalry skirmished at Lowndesborough and Benton, Ala., and there were brief skirmishes at Burke's Station and Arundel's Farm, Va. Sherman's army in North Carolina took up the march once more, moving out toward Raleigh with skirmishing at Boonville, Moccasin Swamp, and Nahunta Station.

Gen. R. E. Lee issued his last general orders. "After four years of arduous service, marked by unsurpassed courage and fortitude, the Army of Northern Virginia has been compelled to yield to overwhelming numbers and resources. . . . By the terms of the agreement officers and men can return to their homes and remain until exchanged. You will take with you the satisfaction that proceeds from the consciousness of duty faithfully performed, and I earnestly pray that a Merciful God will extend to you His blessing and protection. With an increasing admiration of your constancy and devotion to your country, and a grateful remembrance of your kind and generous considerations for myself, I bid you an affectionate farewell."

As General Order No. 9 was being prepared, word came to Gen. Lee that Grant was on his way. Lee went to meet him and the two conferred for some time. Lee hoped there would be no more sacrifice of life; Grant urged Lee to advise surrender of all the Confederate armies. Lee replied that this was up to President Davis. Other officers, including Meade, visited Lee. Memories and curiosity seemed to draw them all together.

April 11, Tuesday

At Mobile the remaining defenses of Forts Huger and Tracy were abandoned, and Gen. Maury began evacuation of the city itself, which was completed by Wednesday morning, April 12. Works were dismantled, stores removed, and only a rear guard remained the night of April 11.

Sherman's troops continued to advance toward Goldsborough, N.C., and entered Smithfield to learn the news of Lee's surrender. A Southern woman heard the wild shouting, and said to her children, "Now father will come home." But the advance was not without some fighting, at Smithfield, near Beulah and Pikeville. Stoneman's Union cavalry, farther west in North Carolina, fought skirmishes at Shallow Ford and near Mocksville. There was Northern scouting from Winchester, Va., to Timber Ridge, W. Va.; also scouting for a couple of days and a skirmish at St. Charles, Ark. Two blockade-runners were captured off Crystal River, Fla.

The Confederate government train arrived at Greensborough, N.C., early in the day to cold response compared to what they had received at Danville, Va. Citizens were concerned about threatened reprisals from Federal troops.

President Lincoln spoke to an enthusiastic crowd from a window of the White House. But it was hardly a victory speech. He expressed the hope for "a righteous and speedy peace" and then discussed reconstruction. He admitted the future was "fraught with great difficulty." A beginning had to be made with "disorganized and discordant elements," and he mentioned the conflict of opinion in the North as to reconstruction. The President went on to defend his policy in setting up a new state government in Louisiana. He conceded that the seceded states "are out of their proper practical relation with the Union; and that the sole object of the government, civil and military, in regard to those States is to again get them into that proper practical relation." Mr. Lincoln considered discussion of whether the states had left the Union immaterial. He did say he would prefer to have Louisiana give the elective franchise to "the very intelligent" Negro and to Negro soldiers. Lincoln admitted the difficulties of reconstruction and desired that plans be kept flexible. It was a serious, anxious speech, full of the future—and it was to be his last.

April 12, Wednesday

SURRENDER OF MOBILE, ALABAMA.

The final major city of the Confederacy fell. Federal troops of Gen. E. R. S. Canby entered Mobile, Ala., following Confederate evacuation during the night of April 11. The capture came much too late to have any effect upon the war. Confederate commander D. H. Maury had removed what supplies he could, burned the cotton, and sent a message to the Union fleet informing them that Confederates were leaving. Maury's force reached Meridian, Miss., unopposed and began refitting with the hope of joining Johnston in North Carolina. The defenses of Mobile had been strong, but the Confederates were unable to man them in view of their slim numbers and the Federals' overpowering strength. Federal losses numbered 232 killed, 1303 wounded, and 43 missing for 1578 casualties in the various operations against Mobile.

James Harrison Wilson's cavalry occupied Montgomery, Ala., after a skirmish on the Columbus Road. Sherman's army was nearing Raleigh, N.C., in its renewed advance against Johnston, with actions near Raleigh and at Swift Creek. Farther west, Stoneman's Federal cavalry moved toward Salisbury and, at Grant's Creek, charged some three thousand Confederate defenders. They captured about thirteen hundred Confederates, and occupied Salisbury. There was a two-day Union expedition from Port Hudson to Jackson, La.; a scout from Tallahassa Mission, Indian Terr.; a five-day scout from Dakota City, Neb. Terr.; and a scout until April 25 from Fort Stanton, N. Mex. Terr.

A ceremony took place at Appomattox Court House. Federal troops formed along the principal street to await the formal laying down of battle flags and arms by the Confederates. Gen. Joshua Chamberlain of Maine described it: "On they come, with the old swinging route step and swaying battleflags. In the van, the proud Confederate ensign. . . . Before us in proud humiliation stood the embodiment of manhood; men whom neither toils and sufferings, nor the fact of death, nor disaster, nor hopelessness could bend from their resolve; standing before us now, thin, worn, and famished, but erect, and with eyes looking level into ours, waking memories that bound us together as no other bond." As the bugle sounded the Federal line shifted to the marching salute of carry arms. Gen. Gordon, riding heavy in spirit, saw the salute, whirled on his horse, dropped the point of his sword to the boot toe and ordered carry arms—"honor answering honor." And then the battle-worn colors of the regiments were folded and laid down until only the Federal colors were against the sky. Memories, tears, victory, defeat blended into one. Of Lee, a Confederate soldier wrote, "We who live today shall never see his like again, and whether our posterity does is problematical."

At Greensborough, N.C., President Davis met with Genls. J. E. Johnston and Beauregard and his Cabinet. The generals felt it was not possible for the army in North Carolina to resist Sherman. Johnston recommended negotiations. But Davis considered further negotiations futile; only surrender would be accepted. Judah Benjamin agreed with Davis, but the others sided with Johnston, so the general was empowered to meet with Sherman.

Mr. Lincoln was now greatly concerned with reconstruction. To Gen. Weitzel at Richmond he wired that if there was no sign of the Virginia legislature convening, the offer should be withdrawn. In another telegraph to Weitzel, Lincoln said Judge Campbell was wrong in assuming Lincoln called the insurgent legislature of Virginia together. The President said, "I have done no such thing. I spoke of them not as a Legislature, but as 'the gentlemen who *acted* as the Legislature of Virginia in support of the rebellion.'" He denied they were the rightful legislature. The President therefore told Weitzel not to let them assemble. Of course, Judge Campbell had understood otherwise and it seems that now, facing opposition in the Cabinet on this policy, Lincoln had thought better of calling the legislature.

April 13, Thursday

The Federal men of Sherman entered Raleigh, N.C., in heavy rain and after skirmishing near Raleigh and at Morrisville, N.C. They were heading toward Johnston's main army and the temporary Confederate capital at Greensborough. Military action elsewhere was simmering down, with skirmishing at Whistler or Eight Mile Creek Bridge and at Wetumpka, Ala. Federal scouts operated about Lexington, Ky. U.S.S. *Ida* fell victim to a torpedo in Mobile Bay, the fifth ship to be lost in five weeks in the area.

Sec. of War Stanton ordered the draft halted and curtailed purchases of war matériel. The number of officers was reduced and many military restrictions removed as first steps in demobilization. President Lincoln conferred with Gen. Grant, Stanton, Welles, and others.

Gen. Johnston left Greensborough to rejoin his army at Hillsborough, N.C.

April 14, Friday

ASSASSINATION.

FEDERAL FLAG RAISED OVER FORT SUMTER, SOUTH CAROLINA.

The event of Good Friday, April 14, 1865, will remain vivid as long as the history of the United States is known. Shortly after 10 P.M. in the presidential box at Ford's Theatre President Abraham Lincoln was shot by actor John Wilkes Booth. It had been a full day for Lincoln, with many callers and a Cabinet meeting, with Gen. Grant in attendance, during which the President told of his recurring dream of a ship "moving with great rapidity toward a dark and indefinite shore." The Cabinet discussed problems of reconstruction, including treatment of Confederate leaders. Callers continued in the afternoon and up to 8:30 P.M., the time Lincoln left for the theater to see a trifling comedy, *Our American Cousin*. Gen. Grant had turned down an invitation to attend, pleading he had to visit his children. It was known that there was some chilliness between Mrs. Lincoln and Mrs. Grant.

At the theater the crowd's cheering stopped the play as the President and his party, including Mrs. Lincoln, Miss Clara Harris, and Maj. H. R. Rathbone, entered the box over the stage. The crowd settled down and the play resumed. One lady reported, "It was while every one's attention was fastened upon the stage that a pistol shot was heard, causing every one to jump & look up at the President's Box merely because that was the direction of the sound and supposing it to be a part of the performance we all looked again upon the stage—when a man suddenly vaulted over the railing of the box—turned back & then leaped to the stage—striking on his heels & falling backward but recovered himself in an instant and started across the stage to behind the scene." John Wilkes Booth brandished a knife and shouted what was said to be "Sic semper tyrannis" as he hobbled across the stage and out into the night, his right leg injured when he leaped to the stage. "Our President! our President is shot! catch him—hang him!"

Bedlam reigned at the theater as men carried the unconscious President across the street to the modest home of William Peterson. There he was put in a rear bedroom. A bullet had gone into the back of the head and lodged near the right eye. Soon the building and streets were full. Medical men, Cabinet members, and congressmen hastened to the Peterson House. Rumors were rife: it was a Confederate raid—murderers were rushing about the streets—many prominent politicians were also assassinated. Truth soon came out that Sec. of State William H. Seward had been stabbed in his bed, where he was recovering from his carriage accident. Only the plaster cast and the courageous action of his son and a male nurse saved the Secretary. It was learned that Lewis Payne (or Paine), a hulking accomplice of Booth, had carried out the Seward stabbing. At the Kirkwood House, Vice-President Andrew Johnson was notified of the attacks. The streets of Washington, still wearing a jubilant air from the recent surrender of Appomattox, now suffered the sudden shock of tragedy. Stunned citizens and troops thronged the avenues. Sec. of War Stanton took charge of the pursuit of Booth and his accomplices as the telegraph wires hummed the awesome news to the nation. Grant was at Baltimore when informed of the tragedy, and he immediately returned to Washington. At the Peterson House, doctors pronounced no hope for the dying President. Mrs. Lincoln came into the room once and was led away in irrepressible grief.

Earlier in the day, at Charleston Harbor, distinguished Northern officers and dignitaries gathered, bands played, and guns thundered from the Northern Navy in salute. In late morning at Fort Sumter, a flag-raising program began. Gen. Robert Anderson, who had lowered the same flag four years earlier, seized the halyards and hoisted the Federal banner once more above the fort that was the very symbol of the war. Henry Ward Beecher gave the oration. For the North it was an occasion of solemn joy ending with fireworks from the fleet at night.

Sherman's forces moved ahead in the rain from Raleigh to Durham Station, N.C. After obtaining permission from President Davis, Gen. Johnston wrote to Sherman asking if he was "willing to make a temporary suspension of active operations," looking toward peace. Sherman, in Raleigh, replied at once that he was willing to confer with Johnston and would limit his advance, expecting Johnston to keep his men in their present position. He suggested the same terms Grant had given Lee. There was some fighting near Morrisville and Sander's Farm, N.C. Near Tuskegee, Ala., Wilson's cavalry skirmished on the Columbus Road. Another skirmish flared at Mount Pleasant, Tenn. C.S.S. *Shenandoah* left the Eastern Caroline Islands in the Pacific and headed for the Kurile Islands in the North Pacific. Still another Union vessel was blown up by a torpedo off Mobile.

April 15, Saturday

PRESIDENT LINCOLN DIES: ANDREW JOHNSON TAKES OATH.

At 7:22 A.M. President Abraham Lincoln died. "Now he belongs to the ages," Sec. of War Stanton is supposed to have intoned to those gathered around the bed in the Peterson House. The Cabinet, except for the injured Seward, formally requested Vice-President Andrew Johnson to assume the office of President. At 11 A.M., at the Kirkwood Hotel, Chief Justice Salmon P. Chase administered the oath in the presence of the Cabinet and several congressmen. Mr. Johnson asked the Cabinet to remain with him, adding, "The course which I have taken in the past, in connection with this rebellion, must be regarded as a guaranty for the future." The nation still had a leader, the process of government went on, the search for the assassins was in full, if somewhat confused, cry. Much of the nation wept openly as the news went out.

Skirmishing broke out near Chapel Hill, N.C., and at McKenzie's Creek near Patterson, Mo. Union scouts operated in Randolph and Pocahontas counties, W. Va.; and Bath and Highland, Va., until April 23.

President Davis, having authorized negotiations by Gen. Johnston, now left Greensborough, N.C., with a cavalry escort. Some officials were on horseback and some in carriages or wagons.

Fugitives John Wilkes Booth and David Herold, one of Booth's accomplices, had escaped to the southeast of Washington and stopped at the home of Dr. Samuel Mudd, where Booth's broken leg was treated.

April 16, Sunday

The North was in deep mourning now, and with it much of the South, if not in mourning, at least felt dismay over the assassination, for it realized that Mr. Lincoln had seemed to understand its position. He had opposed what appeared to be Radical vindictiveness. Federal troops pursued Booth in Maryland. Early in the morning Booth and Herold reached Rich Hill, the home of Samuel Cox, after a harrowing trip through swamps and over meager trails. In Washington Mrs. Lincoln was prostrate with grief and Andrew Johnson was gathering up the reins of the presidency. Radical Republicans were hopeful that the new President would be more amenable to their policies, which included treating the Southern states as conquered territory.

In North Carolina plans were set for a meeting of Johnston and Sherman the following day. James Harrison Wilson's Federal cavalry, well into Georgia now, captured West Point and Columbus. Skirmishing also took place at Crawford, Girard, and Opelika, Ala.

The entourage of carriages and horses of the fleeing Confederate government arrived at Lexington, N.C., but would have to continue on rapidly in view of the approaching Johnston-Sherman negotiations.

April 17, Monday

Genls. William T. Sherman and Joseph E. Johnston met at the Bennett House near Durham Station, N.C. A short time before, Sherman had received news of the assassination of Lincoln. Johnston told Sherman it was a great calamity to the South. In their talks the two generals went further than just surrendering Johnston's army. They discussed terms for an armistice for all the remaining Confederate armies. Sherman later disclaimed going beyond negotiations over Johnston's army, but admitted "it did seem to me that there was presented a chance for peace that might be deemed valuable to the Government of the United States, and was at least worth the few days that would be consumed in reference." They agreed to meet the next day.

Meanwhile, Wilson's Federals wrecked what little Confederate war potential was left at Columbus, Ga., and destroyed the ironclad gunboat C.S.S. *Muscogee* or *Jackson*. There was action at the Catawba River near Morgantown, N.C., and a Union expedition operated until April 30 from Blakely, Ala., to Georgetown, Ga., and Union Springs, Ala.

President Davis and his party were now at Salisbury, N.C., en route toward Charlotte. In Maryland John Wilkes Booth and David Herold were hiding in a cluster of trees while attempting to obtain transportation across the Potomac in the area south of Port Tobacco, Md.

In the evening the body of President Lincoln was taken from the guest chamber of the White House to the East Room, where it lay in state until the funeral on April 19.

April 18, Tuesday

SHERMAN-JOHNSTON MEMORANDUM SIGNED.

After more talk near Durham Station, N.C., Genls. Sherman and Johnston signed a "Memorandum or basis of agreement." This highly controversial document called for an armistice by all armies in the field; Confederate forces were to be disbanded and to deposit their arms in the state arsenals; each man was to agree to cease from war and to abide by state and Federal authority; the President of the United States was to recognize the existing state governments when their officials took oaths to the United States; reestablishment of Federal courts would take place; people were to be guaranteed rights of person and property; the United States would not disturb the people of the South as long as they lived in peace; and a general amnesty for Confederates. The generals recognized that they were not fully empowered to carry out such far-reaching measures and that the necessary authority must be obtained. But it was clear that Sherman was going far beyond what Grant did at Appomattox. He was actually entering into reconstruction policy. He sent the terms to Grant and Halleck, asking approval by the President. Sherman also offered to take charge of carrying out these terms. Later he was to deny vociferously any usurpation of power on his part and to claim that the agreement was according to Mr. Lincoln's wishes as Sherman knew them.

At any rate, the fighting had now ended in North Carolina as well as in Virginia. But there was skirmishing at Pleasant Hill and at the Double Bridges over the Flint River in Georgia as part of Wilson's Union cavalry invasion. Minor skirmishing broke out near Germantown, Tenn., and at Taylorsville, Ky.

President Davis and his disconsolate party slowly moved southward to Concord, N.C. The body of President Lincoln lay in state in the crepe-decorated East Room of the White House. Politics, the search for the assassins, the ending of the war, reconstruction, all were intermingled in sorrow for the President and planning for the future.

April 19, Wednesday

FUNERAL SERVICES FOR PRESIDENT LINCOLN.

President Johnson, the Cabinet, Supreme Court justices, Congress, military figures, and the diplomatic corps in full "court dress" filed into the East Room of the White House. Robert Lincoln represented the family as Mrs. Lincoln and Tad remained sequestered. At the head of the catafalque stood Gen. Grant alone. After the brief services the funeral carriage, escorted by cavalry, infantry, artillery, marines, their banners draped, and the bands playing sorrowful dirges, carried the body past throngs of people to the rotunda of the Capitol. The bells of Washington tolled; the minute guns boomed. Now it was the public's turn, and, until the evening of April 20, they filed past the catafalque in steady streams. Then the body began its last journey, back to Illinois by a long and often agonizing route to burial at Springfield on May 4.

Maj. Gen. John Pope, commanding the Federal Military Division of the Missouri, wrote from St. Louis to Lieut. Gen. E. Kirby Smith, commanding the Confederate Trans-Mississippi Department, suggesting that forces west of the Mississippi surrender on the same terms as those of Lee. Several Federal command changes were made, including Maj. Gen. Halleck being assigned command of the Military Division of the James, which included Virginia and parts of North Carolina not occupied by Sherman. Wilson's cavalry skirmished near Barnesville, Ga. Union expeditions moved from Memphis to Brownsville, Miss., and from Terre Bonne to Pelton's Plantation and Grand Caillou, La. President Davis and his entourage arrived at Charlotte, N.C., which would be their resting place until April 26. Here again suitable quarters were hard to find. Mr. Davis first heard of the assassination of President Lincoln. Confederate Gen. Wade Hampton wrote the President suggesting they withdraw across the Mississippi to continue the fight, an idea which was frequently discussed.

April 20, Thursday

Federal troops of James Harrison Wilson occupied Macon, Ga. Skirmishing occurred near Spring Hill, Mimms Mills on Tobesofkee Creek, Ga.; and at Rocky Creek Bridge, as well as at Montpelier Springs, Ala. The Arkansas legislature ratified the Thirteenth Amendment. Gen. Lee, now in Richmond, wrote Davis, "I believe an army cannot be organized or supported in Virginia," or for that matter east of the Mississippi. He opposed a partisan war and recommended suspension of hostilities and restoration of peace.

April 21, Friday

The body of President Lincoln left Washington en route to Springfield, Ill., the train being stopped often to accommodate immense crowds of mourners.

At Millwood, Va., John Singleton Mosby disbanded his Confederate rangers. There was a Union expedition from Donaldsonville to Bayou Goula, La.; and until April 27 a Federal scout operated from Rolla toward Thomasville, Mo. President Johnson told an Indiana delegation that he did not believe the Southern states had ever left the Union, a position contrary to that held by the Radicals.

April 22, Saturday

Most of the military action now was insignificant, with only the Northern cavalry of James Harrison Wilson active in Georgia and Alabama. Federal troops under him occupied Talladega, Ala. Skirmishes took place at Buzzard Roost, Ga.; at Howard's Gap in the Blue Ridge, N.C.; near Linn Creek and near the mouth of the Big Gravois, Mo. A Union scout from Deer Creek to Sage Creek, Dak. Terr., lasted two days. Gen. Halleck assumed command of the Military Division of the James, and Nathaniel P. Banks resumed command of the Department of the Gulf.

Booth and Herold, after nearly a week out in the open, finally got across the Potomac in a fishing skiff, to Gumbo Creek on the Virginia shore. Plans were now to continue southward. Meanwhile, the search had intensified north of the Potomac. The Lincoln funeral train arrived in Philadelphia from Harrisburg.

April 23, Sunday

Wilson's men fought at Munford's Station, Ala., and Stoneman's Federal cavalry fought an action near Hendersonville, N.C. Otherwise there was an affair near Fort Zarah, Kas., and a scout from Pulaski, Tenn., to Rogersville, Ala. President Davis, at Charlotte, N.C., wrote his wife of the recent disasters and observed that "Panic has seized the country." He continued, "The issue is one which it is very painful for me to meet. On one hand is the long night of oppression which will follow the return of our people to the 'Union'; on the other, the suffering of the women and children, and carnage among the few brave patriots who would still oppose the invader." He wrote of possibly getting across the Mississippi, and concluded, "My love is all I have to offer, and that has the value of a thing long possessed, and sure not to be lost."

April 24, Monday
SHERMAN LEARNS OF REJECTION OF TERMS.

Gen. Grant reached Sherman's headquarters at Raleigh, N.C., and brought with him the news that the President had disapproved Sherman's agreement with Johnston. Sherman was ordered to give forty-eight hours' notice and then resume hostilities if there was no surrender. Sherman was incensed both by the disapproval and by the large amount of material on the subject in the New York papers, including the dispatch of March 3, 1865, from Lincoln to Grant stating that the generals should accept nothing but surrender and should not negotiate peace. Sherman said he never received such a message. The fiery general soon raged against Stanton and Halleck, claiming he had not gone beyond Lincoln's wishes. While historians differ, it does seem that Sherman had gone far beyond strictly military obligations, and that he did try to make a peace agreement. At any rate, Grant was now under orders to direct military movements, but left it up to Sherman to carry them out publicly. Gen. Johnston was given notice of the suspension of the truce at once. At Charlotte, N.C., President Davis approved Johnston's agreement with Sherman, not knowing that it had already been rejected by the Union.

John Wilkes Booth and David Herold crossed the Rappahannock at Port Conway, Va., in their effort to escape Federal pursuers. Lincoln's body lay in state in New York City as thousands of mourners filed past his bier. In military action, skirmishes erupted near Boggy Depot, Indian Terr., and near Miami, Mo.

April 25, Tuesday

Federal cavalry closed in on Booth and Herold. After receiving various leads the officers arrived at the Richard H. Garrett farm south of the Rappahannock in Virginia about 2 A.M. on April 26. In North Carolina troops were preparing to move after Washington had rejected Sherman's agreement with Johnston, but the Confederate general asked Sherman to renew negotiations and Sherman arranged a meeting for April 26. There was a skirmish at Linn Creek, Mo., and a Union scout from Pine Bluff to Rodger's Plantation, Ark. The Lincoln funeral train began the journey to Albany, N.Y.

April 26, Wednesday

SURRENDER OF JOSEPH E. JOHNSTON.
CAPTURE AND DEATH OF JOHN WILKES BOOTH.

Early in the morning Federal troopers surrounded the barn of Richard H. Garrett. Lieut. Col. Everton Conger was in command. Although threatened with hanging, Garrett refused to reveal that there were two fugitives in his barn. To prevent further inquisition, son Jack Garrett informed the officers. The barn was surrounded and the suspects ordered out. Davy Herold surrendered and emerged. Booth was defiant and ranted dramatically. The barn was set afire to force his surrender. As the flames roared, a shot was fired and Booth fell, mortally wounded. Pulled from the burning barn, Booth died, probably about 7 A.M. Sergeant Boston Corbett, a religious fanatic and an unstable man, is generally credited with shooting Booth. Most historians, although there are notable exceptions, feel it was Booth in the barn, that he was shot by Corbett and died on the Garrett porch. But the history of assassinations is hounded by question marks, this one possibly more than others. Booth's body was taken to the Washington Navy Yard for identification, inquest and autopsy aboard U.S.S. *Montauk*. After burial in the Arsenal Penitentiary, the remains were later reburied in Baltimore. Admittedly there was too much War Department secrecy, inefficiency rising out of the trauma of the assassination and the end of the war, and conflicting stories from unreliable witnesses. But despite the many questions and sensational rumors, most historians tend to agree that Booth and the small band he recruited were solely responsible for the assassination of President Lincoln.

At the Bennett House near Durham Station, N.C., Gen. William T. Sherman met again with Gen. Joseph E. Johnston in midafternoon. Final terms of capitulation for troops of Johnston's command were signed following the formula set by Grant at Appomattox. This same day the terms were approved by Grant, now at Raleigh. All arms and public property were to be deposited by Confederates at Greensborough; troops were to give their parole and pledge not to take up arms until released from this obligation; side arms of officers and their private horses and baggage could be retained; and all officers and men were permitted to return to their homes. In a supplement, field transportation was to be loaned to the troops for getting home and for later use; a small quantity of arms would be retained and then deposited in state capitals; horses and other private property were to be retained; troops from Texas and Arkansas were to be furnished water transportation, and surrender of naval forces within the limits of

Johnston's command was also included. Thus the second major army of the Confederate States of America, totaling in all about thirty thousand men, surrendered. There remained two primary Southern forces—those of E. Kirby Smith in the Trans-Mississippi and Richard Taylor in Alabama and Mississippi. But neither could possibly hold out for long now that the main bulwarks of Confederate strength had fallen.

The Confederate Cabinet met with President Davis at Charlotte, N.C., and agreed to leave that day with the aim of getting west of the Mississippi. Att. Gen. George Davis of North Carolina left the group at this time.

Minor operations in the Shenandoah Valley continued until May 5. A four-day Union scout probed from Little Rock to the Saline River, Ark.

April 27, Thursday
Sultana DISASTER.

Hundreds of paroled Federal soldiers were on their way home from Vicksburg after undergoing the privations of Confederate prison camps. Riverboats, heavily loaded, steamed northward. *Sultana,* overcrowded and with defective boilers, was north of Memphis on the Mississippi near Old Hen and Chickens islands. In the darkness of early morning a boiler exploded, hurling soldiers and wreckage high into the air. Fire broke out immediately and the water became full of struggling men, horses, and mules. Some found their way ashore or were picked up, but hundreds died in the catastrophe. Some 2021 passengers, soldiers, and crew were on board. The loss was officially put at 1238 killed, many of them men who had fought in battle and survived life in prison camps. The toll is often put much higher, at 1450 and up to 1900. Although admittedly the boat was overloaded, the *Sultana* disaster was blamed officially on the faulty boilers. It is one of the most lethal ship tragedies on record.

Skirmishes still sputtered on the fringes of the war, this time near James Creek, Mo. Gen. Grant left Raleigh, N.C., after conferring with Sherman. In South Carolina, the fleeing Confederate government lost another Cabinet member when Sec. of the Treasury G. A. Trenholm, too ill to continue, resigned. Postmaster General Reagan succeeded him. The train bearing Lincoln's remains paused at Rochester and Buffalo, N.Y.

April 28, Friday

Sherman left his officers to handle the disbandment of Johnston's army and the preparations for taking his troops north. He then departed for Savannah to take care of affairs in Georgia. Small groups of Confederate soldiers surrendered throughout the South. Jefferson Davis accepted the resignation of G. A. Trenholm as Treasury Secretary. Mrs. Davis was at Abbeville, S.C. In Cleveland, fifty thousand people viewed the coffin of Lincoln.

April 29, Saturday

President Johnson removed restrictions on trade in former Confederate territory east of the Mississippi within military lines. There was a skirmish in Lyon County, Ky. President Davis' party was at Yorkville, S.C., and continuing its flight. The people of Columbus thronged to view Lincoln's body.

April 30, Sunday

A few miles north of Mobile, Ala., Federal Gen. E. R. S. Canby and Confederate Gen. Richard Taylor agreed upon a truce prior to the surrender of Confederate forces in Alabama and Mississippi. Union operations near Brashear City, La., lasted until May 12. The Lincoln funeral train arrived in Indianapolis.

MAY, 1865

It was over. And with the end so much had happened, armies surrendering, a President assassinated, another fleeing the conquerors. The shooting had almost ceased and there was a momentary vacuum everywhere. People began to pick up the pieces, not sure how to put them back together. Two Confederate armies remained, but negotiations were under way for surrender of the primary force left east of the Mississippi and there was confusion, along with a very slight, desperate hope, in the Trans-Mississippi Confederacy of E. Kirby Smith. But most Southern soldiers were going home, bitter, relieved, some of them glad. Many had no homes to go to and began looking westward, or even abroad. In Washington the Radicals were pressuring President Johnson to pursue a vindictive policy. Indications were that the new President would attempt to carry out, in his own way, the policies of the martyred Lincoln.

May 1, Monday

President Johnson ordered the naming of nine army officers to make up the military commission to try the eight accused Lincoln assassination conspirators. It had been ruled by Federal authorities that they were subject to trial before a military commission rather than a civil court. Those accused and held in prison were David E. Herold, who had been with Booth, George A. Atzerodt, Samuel Arnold, Lewis Payne (or Paine), Michael O'Laughlin, Edward Spangler, Mrs. Mary E. Surratt, and Samuel A. Mudd. In Chicago thousands thronged to the courthouse to pay last respects to Lincoln, lying in state.

In the limited military action now going on there was a scout until

May 9 from Ojo de Anaya, N. Mex. Terr., as the Indian troubles continued. President Davis and his fleeing party arrived at Cokesbury, S.C., in what was becoming a more and more desperate flight.

May 2, Tuesday

Maj. Gen. E. R. S. Canby telegraphed Gen. Grant that Confederate Gen. Richard Taylor had accepted the terms for surrender of his forces in Alabama and Mississippi, based on the Appomattox settlement.

President Johnson issued a proclamation accusing President Davis and others of inciting the murder of Lincoln and procuring the actual perpetrators. A $100,000 reward was offered for the arrest of Davis. This accusation is often ascribed to the hysteria resulting from the assassination; no reliable historian has ever connected the Confederate President with the deed. Davis was now at Abbeville, S.C., and the guards carrying the Confederate Treasury turned it over to him and his Cabinet. In a council Davis expressed a wish to try to continue the war, but the others did not agree. By midnight the Confederate refugees left Abbeville. Sec. of the Navy S. R. Mallory officially resigned.

May 3, Wednesday

By daylight President Davis and his party crossed the Savannah River, moving to Washington, Ga. Reluctantly Davis accepted the resignation of Sec. of the Navy S. R. Mallory, one of the two Confederate Cabinet members who had served in the same post since the founding of the Confederacy. Judah Benjamin also departed and eventually escaped to Britain.

The Lincoln funeral train reached its destination, Springfield, Ill.

There was skirmishing on the Missouri River near Boonville, and an affair near Pleasant Hill, Mo. Also there were operations until the sixth about Fort Adams, Miss., and a Union expedition from Rodney to Port Gibson, Miss., until May 6.

May 4, Thursday

SURRENDER OF CONFEDERATE FORCES OF GENERAL RICHARD TAYLOR.

At a conference at Citronelle, Ala., some forty miles north of Mobile, Gen. Richard Taylor surrendered the Confederate forces in the Department of Alabama, Mississippi, and East Louisiana. As in the other surrenders, officers and men retained horses they owned and the men signed paroles. Taylor was allowed to retain control of railways and steamers to transport troops home. Sporadic action continued, with skirmishing at Star House near Lexington, Mo.; a Yankee scout from Pine Bluff to Noble's Farm, Ark.; and a skirmish at Wetumpka, Ala. Meanwhile, the dismal and dwindling procession with President Davis continued southward into Georgia.

Abraham Lincoln was buried at Springfield, Ill.

May 5, Friday

There now remained only the Confederate forces of E. Kirby Smith in the Trans-Mississippi as a major Southern army. President Davis was at Sandersville, Ga. Skirmishing occurred in the Perche Hills, Mo., and at Summerville, Ga. A Union expedition operated until May 13 from Pulaski, Tenn., to New Market, Ala.

Connecticut ratified the Thirteenth Amendment.

May 6, Saturday

The Federal War Department issued orders setting up the military commission to try the alleged Lincoln conspirators. The commission was headed by Maj. Gen. David Hunter, with Brig. Gen. Joseph Holt as judge advocate. A small Federal expedition operated from Richmond to Staunton and Charlottesville, Va.; and another until May 11 from Little Rock to Bayou Meto and Little Bayou, Ark. President Davis, near Sandersville, Ga., was trying to get south of points occupied by Federals. Various cavalry units, now actively pursuing the Confederate leader, scoured the country.

May 8, Monday

PAROLES OF WESTERN CONFEDERATE FORCES ACCEPTED.

The Federal commissioners of E. R. S. Canby accepted the paroles of Richard Taylor's troops in Mississippi, Alabama, and east Louisiana. Canby was under orders to prepare part of an expedition planned by Grant into the Trans-Mississippi, where the last sizable force of Confederates still held out. There was also talk of negotiations in the Trans-Mississippi. Throughout the Confederacy small groups and individual soldiers surrendered or just went home. Near Readsville, Mo., there was a skirmish. Union scouts operated until the tenth in Saline, La Fayette, and Cooper counties, Mo., and until the twentieth from Plum Creek to Midway Station, Neb. Terr. An expedition from Spring Hill, Ala., to Baton Rouge, La., lasted until the twenty-second.

May 9, Tuesday

In Arkansas negotiations were going on at Chalk Bluff on the St. Francis River for the surrender of the men of Brig. Gen. M. Jeff Thompson, the eccentric and brilliant Confederate leader in Missouri and the West. President Johnson recognized Francis H. Pierpoint as governor of Virginia. During the war Pierpoint had headed a Union "restored" state of Virginia in the territory held by Federals. The trial of the eight accused Lincoln assassination conspirators began.

President and Mrs. Davis met near Dublin on the Oconee River in Georgia. Meanwhile, Federal cavalry closed in on the remnant of the Confederate government.

May 10, Wednesday

CAPTURE OF PRESIDENT DAVIS.

PRESIDENT JOHNSON PROCLAIMS ARMED RESISTANCE AT AN END.

Early in the morning Federal troops surprised the encampment of President Davis near Irwinville, Ga. President Davis, Mrs. Davis, Postmaster General Reagan, presidential secretary Burton Harrison, and a few others were taken into custody. There are numerous accounts of the capture and details are contradictory. There were reports of Davis being taken in woman's dress, in various forms of disguise, and of his trying to escape. Many of these stories appear to be exaggerated. Apparently he did wear a waterproof raincoat and had a shawl on due to the rain, and was first found a short distance from his tent in a futile effort to escape the Fourth Michigan Cavalry. Other officials of the Confederacy were taken into custody elsewhere, while a few, Judah Benjamin among them, escaped. With the capture of Davis the Confederate government ceased to exist. Davis was taken to Macon, Ga., and thence to Fort Monroe, Va., where he was imprisoned. At first he was kept in chains in a cell, but eventually conditions improved and his family was allowed to be with him. He was released May 13, 1867, without trial. But in mid-1865 feeling ran high in some quarters. There was talk of trial and execution. There was quarreling over the reward for the capture and considerable criticism of the Union cavalry operations. Rumors had it that Sherman and others actually desired the escape of Davis to avoid future political trouble. Mr. Davis himself maintained a quiet and dignified bearing throughout his capture and incarceration. There is no substantial evidence that any large sum of Confederate treasure was permanently lost. Funds had been dissipated for various purposes, and part of the gold being carried belonged to Richmond banks, to which it was returned.

President Johnson said in a proclamation that "armed resistance to the authority of this Government in the said insurrectionary States may be regarded as virtually at an end. . . ." Therefore the Navy should arrest the crews of commerce raiders still on the high seas and bring them in. He also warned against continued hospitality by foreign powers to Confederate cruisers. The blockade of states east of the Mississippi was partially lifted.

Confederate Maj. Gen. Samuel Jones surrendered forces under his command at Tallahassee, Fla. William Clarke Quantrill, twenty-seven-year-old Confederate guerrilla leader whose depredations had added so much horror to the war in Missouri, was fatally wounded by an irregular force of Federals near Taylorsville in Spencer County, Ky. He and a small group of followers had been looting in Kentucky. Quantrill died on June 6 in Louisville.

May 11, Thursday

Brig. Gen. M. Jeff Thompson surrendered what was left of his famous brigade at Chalk Bluff, Ark., under the same terms as Grant offered Lee.

Small groups continued to surrender east of the Mississippi as well. Federal troops, including many Negroes, moved out from the Gulf Coast area of Brazos Santiago, toward Brownsville, Tex. C.S.S. *Stonewall* arrived at Havana.

May 12, Friday

LAST LAND FIGHT.

In the last land engagement of any significance, Federal troops from Brazos Santiago Post, Tex., under Col. Theodore H. Barrett marched inland toward Brownsville and attacked Palmito Ranch on the banks of the Rio Grande. The camp was taken, but Federals evacuated under pressure. They returned the morning of the thirteenth, again moving toward Palmito Ranch, which had been reoccupied by the Confederates. The Union force was successful in the morning, but in midafternoon of May 13 the Confederates attacked and forced the Union troops to withdraw with considerable casualties. Col. John S. Ford, known as RIP or "Rest in Peace" Ford, led the main Southern drive. The skirmish, known as Palmito Ranch, of course had little bearing on the war. However, it was the last fighting between sizable bodies of men and, ironically, was a Confederate victory.

In Washington the eight accused Lincoln assassination conspirators pleaded not guilty to both specifications and charges before the military commission sitting as their court. Taking of testimony then began. President Johnson appointed Maj. Gen. O. O. Howard to head the Freedmen's Bureau.

May 13, Saturday

At Marshall, Tex., the Confederate governors of Arkansas, Louisiana, Missouri, and a representative of Texas met with E. Kirby Smith and other ranking officers. There was a threat by Jo Shelby and others to arrest Smith unless he continued the war. The governors drew up terms which they advised Smith to accept.

May 14, Sunday

Slight skirmishing on the Little Piney in Missouri, and a three-day Federal expedition from Brashear City to Ratliff's Plantation, La., marked the day.

May 15, Monday

There was a Union scout from Pine Bluff to Johnston's Farm, Ark.

May 17, Wednesday

Maj. Gen. Philip H. Sheridan was assigned to general Federal command west of the Mississippi River and south of the Arkansas River. With his reputation for destruction in the Shenandoah, this appointment angered many Southerners. May 17–20 scattered Confederate troops in Florida surrendered to Brig. Gen. Israel Vogdes.

May 18, Thursday
A Yankee scout operated from Lebanon to Warsaw, Mo.

May 19, Friday
Confederate raider *Stonewall* surrendered at Havana, Cuba. There was a Federal scout until May 22 from Kingsville, Mo.

May 20, Saturday
What little military action continued involved Federals versus guerrillas on the Blackwater, near Longwood, Mo.

May 22, Monday
President Johnson removed commercial restrictions on Southern ports except Galveston, La Salle, Brazos Santiago or Point Isabel, and Brownsville, Tex. There was a minor skirmish at Valley Mines, Mo. President Davis was imprisoned in a cell at Fort Monroe.

May 23, Tuesday
GRAND REVIEW OF THE ARMY OF THE POTOMAC IN WASHINGTON.

The Grand Armies of the Republic passed in a last review. From the Capitol to the White House crowds lined the streets, children sang patriotic songs, and the men marched. In the bright summer air the Army of the Potomac had come home to the appreciation of the nation. For the first time since that sad April day the flag at the White House was at full staff. Regiment by regiment, brigade by brigade, division by division, corps by corps, the conquerors came. There were the dashing horsemen of the cavalry, the long lines of blue-clad infantry, the cries of the crowd for their heroes. There were the engineers and pioneers with "the implements of their branch," the Irish Brigade with sprigs of green in their hats, the ambulances, the artillery, the Zouaves in their flashy uniforms. It was a march of victory and triumph; yet unseen thousands of others were there —those who had fallen on ten thousand fields. The war *was* over.

The pro-Union government of Virginia was established now in Richmond. There was a minor skirmish near Waynesville, Mo.; Union scouting from Thibodeaux to Lake Verret, La.; a scout until May 26 from Warrensburg, Mo., to the mouth of Coal Camp Creek; and until the twenty-seventh a scout from Pine Bluff to Monticello, Ark.

May 24, Wednesday
GRAND REVIEW OF SHERMAN'S ARMY IN WASHINGTON.

For the second straight day the troops paraded in review in Washington.

This time it was the men of the West. Sherman's men were more ragged, more loose in their marching, more rough-cut than those of the Army of the Potomac. In the rear of some units were the typical "Sherman's bummers," complete with mules laden with camp equipage and the spoils of foraging. Negro followers joined in with camp pets, adding a less formal air to the Grand Review. Evidence seems firm now that Gen. Sherman, halting at the White House reviewing stand, shook hands with President Johnson but refused the hand of Sec. of War Stanton because of their disagreement over the surrender of Gen. Johnston.

Sporadic shooting still went on, mainly Federals against guerrillas, as near Rocheport, Mo. There was a Union scout from Napoleonville to Bayou St. Vincent, La.

May 25, Thursday

With the reviews over in Washington, troops dispersed and most of them hurried home. Confederates evacuated Sabine Pass, Tex., and there was an expedition by Federals from Bayou Beouf to Bayou De Large, La., until the twenty-seventh. Twenty tons of captured Confederate powder "shook the foundations" of Mobile, Ala., when it exploded in a warehouse being used as an arsenal. The powder blast set off numerous other explosions. Boats at the dock, warehouses, and other buildings were left in ruins. Possibly three hundred people were casualties. Property loss was put at $5,000,000.

May 26, Friday

SURRENDER OF ARMY OF TRANS-MISSISSIPPI.

At New Orleans Lieut. Gen. S. B. Buckner, acting for Gen. E. Kirby Smith, Confederate commander of the Trans-Mississippi Department, entered into a military convention with Federal Maj. Gen. Peter J. Osterhaus, representing Maj. Gen. E. R. S. Canby. Under the terms of the surrender all resistance would cease, and officers and men would be paroled under terms similar to those of the Appomattox surrender. Gen. Smith approved the convention June 2 at Galveston. Thus the last significant army of the Confederacy surrendered. Some troops, including part of Jo Shelby's command, refused the terms and scattered to Mexico, the Far West, or just went home.

May 27, Saturday

Very minor skirmishing was reported in Chariton County, Mo., particularly at Switzler's Mill. President Johnson ordered most persons imprisoned by military authorities to be discharged.

May 29, Monday

AMNESTY PROCLAMATION OF PRESIDENT JOHNSON.

By presidential proclamation Andrew Johnson granted amnesty and pardon to all persons who directly or indirectly participated in "the existing rebellion," with a few exceptions. All property rights were restored except as to slaves and in special cases. Of course an oath was required that such persons would "henceforth" fully support, protect, and defend the Constitution and abide by the laws. This oath was opposed by the Radicals, who wanted an oath that could be taken only by those who had never directly or indirectly voluntarily supported the Confederacy. Johnson's proclamation followed the pattern laid down by Lincoln except that persons who participated in the rebellion and had had taxable property of over $20,000 were excluded from amnesty. Others excepted were those who held civil or diplomatic offices; those who left U.S. judicial posts; officers above the rank of colonel in the Army or lieutenant in the Navy; all who left Congress to join the South; all who resigned from the U. S. Army or Navy "to evade duty in resisting the rebellion"; all those who mistreated prisoners of war; all who were educated in the U.S. military or naval academies; governors of states in insurrection; those who left homes in the North to go South; those engaged in commerce destroying; and those who had violated previous oaths. But any person belonging to these excepted classes could apply to the President where "such clemency will be liberally extended as may be consistent with the facts of the case and the peace and dignity of the United States." Johnson was liberal in granting such clemency. The proclamation set the tone of the President for a moderate reconstruction policy. In another proclamation William W. Holden was appointed provisional governor of North Carolina.

There were operations in Texas and on the Rio Grande by the Federal Army for most of the rest of 1865 against guerrillas and former Confederates escaping into Mexico. Also there were scattered operations in Johnson County, Mo.

May 31, Wednesday
A Federal military expedition operated from Barrancas to Apalachicola, Fla., until June 6.

AFTERMATH

The War was over and the Peace begun. All the major forces of the Confederate States of America had surrendered, and President Davis was in prison. All that was left was bitterness and a few insignificant pockets of resistance. A new President in Washington was wrestling with reconstruction, as it was called, and facing rising impatience with his policies, which, like those of Lincoln, were more restoration than reconstruction. The armies of the Union had marched in Grand Review and then most of them went home except for those needed in occupation duties. The people now were asking in massive chorus—what next? Personal life could be taken up again and if there were no opportunities at home, there were plenty to the westward. There must be a blending of the way of life of 1860 and the new ways of 1865. There was the problem of the freed slave. Was the Negro a full citizen? How could or should he be brought into the stream of national life? Slavery was in effect actually abolished as the Thirteenth Amendment to the Constitution received approval by most states. What would the new United States be like? The headlines of battles appeared no more; the bulletin boards with their chilling casualty lists had ceased.

June 1, Thursday

A Federal military expedition operated through Pocahontas and Pendleton counties, W. Va., and Highland County, Va. It was a day of humiliation and prayer in honor of Abraham Lincoln.

June 2, Friday

Confederate Gen. E. Kirby Smith at Galveston officially accepted the surrender terms made May 26 at New Orleans.

Lambdin P. Milligan and W. A. Bowles, condemned to be executed this day, were reprieved and sentenced to life imprisonment. Proceedings had been instituted in the Federal courts to reverse their conviction by military court-martial on charges of conspiring against the United States, giving aid and comfort to rebels, and inciting insurrection. Milligan, a prominent Indiana leader of the Copperheads, was arrested Oct. 5, 1864. On Dec. 17, 1866, the U. S. Supreme Court in *ex parte* Milligan unanimously ruled that Milligan be released. A majority held that neither the President nor Congress had the power to order military commissions to try civilians outside the actual theater of war. A minority held that Congress had such power.

The British government officially withdrew belligerent rights from the Confederacy. President Johnson lifted military restrictions on trade in the United States except on contraband of war.

June 3, Saturday

Southern naval forces on the Red River officially surrendered.

June 6, Tuesday

Citizens of Missouri ratified a new state constitution abolishing slavery. Guerrilla chieftain William Clarke Quantrill died in Louisville, Ky., of wounds received May 10. Confederate prisoners of war who were willing to take the oath of allegiance were declared released by President Johnson. Officers above the rank of army captain or navy lieutenant were excepted.

June 8, Thursday
The Sixth Army Corps, which had missed the big review, had its own parade in Washington.

June 9, Friday
Another serious explosion of ammunition occurred. At Chattanooga, Tenn., an ordnance building blew up when set afire by a locomotive on a siding nearby. Casualties were put at about ten.

June 13, Tuesday
President Johnson appointed William L. Sharkey provisional governor of the state of Mississippi. His duties were to include the early convening of a convention of loyal citizens to alter or amend the state constitution and set up a new regular state government. In another proclamation the President declared trade open east of the Mississippi except for contraband of war. He also declared Tennessee, which had adopted a constitution and reorganized its government after suppressing the rebellion, restored and the inhabitants free of all disabilities and disqualifications.

June 17, Saturday
President Johnson named James Johnson provisional governor of Georgia and Andrew J. Hamilton provisional governor of Texas, continuing his policy of attempting to restore representative pro-Union government to the states as soon as possible.

June 21, Wednesday
Lewis E. Parsons was named provisional governor of Alabama by President Johnson.

June 22, Thursday
C.S.S. *Shenandoah* in the Bering Sea captured two whaling vessels.

June 23, Friday
President Johnson declared the Federal blockade of the Southern states, in existence since April, 1861, at an end. At Doaksville, near Fort Towson in the Indian Territory, Cherokee leader Brig. Gen. Stand Watie surrendered the Cherokee, Creek, Seminole, and Osage Battalion to Lieut. Col. Asa Mathews. As the Indian general signed, with picturesque black hair falling to his shoulders, he represented the last formal submission of any sizable body of Confederate troops. Rear Admiral Samuel F. Du Pont died suddenly at Philadelphia.

June 24, Saturday
Commercial restrictions were removed from states and territories west of the Mississippi River by President Johnson.

June 26, Monday
Six whalers were captured in the Bering Sea by C.S.S. *Shenandoah.*

June 28, Wednesday
C.S.S. *Shenandoah* took eleven whalers in the Bering Sea, last day of the cruiser's operations.

June 30, Friday
LINCOLN CONSPIRATORS CONVICTED.

After a lengthy trial the military commission sitting in Washington found all eight alleged Lincoln assassination conspirators guilty. Dr. Samuel Mudd, Samuel Arnold, and Michael O'Laughlin received life sentences, while Edward Spangler was given six years. David Herold, Lewis Payne, George A. Atzerodt, and Mary E. Surratt were sentenced to be hanged. An outcry went up over the decision to execute Mrs. Surratt and several efforts were made to have the sentence changed, but to no avail. President Johnson named Benjamin F. Perry provisional governor of South Carolina.

July 1, Saturday
New Hampshire ratified the Thirteenth Amendment.

July 7, Friday
EXECUTION OF LINCOLN CONSPIRATORS.

On a hot, oppressive midsummer day in Washington a large crowd gathered in the Arsenal grounds at the Old Penitentiary Building. Four graves were dug, four prisoners brought in, and four hanged. Lewis Payne, George A. Atzerodt, David Herold, and Mrs. Mary E. Surratt were executed for their roles in the assassination of Abraham Lincoln. Until the very last it was hoped by some that there would be presidential intervention in the case of Mrs. Surratt, but it was not forthcoming. The four other convicted conspirators were taken to Fort Jefferson on Dry Tortugas off Key West, Fla. There, in 1867, Michael O'Laughlin died of yellow fever. Because of his role as a doctor in the epidemic, Samuel Mudd was pardoned in 1868, and in 1869 Edward Spangler and Samuel Arnold were also pardoned.

July 13, Thursday
William Marvin was named provisional governor of Florida by President Johnson.

July 24, Monday

Ford's Theatre in Washington was rented by the United States Government for $1500 a month. The building was purchased by the government for $88,000 in July, 1866. It was turned into offices of the Adjutant General's Department. On June 9, 1893, a section of the front of the building collapsed, killing twenty-two and injuring sixty-five.

August 2, Wednesday

C.S.S. *Shenandoah* under Lieut. Waddell, en route from the Arctic toward San Francisco, learned from a British bark that the war was over.

August 29, Tuesday

President Johnson proclaimed that even articles declared as contraband of war could now be traded with states "recently declared in insurrection." The proclamation would take effect Sept. 1.

September 14, Thursday

At Fort Smith, Ark., representatives of the Cherokees, Creeks, Choctaws, Chickasaws, Osages, Seminoles, Senecas, Shawnees, and Quapaws signed a treaty of loyalty with the United States, and renounced all Confederate agreements. Additional Indian groups later did the same. On Sept. 21 a treaty was signed with the Choctaws and Chickasaws calling for peace and friendship and abolishing slavery.

October 11, Wednesday

Confederate Vice-President Alexander H. Stephens, Cabinet members John H. Reagan and George A. Trenholm, Gov. Charles Clark of Mississippi and Asst. Sec. of War John A. Campbell were paroled by President Johnson. All had been held in prison since the collapse of their country.

October 12, Thursday

Martial law was ended in Kentucky by presidential proclamation.

November 6, Monday

Confederate cruiser *Shenandoah* was surrendered by Lieut. James Waddell to British officials at Liverpool.

November 10, Friday

Capt. Henry Wirz, who commanded the notorious Andersonville, Ga., Confederate prison, was hanged after conviction by a military commission on charges of cruelty to Federal prisoners of war.

695

November 13, Monday
The Thirteenth Amendment was ratified by South Carolina.

December 1, Friday
President Johnson revoked the suspension of the privilege of the writ of habeas corpus for all of the United States except former Confederate states, the District of Columbia, and New Mexico and Arizona territories.

December 2, Saturday
The Alabama legislature ratified the Thirteenth Amendment.

December 4, Monday
The legislature of North Carolina accepted the Thirteenth Amendment, but the Mississippi legislature rejected it.

December 5, Tuesday
The Georgia legislature approved the Thirteenth Amendment.

December 11, Monday
Oregon ratified the Thirteenth Amendment.

December 18, Monday
The Thirteenth Amendment to the U. S. Constitution abolishing slavery was declared in effect by Sec. of State Seward after approval by twenty-seven states.

1866

April 2, Monday
"Now, therefore, I, Andrew Johnson, President of the United States, do hereby proclaim and declare that the insurrection which heretofore existed in the States of Georgia, South Carolina, Virginia, North Carolina, Tennessee, Alabama, Louisiana, Arkansas, Mississippi, and Florida is at an end and is henceforth to be so regarded." Texas only was omitted, its government not yet formed.

August 20, Monday
In a new proclamation President Johnson declared the insurrection at an end in Texas: "I do further proclaim that the said insurrection is at an end

and that peace, order, tranquility, and civil authority now exist in and throughout the whole of the United States of America."

The Civil War was over and the painful days of reconstruction had begun. But, as in all history, the cataclysm of 1861–65 would color subsequent events. Laws, politics, economics, social mores, the people of all the states were altered irrevocably and for generations to come by the years of war.

SPECIAL STUDIES

THE PEOPLE OF WAR

To wage warfare requires organized, mass efforts of the people. The American Civil War was the greatest such effort seen in this nation up to that time and, in some ways, since. A substantial percentage of the populace was affected: almost every family had a member or members in the armed forces of the warring powers. Therefore, the mere figures of numbers in the armies and navies, and, inevitably, casualties, are a revealing part of history and far from lifeless statistics.

The first U.S. national census of 1790 showed the total population to be 3,929,214. Of this total 1,961,174 lived in the eight slaveholding states of the South. Of these 657,327 were slaves and 32,457 free Negroes. In the nine Northern states the population was 1,968,040, of whom 27,070 were free Negroes, while 40,354 were still slaves. Thus the all-over population balance North and South was fairly equal near the end of the eighteenth century.

Population increases ranged from 32.67 per cent to 36.45 percent every ten years through 1850. But the balance changed. In 1850, out of a total of 23,191,876, there were in the North (including territories) 13,527,220 persons compared to 9,664,656 in the South (fifteen slave states), of whom 3,204,051 were slaves.

In the ten years between 1850 and 1860 the total population jumped to 31,443,321. The North in 1860 numbered 19,127,948, of whom 225,967 were free Negroes and 64 still were slaves. In the South (slave states) there were 12,315,373 people, of whom 3,953,696 were slaves and 262,003 free Negroes. Thus just before the Civil War the slave South had a white population of 8,099,674 compared to 18,901,917 in the North. The eleven states that fully seceded counted a total population of 9,103,332, of whom 5,449,462 were white, 3,521,110 slaves, and 132,760 free Negroes. To this total were added those sympathetic to the Confederacy in Missouri, Kentucky, Maryland, and Delaware as well as a few in the District of Columbia and the territories. Probably something over 6,000,000 white Americans, therefore, can be said to have lived in Confederate territory or to have been sympathetic to the Southern cause.

This 6,000,000 compares to 18,810,123 whites in the non-slavery Northern states and territories, to which must be added pro-unionists in the border areas and the Negroes who supported the North in the Army or in other ways. It thus can be said that over 20,000,000 Northerners faced over

6,000,000 Southerners. As more-than-interested spectators, and occasionally participants, were the nearly 4,000,000 slaves.

1860 Population by States and Regions[1]

States, etc.	Total	White	Free Negro	Slave
NORTH (free states)				
California	379,994	375,908	4,086	
Colorado Territory	34,277	34,231	46	
Connecticut	460,147	451,520	8,627	
Dakota Territory	4,837	4,837		
Illinois	1,711,951	1,704,323	7,628	
Indiana	1,350,428	1,339,000	11,428	
Iowa	674,913	673,844	1,104	
Kansas Territory	107,206	106,579	625	2
Maine	628,279	626,952	1,327	
Massachusetts	1,231,066	1,221,464	9,602	
Michigan	749,113	742,314	6,799	
Minnesota	172,023	173,596	259	
Nebraska Territory	28,841	28,759	67	15
Nevada Territory	6,857	6,812	45	
New Hampshire	326,073	325,579	494	
New Jersey	672,035	646,699	25,318	18
New York	3,880,735	3,831,730	49,005	
Ohio	2,339,511	2,302,838	36,664	
Pennsylvania	2,906,215	2,849,266	56,849	
Oregon	52,465	52,337	128	
Rhode Island	174,620	170,658	3,952	
Utah Territory	40,273	40,214	30	29
Vermont	315,098	314,389	709	
Washington Territory	11,594	11,564	30	
Wisconsin	775,881	774,710	1,171	
Total	19,034,434	18,810,123	225,973	64
BORDER				
Delaware	112,216	90,589	19,829	1,798
District of Columbia	75,080	60,764	11,131	3,185
Kentucky	1,155,684	919,517	10,684	225,483
Maryland	687,049	515,918	83,942	87,189
Missouri	1,182,012	1,063,509	3,572	114,931
New Mexico Territory	93,516	93,431	85	
Total	3,305,557	2,743,728	129,243	432,586

[1] Due to Census Bureau adjustments there is a small discrepancy between the total population in Northern states for 1860 and the total of whites, free Negroes, and slaves. In the above table white includes taxed Indians and Chinese. Population figures are from the various reports of the United States Census Bureau; *National Almanac,* 1863, George W. Childs, Philadelphia, 1863, pp. 307–10; *Historical Statistics of the United States, Colonial Times to 1957,* A Statistical Abstract Supplement, U. S. Department of Commerce, Bureau of the Census, U. S. Government Printing Office, Washington, 1960, pp. 1–13.

States, etc.	Total	White	Free Negro	Slave
SOUTH (seceded states)				
Alabama	964,201	526,431	2,690	435,080
Arkansas	435,450	324,191	144	111,115
Florida	140,424	77,747	932	61,745
Georgia	1,057,286	591,588	3,500	462,198
Louisiana	708,002	357,629	18,647	331,726
Mississippi	791,305	353,901	773	436,631
North Carolina	992,622	631,100	30,463	331,059
South Carolina	703,708	291,388	9,914	402,406
Tennessee	1,109,801	826,782	7,300	275,719
Virginia	1,596,318	1,047,411	58,042	490,865
Texas	604,215	421,294	355	182,566
Total	9,103,332	5,449,462	132,760	3,521,110

Slavery

As the population grew, so did slavery, though at a somewhat lower rate. In 1800 the increase since 1790 in slaves was 27.97 per cent compared to a total population rise of 35.02 per cent. In 1860 slave population increase over 1850 was 23.38 per cent, while the national percentage was 35.58 per cent. The number of free Negroes had swelled rapidly.

Manumission of slaves occurred, but totaled a small percentage of the number of slaves. In 1850 the census showed that out of 3,200,364 slaves, 1467 had been manumitted: one in 2181 slaves. In 1860 figures of the census show the slave total at 3,953,696 with 3018 freed, for one out of 1309. According to the census figures of 1860 there were 803 fugitive slaves compared to 1011 in 1850. It may be assumed, however, that not all fugitive slaves or freed slaves were accurately counted.[2]

As to slaveholders, there were 385,00 in the South in 1860, including some who were Negroes. Three quarters of the free Southern population had no direct connection with slavery through their families or as owners. But in South Carolina and Mississippi about half of all white families owned slaves. As to the numbers held by each owner, 88 per cent held less than twenty, 72 per cent less than ten, and nearly 50 per cent less than five. The so-called aristocratic planters were limited to about 10,000 families who were large slaveholders. In the deep South, however, large slaveholdings were more numerous than in the middle South or in the border states.[8]

[2] *National Almanac*, 1863, p. 312.
[8] Census Reports. See also Stampp, Kenneth, *The Peculiar Institution, Slavery in the Ante-Bellum South*, Alfred A. Knopf, New York, 1956, pp. 29–33.

Immigration

The influx of foreign peoples continued into the United States, Civil War or no Civil War. In the first two years of the conflict the number of aliens arriving in the Federal Union declined from 1860, but by 1863 it surpassed immediate prewar years. However, it was by no means as high as in the 1850s and late 1840s. Scores of agents went to England and Ireland during the war to engage hands for factories and farms. One paper reported in 1864, "Not only villages, but whole counties in Ireland, England will be emptied of their able bodied industrial population."

Number of Alien Passengers Arriving in the United States

1859	121,282	1862	91,985	1865	248,120
1860	153,640	1863	176,282	1866	318,568
1861	91,918	1864	193,418	1861–1865	801,723

Of these 801,723 for the years 1861–65, the distribution by major countries was: Germany, 233,052; Ireland, 196,359; England (less Scotland), 85,116; China, 24,282; France, 14,017; Scotland, 10,156; Norway-Sweden, 11,493.[4]

Cities

The nation was of course far more rural in 1860 than a century later, and the large cities did not play such a preponderant political role, though there were centers of industry, trade, and culture. There were only nine cities with more than 100,000 inhabitants[5]: New York, 805,651; Philadelphia, 562,529; Brooklyn, 266,661; Baltimore, 212,418; Boston, 177,812; New Orleans, 168,675; Cincinnati, 161,044; St. Louis, 160,773; Chicago, 109,260. There were only seven cities with over 50,000, none of them in the Confederacy: Buffalo, 81,129; Newark, 71,914; Louisville, 68,033; Albany, 62,-367; Washington, 61,122; San Francisco, 56,802; and Providence, 50,666.

Thus New Orleans was the only large-sized city in the Confederate States. Other Southern centers were Charleston, S.C. with 40,578; Richmond, 37,910; Montgomery, 35,967; Mobile, 29,508; Memphis, 22,623; and Savannah, 22,292.

---

[4] Census figures up to 1868 included all alien passengers arriving in the United States, not just immigrants. For full figures, see *Immigration into the United States,* Monthly Summary of Commerce and Finance of the United States, June, 1903, No. 12, Series 1902–103, Government Printing Office, Washington, 1903, pp. 4336–40; *Historical Statistics of the United States,* pp. 56–59.
[5] *National Almanac,* 1863, p. 310.

MEN AT WAR

When it came to counting the numbers of men available for war, the North again was predominant in its advantages. Putting the 1860 white population of the Northern free states and territories at 18,810,123, the eleven seceding states had 5,449,462 whites. In the border states of Delaware, Kentucky, Maryland, Missouri, the District of Columbia, and New Mexico Territory, there were 2,743,728 whites. Estimating broadly, the Confederacy may well have had between 6,000,000 and 7,000,000 white residents, while the North could boast over 20,000,000.

There were 2,800,969 white males in the eleven seceding states and 11,068,465 in the rest of the nation in 1860. Assuming that at least a half million border-state white males out of 1,294,194 were pro-Confederate, the Southern white male potential might be put at close to 3,500,000. The Northern white male potential might be put at 10,500,000, deducting the half million estimated for the border states. Then too, the North had Negroes to draw on as soldiers. Of these white male populations a large percentage were children, elderly, physically incapacitated for service, otherwise exempt, or unavailable.

Census figures for 1860 put the supposed "military population" available at: white males between eighteen and forty-five at 1,064,193 for the seceding states and 4,559,872 for the rest of the nation. Adjustment, however, must be made for the border states, and for those unfit for duty due to various infirmities or otherwise exempt. Rejections for assorted reasons are put by some at 20 per cent, though they may have been less. A reasonable assumption may then be drawn that the Confederacy had something around 1,000,000 males available for military service in 1861, including some border-staters, while the North had perhaps slightly under 3,500,000, plus the Negro potential. With few exceptions the "numbers game" as to exact totals of men in the armies, casualties, and other manpower figures cannot be exact. There are too many imponderables entering into the counts. Numerous studies have been made, but their conclusions often conflict.[1]

---

[1] *National Almanac*, 1863, p. 309; Fox, William F., *Regimental Losses in the American Civil War, 1861–1865*, Albany Publishing Co., Albany, N.Y., 1889, p. 552.

Size of the Armies

There is no accurate means of determining just how many individuals served in the armed forces of either the Federal or Confederate armies. Many educated estimates utilizing official and unofficial figures are available. The figures herein accepted are the result of an extensive study of these estimates.

Total enlistments in the Federal forces are officially put at 2,778,304, including, in the Army, 2,489,836 whites, 178,975 Negroes, 3530 Indians, and 105,963 in the Navy and Marines. Some scholars do not even accept these figures as authoritative and it must be borne in mind that many thousands who are included enlisted more than once. Also included are troops whose period of service varied from a few days to the duration. The important question is how many *individuals* served in the armed forces. Estimates run from 1,550,000 to 2,200,000 Federals. Probably something over 2,000,000 would be as accurate a figure as possible on total individuals in the Federal armed forces.

For the Confederates, figures are even more in dispute. Estimates of total Confederate enlistments run from 600,000 to 1,400,000. Many Confederate scholars count 600,000 total individuals. After considering the numerous surveys made, perhaps 750,000 individuals would be reasonably close. Thus it can be said that Federals, counting Negro troops, outnumbered the Confederates about three to one in number of individuals.

As to the navies, the Federals totaled 132,554 enlistments (105,963 credited to states, plus other sailors not so credited). For the Confederate Navy, in 1864 enlisted men totaled 3674, plus officers and marines, but no reliable totals are available.[2]

---

[2] *The War of the Rebellion: A Compilation of the Official Records of the Union and Confederate Armies,* Government Printing Office, Washington, 1880–1901 (Hereafter referred to as *O.R.,* Series I meant unless otherwise indicated), Series III, Vol. IV, p. 1270; Fox, *Regimental Losses,* pp. 533–37; *Official Records of the Union and Confederate Navies in the War of the Rebellion,* Government Printing Office, Washington, 1894–1927 (hereafter referred to as *Navy O.R.,* Series I meant unless otherwise indicated), Series II, Vol. II, p. 633. For sizes of Union and Confederate armies a survey was made of more than twenty-five studies and opinions. The above is the author's evaluation of these figures.

Comparative Strength of Armies[3]

Date	Union Total	Union Present	Union Absent	Conf. Present Duty	Conf. Aggregate Present	Conf. Present & Absent	Conf. Absent
Jan. 1, '61	16,367	14,663	1704				
	Regulars	Regulars	Regulars				
July 1, '61	186,751	183,588	3163				
Dec. 31, '61				209,852	258,680	326,768	68,088
Jan. 1, '62	575,917	527,204	48,713				
Mar. 31, '62	637,126	533,984	103,142				
June 30, '62				169,943	224,146	328,049	103,903
Dec. 31, '62				253,208	304,015	449,439	145,424
Jan. 1, '63	918,191	698,802	219,389				
Dec. 31, '63				233,586	277,970	464,646	186,676
Jan. 1, '64	860,737	611,250	249,487				
June 30, '64				161,528	194,764	315,847	121,083
Dec. 31, '64				154,910	196,016	400,787	204,771
Jan. 1, '65	959,460	620,924	338,536				
1865				125,994	160,198	358,692	198,494
March 31, '65	980,086	657,747	322,339				
May 1, '65	1,000,516						

The figures show more completely than any text the disparity between the armies. The Federals at the start of 1862 had a two-to-one advantage which steadily mounted until the end of 1864 when the Union advantage in numbers present was over three to one. Also of great importance are the absentee figures. While continually high in the Federal forces, rising on January 1, 1865, to over a third of the total, the Confederate figures are much higher. At the end of 1864, the Southern absent totaled more than 50 per cent, and was of course much more important as the total available forces were so low. In addition, for much of the war a large Confederate force was in the Trans-Mississippi region, where it could not contribute to eastern operations.

The Men

Although many of those in both armies were mere youngsters in age at the time of their enlistments, they soon became men.

[3] Sources: Union figures from Kreidberg, Marvin A., and Merton G. Henry, *History of Military Mobilization in the United States Army 1775–1945*, Department of the Army, Washington, 1955, p. 95, and *Provost Marshal General's Report*, Washington, 1866, I, p. 102. Confederate figures from *O.R.*, Series IV, Vol. I, pp. 822, 1176, Vol. II, pp. 278, 380, 1073, Vol. III, pp. 520, 989, 1182.

All but 1.5 per cent of the enlisted men in the Federal Army were between 18 and 46 at the time of their enlistment; and all but 3.3 per cent of the officers fell into that age bracket. The average age was slightly under 26 years (25.8083) at time of enlistment.

There were 127 Northern soldiers recorded as being age 13; 330 age 14; 773 age 15; 2758 age 16; 6425 age 17; 133,475 age 18; 90,215 age 19; 71,058 age 20; 97,136 age 21. From there on it gradually went down to 7012 age 45; 967 age 46; and 2366 age 50 or over.[4]

As to physical characteristics, the average height of the Federal soldier was put at 5 feet, 8¼ inches. The tallest man authentically recorded was said to be Capt. Van Buskirk of the Twenty-seventh Indiana, who stood 6 feet, 10½ inches. The shortest man as far as records go was a member of the 192nd Ohio, and at the age of 24 he measured 3 feet, 4 inches in height.

Incomplete records indicate the average weight was 143½ pounds. About 13 per cent had black hair, 25 per cent dark hair, 30 per cent brown, 24 per cent light, 4 per cent sandy, 3 per cent red, and 1 per cent gray hair. Forty-five per cent of the Yankees had blue eyes, 24 per cent gray, 13 per cent hazel, 10 per cent dark, and 8 per cent black.

In prewar occupations some 48 per cent of the Yankees were farmers, 24 per cent mechanics, 16 per cent laborers, 5 per cent in "commercial pursuits," 3 per cent professional men, and 4 per cent miscellaneous.

As to nativity of Northerners, basing the Army on a total of 2,000,000, about three fourths were native Americans. Of the 500,000 foreign-born, about 175,000 were from Germany, 150,000 from Ireland, 50,000 from England, 50,000 from British America, and 75,000 from other countries.[5]

The vast majority of soldiers on both sides were volunteers. There were 16,367 in the Regular Army in 1861. This increased to 25,463 by January 1, 1863, and then dropped to 21,669 by March 31, 1865. There was a militia (on paper at least) in most states, but as an actual force it had before the war fallen into ineffectual decay and cannot be said to have been more than an institution for occasional parades, festivals, or social events.

In the North the draft act of 1863 resulted in four different enrollments: July, 1863; March, 1864; July, 1864; and December, 1864. These drafts resulted in a total of 249,259 men being held to service. Of this total, some 86,724 paid commutation to be relieved of service, which brought in $26,366,316.78. There were actually 162,535 men raised by the draft. Of this total only 46,347 men were held to personal service; 116,188 furnished substitutes. Thus the draft provided only about 6 per cent of

[4] From *Ages of U.S. Volunteer Soldier*, U. S. Sanitary Commission, New York, 1866, pp. 5–6.
[5] Fox, *Regimental Losses*, pp. 62–63.

the total Federal enlistments in the Army. Nevertheless the draft's main effect seems to have been to stimulate enlistments of volunteers who made up the great bulk of the manpower.

In July of 1862, the Federal Congress authorized the acceptance of Negroes for labor and military service. The first major recruiting began in Louisiana in September of 1862. A few units were organized by states, but for the most part they were considered Federal troops. A total of 178,892 Negroes officially served in the Union Army, of whom 134,111 were from slave states, with some 93,346 of these from seceded states. They participated in 166 regiments including 145 infantry regiments, 12 regiments of heavy artillery, 1 regiment of light artillery, 1 of engineers, and 7 cavalry regiments. Losses in Negro troops were 2751 men killed or mortally wounded; 29,618 died of disease. Among the 7122 white officers, 143 were killed or mortally wounded and 138 died of disease.[6]

In the Confederacy problems of manpower were inherently much greater. Here, as in the North, conscription undoubtedly served to keep men in the Army and to stimulate enlistments and reenlistments far more effectively than it did to provide manpower directly. Furthermore, national conscription was contrary to the theories of local and personal autonomy that formed the spiritual background of the Confederacy. Conflicts with state and local authorities, large exemptions, and substitutions all contributed to the conscription problem. Records are not available as to the effects of conscription in the Confederacy, but its impact both for good and evil is readily apparent. The inescapable fact is that the South urgently needed skilled manpower at home to keep the economy rolling; at the same time the Confederacy desperately needed men for the armies. With too few men to meet both needs, the two necessities could not be reconciled.

The Confederate Congress in an act of April 16, 1862, adopted conscription, which included substitution. This was the first military draft in the history of the United States. The substitution measure was repealed December 28, 1863. An act of February 17, 1864, authorized use of Negroes, free and slave, as laborers in units designed for manifold duties. It was not until March 13, 1865, and after much debate, that provision was made for the use of slaves as soldiers. The move came far too late to be of significance militarily.

Incomplete reports show that 81,993 conscripts were drafted in the

---

[6] Kreidberg and Henry, *Military Mobilization,* pp. 92, 95, 108, 114; Wiley, Bell I., *Southern Negroes 1861–1865,* Rinehart & Company, New York, 1938, p. 311; *O.R.,* Series III, Vol. IV, pp. 1269–70, Vol. V, p. 662; *PMG Report,* I, pp. 68–69, 95, 102; Fox, *Regimental Losses,* p. 533; Dyer, Frederick H., *A Compendium of the War of the Rebellion,* The Dyer Publishing Company, Des Moines, Iowa, 1908, p. 18.

Confederate states east of the Mississippi from April 16, 1862, until early 1865.[7]

Much is often made of the supposition that a disproportionately large number of West Point graduates went South. While it is of course true that many exceptionally capable officers did follow their states into secession, a majority of trained officers stayed with the Union. Of the 1249 known living graduates when the war commenced, 89 per cent served in either the Union or Confederate armies. Of this 89 per cent nearly three fourths were in the Federal armies. While figures vary, it is recorded that 296 West Point graduates joined the Confederacy. Of these over 13 per cent were born in the North and over 11 per cent appointed from the free states.

Of the 1098 officers in the Regular Army at the outbreak of the war, one record lists 286 who resigned and joined the Confederacy. Of this number 187 were West Point graduates, and 99 non-West Pointers. Of those who did go with the South, 26 were appointed from the North, including 16 West Point graduates. One estimate states that out of 350 West Point graduates from slave states who were in military service at the beginning of the war, 162 remained with the North and 168 went South. Of the Regular Army enlisted men, only 26 are recorded as having joined the South, a surprisingly low figure.[8]

Casualties

Statistics can never measure the true loss in any war, but casualty totals include life and death figures and must be considered. Used in perspective they can give added meaning to any conflict. In the Civil War exact totals in most categories are impossible to ascertain and there

---

[7] *O.R.*, Series IV, Vol. III, p. 1101.

[8] As usual there are many discrepancies in the sources. We have tried to analyze and balance the following: Upton, Emory, *The Military Policy of the United States,* Government Printing Office, Washington, 1912, pp. 238–39; Heitman, Francis B., *Historical Register and Dictionary of the United States Army,* Government Printing Office, Washington, 1903, Vol. II, pp. 180–84; *The Centennial of the United States Military Academy at West Point, New York,* Government Printing Office, Washington, 1904, Vol. I, pp. 635, 638; Cullum, George Washington, *Biographical Register of Officers and Graduates of the U.S. Military Academy,* D. Van Nostrand, New York, 1868, Vol. I, p. 6; Eliot, Ellsworth, Jr., *West Point in the Confederacy,* G. A. Baker & Co., Inc., New York, 1941, p. xv; Ambrose, Stephen E., *Duty, Honor, Country, A History of West Point,* The Johns Hopkins Press, Baltimore, 1966, p. 180; Kreidberg and Henry, *History of Military Mobilization,* pp. 115–16; for careful analysis of numbers of generals and other statistical information, see introductions to Warner, Ezra J., *Generals in Gray* and *Generals in Blue,* Louisiana State University Press, 1959 and 1964.

has been much argument and controversy involving them. Herein we have used all major studies of numbers and losses and in many cases have had to draw our own conclusions. But in broad terms the figures can be said to be within reasonable range of the truth. Exact counting was difficult then; it is, to understate the matter, impossible today.

FEDERAL

Total Federal army deaths from all causes are put at 360,222 by the War Department.[9] Total battle deaths, both killed in action and mortally wounded, numbered 110,100. Of these 67,088 died in battle and 43,012 were mortally wounded.[10]

Disease claimed 224,580, although the exact figure is in dispute.[11] Of the total deaths in the Federal forces, some 30,192 died while prisoners of war.[12] Of the Federal army deaths not attributed to battle or disease, there are recorded 4114 killed in accidents, 4944 drowned, 520 murdered, 104 killed after capture, 391 dead by suicide, 267 executed by Federal authorities, 64 executed by the enemy, 313 dead of sunstroke; others, 2043; and causes not stated, 12,121.[13]

Wounded figures on either side are somewhat conjectural, depending upon what is considered to constitute being wounded. Also many men were wounded more than once. The Federal army wounded are put at 275,175.[14]

In the Navy 1804 are listed as killed or mortally wounded, with 3000 dying of disease and accidents, and 2226 wounded. The dead include 342

---

[9] *O.R.*, Series III, Vol. V, p. 665, uses the figure of 359,528 for total deaths. This later was increased due to knowledge of additional prisoner deaths. *Battles and Leaders of the Civil War*, The Century Co., New York, 1884, 1888, Vol. IV, p. 767. Dyer, *Compendium*, p. 18. For breakdown purposes, however, the 359,528 figure is the one most frequently used.

[10] Dyer, *Compendium*, pp. 12, 18. Other sources make battle deaths 110,070, including *Battles and Leaders*, Vol. IV, p. 767. Early War Department figures, *O.R.*, Series III, Vol. V, p. 665, give 107,787, but this was adjusted upward later. Most authorities accept the 110,070 figure or the 110,100 figure.

[11] Dyer, *Compendium*, p. 18, gives 224,580. *O.R.*, Series III, Vol. V, p. 665, has 221,498; *Battles and Leaders*, Vol. IV, p. 767, gives 224,578; and other figures range from 199,720 to 250,000 in deaths from disease.

[12] *Battles and Leaders*, Vol. IV, p. 767.

[13] Dyer, *Compendium*, p. 18, from *Records of the Adjutant General's Office*.

[14] Rhodes, James Ford, *History of the United States, 1850–1877*, The Macmillan Co., New York, 1919, Vol. V, p. 187; Livermore, Thomas L., *Numbers and Losses in the Civil War*, Houghton, Mifflin and Co., Boston, 1901, 2nd ed., p. 9; Fox, *Regimental Losses*, p. 47.

who were scalded to death during action and 308 men drowned in action.[15]

Thus the total Federal casualties in the Army and Navy, including dead from all causes and wounded, come to 642,427.

CONFEDERATE

Casualties for the Confederacy are subject to more controversy than the Federal. Probably the best and most accepted estimate is 94,000 Confederates killed in battle or mortally wounded, while 164,000 died of disease.[16] Total deaths thus came to 258,000. One incomplete record puts wounded at 194,026.[17] Estimates of Confederates who died in Northern prisons are put at 26,000 to 31,000.

Total deaths in the Civil War for both sides may be placed at least at 623,026, with a minimum of 471,427 wounded, for a total casualty figure of 1,094,453.[18]

Other Wars[19]

War	U. S. Armed Forces	Total Casualties Dead & Wounded	Total Deaths	Battle Deaths	Wounded, Not Mortal
Revolution	not over 250,000	10,623	——	4435	6188
War of 1812	286,730	6765	——	2260	4505
Mexican War	115,874 (Army)	17,435 (Army & Navy)	13,283	1733 (Army & Navy)	4152 (Army & Navy)
Spanish-American War	306,760	4108	2446	385	1662
	4,743,826	320,710	116,708	53,513	204,002
World War I	4,057,101 A	300,041 A	106,378 A	50,510 A	193,663 A
	599,051 N	8106 N	7287 N	431 N	819 N
	78,839 M	12,371 M	2851 M	2461 M	9520 M
	8835 CG	—— CG	192 CG	111 CG	——

[15] Fox, *Regimental Losses*, p. 537.

[16] Fox, *Regimental Losses*, p. 554; Livermore, *Numbers and Losses*, pp. 63–64; Rhodes, *History of the U.S.*, Vol. V, p. 187.

[17] *Southern Historical Society Papers*, Vol. VII, June, 1879, "Confederate Losses During the War,—Correspondence Between Dr. Joseph Jones and General Samuel Cooper," pp. 287–90. Confederate Navy losses are unavailable.

[18] The total casualty figures are only approximate, as many uncertainties enter in. We repeat that all the figures herein used seem to be the best available, and nearly all are open to question as to exactness. Some authorities will disagree with our conclusions, but we believe no one has the correct answer in all cases.

[19] Kreidberg and Henry, *Military Mobilization*, pp. 706–7; *World Almanac*, 1967, p. 705; Correspondence, Directorate of Defense Information, Defense Department, Washington, referred author to *World Almanac* figures. ("A" in chart stands for Army; "N" for Navy; "M" Marines; "CG" Coast Guard; "AF" Air Force.)

	U. S. Armed Forces	Total Casualties Dead & Wounded	Total Deaths	Battle Deaths	Wounded, Not Mortal
World War II	16,363,659	1,078,162	407,316	292,131	670,846
	11,260,000 A	884,135 A	318,274 A	234,874 A	565,861 A
	4,183,466 N	100,392 N	62,614 N	36,950 N	37,778 N
	669,100 M	91,718 M	24,511 M	19,733 M	67,207 M
	241,093 CG	——— CG	1917 CG	574 CG	———
Korean War	5,764,143	157,530	54,246	33,629	103,284
	2,834,000 A	114,729 A	37,133 A	27,704 A	77,596 A
	1,177,000 N	6077 N	4501 N	1576 N	1576 N
	424,000 M	29,272 M	5528 M	4267 M	23,744 M
	1,285,000 AF	7452 AF	7084 AF	1200 AF	368 AF
	44,143 CG	———			———

Disease

Disease in the Civil War claimed a far deadlier toll than the battle-field. Of the many and varied death-dealing diseases a final summation shows that diarrhea and dysentery claimed 44,558 Union army lives. They were declared "the most important" causes of mortality from disease in the Army. The several varieties of "camp fever" such as typhoid, typhus, common continued, remittent, and typhomalarial fevers took 40,656 lives. Following these was pneumonia with 19,971 deaths. Among other leading causes of death were smallpox and varioloid, measles, consumption, and intermittent fevers. The biggest cause of discharge for disability was consumption, with 20,995.[20]

For the Confederate armies total figures on disease are unavailable. However, Bell Irvin Wiley in his authoritative *Life of Johnny Reb* arrives at the conclusion that for every soldier killed in battle or of mortal wounds, there were three deaths from disease. New recruits were prone to measles, as in the Federal armies. As in the Northern Army, dysentery and diarrhea were the most common diseases, with many fatalities. Malaria also struck heavily, as did typhoid, which was said to have been responsible for a fourth of the deaths from disease. Smallpox became particularly virulent as the war progressed. Pneumonia was very frequent as well.[21]

---

[20] Disease casualties in Union armies are taken from the monumental study *The Medical and Surgical History of the War of the Rebellion,* Washington, 1875, Medical Volume, Part First and Appendix, p. XLIII.
[21] Wiley, Bell Irvin, *The Life of Johnny Reb,* Bobbs-Merrill, Indianapolis, 1943, pp. 244–69. It would be difficult indeed to improve on this account.

The Chances of War

The Civil War was hard on officers as well as on the men. Figures show that of 583 general officers in the Union Army 47 were killed in action or died of wounds and 18 died of disease or as the result of accidents. Thus, 8 per cent were killed in action or mortally wounded.

For the Confederates, of 425 general officers 77 were killed in action or mortally wounded and 15 died of disease or accident. Thus 18 per cent of Confederate generals were killed or mortally wounded in action.[22]

Among the leading Federal officers killed were Maj. Gen. James B. McPherson, commander of the Army of the Tennessee, killed in the Battle of Atlanta; Maj. Gen. Joseph K. F. Mansfield, Antietam; Maj. Gen. John F. Reynolds, Gettysburg; Maj. Gen. John Sedgwick, Spotsylvania. Fourteen division commanders were killed or mortally wounded, including Maj. Gen. Philip Kearny at Chantilly.

The most prominent Confederate death was Lieut. Gen. Thomas J. Jackson, mortally wounded at Chancellorsville. Gen. Albert Sidney Johnston in Confederate command at Shiloh or Pittsburg Landing was killed during the battle. Other well-known Southern fatalities were Lieut. Gen. Leonidas Polk at Pine Mountain; Lieut. Gen. Ambrose P. Hill at the fall of Petersburg; Maj. Gen. J. E. B. Stuart at Yellow Tavern; Maj. Gen. Patrick R. Cleburne at Franklin, Tenn. It was a tragic and irreparable loss of talent and leadership on both sides.[23]

As to an individual's chances in the war, one estimate for the entire Union Army figures 1 out of approximately 65 men was killed in action; 1 of 56 died of wounds; 1 of 13.5 died of disease; 1 of 10 was wounded in action; 1 of 15 was captured or reported missing; 1 of 7 captured died in prison.

On the other hand, chances went down appreciably for those actually engaged. Here the odds are put at 1 out of every 42.7 effective and actively engaged men killed in battle; 1 out of every 38.1 effectives died of wounds; 1 out of every 10.2 actively engaged was captured; 1 out of every 6.7 effective was wounded.[24] But it should be borne in mind that these are really only approximate, as many factors entered in to increase or decrease the odds.

[22] The outstanding modern studies of Civil War generals are Ezra J. Warner's *Generals in Gray*, Louisiana State University Press, Baton Rouge, 1959, and *Generals in Blue*, Louisiana State University Press, Baton Rouge, 1964. For analysis of casualties see *Generals in Blue*, p. xxi. Warner makes use of Wright, Marcus J., *Memorandum Relative to the General Officers in the Armies of the United States during the Civil War, 1861–1865*, War Dept., Washington, 1906.

[23] Fox, *Regimental Losses*, pp. 40–45, 571–72.

[24] Phisterer, Frederick, *Statistical Record of the Armies of the United States*, Charles Scribner's Sons, New York, 1883, pp. 71–72.

Desertion

Desertion on both sides in the Civil War was an evil that was widespread and never really controlled. Total figures are only indicative of the approximate number of desertions. Some reported as deserters were not, for various reasons, whereas a good many deserters were undoubtedly never reported.

The major study of desertion in the Civil War presents a figure of 200,000 Union desertions compared to 104,000 desertions in the Confederate Army.[25] It should be remembered that the Confederate Army numbered far, far fewer than the Union Army, and the South could much less afford such debilitation.

In the Union Army desertions averaged 4647 a month in 1863; 7333 in 1864; 4368 in 1865. The report of the Deserters' Branch of the Provost Marshal General's Office puts total desertions at 278,644. This has been scaled down to the 200,000 estimate upon investigation of the figures by the provost marshal general. From May 1, 1863, to Dec. 31, 1865, 77,181 Union Army deserters were arrested. Many others, it may be assumed, were never found.[26]

Reports make it clear that Federal troops from large cities had a higher rate of desertion than those from rural areas. States leading in desertion were Kansas, Connecticut, New Hampshire, New Jersey, California, and New York. The high California rate is explained by the fact that many of the state's troops actually were recruited in large eastern cities or in San Francisco. Kansas had more than half of its male population in service and there was a somewhat lax state of discipline in border regiments.[27]

Figures indicate that as penalties became more severe, with the death sentence sometimes imposed, desertion declined. Total Union executions are put at 267, with 147 of those for desertion, but this may not be complete.[28] Other executions were 67 for murder, 19 for mutiny, 23 for rape, and 11 miscellaneous.

[25] Lonn, Ella, *Desertion During the Civil War,* The Century Company, New York, 1928, p. 226. This primary study of desertion examines the situation thoroughly. *O.R.,* Series III, Vol. V, p. 677, report of Provost Marshal General James B. Fry.
[26] Report of Maj. T. A. Dodge, *O.R.,* Series III, Vol. V, pp. 757–58. Dodge puts total at 278,644. Provost Marshal General Fry, report, *O.R.,* Series III, Vol. V, p. 677, puts total at 268,530, but says this should be reduced 25 per cent to 201,397.
[27] Fry's report, *O.R.,* Series III, Vol. V, pp. 668–69.
[28] Lonn, *Desertion,* p. 212; "U. S. Soldiers Executed by U. S. Military Authorities During the Late War 1861–1866," National Archives, Washington.

While the situation improved somewhat at the North during the last year or so of the war, it worsened rapidly at the South. What is more, the deserters often carried off equipment as irreplaceable as they were themselves. Hundreds of messages in the *Official Records* testify to the seriousness of desertion, particularly in the desperate last months of the war. Parts of western North Carolina, Alabama, Mississippi, and Florida, especially, were sanctuaries for deserters. Desertion certainly affected the morale of the South seriously as the chances of victory clearly declined. In southwestern Virginia there apparently was even an organized association of deserters. In February of 1865 Gen. Lee wrote that unless the increase in desertion could be stemmed it "will bring us calamity."[29]

Prisoners

As in all Civil War statistical studies, the number of prisoners is subject to doubt. According to the U. S. Record and Pension Office 211,411 Union soldiers were captured by the Confederates during the war. Of this total 16,668 were paroled on the field and 30,218 died while in prison. Confederate soldiers captured by the Union numbered 462,634. Of this total 247,769 were paroled on the field, mainly in various surrenders, and 25,976 died in prison. The mortality rate was a little over 12 per cent in Northern prisons holding Confederates and 15.5 for Yankees in Southern prisons. If these figures are close to accurate, some 214,000 Confederate Soldiers were in Northern prison camps and 194,000 Federal soldiers in Southern camps.[30]

An "Andersonville complex" seems to exist regarding Civil War prisons. It is synonymous in print and on the screen with all that was reprehensible in wartime prisons. Ofttimes it is the first and only Civil War prison mentioned. While no one should make light of the abominable conditions at Andersonville, Ga., at the same time one cannot ignore the harshness of life in Northern camps at Elmira, N.Y., Johnson's Island in Lake Erie, or Camp Douglas, Chicago. There has been little historical objectivity shown in most writing on Civil War prisons. Andersonville is even enlarged upon, with some authors making it exist for the

[29] *O.R.,* Series I, Vol. XLVI, Part II, p. 1265.
[30] Report of F. C. Ainsworth, Chief of the Record and Pension Office, as given in Rhodes, *History,* Vol. V, pp. 507–8. Hesseltine, William B., *Civil War Prisons,* Ohio State University Press, Columbus, Ohio, 1930, p. 256. Hesseltine's work is the leading study of Civil War prisons. He accepts the figures given by Ainsworth but with some reservations. *O.R.,* Series II, Vol. VIII, pp. 946–48, Commissary General of Prisoners, E. A. Hitchcock, to Sec. of War Stanton, July 18, 1866, gives number of Confederate prisoners held at the North as about 220,000, and Federal prisoners held in the South at 126,950. No breakdown of deaths in prisons is possible.

whole war, whereas it really was in operation from February, 1864, to the end of the war.

Primary Confederate prisons were Libby and Belle Isle at Richmond; Danville, Lynchburg, and Petersburg, Va.; Salisbury, N.C.; Charleston and Columbia, S.C.; Florence, Ala.; Millen, Macon or Camp Oglethorpe, Atlanta, Savannah, and Andersonville, Ga.; Cahaba or Castle Morgan, Tuscaloosa, and Mobile, Ala.; New Orleans, La.; Camps Groce and Ford, Tex.

Principal Northern prisons included those at Alton, Rock Island and Springfield and Camp Douglas near Chicago, Ill.; Camp Chase at Columbus and Johnson's Island, Ohio; Camp Morton, Ind.; Elmira, N.Y.; Fort Delaware, Del.; Point Lookout, Md.; New Orleans, La.; Louisville, Ky.; St. Louis, Mo.; and the Old Capitol in Washington.[31]

Lack of Federal recognition of the Confederacy as a nation infinitely complicated the subject of prisoner exchange. In July, 1862, a cartel was arranged for exchange which operated until late December, 1862, when the Union ordered it discontinued for several reasons, including the status of Negro soldiers. Special exchanges were carried out, however, until late May, 1863. In April, 1864, Grant clamped down on exchanges. The Confederacy soon proposed various exchange plans. It was not until late January, 1865, that a man-for-man exchange was accepted by the North. Grant realized the deleteriousness of the manpower shortage on the Southern military capacity.[32]

The Regiment

Perhaps in no other war was the "esprit" of the regiment more vital or apparent than in the Civil War. The regiment became a second home; usually the men were from the same area, and they often had known each other in civilian life. While there was pride in nation, army, corps, division, and brigade, it was the regiment which usually counted most.

For the Union, 3559 separate units included regiments, separate battalions, companies, or batteries. Of this total 2144 were infantry regiments, 272 cavalry regiments, 61 of heavy artillery, 13 of engineers, 9 light infantry battalions, and 432 separate batteries.[33]

---

[31] For lists of prisons in the North, with populations at various times, see *O.R.,* Series II, Vol. VIII, pp. 987–1004; for a mere listing of primary prisons in the South see ibid., p. 1004.

[32] For summary of exchange policy see Rhodes, *History,* Vol. V, pp. 485–86, 499–501; also Hesseltine, *Civil War Prisons, passim.*

[33] Dyer, *Compendium,* p. 39. Other sources based on volunteers and militia arrive at 2888 units including 1668 infantry regiments, 232 cavalry regiments, 8

Among the Northern infantry regiments the Fifth New Hampshire suffered the most in total killed or dead of wounds—295, including 18 officers. The Eighty-third Pennsylvania was second with 282, including 11 officers; followed by the Seventh Wisconsin with 281; Fifth Michigan with 263; Twentieth Massachusetts, 260; Sixty-ninth New York, 259; and Twenty-eighth Massachusetts, 250. In percentage of those killed and dead of wounds to those enrolled, however, the list is different, with 23 regiments having 15 per cent or more losses. The Second Wisconsin with 1203 men enrolled lost 238 killed for 19.7 per cent, followed by the First Maine Heavy Artillery with 423 killed out of 2202 enrolled, for 19.2 per cent. The Fifty-seventh Massachusetts had 201 killed or mortally wounded out of 1052 for 19.1 per cent.

While figures are often disputed, the largest number of killed or mortally wounded suffered by any one unit in any one engagement for the North seems to have been the First Maine Heavy Artillery with 210 fatalities at Petersburg, June 18, 1864. In fact, heavy artillery appears to have suffered considerably. Second is the Eighth New York Heavy Artillery with 207 fatalities at Cold Harbor in June, 1864. In infantry regiments the Fifth New York had 117 fatalities at Second Bull Run or Manassas; followed by the Fifteenth New Jersey with 116 at Spotsylvania; Forty-ninth Pennsylvania, 109 at Spotsylvania; Fifteenth Massachusetts, 108 at Antietam; First Kansas at Wilson's Creek, Mo., 106; First Missouri at Wilson's Creek, 103; Ninth Illinois at Shiloh or Pittsburg Landing, 103; Eighteenth U. S. Infantry, Stone's River or Murfreesboro, 102; Eleventh Illinois, Fort Donelson, 102.

As to percentage of a regiment killed or mortally wounded in any one engagement, the leader was the First Minnesota, which had 262 engaged, lost 50 dead and 174 wounded (25 of whom died later) for 224 casualties at Gettysburg July 2. Thus, fatalities number 75, or over 28 per cent. Next was the Fifteenth New Jersey at Spotsylvania, which lost 116 killed or mortally wounded out of 432, a loss of 26 per cent in the several days of that battle. At Cold Harbor the Twenty-fifth Massachusetts had 310 reported for duty. Of that number 74 were killed or mortally wounded for 24 per cent plus 118 more wounded and 28 missing. Several other regiments suffered 20 per cent fatalities or more in single battles.[34]

One sound compilation gives for the Confederates 1526 units including regiments, legions, battalions, companies, and batteries. By this count there

---

light artillery, and 44 heavy artillery. *O.R.,* Series III, Vol. V, p. 1029; Phisterer, *Statistical Record,* pp. 22–23.

[34] Fox, *Regimental Losses,* pp. 2–3, 8, 16–17, 26–34; Fox, William F., "The Chances of Being Hit in Battle," *The Century Magazine,* Vol. XXXVI, No. I, May, 1888, pp. 93–106.

were included 642 infantry regiments, 137 cavalry regiments, 16 artillery regiments, and 227 batteries.[35]

Of course, these figures do not give true numerical strength, any more than they do in the Federal forces; regiments varied from as many as 1200 members to only a handful at various times and places on both sides.

Southern losses were often extreme. For instance, the Twenty-sixth North Carolina had some 880 men at the start of Gettysburg. There were 86 reported killed, 502 wounded (including mortally wounded), and 120 missing, for a total of 708. The Sixth Alabama at Fair Oaks or Seven Pines, out of about 632 engaged, lost 91 killed, 277 wounded, and 5 missing for 373. The Fourth North Carolina lost 77 killed, 286 wounded, and 6 missing for 369 out of 678, also at Fair Oaks. The First South Carolina Rifles at Gaines' Mill suffered 81 killed, 234 wounded, and 4 missing for 319 of 537 engaged.

As to percentages of losses to numbers present, incomplete records put the First Texas at the top with 226 present at Antietam or Sharpsburg with 45 killed and 141 wounded (including mortally wounded) for 82.3 per cent. The Twenty-first Georgia lost 38 killed and 146 wounded out of 242 for 75 per cent casualties at Second Manassas or Bull Run. Then comes the Twenty-sixth North Carolina at Gettysburg, as mentioned above, with 86 killed and 502 wounded out of 880, for 71.7 per cent. In addition there were 120 missing. At Shiloh or Pittsburg Landing the Sixth Mississippi suffered 70.5 per cent losses with 61 killed and 239 wounded out of 425. The Eighth Tennessee at Stone's River or Murfreesboro had 41 killed and 265 wounded out of 444 for 68.2 per cent. Closely following was the Tenth Tennessee at Chickamauga with 328 present, 44 killed, and 180 wounded for 68 per cent.[36]

Over Ten Thousand Fights

The Civil War is replete with familiar names of great battles—Gettysburg, Vicksburg, and the like. But the war was much more than just these tremendous extravaganzas of military drama and death. There were "fights" of one kind or another at thousands of other places, many of them forgotten completely today. To those taking part in these so-called minor engagements, they were just as important as the well-known ones.

While the exact total can certainly be disputed, the best available rec-

---

[35] Compilation is by Col. Henry Stone of the Military Historical Society of Massachusetts and appears in Livermore, *Numbers and Losses,* pp. 26–30. Other counts give lower figures, such as Fox, *Regimental Losses,* pp. 552–53, and Col. Charles C. Jones, *Southern Historical Society Papers,* Vol. XX, p. 119.

[36] Fox, *Regimental Losses,* pp. 555–58.

ord gives a total of 10,455 military actions of one degree or another during the Civil War. These can be further subdivided into[87]:

29	Campaigns	26	Sieges
76	Battles	64	Raids
310	Engagements	727	Expeditions
46	Combats	252	Reconnaissances
1026	Actions	434	Scouts
29	Assaults	639	Affairs
6337	Skirmishes	82	Occupations
299	Operations	79	Captures

By states the leading theaters of war were:

1. Virginia 2154 military events
2. Tennessee 1462
3. Missouri 1162
4. Mississippi 772
5. Arkansas 771
6. West Virginia 632
7. Louisiana 566
8. Georgia 549
9. Kentucky 453
10. Alabama 336
11. North Carolina 313
12. South Carolina 239
13. Maryland 203
14. Florida 168
15. Texas 90
16. Indian Territory 89
17. California 88
    (largely against Indians)
18. New Mexico Territory 75

The Navies and Blockade

When the Civil War began the North had a Navy of 90 ships; the Confederacy had no navy at all, and few assets with which to develop one. Of the 90 Union vessels 50 were old sailing types, some never completed, some laid up. There were about 35 available modern vessels and only three steamships immediately ready for blockading. Naval manpower totaled 7600. Through the necessities of wartime, with energy, administrative skill, and inventiveness, the Federal Navy grew to tremendous size and capabilities. There were 51,500 men in the Navy at the close of the war plus 16,880 employed in government navy yards. The Navy constructed 208 vessels and purchased 418 during the war. On Jan. 1, 1865, before operations were reduced, there were 471 ships with 2455 guns on blockade duty alone.[88]

Main operations of the Federal Navy were devoted to the blockade, the river war, tracking down Confederate cruisers on the high seas,

[87] Dyer, *Compendium,* p. 582.
[88] Report of Sec. of the Navy Gideon Welles, Dec. 2, 1861, *Congressional Globe,* 37th Congress, 2nd Session, Appendix, p. 20; Welles report of Dec. 4, 1865, *Congressional Globe,* 39th Congress, 1st Session, Appendix, p. 21.

and cooperating with the Army in offensive actions such as at Port Royal, New Orleans, Mobile, and Wilmington. Principal activities of the makeshift but nevertheless amazing Confederate Navy were in fitting out cruisers to raid Northern commerce, coastal and river defense, and attempting to break the blockade.

Confederate navy figures are much more difficult to ascertain than Federal. Possibly some 500 vessels of one kind or another served in the Confederate Navy, though many of them were small, converted from river steamers or coastal sailing vessels, and nearly all suffered from inferior armament or armor and inadequate engines or construction. But no finer example of building a viable, skillful naval force from virtually nothing can be found.[39]

Many and long are the discussions over the effectiveness of the blockade. Most authorities of Civil War days and historians since feel the blockade of 3500 miles of Confederate coastline on the Atlantic and Gulf coasts was a decisive factor in Northern victory. Others, primarily the late Dr. Frank Owsley, believe it was ineffective. Both schools of thought are apt to use the same figures to prove their points.

There were many violations of the blockade, to be sure. It was not a solid line of Yankee ships offshore. At the same time it seems clear that with the Confederacy's lack of economic self-sufficiency the strictures on shipping made the over-all situation much worse. Then too, one has to consider what foreign and even Northern shipping into the South might have been without the blockade—a great merchant fleet that never sailed. Dr. Owsley places captures of blockade-runners at one in ten in 1861; one out of eight in 1862; one in four in 1863; one in three for 1864; and one out of two in 1865 after most Southern ports were captured. He estimates total violations at 8200.

On the other hand, Sec. of the Navy Welles reported that Federals captured or destroyed 1504 blockade-runners. About 150 small blockade-runners remained at large at war's end. When one considers the Southern Confederacy as a fortress besieged, it becomes clear that, while not perfect, the blockade was a tremendous tool of warfare.[40]

Every successful running of the blockade or capture could not be mentioned in this volume. Almost every day saw one or more actions at sea—evasions of the blockade, chases, and captures.

Steam power was taking over from sail as the major maritime motive power at the start of the war. This trend continued, with improvements

---

[39] For more detailed, yet not conclusive statistics, see *Official Records of the Union and Confederate Navies in the War of the Rebellion,* Series II, Vol. I, pp. 247ff.; *Civil War Naval Chronology,* Part VI, Navy Dept., Washington, 1966, pp. 182ff.

[40] Owsley, Frank Lawrence, *King Cotton Diplomacy,* Second Edition, University of Chicago Press, Chicago, 1959, p. 285; Welles report, Dec. 4, 1865, *Congressional Globe,* 39th Congress, 1st Session, Appendix, p. 25.

in marine engines. There were advancements in armament, in river tactics, in landing operations, and in the development of ironclads and iron vessels. C.S.S. *Merrimack* or *Virginia* was a prime example of iron armor over a wooden hull, producing an ironclad. U.S.S. *Monitor,* followed by a host of similar vessels, despite its defects, was a further step, being an almost entirely iron vessel. Civil War navies were aided by the Industrial Revolution, and in turn helped spur vast changes in the world's ships and shipping for both peaceful and war purposes.

ECONOMICS OF WAR

It was clear to everyone that the economic assets as well as the manpower advantage lay with the Northern states. But actually how great was the advantage? What do the figures show?

Agriculture

In compiling figures we have made use of the U. S. Census of 1860 and given total U.S., and then the North as compared with the eleven seceded states. Missouri and Kentucky are counted in the North, as are the territories. West Virginia later seceded from Virginia, which makes the statistics given general, rather than specific:

	Total U.S.	*North*	*South*
Improved farmland, acres	163,261,389	106,171,756	57,089,633
Unimproved farmland, acres	246,508,244	106,486,777	140,021,467
Cash value of farms, $	6,650,872,507	4,779,933,587	1,870,938,920
Cash value of improvements and machinery, $	247,027,496	163,033,703	83,993,793
Horses	6,115,458	4,417,130	1,698,328
Asses and mules	1,129,553	328,890	800,663
Milch cows	8,728,862	6,037,367	2,691,495
Working oxen	2,240,075	1,383,430	856,645
Other cattle	14,671,400	7,744,123	6,927,277
Sheep	23,317,756	18,304,727	5,013,029
Swine	32,555,267	17,024,709	15,530,558
Value of livestock, $	1,107,490,216	716,527,942	390,962,274
Value of animals slaughtered, $	212,871,653	131,389,352	81,482,301
Wheat, bushels	171,183,381	139,816,487	31,366,894
Indian corn, bushels	830,451,707	549,786,693	280,665,014

	Total U.S.	North	South
Rye, bushels	20,976,286	18,803,253	2,173,033
Oats, bushels	172,554,688	152,634,280	19,920,408
Rice, lbs.	187,140,173	38,313	187,101,860
Tobacco, lbs.	429,390,771	230,369,341	199,021,430
Ginned cotton bales, 400 lbs. each	5,198,077	5,332½	5,192,744½
Wool, lbs.	60,511,343	50,761,641	9,749,702
Peas and beans, bushels	15,188,013	3,632,317	11,555,696
Irish potatoes, bushels	110,571,201	103,993,003	6,578,198
Sweet potatoes, bushels	41,606,302	7,896,726	33,709,576
Barley, bushels	15,635,119	15,454,812	180,307
Buckwheat, bushels	17,664,914	17,128,802	536,112
Value of orchard products, $	19,759,361	16,902,343	2,857,018
Value of market garden products, $	15,541,027	13,449,745	2,091,282
Tons of hay	19,129,128	18,059,845	1,069,283
Value of homemade manufactures, $	24,358,222	10,055,922	14,302,300

Thus it is obvious that the North had dramatic leads in most important categories except specialized local crops such as cotton and rice. The fact that there was much more improved farmland in the North and that the cash value of farms was more than twice as great as that of the South is vitally important. In the field of homemade manufactures the South still led, a point indicative of the local nature of their industry and commerce. From these figures alone it is amazing that the South could support a war at all; cotton could not be eaten or cast into bullets or machined into guns or marine engines.

As the war progressed the Confederacy had some good growing seasons and acreage in cotton was reduced in order to plant food crops. But at the same time the Southern territory shrank, and with it the agricultural potential. Accurate comparison figures for Southern agriculture during the war do not exist, but it is obvious that the peacetime disparity with the North only became infinitely greater. Despite the manpower drain for the armies, the figures show that Northern agricultural output was sustained and in many cases actually showed strong increases for some war years. The larders of the North remained well filled.[1]

[1] Gates, Paul W., *Agriculture and the Civil War*, Alfred A. Knopf, New York, 1965, covers the entire agricultural picture. Pp. 103–4 present some admittedly suspect wartime Southern crop production figures. *National Almanac*, 1863, pp. 316–21.

Transportation and Commerce

In the areas of commerce, imports and exports, as well as transportation, the eleven Confederate states were far behind their Northern and border-state brethren. From July 1, 1860, to June 31, 1861, United States exports totaled $249,344,913 according to incomplete returns. Of the figures for exports eight Confederate states had only $27,145,466 of the total, with no figures given for Tennessee, Arkansas, and Mississippi, and incomplete totals from other states. This gives the Northern states a figure of $222,199,477, with New York alone having $158,606,518.

As to imports, the total for the twenty-five states reporting was $335,-650,153. Eight Southern states could make up only $14,654,129 of the total. Again Arkansas, Tennessee, and Mississippi are missing. Of the Southern total Louisiana had $11,960,869 of the imports, showing clearly the importance of New Orleans.

In shipping, a total of 11,079 American vessels cleared U.S. ports for the year ending June 30, 1861. Of these 819 were from 8 Southern seaport states. Tonnage totaled 4,889,313, with 286,445 tons of this from the South. Foreign vessels clearing the United States totaled 10,586, with 220 of these from the South. The total number of ships, foreign and U.S., clearing from the country and coming into the country in the year ending June 30, 1861, totaled 43,625, with only 1975 of these coming in and out of the South. Total tonnage of all these movements was 14,-392,826 tons, of which 737,901 tons moved in and out of Southern ports.[2]

While railroads spread rapidly in the decade or so before the Civil War and hooked up many cities, the primary growth again had been in the North. In 1850 the nation boasted only 9021 miles of railroads, which had grown to 30,626 miles by the end of 1860. Of this 1860 mileage, 8541 was in the seceded states with over 22,000 in the North and border areas. Virginia led the South with 1771 miles, but in the North, Ohio had 2900, Illinois 2867, and New York 2701.[3] Not only were there more miles of track in the North but more connecting lines, making for better long-distance traveling and hauling. In the South the only route east to west from Richmond to the Mississippi was via Chattanooga and across southern Tennessee to Memphis; all other routes were very roundabout. Of course, as the war went on, Confederate railroads were captured, broken, and disrupted. Locomotives, rails, and all equip-

[2] *National Almanac,* 1863, pp. 165–66.
[3] *Historical Statistics of the United States,* p. 427; *U. S. Census 1860,* Miscellaneous, p. 333; Randall, James G., *The Civil War and Reconstruction,* D. C. Heath and Co., Boston, 1937, pp. 82–84.

ment were hard or impossible to replace and the already inadequate transport system fell apart. By the same token the virtually uninvaded North was able to transport men and equipment for war without very much disruption and was also able to maintain commerce and trade. Nevertheless the South on the worn-out equipment made at least two spectacular movements of large bodies of troops, complicated by several changes of gauge. The North, too, did well in moving troops, particularly from Virginia to Chattanooga in 1863, and were also handicapped by the lack of a uniform gauge. While military railroads had been specially constructed in the Crimean War by the British to a small extent, the American Civil War was the first true railroad war both in use of domestic lines and in construction of special military roads, such as that by the North at Petersburg.

Most neglected among the many heroes of the Civil War are the horses and mules which served by the hundreds of thousands in many ways, large numbers of which suffered painfully and died in service. Total U.S. horse population in 1860 was put by the census at 6,115,458, of which only 1,698,328 were in the seceding states. On the other hand, the South was much ahead in mule power, with 800,663 against the North's 328,890 for a total of 1,129,553. Working oxen were still important and the country had some 2,240,075, of which 856,645 were in the South.

Not only were horses vital for the cavalry of both armies and for the use of officers, but horses and mules were the main motive power for hauling supplies, ammunition, food, and guns. "Trains" were horse-drawn wagon trains, whereas "the cars" generally meant railroads. The demand of the war for livestock greatly increased breeding. In the North the government furnished the cavalry mounts and remounts, whereas in the South the soldier was expected to furnish his own. This policy further strained the Confederate economy as the horses were needed at home as well as in the Army. Replacement of killed, wounded, or diseased horses became a vexing problem to the South and contributed to the decline of their once magnificent cavalry. For example, on July 3, 1863, the Confederate Army had over 6000 convalescent horses in the Army of Northern Virginia. In the middle of the war it required about 500 new horses a day to replenish the Federal services. At the start of the war a good horse cost about $125; by the end the price was up to $185. The service of the average cavalry horse at the North lasted only four months. Obtaining huge amounts of hay and other feed for the immense numbers of horses both for cavalry and trains was a never-ending logistical challenge.

Despite the ascendancy of the railroads, the horse remained the backbone of short-haul operations, a necessity for cavalry and the artillery, essential to army supply, and, in short, an indispensable soldier in the war.[4]

General Sherman was to say, "the value of the magnetic telegraph in war cannot be exaggerated." It was developed into an extremely valuable field instrument as well as for long-distance communication. Authorities in Washington often held "talks" of telegraph with commanders in the West and ofttimes hastily strung wires carried battlefield orders and information. A lack of operators and equipment handicapped the South, but at the North the telegraph was put to full use. The United States Military Telegraph grew to 15,389 miles of line constructed during the war, plus all the existing lines. The Telegraph Office of the War Department in Washington became the nerve center of the war. The telegraph had seen active service in the Crimea, but in the American Civil War it proliferated and gained an impetus in its wartime use that carried over into civilian development in the postwar years.[5]

Riverboat traffic, long a medium for heavy, cheap transport, also went to war, carrying not only the usual civilian products in the North but military supplies and, of course, troops. A large proportion of the riverboats, captains, and pilots stayed with the North and for most of the war the Federals had the advantage of the principal river waterways. Then too, in the novel and typically American mode of warfare developed during the conflict, the river gunboat came into being. The chronology of the war shows the extent of its contribution to both sides, particularly to the North.

Without the technology of the railroads, telegraph, and riverboats, the American Civil War would have differed little from previous wars. These innovations combined to weld a transport and communications network of a relatively modern nature and at the same time worked hand in hand with the older and sometimes more reliable horse and wagon.

Industry and Business

The preponderant advantages of industrial production lay with the North. The South had never been industrial and what firms existed were largely small and local in extent. The cotton regions especially had depended on this staple as a bargaining agent in exchange for Northern

---

[4] *U. S. Census 1860; O.R.,* Series IV, Vol. II, pp. 615–16, Vol. IV, p. 1212, Vol. V, pp. 220–21; *National Almanac,* 1863, pp. 316–20.
[5] Sherman, William T., *Memoirs,* Two vols., D. Appleton & Company, New York, 1875, Vol. II, p. 398; Plum, William R., *The Military Telegraph During the Civil War in the United States,* two vols., Jansen, McClurg & Co., Chicago, 1882, Vol. I, p. 62.

industrial products. Southern industry was in no position to fight a war; and the situation became worse as the Confederacy shrank in size.

As of the fiscal year ending June 1, 1860, there were 128,300 industrial establishments recorded for the country as a whole. Of these only 18,026 were in the seceding states, while New England alone had 19,514. Thus the North, including the Far West, had 110,274 establishments. For the South, Virginia led with 4890 industrial firms. New York with 23,236 and Pennsylvania with 21,000 each had more industry than the entire South.

Even more important are the figures on capital invested in "real and personal estates in the business." With a national total of $1,050,000,000, the South had only $100,665,000. Pennsylvania, New York, and Massachusetts each surpassed the entire Confederacy. The "Value of annual product" for the nation's industry totaled $1,900,000,000. Of this the Confederacy had $145,350,000, or a little over 7.5 per cent. Again, New York, Pennsylvania, and Massachusetts each surpassed the entire product value of the new nation. Virginia with $51,300,000 led the eleven Southern states. In almost every industrial field, from production to raw products such as minerals, the North led. Of course there was considerable coal production in western Virginia, but that was soon lost to the Confederacy as was the developing iron industry in Tennessee.[6]

Cost of War

No war can ever be accurately evaluated in dollars-and-cents costs. And even if one does total up all the known expenditures, the results are apt to be highly inaccurate. On the other hand, such figures are at least indicative of a portion of the cost of warfare.

In January of 1863, with the war not half over and ever increasing in tempo, the daily cost of war for the North was put at $2,500,000 a day.[7]

Total Federal expenditures for the land operations of the war itself are put at $2,713,568,000; for the naval war: $314,223,000. Total strictly war costs: $3,027,791,000. This is, of course, only a portion of the actual monetary cost. On the Federal level there were pensions, interest, and continuing expenditures arising out of the war. One estimate was made in 1879 that expenditures growing out of the war up to that time came to $6,190,000,000. The extensive costs of raising men, supplies, armaments, etc., by the individual states must also be considered.

In 1860 Federal receipts were $56,054,000 and expenditures $63,201,000,

[6] *U. S. Census,* 1860; *National Almanac,* 1863, pp. 322–25.
[7] *Congressional Globe,* 37th Congress, 3rd Session, Part I, p. 286.

for a deficit. In 1865 receipts from taxes and miscellaneous sources came to $322,000,000, while expenditures for war and running the government were $1,295,100,000 for a deficit of $973,100,000. Much of the war expenditure was financed by paper money issues and loans. However, about 20 per cent of the Federal receipts by 1865 came from the nation's first income tax enacted August 2, 1861.[8]

For the Confederacy any attempt to arrive at total figures is much more complicated. One has to contend with lack of reports, the tremendous devaluation of Confederate money, and other difficulties. The Confederate government attempted to finance the war primarily through bonds and treasury notes, a policy which was partially unsuccessful but probably necessary. It also had to establish a national currency. There were four principal tax acts, none of which were really successful: a direct war tax of fifty cents upon each $100 of evaluation of certain kinds of property including real estate and slaves, enacted August 19, 1861; the act of April 24, 1863, a more stringent property tax, license tax, gross sales tax on some businesses, an income tax, plus a tax in kind of one tenth of the agricultural production of 1863. In 1864 this law was made more widespread and as late as March, 1865, a final act further increased the tax burden, but had little effect due to the end of the war.[9]

For the period of February 18, 1861, to October 1, 1863, total receipts of the Confederate government are put at $2,311,399,776. Total expenditures are put at $2,099,808,707, including $1,356,784,244 for running the land war and $93,045,954 for the naval war.[10]

For the war as a whole the funded debt of the Confederacy totaled $712,046,420. A total of $1,554,087,354 was issued in treasury notes. Tariffs and taxes collected came to $207,515,333.13, plus seizures, impressments, confiscations, and donations of $514,379,376.15.[11]

Inflation was a problem in both North and South, but particularly in the Confederacy, where devaluation of the treasury notes was almost disastrous. One dollar in gold at Richmond in May, 1861, cost $1.10 in Confederate currency. By January, 1862, it was only $1.25; but by the end of 1862 the price stood at $3. From there on the currency depreciated rapidly, with one dollar of gold in June, 1863, bringing $7 to $8, and by the beginning of 1864, $20 to $20.50. In the middle of 1864

---

[8] Dewey, Davis Rich, *Financial History of the United States,* Longman's, Green and Co., New York, 1934, pp. 267, 299, 329–30.

[9] Hawk, Emory C., *Economic History of the South,* Prentice-Hall, Inc., New York, 1934, pp. 410–13.

[10] Ibid., p. 414.

[11] Todd, Richard C., *Confederate Finance,* University of Georgia Press, Athens, 1954, pp. 84, 110–20, 156, 174, 194. Todd uses figures from the Papers and Compilations of Raphael P. Thian, Duke University Library.

the ratio dropped a little but by December, 1864, it was $34 to $49, and by March, 1865, it was $60 to $70 in Confederate money for one dollar in gold.

At the North in January, 1862, a dollar in gold compared with $1.03 in U.S. currency and by the end of 1862 stood at $1.32. By the beginning of 1864 it had gone to $1.55 and continued to rise to $2.06 in June, 1864. The ratio reached a peak of $2.59 in July and August, 1864, and then began dropping, although there were a few fluctuations. By March, 1865, a dollar in gold cost $1.79, and by April $1.46 in currency. However, throughout the war the United States had the decided advantage financially, the dollar being a stable medium long in existence, whereas the Confederacy had to issue new money with dubious backing.[12]

[12] Todd, ibid., p. 198, from a compilation by William B. Isaacs and Co., Bankers, Richmond, in the James H. Hamond Papers, Library of Congress.

ACKNOWLEDGMENTS

No author writes a book alone. He is aided directly by many persons, and indirectly by those who, over the years, have helped him. In addition, in a volume such as this, the author owes a primary debt to those who created the history of the Civil War period by living through it. But more specifically, the author wishes to thank all those who have furnished the bits and pieces of the puzzle that is the history of the era. These include the hundreds of students and scholars who have corrected various inaccuracies or suggested through their work sources of information. Then too, there are those who aided in various ways this specific volume. They include Bruce Catton, Allan Nevins, Ralph Newman, John Y. Simon, and various scholars, professional and non-professional, throughout the country. Special mention must be made of those who read portions of the manuscript, James I. Robertson, Jr., and Bell I. Wiley, though of course they are in no way responsible for any errors of commission or omission I may have made. Mrs. Florence Long, my mother, assisted in preparation of the bibliography. Editors do not always receive sufficient mention of their responsibility in any book, and I particularly wish to thank Lucia Staniels, Sam Vaughan, and Walter Bradbury of Doubleday.

E. B. LONG

BIBLIOGRAPHY

The following is the complete bibliography of specific sources used directly in the research notes for Bruce Catton's *Centennial History of the Civil War,* published by Doubleday, 1961, 1963, 1965. Countless other works were consulted. The notes were prepared by E. B. Long and have been deposited by the publisher in the Manuscript Division of the Library of Congress for the use of scholars.

In the *Centennial History* it was possible to print only about 50 per cent of the bibliography. Therefore, the author of this book believes it would be a service to present the complete listing. Section I is a bibliography of special sources used in the *Civil War Day by Day*. Section II is the manuscript collections used in the *Centennial History*. Section III lists the individual newspapers consulted. Section IV enumerates books, pamphlets, and periodicals. Again we wish to thank the staffs of the scores of libraries and private collections who made it possible to consult obscure manuscripts and printed sources.

SECTION I – THE CIVIL WAR DAY BY DAY

In the interrelated preparation of the *Civil War Day by Day* and the Research Notes for the *Centennial History of the Civil War* hundreds of volumes were consulted. There were, however, compilations and other volumes that applied directly and especially to this volume. These include:

Ages of U. S. Volunteer Soldiers, prepared by U. S. Sanitary Commission, New York, 1866.

AMBROSE, STEPHEN E., Duty, Honor, Country, A History of West Point, Baltimore, 1966.

American Annual Cyclopaedia and Register of Important Events of the Year 1861. Also issues for 1862, 1863, 1864, and 1865, New York, 1866.

Battles and Leaders of the Civil War, four vols., New York, 1884, 1886.

BOATNER, MARK MAYO, III, The Civil War Dictionary, New York, 1959.

CARNAHAN, J. WORTH, Manual of the Civil War, Washington, 1899.

Centennial of the United States Military Academy At West Point, two vols., New York, 1904.

Chronicles of the Great Rebellion Against the United States of America, Philadelphia, n.d.

Civil War Naval Chronology 1861–1865, six parts, Washington, 1961, 1962, 1963, 1964, 1965, 1966.

"Confederate Losses During the War," *Southern Historical Society Papers,* Vol. VII, June, 1879.

Congressional Globe, various issues, Washington.

CULLUM, GEORGE WASHINGTON, Biographical Register of Officers and Graduates of the U. S. Military Academy, New York, 1869.

DEWEY, DAVIS RICH, Financial History of the United States, New York, 1934.

Dictionary of American Biography, edited by Allen Johnson, twenty vols., New York, 1946.

DYER, FREDERICK H., A Compendium of the War of the Rebellion, Des Moines, Iowa, 1908.

Eighth and Ninth Census Reports, 1860 and 1870, Washington, 1862 and 1872.

ELLSWORTH, ELIOT, JR., West Point in the Confederacy, New York, 1941.

Evening Journal Almanac, 1863, Albany, N.Y., 1863.

FOX, WILLIAM F., "The Chances of Being Hit in Battle," *Century Magazine,* Vol. XXXVI, No. I, May, 1888.

————, Regimental Losses in the American Civil War, 1861–1865, Albany, N.Y., 1889.

GATES, PAUL W., Agriculture and the Civil War, New York, 1965.

HAWK, EMORY C., Economic History of the South, New York, 1934.

HEITMAN, FRANCIS B., Historical Register and Dictionary of the United States Army, 1789–1903, two vols., Washington, 1903.

HESSELTINE, WILLIAM B., Civil War Prisons, Columbus, Ohio, 1930.

Historical Statistics of the United States, Colonial Times to 1957, A Statistical Abstract Supplement, Bureau of the Census, Washington, 1960.

HITCHCOCK, BENJAMIN W., Hitchcock's Chronological Record of the American Civil War, New York, 1866.

Immigration Into the United States, Monthly Summary of Commerce and Finance of the United States, June 1903, No. 12, Series 1902–1903, Washington, 1903.

KELLER, HELEN REX, The Dictionary of Dates, two vols., New York, 1934.

KENNEDY, JOSEPH C. G., Preliminary Report on the Eighth Census, reprinted as, The United States on the Eve of the Civil War As Described in the 1860 Census, Washington, 1963.

KREIDBERG, MARVIN A., and MERTON G. HENRY, History of Military Mobilization in the United States Army 1775–1945, Department of the Army Pamphlet No. 20–212, Washington, June, 1955.

LINCOLN, ABRAHAM, The Collected Works of, edited by Roy Basler, eight vols., New Brunswick, N.J., 1953.

Lincoln Day by Day, A Chronology, 1808–1865, editor in chief, Earl Schenck Miers, with C. Percy Powell, three vols., Washington, 1960.

LIVERMORE, THOMAS L., Numbers and Losses in the Civil War in America 1861–65, 2nd edition, Boston, 1901.

LONG, E.B., "Chronological Outline of the Civil War," ms., prepared for use by Bruce Catton in writing *Centennial History of the Civil War.*

LONN, ELLA, Desertion During the Civil War, New York, 1928.

LOSSING, BENJAMIN, A History of the Civil War, New York, 1912.

MCPHERSON, EDWARD, The Political History of the United States of America During the Great Rebellion, Washington, 1865.

Medical and Surgical History of the War of the Rebellion, three vols. in six parts, Washington, 1877–88.

National Almanac and Annual Record for the Year 1863, also 1864, Philadelphia, 1863, 1864.

NEWMAN, RALPH, and E. B. LONG, The Civil War Digest, New York, 1965, 1960.

Official Records of the Union and Confederate Navies in the War of the Rebellion, thirty vols. and index, Washington, 1896–1927.

OWSLEY, FRANK LAWRENCE, King Cotton Diplomacy, 2nd edition, Chicago, 1959.

PHISTERER, FREDERICK, Statistical Record of the Armies of the United States, Campaigns of the Civil War, Supplementary Volume, New York, 1883.

Photographic History of the Civil War, Francis Trevelyan Miller, editor in chief, ten vols., New York, 1911.

PLUM, WILLIAM R., The Military Telegraph During the Civil War in the United States, two vols., Chicago, 1882.

PRATT, HARRY E., Abraham Lincoln Chronology 1809–1865, Springfield, 1957.

RANDALL, JAMES G., and DAVID DONALD, The Civil War and Reconstruction, Boston, 1961.

Rebellion Record, A Diary of American Events, edited by Frank Moore, eleven vols. and supplement, New York, 1862–69.

Report of the Provost Marshal General, full title, "Final Report Made to the Secretary of War by the Provost Marshal General of the Operations of the Bureau of the Provost Marshal General of the United States from the Commencement of the Business of the Bureau, March 17, 1863, to March 17, 1866, the Bureau Terminating by Law August 28, 1966, Messages and Documents, War Department 1865–1866," three vols., Washington, 1866.

RHODES, JAMES FORD, History of the United States from the Compromise of 1850 to the Final Restoration of Home Rule in the South in 1877, seven vols., New York, 1892–1906.

ROWLAND, DUNBAR, Jefferson Davis, Constitutionalist, His Letters, Papers, and Speeches, ten vols., Jackson, Miss., 1923.

SHERMAN, WILLIAM T., Memoirs, two vols., New York, 1875.

SIMON, JOHN Y., Ulysses S. Grant Chronology, Columbus, Ohio, 1963.

STAMPP, KENNETH, The Peculiar Institution, Slavery in the Ante-Bellum South, New York, 1956.

STRAIT, NEWTON A., Alphabetical List of Battles 1754–1900, Washington, 1900.

STRICKLER, THEODORE D., When and Where We Met Each Other On Shore and Afloat, Philadelphia, 1899.

TODD, RICHARD C., Confederate Finance, Athens, Ga., 1954.

Tribune Almanac and Political Register for 1865, New York, 1865.

Union Army, eight vols., Madison, Wis., 1908.

"U. S. Soldiers Executed by the U. S. Military Authorities During the Late War 1861–1865," ms., National Archives, Washington.

UPTON, EMORY, The Military Policy of the United States, Washington, 1912.

WARINNER, N. E., A Register of Military Events in Virginia 1861–1865, Virginia Civil War Commission, Richmond, 1959.

WARNER, EZRA J., Generals in Blue, Baton Rouge, La., 1964.

———, Generals in Gray, Batan Rouge, La., 1959.

War of the Rebellion, A Compilation of the Official Records of the Union and Confederate Armies, seventy vols. in one hundred twenty-eight parts, and atlas, Washington, 1880–1901.

War Record, Alphabetical List of the Battles of the Civil War with Dates, n.p., n.d.

WILEY, BELL IRVIN, The Life of Johnny Reb, Indianapolis, 1943.

——, Southern Negroes 1861–1865, New York, 1938.

WRIGHT, MARCUS J., Memorandum Relative to the General Officers in the Armies of the United States During the Civil War, 1861–1865, Washington, 1906.

SECTION II – MANUSCRIPT COLLECTIONS, CENTENNIAL HISTORY OF THE CIVIL WAR

ABBOTT, A. T., Diary, Library of Congress.

ABBOTT, L., Letters, Massachusetts Commandery of the Military Order of the Loyal Legion Papers, Houghton Library, Harvard University.

ALBERT, CHARLES, Journal, Library of Congress.

ADAMS, CHARLES F., JR., Diary, Massachusetts Historical Society.

ADAMS, DANIEL W., Letters, Battles and Leaders of the Civil War, extra illustrated, Huntington Library.

ADAMS, RICHARD H., JR., Diary of, courtesy Mrs. Robert D. Fitting, Midland, Texas.

AFFELD, C. M., Notes, Vicksburg National Military Park.

Affleck, Papers, Louisiana State Department of Archives, Louisiana State University.

AGNEW, SAMUEL ANDREW, Diary, Southern Historical Collection, University of North Carolina.

Alcorn, Papers, Southern Historical Collection, University of North Carolina.

ALEXANDER, E. P., Letter, Palmer Collection, Western Reserve Historical Society.

——, Papers, Library of Congress.

——, Papers, Southern Historical Collection, University of North Carolina.

ALISON, JOSEPH DILL, Diary, Southern Historical Collection, University of North Carolina.

ALLAN, COL. WILLIAM, Collection, Southern Historical Collection, University of North Carolina.

ALLAN, WILLIAM, Conversations with Lee, William Allan Collection, Southern Historical Collection, University of North Carolina.

ALLEN, ISAAC JACOBSON, Papers and Autobiography, Library of Congress.

ALVORD, AUGUSTUS, Letters, Library of Congress.

American Civil War, Ledger of British Naval Orders, Boston Public Library.

AMMEN, JACOB, Diary, Illinois State Historical Library.

ANDERSON, Letters, the A. Conger Goodyear Collection, Yale University Library.

ANDERSON, E. C., Papers, Georgia Historical Society.

ANDERSON, ROBERT, Papers, Library of Congress.

——, Papers, Miscellaneous Letters, New York Public Library.

——, Retirement Hearing Notebooks, Massachusetts Commandery of the Military Order of the Loyal Legion, Houghton Library, Harvard Library.

ANDERSON, MRS. ROBERT, Account of Visit to Fort Sumter, as recorded by Benson J. Lossing, the A. Conger Goodyear Collection, Yale University Library.

Bibliography

ANDREW, JOHN A., Papers, Massachusetts Historical Society.

Arkansas Manuscript Collection, John A. Larson Memorial Library, Little Rock University.

ARNOLD, ISAAC N., The Life of Abraham Lincoln, extra illustrated, Huntington Library.

——, Papers, Chicago Historical Society.

ATKINSON, MRS. E. K., Letters, Southern Historical Collection, University of North Carolina.

ATWATER, M. B., Reminiscences, State Historical Society of Wisconsin.

AUGUR, C. C., Collection, Illinois State Historical Library.

BABCOCK, ORVILLE E., Papers, Chicago Historical Society.

BADEAU, ADAM, Letter, Princeton University Library.

——, Military History of Ulysses S. Grant, three volumes, D. Appleton and Co., New York, 1868. Extra illustrated, Huntington Library. Clippings and notations re Grant's Memoirs.

——, Typescript of Letter to *Century Magazine,* Palmer Collection, Western Reserve Historical Society.

BAILEY, Family Papers, Civil War Letters, Stanford University Libraries, Division of Special Collections.

BAILEY, J. B., The Story of a Confederate Soldier, 1861–65, Texas State Archives.

Baird Papers, Edward Carey Gardiner Collection, The Historical Society of Pennsylvania.

BALFOUR, MISS, Diary, Mississippi Department of Archives and History.

BANKS, NATHANIEL, Papers, Essex Institute Library, Salem, Massachusetts, now transferred to Library of Congress.

BARLOW, FRANCIS CHANNING, Papers, Massachusetts Historical Society.

BARLOW, S. L. M., Autograph Collection, Huntington Library.

——, Papers, Huntington Library.

BARSTOW, WILSON, Papers, Library of Congress.

BARTON, CLARA, Letter, Battles and Leaders of the Civil War, extra illustrated, Huntington Library.

BATE, WILLIAM, Letter, Battles and Leaders of the Civil War, extra illustrated, Huntington Library.

BATEMAN, WARNER M., Papers, Western Reserve Historical Society.

BATES, DAVID HOMER, Diary and Daily Journal, Stern Collection, Rare Book Room, Library of Congress.

BATES, EDWARD, Expression of Patriotism, Miscellaneous Collection, Huntington Library.

——, File, Chicago Historical Society.

BATES, SAMUEL PENNIMAN, Collection, Pennsylvania Historical and Museum Collection.

Battles and Leaders of the Civil War, extra illustrated, Huntington Library.

BEARSS, EDWIN C., Maps of Pea Ridge, and Vicksburg.

BEAUREGARD, Letters, Palmer Collection, Western Reserve Historical Society.

BEAUREGARD, P. G. T., Letter, Miscellaneous Collection, Huntington Library.

——, Letter to Davis May 15, 1864. Battles and Leaders of the Civil War, extra illustrated, Huntington Library.

——, Papers, Columiba University Library.

——, Papers, Manuscript Department, Duke University Library.

——, Papers, Virginia State Library.

——, Papers, Virginia State Library.

BEDFORD, WIMER, Diary, Library of Congress.

BEETHAN, ASA, Letters, Library of Congress.

BENHAM, D. W., Letters, Columbia University Library.

BENNETT, JAMES GORDON, Papers, Library of Congress.

BENSON, BERRY G., Reminiscences and Diary, Southern Historical Collection, University of North Carolina.

BERKELEY, HENRY ROBINSON, Diary, Virginia State Historical Society.

BERKELEY, WILLIAM NOLAND, War Letters of a Confederate to his Wife 1861–1865, Alderman Library, University of Virginia.

BIDWELL, Papers, Bancroft Library, University of California.

Biegler's Settlement, German Farmers' Protest, Fayette County, Texas, Army Records, National Archives.

BIGGS, CAPT. HERMAN, Papers, Southern Historical Collection, University of North Carolina.

"Billie" of 38th Alabama, Letters to his Mother, Department of Lincolniana, Lincoln Memorial University.

BINCKLEY, JOHN MILTON, Papers, Library of Congress.

BINGHAM, HENRY H., Memoirs, Palmer Collection, Western Reserve Historical Society.

BIONDI, EUGENE, Reminiscences, Bancroft Library, University of California.

BISHOP, CHARLES WILLIAM, Log of a Cruise in the Gunboat Fort Royal in 1862, Yale University, Historical Manuscripts Division.

BLACK, JEREMIAH SULLIVAN, Papers, Library of Congress.

Blair Family Papers, Library of Congress.

Blair Papers, Library of Congress.

BLAIR, FRANCIS P., Papers, Library of Congress.

BLAIR, MONTGOMERY, Papers, A. Conger Goodyear Collection, Yale University Library.

Blair-Lee Papers, Princeton University Library.

BONSELL, MRS. REBECCA WRIGHT, Narrative to C. C. Coffin, Houghton Library, Harvard University.

BORGLUM, GUTZON, Papers, Library of Congress.

BOULWARE, J. R., Diary, Virginia State Library.

BOURLIER, EMILE, Letters, Palmer Collection, Western Reserve Historical Society.

BOYKIN, Papers, Southern Historical Collection, University of North Carolina.

BOYLE, JOHN, Papers, Library of Congress.

BOYLE, MRS. JOHN, Letters, Library of Congress.

BOYNTON, H. V., Papers, New York Public Library.

BRADFORD, JEFF D., Letter, Confederate Memorial Literary Society.

BRADLEE and SEARS, Letters, Western Reserve Historical Society.

BRAGG, BRAXTON, Accounts of his Services After Leaving Army of Tennessee, Palmer Collection, Western Reserve Historical Society.

——, Letter to Jefferson Davis, Palmer Collection, Western Reserve Historical Society.

——, Letters, Palmer Collection, Western Reserve Historical Collection.

———, Letters to Davis, July 18, 1864, Battles and Leaders of the Civil War, extra illustrated, Huntington Library.

———, Letters to his Wife, Library of Congress.

———, Papers, Duke University.

———, Papers, Huntington Library.

———, Papers, Missouri Historical Society, St. Louis.

BRAGG, MRS. BRAXTON, Letters to her Husband, Eugene C. Barker Texas History Center, University of Texas.

BRAGG, EDWARD S., Papers, Wisconsin State Historical Society Library.

BRAGG, THOMAS, Diary, Southern Historical Collection, University of North Carolina.

BRANNIGAN, FELIX, Letters, Library of Congress.

BRAXTON, FANNIE PAGE (HUME), Diary, Virginia State Historical Society.

BRAYMAN, MASON, Collection, Chicago Historical Society.

BRECKINRIDGE, JOHN C., Papers, Chicago Historical Society.

———, Papers, Filson Club.

BRIGHT, JOHN, Letter, A. Conger Goodyear Collection, Yale University Library.

BROADHEAD, JAMES O., Papers, Missouri Historical Society.

BROCK, Collection, Huntington Library.

BROOKE, WILLIAM RAWLE, War Letters, War Library and Museum, Military Order of the Loyal Legion of the United States, Philadelphia.

BROWN, ALEXANDER GUSTAVUS, Letters, Virginia Historical Society.

BROWN, CAMPBELL, Notes on Tennessee Iron Manufacture, Tennessee State Library and Archives.

———, Papers, Manuscript Department, Duke University Library.

———, Papers, Southern Historical Collection, University of North Carolina.

BROWN, G. CAMPBELL, Letters, Eldridge Collection, Huntington Library.

BROWN, JOHN, Diary, J. N. Heiskell Collection, Little Rock, Arkansas.

———, Papers, Chicago Historical Society.

BROWN, JOSEPH E., Papers, Massachusetts Commandery of the Military Order of the Loyal Legion of the United States, Houghton Library, Harvard University.

BUCHANAN, ADMIRAL FRANKLIN, Letterbook, Southern Historical Collection, University of North Carolina.

BUCHANAN, JAMES, Letter, Andre de Coppet Collection, Princeton University Library.

———, Miscellaneous File—President—New York Public Library.

———, Papers, Historical Society of Pennsylvania, Philadelphia.

———, Papers, Library of Congress.

———, Papers, Pennsylvania Historical and Museum Commission, Division of Public Records, Harrisburg, Pennsylvania.

BUEGEL, JOHN T., Diary, J. N. Heiskell Collection, Little Rock, Arkansas.

BULLEN, SULLIVAN, Letters, Chicago Historical Society.

BULLOCK, C. SEYMOUR, Papers, Southern Historical Collection, University of North Carolina.

BURDICK, E. D., Extracts from Diary of, Hardin Collection, Chicago Historical Society.

BURGESS, WILLIAM WALLACE, Papers, Alderman Library, University of Virginia.

BURNHAM, J. HOWARD, Letters, J. N. Heiskell Collection, Little Rock, Arkansas.

BURRUS, JOHN C. AND FAMILY, Papers, George Lester Collection, Department of Archives, Louisiana State University.

BURT, ELIZABETH JOHNSTON, Papers, Library of Congress.

BUTLER, BENJAMIN F., File, Eldridge Collection, Huntington Library.

——, Letter, Alderman Library, University of Virginia.

——, Letter, Ohio Historical Society.

——, Letter, Ralph G. Newman Collection.

——, Papers, Library of Congress.

BUTLER, WILLIAM, Papers, Chicago Historical Society.

CADWALLADER, SYLVANUS, Papers, Illinois State Historical Library.

CALHOUN, JAMES M., Petition of the Mayor of Atlanta to General Sherman, 1864. Dearborn Collection, Houghton Library, Harvard University.

CALL, R. K., Letters, Huntington Library.

CAMELS, Correspondence regarding, Old Army Record Group 107, Secretary of War Inventory, National Archives.

CAMERON, SIMON, Papers, Library of Congress.

——, Papers, Pennsylvania Historical and Museum Commission, microfilm from Historical Society of Dauphin County, Harrisburg, Pennsylvania.

CAMPBELL, GEORGE WASHINGTON, Papers, Library of Congress.

CAMPBELL, GIVEN, Narrative of Last March of Jefferson Davis, Library of Congress.

CAMPBELL, JOHN A., Letters, Alabama Department of Archives and History.

——, Letters, the A. Conger Goodyear Collection, Yale University Library.

——, Manuscript, Confederate Memorial Library Society, Richmond.

CAMPBELL, J. C., Letter, Division of Special Collections, Stanford University Library.

CAMPBELL, RICHARD, Letters. Mississippi State Department of Archives and History.

Campbell-Colston Papers, Southern Historical Collection, University of North Carolina.

CARROLL, ANNA ELLA, Papers, Maryland Historical Society.

CARTER BROTHERS, Four Brothers in Blue or Reveries of the Rebellion, Typescript of Extracts from Letters of the Carter Brothers in the Army of the Potomac, Huntington Library.

Cavalry Officer, Federal, name unreadable, letter, Virginia State Library.

CHAMBERLAIN, JOSHUA L., Papers, Library of Congress.

CHAMBERS, ROWLAND, Diaries, Louisiana State University, Department of Archives.

CHAMPION, Family Papers, Champion Family Private Papers, Vicksburg, Miss.

CHANCELLORSVILLE, SUE M., Personal Recollections of the Battle of Chancellorsville, Alderman Library, University of Virginia.

CHANDLER, ZACHARIAH, Papers, Library of Congress.

CHAPMAN, D. P., Letters, Huntington Library.

CHARLESTON, S.C., Board of Health, Daily Meteorological Observations, National Archives.

CHASE, LUCIEN P., Letter, Chicago Historical Society.

CHASE, SALMON P., Miscellaneous File, Huntington Library.
———, Papers, Chicago Historical Society.
———, Papers, New York Historical Society.
———, Papers, New York Public Library.
———, Papers, Pennsylvania Historical Society.
CHASE, COL. W. H., Papers, Palmer Collection, Western Reserve Historical Society.
CHEW, FRANCIS T., Reminiscences, Southern Historical Collection, University of North Carolina.
CHISOLM, COL. A. R., Journal of Events Before and During the Bombardment of Fort Sumter, Palmer Collection, Western Reserve Historical Society.
Chivington Collection, Bancroft Library, University of California.
CISCO, JOHN F., Treasury Department Records, National Archives.
Civil War Collection, Alderman Library, University of Virginia.
Civil War Collection, G. A. R. Room, Chicago Public Library.
Civil War Collection, Ohio State Museum.
Civil War Letters, Barker Texas History Center, University of Texas.
CLARKE, Papers, Houghton Library, Harvard University.
CLAY, C. C., Papers, Duke University Library.
CLARKE, Papers, Houghton Library, Harvard University.
CLAY, C. C., Papers, Duke University Library.
CLEMENS, SHERRARD, Letters, Palmer Collection, Western Reserve Historical Society.
Clendenen Family Letters, Huntington Library.
CLUNE, HENRY, Letter, Collection Shiloh National Military Park.
COBB, HOWELL, Papers, Duke University Library.
COBB, T. R. R., Letters, The Historical Society of Pennsylvania.
COBBETT, J. P., Scrapbook, E. B. Long Collection.
COCHRAN, W. G., Political Experiences of J. D. Cox, Western Reserve Historical Society.
COGGESHELL, WILLIAM T., Diary, Illinois State Historical Library, gift of Mrs. Foreman M. Lebold.
COLLIER, ELIZABETH, Diary, Southern Historical Collection, University of North Carolina.
Commission Appointed for the Manufacture and Purchase of Arms and Munitions of War for the Virginia State Legislature, Letterbook, Huntington Library.
Confederate Papers, Eugene C. Barker Texas History Center, University of Texas.
Confederate State Documents, Boston Public Library.
CONLEY, ALEXANDER W., Letters, Huntington Library.
CONLEY, JAMES M., Collection, Ohio State Museum.
COOK, LILLIAN M., Diary, Virginia State Historical Society.
Cooke Family Papers, Virginia State Historical Society.
COOKE, JAY, Collection, Pennsylvania Historical Society.
COOKE, JOHN ESTEN, Diary, Alderman Library, University of Virginia.
CORMIER, CHARLES, Letter, Louisiana Historical Association, Confederate Memorial Hall, New Orleans.
COX, JACOB D., Collection, Library of Congress.

——, Comments on McClellan's Own Story in Cox's Copy of the Book, Oberlin College Oberlin, Ohio.

——, Letter, Battles and Leaders of the Civil War, extra illustrated, Huntington Library.

CRAM, GEORGE F., Letters, Loring Armstrong Collection.

CRAMER, CHARLES, Letter, Civil War Letters, Eugene C. Barker Texas History Center, University of Texas.

CRAMPTON, BENJAMIN, Papers, Maryland Historical Society.

CRAWFORD, ABEL N., Tennessee State Library and Archives.

CRAWFORD, N. W., Letter, Western Reserve Historical Society.

CRAWFORD, SAMUEL W., Papers, A. Conger Goodyear Collection, Yale University Library.

CRITTENDEN, JOHN, Civil War Letters to his Wife, Eugene C. Barker Texas History Center, University of Texas.

CROFFUT, W. A., Papers, Library of Congress.

CROSSLY, SYLVANUS, Diary of an Escape from the Confederate Army, Library of Congress.

CURTIS, SAMUEL RYAN, Papers, Huntington Library.

CUSHING, CALEB, Correspondence, Nevins' Notes.

CUSTIS, MARY LEE, Letters, Virginia State Historical Society.

DAHLGREN, JOHN A., Letters, Newberry Library.

——, Papers, Manuscripts from Goodspeed's Catalog 510, 1962.

DANA, CHARLES A., Allan Nevins' Notes.

——, Papers, Duke University Library.

——, Papers, Library of Congress.

DANA, N. J. T., Letter, Miscellaneous File, Huntington Library.

Dana, Richard Henry and Family Papers, Massachusetts Historical Society.

DANLEY, C. G., Letters, J. W. Heiskel Collection, Little Rock, Arkansas.

DAVIS, DAVID, Papers, Chicago Historical Society, including photocopies deposited by Willard King.

——, Papers, Illinois State Historical Library.

DAVIS, JEFFERSON, Letter, The Historical Society of Pennsylvania.

——, Letter, Nevins' Notes.

——, Letter, Philip D. and Elsie O. Sang Collection, River Forest, Illinois.

——, Letter, Rosenbach Foundation, Philadelphia.

——, Letter, A. Conger Goodyear Collection, Yale University Library.

——, Letter to Bragg, Lincoln National Life Foundation, Fort Wayne, Indiana.

——, Letters, Confederate Memorial Literary Society.

——, Letters, Confederate Papers, Eugene C. Barker Texas History Center, University of Texas.

——, Letters, Virginia Southern Historical Society.

——, Letters to his Wife, National Archives.

——, Letters to Marcus Wright (typed), Palmer Collection, Western Reserve Historical Society.

——, Papers, Chicago Historical Society.

——, Papers, Louisiana Historical Association.

——, Papers, New York Historical Society.

——, Papers, Palmer Collection, Western Reserve Historical Society.

———, Papers, Yale University Library.

———, Post War Manuscripts, Confederate Memorial Hall, New Orleans, Louisiana.

———, Reagan Papers, Dallas Historical Society.

DAVIS, JEFFERSON and BEAUREGARD, P. G. T., Correspondence, A. Conger Goodyear Collection, Yale University Library, Historical Manuscripts Division.

DAVIS, LAWSON L., Account of Mumford Flag Incident, Louisiana Historical Association.

DAVIS, VARINA, Letters, Autograph Collection, Barlow Papers, Huntington Library.

DAVIS, W. M., Collection, The Historical Society of Pennsylvania.

DAWES, RUFUS, Papers, Courtesy Rufus D. Beach, Evanston, Illinois, and Ralph G. Newman.

DEACON, WILL R., Letter, Lincoln Room, Lincoln Memorial Library.

Dearborn Collection, Houghton Library, Harvard University.

Decatur House Papers, Library of Congress.

DE COPPET, ANDRE, Collection, Princeton University Library.

DELANO, EUGENE, Notes, Nevins' Notes.

DE LONNE, MRS. W., Manuscript, Mississippi State Department of Archives and History.

DE SAUSSURE, WILLIAM GIBBES, Order Book, Southern Historical Collection, University of North Carolina.

DINWIDDIE, JAMES L., Letters to his wife, 1862, Virginia State Library.

DIX, JOHN A., Broadsides, Valentine Museum, Richmond, Virginia.

DOBBENS, PETER B., Letter, Collection Shiloh National Military Park.

DODGE, THEODORE A., Letters, Library of Congress.

DOOLITTLE, JAMES R., Papers, State Historical Society of Wisconsin.

DOUBLEDAY, ABNER, Letter, Palmer Collection.

———, Letters, Battles and Leaders of the Civil War, extra illustrated, Huntington Library.

DOUBLEDAY, ABNER, and MRS. DOUBLEDAY, Sketch of his life, Battles and Leaders of the Civil War, extra illustrated, Huntington Library.

DOUGLAS, HENRY KYD, Papers, Manuscript Department, Duke University Library.

DOUGLAS, STEPHEN A., Letter, Philip D. and Elsie O. Sang Collection, River Forest, Illinois.

———, Papers, Chicago Historical Society.

———, Papers, Illinois State Historical Library.

DRAKE, CHARLES D., Autobiography, Missouri State Historical Society, St. Louis.

DRAYTON, A. L., Diary, Library of Congress.

Dreer Collection, Letters of Union Generals, Vol. II, The Historical Society of Pennsylvania.

DRENNAN, WILLIAM AUGUSTUS, Diary, Mississippi State Department of Archives and History.

DUBARRY, HELEN PRATT, Papers, Illinois State Historical Library.

DUBELLET, PAUL PECQUET, The Diplomacy of the Confederate Cabinet of Richmond and its Agents Abroad, Being Memorandum Notes taken in Paris during the Rebellion of the Southern States from 1861 to 1865, Library of Congress.

DUBOSE, D. M., Letter, Palmer Collection, Western Reserve Historical Society.

DUDLEY, THOMAS HAINES, Papers, Huntington Library.

DUGANNE, W. T., The Story of the Confederate Navy, unpublished manuscript.

DUKE, MORGAN, Papers, Southern Historical Collection, University of North Carolina.

DU PONT, S. F., Miscellaneous Papers, Massachusetts Historical Society.

DUVAL, THOMAS HOWARD, Diaries, Eugene C. Barker Texas History Center, University of Texas.

EADS, JAMES B., Papers, Missouri Historical Society.

EARLY, J. A., Letter, Virginia Historical Society.

EARLY, JUBAL, Letters, Battles and Leaders of the Civil War, extra illustrated, Huntington Library.

Eldridge Collection, Huntington Library.

ELIOT, WILLIAM GREENLEAF, Papers, Missouri Historical Society.

ELLIS, E. J., and FAMILY, Papers, Department of Archives, Louisiana State University.

ELLSWORTH, ELMER EPHRAIM, Papers, Chicago Historical Society.

ELSEFFER, LOUIS, Papers, Library of Congress.

EMERSON, RALPH WALDO, manuscript remarks, Sumner Autographs, Houghton Library, Harvard University.

EMERY, JOSE, Papers, Duke University Library.

ENGLAND, JOHN, Letter, Palmer Collection, Western Reserve Historical Society.

ENGLISH, EDMUND, Papers, Huntington Library.

Eno Collection, Arkansas History Commission.

EPPES, R. F., Letters, Southern Historical Collection, University of North Carolina.

EPPES, RICHARD, Papers, Alderman Library, University of Virginia.

EVANS, CHESLEY D., Letters, 1860–1861, Southern Historical Collection, University of North Carolina.

EVANS THOMAS, Civil War Diary and Memoirs, Library of Congress.

———, Reminiscences, Ohio State Museum, Civil War Collection.

EVERETT, EDWARD, Papers, Massachusetts Historical Society.

EVERETT, J. M., Papers, Georgia Historical Society.

EWELL, RICHARD S. and OTHERS, Letter to Grant re Assassination, National Archives, Washington.

EWING, CHARLES, Family Papers, Library of Congress.

EWING, THOMAS, Letter, Duke University Library.

Fairchild Papers, State Historical Society of Wisconsin.

FAIRFAX, A. B., Letters, Barker Texas History Center, University of Texas.

FARRAGUT, DAVID GLASGOW, Letter, Battles and Leaders of the Civil War, extra illustrated, Huntington Library.

———, Papers, David H. Annan Collection.

FENTON, JAMES, Recollections, Western Reserve Historical Society.

FESSENDEN, SAMUEL, Miscellaneous Papers, Huntington Library.

FESSENDEN, WILLIAM PITT, Papers, Palmer Collection, Western Reserve Historical Society.

FISHBURNE, C. D., Recollections, Southern Historical Collection, University of North Carolina.

FISK, ISABEL, Diary, Tulane University, Department of Archives.

Flanagin Papers, Arkansas History Commission.

FLOYD, JOHN B., Letter, Battles and Leaders of the Civil War, extra illustrated, Huntington Library.

———, Papers, Duke University Library.

FONTAINE, MARY A., Letters, Confederate Memorial Literary Society, Richmond.

FORBES, HENRY C., Papers, Chicago Historical Society.

FORBES, JAMES MONROE, Letter, Huntington Library.

FOSTER, JOHN G., Letter, Battles and Leaders of the Civil War, extra illustrated, Huntington Library.

FOX, G. V., Correspondence, New York Historical Society.

———, Letters and Papers, A. Conger Goodyear Collection, Yale University Library.

FRANKLIN, Battle of, Diary of an Unidentified Michigan Cavalryman, Library of Congress.

FRANKLIN, W. B., Papers, Library of Congress.

Fredericksburg, Personal Recollections of the First Battle of, Fought on December 13, 1862, as seen from an Artillery Position on the Hill at Hamilton's Crossing, no author, Littlefield Collection, Eugene C. Barker Texas History Center, University of Texas.

FRÉMONT, JESSE BENTON, Papers, Chicago Historical Society.

FRÉMONT, JOHN CHARLES, Papers, Bancroft Library, University of California.

FRENCH, SAMUEL LIVINGSTON, The Army of the Potomac, Vol. II, Palmer Collection, Western Reserve Historical Society.

FRONEBERGER, J., Mrs. Duilio Giannitrapani Collection, Oak Park, Illinois.

FULLER, JOSEPH PRYOR, Diary and Letters, Library of Congress.

GALE, WILLIAM D., Papers, Southern Historical Collection, University of North Carolina.

GAMBLE, H. R., Papers, Missouri Historical Society, St. Louis.

GARDINER, EDWARD CAREY, Collection, The Historical Society of Pennsylvania.

GARFIELD, JAMES A., Letter to his Brother, Battles and Leaders of the Civil War, extra illustrated, Huntington Library.

———, Papers, Library of Congress.

GARLAND, HAMLIN, Papers, University of Southern California, American Literature Collection.

GATES, F. S., Letter, Collection Shiloh National Military Park.

GATES, PHILIP THURSTON, Papers, Filson Club.

GAY, SIDNEY HOWARD, Papers, Columbia University.

GAYARRE, CHARLES, Papers, Grace King Collection, Department of Archives, Louisiana State University.

Gettysburg Address, Text of, Associated Press Photostat, Lincoln National Life Foundation, Fort Wayne, Indiana.

GIBSON, S. J., Papers, Library of Congress.

GILLESPIE, JOSEPH, Papers, Chicago Historical Society.

GILLETTE, JAMES, Papers, Nevins' Notes.

GILMER, JEREMY F., Papers, Southern Historical Collection, University of North Carolina.

GILPIN, E. E., Papers, Library of Congress.

GILPIN, SAMUEL J. B. V., Diary, Library of Congress.

GILPIN, WILLIAM, A Pioneer of 1842, Bancroft Library, University of California.

Gilpin Papers, Bancroft Library, University of California.

GIRAUD, PIERRE, Letter, Philip D. and Elsie O. Sang Collection, River Forest, Illinois.

GLUD, ANNA HUNDLEY, The Drummer Boy, Account, Bancroft Library, University of California.

GOLDSBOROUGH, LOUIS M., Papers, Duke University Library.

Goodspeed's Catalog 510, late 1862, Manuscripts.

GOODYEAR, A. CONGER, Collection, Yale University Library, Political Associates of Abraham Lincoln.

Gordon Family Papers, Georgia Historical Society.

GOREE, THOMAS J., Papers, Louisiana State University, Department of Archives.

GORGAS, J., Paper, Confederate Papers, Eugene C. Barker History Center, University of Texas.

GOURDIN, ROBERT, Papers, Duke University Library.

GOWEN, W. R., Diary, Archives Division, Texas State Library.

GRAHAM, HENRY, Journal, 1862–1863, Library of Congress.

GRANT, ULYSSES S., Letter, California Historical Society, San Francisco.

——, Letter, May 22, 1863, Miscellaneous Collection, Huntington Library.

——, Letter, President file, J. P. Morgan Library.

——, Letter, Philip D. and Elsie O. Sang Collection, River Forest, Illinois.

——, Letter, Andre de Coppett Autograph Collection, Princeton University Library.

——, Letter, Rutgers University Library, through the U. S. Grant Association.

——, Letter to his Father, June 13, 1863, Rosenbach Foundation, Philadelphia.

——, Letters, John Hay Library, Brown Library University.

——, Letters, Massachusetts Historical Society.

——, Letters, Princeton University Library, through the Ulysses S. Grant Association.

——, Letters, Rosenbach Foundation, Philadelphia.

——, Letters, University of Virginia, through the Ulysses S. Grant Association.

——, Letters, Palmer Collection, Western Reserve Historical Society.

——, Letters and Papers, Illinois State Historical Library.

——, Notebook, Rosenbach Foundation, Philadelphia.

——, Papers, Chicago Historical Society.

——, Papers, Huntington Library.

——, Papers, Library of Congress.

——, Papers, New York Historical Society.

——, Papers, Ulysses S. Grant Association, Southern Illinois University.

Grant to Halleck, Collection, Illinois State Historical Library.

Grant-Washburne Papers, Illinois State Historical Library.

GRATZ, SIMON, Autograph Collection, The Historical Society of Pennsylvania.

GRAY, JUSTICE HORACE, Papers, Library of Congress.

GRAY, WILLIAM GRANVILLE, Papers, Valentine Museum, Richmond.

GREELEY, HORACE, Papers, Chicago Historical Society.

——, Papers, Library of Congress.

Greeley-Colfax Correspondence, New York Public Library.

GREENE, SAMUEL DANA, Letter to Parents, Dana Papers, Massachusetts Historical Society.

GREENHOW, ROSE O'NEAL, Papers, Duke University Library.

GRIMBALL, JOHN BERKLEY, South Carolina Historical Society, Charleston, South Carolina.

GRONER, J. A., Letters, Southern Historical Collection, University of North Carolina.

Groner Collection, Southern Historical Collection, University of North Carolina.

HALLECK, H. W., General's Papers and Books, Special Civil War Collection, Adjutant General's Office, National Archives.

———, Letter, Battles and Leaders of the Civil War, extra illustrated, Huntington Library.

———, Papers, Chicago Historical Society.

———, Papers, Eldridge Collection, Huntington Library.

HAMLIN, COL. A. C., Collection, Massachusetts Commandery of the Military Order of the Loyal Legion of the United States, Papers, Houghton Library, Harvard University.

HAMPTON, JUSTIN C., Letters, Eugene C. Barker Texas History Center, University of Texas.

HANAFORD, FRANK, Papers, G. E. Hanaford Collection.

HANCOCK, WINFIELD S., Letters, Massachusetts Commandery of the Military Order of the Loyal Legion of the United States, Papers, Houghton Library, Harvard University.

HANKS, O. T., Reminiscences, "Account of Civil War Experience," Eugene C. Barker Texas History Center, University of Texas.

HARD, HANSON, Account of Journey while Prisoner of War, Library of Congress.

HARDAWAY, R., Letter, J. Ambler Johnston Private Collection, Richmond, Virginia.

HARDEE, WILLIAM JOSEPH, Letters, Palmer Collection, Western Reserve Historical Society.

———, Papers, Library of Congress.

Hardin Collection, Chicago Historical Society.

HARPER, W. P., Diary, Louisiana Historical Association, Confederate Memorial Hall.

HARRINGTON, GEORGE, Papers, Huntington Library.

———, Papers, Library of Congress.

HARRIS, ADDIE, Papers, Manuscript Literary Section, New York State Library.

HARRIS, NAT. H., Papers, Southern Historical Collection, University of North Carolina.

HARRIS, WILLIAM HAMILTON, Diary, Virginia State Historical Society.

HARRISON, BENJAMIN, Papers, Library of Congress.

HARRISON, BURTON W., Papers, Library of Congress.

HARRISON, WILLIAM SOUTHALL, JR., Letter, May 8, 1863, Virginia State Historical Society.

HASKELL, A. C., Papers, Southern Historical Collection, University of North Carolina.

HASKELL, FRANK A., Papers, State Historical Society of Wisconsin.

HASKINS, A. H., Diary, Mississippi Department of Archives and History.

HASKINS, NANNIE E., Diary, Tennessee State Library and Archives.

HATCH, EDWARD, Letters, Battles and Leaders of the Civil War, extra illustrated, Huntington Library.

HATCH, O. M., Papers, Illinois State Historical Library.

HAWES, SAMUEL HORACE, Diary, Virginia State Historical Society.

HAWLEY, J. R., Papers, Library of Congress.

HAY, JOHN, Papers, Illinois State Library.

———, Papers, Library of Congress.

HAYES, RUTHERFORD B., Diary, Ohio State Museum.

HAYS, JOHN, An Account of the Wounding of General Jackson at Chancellorsville, written by a Federal Officer, Carlisle, Pennsylvania, *Evening Herald,* October 8, 1910, Massachusetts Commandery of the Military Order of the Loyal Legion of the United States, Papers, Houghton Library, Harvard University.

HAZELTON, GARY W., Manuscript, Abraham Lincoln, Edward S. Bragg Papers, Palmer Collection, Western Reserve Historical Society.

HAZEN, W. B., Account of the Battle of Chickamauga and Missionary Ridge, Palmer Collection, Western Reserve Historical Society.

HEINTZELMAN, Diary, Library of Congress.

HEINTZELMAN, S. P., Letter, Eldridge Collection, Huntington Library.

HENNEBERRY, JAMES E., Journal, Chicago Historical Society.

HENRY, ANSON G., Papers, Illinois State Historical Library.

Henry Family Papers, Library of Congress.

HICKS, GOVERNOR, Papers, Maryland Historical Society.

HILL, A. C., Letters, Eugene C. Barker Texas History Center, University of Texas.

HILL, D. H., Papers, Virginia State Library.

HILL, JOHN LYON, Diary, Virginia State Historical Society.

HILL, JOSEPH, Diary, Southern Historical Collection, University of North Carolina.

HITCHCOCK, E. A., Papers, Missouri Historical Society, St. Louis.

HOBBS, CHARLES A., Diary and Letters, Vicksburg National Military Park.

HOGAN, THOMAS, Letters, Civil War Papers, Missouri Historical Society, St. Louis.

HOLFORD, LYMAN C., Diary 1861–1864, Library of Congress.

HOLT, JOSEPH, Letter, A. Conger Goodyear Collection, Yale University Library.

———, Papers, Library of Congress.

HOOD, CHARLES C., Diary, Library of Congress.

HOOD, HENRY EWELL, Letters, Tennessee State Historical Society.

HOOD, JOHN BELL, Letter, Palmer Collection, Western Reserve Historical Society.

———, Notes for Plan of Operation, Battles and Leaders of the Civil War, extra illustrated, Huntington Library.

HOOKER, JOSEPH, Letter, Civil War Institute, Gettysburg College.

———, Letter, Battles and Leaders of the Civil War, extra illustrated, Huntington Library.

———, Letter, Massachusetts Commandery of the Military Order of the Loyal Legion of the United States, Papers, Houghton Library, Harvard University.

———, Letter, Group 94, AGO Checklist entry 108, War Records, Old Army, National Archives.

———, Papers, Huntington Library.

HORNER, HARLAN HOYT, Lincoln Answers the Albany and Ohio Democrats in re Vallandigham, New York Civil War Centennial Commission.

HOTCHKISS, JED., Papers, Alderman Library, University of Virginia.

———, Papers and Maps, Library of Congress.

HOWARD, O. O., Letter, Philip D. and Elsie O. Sang Collection, River Forest, Illinois.

———, Papers, Lincoln Memorial University, Department of Lincolniana, gift of Justin C. Turner, Los Angeles.

HOWARD, W. A., Letter, Shiloh Military Park Collection.

HUGER, BENJAMIN, Papers, Chicago Historical Society.

HUMPHREYS, A. A., Collection, The Historical Society of Pennsylvania.

HUNT, R. C., Extracts from Diary, Vicksburg National Military Park.

HUNTER, JOHN, JR., Diary, Confederate Memorial Literary Society.

HUNTER, R. M. T., Papers, Alderman Library, University of Virginia.

HUNTER, WILLIAM F., JR., Papers, Ohio State Museum.

HURLEY, W. N., Letters, Civil War Letters, Eugene C. Barker Texas History Center, University of Texas.

HURST, TEMPLETON BRANDON, Diary, Pennsylvania Historical and Museum Commission, Division of Public Records.

INSKEEP, JOHN D., Diary, Ohio Historical Society.

Irregular Books, 1861–1865, Registers of Letters Received, Record Group 107, Secretary of War Inventory 28, War Records, Old Army, National Archives.

JACKSON, EDGAR ALLEN, Letters of, Virginia State Library.

JACKSON, JOHN R., Journal, Library of Congress.

JACKSON, T. J., Letter, Simon Gratz Autograph Collection, The Historical Society of Pennsylvania.

———, Papers, Southern Historical Collection, University of North Carolina.

JAMES, ROBERT EDWIN, Papers, Library of Congress.

JENKINS, H. H., Pocket Diary, Huntington Library.

"John," Letter to "Dear Mother," Confederate Soldier at Gettysburg, Virginia State Library.

"John J.," Letter to Chase, Treasury Departments Records, National Archives.

JOHNSON, BRADLEY T., Letter, Massachusetts Commandery of the Military Order of the Loyal Legion of the United States, Papers, Houghton Library, Harvard University.

JOHNSON, CHARLES JAMES, Papers, Louisiana State Department of Archives, Louisiana State University.

JOHNSTON, ALBERT SIDNEY, Papers, Chicago Historical Society.

———, Scrap Book, Barker Texas History Center, University of Texas.

JOHNSTON, J. AMBLER, Papers, Private Collection.

JOHNSTON, J. STODDARD, Papers, Filson Club, Louisville, Kentucky.

JOHNSTON, JOSEPH E., Letter, Palmer Collection, Western Reserve Historical Society.

———, Papers, Chicago Historical Society.

———, Papers, Manuscript Department, Duke University Library.

———, Papers, Huntington Library.

———, Telegraphic Circular, Greensboro, North Carolina, April 30, 1865, Miscellaneous Collection, Huntington Library.

JONES, JOHN E., Letter, Battles and Leaders of the Civil War, extra illustrated, Huntington Library.

JORDAN, THOMAS, Memorandum, Battles and Leaders of the Civil War, extra illustrated, Huntington Library.

Journal Magnolia Plantation, Southern Historical Collection, University of North Carolina.

"Justius," Letter, Autograph Collection, S. L. M. Barlow Papers, Huntington Library.

KAUTZ, ALBERT, manuscript, Bancroft Library.

KAY, WILLIAM K., Study on Sunken Road at Shiloh, Shiloh National Military Park Collection.

KEARNY, THOMAS, Papers, Brady Memorial Library, Manhattanville College of the Sacred Heart, New York.

KEATINGS, HARRIETTA C., Narrative of the Burning of Georgia, Library of Congress.

KEIFER, JOSEPH WARREN, Letters, Library of Congress.

KELAHER, JAMES, Papers, Huntington Library.

KELLER, JAMES M., Papers, Arkansas History Commission.

KELLOGG, R. M., Papers, Civil War Collection, Ohio State Museum.

KENNEDY, FRANCIS MILTON, Diary, Southern Historical Collection, University of North Carolina Library.

KEPNER, JOHN PRICE, Letters and Diary, Maryland Historical Society.

KERR, WILLIAM C., Letters, Huntington Library.

KEYSER, WILLIAM, Letters and Diary, Maryland Historical Society.

KING, GRACE, Collection, Louisiana State Department of Archives, Louisiana State University.

KING, HORATIO, Papers, Library of Congress.

KING, WILLIAM, Diary, Historical Collection, University of North Carolina.

KLOEPPEL, M. HENRY, Diary, Library of Congress.

LADUC, WILLIAM GATES, Memoirs, Huntington Library.

LAKE, CHARLES H., Letter, J. W. Heiskell Collection.

LAKE, DELOS W., Letters, Huntington Library.

LAMON, WARD HILL, Letters, Chicago Historical Society.

LAMOUNTAIN, J., Report, Check list entry 168, Record Group 94, AGO, War Records, Old Army, National Archives.

LANDER, FREDERICK W., Papers, Library of Congress.

LANGHORNE, SAMUEL, Papers, Virginia Historical Society.

LANPHIER, Papers, Illinois State Historical Library.

LARNED, DANIEL REED, Papers, Library of Congress.

LATTA, JAMES W., Diaries, 1862–1865, Library of Congress.

LAW, E. M., Papers, Southern Historical Collection, University of North Carolina.

LAWRENCE, G. E., Massachusetts Commandery of the Military Order of the Loyal Legion of the United States, Houghton Library, Harvard University.

LEE, Family Papers, Brock Collection, Huntington Library.

LEE, HENRY, Papers, Massachusetts Historical Society.

LEE, MRS. HUGH (Mary Greenhow), Diary, Maryland Historical Society.

———, Papers, Maryland Historical Society.

LEE, MARY CUSTIS, Letters, Rosenbach Foundation, Philadelphia.

LEE, ROBERT E., Col. William Allen's Conversations with General Robert E. Lee, Allen Collection, Southern Historical Collection, University of North Carolina.

——, Letter, Battles and Leaders of the Civil War, extra illustrated, Huntington Library.

——, Letter, Miscellaneous Collection, Huntington Library.

——, Letter, Lincoln National Life Foundation.

——, Letter, Confederate Papers, Eugene C. Barker Texas History Center, University of Texas.

——, Letters, Eldridge Collection, Huntington Library.

——, Letters, Maryland Historical Society, Baltimore.

——, Letters, Philip D. and Elsie O. Sang Collection, River Forest, Illinois.

——, Letters, Andre de Coppet Collection, Princeton University Library.

——, Letters, Palmer Collection, Western Reserve Historical Society.

——, Letters to Jefferson Davis, Andre de Coppet Collection, Princeton University Library.

——, Letters to Markie, Huntington Library.

——, Papers, Chicago Historical Society.

——, Papers, Manuscript Department, Duke University Library.

——, Papers, Library of Congress.

——, Papers, Missouri Historical Society.

——, Papers, New York Historical Society.

——, Papers, New York Public Library.

——, Papers, Southern Historical Collection, University of North Carolina.

LEE, STEPHEN DILL, Papers, Civil War Journal, Southern Historical Collection, University of North Carolina.

Lee Headquarters, Papers, Virginia State Historical Society.

LEET, EDWIN, Letters, Department of Archives, Louisiana State University.

LELAND, EDWIN ALBERT, Organization and Administration of the Louisiana Army During the Civil War, A Thesis, Tulane University, New Orleans, 1938, unpublished.

LEMON, JOHN G., Diary, Huntington Library.

LESTER, GEORGE, Collection, Louisiana State Department of Archives, Louisiana State University.

LETCHER, JOHN, Confederate Broadside, Virginia State Historical Society.

——, Papers, Library of Congress.

LIEBER, FRANCIS, Collection, Huntington Library.

LIGHTFOOT, EMMIE CRUMP, Papers, Confederate Memorial Literary Society, Richmond.

LINCOLN, ABRAHAM, File, Huntington Library.

——, New/Not in Collected Works File, Illinois State Historical Library.

——, North and South, A. Conger Goodyear Collection, Yale University Library.

——, Note, November 18, 1863, Battles and Leaders of the Civil War, extra illustrated, Huntington Library.

——, Papers, New York Historical Society.

——, Unpublished File, John Hay Library, Brown University.

LINCOLN, ROBERT TODD, Papers, Library of Congress, Microfilm in Chicago Historical Society.

Lincoln Collection, Chicago Historical Society.

Littlefield Collection, Eugene C. Barker History Center, University of Texas.

LOGAN, JOHN A., Memorial Collection, Illinois State Historical Library.

Logan Family Papers, Yale University Library.

LONG, E. B., Private Collection.

LONGSTREET, JAMES, Letters, Battles and Leaders of the Civil War, extra illustrated, Huntington Library.

———, Letters to Colonel Latrobe and Fitz John Porter, courtesy Ralph Newman, Chicago.

———, Papers, Manuscript Department, Duke University Library.

LORD, MRS. W. W., Journal kept during the siege of Vicksburg, May and June, 1863.

LOWE, T. S. C., Aeronautic Report, Record Group 94, AGO Checklist entry 126, National Archives.

LUBBOCK, FRANCIS R., Letters, Civil War Letters, Eugene C. Barker Texas History Center, University of Texas.

MCCARTER, Journal, Library of Congress.

MCCLELLAN, GEORGE B., Letter, Philip D. and Elsie O. Sang Collection, River Forest, Illinois.

———, Letters, Battles and Leaders of the Civil War, extra illustrated, Huntington Library.

———, Letters, Eldridge Collection, Huntington Library.

———, Papers, Library of Congress.

———, Papers, New York Historical Society.

———, Papers, Huntington Library.

MCCLELLAN, HENRY BRAINERD, Papers, Virginia State Historical Society.

MCCLERNAND, JOHN A., Papers, Illinois State Historical Library.

MCCOOK, Family Papers, Library of Congress.

MCCONNELL, CHARLES, Papers, Western Reserve Historical Society.

MCCORMICK, C. C., Diary and Letters, Pennsylvania Historical and Museum Commission.

MCCORMICK, THOMAS RASOR, Reminiscences, Mississippi Department of Archives and History.

MCDOWELL, IRVIN, Letter, Autograph Collection, S. L. M. Barlow Papers, Huntington Library.

MCGRATH, W., Letter, Library of Congress.

MCGUIRE, DR. HUNTER, The Seven Days Fighting Around Richmond, Hotchkiss Papers, Alderman Library, University of Virginia.

MCGUIRE, O., Diary of a Southern Refugee, Nevins' Notes.

MCKOWEN, JOHN, Papers, Department of Archives, Louisiana State University.

MCLAWS, LAFAYETTE, Letter, Simon Gratz Autograph Collection, The Historical Society of Pennsylvania.

———, Letters, Palmer Collection, Western Reserve Historical Society.

———, Papers, Southern Historical Collection, University of North Carolina.

MCRAE, JOHN, Letterbooks, State Historical Society of Wisconsin.

MACKALL, W. W., Papers, Southern Historical Collection, University of North Carolina.

MACKEY, JAMES TASWELL, Diary, Confederate Memorial Literary Society.

MACRAE, HUGH, Papers, Manuscript Department, Duke University Library.

MADIGAN, THOMAS F., Collection, Nevins' Notes.

MALLORY, S. R., Diary and Papers, Southern Historical Collection, University of North Carolina.

MAN, FREDERICK H., Letters, Museum of the City of New York.

MANN, ISAAC, Letters to his Wife, Huntington Library.

MANN, MARIA R., Letters, Library of Congress.

MARBLE, MANTON, Papers, Library of Congress.

MARSHALL, CHARLES, Letters, Battles and Leaders of the Civil War, extra illustrated, Huntington Library.

MARTIN, S. F., Letter, Civil War Papers, Missouri Historical Society.

Massachusetts Commandery of the Military Order of the Loyal Legion of the United States, Papers, Houghton Library, Harvard University.

MAURY, BETTY HERNDON, Diary, Library of Congress.

MAURY, MATTHEW FONTAINE, Papers, Library of Congress.

MAY, RICHARD EDWARDS, Letters and Papers, Huntington Library.

MAYO, JOSEPH, Broadside, "To Arms," June 27, 1863, Valentine Museum.

MEAD, DR., Memoir of a Medical Officer, Alderman Library, University of Virginia.

MEADE, GEORGE G., Letter, Rosenbach Foundation, Philadelphia.

———, Letter to Grant, May 21, 1864, Battles and Leaders of the Civil War, extra illustrated, Huntington Library.

———, Papers, The Historical Society of Pennsylvania.

MEADOWS, T. P., Mrs. J. D. Otis Collection, Oak Park, Illinois.

MECKLIN, A. H., Diary, Mississippi Department of Archives and History.

MEDARY, SAMUEL, Papers, Ohio State Museum.

MEIGS, MONTGOMERY, Papers, Library of Congress.

———, Pocket Diaries, Library of Congress.

MELHORN, JOHN WESLEY, Civil War Diary, Stanford University Libraries, Division of Special Collections, Palo Alto, California.

MEMMINGER, CHRISTOPHER G., Letters, Rosenbach Foundation, Philadelphia.

———, Papers, Southern Historical Collection, University of North Carolina.

Memorandum for the Commanders of the Corps and of the Reserve, April 3, 1862, by Command of General A. S. Johnston, Palmer Collection, Western Reserve Historical Society.

MERCER, DR., Letter, Autograph Collection, Barlow Papers, Huntington Library.

MERCER, GEORGE A., Diary, Southern Historical Collection, University of North Carolina.

MERRYWEATHER, GEORGE, Letters, John Merryweather Collection.

MERWIN, JAMES B., Diary, Library of Congress.

Meteorological Registers, Naval Observatory, Washington; Weather Bureau Records, Agriculture and General Branch, National Resources Division, National Archives.

MILES, WILLIAM PORCHER, Letters, New York Public Library.

————, Letters, A. Conger Goodyear Collection, Yale University Library.

————, Papers, Southern Historical Collection, University of North Carolina.

MILLER, WILLIAM E., Letter, William Rawle Brooke Papers, Commandery of the Military Order of the Loyal Legion of the United States, Philadelphia.

MILLS, MRS. CHARLES E., Papers, Dallas Historical Society.

MILLS, L. W., Collection, Shiloh National Military Park.

Miscellaneous Collection, Huntington Library.

Miscellaneous Letters, XXI, Massachusetts Historical Society.

Miscellaneous Papers, Huntington Library.

Miscellaneous Soldiers' Letters, Duke University Library.

MITCHELL, ARCHIBALD, A Journal Kept By, Louisiana Historical Association.

MITCHELL, C. D., Extracts from Field Notes of the Civil War, Library of Congress.

MITCHELL, JOHN K., Papers, Virginia State Historical Society.

MONTGOMERY, JAMES H., Diary, Library of Congress.

MOORE, CHARLES, JR., Diary, 1861–1862, Louisiana Historical Association.

MOORE, ORLANDO HURLEY, Papers, Bancroft Library, University of California.

MOORE, THOMAS O., Papers, Louisiana State Department of Archives, University of Louisiana.

MORDECAI, EMMA, Diary, Southern Historical Collection, University of North Carolina.

————, Letters, Confederate Memorial Literary Society.

MORGAN, EDWIN D., Papers, New York Library.

MORSE, CHARLES F., Papers, Massachusetts Historical Society.

MORSE, SAMUEL F. B., Correspondence with Benson J. Lossing, Palmer Collection, Western Reserve Historical Society.

————, Papers, Library of Congress.

————, Papers, Massachusetts Historical Society.

MOSBY, JOHN B., Papers, Duke University Library.

MOTLEY, JOHN LOTHROP, Letters, Miscellaneous Papers, Massachusetts Historical Society.

MULLEN, JOSEPH, JR., Diary, Confederate Memorial Literary Society.

MULLIGAN, COL. JAMES A., Diary and Journal, Chicago Historical Society.

MUMFORD, THOMAS T., Five Forks—The Waterloo of the Confederacy, Virginia State Historical Society.

————, Papers, Duke University Library.

MYERS, W. E., Letter, Louisiana Historical Association.

NEVINS, ALLAN, Research notes and manuscripts.

NEWBURGER, A., Diary, Library of Congress.

Newhall Family Letters, Boston Public Library.

NICHOLSON, JOHN PAGE, Collection, Huntington Library.

NICOLAY, JOHN, Papers, Library of Congress.

Nicolay-Hay Papers, Illinois State Historical Library, Springfield.

NORRIS, WILLIAM, Papers, University of Virginia.

Now or Never, To Arms! To Arms! Broadsides, Arkansas History Commission.

OLDHAM, KIE, Collection, Arkansas History Commission.

OLDHAM, W. S., Letters, Ryder Collection, Tufts University Library.

———, Memoirs, Barker Texas History Center, University of Texas.

OLIVER, J. R., Typewritten Statement on Wounding of J. E. B. Stuart, Palmer Collection, Western Reserve Historical Society.

OLMSTEAD, CHARLES HART, Reminiscences, Georgia Historical Society.

OLMSTEAD, F. L., Papers, Library of Congress.

ORD, E. O. C., Papers, Bancroft Library, University of California.

O'RORKE, PATRICK HENRY, Papers, Manhattanville College of the Sacred Heart, Brady Memorial Library, Purchase, New York.

PALMER, JOHN M., Papers, Colorado Historical Society.

———, Papers, Illinois State Historical Library.

PALMER, WILLIAM P., Civil War Collection, Western Reserve Historical Society, Cleveland.

PARKER, ELY S., Narrative of Appomattox, Benjamin Harrison Papers, Library of Congress.

PARRY, DR. H. C., Letters made available by Dr. Edward Owen Parry, Devon, Pennsylvania.

PARSONS, LOUIS B., Papers, Illinois State Historical Library.

PATRICK, MARSENA, Diaries, Library of Congress.

PATTERSON, JOHN, Letters, Arkansas Manuscript Collection, John A. Larson Memorial Library, Little Rock University.

PATTON, W. J., Diary, Tennessee Historical Society.

Payroll of Slaves Employed by the Commonwealth of Virginia, Virginia State Library.

PEARCE, GENERAL N. B., Reminiscences of, Arkansas History Commission.

PEMBERTON, JOHN C., Letter to Jefferson Davis, January 5, 1863, Battles and Leaders of the Civil War, extra illustrated, Huntington Library.

———, Manuscript, New York Public Library.

———, Papers, Southern Historical Collection, University of North Carolina.

PENDLETON, EDWARD C., Diary, Library of Congress.

———, Manuscript, Library of Congress.

PENDLETON, WILLIAM NELSON, Papers, Southern Historical Collection, University of North Carolina.

PERHAM, AURESTUS S., Papers, Library of Congress.

Personal Papers, Miscellaneous, Library of Congress.

PETTUS, JOHN J., Correspondence, Mississippi State Archives.

PHELPS, CHARLES R., Letters, Alderman Library, University of Virginia.

PHILLIPS, EUGENIA, A Southern Woman's Story of her Imprisonment During the War of 1861–1862, Library of Congress.

PHILLIPS, GEORGE E., Collection, Huntington Library.

PHILLIPS, WENDELL, Papers, Library of Congress.

PICARD, JACOB, Life of Sigel, Nevins' Notes.

PICKENS, F. W., Letters, A. Conger Goodyear Collection, Yale University Library.

———, Papers, Chicago Historical Society.

———, Papers, Duke University Library.

Pickens-Bonham Papers, Library of Congress.

PICKETT, GEORGE E., Letter to Beauregard, May 9, 1864, Battles and Leaders of the Civil War, extra illustrated, Huntington Library.

———, Letters, Palmer Collection, Western Reserve Historical Society.

———, Papers, Manuscript Department, Duke University Library.

———, Papers, Library of Congress.

PIERCE, FRANKLIN, Letter, Massachusetts Commandery of the Military Order of the Loyal Legion of the United States, Houghton Library, Harvard University.

PIERCE, NATHANIEL G., Letters, Arkansas Manuscript Collection, John A. Larson Memorial Library, Little Rock University.

PINKERTON, ALLAN, Papers, Library of Congress.

PIPKIN, L. M., Four Papers on the Civil War, Louisiana State Museum, Library, and Historian's Office, Military Department, State of Louisiana.

PLEASONTON, ALFRED, Papers, Private Collection, Pleasonton Family, Courtesy Ralph Newman, Chicago.

Political Associates of Abraham Lincoln, A. Conger Goodyear Collection, Yale University Library.

POLK, LEONIDAS, Letter, Palmer Collection, Western Reserve Historical Society.

POLK, TRISTAN, Letter, Confederate States Army Collection 1861–1867, Department of Archives, Louisiana State University.

Pollard Collection, Western Reserve Historical Society.

POPE, JOHN, Letters, Isaac N. Arnold, Abraham Lincoln, extra illustrated, Huntington Library.

———, Letters, Battles and Leaders of the Civil War, extra illustrated, Huntington Library.

———, Papers, Chicago Historical Society.

———, Papers, New York Historical Society.

PORTER, ALBERT QUINCY, Diary, Library of Congress.

———, Diary, 1865, Mississippi Department of Archives and History.

PORTER, D. D., Papers, Eldridge Collection, Huntington Library.

———, Papers, Huntington Library.

PORTER, FITZ JOHN, Letter, Western Reserve Historical Society.

———, Papers, Massachusetts Historical Society.

PORTER, WILLIAM D., Journal and Letters, Boston Public Library.

PRESCOTT, ALBERT E., Notes Describing Grand Review, Miscellaneous Collection, Huntington Library.

Prisoner at Johnson's Island, no author, Louisiana Historical Association.

PURDY, GEORGE, Letter, Charles Shedd Collection, Pittsburg Landing, Tennessee.

QUINCY, SAMUEL M., Papers, Massachusetts Historical Society.

Rabb Family Papers, Barker Texas History Center, University of Texas.

RAMSEUR, S. D., Papers, Southern Historical Collection, University of North Carolina.

RANDOLPH, W. J., Recollections, Palmer Collection, Western Reserve Historical Society.

RAWLINS, JOHN A., Letter to U. S. Grant, Palmer Collection, Western Reserve Historical Society.

———, Papers, Chicago Historical Society.

RAY, CHARLES H., Letters, Huntington Library.

RAYMOND, HENRY J., Letter, A. Conger Goodyear Collection, Yale University Library.

RAYNOR, WILLIAM N., Diary, Vicksburg National Military Park.

REAGAN, JOHN H., Letter, Massachusetts Commandery of the Military Order of the Loyal Legion of the United States, Papers, Houghton Library, Harvard University.

———, Papers, Texas State Library Archives Division, Austin, Texas.

Register of Officers Arriving in Washington, 1861, National Archives.

REICHHELM, PAUL E., Journal, Library of Congress.

REYNOLDS, JOHN F., Letter, Battles and Leaders of the Civil War, extra illustrated, Huntington Library.

REYNOLDS, THOMAS O., Papers, Library of Congress.

RICHARDSON, HENRY A., Palmer Collection, Western Reserve Historical Society.

RIDDLE, ALBERT G., Papers, Western Reserve Historical Society.

RING, G. P., Diary, Louisiana Historical Collection.

RIVES, W. C., Papers, University of Virginia Library.

ROBINSON, J. G., Letters, Malvin Hoffmann Collection, Chicago.

ROBINSON, WILLIAM CULBERTSON, Letters, Illinois State Historical Library.

ROCKWELL, J. H., The Death Blow to the Confederacy, E. B. Long files.

ROMAN, ALFRED, Papers, Library of Congress.

ROMBAUER, ROBERT J., Missouri Historical Society.

ROPES, LIEUTENANT HENRY, Letters, Boston Public Library, Rare Book Room.

ROSE, LUTHER A., Diary, Library of Congress.

ROSECRANS, WILLIAM S., Battles and Leaders of the Civil War, extra illustrated, Huntington Library.

———, Papers, UCLA Library.

ROSIN, WILBERT HENRY, Hamilton Rowan Gamble, Missouri's Civil War Governor, unpublished dissertation, University of Missouri, 1960.

ROSS, LAWRENCE SULLIVAN, Letters, Barker Texas Historical Center, University of Texas.

ROSS, LEVI ADOLPHUS, Papers, Illinois State Historical Library.

ROSS, ROBERT, Letters, Eugene C. Barker Texas Historical Center, University of Texas.

ROSSER, THOMAS L., Papers, Alderman Library, University of Virginia.

ROY, JOHN, Diary, Louisiana State Department of Archives, Louisiana State University.

RUFFIN, EDMUND, Diaries, Library of Congress.

RUTHERFORD, HARRY J., Letter, Lincoln Memorial University, Harrogate, Tennessee.

Ryder Collection, Tufts University Library.

SAINT JOHN, BELA T., Diary, Bancoft Library, University of California.

SALE, JOHN F., Letters, Virginia State Library, Richmond.

SALTER, GOERGE W., Letter, John Hay Library, Brown University.

SANBORN, FRANK A., Manuscript, Chicago Historical Society.

SANBORN, FRED G., Scrapbook, Library of Congress.

Sanitary Report of the Condition of the Prostitutes of Nashville, Tennessee, Palmer Collection, Western Reserve Historical Society.

SAUNDERS, JAMES E., Letter, Confederate Papers, Eugene C. Barker Texas Historical Center, University of Texas.

SCALES, CORDELIA LEWIS, Papers, Mississippi Department of Archives and History.

SCHOFIELD, JOHN W., Letter, Battles and Leaders of the Civil War, extra illustrated, Huntington Library.

SCHOOLCRAFT, HENRY ROWE, Papers, Library of Congress.

SCHURZ, CARL, Papers, State Historical Society of Wisconsin.

SCOTT, WINFIELD, Letter, Greer Collection, the Historical Society of Pennsylvania.

Scrapbook of Unidentified Letters, Huntington Library.

SEWARD, FANNY, Papers, Rush Rees Library, University of Rochester.

SEWARD, WILLIAM H., Papers, Chicago Historical Society.

———, Papers, Library of Congress.

———, Papers, Rush Rees Library, University of Rochester, Rochester, New York.

SHARP, HENRY T., Papers, 1865–1933, Southern Historical Collection, University of North Carolina.

SHAW, ROBERT GOULD, Letters privately held, Nevins' Notes.

SHEDD, CHARLES, Soldier Letter Collection, Pittsburg Landing, Tennessee.

SHELLENBARGER, JOHN K., Papers, Library of Congress.

SHERIDAN, PHILIP H., Papers, Library of Congress.

SHERMAN, WILLIAM TECUMSEH, Letter, Battles and Leaders of the Civil War, extra illustrated, Huntington Library.

———, Letter July 21, 1863, Mississippi Department of Archives and History.

———, Letter to David D. Porter, June 14, 1863, Rosenbach Foundation, Philadelphia.

———, Letter to Silas F. Miller, Papers, Filson Club, Photostats of originals owned by John Mason Brown.

———, Letters, Andre de Coppet Collection, Princeton University Library.

———, Papers, Duke University Library.

———, Papers, Huntington Library.

———, Papers, Illinois State Historical Library.

———, Papers, Library of Congress.

———, Papers, Ohio State Museum.

———, Personal Copies with Sherman's handwritten comments, of Bowman and Irwin, Sherman and his Campaigns; H. V. Boynton, Sherman's Historical Raid, and Sherman's Memoirs, Northwestern University Library.

———, Report from Acworth, Georgia, Battles and Leaders of the Civil War, extra illustrated, Huntington Library.

———, Sherman's Reply to the Mayor of Atlanta, September 12, 1864. Dearborn Collection, Houghton Library, Harvard University.

Shiloh National Military Park Collection.

SHINER, MICHAEL, Diary 1813–1869, Library of Congress.

SHREVE, GEORGE W., Reminiscences of the History of the Stuart Horse Artillery, C.S.A., Virginia State Library.

SHULER, N., Diaries, Library of Congress.

SICKLES, DANIEL W., Papers, Manuscript Department, Duke University Library.

SIGEL, FRANZ, Letters, Eldridge Collection, Huntington Library.

———, Papers, Western Reserve Historical Society.

SIMON, MAURICE KAVANAUGH, Diary, Eugene C. Barker Texas History Center, University of Texas.

SIMPSON, WILLIAM DUNLOP, Papers, Duke University Library.

SMITH, B. H., Papers, Brock Collection, Huntington Library.

SMITH, CALEB B., Letter, Miscellaneous Papers, Huntington Library.

SMITH, E. KIRBY, Letter, Palmer Collection, Western Reserve Historical Society.

———, Letterbooks, Southern Historical Collection, University of North Carolina.

———, Papers, Southern Historical Collection, University of North Carolina.

SMITH, FRANKLIN, Papers, Duke University Library.

SMITH, G. W., Papers, Duke University Library.

SMITH, OSCAR, Papers, Library of Congress.

SMITH, SPOONER, Papers, Huntington Library.

SMITH, W. F., Papers, Walter Wilgus Private Collection.

SMYTHE, AUGUSTINE, Letters, South Carolina Historical Society, Charleston.

SOLOMON, CLARA E., Diary of a New Orleans Girl, 1861–1862, Louisiana Department of Archives, Louisiana State University.

SOWERS, ISAAC M., Diary, Library of Congress.

Special Civil War Collection, Generals' Papers and Books, Halleck, National Archives.

SPRAGUE, HOMER B., Diary, Library of Congress.

SPRING, JOHN VALENTINE, Papers, J. N. Heiskell Collection.

SPRINGER, WILLIAM MCKENDREE, Papers, Chicago Historical Society.

STANBERY, HENRY, Papers, Ohio Historical Society.

STANTON, EDWIN M., Letter, May 5 or 6, 1863, Ralph G. Newman Collection, Chicago.

———, Letters, John Hay Library, Brown University.

———, Papers, Library of Congress.

STAPP, JOSEPH D., Letters, Virginia State Historical Society.

STEARNS, HANNAH, Papers, Houghton Library, Harvard University.

STEPHENS, ALEXANDER, Papers of, Manhattanville College of the Sacred Heart, Brady Memorial Library, Purchase, New York.

STEPHENSON, R. RANDOLPH, Letters, Massachusetts Commandery of the Military Order of the Loyal Legion of the United States, Houghton Library, Harvard University.

STEVENSON, C. L., Letters, Battles and Leaders of the Civil War, extra illustrated, Huntington Library.

STEWART, ALEXANDER P., Letter, Battles and Leaders of the Civil War, extra illustrated, Huntington Library.

STEWART, WILLIAM N., The Charge of the Crater, Personal Statements by Participants, Confederate Memorial Literary Society, Richmond.

———, Diary, Southern Historical Collection, University of North Carolina.

STILES, JOSEPH CLAY, Papers, Huntington Library.

STOKES, THOMAS, Charges and Specifications against Captain, Confederate Papers, Eugene C. Barker Texas History Center, University of Texas.

STOUT, DR. S. N., Reminiscences, Palmer Collection, Western Reserve Historical Society.

STRINGFELLOW, FRANK, Papers, Virginia State Historical Society, Richmond.

STODDER, LOUIS N., Letter, E. B. Long Papers.

STRONG, GEORGE TEMPLETON, Diary, Nevins' Notes.

STUART, EDWARD, Letters, Mississippi State Department of Archives and History.

STUART, J. E. B., Memoranda of Operations of Second Battle of Manassas or Groveton, Ryder Collection, Tufts University Library.

———, Message May 11, 1864, Battles and Leaders of the Civil War, extra illustrated, Huntington Library.

———, Papers, Chicago Historical Society.

———, Papers, Duke University Library.

———, Papers, Huntington Library.

———, Papers, State Historical Society of Wisconsin.

———, Papers, Yale University Library.

STUART, OSCAR J. E. and Family, Papers, Mississippi State Department of Archives and History.

SUBLETT, EMMIE, Letters, Confederate Memorial Literary Society, Richmond.

SUMNER, CHARLES, Papers, Houghton Library, Harvard University.

———, Papers, Huntington Library.

Sumter, Fort, Celebration Scrapbook, Massachusetts Commandery of the Military Order of the Loyal Legion of the United States, Papers, Houghton Library, Harvard University.

"Susie," letter to "Cos: Edith," Alderman Library, University of Virginia.

SWEENEY, THOMAS W., Papers, Huntington Library.

SYKES, GEORGE, Letter, Barlow Papers Autograph Collection, Huntington Library.

"Synopsis of the Agreement between Generals Johnston and Sherman," Palmer Collection, Western Reserve Historical Society.

TAGGART, JOHN, Diary and Letters of, Pennsylvania Historical and Museum Commission.

TARBELL, IDA M., Papers, Allegheny College, Nevins' Notes.

Tarleton Family Papers, Yale University Papers.

TAYLOR, CALVIN and Family, Papers, Louisiana State Department of Archives, Louisiana State University.

TAYLOR, ERASMUS, Civil War Memoirs, Alderman Library, University of Virginia.

Telegram on opening of War from Charleston, Chicago Historical Society.

THAYER, ELI, Papers, Widner Library, Harvard University.

THOMAS, GEORGE H., Letter, Battles and Leaders of the Civil War, extra illustrated, Huntington Library.

THOMPSON, GILBERT, Journal, Library of Congress.

THOMPSON, M. JEFF., Letter, Battles and Leaders of the Civil War, extra illustrated, Huntington Library.

———, Reminiscences of Battle of Memphis, Southern Historical Collection, University of North Carolina.

THOMSON, ARCHIBALD N., Recollections of the Pursuit of Jefferson Davis, Palmer Collection, Western Reserve Historical Society.

THOMSON, RUFFIN, Papers, Southern Historical Collection, University of North Carolina.

THORNTON, HENRY INNES, Papers, California Historical Society.

TILLINGHAST, WILLIAM NORWOOD, Papers, Duke University Library.

TITLOW, JEROME, Papers, Library of Congress.

TOD, GOVERNOR, Collection, Letters Concerning Morgan's Raid, Ohio State Museum.

TOOMBS, ROBERT, Letters, Palmer Collection, Western Reserve Historical Society.

TORRENCE, ADAM, Family Correspondence 1861–1865, Pennsylvania Historical and Museum Commission.

TOWLE, GEORGE W., Personal Recollections, Bancroft Library, University of California.

TRASK, W. I., Journal, Mr. and Mrs. Gordon W. Trask Collection, Oak Park, Illinois.

TURNBO, E. C., History of the Twenty-seventh Arkansas Confederate Regiment, unpublished book manuscript, J. W. Mitchell Collection, Little Rock.

TURNER, ROBERT H., Recollections of the Virginia Convention of 1861, Virginia State Historical Society, Richmond.

TWAIN, MARK, Papers, University of California Library.

U. S. Soldiers Executed by the U. S. Authorities During the Late War, 1861–1866, Old Army Section, War Records Division, National Archives.

Unsigned Letter, Annapolis, Maryland, December, 1861, Virginia State Library.

Unsigned Memorandum, Virginia in 1861, Western Reserve Historical Society.

URQUHART, MRS. ROBERT DOW, Journal, Tulane University Library.

USHER, JOHN P., Letter, Personal Papers, Miscellaneous, Library of Congress.

USINA, N. P., Letter, Georgia Historical Society.

VALENTINE, R. A., Papers, Valentine Museum, Richmond.

Valentine Family Letters, Valentine Museum, Richmond.

VAN BRUNT, HARRY, Letters, Massachusetts Commandery of the Military Order of the Loyal Legion of the United States, Papers, Houghton Library, Harvard University.

VAN DEUSEN, DELOS, Letters, Huntington Library.

VAN DORN, EARL, Letters, Battles and Leaders of the Civil War, extra illustrated, Huntington Library.

VAN LEW, ELIZABETH, Papers, New York Public Library.

VEALE, WILLIAM, Letter, Massachusetts Commandery of the Military Order of the Loyal Legion of the United States, Papers, Houghton Library, Harvard University.

VEIL, CHARLES M., Letter, Civil War Institute, Gettysburg, Pennsylvania.

VENABLE, C. S., Papers, Barker Texas Historical Center, University of Texas.

Virginia General Assembly, Journal of Secret Session of the Senate, Brock Collection, Confederate States, Huntington Library.

WADDEL, JOHN NEWTON, Diaries, 1862–1864, Library of Congress.

WADE, BENJAMIN, Papers, Library of Congress.

WALKER, C. I., War Letters of, Confederate Papers, Barker Texas History Center, University of Texas.

WALKER, CORNELIUS, Diary, Confederate Memorial Literary Society, Richmond.

——, Papers, Confederate Memorial Literary Society, Richmond.

WALKER, W. H., Manuscript, Palmer Collection, Western Reserve Historical Society.

WALLACE, FRANCES N., Diary, Southern Historical Collection, University of North Carolina.

WALLACE, LEW, Letters, Palmer Collection, Western Reserve Historical Society.

WALLACE-DICKEY, Papers, Illinois State Historical Library.

WALTHALL, WILLIAM T., Papers, Mississippi State Department of Archives and History.

WARE, THOMAS L., Diary, Southern Historical Collection, University of North Carolina.

WARING, JOSEPH FREDERICK, Diary, Southern Historical Collection, University of North Carolina.

WARREN, G. K., Papers, New York State Library.

WASHBURN, C. C., Papers, State Historical Society of Wisconsin.

WASHBURNE, ELIHU, Papers, Library of Congress.

Wayne-Stites-Anderson Papers, Georgia Historical Society.

WEBB, ALEXANDER STEWART, Papers, Collection, Historical Manuscripts Division, Yale University Library.

WEBB, LOUIS HENRY, Diary, Southern Historical Collection, University of North Carolina.

WEITZEL, G., Letter, Battles and Leaders of the Civil War, extra illustrated, Huntington Library.

WELLES, GIDEON, Article, Lincoln and Reconstruction, John Hay Library, Brown University.

———, Draft of an Article, *The Collector*.

———, Expressions of Patriotism, Miscellaneous Collection, Huntington Library.

———, Papers, Huntington Library.

———, Papers, Illinois State Historical Library.

———, Papers, Library of Congress.

———, Papers, New York Library.

WENTWORTH, EDWIN OBERLIN, Correspondence, 1862–1864, Library of Congress.

WHEELER, JOSEPH, Letter to Bragg, Palmer Collection, Western Reserve Historical Society.

WHITE, HORACE, Papers, Illinois State Historical Library.

WHITE, JOHN CHESTER, Civil War Journal, Library of Congress.

WIGFALL, LOUIS T., Papers, Library of Congress.

Wigfall Family Papers, Library of Congress.

Wigfall Family Papers, Barker Texas History Center, University of Texas.

WIGHT, CHARLES COPELAND, Diary, Virginia State Historical Society.

Wight Family Papers, Virginia State Historical Society.

WILLIAMS, ALPHEUS, Letters, Huntington Library.

WILLIAMS, DAVID C., Papers, the Clara Eno Collection, Arkansas History Commission, Little Rock.

WILLIAMS, GEORGE, Letters, Courtesy of his grandson Ray Williams, Cleveland.

Williams-Chesnut-Manning Papers, Southern Historical Collection, University of North Carolina.

WILLS, DAVID, Typed Memo from Wills to John G. Nicolay, Lincoln National Life Foundation.

WILSON, WILLIAM B., manuscript, Lincoln File, Huntington Library.

WINSLOW, JOHN A., Papers, New York Historical Society.

WINTHROP, ROBERT C., Collection, Massachusetts Historical Society, Boston.

WIRZ, HENRY, Last Letter to his Wife, Yale University Library.

WISE, HENRY A., Miscellaneous Papers, Massachusetts Historical Society.

———, Papers, New York Historical Society.

WOOD, JOHN TAYLOR, Diary, Southern Historical Collection, University of North Carolina.

WOODMAN, HORATIO, Papers, Massachusetts Historical Society.

WOODWELL, CHARLES R., Diary, Library of Congress.

WORDEN, JOHN L., Statement, Palmer Collection, Western Reserve Historical Society.

WYCKOFF, ELIAS, Correspondence, Department of Archives, Louisiana State University.

YANCEY, WILLIAM L., Papers, Library of Congress.

YATES, RICHARD, Papers of, Illinois State Historical Library.

YOUNG, A. P., Papers, courtesy of Robert F. Evans and Ralph Newman, Chicago.

Young-Kerr Letters, Huntington Library.

SECTION III – NEWSPAPERS, CENTENNIAL HISTORY OF THE CIVIL WAR

Arkansas Gazette, Little Rock, Arkansas.
Arkansas True Democrat, Little Rock, Arkansas.
Atlanta *Daily Herald.*
Berryville (Virginia) *Conservator.*
Boston *Herald.*
Campaign Plain Dealer and Popular Sovereignty Advocate.
Carlisle (Pennsylvania) *Evening Herald.*
Charleston *Daily Courier.*
Charleston *Mercury.*
Chicago *Democrat.*
Chicago *Morning Post.*
Chicago *Times.*
Chicago *Tribune.*
Cincinnati *Daily Commercial.*
Cincinnati *Daily Inquirer.*
Cincinnati *Gazette.*
Cleveland *Plain Dealer.*
Dallas *Morning News.*
Danbury (Connecticut) *Times.*
De Bow's Review.
Frankfort (Kentucky) *Commonwealth.*
Hannibal *Daily Messenger.*
Harper's Weekly.
Hartford *Courant.*
Houston *Post-Dispatch.*
Illustrated London News.
Indianapolis *Sunday Star.*
Irish Times (The Cobbett Scrapbooks).
Jackson (Mississippi) *State Times.*

Kansas City (Missouri) *Star.*
Kansas City *Times.*
Lafayette (Indiana) *Journal and Courier.*
Lexington (Virginia) *Gazette.*
Lexington (Kentucky) *Observer and Reporter.*
The Liberator.
London *Press* (The Cobbett Scrapbooks).
London *Times* (The Cobbett Scrapbooks).
Manchester (England) *Examiner* (The Cobbett Scrapbooks).
Manchester (England) *Guardian* (The Cobbett Scrapbooks).
Montgomery (Alabama) *Daily Mail.*
Montgomery *Daily Post.*
Montgomery *Weekly Advertiser.*
Montgomery *Weekly Confederation.*
Montgomery *Weekly Mail.*
Montgomery *Weekly Post.*
Natchez (Mississippi) *Courier.*
National Intelligencer, Washington.
New York *Daily Tribune.*
New York *Herald.*
New York *Herald-Tribune.*
New York *Leader.*
New York *Times.*
New York *Times Book Review.*
New York *Weekly Tribune.*
Philadelphia *Public Ledger.*
The Railsplitter, Cincinnati.
Richmond *Dispatch.*
Richmond *Enquirer.*
Richmond *Examiner.*
Richmond *Sentinel.*
Richmond *Whig.*
Richmond *Whig and Public Advertiser.*
Sacramento (California) *Daily Union.*
Sheffield (England) *Daily Telegraph* (The Cobbett Scrapbooks).
Southern Literary Messenger.
Southern Watchman, Athens, Georgia.
Spirit of the South, Eufula, Alabama.
Springfield (Massachusetts) *Republican.*
Squatter Sovereign, Havana, Illinois.
Terre Haute (Indiana) *Daily Express.*
Vicksburg *Post.*
Vicksburg *Sunday Post.*
Washington, D.C., *Daily Chronicle.*
Washington (Arkansas) *Telegraph.*
West Virginia Hillbilly.
Winchester (Virginia) *Times.*
Wooster (Ohio) *Republican.*

SECTION IV—BOOKS, PAMPHLETS, AND PERIODICALS, CENTENNIAL HISTORY OF THE CIVIL WAR

ABBOTT, JOHN S. C., The History of the Civil War in America, two vols., Springfield, Massachusetts, 1866.

ABBOTT, MARTIN, "The First Shot at Fort Sumter," *Civil War History,* March, 1957.

ADAMS, BROOKS, "The Seizure of the Laird Rams," *Proceedings of the Massachusetts Historical Society,* Vol. XLV, Dec., 1911.

ADAMS, CHARLES FRANCIS, Charles Francis Adams, by his Son, American Statesmen, Boston, 1900.

———, Memorial Address of Charles Francis Adams of Massachusetts on the Life, Character and Services of William H. Seward, New York, 1873.

———, Richard Henry Dana, A Biography, Boston, 1890.

———, Studies Military and Diplomatic 1775–1865, New York, 1911.

———, Trans-Atlantic Historical Solidarity, Lectures Delivered Before the University of Oxford in Easter and Trinity Terms 1913, Oxford, 1913.

———, "The Trent Affair, 1861–1862," *Proceedings of the Massachusetts Historical Society,* Vol. XLV, October, 1911–June, 1912, Boston, 1912.

ADAMS, EPHRAIM DOUGLASS, Great Britain and the American Civil War, two vols., Gloucester, Massachusetts, 1957.

ADAMS, HENRY, The Education of Henry Adams, Boston, 1918.

———, "Great Secession Winter of 1860–1861," *Proceedings of the Massachusetts Historical Society,* Vol. XLIII, Boston, 1910.

ADAMS, JOHN, and JOHN QUINCY, Selected Writings of John and John Quincy Adams, edited by Adrienne Koch and William Peden, New York, 1946.

Adams Letters, A Cycle of, 1861–1865, edited by Worthington Chauncey Ford, two vols., Boston, 1920.

Ages of U.S. Voluntary Soldiers, U. S. Sanitary Commission Statistical Bureau, New York, 1866.

ALEXANDER, E. P., "The Great Charge and Artillery Fighting at Gettysburg," Battles and Leaders.

———, "Lee at Appomattox, Personal Recollection of the Break-up of the Confederacy," *Century Mazazine,* Vol. LXIII, No. 6, April, 1902.

———, "Letter on Gettysburg," *Southern Historical Society Papers,* Vol. IV, July to December, 1877.

———, "Longstreet at Knoxville," Battles and Leaders.

———, Military Memoirs of a Confederate, New York, 1907.

ALLAN, WILLIAM, The Army of Northern Virginia in 1862, Boston, 1892.

———, "First Maryland Campaign," *Southern Historical Society Papers,* Vol. XIV, January to December, 1886.

———, "General Lee's Strength and Losses at Gettysburg," *Southern Historical Society Papers,* Vol. IV, July to December, 1877.

———, History of the Campaigns of T. J. (Stonewall) Jackson in the Shenandoah Valley of Virginia, Philadelphia, 1890 and 1912.

——, "Letter on Gettysburg," *Southern Historical Society Papers,* Vol. IV, July to December, 1877.

——, "A Reply to General Longstreet," Battles and Leaders.

——, "Stonewall Jackson's Valley Campaign," The Annals of the War, Philadelphia, 1879.

——, "Strategy of the Campaign of Sharpsburg or Antietam," Vol. III, The Military Historical Society of Massachusetts Papers, Boston, 1895.

Alleged Assault on Sumner (Senator), Report No. 182, House of Representatives, 34th Congress, 1st Session, Washington, 1862.

ALLEN, CHARLES J., "Some Accounts and Recollections of the Operations Against the City of Mobile and its Defenses, 1864," Glimpses of the Nation's Struggle, Vol. I, Minnesota Commandery of the Military Order of the Loyal Legion of the United States, St. Paul, Minnesota, 1887.

ALMY, JOHN J., "Incidents of the Blockade," War Paper No. 9, District of Columbia Commandery of the Military Order of the Loyal Legion of the United States, Washington, 1892.

AMBROSE, D. LEIB, History of the Seventh Regiment Illinois Volunteer Infantry, Springfield, Illinois, 1866.

AMBROSE, STEPHEN LEE, Halleck, Lincoln's Chief of Staff, Baton Rouge, 1962.

American Annual Cyclopaedia and Register of Important Events of the Years 1861–1865, New York, 1866, five vols. (known as Appleton's Cyclopaedia).

American Military History 1807–1953, Department of the Army ROTC Manual, ROTCM145–20, Department of the Army, July, 1956.

AMES, ADELBERT, "The Capture of Fort Fisher," Military Historical Society of Massachusetts, Papers, Vol. IX, Boston, 1912.

AMES, H. V., State Documents on Federal Relations, Philadelphia, 1908.

AMES, JOHN W., "In Front of the Stone Wall at Fredericksburg," Battles and Leaders.

AMMEN, DANIEL, The Atlantic Coast, The Navy in the Civil War, Vol. II, New York, 1863–65.

——, "Du Pont and the Port Royal Expedition," Battles and Leaders.

ANDERSON, ARCHER, "Address on the Campaign and Battle of Chickamauga," *Southern Historical Society Papers,* Vol. IX, No. 9, September, 1881.

ANDERSON, BERN, By Sea and By River, The Naval History of the Civil War, New York, 1962.

ANDERSON, CARTER E., "Train Running for the Confederacy," *Locomotive Engineering,* August and October, 1892, courtesy of J. Ambler Johnston, Richmond, Virginia.

ANDERSON, GALUSHA, A Border City in the Civil War, Boston, 1908.

ANDERSON, LATHAM, "Canby's Service in the New Mexican Campaign," Battles and Leaders.

ANDERSON, OSBORNE P., A Voice from Harper's Ferry, Boston, 1861.

ANDERSON, ROBERT, An Artillery Officer in the Mexican War 1846–1847, Letters of Robert Anderson, Captain Third Artillery, U.S., New York, 1911.

——, Fort Sumter Memorial, New York, 1915.

ANDERSON, THOMAS MCARTHUR, The Political Conspiracies Preceding the Rebellion or the True Stories of Sumter and Pickens, New York, 1882.

ANDREANO, RALPH LOUIS, "A Theory of Confederate Finance," Civil War History, Vol. II, No. 4, December, 1956.

ANDREAS, ALFRED T., "The 'Ifs and Buts' of Shiloh," Military Essays and Recollections, Illinois Commandery of the Military Order of the Loyal Legion of the United States, Vol. IV, Chicago, 1891.

ANDREWS, C. G., History of the Campaign of Mobile, including the Cooperative Operations of General Wilson's Cavalry in Alabama, New York, 1867.

ANDREWS, ELIZA FRANCES, The War-time Journal of a Georgia Girl, 1864–1865, New York, 1908.

ANDREWS, J. CUTLER, The North Reports the Civil War, Pittsburgh, Pennsylvania, 1959.

ANGLE, PAUL M. Here I Have Lived, A History of Lincoln's Springfield, 1821–1865, New Brunswick, 1935.

———, Lincoln in the Year 1858, Springfield, 1926.

ANGLE, PAUL M., and MIERS, EARL SCHENCK, Tragic Years 1860–1865, two vols., New York, 1960.

Annals of the War written by Leading Participants North and South, Philadelphia, 1879.

ANSPACH, FREDERICK, The Sons of the Sires, A History of the Rise, Progress, and Destiny of the American Party, and Its Probable Influence on the Next Presidential Election, Philadelphia, 1855.

"Appomattox Court House, Reminiscences of Lee and Gordon at, by a Private," *Southern Historical Society Papers,* Vol. III, No. 1, January, 1880.

ARMISTEAD, DRURY L., "The Battle in which General Johnston was Wounded," *Southern Historical Society Papers,* Vol. XVIII, 1890.

Army of the Potomac, Report of the Joint Committee on the Conduct of the War, Part I, Washington, 1863.

Army of the Potomac under General Grant, map prepared by Richmond and Virginia Prison Civil War Round Tables.

ARNOLD, ISAAC M., The Life of Abraham Lincoln, Chicago, 1885.

———, Reconstruction: Liberty the Cornerstone and Lincoln the Architect, n.p., n.d.

As They Saw Forrest, Some Recollections and Comments of Contemporaries, edited by Robert Selph Henry, Jackson, Tennessee, 1956.

ATKINSON, J. H., "Forty Days of Disaster," *Arkansas Democrat Magazine,* December 28, 1958.

———, "The Unusual Battle at Poison Spring," *Arkansas Democrat Magazine,* June 29, 1958.

Atlas of the Battlefield of Antietam, Prepared Under the Direction of the Antietam Battlefield Board, Washington, 1904.

Atlas to Accompany the Official Records of the Union and Confederate Armies, three vols., Washington, 1891–95.

AUCHAMPAUGH, PHILIP GERALD, James Buchanan and His Cabinet on the Eve of Secession, Lancaster, Pennsylvania, 1926.

AYER, I. WINSLOW, The Great Treason Plot in the North During the War, Most Dangerous, Perfidious, Extensive and Startling Plot Ever Devised: Imminent Hidden Perils of Republic, Astounding Developments Never Before Published, Chicago, 1896.

AYER, JAMES T., The Diary of, edited by John Hope Franklin, Springfield, Illinois, 1947.

BACHE, RICHARD MEADE, Life of General George Meade, Philadelphia, 1897.

BACON, GEORGE S., "One Night's Work, April 20, 1862," *Magazine of American History*, March, 1886.

BADEAU, ADAM, Military History of Ulysses S. Grant, three vols., New York, 1868.

BAILEY, JAMES MONTGOMERY, Civil War Letters from Danbury, Connecticut, *Times* (signed H. P. Manton), Franklin J. Meine Collection, n.d.

BAKER, MARION A., "Farragut's Demands for the Surrender of New Orleans," Battles and Leaders.

BALLARD, COLIN R., The Military Genius of Abraham Lincoln, Cleveland, 1952.

BALTZ, JOHN D., Hon. Edward D. Baker, Lancaster, Pennsylvania, 1888.

BANCROFT, FREDERIC, Calhoun and the South Carolina Nullification Movement, Baltimore, 1928.

———, The Life of William H. Seward, New York, 1900.

BARBEE, DAVID RANKIN, "The Capture of Jefferson Davis," *Tyler's Quarterly Review and Genealogical Magazine*, July, 1947.

BARBEE, DAVID R., and MILLEDGE, L. BONHAM, JR., "Fort Sumter Again," *Mississippi Valley Historical Review*, XXVIII, 1941.

BARINGER, WILLIAM E., Campaign Technique in Illinois—1860, Springfield, 1932.

———, A House Dividing; Lincoln as President Elect, Springfield, 1945.

———, Lincoln's Rise to Power, Boston, 1937.

BARKER, WALTER B., "Two Anecdotes of General Lee," *Southern Historical Society Papers*, Vol, XII, Nos. 7, 8, and 9, August–September, 1884.

BARNARD, J. G., The C.S.A. and the Battle of Bull Run, A Letter to an English Friend, New York, 1862.

———, The Peninsular Campaign and its Antecedents, as Developed by the Report of Major General George B. McClellan and Other Published Documents, New York, 1864.

———, A Report on the Defenses of Washington to the Chief of Engineers, U. S. Army, Professional Papers of the Corps of Engineers, U. S. Army, No. 20, Washington, 1871.

BARNES, FRANK, Fort Sumter National Monument, South Carolina, National Park Service Historical Handbook Series No. 12, Washington, D.C., 1952, reprint 1961.

BARNES, THURLOW WEED, Memoir of Thurlow Weed, two vols., Boston, 1884.

BARRETT, EDWIN S., What I Saw at Bull Run, Boston, 1886.

BARRETT, JOHN G., The Civil War in North Carolina, Chapel Hill, 1963.

———, Sherman's March Through the Carolinas, Chapel Hill, 1956.

BARTLETT, JOHN, "The 'Brooklyn' at the Passage of the Forts," Battles and Leaders.

BASLER, ROY, Abraham Lincoln, His Speeches and Writings, Cleveland, 1946.

BASLER, ROY, editor, The Collected Works of Abraham Lincoln, eight vols., New Brunswick, New Jersey, 1963.

BASSETT, JOHN SPENCER, Anti-Slavery Leaders of North Carolina, Baltimore, 1898.

BATES, DAVID HOMER, Lincoln in the Telegraph Office, New York, 1907.

Bibliography

BATES, EDWARD, The Diary of Edward Bates, Washington 1859–1866, edited by Howard K. Beale, Washington, 1933.

BATES, SAMUEL P., The Battle of Chancellorsville, Meadville, Pennsylvania, 1892.

———, "Hooker's Comments on Chancellorsville," Battles and Leaders.

BATTINE, CECIL, The Crisis of the Confederacy, A History of Gettysburg and the Wilderness, London, 1908.

"Battle of Petersburg," Report of the Joint Committee on the Conduct of the War, Vol. I, Washington, D.C., 1865.

"Battle of Winchester," Report of the Joint Committee on the Conduct of the War, Part III, Washington, 1863.

Battles and Leaders of the Civil War, Robert Underwood Johnson, and Clarence Clough Buel, editors, four vols., New York, 1887 (cited as Battles and Leaders).

BEACH, WILLIAM H., The First New York (Lincoln) Cavalry, New York, 1902.

BEALE, H. K., What Historians Have Said About the Causes of the Civil War, Theory and Practice in Historical Study, New York, 1946.

BEAMAN, CHARLES C., JR., The National and Private "Alabama Claims" and their "Final and Amicable Settlement," Washington, 1871.

BEARD, CHARLES A. and MARY B., The Rise of American Civilization, New York, 1947.

BEARSS, EDWIN C., "Battle of Chickasaw Bayou," Vicksburg Sunday Post, November, 13, 1960, and January 29, 1961.

———, "Cavalry Operations in the Battle of Stone River," Tennessee Historical Quarterly, Vol. XIX, Nos. 1 and 2, March and June, 1960.

———, "Civil War Operations in and Around Pensacola," Florida Historical Quarterly Pamphlet.

———, Decision in Mississippi, Jackson, Mississippi, 1962.

———, "Destruction of the Cairo," Vicksburg Sunday Post, September 18 and 25, 1960.

———, "Federal Attempts to Cut Supply Lines," series of ten articles in Vicksburg Sunday Post, February–April, 1961.

———, "First Day at Pea Ridge, March 9, 1862," Arkansas Historical Quarterly, Vol. XVII, No. 2, Summer, 1958.

———, "Jackson Campaign," Jackson, Mississippi, State Times, July 31 and August 7, 1960.

———, Maps of Pea Ridge and Vicksburg.

———, "Unconditional Surrender, The Fall of Fort Donelson," Tennessee Historical Quarterly, March and June, 1962.

BEATTY, JOHN, Memoirs of a Volunteer, 1861–1865, New York, 1946.

BEAUREGARD, P. G. T., "Battle of Bull Run, Battles and Leaders.

———, "Campaign of Shiloh," Battles and Leaders.

———, Commentary on the Campaign and Battle of Manassas of July, 1861. Together with a Summary of the Art of War, New York, 1891.

———, "Defense of Charleston," Battles and Leaders.

———, "Defense of Drewry's Bluff," Battles and Leaders.

———, "Four Days of Battle at Petersburg," Battles and Leaders.

———, "Letter of General P. G. T. Beauregard to General G. M. Wilcox, The Wilderness Campaign, May–June, 1864," Vol. IV, Military Historical Society of Massachusetts Papers, Boston, 1906.

———, "Narrative by General Beauregard," *Southern Historical Society Papers,* Vol. V, No. 4, April, 1878.

———, "Torpedo Service in Charleston Harbor," *Annals of the War* and *Southern Historical Society Papers,* Vol. V, Nos. 1 and 2, January and February, 1878.

———, "Torpedo Service in the Harbor and Water Defenses of Charleston," *Southern Historical Society Papers,* Vol. V, No. 4, April, 1878.

BEDFORD, H. L., "Fight Between the Batteries and Gunboats at Fort Donelson," *Southern Historical Society Papers,* Vol. XIII, January–December, 1885.

BEE, E. P., "Battle of Pleasant Hill, An Error Corrected," *Southern Historical Society Papers,* Vol. VIII, No. 4, April 1, 1880.

BEEBE, GILBERT J., A Review and Refutation of Helper's "Impending Crisis," Middleton, New York, 1860.

BEECHAM, R. K., Gettysburg, The Pivotal Battle of the Civil War, Chicago, 1911.

BEECHER, HENRY WARD, Oration at the Raising of "The Old Flag" at Fort Sumter, Manchester, 1865.

BELKNAP, GEORGE E., "The 'New Ironsides' off Charleston," *The United Service,* Vol. I, No. 1, January, 1879.

———, "Recollections of a Bummer," E. R. Hutchins, The War of the Sixties.

———, "Reminiscence of the Siege of Charleston," Naval Actions and History, 1799, 1898, Vol. XII, Military Historical Society of Massachusetts Papers, Boston, 1902.

BELL, HERBERT G. H., Lord Palmerston, two vols., London, 1936.

BENEDICT, C. G., Vermont in the Civil War, Vols. I and II, Burlington, 1888.

BENJAMIN, CHARLES F., "Hooker's Appointment and Removal," Battles and Leaders.

BENJAMIN, L. N., The St. Albans Raid, Montreal, 1865.

BENNETT, A. J., The Story of the First Massachusetts Light Battery, Attached to the Sixth Army Corps, Boston, 1886.

BENNETT, FRANK M., The Steam Navy of the United States, two vols., Pittsburgh, 1897.

BENNETT, LYMAN G., and WILLIAM M. HAIGH, History of the Thirty-sixth Regiment, Illinois Volunteers, Aurora, Illinois, 1876.

BENTON, THOMAS HART, Historical and Legal Examination of that part of the Decision of the Supreme Court of the United States in the Dred Scott Case, which declared the Unconstitutionality of the Missouri Compromise Act, and the Self-extension of the Constitution to Territories, Carrying Slavery Along with it, New York, 1857.

BERGER, JOHN, "The Private History of a Campaign that Failed," *Civil War History,* March, 1955.

BERNARDO, C. JOSEPH, and EUGENE H. BACON, American Military Policy, Its Development since 1775, Harrisburg, 1955.

BERNARD, GEORGE S., War Talks of Confederate Veterans, Petersburg, Virginia, 1892.

BERNARD, MONTAGUE, A historical Account of the Neutrality of Great Britain During the American Civil War, London, 1870.

BESSE, S. B., C.S. Ironclad Virginia with Data and References for a Scale Model, Newport News, Virginia, 1937.

———, U.S. Ironclad Monitor with Data and References for a Scale Model, Newport News, Virginia, 1936.

BETTS, S. R., Opinion of the Hon. Samuel R. Betts in the Cases of the Hiawatha and other vessels captured as prizes, two vols., New York, 1861.

BEVERIDGE, ALBERT J., Abraham Lincoln 1809–1858, two vols., Boston, 1928.

BEVIER, R. S., History of the First and Second Missouri Brigades, 1861–1865, St. Louis, 1879.

BICKMAN, WILLIAM D., "W.D.B.," Rosecrans' Campaign with the Fourteenth Army Corps or the Army of the Cumberland, a Narrative of Personal Observations with an appendix consisting of Official Reports of the Battle of Stone River, Cincinnati, 1863.

BIDDLE, JAMES C., "General Meade at Gettysburg," Annals of the War.

BIERCE, AMBROSE, Ambrose Bierce's Civil War, Chicago, 1956.

BIGELOW, JOHN, France and the Confederate Navy 1862–1868, New York, 1868.

———, Retrospection of an Active Life, two vols., New York, 1909.

———, The Peach Orchard, Gettysburg, July 2, 1863, Minneapolis, 1919.

BIGELOW, JOHN, JR., The Campaign of Chancellorsville, A Strategical and Tactical Study, Yale University Press, 1910.

BILL, ALFRED HOYT, The Beleaguered City, New York, 1946.

BILLINGS, JOHN D., The History of the Tenth Massachusetts Battery of Light Artillery in the War of the Rebellion, 1862–1865, Boston.

BISHOP, J. LEANDER, A History of American Manufactures from 1608 to 1860, three vols., Philadelphia, 1868.

BISHOP, JIM, The Day Lincoln Was Shot, New York, 1956.

BISSELL, J. W., "Sawing out the Channel above Island Number Ten," Battles and Leaders.

BLACK, ROBERT C., III, The Railroads of the Confederacy, Chapel Hill, 1952.

BLACKFORD, CHARLES M., "The Campaign and Battle of Lynchburg," *Southern Historical Society Papers*, Vol. XXX, 1902.

BLACKFORD, SUSAN LEIGH, Letters from Lee's Army, New York, 1947.

BLACKFORD, W. W., War Years with Jeb Stuart, New York, 1945.

BLACKWELL, SARAH ELLEN, A Military Genius, Life of Anna Ella Carroll of Maryland, Vol. I, Washington, 1891.

BLAINE, JAMES G., Twenty Years of Congress, two vols., Norwich, Connecticut, 1886.

BLAIR, CARVEL HALL, "Submarines of the Confederate Navy," United States Naval Institute Proceedings, October, 1952.

BLAIR, MONTGOMERY, "Opening of the Mississippi," *The United Service*, January, 1881.

BLAKE, HENRY N., Three Years in the Army of the Potomac, Boston, 1865.

"Blockade Runners of the Confederacy," no author, *Century Magazine*, Vol. XIX, June, 1869.

BLODGETT, EDWARD E., "The Army of the Southwest and the Battle of Pea Ridge," Military Essays and Recollections, Illinois Commandery of the Military Order of the Loyal Legion of the United States, Vol. II, Chicago, 1894.

BLOODGOOD, J. D., Personal Reminiscences of the War, New York, 1893.

BLOSS, JOHN M., "Antietam and the Lost Dispatch," War Talks in Kansas,

Kansas Commandery of the Military Order of the Loyal Legion of the United States, Vol. I, Kansas City, 1906.

BOATNER, MARK MAYO, III, The Civil War Dictionary, New York, 1959.

BOLLES, CHARLES E., "General Grant and the News of Mr. Lincoln's Death," *Century Magazine,* Vol. XL, No. 2, June, 1890.

BONHAM, MILLEDGE L., "The British Consuls in the Confederacy," Studies in History, Economics and Public Law, Vol. XLIII, No. 3, New York, 1911.

BOOTH, EDWIN, "Edwin Booth and Lincoln," *Century Magazine,* Vol. LXXVII, No. 6, April, 1909.

Boston Slave Riot, and Trial of Anthony Burns, no author, Boston, 1854.

BOTTS, JOHN MINOR, The Great Rebellion; Its Secret History, Rise, Progress and Disastrous Failure, New York, 1886.

BOUCHER, C. S., The Nullification Controversy in South Carolina, Chicago, 1916.

BOWDITCH, WILLIAM I., The Rendition of Anthony Burns, Boston, 1854.

BOWEN, JAMES L., "Edwards' Brigade at the Bloody Angle," Battles and Leaders.

———, History of the Thirty-Seventh Regiment Massachusetts Volunteers, in the Civil War of 1861–1865, Holyoke, Massachusetts, and New York City, 1884.

BOWMAN, S. M., and R. B. IRWIN, Sherman and his Campaigns, New York, 1865.

BOYKIN, EDWARD, Ghost Ship of the Confederacy, New York, 1957.

BOYKIN, EDWARD M., The Falling Flag, Evacuation of Richmond, Retreat and Surrender at Appomattox, New York, 1874.

BOYNTON, CHARLES B., The History of the Navy During the Rebellion, 2 vols., New York, 1867.

BOYNTON, H. V., "The Battles about Chattanooga, Lookout Mountain and Missionary Ridge," Vol. VII, The Military Historical Society of Massachusetts Papers, Boston, 1906.

———, "The Chickamauga Campaign," Vol. VII, Military Historical Society of Massachusetts Papers, Boston, 1908.

———, Compiler, Dedication of the Chickamauga and Chattanooga National Military Park, September 18–20, 1895, Washington, 1896.

———, Sherman's Historical Raid, The Memoirs in the Light of the Records, Cincinnati, 1875.

BRADLEE, FRANCIS B. C., Blockade Running During the Civil War and the Effect of Land and Water Transportation on the Confederacy, Salem, Massachusetts, 1925.

BRADLEY, CHESTER D., "President Lincoln's Campaign Against the *Merrimac,*" *Journal of the Illinois State Historical Society,* Spring, 1958.

BRADLOW, EDNA and FRANK, Here Comes the Alabama, Cape Town and Amsterdam, 1958.

BRAGG, BRAXTON, "General Bragg's Comments on Missionary Ridge," Battles and Leaders.

———, "Letter to his Brother," *Southern Historical Society Papers,* Vol. X, 1882.

BRAINERD, WESLEY, "The Pontoniers at Fredericksburg," Battles and Leaders.

BRECKINRIDGE, W. C. P., "The Opening of the Atlanta Campaign," Battles and Leaders.

BREIHAN, CARL W., The Complete and Authentic Life of Jesse James, New York, 1953.

BRIDGES, HAL, "A Lee Letter on the Lost Dispatch and the Maryland Campaign of 1862," *Virginia Magazine of History,* April, 1958.

———, Lee's Maverick General: David Harvey Hill, New York, 1961.

Brief History of Fort Macon, State of North Carolina Department of Conservation and Development, Division of State Parks.

British and Foreign State Papers, 1860–1861, Vol. LI, also 1861–1862, Vol. LII, Compiled by the Librarian and Keeper of the Papers, Foreign Office, London, 1868.

BRITTON, WILEY, The Civil War on the Border, two vols., New York, 1904.

———, Résumé of Military Operations in Missouri and Arkansas, 1864–1865, Battles and Leaders.

———, "Union and Confederate Indians in the Civil War," Battles and Leaders.

BROOKE, JOHN M., The Virginia or Merrimac; Her Real Projector, William Ellis Jones, Richmond, 1891.

BROOKS, NOAH, Castine Letters, Sacramento Union, 1862–1863, Bancroft Library, University of California.

———, "Two War-Time Conventions," *Century Magazine,* April, 1895, XXVII.

———, Washington in Lincoln's Time, edited by Herbert Mitgang, New York, 1956.

BROOKS, R. P., "Conscription in the Confederate States of America," 1862–1865, *Bulletin of the University of Georgia,* Vol. XVII, No. 4, March, 1917.

BROTHERHEAD, W., General Frémont and the Injustice done him by Politicians and Envious Military Men, Philadelphia, 1862.

BROWN, D. ALEXANDER, Grierson's Raid, Urbana, 1954.

BROWN, E. R., The Twenty-Seventh Indiana Volunteer Infantry in the War of the Rebellion, 1861 to 1865, by a Member of Company C., Monticello, Indiana, 1899.

BROWN, GEORGE WILLIAM, Baltimore and the Nineteenth of April, 1861, Baltimore, 1887.

BROWN, ISAAC N., "The Confederate Gun-Boat Arkansas," Battles and Leaders.

BROWN, JUNIUS H., Four Years in Secessia, Hartford, 1865.

BROWN, WALTER LEE, "Pea Ridge; Gettysburg of the West," *The Arkansas Historical Quarterly* Vol. XV, No. 1, Spring, 1956.

BROWNE, FRANCIS FISHER, The Every-Day Life of Abraham Lincoln, Chicago, 1913.

BROWNE, JOHN M., "The Duel Between the 'Alabama' and the 'Kearsarge,'" Battles and Leaders.

BROWNING, ORVILLE H., The Diary of, Edited by Theodore Calvin Pearse and James G. Randall, Springfield, 1927.

BROWNLEE, RICHARD S., Grey Ghosts of the Confederacy, Guerilla Warfare in the West, 1861–1865, Baton Rouge, 1958.

BROWNLOW, W. G., Sketches of the Rise, Progress and Decline of Secession, Philadelphia, 1862.

BRUCE, GEORGE A., "The Donelson Campaign, Campaigns in Kentucky and Tennessee 1862–1864," Military Historical Society of Massachusetts Papers, Vol. VII, Boston, 1908.

————, "General Buell's Campaign Against Chattanooga, The Mississippi Valley; Tennessee, Georgia, Alabama, 1861–1864," Military Historical Society of Massachusetts Papers, Vol. VIII, Boston, 1910.

————, "General Butler's Bermuda Campaign," Vol. IX, Military Historical Society of Massachusetts Papers, Boston, 1912.

————, "Petersburg, June 15– Fort Harrison, September 29; A Comparison," Vol. XIV, Military Historical Society of Massachusetts Papers, Boston, 1912.

————, The Twentieth Regiment of Massachusetts Vounteer Infantry, 1861–1865, Boston, 1906.

BRUCE, H. W., "Some Reminiscences of the Second of April, 1865," *Southern Historical Society Papers,* Vol. IX, No. 5, May, 1881.

BRUCE, ROBERT V., Lincoln and the Tools of War, Indianapolis, 1956.

BRYANT, EDWIN E., History of the Third Regiment of Wisconsin Veteran Volunteer Infantry, 1861–1865, Madison, Wisconsin, 1891.

BUCHANAN, JAMES, The Administration on the Eve of the Rebellion, London, 1865.

BUCK, IRVING A., Cleburne and his Command, and Thomas Robson Hay, Pat Cleburne, Stonewall Jackson of the West, Jackson, Tennessee, 1959.

————, "Cleburne and his Division at Missionary Ridge and Ringgold," *Southern Historical Society Papers,* Vol. XI, No. 11, November, 1883.

BUCKINGHAM, J. S., The Slave States of America, London, about 1842.

BUELL, AUGUSTUS, The Cannoneer, Recollections of Service in the Army of the Potomac, Washington, 1890.

BUELL, DON CARLOS, "East Tennessee and the Campaign of Perryville," Battles and Leaders.

————, "Operations in North Alabama," Battles and Leaders.

BULLOCH, JAMES D., The Secret Service of the Confederate States in Europe or How the Confederate Cruisers were Equipped, two vols., London, 1883.

"Bull Run-Ball's Bluff," Report of the Joint Committee on the Conduct of the War, Part II, Washington, 1863.

BURCH, JOHN F., Charles W. Quantrell, as told by Captain Harrison Trow, Vega, Texas, 1923.

BURGESS, JOHN W., The Middle Period, 1817–1858, New York, 1905.

BURNS, W. S., "A. J. Smith's Defeat of Forrest at Tupelo," Battles and Leaders.

BURNSIDE, A. E., "The Burnside Expedition," Battles and Leaders.

"Burnside Expedition," Report of the Joint Committee on the Conduct of the War, Part III, Washington, 1863.

BURRAGE, HENRY S., "Burnside's East Tennessee Campaign," Vol. VIII, Military Historical Society of Massachusetts Papers, Boston, 1910.

BUSHNELL, HORACE, Reverses Needed. A Discourse Delivered on the Sunday After the Disaster of Bull Run, in the North Church, Hartford, 1861.

BUSHNELL, REV. SAMUEL, The Story of the Monitor and the Merrimac, n.p., n.d.

BUSHONG, MILLARD E., Old Jube, Boyce, Virginia, 1955.

BUTLER, BENJAMIN, Butler's Book, Boston, 1892.

BUTLER, BENJAMIN F., Private and Official Correspondence of Gen. Benjamin F. Butler During the Period of the Civil War, five vols., Norwood, Massachusetts, 1917.

BUTLER, M. C., "The Cavalry Fight at Trevilian Station," Battles and Leaders.

BUTTS, FRANCIS B., "The Loss of the 'Monitor,'" Battles and Leaders.

BYERS, S. H. M., "Sherman's Attack at the Tunnel," Battles and Leaders.

———, What I Saw in Dixie or Six Months in Rebel Prisons, Danville, New York, 1868.

BYRNE, FRANK L., "Libby Prison, A Study in Emotions," *Journal of Southern History*, Vol. XXIV, No. 4, November, 1958.

CABELL, SEARS WILSON, The Bulldog, Longstreet at Gettysburg and Chickamauga, Atlanta, 1938.

CABLE, GEORGE, "New Orleans Before the Capture," Battles and Leaders.

CADWALLADER, SYLVANUS, Three Years with Grant, edited by Benjamin P. Thomas, New York, 1955.

Calendar of the Ryder Collection of Confederate Archives at Tufts College, Historical Records Survey, Division of Professional and Service Projects, Work's Progress Administration, Boston, Massachusetts, 1940.

CALHOUN, JOHN C., Works of John C. Calhoun, six vols., Edited by Richard K. Cralle, New York, 1883.

CALLAHAN, JAMES MORTON, The Diplomatic History of the Southern Confederacy, Springfield, Massachusetts, 1957.

CALLENDER, ELIOT, "What a Boy Saw on the Mississippi," Military Essays and Recollections, Vol. I, Illinois Commandery of the Military Order of the Loyal Legion of the United States, Chicago, 1891.

CAMERON, WILLIAM E., "The Career of General A. P. Hill," Annals of the War.

Campaigns in Kentucky and Tennessee, 1862–1864, The Military Historical Society of Massachusetts Papers, Vol. VII, Boston, 1908.

Campaigns in Virginia, 1861–1862, The Military Historical Society of Massachusetts Papers, Vol. I, Boston, 1896.

Campaigns in Virginia, Maryland and Pennsylvania, 1862–1863, The Military Historical Society of Massachusetts Papers, Vol. III, Boston, 1895.

CAMPBELL, JAMES E., "Sumner-Brooks-Burlingame—or—the Last of the Great Challenges," Ohio Archaeological and Historical Publications, Vol. XXXIV, Columbus, 1926.

CAMPBELL, JOHN, The Administration and the Confederate States—Letters and correspondence between the Hon. John A. Campbell and Hon. William H. Seward, all of which was laid before the Provisional Congress on Saturday by President Davis, Richmond, 1861.

———, "Papers of the Hon. John A. Campbell—1861–1865," *Southern Historical Society Papers*, October, 1917.

———, "A view of the Confederacy from the Inside," *Century Magazine*, Vol. XXXVII, No. 6, October, 1889.

CAMPBELL, MARY R., Tennessee and the Union, 1847–1861, Reprinted from the East Tennessee Historical Society's Publication, No. 10, 1938.

CAPERS, GERALD M., JR., The Biography of a River Town, Memphis, Its Heroic Age, Chapel Hill, 1939.

CAPRON, THADDEUS B., "War Diary," *Journal of the Illinois State Historical Society*, Vol. XII, No. 3, October, 1919.

"Capture of Fort Pillow, Vindication of General Chalmers by a Federal Officer," *Southern Historical Society Papers*, Vol. VII, No. 9, September, 1879.

CARMAN, E. A., "General Hardee's Escape from Savannah," District of Columbia, Commandery of the Military Order of the Loyal Legion of the United States, War Paper No. 13, Washington, 1898.

CARMAN, HARRY J., and Reinhard Luthin, Lincoln and the Patronage, New York, 1963.

CARNATHAN, W. J., "The Proposal to Reopen the African Slave Trade in the South, 1854–1860," *South Atlantic Quarterly,* October, 1926.

CARNES, W. W., "Chickamauga," *Southern Historical Society Papers,* Vol. XIV, January–December, 1886.

CARPENTER, F. B., Six Months in the White House, Watkins Glen, New York, 1961.

CARR, JOSEPH B., "Operations of 1861 About Fort Monroe," Battles and Leaders.

CARROL, J. F., "The Burning of Columbus, North Carolina—Report of the Committee of Citizens Appointed to Collect Testimony," *Southern Historical Society Papers,* Vol. VIII, No. 8, 1880.

CARROLL, ANNA ELLA, The Great American Battle; or, The Contest Between Christianity and Political Romanism, New York, 1856.

———, The Star of the West; or, National Men and National Measures, James French and Company, Boston, 1857.

CARROLL, JOSEPH CEPHAS, Slave Insurrections in the United States, 1860–1863, Boston, 1938.

CARSE, ROBERT, Department of the South, Hilton Head Island in the Civil War, Columbia, South Carolina, 1961.

CARSON, JAMES PETIGRU, Life, Letters and Speeches of James Louis Petigru, The Union Man of South Carolina, Washington, 1920.

CARY, CLARENCE FAIRFAX, The War Journal of Midshipman Cary, edited by Brooks Thompson and Frank Lawrence Owsley, Jr., *Civil War History,* Vol. IX, No. 2, June, 1963.

CASKEY, WILLIE MAVIS, Secession and Restoration of Louisiana, University, Louisiana, 1938.

CASLER, JOHN O., Four Years in the Stonewall Brigade, Guthrie, Oklahoma, 1893, also Marietta, Georgia, 1950.

CASSELMAN, A. B., "Did the Confederate Army Number 1,650,000?", *Current History,* Vol. XVIII, No. 5, 1923.

———, "How Large was the Confederate Army?", *Current History,* Vol. XVII, No. 4. January, 1923.

CASTEL, ALBERT, "The Fort Pillow Massacre: A Fresh Examination of the Evidence," *Civil War History,* Vol. IV, No. 1, March, 1958.

CASTINE (Noah Brooks), Letters of, Sacramento *Daily Union,* n.d.

CATTON, BRUCE, Glory Road, Garden City, New York, 1952.

———, Grant Moves South, Boston, 1960.

———, Mr. Lincoln's Army, Garden City, New York, 1951.

———, "Sheridan at Five Forks," *The Journal of Southern History,* Vol. XXX, No. 3, August, 1955.

———, A Stillness at Appomattox, Garden City, New York, 1953.

———, This Hallowed Ground, Garden City, New York, 1950.

"Causes of the Defeat of General Lee's Army at the Battle of Gettysburg," *Southern Historical Society Papers,* Vol. IV, No. 2, August, 1877.

Census Reports, United States, various.

CHADWICK, FRENCH ENSOR, Causes of the Civil War, 1859–1861, New York, 1906.

CHALMERS, JAMES R., "Forrest and his Campaign," *Southern Historical Society Papers,* Vol. VII, No. 9, September, 1879.

CHAMBERLAIN, JOSHUA L., Military Operations on the White Oak Road, Virginia, March 31, 1865, Portland, Maine, 1897.

———, The Passing of the Armies, New York, 1918.

CHAMBERLAIN, W. N., "Hood's Second Sortie at Atlanta," Battles and Leaders.

CHAMBERS, LENOIR, Stonewall Jackson, two vols., New York, 1959.

Chancellorsville Source Book, Fort Leavenworth, Kansas, 1937.

CHANDLER, ALBERT, "Military Telegraph Under Lincoln," *Sunday Magazine,* June 17, 1906.

CHANNING, EDWARD, A History of the United States, Vol. VI, New York, 1925.

———, The United States of America, New York, 1897.

"Charleston, Operations Against," Report of the Joint Committee on the Conduct of the War, Vol. III, Washington, 1865.

"Charleston Under Arms," *The Atlantic Monthly,* April, 1861.

CHASE, SALMON P., Diary and Correspondence of, Annual Report of the American Historical Association for the Year 1902, Vol. XX, Washington, 1903.

———, Inside Lincoln's Cabinet; The Civil War Diaries of Salmon P. Chase, edited by David Donald, New York, 1954.

CHEATHAM, B. F., "General Cheatham at Spring Hill," Battles and Leaders.

Cheat Mountain; or, Unwritten Chapter of the Late War, By a Member of the Bar, Fayetteville, Tennessee, Nashville, 1885.

CHENEY, NEWEL, History of the Ninth Regiment New York Volunteers Cavalry, War of 1861–1865, Jamestown, New York, 1901.

CHESNUT, MARY B., A Diary from Dixie, New York, 1922, edited by Isabella B. Martin and Mary Lockett Avary, New York, 1929.

CHESTER, COLBY M., "Chasing the Blockaders," War Papers No. 94, District of Columbia Commandery of the Military Order of the Loyal Legion of the United States, Washington, 1913.

CHESTER, JAMES, "Inside Sumter in 1861," Battles and Leaders.

CHETLAIN, AUGUSTUS L., "The Battle of Corinth, October 3 and 4, 1862," Military Essays and Recollections, Vol. II, Illinois Commandery of the Military Order of the Loyal Legion of the United States, Chicago, 1891.

———, "Recollections of General U. S. Grant," Military Essays and Recollections, Vol. I, Illinois Commandery of the Military Order of the Loyal Legion of the United States, Chicago, 1891.

Chicago Copperhead Convention, The Treasonable and Revolutionary Utterances of the Men who composed it, n.d., n.p.

CHILDS, ARNEY ROBINSON, The Private Journal of Henry William Ravenal, Columbia, South Carolina, 1947.

CHISOLM, A. R., "Beauregard's and Hampton's Orders on evacuating Columbia," *Southern Historical Society Papers,* Vol. VII, No. 5, 1879.

———, "The Failure to Capture Hardee," Battles and Leaders.

———, "The Shiloh Battle Order and Withdrawal Sunday Evening," Battles and Leaders.

CHITTENDEN, L. E., Recollections of President Lincoln and his Administration, New York, 1891.

———, A Report of the Debates and Proceedings in the Secret Sessions of the Confederate Convention, for Proposing Amendments to the Constitution of the United States, held in Washington, D.C., in February A.D., 1861, New York 1864.

Chronicles of the Great Rebellion, Philadelphia, n.d.

CHURCH, WILLIAM CONANT, The Life of John Ericsson, two vols., London, 1890.

———, Ulysses S. Grant and the Period of National Preservation and Reconstruction, New York, 1926.

CIST, HENRY M., The Army of the Cumberland, Campaigns of the Civil War, New York, 1890.

Civil War History, various special issues.

Civil War Times Illustrated, various issues.

CLAIBORNE, JOHN HERBERT, "Last Days of Lee and his Paladins," War Talks of Confederate Veterans, Petersburg, Va., 1892.

CLARK, CHARLES, The Trent and San Jacinto; Being the Substance of a Paper on This Subject, Read Before the Juridical Society, on the 16th December, 1861, London, 1862.

CLARK, VICTOR S., History of Manufactures in the United States, two vols., New York, 1929.

CLARK, WALTER, Histories of the Several Regiments and Battalions from North Carolina in the Great War 1861–1865, Raleigh, 1901.

CLARKE, JAMES FREEMAN, A Discourse on Christian Politics, Boston, 1854.

Clarke's Confederate Household Almanac for the Year 1863, Vicksburg, Mississippi, 1863.

CLAY, HENRY, Speech of the Hon. Henry Clay of Kentucky, On Taking up his Compromises. Resolutions on the Subject of Slavery as reported by the *National Intelligencer,* New York, 1850.

CLEAVES, FREEMAN, Meade of Gettysburg, Norman, Oklahoma, 1860.

CLEMENS, WILL M., Mark Twain, Chicago, 1894.

CLEMENT, EDWARD HENRY, "The Bull Run Rout," in *Proceedings of the Massachusetts Historical Society,* March, 1909, Cambridge, 1909.

COBB, THOMAS R. R., The Correspondence of Thomas Reade Rootes Cobb, 1860–1862, Washington, 1907.

———, "Member of the Secession Convention of Georgia, of the Provisional Congress, and a Brigadier-General of the Confederate States Army, Extracts from Letters to his Wife, February 3, 1861–December 10, 1866," *Southern Historical Society Papers,* Vol. XXVIII, Richmond, 1900.

COCKE, PRESTON, The Battle of New Market, and the Cadets of the Virginia Military Institute, May 15, 1864, By A V.M.I. New Market Cadet, May 13, 1914. n.p.

COCKRELL, MONROE F., editor, The Last Account of the Battle of Corinth and Court-Martial of General Van Dorn, by an unknown author, Jackson, Tennessee, 1955.

CODDINGTON, D. S., The Crisis and the Man, n.p., n.d.

COFFIN, CHARLES CARLETON, "Antietam Scenes," Battles and Leaders.

———, The Boys of '61, Boston, 1881.

———, Drum-Beat of the Nation, New York, 1888.

———, Four Years of Fighting, Boston, 1866.

———, My Days and Nights on the Battlefield, Boston, 1887.

COGGINS, JACK, Arms and Equipment of the Civil War, New York, 1962.

COHEN, VICTOR H., "Charles Sumner and the *Trent* Affair," *The Journal of Southern History,* Vol. XXII, No. 2, May, 1956.

COHN, DAVIS L., The Life and Times of King Cotton, New York, 1956.

COIT, MARGARET L., John C. Calhoun, American Patriot, Boston, 1950.

COLBY, C. E., Civil War Weapons, New York, 1952.

COLE, ARTHUR CHARLES, The Irrepressible Conflict 1850–1865, New York, 1934.

COLEMAN, MRS. A. M. B., The Life of John J. Crittenden, two vols., Philadelphia, 1871.

COLGROVE, SILAS, "The Finding of Lee's Lost Order," Battles and Leaders.

COLLINS, JOHN L., "A Prisoner's March from Gettysburg to Staunton," Battles and Leaders.

———, "When Stonewall Jackson Turned our Right," Battles and Leaders.

COLSTON, R. E., "Lee's Knowledge of Hooker's Movements," Battles and Leaders.

———, "Watching the 'Merrimac,'" Battles and Leaders.

COLTON, CALVIN, The Life and Times of Henry Clay, two vols., New York, 1846.

COLTON, RAY C., The Civil War in the Western Territories, Norman, Oklahoma, 1959.

COMMAGER, HENRY STEELE, The Blue and the Gray, two vols., Indianapolis, 1950.

———, Documents of American History, New York, 1949.

COMTE DE PARIS, History of the Civil War in America, four vols., Philadelphia, 1876.

Confederate Flags, Richmond, n.d.

Confederate Military History, twelve vols., Atlanta, Georgia, 1899.

Confederate States Almanac and Repository of Useful Knowledge for 1862, Vicksburg, Mississippi, 1862.

Confederate States Almanac and Repository of Useful Knowledge for the Year 1865, compiled by H. C. Clarke, Mobile, Alabama, 1865.

Confederate States Almanac for the Year of our Lord 1864, Being Bessestile, or Leap and the fourth year of the Independence of the Confederate States of America, Macon, Georgia, and Mobile, Alabama, 1864.

Confederate Veteran, various issues.

CONGER, A. L., The Rise of Ulysses S. Grant, New York, 1931.

Congressional Globe, Washington, D.C., various volumes.

CONNOLLY, JAMES AUSTIN, Major Connolly's Letters to his wife, 1862–1865, Transactions of the Illinois State Historical Society, 1928, Springfield, 1928.

———, Three Years in the Army of the Cumberland, The Letters and Diary of Major James A. Connolly, edited by Paul M. Angle, Bloomington, Indiana, 1959.

CONNOLLEY, WILLIAM E., Quantrill and the Border Wars, New York, 1956.

———, A Standard History of Kansas and Kansans, Chicago, 1918.

———, Wild Bill and his Era, the Life and Adventures of James Butler Hickok, New York, 1933.

CONNOR, HENRY G., John Archibald Campbell, Boston, 1920.

CONRAD, DANIEL B., "Capture of the C.S. Ram *Tennessee* in Mobile Bay, August, 1864," *Southern Historical Society Papers,* Vol. XIX, 1891.

CONWAY, MONCURE DANIEL, Autobiography, Memories, and Experiences, Boston and New York, 1904.

CONWAY, WILLIAM B., "Talks with General J. A. Early," *Southern Historical Society Papers,* Vol. XXX, 1902.

CONYNHAM, DAVID F., Sherman's March Through the South with Sketches and Incidents of the Campaign, New York, 1865.

COOKE, JOHN ESTEN, Wearing of the Gray, edited by Philip Van Dorn Stern, Indiana University Press, Bloomington, 1959.

COOKE, P. ST. GEORGE, "The Charge of Cooke's Cavalry at Gaines's Mill," Battles and Leaders.

COPELAND, MELVIN THOMAS, The Cotton Manufacturing Industry of the United States, Cambridge, 1912.

"The Copperheads and Lake Erie Conspiracy," Ohio Handbook of the Civil War, Columbus, 1961.

The Copperheads' Prayer; Containing Remarkable Confessions; by a Degenerate Yankee, Chicago, 1864.

"Correspondence between General A. S. Johnston and Governor Isham G. Harris," *Southern Historical Society Papers,* Vol. IV, No. 4, October, 1877.

"Correspondence Relating to Chickamauga and Chattanooga," Vol. VIII, Military Historical Society of Massachusetts Papers, Boston, 1910.

Correspondence Relative to the Case of Messrs. Mason and Slidell, n.a., n.p., n.d.

Correspondence of Robert Toombs, Alexander Stephens and Howell Cobb, edited by Ulrich Bonnell Phillips, Vol. II, Annual Report of the American Historical Association, Washington, 1913.

Corruptions and Frauds of Lincoln's Administration, New York, 1864.

CORTISSOZ, ROYAL, The Life of Whitelaw Reid, two vols., New York, 1921.

COSTI, MICHELE, Memoir of the Trent Affair, London, 1865.

COUCH, DARIUS M., "The Chancellorsville Campaign," Battles and Leaders.

———, "Sumner's Right Grand Division," Battles and Leaders.

COULTER, E. MERTON, The Civil War and Readjustment in Kentucky, Chapel Hill, 1926.

———, "Commercial Intercourse with the Confederacy in the Mississippi Valley, 1861–1865," *The Mississippi Valley Historical Review,* Vol. V, No. 4, March, 1919.

———, The Confederate States of America 1861–1865, A History of the South, Vol. VII, Baton Rouge, 1950.

COUPER, WILLIAM, Virginia Military Institute Seventy-fifth Anniversary of the Battle of New Market, May 18, 1939, n.d., n.p.

COWLEY, CHARLES, Leaves from a Lawyer's Life Afloat and Ashore, Lowell, Massachusetts, 1879.

COWTAN, CHARLES W., Services of the Tenth New York Volunteers (National Zouaves), in the War of the Rebellion, New York, 1882.

COX, JACOB D., Atlanta, Campaigns of the Civil War, New York, 1882.

———, "Battle of Antietam," Battles and Leaders.

———, "Forcing Fox's Gap and Turner's Gap," Battles and Leaders.

———, The March to the Sea, Franklin and Nashville, Campaigns of the Civil War, New York, 1913.

———, "McClellan in West Virginia," Battles and Leaders.

———, Military Reminiscences of the Civil War, two vols., New York, 1900.

———, "War Preparations in the North," Battles and Leaders.

COX, SAMUEL S., Three Decades of Federal Legislation, 1855 to 1865, San Francisco, California, 1885.

CRAFT, DAVID, History of the One Hundred Forty-First Regiment, Pennsylvania Volunteers, 1862–1865, Towanda, Pennsylvania, 1885.

CRAMER, JOHN HENRY, Lincoln Under Enemy Fire, Baton Rouge, 1948.

CRAVEN, AVERY, The Coming of the Civil War, New York, 1942, also 2nd revised edition, New York, 1957.

———, "Coming of the War Between the States; An Interpretation," *The Journal of Southern History,* Vol. II, No. 3, August, 1936.

———, Edmund Ruffin, Southerner, New York, 1932.

———, The Growth of Southern Nationalism 1848–1861, Baton Rouge, 1953.

———, The Repressible Conflict 1830–1861, University, Louisiana, 1939.

———"Slavery and the Civil War," *The Southern Review,* Vol. IV, 1938–39.

CRAWFORD, SAMUEL WYLIE, The Genesis of the Civil War; The Story of Sumter 1860–1861, New York, 1887.

CRAWFORD, W. T., "The Mystery of Spring Mill," Civil War History, Vol. I, No. 11, June, 1955.

CRENSHAW, OLLINGER, The Slave States in the Presidential Election of 1860, Baltimore, 1945.

CRISWELL, ROBERT, Uncle Tom's Cabin Contrasted with Buckingham Hall, the Planter's Home, or a Fair View of Both Sides of the Slavery Question, New York, 1852.

CRITTENDEN, THOMAS L., "The Union Left at Stone's River," Battles and Leaders.

CROCKER, LUCIAN B., "Episodes and Characters in an Illinois Regiment," Military Essays and Recollections, Illinois Commandery of the Military Order of the Loyal Legion of the United States, Vol. I, Chicago, 1891.

CROLY, HERBERT, The Promise of American Life, New York, 1914.

CROOK, GEORGE, General George Crook, His Autobiography, edited and annotated by Martin F. Schmitt, Norman, Oklahoma, 1946.

CROSS, NELSON, Life of General Grant: His Political Record, New York, 1872.

CROTTY, D. G., Four Years Campaigning in the Army of the Potomac, by Color Sergeant D. G. Crotty, Third Michigan Volunteer Infantry, Grand Rapids, Michigan, 1874.

CROWNINSHIELD, BENJAMIN W., "Cavalry in Virginia," Vol. XXII, Military Historical Society of Massachusetts Papers, Boston, 1912.

———, "Cedar Creek," Vol. VI, Military Historical Society of Massachusetts Papers, Boston, 1907.

———, A History of the First Regiment of Massachusetts Cavalry Volunteers, Boston and New York, 1891.

CROWNOVER, SIMS, The Battle of Franklin, reprinted from *Tennessee Historical Quarterly,* Vol. XIV, No. 4, December, 1955.

CRUMMER, WILBUR G., With Grant at Fort Donelson, Shiloh and Vicksburg, Oak Park, Illinois, 1915.

CUDWORTH, WARREN H., History of the First Regiment Massachusetts Infantry, Boston, 1866.

CULLEN, JOSEPH P., Richmond National Battlefield Park, Virginia, National Park Service Historical Handbook Series No. 33, Washington, 1961.

CUNNINGHAM, EDWARD, The Port Hudson Campaign 1862–1863, Baton Rouge, 1963.

CURRY, J. L. M., Civil War History of the Government of the Confederate States with some personal reminiscences, Richmond, 1901.

CURTIS, FRANCIS, The Republican Party, New York, 1904.

CURTIS, GEORGE TICKNOR, Life of James Buchanan, two vols., New York, 1883.

CURTIS, NEWTON MARTIN, From Bull Run to Chancellorsville; The Story of the Sixteenth New York Infantry, New York, 1906.

CURTIS, SAMUEL PRENTIS, "The Army of the South-West, and the First Campaign in Arkansas," The Annals of Iowa, Vols. IV–VI.

CUSHING, W. B., "The Destruction of the 'Albemarle,'" Battles and Leaders.

CUTTS, J. MADISON, A Brief Treatise upon Constitutional and Party Questions, The History of Political Parties, as I received it Orally from the Late Senator Stephen A. Douglas, of Illinois, New York, 1866.

DABNEY, R. L., Life and Campaigns of Lieut.-General Thomas J. Jackson, New York, 1866.

DABNEY, REV. R. L., D.D., "Memoirs of a Narrative Received of Colonel John R. Baldwin, of Staunton, touching the origin of the War," *Southern Historical Society Papers*, Vol. I, No. 6, June, 1876.

DAHLGREN, JOHN A., Memoir of, Boston, 1882.

DALTON, JOHN CALL, John Call Dalton, M.D., U.S.V., Cambridge, Massachusetts, 1892.

DALY, R. W., How the *Merrimac* Won, New York, 1957.

DALZELL, GEORGE W., The Flight from the Flag, Chapel Hill, 1940.

DANA, CHARLES A., Recollections of the Civil War, New York, 1898.

DANIEL, JOHN A., "General Jubal A. Early, Memorial Address from Richmond Dispatch, December 14, 1894," *Southern Historical Society Papers*, Vol. XXII, 1894.

DANNETT, SYLVIA G. L., "Rebecca Wright—Traitor or Patriot," Lincoln *Herald*, Fall, 1963.

DARROW, MRS. CAROLINE BALDWIN, "Recollections of the Twiggs Surrender," Battles and Leaders.

DAVENPORT, ALFRED, Camp and Field Life of the Fifth New York Volunteer Infantry, New York, 1879.

DAVIDSON, JAMES WOOD, "Who Burned Columbia?—A Review of General Sherman's Version of the Affair," *Southern Historical Society Papers*, Vol. VII, No. 4, April, 1879.

DAVIS, BURKE, Nine April Days, New York, 1959.

DAVIS, CHARLES E., Three Years in the Army, The Story of the Thirteenth Massachusetts Volunteers from July 16, 1861, to August 1, 1864, Boston, 1894.

DAVIS, CHARLES W., "New Madrid and Island No. 10," Military Essays and Recollections, Illinois Commandery of the Military Order of the Loyal Legion of the United States, Vol. I, Chicago, 1891.

DAVIS, GEORGE B., The Antietam Campaign, Vol. III, The Military Historical Society of Massachusetts Papers, Boston, 1895.

DAVIS, JEFFERSON, Calendar of the Jefferson Davis Postwar Manuscripts in the Louisiana Historical Association Collection, New Orleans, 1943.

——, "Lord Wolseley's Mistakes," *The North American Review,* October, 1889.

——, "The Peace Commission—Letter from Ex-President Davis," *Southern Historical Society Papers,* Vol. IV, July–December, 1877.

——, "The Peace Conference of 1865, An Unpublished Letter from Jefferson Davis, *Century Magazine,* Vol. LXXVII, No. 1, September, 1908.

——, Relations of States, Speech of the Honorable Jefferson Davis of Mississippi, Speech of May 7th, 1860, Baltimore, 1860.

——, The Rise and Fall of the Confederate Government, two vols., New York, 1881.

DAVIS, JULIE, The Shenandoah, Rivers of American Series, New York, 1945.

DAVIS, ROBERT STEWART, "Three Months Around Charleston Bar; or the Great Siege as we saw it," *United Service Magazine,* Vol. I, No. 2, February, 1864.

DAVIS, VARINA, Jefferson Davis, A Memoir by his Wife, two vols., New York 1890.

DAVIS, W. W. H., "The Siege of Morris Island," Annals of the War, Philadelphia, 1879.

DAWES, EPHRAIM C., "The Battle of Shiloh," Vol. VII, The Military Historical Society of Massachusetts Papers, Boston, 1908.

DAWES, RUFUS, Service with the Sixth Wisconsin Volunteers, Marietta, Ohio, 1890.

"Deaths of Generals Cleburne and Adams," Battles and Leaders.

DeBow's Review, various issues.

DEBRAY, X. R., "A Sketch of DeBray's Twenty-sixth Regiment of Texas Cavalry," *Southern Historical Society Papers,* Vol. XIII, January–December, 1885.

DEFONTAINE, FELIX GREGORY, "Shoulder to Shoulder," *Century Magazine,* Vol. XIX, September, 1889.

DEFOREST, JOHN WILLIAM, A Volunteer's Adventures, edited by James M. Croushore, New Haven, 1946.

DELEON, T. G., Four Years in Rebel Capitals, Mobile, Alabama, 1890.

DERBY, W. P., Bearing Arms in the Twenty-seventh Massachusetts Regiment of Volunteer Infantry during the Civil War, 1861–1865, Boston, 1883.

DERRY, JOSEPH T., Georgia, Confederate Military History, Vol. IV, Atlanta, Georgia, 1889.

DETROBRIAND, REGIS, Four Years with the Army of the Potomac, Boston, 1889.

DEWEY, DAVIS RICH, Financial History of the United States, New York, 1934.

DEWEY, GEORGE, Autobiography, New York, 1913.

Diary of a Public Man, and a Page of Political Correspondence Stanton to Buchanan, edited by F. Louriston Bullard, New Brunswick, New Jersey, 1946.

DICKENS, CHARLES, American Notes, The Biographical Edition of the Works of Charles Dickens, Philadelphia, n.d.

DICKERT, D. AUGUSTUS, History of Kershaw's Brigade, Newberry, South Carolina, 1899.

DICKISON, J. J., Florida, Confederate Military History, Vol. XI, Atlanta, Georgia, 1899.

Dictionary of American Biography, twenty-two vols., New York, 1946.

Dictionary of American History, Adams, James Truslow, editor, six vols., New York, 1941.

DILLAHUNTY, ALBERT, Shiloh National Military Park, Tennessee, National Park Service Handbook Series No. 10, Washington, D.C., 1955.

DIMITRY, JOHN, Louisiana, Confederate Military History, Vol. X, Atlanta, Georgia, 1899.

DIMON, THEODORE, "A Federal Surgeon at Sharpsburg," edited by James I. Robertson, *Civil War History*, Vol. XL, No. 11, June, 1960.

DINKINS, JAMES, "An August Sunday Morning in Memphis," in Henry, As They Saw Forrest.

DIX, JOHN ADAMS, Memoirs of John Adams Dix, compiled by his son, Morgan Dix, two vols., New York, 1883.

DIXON, MRS. ARCHIBALD, True History of the Missouri Compromise and its Repeal, Cincinnati, n.d.

DOAN, ISAAC, Reminiscences of the Chattanooga Campaign, Richmond, Indiana, n.d.

DODD, DOROTHY, Fort Pickens, Folder of Florida Park Service, Tallahassee, Florida, n.d.

DODD, WILLIAM E., Jefferson Davis, Philadelphia, 1907.

DODGE, GRENVILLE M., The Battle of Atlanta and other Campaigns, Addresses, etc., Council Bluffs, Iowa, 1910.

———, Personal Recollections of General Grant and his Campaigns in the West; Personal Recollections of the War of the Rebellion; Addresses delivered before the Commandery of the State of New York, Military Order of the Loyal Legion of the United States; second series edited by A. Noel Blakeman, Vol. III, New York, 1903.

———, Personal Recollections of President Abraham Lincoln, General Ulysses S. Grant and General William T. Sherman, Council Bluffs, Iowa, 1914.

DODGE, THEODORE A., "The Battle of Chancellorsville," *Southern Historical Society Papers*, Vol. XIV, January–December, 1886.

———, The Romance of Chancellorsville, Vol. III, Military Historical Society of Massachusetts Papers, Boston, 1903.

DODGE, WILLIAM SUMNER, History of the Old Second Division, Army of the Cumberland, Chicago, 1864.

DONALD, DAVID, Inside Lincoln's Cabinet; The Civil War Diaries of Salmon P. Chase, New York, 1954.

DONNELLY, RALPH W., "Confederate Copper," *Civil War History*, Vol. I, No. 4, December, 1955.

DORNBLASTER, T. F., Sabre Strokes of the Pennsylvania Dragoons in the War of 1861–1865, Philadelphia, 1884.

DORSEY, GUS W., "Fatal Wounding of General J. E. B. Stuart," *Southern Historical Society Papers*, Vol. XXX, 1902.

DOUBLEDAY, ABNER, Chancellorsville and Gettysburg, Campaigns of the Civil War, Vol. VI, New York, 1882.

———, From Moultrie to Sumter, Battles and Leaders.

———, Reminiscences of Forts Sumter and Moultrie in 1860–1861, New York, 1876.

DOUGLAS, HENRY KYD, I Rode with Stonewall, Chapel Hill, 1940.

———, "Stonewall Jackson in Maryland," Battles and Leaders.

DOUGLAS, STEPHEN A., "The Dividing Line between Federal and Local Authority, Popular Sovereignty in the Territories," *Harper's New Monthly Magazine,* September, 1859.

———, Kansas-Utah-Dred Scott Decision, Speech delivered at Springfield, Illinois, June 12, 1857, Springfield, 1857.

DOWDEY, CLIFFORD, Death of a Nation; The Story of Lee and His Men at Gettysburg, New York, 1958.

———, Experiment in Rebellion, Garden City, 1946.

———, Lee's Last Campaign, Boston, 1960.

DOWNEY, FAIRFAX, Clash of Cavalry; The Battle of Brandy Station, New York, 1959.

———, The Guns at Gettysburg, New York, 1958.

———, Storming of the Gateway, Chattanooga, 1863, New York, 1960.

DOYLE, JOSEPH B., In Memoriam Edwin McMasters Stanton, Steubenville, Ohio, 1911.

DRAYTON, PERCIVAL, "Naval Letters from Captain Percival Drayton," *Bulletin of the New York Public Library,* Vol. X, No. 11, November, 1906.

Dred Scott in the United States Supreme Court, The Case of, The Full Opinion of Chief Justice Taney and Justice Curtis, New York, 1860.

DUBERMAN, MARTIN B., Charles Francis Adams, 1807–1866, Boston, 1961.

DUBOSE, J. W., The Life and Times of William Lowndes Yancey, two vols., New York, 1942.

DUFOUR, CHARLES L., The Night the War Was Lost, Garden City, New York, 1960.

DUKE, BASIL W., A History of Morgan's Cavalry, Bloomington, Indiana, 1961.

———, "Morgan's Cavalry During the Bragg Invasion," Battles and Leaders.

———, "Morgan's Indiana and Ohio Raid," Annals of the War.

———, Reminiscences of General Basil W. Duke, C.S.A., Garden City, New York, 1911.

DUMOND, DWIGHT L., Antislavery Origins of the Civil War in the United States, Ann Arbor, 1939.

———, The Secession Movement 1860–1861, New York, 1931.

———, Southern Editorials on Secession, Washington, 1931.

DUPONT, N. A., The Campaign of 1864 in the Valley of Virginia and the Expedition to Lynchburg, New York, 1925.

DUPUY, R. ERNEST, and TREVOR N. DUPUY, Military Heritage of America, New York, 1956.

DURKIN, JOSEPH T., Stephen R. Mallory, Confederate Navy Chief, Chapel Hill, 1954.

DYER, FREDERICK H., A Compendium of the War of the Rebellion, Des Moines, 1908.

DYER, JOHN P., The Gallant Hood, Indianapolis, 1930.

EADS, JAMES B., Recollections of Foote and the Gun Boats, Battles and Leaders.

EARLE, JOHN JEWETT, The Sentiment of the People of California with Respect to the Civil War, Annual Report of the American Historical Association, Washington, 1908.

EARLY, JUBAL A., "The Advance on Washington in 1864," *Southern Historical Society Papers*, Vol. IX, Nos. 7 and 8, July and August, 1881.

———, Autobiographical Sketch and Narrative of the War between the States, Philadelphia, 1912.

———, Early's March to Washington, Battles and Leaders.

———, "Letter from General J. A. Early, Barbara Fritchie—Refutation of Whittier's myth," *Southern Historical Society Papers*, Vol. VII, No. 9, September, 1879.

———, "Letter on Gettysburg," *Southern Historical Society Papers*, Vol. IV, No. 2, August, 1877.

———, "Relative Strength of the Armies of Generals Lee and Grant," *Southern Historical Society Papers*, Vol. II, July, 1876.

———, "Stonewall Jackson," *Southern Historical Society Papers*, Vol. VI, No. 6, December, 1878.

———, "Winchester, Fisher's Hill and Cedar Creek," Battles and Leaders.

"Early, Jubal A., Recollections of, by one who followed him," *Century Magazine*, Vol. LXX, May–October, 1905.

EATON, CLEMENT, A History of the Old South, New York, 1949.

———, A History of the Southern Confederacy, New York, 1954.

EBERT, VALERIUS, "Letter from Mrs. Fritchie's nephew," *Southern Historical Society Papers*, Vol. VII, No. 9, September, 1879.

ECKENRODE, H. J., Jefferson Davis, President of the South, New York, 1923.

ECKENRODE, H. J., and BRYAN CONRAD, George B. McClellan, the Man Who Saved the Union, Chapel Hill, 1941.

Economic Trends of War and Reconstruction, n.a., New York, 1918.

EDMANDS, THOMAS F., "Operations in North Carolina, 1861–1862," Vol. IX, The Military Historical Society of Massachusetts Papers, Boston, 1912.

EDWARDS, JOHN N., Shelby and his Men; or, The War in the West, Cincinnati, 1867.

EDWARDS, WILLIAM E., Civil War Guns, The Stackpole Company, Harrisburg, Pennsylvania, 1962.

EGGLESTON, GEORGE CARY, A Rebel's Recollections, introduction by David Donald, Bloomington, Indiana, 1959.

EISENDRATH, JOSEPH L., JR., "Chicago's Camp Douglas," *Journal of the Illinois Historical Society*, Vol. LXIX, No. 1, Spring, 1960.

EISENSCHIML, OTTO, The Celebrated Case of Fitz John Porter, Indianapolis, 1950.

———, In the Shadow of Lincoln's Death, New York, 1940.

———, "Sherman, Hero or War Criminal," *Civil War Times Illustrated*, Vol. II, No. 9, January, 1964.

———, The Story of Shiloh, Chicago, 1940.

———, Why the Civil War? Indianapolis, 1958.

———, Why Was Lincoln Murdered? Boston, 1937.

EISENSCHIML, OTTO, and E. B. LONG, As Luck Would Have It, Indianapolis, 1948.

EISENSCHIML, OTTO, and RALPH NEWMAN, The American Iliad, Vol. I, The Civil War, New York, 1956.

ELIOT, ELLSWORTH, JR., West Point in the Confederacy, New York, 1941.

ELLET, ALFRED W., "Ellet and his Steam Rams at Memphis," Battles and Leaders.

ELLICOTT, JOHN N., The Life of John Ancrum Winslow, New York, 1902.

ELLIOTT, GILBERT, "The Career of the Confederate Ram Albemarle, Her Construction and Service," *Century,* Vol. XXXVIII, May–October, 1889.
——, "The First Battle of the Confederate Ram 'Albemarle,'" Battles and Leaders.
ELLIOTT, ISAAC N., History of the Twenty-third Regiment, Illinois Veterans Volunteer Infantry, Gibson City, Illinois, 1902.
ELLIS, MRS. L. E., "The Chicago 'Times' during the Civil War," Transactions for the year 1932, Illinois State Historical Society, Springfield.
"Ellsworth Requiem March" sheet music, Root and Cady, Chicago.
ELY, ALFRED, Journal of Alfred Ely, a Prisoner of War in Richmond, edited by Charles Laman, New York, 1862.
EMERSON, EDWIN, JR., A History of the Nineteenth Century Year by Year, three vols., New York, 1902.
English Merchant, An, Two Months in the Confederate States including a visit to New Orleans under the domination of General Butler, London, 1865.
ERICSSON, JOHN, "The Building of the 'Monitor,'" Battles and Leaders.
——, "The Early Monitors," Battles and Leaders.
ERSKINE, JOHN, Leading American Novelists, New York, 1910.
ESPOSITO, COLONEL VINCENT J., Atlas to Accompany Steele's American Campaigns, West Point, New York, 1953.
EVANS, A. W., "Canby at Valverde," Battles and Leaders.
EVANS, CLEMENT A., Confederate Military History, twelve vols., Atlanta, 1899.
EVERHART, WILLIAM G., Vicksburg National Military Park, Mississippi, National Park Service Historical Handbook, Series No. 21, Washington, 1954.
"Exchange of Prisoners," Report of the Joint Committee on the Conduct of the War, Vol. III, 1865, Washington, 1868.
FAIRBAIRN, CHARLOTTE JUDD, Historic Harper's Ferry, Ranson, West Virginia.
FAIRCHILD, C. B., History of the Twenty-Seventh Regiment New York Volunteers, Binghamton, New York, 1888.
FAIRCHILD, J. H., Its Origin, Progress and Results, Oberlin, Ohio, 1869.
FAIRFAX, D. MACNEILL, "Captain Wilkes' Seizure of Mason and Slidell," Battles and Leaders.
FARBER, JAMES, Texas, C.S.A., New York, 1947.
FARRAGUT, LOYALL, The Life of David Glasgow Farragut, First Admiral of the United States Navy, embodying his Journal and Letters, New York, 1879.
FEHRENBACHER, DON G., Chicago Giant, A Biography of Long John Wentworth, Madison, Wisconsin, 1957.
FEIGHT, HENRY B., "When Ohioans Rebelled Against Draft Act of 1863," Cleveland *Plain Dealer,* August 27, 1933.
FIELD, C. W., "Campaign of 1864 and 1865," *Southern Historical Society Papers,* Vol. XIV, January–December, 1886.
FISKE, JOHN, The Mississippi Valley in the Civil War, Boston, 1900.
FITCH, MICHAEL HENDRICK, The Chattanooga Campaign, Madison, Wisconsin, 1911.
FITE, EMERSON DAVID, The Presidential Campaign of 1860, New York, 1911.
——, Social and Industrial Conditions in the North during the Civil War, New York, 1950.
FITTS, ALBERT N., "The Confederate Convention," *The Alabama Review,* April, 1949, and July, 1949.

FITZGERALD, W. NORMAN, JR., President Lincoln's Blockade and the Defense of Mobile, Madison, Wisconsin, 1954.

FITZHUGH, LESTER N., "Saluria, Fort Esperanza and Military Operations on the Texas Coast, 1861–1864," *The Southwestern Quarterly*, Vol. LXI, No. 1, July, 1957.

Flags of the Confederate States of America, by authority of the United Confederate Veterans, 1907.

FLETCHER, MISS A., Within Fort Sumter; or, A view of Major Anderson's Garrison Family for One Hundred and Ten Days, New York, 1861.

FLETCHER, WILLIAM ANDREW, Rebel Private Front and Rear, preface by Bell Irvin Wiley, Austin, 1954.

FLOWER, FRANK A., Edwin McMasters Stanton, The Autocrat of Rebellion, Emancipation and Reconstruction, Akron, Ohio, 1905.

FOOTE, H. S., Casket of Reminiscences, Washington, 1874.

———, War of the Rebellion, New York, 1868.

FOOTE, JOHN A., "Notes on the Life of Admiral Foote," Battles and Leaders.

FORCE, M. F., From Fort Henry to Corinth, Campaigns of the Civil War, New York, 1908.

FORD, ANDREW E., The Story of the Fifteenth Regiment, Massachusetts Volunteer Infantry in the Civil War, 1861–1864, Clinton, 1898.

FORD, HARVEY S., "Van Dorn and the Pea Ridge Campaign," *The Journal of the American Military Institute*, Vol. III, No. 4, Winter, 1939.

FORMBY, JOHN, The American Civil War, two vols., New York, 1910.

FORNELL, EARL W., "The Civil War Comes to Savannah," *The Georgia Historical Quarterly*, Vol. XLIII, No. 3, September, 1959.

FORRESTER, IZOLA, This One Mad Act, The Unknown Story of John Wilkes Booth and his Family, Boston, 1937.

FORSYTH, GEORGE A., Thrilling Days in Army Life, New York, 1900.

Fort Donelson National Military Park, pamphlet, Washington, 1954.

"Fort Fisher Expedition," Report of the Joint Committee on the Conduct of the War, Vol. II, 1865.

Fort Fisher State Historic Site, State Department of Archives and History, Raleigh, North Carolina, n.d.

Fort Henry and Fort Donelson Campaigns, February, 1862, Source Book, Fort Leavenworth, Kansas, 1923.

"Fort Hudson, Fortifications and Siege of," Compiled by the Association of Defenders of Fort Hudson, *Southern Historical Society Papers*, Vol. XIV, January–December, 1886.

"Fort Pillow Massacre," Report of the Joint Committee on the Conduct of the War, Washington, 1864.

"Forts, Arsenals, Arms," Report No. 85, February 18, 1861, House Reports 36th Congress, 2nd Session, three vols., Washington, 1861.

FOWLER, ROBERT E., "The Other Gettysburg Address," *Civil War Times Illustrated*, November, 1962.

FOX, GUSTAVUS VASA, Confidential Correspondence of Gustavus Vasa Fox, two vols., New York, 1918.

FOX, WILLIAM F., Regimental Losses in the American Civil War, 1861–1865, Albany, New York, 1889.

————, Slocum and his Men, In Memoriam Henry Warner Slocum, 1826–1894, Albany, 1904.

FRANK, SEYMOUR J., "The Conspiracy to Implicate the Confederate Leaders in Lincoln's Assassination," *The Mississippi Valley Historical Review*, Vol. XL, No. 6, March, 1954.

FRANKLIN, JOHN HOPE, The Emancipation Proclamation, New York, 1963.

————, From Slavery to Freedom, New York, 1952.

FRANKLIN, W. B., "The First Great Crime of the War," Annals of the War.

————, "Notes on Crampton's Gap and Antietam," Battles and Leaders.

————, "Rear-Guard Fighting during the Change of Base," Battles and Leaders.

————, "The Sixth Corps at the Second Bull Run" Battles and Leaders.

FREDERICK, GILBERT, The Story of a Regiment, being a record of the military services of the Fifty-seventh New York, Chicago, 1895.

Fredericksburg and Spotsylvania County National Military Park, Virginia, United States Department of the Interior, 1942.

FREE, GEORGE D., History of Tennessee, Nashville, 1895, 1896.

FREEMAN, DOUGLAS SOUTHALL, "An Address," *Civil War History*, Vol. X, No. 1, March, 1935.

————, A Calendar of Confederate Papers, Richmond, Virginia, 1908.

————, R. E. Lee, A Biography, four vols., New York, 1934.

————, Lee's Lieutenants, three vols., New York, 1944.

FREEMAN, DOUGLAS SOUTHALL, and GRADY MCWHINEY, editors, Lee's Dispatches, New York, 1957.

FREMANTLE, JAMES ARTHUR LYON, The Fremantle Diary, edited by Walter Lord, Boston, 1954.

FRÉMONT, JESSIE BENTON, The Story of the Guard; A Chronicle of the War, Boston, 1863.

FRÉMONT, JOHN C., In Command in Missouri, Battles and Leaders.

FRY, JAMES B., McDowell and Tyler in the Campaign of Bull Run, New York, 1884.

————, Military Miscellanies, New York, 1889.

————, Operations of the Army under Buell from June 10th to October 30, 1862, and the Buell Commission, New York, 1884.

FUESS, CLAUDE MOORE, Daniel Webster, Boston, 1930.

FULLER, J. F. C., The Generalship of Ulysses S. Grant, New York, 1929.

————, Grant and Lee: A Study in Personality and Generalship, New York, 1933.

FULLERTON, J. S., "The Army of the Cumberland at Chattanooga," Battles and Leaders.

————, "Reenforcing Thomas at Chickamauga," Battles and Leaders.

FUNKHOUSER, E. D., "Storming of Fort Stedman or Mares Hill, Front of Petersburg, Virginia, March 25, 1865," E. H. Hutchins, The War of the 'Sixties, New York, 1912.

FURNESS, WILLIAM ELIOT, "The Battle of Olustee, Florida, February 20, 1864," Vol. XX, Military Historical Society of Massachusetts Papers, Boston, 1912.

FUTCH, OVID, "Prison Life at Andersonville," *Civil War History*, Vol. VIII, No. 2, June, 1962.

Future of the Country, A, by a Patriot, n.p., 1864.

GALBREATH, C. B., "John Brown," *Ohio Archaeological and Historical Quarterly,* July, 1921.

GALLOWAY, G. NORTON, "Hand-to-hand Fighting at Spotsylvania," Battles and Leaders.

GAMBRELL, HERBERT P., "Rams Versus Gunboats," *Southwest Review,* Vol. XXVIII, October, 1937.

GAMMAGE, W. L., The Camp, the Bivouac and the Battlefield, Little Rock, Arkansas, 1958.

GANOE, WILLIAM ADDELMAN, The History of the United States Army, New York, 1932.

GARDNER, ASA BIRD, Argument on Behalf of Lieutenant General Philip W. Sheridan, U.S.A., Respondent, before the Court of Inquiry, in the Case of Lieutenant Colonel and Bvt. Major General Gouverneur K. Warren, Applicant, Chicago, 1881.

GARRET, WILLIAM, Public Men of Alabama, Atlanta, Georgia, 1872.

GARRETT, W. R., and GOODPASTURE, A. V., History of Tennessee, Nashville, 1900.

"General Warren at Five Forks and the Court of Inquiry," Battles and Leaders.

"Gettysburg, Causes of the Defeat of General Lee's Army at the Battle of," by various authors, *Southern Historical Society Papers,* Vol. IV, July–December, 1877, and Vol. V, January–June, 1878.

GIBBON, JOHN, "Personal Recollections of Appomattox," *Century Magazine,* Vol. LXIII, No. 6, April, 1902.

GIFT, GEORGE W., "The Story of the Arkansas," *Southern Historical Society Papers,* Vol. XII, Nos. 1–5, January–May, 1884.

GIHON, JOHN H., History of Kansas, 1857.

GILBERT, CHARLES C., "On the Field of Perryville," Battles and Leaders.

GILBERT, J. WARREN, The Blue and the Gray, Gettysburg, 1952.

GILBERTSON, CATHERINE, Harriet Beecher Stowe, New York, 1937.

GILLMORE, QUINCY A., "The Army Before Charleston in 1863," Battles and Leaders.

———, Engineer and Artillery Operations against the defense of Charleston Harbor in 1863, New York, 1863.

———, "Siege and Capture of Fort Pulaski," Battles and Leaders.

GILMAN, J. H., "With Slemmer in Pensacola Harbor," Battles and Leaders.

Gladstone and Palmerston, being the Correspondence of Lord Palmerston with Mr. Gladstone 1851–1856, edited by Philip Guedalla, New York, 1928.

GLONEL, JAMES F., "Lincoln, Johnson and the Baltimore Ticket," *The Abraham Lincoln Quarterly,* Vol. VI, No. 5, March, 1951.

GLOVER, GILBERT GRAFFENRIED, Immediate Pre-Civil War Compromise Efforts, Nashville, 1934.

GOBRIGHT, L. A., Recollections of Men and Things at Washington During the Third of a Century, Philadelphia, 1869.

GOING, CHARLES BUXTON, David Wilmot, Free-Soiler, New York, 1924.

GOLDSBOROUGH, W. W., The Maryland Line in the Confederate States Army, Baltimore, 1869.

GOODWIN, CARDINAL, John Charles Frémont, An Explanation of His Career, Stanford University, California, 1930.

GOOLRICK, JOHN T., Fredericksburg, America's Most Historic City, Fredericksburg, 1948.

GORDON, A. C., "Hard Times in the Confederacy," *Century Magazine,* Vol. XXXVI, No. 5, September, 1888.

GORDON, GEORGE H., History of the Campaigns of the Army of Virginia, Boston, 1889.

——, A War Diary of Events in the War of the Great Rebellion in 1863–1865, Boston, 1885.

GORDON, GENERAL JOHN B., Reminiscences of the Civil War, New York, 1904.

GORGAS, JOSIAH, The Civil War Diary of General Josiah Gorgas, edited by Frank E. Vandiver, University, Albama, 1947.

——, "Notes on the Ordnance Department of the Confederate Government," *Southern Historical Society Papers,* Vol. XII, Nos. 1 and 2, January and February, 1884.

GORHAM, GEORGE O., Life and Public Service of Edwin M. Stanton, two vols., Boston, 1899.

GOSS, WARREN LEE, "Yorktown and Williamsburg," Battles and Leaders.

GOVAN, GILBERT E., and JAMES W. LIVINGOOD, The Chattanooga Country, 1540–1951, New York, 1956.

——, A Different Valor, The Story of General Joseph E. Johnston, C.S.A., Indianapolis, 1956.

"Government Contracts," House Report No. 2, two vols., 37th Congress, 2nd Session, Washington, 1862.

GRACIE, ARCHIBALD, The Truth about Chickamauga, Boston, 1911.

GRAHAM, MATTHEW J., The Ninth Regiment New York Volunteers, Nevins' Notes.

GRANT, FREDERICK DENT, "With Grant at Vicksburg," *Outlook,* July 2, 1898.

GRANT, ULYSSES S., "Chattanooga," Battles and Leaders.

——, "General Grant on the Siege of Petersburg," Battles and Leaders.

——, Letters of Ulysses S. Grant to his father and his youngest sister, 1857–1876, edited by his nephew, James Grant Cramer, New York, 1912.

——, Personal Memoirs, two vols., New York, 1885.

——, Personal Memoirs of General Grant, edited by E. B. Long, Cleveland, 1952.

——, "Preparing for the Campaigns of 1864," Battles and Leaders.

——, Report of Lieutenant General U. S. Grant of the Armies of the United States 1864–1865, n.p., n.d.

——, "The Vicksburg Campaign," Battles and Leaders.

GRANT, ULYSSES S., and JOHN C. PEMBERTON, "The Terms of Surrender," Battles and Leaders.

GRAVES, THEODORE THATCHER, "The Occupation," Battles and Leaders.

GRAY, JOHN CHAPMAN, and JOHN CODMAN ROPES, War Letters 1862–1865, Boston, 1927.

GRAY, WOOD, The Hidden Civil War, The Story of the Copperheads, New York, 1942.

GRAYSON, A. J., History of the Sixth Indiana Regiment in the Three Months' Campaign in Western Virginia, Madison, Indiana, 1875.

Great Indiana-Ohio Raid, by Brigadier John Hunt Morgan and his men, July, 1863, edited by Don G. John, Louisville, Kentucky, n.d.

GREELEY, HORACE, The American Conflict, two vols., Hartford, 1867.

———, "Greeley's Estimate of Lincoln," *Century Magazine*, Vol. XLII, No. 3, July, 1891.

GREELEY, HORACE, and JOHN F. CLEVELAND (compilers), A Political Textbook for 1860, New York, 1860.

GREEN, ANNA MACLAY, "Civil War Public Opinion of General Grant," *Journal of the Illinois State Historical Society*, Vol. XXII, No. 1, April, 1929.

GREEN, JOHN WILLIAM, Johnny Green of the Orphan Brigade; The Journal of a Confederate Soldier, A. D. Kirwin, editor, Lexington, 1956.

GREENAWALT, JOHN G., "The Capture of Fort Henry and Fort Donelson, February, 1862," War Papers No. 87, Commandery of the District of Columbia of the Military Order of the Loyal Legion of the United States, Washington, D.C., 1912.

GREENE, FRANCIS VINTON, The Mississippi, Campaigns of the Civil War, New York, 1882.

GREENE, JACOB L., Franklin at Fredericksburg 1862, Hartford, 1900.

GREENE, S. DANA, "In the 'Monitor' Turret," Battles and Leaders.

GREGG, D. M'M., "The Union Cavalry at Gettysburg," Annals of the War.

GREGORY, EDWARD S., "Vicksburg during the Siege," Annals of the War.

GRIERSON, FRANCIS, The Valley of Shadows, New York, 1913.

Grimes, Absalom, Confederate Mail Runner, edited from Captain Grimes's Own Story by M. M. Quaife, New Haven, 1926.

GUE, BENJAMIN F., History of Iowa, Vol. II, New York, 1903.

GUEGAN, J. A., JR., The Story of the Battle of Lexington, Lexington, Missouri, 1955.

GUERRANT, EDWARD O., "Marshall and Garfield in Eastern Kentucky," Battles and Leaders.

———, "Operations in East Tennessee and Southwest Virginia," Battles and Leaders.

Guide to the Manuscripts in the Historical Collection of the University of North Carolina, Chapel Hill, 1941.

"Gulf, Operations in the Department of," Report of the Joint Committee on the Conduct of the War, Vol. III, Washington, 1865.

GUROWSKI, ADAM, Diary, three vols., Boston, 1862.

HAGOOD, JOHNSON, Memoirs of the War of Secession, Columbia, South Carolina, 1910.

HAIGHT, THERON WILBER, Three Wisconsin Cushings, Wisconsin's History Commission, Madison, 1910.

HALL, GRANVILLE DAVISSON, Lee's Invasion of Northwest Virginia in 1861, Chicago, 1911.

———, The Rending of Virginia, Chicago, 1902.

HALL, MARTIN HARDWICK, Sibley's New Mexico Campaign, Austin, Texas, 1960.

HALSTEAD, MURAT, Caucuses of 1860, A History of the National Political Conventions, Columbus, 1860.

HAMERSLY, LEWIS R., The Records of Living Officers of the United States Navy and Marine Corps, Philadelphia, 1860.

———, The Records of Living Officers of the United States Navy and Marine Corps with a History of Naval Operations during the Rebellion of 1861–1865, Philadelphia, 1870.

HAMILTON, CHARLES S., "The Battle of Iuka," Battles and Leaders.

———, "Hamilton's Division at Corinth," Battles and Leaders.

HAMILTON, HOLMAN, Zachary Taylor, Soldier in the White House, Indianapolis, 1951.

HAMILTON, SCHUYLER, "Comments on Colonel Bissell's Papers," Battles and Leaders.

HAMLIN, AUGUSTUS CHOATE, The Battle of Chancellorsville, Bangor, Maine, 1896.

———, "Who Captured the Guns at Cedar Creek?" Vol. VI, Military Historical Society of Massachusetts Papers, Boston, 1907.

HAMLIN, CHARLES EUGENE, The life and Times of Hannibal Hamlin, Cambridge, 1899.

HAMLIN, PERCY GATLING, Old Bald Head (General R. S. Ewell), Strasburg, Virginia, 1940.

HAMMOND, M. B., The Cotton Industry, New York, 1897.

HAMPTON, WADE, The Battle of Bentonville, Battles and Leaders.

———, "Letter from General Hampton on the Burning of Columbia," *Southern Historical Society Papers,* Vol. VII, No. 3, March, 1879.

HANCOCK, HAROLD, "Civil War Comes to Delaware," *Civil War History,* December, 1956.

HANCOCK, WINFIELD, "Letter to Fitzhugh Lee," *Southern Historical Society Papers,* Vol. V, No. 4, April, 1878.

HANNA, A. J., Flight into Oblivion, Richmond, 1938.

HANNAFORD, E., The Story of a Regiment; A History of the Campaigns and Associations in the Field of the Sixth Regiment, Ohio Volunteer Infantry, Cincinnati, 1868.

Hansard's Parliamentary Debates, Third Series, Vol. CLXXX, March 19, 1861–May 17, 1861, London, 1861.

HANSON, ARTHUR O., The Hooker Letter, An Analysis, Lincoln Fellowship of Wisconsin, Historical Bulletin No. 11, Madison, 1953.

HANSON, E. HUNN, "Forrest's Defeat of Sturgis at Brice's Cross-Roads," Battles and Leaders.

HANSON, JOSEPH MILLS, Bull Run Remembers, Manassas, Virginia, 1953.

HAPPEL, RALPH, Appomattox Court House, National Historical Park, Virginia National Park Service, Washington, D.C., 1955.

HARDIN, MARTIN D., "The Defense of Washington against Early's Attack in June, 1864," Military Essays and Recollections, Vol. II, Illinois Commandery of the Military Order of the Loyal Legion of the United States, Chicago, 1894.

HARKNESS, DIXON J., "The Expeditions against Fort Fisher and Wilmington," Military Essays and Recollections, Vol. II, Illinois Commandery of the Military Order of the Loyal Legion of the United States, Chicago, 1894.

HARMON, GEORGE B., Douglas and the Compromise of 1850. Aspects of Slavery and Expansion 1848–1860, Lehigh University, 1929.

HARPER, CHANCELLOR, GOVERNOR HAMMOND, Dr. Simms and Professor Dew, The Pro-Slavery Argument, Charleston, 1852.

HARPER, ROBERT S., Lincoln and the Press, New York, 1951.

———, Ohio Handbook of the Civil War, Ohio Historical Society, Columbus, 1961.

Harper's Encyclopedia of United States History, ten vols., New York, 1907.

"Harper's Ferry, Invasion at," Senate Report No. 278, 36th Congress, 1st Session 1859–1860, Washington, 1860.

Harper's Ferry Affair, The Press upon, pamphlet, Boston *Journal,* Saturday, October 29, 1859.

HARRELL, JOHN N., Arkansas, Confederate Military History, Vol. X, Atlanta, Georgia, 1899.

HARRINGTON, FRED HARVEY, Fighting Politician, Major General N. P. Banks, Philadelphia, 1946.

HARRIS, THOMAS L., The Trent Affair including a review of English and American Relations at the Beginning of the Civil War, Indianapolis, 1896.

HARRIS, W. A., The Record of Fort Sumter, Columbia, South Carolina, 1862.

HARRISON, BURTON N., "The Capture of Jefferson Davis," *Century Magazine,* Vol. XXVII, No. 1, November, 1883.

HART, ALBERT BUSHNELL, American History told by Contemporaries, Vol. III, New York, 1901.

———, Slavery and Abolition 1831–1841, The American Nation: A History, Vol. XVI, New York, 1906.

HART, B. H. LIDDELL, Sherman, Soldier, Realist, American, New York, 1929.

HARTJE, ROBERT G., "A Confederate Dilemma Across the Mississippi," *The Arkansas Historical Quarterly,* Vol. XVII, No. 2, Summer, 1958.

———, "Van Dorn Conducts a Raid on Holly Springs and Enters Tennessee," *Tennessee Historical Quarterly,* Vol. XVIII, No. 2, June, 1959.

HARTRANFT, JOHN F., "The Recapture of Fort Stedman," Battles and Leaders.

HARVEY, PETER, Reminiscences and Anecdotes of Daniel Webster, Boston, 1867.

HARWELL, RICHARD BARKSDALE, Songs of the Confederacy, New York, 1951.

HASCALL, MILO S., "Personal Recollections," Vol. IV, Military Essays and Recollections, Illinois Commandery of the Military Order of the Loyal Legion of the United States, Chicago, 1907.

HASKELL, FRANK A., The Battle of Gettysburg, Boston, 1958.

HASKELL, JOHN, The Haskell Memoirs, edited by Gilbert M. Govan and James W. Livingood, New York, 1960.

HASSLER, WARREN W., JR., General George B. McClellan, Shield of the Union, Baton Rouge, 1957.

HASSLER, WILLIAM WOODS, A. P. Hill, Lee's Forgotten General, Richmond, 1957.

———, "The Slaughter Pen at Bristoe Station," *Civil War Times Illustrated,* Vol. I, No. 2, May, 1952.

"Hatteras Inlet Expedition," Report of the Joint Committee on the Conduct of the War, Part III, Washington, 1863.

HAVEN, FRANKLIN, JR., "The Conduct of McClellan at Alexandria in August, 1862," Vol. II, The Military Historical Society of Massachusetts Papers, Boston, 1895.

HAWK, EMORY Q., Economic History of the South, New York, 1934.

HAWKINS, RUSH C., "Early Coast Operations in North Carolina," Battles and Leaders.

———, "Why Burnside did not renew the attack at Fredericksburg," Battles and Leaders.

HAWLEY, JOSEPH R., "Comments on General Jones's paper by Joseph T. Hawley, Brevet Major General U.S.C.," Battles and Leaders.

HAY, JOHN, Letters of John Hay and Extracts from Diary, Washington, 1908, printed but not published.

———, Lincoln and the Civil War in the Diaries and Letters of John Hay, selected by Tyler Dennett, New York, 1939.

———, "A Young Hero; Personal Reminiscences of Colonel E. E. Ellsworth," *McClure's Magazine,* March, 1896.

HAY, THOMAS ROBSON, "Hood's Tennessee Campaign," Battles and Leaders.

HAYES, JOHN D., "Decision at Drewry's Bluff," *Civil War Times,* Vol. III, No. 2, May, 1961.

HAYNES, MARTIN A., A History of the Second Regiment, New Hampshire Volunteer Infantry in the War of the Rebellion, New Hampshire, 1892.

HAYS, GILBERT A., Under the Red Patch, Story of the 63rd Regiment Pennsylvania Volunteers, Pittsburgh, 1908.

HAYS, ROBERT D., and RICHARD L. FARRELLY, JR., Fort Gaines Under Two Flags 1861–1865 and the Battle of Mobile Bay, Dauphin Island, Alabama, 1955.

HAZARD, R. G., Our Resources, London, 1864.

HAZEN, W. E., A Narrative of Military Service, Boston, 1885.

HEAD, THOMAS A., Campaigns and Battles of the Sixteenth Regiment Tennessee Volunteers, Nashville, Tennessee, 1885.

HEADLEY, JOHN W., Confederate Operations in Canada and New York, New York, 1906.

HEATON, N., "Personal Recollections of Sherman's March to the Sea," Hutchins, E. R., The War of the Sixties, New York, 1912.

HEBERT, WALTER E., Fighting Joe Hooker, Indianapolis, 1944.

HEDLEY, F. Y., Marching Through Georgia, Pen Pictures of Everyday Life in General Sherman's Army from the beginning of the Atlanta Campaign until the close of the War, Chicago, 1890.

HEITMAN, FRANCIS B., Historical Register and Dictionary of the United States Army, two vols., Washington, 1903.

HELPER, HINTON ROWAN, The Impending Crisis of the South; How to Meet it, New York, 1857.

———, The Land of Gold, Baltimore, 1855.

———, The Negroes in Negroland, New York, 1868.

———, Nojoque, Question for a Continent, New York, 1867.

———, Noonday Exigencies in America, New York, 1871.

HEMSTREET, WILLIAM, "Little Things about Big Generals," Addresses delivered before the Commandery of the State of New York, of the Military Order of the Loyal Legion of the United States, second series, edited by A. Noel Blakeman, Vol. III, New York, 1903.

HENDERSON, G. F. R., The Civil War, A Soldier's View, A Collection of Civil War Writings by Colonel G. F. R. Henderson, edited by Jay Luvaas, Chicago, 1958.

———, Stonewall Jackson and the American Civil War, New York, 1949.

HENDRICK, BURTON J., Statesmen of the Lost Cause, New York, 1939.

HENRY, ROBERT SELPH, As They Saw Forrest, Jackson, Tennessee, 1958.

——, "Chattanooga and the War," *Tennessee Historical Quarterly,* Vol. XIX, No. 3, September, 1960.

——, First with the Most Forrest, Indianapolis, 1944.

——, The Story of the Confederacy, New York, 1943.

——, The Story of Reconstruction, Indianapolis, 1938.

HERNDON, WILLIAM H., and JESSE W. WEIK, Life of Lincoln, edited by Paul M. Angle, Cleveland, 1949.

HESSELTINE, WILLIAM BEST, Civil War Prisons: A Study in War Psychology, Columbus, Ohio, 1930.

——, Lincoln and the War Governors, New York, 1948.

——, Lincoln's Plan of Reconstruction, Confederate Centennial Studies, No. 13, Tuscaloosa, Alabama, 1960.

——, The South in American History, New York, 1951.

——, Ulysses S. Grant, Politician, New York, 1935.

HESSELTINE, WILLIAM BEST, and HAZEL C. WOLFE, The Blue and the Gray on the Nile, Chicago, 1961.

HETH, HENRY, "Letter on Gettysburg," *Southern Historical Society Papers,* Vol. IV, No. 4, October 1877.

HEYSINGER, ISAAC W., Antietam and the Maryland and Virginia Campaigns of 1862, New York, 1912.

HIGGINSON, THOMAS WENTWORTH, Army Life in a Black Regiment, Boston, 1900.

——, "The First Black Regiment," *Outlook,* July 2, 1898.

——, Letters and Journals, 1921.

HILL, D. H., "Battle of South Mountain or Boonsboro," Battles and Leaders.

——, "Chickamauga, The Great Battle of the West," Battles and Leaders.

——, "Lee's Attacks North of the Chickahominy," Battles and Leaders.

——, "The Lost Dispatch," *The Land We Love,* Vol. IV, February, 1868.

——, "The Lost Dispatch, Letter from General D. H. Hill," *Southern Historical Society Papers,* Vol. XIII, January–December, 1885.

——, "McClellan's Change of Base and Malvern Hill," Battles and Leaders.

HILL, D. H., JR., North Carolina, Confederate Military History, Vol. IV, Atlanta, 1899.

HILL, FREDERICK STANHOPE, Twenty Years at Sea, Boston, 1893.

HILL, JIM DAN, Sea Dogs of the Sixties, Minneapolis, 1935.

HINKLEY, JULIAN WISNER, A Narrative of Service with the Third Wisconsin Infantry, Madison, 1912.

HINMAN, WILBUR F., The Story of the Sherman Brigade, n.p., 1897.

HINN, RICHARD J., John Brown and His Men, New York, 1904.

Historic Harper's Ferry, pamphlet, Baltimore, n.d.

Historic Lexington, Anderson House and Lexington Battlefield Foundation, pamphlet, Lexington, Missouri, 1958.

Historic New Berne, Guide Book, New Berne, North Carolina, 1954.

History of America in Documents, Part III, The Pre-Civil War Period to the Twentieth Century, Philadelphia, 1951.

History of La Fayette County, Missouri, n.a., Missouri Historical Society, 1881.

History of Tennessee, n.a., Nashville, 1887.

HITCHCOCK, ETHAN ALLEN, Fifty Years in Camp and Field, New York, 1909.

HITCHCOCK, HENRY, Marching with Sherman, Passages from Letters and Campaigns, Diaries of Henry Hitchcock, edited by M. A. DeWolfe Howe, New Haven, Connecticut, 1927.

HITCHCOCK, N. H., "Recollections of a Participant in the Charge," Battles and Leaders.

Hitchcock's Chronological Record of the American Civil War, New York, 1866.

HITE, CORNELIUS, "The Size of the Confederate Army," *Current History,* Vol. VIII, No. 2, May, 1923.

Hobart-Hampton, Augustus Charles, Hobart Pasha, Blockade Running, Slave Hunting and War and Sport in Turkey, edited by Horace Kephart, New York, 1915.

HODDER, FRANK HEYWOOD, Genesis of the Kansas-Nebraska Act, Madison, Wisconsin, 1912.

———, Some Aspects of the English Bill for the Admission of Kansas, Washington, 1908.

HOEHLING, A. A., Last Train from Atlanta, New York, 1958.

HOGAN, J. T., "Reminiscences of the Siege of Vicksburg," *Southern Historical Society Papers,* Vol. XI, Nos. 4 and 5, April and May, 1883; Vol. XI, No. 7, July, 1883; and Vol. XI, No. 11, November, 1883.

HOKE, JACOB, The Great Invasion of 1863; or General Lee in Pennsylvania, New York, 1959.

HOLCOMBE, RETURN IRA, and ADAMS, An Account of the Battle of Wilson's Creek or Oak Hills, Springfield, Missouri, 1883.

HOLDEN, EDGAR, "The Albemarle and the Sassacus," Battles and Leaders.

HOLLAND, CECIL FLETCHER, Morgan and His Raiders, New York, 1942.

HOLLISTER, OVANDO J., Boldly They Rode, Lakewood, Colorado, 1949.

HOLLOWAY, J. M., History of Kansas, Lafayette, Indiana, 1888.

HOLMES, OLIVER WENDELL, JR., Touched with Fire, Letters and Diary of Oliver Wendell Holmes, Jr., edited by Mark DeWolfe Howe, Cambridge, Massachusetts, 1946.

HOLST, DR. H. VON, John C. Calhoun, Boston, 1883.

HOLT, ALBERT C., The Economic and Social Beginnings of Tennessee, Nashville, 1923.

HOLZMAN, ROBERT S., Stormy Ben Butler, New York, 1954.

HOMANS, JOHN, "The Red River Expedition," Vol. VIII, Military Historical Society of Massachusetts Papers, Boston, 1910.

HOOD, J. B., Advance and Retreat, New Orleans, 1880.

———, "The Defense of Atlanta," Battles and Leaders.

———, "Invasion of Tennessee," Battles and Leaders.

HOOKER, CHARLES E., Mississippi, Confederate Military History, Vol. VII, Atlanta, 1899.

HOPKINS, ARCHIBALD, Letters from the Civil War Front, *The Military Engineer,* Vol. XX, No. 112, July–August, 1928.

HOPKINS, VINCENT C., S.J., Dred Scott's Case, New York, 1951.

HOPLEY, CATHERINE S., Life in the South from the Commencement of the War by a Blockaded British Subject, two vols., London, 1863.

HOPPIN, JAMES MASON, Life of Admiral Foote, Rear Admiral United States Navy, New York, 1894.

HOPPIN, WILLIAM W., The Peace Conference of 1861, Providence, Rhode Island, 1903.

HORAN, JAMES D., Confederate Agent, New York, 1954.

HORN, STANLEY, The Army of Tennessee, Indianapolis, 1941.

———, The Decisive Battle of Nashville, Baton Rouge, 1959.

———, Gallant Rebel, The Fabulous Cruise of the Shenandoah, New Brunswick, New Jersey, 1949.

———, "Most Decisive Battle of the War," *Civil War Times,* Vol. III, No. 8, December, 1961.

HOSES, LEWIS M., "The Campaign of Selma," Sketches of War History 1861–1865, Ohio Commandery of the Military Order of the Loyal Legion of the United States, Vol. I, Cincinnati, Ohio, 1888.

HOTCHKISS, JED., Virginia, Vol. III, Confederate Military History, Atlanta, 1899.

HOTCHKISS, JED., and WILLIAM ALLAN, The Battlefields of Virginia, Chancellorsville, New York, 1867.

HOUGHTON, CHARLES B., "In the Crater," Battles and Leaders.

HOUSTON, DAVID FRANKLIN, A Critical Study of Nullification in South Carolina, Cambridge, 1896.

HOWARD, JOHN RAYMOND, Remembrance of Things Past, A Familiar Chronicle of Kinsfolk and Friends Worthwhile, New York, 1925.

HOWARD, MCHENRY, "Notes and Recollections of the Opening of the Campaign of 1864," Vol. IV, Military Historical Society of Massachusetts Papers, Boston, 1905.

———, Recollections of a Maryland Confederate Soldier and Staff Officer under Johnston, Jackson and Lee, Baltimore, 1914.

HOWARD, OLIVER OTIS, Autobiography of Oliver Otis Howard, two vols., New York, 1907.

———, "The Eleventh Corps at Chancellorsville," Battles and Leaders.

———, "Sherman's Advance from Atlanta," Battles and Leaders.

———, "The Struggle for Atlanta," Battles and Leaders.

HOWE, D. WATSON, "On the Field of Fredericksburg," Annals of the War.

HOWE, DANIEL WAIT, Political History of Secession, New York, 1914.

HUBBARD, JOHN MILTON, "Private Hubbard's Notes," from R. S. Henry, As They Saw Forrest, Jackson, Tennessee, 1958.

HUEY, PENNOCK, J. EDWARD CAMPBELL, and ANDREW B. WELLS, "The Charge of the Ninth Pennsylvania Cavalry," Battles and Leaders.

HUGHES, M. C., JR., "Hardee's Defense of Savannah," *The Georgia Historical Quarterly,* Vol. XLVII, No. 2, March, 1963.

HULSTON, JOHN F., "West Point at Wilson's Creek," *Civil War History,* Vol. I, No. 4, December, 1955.

HUMPHREYS, ANDREW A., The Virginia Campaign of '64 and '65, New York, 1883.

HUNDLEY, D. R., Social Relations in our Southern States, New York, 1860.

HUNT, AURORA, The Army of the Pacific, Its Operations in California, Texas, Arizona, New Mexico, Utah, Nevada, Oregon, Washington, Plains' Region, Mexico, etc., 1860–1865, Glendale, California, 1951.

HUNT, H. J., "The First Day at Gettysburg," Battles and Leaders.

———, "The Second Day at Gettysburg," Battles and Leaders.

——, "The Third Day at Gettysburg," Battles and Leaders.

HUNTER, R. W., "Men of Virginia at Ball's Bluff, *Southern Historical Society Papers,* Vol. XXXIV, 1906.

HUNTER, R. M. T., "The Peace Commission of 1865," *Southern Historical Society Papers,* Vol. III, No. 4, April, 1877.

HUNTINGTON, JAMES F., "The Artillery at Hazel Grove," Battles and Leaders.

——, "The Battle of Chancellorsville," Vol. III, Military Historical Society of Massachusetts Papers, Boston, 1905.

——, "Operations in the Shenandoah Valley from Winchester to Port Republic, March 10 to June 9, 1862," Vol. I, Military Historical Society of Massachusetts Papers, Boston, 1895.

HUNTON, EPPA, Autobiography, Richmond, Virginia, 1933.

HUSE, CALEB, The Supplies for the Confederacy, How they were obtained in Europe and how paid for, Boston, 1904.

HUSSEY, GEORGE, and WILLIAM DODD, History of the Ninth Regiment N.Y.S.M.-N.G.S., New York (Eighty-third New York Volunteers), New York, 1889.

HUTCHINS, E. R., The War of the Sixties, New York, 1912.

IMBODEN, JOHN D., "The Battle of New Market, Virginia, May 15, 1864," Battles and Leaders.

——, "The Confederate Retreat from Gettysburg," Battles and Leaders.

——, "Fire, Sword and the Halter," Annals of the War.

——, "Jackson at Harper's Ferry in 1861," Battles and Leaders.

——, "Stonewall Jackson in the Shenandoah," Battles and Leaders.

INGERSOLL, L. D., A History of the War Department of the United States, Washington, 1879.

INGRAHAM, CHARLES A., Ellsworth and the Zouaves of '61, Chicago, 1925.

"Invasion of New Mexico," Report of the Joint Committee on the Conduct of the War, Part III, Washington, 1863.

IOBST, RICHARD, Battle of New Berne, Raleigh, North Carolina, 1962.

IRWIN, RICHARD B., "Ball's Bluff and the Arrest of General Stone," Battles and Leaders.

——, "The Capture of Fort Hudson," Battles and Leaders.

——, "The Case of Fitz John Porter," Battles and Leaders.

——, "Land Operations Against Mobile," Battles and Leaders.

——, "Military Operations in Louisiana in 1862." Battles and Leaders.

——, "The Red River Campaign," Battles and Leaders.

——, "The Removal of McClellan," Battles and Leaders.

Issues of the Campaign, Shall the North Vote for a Disunion Peace, Chicago *Tribune* Campaign Document No. 2, 1864.

JACKSON, HUNTINGTON W., "The Battle of Chancellorsville," Military Essays and Recollections, Vol. II, Illinois Commandery of the Military Order of the Loyal Legion of the United States, Chicago, 1894.

——, "Sedgwick at Fredericksburg and Salem Heights," Battles and Leaders.

JACKSON, JAMES W., Life of, The Alexandria Hero, the Slayer of Ellsworth, the First Martyr in the Cause of Southern Independence, Richmond, 1862.

JACKSON, MARY ANNA, Life and Letters of General Thomas J. Jackson, New York, 1892.

——, Memoirs of Stonewall Jackson, Louisville, 1895.

JAMES, ALFRED P., "The Strategy of Concentration as used by the Confederate Forces in the Mississippi Valley in the Spring of 1862," Mississippi Valley Historical Association Proceedings, Vol. X, Part 2, 1919–20.

JAMES, MARQUIS, The Raven, A Biography of Sam Houston, Indianapolis, 1929.

JEFFERSON, THOMAS, Notes on the State of Virginia, Newark, 1801.

JENNINGS, ARTHUR H., "Confederate Forces in the Civil War," *Current History,* Vol. XX, No. 1, April, 1924.

JERVEY, THEODORE D., "Charleston during the Civil War," Annual Report of the American History Association for the Year 1913, Vol. I, Washington, 1915.

JOHN, DON D., The Great Indiana-Ohio Raid by Brigadier General John Hunt Morgan and his Men, Louisville, Kentucky, n.d.

JOHN, EVAN, Atlantic Impact 1861, New York, 1952.

John Brown Invasion, n.a., Boston, 1860.

JOHNSON, ADAM R., The Partisan Rangers of the Confederate States Army, edited by William J. Davis, Louisville, Kentucky, 1904.

JOHNSON, ALLEN, Stephen A. Douglas, A Study in American Politics, New York, 1908.

JOHNSON, BRADLEY T., "Memoirs of the First Maryland Regiment," *Southern Historical Society Papers,* Vol. X, Nos. 1, 2, 4, January and February, 1882, and April, 1882.

——, "My Ride Around Charleston in 1864," *Southern Historical Society Papers.* Vol. XXX, 1902.

JOHNSON, BRADLEY T., and HENRY KYD DOUGLAS, "Stonewall Jackson's Intentions at Harper's Ferry," *Southern Historical Society Papers,* Vol. IV, No. 4, October, 1877.

JOHNSON, CHARLES B., The Presidential Campaign of 1860, Springfield, 1927.

JOHNSON, JOHN, "The Confederate Defense of Fort Sumter," Battles and Leaders.

——, The Defense of Charleston Harbor including Fort Sumter and the Adjacent Islands, 1863–1865, Charleston, 1890.

JOHNSON, LUDWELL H., Red River Campaign, Politics and Cotton in the Civil War, Baltimore, 1958.

JOHNSON, RICHARD W., Memoir of Major General George M. Thomas, Philadelphia, 1881.

JOHNSON, ROSSITER, Campfire and Battlefield, History of the Conflict and Campaigns of the Great Civil War in the United States, New York, n.d.

JOHNSON, W. FLETCHER, Life of William Tecumseh Sherman, Late Retired General U.S.A., Philadelphia, 1891.

Johnsonville, Battle of, Tennessee Historical Commission and Nashville *Banner,* Nashville, n.d.

JOHNSTON, A. S., "Correspondence Between General A. S. Johnston and Governor Isham G. Harris," *Southern Historical Society Papers,* Vol. IV, No. 4, October, 1877.

——, "Letter to General Cooper," *Southern Historical Society Papers,* Vol. III, No. 3, March, 1877.

JOHNSTON, CHARLES, "Attack on Fort Gilmer," *Southern Historical Society Papers,* Vol. I, No. 6, June, 1876.

797

JOHNSTON, J. D., "The Battle of Mobile Bay," *Southern Historical Society Papers*, Vol. IX, No. 10, 1881.

——, "The Ram Tennessee at Mobile Bay," Battles and Leaders.

JOHNSTON, JOSEPH E., "Jefferson Davis and the Mississippi Campaigns," Battles and Leaders.

——, "Manassas to Seven Pines," Battles and Leaders.

——, Narrative of Military Operations, New York, 1874.

——, "Responsibilities of the First Bull Run," Battles and Leaders.

——, "Opposing Sherman's Advance to Atlanta," Battles and Leaders.

JOHNSTON, R. M., Bull Run, Its Strategy and Tactics, Boston, 1913.

JOHNSTON, RICHARD MALCOLM, and WILLIAM HAND BROWN, Life of Alexander H. Stephens, Philadelphia, 1878.

JOHNSTON, ROBERT UNDERWOOD, and C. C. BUEL, Battles and Leaders of the Civil War, four vols., New York, 1887.

JOHNSTON, WILLIAM PRESTON, "Albert Sidney Johnston at Shiloh," Battles and Leaders.

——, The Life of General Albert Sidney Johnston, New York, 1878.

JOINVILLE, PRINCE DE, The Army of the Potomac, its Organization, its Commander and its Campaign with notes by William Henry Hurlbert, New York, 1862.

JONES, ARCHER, Confederate Strategy from Shiloh to Vicksburg, Baton Rouge, 1961.

——, "The Gettysburg Decision," *Virginia Magazine of History and Biography*, June, 1960.

JONES, CATESBY ap R., "Services of the Virginia (Merrimac)," *Southern Historical Society Papers*, Vol. XI, Nos. 2 and 3, February and March, 1883.

JONES, CHARLES C., The Siege of Savannah, Albany, 1874.

JONES, EVAN ROWLAND, Lincoln, Stanton and Grant, London, 1875.

JONES, IREDELL, "Letters from Fort Sumter in 1862, 1863," *Southern Historical Society Papers*, Vol. XII, No. 5, March, 1884.

——, compiler, "The Kilpatrick-Dahlgren Raid against Richmond," *Southern Historical Society Papers*, Vol. XXII, January–December, 1895.

JONES, J. WILLIAM, Christ in the Camp or Religion in the Confederate Army, Atlanta, 1904.

——, "Reminiscences of the Army of Northern Virginia," *Southern Historical Society Papers*, Vol. IX, Nos. 7 and 8, July and August, 1881.

——, "Reminiscences of the Army of Northern Virginia, How Frémont and Shields caught Stonewall Jackson," *Southern Historical Society Papers*, Vol. IX, No. 6, June, 1881.

JONES, JAMES F., "The Battle of Atlanta and McPherson's Successor," *Civil War History*, Vol. VII, No. 4, December, 1961.

JONES, JENKIN LLOYD, An Artilleryman's Diary, Wisconsin Historical Commission, Madison, February, 1914.

JONES, JOHN BEAUCHAMP, A Rebel War Clerk's Diary, two vols., Philadelphia, 1886.

——, A Rebel War Clerk's Diary, condensed, edited and annotated by Earl Schenck Miers, New York, 1958.

JONES, JOSEPH, "Confederate Losses during the War—correspondence between Dr. Joseph Jones and General Samuel Cooper, *Southern Historical Society Papers,* Vol. VII, No. 6, June, 1879.

JONES, ROBERT HUGH, The Civil War in the Northwest, Nebraska, Wisconsin, Iowa, Minnesota, and the Dakotas, Norman, Oklahoma, 1960.

JONES, SAMUEL, "The Battle of Olustee or Ocean Pond, Florida," Battles and Leaders.

——, The Siege of Charleston and the Operations of the South Atlantic Coast in the War Among the States, New York, 1911.

JONES, STACY V., "GOP, Centenarian," New York *Times Magazine,* February 19, 1956.

JONES, VIRGIL CARRINGTON, The Civil War at Sea, three vols., New York, 1960, 1961, 1962.

——, Nine Hours Before Richmond, New York, 1957.

——, Ranger Mosby, Chapel Hill, 1944.

JORDAN, DONALDSON, and EDWIN J. PRATT, Europe and the American Civil War, Boston, 1931.

JORDAN, THOMAS, "Letter to the Savannah Republican," *Southern Historical Society Papers,* Vol. VIII, Nos. 8 and 9, August and September, 1880.

——, "Notes of a Confederate Staff Officer at Shiloh," Battles and Leaders.

——, "Recollections of General Beauregard's Service in West Tennessee, in the Spring of 1862," *Southern Historical Society Papers,* Vol. VIII, Nos. 8 and 9, August and September, 1880.

——, "Sea Coast Defenses of South Carolina and Georgia," *Southern Historical Society Papers,* Vol. I, No. 6, June, 1876.

Journal of the Congress of the Confederate States of America, 1861–1865, seven vols., Washington, 1904–5.

Journal of the Convention of the People of South Carolina held 1860–1861, Charleston, 1861.

JUDD, DAVID W., The Story of the Thirty-Third N.Y.S. Volunteers, Rochester, New York, 1864.

JULIAN, ALLEN P., "From Dalton to Atlanta, Sherman vs. Johnston," *Civil War Times Illustrated,* Vol. XXI, No. 4, July, 1964.

——, Historic Fort McAllister, 1958.

"Kansas Affairs," House Report No. 200, 34th Congress, 1st Session, Vol. II, Washington, 1856.

"Kansas Constitution," House Report No. 377, 35th Congress, 1st Session, Vol. III, Washington, 1858.

KAUTZ, ALBERT, "Incidents of the Occupation of New Orleans," Battles and Leaders.

KEAN, ROBERT GARLICK HILL, Inside the Confederate Government, The Diary of Robert Garlick Hill Kean, edited by Edward Younger, New York, 1957.

KELEHER, WILLIAM A., Turmoil in New Mexico, 1846–1863, Santa Fe, New Mexico, 1952.

KELL, JOHN MCINTOSH, "Cruise and Combats of the 'Alabama,'" Battles and Leaders.

KELLER, ALLAN, Thunder at Harper's Ferry, Englewood, New Jersey, 1958.

KELLER, HELEN REX, The Dictionary of Dates, two vols., New York, 1934.

KELLEY, WILLIAM D., Lincoln and Stanton, New York, 1885.

KELLOGG, J. H., War Experiences and the Story of the Vicksburg Campaign from Milliken's Bend to July 4, 1853, n.p., 1913.

KELLOGG, SANFORD, The Shenandoah Valley and Virginia 1861–1865, A War Study, Washington, 1903.

KELLY, ALFRED H., and WINFRED A. HARBISON, The American Constitution, Its Origins and Development, two vols., New York, 1948.

KELLY, R. M., "Holding Kentucky for the Union," Battles and Leaders.

KENNEDY, ELIJAH R., The Contest for California in 1861, How Colonel E. D. Baker saved the Pacific States to the Union, Boston, 1912.

KENNON, L. W. V., "The Valley Campaign of 1864, A Military Study," annotated by Hazard Stevens, Vol. VI, Military Historical Society of Massachusetts Papers, Boston, 1907.

KERBY, ROBERT LEE, The Confederate Invasion of New Mexico and Arizona, 1861–1865, Los Angeles, 1958.

KERSHAW, J. B., "Kershaw's Brigade at Fredericksburg," Battles and Leaders.

———, "Richard Kirklin, the Human Hero of Fredericksburg," *Southern Historical Society Papers,* Vol. VIII, No. 4, April, 1880.

KEY, WILLIAM, The Battle of Atlanta and the Georgia Campaign, New York, 1958.

KILLEBREW, J. B., Life and Character of James Cartwright Warner, Nashville, 1891.

———, Resources of Tennessee, First and Second Reports of the Bureau of Agriculture for the State of Tennessee, Introduction to the Resources of Tennessee, Nashville, 1894.

KILMER, GEORGE L., "The Dash Into the Crater," *Century Magazine,* Vol. XXXIV, No. 5, September, 1887.

———, "Gordon's Attack at Fort Stedman," Battles and Leaders.

KIMBALL, NATHAN, "Fighting Jackson at Kernstown," Battles and Leaders.

KIMBALL, WILLIAM J., "The Bread Riot in Richmond in 1863," *Civil War History,* Vol. VII, No. 2, June, 1961.

KING, CHARLES, "In Vindication of General Rufus King," Battles and Leaders.

KING, DAVID H., History of the Ninety-Third Regiment, New York Volunteer Infantry, Milwaukee, Wisconsin, 1895.

KING, HORATIO, "James Buchanan," *The Galaxy,* October, 1870.

———, "The Trent Affair," *Magazine of American History,* March, 1886.

KING, JOSEPH R., "The Fort Fisher Campaigns 1864–1865," United States Naval Institute Proceedings, August, 1961.

KING, WILLARD, Lincoln's Manager, David Davis, Cambridge, Massachusetts, 1960.

KINNEY, JAMES C., "An August Morning with Farragut," *Scribner's Magazine,* Vol. XXII, No. 2, June, 1881.

———, "Farragut at Mobile Bay," Battles and Leaders.

KINSLEY, PHILIP, The Chicago *Tribune,* Its First Hundred Years, Vol. I, 1847–1865, New York, 1943.

KIRKE, EDMUND, Down in Tennessee and Back by Way of Richmond, New York, 1864.

KIRKLAND, CAROLINE, Chicago Yesterdays, A Sheaf of Reminiscences, Chicago, 1919.

KIRKLAND, EDWARD CHASE, The Peacemakers of 1864, New York, 1927.

KLEMENT, FRANK L., "'Brick' Pomeroy, Copperhead and Curmudgeon," *Wisconsin Magazine of History,* Winter, 1951.

———, The Copperheads in the Middle West, Chicago, 1960.

KNIFFEN, GILBERT C., "The Battle of Stone's River," Battles and Leaders.

———, "The Last Tennessee Campaign, September, 1863," Vol. VII, Military Historical Society of Massachusetts Papers, Boston, 1908.

———, "Manoeuvering Bragg out of Tennessee," Battles and Leaders.

KNOX, THOMAS W., Camp-Fire and Cotton-Fields, Southern Adventure in Time of War, New York, 1865.

KOERNER, GUSTAVE, Memoirs of Gustave Koerner, 1809–1896, two vols., edited by Thomas J. McCormack, Cedar Rapids, Iowa, 1909.

KORN, BERTRAM W., American Jewry and the Civil War, Philadelphia, 1951.

KORNGOLD, RALPH, Thaddeus Stevens: A Being Darkly Wise and Rudely Great, New York, 1955.

KREIDBERG, MARVIN A., and MERTON G. HENRY, History of Military Mobilization in the United States Army, 1775–1945, Washington, July, 1955.

KREUTZER, WILLIAM, The Ninety-Eighth New York Volunteers in the War of 1861, Philadelphia, 1878.

KULL, IRVING S., and NELL M. KULL, A Short Chronology of American History, New Brunswick, New Jersey, 1952.

KURTZ, WILBUR G., The Atlanta Cyclorama, Published by the City of Atlanta, Atlanta, 1954.

———, "The Battles Around Atlanta: Hood versus Sherman," *Civil War Times Illustrated,* Vol. III, No. 4, July, 1964.

———, Map of Atlanta showing Major Engagements of Summer of 1864, Atlanta Chamber of Commerce, 1938.

LAMB, WILLIAM, "The Defense of Fort Fisher," Battles and Leaders.

———, "Defense at Fort Fisher, North Columbia," Vol. IX, Military Historical Society of Massachusetts Papers, Boston, 1912.

LAMERS, WILLIAM E., The Edge of Glory, A Biography of General William S. Rosecrans, New York, 1961.

LAMON, WARD HILL, Recollections of Abraham Lincoln 1847–1865, edited by Dorothy Lamon, Chicago, 1895.

LANDRY, ERNEST ADAM, The History of Forts Jackson and St. Philip with Special Emphasis on the Civil War Period, Thesis, Louisiana State University, Baton Rouge, Louisiana.

Land We Love, The, various issues.

LANE, JAMES M., "History of Lane's North Carolina Brigade," *Southern Historical Society Papers,* Vol. VIII, Nos. 10, 11, and 12, October, November, and December, 1880.

LANG, THEODORE F., Loyal West Virginia from 1861 to 1865, Baltimore, 1895.

LANGDON, LOOMIS L., "The Stars and Stripes in Richmond," *Century Magazine,* Vol. XL, No. 2, June, 1890.

LARNED, J. G., History for Ready Reference, Springfield, Massachusetts, 1901.

LATTIMORE, RALSTON B., Fort Pulaski, National Monument, Georgia, National Park Service Historical Handbook Series No. 18, Washington, D.C., 1954.

LAW, E. M., "From the Wilderness to Cold Harbor," Battles and Leaders.

———, "On the Confederate Right at Gaines' Mill," Battles and Leaders.

———, "The Struggle for Round Top," Battles and Leaders.

LAWTON, EBA ANDERSON, Major Robert Anderson and Fort Sumter 1861, New York, 1911.

LAY, COLONEL J. F., "Reminiscences of the Powhatan Troop of Cavalry in 1861," *Southern Historical Society Papers*, Vol. VIII, 1880.

"Leading Confederates on the Battle of Gettysburg," *Southern Historical Society Papers*, Vol. V, Nos. 1 and 2, January and February, 1878.

LEAKE, JOSEPH B., "Campaign of the Army of the Frontier," Military Essays and Recollections, Vol. II, Illinois Commandery of the Military Order of the Loyal Legion of the United States, Chicago, 1891.

———, "Campaign of the Army of the Frontier," Military Essays and Recollections, Vol. II, Illinois Commandery of the Military Order of the Loyal Legion of the United States, Chicago, 1894.

LECONTE, EMMA, When the World Ended, edited by Earl Schenck Miers, New York, 1957.

LEDDY, ROBERT, "The First Shot on Fort Sumter," *The South Carolina Historical and Genealogical Magazine*, July, 1911.

LE DUC, WILLIAM G., "The Little Steamboat that Opened the Cracker Line," Battles and Leaders.

LEE, ALVID, "The Battle of Cross Keys, Campaigning in the Mountain Department," *Magazine of American History*, May, 1886.

LEE, CASENOVE G., "Relative Numbers of the United States and Confederate States Armies," *Southern Historical Society Papers*, Vol. XXXII, 1904.

LEE, FITZHUGH, "Chancellorsville," *Southern Historical Society Papers*, Vol. VII, No. 10, December, 1879.

———, General Lee, New York, 1894.

———, "Reply to Longstreet," *Southern Historical Society Papers*, Vol. V, No. 4, April, 1878.

———, Speech of General Fitzhugh Lee at A.N.V. Banquet, October 25th, 1875.

LEE, ROBERT E., "General Lee's Farewell Address to his Army, including comments by Charles Marshall," Battles and Leaders.

———, Lee's Dispatches to Jefferson Davis, edited by Douglas Southall Freeman and Grady McWhiney. New York, 1957.

———, "Letter of R. E. Lee to Governor John Letcher," *Southern Historical Society Papers*, Vol. I, No. 6, June, 1876.

———, Recollections and Letters of General Robert E. Lee, New York, 1904, also Garden City, New York, 1924.

———, The Wartime Papers of, edited by Clifford Dowdey, Virginia Civil War Commission, Boston, 1861.

LEE, STEPHEN D., "The First Step in the War," Battles and Leaders.

———, "Letter on Fort Sumter," *Southern Historical Society Papers*, November, 1883.

———, "Sherman's Meridian Expedition and Sooy Smith's Raid to West Point," *Southern Historical Society Papers*, Vol. VIII, No. 2, February, 1880.

LEECH, MARGARET, Reveille in Washington, Garden City, New York, 1945.

LEFLER, HUGH TALMADGE, Southern Sketches, No. I, Hinton Rowan Helper, Advocate of a White America, Charlottesville, Virginia, 1935.

LEIB, CHARLES, Nine Months in the Quartermaster's Department; or the Chances of Making a Million, Cincinnati, 1862.

LEIGH, BENJAMIN WATKINS, "Letter May 12, 1863 from camp near Hamilton's Crossing, Spotsylvania Courthouse, Virginia," *Southern Historical Society Papers*, Vol. IV, No. 5, November, 1877.

LELAND, EDWIN ALBERT, Organization and Administration of the Louisiana Army during the Civil War, Thesis, Tulane University, New Orleans, 1938.

LETCHER, JOHN, "Official Correspondence of Governor John Letcher," *Southern Historical Society Papers*, Vol. I, No. 6, June, 1876.

Letters of Loyal Soldiers and how Douglas Democrats will vote, n.p., n.d.

LEVIN, L. C., Speech of Mr. L. C. Levin of Pennsylvania on the Subject of Altering the Neutralization Laws, n.p., 1845.

LEWIS, CHARLES LEE, Admiral Franklin Buchanan, Baltimore, 1929.

——, David Glasgow Farragut, two vols., Annapolis, 1943.

LEWIS, LLOYD, Captain Sam Grant, Boston, 1950.

——, Sherman, Fighting Prophet, New York, 1932.

LIDDELL HART, B. H., Sherman, Soldier, Realist, American, New York, 1929.

Life and Reminiscences of General W. T. Sherman, n.a., Baltimore, 1881.

LINCOLN, ABRAHAM, The Collected Works of, edited by Roy Basler, eight vols., New Brunswick, New Jersey, 1953.

Lincoln Catechism, The, Whereby the Eccentricities and Beauties of Despotism are fully set forth, New York, 1864.

Lincoln Day by Day, A Chronology, 1808–1865, three vols., Earl Schenck Miers, editor in chief, C. Percy Powell, Washington, 1960.

Lincoln's Treatment of Grant, New York, 1864.

LINDER, USHER F., Reminiscences of the Early Bench and Bar of Illinois, Chicago, 1879.

LINDSLEY, JOHN BERRIEN, editor, The Military Annals of Tennessee, Nashville, 1886.

LIVERMORE, MARY A., My Story of the War, Hartford, Connecticut, 1888.

LIVERMORE, THOMAS L., "The Conduct of Generals McClellan and Halleck in August, 1862 and the Case of Fitz-John Porter," Vol. II, Military Historical Society of Massachusetts Papers, Boston, 1895.

——"The Failure to take Pittsburgh June 15, 1864," Vol. V, Military Historical Society of Massachusetts Papers, Boston, 1906.

——, "The Generalship of the Appomattox Campaign," Vol. VI, Military Historical Society of Massachusetts Papers, Boston, 1907.

——, "The Gettysburg Campaign," Vol. XIII, Military Historical Society of Massachusetts Papers, Boston, 1913.

——, "Grant's Campaign against Lee," Vol. IV, Military Historical Society of Massachusetts Papers, Boston, 1906.

——, "The Mine Run Campaign, November, 1863," Vol. XIV, Military Historical Society of Massachusetts Papers, Boston, 1905.

——, Number and Losses in the Civil War in America 1861–1865, 2nd edition, Boston, 1902.

————, "The Siege and Relief of Chattanooga," Vol. VIII, Military Historical Society of Massachusetts Papers, Boston, 1910.

LIVERMORE, WILLIAM R., The Story of the Civil War, The Campaigns of 1863, New York, 1913.

————, "The Vicksburg Campaign," Vol. IX, Military Historical Society of Massachusetts Papers, Boston, 1912.

LLOYD, ARTHUR YOUNG, The Slavery Controversy, Chapel Hill, 1939.

LOBDELL, JARED C., "Nathaniel Lyon and the Battle of Wilson's Creek," *The Bulletin,* Missouri Historical Society, October, 1960.

LOCKETT, S. H., "The Defense of Vicksburg," Battles and Leaders.

————, "Surprise and Withdrawal at Shiloh," Battles and Leaders.

London *Times,* Uncle Tom in England; The London *Times* on *Uncle Tom's Cabin,* A Review from the London *Times* of Friday, September 3, 1852, pamphlet, New York, 1852.

LONG, A. L., "Lee's West Virginia Campaign," Annals of the War.

————, "Letter on Gettysburg," *Southern Historical Society Papers,* Vol. IV, No. 1, July, 1877.

————, Memoirs of Robert E. Lee, New York, 1887.

————, "Sea Coast Defenses of South Carolina and Georgia," *Southern Historical Society Papers,* Vol. I, No. 2, February, 1896.

LONG, E. B., "Dear Julia, Two Grant Letters," *Civil War History,* Vol. I, No. 1, March, 1955.

————, "Our Forgotten War with Japan," *Blue Book,* May, 1950.

LONG, JOHN SHERMAN, "The Gosport Affair, 1861," *The Journal of Southern History,* May, 1937.

LONGSTREET, JAMES, "The Battle of Fredericksburg," Battles and Leaders.

————, From Manassas to Appomattox, Philadelphia, 1896.

————, "General James Longstreet's Account of the Campaign and Battle (Gettysburg)," *Southern Historical Society Papers,* Vol. V, No. 1–2, January–February, 1877.

————, "Lee in Pennsylvania," Annals of the War.

————, "Lee's Invasion of Maryland," Battles and Leaders.

————, "Lee's Right Wing at Gettysburg," Battles and Leaders.

————, "Our March against Pope," Battles and Leaders.

————, "The Seven Days," Battles and Leaders.

LONN, ELLA, Desertion During the Civil War, New York, 1928.

————, Salt as a Factor in the Confederacy, New York, 1933.

LORD, FRANCIS A., Civil War Collector's Encyclopedia, Harrisburg, Pennsylvania, 1963.

LORD, WILLIAM W., JR., "A Child at the Siege of Vicksburg," *Harper's Monthly Magazine,* Vol. CXVII, No. 703, December, 1908.

LOSSING, BENSON J., Pictorial History of the Civil War, three vols., Hartford, 1863.

LOTHROP, THORNTON KIRKLAND, William Henry Seward, Boston, 1896.

LUFF, WILLIAM M., "March of the Cavalry from Harper's Ferry, September 14, 1862," Military Essays and Recollections, Vol. II, Illinois Commandery of the Military Order of the Loyal Legion of the United States, Chicago, 1894.

LUNT, DOLLY SUMNER, Mrs. Thomas Burge, A Woman's Wartime Journal, An Account of the Passage over Georgia Plantation of Sherman's Army on the March to the Sea, New York, 1918.

LUTHIN, REINHARD, The First Lincoln Campaign, Cambridge, 1944.

LUVAAS, JAY, "Bentonville—Last Chance to Stop Sherman," *Civil War Times Illustrated*, Vol. II. No. 6, October, 1963.

——, "The Fall of Fort Fisher," *Civil War Times Illustrated*, Vol. III, No. 5, August, 1964.

——, "Johnston's Last Stand—Bentonville," *The North Carolina Historical Review*, Vol. XXXIII, No. 5, July, 1958.

LYKES, RICHARD WAYNE, Petersburg National Military Park, Virginia, National Park Service Historical Handbook No. 13, Washington, 1961.

LYMAN, THEODORE, "Crossing of the James and Advance on Petersburg," Vol. V, Military Historical Society of Massachusetts Papers, Boston, 1908.

——, Meade's Headquarters, 1863–1865, Letters of Colonel Theodore Lyman from the Wilderness to Appomattox, selected and edited by George G. Agassiz, Boston, 1922.

——, "Operations of the Army of the Potomac, June 5–15, 1864," Vol. V, Military Historical Society of Massachusetts Papers, Boston, 1906.

——, Review of the Reports of Colonel Haven and General Weld, Vol. II, Military Historical Society of Massachusetts Papers, Boston, 1895.

——, "Uselessness of the Maps Furnished to Staff of the Army of the Potomac Previous to the Campaign of 1864," Vol. IV, Military Historical Society of Massachusetts Papers, Boston, 1905.

LYSTER, HENRY F., Recollections of the Bull Run Campaign after Twenty-seven Years, A Paper read before the Michigan Commandery of the Military Order of the Loyal Legion of the United States, February 1st, 1887, Detroit, 1888.

LYTLE, ANDREW NELSON, Bedford Forrest and his Critter Company, New York, 1931.

MCALLISTER, ROBERT, "McAllister's Brigade at the Bloody Angle," Battles and Leaders.

MCBRIDE, ROBERT, Civil War Ironclads, Philadelphia, 1962.

MCCABE, JAMES D., JR., Life and Campaigns of General Robert E. Lee, Atlanta, 1866.

MCCABE, W. GORDON, "Defense of Petersburg," *Southern Historical Society Papers*, Vol. II, No. 6, December, 1876.

MCCALEB, WALTER, The Conquest of the West, New York, 1949.

MCCARTHY, CARLTON, "Origin of the Confederate Battle Flag," *Southern Historical Society Papers*, January–December, 1880.

MCCARTNEY, CLARENCE EDWARD, Little Mac, Philadelphia, 1940.

MCCAUSLAND, JOHN, "The Burning of Chambersburg," Annals of the War.

MCCLELLAN, CARSWELL, The Personal Memoirs and Military History of Ulysses S. Grant versus the Record of the Army of the Potomac, Boston, 1887.

MCCLELLAN, GEORGE B., "From the Peninsula to Antietam," Battles and Leaders.

——, McCellan's Own Story, New York, 1887.

——, The Mexican War Diary of General George B. McClellan, edited by William S. Myers, Princeton, New Jersey, 1917.

——, "The Peninsular Campaign," Battles and Leaders.

——, Report on the Organization and Campaigns of the Army of the Potomac, New York, 1864.

MCCLELLAN, H. B., I Rode with Jeb Stuart, Introduction and Notes by Burke Davis, Bloomington, 1958.

MCCLURE, A. K., Abraham Lincoln and Men of War Times, Philadelphia, 1892.

MCCLURG, ALEXANDER C., "The Last Chances of the Confederacy," Military Essays and Recollections, Vol. I, Illinois Commandery of the Military Order of the Loyal Legion of the United States, Chicago, 1891.

MCCORDOCK, ROBERT STANLEY, The Yankee Cheese Box, Philadelphia, 1938.

MCCORMICK, ROBERT R., The War Without Grant, New York, 1950.

MCCRADY, EDWARD, JR., "Gregg's Brigade of South Carolinians in the Second Brigade of Manassas," *Southern Historical Society Papers,* Vol. XIII, January–December, 1885.

MCCULLOCH, HUGH, Men and Measures of Half a Century, New York, 1888.

MCDONALD, MRS. CORNELIA (Peake), A Diary with Reminiscences of the War and Refugee Life in the Shenandoah Valley, 1860–1865, Nashville, 1935.

MCDOUGALL, MARION GLEASON, Fugitive Slaves (1819–1865), Boston, 1891.

MCELROY, JOHN, The Struggle for Missouri, Washington, 1913.

———, This was Andersonville, edited by Roy Meredith, New York, 1957.

MCGOWAN, J. E., "Morgan's Indiana and Ohio Raid," Annals of the War.

MCGREGOR, JAMES C., The Disruption of Virginia, New York, 1922.

MCKEE, IRVING, "Ben Hur" Wallace, The Life of General Lew Wallace, Berkeley, California, 1947.

MCKEE, JAMES COOPER, Narrative of the Surrender of a Command of United States Forces at Fort Fillmore, New Mexico, in July, A.D. 1861, at the Breaking out of the Civil War Between the North and the South, March, 1878.

MCKEE, THOMAS H., The National Conventions and Platforms of all Political Parties 1789 to 1905, Baltimore, 1906.

MCKIM, RANDOLPH, The Numerical Strength of the Confederate Army, New York, 1912.

———, A Soldier's Recollections, New York, 1910.

MCKINNEY, FRANCIS F., Education in Violence, The Life of George H. Thomas and the History of the Army of the Cumberland, Detroit, 1961.

MCKITRICK, ERIC L., Andrew Johnson and Reconstruction, Chicago, 1960.

MCLAWS, LAFAYETTE, "The Confederate Life at Fredericksburg," Battles and Leaders.

MCMAHON, M. T., "Cold Harbor," Battles and Leaders.

———, "The Death of General John Sedgwick," Battles and Leaders.

———, "From Gettysburg to the Coming of Grant," Battles and Leaders.

MCMASTER, F. W., "The Battle of the Crater, July 30, 1864," *Southern Historical Society Papers,* Vol. X, No. 3, March, 1882.

MCMASTER, JOHN BACH, A History of the People of the United States during Lincoln's Administration, New York, 1927.

———, A History of the People of the United States from the Revolution to the Civil War, 8 vols., New York, 1900.

MCPHERSON, EDWARD, The Political History of the United States of America during the Great Rebellion, Washington, 1865.

MCWHINEY, GRADY, "Controversy in Kentucky, Braxton Bragg's Campaign of 1862," *Civil War History,* Vol. VI, No. 1, March, 1960.

MACARTNEY, CLARENCE EDWARD, Little Mac; The Life of General George B. McClellan, Philadelphia, 1940.

Magazine of American History, various issues.

MAGRUDER, ALLAN B., "A Piece of Secret History, President Lincoln and the Virginia Convention of 1861," *Atlantic Monthly*, April, 1875.

MAHAN, A. T., Admiral Farragut, New York, 1916.

———, The Gulf and Inland Waters, The Navy in the Civil War, Vol. III, New York, 1883–85.

MALIN, JAMES C., John Brown and the Legend of 'Fifty-six, Philadelphia, 1942.

———, The Nebraska Question, 1852–54, Ann Arbor, Michigan, 1953.

MANN, ALBERT N., History of the Forty-Fifth Regiment of Massachusetts Volunteer Militia, The Cadet Regiment, Boston, 1908.

MANTON, H. J., (pseudonym for James Montgomery Bailey), Letters, Danbury, Connecticut, *Times*, n.d.

Manufactures of the United States in 1863, compiled from the original returns of the Eighth Census, Washington, 1865.

Maps, Selected Civil War Coast and Geodetic Survey, United States Department of Commerce, Washington, 1961.

MARGREITER, JOHN L., "Union Heroism at Pilot Knob Saved St. Louis from Attack," *Civil War Times Illustrated*, Vol. II, No. 9, January, 1964.

MARSHALL, ALBERT C., Army Life, from a Soldier's Journal, Joliet, Illinois, 1883.

MARSHALL, CHARLES, An Aide-de-Camp of Lee, being the papers of Colonel Charles Marshall, sometime Aide-de-Camp, Military Secretary and Assistant Adjutant General on the Staff of Robert E. Lee 1862–1865, edited by Sir Frederick Maurice, Boston, 1927.

MARSHALL, JOHN A., American Bastile, Philadelphia, 1864.

MARTHON, JOSEPH, "The Lashing of Admiral Farragut in the Rigging," Battles and Leaders.

MARTIN, T., "From Gettysburg to the Coming of Grant," Battles and Leaders.

MARTIN, THEODORE, The Life of His Royal Highness, The Prince Consort, five vols., New York, 1880.

MARTIN, W. T., "A Defense of General Bragg's Conduct at Chickamauga, *Southern Historical Society Papers*, Vol. XI, Nos. 4 and 5, April and May, 1883.

MARTYN, CARLOS, Wendell Phillips, The Agitator, New York, 1890.

MARVIN, EDWIN E., Fifth Regiment Connecticut Volunteers, published for the reunion, Association of the Regiment, Hartford, Connecticut, 1889.

MARX, KARL, and FREDERICK ENGELS, The Civil War in the United States, New York, 1937.

MASON, GEORGE, "Shiloh," Military Essays and Recollections, Vol. I, Illinois Commandery of the Military Order of the Loyal Legion of the United States, Chicago, 1891.

MASON, W. ROY, "Marching on Manassas," Battles and Leaders.

———, "Notes of a Confederate Staff Officer," Battles and Leaders.

"Massacre of Cheyenne Indians," Report of the Joint Committee on the Conduct of the War, Washington, D.C., 1865.

MASSEY, MARY ELIZABETH, Ersatz in the Confederacy, Columbia, South Carolina, 1952.

MAURICE, SIR FREDERICK, editor, An Aide-de-Camp of Lee, being the papers of Colonel Charles Marshall etc., Boston, 1927.

MAURY, D. H., "The Defense of Mobile in 1865," *Southern Historical Society Papers*, Vol. III, No. 1, January, 1877.

———, "Recollections of the Elkhorn Campaign," *Southern Historical Society Papers*, Vol. II, No. 4, October 1876.

———, "Recollections of Campaign against Grant in North Mississippi in 1862–1863, *Southern Historical Society Papers*, Vol. XIII, January–December, 1885.

———, "Sketch of General Richard Taylor," *Southern Historical Society Papers*, Vol. VII, No. 7, July, 1879.

———, Van Dorn, the Hero of Mississippi, Philadelphia, 1879.

MAURY, R. L., "The Battle of Williamsburg and the Charge of the Twenty-fourth Virginia of Early's Brigade," *Southern Historical Society Papers*, Vol. VIII, Nos. 6, 7, June–July, 1880.

MAXWELL, WILLIAM QUENTIN, Lincoln's Fifth Wheel, New York, 1956.

MEADE, GEORGE, The Life and Letters of George Gordon Meade, two vols., New York, 1913.

———, With Meade at Gettysburg, Philadelphia, 1930.

MEADOR, L. E., History of the Battle of Wilson Creek, Wilson Creek Camp No. 30, Department of Missouri, Sons of Union Veterans of the Civil War, Springfield, Missouri, 1938.

MEAGHER, FRANCIS F., "Last Days of the Sixty-ninth in Virginia," *The Irish American Historical Journal*, 1861.

MEARNS, DAVID C., The Lincoln Papers, two vols., Garden City, New York, 1948.

MEARNS, DAVID C., and LLOYD A. DUNLOP, Long Remembered, The Library of Congress, Washington, 1963.

Medical and Surgical History of the War of the Rebellion, prepared under direction of Surgeon General Joseph K. Barnes, six vols., Washington, 1875.

MEIGS, M. C., "The Relations of President Lincoln and Secretary Stanton to the Military Commanders in the Civil War," *The American Historical Review*, Vol. XXVI, No. 2, January, 1921.

MEMMINGER, R. W., "The Surrender of Vicksburg, A Defense of General Pemberton," *Southern Historical Society Papers*, Vol. XXI, Nos. 7, 8, 9, July and August, 1884.

MENEELY, A. HOWARD, The War Department, 1861, A Study in Mobilization and Administration, New York, 1928.

MEREDITH, ROY, Storm over Sumter, New York, 1957.

MEREDITH, WILLIAM T., "Farragut's Capture of New Orleans," Battles and Leaders.

MERRILL, JAMES M., "Personne Goes to Georgia; Five Civil War Letters, (of Felix Gregory DeFontaine)," *The Georgia Historical Quarterly*, Vol. XLIII, No. 2, June, 1959.

MERRILL, SAMUEL, The Seventieth Indiana Volunteer Infantry, Indianapolis, 1900.

MERRITT, DIXON L., A History of Tennessee and Tennesseans, Chicago, 1913.

MERRITT, WESLEY, "Note on the Surrender of Lee," *Century Magazine*, Vol. LXIII, No. 6, April, 1902.

MICHIE, PETER S., General McClellan, New York, 1901.

MIERS, EARL SCHENCK, The General Who Marched to Hell, New York, 1951.
———, The Great Rebellion, Cleveland, 1958.
———, The Web of Victory, New York, 1955.
MIERS, EARL SCHENCK, and RICHARD A. BROWN, Gettysburg, New Brunswick, 1948.
Military Essays and Recollections, Illinois Commandery of the Military Order of the Loyal Legion of the United States, four vols., Chicago, 1891–92.
Military Historical Society of Massachusetts Papers, fourteen vols., Boston, various dates.
MILLER, EMILY VAN DORN, editor, A Soldier's Honor, with Reminiscences of Major-General Earl Van Dorn by his Comrades, New York, 1902.
MILLER, FRANCIS TREVELYAN, The Photographic History of the Civil War, ten vols., New York, 1911.
MILLER, SAMUEL H., "Yellow Tavern," *Civil War History,* Vol. II, No. 1, March, 1956.
MILLER, WILLIAM E., "The Cavalry Battle near Gettysburg," Battles and Leaders.
MILLS, J. HARRISON, Chronicles of the Twenty-first Regiment, New York State Volunteers, Buffalo, New York, 1863.
MILLS, WILLIAM HOWARD, "Chancellorsville," *The Magazine of American History,* Vol. XV, No. 4, April, 1866.
MILTON, GEORGE FORT, Abraham Lincoln and the Fifth Column, New York, 1942.
———, The Age of Hate, Andrew Johnson and the Radicals, New York, 1930.
———, The Eve of Conflict, Boston, 1934.
MINDIL, GEORGE W., The Battle of Fair Oaks, A Reply to General Joseph B. Johnston, Philadelphia, 1874.
MINNIGH, L. W., Gettysburg, What They Did Here, Gettysburg, 1924.
"Mississippi Valley, Tennessee, Georgia, Alabama 1861–1864," Vol. VIII, Military Historical Society of Massachusetts Papers, Boston, 1910.
Mr. Lincoln's Arbitrary Arrests, New York, 1864.
MITCHELL, MARY BEDINGER, "A Woman's Recollections of Antietam," Battles and Leaders.
MITCHELL, BRIGADIER GENERAL WILLIAM A., Outlines of the World's Military History, Harrisburg, 1940.
Mixed Commission on American and British Claims, Wood and Heyworth vs. United States, No. 103; Cowan Graveley vs. United States, No. 292, n.p., n.d.
MOLLOY, ROBERT, Charleston, A Gracious Heritage, New York, 1947.
MONAGHAN, JAY, Civil War on the Western Border, 1854–1865, Boston, 1955.
———, "Custer's Last Stand, Trevilian Station, 1864," *Civil War History,* Vol. VIII, No. 3, September, 1962.
———, Diplomat in Carpet Slippers, Indianapolis, 1945.
———, Swamp Fox of the Confederacy, The Life and Military Services of Jeff Thompson, Tuscaloosa, Alabama, 1956.
"Monitor and Merrimack," Report of the Joint Committee on the Conduct of the War, Part III, Washington, 1863.
MONNETT, HOWARD N., Action Before Westport, 1864, Kansas City, 1954.

———, "The Battle of Westport," Kansas City *Star,* April 23, 1961.

———, "The Confederate Advance to Lexington, 1864," *Missouri Historical Society Bulletin,* April, 1963.

———, "The Origin of the Confederate Invasion of Missouri, 1864," *Missouri Historical Society Bulletin,* October, 1951.

———, "Retreat from Westport," *The Trail Guide,* Kansas City Posse, The Westerners, Vol. VII, No. 3, September, 1962.

MONROE, COLONEL J. ALBERT, "The Rhode Island Artillery at the First Battle of Bull Run," Personal narratives of the Battles of the Rebellion, being papers read before the Rhode Island Soldiers and Sailors Historical Society, No. 1, Providence, 1878.

MONTGOMERY, JAMES STUART, The Shaping of a Battle: Gettysburg, Philadelphia, 1959.

MOONEY, CHASE C., "Some Institutional and Statistical Aspects of Slavery in Tennessee," *Tennessee Historical Quarterly,* Vol. I.

MOORE, ALBERT BURTON, Conscription and Conflict in the Confederacy, New York, 1924.

MOORE, AVERY C., Destiny's Soldier (General Albert Sidney Johnston), San Francisco, 1958.

MOORE, FRANK, The Civil War in Song and Story, 1860–1865, New York, 1889.

———, The Rebellion Record; A Diary of American Events, eleven vols. and supplement, New York, 1861, 1868.

MOORE, GLOVER, The Missouri Controversy 1819–1820, Lexington, 1953.

MOORE, J. R., "With Jackson at Hamilton's Crossing," Battles and Leaders.

MOORE, JOHN C., Missouri, Confederate Military History, Atlanta, 1899.

MOORMAN, MARCELLUS N., "Narrative of Events and Observations connected with the Wounding of General T. J. (Stonewall) Jackson, *Southern Historical Society Papers,* Vol. XXX, 1902.

MORAN, BENJAMIN, The Journal of Benjamin Moran 1857–1865, two vols., edited by Sarah Agnes Wallace and Frances Elma Gillespie, Chicago, 1948.

MORGAN, GEORGE W., "The Assault on Chickasaw Bluffs," Battles and Leaders.

———, "Cumberland Gap," Battles and Leaders.

MORGAN, JAMES MORRIS, Recollections of a Rebel Reefer, London, 1918.

"Morgan's Ohio Raid," n.a., Battles and Leaders.

MORRIS, JEROME, The Brief Belligerence of Fort Macon, Raleigh, North Carolina, 1962.

MORSE, JOHN T., JR., Abraham Lincoln, two vols., Boston, 1924.

———, John Quincy Adams, Boston, 1890.

MORSE, SAMUEL FINLEY BREESE, Imminent Dangers to the Institutions of the United States through foreign immigration and the present state of the naturalization laws, New York, 1854.

MORTON, CHARLES, "Opening of the Battle of Shiloh," War Papers No. 80, Commandery of the District of Columbia of the Military Order of the Loyal Legion of the United States, 1912.

MOSBY, JOHN S., "A Bit of Partisan Service," Battles and Leaders.

———, The Memoirs of Colonel John S. Mosby, edited by Charles Wells Russell, Bloomington, Indiana, 1959.

MOSGROVE, GEORGE DALLAS, Kentucky Cavaliers in Dixie, edited by Bell Irwin Wiley, Jackson, Tennessee, 1957.

MOSS, M. HELEN PALMES, "Lincoln and John Wilkes Booth as seen on the day of the assassination," *Century Magazine,* Vol. LXXVII, No. 6, April, 1909.

MUDD, JOSEPH A., "What I Saw at Wilson's Creek," *Missouri Historical Review,* Vol. VII, January, 1913.

MUIR, ANDREW FOREST, "Dick Dowling and the Battle of Sabine Pass," *Civil War History,* Vol. IV, No. 4, December, 1958.

MULHANE, L. W., Memorial of Major-General William Stark Rosecrans, private, 1898.

MULLAN, JAMES M., "Last Days of Johnston's Army," *Southern Historical Society Papers,* Vol. XVIII, January–December, 1890.

MULLIGAN, JAMES A., "The Siege of Lexington," Battles and Leaders.

MUNFORD, T. T., "Reminiscences of Jackson's Valley Campaign," *Southern Historical Society Papers,* Vol. VII, No. 11, November, 1879.

MURPHY, D. F., Proceedings of the National Union Convention held in Baltimore, June 7 and 8, 1864, New York, 1864.

MURPHY, HARMON KING, "The Northern Railroads and the Civil War," *Mississippi Valley Historical Review,* Vol. V, No. 3, December, 1918.

MYERS, WILLIAM STARR, General George Brinton McClellan, New York, 1934.

Narrative of Privations and Sufferings of United States Officers and Soldiers while Prisoners of War in the Hands of the Rebel Authorities, United States Sanitary Commission, Boston, 1864.

NASH, HOWARD P., JR., "The CSS *Alabama;* Roving Terror of the Seas," *Civil War Times Illustrated,* August, 1963.

NASON, ELIAS, The Life and Times of Charles Sumner, Boston, 1874.

National Almanac and Annual Record for the year 1863, Philadelphia, 1863; also issue of 1864.

Native American, The; A Gift for the People. Philadelphia, 1845.

"Negotiations for the Building of the 'Monitor,'" Battles and Leaders.

NELSON, A. H., The Battles of Gettysburg and Chancellorsville, Minneapolis, 1899.

NEVINS, ALLAN, The Emergence of Lincoln, two vols., New York, 1950.

——, Frémont, Pathmaker of the West, New York, 1955.

——, "He Did Hold Lincoln's Hat," *American Heritage,* Vol. X, No. 2, February, 1959.

——, The Ordeal of the Union, two vols., New York, 1947.

——, The War for the Union, two vols., New York, 1960.

NEVINS, ALLAN, and H. S. COMMAGER, The Pocket History of the United States, New York, 1951.

NEWELL, J. E., Ours, Annals of the Tenth Regiment Massachusetts Volunteers, Boston, 1875.

NEWHALL, F. C., The Battle of Beverly Ford, Annals of the War.

NEWMAN, RALPH G., "The Douglas Deal Lincoln Spurned," Chicago *Tribune Magazine,* October 4, 1964.

NEWMAN, RALPH G., and E. B. LONG, The Civil War, Vol. II, The Picture Chronicle of the Events, Leaders and Battlefields of the War, New York, 1956; also published as Civil War Digest, New York, 1960.

NEWTON, LORD, Lord Lyons, A Record of British Diplomacy, two vols., London, 1913.

NEWTON, VIRGINIUS, The Confederate Ram Merrimac or Virginia, Richmond, 1892.

NICHOLS, ALICE, Bleeding Kansas, New York, 1954.

NICHOLS, EDWARD J., Towards Gettysburg: A Biography of General John F. Reynolds, University Park, Pennsylvania, 1953.

NICHOLS, GEORGE WARD, The Story of the Great March from the diary of a Staff Officer, New York, 1885.

NICHOLS, ROY FRANKLIN, The Disruption of American Democracy, New York, 1948.

———, "The Kansas-Nebraska Act: A Century of Historiography," *Mississippi Valley Historical Review*, September, 1956.

NICOLAY, HELEN, Lincoln's Secretary, A Biography of John C. Nicolay, New York, 1949.

NICOLAY, JOHN G., The Outbreak of Rebellion, New York, 1882.

NICOLAY, JOHN G., and JOHN HAY, Abraham Lincoln, A History, ten vols. New York, 1866, 1890, 1914.

———, "Blair's Mexican Project," *Century Magazine*, Vol. XXXVIII, No. 6, October, 1889.

———, "The Hampton Roads Conference," *Century Magazine*, Vol. XXXVIII, No. 6, October, 1889.

———, "The Thirteenth Amendment," *Century Magazine*, Vol. XXXVIII, No. 6, October, 1889.

Niles Register, Baltimore, various issues.

NISBET, JAMES COOPER, Four Years on the Firing Line, edited by Bell Irwin Wiley, Jackson, Tennessee, 1963.

NOBLE, JOHN W., "Battle of Pea Ridge or Elkhorn Tavern," War Papers of the Missouri Commandery of the Military Order of the Loyal Legion of the United States, Vol. I, St. Louis, 1892.

NOEL, THEOPHILUS, Autobiography and Reminiscences of, Chicago, 1904.

NORTON, OLIVER WILLIAM, The Attack and Defense of Little Round Top, Gettysburg, July 2, 1863, New York, 1913.

NOURSE, HENRY, "The Burning of Columbus, South Carolina," Vol. IX, Military Historical Society of Massachusetts Papers, Boston, 1912.

OAKLEY, DANIEL, "Marching Through Georgia and The Carolinas," Battles and Leaders.

OBERHOLTZER, ELLIS PAXTON, Jay Cooke, Financier of the Civil War, two vols., Philadelphia, 1907.

O'BRIEN, J. EMMET, "Telegraphing in Battle," *The Century Illustrated Monthly*, Vol. XXXVIII, No. 5, September, 1889.

O'CONNOR, RICHARD, Hood, Cavalier General, New York, 1949.

———, Sheridan, The Inevitable, Indianapolis, 1963.

O'CONNOR, THOMAS H., "Lincoln and the Cotton Trade," *Civil War History*, Vol. VII, No. 1, March, 1961.

Official Proceedings of the Democratic National Convention held in 1860 at Charleston and Baltimore, Cleveland, 1860.

Official Records of the Union and Confederate Navies in the War of the Rebellion, thirty vols. plus index, Washington, 1896.

O'FLAHERTY, DANIEL, General Jo Shelby, Undefeated Rebel, Chapel Hill, North Carolina, 1954.

OLDROYD, OSBORN N., A Soldier's Story of the Siege of Vicksburg, Springfield, 1885.

OLMSTEAD, CHARLES H., "The Memoirs of," edited by Lilla Mills Hawes, *The Georgia Historical Quarterly*, Vol. XLIV, No. 3, September, 1960.

———, "Reminiscences of Service in Charleston Harbor in 1863," *Southern Historical Society Papers*, Vol. XI, Nos. 2 and 3, February and March, 1885.

OLMSTEAD, FREDERICK LAW, A Journey in the Seaboard Slave States in the years 1853–1854 with remarks on the economy, New York, 1905.

OPDYKE, EMERSON, "Notes on the Chickamauga Campaign," Battles and Leaders.

"Opposing Forces," Various battles, Battles and Leaders.

"Ordnance and Ordnance Stores, report to the commission on ordnance and ordnance stores made to the War Department," Senate Executive Document No. 72, 37th Congress, 2nd Session, Vol. VI, Washington, 1862.

OSBORN, HARTWELL, and OTHERS, Trials and Triumphs, The record of the Fifty-Fifth Ohio Volunteer Infantry, Chicago, 1904.

OSBORNE, WILLIAM H., The History of the Twenty-Ninth Regiment of Massachusetts Volunteer Infantry in the Late War of the Rebellion, Boston, 1897.

OSBURN, FRANCIS A., "Bermuda Hundred, June 16 and 17, 1864," Vol. V, Military Historical Society of Massachusetts Papers, Boston, 1906.

OTIS, EPHRAIM, "A Recollection of the Kentucky Campaign of 1862," Vol. VII, Military Historical Society of Massachusetts Papers, Boston, 1908.

OULD, ROBERT, "The Exchange of Prisoners," Annals of the War.

OVERDYKE, W. DARRELL, The Know Nothing Party in the South, Baton Rouge, Louisiana, 1903.

OWEN, WILLIAM M., In Camp and Battle with the Washington Artillery, Boston, 1885.

OWSLEY, CLIFFORD D., "Genesis of World's Greatest Speeches," *Lincoln Herald*, Fall, 1962.

OWSLEY, FRANK LAWRENCE, King Cotton Diplomacy, Chicago, 1931; also Chicago, 1959.

———, Plain Folk of the Old South, Baton Rouge, Louisiana, 1949.

PAGE, RICHARD L., "The Defense of Fort Morgan," Battles and Leaders.

PALFREY, FRANCIS W., "After the Fall of Yorktown," Vol. I, Military Historical Society of Massachusetts Papers, Boston, 1895.

———, The Antietam and Fredericksburg Campaigns of the Civil War, New York, 1862.

———, "The Battle of Antietam," Vol. III, Military Historical Society of Massachusetts Papers, Boston, 1895.

———, "The Battle of Malvern Hill," Vol. I, Military Historical Society of Massachusetts Papers, Boston, 1895.

———, "The Seven Days Battles to Malvern Hill," Vol. I, Military Historical Society of Massachusetts Papers, Boston, 1895.

Bibliography

PALFREY, JOHN C., "General Sherman's Plans After the Fall of Atlanta," Vol. VIII, Military Historical Society of Massachusetts Papers, Boston, 1910.

———, "Port Hudson," Vol. VIII, Military Historical Society of Massachusetts Papers, Boston, 1910.

———, "The Siege of Yorktown," Vol. I, Military Historical Society of Massachusetts Papers, Boston, 1910.

Papers of the Military Historical Society of Massachusetts, fourteen vols., Boston, various dates.

PARIS, THE COMTE DE PARIS, History of the Civil War in America, four vols., Philadelphia, 1875–88.

PARK, ROBERT E., "Diary," *Southern Historical Society Papers,* Vol. II, No. I, July, 1876.

PARKER, FOXHALL A., "The Battle of Mobile Bay," Vol. XII, Military Historical Society of Massachusetts Papers, Boston, 1902.

PARKER, JOEL, International Law, Case of the Trent, Capture and Surrender of Mason and Slidell, Cambridge, 1862.

PARKER, JOHN L., Henry Wilson's Regiment, History of the Twenty-Second Massachusetts Infantry; The Second Company Sharpshooters and the Third Light Battery in the War of the Rebellion, Boston, 1887.

PARKER, WILLIAM HARWAR, The Confederate States Navy, Confederate Military History, Vol. XII, Atlanta, 1883.

———, Recollections of a Naval Officer 1861–1865, New York, 1883.

PARKS, JOSEPH HOWARD, "A Confederate Trade Center under Federal Occupation, Memphis 1862–1865," *Journal of Southern History,* Vol. VII, No. 3, August, 1941.

———, General Edmund Kirby Smith, C.S.A., Baton Rouge, 1954.

———, General Leonidas Polk, C.S.A., The Fighting Bishop, Baton Rouge, 1962.

PARKS, JOSEPH HOWARD, and STANLEY J. FOLMSBEE, The Story of Tennessee, Oklahoma City, 1954.

PARSONS, H. C., "Farnsworth's Charge and Death," Battles and Leaders.

PARSONS, BREV. MAJOR GENERAL LEWIS B., Reports to the War Department, St. Louis, 1867.

PARTON, JAMES, General Butler in New Orleans, New York, 1864.

PATRICK, REMBERT W., The Fall of Richmond, Baton Rouge, 1960.

———, Jefferson Davis and his Cabinet, Baton Rouge, 1944.

PATTERSON, JAMES, Unionism and Reconstruction in Tennessee, Chapel Hill, 1934.

PATTERSON, ROBERT, A Narrative of the Campaign in the Valley of the Shenandoah 1861, Philadelphia, 1865.

PATTON, JOHN M., "Reminiscences of Jackson's Infantry (Foot Cavalry)," *Southern Historical Society Papers,* Vol. VIII, No. 3, March, 1880.

PAXTON, A. G., The Vicksburg Campaign, A Story of Perseverance, n.p., 1959.

PEABODY, FRANK, "Crossing of the James and First Assault upon Petersburg, June 12–15, 1864," Vol. V, Military Historical Society of Massachusetts Papers, Boston, 1906.

———, "Some Observations Concerning the Opposing Forces at Petersburg on June 15, 1864," Vol. V, Military Historical Society of Massachusetts Papers, Boston, 1906.

PEARCE, N. B., "Arkansas Troops in the Battle of Wilson's Creek," Battles and Leaders.

PECK, ROBERT MORRIS, "Rough Riding on the Plains," *National Tribune,* Washington, D.C., August 29, 1901 (furnished by Mrs. Raymond Millbrook of Detroit).

PECKHAM, JAMES, General Nathaniel Lyon and Missouri in 1861, New York, 1866.

PEIRSON, CHARLES L., "The Mine Run Affair," Vol. XIV, Military Historical Society of Massachusetts Papers, Boston, 1918.

PEISSNER, ELIAS, The American Question in its National Aspect, New York, 1861.

PELET, J. C., "Story of Andersonville Prison in Defense of Captain Wirz," Manatee River *Journal,* July 13, 1913.

PEMBERTON, JOHN C., Pemberton, Defender of Vicksburg, Chapel Hill. 1942.

PENNYPACKER, ISAAC E., General Meade, New York, 1901.

PENROSE, CHARLES B., "Lincoln's Visit to Richmond," *Century Magazine,* Vol. XI, No. 2, June, 1890.

PERKINS, HOWARD CECIL, Northern Editorials on Secession, New York, 1942.

PERLEY POORE, BEN, Perley's Reminiscences of Sixty Years in the National Metropolis, Philadelphia, 1886.

PERRY, B. F., Biographical Sketches of Eminent American Statesmen, Philadelphia, 1887.

Personal Recollections of the War of the Rebellion, Addresses delivered before the Commandery of the State of New York, Military Order of the Loyal Legion of the United States, second series, edited by A. Noel Blakeman, New York, 1897.

"Petersburg, Battle of," Report of the Joint Committee on the Conduct of the War, Vol. I, Washington, 1865.

PETTUS, GEORGE H., "The Confederate Invasion of New Mexico and Arizona," Battles and Leaders.

PHILLIPPE, COMTE DE PARIS, "McClellan Organizing the Grand Army," Battles and Leaders.

PHILLIPS, DINWIDDIE, "Notes on the 'Monitor-Merrimac' Fight," Battles and Leaders.

PHILLIPS, ISAAC N., Abraham Lincoln by Some Men Who Knew Him, edited by Paul M. Angle, Chicago, 1950.

PHILLIPS, JOHN F., "Diary written of the March tells of the Battle of Westport," Kansas City *Star,* October 23, 1925.

PHILLIPS, ULRICH BONNELL, American Negro Slavery, New York, 1918.

———, The Course of the South to Secession, New York, 1939.

———, "The Slavery Issue in Federal Politics," Chapter VII, Vol. IV, The South in the Building of the Nation, Richmond, 1909.

PHILLIPS, WILLIAM, The Conquest of Kansas by Missouri and her Allies, Boston, 1856.

PHISTERER, FREDERICK, Statistical Record of the Armies of the United States, New York, 1883.

PIATT, DONN, Memories of the Men who Saved the Union, New York, 1887.

PICKETT, GEORGE E., Soldier of the South, General Pickett's War Letters to his wife, edited by Arthur Grow Anmun, Boston, 1928.

PICKETT, MRS. LA SALLE CORBELL, "The First United States Flag Raised in Richmond after the War," in R. Johnson, Campfire and Battlefield.

———, Pickett and his Men, Atlanta, 1960.

PIERSON, CHARLES LAWRENCE, Ball's Bluff, An Episode and its Consequences to Some of us, Salem, Massachusetts, 1913.

———, "The Operations of the Army of the Potomac, May–June, 1864," Vol. IV, Military Historical Society of Massachusetts Papers, Boston, 1905.

PIKE, J. S., First Blows of the Civil War, New York, 1879.

PIRTLE, JOHN B., "Defense of Vicksburg in 1862, The Battle of Baton Rouge," *Southern Historical Society Papers*, Vol. VIII, June–July, 1880.

PISANI, CAMILLE FERRI, Prince Napoleon in America, Bloomington, Indiana, 1959.

PITTINGER, WILLIAM, "The Locomotive Chase in Georgia," Battles and Leaders.

PLEASANTS, HENRY J., JR., and GEORGE H. STRALEY, Inferno at Petersburg, Philadelphia, 1961.

PLEASONTON, ALFRED, "The Campaign of Gettysburg," Annals of the War.

———, "The Successes and Failures of Chancellorsville," Battles and Leaders.

PLUM, WILLIAM R., The Military Telegraph During the Civil War in the United States, two vols., Chicago, 1882.

POAGUE, WILLIAM THOMAS, Gunner with Stonewall, Reminiscences of William Thomas Poague, edited by Monroe F. Cockrell, Jackson, Tennessee, 1957.

POATS, RUTHERFORD M., Decision in Korea, New York, 1954.

POE, ORLANDO, "The Defense of Knoxville," Battles and Leaders.

Political Debates between Honorable Abraham Lincoln and Honorable Stephen A. Douglas in the celebrated campaign of 1858 in Illinois, Columbus, 1860.

POLK, JAMES K., The Diary of, edited by Milo M. Quaife, Chicago, 1910.

POLK, W. M., "The Battle of Chickamauga," *Southern Historical Society Papers*, Vol. X, Nos. 1 and 2, January and February, 1862.

———, "General Bragg and the Chickamauga Campaign," *Southern Historical Society Papers*, Vol. XIII, Nos. 7–9, July, August, and September, 1864.

———, "General Polk and the Battle of Belmont," Battles and Leaders.

———, "General Polk at Chickamauga," Battles and Leaders.

———, "The Hated Helper," *South Atlantic Quarterly*, Vol. XXX, 1931.

———, Leonidas Polk, Bishop and General, two vols., New York, 1915.

POLLARD, EDWARD A., The First Year of the War, Richmond, 1862, and New York, 1863.

———, Life of Jefferson Davis, Philadelphia, 1869.

———, The Lost Cause, New York, 1867.

———, Robert Lee and his Lieutenants, New York, 1867.

———, The Second Year of the War, New York, 1864.

———, Southern History of the War, New York, 1866.

POND, GEORGE E., The Shenandoah Valley in 1884, Campaigns of the Civil War, New York, 1883.

POORE, BEN PERLEY, "Life of Burnside," *National Review*, May 18, 1882.

———, The Life and Public Services of Ambrose E. Burnside, Soldier-Citizen-Statesman, Providence, Rhode Island, 1882.

POPE, JOHN, "The Second Battle of Bull Run," Battles and Leaders.

PORTER, CHARLES H., "The Battle of Cold Harbor," Vol. IV, Military Historical Society of Massachusetts Papers, Boston, 1905.

———, "The Fifth Corps at the Battle of Five Forks," Vol. VI, Military Historical Society of Massachusetts Papers, Boston, 1907.

———, "Opening of the Campaign of 1864," Vol. IV, Military Historical Society of Massachusetts Papers, Boston, 1905.

———, "Operations against the Weldon Railroad August 18, 19 and 21, 1864," Vol. V, Military Historical Society of Massachusetts Papers, Boston, 1906.

———, "Operations of Generals Sigel and Hunter in the Shenandoah Valley, May and June, 1864," Vol. VI, Military Historical Society of Massachusetts Papers, Boston, 1907.

———, "The Petersburg Mine," Vol. V, Military Historical Society of Massachusetts Papers, Boston, 1908.

PORTER, CHARLES W., Fort Raleigh National Historic Site, North Carolina, National Park Service Historical Series No. 16, Washington, 1952.

PORTER, DAVID D., Incidents and Anecdotes of the Civil War, New York, 1886.

———, The Naval History of the Civil War, New York, 1886.

———, "The Opening of the Lower Mississippi," Battles and Leaders.

PORTER, HORACE, Campaigning with Grant, New York, 1897

———, "Five Forks and the Pursuit of Lee," Battles and Leaders.

———, "The Surrender at Appomattox Court House," Battles and Leaders.

PORTER, FITZ JOHN, "The Battle of Malvern Hill," Battles and Leaders.

———, "Hanover Court House and Gaines' Mill," Battles and Leaders.

PORTER, JAMES D., Tennessee, Confederate Military History, Vol. VIII, Atlanta, 1899.

PORTER, JOHN L., "The Plan and Construction of the 'Merrimac,'" Battles and Leaders.

"Port Royal Expedition," Report of the Joint Committee on the Conduct of the War, Part III, Washington, 1863.

"Potomac, Army of the," Report of the Joint Committee on the Conduct of the War, Part I, Washington, 1863.

POTTER, DAVID M., Lincoln and His Party in the Secession Crisis, New Haven, 1942.

POTTER, E. B., Sea Power, A Naval History, Englewood Cliffs, New Jersey, 1960.

POTTER, E. B., editor, The United States and World Sea Power, Englewood Cliffs, New Jersey, 1958.

POWE, JAMES HARRINGTON, Reminiscences and Sketches of Confederate Times, by one who lived through them, Harriett Powe Lynch, editor, Columbia, South Carolina, 1909.

POWELL, EDWARD PAYSON, Nullification and Secession in the United States, New York, 1897.

POWELL, MORGAN ALLEN, "Cotton for the Relief of Confederate Prisoners," *Civil War History,* Vol. II, No. 1, March, 1863.

POWELL, WILLIAM H., "The Battle of the Petersburg Crater," Battles and Leaders.

PRATT, FLETCHER, Civil War on Western Waters, Henry Holt and Company, New York, 1956.

———, Stanton, Lincoln's Secretary of War, New York, 1953.

PRATT, HARRY E., Abraham Lincoln Chronology, Springfield, 1953.

PRESSLY, THOMAS J., Americans Interpret their Civil War, Princeton, New Jersey, 1954.

PRICE, DR. HENRY M., "Rich Mountain in 1861," *Southern Historical Society Papers*, Vol. XXVII, 1899.

"Prisoners, Treatment of," Report of the Joint Committee on the Conduct of the War, Vol. III, Washington, 1865.

Proceedings of the First Confederate Congress, Fourth Session, *Southern Historical Society Papers*, Vol. L, edited by Frank Vandiver, The Virginia Historical Society, Richmond, 1953.

PROCTOR, ADDISON G., Lincoln and the Convention of 1860. An Address before the Chicago Historical Society, April 4, 1918, Chicago, 1918.

Proofs for Workingmen of the Monarchic and Aristocratic Designs of the Southern Conspirators and their Northern Allies, n.p., n.d.

Provost-Marshal-General's Report, Final Report made to the Secretary of War by the Provost Marshal General of the Operations of the Bureau of the Provost Marshal General of the United States from the Commencement of the Business of the Bureau, March 17, 1863 to March 17, 1866; the Bureau terminating by law August 29, 1866. Messages and Documents, War Department 1865–1866, Executive Document No. 1, House of Representatives, Thirty-Ninth Congress, 1st Session, Vol. IV, Washington, 1866.

PRYOR, MRS. ROGER A., Reminiscences of Peace and War, New York, 1904.

Pulaski County Historical Review, The, Vol. V, No. 1, Little Rock, Arkansas, March, 1957.

PULLEN, JOHN J., The Twentieth Maine, A Volunteer Regiment in the Civil War, Philadelphia, 1957.

PUTNAM, SALLIE A., In Richmond During the Confederacy, New York, 1961.

———, Richmond During the War, Four Years of personal Observations by a Richmond lady, New York, 1867.

QUARLES, BENJAMIN, Lincoln and the Negro, New York, 1962.

———, The Negro in the Civil War, Boston, 1953.

Questions and Facts, pamphlets, n.n., n.d., circa 1863.

QUINT, ALONZO, The Potomac and the Rapidan, Boston, 1864.

———, The Record of the Second Massachusetts Infantry, 1861–1865, Boston, 1867.

RAMSDELL, CHARLES W., Behind the Lines in the Southern Confederacy, Baton Rouge, 1944.

———, "General Robert E. Lee's Horse Supply, 1862–1865," *American Historical Review*, Vol. XXXV, 1930.

———, "Lincoln and Fort Sumter," *Journal of Southern History*, August, 1937.

RAMSEY, H. ASHTON, "The Monitor and the Merrimac," *Confederate Veteran*, July, 1907.

RANDALL, JAMES G., Civil War and Reconstruction, Boston, 1937; also second edition with David Donald, Boston, 1961.

———, Constitutional Problems under Lincoln, Urbana, Illinois, 1951.

———, Lincoln the Liberal Statesman, New York, 1947.

———, Lincoln the President, four vols. (Vol. IV, "Last Full Measure," with Richard N. Current), New York, 1945–55.

———, "When War Came in 1861," *Abraham Lincoln Quarterly*, March, 1940.

RANSOM, ROBERT, "Ransom's Division at Fredericksburg," Battles and Leaders.

RAPP, WILLIAM, Letter to his Father, Newberry Library Bulletin, Chicago, May, 1952.

RAY, N.W., Sketch of the Sixth Regiment North Carolina State Troops, n.p., n.d.

RAY, P. ORMAN, The Convention that Nominated Lincoln, Chicago, 1916.

———, "The Genesis of the Kansas-Nebraska Act," Annual Report of the American Historical Association, Washington, 1911.

———, The Repeal of the Missouri Compromise, Cleveland, 1909.

RAYMOND, HENRY J., The Life and Public Services of Abraham Lincoln, New York, 1865.

REA, RALPH R., Sterling Price, The Lee of the West, Little Rock, Arkansas, 1959.

READ, C. W., "Reminiscences of the Confederate States Navy," *Southern Historical Society Papers*, Vol. I, No. 5, May, 1876.

REAGAN, JOHN N., "Flight and Capture of Jefferson Davis," Annals of the War.

———, Memoirs with special reference to Secession and the Civil War, New York, 1906.

REANEY, HENRY, "How the Gun-Boat 'Zouave' aided the 'Congress,'" Battles and Leaders.

"Rebel Prisoners, Treatment of," Report of the Joint Committee on the Conduct of the War, Vol. III, Washington, 1865.

Rebellion Record: A Diary of American Events edited by Frank Moore, eleven vols. and supplement, New York, 1861–68.

"Reconstruction," House Report No. 30, 39th Congress, 1st Session, Part 2, Washington, 1866.

Record of Hon. C. L. Vallandigham on Abolition, The Union and the Civil War, Cincinnati, 1863.

REDPATH, JAMES, Echoes of Harper's Ferry, Boston, 1860.

"Red River Expedition," Report of the Joint Committee on the Conduct of the War, Vol. II, Washington, 1865.

REDWAY, G. W., Fredericksburg, A Study in War, special campaign series No. 3, London and New York, 1906.

REDWOOD, ALLAN C., "Jackson's Foot-Cavalry at the Second Bull Run," Battles and Leaders.

REED, SAM ROCKWELL, The Vicksburg Campaign, Cincinnati, 1882.

"Relief of Telegraph Operators who Served in the War of the Rebellion," Senate Document No. 251, 58th Congress, 2nd Session, 1903–4.

Reminiscences of the Women of Missouri during the 'Sixties, gathered, compiled and published by Missouri Division, United Daughters of the Confederacy, Jefferson City, n.d.

"Repelling Lee's Last Blow at Gettysburg," Battles and Leaders.

Reply to the Address of the Native American Convention Assembled at Harrisburg, Pennsylvania, February, 1845, in a Series of Letters, Philadelphia, 1845.

Reply of the Philadelphia Brigade Association to the Foolish and Absurd Narrative of Lieutenant Frank A. Haskell, The Philadelphia Brigade Association, Philadelphia, 1910.

Report of Committee of Agriculture, 1862, 1863, 1864, 1865, 1866, Washington, various dates.

"Report of Committee on Ordnance and Ordnance Stores," Senate Executive Document ⚹72, 37th Congress, 2nd Session.

"Report of the Joint Committee on the Conduct of the War," three vols., Washington, 1863, and three vols. plus two supplements, Washington, 1865.

Report of the Joint Committee on Reconstruction, at the 1st Session, 39th Congress, Washington, 1866.

Report No. 182, House of Representatives, 34th Congress, 1st Session, Washington, 1856.

Report of Special Committee on the Recent Military Disasters at Forts Henry and Donelson and the Evacuation of Nashville, Richmond, 1862.

"Report on Treatment of Prisoners of War, by the Rebel Authorities, during the War of the Rebellion," House of Representatives, 40th Congress, 3rd Session, Report No. 45, Washington, 1869.

"Returned Prisoners," Report of the Joint Committee on the Conduct of the War, Washington, 1864.

REVERE, JOSEPH W., Keel and Saddle: A Retrospect of Forty Years of Military and Naval Service, Boston, 1872.

———, A Statement of the Case of Brigadier-General Joseph W. Revere, United States Volunteers, tried by court-martial and dismissed from the service of the United States August 10, 1863, New York, 1863.

RHETT, R. BARNWELL, "The Confederate Government at Montgomery," Battles and Leaders.

RHODES, ELISHA H., The First Campaign of the Second Rhode Island Infantry, from personal narratives of the Battles of the Rebellion, being papers read before the Rhode Island Soldiers and Sailors Historical Society, Providence, 1887.

RHODES, JAMES FORD, History of the United States from the Compromise of 1850 to the final restoration of home rule in the South in 1877, eight vols., New York, 1892–1919.

RICE, ALLEN THORNDIKE, Reminiscences of Abraham Lincoln by distinguished Men of his Time, New York, 1888.

RICH, JOSEPH W., The Battle of Shiloh, Iowa City, Iowa, 1911.

RICHARDSON, ALBERT D., A Personal History of Ulysses S. Grant, Hartford, Connecticut, 1868.

———, The Secret Service, The Field, The Dungeon and The Escape, Hartford, Connecticut, 1865.

RICHARDSON, JAMES D., Messages and Papers of the Confederacy, two vols., Nashville, 1905.

———, Messages and Papers of the Presidents, twenty vols., New York, 1897.

RICHARDSON, RALPH, "The Choice of Jefferson Davis as Confederate President," *Journal of Mississippi History*, July, 1955.

RIDDLE, ALBERT GALLATIN, Recollections of War Times, New York, 1895.

RIDDLE, THOMAS J., "Reminiscences of Floyd's Operations in West Virginia in 1861," *Southern Historical Society Papers*, Vol. XI, Nos. 2 and 3, February and March, 1883.

RILEY, GENERAL, Speech of General Riley, edited by Franklin J. Meine, Chicago, 1940.

RIPLEY, EDWARD HASTINGS, Vermont General, The Unusual War Experiences of Edward Hastings Ripley, edited by Otto Eisenschiml, New York, 1960.

RITCHIE, J. EWING, The Life and Times of Viscount Palmerston, two vols., London, n.d.

ROBERTS, A. S., "The Federal Government and Confederate Cotton," *American Historical Review,* Vol. XXXII, No. 2, January, 1927.

ROBERTS, MACLENNAN, The Great Locomotive Chase, New York, 1956.

ROBERTS, O. M., Texas, Confederate Military History, Vol. XI, Atlanta, 1899.

ROBERTSON, WILLIAM B., "The Water-Battery at Fort Jackson," Battles and Leaders.

ROBINS, W. T., "Stuart's Ride Around McClellan," Battles and Leaders.

ROBINSON, CHARLES, The Kansas Conflict, Lawrence, Kansas, 1898.

ROBINSON, WILLIAM M., JR., The Confederate Privateers, New Haven, Connecticut, 1928.

———, "Drewry's Bluff, Naval Defense of Richmond," *Civil War History,* Vol. VII, No. 2, June, 1961.

ROBINTON, MADELINE RUSSELL, An Introduction to the Papers of the New York Prize Court, 1861–1865, New York, 1945.

ROCKWELL, ALFRED P., "The Operations Against Charleston," Vol. IX, Military Historical Society of Massachusetts Papers, Boston, 1912.

———, "The Tenth Army Corps in Virginia, May, 1864," Vol. IX, Military Historical Society of Massachusetts Papers, Boston, 1912.

RODENBOUGH, THEO. F., "Sheridan's Richmond Raid," Battles and Leaders.

———, "Sheridan's Trevilian Raid," Battles and Leaders.

RODGERS, C. R. P., "Du Pont's Attack at Charleston," Battles and Leaders.

ROE, ALFRED S., Monocacy, A Sketch of the Battle of Monocacy, Maryland, July 9th, 1864, Worcester, Massachusetts, 1894.

ROEBLING, WASHINGTON, "Letter to Langhourne M. Williams of Richmond, Virginia," "Letters and Diaries," edited by Eldon E. Billings, *Civil War Times Illustrated,* Vol. I, No. 9, January, 1963.

ROGERS, EARL M., "McClellan's Candidacy with the Army," *Century Magazine,* Vol. XI, No. 6, October, 1890.

ROLAND, CHARLES P., "Albert Sidney Johnston and the Loss of Forts Henry and Donelson," *Journal of Southern History,* February, 1957.

———, "Albert Sidney Johnston and the Shiloh Campaign," *Civil War History,* Vol. IV, No. 4, December, 1958.

———, The Confederacy, Chicago, 1960.

ROMAN, ALFRED, The Military Operations of General Beauregard, 2 vols., New York, 1884.

ROMBAUER, ROBERT J., The Union Cause in St. Louis in 1861, St. Louis, 1909.

ROPES, J. C., The Army Under Pope, Campaigns of the Civil War, Vol. IV, New York, 1881.

———, "The Battle of Cold Harbor," Vol. IV, Military Historical Society of Massachusetts Papers, Boston, 1905.

———, "The Failure to Take Petersburg on June 16–18, 1864," Vol. V, Military Historical Society of Massachusetts Papers, Boston, 1906.

———, "General Sherman," Vol. X, Military Historical Society of Massachusetts Papers, Boston, 1895.

———, "Grant's Campaign in Virginia in 1864," Vol. IV, Military Historical Society of Massachusetts Papers, Boston, 1906.

———, The Story of the Civil War, two vols., New York, 1898.

ROSCOE, THEODORE, The Web of Conspiracy, Englewood Cliffs, New Jersey, 1959.

ROSECRANS, WILLIAM S., "The Battle of Corinth," Battles and Leaders.

———, "The Campaign for Chattanooga," *Century Magazine,* Vol. XXIV, No. 1, May, 1887.

"Rosecrans Campaigns," Report of the Joint Committee on the Conduct of the War, Vol. III, Washington, 1865.

ROSIN, WILBERT HENRY, Hamilton Rowan Gamble, Missouri's Civil War Governor, Dissertation, University of Missouri, Columbia, Missouri, 1960.

ROSKE, RALPH J., and CHARLES VAN DOREN, Lincoln's Commando, the Biography of Commander William B. Cushing, U.S.N., New York, 1957.

ROSS, FITZGERALD, Cities and Camps of the Confederate States, edited by Richard Barksdale Harwell, Urbana, Illinois, 1958.

———, A Visit to the Cities and Camps of the Confederate States, London, 1865.

ROSS, ISHBEL, The General's Wife, The Life of Mrs. Ulysses S. Grant, New York, 1959.

ROTHROCK, MARY U., Discovering Tennessee, Knoxville, Tennessee, 1951.

ROWE, D. WATSON, "On the Field of Fredericksburg," Annals of the War.

ROWLAND, DUNBAR, History of Mississippi, The Heart of the South, Chicago, 1925.

———, Jefferson Davis, Constitutionalist: His Letters, Papers and Speeches, 10 vols., Jackson, Mississippi, 1923.

ROY, T. B., "General Hardee and the Military Operations Around Atlanta," *Southern Historical Society Papers,* Vol. VIII, Nos. 8 and 9, August and September, 1880.

RUSSELL, DON, "Lincoln Raises an Army," *Lincoln Herald,* June, 1948.

RUSSELL, JOHN EARL, Recollections and Suggestions, 1813–1873, Boston, 1875.

RUSSELL, WILLIAM HOWARD, My Diary North and South, New York, 1863.

RUTMAN, DARRETT B., "The War Crimes and Trial of Henry Wirz," *Civil War History,* Vol. VI, No. 2, June, 1960.

ST. JOHN, T. N., "Resources of the Confederacy in 1865," *Southern Historical Society Papers,* Vol. III, No. 3, March, 1877.

SALTONSTALL, WILLIAM G., "Personal Reminiscences of the War, 1861–1865," Vol. XII, Military Historical Society of Massachusetts Papers, Boston, 1902.

SANBORN, F. B., The Life and Letters of John Brown, Liberator of Kansas and Martyr of Virginia, Boston, 1891.

SANDBURG, CARL, The Prairie Years, 2 vols., New York, 1926.

———, The War Years, 4 vols., New York, 1939.

SANDS, FRANCIS P. B., "A Volunteer's Reminiscences of Life in the North Atlantic Blockading Squadron, 1862–1865," War Paper No. 20, Commandery of the District of Columbia of the Military Order of the Loyal Legion of the United States, 1894.

SANGER, DONALD BRIDGMAN, "The Authorship of General Orders No. 29," Transactions of the Illinois State Historical Society for the Year 1933, Springfield, Illinois.

SANGER, DONALD BRIDGMAN, and THOMAS ROBSON HAY, James Longstreet, Baton Rouge, 1952.

Sayler's Creek Battlefield Park, Virginia Department of Conservation and Development, Richmond, 1955.

SCHAFF, MORRIS, The Battle of the Wilderness, Boston, 1910.

——, The Sunset of the Confederacy, Boston, 1912.

SCHARF, J. THOMAS, History of the Confederate States Navy from its Organization to the Surrender of its Last Vessel, New York, 1887.

SCHEIBERT, I., "Letter from," *Southern Historical Society Papers,* Vol. V, Nos. 1 and 2, January and February, 1877.

SCHEIBERT, JUSTUS, Seven Months in the Rebel States during the North American War, 1863, Confederate Centennial Studies, No. 9, Tuscaloosa, Alabama, 1958.

SCHENCK, MARTIN, "Burnside's Bridge," *Civil War History,* Vol. II, No. 4, December, 1956.

——, Up Came Hill, The Story of the Light Division and Its Leaders, Harrisburg, Pennsylvania, 1958.

SCHERER, JAMES A. B., Cotton as a World Power, New York, 1916.

SCHOFIELD, JOHN M., Forty-Six Years in the Army, New York, 1897.

SCHUCKERS, J. W., The Life and Public Services of Salmon Portland Chase, New York, 1874.

SCHULER, LOUIS J., Last Battle in the War Between the States, Brownsville, Texas, 1960.

SCHURZ, CARL, Henry Clay, Boston, 1899.

——, The Reminiscences of Carl Schurz, three vols., New York, 1907.

SCHWAB, JOHN CHRISTOPHER, The Confederate States of America, 1861–1864; A Financial and Industrial History of the South during the Civil War, New York, 1901.

SCOTT, WINFIELD, Memoirs of Lieutenant General Scott, LL.D., written by himself, New York, 1864.

SCROGGS, JACK B., "Arkansas in the Secession Crisis," *The Arkansas Historical Quarterly,* Autumn, 1953.

SCRUGGS, JOHN, A Touching Incident of General McPherson, Altamont, Tennessee, n.d.

SEILHEIMER, GEORGE O., "The Historical Basis of Whittier's 'Barbara Frietchie,'" Battles and Leaders.

SEITZ, DON C., Braxton Bragg; General of the Confederacy, Columbia, South Carolina, 1924.

SELFRIDGE, THOMAS O., JR., Memoirs of, New York, 1924.

——, "The Navy at Fort Fisher," Battles and Leaders.

——, "The Navy in the Red River," Battles and Leaders.

——, "The Story of the Cumberland," Vol. XII, Military Historical Society of Massachusetts Papers, Boston, 1902.

SELLERS, JAMES LEE, "The Make-up of the Early Republican Party," Transactions of the Illinois State Historical Society, Springfield, Illinois, 1930.

SEMMES, RAPHAEL, Memoirs of Services Afloat During the War Between the States, Baltimore, 1869.

SEMPLE, ELLEN CHURCHILL, American History and its Geographic Conditions, Boston, 1903.

SENOUR, F., Major General William T. Sherman and his Campaigns, Chicago, 1865.

SEWARD, FREDERICK W., Reminiscences of a War-time Statesman and Diplomat, 1830–1915, New York, 1916.

——, Seward at Washington, 1861–1872, three vols., New York, 1891.

SEWARD, WILLIAM H., The Irrepressible Conflict, New York, 1858.

——, Speech Delivered by William H. Seward at St. Paul, September 18, 1860, Albany, 1860.

SHAFFER, DALLAS B., The Battle at Droop Mountain, West Virginia, West Virginia Department of Natural Resources, Division of Parks and Recreation, n.d.

SHALER, NATHANIEL S., "The Kentucky Campaign of 1862," Vol. VII, Military Historical Society of Massachusetts, Boston, 1908.

SHANKS, HENRY T., The Secession Movement in Virginia 1847–1861, Richmond, 1934.

SHANNON, FRED ALBERT, The Organization and Administration of the Union Army 1861–1865, two vols., Cleveland, 1928.

SHEAHAN, JAMES W., The Life of Stephen A. Douglas, New York, 1860.

SHEPARD, MISS JULIA ADELAIDE, "Lincoln's Assassination Told by an Eye-witness," *Century Magazine*, Vol. LXXVII, No. 6, April, 1909.

SHERER, JAMES A. B., Cotton as a World Power, New York, 1916.

SHERIDAN, PHILIP H., "Last Days of the Rebellion," Military Essays and Recollections, Vol. I, Illinois Commandery of the Loyal Legion of the United States, Chicago, 1891.

——, Personal Memoirs of, two vols., New York, 1888.

SHERMAN, JOHN. Recollections of Forty Years in the House, Senate and Cabinet, two vols., Chicago, 1895.

SHERMAN, WILLIAM T., "General Sherman and the March to the Sea," *Century Magazine*, Vol. XXXIV, new series Vol. XII, May–October, 1887.

——, "The Grand Strategy of the Last Year of the War," Battles and Leaders.

——, Home Letters of General Sherman, edited by M. A. DeWolfe Howe, New York, 1909.

——, Letters, Correspondence Between General and Senator Sherman from 1837 to 1891, Rachel Sherman Thorndike, editor, London, 1894.

——, Memoirs of General Sherman, two vols., New York, 1875.

"Sherman-Johnston Surrender," Report of the Joint Committee on the Conduct of the War, Vol. III, Washington, D.C., 1865.

SHIELDS, MCILWAINE, Memphis Down in Dixie, New York, 1948.

SHOEMAKER, FLOYD C., "Figures of Battle of Westport," unidentified clipping, E. B. Long files.

SHYROCK, R. H., Georgia and the Union in 1850, Durham, 1926.

"Sidelights at Gettysburg," Lincoln Lore, Bulletin of the Lincoln National Life Foundation, No. 1473, November, 1960.

SIEBERT, WILBUR H., The Underground Railway from Slavery to Freedom, New York, 1899.

Siege and Battle of Lexington, n.a., n.p., n.d., pamphlet.

"Siege of Cincinnati," *Atlantic Monthly*, February, 1863.

SIGEL, FRANZ, "The Flanking Column at Wilson's Creek," Battles and Leaders.

———, "The Pea Ridge Campaign," Battles and Leaders.

———, "Sigel in the Shenandoah Valley in 1864," Battles and Leaders.

SIMMS, WILLIAM GILMORE, Sack and Destruction of Columbia, Its Memorabilia, Columbia, South Carolina, 1905.

SIMON, JOHN Y., Ulysses S. Grant Chronology, Ohio Historical Society for Ulysses S. Grant Association and Ohio Civil Centennial Commission, Columbus, Ohio, 1963.

SITTERSON, JOSEPH CARLYLE, The Secession Movement in North Carolina, Chapel Hill, 1939.

SLOCUM, ELIHU, The Life and Services of Major General Henry Warner Slocum, Toledo, Ohio, 1913.

SLOCUM, HENRY W., "Final Operations of Sherman's Army," Battles and Leaders.

———, "Sherman's March from Savannah to Bentonville," Battles and Leaders.

SMITH, A. P., History of the Seventy-sixth Regiment New York Volunteers; What it endured and Accomplished, Cortland, New York, 1867.

SMITH, D. E., Huger, A Charlestonian's Recollection, Charleston, South Carolina, 1950.

SMITH, DONNAL V., Chase and Civil War Politics, Ohio Archaeological and Historical Society, Columbus, Ohio, 1931.

SMITH, E. KIRBY, "The Defense of the Red River," Battles and Leaders.

SMITH, EDWARD CONRAD, The Borderland in the Civil War, New York, 1927.

SMITH, ERNEST ASHTON, The History of the Confederate Treasury, Harrisburg, Pennsylvania, 1901.

SMITH, GEORGE E., and ORSON B. CURTIS, "In the Ranks at Fredericksburg," Battles and Leaders.

SMITH, GUSTAVUS W., Confederate War Papers, New York, 1884.

———, Generals Johnston and G. T. Beauregard at the Battle of Manassas, New York, 1892.

———, "The Georgia Militia About Atlanta," Battles and Leaders.

———, "The Georgia Militia During Sherman's March to the Sea," Battles and Leaders.

———, "Two Days of Battle at Seven Pines," Battles and Leaders.

SMITH, HAROLD F., "The 1861 Struggle for Lexington, Missouri," *Civil War History*, Vol. VII, No. 2, June, 1961.

SMITH, HENRY E., and ERASMUS D. KEYES, "The Rear Guard at Malvern Hill," Battles and Leaders.

SMITH, J. L., Philadelphia's Corn Exchange Regiment, History of the 118th Pennsylvania Regiment Volunteers—from Antietam to Appomattox, Philadelphia, 1888.

SMITH, JAMES E., A Famous Battery and its Campaigns 1861–1864, Fourth New York Independent Battery, Washington, 1892.

SMITH, JAMES POWER, "General Lee at Gettysburg," Vol. V, Military Historical Society of Massachusetts Papers, Boston, 1906.

———, "Stonewall Jackson and Chancellorsville," Vol. V., Military Historical Society of Massachusetts Papers, Boston, 1906.

———, "Stonewall Jackson's Last Battle," Battles and Leaders.

SMITH, PAUL TINCHER, "Militia of the United States from 1846 to 1860," *Indiana Magazine of History*, Vol. XV, March, 1919.

SMITH, THEODORE CLARKE, The Life and Letters of James Abram Garfield, two vols., New Haven, 1928.

———, Parties and Slavery, 1850–1859, The American Nation: A History, Vol. XVIII, New York, 1906.

SMITH, W. L. G., Life at the South, or "Uncle Tom's Cabin" as it is, Buffalo, 1852.

SMITH, WILLIAM ERNEST, The Francis Preston Blair Family in Politics, two vols. New York, 1933.

SMITH, WILLIAM FARRAR, "Butler's Attack on Drewry's Bluff," Battles and Leaders.

———, "The Eighteenth Corps at Cold Harbor," Battles and Leaders.

———, "Franklin's Left Grand Division," Battles and Leaders.

———, From Chattanooga to Petersburg Under Generals Grant and Butler; A Contribution to the History of the War, and a Personal Vindication, Boston, 1893.

———, "An Historical Sketch of the Military Operations Around Chattanooga, Tennessee September 22 to November 27, 1863," Vol. VIII, Military Historical Society of Massachusetts Papers, Boston, 1910.

———, "The Military Situation in Northern Virginia, from the 1st to the 14th of November, 1862," Vol. III, Military Historical Society of Massachusetts Papers, Boston, 1895.

———, "The Movement Against Petersburg, June, 1864," Vol. V, Military Historical Society of Massachusetts Papers, Boston, 1906.

———, "Shiloh," *Magazine of American History,* April, 1886.

SMITH, WILLIAM FARRAR, and HENRY M. CIST, "Comments on General Grant's 'Chattanooga,'" Battles and Leaders.

SNEAD, THOMAS L., "The Conquest of Arkansas," Battles and Leaders.

———, "The Conquest of Missouri," Battles and Leaders.

———, The Fight for Missouri, New York, 1886.

———, "The First Year of the War in Missouri," Battles and Leaders.

———, "With Price East of the Mississippi," Battles and Leaders.

Soldier Life in the Union and Confederate Armies, excerpts from "Hardtack and Coffee" by John D. Billings and "Soldier Life in the Army of Northern Virginia" by Carlton McCarthy, edited by Philip Van Dorn Stern, Bloomington, Indiana, 1961.

Soldier in Our Civil War, The, two vols., New York, 1890.

SOLEY, JAMES RUSSELL, The Blockade and the Cruisers, The Navy in the Civil War, Vol. I, New York, 1883, 1885.

———, "The Confederate Cruisers," Battles and Leaders.

———, "Early Operations in the Gulf," Battles and Leaders.

———, "Early Operations on the Potomac River," Battles and Leaders.

———, "Gulf Operations in 1862 and 1863," Battles and Leaders.

———, "Minor Operations of the South Atlantic Squadron under Du Pont," Battles and Leaders.

———, The Naval Brigade, Vol. XII, Military Historical Society of Massachusetts Papers, Boston, 1902.

———, "Naval Operations in the Vicksburg Campaign," Battles and Leaders.

———, "The Navy in the Peninsular Campaign," Battles and Leaders.

SORRELL, G. MOXLEY, Recollections of a Confederate Staff Officer, edited by Bell I. Wiley, Jackson, Tennessee, 1958.

"South Atlantic Blockading Squadron," Battles and Leaders.

Southern Historical Society Papers, Richmond, Virginia, various issues and dates.

Southern Literary Messenger, July and August, 1862.

SPARKS, EDWIN ERLE, The Lincoln-Douglas Debates of 1858, Springfield, 1908.

SPAULDING, OLIVER LYMAN, JR., The Bombardment of Fort Sumter, 1861, Washington, 1915.

SPEAR, ELLIS, "The Hoe Cake of Appomattox," War Paper No. 93, Commandery of the District of Columbia of the Military Order of the Loyal Legion of the United States, 1913.

SPEED, THOMAS, The Union Cause in Kentucky, 1860–1865, New York, 1907.

SPICER, WILLIAM A., Replacing the Flag upon Sumter; from the narrative of William A. Spicer, Raising of the Flag on Fort Sumter, Fort Sumter Memorial, New York, 1915.

Spirit of the Chicago Convention, Chicago, 1864.

SPRENGER, GEORGE F., Concise History of the Camp and Field of the 122nd Regiment Pennsylvania Volunteers, Lancaster, Pennsylvania, 1885.

SPRINGER, LEVERETT WILSON, Kansas, New York, 1894.

SPRUNT, JAMES, Chronicles of the Cape Fear River, Raleigh, 1914.

——, Derelicts, Baltimore, also Wilmington, North Carolina, 1920.

——, Tales and Traditions of the Lower Cape Fear 1861–1895, Wilmington, North Carolina, 1896.

STACKPOLE, EDWARD J., Chancellorsville, Lee's Greatest Battle, Harrisburg, Pennsylvania, 1958.

——, Drama on the Rappahannock, The Fredericksburg Campaign, Harrisburg, Pennsylvania, 1957.

——, From Cedar Mountain to Antietam, Harrisburg, Pennsylvania, 1959.

——, Sheridan in the Shenandoah, Harrisburg, Pennsylvania, 1961.

——, They Met at Gettysburg, Harrisburg, Pennsylvania, 1936.

STACKPOLE, J. LEWIS, The Department of North Carolina under General Foster July, 1862, to July, 1863, Vol. IX, Military Historical Society of Massachusetts Papers, Boston, 1912.

STAMPP, KENNETH M., And The War Came, Baton Rouge, 1950.

——, The Peculiar Institution, New York, 1956.

STANLEY, DAVID S., "The Battle of Corinth," Personal Recollections of the War of the Rebellion, addresses delivered before the Commandery of the State of New York, Military Order of the Loyal Legion of the United States, second series, edited by E. Noel Blakeman, Vol. II, New York, 1897.

——, "An Order to Charge at Corinth," Battles and Leaders.

STANTON, EDWIN M., "A Page of Political Correspondence, Unpublished Letters of Mr. Stanton to Mr. Buchanan," *The North American Review,* November, 1879.

STANWOOD, EDWARD, A History of the Presidency from 1788 to 1897, two vols., Boston, 1912.

Statistical Record of the Progress of the United States 1800–1906, Washington, 1906.

STEARNS, REV. E. J., Notes on "Uncle Tom's Cabin"; being a logical answer to the Allegations and Inferences against Slavery as an Institution, Philadelphia, 1853.

STEDMAN, EDMUND C., The Battle of Bull Run, New York, 1861.

STEDMAN, WILLIAM P., "Pursuit and Capture of Jefferson Davis by an Eye Witness," *Century Magazine*, Vol. XXXIX, No. 4, February, 1890.

STEELE, MATTHEW FORNEY, American Campaigns, two vols., Washington, 1951.

STEERE, EDWARD, "Rio Grande Campaign Logistics," *Military Review*, November, 1953.

———, The Wilderness Campaign, Harrisburg, Pennsylvania, 1960.

STENBERG, RICHARD R., "The Motivation of the Wilmot Proviso," *Mississippi Historical Review*, March, 1932.

STEPHEN, L., The Times on the American War: A Historical Study, London, 1865.

STEPHEN, ALEXANDER H., A Constitutional View of the Late War Between the States, two vols., Philadelphia, 1870.

STEPHENSON, NATHANIEL W., The Day of the Confederacy; A Chronicle of the Embattled South, New Haven, 1920.

STERN, PHILIP VAN DORN, An End to Valor, Boston, 1958.

———, The Man Who Killed Lincoln, New York, 1939.

STEVENS, CHARLES EMERY, Anthony Burns, A History, Boston, 1856.

STEVENS, HAZARD, "The Battle of Cedar Creek," Vol. VI, Military Historical Society of Massachusetts Papers, Boston, 1907.

———, "The Battle of Sailor's Creek," Vol. VI, Military Historical Society of Massachusetts Papers, Boston, 1907.

———, Life of Isaac Ingalls Stevens, two vols., 1900.

———, "Military Operations in South Carolina in 1862 against Charleston, Port Royal Ferry, James Island and Secessionville, Vol. IX, Military Historical Society of Massachusetts Papers, Boston, 1912.

———, "The Siege of Suffolk, April 11–May 3, 1863," Vol. XX, Military Historical Society of Massachusetts Papers, Boston, 1912.

———, "The Storming of the Lines of Petersburg by the Sixth Corps, April 2, 1865," Vol. VI, Military Historical Society of Massachusetts Papers, Boston, 1907.

STEVENS, THOMAS M., "The Boat Attack on Sumter," Battles and Leaders.

STEVENS, W. C., The Shenandoah and Its Byways, New York, 1951.

STEVENSON, ALEXANDER F., "The Battle of Stone's River near Murfreesboro, Tennessee," Boston, 1884.

STEWART, REV. A. M., Camp, March, and Battlefields; or three years and a half with the Army of the Potomac, Philadelphia, 1865.

STEWART, GEORGE R., Pickett's Charge, Boston, 1959.

STEWART, LUCY SHELTON, The Reward of Patriotism, New York, 1930.

STICKLES, ARNDT, Simon Bolivar Buckner, Borderland Knight, Chapel Hill, North Carolina, 1940.

STILES, ISRAEL N., "The 'Merrimac' and the 'Monitor,' Military Essays and Recollections," Vol. I, Illinois Commandery of the Military Order of the Loyal Legion of the United States, Chicago, 1891.

STILL, JOHN B., "Blitzkrieg, 1863; Morgan's Raid and Rout," *Civil War History,* Vol. III, No. 3, September, 1957.

STILLWELL, LUCILLE, John Cabell Breckinridge, Caldwell, Idaho, 1936.

STINE, J. B., History of the Army of the Potomac, Washington, 1893.

STINSON, THOMAS A., "War Reminiscences from 1862 to 1865," in E. R. Hutchins, The War of the Sixties.

STIRLING, JAMES, Letters from the Slave States, London, 1857.

STOCKWELL, ELISHA, JR., Private Elisha Stockwell, Jr., Sees the Civil War, edited by Byron E. Abernathy, Norman, Oklahoma, 1958.

STODDARD, HENRY LUTHER, Horace Greeley, New York, 1946.

STONE, CHARLES P., "Washington on the Eve of the War," Battles and Leaders.

STONE, HENRY, "The Atlanta Campaign, Part I, Opening of the Campaign," Vol. VIII, Military Historical Society of Massachusetts Papers, Boston, 1910.

——, "The Battle of Franklin, Tennessee, November 30, 1864," Vol. VII, Military Historical Society of Massachusetts, Boston, 1909.

——, "The Battle of Shiloh," Vol. VII, Military Historical Society of Massachusetts Papers, Boston, 1908.

——, "The Operations of General Buell in Kentucky and Tennessee in 1862," Vol. VII, Military Historical Society of Massachusetts Papers, Boston, 1908.

——, "Repelling Hood's Invasion of Tennessee," Battles and Leaders.

STORRICK, W. C., Gettysburg, The Place, The Battle, The Results, Harrisburg, Pennsylvania, 1932.

Story of the General, Issued by the Passenger Department of the Nashville, Chattanooga and St. Louis Railway, Nashville, Tennessee, n.d., pamphlet.

STOVALL, PLEASANT A., Robert Toombs, New York, 1892.

STOWE, HARRIETT BEECHER, A Key to "Uncle Tom's Cabin," Boston, 1853.

——, Uncle Tom's Cabin, two vols., Boston, 1852.

STRAIT, NEWTON A., Alphabetical List of Battles, Washington, D.C., 1900.

STRIPP, FRED, "The Other Gettysburg Address," *Civil War History,* Vol. I, No. 2, June, 1955.

STRODE, HUDSON, Jefferson Davis, three vols., New York, 1955, 1959, 1964.

STRONG, GEORGE TEMPLETON, The Diary of, four Vols., New York, 1952.

——, Diary of the Civil War 1860–1865, edited by Allan Nevins, New York, 1962.

STRONG, WILLIAM H., "The Death of General James B. McPherson," Military Essays and Recollections, Vol. III, Illinois Commandery of the Military Order of the Loyal Legion of the United States, Chicago, 1891.

STROTHER, D. H., "Personal Recollection of the War by a Virginian, Antietam," *Harper's New Monthly Magazine,* Vol. XXXVI, February, 1868.

——, A Virginia Yankee in the Civil War, the diaries of David Hunter Strother, edited and with an introduction by Cecil E. Eby, Jr., Chapel Hill, 1961.

——, "With Sigel at New Market; The History of Colonel D. H. Strother," edited by Cecil D. Eby, Jr., *Civil War History,* Vol. VI, No. 1, March, 1960.

STROUPE, HENRY SMITH, The Religious Press in the South Atlantic States, 1802–1865, Doctoral Dissertation, Duke University Library, 1942.

STRYKER, LLOYD PAUL, Andrew Johnson, A Study in Courage, New York, 1930.

Bibliography

STRYKER, WILLIAM S., "The Swamp Angel," Battles and Leaders.

STUART, J. E. B., "The Death of a General, by a private of the Sixth Virginia Cavalry," Battles and Leaders.

SULIVANE, CLEMENT, "The Evacuation," Battles and Leaders.

SULLIVAN, JAMES R., Chickamauga and Chattanooga Battlefields, National Park Service Handbook Series No. 25, Washington, 1956.

Sumter, Battle of Fort and First Victory of the Southern Troops, n.a., Charleston, 1861.

Supplemental Report of the Joint Committee on the Conduct of the War, two vols., Washington, 1866.

Survivors' Association, History of the Corn Exchange Regiment 118th Pennsylvania Volunteers, Philadelphia, 1888.

SWAN, WILLIAM W., "Battle of the Wilderness," Vol. IV, Military Historical Society of Massachusetts Papers, Boston, 1905.

——, "The Five Forks Campaign," Vol. VI, Military Historical Society of Massachusetts Papers, Boston, 1907.

SWANBERG, W. A., First Blood; The Story of Fort Sumter, New York, 1957.

SWIGGETT, HOWARD, The Great Man, New York, 1953.

——, The Rebel Raider; A Life of John Hunt Morgan, Indianapolis, 1934.

SWINTON, WILLIAM, Campaigns of the Army of the Potomac, New York, 1882.

SYKES, E. T., "A Cursory Sketch of General Bragg's Campaigns," Southern Historical Society Papers, Vol. XI, No. 11, November, 1883.

SYNDOR, CHARLES S., The Development of Southern Sectionalism 1819–1848, Baton Rouge, 1948.

TAFT, ROBERT, "Review of Bleeding Kansas by Alice Nichols," Mississippi Valley Historical Review, December, 1954.

TALCOTT, T. M. R., "From Petersburg to Appomattox," Southern Historical Society Papers, Vol. XXXII, January and February, 1904.

——, Stuart's Cavalry in the Gettysburg Campaign, Richmond, 1909.

Tales of Old Fort Monroe, No. 5, Committee for the Fort Monroe Casemate Museum, Newport News, Virginia, n.d.

TALIAFERRO, W. B., "Jackson's Raid Around Pope," Battles and Leaders.

TANNER, JAMES, "Letter to Henry F. Walsh," Abraham Lincoln Quarterly, December, 1942.

TARBELL, IDA M., The Life of Abraham Lincoln, four vols., New York, 1909.

TAUSSIG, F. W., "Results of Recent Investigations of Prices in the United States," Yale Review, Vol. II, No. 3, November, 1893.

TAYLOR, BENJAMIN F., Mission Ridge and Lookout Mountain with Pictures of Life in Camp and Field, New York, 1872.

TAYLOR, EMERSON CLIFFORD, Gouverneur Kemble Warren, The Life and Letters of an American Soldier, 1830–1883, Boston, 1932.

TAYLOR, JESSE, "The Defense of Fort Henry," Battles and Leaders.

TAYLOR, RICHARD, Destruction and Reconstruction, edited by Richard Harwell, New York, 1955.

——, "The Last Confederate Surrender," Southern Historical Society Papers, Vol. XXI, January–June, 1877.

TAYLOR, THOMAS E., Running the Blockade; A Personal Narrative of Adventures, risks, and escapes during the American Civil War, London, 1896.

TAYLOR, WALTER H., Four Years with General Lee, New York, 1878.

TEEL, T. T., "Sibley's New Mexico Campaign," Battles and Leaders.

TEMPLE, OLIVER P., East Tennessee and the Civil War, Cincinnati, 1899.

Tennessee, A Guide to the State, American Guide Series, New York, 1945.

THOMAS, BENJAMIN P., Abraham Lincoln, New York, 1952.

THOMAS, BENJAMIN P., and HAROLD M. HYMAN, Stanton, the Life and Times of Lincoln's Secretary of War, New York, 1962.

"Thomas, George H., Report of," Supplemental Report, Vol. I, Report of the Joint Committee on the Conduct of the War, Washington, 1866.

THOMAS, HENRY GODDARD, "The Colored Troops at Petersburg," Battles and Leaders.

THOMASON, JOHN W., JR., Jeb Stuart, New York, 1948.

THOMPSON, DAVID L., "With Burnside at Antietam," Battles and Leaders.

THOMPSON, JNO. R., "The Burial of Latane and extract from private letter," *Southern Literary Messenger,* July and August, 1862.

THOMPSON, JOSEPH DIMMIT, "The Battle of Shiloh; from the letters and diary of Joseph Dimmit Thompson, John G. Biel, editor, *Tennessee Historical Quarterly,* Vol. XVII, No. 3, Sept., 1958.

THOMPSON, ROBERT LUTHER, Wiring a Continent: The History of the Telegraph Industry in the United States 1832–1866, Princeton, New Jersey, 1947.

THOMPSON, SAMUEL BERNARD, Confederate Purchasing Operations Abroad, Chapel Hill, 1935.

THURSTON, GATES F., "The Crisis at Chickamauga," Battles and Leaders.

TICKNOR, GEORGE, Life, Letters, and Journals of George Ticknor, two vols., Boston, 1876.

TILBERG, FREDERICK, Antietam, National Park Service Historical Handbook Series No. 31, Washington, 1960, revised 1961.

———, Gettysburg National Military Park, National Park Service Historical Handbook Series No. 9, Washington, D.C., 1950.

TILLEY, JOHN SHIPLEY, Lincoln Takes Command, Chapel Hill, 1941.

TILTON, CLINT CLAY, "Lincoln and Lamon; Partners and Friends," Transactions of the Illinois State Historical Society for the Year 1913.

"Time of Longstreet's Arrival at Greentown," Battles and Leaders.

TODD, HERBERT E., The Building of the Confederate States Navy in Europe, A Summary of a Thesis, Vanderbilt University, Department of History, 1940, Nashville, 1941.

TODD, RICHARD CECIL, Confederate Finance, Athens, Georgia, 1954.

TODD, WILLIAM, The Seventy-ninth Highlanders, New York Volunteers, Albany, N.Y., 1886.

TOLBERT, FRANK X., "War's Last Land Battle," Dallas *Morning News,* July 7, 1959.

TOMPKINS, ELLEN WILKINS, editor, "The Colonel's Lady, some letters of Ellen Wilkins Tompkins, July to December, 1861," *Virginia Magazine of History and Biography,* Vol. 69, No. 4, October, 1961.

TOOMBS, ROBERT, ALEXANDER H. STEPHENS, and HOWELL COBB, The Correspondence of Robert Toombs, Alexander H. Stephens and Howell Cobb, Washington, 1911.

TOOMBS, SAMUEL, Reminiscences of the War Comprising a Detailed Account of the Thirteenth Regiment New Jersey Volunteers in Camp, on the Road, and in Battle, Orange, New Jersey, 1878.

TOWLE, G. W., "Glances from the Senate Gallery," *Cincinnati Monthly,* Vol. II, July–December, 1862.

TOWNSEND, E. D., Anecdotes of the Civil War in the United States, New York, 1884.

TOWNSEND, GEORGE ALFRED, Campaigns of a Non-combatant, New York, 1868.

"Trade Regulations," Report of the Joint Committee on the Conduct of the War, Vol. III, Washington, 1865.

"Trade with Rebellious States," House Report No. 24, 38th Congress, 2nd Session, Washington, 1864–65.

TREADGILL, JOHN, "A Scene of Interest in front of Fort Hell," E. R. Hutchins, The War of the Sixties, New York, 1912.

"Treatment of prisoners during the War between the States," *Southern Historical Society Papers,* Vol. I, Nos. 3 and 4, March and April, 1876.

"Treatment of Rebel Prisoners," Report of the Joint Committee on the Conduct of the War, Vol. III, 1865, Washington, 1865.

TREVELYAN, GEORGE MACAULAY, History of England, London, 1926.

TREXLER, HARRISON A., The Confederate Ironclad Virginia (Merrimac), Chicago, 1936.

———, "The Confederate Navy Department and the Fall of New Orleans," *Southwest Review,* Vol. XIX.

TREZEVANT, D. H., The Burning of Columbia, South Carolina, A Review of Northern Assertions and Southern Facts, Columbia, South Carolina, 1869, reprint Marietta, Georgia, 1958.

TUCKER, GLENN, Chickamauga, Bloody Battle in the West, Indianapolis, 1961.

———, Hancock the Superb, Indianapolis, 1960.

———, High Tide at Gettysburg, Indianapolis, 1958.

———, "Jeb Stuart Learned on Fleetwood Hill Federals Could Fight on Horseback, Too," *Civil War Times,* Vol. II, No. 8, December, 1960.

———, "Longstreet, Culprit or Scapegoat," *Civil War Times Illustrated,* Vol. I, No. 1, April, 1962.

TUNNARD, W. H., A Southern Record, The History of the Third Regiment of Louisiana Infantry, Baton Rouge, Louisiana, 1866.

Tupelo National Battlefield Site, Mississippi, United States Department of the Interior, 1946.

TURCHIN, JOHN B., Chickamauga, Chicago, 1888.

TURNER, EDWARD RAYMOND, The New Market Campaign, May, 1864, Richmond, 1912.

TURNER, F. P., "Grant is the King of Virginia," song sheet.

TURNER, FREDERICK JACKSON, The Frontier in American History, New York, 1920.

TURNER, GEORGE EDGAR, Victory Rode the Rails; The Strategic Place of the Railroads in the Civil War, Indianapolis, 1953.

TURNER, W. E., Maps Showing Roads Used by General Lee in his Retreat from Richmond and Petersburg and General Grant's Advance on Appomattox, 1953.

TUTHILL, RICHARD S., "An Artilleryman's Recollections of the Battle of Atlanta,

Military Essays and Recollections," Vol. I, Illinois Commandery of the Military Order of the Loyal Legion of the United States, Chicago, 1907.

TUTTLE, CHARLES R., A New Centennial History of the State of Kansas, Madison, Wisconsin, 1867.

TUTWILER, HALL, "Letter to his Sister Nettie," *The Virginia Magazine*, Virginia Historical Society, Richmond, April, 1863.

TWAIN, MARK, "The Private History of a Campaign that Failed," *Century Magazine*, Vol. XXI, No. 2, December, 1885.

TWITCHELL, RALPH EMERSON, The Leading Facts of New Mexican History, two vols., Cedar Rapids, Iowa, 1912.

UNDERWOOD, J. L., The Women of the Confederacy, New York and Washington, 1908.

Union, The, Being a Condemnation of Mr. Helper's Scheme, n.p., n.d.

Union Army, The, eight vols., Madison, Wisconsin, 1908.

United States Statutes at Large, various volumes.

UPSON, THEODORE F., With Sherman to the Sea, edited by Oscar O. Winther, Bloomington, Indiana, 1958.

UPTON, EMORY, The Military Policy of the United States, Washington, 1912.

UPTON, LUCILLE MORRIS, Battle of Wilson's Creek, Springfield, Missouri, n.d.

URQUHART, DAVID, "Bragg's Advance and Retreat," Battles and Leaders.

VAGTS, ALFRED, Landing Operations, Harrisburg, Pennsylvania, 1946 and 1952.

VAIL, I. E., "Three Years of the Blockade," *The United Service*, A Monthly Review of Military and Naval Affairs, Vol. V, 1861, Philadelphia, August–September, 1881.

VALLANDIGHAM, C. L., Speeches, Arguments and Addresses and letters of Clement L. Vallandigham, New York, 1864.

——, Biographical Memoir of, by his brother, New York, 1864.

Vallandigham Song Book, Songs for the Times, n.p., n.d.

VANCE, WILSON J., Stone's River, The Turning Point of the Civil War, New York, 1914.

VAN DEUSEN, GLYNDON G., Thurlow Weed, New York, 1947.

VANDIVER, FRANK E., Confederate Blockade Blockade Running Through Bermuda 1861–1865, Austin, 1947.

——, Jubal's Raid: General Early's Famous Attack on Washington in 1864, New York, 1960.

——, Mighty Stonewall, 1957.

——, Ploughshares into Swords; Josiah Gorgas and Confederate Ordnance, Austin, 1952.

——, Rebel Brass; The Confederate Command System, Baton Rouge, 1956.

VAN HORNE, THOMAS B., History of the Army of the Cumberland, two vols. and atlas, Cincinnati, 1875.

——, The Life of Major General George H. Thomas, New York, 1882.

VAN SANTWOOD, C., The One Hundred and Twentieth Regiment New York State Volunteers, Roundout, New York, 1894.

VENABLE, C. S., "The Campaigns from the Wilderness to Petersburg," *Southern Historical Society Papers*, Vol. XIV, January–December, 1886.

——, "General Lee in the Wilderness Campaign," Battles and Leaders.

Vidette, The, Occasional Newspapers published by John Hunt Morgan's Command, Southern Historical Society Collection, University of North Carolina, Chapel Hill.

VILAS, WILLIAM FREEMAN, A View of the Vicksburg Campaign, Madison, August, 1908.

VILLARD, HENRY, Lincoln on the Eve of '61, edited by Harold G. and Oswald Garrison Villard, New York, 1941.

———, Memoirs of Henry Villard, Journalist and Financier 1835–1900, two vols., Boston, 1904.

VILLARD, OSWALD GARRISON, John Brown, 1800–1859, Boston, 1910.

VILLIERS, BROUGHAM, and W. H. CHESSON (Villiers is F. J. Shaw), Anglo-American Relations 1861–1865, New York, 1920.

VINCENT, THOMAS M., "The Battle of Bull Run, July 21, 1861," Commandery of the District of Columbia of the Military Order of the Loyal Legion of the United States, War Paper No. 58, 1905.

Virginia Campaign of 1862, Under General Pope, Vol. II, Military Historical Society of Massachusetts Papers, Boston, 1895.

"Visitor to Charleston," *Atlantic Monthly,* April, 1861.

VON ABELE, RUDOLPH, Alexander H. Stephens, New York, 1948.

VON BORCKE, HEROS, Memoirs of the Confederate War for Independence, two vols., New York, 1938.

WADE, WILLIAM W., "The Man who Stopped the Rams," *American Heritage,* Vol. XIV, No. 3, April, 1963.

WAINWRIGHT, CHARLES S., A Diary of Battle, The Personal Journals of Colonel Charles S. Wainwright 1861–1865, edited by Allan Nevins, New York, 1962.

WAIT, HORATIO L., "The Blockade of the Confederacy," *Century Magazine,* Vol. LVI, No. 6, October, 1896.

———, "The Blockading Service," Military Essays and Recollections, Vol. II, Illinois Commandery of the Military Order of the Loyal Legion of the United States, Chicago, 1891.

———, "Reminiscences of Fort Sumter," Military Essays and Recollections, Vol. I, Illinois Commandery of the Military Order of the Loyal Legion of the United States, Chicago, 1891.

WALCOTT, CHARLES F., "The Battle of Chantilly," Military Historical Society of Massachusetts Papers, Boston, 1895.

———, History of the Twenty-first Regiment Massachusetts Volunteers in the War for the Restoration of the Union 1861–1865, Boston, 1882.

WALKE, HENRY, "The Gun Boats at Belmont and Fort Henry," Battles and Leaders.

———, Naval Scenes and Reminiscences of the Civil War in the United States on the Southern and Western Waters during the years 1861, 1862 and 1863, New York, 1877.

———, "The Western Flotilla at Fort Donelson, Island No. 10, Fort Pillow and Memphis," Battles and Leaders.

WALKER, F. A., "The expedition to the Boydton Plank Road, October, 1864," Vol. V., Military Historical Society of Massachusetts Papers, Boston, 1906.

———, History of the Second Army Corps in the Army of the Potomac, New York, 1886.

———, "Meade at Gettysburg," Battles and Leaders.

———, "Ream's Station," Vol. V, Military Historical Society of Massachusetts Papers, Boston, 1906.

WALKER, FRANCIS A., and HENRY J. HUNT, "General Hancock and the Artillery at Gettysburg," Battles and Leaders.

WALKER, GEORGE, The Wealth, Resources and Public Debt of the United States, London, 1865.

WALKER, JOHN G., "Jackson's Capture of Harper's Ferry," Battles and Leaders.

———, "Sharpsburg," Battles and Leaders.

WALKER, PETER F., "Command Failure; The Fall of Forts Henry and Donelson, Tennessee," *Tennessee Historical Quarterly,* Vol. XVI, No. 4, December, 1957.

———, Vicksburg, A People at War 1860–1865, Chapel Hill, 1960.

WALLACE, ISABEL, Life and Letters of General W. H. L. Wallace, Chicago, 1909.

WALLACE, J. S., Sketch of the Life and Public Services of Edward D. Baker, Springfield, 1870.

WALLACE, LEW, An Autobiography, two vols., New York, 1906.

———, "The Capture of Fort Donelson," Battles and Leaders.

WALPOLE, SPENCER, The Life of Lord John Russell, two vols., London, 1889.

WALTHALL, W. T., "The True Story of the Capture of Jefferson Davis," *Southern Historical Society Papers,* Vol. V, No. 3, March, 1878.

WALTON, J. B., "Letter from," *Southern Historical Society Papers,* Vol. V, Nos. 1, 2, 1878.

"War Claims at St. Louis," Executive Documents of the House of Representatives, 37th Congress, 2nd Session, 1861–1862, Vol. VII, Washington, 1862.

WARD, JOHN SHIRLEY, "Did the Federals Fight Against Superior Numbers?" *Southern Historical Society Papers,* Vol. XX, January–December, 1892.

WARDEN, ROBERT B., An Account of the Private Life and Public Services of Salmon Portland Chase, Cincinnati, 1874.

WARDER, T. B., and JAS. M. CATLETT, Battle of Young's Branch; or Manassas Plain, Richmond, 1862.

WARE, E. F., The Lyon Campaign in Missouri, being a history of the First Iowa Infantry, Topeka, Kansas, 1907.

WARING, GEORGE E., "The Sooy Smith Expedition (February, 1862)," Battles and Leaders.

WARLEY, A. F., "Notes on the Destruction of the 'Albemarle,'" Battles and Leaders.

———, "The Ram 'Manassas' at the Passage of the New Orleans Forts," Battles and Leaders.

WARNER, EZRA J., Generals in Blue, Baton Rouge, 1964.

———, Generals in Gray, Baton Rouge, 1959.

War of the Rebellion, The, A Compilation of the official records of the Union and Confederate Armies, seventy vols., in one hundred twenty-eight parts, Washington 1880–1901, and atlas.

WARREN, CHARLES, The Supreme Court in United States History, two vols., 1923.

WARREN, G. K., Proceedings, Findings and Opinions of the Court of Inquiry Convened by Order of the President of the United States in Special Orders

No. 277, Headquarters of the Army, Adjutant General's Office, Washington D.C., December 9, 1879. In the Case of Gouverneur K. Warren, late Major General United States Volunteers Commanding the Fifth Army Corps in the Campaign of Five Forks, Virginia, 1865. Three parts with maps, Washington, 1883.

WARREN, LOUIS A., Lincoln's Gettysburg Declaration, "A New Birth of Freedom," Lincoln National Life Foundation, Fort Wayne, Indiana, 1964.

WARREN, ROBERT PENN, John Brown, the Making of a Martyr, New York, 1929.

War of the Sixties, E. R. Hutchins, compiler, New York, 1912.

War Talks of Confederate Veterans, edited by George S. Bernard, Petersburg, Virginia, 1892.

WASHBURN, GEORGE N., A Complete History and Record of the 108th Regiment New York Volunteers from 1862 to 1894, Rochester, 1894.

WATKINS, JAMES L., King Cotton, A Historical and Statistical Review 1790 to 1906, New York, 1908.

WATSON, ELMO SCOTT, "The Big Parade 1865 Model," Feature Story for Western Newspaper Union.

WATSON, JOHN C., "Farragut and Mobile Bay, Personal Reminiscences," Commandery of the District of Columbia, Military Order of the Loyal Legion of the United States, War Paper 98, 1916.

——, "The Lashing of Admiral Farragut in the Rigging," Battles and Leaders.

WATSON, WILLIAM, Life in the Confederate Army, London, 1887.

WAYLAND, JOHN W., Stonewall Jackson's Way, Staunton, Virginia, 1956.

WEBB, ALEXANDER S., The Peninsula, McClellan's Campaign of 1862, Campaigns of the Civil War, Vol. III, New York, 1881.

WEBB, ELIZABETH YATES, "Cotton Manufacturing in North Carolina 1861–1865," *North Carolina Historical Review*, April, 1932.

WEBB, W. L., Battles and Biographies of Missourians of the Civil War Period of our State, Kansas City, Missouri, 1900.

WEBER, THOMAS, The Northern Railroads in the Civil War 1861–1865, New York, 1962.

WEED, THURLOW, Diplomatic Incidents, A Chapter from the Autobiography of Mr. Thurlow Weed, *Galaxy*, Vol. X, July, 1871.

WEIGLEY, RUSSELL F., Quartermaster General of the Union Army; A biography of M. C. Meigs, New York, 1959.

WELCH, SPENCER GLASGOW, A Confederate Surgeon's Letters to his Wife, Marietta, Georgia, 1954.

WELD, STEPHEN M., "The Conduct of General McClellan at Alexandria in August, 1862," Vol. II, Military Historical Society of Massachusetts Papers, Boston, 1895.

——, "The Petersburg Mine," Vol. V, Military Historical Society of Massachusetts Papers, Boston, 1906.

WELLES, E. L., "Who Burnt Columbia? Testimony of a Confederate Cavalryman," *Southern Historical Society Papers*, Vol. X, No. 3, March, 1882.

WELLES, GIDEON, "Admiral Farragut and New Orleans," *Galaxy*, November, 1871.

——, "Capture and Release of Mason and Slidell," *Galaxy*, May, 1873.

——, Diary of Gideon Welles, three vols., Boston, 1909–11.

——, "First Iron-Clad Monitor," Annals of the War, Philadelphia, 1879.

——, "Fort Sumter," *Galaxy,* November, 1870.

——, "Lincoln and Seward," New York, 1874.

——, "Nomination and Election of Abraham Lincoln," *Galaxy,* September, 1876.

WELLMAN, MANLY WADE, Giant in Gray, A Biography of Wade Hampton of South Carolina, New York, 1949.

WELLMAN, PAUL I., The Indian Wars of the West, New York, 1954.

——, "Missourians Stage a Private Fight in Deadly Battle of Lone Jack," Kansas City, Missouri, *Times,* August 18, 1938.

WENDER, HERBERT, Southern Commercial Conventions 1837–1859, Baltimore, 1930.

WERSTEIN, IRVING, July, 1863, New York, 1950.

WEST, RICHARD S., JR., Gideon Welles, Lincoln's Navy Department, Indianapolis, 1943.

——, Mr. Lincoln's Navy, New York, 1957.

——, "The Morgan Purchases," *United States Naval Institute Proceedings* Vol. 66, No. 443, January, 1940.

——, The Second Admiral, A life of David Dixon Porter 1813–1891, New York, 1937.

WESTCOTT, THOMPSON, Chronicles of the Great Rebellion, Philadelphia, 1867.

"Western Department or Missouri-Miscellaneous," Report of the Joint Committee on the Conduct of the War, Part III, Washington, 1863.

West Virginia, A Guide to the Mountain State, American Guide Series, New York, 1941.

WEYGANT, GEORGE H., History of the One Hundred Twenty-fourth Regiment of New York State Volunteers, Newburgh, New York, 1877.

WEYMOUTH, H. G. O., "The Crossing of the Rappahannock by the Nineteenth Massachusetts," Battles and Leaders.

WHAN, VORIN E., JR., Fiasco at Fredericksburg, State College, Pennsylvania, 1961.

WHEELER, LIEUTENANT GENERAL JOSEPH, Alabama, Vol. VII, Confederate Military History, Atlanta, Georgia, 1899.

——, "An Effort to Rescue Jefferson Davis," *Century Magazine,* Vol. LVI, No. 1, May, 1898.

——, "Bragg's Invasion of Kentucky," Battles and Leaders.

WHELESS, JOHN F., "The Confederate Treasure," *Southern Historical Society Papers,* Vol. X, No. 3, March, 1882.

WHERRY, WILLIAM M., The Campaign in Missouri and the Battle of Wilson's Creek, 1861, St. Louis, Missouri, 1880.

——, "Wilson's Creek and the Death of Lyon," Battles and Leaders.

WHITBRIDGE, ARNOLD, "The *Alabama* 1862–1864," *History Today,* March, 1965.

WHITE, E. V., The First Iron-clad Naval Engagement in the World, Portsmouth, Virginia, 1904.

——, History of the Battle of Ball's Bluff, Leesburg, Virginia, n.d.

WHITE, HENRY ALEXANDER, "Lee's Wrestle with Grant in the Wilderness 1864," Vol. IV, Military Historical Society of Massachusetts Papers, Boston, 1905.

WHITE, JOHN CHESTER, "Military Prisons; North and South," Vol. XIV, Military Historical Society of Massachusetts Papers, Boston, 1918.

WHITE, JULIUS, "The Capitulation of Harper's Ferry," Battles and Leaders.

WHITE, LAURA A., Robert Barnwell Rhett; Father of Secession, New York, 1931.

WHITE, RUTH, Yankee from Sweden, New York, 1960.

WHITE, WILLIAM CHAPMAN, and RUTH WHITE, Tin Can on a Shingle, New York, 1957.

WHITFORD, WILLIAM CLARKE, Colorado Volunteers in the Civil War; The New Mexico Campaign in 1862, Denver, 1906.

WHITMAN, WALT, The Complete Writings of Walt Whitman, ten vols., New York, 1902.

———, The Gathering of the Forces, New York, 1920.

WHITNEY, THOMAS R., A Defense of the American Policy as opposed to the encroachments of Foreign Influence, and especially to the Interference of the Papacy in the Political Interests and Affairs of the United States, New York, 1856.

Who Burnt Columbia? Part I, Official Deposition of William Tecumseh Sherman and General O. O. Howard, filed in certain claims vs. United States, pending before "The Mixed Commission on British and American Claims," Charleston, South Carolina, 1873.

WIGHT, AMBROSE S., "The Flag First Hoisted at Mobile," *Century Magazine,* Vol. XLI, No. 1, November, 1890.

WIGHTMAN, JOHN T., A Discourse Delivered in the Methodist Episcopal Church South, Yorkville, South Carolina, July 28, 1861, The Day of the Thanksgiving for the Victory at Manassas, Portland, Maine, 1871.

WILBOURN, E. R., "Letter (re death of Jackson at Chancellorsville)," *Southern Historical Papers,* Vol. VI, No. 6, December, 1878.

WILCOX, C. M., "Lee and Grant in the Wilderness," Annals of the War.

———, "Letter on Gettysburg," *Southern Historical Society Papers,* Vol. IV, July–December, 1877.

WILCOX, CHARLES R., "With Grant at Vicksburg, from Captain Wilcox's Diary, edited by Edgar L. Erickson," *Journal of the Illinois State Historical Society,* January, 1938.

WILDER, DANIEL WEBSTER, The Annals of Kansas, Topeka, 1857.

WILEY, BELL IRVIN, The Life of Billy Yank, Indianapolis, Indiana, 1951, 1952.

———, The Life of Johnny Reb, Indianapolis, Indiana, 1943.

———, The Plain People of the Confederacy, Baton Rouge, 1944.

———, Southern Negroes 1861–1865, New York, 1938.

WILKES, GEORGE, The Great Battle, New York, 1861.

WILKINSON, J., The Narrative of a Blockade Runner, New York, 1887.

WILLCOX, ORLANDO B., "The Capture," *Century Magazine,* Vol. XLI, No. 3, January, 1891.

WILLEY, WILLIAM P., An Inside View of the Formation of the State of West Virginia, Wheeling, West Virginia, 1901.

WILLIAMS, ALPHEUS B., From the Cannon's Mouth; The Civil War Letters of General Alpheus S. Williams edited by Milo M. Quaife, Detroit, Michigan, 1959.

WILLIAMS, MRS. ELLEN, Three Years and a Half in the Army; or the History of the Second Colorado, New York, 1895.

WILLIAMS, K. P., Lincoln Finds a General, five vols., New York, 1949, 1952, 1956, 1959.

———, "The Tennessee River Campaign and Anna Ella Carroll," *Indiana Magazine of History*, Vol. XLVI, No. 2, September, 1960.

WILLIAMS, T. HARRY, "Investigations 1862," *American Heritage*, Vol. VI, No. 1, December, 1954.

———, Lincoln and His Generals, New York, 1952.

———, Lincoln and the Radicals, Madison, Wisconsin, 1941.

———, P. G. T. Beauregard, Napoleon in Gray, Baton Rouge, 1954.

———, With Beauregard in Mexico, Baton Rouge, 1956.

WILLSON, BECKLES, John Slidell and the Confederates in Paris (1862–1865), New York, 1932.

WILSHIN, FRANCIS F., Manassas (Bull Run) National Military Park, National Park Service Historical Handbook Series No. 15, Washington, D. C., 1955.

WILSON, HILL PEEBLES, John Brown, Soldier of Fortune, A Critique, Boston, 1913.

WILSON, JAMES HARRISON, The Life of John A. Rawlins, New York, 1916.

———, Under the Old Flag, two vols., New York, 1912.

———, "The Union Cavalry in the Hood Campaign," Battles and Leaders.

WILSON, RUFUS ROCKWELL, Intimate Memoirs of Lincoln, Elmira, New York, 1945.

WILSON, WOODROW, Division and Reunion, New York, 1912.

"Wilson's Raid Through Alabama and Georgia," Battles and Leaders.

WILTSE, CHARLES H., John C. Calhoun, Nullifier, 1829–1839, Indianapolis, 1949.

WINTHROP, THEODORE, "The New York Seventh Regiment, Our March to Washington," *Atlantic Monthly*, June, 1861.

WISE, JOHN S., The End of an Era, Boston, 1901.

———, "The West Point of the Confederacy, Boys in Battle at New Market, Virginia, May 15th, 1864," unidentified magazine, Vol. XXXVIII.

WITHERSPOON, WILLIAM, "Tishomingo Creek or Bryce's Crossroads," Jackson, Tennessee, 1908, reprinted in Robert Selph Henry, As They Saw Forrest.

WOLFE, SAMUEL M., Helper's Impending Crisis Dissected, Philadelphia, 1860.

WOOD, JOHN TAYLOR, "The First Fight of Iron-clads," Battles and Leaders.

WOOD, ROBERT C., Confederate Handbook, New Orleans, 1900.

WOOD, THOMAS J., "The Battles of Missionary Ridge," Sketches of War History, Vol. IV, Ohio Commandery of the Military Order of the Loyal Legion of the United States, Cincinnati, 1896.

WOOD, WILLIAM NATHANIEL, Reminiscences of Big I, edited by Bell I. Wiley, Jackson, Tennessee, 1956.

WOODBURN, JAMES A., The Historical Significance of the Missouri Compromise, Washington, 1893.

WOODS, J. T., Services of the Ninety-sixth Ohio Volunteers, Toledo, Ohio, 1874.

WOODWARD, E. M., History of the Third Pennsylvania Reserve, Trenton, New Jersey, 1885.

WOODWARD, S. L., "Grierson's Raid, April 17th to May 26, 1863," *Journal of the United States Cavalry Association*, Vol. XXV, No. 52, April, 1904.

WOOTEN, JOHN MORGAN, A History of Bradley County, Tennessee, n.p., 1949.

WORDEN, J. L., SAMUEL GREENE, and H. ASHTON RAMSAY, The Monitor and the Merrimac, New York, 1912.

WORLEY, TED R., "The Arkansas Peace Society of 1861; A Study in Mountain Unionism," *Journal of Southern History*, November, 1958.

———, editor, At Home in Confederate Arkansas, Letters to and from Pulaski Counties, 1861–1865, Little Rock, Arkansas, 1955.

WORSHAM, JOHN H., One of Jackson's Foot Cavalry, New York, 1912.

WORTH, JONATHAN, the Correspondence of Jonathan Worth, edited by J. G. de Roulhac Hamilton, two vols., Raleigh, 1902.

WORTHINGTON, GLENN H., Fighting for Time, or the Battle that Saved Washington and Mayhap the Union, Baltimore, Maryland, 1932.

"Wounding of Lieutenant General T. J. Jackson," Anonymous (said by Freeman to be J. G. Morrison), *The Land We Love*, Vol. I, No. 21, July, 1886.

WRIGHT, CRAFTS J., Official Journal of the Conference Convention held at Washington City, February, 1861, Washington, 1861.

WRIGHT, MRS. D. GIRARD, A Southern Girl in '61, New York, 1905.

WRIGHT, HOWARD G., Port Hudson, The History from an Interior Point of View, Baton Rouge, 1961.

WRIGHT, J. MONTGOMERY, "Notes of a Staff Officer at Perryville," Battles and Leaders.

WRIGHT, REBECCA, The Loyal Girl of Winchester, n.a., n.d.

WYETH, JOHN ALLEN, That Devil Forrest, Life of General Nathan Bedford Forrest, New York, 1959.

———, With Sabre and Scalpel, New York, 1914.

YANCEY, WILLIAM L., Speech of the Honorable William L. Yancey delivered in the National Democratic Convention, 1860, Washington, n.d.

YARYAN, JOHN LEE, "Stone's River," War Papers, Indiana Commandery of the Military Order of the Loyal Legion of the United States, Vol. I, Indianapolis, 1898.

YEARNS, WILFRED BUCK, The Confederate Congress, Atlanta, 1960.

YOUNG, BENNETT H., Confederate Wizards of the Saddle, Being Reminiscences and Observations of One Who Rode With Morgan, Boston, 1914, and Kennesaw, Georgia, 1959.

YOUNG, JESSE BOWMAN, The Battle of Gettysburg, A Comprehensive Narrative, New York, 1913.

YOUNG, JOHN RUSSELL, Around the World With General Grant, two vols., New York, 1879.

YOUNG, MRS. M. J., A Remarkable Plea to the Soldiers of the Trans-Mississippi, A Southern Woman Glories in Rebellion, in E. R. Hutchins, The War of the Sixties.

YOUNG, WILLIAM, Young's History of La Fayette County, Missouri, Indianapolis, 1910.

INDEX BY DATES

The following subject index *keyed to dates* is designed to provide a guide to THE CIVIL WAR DAY BY DAY itself, and at the same time serve as a ready reference to dates and sequence of all major, and many of the minor, events of the Civil War period. Individuals have been identified as Federal or Confederate by use of (C) and (F) after their names. Other abbreviations are:

action—act.
affair—aff.
Army of Northern Virginia—A.N.Va.
Army of the Potomac—A. of P.
artillery—art.
assault—ass.
attack—att.
battle—Bat.
bombardment—bomb.
Bridge—Br.,
campaign—camp.
captured—capt.
cavalry—cav.
combat—comb.
Confederate—Conf.
Congress—Cong.
Creek—Cr.
demonstration—demon.
descent—desc.
District—Dist.
engagement—eng.
evacuation—evac.
expedition—exped.
Federal—Fed.
Ferry—Fy.

Ford—Fd.
Fort—ft.
government—govt.
headquarters—hdqrs.
Indians, fight with—(Ind.)
Indian Territory—I.T.
infantry—inf.
Island—I.
Landing—Ldg.
legislature—leg.
mentioned—ment.
occupation—occup.
operations—oper.
prisoners, U.S.—are Federal prisoners in the Confederacy
prisoners, Conf.—are Confederate prisoners in the U.S.
railway—ry.
reconnaissance—recon.
regiment—regt.
River—R.
Road—Rd.
scout—sc.
skirmish—sk.
Squadron—Squad.

Following the main date index is a brief index to the Special Studies section.

INDEX

Abingdon, Va.: (1863) death of J. B. Floyd at, Aug. 26; (1864) Morgan retreats to, June 12; sk. near, Dec. 15

Abolition: *See* Emancipation

Abolitionists: (1861) Rochester, N.Y., meeting broken up, Jan. 12; abolition bills in Cong., Dec. 5

Accomack Co., Va.: (1861) Oct. 14

Accotink, Va.: (1863) aff., Oct. 17; (1864) aff. near, Jan. 12; aff., July 15

Acton, Minn.: (1862) Sioux uprising, Aug. 17

Acworth, Ga.: (1864) act., June 2; Fed. cav. enters, June 3; eng., June 4; sk., June 5; act., June 8; act., June 10; sk. near, June 12; sks., June 18, 30, Oct. 4

Adairsville, Ga.: (1864) Atlanta Camp., May 15, 17, 18; act., July 7

Adams, Charles Francis (F): (1861) Lincoln appoints minister to Britain, Mar. 18; tries to prevent C.S.A. recognition, May 13; contact with British govt. limited, May 21; (1862) discussion of mediation forbidden, Aug. 2; (1863) "Laird Rams" crisis, Sept. 5; (1864) on Grant's Va. losses, June 3

Adams, John (C): (1864) killed at Franklin, Tenn., Nov. 30

Adams, Ft., Miss.: (1863) Fed. exped. from, Oct. 14; (1864) Fed. exped. to, Oct. 5; (1865) oper. around, May 3

Adams, U.S.S.: (1864) eng. with Greene's raiders, June 2

Adamstown, Md.: (1864) sk., Oct. 14

Adamsville, Tenn.: (1862) sk. near, Mar. 31

Adirondack, U.S.S. (sloop): (1862) wrecked, Aug. 23

Adjutant General's Office, U.S.: (1863) organizing of Negro troops, May 22

Admiral: *See* Rear Admiral

Adobe, Ft., N. Mex. Terr.: (1864) eng. (Ind.), Nov. 25

Aenon Church, Va.: (1864) comb., May 28

Africa: (1862) colonization of Negroes, Mar. 6

African Brigade: (1863) at Vicksburg, June 7

African Slave Trade: *See* Slave Trade

Agnew's Fy., Tenn.: (1862) Fed. recon. to, Mar. 25

Agriculture, Dept. of, U. S.: (1862) Lincoln approves establishment of, May 15; (1864) development of, Dec. 6

Agua Fria, N. Mex. Terr.: (1865) oper. about, Mar. 31

Aiken, S.C.: (1865) act., Feb. 11

Alabama: (1860) offers troops to S.C., Dec. 27; (1861) takes over U. S. Arsenal at Mt. Vernon, Jan. 4; takes Fts. Morgan and Gaines, Jan. 5; State Convention meets, Jan. 7; secedes, Jan. 11; ratifies Conf. Constitution, Mar. 13; (1862) Bragg quote, Ala. "is redeemed," Sept. 5; Davis to Seddon re north Ala., Dec. 18; (1863) use of slaves in armies approved, Sept. 2; Thomas H. Watts elected gov. of, Sept. 8; (1865) Lewis E. Parsons appointed provisional gov. of, June 21; ratifies Thirteenth Amendment, Dec. 2

Alabama, C.S.S. (also known as *Enrica*): (1862) cruiser launched, May 15; leaves Liverpool, July 29; commissioned cruiser in Conf. Navy, Aug. 24; depredations, burns *Elisha Dunbar*, Sept. 18; takes prizes, Oct. 3; sinks *Manchester*, Oct. 11; raids seas, Oct. 23; (1863) sinks U.S.S. *Hatteras*, Jan. 11; seizes ship off San Domingo, Jan. 26; takes whalers off Brazil, Apr. 15; takes prizes off Bahia, Brazil, May 25; ment., July 16; captures bark off Cape of Good Hope, Aug. 6; prizes near Straits of Malacca, Dec. 26; (1864) arrives at Capetown, S.A., Mar. 20; arrives at Cherbourg, June 11; *Kearsarge* arrives at Cherbourg, June 14; destroyed by *Kearsarge*, June 19; Alabama Claims, Apr. 7

Alabama, Mississippi, and East Louisiana, Dept. of (C): (1864) S. D. Lee assumes command of, May 9; Maury to command, July 26; Richard Taylor to command, Aug. 15; Taylor assumes command of, Sept. 6; (1865) Taylor surrenders, May 4

Alabama Claims: (1865) Apr. 7

Alabama Rd., Miss.: (1862) Fed. recon. on, May 10

Alabama and West Florida, Dept. of (C): (1861) Bragg given command of, Oct. 14

Alamo, The: (1863) ment., Sept. 8

Alamo, U.S. (steamer): (1864) guerrilla attack on, Nov. 29

Albany, Ky.: (1861) aff., Sept. 23; sk., Sept. 29; (1863) sk. near, Aug. 18

Albany, Mo.: (1864) sk., Oct. 26

Albany, N.Y.: (1861) Lincoln addresses legislature, Feb. 18; (1865) Lincoln's funeral train en route to, Apr. 25

Albatross, U.S.S.: (1863) passage of Port Hudson batteries, Mar. 14; off Natchez, Mar. 17; passage of Grand Gulf batteries, Mar. 19; attacks Warrenton, Miss., batteries, Mar. 23; passes Grand Gulf batteries, Mar. 31; damaged at Ft. De Russy, May 4

Albemarle, C.S.S.: (1864) ment., Apr. 17; ram attacks Plymouth, N.C., sinks U.S.S. *Smithfield*, Apr. 19; menaces Fed. position in N.C., May 4; engages Fed. fleet in Roanoke R., May 5; attempt to destroy fails, May 25; sinking of, Oct. 27

Albemarle Canal (also known as Chesapeake and Albemarle Canal, Dismal Swamp Canal): (1862) Fed. exped. from North R., N.C., to, Feb. 13; blocked by Feds., Apr. 23

Albemarle and Chesapeake Canal: *See* Albemarle Canal

Albemarle Co., Va.: (1864) Custer's cavalry active in, Feb. 2, Custer's raid into, Feb. 28, 29, Mar. 2

Albemarle Sound, N.C.: (1864) sks. along, May 4; Feds. control, May 5

Albert, Prince: (1861) dies, diplomacy of in *Trent* Aff., Dec. 14

Albion (blockade-runner): (1861) captured, Dec. 1

Albuquerque, N. Mex. Terr.: (1862) abandoned by Feds., Mar. 2; sk. as Sibley retreats, Apr. 8; Conf. evacuation of, Apr. 12

Alder Gulch (or Virginia City, Mont. Terr.): (1863) gold discovered at, May 26

Aldie, Va.: (1862) Fed. recon. toward, Sept. 16; Fed. recon. to, Oct. 8; (1863) sk. near, Mar. 2; Fed. sc. to, May 27; sk., June 17; sk. near, June 18, 22; Mosby's oper. near, July 28; Fed. sc. to, Aug. 15; (1864) sk. near, Feb. 5; Fed. sc. to, Mar. 28; sk. near, July 6; (1865) Fed. sc. to, Feb. 15

Alert (blockade-runner): (1861) capt., Oct. 6

Alexander, Edward Porter (C): (1861) use of signal flags at Bull Run, July 21

Alexander's Br., Ga.: (1863) sk., Sept. 18

Alexander's Cr., La.: (1864) sk. at, near St. Francisville, Oct. 5

Alexandria (Conf. vessel): (1863) seized by British, April 6

Apr. 12; sk. on, Apr. 17; Grierson's Raid crosses, May 1; Fed. exped. to, Sept. 24; (1864) oper. on, July 3; sk. at Benton's Fy. on, July 25; Fed. exped. to, Oct. 2; sk. on, Dec. 12; (1865) sk. on, Mar. 18; Fed. exped. to, Mar. 26

Amite R. and Jackson R.R.: (1863) oper. on, May 9

Amnesty, Federal: (1862) Lincoln grants to political prisoners who take oath, Feb. 15; (1863) proclamation of, for deserters, Mar. 10; Lincoln's Proclamation of Amnesty and Reconstruction, Dec. 8; (1864) Lincoln clarifies position on, Mar. 26

Amnesty and Reconstruction, Proclamation of: (1863) Lincoln issues, Dec. 8; (1865) Johnson's, May 29

"Anaconda Plan": (1861) May 3

Anderson, Charles D. (C): (1864) censored for surrender of Ft. Gaines, Aug. 7

Anderson, G. W. (C): (1864) fall of Ft. McAllister, Dec. 13

Anderson, Richard Heron (C): (1861) Santa Rosa I., landing, Oct. 9; (1864) moves toward Spotsylvania Court House, May 7; Bat. of Spotsylvania Court House, May 8, 10, 12; Bat. of Cold Harbor, June 1, 3; ordered to Petersburg, June 17; att. against Sheridan, Aug. 21; eng. at Berryville, Va., Sept. 3; joins Lee, Sept. 14, 16; (1865) eng. at Sayler's Cr., Va., Apr. 6

Anderson, Robert (F): (1860) background, Nov. 15; asks to garrison, strengthen Ft. Sumter, Castle Pinckney, warns S.C. secession imminent, Nov. 23; reports to Wash., Dec. 10; transfers garrison from Moultrie to Sumter, Dec. 26, 27; raises U.S. flag on Sumter, Dec. 27; Buchanan refuses to disavow his move to Sumter, Dec. 31; (1861) status of Ft. Sumter, Jan. pg.; protests *Star of the West* firing, Jan. 9; ordered to act defensively, Jan. 10; refuses to surrender Sumter, Jan. 11; temporary "truce" with Gov. Pickens, Jan. 13; communicates with Wash., Feb. 28; requests decision on evac., Mar. 1; requests reinforcements, Mar. 4, 9; defensive plans, Mar. 16; Pres. Davis' concern for Sumter, Mar. 18; talks with G. V. Fox, Mar. 21; reinforcing exped., Apr. 4; communication with Charleston cut off, Apr. 7; refuses to evacuate Sumter, Apr. 11; Sumter fired upon, Apr. 12; agrees to surrender, Apr. 13; surrenders Sumter, Apr. 14; on evils of secession, Apr. 14; arrives in N.Y., Apr. 18; invited to White Rouse, May 1; recruiting duty in Ky., western Va., May 7; Lincoln to, May 14; confers with Lincoln, Aug. 13; commands Dept. of the Cumberland, Aug. 15; to raise Ky. troops, Sept. 20; Sherman supersedes in Dept. of Cumberland, Oct. 8; (1865) attends flag raising on Sumter, Apr. 14

Anderson, William C. "Bloody Bill" (C): (1864) invades Centralia, Mo., Sept. 27; death of in Oct. ambush, Sept. 27; Oct. 26

Anderson, Camp, Calif.: (1864) Fed. sc. from to Bald Mt., Aug. 8

Anderson, Ft., Ky.: (1864) Forrest attacks, Mar. 25

Anderson, Ft., N.C.: (1865) bombardment of, Feb. 18; capt., Feb. 19; *Thorn* destroyed, Mar. 4

Anderson's Cross Roads, Tenn.: (1863) sk., Oct. 2

Andersonville (Camp Sumter), Ga.: (1864) in operation, Feb. 27; reports of attempt to free prisoners in, Dec. 1; (1865) execution of Wirz, Nov. 10

Andracita, British schooner: *See J. W. Wilder*

Andrew, John A., gov. of Mass. (F): (1864) Lincoln asks home for Negroes in Mass., Feb. 18

Andrews, James J. (F): (1862) locomotive chase, Apr. 12

Angley's Post Office, S.C.: (1865) sk., Feb. 4

Anglo-American, U.S.S.: (1862) eng. with Port Hudson batteries, Aug. 29

Annandale, Va.: (1861) sk., Dec. 2; (1863) Fed. wagon train captured, Aug. 11; sk., Oct. 18; aff., Oct. 22; (1864) aff., Mar. 16; sk., Aug. 24

Annapolis, Dept. of: (1861) B. F. Butler assigned command, Apr. 27; Cadwalader supersedes Butler, May 15

Annapolis, Md.: (1861) Fed. troops at, Apr. 19; (1864) Constitutional Convention meets in, Apr. 27

"Annie Laurie"; (1865) sung by Pickett's men, Apr. 1

Antelope Cr., Calif.: (1865) Fed. exped. to, Apr. 5

Anthony's Hill (or King's Hill), Tenn.: (1864) act., Dec. 25

Antietam, Bat. of (or Sharpsburg): (1862) lost order of, Sept. 13; South Mt., Sept. 14; pre-bat. moves, Sept. 15, 16; Bat. of, Sept. 17; aftermath, Sept. 18, 19, 20, 22; Emancipation Proclamation, Sept. 22; ment., Oct. 1, 25, 26; Lee licks wounds after, Nov. 1; McClellan's slowness after, Nov. 5; (1863) ment., Mar. 21, July 12

Antietam, lost order of: *See* Lee's lost order

Antietam, Md.: (1864) aff., July 6

Antietam Br., Md.: (1864) sk. (Early's raid), July 8

Antietam Cr., Md.: (1862) Lee's line west of, Sept. 15; Lee gathers forces on, Sept. 16; Bat. of Antietam, Sept. 17

Antietam Fd., Md.: (1861) Sept. 15; (1864) sk., Aug. 4

Antietam Iron Works, Md.: (1861) sk., Aug. 27

Antioch Church, Tenn.: (1863) Fed. exped. to, May 26

Antoine (or Terre Noir Cr.), Ark.: (1864) sks. (Camden exped.), Apr. 2

Apache Canyon, N. Mex. Terr.: (1862) eng., Mar. 26

Apache Pass, N. Mex. Terr.: (1862) sk. (Ind.), July 15

Apaches: (1861) ambush Conf. detachment, Aug. 12; (1862) sk. with Fed. troops at Apache Pass, N. Mex. Terr., July 15

Apalachicola, Fla.: (1861) blockaded, June 7; (1862) surrenders, Apr. 3; (1865) Fed. exped. to, May 31

Apalachicola Arsenal, Fla.: (1861) taken by state, Jan. 6

Apalachicola R., Fla.: (1862) blockade-runner captured on, Oct. 15

Appomattox Court House, Va.: (1864) ment., May 4; (1865) camp., Mar. 29, 30, 31, Apr. 1, 2, 3, 4, 5, 6, 7, 8; surrender A.N.Va., Apr. 9; paroling of Conf., Apr. 10; surrender ceremony, Apr. 12

Appomattox R., Va.: (1864) ment., May 17; attempt to put Fed. lines on, June 21; Fed. drive to reach, Sept. 29; (1865) Fed. army south of, Apr. 1; Lee heads for, Apr. 5, 6; Lee crosses, Apr. 7

Appomattox Station, Va.: (1865) Sheridan blocks Lee at, Apr. 7; eng., Apr. 8; eng. near, Apr. 9

Aquia Cr., Va. (*See also* Aquia Ldg.): (1861) Fed. bomb. at, May 29; Conf. batteries shelled, May 31, June 1; (1862) McClellan's possible movement via, Mar. 8; Lincoln meets McDowell at, May 23; Burnside arrives at, Aug. 4; A. of P. corps move toward, Aug. 14; A. of P. moves toward, Aug.

16, 20; A. of P. lands at, Aug. 27; Feds. evacuate, Sept. 6; Lincoln confers with Burnside at, Nov. 27; (1863) sk. on at Wiggenton's Mill, Feb. 6; Lincoln leaves from, Apr. 10; Lincoln visits, Apr. 19

Aquia District, Conf.: (1861) Holmes commands, Oct. 22

Aquia Ldg., Va. (*See also* Aquia Cr.): (1862) A. of P. ordered back to, Aug. 3

Aransas Bay, Tex.: (1862) eng., Feb. 22; Fed. launches capt., Apr. 22; oper. in, July 7

Aransas Pass, Tex.: (1862) oper., Feb. 11; U.S.S. *Arthur* captures C.S.S. *Breaker*, Aug. 12; (1863) Conf. battery capt., Nov. 17

Arapahoes: (1864) Sand Cr. massacre, Nov. 29

Arbuckle, Ft., I.T.: (1861) evacuated by Feds., May 4; Conf. occup., May 5

Arcadia, Mo.: (1864) sk., Sept. 7

Arcadia Valley, Mo.: (1864) sk., Sept. 26

Archer, C.S.S. (schooner): (1863) descent on Portland, Me., June 26

Arizona, Territory of, Conf. (*See also* Arizona Territory): (1862) formed, Jan. 18

Arizona Territory (*See also* Arizona, Territory of, Conf.): (1861) pro-Confs. declare out of Union, Mar. 16; Sibley commands Conf. forces in, Dec. 14; (1863) separated from N. Mex. Terr., Feb. 24; (1864) Fed. oper. in, Feb. 1; sc. in, July 6; Fed. exped. in, Dec. 10, 26

Arkadelphia, Ark.: (1863) sk., Feb. 15; Price's withdrawal to, Sept. 10; "Jo" Shelby's raid into Ark. and Mo., Sept. 22; Feds. occupy, Oct. 28; (1864) sk., Mar. 20; sk. (Camden exped.), Mar. 29; sk. near (Camden exped.), Mar. 31; sk. (Camden exped.), Apr. 1

Arkansas: (1861) votes referendum on secession, Jan. 16; Little Rock Arsenal seized, Feb. 8; U.S. stores seized, Feb. 12; votes down secession, to hold referendum, Mar. 18; legislature votes secession, May 6; admitted to Confederacy, May 18; U. S. Senate expels sens., July 11; Polk commands Conf. troops, Sept. 2; ment., Sept. 20; recruiting in, Sept. 22; in Fed. Dept. of the Mo., Nov. 9; (1862) in Conf. Trans-Miss. Dept., May 26; Fed. mil. gov. appointed, July 18; gov. asks Davis for aid, July 28; Davis to Holmes on, Oct. 21; (1863) Davis on morale in, Nov. 6; Davis on loss of, Nov. 19; (1864) pro-Union constitution ratified, anti-slavery measure, Jan. 19; Lincoln orders elections in, Jan. 20; provisional pro-Union gov. elected, Jan. 22; Lincoln on governing, Jan. 27; ratifies pro-Union constitution, ends slavery, Mar. 18; pro-Union govt. inaugurated, Apr. 11; reconstruction in, July 4; Fed. scs. in, Sept. 6; (1865) ratifies Thirteenth Amendment, Apr. 20

Arkansas, C.S.S. (ram): (1862) attacks Fed. fleet on Yazoo, Miss. rs., July 15; at Vicksburg, July 16; Fed. att. on, July 22; misses Baton Rouge eng., Aug. 1; faulty engines, Aug. 5; attacked, abandoned, destroyed, Aug. 6

Arkansas, Dept. of, Fed.: (1864) Steele assumes command of, Jan. 30; Sherman in over-all command of, Mar. 12

Arkansas, District of, Conf.: (1863) Holmes assumes command of, Mar. 18

Arkansas Post, Ark.: (1862) Fed. exped. against, Nov. 16; (1863) McClernand moves toward, Jan. 4; eng., Jan. 10; surrenders, Jan. 11; (1864) Fed. exped. to, Oct. 13

Arkansas R.: (1862) Van Dorn retreats toward, Mar. 8; (1863) McClernand's move up, Jan. 4; eng. at Arkansas Post, Jan. 10; Fed. sc. to from Fayette-ville, Feb. 5; sc. to Booth's Ranch on, Sept. 13; (1864) sk. on, Apr. 6; Shelby's camp. north of, May 13; Shelby assumes command of troops north of, May 27; U.S.S. *Miller* captured on, Aug. 17; Conf. guerrilla attack on *Alamo,* Nov. 29; (1865) Fed. oper. against Indians on, Jan. 28; Fed. exped. on, Feb. 8; Fed. sc. to, Feb. 17

Arkansas True Democrat: (1861) on Lincoln's first inaugural, Mar. 4

Arlington, Va.: (1862) Pope at, Sept. 5

Arlington Mills, Va.: (1861) sk., June 1

Armies of the Union: (1864) concerted move ordered, Apr. 9

Armistead, Lewis Addison (C): (1863) Bat. of Gettysburg, July 3

Armstrong, William "Duff": (1863) Lincoln gives honorable discharge to, Sept. 18

Armstrong's Farm, Va.: (1864) comb., May 30

Armstrong's Fy., Tenn.: (1864) sk., Jan. 21

Armstrong's Mill, Va.: (1865) *See* Hatcher's Run, Bat. of, Feb. 5, 6, 7

Armuchee Cr., Ga.: (1864) sk., May 15

Army, Conf.: *See* individual names of armies; major camps. and bats.; com-manders such as Lee, Bragg, A. S. Johnston, J. E. Johnston, Beauregard, Van Dorn, E. K. Smith

Army, U. S.: *See* individual names of armies; major camps. and bats.; com-manders such as Winfield Scott, McClellan, Halleck, Grant, W. T. Sherman, Meade, Hooker, Burnside, Pope

Arnold, Samuel (*See also* Lincoln, assassination of): (1865) imprisoned as Lincoln conspirator, May 1; judged guilty, gets life imprisonment, June 30; imprisonment, pardon, July 7

Arnoldsburg, W. Va.: (1862) sk., May 6

Arnoldsville, Mo.: (1864) sk., June 1

Arrington's Depot, Va.: (1864) Fed. raid on, June 11

Arrowfield Church (or Swift Cr.), Va.: (1864) eng. (south side James oper.), May 9

Arrow Rock, Mo.: (1862) sk., July 29; sk. near, Oct. 12; (1863) defeat of Shelby at, Oct. 13; (1864) Conf. guerrilla att. on, July 20

Arthur, U.S.S.: (1862) captures *Breaker,* Aug. 12

Arundel's Farm, Va.: (1865) sk., Apr. 10

Ashby, Turner (C): (1862) 1st bat. of Kernstown, Va., Mar. 23; killed, June 6

Ashbysburg, Ky.: (1862) sk., Sept. 25

Ashby's Gap, Va.: (1862) sks., Sept. 20, 22; (1863) in Gettysburg Camp., June 15; sks., July 11, 20; (1864) sk., July 19

Ash Cr., near Ft. Larned, Kas.: (1864) sk. at, Nov. 13

Ashepoo R., S.C.: (1861) Fed. oper. on, Dec. 12; (1864) sk. on, May 16; Fed. exped. up, May 25; U.S. *Boston* destroyed on, May 26

Asheville, N.C.: (1865) Fed. exped. to, Apr. 3

Ashland, Tenn.: (1863) aff., Jan. 8

Ashland, Va.: (1862) Conf. supplies destroyed at, May 28; sk. near, June 25; (1863) sk. near, May 3; (1864) comb., May 11; cav. eng., May 30; comb., June 1; (1865) sk. near, Mar. 15

Ashland Church, Va.: (1863) sk., May 4

Ashley, James Mitchell (F): (1865) brings up Thirteenth Amendment in House, Jan. 6

Ashley, Mo.: (1862) sk., Aug. 28

Ashley's Mills (or Fy. Ldg.), Ark.: (1863) sk., Sept. 7

Ashley's Station, Ark.: (1864) act., Aug. 24

Ashton, England: (1863) neutrality policy urged in, Jan. 21

Ashton, La.: (1864) sk., May 1

Ashwood, Miss.: (1864) sk., June 25

Ashwood Ldg. La.: (1864) sk., May 4

Aspinwall, William Henry (F): (1862) gives War Dept. his profits, July 16

Assassination of Lincoln: *See* Lincoln, assassination of

Atchafalaya, La.: (1863) sk., June 4; (1864) sks., July 21, Oct. 5

Atchafalaya R., La.: (1863) sk. at Morgan's Fy. on, Sept. 7; sk. on, Sept. 8; (1864) Red R. Camp., May 19; Fed. exped. to, May 30; sk. at Morgan's Fy. on, Aug. 25; Fed. exped. to, Dec. 16

Atchison, Kas.: (1862) oper., sk., Jan. 20

Athens, Ala.: (1862) oper., May 1; sks., May 8, Aug. 6; (1864) att. on, Jan. 26; Fed. sc. from, Mar. 30; sk., Sept, 23; Forrest capt., Sept. 24; sk., Oct. 1

Athens, Ky.; (1863) aff., Fed. 23

Athens, Mo.: (1861) sk., Aug. 5

Athens, O.: (1863) sk. (Morgan's raid), July 24

Athens, Tenn.: (1863) sks., Sept. 10, 25, 27; (1864) Confs. pursued from, Aug. 1; (1865) Conf. atts. on, Feb. 16; oper. near, Mar. 2

Atkins' Mill, Tenn.: (1862) sk., Apr. 26

Atlanta, C.S.S. (*See also* C.S.S. *Fingal*): (1861) Nov. 12; (1863) capt. by *Weehawken*, June 17

Atlanta, Ga. (*See also* Atlanta Camp.): (1862) great locomotive chase, Apr. 12; (1863) ry. route to Chattanooga, Sept. 2; Davis' arrival in, Oct. 9; Davis in, Oct. 29; (1864) Conf. evac. of, Sept. 1; Fed. troops enter city, Sept. 1, 2; Sherman's rule of begins, Sept. 3, 4; Sherman orders evac. of, Sept. 7; Davis on recovery of, Sept. 18; Fed. exped. from to Flat Cr., Oct. 11; Sherman to return to, Oct. 28; destroyed, Nov. 12; ment., Dec. 26

Atlanta Camp.: (1864) May 1, 2, 4, 7, (Sherman begins camp.), 8, 9 (Snake Cr. Gap), 10, 12 (Johnston evacuates Dalton, Ga.), 13, 14–15 (bat., Resaca), 17, 18, 19, 20, 21, 22, 23, 24; May 25–June 1 (New Hope Church); May 26, 27, 28, 29, 30 (summary); June 1 (Allatoona Pass), 2, 3, 4, 5, 6, 8, 9, 10, 11, 12, 13, 14 (Conf. Gen. Polk killed), 15, 16, 17, 18, 19, 20, 21, 23, 24, 25, 26, 27 (Bat. of Kennesaw Mt.); July 2, 3, 4, 5, 6, 7, 8, 9, 10, 12, 13, 15, 16, 17 (Hood replaces J. E. Johnston in command Army of Tenn.), 18, 19, 20 (Bat. of Peachtree Cr.), 21, 22 (Bat. of Atlanta), 23, 26 (Stoneman raid), 27 (Fed. ry. raids), 28 (Bat. of Ezra Church); Aug. 3, 4 (Feds. crossing Utoy Cr.), 5, 6 (ass. Utoy Cr.), 9, 10, 14, 16 (Kilpatrick's raid around), 17, 19 (Fed. recon. toward), 25 (Jonesborough flank movements), 26, 27, 28 (Sherman advances), 29 (Feds. prepare move toward Jonesborough), 30, 31 (Bat. of Jonesborough); Conf. evac. of, Sept. 1; Fed. troops enter, Sept. 2; Sherman begins occup. of, Sept. 3; Lincoln proclaims days of celebration for victory, Sept. 3; U.S. troops rest, Sept. 4; Sherman orders evac. of, Sept. 7; Feds. harassed by cav., Sept. 20; victory at helps Lincoln's camp., Sept. 22; front quiet, Sept. 28; Conf. moves on ry. supply lines, Oct. 1, 2, 3, 4; eng. at Allatoona, Ga., Oct. 5; sk. near, Nov. 6; Davis on, Nov. 7; Sherman to move back to, Nov. 10, 11; Sherman destroys Atlanta, Nov. 12, 14; Sherman prepares to march to sea, Nov. 14; march to sea begins, Nov. 15, 16, 17

Atlanta-Chattanooga rail line: *See* Chattanooga-Atlanta R.R.

Atlanta and Decatur R.R.; (1864) Johnston's defenses on, July 16

Atlanta and West Point R.R.: (1864) McCook's raid on, July 27

Atlantic coast (*See also* individual operations): (1861) blockade of, Apr. 19; exped. to Atlantic ports considered, Oct. 12; (1862) Fed. base on, Feb. 8; (1864) C.S.S. *Tallahassee* raids alarm, Aug. 12

Atlee's Station, Va.: (1862) sk., June 26

Atrocities: (1862) supposed Union, Aug. 1; (1864) Ft. Pillow massacre, Apr. 12; Lincoln confers on, May 3; Sand Cr. massacre, Nov. 29

Attorney General, C.S.A.: (1861) Judah F. Benjamin, Feb. 19; Thomas Bragg, Nov. 21; (1862) Thomas H. Watts replaces Bragg, Mar. 18; (1863) George Davis replaces Watts, Dec. 31

Attorney General, U.S. (*See also* Cabinet, presidential, U.S.): (1860) Jeremiah Sullivan Black, Nov. 9: Edwin M. Stanton named, Dec. 20; Stanton gives Buchanan advice, Dec. 30; (1861) Edward Bates named, Mar. 4; Sen. confirms appt., Mar. 5; (1864) Bates resigns, Nov. 25; James Speed named, Dec. 1

Atzerodt, George A.: (1865) assassination conspirator, imprisoned, May 1; found guilty, June 30; hanged, July 7

Aubrey, Kas.: (1862) sk. near, Mar. 12

Auburn, N.Y.: (1863) ment., Nov. 3

Auburn, Tenn.: (1863) Fed. recon. to from Murfreesboro, Jan. 25; Fed. exped. from to Murfreesboro, Feb. 3; sk. near, Feb. 15

Auburn, Va.: (1863) sk. near, Oct. 1; Oct. 13 (Bristoe Camp.)

Augur, Christopher Columbus (F): (1863) commands Dept. of Wash. D.C., Oct. 14

Augusta, Ark.: (1862) Fed. recon. toward, June 23; (1864) Fed. expeds. to, Apr. 22, Aug. 27; Fed. sc. to, Nov. 22; (1865) Fed. exped. to, Jan. 4

Augusta, Ga.: (1864) ment., Oct. 2; Davis speaks in, Oct. 5; (1865) Conf. troops near, Feb. 11

Augusta, Ga., *Constitutionalist*: (1863) on problems of Confs., Oct. 2

Augusta, Ky.: (1862) sk., Sept. 27

Augusta Co., Va.: (1862) oper., Nov. 5

Augusta R.R., Ga.: (1864) Sherman's troops on, Dec. 3

Austin, Miss.: (1863) burned, May 24; sk. near, May 28

Austin, Tex.: (1861) Tex. convention votes secession at, Feb. 1; convention votes for Confederacy, Feb. 11

Austin, Tunica Co., Miss.: (1862) sk., Aug. 2

Auxvasse Cr., Callaway Co., Mo.: (1862) sk., Oct. 16

Averasborough, N.C.: (1865) Bat. of, Mar. 16; aftermath, Mar. 17

Averell, William Woods (F): (1863) Bat. of Kelly's Fd., Va., Mar. 17; exped. into W. Va., Aug. 5, 6 (sk. at Moorefield), 19, 24, 25; exped. toward Lewisburg, W. Va. (Beverly exped.), Nov. 1, 3, 4, 5, 6, 7, 8, 10, 13,

16, 17 (*See also* W. Va., Va. and Tenn. R.R. raid); r.r. raids in Va., Dec. 8, 10, 11, 12, 13, 16, 19, 25; cav. exped. against Va. and Tenn. R.R., May 5; to aid in Lynchburg Camp., June 3, 8; eng. at Stephenson's Depot, Va., July 20; pursues Early in Pa., July 30; pursues McCausland after Chambersburg, July 31

Averell, Camp, Va.: (1865) Fed. exped. from into Loudoun Co., Feb. 18

Avoyelles (or Marksville Prairie), La.: (1864) sk., May 15

Ayletts, Va.: (1863) sk., May 4; Fed. exped. to, June 4

Azores: (1862) *Alabama* commissioned near, Aug. 24

Babbitt, Camp: (1863) Fed. exped. to Keysville, Calif., Apr. 12

Back Bay, Va.: (1863) salt works destroyed, Sept. 30

Backbone, I.T. (1864) act., Aug. 27

Backbone Mt., Ark.: *See* Devil's Backbone

Back Cr. Br., W. Va.: (1864) sk., July 27

Back R., Va.: (1861) sk., July 24

Back R. Rd., Va.: (1861) aff., July 19

Back Rd., Va.: (1864) sk. on, near Strasburg, Oct. 7

Bacon Cr., Ky.: (1862) sks., Dec. 26, Dec. 28

Bagdad, Fla.: (1862) Fed. recon. to, from Pensacola, Aug. 7

Bahamas (*See also* Nassau): (1861) Dec. 1; (1862) Mar. 22; Apr. 28; blockade-runner captured, Aug. 3

Bahia, Brazil: (1963) *Alabama* takes prizes off, May 25; (1864) U.S.S. *Wachusett* captures C.S.S. *Florida* at, Oct. 7

Bailey, Joseph (F): (1864) constructs dams on Red R., May 9

Bailey's Cr., Va.: (1864) comb., Aug. 13

Bailey's on Crooked Cr., Ark.: (1864) aff., Jan. 23

Bailey's Cross Roads, Va.: (1861) sk., Aug. 28

Bainbridge, Tenn.: (1864) Hood reaches, Dec. 25; Hood crosses Tenn. R. at, Dec. 26, 27

Bainbridge Fy., Ala.: (1864) sk., Jan. 25

Baird's Mills, Tenn.: (1862) Fed. recon., with sk., Nov. 29

Baker, Edward Dickinson (F): (1861) killed at Ball's Bluff, Oct. 21; funeral, Lincoln attends, Oct. 24; N.Y. obsequies, Nov. 11; Sen. memorial services, Dec. 11

Bakeries, army: (1862) Lincoln orders removed from Capitol basement, Oct. 14

Baker's Cr., Miss. (or Champion's Hill): (1863) bat., May 16; sk. near, July 7; (1864) sk. on, Feb. 5

Baker's Springs, Ark.: (1864) Fed. sc. to, Jan. 21

Bald (or Leggett's) Hill, Ga.: (1864) eng., July 20–21

Bald Hill, Manassas, Va.: (1862) 2nd Bat. Bull Run, Aug. 30

Bald Mt., Calif.: (1864) Fed. sc. to, Aug. 8

Bald Spring Cañon, Eel R., Calif.: (1864) sk. (Humboldt oper.), Mar. 22

Baldwin, John B. (C): (1861) Lincoln holds secret meeting with, Apr. 4

Baldwin, Fla.: (1864) Fed. raid toward, July 23; sks., Aug. 10

Baldwin, Ft., Va.: (1865) delays Fed. advance, Apr. 2

Baldwin's Fy., Big Black R., Miss.: (1863) sk., May 13; sk., Sept. 11; Fed. sc. to, Nov. 1; (1864) Fed. sc. to, Jan. 14

Baldwyn, Miss.: (1862) Fed. recon. toward, June 3; recon. from Booneville toward, June 6; Fed. recon. continues to, June 9; sk. near at Clear Creek, June 14; sk., Oct. 2

Ballahock, Bear Quarter Rd., Va.: (1864) sk., Feb. 29

Un Ballo in Maschera: (1861) Lincoln sees opera in N.Y., Feb. 20

Balloons, C.S.A.: (1862) made of silk dresses, July 4; C.S.S. *Teaser* captured while trying to launch balloon, July 4

Balloons, U.S.: (1861) Prof. Lowe demonstrates for Lincoln, June 17; Lowe observes Conf. troops, June 23; at Fort Monroe, July 25; ascension from Fed. ship deck, Aug. 3; Lincoln observes, Oct. 4; Lowe's use of "Balloon-Boat," Nov. 11

Ball's Bluff, Va., Bat. of (or Leesburg, Harrison's I., Conrad's Fy.): (1861) camp., Oct. 20; bat., Oct. 21; news of, Oct. 22, Nov. 11; Conf. discontent with, Dec. 2; and Committee on Conduct of the War, Dec. 9, Dec. 11; (1862) Gen. Stone imprisoned, Feb. 9

Ball's Cross Roads, Va.: (1861) sk., Aug. 27

Ball's Fy., Ga.: (1864) sk., Nov. 23

Ball's Mill, W. Va.: (1863) sk., Aug. 27

Ball's Mills, Mo.: (1861) sk., Aug. 28

Baltic, steamer, Fed.: (1861) sails for Ft. Sumter, Apr. 9; unable to resupply ft., Apr. 13; arrives at Newport, R.I., May 9

Baltic Sea: (1863) Russian Navy visits U.S., Sept. 23, Dec. 19

Baltimore, Md.: (1861) Lincoln warned of assassination plot, Feb. 21; travels safely through, Feb. 23; secessionists meet, Apr. 17; seccessionist flag raised, Apr. 18; riots, Apr. 19–20; U.S. troops bypass, Apr. 20; Gen. Butler takes Federal Hill, May 13; Butler extends control of, May 13; contraband of war seized, Aug. 3; (1862) hdqrs. Middle Military Dept., Mar. 22; arrests of draft evaders, Aug. 8; McClellan protects, Sept. 7; (1863) sale of "secession music" banned in, March 7; sale of Conf. pictures banned, Mar. 11; anxiety over Lee's invasion, June 15, 20; (1864) Sanitary Fair in, Apr. 18; National Union Convention, June 7–8; U.S. troops arrive in, July 7; U.S. troops prepare to confront Early's raiders, July 8; panic in, July 9; Lincoln's hopes for safety of, July 10; Early threatens, July 11

Baltimore, Md., Police Board: (1861) members arrested, July 1

Baltimore Convention: *See* National Union Party Convention and Republican party

Baltimore Crossroads, Va.: (1862) sk., May 13; (1863) sk., July 1–2

Baltimore & Ohio R.R.: (1861) May 5; allowed to operate by Conf., Jackson seizes rolling stock, May 14; McClellan orders troops to protect, May 26; Grafton occupied to protect r.r., May 30; obstructing boulder blasted, June 15; (1862) Jackson aims to break up, Jan. 3; (1863) Conf. raid on, Apr. 21; (1864) Conf. raid on, Feb. 11; Conf. raid on, May 5; Early attacks, July 26; threat to, Sept. 14; Early advances toward, Sept. 17; Mosby wrecks, robs train, Oct. 13; Rosser wrecks r.r. bridge on, Nov. 28

Baltimore Riots: (1861) Apr. 19, 20; casualties receive military honors at Boston, May 1

Baltimore Store, Va.: (1863) sk., July 2; (1864) sk. near, Feb. 6

Bangor, Me.: (1861) habeas corpus suspension authorized between Bangor and Wash., Oct. 14

Bank robberies: (1864) in Mt. Sterling, Ky., June 8; St. Albans, Vt., raid on, Oct. 19

Banks, Nathaniel Prentiss (F) (*See also* Red R. Camp.): (1861) ordered arrest of George P. Kane, June 27; named to command Dept. of the Shenandoah, July 21; takes command Shenandoah, July 25; commands Potomac Valley area, Oct. 20; (1862) troops occupy Harper's Ferry, Feb. 24; advancing up Shenandoah, Mar. 5; sk. at Winchester, Mar. 7; follows withdrawing Jackson up valley, Mar. 11; ordered to protect capital, Mar. 19; weakened, Mar. 20; returned to valley to protect Wash., Mar. 23; follows withdrawing Jackson, Apr. 1; Fifth Army corps put into Dept. of the Shenandoah, Apr. 4; Jackson leaves valley mainly to, Apr. 18; troops concentrating at Harrisonburg, New Market, Apr. 26; falls back before Jackson, May 6; Jackson moves against, May 12; threatened by Jackson, May 13; uncertain on Jackson's moves, May 18; Jackson operating against, May 20; pulls Fed. force north in Shenandoah, May 21; threatened by Fed. defeat at Front Royal, May 23; Jackson attempts unsuccessfully to cut off retreat, May 24; orders trains north toward Williamsport, Md., May 24; defeated at Bat. of Winchester, May 25; pulls back, May 26; Lincoln to McClellan re Banks' apparent safety at Williamsport, Md., May 26; crosses Potomac at Williamsport, Md., May 27; troop strength, May 29; Lincoln urges to destroy Jackson, May 30; to be part of new Army of Va. under Pope, June 17; Bat. of Cedar Mt., Aug. 9; assumes command Wash. defenses, Sept. 8; Heintzelman succeeds, Oct. 26; named to command Dept. of the Gulf, Nov. 8; assumes command Dept. of the Gulf, Dec. 16; (1863) unsent letter of Lincoln to Butler, Jan. 23; move to cooperate with Grant at Vicksburg, Mar. 7; cooperates with riverboats in passage of Port Hudson batteries, Mar. 14; att. on Ft. Bisland, Apr. 12; eng. Ft. Bisland, Apr. 13; occupies Franklin, La., Apr. 15; advance into La., May 5; Port Hudson movement begins, May 14; across from Port Hudson, May 17; troops gather, May 20; siege of Port Hudson, May 21, 22, 23, 24, 25, 26, 27, June 2, 3, 8, 14, 26, 28, July 1, 2, 3, 4,; surrender of Port Hudson, July 7; ceremony, July 9; ment., July 13; Lincoln to, Aug. 5; Sabine Pass exped., Sept. 4; Grant confers with, Sept. 4; att. on Sabine Pass, Sept. 8; begins Bayou Teche Camp., Oct. 3; Bayou Teche Camp., Oct. 4, 14, 16, 18, 21; sk. at Washington, La., Oct. 24; Bayou Teche Camp., Oct. 27, 30; sk. at Washington, La., Oct. 31; Bayou Teche Camp., Nov. 1, 2; Rio Grande exped., Oct. 27, Nov. 2, 6; Lincoln to, Nov. 5; enters Corpus Christi, Tex., Nov. 16; Rio Grande exped., Nov. 22; Lincoln to, Dec. 24; (1864) Lincoln to on La. govt., Jan 13; Lincoln to on voting in La., Jan. 31; Red R. Camp., Feb. 29, Mar. 10, 11, 12, 14 (capt. of Ft. De Russy), 15, 16 (occ. of Alexandria), 21, 28, Apr. 3, 4, 5, 7, 8 (Bat. of Sabine Crossroads), 9 (eng. at Pleasant Hill); gives up attempt to take Shreveport, Apr. 9, 10; ordered to move on Mobile, Ala., Apr. 9; at Grand Ecore, La., Apr. 11; ment., Apr. 13; withdrawing from Red R., Apr. 21, 25, 26, May 13, 19, 21; Lincoln to on La. constitution, Aug. 9; (1865) resumes command Dept. of the Gulf, Apr. 22

Banks, National: (1863) Lincoln signs act for, Feb. 25

Banks' Ford, Va.: (1863) May 4

Bannock Indians: (1863) Bat. of Bear R. or Battle Cr., Ut. Terr., Jan. 29

Baptist: *See* Southern Baptist Convention

Barataria, U.S.S.: (1863) capt., Apr. 7

Barbed wire: (1864) forerunner of, May 15

Barbee's Cross Roads, Va.: (1863) sk., July 25; Fed. sc. to, Aug. 24; sk., Sept. 1

Barber's Fd., St. Mary's R., Fla.: (1864) sk., Feb. 10

Barber's Plantation, Fla.: (1864) Fed. troops march from (Bat. of Olustee), Feb. 20

Barboursville, Ky.: (1861) act., Sept. 19; (1862) sk., Sept. 8; (1863) sk., Apr. 27; (1864) sk., Feb. 8

Barboursville, W. Va.: (1861) act. near, July 13; sk., July 16

Bardstown, Ky.: (1862) Bragg moves to, Sept. 21; Buell moves toward, Oct. 2; sk. near, Oct. 4; Buell occupies, Oct. 6; sk., Oct. 19; (1863) taken by Morgan, July 5; (1864) sk., Aug. 1

Bardstown Pike (or Rd.), Ky.: (1862) sk. on near Mt. Washington, Oct. 1; sk. on, Oct. 9

Barhamsville, Va.: *See* Eltham's Ldg.

Barker's Mill, Whippy Swamp, S.C.: (1865) sk., Feb. 2

Barksdale, William (C): (1862) att. on pontoon bridge builders at Fredericksburg, Dec. 11

Barnesville, Ga.: (1865) sk., Apr. 19

Barnesville, Md.: (1862) sk., Sept. 9

Barnett's Corners, Miss.: (1862) sk., Sept. 19

Barnett's Fd., Va.: (1862) sk., Aug. 1

Barnum's Museum: (1864) plot to burn, Nov. 24

Barnwell, S. C.: (1865) sk. near, Feb. 6

Barnwell's I., S.C.: (1862) sk., Feb. 10; (1863) July 30

Baron De Kalb, U.S.S. (gunboat): (1863) seizes munitions at Devall's Bluff, Ark., Jan. 16

Barrancas, Fla.: (1864) Fed. exped. from, July 21; Fed. exped. from to Marianna, Fla., Sept. 18; Fed. exped. from to Pine Barren Ridge, Nov. 16; Fed. exped. from to Pollard, Ala., Dec. 13; (1865) Fed. exped. from to Milton, Feb. 19, Feb. 22; fed. exped. from to Apalachicola, May 31

Barrancas, Ft., at Pensacola, Fla.: (1861) fires on men approaching, Jan. 8; taken over by Fla. troops, Jan. 12; bomb. of, Nov. 22, 23; (1862) bomb. of, Jan. 1; (1864) Fed. exped. from, Aug. 13

Barrancas Barracks at Pensacola, Fla.: (1861) garrison of to Ft. Pickens, Jan. 10; capt. by Fla. troops, Jan. 12

Barren, Ft., I.T.: (1863) sk. near, Dec. 18

Barren Mound, Ky.: (1862) sk., Oct. 15

Barre's Ldg., La.: (1863) Fed. exped. to, Apr. 21; oper. near, May 21; steamer attacked near, May 22; sk., Oct. 21

Barrett, Theodore H. (F): (1865) sks. at Palmito Ranch, May 12, 13

Barry, Mo.: (1862) sk., Aug. 14

Barry Co., Mo.: (1862) sk. at Keetsville in, Feb. 25; (1864) sks. in, Oct. 8, 18, 29

Barton Co., Mo.: (1863) 4-day Fed. sc. in, Feb. 19

Barton's Station, Ala.: (1863) sks., Apr. 17, Oct. 20, 26, 31

Bartow, Francis S. (C): (1861) Ga. secession leader, Jan. 19; killed 1st Bull Run Bat., July 21

Bass' Plantation, Ark.: (1865) Fed. exped. to, Mar. 17

Batchelder's Cr., N.C.: (1862) sk., Apr. 29; (1863) sk., Feb. 10; Fed. exped. from, Feb. 12; sk., May 20; (1864) sk. on (New Berne exped.), Feb. 1; Fed. exped. from, June 20

Bates, Edward (F): (1861) Lincoln names Attorney General of U.S., Mar. 4; on relieving Ft. Sumter, Mar. 15, 29; (1862) makes out Supreme Court commission for David Davis, Oct. 17; to enforce Confiscation Act, Nov. 13; (1864) resigns from Cabinet, Nov. 24; resignation effective, Dec. 1

Bates Co., Mo.: (1863) Fed. sc. in, May 3, aff. in, May 18; General Orders No. 11, Aug. 25; Fed. sc. in, Sept. 27; oper. in, Oct. 3

Bates' Fy., Congaree R., S.C.: (1865) sk., Feb. 15

Bates House, Indianapolis, Ind.: (1861) Lincoln speaks at, Feb. 11

Bates Township, Ark.: (1863) sk., Nov. 2

Batesville, Ark.: (1862) sk., May 3; Fed. sc. from to Fairview, June 16; sk. near, July 14; (1863) Marmaduke driven out of, Feb. 4; Fed. sc. to, Dec. 26; (1864) Fed. sc. from to near Searcy Ldg., Jan. 30; Fed. exped. from, Feb. 12; capture of wagon train near, Feb. 19; Fed. exped. to, Feb. 29; Fed. exped. from to Wild Haws, Strawberry Cr., Ark., Mar. 10; Fed. exped. from to West Point, Grand Glaize, Searcy Ldg., Mar. 15; Fed. exped. to, Mar. 19; Fed. exped. from to Coon Cr., Devil's Fork of Red R., Mar. 24; Fed. sc. from to Fairview, Mar. 25

Bath, W. Va.: (1862) sk., Jan. 3; Jackson's troops occupy, Jan. 4, 5; (1863) sk., Sept. 7

Bath Co., Ky.: (1863) sk. in, June 13; (1864) sk. in, Jan. 13; (1865) sk., Mar. 26

Bath Co., Va.: (1862) oper. in, Nov. 5; (1865) Fed. sc. in, Apr. 15

Bath Springs, Miss.: (1863) sk., Jan. 1

Baton Rouge, La.: (1862) 3-day exped. from, June 7; Fed. exped. to cut canal at Swampy Toe, June 20; gunboats guard river, July 24; eng. at, Aug. 5; sk., Aug. 20; Feds. evacuate, Aug. 21; (1863) Banks moves to, Mar. 1; Grierson's raid, May 1, 2; Banks moves to att. Port Hudson, May 14; siege of Port Hudson, May 21; sk. near, Sept. 19; exped. from to New and Amite rs., Sept. 24; Fed. exped. from, Sept. 24; oper. near, Sept. 25; (1864) sk. near, Mar. 3, 8, Apr. 15, May 3; oper. around, July 3; ment., July 29; Fed. exped. from to Clinton, Camp Moore, Oct. 5; Fed. exped. from against Mobile and Ohio R.R., Nov. 27; Fed. exped. from to Clinton, Dec. 23; (1865) Fed. exped. from to Jackson, Clinton, Mar. 1; Fed. exped. from to Clinton, Comite R., Mar. 30; Fed. exped. to, May 8

Baton Rouge Arsenal and Barracks, U.S.: (1861) seized by La. troops, Jan. 10

Battery Cheves, James I., S.C.: (1863) magazine explosion, Sept. 15

Battery Gregg, S.C.: (1863) bombarded, Aug. 17; small boat atts. on fail, Sept. 5; evacuated, Sept. 6; Fed. occup. of, Sept. 7

Battery Huger, Hill's Point, Va.: (1863) capture of, Apr. 19

Battery I., S.C.: (1862) aff., May 21; (1864) Fed. demon. on, Apr. 15

Battery Simkins, Charleston Harbor, S.C.: (1864) att. on, July 10; (1865) att. on, Feb. 11

Battery Wagner (or Ft.), Charleston Harbor, S.C.: (1863) siege of, July 10; 1st ass. on, July 11; Conf. sortie from, July 14; 2nd ass. on, July 18; bomb. of, July 24; Fed. att. on planned, Aug. 1; bomb. of, Aug. 4; defenses strengthened, Aug. 5; Fed. offensive preparations, Aug. 8; firing on Fed. work parties, Aug. 11; bomb. of Sumter, Aug. 17, 18, 19, 20, 21, 22, 23, 24, 25, 26 (rifle pits capt.), Sept. 1, 2, 3, 5, 6 (evac. of); Fed. occup. of, Sept. 7

Battle: *See* individual battle names

"Battle Above the Clouds," Bat. of Lookout Mt., Tenn.: (1863) Nov. 24

Battle Cr., Tenn.: (1862) sks., June 21, July 5; Fed. att. on Ft. McCook at, Aug. 27

Battle Cr. or Bear R., Bat. of, Ut. Terr.: (1863) Jan. 29

"Battle Hymn of the Republic": (1862) Feb. page

Battle Mt., Va.: (1863) sk., July 24

Baxter Springs, Kas.: (1863) Fed. exped. from to Grand R., July 27; act., Oct. 6

Baylor, John R. (C): (1861) sk. at Mesilla, N. Mex. Terr., July 25; "Buffalo Hunt," July 25; takes Ft. Fillmore, July 26; Lynde surrenders troops to, July 27

Bayou Bartholomew, Ark.: (1865) Fed. sc. to, Apr. 1

Bayou Bernard, near Ft. Gibson, I.T.: (1862) sk., July 27

Bayou Boeuf, Ark.: (1863) sk. at Meriwether's Fy., Dec. 13

Bayou Boeuf, La.: (1863) Fed. exped. to, Apr. 29; (1864) sk. (Red R. Camp.), May 7; (1865) Fed. sc. from to Bayou Chemise, Mar. 24; Fed. exped. from to Bayou De Large, May 25

Bayou Boeuf Crossing, La.: (1863) Fed. forces captured at, June 24

Bayou Boeuf Rd., La.: (1863) sk., Apr. 22

Bayou Bonfouca, La.: (1862) sk., Nov. 21; (1865) Fed. exped. to, Jan. 31

Bayou Bourdeau, La.: (1863) sk., Nov. 2; eng. near Grand Coteau, Nov. 3

Bayou Cache, Ark.: (1862) sk., July 6

Bayou Chemise, La: (1865) Fed. sc. to, Mar. 24

Bayou City, La.: (1865) Fed. exped. to, Apr. 2

Bayou Courtableau, La.: (1863) sk., May 22

Bayou De Glaize (or Norwood's Plantation, Old Oaks or Yellow Bayou), La.: (1864) sk., May 17; eng., May 18

Bayou De Large, La.: (1865) Fed. exped. to, May 25

Bayou De Paul (Carroll's Mill), La.: (1864) sk. (Red R. Camp.), Apr. 8

Bayou des Allemands, La.: (1862) sk., June 20; aff., Sept. 4

Bayou des Arc, Ark.: (1862) Fed. exped. from Searcy Ldg. to, May 27

Bayou De View, Ark.: (1862) sk., July 7; (1864) pursuit of Confs. to, June 26

Bayou Fordoche Rd., La.: (1864) sk., May 29

Bayou Fourche, Ark.: (1863) eng., Sept. 10

Bayou Goula, La.: (1863) Conf. raid on, June 19; (1865) sk. near, Jan. 24; Fed. sc. from to Grand R., Jan. 28; Fed. expeds. to, Feb. 14, Mar. 23

Bayou Grand, Fla.: (1864) aff., Jan. 25

Bayou Grand Caillou, La.: (1864) Fed. exped. to, Nov. 19

Bayou Grossetete, La.: (1864) aff., June 19

Bayou La Fourche, La.: (1863) eng. on near Donaldsonville, July 12

Bayou Lamourie, La.: (1864) sk. (Red R. Camp.), May 6; sk., May 12

Bayou Liddell, La.: (1864) sk., Oct. 15

Bayou Macon (or Pin Hook), La.: (1863) sk., May 10; (1864) Fed. exped. to, Nov. 6

Bayou Manchac, La.: (1864) Fed. exped. to, Oct. 2

Bayou Meto, Ark.: (1863) sk., Aug. 26; act. (Reed's Br.), Aug. 27; sk. on, at Shallow Fd., Aug. 30; sk. near, Sept. 23; (1865) Fed. scs. to, Feb. 22, May 6

Bayou Meto Br., Ark.: (1863) sk. near, Sept. 23

Bayou Pierre, La.: (1864) sks., May 2

Bayou Pierre, North Fork, Miss.: (1863) sk. on, May 3

Bayou Pierre, South Fork, Miss.: (1863) sk. on, May 2

Bayou Pigeon, La.: (1865) Fed. exped. to, Mar. 20

Bayou Planton, La.: (1865) Fed. exped. to, Jan. 30

Bayou Portage, Grand Lake, La.: (1863) aff., Nov. 23; (1864) Fed. exped. to, Nov. 17

Bayou Rapides, La.: (1864) sk. (Red R. Camp.), Mar. 20

Bayou Rapides Br. near McNutt's Hill, La.: (1864) sk. (Red R. Camp.), Apr. 26

Bayou Robert, La.: (1864) sk. (Red R. Camp.), May 8

Bayou Saline, Ark.: (1864) sk. (Red R. Camp.), Apr. 14

Bayou Sara, La.: (1862) affs., Aug. 10, 23; (1863) Banks approaches, May 21; Banks crosses Miss. R. near, May 23; sk. near, Nov. 9; (1864) Fed. expeds. to, Sept. 6, Oct. 3; sks., Oct. 4; sks. near, Oct. 9

Bayou Sara Rd., La.: (1863) oper., May 18

Bayou Sorrel, La.: (1865) Fed. exped. to, Jan. 21

Bayou Teche, La. (*See also* Teche Country operations): (1863) gunboat *Cotton* destroyed, eng., Jan. 14; att. on Ft. Bisland, Apr. 12; eng. at Ft. Bisland, Apr. 13; Feds. occupy Ft. Bisland, Apr. 14; steamer attacked on, May 22; sk., July 27

Bayou Teche operations: *See* Teche Country operations

Bayou Tensas, La.: (1863) sk., May 9; sk., Aug. 10; (1864) sk., July 30; sk. near, Aug. 26

Bayou Tunica (or Tunica Bend), La.: (1863) sk., Nov. 8

Bayou Vermillion, La.: (1863) act., Apr. 17

Bayou Vidal, La.: (1863) sk. near, Apr. 7; sk. on, Apr. 15

Bayport, Fla.: (1863) Fed. oper. in, Apr. 3; (1864) Fed. raid on, July 7

Bay St. Louis, Miss.: (1863) sk., Nov. 17; (1865) Fed. exped. to, Mar. 28

Bay Springs, Miss.: (1862) Fed. exped. from Rienzi to, Aug. 19; (1863) sk. near, Oct. 26

Beach Cr. Br., Tenn.: (1862) destruction of, Mar. 13

Beach Fork, Ky.: (1862) sk., Oct. 6

Beachtown, Ga.: (1864) act., July 22

Bealer's Fy., Little Red. R., Ark.: (1864) sk., June 6

Bealeton Station (or Bealeton), Va.: (1863) sk., Mar. 17; sk. near, Oct. 22; sks., Oct. 24, 25; sk. near, Oct. 27; Fed. exped. from toward Thoroughfare Gap, Nov. 21; Fed. exped. from to Luray, Va., Dec. 21; (1864) Fed. exped. from to Front Royal, Jan. 1; (1865) Fed. oper. about, Mar. 3

Beall, John Yates (C): (1863) captures Chesapeake Bay schooner, Sept. 19; (1864) captures *Philo Parsons,* plans to free Johnson's I. prisoners in Lake Erie, Sept. 19

Bean's Station, Tenn.: (1863) scs. and sks., Dec. 9; eng. (Knoxville Camp.), Dec. 14; sk., Dec., 15; sk., Dec. 18; (1864) sk., June 14; sk. at Thorn Hill near, Oct. 10

Bear Cr., Ala.: (1862) Fed. exped. to, Apr. 12

Bear Cr., Miss.: (1863) act. near, June 22; sk. at near Canton, July 17

Bear Cr., Johnson Co., Mo.: (1863) sk., Feb. 5

Bear Cr., Tenn.: (1863) sks., Mar. 3, Oct. 3

Bear Cr. Station, Ga.: (1864) sk., Nov. 16

Bear Inlet, N.C.: (1863) destruction of salt works on, Dec. 25; (1864) Fed. exped. to, Mar. 25

Bear Quarter Rd., Va.: (1864) sk. on, Feb. 29

Bear R., Id. Terr.: (1863) Fed. sc. to, May 5

Bear R. or Battle Cr., Ut. Terr.: (1863) eng., Jan. 29

Bear Skin Lake, Mo.: (1863) sk., Sept. 7

Bear Wallow, Ky.: (1862) sk., Sept. 19; sk., Dec. 25

Beardstown, Tenn.: (1864) sk., Sept. 27

Beatty's Mill, Ark.: (1864) sk. near, Sept. 1

Beaufort, N.C.: (1862) Ft. Macon near, Mar. 23; Ft. Macon surrenders, Apr. 25; commerce allowed, May 12; (1864) sks. at Gale's Cr., Bogue Sound Blockhouse, Newport Barracks, Feb. 2; Fed. exped. from to Bogue and Bear Inlet, Mar. 25; 1st Ft. Fisher exped. vessels rendezvous at, Dec. 23; (1865) 2nd Fed. exped. to Ft. Fisher rendezvous at, Jan. 8; Fed. fleet delayed, Jan. 11

Beaufort, S.C.: (1861) Beauregard's command enlarged to include, Mar. 18; Fed. recon. in area, Nov. 8; capt., Nov. 9; Fed. exped. around, Dec. 6; (1862) Gen. O. Mitchel dies at, Oct. 30; (1863) freedmen celebrate Emancipation Proclamation, Jan. 1; Fed. exped. from, up St. Mary's R., Jan. 23; (1865) troops of Howard transferred to, Jan. 3; troops of Sherman move to, Jan. 14; Sherman embarks for, Jan. 21; Sherman en route to, Jan. 22; Carolina Camp., Feb. 1

Beaulieu, Ft., Ga.: (1864) Fed. naval att. on, Dec. 14

Beaumont, Tex.: (1862) r.r. depot destroyed, Oct. 2; (1863) Sabine Pass exped., Sept. 8

Beauregard, Pierre Gustave Toutant (C): (1861) named by Pres. Davis to command at Charleston, S.C., Mar. 1; assumed command at Charleston Harbor, Mar. 3; command enlarged to include Beaufort, S.C., area, Mar. 18; confers with Col. Ward Hill Lamon, Mar. 25; stops intercourse between Sumter and Charleston, Apr. 7; orders military forces to stations, Apr. 8; ordered to demand evacuation of Sumter, or reduce it if sure of resupply, Apr. 10; Beauregard demands evacuation of Ft. Sumter, Apr. 11; three emissaries refuse Anderson's terms, Apr. 12; surrender of Ft. Sumter arranged, Apr. 13; named to command Alexandria Line, Conf. troops in northern Va., May 31, June 2; "Beauty and booty," June 5; and Wash. offensive, July 2; strategy at Manassas, July 16; "on line of Bull Run," July 17; at Manassas, July 18; July 19; plan for attack, July 20; Bat. of Manassas, July 21; appointed gen., Aug. 31; strategy conference, Oct. 1; Ball's Bluff Camp., Oct. 20; relations with Davis, Oct. 20; commands Dist. of the Potomac, Oct. 22; Oct. 25; Davis to Beauregard re Manassas report, Oct. 30; Manassas follow-up, Nov. 3; quarrel with Davis, Nov. 4; (1862) ordered to western command under A. S. Johnston, Jan. 26; confers with Johnston, Hardee at Bowling Green, Ky., Feb. 7; concentrating at Island No. 10, Ft. Pillow, Tenn., Corinth, Miss., Mar 1; assumes command, Army of the Miss., Mar. 5; troops meet with Johnston's, Mar. 26; takes command at Shiloh, Apr. 6, 7; withdraws to Corinth, Apr. 8; Davis asks govs. for troops for, Apr. 10; Halleck to advance on, Apr. 28; troop strength, Apr. 29; calls for defense of Corinth, May 2; army skirmishes with Feds. near Corinth, May 22; outnumbered, orders pull-out toward Tupelo, May 29; skillfully evacuates Corinth, May 30; aff. near Rienzi, June 2; Pope probes against, June 4; succeeded by Bragg, June 17; Davis on "what Beauregard has abandoned in the West," June 21; assigned to Dept. of S.C. and Ga., Aug. 29; commands Dept. of S.C. and Ga., Sept. 24; middle and east Fla. in command, Oct. 7; (1863) warns against attacks on Charleston or Savannah, Feb. 18; Davis asks for reinforcements, June 25; Davis to Johnston re, July 11; orders James I. defense lines shortened, Aug. 11; decision to hold Sumter, Aug. 26; Davis to, Aug. 27; evac. of Ft. Wagner, Sept. 6; (1864) assigned command of Dept. of N.C. and Southern Va., Apr. 18; superseded by Jones in Dept. of S.C., Ga., Fla., Apr. 20; (*See also* Benjamin F. Butler) Butler's south side of James oper. against, May 9, 12; eng. at Ft. Darling or Drewry's Bluff, May 16; pushes Butler, May 17, 18; Davis to Lee re, May 19; outnumbered, May 28; Lee urges to move in front of Richmond, June 1; throws back Butler's att., June 9; holds against Hancock's att., June 15; Fed. att. on Petersburg, Va., June 16, 17; convinces Lee Grant had crossed James, June 17; Davis considers for post, Sept. 28; to command western depts., Oct. 2; hears Davis speech, Oct. 5; assumes command Mil. Div. of the West, east of the Miss., Oct. 17; Davis to, Nov. 30; at Savannah, urges evacuation of, Dec. 18, 20; Davis to, Dec. 20; (1865) ment., Jan. 13; takes temporary command of Army of Tenn., Jan. 14; given command in S.C., Ga., Fla., Jan. 16; Davis to on taking command, Feb. 4; counsels evac. of Charleston, Feb. 11; troop strength of, Feb. 13; Lee to Stephens on, Feb. 13; leaves Columbia, S.C., Feb. 16; ordered to report to J. E. Johnston, Feb. 22; conference with Davis, other gens., Apr. 12

Beauregard, Ft., La.; (1863) Fed. gunboat attack on, May 10
Beauregard, Ft., S.C.: (1861) capt., Nov. 7
Beaver Cr., Kas.: (1864) Fed. exped. to, Apr. 14
Beaver Cr., Ky.: (1863) Fed. exped. from into Va., July 3
Beaver Cr. (Benevola), Md.: (1863) sk., Gettysburg Camp., July 9
Beaver Cr., Mo.: (1862) sk., Nov. 24
Beaver Cr., N.C.: (1864) sk., Apr. 17
Beaver Cr. Swamp, Tenn.: (1863) Fed. sc. in, Apr. 2
Beaver Dam Church, Va.: (1862) sk., Dec. 1
Beaver Dam Cr. (*See* Mechanicsville): June 26, 1862
Beaver Dam Station, Va.: (1862) Fed. exped. destroys stores at, July 19;

(1864) sk., Feb. 29; comb. (Sheridan's exped.), May 9, 10; (1865) sk., Mar. 13

Beaver Pond Cr. (or Tabernacle Church), Va.: (1865) sk., Apr. 4

Beaver Station, Mo.: (1863) sk. at Ft. Lawrence, Jan. 6

Beckley (or Raleigh Court House), W. Va.: (1861) Feds. occupy, Dec. 28

Bee, Barnard Elliott (C): (1861) at 1st Bull Run, Bat. of, shouted, "Look! There is Jackson standing like a stone wall!", mortally wounded, July 21

Bee Cr., Mo.: (1864) aff. on, May 2

Beech Cr., W. Va.; (1862) sk., Aug. 6

Beecher, Henry Ward (F): (1865) orates at Ft. Sumter flag raising, Apr. 14

Beech Fork, Calhoun Co., W. Va.: (1863) sk., Sept. 8

Beech Grove, Ky.: (1862) reports of Fed. advance, Jan. 16; Bat. of, also known as Mill Springs, Logan's Cross Roads, Fishing Cr., or Somerset, Jan. 19

Beech Grove, Tenn.: (1863) sk., Tullahoma Camp., June 26

Beersheba, Tenn.: (1863) sk. near, Oct. 3

Beersheba Springs, Tenn.: (1864) sk., Mar. 19

Bell, John: (1860) defeated in 1860 election as pres. candidate, Nov. 6; opposed to subjugation of South, Apr. 23

Bellefonte, Ark.: (1864) Fed. sc. to, Mar. 29

Belle Grove, Va.: (1864) Bat. of (or Cedar Creek), Oct. 19

Belle Plain, Va.: (1862) Lincoln confers with Burnside at, Nov. 26; (1863) Fed. 3-day exped. from, Feb. 12; Fed. exped. from, Mar. 3; Fed. exped. from, Mar. 25; Fed. exped. from, Apr. 22

Belle R., La.: (1864) Fed. exped. to, Oct. 22

Beller's Mill, W. Va.: (1861) sk., Sept. 2

Belle Saint Louis (U.S. steamer): (1864) Conf. guerrilla att., Oct. 27

Bellington, W. Va.: (1861) sk., July 7

Bell Mines, Ky.: (1864) sk., July 13

Bell's Mills, Tenn.: (1864) act., Dec. 4, 6

Bells, Southern: (1862) confiscated bells sold in Boston, July 30

Belmont, August (F): (1864) addresses Democratic Convention, Aug. 29

Belmont, Miss.: (1863) sk., June 18

Belmont, Mo.: (1861) act., Sept. 3; sk. near, Sept. 26; eng., Nov. 7

Benevola (Beaver Cr.), Md.: (1863) sk. (Gettysburg Camp.), July 9

Benham, Henry Washington (F): (1862) eng. of Secessionville, S.C., June 16

Benjamin, Judah Philip (C): (1860) speaks in U. S. Sen. for peaceful separation, Dec. 31; (1861) withdraws from U. S. Sen., Feb. 4; Attorney General, C.S.A., Feb. 19; named Sec. of War, C.S.A., Nov. 21; (1862) cracks down on speculators, Feb. 4; named Sec. of State, C.S.A., Mar. 18; (1865) conference with Davis, Apr. 12; leaves Pres., May 3; escape of, May 10

Bennett House (or Place), near Durham, N.C.: (1865) scene of Johnston-Sherman meeting, Apr. 17; Johnston surrenders at, Apr. 26

Bennett's Bayou, Ark.: (1865) Fed. oper. about, Feb. 16

Bennett's Bayou, Mo.: (1863) Fed. sc., Aug. 23

Bennight's Mills, Mo.: (1861) sk., Sept. 1

Benn's Church, Va.: (1864) sk. near, Jan. 29

Bent Creek, Tenn.: (1864) sk., Mar. 14

Benton, Ala.: (1865) sk. near, Apr. 10
Benton, Ark.: (1863) Fed. exped. from, Nov. 10; (1864) sk. near, July 6; aff., July 25; sk., Aug. 18; Fed. sc. to, Nov. 27
Benton, Mo.: (1861) Fed. exped. from Cape Girardeau to, Aug. 7; (1862) Fed. exped. to, Jan. 15
Benton Co., Ark.: (1864) sk. in, Oct. 20
Benton Rd., Ark.: (1864) sk. (Red R. Camp.), Mar. 23; sk. on, July 19; (1865) sk. on, near Little Rock, Jan. 22
Benton's Cross Roads, N.C.: (1865) sk. near, Mar. 18
Benton's Fy., Amite R., La.: (1864) sk. near, July 25
Bentonville, Ark.: (1862) sk., Feb. 18; (1863) sk., Aug. 15; sk., Sept. 4; (1865) sk., Jan. 1
Bentonville, N.C.: (1865) Slocum's troops south of, Mar. 18; Bat. of, Mar. 19–21; aftermath, Mar. 22
Benvard's Mills, Va.: (1865) Fed. sc. from to South Quay, Jan. 2
Berkeley Plantation, Harrison's Ldg., Va.: (1862) A. of P. withdraws to, July 1
Berkley, Pa., Luzerne Co.: (1862) troops put down draft opposition, Oct. 17
Berlin (now Brunswick), Md.: (1861) sk., Sept. 29; (1862) sk., Sept. 4; (1863) Lee at, July 19
Berlin, O.: (1863) sk., July 17
Bermuda Hundred, Va.: (1864) Butler lands at, May 5–6; ment., May 12; Bat. of Drewry's Bluff or Ft. Darling, May 16; Butler back at, May 17; investment of Butler at, May 18, 20; W. F. Smith at, June 14; ment., June 15; act., June 15–16; Fed. exped. withdraws to, Aug. 16, 20; Fed. sc. from, Nov. 1; (1865) preparation for Ft. Fisher exped., Jan. 3; Ft. Fisher exped. embarks from, Jan. 4; Fed. exped. from, Feb. 11
Bernard's Mills, Va.: (1864) Fed. exped. from, Oct. 15
Berry Co., Tenn.: (1864) sk., Apr. 29
Berry's Fy., Va.: (1863) May 16; sk. near, July 20
Berry's Fd., Va.: (1864) sk., July 19
Berryville, Ark.: (1862) recon., Mar. 3; (1863) Fed. sc. from Elkhorn, Ark., to, Jan. 8; Fed. exped. to, Nov. 10
Berryville, Va.: (1862) sk., May 24; Fed. recon. to, Nov. 28; (1863) sk., June 6; Ewell occupies, June 13; Rodes moves from, June 14; sk., Oct. 17–18; (1864) Early near, July 17; sk., July 19–20; sk. near, July 22; aff., Aug. 13; Sheridan withdraws toward, Aug. 14; Sheridan leaves rear guard at, Aug. 17; Sheridan leaves, Aug. 18; sk., Aug. 20; sk. near, Aug. 21; Sheridan moves troops toward, Aug. 30–Sept. 3; sk., Sept. 4; aff. near, Sept. 13
Berryville and Winchester Pike, Va.: (1864) sk. on, Aug. 19; 3rd Bat. of Winchester, Sept. 19
Berthold, Ft., Dak. Terr.: (1862) Sioux-miners fight, Oct. 10
Bertrand, Mo.: (1861) sk. near, Dec. 11
Berwick, La.: (1863) oper. near, May 21; sk., June 1; (1864) sk., Apr. 26; aff., May 1; Fed. recon. from, Aug. 2
Berwick Bay, La.: (1862) naval oper., Nov. 1; (1863) sk., Apr. 9; start of Bayou Teche Camp., Oct. 3
Bethel, Tenn.: (1862) May 9
Bethel Church, Va. (*See* Big Bethel): June 10, 1861

Blair, Montgomery (F): (1861) named Postmaster General, Mar. 4; opposes evac. of Ft. Sumter, Mar. 15; still opposes evac., Mar. 29; May 26; ends postal ties with South, May 31; protests *Trent* Aff., Nov. 16; (1862) offers to resign, Dec. 19; (1864) Lincoln advised to drop from Cabinet, Sept. 3; pressure to remove, Sept. 16; Lincoln asks to resign, Sept. 23; replaced by Wm. Dennison, Sept. 24

Blair Family (F): (1861) urges removal of Frémont, Sept. 9; (1864) Early burns home at Silver Spring, Md., July 11; controversial, Sept. 24

Blair's Ldg., La.: (1864) eng., Apr. 12

Blakely, Ala.: (1865) sk. near, Apr. 1; Fed. sc. from, Apr. 7; Fed. exped. from, Apr. 17

Blakely, Ft., Ala.: (1865) siege of, Apr. 2; carried by ass., Apr. 9

Blakely R., Ala.: (1865) U.S.S. *Osage* sunk, Mar. 29

Blake's Farm, W. Va.: (1861) sk., Nov. 10

Blandville, Ky.: (1862) Grant's recon. near, Jan. 14; Confs. carry off records, Jan. 23

Blakeny's, S.C.: (1865) sk., Mar. 3

Blenker, Louis (Ludwig) (F): (1862) division sent to Frémont, Mar. 31

Blick's Station, Va.: (1864) comb., Aug. 18

Bliss, P. P. (F): (1864) evangelist author of hymn, Oct. 5

Bliss, Ft., Tex.: (1861) surrendered by Feds., Mar. 31

Blockade, U.S. (*See also* Blockade-runners): (1860) coaling stations in Fla., Nov. 15; (1861) declared by Lincoln, Apr. 19; implemented, Apr. 26; extended, Apr. 27; James R., Hampton Rds., May 2; increases, May 9; off Charleston, May 10; mouth of Rappahannock, May 18; at Mobile, May 26; at New Orleans, May 26; Apalachicola, Fla., June 7; strategy, June 27; off Galveston, July 3; effective, July 31; Aug. 5; Ocracoke Inlet closed, Sept. 17; blockading squadrons, Sept. 19; disrupted at mouth of Miss., Oct. 12; tightens, Oct. 17; Port Royal capture aids, Nov. 7; act. at Savannah, Nov. 26; off Charleston, Dec. 11; tightening, Dec. 15; temporarily lifted at Savannah, Dec. 26; (1862) fall of Ft. Pulaski strengthens, Apr. 11; commerce allowed at Beaufort, N.C., Port Royal, S.C., New Orleans, May 12; Confederacy asks Napoleon III for aid in breaking, July 16; developing, Aug 3; continuing, Oct. 27; (1863) captures, Jan. 21; 2 blockaders seized, Jan. 21; Confs. attack blockaders off Charleston, Jan. 31; Confs. declare blockade lifted, Jan. 31; *Britannia* runs into Wilmington, N.C., May 15; vessels seized, Nov. 5; at Wilmington, Nov. 6; Lincoln reports on, Dec. 8, 9; *Minna* taken off Charleston, Dec. 9; (1864) on Atlantic coast, Jan. 10; off N.C., Jan. 11; (1865) partially lifted, May 10; Johnson removes most restrictions, May 22; declared ended, June 23

Blockade-runners: (1861) Apr. 19; June 18; off Galveston, July 4; 4 taken off Cape Hatteras, Sept. 8; Ocracoke Inlet closed, Sept. 17; capt. by *Connecticut*, Nov. 17; near North Edisto, S.C., Nov. 25; *Albion* capt. off Charleston, Dec. 1; 2 capt., Dec. 15; vessels sunk off Charleston to impede, Dec. 20; off Cape Fear, N.C., Dec. 25; (1862) attack on, Cedar Keys, Fla., Jan. 16; Fed. sink hulks in Charleston Harbor, Jan. 20; *Andracita* or *J. W. Wilder* run ashore, Jan. 20; stopped off mouth Miss. R., Jan. 24; *Columbia* capt. off Bahamas, another off Charleston, Aug. 3; capt.

up Apalachicola R., Fla., Oct. 15; capt., Oct. 27; 3 capt. off N.C., Dec. 3; (1863) U.S.S. *Quaker City* capt., Jan. 4; 3 break into Charleston, Feb. 7; *Peterhoff* seized, Feb. 25; 4 evade at Wilmington, Apr. 23; U.S.S. *DeSoto* captures 4, Apr. 24; 2 arrive at Charleston, May 20; capt., May 20; capt., Nov. 5; *Minna* taken, Dec. 9; (1864) British *Presto* destroyed, Feb. 2; U.S.S. *Florida* destroys 2, Feb. 10; ment., Mar. 5; escape from Galveston, Apr. 30; Mobile closed to, Aug. 6; Wilmington last Conf. open port, Aug. 23; trade lucrative, Oct. 22; C.S.S. *Olustee* runs, Oct. 30; (1865) at Wilmington, Jan. 12

Blood's, Tenn. (or Insane Asylum or Cox's Hill): (1863) sk., Jan. 3

"Bloody Angle of Spotsylvania": (1864) May 12

"Bloody Lane": (1862) at Antietam, Sept. 17

"Bloody Pond": (1862) at Shiloh, or Pittsburg Ldg., Apr. 6

"Bloody Ridge": (1861) at Wilson's Creek, Aug. 10

Bloomery, W. Va.: (1862) sk., Feb. 14

Bloomery Gap, W. Va.: (1864) aff., Mar. 28

Bloomfield, Ky.: (1862) sk., Oct. 18; (1864) sk., Nov. 5

Bloomfield, Mo.: (1862) Fed. exped. to, Jan. 15; sks., May 10, July 29; aff., Aug. 24; sk., Aug. 29; act., Sept. 11; (1863) aff., Jan. 27; capt., Mar. 1; Fed. exped. from, Mar. 9; aff., Apr. 20; sks., Apr. 30, May 12; mutiny, Oct. 22; att. on, Nov. 29; (1864) aff., Apr. 1; Fed. scs. from, May 6; Fed. exped. to, May 16; sk., July 14; (1865) Fed. exped. from, Jan. 4, Mar. 3

Bloomington, Tenn.: (1863) sk., Feb. 27

Bloomington, W. Va.: (1864) raid near, May 5

Blount Co., Tenn.: (1864) sk., July 20

Blount's Cr., N.C.: (1864) aff. near, Apr. 5

Blount's Mills, N.C.: (1863) sk., Apr. 9

Blount's Plantation, Ala.: (1863) act., May 2

Blountsville, Ala.: (1863) sk., May 1

Blountsville, Tenn.: (1863) eng., Sept. 22; sk., Oct. 14

Blountsville Rd., Tenn.: (1862) Confs. captured on, Dec. 29

Blue Bird Gap, Ga.: (1863) sk., Sept. 11

Blue Cr., W. Va.: (1861) sk., Sept. 1

Blue Mills, Mo.: (1861) sk., July 24

Blue Mills Ldg., Mo.: (1861) act., Sept. 17

Blue Pond, Ala.: (1864) sk., Oct. 20

Blue Ridge Mts.: (1862) Apr. 30; A. of P. east of, Oct. 28; Feds. occupy Snicker's Gap, Nov. 2; (1863) Lee crosses, June 12; Stuart holds approaches, June 18; act. at Middleburg, June 19; A. of P. heads to passes, July 19, 20, 21; Feds. attempt to cross at Manassas Gap, July 21, 22, 23; Fed. exped., Aug. 1; Fed. recon. to, Nov. 18; (1864) Early's force in, Sept. 25; (1865) sk., Apr. 22

Blue R., Mo.: (1864) aff., May 21

Blue Rock Station, Calif.: (1864) sk., Mar. 17

Blue's Br., S.C.: (1865) sk., Mar. 8

Blue's Gap, W. Va.: *See* Hanging Rock Pass, W. Va.

Blue's House, W. Va.: (1861) sk., Aug. 26

Blue Springs, Mo.: (1862) sk., Jan. 29; (1863) sk., Mar. 22

Blue Springs, Tenn.: (1863) sks., Oct. 5, 7, 10

Blue Stone, W. Va.: (1862) sk., Aug. 13

Blue Stone R., W. Va.: (1862) sk., Feb. 8

Blue Sulphur Rd., W. Va.: (1863) sk. on, Dec. 14

Bluffton, S.C.: (1862) oper., Mar. 20; (1863) Fed. exped. to, June 4

Blunt, James G. (F): (1862) assumes command Dept. of Kas., May 1; at Cane Hill, Nov. 28; Bat. of Prairie Grove, Ark., Dec. 7; Army of the Frontier, Dec. 28; (1863) eng. at Elk Cr., I.T., July 17; (1864) act. at Lexington, Mo., Oct. 19; Price plans attack, Oct. 22; Bat. of Westport, Mo., Oct. 23; pursuit of Price, Oct. 24; eng. at Newtonia, Mo., Oct. 28

Blythe's Fy. on Tenn. R., Tenn.: (1863) sk., Nov. 13

Boatswain Swamp, Va.: (1862) June 26

Bob's Cr., Mo.: (1862) sk., Mar. 7

Bobo's Cross Roads, Tenn.: (1863) sk., July 1

Boca Chica Pass, Tex.: (1864) sk., Oct. 14

Boggy Depot, I.T.: (1865) sk., Apr. 24

Bogue Chitto Cr., Miss.: (1863) act., Oct. 17

Bogue Inlet, N.C.: (1864) Fed. exped. to, Mar. 25

Bogue Sound Blockhouse, N.C.: (1864) sk., Feb. 2

Boileau, A. D. (F): (1863) arrested, Jan. 27

Boiling Fork, Tenn.: (1863) sk. (Tullahoma Camp.), July 3

Boiling Springs, Tenn.: (1864) sk., Apr. 19

Boise, Ft., Id. Terr.: (1864) Fed. exped. from, July 20; Fed. exped. against Inds., Aug. 27; (1865) Fed. oper. around, Feb 1

Boles' Farm, Mo.: (1862) sk., July 23

Bolivar, Ala.: (1862) sk., Apr. 28

Bolivar, Miss.: (1862) att. of Fed. gunboat, Sept 19

Bolivar, Mo.: (1862) aff., Feb. 8

Bolivar, Tenn.: (1862) Conf. exped. from, July 25; Fed. exped. from, Sept. 20; Ord moves from, Oct. 5; Fed. advance from, Oct. 31; sk., Dec. 24; (1863) Fed. sc. to, Jan. 25; Conf. att., Mar. 21; Fed. exped. from, May 26; sk., July 10; (1864) aff., Feb. 6; sk., Mar. 29, May 2

Bolivar Heights, W. Va.: (1862) Fed. recon. from, Oct. 6; Nov. 9; Nov. 26; Dec. 2; (1864) sk., July 2

Bollinger Co., Mo.: (1864) sk., Jan. 14; (1865) Fed. sc., Mar. 9

Bollinger's Mill, Mo.: (1862) sk., July 26

Bolton (Depot or Station), Miss.: (1863) eng., July 5; sk., July 8; sk., July 16; (1864) sk., Feb. 4

Bombshell, C.S.S.: (1864) capt., May 5

Bonds, Conf.: (1863) Erlanger Loan, Jan. 29

Bonds, U.S.: (1863) Jay Cooke agent for, Mar. 3; (1864) Treasury to issue, Mar. 3

Bonham, Milledge L. (C): (1861) succeeded by Beauregard, June 2; (1863) as gov. asks S.C. leg. to halt speculation, Apr. 3; Davis to, July 10, Aug. 6

Bonnet Carré, La.: (1862) sk., Oct. 19; (1863) Fed. exped. from, Mar. 21; (1865) Fed. exped. from, Mar. 26

"Bonnie Blue Flag": (1861) possible origin of song, Jan. 9

Botts, John Minor: (1861) confers with Lincoln on Va. loyalty, Apr. 7; (1862) arrested, Mar. 1

Boutte Station, La.: (1862) aff., Sept. 4

Bovina Station, Miss.: (1863) Fed. sc. from, Nov. 1

Bowen, John Stevens (C): (1863) Bat. of Port Gibson, Miss., May 1

Bowers' Mill (or Oregon), Mo.: (1863) sk., Oct. 4

Bowie, Ft., Ariz. Terr.: (1863) sk., Apr. 25

Bowling Green, Ky.: (1861) Confs. occupy, Sept. 18; Conf. defense line, Sept. 19; Oct. 28; (1862) sk. near, Feb. 1; Johnston, Beauregard, Hardee confer, Feb. 7; Confs. evacuate, Feb. 11; fire, Feb. 13; Conf. rear guard leaves, Feds. occupy, Feb. 14; Feds. move toward Nashville from, Feb. 19, 22; Mar. 1; Buell reaches, Sept. 14; (1863) Fed. exped. from, May 6

Bowling Green Rd., Ky.: (1862) sk. on, Sept. 17

Bowling Green Rd., near Fredericksburg, Va.: (1862) sk., May 11

Bowman's Place, W. Va.: (1861) sk., June 29

Box Fd., Hatchie R., Miss.: (1862) sk. near, Oct. 7

Boyce's Br., La.: (1863) sk., May 14

Boyce's Plantation, La.: (1864) sk. (Red R. Camp.), May 6

Boyd, Belle (C): (1862) Conf. spy capt., sent to Wash., July 29; released, Aug. 28; (1863) in prison, Aug. 1; released, Dec. 1

Boyd's Ldg., S.C.: (1864) sk. near, Nov. 29

Boyd's Station, Ala.: (1865) sk. near, Mar. 10, 15

Boyd's Trail, Ga.: (1864) sk. (Atlanta Camp.), May 9

Boydton Plank Rd., Va.: (1864) eng., Oct. 27; (1865) Bat. of Hatcher's Run, Feb. 5, 6, 7; A. P. Hill killed near, Apr. 2

Boydton Rd., Va.: (1865) sk., Mar. 29; act., Mar. 31

Boykin, Edward M. (C): (1865) on Lee's surrender, Apr. 9

Braddock's Farm, near Welaka, Fla.: (1865) act., Feb. 5

Braddock's Point, S.C.: (1861) Fed. exped. to, Nov. 10

Bradford, William F. (F): (1864) Confs. capture Ft. Pillow, Apr. 12

Bradfordsville, Ky.: (1865) sk., Feb. 8

Brady, Ft., Va.: (1865) act., Jan. 23

Bradyville, Tenn.: (1863) sk., Feb. 16, Mar. 1; recon. from, Mar. 26; sk. (Tullahoma Camp.), June 24

Bradyville Pike, Tenn.: (1863) sk., May 17

Bragg, Braxton (C): (1861) assumes command Fla. forces, Mar. 11; forbids supplying Ft. Pickens, Mar. 18; asks permission to fire, Apr. 7; permits Worden visit, Apr. 10; commands Dept. of Ala. and West Fla., Oct. 14; Nov. 21; (1862) commands corps, Army of the Miss., Mar. 29; named command Western Dept., June 17; assumes command, June 27; shifts army to Chattanooga, July 23; crosses Tenn. R., Aug. 21; begins fall campaign, Aug. 27; moves into central Tenn., Aug. 28; marches north, Sept. 2; proclaims Tenn. restored, Sept. 5; Lincoln asks where is Bragg, Sept. 7; moves toward Ky., Davis writes, Sept. 7; siege of Munfordville, Ky., Sept. 14, 15, 16; proclamation, Sept. 18; opposed by Buell, Sept. 19; moves to Bardstown, Sept. 21; Ky. Camp., Oct. 1; Bat. of Corinth removes pressure, Oct. 4; attends inaugural of Conf. gov. Ky., Oct. 4; pulls back from Bardstown, toward Harrodsburg, Oct. 5, 6; Conf. army divided,

Oct. 7; Bat. of Perryville, Ky., Oct. 8; retreats south, Oct. 10, 13; moves toward Cumberland Gap, Oct. 16; arrives Cumberland Gap, Oct. 19; makes good escape, Oct. 22; passes Cumberland Gap, Oct. 23, 24; evacuates Ky., Oct. 26; escapes intact, Nov. 1; resumes command Army of the Miss., Nov. 7; moves toward Murfreesboro, Tenn., Nov. 13; concentrates at Tullahoma, Nov. 14; Army of Tenn. constituted, Nov. 20; sends out Forrest, Nov. 21; J. E. Johnston to supervise, Nov. 24; 3 corps move to Murfreesboro, Nov. 24; Dec. 1; Davis reviews army, Dec. 13; at Murfreesboro, Dec. 26, 27; Bat. of Murfreesboro, Dec. 31; (1863) respite, Jan. 1; bat. resumes, Jan. 2; withdraws from Murfreesboro, Jan, 3, 4; Davis to, Jan. 15; Davis orders Johnston to investigate, Jan. 21; Davis' lack of confidence in, Feb. 19; Davis to, May 22; in Tenn., May 24; Rosecrans faces, May 31; confirmed, June 10; Davis to, June 13; Tullahoma Camp., June 23, 24, 25, 27, July 1, 2, 3, 7, 11; Davis to Johnston, July 11; corps command change, July 19; Dept. of E. Tenn., merged into command, July 25; calls for troops, Aug. 16; Davis seeks troops for, Aug. 22; troops sent to, Sept. 1; Rosecrans' advance cont., Sept. 1, 2, 4; Davis to, Sept. 5; threat to, Sept. 5, 8; evacuates Chattanooga, Sept. 9; Longstreet's corps to aid, Sept. 9, 10; orders attack, Sept. 11, 13; concentrates, Sept. 15; Lee on, Sept. 16; fails to halt Fed. concentration, Sept. 17; plans advance, Sept. 18; Bat. of Chickamauga, Sept. 19, 20; aftermath, Sept. 21, 22; Davis to, Sept. 28; Oct. 3; Davis visits, Oct. 6, 9, 10, 13, 14; siege of Chattanooga weakened, Oct. 27; Forrest, Oct. 29; siege of Chattanooga, Nov. 1; Davis to, Nov. 1; ill feelings, Nov. 8; Davis to, Nov. 11; Davis asks help for Bragg, Nov. 20; sends Buckner to Longstreet in Tenn., Nov. 22; Bat. of Chattanooga, Lookout Mt., Missionary Ridge, Nov. 23, 24, 25; aftermath, Nov. 26; Davis orders concentration, Nov. 27; asks to resign, Nov. 28; gathers forces, Nov. 30; relieved, Nov. 30; dispute, Dec. 1; turns army over to Hardee, Dec. 2; Dec. 16; (1864) Davis summons, Jan. 27; charged with military oper. of armies, Feb. 24; Davis sends to Ga., July 9, 13; sent to Wilmington, Oct. 15; ordered to Ga., Nov. 22; (1865) Ft. Fisher exped., Jan. 12, 13, 14, 15, 16; orders evacuation of Wilmington, Feb. 21, 22; Bat. of Kinston, N.C., Mar. 8, 9, 10; retreats, moves to join Johnston, Mar. 10

Bragg, Thomas (C): (1861) named Attorney General, Nov. 21; (1862) replaced, Mar. 18

Bragg's Farm, near Whaley's Mill, Mo.: (1862) sk., Sept. 13

Braine, John C. (C): (1863) seizure of *Chesapeake*, Dec. 8

Braintree, Mass.: (1861) pro-secessionist run out of, Oct. 28

Branch, Lawrence O'Bryan (C): (1862) defends New Berne, N.C., Mar. 14

Branchville, Ark.; (1864) sk., Jan. 19; aff., Mar. 27

Branchville, S.C.: (1865) Confs. at, Feb. 11; Sherman mentions, Feb. 14

Brandenburg, Ky.: (1862) sk., Sept. 12; (1863) Morgan crosses Ohio R., July 8; Morgan's raid, July 9

Brander's (or Brandon) Br., Va.: (1864) sk., May 9

Brandon, Miss.: (1863) act., July 19; Dec. 16; (1864) sk., Feb. 7

Brandy Station, (or Fleetwood) Va.: (1862) sk., Aug. 20; (1863) sk., Apr. 29; Bat. of, June 9; act., Aug. 1; sks., Aug. 4, 9, Sept. 8, Sept. 13, Oct. 11, 12, Nov. 8

Brandyville Pike, Tenn.: (1863) sk., Jan. 23

Brashear City, La.: (1863) sk., June 21; capt., June 23; Feds. retake, July 22; (1864) Fed. exped. from, Feb. 3; Oct. 22; Nov. 17; (1865) Fed. exped. from, Jan. 16, Jan. 21; Feb. 10; Mar. 20; Mar. 25; Apr. 2; Fed. oper., Apr. 30; Fed. exped. from, May 14

Brawley Forks, Tenn.: (1865) sk., Mar. 25

Braxton Co., W. Va.: (1861) sk., Dec. 29; (1864) Fed. sc., May 15

Brazil: (1861) recognizes Confederacy as belligerent, Aug. 1

Brazil Cr., I.T.: (1863) sk., Oct. 11

Brazos, Tex.: (1864) *Stingaree* capt., May 22

Brazos I., Tex.: (1863) Banks occupies, Nov. 2

Brazos Santiago, Tex.: (1861) U.S. property seized, Feb. 21; (1864) oper., Aug. 4; sk., Sept. 6; (1865) Fed. exped. from, May 11, 12; sk., Palmito Ranch, May 12; port restrictions cont., May 22

Bread: (1863) price of in Charleston, S.C., Feb. 25; Richmond riots, Apr. 2

Breaker, C.S.S.: (1862) capt., Aug. 12

Breaux Br., La.: (1863) Fed. exped. to, Apr. 17

Breckinridge, John Cabell (C): (1860) pres. candidate, Nov. page; defeated in election, Nov. 6; named Com. of Thirteen, Dec. 20; (1861) swears in Hamlin as Vice-Pres., Mar. 4; denounces Lincoln's call for troops, Apr. 20; expelled by U. S. Senate, Dec. 4; (1862) eng. at Baton Rouge, Aug. 5; assumes command Army of Middle Tenn., Oct. 28; joins Bragg, Nov. 13; (1863) at Murfreesboro, Jan. 2; Bat. of Chickamauga, Sept. 20; supersedes D. H. Hill command Second Corps, Nov. 8; (1864) assigned command Trans-Allegheny Dept., Feb. 25; assumes command Dept. of Western Va., Mar. 5; moves into Shenandoah, May 14; Bat. of New Market, Va., May 15; succeeded by Jones, May 26; opposes Hunter, June 10; invests Lynchburg, June 16; Early joins, June 17; 2nd Bat. of Kernstown, July 24; 3rd Bat. of Winchester, Sept. 19; advances into east Tenn., Nov. 4, 14, 16, 17; (1865) named Conf. Sec. of War, Feb. 6; Lee to, Feb. 21, Mar. 9; informs Davis of danger, Apr. 8

Breckinridge Co., Ky.: (1864) Fed. sc., May 5

Breckinridge, Mo.: (1864) aff., June 9

Breckinridge, Ft., N. Mex. Terr.: (1861) abandoned by Feds., July 10

Brentsville, Va.: (1862) Fed. sc., Dec. 21; (1863) sks., Oct. 14, Nov. 26, 29; (1864) aff., Feb. 14; (1865) Fed. sc., Feb. 6

Brentwood, Tenn.: (1862) sk., Sept. 19; (1862) sk., Dec. 9, 25; (1863) Forrest raids, Mar. 25

Brentwood Hills, Nashville, Tenn.: (1864) Bat. of Nashville, Dec. 15

Brest, France: (1864) C.S.S. *Florida* leaves, Feb. 10

Breweries: (1862) Butler closes, Nov. 8

Brice's Cross Roads (or Guntown, or Tishomingo Cr.), Miss.: (1864) Bat. of, June 10; aftermath, June 11, 12

Bridge Cr., Miss.: (1862) sk., May 27

Bridgeport, Ala.: (1862) sks., Apr. 23, 27, 29, Aug. 27; (1863) att. on steamer, July 27; occupied by Feds., July 29; Feds. cross Tenn. R., Sept. 4; Feds. arrive, Oct. 2; Fed. recon. from, Oct. 20; Grant in, Oct. 21; Hooker crosses Tenn. R., Oct. 26; Cracker Line, Oct. 27; Sherman at, Nov. 15; (1864) Fed. sc., Mar. 31; Fed. recon. from, Apr. 12

Brown, Ft., Tex.: (1861) Feds. surrender, Mar. 20

Brownell, Francis E. (F): (1861) shoots Ellsworth's killer, May 24

Brown Hill, Ky.: (1862) sk., Oct. 7

Brownlow, William Gannaway (F): (1861) Knoxville, Tenn., *Whig* suppressed, ed. Brownlow charged with treason, Oct. 24; (1865) elected gov. of Tenn. as unionist, Mar. 4; inaugurated, Apr. 7

Brownsburg, Va.: (1864) sk., June 10

Brown's Fy., Ala.: (1864) oper., Feb. 19

Brown's Fy., Tenn. R.: (1863) "cracker line," Oct. 24, 27; Sherman moves to cross Tenn. R. at, Nov. 21

Brown's Fy., Va.: (1864) sk., May 12

Brown's Gap, Va.: (1864) sk., Sept. 26

Brown's Pass, Va.: (1864) Early forced back in, Sept. 25

Brown's Plantation, Miss.: (1862) sk., Aug. 11

Brown's Spring, Mo.: (1862) sk., July 27

Brownsville, Ark.: (1863) sks., July 25, Aug. 25, Sept. 12; aff., Sept. 12; aff., Sept. 16; (1864) Fed. scs. from, Jan. 17, June 27; sks., July 13, 30, Sept. 4; Fed. exped. from, Oct. 26; (1865) Fed. exped. from, Jan. 4

Brownsville, Ky.: (1861) sk., Nov. 20

Brownsville, Md.: (1864) aff., July 7

Brownsville, Miss.: (1863) sks., Oct. 15, 22; (1864) sks., Mar. 3, 7, Sept. 28; (1865) Fed. exped., Apr. 19

Brownsville, Tenn.: (1862) Conf. raid, July 19; recon. from, Aug. 10

Brownsville, Tex.: (1863) capt. by Banks, Nov. 6; (1864) Lincoln proclaims blockade lifted, Feb. 10; Conf. reoccupation, July 20; (1865) Fed. exped. to, May 11; port restrictions maintained, May 22

Broxton's Br., Salkehatchie R., S.C.: (1865) sk., Feb. 2

Brucetown, Va.: (1864) sk., Sept. 7

Bruinsburg, Miss.: (1863) Vicksburg Camp., Apr. 29, May 1, May 2

Brunswick, Ga.: (1863) aff., June 8

Brunswick, Md.: *See* Berlin, Md.

Brunswick, Mo.: (1861) sk., Aug. 17; (1864) aff., Sept. 6; sk., Oct. 11

Brush Cr., Mo.: (1864) Bat. of Westport, Oct. 23

Brush Mt., Ga.: (1864) Johnston at, June 4; comb., June 15

Brushy Cr., Ark.: (1864) sk., Apr. 7

Bryan Court House, Ga.: (1864) sk., Dec. 8

Bryant's Plantation, Fla.: (1864) sk., Oct. 21

Buchanan, Franklin (C): (1861) resigns U. S. Navy to go South, Apr. 22; (1862) commands C.S.S. *Virginia (Merrimack)*, wounded, Mar. 8; (1864) Pres. Davis to, Feb. 19; Bat. of Mobile Bay, Aug. 5

Buchanan, James: (1860) as President powerless to prevent secession, Cabinet split, proposals, Nov. 9; asks Attorney General opinion, Nov. 20; State of Union message, Dec. 4; names Philip F. Thomas Sec. of Treasury, Dec. 8; meets S.C. delegation, Dec. 8; moves to prepare military, Dec. 10; S.C. delegation presents memo, Dec. 10; names Jeremiah S. Black Sec. of State, Dec. 17; appoints Edwin M. Stanton Attorney General, reaction to S.C. secession, Dec. 20; South protests shift of troops to Ft. Sumter, Buchanan expresses surprise over move, hopes to confine secession, Dec. 27; receives

fense of Ohio R. cities, Oct. 1; presses toward Bardstown, Ky., Oct. 2; Corinth Camp., keeps reinforcements from, Oct. 4; follows Bragg, Oct. 5; occupies Bardstown, Oct. 6; nears Perryville, Ky., Oct. 7; Bat. of Perryville, Ky., Oct. 8; Bragg escapes, Oct. 22; replaced by Rosecrans, Oct. 24, 30; ment., Dec. 18

Buell's Fd., Tenn.: (1863) sk., Sept. 28

Buffalo, N.Y.: (1861) Lincoln at, Feb. 16, 17; (1865) Lincoln's funeral train pauses at, Apr. 27

Buffalo, W. Va.: (1862) exped. from Point Pleasant to, Sept. 26

Buffalo Hill, Ky.: (1861) sk., Oct. 4

"Buffalo Hunt": (1861) Baylor organizes for Conf. control of Southwest, July 8, 25, Aug. 1

Buffalo Mt., W. Va.: *See* Camp Alleghany

Buffalo Mts., Ark.: (1863) sk., Oct. 24

Buffalo R., Ark.: (1863) Fed. exped. from, Jan. 9; ment., Dec. 16; sk., Dec. 25; (1864) Fed. sc. to, Mar. 13

Buffington, O.: (1863) Morgan heads for, July 18

Buffington I., O.: (1863) Morgan defeated at, July 19

Buford, John (F): (1863) Gettysburg Camp., June 29, July 1; named Maj. Gen., death of, Dec. 16

Buford's Br., S.C.: (1865) sk., Feb. 4

Buford's Gap, Va.: (1864) sk., June 20

Bull I., S.C.: (1863) aff., Jan. 31

Bullitt's Bayou, La.: (1864) sk., Sept. 14

Bulloch, James Dunwody (C): (1861) sent by C.S.A. Navy to Europe to purchase ships and arms, May 9

Bull Pasture Mt., Va.: *See* McDowell, Va.

Bull R., S.C.: (1862) Fed. recon., Feb. 23

Bull Run, Va.: (1861) Beauregard's troops on, July 18; Conf. defenses, July 19; July 20; Bat. of 1st Bull Run or Manassas, July 21; (1862) Bat. of 2nd Bull Run or Manassas, Aug. 29, 30; (1863) Fed. exped., Aug. 1; sk. at McLean's Fd., Oct. 14; Bristoe Camp., Oct. 15, 17, 18

Bull Run Br., Va.; (1862) sk., 2nd Bull Run Camp., Aug. 26; act., Aug. 27

Bull Run Mts., Va.: (1862) 2nd Bull Run Camp., Aug. 26; (1863) Fed. sc., Aug. 14

Bull Run, 1st, Va., Bat. of (or Manassas): (1861) Bull Run or Manassas Camp., July 16–22; bat., July 21; effect of Conf. victory, Aug. 1; Davis on, Aug. 4, Nov. 2; Fed. Cong. discontent, Dec. 1; N.Y. Rep. Alfred Ely freed, Dec. 27; (1862) battlefield ment., Aug. 26, 28

Bull Run, 2nd, Va., Bat. of (or Manassas): (1862) preliminaries under way, Aug. 13; main camp., Aug. 26, 27, 28; bat., Aug. 29, 30; aftermath, Aug. 31; Chantilly, Sept. 1; consternation in east, Sept. 1; Sept. 2; Pope charges against McClellan and Porter, Sept. 3; F. J. Porter charged with disobedience at, Nov. 5; (1863) Porter cashiered from Army, Jan. 10, 21; Oct. 13

Bull's Bay, S.C.: (1861) exped. to considered, Oct. 12

Bull's Gap, Tenn.: (1864) sk., Mar. 15; Fed. exped. from, Apr. 25; sk., Oct. 16

Bulltown, W. Va.: (1863) sk., Oct. 13; (1864) Fed. raid, May 3; sk., Aug. 20

"Bummers": (1864) on Sherman's March to the Sea, Nov. 22

Bunger's Mills, W. Va.: (1864) Averell moves from, June 3

Bunker Hill, W. Va.: (1861) J. E. Johnston's troops fall back to, June 15; (1862) sk., Sept. 3; Fed. recon. to, Dec. 12; (1863) sk., June 13; Lee at, July 16, 20; (1864) sk., Jan. 1; 2nd Bat. of Kernstown, July 24; sk., July 25; Early moves south from, Aug. 10; Early moves toward, Aug. 18, 19; Early moves west of, Aug. 26; Early at, Aug. 27; act., Sept. 2; sk., Sept. 13; Bat. of 3rd Winchester or Opequon Cr., Sept. 18

Burden's Causeway, John's I., S.C.: (1864) act., July 9

Bureau for the Relief of Freedmen and Refugees: *See* Freedmen's Bureau

Burgess' Mill, Va.: (1864) eng., Oct. 27

Burke's Mill, Ga.: (1864) Fed. sc. to, Feb. 18

Burke's Station, Va.: (1861) sk., Dec. 4; (1863) aff., Aug. 7; (1865) sk., Apr. 10

Burkesville, Ky.: (1862) sk., Nov. 8; (1863) Fed. exped. to, June 8; Morgan crosses Cumberland, July 2; (1864) Fed. exped. from, Apr. 18

Burkeville, Va.: (1864) exped. against South Side R.R., June 22; (1865) ment., Feb. 21; Grant's pursuit of Lee, Apr. 3

Burlington, W. Va.: (1861) sk., Sept. 1; (1863) sks., Apr. 6, 26, Aug. 4, Oct. 13, Nov. 16

Burned Church, Ga.: (1864) armies entrenched, May 26; act., May 30

Burnside, Ambrose E. (F) (*See also* East Tenn. Camp.): (1862) commands Dept. of N.C., Jan. 7; Roanoke I. exped. preliminaries, Jan. 11, 13; ment., Jan. 21; threatens Roanoke I., Jan. 22; exped. in difficulty, Jan. 25; lands on Roanoke I., Feb. 7; Bat. of Roanoke I., Feb. 8; lands west side of Neuse R., N.C., Mar. 13; capture of New Berne, N.C., Mar. 14; Mar. 20; sails for A. of P. in Va., July 6; takes command Ninth Army Corps, July 22; arrives Aquia Cr., Aug. 4; Potomac R. collision, Aug. 13; Lincoln asks for news, Aug. 27; Bat. of South Mt., Md., Sept. 14; Bat. of Antietam, Sept. 17; ordered to command A. of P., Nov. 5; told of A. of P. command, Nov. 7; assumes command A. of P., Nov. 9; idolization of McClellan a problem, Nov. 10; Lincoln approves plans, Nov. 14; moves toward Fredericksburg, Va., Nov. 15, 16; hdqrs. near Falmouth, Va., Nov. 19; calls upon Fredericksburg to surrender, Nov. 21; Lincoln confers with, Nov. 26; faces Lee at Fredericksburg, Dec. 2; action increases, Dec. 10; Feds. occupy Fredericksburg, Dec. 11; attack imminent, Dec. 12; Bat. of Fredericksburg, Dec. 13; dissuaded from another attack, Dec. 14; judgment questioned, Dec. 15; army licks wounds, Dec. 16; Lincoln calls to Wash., Dec. 19; confers with Lincoln, Dec. 22; Lincoln to, Dec. 30; meets with Lincoln, Dec. 31; (1863) offers to resign, Jan. 1, 5; Halleck to, Jan. 7; Lincoln to, Jan. 8; "Mud March," Jan. 19, 20, 21, 22, 23, 24; orders removing subordinate gens., Jan. 23; army in winter quarters, Jan. 24; Lincoln awaits arrival, Jan. 24; Lincoln relieves Burnside from command A. of P., Jan. 25; supersedes Wright in command Dept. of the O., Mar. 25; orders death penalty, deportation of Conf. abettors, Apr. 13; Lincoln refuses resignation of over Vallandigham, May 29; suppresses Chicago *Times,* June 1; leaves Ky. for Tenn., Aug. 16; fall of Knoxville, Sept. 2; fall of Cumberland Gap, Sept. 7, 9; Lincoln refuses resignation of, Sept. 11; Lincoln orders to Rosecrans, Sept. 21; difficulty in east Tenn., Sept. 22; Lincoln to, unsent, Sept. 25; Lincoln to, Sept. 27; Lincoln mentions, Oct. 4; continues in command Dept. of the O., Oct. 17; Grant wires, Oct. 20; Bragg sends Longstreet against, Nov. 4, 5; withdraws into Knoxville, Tenn., Nov. 16 (*See* Knoxville, Tenn., Camp.); siege of Knoxville ends, Dec. 6; superseded by John G. Foster, Dec. 9; (1864) Burnside's Ninth Corps moves to Grant, May 4; Bat. of Wilderness, May 5, 6; Bat. of Spotsylvania, May 9, 10, 11, 12, 18; Bat. of the North Anna, May 24; Bat. of Cold Harbor, June 3; Early moves toward, June 6; south of James R., June 16; assault on Petersburg, Va., June 16; troops prepare for mine explosion, July 29; Petersburg mine explosion, July 30

Burnside Br. at Antietam, Md.: (1862) Sept. 17

Burnsville, Miss.: (1862) Fed. exped. to, May 22; (1863). sk., Jan. 3

Burnt Br., near Humboldt, Tenn.: (1862) sk., Sept. 5

Burnt Cross Roads, Ky.: (1862) sk., Oct. 6

Burnt Hickory, Ga.: (1864) sks., May 24, June 13; act., July 4

Burnt Ordinary, Va.: (1862) Fed. recon. to, Dec. 17; (1863) sk., Jan. 19

Burrowsville, Ark.: (1864) Fed. sc. to, Mar. 29

Bush Cr., Mo.: (1863) sk., May 26

Bushwhackers: (1863) Quantrill's sacking of Lawrence, Kans., Aug. 21; (1865) Fed. sc. for, Jan. 2

Bushy Cr. Mo.: (1863) Fed. sc. to, Nov. 24

Bushy Swamp, N.C.: (1865) sk., Mar. 18

Butler, Benjamin F. (F): (1861) and Eighth Mass. at Annapolis, Apr. 20; assigned command Dept. of Annapolis, Apr. 27; occupies Relay House, Md., May 5; takes Federal Hill, Baltimore, May 13; extends rule in Baltimore, May 14; command of Ft. Monroe, May 15; arrives at Ft. Monroe, May 22; recon. to Hampton, Va., May 23; refuses to return slaves, May 24; sends force to Newport News, May 27; War Sec. Cameron directs Butler to put fugitive slaves to work, May 30; Big Bethel, June 10; Butler to Cameron re contrabands, July 30; bans liquor, Aug. 2; Magruder burns Hampton, Va., Aug. 7; Cameron to Butler re slaves, Aug. 8; commands forces to attack Hatteras, Aug. 17; leads Hatteras exped., Aug. 27; commands Dept. of New England, Oct. 1; (1862) to command Dept. of the Gulf, Feb. 23; assumes command Dept. of the Gulf, Mar. 20; below New Orleans, Apr. 17; "reign" in New Orleans begins, May 1; seizes Netherland gold, May 10; issues Order 28, notorious women order, May 15; suspends New Orleans *Bee,* takes over *Delta,* May 16; hanging of Wm. B. Mumford, June 7; New Orleans cleaner under Butler, July 12; confiscates bells meant for Conf. cannon, July 30; assesses secessionists to pay for poor, Aug. 4; Davis on, Aug. 18; orders registration of foreigners, Sept. 13; authorizes Negro regts., Sept. 27; orders pertaining to slaves, Nov. 1; Banks appointed to replace Butler, Nov. 8; Butler closes distilleries, breweries, Nov. 8; bids farewell to people of New Orleans, Dec. 15; Banks supersedes in Dept. of the Gulf, Dec. 16; Butler proclaimed outlaw by Pres. Davis, Dec. 23; (1863) reward offered by Confs., Jan. 1; unsent letter of Lincoln to, Jan. 23; commands Dept. of Va. and N.C., Nov. 11; (1864) orders raid to release prisoners, Feb. 6; Lincoln confirms faith in, Feb. 26; Kilpatrick's raiders join, Mar. 2;

Lincoln to, Mar. 12; ordered to move against Richmond, Apr. 9; threat of invasion by, Apr. 18; south side of James operation, May 4, 5, 6, 7, 8, 9, 12; Sheridan rides toward, May 12; Bat. of Ft. Darling or Drewry's Bluff, May 12, 13; Davis on oper. of, May 14; Sheridan attempts to reach, May 15; defensive line at Drewry's Bluff, May 15; eng. at Drewry's Bluff or Ft. Darling, May 16; attempt to take Petersburg fails, May 16, 17; Beauregard's investment of Butler, May 18, 19, 20, 28, June 1, 9; Grant orders to obstruct James, June 13; W. F. Smith reports to, June 14; att. on Petersburg fails, June 15; act. on Bermunda Hundred front, June 16; Lincoln, Grant visit, June 22; destruction of *Greyhound,* Nov. 27; commands army on Ft. Fisher exped., Dec. 23, 24, 25; Lincoln on, Dec. 30: (1865) Dutch Gap explosion fails, Jan. 1; Lincoln disenchanted with, Jan. 2; ment., Jan. 4; Grant on, Jan. 6; removed from command, Jan. 7; Ord takes command from, Jan. 8

Butler, Mo.: (1861) sk., Nov. 20

Butler, Camp, Springfield, Ill.: (1864) fire at, Jan. 17

Butte-à-la-Rose, La.: (1863) capt., Apr. 20

Buzzard Roost, Ga.: (1864) Fed. demon. to, Feb. 22–25; eng., Feb. 25; demon., May 8; defenses tested, May 9; (1865) sk., Apr. 22

Byhalia, Miss.: (1863) sk. near, Oct. 12; (1864) aff., Feb. 11

Byhalia Rd., Miss.: (1864) sk., July 2.

Byram's Fd., Big Blue R., Mo.: (1864) act., Oct. 22; Bat. of Westport, Oct. 23

Cabell Co., W. Va.: (1863) Fed. Exped. through, Apr. 3; (1864) Fed. sc. in, Mar. 16

Cabin Cr., I.T.: (1863) eng., July 1; sk., July 20; (1864) act., Sept. 19

Cabinet, presidential, C.S.A.: (1861) Cabinet as of Feb. 19, Sec. of State, Robert Toombs, Ga.; Sec. of Treasury, Christopher G. Memminger, S.C.; Sec. of War, LeRoy Pope Walker, Ala.; Sec. of Navy, S. R. Mallory, Fla.; Attorney General, Judah P. Benjamin, La.; Postmaster General, J. H. Reagan, Tex.; statement on Sumter surrender, Apr. 14; R. M. T. Hunter, Va., succeeds Toombs as Sec. of State, July 25; Judah P. Benjamin replaces Walker as Sec. of War, Nov. 21; Thomas Bragg, N.C., succeeds Benjamin as Attorney General, Nov. 21; (1862) Benjamin replaces Hunter as Sec. of State, Mar. 18; George W. Randolph, Va., appointed Sec. of War replacing Benjamin, Mar. 18; Thomas Hill Watts, Ala., replaces Bragg as Attorney General, Mar. 18; George W. Randolph resigns as Sec. of War, Nov. 15; Gustavus W. Smith, temporary Sec. of War, Nov. 17; James A. Seddon, Va., named Sec. of War, Nov. 21; (1863) Watts resigns, Keyes succeeds ad interim, Sept. 9; George Davis, N.C., named Attorney General replacing Thomas H. Watts, Dec. 31; (1864) George Davis confirmed as Attorney General, Jan. 2; Memminger resigns as Sec. of The Treasury, June 21; G. A. Trenholm, S.C., appointed Sec. of the Treasury, July 18; (1865) Seddon resigns as Sec. of War, Feb. 1; John C. Breckinridge, Tenn., named Sec. of War, Feb. 6; evac. of Richmond, Apr. 2; in Danville, Va., Apr. 3, 7; conference with Pres. Davis and gens., Apr. 12; flight continues, Apr. 14, 15, 16, 17, 18, 19, 23, 26; Attorney General Davis leaves Pres. Davis, Apr. 26; Trenholm resigns Treasury, Apr. 29; flight, May 1; Mallory resigns

Navy Dept., May 2; Mallory resignation accepted, May 3; Benjamin, Sec. of State, leaves Davis, May 3; flight continues, May 4; Postmaster General Reagan captured with Pres. Davis near Irwinville, Ga., May 10

Cabinet, presidential, U.S., Buchanan's administration: (1860) split over seccession, Nov. 9; Sec. of Treasury Howell Cobb resigns, Dec. 8; Philip F. Thomas, Md., named Sec. of Treasury, Dec. 8; Sec. of State Lewis Cass resigns, Dec. 12; Attorney Gen. Jeremiah Sullivan Black succeeds Cass as Sec. of State, Dec. 20; Edwin M. Stanton, Pa., succeeds Black as Attorney General, Dec. 20; Cabinet votes on proposal to remove all U.S. forces from Charleston Harbor, Dec. 27; Sec. of War John B. Floyd resigns, Dec. 29; Stanton and Black give Buchanan document of advice on crisis, Dec. 30; Joseph Holt, Ky., named temporary Sec. of War, Dec. 31; (1861) Cabinet hears S.C. commissioners' letter, approves reinforcing Ft. Sumter, Jan. 2; John A. Dix, N.Y., succeeds Philip F. Thomas as Sec. of the Treasury, Jan. 11; Joseph Holt named Sec. of War, Jan. 18; Horatio King, Me., named Postmaster General succeeding Holt, Feb. 1; Lincoln calls on Cabinet, Feb. 23

Cabinet, presidential, U.S., Lincoln's administration: (1860) posts becoming of interest, Nov. 16; posts discussed with Hamlin, Nov. 21; Cabinet appointments discussed, Dec. 12; Lincoln works on appointments, Dec. 29; Lincoln confers with Simon Cameron, Dec. 30; (1861) Lincoln and Salmon P. Chase confer, Jan. 4; William H. Seward accepts post as Sec. of State in new Cabinet, Jan. 10; negotiations continue on Cabinet, Feb. 4; difficulties with appointments, Mar. 2; Simon Cameron accepts post as Sec. of War, Mar. 1; Cabinet as of Mar. 4, 1861, Sec. of State, William H. Seward, N.Y.: Sec. of Treasury, Salmon P. Chase, O.; Sec. of War, Simon Cameron, Penn.; Sec. of Navy, Gideon Welles, Conn.; Sec. of Interior, Caleb B. Smith, Ind.; Attorney General, Edward Bates, Mo.; Postmaster General, Montgomery Blair, Md.; Sen. confirms appointments, Mar. 5; meets with Lincoln to consider Sumter reinforcement, Mar. 9; discusses Sumter crisis, Mar. 14; Lincoln requests opinions on provisioning Ft. Sumter, Mar. 15, 16; meets on crisis, Mar. 26; reverses stand on Ft. Sumter, Mar. 29; meets on crisis, Apr. 3; long night session on crisis, Apr. 14; meets, Apr. 18; decision on war expenses, June 6; strategy meeting, June 29; meets on 1st Bull Run defeat, July 21; confers with Lincoln on McClellan memorandum, Aug. 3; discusses Frémont, Sept. 15; hears Frémont reports, Sept. 18; meets with McClellan, Sept. 27; meets, Oct. 1; considers Frémont's removal, Oct. 7; meets, Oct. 9, 22; visits resigned Gen. Scott, Nov. 1; voices approval of *Trent* Aff., Nov. 15; discusses *Trent* Aff., Dec. 18; decides seizure of Mason, Slidell illegal, surrenders commissioners, Dec. 26; (1862) Cameron resigns as Sec. of War, Jan. 11; Cabinet meets with Lincoln, Jan. 13; Edwin M. Stanton of Pa. appointed Sec. of War, Jan. 13; Stanton confirmed, Jan. 15; War Order No. 3 command changes, Mar. 11; discusses McClellan, Apr. 9; discusses possible use of Negroes as soldiers, July 21; discussions, Sept. 4; preliminary Emancipation Proclamation, Sept. 20; colonization of Negroes, Sept. 26; Seward resigns, Dec. 17; Republican sens. meet with Lincoln concerning Cabinet, Dec. 18; crisis in Cabinet, Dec. 19; crisis over, Dec. 20; (1863) Caleb Smith resigns as Attorney General, Jan. 8; John P. Usher, Ind., confirmed as Sec. of Interior, Jan. 8; Lincoln confers with, Apr. 11; Chase offers resignation, May 11; debates possible peace negotiations, July 4; rejects peace conference, July 6; confers with Meade, Aug. 14; conference on strategy, Sept. 23

(1864) meets without Chase, Feb. 23; confers on Ft. Pillow, May 3; Salmon P. Chase resigns again as Sec. of Treasury and Lincoln accepts, June 30; William Pitt Fessenden, Me., named to replace Chase as Sec. of Treasury, July 1; Lincoln's memo on tenure, July 14; Lincoln has members sign memo without reading it, Aug. 23; Lincoln advised to drop Blair, Sept. 3; concerned over cotton trading, Sept. 9; pressure to remove Blair, Stanton, Sept. 17; Lincoln asks Blair to resign as Postmaster General, Sept. 23; William Dennison, O., named Postmaster General, Sept. 24; Dennison joins Cabinet, Oct. 4; Lincoln opens "sealed" document signed by secretaries, Nov. 11; Bates resigns as Attorney General, Nov. 24; James Speed, Ky., appointed Attorney General, Dec. 1; Lincoln indicates to Cabinet Butler's impending removal, Dec. 30; (1865) Lincoln proposes compensated emancipation, Feb. 5; considers congressional bills, Mar. 3; Fessenden resigns as Sec. of Treasury, Mar. 5; Hugh McCulloch, Ind., asked by Lincoln to be Sec. of Treasury, Mar. 5; named, Mar. 6; Sec. of Interior Usher offers to resign, Mar. 8; Lincoln accepts Usher's resignation, Mar. 9; President names Sen. James Harlan, Ia., Sec. of Interior, Mar. 9; Sec. of State Seward injured, son Frederick, Asst. Sec., assumes post temporarily, Apr. 5; opposition to Va. legislature convening, Apr. 12; Lincoln confers with Cabinet, Apr. 13, 14; Cabinet and assassination of Lincoln, Apr. 14; asks Johnson to assume presidency, Apr. 15; Johnson asks Cabinet to remain, Apr. 15; at Lincoln's funeral, Apr. 19

Cabin Point, Va.: (1864) sk., Aug. 5

Cacapon Mt., W. Va.: (1863) sk., Aug. 6

Cache R., Ark.: (1862) act. at, July 7

Cackleytown, W. Va.: (1863) sk. near, Nov. 4

Caddo Gap, Ark.: (1863) Fed. sc. to, Dec. 2; (1864) sks., Jan. 26, Feb. 12, 16

Caddo Mill, Ark., (1863) sk., Dec. 14

Cadwalader, George (F): (1861) replaces Butler in Dept. of Annapolis, May 15; and *ex parte* Merryman, May 27

Cahawba R., Ala.: (1865) sk. on at Fike's Fy., Apr. 7

Cainsville, Tenn.: (1863) sk. near, Feb. 15

Cairo, Ill.: (1861) Ill. troops arrive at, Apr. 22; guns planted at, June 1; Lincoln proposes movement from, July 27; Frémont arrives at, Aug. 12; ment., Aug. 19; recon. from, Sept. 8; Conf. camp at Charleston broken up, Oct. 2; recon. from, Oct. 7; eng. at Belmont, Nov. 7; (1862) ment., Jan. 1; ment., Jan. 9; Fed. recon. into Ky. from, Jan. 10; Fed. recon. from, Jan. 15; Fed. recon. returns, Jan. 21; Lincoln's War Order No. 1, Jan. 27; troop transports move from, Feb. 3; Fed. exped. from to Eastport, Miss., Feb. 15; tornado, Apr. 2; (1863) Grant ordered to, Oct. 16; (1864) cold wave reaches, Jan. 1

Cairo, District of, Fed.: (1862) W. T. Sherman assigned to command, Feb. 14; Grant assumes command, July 17

Cairo, U.S.S. (ironclad): (1862) sunk on Yazoo R., Dec. 12

Cairo Station, W. Va.: (1863) aff., May 7

Calais, France: (1864) C.S.S. *Rappahannock* held at, Aug. 2
Calcasieu Pass, La.: (1864) oper. in, May 6
Caleb Cushing, U.S.S. (revenue cutter): (1863) seized at Portland, Me., June 26
Caledonia, La.: (1863) sk., May 10
Caledonia, Mo.: (1864) sks., Sept. 12, 28
Caledonia Iron Works (or Stevens' Furnace), Pa.: (1863) sk., July 5
Calfkiller Cr., near Sparta, Tenn.: (1863) sk., Aug. 17
Calhoun (Conf. privateer): (1861) captures *Ocean Eagle,* May 15
Calhoun, Ga.: (1864) Johnston heads for, May 15; Johnston pulls back from, May 17; sk., June 10
Calhoun, Ky.: (1862) sk., Nov. 25
Calhoun, Mo.: (1864) guerrilla raid on, June 12
Calhoun, Tenn.: (1863) sks., Sept. 18, 25, 26; act., Dec. 28
Calhoun Co., W. Va.: (1863) sk. at Beech Fork in, Sept. 8
Calico Rock, Ark.: (1862) sk., May 26
California: (1861) pro-secessionist, independence movements, May 11; legislature pledges support to Union, May 17; pro-Confederates in, Oct. 5; (1862) Republican victories in, Nov. 4; (1863) gold mining in, May 26
California, Mo.: (1864) sk., Oct. 9
"California Column": (1862) Carleton's exped., Apr. 13, May 4
California Home Guards: (1861) organized, Aug. 12
California House, Mo.: (1864) aff. near, Feb. 12
Callaway Co., Mo.: (1862) sc., Sept. 4; sk. at Auxvasse Cr., Oct. 16; (1864) Fed. sc. in, Nov. 6
Callaghan's Station, Va.: (1864) aff., May 4
Camargo Cross-Roads, Miss.: (1864) sk., July 13
Cambridge, Mo.: (1862) sc., June 4
Camden, Ark.: (1864) sk. (Camden exped.), Apr. 15, 20; Conf. demon. on, Apr. 23; sk. near, Apr. 24; Steele retreat from, Apr. 26, 29; (1865) Fed. sc. toward, Jan. 26
Camden, Ark., exped. (*See also* Steele, Frederick; Red. R. Camp.): (1864) Mar. 23 (advance from Little Rock), 25 (sk. Rockport), 27; Apr. 1 (sk. Arkadelphia), 3 (Elkin's Fy.), 6 (at the Little Mo. R.), 9, 10 (head back), 13, 14 (sk. Dutch Mills, White Oak Cr.), 15 (sk. Camden), 16, 17 (Red Mt.), 18 (Poison Springs), 20 (Camden), 23, 24 (Camden), 26, 28 (Princeton), 29, 30; May 3 (arrives at Little Rock)
Camden, S.C.: (1865) sk. near, Feb. 22, 23; sk., Feb. 24; Fed. troops occupy, Feb. 25; Fed. exped. to, Apr. 5
Camden Co., N.C.: (1862) sk. at South Mills, Apr. 19; (1863) Fed. exped. to, Aug. 5
Camden Court House, N.C. (1863) sk. near, Oct. 17; Fed. exped. to, Dec. 5
Camden Point, Mo.: (1864) act., July 13; sk. near, July 22
Cameron, Simon (F): (1860) confers with Lincoln, Dec. 30; (1861) accepts post as Sec. of War, Mar. 1, 4; against provisioning Sumter, Mar. 15; signs letter to Anderson, Apr. 4; accepts aid of Dorothea Dix, May 29; on fugitive slaves, May 30; approves Sanitary Commission, June 8; reports on McDowell's army, July 20; to Butler re Negroes, Aug. 8; on Western

inspection trip, Oct. 7; (1862) charges against, Jan. 10; resigns, Jan. 11; minister to Russia, Jan. 11, 13; (1863) resigns as minister to Russia, Feb. 23

Camp: *See* individual names

Campbell, John Archibald (C): (1861) on Lincoln's inaugural address, Mar. 4; intermediary for Conf. commissioners, Mar. 8; contact with Seward for commissioners, Mar. 31; resigns from Supreme Court, May 2; (1865) commissioner to Hampton Rds. Peace Conference, Jan. 28, Feb. 2, 3; Lincoln confers with, Apr. 4, 5; misunderstanding over Va. legislature, Apr. 12; imprisonment, parole of, Oct. 11

Campbell's Station, Tenn.: (1863) eng., Nov. 16

Campbellsville, Tenn.: (1864) act., Nov. 24

Campbellton, Ga.: (1864) acts., July 4, 10; sks., July 12, 18, 28; aff., Sept. 10

Camp Cole, Mo.: (1863) sk., June 8

Camp Cr., Ga.: (1864) comb., Aug. 18; sk., Sept. 30

Camp Cr., W. Va.: (1862) sk., May 1

Camp Grover, Mo.: (1865) Fed. sc. from to Texas Prairie, Jan. 12

Campti, La.: (1864) sk., Apr. 4

Canada: (1861) and *Trent* Aff., Dec. 20; (1862) St. Croix *Herald* wrecked, July 28; draft evaders flee to, Aug. 9; (1863) Vallandigham in, June 11; Vallandigham runs campaign from, Oct. 13; (1864) Davis names commissioners to, Apr. 27; Northwest Conspiracy in, June 8; return of Vallandigham from, June 15; Young authorized to organize Conf. raiders in, June 16; peace feeler letter to Greeley, July 5; St. Albans, Vt., raid operated from, Oct. 19; reports of conspiracy in, Nov. 2; plot to burn N.Y., Nov. 25; (1865) Lord Russell protests St. Albans raid, Feb. 13

Cañada Alamosa, N. Mex. Terr.: (1861) sk., Sept. 25

Canadian R., N. Mex. Terr.: (1862) Fed. exped. from Ft. Union to, Oct. 9; (1864) eng. at Adobe Ft. on, Nov. 25

Canal boats, Union: (1862) for A. of P., Feb. 28

Canals: (1862) Albemarle Canal (or Chesapeake and Albemarle Canal, Dismal Swamp Canal), Feb. 13; Apr. 23; Island No. 10 canal, Apr. 4; (1862) Swampy Toe or Williams Canal at Vicksburg, June 20, 25, 27; July 22; (1863) Mar. 5

Canby, Edward Richard Sprigg (F): (1861) commands Fed. Dept. of N. Mex., June 11; Nov. 9; (1862) eng. at Valverde, N. Mex. Terr., Feb. 21; defeats Confs. retreating from Santa Fe, Aug. 7; superseded by Carleton, Sept. 18; (1864) assumes command Mil. Div. of West Miss., May 11; Lincoln to on govt. policy in La., Dec. 12; (1865) Mobile Camp., Mar. 17, 25; Apr. 12 (surrender of Mobile); agrees on truce with Richard Taylor, Apr. 30; Taylor's surrender, May 2, 4; preparing exped. into Trans-Miss., May 8; accepts surrender of Army of the Trans-Miss., May 26

Canby, Ft., N. Mex. Terr.: (1864) exped. from to Cañon de Chelly, Jan. 6

Cane Cr., Ala.: (1863) sks., Oct. 20, 26

Cane Hill (or Boston Mts.), Ark.: (1862) sks. near, Nov. 9, 25; Blunt attacks Marmaduke at, Nov. 28; oper. about, Dec. 4; sk. near, Dec. 20; (1864) sk., Nov. 6

Cane Patch, near Murrell's Inlet, S.C.: (1864) salt works destroyed at, Apr. 21

Cane R., La.: (1864) eng. at Red R. junction (Red. R. Camp.), Apr. 26

Cane R. Crossing (or Monett's Fy.), La.: (1864) eng., Apr. 23
Caney Bayou, Tex.: (1864) bomb. of Conf. works at, Jan. 8; aff., Feb. 7
Caney Ft., Tenn.: (1863) aff. near, May 9
Cannon's Bridge, South Edisto R., S.C.: (1865) Fed. recon. to, Feb. 7; sk., Feb. 8
Canoe Cr., Fla.: (1865) act., Mar. 25
Canoe Station, Ala.: (1865) Fed. column reaches, Mar. 27
Cañon de Chelly, N. Mex. Terr.: (1863) Carson's operations in area of, Aug. 20; (1864) Fed. exped. against Navajos to, Jan. 6
Cañon Station, Nev. Terr.: (1863) aff., June 23
Canton, Ky.: (1864) sk., Aug. 22
Canton, La.: (1864) ment., June 7
Canton, Miss.: (1863) sk. (Jackson Camp.), July 12; sk. near, July 17; Fed. exped. toward, Oct. 14, 15; (1864) sks. near, Feb. 24, 26; sk., Mar. 2
Canton, O.: (1861) suppression of newspapers in, Aug. 22
Canyon City, Ore.: (1864) Fed. exped. from Camp Lincoln to Harney Valley, Mar. 24
Cape Canaveral, Fla.: (1861) Brit. blockade-runner capt. off, Nov. 17
Cape Cod: (1862) Jan. 1; (1863) *Chesapeake* seized, Dec. 8
Cape Fear, N.C.: (1861) blockade-runners capt. off, Dec. 15, 25
Cape Fear and defenses of Wilmington, N.C., Dist. of: (1863) W. H. C. Whiting assigned to command, Sept. 26
Cape Fear R., N.C.: (1863) Fed. recon. on, Nov. 13; (1864) C.S.S. *Raleigh* engages Fed. vessels, is destroyed off mouth of, May 7; 1st Fed. Ft. Fisher exped. fails, Dec. 25 (*See also* Fisher, Ft., N.C.); (1865) 2nd att. on Ft. Fisher, Jan. 13, 14, 15; bomb. of Ft. Anderson on, Feb. 18, 19; drive on Wilmington, Feb. 20, 22
Cape Girardeau, Mo.: (1861) Fed. exped. from to Price's Ldg., Commerce, Benton, Hamburg, Mo., Aug. 7; Grant assumes command at, Sept. 1; Fed. oper. from, Oct. 18; Nov. 2; (1862) Fed. recon. from to Jackson, White-water, Dallas, Mo., Apr. 2; (1863) act., Apr. 26; Fed. sc. from, Aug. 9; Fed. exped. from to Pocahontas, Ark., Aug. 17; Fed. exped. from to Doniphan, Mo., Pocahontas, Ark., Oct. 26; (1864) sk. near, Feb. 5; Fed. exped. from, Nov. 16; sk. in Cypress Swamp near, Dec. 14; Fed. exped. from to Cherokee Bay, Ark., St. Francis R., Dec. 20; (1865) Fed. exped. from to Eleven Points R., Ark., Jan. 24; Fed. sc. from into Bollinger, Wayne, Stoddard cos., Mar. 9
Cape of Good Hope: (1863) *Alabama* captures bark near, Aug. 6
Cape Hatteras (*See also* Outer Banks of N.C.): (1861) Butler command of ment., Aug. 17; Fed. oper. against, Aug. 26; Fed. att. on forts, Aug. 27; fts. fall to Feds., Aug. 28; blockade-runners taken off, Sept. 8; Port Royal exped., Oct. 29; Nov. 1; blockade-runners capt. off, Dec. 15; (1862) *Monitor* sinks off, Dec. 30, 31; (1863) *Tacony* capt. by C.S.S. *Clarence* off, June 12; (1864) Fed. fleet scattered off, Dec. 23
Cape Henry, Va.: (1862) Fed. lightship crew capt., Jan. 24; (1863) *Maple Leaf* taken over by prisoners, June 10
Cape Lookout Lights, N.C.: (1864) Conf. destruction of, Apr. 2
Caperton's Fy., Ala.: (1863) sk., Aug. 29; (1864) Fed. sc. to, Mar. 28; aff., Mar. 29; Fed. sc. to, Mar. 31

Capetown, S. Africa: (1864) *Alabama* at, Mar. 20

Capital, Confederacy: (1861) C.S.A. Cong. votes to move to Richmond, May 20, 21; (1865) fall of Richmond, Apr. 3

Capitol, U.S.: (1861) troops quartered in, Apr. 19, 27; (1862) Lincoln orders bakeries removed from, Oct. 14

Carleton, James Henry (F): (1861) commands Fed. Dist. of South Calif., Oct. 14; (1862) exped., Apr. 13; "Calif. Column," May 4; commands Dept. of N. Mex., Sept. 18

Carlisle, England: (1863) mass meetings support Emancipation Proclamation, Feb. 19

Carlisle, Pa.: (1863) Ewell's troops from, July 1

Carmel Church, Va.: (1862) Fed. cav. raid, July 23

Carnifix Fy., W. Va.: (1861) Rosecrans moves against Confs. near, Sept. 9; eng., Sept. 10; effects of, Sept. 11

Carolina Camp.: *See* Sherman, W. T.

Carondelet, Mo.: (1861) *St. Louis* launched, Oct. 12

Carondelet, U.S.S.: (1862) bomb. at Ft. Donelson, Feb. 13; runs Island No. 10 batteries, Apr. 4; at Island No. 10, Apr. 7; damaged at Bat. of Memphis, June 6

Carr, Eugene Asa (F): (1862) assumes command Army of the Southwest, Oct. 7

Carrick's Fd., W. Va: *See* Corrick's Fd.

Carrion Crow Bayou, La.: (1863) sks., Oct. 14, 18 (Teche oper.), Nov. 3, 11, 18

Carroll Co., Mo.: (1862) Fed. oper. in, July 27; (1863) sk. in, Apr. 1; (1864) oper. in, Aug. 12

Carroll's Mill (or Bayou De Paul), La.: (1864) sk. (Red. R. Camp.), Apr. 8

Carrollsville, Miss.: (1862) Fed. recon. toward, June 3

Carrollton, Ark.: (1863) sk., Jan. 10; Fed. sc. from, Apr. 3; Fed. exped. to, Nov. 10; (1864) sk., Mar. 13

Carrollton, La.: (1862) Fed. exped. from, Sept. 21; (1863) Thirteenth Army Corps sent to, Aug. 10; Fed. expeds. from, Sept. 24

Carrollton, Mo.: (1862) sk., Aug. 1; (1864) surrenders to Price, Oct. 17

Carrsville, Va.: (1862) sk. near, Oct. 15; aff. near, Nov. 17; (1863) sk. near, May 12

Carson, Christopher "Kit" (F): (1863) oper. against Navajos, Aug. 20; (1864) exped. from Ft. Canby to Cañon de Chelly, Jan. 6

Carter, John Carpenter (C): (1864) mortally wounded at Bat. of Franklin, Nov. 30

Carter, Samuel Powhatan (F): (1862) cav. exped. into upper Tenn. Valley, Dec. 26, 29

Carter Co., Ky.: (1863) sk. in, Aug. 27

Carter Cr. Pike, Tenn.: (1863) sk. on, Apr. 2, 27

Carter Cr. Rd., Tenn.: (1863) Fed. recon. on, Feb. 21

Carter House, Franklin, Tenn.: (1864) Bat. of Franklin, Nov. 30

Carter's Cr. Station, Tenn.: (1864) capture of blockhouses by Forrest, Oct. 1

Carter's Depot, Tenn.: (1862) capture of, Dec. 30; (1863) sks., Sept. 20, 22

Carter's Run, Va.: (1863) sk., Sept. 6

Carter's Station, Tenn.: (1864) sks., Sept. 30

Cartersville, Ga.: (1864) Johnston retires through, May 19, 20 (act.), 21 (Sherman near); sk. near, July 24; sk., Sept. 20

Carthage, Mo.: (1861) eng., July 5; (1862) sk., Nov. 27; (1863) sk., Jan. 13; sk. near, May 16; sks., June 27, Sept. 6, Oct. 2, 18 (Shelby's raid); (1864) Fed. sc., May 18; sk., Sept. 22

Carthage, Tenn.: (1862) Morgan's 2nd Ky. raid, Dec. 21; (1863) sk., Jan. 23; Fed. exped. to, Apr. 1, Oct. 10

Carthage Rd., Tenn.: (1862) sk. on near Hartsville and Rome, Nov. 28

Caruthersville, Mo.: (1864) Fed. exped. to, July 5; sk. near, Dec. 30

Caseyville, Ky.: (1861) exped. to by Forrest, Nov. 24

Cashtown, Pa.: (1862) Stuart's Chambersburg raid, Oct. 9; (1863) June 28

Cass, Lewis (F): (1860) favors Union, Nov. 9; resigns from Cabinet as Sec. of State, Dec. 12

Cass Co., Mo.: (1861) Nov. 16; (1862) Fed. exped. through, Sept. 8; (1863) Fed. sc. in, May 3; General Orders No. 11, Aug. 25; Fed. exped. into, Aug. 28; (1864) Fed. sc. in, Aug. 25

Cassville, Ark.: (1863) Fed. sc. from, May 21

Cassville, Ga.: (1864) Atlanta Camp., May 17, 18, 19, 20, 21, 22 (act.), 23, 24 (sk.), 27 (sk.), June 20 (sk.)

Cassville, Mo.: (1862) sks., June 11, Sept. 21; oper. about, Nov. 17; (1863) sk., July 4; Fed. sc. to Huntsville, Ark., July 18; aff. near, July 27; (1864) Fed. sc. from, June 9, 20; Fed. exped. from, Aug. 23

Cassville, W. Va.: (1861) Sept. 23

Castle Pinckney, Charleston Harbor, S.C.: (1860) Anderson favors garrisoning, Nov. 23; S.C. claims, Dec. 22; S.C. seizes, fortifies, Dec. 26, 27

Castor R., Mo.: (1863) sk., Apr. 29; aff. near, Aug 1

Caswell, Ft., N.C.: (1861) occup. of by citizens, Jan. 10; seized by state troops, Apr. 16; (1863) eng., Feb. 23; (1865) destroyed, abandoned, Jan. 16

Catawba Mts., Va.: (1864) sk., June 21

Catawba R., N.C.: (1865) act. near Morgantown, Apr. 17

Catawba R., S.C.: (1865) Twentieth Corps (Fed.) reaches, Feb. 22, 23

Catherine Furnace, Va.: (1863) Bat. of Chancellorsville, May 2

Catlett's Gap, Pigeon Mt., Ga.: (1863) sk., Sept. 15

Catlett's Station, Va.: (1862) Stuart Captures Pope's baggage train, Aug. 22; sk., Sept. 26; sk. near, Oct. 19; Burnside moves hdqrs. to, Nov. 16; Fed. sc. to, Dec. 21; (1863) Fed. recon. to, Jan. 8; aff. near, Oct. 6; sks., Oct. 6, 14, 19, 30, Nov. 1; Conf. sc. around, Nov. 3; sk., Nov. 27; aff. near, Dec. 14; (1864) aff. near, Apr. 16;

Cato, Kas.: (1862) sk. near, Nov. 8

Catoctin Cr., Md.: (1863) sk., June 17

Catoctin Mt., Md.: (1862) sk., Sept. 13; (1864) aff., July 7

Caton, Ga.: (1864) sk., Aug. 22

Catoosa Springs, Ga.: (1864) sk., May 3

Catoosa Station (or Platform), Ga.: (1864) sk., Feb. 23, 27 (near)

Catskill, U.S.S.: (1863) siege of Ft. Wagner, July 10

Cattle raid: (1864) by Wade Hampton, Sept. 15, 16

"Cavalier of Dixie": *See* Stuart, Jeb

Cave City, Ky.: (1862) aff., May 11; sk. near, Sept. 18

Cave Spring, Md.: (1864) Conf. cav. crosses Potomac near, July 29
Cedar Bayou, Tex.: (1863) sk., Nov. 23
Cedar Bluff, Ala.: (1863) Streight's raiders surrender to Forrest, May 3; (1864) Fed. sc. around, July 28
Cedar Bluffs, Colo. Terr.: (1864) sk., May 3
Cedar Church, near Shepherdsville, Ky.: (1862) sk., Oct. 3
Cedar Co., Mo.: (1862) sk., Aug. 12; (1863) sk. (Shelby's raid), Oct. 17
Cedar Cr., Fla.: (1864) sks., Mar. 1, Apr. 2
Cedar Cr., Mo.: (1862) sk. on, Oct. 5
Cedar Cr., Va.: (1864) Early moves toward, Aug. 11; Early entrenches on, Aug. 12; sk. along, Aug. 12; Early stiffens resistance at, Aug. 13; sk., Aug. 15; Sheridan withdraws from, Aug. 15, 16; Early moves north from, Aug. 17; ment., Oct. 1; Sheridan at, Oct. 13; sk., Oct. 13; Conf. recon., Oct. 18; Bat. of, Oct. 19, 20; act., Nov. 12
Cedar Cr., Va., Bat. of: (1864) Oct. 19; aftermath, Oct. 20
Cedar Cr. Valley, Va.: (1863) recon. from, Apr. 12
Cedar I., N.C.: (1863) schooners capt. near, July 20
Cedar Keys, Fla.: (1862) Fed. naval att. on, Jan. 16; (1865) sk., Feb. 16
Cedar Mt., Va., Bat. of (or Slaughter Mt., Cedar Run, Cedar Run Mt., Southwest Mt.): (1862) Aug. 9
Cedar Point, N.C.: (1863) Fed. exped. to, Mar. 7; Fed. exped. to, July 13; sk., Dec. 1
Cedar Run, Va.: (1862) sk., Aug. 10
Cedar Run (or Cedar Run Mt.), Va.: (1862) bat., Aug. 9
Cedar Run Church, Va.: (1864) aff., Oct. 17
Cedarville, Va.: (1863) sks., June 12; (1864) Sept. 20
Celeste (Fed. transport steamer): (1864) att. on, Sept. 4
Celina, Ky.: (1863) sk., Apr. 19; Fed. exped. to, Apr. 26
Celina, Tenn.: (1865) sks., Mar. 19, 22
Cemetery Hill at Gettysburg: (1863) Bat. of Gettysburg, July 1, 2
Cemetery Ridge at Gettysburg: (1863) Bat. of Gettysburg, July 1, 2, 3
Centerville, Ala.: (1865) sk., Apr. 1
Centerville, W. Va.: (1864) sk. near, Sept. 14
Central America: (1862) colonization of Negroes in, Mar. 6, Aug. 14
Central Division of Ky., Conf.: (1861) Buckner commands, Sept. 18
Centralia, Mo.: (1864) aff., Sept. 7; aff. (massacre), Sept. 27
Central Ky., Army of: (1861) A. S. Johnston commands, Oct. 28
Central Pacific R.R. (*See also* Union Pacific R.R.): (1862) Lincoln signs bill for Pacific route, July 1; (1863) ground broken for, Feb. 22
Centre, Ala.: (1863) sk., near, May 2
Centre Cr., Mo.: (1863) sk. at ment., May 6; Fed. sc. to, May 13; (1865) sk., Feb. 20
Centre Star, Ala.: (1864) sk., May 15
Centreville, La.: (1863) sk., May 25
Centreville, Mo.: (1861) recon. to, Aug. 2; (1863) act. around, Dec. 23; (1864) sk. near, Nov. 12
Centreville, Tenn.: (1863) sk., Nov. 2; (1864) sk., Sept. 29
Centreville, Va.: (1961) Bull Run Camp., July 16, 18, 20, 21 (bat.); Conf.

strategy conference at, Oct. 1; (1862) J. E. Johnston pulls out of, Mar. 9; Bat. of Groveton or Brawner's Farm, Aug. 28; 2nd Bull Run bat., Aug. 30; Pope gathers army at, Aug. 31; Sept. 1; Fed. expeds. from, Sept. 25, 29; (1863) Fed. sc. from, Feb. 27; Aug. 15; sk. near, Sept. 22; ment., Oct. 13; Meade prepares lines around, Oct. 14; sk. near, Oct. 14; (1865) Fed. oper. about, Mar. 3

Chacahoula Station, La.: (1863) sk., June 24

Chadbourne, Ft., Tex.: (1861) abandoned by Feds., Mar. 23

Chaffin's Bluff, Va.: (1863) Union control of James R. to, July 14; (1864) Fed. exped. aims for, Aug. 15

Chaffin's Farm, Va.: (1864) Bat. of, Sept. 29, 30

Chain Bridge, Washington, D.C.: (1861) Fed. recon. from, Sept. 11

Chalk Bluff, Ark.: (1863) Fed. exped. to, Mar. 9; sk., Apr. 1; Fed. exped. to, Apr. 21; Marmaduke's raid, sk., May 1; (1865) surrender negotiations with M. Jeff Thompson at, May 9; surrender of Thompson, May 11

Chalmers, James Ronald (C): (1863) raid, Oct. 4, 5, 6, 11, 12, 13

Chamber of Commerce: (1862) St. Louis pro-Union members leave, Jan. 9; (1863) Cincinnati members expelled, July 20; N. Y. Chamber estimates loss to Conf. raiders, July 22

Chamberlain, Joshua (F): (1865) description of Appomattox Camp., Apr. 12

Chambersburg, Pa.: (1862) Stuart's raid to, Oct. 9, 10; Stuart destroys equipment at, Oct. 11; (1863) in Gettysburg Camp., June 15, 27, 30; Lee's trains retreat through, July 5; (1864) Conf. capture, burning of, July 30, 31

Chambersburg Pike, Pa. (1863) Bat. of Gettysburg, July 1

Chambersburg raid: (1864) *See* Early, Jubal, and McCausland, John

Champion's Hill, Miss. (or Baker's Cr.): (1863) Bat. of, May 16; (1864) sk., Feb. 4

Chancellorsville, Va.: (1863) camp., Apr. 27, 28, 29, 30; Bat. of, May 1, 2, 3, 4; repercussions of, May 5, 6; death of Jackson, May 10; follow-up, May 7, 13, 14; bat. ment., May 31; (1864) sk. near, May 4, ment., May 7

Chandler, Zachariah (F): (1862) presents Mich. resolution on war, Feb. 3; (1864) advice to Lincoln on dropping Blair from Cabinet, Sept. 3; pressure on Frémont to resign, Sept. 17

Chantilly, Va.: (1862) Jackson, Longstreet move near, Aug. 31; Bat. of Chantilly (or Ox Hill), Sept. 1; Conf. forces gather near, Sept. 2; Fed. recon. from, Nov. 28; (1863) sk., Feb. 10; sk. near, Feb. 25; sk. near, Mar. 23; sk. near (Bristoe Camp.), Oct. 17

Chapel Hill, Mo.: (1862) Fed. exped. toward, July 6; Fed. exped. against guerrillas, Oct. 24; (1864) Fed. exped. to, July 29

Chapel Hill, N.C. (1865) sk., Apr. 15

Chapel Hill, Tenn.: (1863) exped. from, Mar. 3; sk. near, Apr. 13

Chapel Hill Pike, Tenn.: (1863) recon. on, Apr. 29

Chaplains, Conf.: (1863) ment., Dec. 18; (1864) exchange of, Sept. 3

Chaplains, Fed.: (1861) Lincoln re, Oct. 21; (1864) exchange of, Sept. 3

Chaplin Hills, Ky., Bat. of (or Perryville): (1862) Oct. 8

Chaplintown, Ky.: (1865) sk. near, Jan. 30

Chapman, J. M.: See J. M. Chapman

19; treaty with C.S.A., Oct. 4; eng. with Creeks, Nov. 19; oppose Creeks, Dec. 29; (1863) for Union, Feb. 26; (1865) loyalty treaty, Sept. 14

Cherokee Station, Ala.: (1863) sk., Apr. 17; act., Oct. 21; sk., Oct. 29

Cherry, W. Va.: (1861) sk., Dec. 25

Cherry Cr., Miss.: (1864) sk., July 10

Cherry Grove, Schuyler Co., Mo.: (1862) sks., June 26, July 1

Cherry Grove, Va.: (1864) Conf. outpost capt., Mar. 30

Cherrystone Point, Va.: (1864) Conf. raid, Mar. 5

Chesapeake (Fed. steamer): (1863) seized, Dec. 8

Chesapeake and Albemarle Canal: *See* Albemarle Canal

Chesapeake Bay: (1861) Fed. troops embarked at, Apr. 19; May 31; (1862) Apr. 1, 14; salt works on destroyed, Nov. 22; (1863) schooner capt. in, Sept. 19

Chesapeake and Ohio Canal: (1861) sks. on, Nov. 8, Dec. 8, 11; Jackson's oper. on, Dec. 17; (1862) Jackson's plans against, Jan. 3; (1864) Early's threat to, Sept. 14

Cheshire, O.: (1863) sk. near (Morgan's raid), July 20

Chesnessex Cr., Va.: (1863) Oct. 9

Chesnut, James, Jr. (C): (1860) resigns from Sen., Nov. 10; (1861) emissary to Sumter, Apr. 11, 12

Chesser's Store (or Dry Ridge or Dog Walk), Ky.: (1862) Oct. 9

Chester, O.: (1863) Morgan's raid, July 18

Chesterfield, C.S.S.: (1863) att. on, Aug. 2

Chesterfield, S.C.: (1865) sk., occup. of, Mar. 2

Chesterfield Br., Va.: (1964) Bat. of North Anna R., May 24

Chester Gap, Va.: (1863) cav. fight in, July 21; act. in, July 22; sk., July 23

Chester Station, Va.: (1864) act., May 10

Chew, Robert S. (F): (1861) emissary to Sumter, Apr. 6, 8

Chewalla, Tenn.: (1862) Oct. 4; sk. near, Oct. 5

Cheyennes: (1864) Sand Cr. massacre, Nov. 29

Chicago, Ill.: (1860) Lincoln meets Hamlin in, Nov. 21; (1861) Union mass meeting, Jan. 6; (1864) Democratic National Convention meets in, Aug. 29, 30; Chicago conspiracy, Nov. 6; (1865) celebrates Lee's surrender, Apr. 9; Lincoln lies in state in, May 1

Chicago conspiracy: (1864) Nov. 6

Chicago *Times:* (1863) circulation halted, Feb. 8, 17; suppression of, June 1, 4

Chickahominy R., Va.: (1862) Johnston retreats across, May 15; oper. along, May 20; Fed. advance on, May 21; McClellan on, May 22; Fed. exped. from, May 25; McClellan inactive on, May 26; sk. near Seven Pines, May 29; Bat. of Seven Pines or Fair Oaks, May 31, June 1; Fed. recon. from, June 3; McClellan on, June 4; heavy rains on, June 5; Fed. recon. on, June 7; June 8; act. quiet on, June 10; Stuart crossing, June 13, 14; sk. light on, June 21, 23; Bat. of Mechanicsville, June 26; Bat. of Gaines' Mill, 1st Cold Harbor, or the Chickahominy, June 27; Bat. of Savage's Station, June 29; (1863) sk. on, Aug. 25; (1864) ment., Feb. 7; Kilpatrick's Richmond raid, Mar. 1; Sheridan along, May 12; Lee north of, May 28, 30; Lee orders troops to, June 1; Bat. of Cold Harbor, June 1, 2, 3; ment., June 13; sk. at Jones Br., June 23

Chicamacomico, N.C.: (1861) aff., Oct. 4

Chickamauga Camp. (*See also* Bragg, Braxton; Rosecrans, William S.): (1863) Aug. 16, 20, 21, 22, 29, 30, 31, Sept. 1, 2, 3, 5, 6, 8, 9, 10, 11, 12, 13, 14, 15, 17, 18, 19; Bat. of Chickamauga, Sept. 19, 20, 21 (summary of), 22 (windup); Lincoln on, Sept. 24; court of inquiry on, Sept. 28; Polk's role argued, Oct. 3; Davis tours area, Oct. 13; ment., Oct. 17, Dec. 9; (1864) ment., May 7

Chickamauga Cr., Ga. (*See also* West Chickamauga Cr.): (1863) Army of the Cumberland on, Sept. 16; Bat. of Chattanooga, Nov. 23; Bat. of Missionary Ridge, Nov. 25; (1864) sks., Jan. 30, May 3

Chickamauga Station, Tenn.: (1863) sk., Nov. 26

Chickasaw, Ala.: (1862) Fed. exped. to, Apr. 1; Fed. gunboat recon. to, Apr. 3

Chickasaw, U.S.S.: (1864) bomb. of Fts. Powell, Gaines, Aug. 6

Chickasaw Bayou, Miss.: (1862) assault by Sherman on, Dec. 29; aftermath, Dec. 30, 31; (1863) Jan. 1

Chickasaws: (1861) Apr. 30; treaty with C.S.A., July 12; oppose Creeks, Dec. 29; (1865) treaty with U.S., Sept. 14

Chicora, C.S.S. (gunboat): (1863): att. on blockade, Jan. 31

Chicotville, La.: (1863) Fed. exped. to, Apr. 29

Chimneys, the, Va.: (1864) ass. on, Sept. 10

Chincoteague Inlet, Va.: (1861) Oct. 5; Conf. ships burned, Oct. 27

Chincoteague I., Va.: (1861) citizens take oath, Oct. 14

Chiricahua Mts., Ariz. Terr.: (1863) sks. in, Sept. 8

Chiriqui Improvement Co.: (1861) confers with Lincoln on colonization, Apr. 10

Chisholm, Jesse (F): (1861) Union troop guide, Chisholm Trail, May 31

Chisholm Trail: (1861) May 31

Chisolm's I., S.C.: (1861) sk., Dec. 17

Chisolm, Alexander Robert (C): (1861) emissary to Sumter, Apr. 11, 12

Chivington, John Milton (F): (1862) eng. at Apache Canyon, Mar. 26; eng. of Glorieta or Pigeon's Ranch, Mar. 28; (1864) Sand Cr. massacre, Nov. 29

Choctaw, U.S.S.: (1863) in Milliken's Bend att., June 7

Choctawatchie Bay, Fla.: (1863) Conf. salt works destroyed, Dec. 10

Choctaw Indian Nation: (1861) adheres to Southern states, Feb. 7; treaty with C.S.A., July 12; oppose Creeks, Dec. 29; (1863) sks. in, Oct. 7, Nov. 9; (1865) treaty with U.S., Sept. 14

Chowan R., N.C.: (1863) Fed. recon. down, June 5; Fed. exped. up, Nov. 4; (1864) oper. about, Dec. 11

Christiana, Tenn.: (1863) sk., Tullahoma Camp., June 24; aff., Oct. 6

Christianburg, Ky.: (1863) aff., July 1

Christmas: (1860) Eve, Dec. 24; Dec. 25; (1861) Dec. 24; Lincolns entertain, Dec. 25; (1862) Lincoln visits wounded, Dec. 25; (1863) Dec. 25; (1864) Dec. 25

Christmas gift: (1864) Sherman presents Savannah to Lincoln, Dec. 22

Chuckatuck, near Suffolk, Va.: (1863) aff., Apr. 23; sk., May 2

Chulahoma, Miss.: (1862) sk., Nov. 30

Chunky Cr., Miss.: (1864) sk. near, Feb. 13

toward, Nov. 15; Fed. exped. to, Nov. 26; (1863) Fed sc. from, May 20; sk., Oct. 28

Clarkton, Mo.: (1862) sk., Oct. 23; Fed. exped. to, Dec. 17

Clay, Cassius Marcellus (F): (1862) replaced as minister to Russia, Jan. 13

Clay, Clement Claiborne, Jr. (C): (1861) resigns from U. S. Sen., Jan. 21; (1864) commissioner to Canada, Apr. 27

Clay Co., Mo.: (1863) sk. in, May 19; (1864) sk. in, July 4

Clay Co., W. Va.: (1861) sk. in, Dec. 29

Clay Village, Ky.: (1862) sk. near, Oct. 4

Claysville, Ala.: (1864) sk., Mar. 14

Clear Cr., Ark.: (1862) sk. on, Aug. 19; (1864) sk., Jan. 22; (1865) sk., Feb. 11

Clear Cr., Ga.: (1864) act., July 30

Clear Cr., Miss.: (1862) sk., June 14

Clear Cr., Mo.: (1862) sk. near Taberville, Aug. 2; (1863) aff. near Ball Town, Aug. 8

Clear Fork, Mo: (1864) sk. on, July 16

Clear Lake, Ark.: (1865) Fed. sc. to, Mar. 10

Clear Spring, Md.: (1863) sks., July 10; (1864) July 29

Cleburne, Patrick Ronayne (C): (1863) Bat. of Missionary Ridge, Nov. 25; pursuit of Bragg, Nov. 26; (1864) eng. at Leggett's or Bald Hill, Ga., July 21; at Spring Hill, Tenn., Nov. 29; killed Bat. of Franklin, Nov. 30

Clergy, Conf.: (1861) plead Conf. cause, Apr. 21; (1862) ordered to ride guerrilla-attacked trains, Aug. 8

Clergy, U.S.: (1861) plead Union cause, Apr. 21

Cleveland, O.: (1861) Lincoln at, Feb. 15; (1864) Radical Republican Convention, May 31; (1865) Lincoln's funeral train stops at, Apr. 28

Cleveland, Tenn.: (1863) sks., Sept. 18, Oct. 9, Nov. 24, Dec. 22, 29; (1864) sk., Apr. 2; sk. near, Apr. 13

Cleveland Radical Republican Convention: (1864) nominates Frémont, May 31; favors confiscation, June 8

Clifton, Tenn.: (1862) Forrest crosses Tenn. R. at, Dec. 15; (1863) sk., Jan. 1; Jan. 2; sk., Jan. 10; Fed. exped. to, Feb. 17; (1864) sks., July 22, 30, Aug. 30; (1865) Schofield leaves for N.C., Jan. 15

Clifton, Ft., Va.: (1864) eng. (south side James oper.), May 9

Clinch Mt., Tenn.: (1863) sks., Oct. 27, Dec. 6; capture of Fed. wagon train near, Dec. 14; (1864) sks., Oct. 1, 18; (1865) Fed. exped. to, Jan. 28

Clinch Mt. Gap. Tenn.: (1863) sk. (Knoxville Camp.), Dec. 14

Clinch R., Tenn.: (1863) sk. at Walker's Fd., Dec. 5; sk., Dec. 21

Clinton, Ark.: (1864) Fed. sc. from, June 4

Clinton, Ga.: (1864) comb., July 30; sks., Nov. 20, 21

Clinton, Ky.: (1863) Fed. exped. from, July 22; (1864) Conf. raid on, Mar. 10; Fed. sc. to, Mar. 30

Clinton, La.: (1863) Fed. exped. to, June 3; (1864) aff., May 1; Fed. exped. near, July 17; Fed. exped. from, Aug. 23; Fed. exped. to, Oct. 5; sk., Nov. 15; Fed. exped. to, Dec. 23; (1865) Fed. expeds. to, Mar. 1, 30

Clinton, Miss.: (1863) McClernand's forces move toward, May 13; sks. near, July 8, 9; sk. (Jackson Camp.), July 16; Oct. 18; (1864) sks., Feb. 5, Apr. 3

Clinton, Mo.: (1862) sk., Mar. 30

Cole Camp, Mo.: (1861) sk., June 19; (1862) sk., Oct. 5; (1863) sk. near, Oct. 9

Cole Co., Mo.: (1864) sk., Oct. 6

Colesburg, Ky.: (1865) att. on Ft. Jones near, Feb. 18

Cole's I., S.C.: (1862) bomb. of, May 20

College Grove, Tenn.: (1863) sk. near, Mar. 19; aff. near, Apr. 26

Collierville, Tenn.: (1863) sk. near, Jan. 28; Fed. exped. from, Mar. 8; sk., May 20; act., Oct. 11; act., Nov. 3; sk., Dec. 27; (1864) sk. near, Jan. 13; Fed. sc. from, Jan. 14; Smith moves beyond, Feb. 11; sk. near, June 13; sk., June 23; sk. on Byhalia Rd., July 2; sks. near, July 24, Nov. 15

Collins, Napoleon (F): (1864) captures C.S.S. *Florida,* Oct. 7

Colonization of Negroes: (1861) Chiriqui Improvement Co., Apr. 10; (1862) ment. in Cong., Jan. 9; Lincoln favors, Mar. 6, July 17, Aug. 14; Lincoln, Cabinet discuss, Sept. 26; in Lincoln's message to Cong., Dec. 1; on Haiti, Dec. 31; (1864) Lincoln returns Haiti colonists, Feb. 1

Colorado, Camp, Tex.: (1861) abandoned by Feds., Feb. 26

Colorado, U.S.S.: (1861) destroys *Judah,* Sept. 14

Colorado Territory: (1861) formed, Feb. 28; (1864) enabling act for, Mar. 21; Fed. oper. against Inds. in, Nov. 5; Sand Cr. massacre, eng., Nov. 29

Colorado Territory troops: (1862) at Apache Canyon, Mar. 26; at Glorieta or Pigeon's Ranch, Mar. 28

Colored troops: *See* Negro soldiers

Colt, Samuel: (1861) revolving rifles, May 1

Columbia (Brit. blockade-runner): (1862) capture of, Aug. 3

Columbia, Ark.: (1864) Conf. raiders near, June 1

Columbia, Ky.: (1863) sk., June 29; sk. (Morgan's raid), July 3; Fed. scs. from, Dec. 5

Columbia, La.: (1864) sk., Feb. 4

Columbia, Mo.: (1861) exped., Sept. 2; (1862) sk. near, Oct. 2; (1863) sk. near, Jan. 21; (1864) sks., June 17, Aug. 16; (1865) sk., Feb. 12

Columbia, Pa.: (1863) sk. near (Early's ride), June 28

Columbia, S.C.: (1864) Davis at, Oct. 3; (1865) Sherman heads for, Jan. 19, 21, Feb. 1, 3, 14, 15, 16; Fed. troops arrive at, Feb. 16; Fed. capture of, burning of, Feb. 17, 18, 19

Columbia, Tenn.: (1862) sk. near, July 17; sks., Sept 9, 10; Forrest leaves from, Dec. 11, 15; (1864) sk. near, Oct. 2; Schofield moves to, Nov. 22, 23, 24; sks. in front of, Nov. 24; Schofield entrenching, Nov. 25; Hood delayed, Nov. 25; Hood arrives, Nov. 26; Schofield moves north of, Nov. 27; Army of Tenn. occupies, Nov. 28; "Spring Hill aff.," Nov. 29; Hood withdraws toward, Dec. 17, 18, 19, 20; sk. near, Dec. 20; Hood marching south from, Dec. 21; sks. near, Dec. 22, 23

Columbia, U.S.S.: (1863) runs aground, capt., burned, Jan. 13

Columbia, Va.: (1865) Sheridan occupies, Mar. 9

Columbia Br., Va.: (1862) sk., May 5; Fed. recon. from, July 22

Columbia Furnace, Va.: (1864) sk. near, Oct. 7

Columbia Pike, Tenn.: (1863) sk. on, Apr. 1

Columbia Rd., Tenn.: (1863) Fed. recon. on, Feb. 21

Columbus, Ga.: (1864) Fed. raid on r.r., July 10; (1865) Fed. capture of, Apr. 16

Columbus, Ky.: (1861) Ky. neutrality, June 12; Conf. troops en route to, Sept. 3; gunboat, battery duel, Sept. 4; Conf. western defense line, Sept. 19; Fed. recon. toward, Sept. 22; eng. at Belmont, Mo., Nov. 7; Conf. gun explodes, Nov. 11; Conf. fears for safety of, Nov. 21; (1862) Lincoln urges drive on, Jan. 1; Grant prepares move toward, Jan. 9; sk. near, Jan. 9; recon. by Grant toward, Jan. 10; gunboat eng. near, Jan. 11; Conf. encampments shelled, Jan. 14; Conf. defense line, Jan. 19; Fed. recon. threat, to, Jan. 21; last Conf. bastion on Miss. R., Feb. 11; Conf. evac. of, Feb. 20, Mar. 2; troops from concentrated, Mar. 1; Feds. occupy, Mar. 3; Fed. exped. from, Sept. 28; (1863) Fed. expeds. from, Mar. 12, Aug. 1; (1864) att. on Union pickets, Mar. 6; sk., Mar. 27; Fed. sc. from, Mar. 30; Porter's gunboats at, Apr. 11; sk., Apr. 13; Fed. sc. from, July 17

Columbus, Miss.: (1863) Davis to citizens of, May 8

Columbus, Mo.: (1862) sks., Jan. 5, July 23

Columbus, O.: (1861) Lincoln alleges "nothing going wrong," Feb. 13; (1863) Vallandigham's speech in, May 5; protests over Vallandigham's arrest, May 23; Morgan imprisoned in, July 26; Morgan's escape, Nov. 27; (1865) Lincoln lies in state in, Apr. 29

Columbus, O., *Crisis:* (1863) office of damaged, Mar. 5

Columbus Rd., Ala.: (1865) sks. on, Apr. 12, 14

Colwell's Fd., Tenn.: (1863) sk., Nov. 19

Comanche Pass, N. Mex. Terr.: (1862) act., Mar. 3

Combahee Fy., S.C.: (1865) sk., Feb. 5

Combahee R., S.C.: (1863) Fed. raid on, June 2; Fed. telegraph party capt. on, Sept. 13; (1865) sk. on, Jan. 28

Comet: (1861) appears, June 30

Comite R., La.: (1863) sks. on, Mar. 9, May 2; (1864) Fed. exped. to, Aug. 23; (1865) Fed. exped. to, Mar. 30

Commerce, Miss.: (1863) att. on Fed. transports, June 17

Commerce, Mo.: (1861) Fed. exped. to, Aug. 7; descended on by M. Jeff Thompson, Dec. 29; (1862) Feb. 23; Fed. forces move from, Feb. 28

Commercial (U.S. transport): (1864) att. on, Sept. 4

Commercial restrictions: (1865) removed west of Miss. R., June 24

Commissary Dept., C.S.A.: (1865) Lee complains of, Jan. 27

Commissioner of Immigration: *See* Immigration, Commissioner of

Commissioners to Britain, Conf.: (1861) named, Mar. 16; received, May 3; *Trent* Aff., Nov. 8

Committee on the Conduct of the War: *See* Joint Committee on the Conduct of the War

Committee on Federal Relations, Mo. State Convention: (1861) Mar. 9

Committee of Thirteen, U. S. Sen.: (1860) Crittenden Compromise referred to, Dec. 18; to look into country's condition, Dec. 20, 31; (1861) unable to approve compromise, Jan. 14

Committee of Thirty-three, U. S. House of Representatives: (1860) named, Dec. 4; submits plans of compromise, Dec. 12; (1861) proposals submitted, Jan. 14; chairman, Jan. 14; Corwin amendment on slavery passes House, Feb. 28

Commodity prices: (1863) in C.S.A., Feb. 25

Commodore Barney, U.S.S.: (1863) damaged, Aug. 5
Commodore Jones, U.S.S.: (1864) sunk, May 6
Como, Tenn.: (1863) sk., Sept. 19
Como Ldg., La.: (1864) att. on Fed. gunboats, June 15
Compensated emancipation: *See* Emancipation
Compton's Fy., or Little Compton, Grand R., Mo.: (1862) sk., Aug. 11
Conchas Springs, N. Mex. Terr.: (1863) sk. with Inds., July 29
Concho R., Tex.: (1865) act. at Dove Cr., Jan. 8
Concord, N.H.: (1861) *Democratic Standard* office mobbed, Aug. 8
Concordia, La.: (1864) sk., July 22
Concordia Bayou, La.: (1864) sk. Aug. 5
Condor (British blockade-runner): (1864) aground, Mrs. Greenhow perishes, Oct. 1
Conestoga, U.S.S. (gunboat): (1861) Aug. 12; eng. at Lucas Bend, Mo., Sept. 10; takes prizes, Sept. 16; attacks Saratoga, Ky., Oct. 26; (1863) captures steamers, Feb. 12
Confederacy, recognition of: *See* Recognition of Confederacy
Confederacy, Southern: *See* Confederate States of America
Confederate commissioners: *See Trent* Affair; Mason, James M.; Slidell, John
Confederate commissioners to Wash.: (1861) Feb. 27; attempt to open relations, Mar. 6; try to reach Seward, Mar. 8; correspondence with Seward released, Mar. 20; rumor Sumter to be evacuated, Apr. 8; leave Wash., Apr. 11
Confederate gens.: (1863) sale of pictures banned, Mar. 11
Confederate States of America (*See also* Congress, C.S.A.; Davis, Jefferson): (1860) Southern Confederacy proposed, Nov. 7; S.C. secession convention calls for, Dec. 24; (1861) sentiment for, Jan. 15; convention of seceded states, Feb. 4, 5, 7; Provisional Constitution adopted, Feb. 8; Pres., Vice-Pres. chosen, Feb. 9; Provisional Cong. declares all U.S. laws in force, Feb. 9; Davis accepts provisional presidency, Feb. 10; Stephens inaugurated, Feb. 11; Davis inaugurated Provisional Pres., Feb. 18; assumes control at Charleston, Mar. 1; Great Britain recognizes as belligerent, May 6, 13; vote to move capital, May 20; Spain recognizes as belligerent, June 17; concludes treaty with Creeks, July 10; Brazil recognizes as belligerent, Aug. 1; admits Mo. to Confederacy, Aug. 19; treaty with Great Osage Ind. tribe, Oct. 2; Davis elected Pres., regular Cong. elected, Nov. 6; year's end, Dec. 31; (1862) inauguration of Davis, Feb. 22; Davis' message to Cong., Aug. 18; Davis on fight for independence, Sept. 7; (1863) Erlanger loan, Jan. 29; announces blockade "lifted," Jan. 31; Erlanger opens loan to, Mar. 18; (1864) vessel capacity for govt. shipments, Mar. 5; plans to thwart Sherman, Dec. 10; (1865) ceases to exist, May 10
Confederate States of America, recognition of: *See* Recognition of Confederacy
Confederate treasure: (1865) rumors of loss of, May 10
Confiscation (*See also* Confiscation Acts): (1861) Frémont's order, Aug. 30; (1862) property seizures in St. Louis, Jan. 23; seizure for military use, July 22; (1864) Radical Republicans favor, June 8; Lincoln discusses with Geo. W. Julian, July 2; (1865) Lincoln disturbed over, Feb. 12
Confiscation acts: 1st, (1861) Aug. 6; (1862) 2nd approved by Lincoln, July 17;

ment. in Emancipation Proclamation, July 22; promulgated by Lincoln, July 25; Lincoln charges Bates with enforcement of, Nov. 13

Congaree Cr., S.C.: (1865) sk., Feb. 15

Congaree R., S.C.: (1865) Sherman crosses, Feb. 14, 16

Conger, Everton (F): (1865) Booth's capture, Apr. 26

Congress, U. S. (36th) (*See also* House of Representatives, U. S.; Senate, U. S.; Committee of Thirteen; Committee of Thirty-three; Joint Committee on the conduct of the War): (1860) election returns, Nov. 6; Southern sens. resign, Nov. 10; lame-duck session convenes, Dec. 3; Committee of Thirty-three, Dec. 4; State of the Union message, Dec. 4; (1861) committee to consider compromise plans, Crittenden suggests referendum, Jan. 3; Buchanan sends special message to, Jan. 8; authorizes $25 million loan, Feb. 8; $10 million loan authorized, Morrill Tariff Act approved, Nev., Dak. Terrs. set up, Mar. 2; amendment to bar interference with slavery introduced, Mar. 2; Buchanan message to, troops ordered to defend Wash., Mar. 2

(37th) (1861) special 1st session convenes, July 4; Lincoln's message to, July 4, 5; elects speaker, July 4; Sen. expels sens., July 11; $250 million loan, July 17; Crittenden Resolution, July 22, 25; state indemnification act approved, July 27; July 29; acts on attempted overthrow of govt. approved, July 31; first income tax measure passes, Aug. 2; higher tariffs, Aug. 2; acts for ship construction, army organization, Aug. 3; $20 million tax measure passed, Aug. 5; enlistment of seamen authorized, Aug. 5; bonds issued, tariff increase, Aug. 5; adjourns, approves pres. acts, orders, and proclamations, Aug. 6; bills on freeing slaves, pay increase for privates, confiscation of Rebel property, Aug. 6

2nd session convenes, Dec. 2; Lincoln's message to, Dec. 3; slavery abolition bills, Dec. 5; approves Joint Committee on the Conduct of the War, Dec. 9, 10; increases duties, Dec. 24; (1862) petitions for abolition, Jan. 9; gives Lincoln authority to seize telegraph, railroads, Jan. 31; petitions on prosecution of war, Feb. 3; discusses slavery, Mar. 10; Atlantic fisheries act, Mar. 15; compensated emancipation, Mar. 24; House committee on emancipation, colonization of Negroes, Apr. 7; emancipation in Wash. D.C., Apr. 11, 16; Lincoln to on compensated emancipation, July 14; Sen. passes bill creating W. Va., July 14; Lincoln signs bills creating grade of rear adm., increasing tariffs, forbidding conflict of interests, July 16; Confiscation Act signed, July 17; legislative-executive power struggle appears, July 17; adjourns, July 17; 3rd session convenes, Dec. 1; Lincoln's message to, Dec. 1; (1863) payment of armed forces, Jan. 17; Conscription Act passed, Feb. 25; special session of Sen. called for March, Feb. 28; Mar. 1; confirms military appointments, Mar. 2; first Fed. draft act, Mar. 3; adjourns, Mar. 4

(38th) (1863) 1st session convenes, Dec. 7; Lincoln's message to, Dec. 8; Lincoln's plan for Bureau of Emancipation, Dec. 17; (1864) Lincoln to, Jan. 5; House bill to revive rank of lieut. gen., Feb. 1, 24, 29; compensation to masters of slave volunteers, Feb. 24; enabling act for Nev., Colo., Mar. 21; "radical" members urge Meade's removal, Mar. 23; resolution barring Mexican monarchy, Apr. 4; Sen. passes joint resolution abolishing slavery, approves Thirteenth Amendment, Apr. 8; Neb. Terr. enabling act, Apr. 19; "In God We Trust" coin motto approved, Apr. 22; duties raised, Apr. 29; Wade-Davis reconstruction bill, May 4, July 4, 8; Postal Money Order System Act, May 17; Bureau of Currency approved by Lincoln, June 3; House defeats abolition resolution, June 15; public land grants for r.r.'s, telegraph, July 2; Northern Pacific R.R. chartered, July 2; adjourns, July 4; Wade-Davis Manifesto, Aug. 5; Lincoln challenges powers of, Aug. 5; Republican gains in, Oct. 11; convenes 2nd session, Dec. 5; Lincoln on readmission of members of, Dec. 6; Lincoln's message to, Dec. 6; Lincoln-Radical schism on reconstruction, Dec. 18; establishes rank of vice-adm., Dec. 21; (1865) Thirteenth Amendment, Jan. 6, 10, 31 (passes); reconstruction policy of, Feb. 3; resolution bars Southern states from electoral college, Feb. 8; establishes Freedmen's Bureau, adjourns, Mar. 3; Sen. meets in special session, Mar. 4; Sen. adjourns, Mar. 11

Congress, U.S.S. (wooden frigate): (1862) opposes *Merrimack,* Mar. 8

Congress of the Confederate States of America: (1861) forerunner of, Feb. 4; Provisional Constitution adopted by convention of seceded states, Feb. 8; Provisional Pres. chosen, Feb. 9; declares all U.S. laws in force, with exceptions, Feb. 9; Davis accepts presidency, Feb. 10; names Peace Commission, Feb. 12; authority over forts, Feb. 12; authorizes contracts, Feb. 20; declares Miss. R. navigation open, Feb. 21; authorizes loan, Feb. 28; admits Tex. to Confederacy, Mar. 2; "Stars and Bars," Mar. 4; Mallory confirmed as Sec. of Navy, Mar. 4; internal issues considered, sessions secret, Mar. 6; Reagan confirmed as Postmaster General, Mar. 6; authorizes treasury notes, Army, Mar. 9; Constitution adopted, Mar. 11; govt. organized, prepares for war, Mar. 15; Provisional Cong. adjourns, Mar. 16; 2nd session Provisional Cong. meets, Apr. 29; bill to accept volunteers, May 9; purchasing abroad, May 10; day of fasting and prayer, May 14; admits Tenn. to Confederacy, May 16; Arkansas admitted to Confederacy, May 18; votes to move capital to Richmond, May 30; capital move discussed, May 21; convenes in Richmond, July 20; day of thanksgiving, July 22; acts re volunteers, enemy aliens, public defense, Aug. 8; admits Mo. to Confederacy, authorizes loan, Aug. 19; increases artillery, Aug. 20; commissioners to Europe authorized, Aug. 21; aid to Mo., Aug. 21; appoints full gens., Aug. 31; adjourns, Aug. 31; elected, Nov. 6; 5th session convenes, Nov. 18; officially admits Mo. to C.S.A., Nov. 28; admits Ky. to C.S.A., Dec. 10

(1862) Provisional Cong. adjourns, Feb. 17; 1st Cong. of C.S.A. convenes, Feb 18; electoral vote, frees prisoners of war, Feb. 19; Davis' message to, Feb. 25; Simms' declaration on defense, Feb. 26; gives Davis power to suspend habeas corpus, Feb. 27; stipulates destruction of crops, property, Mar. 6; Senate passes conscription bill, Apr. 9; Davis approves Conscription Act, Apr. 16; adjourns, Apr. 21; 2nd session convenes, Aug. 18; debates propriety of Northern invasion, Sept. 12; 2nd Conscription Act, Sept. 27; organizes military courts, Oct. 9; draft exemptions enlarged, Oct. 11; adjourns, renews suspension of habeas corpus, Oct. 13

(1863) 3rd session, 1st Conf. Cong. convenes at Richmond, Davis' State of the Confederacy message, Jan. 12; debates Emancipation Proclamation, Jan. 19; authorizes European loan, Jan. 29; provides for funding of treasury notes, Feb. 20, Mar. 23; authorizes property impressment, Mar. 26; acts on minors holding commissions, AWOL soldiers, Apr. 16; volunteer Navy established, Apr. 18; "tax in kind," Apr. 24; bonds, stocks authorized, Apr. 27; Provisional Navy, May 1; authorizes construction of ships in Europe, delegates from Ind. nations, May 1; adopts national flag, May 1; punishment for white officers of Negro troops, May 1; adjourns, May 1; 4th session, 1st Cong., convenes, Dec. 7; end use of substitutes, makes tax in kind changes, Dec. 28

(1864) Davis recommends habeas corpus suspension, Feb. 3; bans luxuries, U.S. paper money, regulates exports, Feb. 6; suspends habeas corpus conditionally, Feb. 17; 4th session, 1st Cong. adjourns, Feb. 17; 1st session, 2nd Cong. convenes, May 2; authorizes military service for men 17–18 and 45–50, June 10; adjourns, June 14; levies taxes, June 14; 2nd session, 2nd Cong. convenes, Nov. 7

(1865) Davis signs General-in-Chief act, Jan. 23; prisoner exchange offer, Jan. 24; act to make Lee General-in-Chief, Feb. 6; Hampton Roads report, Feb. 6; House authorizes use of slaves as soldiers, Feb. 20; Sen. postpones slave-soldier bill, Feb. 21; approves revision in flag, Mar. 4; Senate approves Negro soldiers, Mar. 8; Negro troop issue, Mar. 10; approves use of Negro troops, Mar. 13; message of Davis to, Mar. 13; denies lack of action, Mar. 16; adjourns, contention with Davis, Mar. 18

Congressional elections: (1862) Democratic gains, Oct. 14
Connecticut: (1865) ratifies Thirteenth Amendment, May 5
Connecticut, U.S.S.: (1862) captures Brit. blockade-runner, Nov. 17
Conrad's Fy., Md.: (1861) occup. of, June 15; sk., June 17; Ball's Bluff Camp., Oct. 20, 21 (bat.)
Conrad's Fy., Va.: (1862) Oct. 4
Conrad's Mill, W. Va.: (1861) in Cheat Mt. Camp., Sept., 11
Conrad's Store, Va.: (1862) Jackson leaves for, Apr. 18; May 6
Conscription, C.S.A.: (1862) Sen. passes conscription bill, Apr. 9; Davis approves act, Apr. 16; Cong. declares exemptions, Apr. 21; stricter observance of, July 14; in S.C., Sept. 1; 2nd Conscription Act, Sept. 27; Davis to Lee on, Sept. 28; exemptions expanded, Oct. 11; (1863) draft law tightened, May 1; Davis calls for enrollment, July 18; end use of substitutes, Dec. 28; (1864) opposition to in N.C., Jan. 18; Davis on, Dec. 18
Conscription, U.S.: (1862) Lincoln signs militia draft act, July 17; Lincoln issues militia draft order, Aug. 4; avoidance of draft, Aug. 9; draft in Pa., other states, Oct. 16; opposition to, Oct. 17; (1863) Conscription Act passed by Cong., signed, Feb. 16, 25, Mar. 3; Lincoln on alien eligibility, May 8; opposition to in O., June 16; begins in R.I., elsewhere, opposition to, July 7; in Mass., July 8; draft riots in N.Y., elsewhere, July 13, 14, 15; Lincoln on, Aug. 11, 16; draft in N. Y. City resumes, Aug. 19; (1864) Lincoln orders 500,000 draft, Feb. 1; Navy draft order, Mar. 14
Constellation, U.S.S.: (1861) captures slave ship, May 21
Constitution, Confederate: (1861) Provisional Constitution adopted, Feb. 8, Mar. 11; ratification of, Mar. 11; state ratification of, Mar. 13, 21, 25, 29, Apr. 22

O., June 15; at Democratic Convention, Aug. 30, 31; Lincoln's concern over votes of, Oct. 13; in plot to burn New York, Nov. 25

Corbett, Boston (F): (1865) shooting of Booth, Apr. 26

Corbin's Br., Va.: (1864) comb. (Spotsylvania), May 8

Corbin's Cross Roads, Va.: (1863) sk., Sept. 1

Core Cr., N.C.: (1862) sk., Nov. 18; (1863) sk., Apr. 17; sc. to, June 17; (1864) Fed sc. from, Dec. 10

Corinth, Miss.: (1862) Conf. concentration, Mar. 1; A. S. Johnston's troops move to, Mar. 5, 18, 24; Mar. 29; Apr. 2; Conf. advance to Shiloh, Apr. 3; sk. at Monterey, Tenn., Apr. 3; Apr. 4; Beauregard withdraws to, Apr. 8; Feds. to move against, Apr. 11; Apr. 17; Halleck to move on, Apr. 28, 29; defense of, May 2; sk. near, May 3; Halleck moving toward, May 3, 4, 6, 11; Fed. recon. toward, May 8; sk., May 9; May 10; sk. near, May 14; act. near, May 15; sks., May 17, 19, 21, 22, 24, 27 28; comparison of forces near, May 29; Beauregard evacuates, May 30; June 2; effects of fall of, June 3; Fed. recon. near, June 3; Pope probes against Beauregard, June 4; Fed. recon. near, June 6; Fed. recon. near, June 9; Grant second in command in Camp. of, June 10; sk. near, June 11; act., July 1; ment., July 11; Aug. 11; sk. near, Aug. 28; Iuka occup., Sept. 14; drive on Iuka, Sept. 19; Van Dorn marches toward, Sept. 29; Conf. move in on, Oct. 2; Bat. of, Oct. 3, 4; pursuit of Van Dorn, Oct. 5; "Union Brigade" camp att., Oct. 5; Feds. move from toward Grand Junction, Oct. 31; Fed. exped. from, Dec. 9; Fed. r.r. raid, Dec. 13; (1863) Fed. expeds. from, Apr. 15, May 26, Sept. 11, 27; sks., June 11, Aug. 16, Nov. 2, 12, Dec. 23; (1864) Fed. evac. of, Jan. 25; Bat. of Brice's Cross Roads, June 10; Forrest raid leaves from, Oct. 19, Nov. 4, 9, 10; ment., Nov. 14; (1865), sk., Jan. 19

Corinth Camp.: *See* Corinth, Miss.

Corinth Rd., Miss.: (1862) recon. by Feds., Apr. 13; sk., Apr. 24

Cornersville Pike, Tenn.: (1864) aff. on, Jan. 28

Cornfield: (1862) at Antietam, Sept. 17

Corn's Farm, Franklin Co., Tenn.: (1865) aff., Feb. 6

Corpus Christi, Tex.: (1862) *Elma* and *Hannah* burned, Aug. 12; Fed. naval bomb. of, Aug. 16; in Fed. hands, Oct. 15; (1863) Feds. occupy, Nov. 16; Feds. capture battery near, Nov. 17; (1864) affs., Mar. 17, 22

Correspondence with "Rebel govt.": (1863) forbidden, Feb. 25

Corrick's Fd., W. Va.: (1861) act., July 13; ment., July 14; (1865) Fed. sc. to, Mar. 14

Corse, John Murray (F): (1864) Oct. 5

Corwin, Thomas: (1861) chairman, House Committee of Thirty-three, Jan. 14; slavery amendment of, Feb. 28

Corydon, Ind.: (1863) sk., July 9; ment., July 10

Cosby Cr., Tenn.: (1864) sk., Jan. 13

Cotile Bayou, La.: (1863) sk. on, May 14

Cotile Ldg., La.: (1864) sk. (Red R. exped.), Apr. 25

Cotton: (*See also* Trade with enemy): (1861) Nov. 28; burned, Nov. 29, Dec. 9; (1862) auction of, Jan. 10; C.S.A. offers France cotton for aid against blockade, July 16; Lincoln on purchase of, Oct. 22; (1863) Lincoln on shortage of, Jan. 19; Davis on, Jan. 27; Apr. 10; Augusta *Constitutionalist* on, Oct. 2; (1864) trading, Jan. 19; export of regulated in C.S.A., Feb. 6; trading, Feb. 28, Sept. 9; Lincoln on, Dec. 12

Cotton, C.S.S. (gunboat): (1863) destroyed, Jan. 14

Cotton Cr., Fla.: (1865) sk., Mar. 25

Cotton Hill, W. Va.: (1861) sks., Oct. 13, 31, Nov. 1, 10, 12

Cotton Plant, Ark.: (1862) sk., May 14; (1864) affs., Apr. 21, 22; Fed. exped. to, Oct. 26

Cotton Port Fd., Tenn.: (1863) sk., Sept. 30

Cotton R. Br., Ga.: (1864) sk., Nov. 16

Cottonwood, Kas.: (1863) exped. to, Apr. 10

Couch, Darius Nash (F): (1863) given corps command, Feb. 5; Bat. of Chancellorsville, May 3; assumes command Dept. of the Susquehanna, June 10

Counterfeiting: (1862) in St. Louis, Apr. 10

Courtland, Ala.: (1862) sk., July 25; (1863) Fed. exped. to, Apr. 15; (1864) aff., Mar. 8; Fed. cav. oper. to, July 25; Hood heads for, Oct. 29

Courtney's Plantation, Miss.: (1863) sk., Apr. 11

Courts-martial: (1864) Lincoln reviews, Apr. 14, 21

Couthard's Ldg., Va.: (1864) Sheridan crosses James at, June 26

Cove Cr., Ark.: (1862) sk., Nov. 8

Cove Gap, W. Va.: (1864) sk., June 23

Cove Mt. (or Grassy Lick), Va.: (1864) eng., May 10

Cove Point, Md.: (1864) aff., Aug. 22

Cove Springs, Ga.: (1864) sk., July 8

Covington, Ga.: (1864) Garrard cav. raid to, July 22

Covington, Ky.: (1862) martial law declared in, Sept. 2; sk., Sept. 10; E. Kirby Smith before, Sept. 15; (1863) Fed. troops arrive at, Aug. 12, 20

Covington, La.: (1862) sk., July 27

Covington, Tenn.: (1863) Fed. exped. to, Mar. 8

Covington, Va.: (1863) sk., Nov. 9; (1864) aff., June 2

Cowan, Tenn.: (1863) aff., Oct. 9

"Cowboys": (1864) Hampton's cattle raid, Sept. 16

Cow Cr., Kas.: (1864) sks., Nov. 14, 28, Dec. 4

Cow Fd. Cr., Fla.: (1864) sk., Apr. 2

Cowpen Fd., S.C.: (1865) sk., Feb. 6

Cowpen Ldg., N.C.: (1865) U.S. steamers burned, Apr. 5

Cowskin Bottom, I.T.: (1864) aff., Jan. 23

Cox, Jacob Dolson (F): (1861) movement to Charleston, W. Va., July 11; moves up Great Kanawha Valley, July 12; advance into W. Va., July 17; attacks Conf. rear, July 24; Charleston, W. Va., occup., July 25; near Gauley Br., July 30; in Kanawha Valley, Sept. 9; (1862) assumes command Fed. Dist. of W. Va., Oct. 13; (1864) rumors of actions by, Oct. 5; reaches Columbia, Nov. 24; Bat. of Franklin, Tenn., Nov. 30; (1865) drive toward Wilmington, N.C., Feb. 19; heads Fed. base at New Berne, Mar. 7; Bat. of Kinston, N.C., Mar. 8, 9, 10; occup. of Kinston, Mar. 14; to join Sherman, Mar. 14

Cox, Samuel: (1865) Booth, Herold reach home of, Apr. 16

Cox, Samuel S. (F): (1865) on govt. power, Jan. 12

Cox's Br., Neuse R., N.C.: (1865) sk., Mar. 23

for, Jan. 7; Buchanan advocates, Jan. 8; defeated in Cong., Jan. 16, Feb. 27, Mar. 7

Crittenden resolution: (1861) July 22

Croatan, N.C.: (1864) Fed. outpost surrenders, May 4

Crook, George (F): (1864) heads toward Lynchburg, May 30; augments Hunter, June 8; eng. at Snicker's Fy., July 17; 2nd Bat. of Kernstown, July 24; retreat from Kernstown, July 25, 26; assigned command Dept. of W. Va., Aug. 30; Bat. of Fisher's Hill, Sept. 22

Crook, Ft., Calif.: (1861) Fed. scs. from, Aug. 3, 15

Crooked Cr., Ark.: (1863) sk. on, Mar. 31; act., Apr. 30; (1864) aff., Jan. 23; sk., Feb. 5

Crooked Cr., Kas.: (1865) Fed. sc. to, Mar. 9

Crooked Cr., Mo.: (1862) sk. on, Aug. 24

Crooked R., Fla.: (1862) aff., May 20

Crooked Run, Va.: (1863) sk., Sept. 18

Crook's Run, Va.: (1863) sk., Apr. 29

Cross Bayou, La.: (1864) sk., July 4

Cross Hollow, Ark.: (1862) sk., Oct. 18; (1863) sks., Mar. 30, 31; (1864) Fed. sc. to, June 9

Cross Keys, Va.: (1862) Bat. of, June 8

Cross Lanes, W. Va.: (1861) act., Aug. 26

Cross Timbers, Mo.: (1862) sk., July 28; (1863) sk. (Shelby's raid), Oct. 15

Crossville, Tenn.: (1863) aff., Dec. 9

Crowley's Ridge (or Taylor's Cr.), Ark.: (1863) sk., May 11

Crow's House, Va.: (1865) act., Mar. 31

Crows Station, Mo.: (1862) sk., May 26

Crow's Valley (or Rocky Face Ridge), Ga.: (1864) sk., Feb. 24

Cruisers, Conf. (*See also* individual ships): (1865) Johnson warns foreign powers against giving hospitality to, May 10

Crump's Cr., Va.: (1864) comb., May 28

Crump's Cross Roads (or Baltimore Cross Roads), Va.: (1863) sk., July 2

Crump's Hill, La.: (1864) sk. (Red R. Camp.), Apr. 2

Crump's Ldg., Tenn. (*See also* Shiloh, Bat. of): (1862) Fed. oper. from, Mar. 9; Grant orders Wallace's division to Shiloh, Apr. 6

Crystal R., Fla.: (1865) blockade-runners capt. off, Apr. 11

Crystal Springs, Miss.: (1863) Fed. cav. raid near, May 11

Cuba: (1861) Conf. prize ships, July 6; *Trent* Aff., Nov. 8; (1865) C.S.S. *Stonewall* at, May 11; surrender of *Stonewall*, May 19

Cuba, Mo.: (1864) sk., May 13; aff., Sept. 29

Cubero, N. Mex. Terr.: (1862) Confs. capture, Mar. 3

Cub Run, Va.: (1863) sk., Jan. 5

Cub Run Br., Va.: (1861) 1st Bull Run, Bat., of, July 21

Culpeper Court House, Va. (or Culpeper): (1862) Fed. recon. to, July 12; Fed. recon. from, July 28; Bat. of Cedar Mt., Aug. 9; Longstreet arrives at, Nov. 3; Conf. base at, Nov. 19; (1863) Lee moves toward, June 4, 6; Longstreet moves from, June 15; Lee's retreat to, July 23; Longstreet arrives at, July 24; Conf. forces move toward, July 26; Lee at, July 28; Meade occupies, Sept. 13; cav. sk., Sept. 19; sks., Oct. 1, 11, Nov. 8; aff., Dec. 18; sk., Dec.

Cunningham's Bluff, S.C.: (1863) sk. near, Nov. 24
Cunningham's Cross Roads, Pa.: (1863) sk., July 5
Curlew, U.S.S.: (1864) Greene's raid on, May 25
Currency, comptroller of, U.S. (*See also* Treasury, comptroller of): (1863) Feb. 25
Currency, U.S. (*See also* Currency Act): (1863) shortage of, Feb. 20; national currency established, Feb. 25; Cong. authorizes fractional currency, Mar. 3; (1864) circulation banned in C.S.A., Feb. 6
Currency Act, U.S. (*See also* Currency Bureau of Treasury): (1862) use of postage stamps for currency authorized, July 17; stamps issued, Aug. 21
Currency Bureau of Treasury, U.S.: (1863) established, Feb. 25; (1864) 2nd act establishing, June 3
Current Hills, Mo.: (1861) Fed. exped., Dec. 5
Current R., Mo.: (1862) Fed. sc. to, Aug. 24; (1863) Fed. sc. to, Apr. 18
Currioman Bay, Va.: (1863) Fed. exped. to, Feb. 12
Currituck Beach, N.C.: (1863) salt works destroyed, Feb. 2
Currituck Br., Va.: (1864) sk., Sept. 9
Currituck Co., N.C.: (1863) Fed. exped. into, Aug. 5
Currituck Sound, N.C.: (1862) Fed. exped., Feb. 20
Curtin, Andrew G. (F): (1862) as Pa. gov. calls for 50,000 men, Sept. 11; Lincoln to, Sept. 16; (1863) calls for 60,000 men, June 26; reelected, Oct. 3
Curtis, Samuel Ryan (F): (1861) Lincoln to re Frémont, Oct. 7; Lincoln sends orders relieving Frémont to, Oct. 24; (1862) pushes Price out of Mo., Mar. 5; entrenched near Pea Ridge, Mar. 6; Bat. of Pea Ridge, Mar. 7; aftermath, Mar. 8; assumes command Dist. of Kas., Apr. 10; arrives at Helena, July 12; assumes command Dept. of Mo., Sept. 24; (1863) Lincoln to, Jan. 10; superseded by Schofield, May 24; (1864) assumes command Dept. of Kas., Jan. 16; commands Army of the Border, Oct. 20; Price's plans to attack army of, Oct. 22; Bat. of Westport, Oct. 23; pursuit of Price, Oct. 24, 26; squabble over leadership, Oct. 26; eng. at Newtonia, Oct. 28; divested of Rosecrans' troops, Oct. 28
Curtis' Cr., Tenn.: (1864) sk., Dec. 19
Cushing, William Barker (F): (1862) captures schooners, Nov. 23; (1864) sinking of *Albemarle,* Oct. 27
Custer, George Armstrong (F): (1864) Albemarle Co., Va., raid, Feb. 28, 29, Mar. 2; Sheridan's exped., May 10; comb. at Trevilian Station, June 11; sk. at Brock's Gap, Va., Oct. 6; eng. at Tom's Brook, Oct. 9; (1865) eng. at Waynesborough, Va., Mar. 2; demands surrender of Confs., Apr. 9
Customs, U.S.: (1861) bill concerning, July 13
Cuyler's Plantation, Ga.: (1864) sk., Dec. 9
Cynthiana, Ky.: (1862) Morgan raids in area, July 14; Morgan captures, July 17; (1864) Morgan captures, June 11
Cypress Bend, Ark.: (1863) Fed. exped. to, Feb. 14
Cypress Br., Ky.: (1861) sk., Nov. 17
Cypress Cr., Ark.: (1864) sks., May 13, Dec. 1
Cypress Cr., La.: (1864) sk., Mar. 8
Cypress Cr. Br., Tenn.: (1862) burned by Confs., May 30
Cypress Swamp, Ga.: (1864) sk., Dec. 7

Danville, Va.: (1865) Conf. leaders head for, Apr. 2; Davis, Cabinet arrive, Apr. 3; capital of Confederacy, Apr. 4, 5, 7, 8, 9

Danville Cross Roads, Ky.: (1862) sk., Oct. 10

Danville R.R., Va.: (1865) Davis, Cabinet take, Apr. 2, 3; Sheridan arrives at, Apr. 4; useless to Lee, Apr. 5

Darbytown, Va.: (1864) eng., July 27

Darbytown Rd., Va.: (1864) engs., Oct. 7, 27

Dardanelle, Ark.: (1864) sks., May 10, 15, Aug. 30; guerrilla att. on Fed. steamer, Nov. 29

Darien, Ga.: (1863) att., June 11; Conf. salt works destroyed, Sept. 22

Dark Corners, Ga.: (1864) sk., July 7

Darkesville, W. Va.: (1862) sk., Dec. 11; (1864) sks., July 3, 19, Sept. 2, 10

Darling, Ft. (or Drewry's Bluff), Va.: (1862) Bat. of Drewry's Bluff, May 15; (1864) Butler's march on canceled, May 5; Bat. of, May 12; eng., May 16

Daufuskie I., S.C.: (1863) Conf. exped. to, Jan. 29

Dauphin I., Ala.: (1864) investment of Ft. Gaines, Aug. 3; Bat. of Mobile Bay, Aug. 5; surrender of Ft. Gaines, Aug. 7, 8; (1865) Fed. feint on Mobile, Mar. 18

Davenport, Va.: (1864) comb., May 9

Davenport Church, Va.: (1864) sk., Dec. 4

Davenport Fd., Va.: (1864) comb., May 9–10

David, C.S.S.: (1863) torpedo boat att. on U.S.S. *New Ironsides*, Oct. 5

David's Fy., La.: (1864) U.S. transport *Emma* capt., May 1; eng., May 4

Davidson, Ft., at Pilot Knob, Mo.: (1864) sk., Sept. 27; Feds. evacuate, Sept. 27

Davies, Camp, Miss.: (1863) sk., Nov. 22

Davis, Charles Henry (F): (1862) commands Fed. fleet Bat. of Plum Run Bend, Tenn., May 10; commands Fed. fleet Bat. of Memphis, June 6; Farragut's fleet joins, July 1; replaced by D. D. Porter, Oct. 1

Davis, David (F): (1862) Lincoln appoints to Supreme Court, Oct. 17

Davis, George (C): (1863) Davis nominates Attorney General, C.S.A., Dec. 31; (1864) confirmed as Attorney General, Jan. 2; (1865) leaves Cabinet in flight, Apr. 26

Davis, Henry Winter (F): (1863) Lincoln to, Mar. 18; (1864) House passes Wade-Davis bill, May 4; Lincoln pocket-vetoes bill, July 4; Wade-Davis Manifesto, Aug. 5

Davis, Jefferson (C): (1860) as U.S. sen. on Committee of Thirteen, Dec. 20; (1861) views on secession in Sen., Jan. 10; leaves U. S. Sen., Jan. 21; chosen Provisional Pres. of C.S.A., Feb. 9; told of election, Feb. 10; departs Brierfield, Miss., for Montgomery, Ala., Feb. 11; en route, speeches, Feb. 11, 12; arrives at Montgomery, Yancey says, "The man and the hour have met," Feb. 16; inaugurated Provisional Pres., C.S.A., Feb. 18; forming Cabinet, Feb. 19; Charleston Harbor situation, Feb. 25; names 3 Conf. commissioners to Wash., Feb. 27; names Beauregard to command Charleston, S.C., area, Mar. 1; names commissioners to Britain, Mar. 16; to Gov. Pickens, Mar. 18; doubts if enemy will retire, Mar. 18; on surrender of Ft. Sumter, Apr. 14; and privateers, Apr. 17; promises aid to Va., Apr. 18; tells Va. to aid Baltimore, Apr. 22; promises aid to Mo., Apr. 23; message to Cong., Apr. 29; approves state of war bill, May 6; bill to accept volunteers, May 9;

concern over troops, invasion of coast, state-C.S.A. relations, Nov. 1; Sec. of War Randolph resigns, Nov. 15; G. W. Smith named temporary Sec. of War, Nov. 17; James A. Seddon appointed Sec. of War, Nov. 21; to govs. on conscription, supplies, Nov. 26; to Pemberton re troops, Dec. 7; to Lee re shortage of forces, Dec. 8; on western tour, Dec. 13; to Seddon re condition of South, Dec. 18; to T. H. Holmes, Dec. 21; proclaims Butler outlaw, Dec. 23; wires for guns at Vicksburg, Dec. 23

(1863) on Confederacy as home of representative govt., Jan. 5; to Lee on atrocities, Jan. 7; to Johnston on holding Miss., Jan. 8; message to Cong., Jan. 12; orders Johnston to investigate Bragg, Jan. 21; to Lee, Jan. 22; to Gov. Brown of Ga., Jan. 27; to Holmes, Jan. 28; to Pemberton re Yazoo Pass, Jan. 29; to Lee on threats to east coast, Feb. 4; to Johnston on Bragg, Feb. 19; concern over Vicksburg, Feb. 19; concern for Trans-Miss., Feb. 26; names Mar. 27 fast day, Feb. 27; to Pemberton, Mar. 10; Richmond bread riots, Apr. 2; counters criticism of Pemberton, Apr. 2; defense of Miss. R., Apr. 3; proclamation, Apr. 10; re Vicksburg, Apr. 22; to Johnston, Apr. 30; to Lee after Chancellorsville, May 4; to Pemberton, May 7; to citizens of Columbus, Miss., May 8; to Pemberton, May 12; concern over Vicksburg, May 13; calls for attack on Feds. at Vicksburg, May 18; illness, May 20; to Bragg, May 22; to Johnston and Pemberton, May 23; to Johnston, May 24; to Lee, May 26, 31; orders Vallandigham treated as "enemy alien," June 2; Brierfield destroyed, June 7; Stephens offers to be mediator, June 12; asks Bragg for reinforcements, June 13; fears loss of Miss. R., June 25

Peace feelers, July 2; awaits war news, July 3; Lee to on defeat, July 4; Lee to, July 7, 8; to Johnston, July 9; to Gov. Bonham, S.C., July 10; to Johnston, July 11; Tex. requests more arms, July 13; to Sen. R. W. Johnson, July 14; to T. H. Holmes, Johnston, July 15; Lee to, July 16; calls for enrollment, July 18; to Lee, July 21; Lee to, July 24; to Lee, July 28; calls for greater exertion, Aug. 1; to Lee re manpower, Aug. 2; to Gov. Bonham, S.C., Aug. 6; Lee offers resignation, Aug. 8; refuses Lee's resignation, Aug. 11; seeks troops for Bragg, Aug. 22; decision to hold Ft. Sumter, Aug. 26; concern over Charleston, and east Tenn., Aug. 27; to Gov. Harris, Tenn., Sept. 1; to Bragg, Sept. 5; to Lee, Sept. 8; detaches Longstreet's corps to aid Bragg, Sept. 9; to Lee, Sept. 16; to Bragg, Sept. 28, Oct. 3; tours war fronts, Oct. 6, 9; with Bragg, Oct. 10; authorizes removal of D. H. Hill, Oct. 13; message to Army of Tenn., Oct. 14; leaves Bragg's army in Ala., Oct. 18; removes Polk, Oct. 23; approves Forrest's Camp., Oct. 29; to Bragg, Nov. 1; visits Charleston, Nov. 2, 4; at Wilmington, N.C., Nov. 6; on morale in Ark., Nov. 6; to Bragg, Nov. 11; concern over situation, Nov. 11; on loss of Ark., Nov. 19; asks Johnston to help Bragg, Nov. 20; advises Bragg to concentrate, Nov. 27; accepts Bragg's resignation, Nov. 30, Dec. 1; Bragg suggests Davis head Army of Tenn., Dec. 2; considers sending Lee west, Dec. 6; message to Cong., Dec. 7; asks Lee to visit, Dec. 8; concern over troop disposition, Dec. 10; differences with Johnston, Dec. 16; to Johnston, Dec. 19, 23; names George Davis Attorney General, Dec. 31

(1864) to Lee on food, Jan. 4; suspends execution, Jan. 7; to Z. B. Vance, gov. of N.C., Jan. 8; on peace prospects, Jan. 8; Fed. plans for att. on Mobile, Jan. 9; to Johnston, Jan. 13, 14; summons Bragg, Jan. 27; on disloyalty, Feb. 3; warns Lee of Feds., Feb. 7; warns Johnston of Sherman, Feb. 11; concern about Meridian Camp., Feb. 15; logistical problems, Feb. 16; reinforcements to Miss., Feb. 17; discontent with admin. of, Feb. 17; to Adm. F. Buchanan, Feb. 19; concern over military situation, Feb. 21; to Johnston, Feb. 23; names Bragg to conduct military oper., Feb. 24; plot to assassinate, Mar. 2; to Longstreet, Mar. 7; to Pemberton, Mar. 11; suspends deserter's execution, Mar. 12; Ga. legislature expresses confidence, Mar. 19; discusses trade, troops, Mar. 26; to Lee re supplies, Apr. 12; to Polk on Negro prisoners, Apr. 22; names commissioner to Canada, Apr. 27; to E. Kirby Smith on Trans-Miss., Apr. 28; to Polk on capt. slaves, Apr. 30; son Joe Davis killed, Apr. 30; message to Cong., May 2; tells Lee of Butler's ldgs., May 5; to Beauregard on danger to Richmond, May 6; to Lee, May 9, 11; death of Jeb Stuart, May 12; promises to sustain Lee, May 13; to Lee re Butler, May 14, 15; re troops to Va., May 15; withdrawal in Ga., May 18; to Lee re Butler, May 19; to Lee on situation, May 20; to Lee re Beauregard, May 28; local forces to protect Richmond, June 1; to citizen of Canton, La., June 7; to Lee re threat to Petersburg, June 9; to E. Kirby Smith, June 13; accepts resignation Sec. of Treasury Memminger, June 21; to Gov. Brown, Ga., June 29

To Johnston, July 7; sends Bragg to Johnston, July 9; to Lee on Johnston "failure," July 12, 13; to Johnston, July 16; Johnston relieved of command, Army of Tenn., Hood takes over, July 17; names George Trenholm Sec. of Treasury replacing Memminger, July 18; Hood-Hardee personality clash, Aug. 7; to Lee re soap, Aug. 10; to Lee re Fed. strategy, Aug. 11; on Weldon R.R., Aug. 20; apprehension over loss of supply lines, Aug. 23; Lincoln to Raymond on possible peace discussions with, Aug. 24; Lee to, urging greater use of Negroes, Sept. 2; tries to gather troops for Ga., Sept. 3; on recovery of Atlanta, Sept. 18; on interstate harmony, Sept. 19; leaves for Ga., Sept. 20; arrives in Macon, Ga., Sept. 22; on Sherman's supply line, Sept. 22; visits Hood, Sept. 25; authorizes Hardee's transfer, Sept. 28; gives Beauregard command of western depts., Oct. 2; at Columbia, S.C., Oct. 3; on combating Sherman, Oct. 3; speech on condition of C.S.A., Oct. 5; returns to Richmond, sends Bragg to command Wilmington, N.C., area, Oct. 15; message to Cong., Nov. 7; to Hood, re beating Sherman in detail, Nov. 7; objects to separate state peace negotiations, Nov. 17; calls out available troops to oppose Sherman, Nov. 18; orders resistance in Ga., Nov. 22, 24; concern over Ga., Nov. 26; to Beauregard on Sherman's march, Nov. 30; Davis attempts to raise troops to oppose Sherman, Dec. 12; lets Lee decide on troops to Sherman, Dec. 14; no troops for Hardee, Dec. 17; to Seddon, Dec. 18; to Beauregard on serious situation, Dec. 20; to E. Kirby Smith re troops, Dec. 24; F. P. Blair, Sr., to re peace, Dec. 30

(1865) to Beauregard re Hood's possible removal, Jan. 2; concern over course of events, Jan. 5; to A. Stephens, Jan. 6; consolidating, recruiting armies, Jan. 11; confers with F. P. Blair, Sr., on peace, Jan. 12; to R. Taylor on faltering fortunes, C.S.A., Jan. 12; to Gov. Brown, Ga., Jan. 15; to Hardee, Jan. 15; Blair's report from Davis on peace efforts, Jan. 16; urges Bragg to retake Ft. Fisher, Jan. 16; to Gov. A. Magrath, S.C., re Sherman, Jan. 17; peace overtures by F. P. Blair, Sr., Jan. 18; urges Lee to take command all Conf. troops, Jan. 18; attempts to recruit troops to oppose Sherman, Jan. 18, 19; Lee to Davis, re General-in-Chief appointment, Jan. 19; signs act authorizing a General-in-Chief, Jan. 23; names committee to hold informal peace talks, Jan. 28; Sen. approves Lee for General-in-Chief, Jan. 31; willingness to have peace talks on basis of separate Confederacy, Jan. 31; to Lee on troop recruitment, Jan. 31; on "hour of necessity," Jan. 31; accepts Seddon's resignation as Sec. of War, Feb. 1; on choosing own Cabinet, Feb. 1; report on Hampton Rds. Peace Conference, Feb. 3; to Beauregard, Feb. 4; names John C. Breckinridge Sec. of War, Feb. 6; on Hampton Rds. Conference, Feb. 6; approves Lee's pardon of deserters, Feb. 9; to Hardee, Feb. 11, 14; on Negro soldiers, Feb. 21; sees realities of command situation, Feb. 22; Lee to on strategy, Feb. 23; "expects hour of deliverance," Mar. 3; E. Kirby Smith offers to resign, Mar. 8; Lee to re Negro troops, Mar. 10; signs bill authorizing Negro troops, Mar. 13; message to Cong., Mar. 13; Lee to, Mar. 14; Cong. rebuts Davis' charges of inaction, Mar. 16; dispute with Cong., Mar. 18; to Lee on defense of Mobile, Mar. 21; Lee to on strategy, Mar. 26; on faction in govt., Mar. 30

Lee to on situation, Apr. 1; to Lee on Negro troops, Apr. 1; evac. of Richmond, Apr. 2; arrives in Danville, Va., Apr. 3; accusations against, Apr. 4; proclamation, Apr. 4; sets up govt. at Danville, Apr. 5, 7; to wife, Apr. 5; gets word of critical situation, Apr. 8; building entrenchments, Apr. 9; hears of Lee's surrender, heads for N.C., Apr. 10; arrives at Greensborough, N.C., Apr. 11; meets with genls., Apr. 12; gives Johnston permission to ask for terms, Apr. 14; leaves Greensborough, N.C., Apr. 15; arrives Lexington, N.C., Apr. 16; at Salisbury, N.C., Apr. 17; goes toward Concord, N.C., Apr. 18; arrives at Charlotte, N.C., Apr. 19; hears of Lincoln's death, Apr. 19; Wade Hampton to, on continuing fight, Apr. 19; Lee to, opposing continuing war, Apr. 20; to wife on future, Apr. 23; approves Sherman-Johnston terms, Apr. 24; meets with Cabinet, Apr. 26; Trenholm resigns as Sec. of Treasury, Apr. 27, 28; reaches Yorkville, S.C., Apr. 29; reaches Cokesbury, S.C., May 1; at Abbeville, S.C., May 2; favors continuing war, May 2; crosses Savannah R. to Washington, Ga., May 3; Sec. of Navy Mallory, Sec. of State Benjamin resign, May 3; flight continues, May 4; at Sandersville, Ga., May 5, 6; meets Mrs. Davis near Dublin, Ga., May 9; capt. by Fed. troops near Irwinville, Ga., May 10; imprisoned in Ft. Monroe, Va., May 22

Davis, Jefferson C. (F): (1862) mortally wounds Gen. Wm. Nelson, Sept. 29; (1865) at Bat. of Bentonville, N.C., Mar. 19, 20, 21

Davis, "Joe" (C): (1864) son of Pres. Davis killed, Apr. 30

Davis, Joseph (C): (1863) plantation of brother of Pres. Davis destroyed, June 7

Davis, Varina (Mrs. Jefferson) (C): (1861) Jan. 21; receives news of husband chosen Pres. C.S.A., Feb. 10; (1862) Davis to, May 13, 19, 28, June 3, 11, 21; (1865) evac. of Richmond, Apr. 2; Davis to, Apr. 5, 23; at Abbeville, S.C., Apr. 28; meets Davis in Ga., May 9; capt. by Fed. troops, May 10

Davis, Ft. Tex.: (1861) abandoned by Feds., Apr. 13; Apache ambush, Aug. 12

Davisborough, Ga.: (1864) sk., Nov. 28

Davis' Bridge on Hatchie R., Tenn.: (1862) sks., Sept. 25, Oct. 1

Davis' Cross Roads, Ga.: (1863) sk., Sept. 11
Davis' Gap., Ala.: (1863) sk., Sept. 1
Davis' Mill, Miss.: (1862) sk., Dec. 21; (1864) sk., June 12
Davis' Mill, Tenn.: (1863) sks., Mar. 14, Apr. 5
Davis' Mill Rd., Tenn.: (1863) sk. near La Grange, Mar. 24
Davison's Fd., near Clinton, La.: (1864) Fed. exped. to, July 17
Daylight, U.S.S.: (1861) sets up blockade at Wilmington, N.C., July 14
Day of fasting, prayer: (Fed.) (1861) Aug. 12, Sept. 26; (1863) Lincoln
 designates Apr. 30 as, Mar. 30; (Conf.) (1861) June 13; (1863) Feb. 27
Day's Gap or Sand Mt., Ala.: (1863) act., Apr. 30
Dayton, William Lewis (F): (1861) Lincoln appoints as minister to France,
 Mar. 18
Dayton, Mo.: (1861) sk., Dec. 23; (1862) nearly destroyed, Jan. 1; (1863) sk.,
 Aug. 10; (1864) sk., Apr. 27
Dayton, O.: (1863) Vallandigham arrested, May 5; (1864) Vallandigham re-
 turns, June 15
Dead Buffalo Lake, Dak. Terr.: (1863) act. with Sioux, July 26
Death sentence: *See* Executions
Debts, repudiation of: (1861) by Ga., Apr. 26; (1865) U. S. Sen. repudiates
 Conf. debts, Feb. 17; Tenn. repudiates Conf. debts, Feb. 22
Decatur, Ala.: (1862) Feds. occupy, Apr. 13; Fed. exped. from, July 12; sk.,
 Aug. 7; (1863) Fed. exped. to, Nov. 14; (1864) sks., Mar. 7, Apr. 13,
 18, 24, 27, 30, May 8; cav. eng., May 26; raid from, July 10; oper. from,
 July 25; demon. against, Oct. 26; Hood leaves Gadsden for, Oct. 28; Hood
 leaves from, Oct. 29; sks., Dec. 27, 28; (1865) sk., Mar. 3
Decatur, Ga.: (1864) Sherman's advance on Atlanta, July 13, 16, 19, 20, 21, 22;
 sks., July 20, 22, 26, 28; Bat. of Atlanta, July 22; Slocum moves to, Nov. 14
Decherd, Tenn.: (1862) Aug. 6; (1863) sk. (Tullahoma Camp.), June 29
Declaration of Immediate Causes, S.C.: (1860) Dec. 24
Declaration of Independence: (1861) Lincoln on, Feb. 22
Dedmon's Trace, Ga.: (1864) Fed. sc. to, Apr. 10
Deep Bottom, Va.: (1864) acts. Four Mile Cr., June 30; eng. (or Darby-
 town, Strawberry Plains, New Market Rd.), July 27; sk., Aug. 1; Fed.
 demon., Aug. 13; (1865) Fed. exped. from, Mar. 28
Deep Cr., Va.: (1864) sk., Feb. 29
Deep Gully, N.C.: (1862) sks., Mar. 31, May 2; (1863) sk., Mar. 30
Deep Run, Va.: *See* Franklin's Crossing
Deep Water, Mo.: (1862) sk., June 11
Deepwater Township, Mo.: (1864) aff., Mar. 27
Deer Cr., Dak. Terr.: (1865) Fed. sc. from, Apr. 22
Deer Cr., Miss.: (1863) sk., Mar. 21; Fed. exped. to, Apr 2; Davis on defense
 of, Apr. 2; (1864) Fed. exped. to, Sept. 21
Deer Cr., Mo.: (1863) sk., Oct. 16
Deer Head Cove, Ga.: (1864) Fed. sc. to, Mar. 29
Deerhound (English yacht): (1864) at *Kearsarge-Alabama* fight, June 19
Deer Park Road, Ala.: (1865) sk., Mar. 25
Delaware: (1861) leg. rejects Confederacy, Jan. 3; Peace Convention urges recog-
 nition of Confederacy, June 27; Lincoln proposes compensated emancipation,
 Nov. 26; (1865) opposes Thirteenth Amendment, Feb. 7

Delaware, Ft., Del.: (1863) *Maple Leaf* incident, June 10
Deloach's Bluff, La.: (1864) sk., destruction of *Eastport,* Apr. 26
De Long, James (F): (1862) as U.S. consul Tangier seizes Sumter officers, Feb. 21
Delta (Fed. steamer): (1864) attacked by guerrillas, Jan. 6
Democratic National Convention: (1864) convenes in Chicago, Aug. 29; platform, Aug. 30; nominates McClellan, Pendleton, Aug. 31; McClellan accepts nomination, disavows "peace plank," Sept. 8
Democratic party: (1860) split aids Republicans, Nov. page; election returns, Nov. 6; (1861) split, June 3; in Confederacy, Nov. 6; (1862) gains in Fed. Cong. elections, Oct. 14; (1863) convention broken up at Frankfort, Ky., Feb. 18; (1864) Chicago convention and McClellan nomination, Aug. 29, 30, 31; (1865) Odell refers to, Jan. 9
Democratic Standard, Concord, N.H.: (1861) office mobbed, Aug. 8
Democrats: (*See also* Democratic National Convention and Democratic party): (1863) protests Vallandigham arrest, May 30; (1864) Blair's support of, Sept. 3; rumors of govt. seizure, Oct. 19
Denmark, Tenn.: (1862) sk. Hatchie Bottom, July 29; (1863) sk., Aug. 3
Dennison, William (F): (1864) notifies Lincoln of pres. nomination, June 9; Lincoln names Postmaster General, Sept. 24; joins Cabinet, Oct. 4
Dennison, Camp, O.: (1863) sk. (Morgan's raid), July 14
Denver, Colo. Terr.: (1861) trans-continental telegraph, Oct. 24; (1864) Sand Cr. massacre, Nov. 29; (1865) Fed. oper. against Inds., Jan. 14
Departments, Conf. and Fed.: *See* under area names
Deportation: (1863) Burnside orders, Apr. 13
De Russy, Ft., La.: (1863) Fed. gunboat att., May 4; Fed. fleet moves to, May 5; (1864) Feds. capture, Mar. 14
Des Allemands, La.: (1863) sk., July 18
Des Arc, Ark.: (1863) capt., Jan. 13
Deserted House, or Kelly's Store, Va.: (1863) sk., Jan. 27; eng., Jan. 30
Desert Station, La.: (1862) sk., Dec. 10
Desertion, Conf.: (1863) Gov. Vance on, May 13; (1865) Lee proposes pardon to, Feb. 9; Lee to War Dept. on, Feb. 24
Desertion, U.S.: (1865) Lincoln proclaims pardon for, Mar. 11
De Soto, U.S.S.: (1863) burned, Feb. 14; captures blockade-runners, Apr. 24
Devall's Bluff, Ark.: (1863) Fed. capture of, Jan. 13; Fed. gunboat at, Jan. 16; sk., Dec. 1; (1864) aff., May 22; act., Aug. 24; Fed. exped. to, Aug. 27; Fed. exped. from, Oct. 16; aff., Nov. 2; Fed. scs. from, Nov. 9, 16, 22; Fed. exped. from, Dec. 7, 13; (1865) Fed. sc. to, Feb. 9
Devaluation, U.S., currency: (1864) greenback at lowest, July 11
Devil's Backbone (or Backbone Mt.), Ark.: (1863) act., Sept. 1
Devil's Den, Gettysburg: (1863) July 2
Devil's Fork, Red R., Ark.: (1864) Fed. exped. to, Mar. 24
Devil's Gap, Tenn.: (1864) act., Dec. 25
Dewey, George (F): (1862) on Farragut, Apr. 24
Diamond Grove, Mo.: (1862) sk., Apr. 14; (1864) sk., Aug. 21
Diamond Grove Prairie, Mo.: (1864) sk., Aug. 1
Diamond Hill, Va.: (1864) sk., June 17

Diana, U.S.S.: (1863) capt. by Confs., Mar. 28

Diascund Br., Va.: (1862) Fed. recon. to, Dec. 17; (1863) sk., June 10, 20

Dickinson, Daniel S. (F): (1864) votes for at Union Party Convention, June 8

Dick Robinson, Camp, Ky.: (1861) established, Aug. 6; Geo. H. Thomas commands, Sept. 10

Dick's Fd., Ky.: (1862) sk., Oct. 12

Dickson Station, Ala.: (1863) Apr. 19; sks., Apr. 23, Oct. 20

Dictatorship: (1863) accusation of by Vallandigham, May 5

Dillingham's Cross Roads (or Duck Branch), S.C.: (1865) sk., Feb. 3

Dinwiddie Court House, Va.: (1864) Fed. recon. toward, Sept. 15; (1865) Appomattox Camp., Mar. 29, 30; eng., Mar. 31

Dinwiddie Rd., Va.: (1864) act. on, Aug. 23

Dirt Town, Ga.: (1863) sk., Sept. 12

Disloyalty, C.S.A.: (1864) Davis deplores, Feb. 3

Disloyalty, U.S. (*See also* Disloyalty, Fed. arrests for; Copperheads; Newspaper suppression): (1862) War Dept. issues orders to suppress, Aug. 8; (1863) Democratic convention in Ky. broken up, Feb. 18; Vallandigham, May 5, 6, 16, 19

Disloyalty, Fed. arrests for: (1861) in Maryland, Sept. 12; Lincoln defends, Sept. 15; Md. prisoners sent to Ft. Lafayette, N.Y., Sept. 20; (1862) Stanton frees most political prisoners, Nov. 22; (1863) Vallandigham's arrest, May 5; disloyalists sent South, May 6; Vallandigham convicted, May 16

Dismal Swamp Canal: *See* Albemarle Canal

Disputanta Station, Va.: (1865) sk. near, Jan. 9

Distilleries: (1862) Butler closes in Dept. of Gulf, Nov. 8

District of Columbia: (1862) Sen. votes to abolish slavery, Apr. 3; House votes slavery abolished in, Apr. 11; Lincoln signs abolition bill, Apr. 16; (1864) militia called up, July 11

Dix, Dorothea (F): (1861) aid accepted by Sec. Cameron, May 29

Dix, John A. (F): (1861) appointed Sec. of Treasury by Buchanan, Jan. 11; commands Dept. of Maryland, July 23; assumes Baltimore command, July 25; (1862) commands Middle Military Dept., Mar. 22; commands at Ft. Monroe, June 1; (1863) commands Dept. of the East, July 18

"Dixie": (1861) played in Britain, Dec. 20; (1865) Pickett's men sing, Apr. 1; at occupation of Richmond, Apr. 3; Lincoln asks for, Apr. 10

Dixon, George E. (C): (1864) commanded *H. L. Hunley,* killed, Feb. 17

Dixon's I., S.C.: (1862) aff. with James I., May 25; (1863) aff., June 21

Doaksville, I.T.: (1865) surrender of Stand Watie, June 23

Dobbins' Fy., Tenn.: (1862) sk. near La Vergne, Dec. 9

Doboy R., Ga.: (1862) Fed. exped. on, and sk., Nov. 18

Dr. Green's Farm, near Lawrenceburg, Ark.: (1863) sk., Nov. 19

Doctor's Cr., Bat. of, Perryville, Ky.: (1862) Oct. 8

Dodd, David O. (C): (1864) executed as Conf. spy, Jan. 8

Dodge, Grenville M. (F): (1863) captures Tuscumbia, Ala., Apr. 24; (1864) Bat. of Atlanta, July 22; named command Dept. of the Mo., Dec. 2; (1865) Lincoln to on violence in Mo., Jan. 15

Doe R., Tenn.: (1861) pro-unionists seized, Nov. 18

"Dog tags": (1864) used at Cold Harbor, June 1

Dog Walk (or Dry Ridge, Chesser's Store), Ky.: (1862) act., Oct. 9

Dogwood Gap, W. Va.: (1861) Conf. troops withdraw toward, Sept. 10

Donaldsonville, La.: (1862) Fed. naval bomb. of, Aug. 9, 10; Fed. exped. to, Sept. 21; eng., Oct. 4; capt. by Fed., Oct. 25; (1863) Conf. att., June 28; eng., July 12; sk., July 13; sk., Sept. 23; (1864) sk., Feb. 8; aff., July 31; Sept. 4; (1865) Fed. sc. from, Jan. 19; Fed. exped. from, Feb. 14; Fed. sc., Mar. 23

Donelson, Ft., Tenn.: (1861) Lloyd Tilghman, Conf., commands, Nov. 21; (1862) Ft. Henry force transfers to, Feb. 6; recon. by Grant, Feb. 7; threat to develops, Feb. 8; Gideon Pillow assumes Conf. command, Feb. 9; Grant builds up army, Feb. 10; Feds. begin march to, Feb. 11; Feds. prepare to attack, Feb. 12; Fed. att. and siege, Feb. 13; Fed. gunboat att., Feb. 14; weather, Feb. 13, 14; Conf. counteroffensive, Feb. 15; surrender of by Confs., Feb. 16; casualty lists, Feb. 20; victory aftermath, Feb. 25; Grant ordered from, Mar. 1; Grant accused of misconduct, Mar. 3; Mar. 11; Grant exonerated, Mar. 15; Apr. 25; sks., Aug. 23, 25; Fed. exped. from, Sept. 5; oper. around, Sept. 18; Fed. exped. from, Oct. 22; (1863) sk., Jan. 2; Forrest attacks, Feb. 3; sk., July 29; aff., Sept. 18; (1864) sk., Oct. 11

Doniphan, Mo.: (1861) Fed. exped. from, Nov. 13; (1862) sk., Apr. 1; (1863) Fed. sc. to, Mar. 19; sk., June 1; Fed. exped. to, Oct 26; (1864) Price's exped., aff., Sept. 19

Doolan's Farm, Va.: (1861) Fed. foragers capt., Nov. 16

Dorchester, Mass.: (1861) votes $20,000 for war, May 6

Double Br., Tenn.: (1862) sk., Nov. 18

Double Brs. over Flint R., Ga.: (1865) sk., Apr. 18

Doubtful Canyon, N. Mex. Terr.: (1864) sk., May 4

Douglas, Stephen A. (F): (1860) defeated in pres. elect., Nov. 6; named to Sen. Committee of Thirteen, Dec. 20; (1861) calls on Lincoln, Feb. 23; talks with Lincoln, Feb. 27; at Lincoln's inauguration, Mar. 4; pledges support of Union, Apr. 14; pro-Union speech to Ill. leg., Apr. 25; death, June 3; funeral, June 7

Douglas, Camp, Chicago, Ill.: (1864) conspiracy to free prisoners, Nov. 6

Douglas, Camp, Ut. Terr.: (1863) Fed. exped. against Inds., Apr. 11; May 5

Douglas Co., Mo.: (1862) Fed. sc. through, Mar. 4; (1864) Fed. sc., June 5

Douglas Ldg., Ark.: (1865) eng., Feb. 22

Douglas' Plantation, Ark.: (1865) Fed. sc. to, Feb. 21

Dove Cr., Concho R., Ark.: (1865) act., Jan. 8

Dover, Ark.: (1864) sk., Mar. 25

Dover, Del.: (1861) convention urges recognition of Confederacy, June 27

Dover, Mo.: (1864) sk., Sept. 10

Dover, N.C.: (1863) sc. to, June 17

Dover, Tenn. (*See also* Donelson, Ft.): (1862) Ft. Donelson near, Feb. 7; Grant's army near, Feb. 12; Conf. genls. confer at, Feb. 15; surrender of Ft. Donelson, Feb. 16; (1863) sk., Jan. 31

Dover, Va.: (1863) sk., June 22

Dover Rd., N.C.: (1863) Fed. recon., Jan. 27

Dover Swamp, N.C.: (1865) Fed. advance, Mar. 7

Dudley Lake, Ark.: (1864) sk., Dec. 16

Duffie, Alfred Napoleon Alexander, "Nattie" (F): (1863) on Averell exped., Nov. 3, 7

Duffield's Station, W. Va.: (1864) sks., June 29, Aug. 27; aff., Oct. 14

Dug Fd. near Jonesborough, Mo.: (1863) sk., Oct. 12

Dug Gap, Ga.: (1864) demon., May 8

Dug Springs, Mo.: (1861) sks., July 25, Aug. 2; Lyon falls back, Aug. 5

Duguidsville, Va.: (1865) sk., Mar. 8

Duke, Basil (C): (1863) captures Mt. Sterling, Ky., Mar. 22; sk., Danville, Ky., Mar. 24; sk., Dutton's Hill, Ky., Mar. 30

Dukedom, Tenn.: (1864) sk., Feb. 28

Dumfries, Va.: (1862) Johnston withdraws, Mar. 7; Fed. recon. to, Mar. 20; Fed. pickets capt., Dec. 2; sks., Dec. 12, 27; (1863) affs., Mar. 15, 29; sk., May 17

Dumfries Cr., Va.: (1861) Conf. schooner burned, Oct. 11

"Dummy" ironclads: (1863) goes past Vicksburg, Feb. 26, Mar. 9

Dunbar's Plantation near Bayou Vidal, La.: (1863) sks., Apr. 7, 15

Duncan, Ft., Tex.: (1861) surrendered by Feds., Mar. 20

Duncanville, S.C.: (1865) sk., Feb. 5

Dunkard Church at Antietam: (1862) Sept. 17

Dunklin Co., Mo.: (1862) Fed. sc. in, Aug. 20; (1865) Fed. exped., Mar. 3

Dunksburg, Mo.: (1864) aff. near, June 27

Dunlap, Tenn.: (1863) sk., Oct. 2

Dunn's Bayou, La.: (1864) eng., May 5

Du Pont, Samuel Francis (F): (1861) commands South Atlantic Blockading Squad., Sept. 18; Sept. 19; on Port Royal exped., Oct. 17; combined command Port Royal exped., Oct. 29; Bat. of Port Royal Sound, Nov. 7; (1863) att. on Charleston, Apr. 7; Lincoln orders to hold position, Apr. 13; relieved of command, July 6; (1865) death of, June 23

Du Pont Powder Works: (1861) powder seized by Feds., June 5

Durham Station, N.C.: (1865) Johnston-Sherman meeting, Apr. 17, 18

Durhamville, Tenn.: (1862) Fed. exped. to, Sept. 28

Dutch Cr., Ark.: (1863) sc. to, Dec. 9

Dutch Cr., Va.: (1864) act., Aug. 13

Dutch Gap, Va.: (1863) *Commodore Barney* damaged near, Aug. 5; (1865) Butler's explosion at fails, Jan. 1

Dutch Hollow, Mo.: *See* Wet Glaize, Mo.

Dutch Mills, Ark.: (1864) sk., Apr. 14

Duties, Fed.: (1864) Cong. raises, Apr. 29

Dutton's Hill, Ky.: (1863) sk., Mar. 30

Dyersburg, Tenn.: (1862) sks., Aug. 7, 18

Dyer's Fd., Ga.: (1863) sk., Sept. 18

Eads, James Buchanan: (1861) U.S. orders ironclads from, Aug. 7

Eagle I., N.C.: (1865) sk., Feb. 21

Eagle Pass, Tex.: (1864) aff., June 19

Eagleport, O.: (1863) sk. (Morgan's raid), July 22

Eagleville, Tenn.: (1863) sks., Mar. 2, 31, Apr. 16; Fed. sc. to, May 3; sk., Dec. 7

Eagleville Pike, Tenn.: (1863) Fed. sc. on, June 10

Early, Jubal Anderson (C): (1863) Chancellorsville Camp., May 1; 2nd Fredericksburg, May 3, 4; Bat. of 2nd Winchester, June 14; moves on York, Pa., surrender of, June 26, 27, 28; Bat. of Gettysburg, July 1, 2; Mine Run Camp., Nov. 27; assigned command Shenandoah Valley Dist., Dec. 15; (1864) temporary command A. P. Hill's corps (Spotsylvania), May 8, 10, 12; Bat. of Cold Harbor, June 3; moves toward Burnside, June 6; to reinforce valley, June 11, 16; Hunter attacks at Lynchburg, June 18; pursues Hunter, June 19, 20, 23; reaches Staunton, June 26; heads into Shenandoah, Wash. aroused, June 28, 30; reaches Winchester, July 2; near Harper's Fy., July 3, 4; raid on Wash., July 5, 6, 7, 8, 9 (Bat. of Monocacy), 10, 11 (burns Blair home); sk. at Ft. Stevens, July 11; retreats from Washington, July 12, 13; crosses Potomac, July 14; at Leesburg, July 15; retreat, July 15, 16; near Berryville, July 17; sks., July 19, 20 (eng. at Stephenson's Depot); near Strasburg, July 22; sk. at Kernstown, July 23; 2nd Bat. of Kernstown, July 24; follows Feds., July 25, 26; rail wrecking, July 26, 27; troops cross Potomac, July 29; capture of Chambersburg, Pa., July 30; still threatens Feds., Aug. 1; Sheridan to oppose, Aug. 1; sk. at Hancock, Md., Aug. 2; McCausland escapes into W. Va., Aug. 3; sk. at Antietam Fd., Aug. 4; sks., Aug. 5; Fed. efforts against, Aug. 7; Sheridan to move toward, Aug. 9; moves near Winchester, Aug. 10, 11; entrenches along Cedar Cr., Aug. 12, 13; Sheridan withdraws, Aug. 14, 15, 16; follows Sheridan, Aug. 17, 18, 19, 20; att. on Sheridan, Aug. 21; demon. against Harper's Fy., Aug. 22; demon. against Sheridan, Aug. 23, 24; threatens invasion of Md., Pa., Aug. 25; divides force, Aug. 25; west of Opequon, Aug. 26; at Bunker Hill, Aug. 27; Sheridan advances, Aug. 28, 29, 30, Sept. 1; pressed to return troops to Lee, Sept. 2; Sheridan moves toward, Sept. 3; pulls army back, Sept. 4; sks. along Opequon Cr., Sept. 5; sks., Sept. 7; Lincoln's concern over valley, Sept. 12; Fed. pressure to defeat rises, Sept. 14; weakened, Sept. 16; advances against B. & O. R.R., Sept. 17; 3rd Bat. of Winchester or Opequon Cr., Sept. 18 (prelim.), 19 (bat.), 20 (aftermath); Bat. of Fisher's Hill, Sept. 21 (prelim.), 22, 23 (retreat); pulls out of valley, Sept. 24, 25; reorganizing, Sept. 26; criticism of, Sept. 26; act. against, Sept. 27, 28; reinforcments, ment., Sept. 29; at Fisher's Hill, Oct. 13; recon. of Sheridan's forces, Oct. 18; Bat. of Cedar Cr., Oct. 19, 20 (aftermath); moves toward Kernstown, Nov. 10; act. at Newtown or Middletown, Cedar Cr., and Ninevah, Nov. 12; troops detached from, Nov. 13; summary of Valley Camp., Nov. 13; troops to Richmond-Petersburg front, Dec. 19; (1865) troop strength, Feb. 27; Sheridan pursues, Mar. 1; defeat at Waynesborough, Mar. 2

Early Grove, Miss.: (1863) Fed. sc. to, Apr. 5

East, Dept. of the, Fed.: (1863) John E. Wool assumes command of, Jan. 12; John A. Dix assumes command of, July 18

East Branch Big Warrior R., Ala.: (1863) sk., May 1

East Macon, Ga.: (1864) sk., Nov. 20

Easton, Pa.: (1861) newspaper raid, Aug. 19

East Point, Ga.: (1864) Fed. recon. to, Aug. 19; Fed. demon., Aug. 26; sks., Aug. 30, Nov. 15

Eastport, Miss.: (1862) Fed. exped. to, Feb. 15; Grant to move to, Mar. 1; Fed. exped. to returns, Mar. 14; Fed. exped. to, Apr. 1; Fed. recon. to, Apr. 3; (1864) boat att. on Forrest, Oct. 10; (1865) Fed. recon. from to Iuka, Jan. 9; Fed. exped. from to Iuka, Feb. 17; Fed. exped. from, Feb. 19

Eastport, Tenn.: (1863) sk., Nov. 1

Eastport, U.S.S. (ironclad gunboat): (1864) destruction of ment., Apr. 15

East R. Br., Fla.: (1865) sk., Mar. 4

East Room of White House: (1861) "Frontier Guards" quartered in, Apr. 18; (1862) ball in, Feb. 5; (1864) Lincoln meets Grant in, Mar. 8; (1865) Lincoln's funeral in, Apr. 19

East Tennessee: *See* Tennessee

East Tennessee, Dept. of, Conf.: (1862) McCown assumes command of, Sept. 1; E. K. Smith resumes command of, Dec. 23; (1863) D. H. Maury assumes command of, Apr. 25; Buckner supersedes Maury, Apr. 27; Buckner assumes command of, May 12; merged into Dept. of Tenn. under Bragg, July 25; (1864) Buckner assumes command of, Apr. 12

East Tenn. and Ga. R.R.: (1863) Fed. raid on, Nov. 24

East Tenn. Camp. (*See also* Burnside, Ambrose E.; Knoxville Camp.): (1863) Aug. 16 (Burnside heads for east Tenn.), 20, 27, 28 (sk. at Jacksborough, Tenn.), 31 (sk. at Winter's Gap), Sept. 2, 5, 6, 7 (Cumberland Gap oper.), 8 (Limestone Station and Telford's Station), 9 (surrender of Cumberland Gap), 10, 11 (sk. near Greenville, Ky.), 12, 18, 20 (sk. Carter's Depot, act. at Zollicoffer, Tenn.), 22, 23, 25, 27, 28 (sk. at Jonesborough, Tenn.), Oct. 2 (sk. Greeneville, Tenn.), 5 (sk. Blue Springs, Tenn.), 6, 8, 9, 10, 11, 12, 14 (sk. Blountsville), 15, 19, Nov. 4 (Longstreet's corps detached from Army of Tenn.)

East Tenn., Southwestern Va. Camp., Fed. (*See also* Stoneman, George): (1864) exped. from Knoxville, Dec. 10, 12, 13, 14, 15, 16

Eatonton, Ga.: (1864) sk., Nov. 21

Eben Dodge (Fed. whaler): (1861) capt., Dec. 8

Ebenezer Church, Ala.: (1865) act., Apr. 1

Ebenezer Cr., Ga.: (1864) sk., Dec. 8

Echols, John (C): (1863) eng. at Droop Mt., Nov. 6

Eddyville, Ky.: (1861) exped. by Forrest to, Nov. 24; (1864) sk., Oct. 17

Edenburg, Va.: (1862) Apr. 1; sk., Apr. 2; (1863) Fed. exped. to, Nov. 15; (1864) sks., Sept. 23, Nov. 7; (1865) Fed. exped. to, Feb. 13; Fed. sc. to, Mar. 17, 20

Eden Station, Ga.: (1864) sk., Dec. 9

Edenton, N.C.: (1862) Feds. capture, Feb. 12; (1863) sk., Feb. 7; Fed. expeds. to, Aug. 11, Oct. 10

Edenton Rd., Va.: (1863) sks. on, Apr. 12, 24

Edgefield, Tenn.: (1862) Fed. exped. from, Nov. 26

Edgefield Junction, Tenn.: (1862) sk., Aug. 19; Fed. recon. toward, Nov. 15

Edina, Mo.: (1861) sk., Aug. 1

Edisto I., S.C.: (1862) occup. by Feds., Feb. 11; aff., Mar. 29; Feds. occupy, Apr. 5; sk., Apr. 19; (1863) sk., June 18

Edisto R. Br., S.C.: (1865) sk., Feb. 7

Edmondson Pike, Tenn.: (1862) sk. on, Dec. 25

Edmonton, Ky.: (1863) sk., June 7

Edwards' Fy., Md.: (1861) Rockville exped., June 10; occup. of, June 15; sks., June 18, July 29, Oct. 4; Ball's Bluff Camp., Oct. 20, 21 (bat.); (1862) sk., Sept. 3; (1863) sk., Aug. 27

Edward's Fy., Miss.: (1864) sk., Feb. 4

Edward's Station, Miss.: (1863) Pemberton near, May 12, 14, 15; Champion's Hill Bat., May 16; sks., June 10, July 1

Eel R., Calif.: (1861) Fed. sc. on (Ind.), May 23; (1864) Humboldt oper. (Fed., Ind.), Mar. 19, 27, 28

Eel R., Calif., north fork: (1864) Fed. sc. to, Sept. 1

Eel R., Calif., south fork: (1861) sk., July 21

Egypt, Miss.: (1864) eng., Dec. 28

Egypt Station, Miss.: (1864) sk., Feb. 19

Eighteenth Corps, U. S. Army: (1864) at Cold Harbor, June 1; to move on Petersburg, June 14; Conf. mine explodes, Aug. 5; Bat. of Ft. Harrison, Sept. 29

Eighth Corps, U. S. Army: (1864) Bat. of Cedar Cr., Oct. 19

Eighth Mass. Regiment: (1861) at Annapolis, Apr. 20

Eighth U. S. Colored Troops: (1864) Bat. of Olustee, Fla., Feb. 20

Eight Mile Cr. Br., Ala.: (1865) sk., Apr. 13

Eight Mile Post, Natchez and Liberty Rd., Miss.: (1864) sk., Sept., 6

Elba I., S.C.: (1862) Fed. recon. to, Mar. 7

Eldrod's Tanyard, DeKalb Co., Ala.: (1865) sk., Jan. 27

Election, presidential: *See* Presidential election

Elections in states, U.S.: (1862) Oct. 14; (1864) Oct. 11

Elections, mid-term, U.S.: (1862) congressional, Oct. 14; Democratic gains in, Nov. 4; Republican control of House, Nov. 4

Electoral College, U.S.: (1861) electoral vote, Feb. 4; (1865) Southern states denied representation in, Feb. 8

Electoral vote: (1860) pres. election, Nov. 6; (1861) Feb. 4; (1864) election, Nov. 8; (1865) official, Feb. 12

Elephants: (1862) Lincoln refuses offer of, Feb. 3

Eleven Points, Mo.: (1862) sks., June 1, Oct. 25

Eleven Points R., Ark.: (1865) Fed. exped. to, Jan. 24

Eleventh Army Corps, Fed.: (1863) Howard commands, Apr. 2; Bat. of Gettysburg, July 1; to aid Rosecrans, Sept. 23; in Nashville, Oct. 1

Eleventh Mass. Infantry: (1861) on White House grounds, June 29

Eleventh N. Y. Infantry: *See* New York Fire Zouaves

Elisha Dunbar (whaler): (1862) capt., burned by *Alabama,* Sept. 18

Elizabeth, W. Va.: (1863) sk., Oct. 27

Elizabeth City, N.C.: (1862) Feds. destroy "Mosquito" fleet, Feb. 10; sk., Dec. 27; (1863) Fed. exped. to, Oct. 10

Elizabeth Court House, W. Va.: (1863) sk., May 16

Elizabethtown, Ark.: (1863) sk., Oct. 1

Elizabethtown, Ky.: (1862) Morgan captures garrison, Dec. 27

Elk Cr., near Honey Springs, I.T.: (1863) cav. eng., July 17

Elk Cr., Neb. Terr.: (1864) sk., Oct. 7

Elk Ft., Tenn.: (1862) sk. (Carter's raid), Dec. 26

Elkhorn, Ark.: (1863) Fed. sc. from, Jan. 8

Elkhorn Tavern, Ark. (*See also* Pea Ridge): (1862) Bat. of, Mar. 7, 8; sk., Oct. 16

Elkin's Fy., Little Mo. R., Mo.: (1864) eng. (Camden exped.), Apr. 3

Elk Mt., W. Va.: (1862) sk., Mar. 19

Elk R., Ala.: (1862) oper., May 1

Elk R., Tenn.: (1862) sks., May 9, 20; (1863) sks., July 1, 2, Oct. 9

Elk R., W. Va.: (1863) sk., Aug. 27

Elk R. Br., Tenn.: (1863) sks., July 2, 14

Elk Run, Va.: (1862) Jackson leaves, Apr. 30; (1863) sk., Apr. 13

Elk Run Valley, Va.: (1862) Jackson leaves for, Apr. 18

Elkwater, W. Va.: (1861) Cheat Mt. Camp., Sept. 11, 12

Ellerson's Mill, Va. (*See also* Mechanicsville, Va.): (1862) June 26

Ellet, Charles Rivers (F): (1863) runs Vicksburg batteries, Feb. 2; captures Conf. vessels, Feb. 3; oper. on Miss. R., Feb. 10; capture of *Queen of the West*, Feb. 14

Ellidge's Mills, Ga.: (1864) Fed. sc. to, Feb. 18

Elliott's Salient, Petersburg Lines: (1864) mine, July 30

Ellis, John Willis (C): (1861) gov. calls N.C. General Assembly, Apr. 26

Ellis, U.S.S. (steamer): (1862) captures schooners, sinks, Nov. 23

Ellis' Br., Miss.: (1864) sk., Feb. 21

Ellis' Fd., Va.: (1862) Fed. exped. to, Dec. 30; (1863) sk., Dec. 3; (1864) affs., Jan. 12, 17, 22, Apr. 17

Ellistown, Miss.: (1864) sk., July 16

Ellisville, Miss.: (1863) sk., June 23

Ellsworth, Elmer Ephraim (F): (1861) Zouaves in Washington, May 2; Lincoln reviews troops, May 7; death of, May 24; funeral, Lincoln on, May 25; grief over death, May 26

Ellsworth, Ft., Kas.: (1865) Fed. sc. from, Jan. 7

Elma, C.S.A. (schooner): (1862) burned, Aug. 12

Elm Cr., Tex.: (1864) sk. on (Ind. oper.), Oct. 13

Elm Springs, Ark.: (1862) Van Dorn beyond, Mar. 5; (1863) sk., July 30

Eltham's Ldg., Va.: (1862) eng., May 7

Ely, Alfred (F): (1861) capture, release of, Dec. 27

Ely's Fd., Va.: (1863) sks., May 2, Dec. 1; (1864) affs., Jan. 13, 17, Feb. 28

Elyton, Ala.: (1865) sks., Mar. 7, 28

Elzey, Arnold (C): (1863) commands Dept. of Richmond, Apr. 1

Emancipation (*See also* Slavery; Slaves; Thirteenth Amendment): (1861) Frémont's unauthorized emancipation proclamation, Aug. 30; Mrs. Frémont's intercession with Lincoln, Sept. 10, 12; Lincoln modifies Frémont's eman. proc., Sept. 12; Lincoln proposes compensated eman. for Del., Nov. 26; (1862) discussed in Cong., Jan. 9; Lincoln calls for by states, Mar. 6; Lincoln on, Mar. 14; Cong. discusses, Mar. 24; Lincoln to Greeley on, Mar. 24; Sen. resolution re, Apr. 2; in D.C., Apr. 3, 11, 16; Hunter's eman. proc., disavowal of by Lincoln, Apr. 12, May 9, 19; Lincoln appeals for, May 19; Lincoln's Eman. Proc. drafts, June 18; Lincoln urges congressmen to support, July 12; Lincoln's message to Cong. on, July 14; Cong. reacts to Lincoln's plan for, July 14; Lincoln approves Confiscation Act, July 17; 1st draft of Eman. Proc., July 22; Lincoln reads Eman. Proc. to Cabinet, July 22; Lincoln prepares preliminary Eman. Proc., Sept. 20; preliminary Eman. Proc. announced, Sept. 22; word of emancipation spreading, Sept. 23; Richmond *Whig* on, Oct. 1; Lincoln will not retract, Nov. 21; Lincoln on in State of Union message, Dec. 1; Lincoln prepares final draft of Eman. Proc., Dec. 30; Lincoln discusses final draft of Eman. Proc. with Cabinet, Dec. 31; (1863) final Eman. Proc. issued, Jan. 1; celebrations over issuance, Jan. 2; Southern reaction to, Jan. 7; Lincoln on Eman. Proc., Jan. 8; Davis on Eman. Proc., Jan. 12; Conf. Cong. debates Eman. Proc., Jan. 19; ratification of Eman. Proc. by mass meeting, Jan. 28; British support of Eman. Proc., Feb. 19; Cherokees abolish slavery, Feb. 26; emancipation in W. Va., Mar. 26; Lincoln on, Aug. 5, Sept. 2, Nov. 5, Dec. 20; Fed. Bureau of proposed, Dec. 17; (1864) in Ark., Jan. 19, 20; in Tenn., Jan. 21; Lincoln favors hiring freed slaves, Jan. 23; Lincoln signs bill compensating Fed. owners, Feb. 24; Lincoln on, Mar. 7; in Ark., Mar. 18; Lincoln on, Apr. 4; in La., Apr. 6, May 11; July 23; Sept. 5; U. S. Sen. passes joint resolution abolishing slavery, Apr. 8; ment., May 31; House rejects anti-slavery amendment, June 15; in Wade-Davis bill, July 4; Lincoln on Wade-Davis pocket veto, July 8; in Md., Oct. 13; (1865) in Tenn., Jan. 9, Feb. 22; passage of Thirteenth Amendment, Jan. 31; Lincoln proposes compensated emancipation if South ceases resistance, Feb. 5; of Negro soldiers' wives, Mar. 3; in Mo., June 6; on Sept. 21 by Chickasaws, Choctaws passed, Sept. 14; Thirteenth Amendment declared in effect, Dec. 18

Emancipation Proclamation: *See* Emancipation

Eminence, Mo.: (1862) sk., June 17

Emma, U.S. (steamer): (1862) plundered, Sept. 23; (1864) capt., May 1

Emmitsburg, Md.: (1862) Stuart's Chambersburg raid, Oct. 11; (1863) Gettysburg Camp., June 29; cav. sk. near, July 4; (1864) aff., July 30

Emmitsburg Rd., Pa.: (1863) Bat. of Gettysburg, July 2, 3

Emory, William Hemsley (F): (1861) evacuates Ft. Washita, I.T., Apr. 30; marches north, May 4; troops join, May 9; (1864) Bat. of Sabine Crossroads, Apr. 8

Enabling Acts, U.S.: (1864) for Nev., Colo., Mar 21; for Neb. Terr., Apr. 19

Enfield rifles: (1862) ment., Aug. 3

England: *See* Great Britain

English Turn, Miss. R.: (1862) eng., Apr. 25

Ennis' Cross Roads, S.C.: (1865) sk., Jan. 27

Enrica: See C.S.S. *Alabama*

Enrollment Act: (1864) some exemption clauses repealed, July 4

Enterprise, Mo.: (1863) sk., Sept. 15; (1864) sk., Aug. 7

Episcopal Church: *See* Protestant Episcopal Church

Ericsson, John (F): (1861) Oct. 4; (1862) *Monitor* launched, Jan. 30

Erie, Lake: (1864) plot to free Johnson I. prisoners, Sept. 19; Conf. capture of Fed. ships, Sept. 19

Erlanger, Emil: (1863) Conf. loan placed through, Jan. 29

Erlanger, House of: (1863) loan to C.S.A., Mar. 18

"Erring sisters": (1860) Nov. 9

Escambia R., Fla.: (1865) sk., Mar. 25

Esperanza, Ft.: (1863) capt., Nov. 22

Essex, U.S.S.: (1862) hit at Ft. Henry, Feb. 6; attacks C.S.S. *Arkansas*, Aug. 6; duels Port Hudson batteries, Sept. 7

Estenaula, Tenn.: (1863) sk., Dec. 24

Estill Springs, Tenn.: (1863) sk., July 2

Ethan Allen, U.S.S.: (1863) destroys salt works, Jan. 9

Etna, Mo.: (1861) sk., July 22

Etowah R., Ga.: (1864) Johnston crosses, May 19, 20; Sherman crosses, May 23; ment., May 24; ment., Nov. 11

Eudora Church, Ark.: (1864) sk., May 9

Eugene (Fed. steamer): (1862) guerrilla att. on, Sept. 23

Eugenia Smith (British schooner): (1861) Conf. agent seized on, Dec. 7

Eunice, Ark.: (1862) Fed. exped. to, Aug. 28; (1863) burned, June 14

Eureka, Boone Co., Mo.: (1862) Fed. exped. to, Sept. 23

Europe: (1861) and Conf. recognition, June 17; (1862) Jan. 1

Evans, Nathan George (Shanks) (C): (1861) Bat. of 1st Bull Run, July 21; Ball's Bluff Camp., Oct. 20; Bat. of Ball's Bluff, Oct. 21; (1862) eng. of Secessionville, S.C., June 16

Evans' I., Tenn.: (1865) Fed. exped. to, Jan. 25

Evansport, Va.: (1862) Johnston pulls out from, Mar. 7

Evansville, Ind.: (1862) Conf. raid near, July 18

Evening Shade, Ark.: (1863) sk., Oct. 7

Everett, Edward (F): (1860) vice-pres. candidate, Constitutional Union, Nov. 6; (1863) speaks at Gettysburg, Nov. 19; praises Gettysburg Address, Nov. 20; (1865) death of, Jan. 15

Evergreen, Ala.: (1865) aff., Mar. 24

Ewell, Richard Stoddert (C): (1862) joins Jackson in Shenandoah, May 20; Lincoln's orders to capture, May 24; Bat. of 1st Winchester, May 25; Bat. of Cross Keys, June 8; Bat. of Port Republic, June 9; (1863) commands corps A.N.Va., May 30; Gettysburg Camp., June 4, 8, 10, 12 (in Shenandoah), 13 (occupies Berryville), 14, 15 (Bat. of 2nd Winchester), 19, 25, 28, 30, July 1, 2, 3 (Bat. of Gettysburg); cleanup operations, July 21; att. at Manassas Gap, July 23; (1864) in van of Lee's move, May 4; Bat. of Wilderness, May 5, 6; Bat. of Spotsylvania, May 8, 10, 12, 18, 19; assigned command of Dept. of Richmond, June 13; (1865) eng. at Sayler's Cr., Va., Apr. 6

Ewing, Thomas, Jr. (F): (1863) issues General Orders No. 11, Aug 25; (1864) evacuates Ft. Davidson, Pilot Knob, Mo., Sept. 27

Exchange, U.S.S.: (1864) aff. with Greene's raiders, June 1

Exchange Hotel, Montgomery, Ala.: (1861) Feb. 16

Executions: (1862) Nathaniel Gordon, Feb. 21; Lincoln requests Sioux uprising records, Nov. 10; Lincoln changes date of Indians' execution, Dec. 16; execution of Inds., Dec. 26; (1863) Lincoln commutes death sentence, Apr. 28; June 9; (1864) Jan. 7; David Dodd, Jan. 8; Lincoln suspends executions, Jan. 20; Lincoln mitigates death sentences, Feb. 26; (1865) execu-

tion of Lincoln conspirators, July 7; execution of Henry Wirz, Nov. 10;
R. C. Kennedy, Nov. 25

Ex parte Merryman: *See* Merryman, John

Ex parte Milligan: *See* Milligan, *ex parte*

Explosions: (1861) Columbus, Ky., Nov. 11; (1862) New Orleans, Mar. 9;
(1863) Richmond, Mar. 13; C.S.S. *Chattahoochee,* May 27; Alexandria, Va.,
June 9; City Point, Aug. 9; (1864) Wash. Arsenal, June 17; (1865) Ft.
Fisher, Jan. 16; Mobile, May 25; Chattanooga, June 9

Fagan, James Fleming: (1864) Price's Mo. raid, Oct. 22

Fagan's Fd. on Saline R., Ark.: (1864) Fed. exped. to, Nov. 17

Fairburn, Ga.: (1864) sk., Aug. 15; Kilpatrick's Fed. raid to, Aug. 16; act.,
Aug. 27; Fed. armies near, Aug. 28; sk., Oct. 2

Fairfax Court House, Va.: (1861) sk., June 1, July 17; McDowell halts
at, July 17; McDowell moves from, July 18 to 1st Bull Run; sk., Nov.
27; Fed. sc. to, Dec. 24; (1862) McClellan holds conference, Mar. 13;
Sept. 1; sk., Sept. 2; Fed. recon. from, Oct. 8; (1863) sks., Jan. 9, 26;
Mosby captures Gen. Stoughton, Mar. 8; aff., Mar. 9; Fed. sc. to, May 27;
sk. on Lawyer's Rd., June 4; Hooker's Fed. army at, June 16; sk., June 27;
Mosby's oper., July 28; exped. to, Aug. 4; Mosby captures wagon train,
Aug. 6; sk. at Coyle's Tavern, Aug. 24; (1865) Fed. scs. from, Feb. 6,
15, Apr. 8

Fairfax Station, Va.: (1864) sks., Aug. 8, Nov. 26

Fairfield, N.C.: (1864) aff., Feb. 16

Fairfield, Pa.: (1863) sk., June 30, July 5

Fairfield, Tenn.: (1863) sk., June 27

Fairfield Gap, Pa.: (1863) cav. sk., July 4

Fair Gardens (or Kelly's Fd.), Tenn.: (1864) eng., Jan. 27

Fair Grounds, Ky.: (1862) sk., Oct. 6

Fairmont, W. Va.: (1863) sk., Jones' raid, Apr. 29

Fairmount, Ga.: (1864) sk., Aug. 14

Fair Oaks, Va.: (1862) sk., May 30; Bat. of (or Seven Pines), May 31, June 1;
Pres. Davis writes on Bat. of, June 1; armies rest after bat., June 2; sks.,
June 8, 18, 27; eng., June 29; (1864) eng., Oct. 27

Fair Oaks Station, Va.: (1862) sk., June 21

Fairview, Ark.: (1862) sk., June 7; Fed. sc. to, June 16; (1864) Fed. sc. to,
Mar. 25; Fed. exped. to, Aug. 27

Falling Cr., N.C.: (1865) sk., Mar. 17, 20

Falling Waters, Md.: (1863) act., July 10

Falling Waters, W. Va.: (1861) sk., July 2; (1863) sk., July 14; (1864) sks.,
July 24, 26

Falls Church, Va.: (1861) balloon observations, June 23; act., Nov. 18;
(1862) sks., Sept. 2, 3; (1863) sk., Aug. 16; (1864) Fed. sc. from, July 18

Falmouth, Ky.: (1862) sk., Sept. 17

Falmouth, Va. (*See also* Fredericksburg): (1862) Burnside at, Aug. 27; Sumner's
Fed. division arrives, Nov. 17; Burnside at, Nov. 19; exped. from, Dec.
30; (1863) Fed. sc. to, Feb. 27; Lincoln reviews troops, Apr. 8; A. of P.
moves out from, Apr. 27; A. of P. at, June 3; sks., Nov. 4, 6

act passed, Feb. 20; Erlanger loan to, Mar. 18; act for funding, issuing treasury notes, Mar. 23; bonds, stock issued, Apr. 27; (1864) Cong. votes taxes, June 14

Financing the war, U.S. (*See also* Taxes, Fed.): (1861) $25 million loan, Feb. 8; $10 million loan, Mar. 2; citizen contributions to war, May 7; Fed. govt. to pay war costs, June 6; state indemnification act, July 27; first income tax law, Aug. 2; Lincoln signs income tax bill, tariff increases, Aug. 5; (1862) Lincoln signs loan and treasury bill, Feb. 26; Lincoln signs revised income tax bill, July 1; (1863) Cong. authorizes loan, Mar. 3; Jay Cooke named agent for U.S. bond sales, Mar. 3; bonds authorized, Mar. 3; Lincoln signs act raising taxes, duties, June 30

Finegan, Joseph (C): (1864) Bat. of Olustee, Fla., Feb. 20

Finegan, Camp, Fla.: (1864) sks., Feb. 8, May 25

Fingal, C.S. (*See also* C.S.S. *Atlanta*): (1861) arrives in Savannah, Nov. 12

Fire rafts: (1863) Davis recommends use of, Apr. 22

First Army Corps, Fed.: (1862) in Dept. of the Rappahannock, Apr. 4; Reynolds assumes command of, Sept. 29; (1863) Bat. of Gettysburg, July 1

First Bull Run: *See* Bull Run, 1st Bat. of

First Fire Zouaves: *See* New York Fire Zouaves

First Manassas, Bat. of: *See* Bull Run, 1st Bat. of

First shot of war: (1861) shots fired at Ft. Barrancas, Jan. 8; *Star of the West* incident, Jan. 9; first shot at Sumter, Apr. 12

First S. C. Inf., Conf.: (1861) captures train at Vienna, Va., June 17

First S. C. Volunteers (African descent) (*See also* S. C. Volunteer Infantry): (1862) in Ga. and Fla. exped., Nov. 3

Fishburn's Plantation, S.C.: (1865) act., Feb. 6

Fisher, Ft., N.C.: (1864) plans to reduce, Oct. 12; exped. against, Dec. 7; Fed. fleet sails for, Dec. 18; 1st Fed. exped. against, and powder boat att. on, Dec. 23; bomb. of, Dec. 24, 25; aftermath, Dec. 28, 29; (1865) 2nd exped. against, Jan. 3, 4 (embarking); ment., Jan. 6; Butler removed, Jan. 7; Fed. fleet, troops rendezvous, Jan. 8; Fed. fleet delayed, Jan. 10; Fed. fleet arrives, Jan. 12; 2nd att. on, Jan. 13, 14; capt., Jan. 15; magazine explodes, Jan. 16; Davis urges Bragg to retake, Jan. 16; news of fall spreads, Jan. 17; Schofield's advance arrives at, Feb. 9

Fisher, Ft., Va.: (1865) act., Mar. 25

Fisheries, Atlantic: (1862) Lincoln approves act on, Mar. 15

Fisher's Hill, Va.: (1863) sk., Apr. 22; (1864) Confs. at, Sept. 20; sk., Sept. 21; Bat. of, Sept. 22; aftermath, Sept. 23; sk. near at Brock's Gap, Oct. 6; eng. near at Tom's Brook, Oct. 9; Bat. of Cedar Cr., Oct. 19; sk., Oct. 20

Fish fry at Five Forks: (1865) Apr. 1

Fishing Cr., Ky.: (1861) sk., Dec. 8; (1862) sk., Jan. 8; Bat. of (also known as Mill Springs, Logan's Cross Roads, Somerset, or Beech Grove), Jan. 19

Fish Lake, Mo.: (1861) sk., Aug. 20

Fitzhugh's Crossing, Va.: *See* Pollock's Mill Cr.

Fitzpatrick, Benjamin (C): (1861) resigns from U. S. Sen., Jan. 21

Five Civilized Indian Tribes: (1861) influenced by Confs., Apr. 30

Five Forks, Va.: (1865) Conf. troops sent to, Mar. 29; sk. near, Mar. 30; Pickett pulls back toward, Mar. 31; Bat. of, Apr. 1

Florida R.R.: (1864) Fed. raid on, Aug. 15

Flour: (1861) cost of, Nov. 16; (1863) cost of in Charleston, Feb. 25

Flour Bluffs, Tex.: (1862) oper. at, Sept. 13

Floyd, John Buchanan (C): (1860) opposes secession, Nov. 9; sends Buell
to Charleston, instructs Anderson, Dec. 11; opposes Sumter shift, Dec. 26;
favors removing Fed. force from Charleston Harbor, Dec. 27; opposes
Stanton on Sumter, Dec. 28: resigns as U. S. Sec. of War, Dec. 29;
charges against, Dec. 29; (1861) orders guns to Southern forts, Jan. 3;
resignation ment., Jan. 18; commands Conf. force in W. Va., Aug. 11;
eng. Carnifix Fy., Sept. 10; disagrees with Gen. Wise, Sept. 25; (1862)
sent orders, Feb. 7; assumes command at Donelson, Feb. 13; Conf. counteroffensive at Donelson, Feb. 15; flees, Feb. 15, 16; arrives at Nashville, Feb.
17; relieved from command, Mar. 11; (1863) death of, Aug. 26

Floyd Co., Ky.: (1862) sk., Dec. 4

Folly I., S.C: (1863) sk., Apr. 10

Fontaine, Mary A. (C): (1865) on fall of Richmond, Apr. 3

Food, hoarding of: (1863) Apr. 3

"Foot Cavalry": *See* Jackson, Thomas Jonathan

Foote, Andrew Hull (F): (1861) to command western gunboat forces, Aug. 26;
(1862) att. on Ft. Henry, Feb. 6; readies gunboats for Ft. Donelson att.,
Feb. 11; wounded, Feb. 14; still ailing, June 6; (1863) death of, June 26

Foote, Henry S. (C): (1863) critical of Davis, Dec. 8

Ford, John S. (RIP, "Rest in Peace" Ford): (1865) sks. at Palmito Ranch, Tex.,
May 12, 13

Ford's Mill, near New Berne, N.C.: (1863) aff., Oct. 30

Ford's Theatre: (1865) assassination of Lincoln, Apr. 14; rented by U.S. govt.,
July 24

Foreign relations, U.S. (*See also* France; Great Britain; "Laird Rams"; Trent
Affair; Seward, William H.): (1863) Lincoln on, Dec. 8

Forest Hill (or Timberville), Va.: (1864) sk., Sept. 24

Forge Br., Va.: (1862) Stuart attempts to cross, June 13; Stuart rebuilds, June
14; Conf. recon. toward, Aug. 17

Forked Deer Cr., Miss.: (1863) sk., Oct. 3

Forked Deer R., Tenn.: (1862) Conf. sc. on, Apr. 26; sk. on, Dec. 20; (1863)
sks. on, July 13, 15

Forks of Beaver, Ky.: (1864) sk., Mar. 31

Forrest, Nathan Bedford (C): (1861) exped. to Caseyville, Eddyville, Ky., Nov.
24; (1862) escapes from Ft. Donelson, Feb. 16; arrives at Nashville, Feb.
17; retreat from Nashville, Feb. 24; captures Murfreesboro, Tenn., July 13;
repulsed on Gallatin Pike, Oct. 20; sent to cut Grant's communications,
Dec. 11; moves into west Tenn. to harass Grant, Dec. 15, 16; defeats
Fed. cav. at Lexington, Dec. 18; ment. by Davis, Dec. 18; att. on r.r. near
Jackson, Dec. 19, 20; withdraws, Dec. 26; eng. at Parker's Store, Dec. 31;
(1863) completes camp., Jan. 2; att. on Ft. Donelson, Feb. 3; Fed. inf.
surrenders near Spring Hill, Tenn., Mar. 4; raids Brentwood, Franklin,
Tenn., Mar. 25; Streight surrenders to, May 3; Lincoln mentions, May
27; act. at Triune, Tenn., June 11; Bat. of Chickamauga, Sept. 19; Davis
approves Miss., Tenn., campaigning, Oct. 29; commands west Tenn., Nov.

14; oper. against Memphis and Charleston R.R., Nov. 28; (1864) defeats W. S. Smith, Jan. 10; defeat of W. S. Smith, Feb. 21; eng. of Okolona, Miss., Feb. 22; harassment of Smith, Feb. 26; exped. into Ky., west Tenn., Mar. 16; capture of Union City, Tenn., Mar. 24; att. on Paducah, Ky., Mar. 25; sk. at Columbus, Ky., Mar. 27; sk. at Bolivar, Tenn., Mar. 29; sks. near Raleigh, Tenn., Apr. 3, 9; sk. near Columbus, Ky., Apr. 11; capture of Ft. Pillow, Tenn., Apr. 12; sk., Columbus, Ky., Apr. 13; sk. at Paducah, Ky., Apr. 14; Sturgis' exped. against, June 1, 4, 7; Bat. of Brice's Cross Roads, June 10; follows Sturgis' retreat, June 12; exped. under A. J. Smith goes after, July 5, 7, 10, 13, 14 (Bat. of Tupelo), 15 (follows Smith's retreat), 16, 23, Aug. 13 (sk. at Hurricane Cr., Miss.), 14 (sk. at Lamar, Miss.); temporary occup. of Memphis, Aug. 21; raid into north Ala. and middle Tenn., Sept. 16, 20, 21, 23, 24 (captures Athens), 25, 26, 27, 29, Oct. 1, 2, 10 (boat att. on); new raid into Tenn. Oct. 19, 22 (at Jackson), 28 (on Tenn. R.), 30 (near Fts. Heiman and Henry), 30, 31 (at Ft. Heiman, puts together "navy"), Nov. 1, 2, 3 (att. on gunboats), 4 (eng. at Johnsonville, Tenn.), 9 (moves toward Corinth), 14, 16 (joins Hood), 21; sk. at Columbia, Tenn., Nov. 24; rumor about, Nov. 27; crosses Duck R., Nov. 28; eng. at Spring Hill, Nov. 29; demon. against Murfreesboro, Dec. 7; (1865) assumes command Dist. of Miss., east La., west Tenn., Jan. 24; sk., Montevallo, Ala., Mar. 30; Selma Camp., Mar. 22, 28, 30, 31, Apr. 1, 2 (fall of Selma); act. at Northport, Apr. 3; sk. at Fike's Fy., Ala., Apr. 7

Forsyth, John (C): (1861) Conf. commissioner to Wash., Feb. 27, Mar. 8; (1865) Davis to, Feb. 21

Forsyth, Mo.: (1861) Fed. exped. to, July 20; sk., July 22; (1862) sk., Aug. 4; Fed. sc. from, Aug. 7; (1863) Fed. sc. from, Dec. 26; (1864) Fed. sc. from, June 5

Fort Frederick, Md.: (1861) sk., Dec. 25

Fort Furnace, Va.: (1862) sk., July 1

Fort Ridgely, Minn.: (1862) Sioux uprising, Aug. 17, 18, 19, 20, 22; Sibley relieves, Aug. 28

Forts: *See* under names except for communities with prefix "Fort"

Fort Scott, Kas.: *See* Scott, Ft., Kas.

Fort Smith, Ark.: (1861) seized by state troops, Apr. 23; (1862) Fed. recon. toward, Nov. 20; (1863) sks., Mar. 5, May 15; Fed. occup. of, Sept. 1: (1864) act. near, July 27, 31; sks., Sept. 1, 11; Fed. exped. to, Sept. 25; sk., Oct. 14; Fed. expeds. to, Nov. 5; sk., Dec 24; (1865) Indian treaty with U.S., Sept. 14

Forty-eighth Pennsylvania Regt., Fed.: (1864) Petersburg Mine, July 30

Forty Hills, Miss.: (1863) sk., May 3

"Forward to Richmond": (1861) Horace Greeley, July 14; in N. Y. *Tribune,* July 16; July 29

Foster, John Gray (F): (1862) captures Kinston, N.C., exped. from New Berne, Dec. 14, 15; (1863) assumes command Dept. of Va. and N.C., July 18; superseded by Butler, Nov. 11; Dept of the O. command, Dec. 9; (1864) superseded, Feb. 9; assumes command Dept. of the South, May 26; Sherman contacts at Savannah, Dec. 13; given command at Savannah, Dec. 13; (1865) Gillmore supersedes, Dept. of the South, Feb. 9

Foster's Ldg., Ohio R.: (1862) *Emma* plundered at, Sept. 23

Foster's Mills, N.C.: (1863) Fed. exped. to, July 26

Foster's Plantation, Va.: (1864) sk., May 18

Fosterville, Tenn.: (1863) sks., June 25, 27, Oct. 6

Fouché-le-Faix Mts., Ark.: (1863) sk., Nov. 11

Fouche Springs, Tenn.: (1864) sk., Nov. 23

Fountain Dale, Pa.: (1863) sk., June 28 (Gettysburg Camp.)

Four Mile, Mo.: (1862) sk., Aug. 23

Four-Mile Cr., Va.: (1864) acts., June 30, July 16, 28, Aug. 13; comb., Oct. 7

Fourteen Mile Cr., I.T.: (1863) sk., Oct. 30

Fourteen Mile Cr., Miss.: (1863) sk., May 12

Fourteenth Corps, U. S. Army: (1863) under Geo. H. Thomas, Jan. 9; (1864) part of Sheridan's left wing, Nov. 9; Sherman rides with, Nov. 16; on Augusta R.R., Dec. 3

Fourth Corps, U. S. Army: (1863) discontinued, Aug. 1; (1864) heads toward Pulaski, Tenn., Oct. 30, Nov. 3

Fourth Mass. Inf.: (1861) at Ft. Monroe, Apr. 20

Fourth Mich. Cav.: (1865) capture of Jefferson Davis, May 10

Fox, E. C. (C): (1864) foils Dahlgren's Richmond raid, Mar. 2

Fox, Gustavus Vasa (F): (1861) Lincoln confers with on Sumter, Mar. 13; plan for provisioning Sumter, Mar. 15; visits Sumter, Mar. 21; informed Sumter to be resupplied, Apr. 4; sails for Sumter, Apr. 9; named Asst. Sec. of Navy, Aug. 1

Fox Cr., Mo.: (1862) sk., Mar. 7

Fox Springs, Ky.: (1863) sk., June 15

Fox's Fd., Va.: (1863) sk., Oct. 13

Fox's Gap, Md.: (1862) Sept. 14

Foy's Plantation, N.C.: (1862) Apr. 7

Fractional currency: *See* Currency

France: (1861) Dayton Fed. minister to, Mar. 18; Conf. commissioner to named, Aug. 24; Dec. 26; (1862) Louis Napoleon on neutrality, Jan. 27; and fisheries act, Mar. 15; Napoleon III receives Conf. commissioner, July 16; (1863) offer of mediation, Feb. 3, 6; C.S.S. *Rappahannock* sails for, Nov. 25; (1865) intervention in North America, Feb. 3

Frankford, W. Va.: (1864) sk., July 4

Frankfort, Ky.: (1861) U.S. flag raised, Sept. 2; (1862) reports of Morgan's raid, July 12; E. K. Smith occupies, Sept. 3; Hawes inaugurated Conf. gov., Oct. 4; Smith in, Oct. 5; Confs. in, Oct. 7, 8; (1863) Dem. convention broken up, Feb. 18; (1864) Morgan demon. on, June 10

Frankfort, Mo.: (1862) sk., June 4

Frankfort, W. Va.: (1861) sk., June 26

Franklin, William Buel (F) (*See also* Teche Country oper.): (1862) eng. Eltham's Ldg., May 7; Bat. of Crampton's Gap, Sept. 14; commands Left Grand Div., A. of P., Nov. 14; in Fredericksburg Camp., Dec. 11, 12, 13 (Bat. of Fredericksburg); nears U. S. Ford, Jan. 19; (1863) Burnside's dismissal order, Jan. 23; removal of, Jan. 25; Fed. exped. to Sabine Pass, Sept. 7, 8 (att. on Sabine Pass)

Franklin, La.: (1863) Banks occupies, Apr. 15; (1864) Fed. forces move from, Mar. 14

Franklin, Miss.: (1865) eng., Jan. 2

Franklin, Mo.: (1864) sk., Oct. 1; aff., Dec. 7

Franklin, Tenn.: (1862) Fed. recon. toward, sk. at Brentwood, Dec. 9; Fed. recon. toward, Dec. 11; sk., Dec. 26; (1863) Fed. exped. to, Jan. 31; Fed. occup. of, Feb. 1; Fed. recons. from, Feb. 21, Mar. 4; Fed. exped. returns, Mar. 12; Forrest raids, Mar. 25; sks., Mar. 31, Apr. 9; eng., Apr. 10; eng., June 4; spies hanged, June 9; sk., July 5; (1864) "Spring Hill aff.," Nov. 29; Bat. of, Nov. 30, Dec. 1 (aftermath); Hood holds road to, Dec. 15; Hood goes through, Dec. 17; act., Dec. 17; (1865) windup Nashville-Franklin Camp., Jan. 4; Fed. scs. near, Jan. 16

Franklin, Va.: (1862) sks., Aug. 31, Oct. 31, Nov. 18, Dec. 2; (1863) sk., Mar. 17

Franklin, W. Va.: (1862) sk., May 5; Feds. withdraw toward, May 8; Jackson moves toward, May 9, 10; Jackson leaves, May 12; Frémont arrives at, May 13; May 15; sk., May 26; (1863) Fed. sc. to, Apr. 11; Averell's raiders near, Aug. 19; (1864) saltpeter works destroyed, Feb. 29; sk., Aug. 19

Franklin Co., Ark.: (1863) sk., Sept. 27

Franklin Cr., Miss.: (1864) sks., Dec. 21, 22

Franklin-Nashville Camp.: *See* Nashville, Tenn.; Thomas, George H.; Hood, John B.; Franklin, Tenn.

Franklin Pike, Tenn.: *See* Franklin Turnpike, Tenn.

Franklin Rd., Ky.: (1862) sk., Sept. 9

Franklin's Crossing (or Deep Run), Va.: (1863) Chancellorsville Camp., Apr. 29; A.N.Va. at, June 5

Franklinton, La.: (1864) Fed. exped. to, Feb. 1

Franklin Turnpike, Tenn.: (1862) sks. on, Dec. 4, 14; (1864) Feds. keep open, Nov. 29; Bat. of Franklin, Nov. 30; Bat. of Nashville, Dec. 15, 16

Fraternization: (1862) at Guntown, Miss., July 10; (1863) at Vicksburg, June 19

Frauds: (1863) U. S. Cong. act to prevent, Mar. 3

Frayser's Farm (White Oak Swamp, etc.), Va.: (1862) Bat. of, June 30

Frederick, Md.: (1861) legislature to convene, Sept. 12; (1862) Feds. evacuate, Sept. 4; Lee moves toward, Sept. 5; Jackson occupies, Sept. 6; Lee at, Sept. 9; sk., Sept. 10; A. of P. moves into, Sept. 12; ment., Sept. 13; (1863) sk., June 21; Gettysburg Camp., June 26, 27, 28; (1864) Early's raid, July 8, 9, 11

Frederick Co., W. Va.: (1863) Fed. sc. in, Dec. 7

Fredericksburg, Ray Co., Mo.: (1864) act., July 17

Fredericksburg, Va.: (1862) Joseph E. Johnston moves toward, Mar. 7; Apr. 18, 20; May 10, 11, 21; Lincoln in, May 22, 23; May 24; Shields, McDowell ordered toward, June 9; Fed. cav. raid from, July 23; Fed. recon. from, July 24; ment., Aug. 3; Stuart's exped. to, Aug. 4; Fed. exped. from, Aug. 5; Fed. exped. from, Aug. 15; evac. by Feds., Aug 31; Sept 6; Dahlgren's raid into, Nov. 9; A. of P. moves toward, Nov. 15, 16; Sumner arrives opposite, Nov. 17; armies converging on, Nov. 18; Longstreet on heights of, Burnside across from, Nov. 19; Lee arrives at, Nov. 20; Burnside asks surrender of, Nov. 21; Jackson en route to, Nov. 21, 24; bomb. agreement, Nov. 22; Jackson's troops on right, Dec. 1; eng. at Port Royal near, Dec. 4; att. imminent, Dec. 10; Feds. occupy, Dec. 11; pontoon brs. at, Dec. 11; Fed. troops crossing into, Dec. 12; Bat. of, Dec. 13; aftermath, Dec. 14, 15, 16, 19; disputes over bat., Dec. 22; (1863) aftereffects of bat., Jan. 1; "Mud March," Jan. 19, 20, 22; A. of P. winters across from, Jan. 24; Pelham's role at Bat. of, Mar. 17; Lincoln visits Hooker at, Apr. 4, 5, 6, 8, 10, 11; Chancellorsville Camp., Apr. 28, 30; Bat. of Chancellorsville, May, 1, 2, 3; 2nd Bat. of Fredericksburg, May 3, 4; armies at, May 24; Lee moves from, June 3, 4; June 5; (1864) May 7; (1865) Fed. exped. to, Mar. 5

Fredericksburg, Bat. of (*See also* Fredericksburg, Va.): (1862) Dec. 13

Frederick's Hall Station, Va.: (1862) Fed. exped. to, Aug. 5

Fredericktown, Mo.: (1861) Fed. oper., Aug. 16; sk., Oct. 17; eng., Oct. 21; (1863) sk., Apr. 22

Freeborn's Cut, Ga.: *See* Wilmington Narrows, Ga.

Free Br., Miss.: (1862) sk., Dec. 3

Free Br., near Trenton, N.C.: (1863) sks., July 6, Dec. 16

Freedmen (*See also* Emancipation; Negroes; Slavery): (1862) entry into W. Va. banned, Feb. 13; (1863) proposal to aid, Dec. 17

Freedmen's Aid Society: (1863) plans for Bureau of Emancipation, Dec. 17

Freedmen's Bureau: (1863) establishment of ment., Dec. 17; (1865) established, Mar. 3; O. O. Howard to head, May 12

Freedmen's Savings and Trust Co.: (1865) established, Mar. 3

Freedom: (1863) Lincoln on, Dec. 8

Freeman's Fd., Va.: (1862) sk., Aug. 21

Freestone Point, Va.: (1861) Conf. bat. duel with ships, Sept. 25

Frémont, Jessie Benton (Mrs. John Charles) (F): (1861) intercedes with Lincoln, Sept. 10; Lincoln to, Sept. 12

Frémont, John Charles (F): (1861) ment., May 16; confers with Lincoln, en route to Mo., July 2; assumes command Western Dept., July 25; in Cairo, Aug. 2; declares martial law, Aug. 14; calls for reinforcements, Aug. 15; emancipation proclamation, confiscation order, Aug. 30; intention to enter Ky., Sept. 3; Lincoln discusses future of, Sept. 5; Lincoln sends Hunter to aid, Sept. 8; removal of urged, Sept. 9; Mrs. Frémont visits Lincoln, Sept. 10; Lincoln to re eman. proc., Sept. 11; eman. proc. modified, Sept. 12; not relieving Mulligan at Lexington, Sept. 13; Cabinet discusses removal of, Sept. 15; arrests Blair, Sept. 15; investigation of command, Sept. 18; sent no aid to Mulligan, Sept. 20; charges of dereliction against, Sept. 20; Lincoln on eman. proc., Sept. 22; closes St. Louis *Evening News*, Sept. 23; Lincoln concerned about, Sept. 30; Lincoln confers on Dept. of West, Oct. 4; moves after Price, Oct. 7; removal considered, Oct. 7; Oct. 22; Lincoln dispatches letter of removal, Oct. 24; Zagonyi occupies Springfield, Oct. 25; to pursue Price, Oct. 27; prisoner agreement, Nov. 1, 7 (Hunter repudiates); relieved of duty, Nov. 2; Hunter supersedes, Nov. 3; Nov. 9; rule of, Nov. 19; (1862) commands Mt. Dept., Mar. 11; assumes command Mt. Dept., Mar. 29; Blenker's division sent to, Mar. 31; Bat. of McDowell, May 8; reaches Franklin, W. Va., May 13; ordered to Shenandoah, May 24; aims to cut off Jackson, May 25, 26; troop strength, May 29; converging with McDowell's forces, May 30; Lincoln urges to destroy Jackson, May 30; Jackson gets between Frémont, McDowell, May 30; approaching Jackson, June 1, 6; Bat. of Cross Keys, June 8; Bat. of Port Republic, June 9; pulls back, June 11; Lincoln's warning to, June 12; Lincoln to, June 15; resigns command, June 17; resignation accepted, June 27; (1864) nominated for Pres., May 31; withdraws from contest, Sept. 17

Fremont's Orchard, Colo. Terr.: (1864) sk., Apr. 12

French, Samuel Gibbs (C): (1863) commands Dept. of South Va., Apr. 1; (1864) eng. of Allatoona, Ga., Oct. 5

French, William Henry (F): (1863) commands Third Corps at Manassas Gap, July 22; Meade blames for delay at Mine Run, Nov. 27

French Point, Mo.: (1863) Fed. sc. to, May 13

French Settlement, La.: (1865) Fed. exped. to, Apr. 2

French's Field, Va.: *See* Oak Grove, Va.

Friar's Point, Miss.: (1862) sk., Sept. 28; (1865) Fed. sc. from, Feb. 10; Fed. exped. to, Feb. 19

Frick's Gap, Ga.: (1864) Fed. sc. to, Feb. 25

Friends, Society of: (1864) Lincoln to Mrs. Gurney, Sept. 4

Frog Bayou, Ark.: (1863) sk., Mar. 19; Fed. exped. to, Nov. 7

Frogtown, Ga.: (1864) act., Aug. 3

Frontier, Army of the, Fed.: (1862) sk., Dec. 28; (1863) Herron supersedes Schofield in command, Apr. 1

Frontier, Dist. of the, Fed.: (1863) McNeil assumes command of, Nov. 2

"Frontier Guards": (1861) Apr. 18

Front Royal, Va.: (1862) Jackson heads toward, May 21, 22; eng., May 23; aftermath, May 24; sk., May 30; sk., May 31; Fed. recon. from, June 29; (1863) Ewell's rear guard at, July 23; Fed. Third Corps moves to, July 24; (1864) Fed. exped. to, Jan. 1; sks., Feb. 20, May 22; eng., Aug. 16; sks., Sept. 21, 23; Sixth Corps moves via, Oct. 10; ment., Oct. 19; sk., Nov. 22

Front Royal Fd., Va.: (1863) oper., May 12

Frost, Daniel Marsh (C): (1861) Camp Jackson aff., May 10

Frying Pan, Va.: (1863) sk., June 4

Frying Pan Church, Va.: (1863) sk., Oct. 17

Fugitive Slave Law: (1861) Lincoln signs act repealing, June 28; July 30; Aug. 8

Fugitive slaves: *See* Slaves, fugitive

Fulton, Mo.: (1861) sk., July 17; Fed. sc. to, Oct. 28; (1862) sks., July 24, 28

Fulton Rd., near Iuka, Miss.: (1862) sk., Sept. 20

Funchal, Madeira: (1864) *Sea King* (C.S.S. *Shenandoah*) leaves for, Oct. 8; commissioning of *Shenandoah,* Oct. 19

Funkstown, Md: (1863) sks., July 7, 10

Furnaces: (1865) destroyed, Mar. 31

Fussell's Mill, Va.: (1864) comb., Aug. 13; Fed. att. on, Aug. 16

Gadsden, Ala.: (1864) Hood moves toward, Oct. 17; Hood marches from, Oct. 22, 28

Gadsden Rd., Ala.: (1864) sk., Oct. 25

Gaines, C.S.S.: (1864) sunk, Aug. 5

Gaines, Ft., Ala.: (1861) state forces take, Jan. 5; (1864) Fed. recon. of, Jan. 20; investment of, Aug. 3; Bat. of Mobile Bay, Aug. 5, 6; surrenders, Aug. 7, 8

Gaines' Cross Roads, Va.: (1862) sks., May 14, 15; (1863) sk., July 21; sk., July 23; sk., Oct. 12

Gaines' Ldg., Ark.: (1862) sk., July 20; (1863) destroyed, June 14; (1864) eng., Aug. 10

Gaines' Mill, Va.: (1862) sk., May 19; Porter withdraws to, June 26; Bat. of (also 1st Cold Harbor, Bat. of the Chickahominy), June 27; McClellan on defeat of, June 28

Gainesville, Ark.: (1864) Fed. sc. to, May 10

Gainesville, Fla.: (1864) Fed. capture of, Feb. 14; act., Fed. r.r. raid, Aug. 15

Gainesville, Va.: (1862) Fed. recon. to, Mar. 20; sk., 2nd Bull Run Camp., Aug. 26; (1863) exped. from, June 7; sks., June 21, Oct. 14; cav. eng. ("Buckland Races"), Oct. 19

Galena, U.S.S.: (1862) damaged, May 15

Gale's Cr. N.C.: (1864) sk., Feb. 2

Gallatin, Tenn.: (1862) Morgan's oper., Mar. 15; Conf. guerrillas capt. near, July 10; Morgan capt., Aug. 12; sks., Aug. 19, Nov. 7, 8; (1863) Fed. exped. from, Oct. 10; (1864) aff. near, Oct. 10

Gallatin Co., Ky.: (1862) oper. against guerrillas in, Oct. 15

Gallatin Pike, Tenn.: (1862) Forrest repulsed on, Oct. 20

Gallatin Rd., Tenn.: (1862) aff., Sept. 6

Galloway's Farm, near Jacksonport, Ark.: (1862) aff., June 2

Galveston, Tex.: (1861) blockaded, July 3; act. off, Aug. 5; (1862) Fed. naval demon. near, May 15; att. on, Oct. 3; Feds. capture, hold briefly, Oct. 5; in Union possession, Oct. 15; Feds. occupy, Dec. 24; (1863) Confs. capture, Jan. 1; bomb., Jan. 10; U.S.S. *Hatteras* sunk off, Jan. 11; bomb., Jan. 29; mutiny at, Aug. 10; (1864) blockade-runners escape from, Apr. 30; (1865) restrictions on, May 27

Galveston Volunteers: (1861) capture *Star of the West,* Apr. 17

Gamble, Camp, Mo.: (1862) Fed. exped. from, Aug. 12

Gamble, Hamilton Rowan (F): (1861) Union gov. of Mo., July 22; inaugurated gov. of Mo., July 31; organizes militia, Nov. 8

Gano, Richard Montgomery (C): (1864) att. on Fed. wagon train, Cabin Cr., I.T., Sept. 19

Gap Mt., Va.: (1864) sk., May 12

Garden Hollow, Mo.: (1863) sk., Aug. 9

Gardner, Franklin (C) (*See also* Port Hudson): (1863) commands at Port Hudson, May 27; surrender of Port Hudson, July 8, 9

Gardner, John L. (F): (1860) relieved of command of Ft. Moultrie, Nov. 15

Garfield, James Abram (F): (1862) eng. at Middle Cr., Ky., Jan. 10; (1865) on slavery, Jan. 12

Garland, Ft., Colo. Terr.: (1863) Fed. sc., Oct. 12; (1864) Fed. sc., Aug. 12

Garlandville, Miss.: (1863) sk., Apr. 24

Garnett, Robert Selden (C): (1861) commands northwest Va. troops, June 8; July 10; eng. at Rich Mt., July 11; retreat from Laurel Hill, July 12; killed, July 13; Aug. 1

Garnett's Farm, Va.: (1862) act., June 28

Garnettsville, Ky.: (1863) Morgan occupies, July 6

Garrard, Kenner (F): (1864) cav. raid to Covington, Ga., July 22, 26, 27

Garrett, Jack: (1865) informs on Booth's whereabouts, Apr. 26

Garrett, Richard H.: (1865) Fed. cav. arrives at farm of, Apr. 25; Booth shot in barn of, Apr. 26

Garrettsburg, Ky.: (1862) sk., Nov. 6

Garrison's Cr., Tenn.: (1863) sk., Oct. 6

Garrott, Ft., Miss.: (1863) 2nd ass. on Vicksburg, May 22

Gassendi (French man-of-war): (1862) Lincoln visits, Apr. 26

Gaston, Ft., Calif.: (1863) sks., Dec. 25, 26

Gates, Ft., Fla.: (1864) Fed. exped. to, Apr. 1

Gates Co., N.C.: (1863) Fed. recon., June 5

Gatesville, N.C.: (1862) Fed. exped. to, May 7

Gatewood's, W. Va.: (1863) sk., Dec. 12

Gatlinburg, Tenn.: (1863) sk., Dec. 10

Gauley, W. Va: (1861) sk., Oct. 23; (1862) sk., Sept. 11

Gauley Br., W. Va.: (1861) July 24; Cox in area of, July 30; sks., Nov. 1, 10

Gaylesville, Ala.: (1864) Sherman halts pursuit of Hood at, Oct. 21, 28

Gayoso, Mo.: (1862) sk., Aug. 4; (1864) sk., Sept. 8

Geary, John White (F): (1863) eng. at Wauhatchie, Tenn., Oct. 28; occup. of Savannah, Dec. 21

Geiger's Lake, Ky.: (1862) sk., Sept. 3

General, The: (1862) Great Locomotive Chase, Apr. 12

General Hunter, U.S.S.: (1864) transport destroyed, Apr. 16

General-in-Chief, Conf.: (1865) Lee assumes duties of, Feb. 6

General-in-Chief, U.S.: (1861) George B. McClellan replaces Winfield Scott, Nov. 1; (1862) McClellan relieved, Mar. 11; Henry W. Halleck named, July 11; (1864) Grant given authority to take command, Mar. 10; official orders naming Grant announced, Halleck to be Chief of Staff, Mar. 12

General Lee (steamer): (1862) capt., Aug. 10

General Orders No. 9; (1865) order, Apr. 10

General Orders No. 11; (1862) against "Jew" peddlers, issued by Grant, Dec. 17; (1863) Lincoln revokes Grant order, Jan. 4; order evacuating western Mo. counties issued by Fed. Gen. Ewing, Aug. 25

General War Orders: *See* War Orders

George Peabody, U.S.S.: (1862) collides with *West Point,* Aug. 13

Georgetown, Ga.: (1865) Fed. exped. to, Apr. 17

Georgetown, Ky.: (1864) Morgan reaches, June 10

Georgetown, S.C.: (1865) Fed. exped. to, Apr. 5

Georgia (*See also* Brown, Joseph Emerson, Gov.): (1860) legislature votes to arm state, Nov. 18; calls convention to consider Southern Confederacy, Dec. 14; offers troops to S.C., Dec. 27; (1861) State Convention votes secession, Jan. 19; seizes U. S. Arsenal, Jan. 24; seizes Oglethorpe Barracks, Ft. Jackson, Savannah, Jan. 25; ratifies C.S.A. constitution, Mar. 16; repudiates Northern debts, Apr. 26; (1862) Fed. exped. along coast of begins, Nov. 3; (1864) legislature votes peace offers stipulating C.S.A. independence be made, Mar. 19; Milledgeville occupied, legislature flees, Nov. 22; (1865) James Johnson appointed provisional gov., June 17

Georgia, C.S.S. (cruiser): (1864) capture of, Aug. 15

Georgia Central R.R.: (1864) sk. on, Dec. 4

Georgia Central R.R. Br., Oconee R., Ga.: (1864) sk., Nov. 23

Georgia coast: (1862) Fed. exped. along, Nov. 13; (1863) Davis to Lee on, Feb. 4

Georgia Ldg., La.: (1862) act., Oct. 27

Georgia militia: (1864) ment., July 16; sks. with Sherman, Nov. 21

Georgia state troops: *See* Georgia militia

Geranium (U.S. tug): (1864) fired on from Ft. Moultrie, Apr. 14

Germanna Fd., Va.: (1863) sks. Apr. 29, Oct. 10, Nov. 18; (1864) A. of P. crosses at, May 4

Germanna Plank Rd., Va.: (1864) Bat. of Wilderness, May 5

German pro-Unionists: (1861) Camp Jackson aff., May 10; (1862) at Pea Ridge, May 7

Germantown, Tenn.: (1863) aff. near, Jan. 27; Fed. sc. from, July 8, 16; capture of Union pickets, July 18; (1865) sks., Mar. 28, Apr. 18

Germantown, Va.: (1862) Sept. 1; (1863) affs., Feb. 26, Nov. 16, Dec. 13, 24; (1864) sk., Jan. 22

Germantown Rd., Tenn.: (1864) sk. on, near Memphis, Dec. 14

Gettysburg, Pa., Camp. (*See also* Lee, R. E.; Meade, George Gordon): (1863) June 3, 4, 5, 6, 8 (Stuart holds cav. review), 9 (Bat. of Brandy Station), 10, 11, 12, 13, 14 (Bat. of 2nd Winchester), 15, 16, 17, 18, 19, 20, 21, 23, 24, 25, 26, 27, 28, 29, 30; Bat. of Gettysburg, July 1, 2, 3; retreat of A.N.Va., July 4, 5, 6; Lincoln on Meade's inaction, July 6, 14; aftermath, July 7, 8, 9, 10, 11, 13, 14, 15, 16, 17, 19, 20, 21, 22, 23, 24, 26, 28, 31, Aug. 1; troops from control N.Y. draft riots, July 13; Lee offers to resign, Aug. 8; Meade confers with Lincoln on, Aug. 14; Buford ment., Dec. 16; ment., Dec. 31; (1864) Lincoln prevents court of inquiry asked by Meade, Mar. 29

Gettysburg Address: (1863) Lincoln works on, Nov. 17, 18; presented and reception of, Nov. 19; Everett praises, Nov. 20

Gettysburg National Cemetery: (1863) Lincoln asked to dedication of, Nov. 2; Lincoln works on address, Nov. 17, 18; Lincoln leaves for, Nov. 18; Lincoln's address at, Nov. 19

Ghent, Ky.: (1864) sk., Aug. 29

Gibbon, John (F): (1862) Bat. of Fredericksburg, Dec. 13

Gibson, Randall Lee (C): (1865) Mobile Camp., Mar. 17, 25

Gibson, Ft., I.T.: (1862) Fed. recon. from, July 14; sk. near, July 27; sk., Oct. 15; (1863) sks., Feb. 28, Apr. 30, May 14; act., May 20; sks., May 22, 28, June 6; demon. on, Dec. 16; sk., Dec. 26; (1864) sk., Apr. 3; (1865) Fed. exped. from, Mar. 18

Gibson's Mill, Indian Cr., Va.: (1864) sk., Feb. 22

Glorieta, N. Mex. Terr. (La Glorieta Pass): (1862) Apache Canyon near, Mar. 26; eng. of, or Pigeon's Ranch, Mar. 28

Gloucester Co., Va.: (1862) Conf. sc. into, July 22; Fed. recon. into, Dec. 11; (1864) Fed. scs. in, Feb. 28, Mar. 28

Gloucester Court House, Va.: (1863) Fed. expeds. to, Apr. 7, July 24; (1864) aff. near, Jan. 29

Gloucester Point, Va.: (1861) shore batteries fire on U.S.S. *Yankee,* May 9; sk., Nov. 16; (1863) Fed. exped. from, Apr. 7; sk., Apr. 9; Fed. recon. from, Apr 12; Fed. exped. from, May 19

God: (1864) Lincoln on purposes of Almighty, Sept. 4

Goggin, Camp, Ky.: (1861) sk. near, Dec. 1

Goings' Fd., W. Va.: (1863) sk., Apr. 6

Gold: (1863) discovered at Alder Gulch, Mont., May 26; (1864) price rising, Jan. 2

Golding's Farm, Va.: (1862) act., June 28

Goldsborough, Louis Malesherbes (F): (1861) commands North Atlantic Blockading Squad., Sept. 19; (1862) commands navy squad., Roanoke exped., Jan. 11; attacks Roanoke I. naval defenders, Feb. 7; relieved of command North Atlantic Blockading Squad., Sept. 2

Goldsborough, N.C.: (1862) Foster's 11-day Fed. exped. from New Berne to, Dec. 11, 12, 15, 16, 17; (1865) Sherman headed for, Feb. 22; Cox orders r.r. repairs toward, Mar. 6; Sherman orders troops toward, Mar. 10, 12, 14, 16, 18; sk. near, Mar. 19; Mar. 23; Sherman, Schofield join at, Mar. 23; sk. near, Apr. 2

Golgotha (or Gilgal) Church, Ga.: (1864) comb., June 15

Goochland Court House, Va.: (1864) Kilpatrick's raid, Feb. 29; Mar. 1; (1865) sk., Mar. 11

Goodlettsville, Tenn.: (1862) sk., Sept. 30

Goodrich's Ldg., La.: (1863) att. on, June 30; (1864) sk., Mar. 24

Goodwin, Ft., Ariz. Terr.: (1864) Fed. exped. to, May 16

Goose Cr., near St. Marks, Fla.: (1864) salt works on destroyed, Feb. 27

Goose Cr., Va.: (1863) sc., July 25

Goose Cr. Salt Works, near Manchester, Ky.: (1862) destroyed by Feds., Oct. 23

Gordon, John Brown (C): (1864) Bat. of Wilderness, May 6; at Spotsylvania, May 10; Bat. of Cedar Cr., Oct. 19; (1865) ordered to attack at Ft. Stedman, Mar. 24, 25 (att.); eng. at Sayler's Cr., Apr. 6; Appomattox eng., Apr. 9; A.N.Va. surrenders, Apr. 9; surrender ceremony, Apr. 12

Gordon, Nathaniel: (1862) hanged as slave trader, Feb 21

Gordon, Ga.: (1864) sk., Nov. 21; Kilpatrick, Howard at, Nov. 22

Gordonsville, Va.: (1862) Jackson advances to, July 13; capt. by Pope, July 17; Pope advances toward before Cedar Mt., Aug. 9; Jackson withdraws to vicinity of, Aug. 11; Lee's army moves toward, Aug. 13, 16; (1864) Lee moves from, May 4; Torbert's exped. toward, Dec. 19; sk. near, Dec. 23

Goresville, Va.: (1864) sk., Nov. 28

Goshen, Ala.: (1864) sk., Oct. 28

Goshen Swamp, N.C.: (1862) aff., Dec. 16

Gosport Navy Yard, Va.: (1861) Lincoln, Scott confer on, Apr. 17; evacuated, Apr. 20

Gouge's Mill, Mo.: (1862) sk., Mar. 26

Gourd Neck, Ala.: (1864) Fed. exped. to, Mar. 2

Government Springs, Ut. Terr.: (1863) sk. near, June 20

Governors, C.S.A. (*See also* individual names, states, Davis, Jefferson): (1862) Davis asks for troops, Apr. 10; response to request for troops, Apr. 11; western govs. ask Davis for more aid, July 28; Davis to on conscription, supplies, Nov. 26; (1863) Lubbock of Tex. asks more arms, July 13; (1864) govs. of N.C., S.C. discuss trade, troop procurement with Davis, Mar. 26; Davis to, Sept. 19; (1865) advise E. K. Smith on surrender terms, May 13; Charles Clark of Miss., imprisonment, parole of, Oct. 11

Governors, provisional, Fed.: (1864) in Ark., Jan. 22; (1865) in N.C., May 29; in Miss., June 13; in Ga., June 17; in Tex., June 17; in S.C., June 30; in Fla., July 13

Governors, U.S. (*See* individual names, states; Lincoln, Abraham): (1861) Lincoln calls for troops, Apr. 14; of western states, Aug. 15; (1862) Lincoln asks for 300,000 men, July 1; Altoona, Pa., conference of, Sept. 24; (1864) Lincoln confers with, Apr. 21; Lincoln asks for 100-day troops, May 21

Gradyville, Ky.: (1861) sk., Dec. 12

Grafton, W. Va.: (1861) Fed. drive toward, May 26; Fed. occup. of, May 30; Fed. forces move out from, June 2; line of att. through, June 3; Fed. forces advance from to Philippi, June 3; sk. near, Aug. 13

Graham's Plantation, La.: (1864) (Red R. Camp.) May 5

Grahamville, S.C.: (1864) eng. at Honey Hill near, Nov. 30

Grampus, No. 2, U.S.S.: (1863) capt., burned, Jan. 11

Granbury, Hiram Bronson (C): (1864) killed at Bat. of Franklin, Nov. 30

Granby, Mo.: (1862) sk., Sept. 24; aff., Oct. 4; (1863) Conf. guerrilla att. on, Mar. 3

Grand Bayou, Fla.: (1864) aff., Aug. 7

Grand Bayou, La.: (1865) Fed. exped. to, Feb. 14

Grand Caillou, La.: (1865) Fed. exped. to, Apr. 19

Grand Coteau, La.: (1863) sk., Oct. 16; eng. near at Bayou Bourbeau, Nov. 3

Grand Divisions, Fed.: (1862) Burnside organizes A. of P. into, Nov. 14; crossing river at Fredericksburg, Dec. 12; at Bat. of Fredericksburg, Dec. 13; (1863) Hooker eliminates, Feb. 5

Grand Ecore, La. (*See also* Red R. Camp.): (1864) sk., Apr. 3; gunboats at, Apr. 8; Banks retreats toward, Apr. 10, 11; Porter reaches, Apr. 13; sk., Apr. 16; Feds. withdrawing from, Apr. 21; sk., Apr. 29

Grand Glaize, Ark.: (1864) Fed. sc. to, Mar. 15

Grand Gulf, Miss.: (1862) aff., May 26; boat, shore battery eng., June 9; sk. at Hamilton's Plantation, June 24; (1863) Farragut passes batteries, Mar. 19, 31; Fed. bomb. of, Apr. 29; Bat. of Port Gibson, May 1; evac. by Confs., May 3; Sherman leaves area, May 7; (1864) sk., Jan. 18; Fed. expeds. to, Feb. 15, July 4, 10; (1865) Fed. exped. to, Mar. 12

Grand Junction, Tenn.: (1862) Fed. exped. from, Sept 20; Fed. troops converge on, start Vicksburg Camp., Oct 31; Grant occupies, Nov 4; Fed. exped. from, Nov. 19; (1863) Conf. att. on train, Mar. 21; Fed. sc. from, Apr. 5; sk., July 30

Grand Lake, La.: (1863) sk. at Bayou Portage, Nov. 23

Grand Pass, Id. Terr.: (1863) sk., July 7

Grand Prairie, Ark.: (1863) sk., Aug. 17

Grand Review: (1865) in Wash., D.C., May 23, 24

Grand R., I.T.: (1862) sk., June 6; Fed. recon. from, July 14

Grand R., Kas.: (1863) Fed. exped. to, July 27

Grand R., La.: (1864) Fed. exped. to, Sept. 26; (1865) Fed. exped. to, Jan. 18; Fed. sc. to, Jan. 28

Grand R., Mo: (1861) sk., Nov. 30; (1862) sks., Aug. 1, 11

Granger, Gordon (F): (1862) assumes command Army of Ky., Oct. 7; (1863) oper. to Duck R., Tenn., Mar. 12; at Chickamauga, Sept. 20; to relieve Burnside at Knoxville, Nov. 27, 28; (1864) Bat. of Mobile Bay, Aug. 5

Granger's Mill, Tenn.: (1863) sk., Dec. 14 (Knoxville Camp.)

Granite City, U.S.S.: (1864) capt., May 6

"Granny" Patterson: *See* Robert Patterson

Granny White Pike, Tenn.: (1862) sk., Mar. 9; (1864) in Bat. of Nashville, Dec. 16

Grant, Ulysses S. (F): (1861) offers services to Union, May 24; appointed brig. gen., July 31; assumes command Dist. of Ironton, Mo., Aug. 8; assumes command in southeast Mo., Sept. 1; Frémont tells intention to enter Ky., Sept. 3; arrives at Cairo, Sept. 4; prepares Paducah exped., Sept. 5; exped. to Paducah, Ky., Sept. 6; eng. at Belmont, Mo., Nov. 7; (1862) prepares recon. in force toward Columbus, Ky., Jan. 9; recon. in force toward Columbus, Jan. 10; recon. near Blandville, Ky., Jan. 14; gunboat recon. on Tenn. R., Jan. 15; Ky. recon. returns, Jan. 21; prepares Ft. Henry Camp., Feb. 1; Ft. Henry Camp., Feb. 3, 4, 5, 6; recon. to Ft. Donelson, Feb. 7; delayed, Feb. 9; prepares for Donelson att., Feb. 10, 11, 12; Ft. Donelson att., Feb. 13, 14, 15 (siege of); assigned to Dist. of West Tenn., command, Feb. 14; "unconditional surrender" of Ft. Donelson, Feb. 16; becomes Northern hero, Feb. 17; looks toward Nashville, Feb. 19; aftermath, Donelson victory, Feb. 25; ordered up Tenn. R., Mar. 1; accused of misconduct, Mar. 3; to stay at Ft. Henry, Mar. 4; advancing army, Mar. 15; exonerated, restored to field command, Mar. 15; at Savannah, Tenn., Mar. 17; A. S. Johnston prepares to oppose, Mar. 24; Johnston orders att. on Pittsburg Ldg., Apr. 2; Conf. att. delayed, Apr. 3, 4; Feds. unaware, Apr. 5; Bat. of Shiloh, Apr. 6, 7; Halleck takes field command, Apr. 11; death of C. F. Smith, Apr. 25; second in command to Halleck, Apr. 29; reassigned to corps, June 10; commands enlarged Dist. of West Tenn., July 16; on employment of slaves, Aug. 11; Bat. of Iuka, Sept. 19; Bat. of Corinth, Oct. 3; effects of Corinth Camp. on, Oct. 4; Lincoln congratulates, Oct. 8; commands new Dept. of the Tenn., Oct. 16; McClernand exped. against Vicksburg ordered, ensuing friction, Oct. 20; assumes command Thirteenth Army Corps and Dept. of the Tenn., Oct. 25; preliminaries of Vicksburg Camp., Oct. 31, Nov. 1; political intrigue against, Nov. 1; recon. from La Grange, Tenn., Nov. 8; Forrest to cut communications of, Nov. 21;

11, 12, 13, 14, 15, 18; as "butcher," May 12; shifts to "left," May 13, 14, 17, 18, 19; orders A. of P. to move left, May 20, 21, 22 (toward Hanover Junction); Camp. of the North Anna, May 23, 24, 25, 26, 27; crossing Pamunkey R., May 28; May 29; along Totopotomoy Cr., May 30; Lee blocks way to Richmond, May 30; moves toward Cold Harbor, May 30; Bat. of Cold Harbor, June 1, 2, 3; Lincoln approves camp., June 3; armies entrenched, June 4

Lynchburg Camp., June 5; proposes truce for burying dead, June 5; quiet at Cold Harbor, June 6; plans James R. crossing, June 7, 10, 11; votes for National Union Party Convention, June 8; move to James, June 12, 13; crossing James, 14, 15; orders for Petersburg att., June 15; Lincoln to, June 15; ass. on Petersburg, June 16, 17; siege of Petersburg, June 18, 19, 20, 21; Lincoln visits, June 21; visits Butler with Lincoln, June 22; Weldon R.R., June 22; Lincoln to, July 10; orders pursuit of Early, July 13; Lincoln to, July 17; strategy against Early, July 22, sends troops north of James, July 26; mine at Petersburg, July 25, 30 (explosion); Lincoln to confer with, July 30, 31; Lincoln to, Aug. 3, 4; confers with Lincoln, Aug. 7; explosion at City Point, Aug. 9; rumors of pres. candidacy, Aug. 12; demon. north bank of James R., Aug. 13; Lincoln to, Aug. 17; refuses prisoner exchange, Aug. 18; Weldon R.R., Aug. 18, 19, 20, 21; Reams' Station, Aug. 25; "dead lock" in Valley, Sept. 12; pressure on to defeat Early, Sept. 14; conference with Sheridan, Sept. 15, 16; orders to desolate Valley, Sept. 24; Bat. of Chaffin's Farm or Ft. Harrison and Bat. of Peebles' Farm, Sept. 29, 30; Lincoln praises, Oct. 21; eng. at Burgess' Mill, Oct. 27; position, strength of forces, Oct. 27; wants Price pursued, Oct. 28; confers with Lincoln, Stanton, Halleck, Nov. 23; hopeful Thomas will attack Hood, Dec. 3; orders Thomas to attack, Dec. 6, 7; on possible removal of Thomas, Dec. 8; replaces Thomas, rescinds order, Dec. 9; orders Thomas to attack, Dec. 11; orders Logan to replace Thomas, Dec. 13; cancels Nashville trip, Dec. 15; Davis on, Dec. 20; Lincoln to, Dec. 28

(1865) asks Butler's removal, Jan. 6; Lincoln asks staff post for son Robert, Jan. 19; agrees to prisoner exchange, Jan. 24; Lincoln to, Feb. 1, 4; Bat. of Hatcher's Run, Feb. 5, 6, 7; orders to Sheridan, Feb. 27; Lee to, Mar. 2; Grant to Lee, Mar. 2; Lincoln's policy for ending war, Mar. 3; Sheridan to join, Mar. 19; Lincoln visits, Mar. 23, 25, 26, 29, Apr. 1; confers with Sheridan, Mar. 26, 29; Lincoln, Sherman confer with on *River Queen*, Mar. 27, 28; Appomattox Camp., Mar. 29 (strategy of), 30, 31, Apr. 2 (evac. of Richmond, fall of Petersburg lines); confers with Lincoln, Apr. 3; pursues Lee, Apr. 3, 4, 5, 6; to Lee on hopelessness of struggle, Apr. 7; Lincoln to, Apr. 7; terms to Lee, Apr. 8; Lee's surrender, Apr. 9; paroling of A.N.Va., Apr. 10; confers with Lee, Apr. 10; confers with Lincoln, Apr. 13; declines invitation to theater, Apr. 14; at Lincoln's funeral, Apr. 19; Sherman-Johnston agreement, Apr. 24; approves Sherman-Johnston surrender terms, Apr. 26; confers with Sherman, leaves Raleigh, Apr. 27

Grant, Camp, Calif.: (1864) Fed. sc. from, Sept. 1
Grant's Cr., N.C.: (1865) sk., Apr. 12
Grant's Fy., Pearl R., Miss.: (1863) sk. (Jackson Camp.), July 16
Grassy Lick (or Cove Mt.), Va.: (1864) eng., May 10

Grassy Mound, Ky.: (1862) sk., Oct. 6
Gravel Hill, Va.: (1864) comb., Aug. 13
Gravelly Fd., Va.: (1865) sk., Apr. 2
Gravelly Run, Va.: (1865) sk. near, Mar. 29; sk. near, Mar. 30
Gravelly Springs, Ala.: (1865) Fed. exped. from, Mar. 1
Grayson, John Breckinridge (C): (1861) commands Dept. of Middle and East Fla., Aug. 21
Graysville, Ga.: (1863) sk., Sept. 10; pursuit of Bragg, Nov. 26
Great Bear Cr., Ala.: (1863) sk., Apr. 17
Great Bethel, Va.: *See* Big Bethel
Great Br., Va.: (1863) Fed. exped. from, Sept. 15; Fed. sc. from, Oct. 13
Great Britain: (1861) C.S.A. recognition discussed, Mar. 12; C.S.A. commissioners to, Mar. 16, May 3; recognizes C.S.A. as belligerent, May 6, 13; C.S.A. sends Bulloch to, May 9; relations with U.S., C.S.A., May 28; closes waters to belligerents' prizes, June 1; *Trent* Aff., Nov. 8, 15, 24, 26, 27, 29, 30; export of ordnance stopped, Dec. 4; mourns death of Prince Albert, Dec. 14; press condemns *Trent* Aff., Dec. 17; demands release of *Trent* commissioners, Dec. 18, 19, 20, 21, 23; Dec. 25, 26 (Conf. commissioners released); (1862) Conf. commissioners arrive, Jan. 30; neutrality of, Jan. 31; lifts prohibition on ordnance shipments, Feb. 5; Atlantic fisheries act, Mar. 15; *Florida (Oreto)* sails from, Mar. 22; signs treaty on slave trade, Apr. 7, July 11; reconciliation in U.S. called for, July 9; House of Commons rejects mediation, July 18; U.S. minister to prohibited from discussing mediation, Aug. 2; meeting advocates recognition of C.S.A., Aug. 7; Palmerston on neutrality, Aug. 8; Napoleon III proposes mediation, Oct. 30
  (1863) British steamer seized, Jan. 6; neutrality urged, Jan. 21; Queen Victoria on intervention, Feb. 5; C.S.A. strives for recognition, Feb. 11; meetings support Eman. Proc., Feb. 19; *Peterhoff* aff., Feb. 25; seizure of *Alexandria,* Apr. 6; Parliament debates vessel seizures, Apr. 25; House of Lords debates rights of shipowners, May 18; meeting praising Stonewall Jackson, June 3; seizures of ships, June 15; Gladstone on North-South reunion, June 30; war claims convention, July 1; neutrality of, July 29; "Laird Rams" detained, Sept. 5; C.S.A. *Rappahannock* sails, Nov. 25; (1864) C.S.S. *Shenandoah* leaves, Oct. 8; Conf. benefit in, Oct. 18; (1865) withdraws belligerent right from C.S.A., June 2
Great Cacapon Br., W. Va.: (1862) sk., Jan. 4
Great Central Fair (for Sanitary Commission), Philadelphia, Pa.: (1864) Lincoln addresses, June 16
Great Falls, Md.: (1861) sks., July 7, Sept. 4; Fed. sc. from, Aug. 25
Great Kanawha R.: (1861) July 11, 12; camp. along, July 13; Cox's advance held up, July 17; July 25; (1862) sk. near falls of, Oct. 31; (1864) capture of *Levi,* Feb. 3
Great Kanawha Valley: *See* Kanawha Valley, W. Va.
Great Lakes: (1865) Lord Russell protests activity on, Feb. 13
Great Locomotive Chase: (1862) Apr. 12
Great Osage Indian Tribe: (1861) treaty with C.S.A., Oct. 2
Great Salt Lake, Ut. Terr.: (1861) Ind. att., Aug. 8

Great Western Station, Springfield, Ill.: (1861) Lincoln's farewell address at, Feb. 11

"Greek Fire": (1864) plot to burn N. Y. City, Nov. 24

Greeley, Horace (F): (1861) "Forward to Richmond," July 14; to Lincoln, July 29; (1862) Lincoln to, Mar. 24; criticizes Lincoln's slavery policy, Aug. 19; Lincoln to on saving Union, Aug. 22; (1864) Canadian peace feelers, July 5, 17; Lincoln to, July 9, Aug. 9

Greenbrier, W. Va.: (1861) sk., Oct. 31

Greenbrier Br., W. Va.: (1863) sk., Sept. 24

Greenbrier Co., W. Va.: (1862) Fed. exped. into, Nov. 9; (1864) ment., June 3

Greenbrier R., W. Va.: (1861) eng., Oct. 3; sk. on, Dec 12; (1862) Fed. sc. from, Aug. 2; sk. Aug. 3; (1863) sk., Dec. 12; (1864) sk., May 20

Greencastle, Pa.: (1863) sks., June 22, July 5

Greene, Colton (C): (1864) raids along Miss. R., May 24, 25, June 1 (aff. with U.S.S. *Exchange*); eng. with Fed. boats, June 2

Greene, Samuel Dana (F): (1862) commands *Monitor*, Mar. 9

Greeneville, Tenn.: (1861) pro-Union meeting in, June 17, 21; (1862) Fed. exped. from, Apr. 6; (1863) sk., Oct. 2; Longstreet moves toward, Dec. 3, 5, 6, 10; (1864) Longstreet at, Mar. 7; sks., Apr. 15, May 30; Fed. sc. to, Aug. 1; Fed. oper. near, Aug. 29; death of John Hunt Morgan, Sept. 4; sk., Oct. 12; (1865) Fed. exped. to, Feb. 20

Greenfield, Mo.: (1863) sk., Oct. 5

Green Hill, Tenn.: (1863) sks., Apr. 6, June 14

Greenhow, Mrs. Rose O'Neal (C): (1861) spy role at 1st Bull Run, July 17; arrested, Aug. 24; (1862) sent beyond Union lines, Apr. 2; (1864) death of, Oct. 1

Greenland Gap, W. Va.: (1863) sk., Apr. 25

Greenleaf Prairie, I.T.: (1863) sks., Nov. 11, 12

Green Oak, Pa.: (1863) sk., July 5

Greenpoint L.I., N.Y.: (1861) *Monitor* keel laid, Oct. 25; (1862) *Monitor* launched, Jan. 30

Green R., Ky.: (1861) Dec. 17; (1863) J. H. Morgan repulsed in eng. on, July 4

Green Spring Run, W. Va.: (1863) sk., Mar. 7; (1864) sk., Aug. 2; aff., Nov. 1

Greensborough, N.C.: (1865) flight of Davis, Apr. 10, 11, 12, 15

Greensburg, Ky.: (1862) sk., Jan. 28

Green's Chapel, Ky.: (1862) sk., Dec. 25

Greenton, Mo.: (1862) Fed. exped. against guerrillas, Oct. 24; (1864) affs., Mar. 29, Nov. 1

Greenton Valley, near Hopewell, Mo.: (1863) aff., Oct. 21

Greenupsburg, Ky.: (1862) Feds. arrive at, Oct. 3

Greenville, Ky.: (1863) sks., Sept. 11, Dec. 3

Greenville, Miss.: (1862) sk., Aug. 23; (1863) Fed. exped. to, Feb. 14; Fed. exped. to, Apr. 2; gunboat act. near, May 2; sks., May 12, 18; Fed. exped. to, June 25; (1864) sks., May 20, 27

Greenville, Mo.: (1861) Fed. exped. from, Nov. 13; (1862) Fed. recon. from, Feb. 23; sk., July 20

Greenville, N.C.: (1863) sks., Nov. 25, Dec. 30

Greenwell Springs Rd., near Baton Rouge, La.: (1863) sks., Sept. 19, Oct. 5
Greenwich, Va.: (1863) sk., May 30; (1864) sk., Mar. 9; aff., Apr. 11
Greenwood, Miss.: (1863) Ft. Pemberton near, Mar. 11; bomb. of Ft. Pemberton, Mar. 13; att. on Fed. gunboats near, May 27
Gregg, David McMurtrie (F): (1864) temporarily supersedes Pleasonton, in command Fed. cav. in Va., Mar. 25; superseded by Sheridan, Apr. 4
Gregg, John (C): (1863) eng. at Raymond, Miss., May 12
Gregg, Maxcy (C): (1861) capture of train at Vienna, Va., June 17
Gregg, Battery, S.C.: *See* Battery Gregg
Gregg, Ft., Va.: (1865) holds out, Apr. 2
Gregory's Ldg., White R., Ark.: (1864) att. on Fed. steamers, Sept. 4
Grenada, Miss.: (1862) Fed. exped. near, Nov. 27; Pemberton at, Dec. 7; Van Dorn moves from, Dec. 20; (1863) Fed. exped. to, Aug. 12
Greyhound, U.S.S. (steamer): (1864) destroyed, Nov. 27
Grider's Fy., Ky.: (1861) sk., Dec. 28
Grierson, Benjamin Henry (F): (1863) raid, Apr. 17, 18, 19, 24, 28, 29, 30, May 1, 2, 3
Grierson's raid: *See* Grierson, Benjamin Henry
Griffin, Charles (F): (1865) commands Warren's Fifth Corps, Apr. 8
Griffinsburg, Va.: (1863) sk., Oct. 11
Grimball's Ldg., S.C. (1863) sk., July 16
Grisson's Br., Tenn.: (1863) sk., Dec. 27
Griswoldville, Ga.: (1864) sks., Nov. 20, 21; eng., Nov. 22
Grossetete, La.: (1864) sk., Feb. 19
Grossetete Bayou, La.: (1864) sk., Apr. 2; (1865) Fed. sc. to, Feb. 7
Ground Squirrel Br. (or Church), Va.: (1864) comb., May 11
Grouse Cr., Calif.: (1864) sk. (Ind.), May 23
Grove Church, Va.: (1862) Fed. recon. to, Dec. 1; (1863) sk., Jan. 26; oper. at, Feb. 5; sks., May 8, Oct. 14, Nov. 19
Groveton (or Brawner's Farm), Va.: (1862) Bat. of, Aug. 28; 2nd Bat. of Manassas or Bull Run, Aug. 29; (1863) sk., Oct. 17
Grubb's Crossroads, Ky.: (1864) sk., Aug. 21
Guard Hill, Va.: (1864) eng., Aug. 16
Guerrillas: (1861) Fed. oper. against in Mo., Sept. 8, Oct. 20, Nov. 1; (1862) Conf., in W. Va., Jan. 12; in western Va., Apr. 8; Fed. exped. against in La., July 5; Conf., capt., July 10; depredations of, July 10; Pope's order on civilian responsibility for, July 10; sk. near Pleasant Hills, Mo., July 11; kill Gen. Robert L. McCook, Aug. 6; Fed. order at Huntsville, Ala., for disloyal ministers to ride guerrilla-attacked trains, Aug. 8; Fed. exped. for from Camp Gamble, Mo., Aug. 12; plunder *Emma* on Ohio R., Sept. 23; driven out of Hawesville, Ind., Oct. 10; oper. against in Ky., Oct. 15; Fed. exped. against in Mo., Oct. 24; camp attacked, Powell Co., Ky., Dec. 26; (1863) burning of Mound City, Ark., Jan. 15; att. U.S. tug *Hercules,* Feb. 17; Fed. exped. against from Memphis, Feb. 17; att. Woodburn, Tenn., Feb. 26; raid Granby, Mo., Mar. 3; attack train in Tenn., Mar. 21; in Mo., May 21; activity, May 23; Quantrill nears Lawrence, Kas., Aug. 20; sacking of Lawrence, Aug. 21; General Orders No. 11, Aug. 25; Fed. expeds. for, Oct. 14, Nov. 10; Fed. restrictions on consorting with, Nov. 15; Fed.

scs. against, Dec. 18; Fed. exped. against, Dec. 28; (1864) Fed. exped. against in Va., Jan. 1; att. on *Delta,* Jan. 6; sc. against, Mar. 20; Fed. sc. against increases, Sept. 9; attack Fed. transport on White R., Oct. 22; att. on *Belle Saint Louis,* Oct. 27; Fed. sc. against, Nov. 13; Fed. activities against, Nov. 16; (1865) oper. against in Ark., Jan. 1; sk. with, May 20

Guiney's Station, Va.: (1863) Jackson at, May 6; death of Jackson, May 10; (1864) May 20; comb., May 21; May 22

Gulf, Dept. of the, Fed.: (1862) constituted, Butler commands, Feb. 23; Butler assumes command, Mar. 20; Banks named to command, Nov. 8; Butler leaves New Orleans, Dec. 15; Banks assumes command of, Dec. 16; (1863) ment., Dec. 24; (1864) S. A. Hurlbut assigned command of, Sept. 23; (1865) Banks resumes command of, Apr. 22

Gulf, Dist. of the, Conf.: (1862) Buckner assumes command of, Dec. 23

Gulf Coast (*See* separate operations; Galveston; Mobile; New Orleans; Sabine Pass): (1861) blockade of, Apr. 19; Sept. 17; Nov. 27; possible Fed. move against, Dec. 3

Gulf of Mexico: (1862) War Order No. 1, Fed. naval force to advance, Jan. 27; (1863) U.S.S. *De Soto* captures blockade-runners, Apr. 24

"Gulf Squadron" (deep South states): (1861) Jan. 7

Gulley's, N.C.: (1865) sk., Mar. 31

Gumbo Creek, Va.: (1865) Booth reaches, Apr. 22

Gum Slough, Mo.: (1863) Fed. exped. to, Mar. 9

Gum Swamp, N.C. (1863) sk., May 20; (1864) Fed. sc. to, Oct. 11; (1865) Cox's force moving in, Mar. 7

Gunboats, river (*See also* individual boats, actions): (1861) Eads' ironclads, Aug. 7; *Tyler, Lexington, Conestoga,* Aug. 12; C.S.S. *Manassas* attacks Fed. squadron, Oct. 12; U.S.S. *Rescue* captures schooner, Nov. 8; Dec. 1; (1862) U.S. gunboats shell Conf. encampments near Columbus, Ky., Jan. 14; Fed. recon. on Tenn. R., Jan. 15; in Ft. Henry Camp., Feb 3, 4, 5, 6; raid up Tenn. R., Feb. 6, 10; Fed. gunboats at Ft. Donelson, Feb. 11, 13, 14; silence Conf. battery at Pittsburg Ldg., Tenn., Mar. 1; arrive at Savannah, Tenn., Mar. 5; recon. from Savannah, Tenn., Apr. 3; ass. on Island No. 10, Apr. 7; C.S.A. building, Apr. 17; Conf. at Bat. of New Orleans, Apr. 24, 25; Fed. demon. against Sewell's Point batteries, May 8; Bat. of Plum Run Bend, Tenn., May 10; Fed. push down Miss. R., June 4; Bat. of Memphis, June 6; *Wissahickon, Itasca* engage Grand Gulf batteries, June 9; Farragut aids Vicksburg exped., June 20; above Vicksburg, June 26; at Baton Rouge eng., Aug. 5; Fed. gunboat flotilla transferred from War to Navy Dept., Oct. 1; (1863) att. on Conf. batteries on Rappahannock R., Va., Feb. 21; *Indianola* surrendered to Confs., Feb. 24; eng. between, and land forces at Pattersonville, La., Mar. 27; 2 Conf. burned, Apr. 14; Fed. att. on Ft. Beauregard, May 10; at siege of Vicksburg, May 22, 27; Conf. att. on Fed. gunboats, May 27; in Sabine Pass att., Sept. 8; (1864) sk. at Paducah, Ky., Apr. 14; in Red R. Camp., Apr. 25, 26, May 5; *Shawsheen* capt., May 7; Conf. att. on, June 15; at Bat. of Mobile Bay, Aug. 5

Gunpowder Br., Va.: (1864) burned, July 10

Guns: *See* Ordnance

Gunter's Br., on North Edisto R., S.C.: (1865) sk., Feb. 14

conduct, Mar. 3; Charles F. Smith to command Tenn. exped., Mar. 4; given command Depts. of Mo., Kas., and part of the O., Mar. 11; assumes command new Dept. of the Miss., Mar. 13; orders Buell to Savannah, Tenn., Mar. 15; restores Grant to command, Mar. 15; takes field command, Apr. 11; enlarging army, Apr. 19; advance on Corinth, Miss., Apr. 28, 29, May 2, 3, 4, 6, 8, 17, 22; troop strength, Apr. 29; Lincoln to, May 11; Beauregard pulls out, May 29; enters Corinth, May 30; studies troop dispositions at Tupelo, June 3; Pope probes against Beauregard, June 4; gives Buell, Grant, Pope army corps, June 10; Lincoln names General-in-Chief, July 11; leaves Western post to be gen. of all U.S. armies, July 16; assumes command, July 23; orders A. of P. to defend Washington, Aug. 3; urges McClellan to send troops to 2nd Bull Run, Aug. 29; confers with Lincoln, McClellan, Sept. 1; Army of Va. consolidated into A. of P., Sept. 5; Lincoln orders McClellan through, Oct. 6; rescinding of Grant's "Jew order," Dec. 17

(1863) Burnside to Lincoln, ment., Jan. 1; revocation of Grant's "Jew order," Jan. 4; to Burnside, Jan. 7; to Grant, Jan. 21; Lincoln confers with, Jan. 24, Apr. 11; visits Aquia Cr., Apr. 19; leaves for A. of P., May 6; confers with Hooker, Lincoln, May 7; confers on Lee's movements, June 5; dispute with Hooker, June 16; gives Meade command A. of P., June 27; Lincoln to, July 6, 7, 29; Lincoln confers with, Sept. 11; Lincoln to, Sept. 15, 19, Oct. 16, 24; (1864) replaced by Grant as General-in-Chief, named Chief of Staff, Mar. 12; defending Wash., July 10, 27; confers with Lincoln, Aug. 7; Curtis protests to, Oct. 28; confers with Lincoln, Stanton, Grant, Nov. 23; Grant to, Dec. 8, 12; (1865) assigned to command Mil. Div. of the James, Apr. 19; assumes command, Apr. 22; Sherman angry with, Apr. 24

Halleck, Ft., Dak. Terr.: (1863) sk., Feb. 20

Hall's Fy., Miss.: (1863) sk., May 13

Hallsville, Mo.: (1861) sk., Dec. 27

Halltown, W. Va.: (1862) sks., Nov. 22, Dec. 20; (1863) sk., July 15; (1864) aff., May 8; Sheridan's move from, Aug. 9, 10; Sheridan to, Aug. 21; Early demon. against, Aug. 23; sk., Aug. 24; Early leaves force at, Aug. 25; sk., Aug. 25; act., Aug. 26

Hambright's Station, Mo.: (1862) sk., June 18

Hamburg, Mo.: (1861) Fed. exped. to, Aug. 7; aff., Aug. 11

Hamden, O.: (1863) sk. (Morgan's raid), July 17

Hamilton, Andrew J.: (1865) provisional gov. of Tex., June 17

Hamilton, N.C.: (1862) capt., July 9

Hamilton, O.: (1863) Morgan heads for, July 13

Hamilton's Fd., on Rolling Fork, Ky.: *See* Johnson's Fy., Ky.

Hamilton's Plantation near Grand Gulf, Miss.: (1862) sk., June 24

Hamlin, Hannibal (F): (1860) elected vice-pres., Nov. 6; meets with Lincoln, Nov. 21; (1861) meets with Lincoln in N.Y., Feb. 20; inaugurated, Mar. 4; (1862) Eman. Proc. draft, June 18; (1864) dropped in 1864 election, June 5; not nominated, June 8

Hamlin, W. Va.: (1864) sk., May 29

Hammond, James, H., Jr. (C): (1860) resigns from Sen., Nov. 10

Hardee, William Joseph (C): (1861) assumes command Central Army of Ky., Dec. 5; (1862) rear guard leaves Bowling Green, Ky., Feb. 14; A. S. Johnston precedes to Nashville, Feb. 15; commands corps, Army of the Miss., Mar. 29; corps command to, Nov. 7; commands Corps, Army of Tenn., Nov. 20; Bat. of Murfreesboro, Dec. 30; (1863) superseded in command, July 19; Polk replaces in Miss., Oct. 23; Bat. of Missionary Ridge, Nov. 25; Bragg's command to, Nov. 30, Dec. 2; superseded, Dec. 16; (1864) Atlanta Camp., May 19, 25, 28 (recon. near Dallas); June 14; Sherman attacks, June 17; Bat. of Peachtree Cr., July 20; att. on McPherson's flank, July 21; Bat. of Atlanta, July 22; problems with Hood, Aug. 7; Bat. of Jonesborough, Aug. 31, Sept. 1; Hood asks removal of, Sept. 25; relieved, to command Dept. of S.C., Ga., and Fla., Sept. 28; hears Davis' speech, Oct. 5; opposes Sherman, Nov. 23, 24; entrenched at Savannah, Ga., Dec. 10; Davis to, Dec. 17; Sherman asks surrender of, Dec. 17, 18 (refusal); evacuates Savannah, Dec. 20; escape of, Dec. 21; heads north, Dec. 22; (1865) Davis mentions, Jan. 12; Davis to, Jan. 15; attempts to recruit, Jan. 19; Sherman's advance, Feb. 1; Davis to, Feb. 11, 14; at Charleston, Feb. 13, 16, 17; Bat. of Averasborough, Mar. 16; Bat. of Bentonville, Mar. 19, 20, 21

Hardin Co., Tenn.: (1864) sk. in, Feb. 9

Hardin Pike, Tenn.: (1864) sk. on near Nashville, Dec. 3

Hard Times Ldg., La.: (1863) Fed. fleet concentrates near, Apr. 16; sk., Apr. 25

Hardy, W. Va.: (1862) Conf. exped. from, Nov. 8

Hardy Co., W. Va.: (1863) Fed. sc., Dec. 7; (1864) Fed. oper. in, Jan. 1, 27

Harlan, James (F): (1865) named Sec. of Interior, Mar. 9

Harney, William Selby (F): (1861) St. Louis command, May 11; proclamation, May 12, 14; relieved, reinstated, May 18; proclamation with Price, May 21; superseded by Lyon, May 31; Harney-Price agreement analysis, May 31

Harney-Price agreement: (1861) May 21, 31

Harper's Fy., W. Va.: (1861) Scott, Lincoln confer on, Apr. 17; U. S. Armory at abandoned, Apr. 18; taken by Va. troops, Apr. 19; Va. volunteers to, under Jackson, May 1; Conf. garrisons reinforced, May 19; J. E. Johnston on holding, June 13; Johnston evacuates, June 14; sks., July 4, 14, Sept., 2, 17, Oct. 11, 16, 20; Jackson's oper. near, Dec. 17; (1862) Fed. batteries shell, Feb. 7; Feds. sent to bridge Potomac, Feb. 8; Fed. troops occupy, Feb. 24; Banks advances from, Mar. 5; Banks ordered back to, Mar. 23; Banks retreats toward, May 25; Jackson to head for, May 26; Jackson demon. near, May 29; Jackson falls back from, May 30; Fed. train capt. near, Aug. 23; Fed. oper. and recon. from, Sept. 3; Fed. forces cut off from Wash., Sept. 7; Lincoln on, Sept. 7; Jackson converging on, Sept. 9, 12; Bat. of Crampton's Gap, Sept. 14; Jackson captures, Sept. 15; A. P. Hill arranges surrender of, Sept. 16; Hill to Antietam, Sept. 17; Fed. troops reoccupy, Sept. 22; Fed. recon. from, Sept. 27; Fed. recon. from, Oct. 1, 16; Lincoln, McClellan confer at, Oct. 1, 2; sk. near, Dec. 12; (1863) Fed. sc. from, Mar. 15; ment., June 14; Feds. escape toward, June 15; menaced by Lee, June 16; evac. of Maryland Heights, June 26, 27; sk., Feds. reoccupy

Maryland Heights, July 7; sk., July 14; Lee at, July 19; Fed. sc. from, Sept. 12, 21; sk. near, Oct. 1; W. Va., Va., and Tenn. R.R. raid operates from, Dec. 10; (1864) Early near, July 3, 4, 5 (decides not to take); Fed. retreat toward after 2nd Kernstown, July 24; Sheridan's move from, Aug. 9, 10; Sheridan pulls back toward, Aug. 21; Early demonstrates against, Aug. 22; act. near, at Halltown, Aug. 26; Early decides not to attack, Aug. 27; Mosby wrecks, robs train near, Oct. 13; (1865) aff., Feb. 3; Fed. sc. from, Mar. 20

Harper's Fy., Dept. of, Fed.: (1861) B. F. Kelley commands, Oct. 22

Harper's Fy. Rifle Factory: (1861) May 1

Harpeth R., Tenn.: (1863) Fed. recon. to, Jan. 13; (1864) Bat. of Franklin, Nov. 30

Harpeth Shoals, Cumberland R., Tenn.: (1863) aff., Jan. 8; U.S.S. *Slidell* capt., Jan. 13

Harriet Lane, U.S.S.: (1861) Apr. 5; to Sumter, Apr. 8; fails to reach Sumter, Apr. 13; shells Pig Point batteries, June 5; (1863) capt. by Confs. at Galveston, Jan. 1

Harrington, George (F): (1864) temporary Sec. of Treasury, June 30

Harris, Clara: (1865) guest of Lincolns at Ford's Theatre, Apr. 14

Harris, Isham Green (C): (1861) as gov. Tenn. leagues state to C.S.A., May 7; requests supplies, Aug. 23; calls for arms, Nov. 2; (1862) leaves Nashville, Feb. 16; Tenn. capital to Memphis, Feb. 20; (1863) Davis to, Sept. 1

Harrisburg, Miss.: (1864) A. J. Smith arrives at, July 13; Bat. of (or Tupelo), July 14, 15

Harrisburg, Pa.: (1861) Lincoln speaks in, Feb. 22; (1862) approach of Conf. troops, Sept. 7; (1863) panic in over Lee's invasion, June 16, 27; sk. near (Gettysburg Camp.), June 30; (1865) Lincoln's funeral train in, Apr. 22

Harrison, Burton (C): (1865) Davis' sc., capt., May 10

Harrison, Mo. (or Leasburg): (1864) sk., Sept. 29

Harrison, O.: (1863) Morgan's raid, July 13

Harrison, Tenn.: (1864) Fed. sc. to, Jan. 21

Harrison, Ft., Va.: (1864) Bat. of (or Chaffin's Farm), Sept. 29, 30

Harrisonburg, La.: (1863) Fed. oper. to, Sept. 1

Harrisonburg, Va.: (1862) Jackson leaves, Apr. 18; sk., May 6; Jackson moving to, June 1; Turner Ashby's death near, June 6; sk., June 7; Lincoln orders Frémont to halt at, June 9; Feds. leave, June 12; (1864) aff., June 4; Sheridan falls back to, Sept. 28; Sheridan harassed near, Oct. 3

Harrison Co., W. Va.: (1863) aff., Apr. 18

"Harrison's Bar letter": (1862) July 7

Harrison's Gap, Ala.: (1864) aff., Apr. 21

Harrison's I., Potomac R.: (1861) Oct. 20; Bat. of Ball's Bluff, Oct. 21

Harrison's Ldg., Va.: (1862) McClellan hdqrs., June 26; A. of P. to, June 28, July 1, 2; act., July 2; sk., July 3; Fed. recon. from, July 4; Lincoln at, July 8; Fed. recons. from, July 10, 11, 29; McClellan ordered to remove sick, wounded from, July 30; Conf. att. on, July 31; evac. of, Aug. 14, 16; (1864) sk., June 14; act., Aug. 4; cattle raid near, Sept. 15

Harrisonville, Mo.: (1861) act., July 18; sk., July 25; (1862) sk., Nov. 3; (1863) sk., Oct. 24

Harrisville, W. Va.: (1863) aff., May 7

Harrodsburg, Ky.: (1862) Bragg moving toward, Oct. 6; eng., Oct. 10; (1864) sk., Oct. 21; (1865) sk., Jan. 29

Hartford, U.S.S.: (1862) passes forts below New Orleans, Apr. 24; (1863) passes Port Hudson batteries, Mar. 14; off Natchez, Mar. 17; passes Grand Gulf batteries, Mar. 19, 31; att. on Conf. batteries at Warrenton, Mar. 23; (1864) Bat. of Mobile Bay, Aug. 5

Hartsville, Tenn.: (1862) Conf. guerrillas capt. near, July 10; sk., Nov. 28; Morgan captures Fed. garrison, Dec. 7; (1863) sks., Apr. 18, 22

Hartsville Rd., Tenn.: (1862) sk., Aug. 19

Hartville, Mo.: (1863) Fed. garrison surrenders to Marmaduke, Jan. 9; eng., Jan. 11; sk., May 23; (1864) sk., Aug. 11

Hartwood, Va.: (1862) Fed. recon. near, Dec. 1

Hartwood Church, Va.: (1862) aff., Nov. 28; (1863) sks., Feb. 25, Aug. 15, 25, 28, Oct. 12, Nov. 5

Harvey Birch (U.S. clipper ship): (1861) seized, Nov. 19

Haskell, Ft., Va.: (1864) sk., Nov. 5

Hatch, John Porter (F): (1864) assumes command Dept. of the South, May 1

Hatcher's Run, Va.: (1864) eng. of Burgess' Mill or Boydton Plank Rd., Oct. 27; sk., Dec. 8; Fed. recon. to, Dec. 9; (1865) Bat. of, Feb. 5, 6, 7; sk. near, Mar. 29; sk. near, Mar. 30; act., Mar. 31; sk., Apr. 2

Hatchie Bottom, Miss.: (1862) aff., July 20

Hatchie Bottom, Tenn.: (1862) sk., July 29

Hatchie R., Miss.: (1862) sk., July 5; Fed. recon. to, Sept. 30; sk., Oct. 7

Hatchie R., Tenn.: (1862) Fed. recon. toward, Aug. 10; sk. on, Sept. 25; Ord intercepts Confs., Oct. 5; (1863) sk. near Bloomington, Feb. 27; Fed. exped. to, Apr. 1; Fed. sc. to, June 16

Hatteras, N.C.: (1861) pro-Union govt. voted, Nov. 18

Hatteras, Ft., N.C.: (1861) duels with U. S. Navy, Aug. 27; surrenders, Aug. 28

Hatteras, U.S.S.: (1863) sunk by *Alabama,* Jan. 11

Hatteras Inlet: (1861) Aug. 27; cleanup oper. at, Aug. 29; Oct. 4; Mansfield in Fed. command, Oct. 5; (1862) Roanoke exped., Jan. 13, 22, 25, Feb. 7

Haughton's Mill, N.C.: (1862) sk., Apr. 27

Havana, Cuba: (1861) Nov. 8; (1865) C.S.S. *Stonewall* arrives, May 11; *Stonewall* surrenders, May 19

Havelocks: (1861) sent to Lincoln, Aug. 3

Haverhill, Mass.: (1861) editor attacked, Aug. 19

Hawaiian Is.: (1861) neutrality of, Aug. 26

Hawes, Richard (C): (1862) gov. of Ky., Oct. 4

Hawesville, Ind.: (1862) guerrillas driven out, Oct. 10

Hawk's Nest, W. Va.: (1861) sks., Aug. 20, Sept. 2

Haw's Shop, Va.: (1862) sk. (Stuart's ride around McClellan), June 13; (1864) comb., May 28; act., June 3

Hawthorne, Nathaniel: (1864) death of, May 19

Haxall (or Haxall's) Ldg., Va.: (1864) ment., May 12, 17

Hay, John Milton (F): (1861) visits McClellan, Nov. 13; (1863) Lincoln writes doggerel for, July 19; (1864) Lincoln to, June 7; on N.Y. peace mission, July 16

Haymarket, Va.: (1862) sks., Aug. 26, 28; (1863) sks., June 21, Oct. 19

Hayne, J. W. (C): (1861) S.C. envoy to Wash., Jan. 13

Haynes' Bluff, Miss.: (1862) Sherman's exped. advancing toward, Dec. 26; (1863) Fed. demon. against, Apr. 29; Fed. capture of, May 18; sk., May 23; Fed. expeds. from, May 26, June 2

Hays, William (F): (1863) superseded in command, Second Corps, Aug. 16

Hay's Fy., near Dandridge, Tenn.: (1863) act., Dec. 24

Hay Station No. 3, near Brownsville, Ark.: (1864) sk., July 30

Hazard Powder Co.: (1861) powder seized, June 5

Hazel Bottom, Mo.: (1862) sk., Oct. 14

Hazel Grove at Chancellorsville, Va.: (1863) May 3

Hazel R., Va.: (1863) sks., Sept. 27, Oct. 7

Hazen, William Babcock (F): (1864) fall of Ft. McAllister, Dec. 13

Hazen's Farm, near Devall's Bluff, Ark.: (1864) aff., Nov. 2

Hazle Green, Ky.: (1863) sks., Mar. 9, 19

Head of Passes, La.: (1861) *Manassas* att. on Union squadron, Oct. 12

Heathsville, Va.: (1863) Fed. exped. to, Feb. 12

Hébert, Paul Octave (C): (1861) commands Tex. forces, Aug. 14; commands Dept. of Tex., Sept. 18

Hedgesville, W. Va.: (1863) sk., July 18; aff., Oct. 15

Heiman, Ft., Ky.: (1862) occup., Feb. 5; sk., Feb. 13; (1863) Fed. sc. from, May 26; (1864) Forrest near, Oct. 30, 31

Heintzelman, Samuel Peter (F): (1862) Bat. of Fair Oaks or Seven Pines, May 31; eng. at Oak Grove, June 25; commands Wash. defenses, Sept. 9, Oct. 26; (1863) commands re-created Dept. of Wash., Feb. 7; superseded by C. C. Auger, Oct. 14

Helena, Ark.: (1862) Curtis arrives at, July 12; sk. near, July 14; Fed. expeds. from, July 23, 24, 28, Aug. 4; C.S.A. controls Miss. R., to Baton Rouge, La., Aug. 5; Fed. exped. from, Aug. 5; sk., Aug. 11; Fed. gunboat exped. from, Aug. 16; Fed. exped. from, Aug. 28; sk., Sept. 19; Fed. expeds. from, Sept. 26; sks., Oct. 11, 18, 20; Davis on recapture of, Oct. 21; sks., Oct. 22, 25; oper. from, Nov. 5; Fed. exped. from, Nov. 16; aff., Dec. 14; sk., Dec. 23; (1863) aff., Jan. 1; sk. near, Jan. 12; Fed. expeds. from, Jan. 13, Mar. 5, 6, May 23; sk., May 25; Conf. att. on, July 4; Steele commands Fed. forces in Ark., Aug. 5; Steele's march begins, Aug. 10; fall of Little Rock, Sept. 10; Fed. exped. from, Nov. 14; (1864) Fed. expeds. from, Feb. 4, 13, 20, July 13; Fed. sc. from, Aug. 22; Fed. exped. from, Aug. 29; Fed. scs. from, Sept. 9, 22; (1865) Fed. exped. from, Jan. 11; Fed. sc. from, Feb. 8; Fed. exped. from, Feb. 19; Fed. sc. from, Feb. 24

Helena Rd., Miss.: (1863) sk. on, June 21

Hell: (1862) warfare described as, May 25; soldier quote on, Dec. 13

Helm, Ben Hardin (C): (1863) death of, Sept. 22; widow visits Lincoln, Dec. 13

Helm, Emily Todd: (1863) visits Lincolns, Dec. 13; takes oath, Dec. 14

Hemp bales, Bat. of the, at Lexington, Mo.: (1861) Sept. 20

Henderson, John B. (F): (1864) proposes abolition by amendment, Jan. 11

Henderson, Ky.: (1862) sks., June 30, Sept. 14; (1864) sk., Sept. 25

Henderson Co., Ky.: (1862) sk., Nov. 1

Henderson's Gap, Ga.: (1863) recon. from, Sept. 13

Henderson's Hill, La.: (1864) aff., Mar. 21
Henderson's Mill, Tenn.: (1863) sk., Oct 11
Henderson's Station, Tenn.: (1862) capt., Nov. 25
Henry, Ft., Tenn.: (1861) Tilghman named to command, Nov. 21; (1862) Fed. recon., Jan. 15; demon. by Feds. against, Jan. 17; shelled, Jan. 22; Grant prepares offensive, Feb. 1; exped. readies, Feb. 2; gunboat fleet heads toward, Feb. 3; troops land north of, Feb. 4, 5; defense, surrender of, Feb. 6; Grant near, Feb. 7; news of fall of, Feb. 8; ment., Feb. 10; Fed. advance from, Feb. 11; ment., Feb. 14; Grant hurries to, Mar. 1; C. F. Smith commands exped. from, Mar. 3; Grant at, Mar. 4; oper., Sept. 18; (1863) Fed. exped. from, Jan. 16; (1864) Forrest near, Oct. 30
Henry Co., Ky.: (1862) oper. against guerrillas, Oct. 15
Henry Co., Mo.: (1862) sk., Feb. 24; oper., Mar. 18; (1863) Fed. exped. into, Aug 28
Henry Dodge (U.S. revenue cutter): (1861) seized, Mar. 2
Henry House Hill, Va.: (1861) Bat. of 1st Bull Run, July 21; (1862) Bat. of 2nd Bull Run, Aug. 30
Henrytown, Mo.: (1861) act. of Wet Glaize, near, Oct. 13
Henryville, Tenn.: (1864) sk., Nov. 23
Hercules, U.S. (tug): (1863) att. on, Feb. 17
Hermann, Mo.: (1864) sk., Oct. 3
Hermitage, The, La.: (1865) Fed. exped. from, Apr. 2
Hermitage Fd., Tenn.: (1862) sk., Oct. 20
Hermitage Plantation near Morganza, La.: (1864) oper. near, Dec. 14
Hernando, Miss.: (1862) Fed. expeds. to, June 21, Sept. 8; (1863) sk., Mar. 15; Fed. expeds. to, May 23, 26; Fed. sc. toward, May 28; act. near, June 19; Fed. expeds. to, Aug. 16, Oct. 10; Fed. sc. to, Nov. 19; (1864) sk., Oct. 15
Hernando Rd., Tenn.: (1865) Fed. sc. on, Feb. 7
Herndon Station, Va.: (1863) aff., Mar. 17
Herold, David E.: (1865) accomplice of Booth, Apr. 15; flight, Apr. 16, 17, 22, 24, 25; capture, Apr. 26; imprisonment, May 1; death sentence, June 30; hanged, July 7
Herring Creek, near Harrison's Ldg., Va.: (1862) sk. near, July 3; (1864) sk., July 17
Herr Ridge, Pa.: (1863) in Bat. of Gettysburg, July 1
Herron, Francis Jay (F): (1862) Bat. of Prairie Grove, Ark., Dec. 7; (1863) in command Army of the Frontier, Apr. 1; (1864) assumes command on Rio Grande, Jan. 3
Hertford, N.C.: (1863) sk., Dec. 10
Heth, Henry (C): (1863) Bat. of Gettysburg, July 3; (1864) Bat. of the Weldon R.R., Aug. 18; eng. of Burgess' Mill, Oct. 27
Hickman, Ky.: (1861) Confs. en route to, Sept. 3; battery-gunboat duel, Sept. 4; (1863) Fed. occup. of, July 15; Fed. exped. to, Aug. 1; (1864) Fed. sc. to, July 17
Hickman Co., Tenn.: (1864) Fed. sc. in, May 2
Hickory Forks, Va.: (1863) Fed. recon. to, Apr. 12; Fed. exped. beyond, Apr. 27
Hickory Grove, Mo.: (1862) sks., Aug. 23, Sept. 19

Hilton Head I., S.C.: (1861) occup., Nov. 7; Fed. recon., Nov. 8; Fed. expeds. from, Nov. 10, Dec. 6; Fed. threat to Charleston from, Dec. 11; Dec. 17; (1862) Fed. Dept. of the South hdqrs., Mar. 15; Fed. oper. from, Mar. 20; Hunter assumes command Dept. of the South, Mar. 31; aff., June 13; Fed. land-sea exped. from, Sept. 30; (1863) monitors reported leaving, Mar. 25; Negro troops leave for, May 28; (1864) Fla. exped. moves from, Feb. 5; troops from to Honey Hill, Nov. 30; (1865) Sherman pauses at, Jan. 21

Hindman, Thomas Carmichael (C): (1862) assumes command Trans-Miss. Dist., May 31; Bat. of Prairie Grove, Dec. 7

Hindman, Ft. (or Arkansas Post), Ark.: (1863) McClernand moves toward, Jan. 4; eng., Jan. 10; surrenders, Jan. 11

Hinesville, Ga.: (1864) sk., Dec. 16

History: (1862) "We cannot escape . . ." Lincoln, Dec. 1

H. L. Hunley, C.S.S. (submarine): (1863) sinks, Aug. 29; raised, sinks, Oct. 15; (1864) sinks *Housatonic,* Feb. 17

Hockingport, O.: (1863) sk. (Morgan's raid), July 20

Hodgenville, Ky.: (1861) sk., Oct. 23

Hodge's Plantation, La.: (1864) sk., Sept. 11

Hoffman, Henry W.: (1864) Lincoln to, Oct. 10

Hogan's, Va.: (1862) sk., May 23

Hog Eye, Ark.: (1863) sk., Sept. 4

Hog I., Bates Co., Mo.: (1863) aff., May 18

Hog Jaw Valley, Ala.: (1865) sk. at Ladd's House, Feb. 3

Hog Mt., Ala.: (1863) act., Apr. 30

Hog Point, Miss.: (1863) Conf. oper. against U.S. gunboats, Nov. 18

Hoke, Robert Frederick (C): (1864) att. on Plymouth, N.C., Apr. 17, 18, 19, 20 (capt.); (1865) capture of Ft. Fisher, Jan. 15

Hoke's Run, W. Va.: (1861) sk., July 2

Holden, W. W. (F): (1863) newspaper offices pillaged, Sept. 10; (1865) provisional gov. of N.C., May 29

Holden, Mo.: (1864) oper. near, Aug. 2

"Hold the Fort, for We Are Coming": (1864) Oct. 5

Hollins, George N. (C): (1861) seizes *St. Nicholas,* June 28

Hollow Tree Gap, Tenn.: (1864) act., Dec. 17

Holly, Ft., Va.: (1864) sks., Dec. 10

Holly Springs, Miss.: (1862) sk., July 1; Conf. exped. from, July 25; Fed. sc. toward, Sept. 5; Fed. troops seize, Nov. 13; sk., Nov. 28; Grant issues "Jew order" from, Dec. 17; Holly Springs raid, Dec. 20; (1863) Feds. evacuate, Jan. 9; sks., June 16, Sept. 7, Nov. 5; (1864) sks., Feb. 12, Apr. 17, May 24; aff., Aug. 28

Hollywood Cemetery, Richmond, Va.: (1862) Pres. Tyler buried, Jan. 18

Holman's Br., S.C.: (1865) sk., Feb. 9

Holmes, Oliver Wendell, Jr. (F): (1864) admonishes Lincoln at Ft. Stevens, July 12

Holmes, Theophilus Hunter (C): (1861) commands Aquia Dist., Oct. 22; (1862) assigned to command Trans-Miss. Dept., July 16; assumes command, July 30; Davis to, Oct. 21, Dec. 21; (1863) Davis to, Feb. 26; assumes command Dist. of Ark., Mar. 18; Davis to, July 14; ment., Aug. 13; (1864) Price supersedes, Mar. 16

Holmes Co., O.: (1863) opposition to draft, war, June 16

Holston R., Tenn.: (1862) br. destroyed, Dec. 30; (1863) sks. at Leiper's Fy., Oct. 28, 30; sk. at Farley's Mill, Dec. 13; (1864) Stoneman's southwest Va. exped., Dec. 13

Holt, Joseph (F): (1860) as Postmaster General opposes secession, Nov. 9; Dec. 27; named temporary Sec. of War, Dec. 31; (1861) named Sec. of War, Jan. 18; orders Twiggs dismissal, Mar. 1; Anderson message on Sumter reinforcements, Mar. 4; emissary to Frémont, Sept. 13; (1864) appointed judge advocate general, Sept. 3; refuses attorney generalship, Nov. 26; (1865) judge advocate in conspiracy trial, May 6

Holt, Ft., Ky.: (1861) gunboat demon. near, Dec. 1

Holy See, Rome: (1863) Conf. agent to appointed, Sept. 24

Home Guards, Mo.: (1861) Camp Jackson aff., May 10; Cole Camp sk., June 19

Homestead Act: (1862) Lincoln signs, May 20

Homochitto R., Miss.: (1864) Fed. exped. to, Oct. 5

Honey Cr., Mo.: (1863) aff. on, Oct. 19; (1864) sk., May 30

Honey Hill, S.C.: (1864) eng., Nov. 30

Honey Springs, I.T.: (1863) cav. eng., July 17

Hood, John Bell (C): (1862) at Gaines' Mill, June 27; (1863) Gettysburg Camp., June 8; (1864) Bat. of Resaca, May 15; Atlanta Camp., May 19, 25, June 22; replaces Johnston in Ga., July 17; commands Army of Tenn., July 18; plans att., July 19; Bat. of Peachtree Cr., July 20; defends Atlanta, July 21; Bat. of Atlanta, July 22; Bat. of Ezra Church, July 28; Aug. 3, 4; problems with Hardee, Aug. 7; Sherman plans moves against, Aug. 9; Aug. 14, 15, 18, 21, 25, 26 (Hood's lines endangered), 27, 28, 29, 30 (prepares to attack), 31 (Bat. of Jonesboro), Sept. 1 (evac. of Atlanta), 2, 3, 4 (resting troops), 7 (Sherman orders evac. of Atlanta); Davis to confer with, Sept. 22; confers with Davis, asks Hardee's removal, Sept. 25; transfer of Hardee, Sept. 28; moves against supply lines, Oct. 1; Western & Atlantic R.R. broken, Oct. 2; Beauregard to command Western depts., Oct. 2; Davis on, Oct. 3; holds r.r., Oct. 4, 5; moves toward Ala., Oct. 7, 15; sk. near Rome, Ga., Oct. 10; below Rome, Oct. 11; sk., Ship's Gap, Ga., Oct. 16; Sherman halts pursuit of, Oct. 21; seeks route to Tenn., Oct. 22; sks., Oct. 25; near Courtland (by Oct. 30), Oct. 26; moves across Ala., Oct. 28, 29; Fed. opposition grows, Oct. 30; expects Forrest to join him, Oct. 30; at Tuscumbia, Oct. 31

Nashville defenses, Nov. 3; Forrest heads toward, Nov. 4; move into Tenn. by expected, Nov. 9; Thomas to halt, Nov. 9; advance into Tenn. delayed, Nov. 18; moves out to Tenn., Nov. 21; attempts to divide Feds., Nov. 21; advance into Tenn., Nov. 22, 23; Schofield beats to Columbia, Tenn., Nov. 24, 25; at Columbia, Nov. 26, 27, 28; Spring Hill aff., Nov. 29; Bat. of Franklin, Nov. 30; Davis mentions, Nov. 30; en route to Nashville, Dec. 1; positions at Nashville, Dec. 2; Thomas prepares att. on, Dec. 4; demon. against Murfreesboro, Tenn., Dec. 5; Thomas ordered to attack, Dec. 2, 6, 7, 8, 10, 11, 12, 13 (sleet storm), 14; Bat. of Nashville, Dec. 15, 16; withdrawal from Nashville, Dec. 17, 18, 20 (across Duck R.); retreats toward Pulaski, Tenn., Dec. 21; sk. on Duck R., Dec. 22; sk. at Warfield's, Dec. 23; Thomas pursues, Dec. 23, 24, 25, 26, 27; (1865) Davis on possible removal of, Jan. 2; moves to Tupelo, Jan. 9; Davis on, Jan. 12; resigns command, Jan. 13; defeat at Nashville ment., Jan. 23

Hood's Texas Brigade: (1862) at Gaines' Mill, June 27

Hooker, Joseph (F): (1862) Bat. of Williamsburg, May 5; Bat. of South Mt., Sept. 14; commands corps, Nov. 5; takes command of Fifth Corps, Nov. 10; commands Center Grand Div., A. of P., Nov. 14; Bat. of Fredericksburg, Dec. 13; (1863) nears U. S. Ford, Jan. 19; Burnside's order dismissing, Jan. 23; Lincoln names to command A. of P., Jan. 25; takes command, A. of P., Lincoln's advice to, Jan. 26; meets with Lincoln, Jan. 26; Lincoln visits, Apr. 3, 4, 5, 6, 8, 10, 11; proposes outflanking Lee, Apr. 12; Fed. cav. attacks, Apr. 14; Lincoln to, Apr. 15, 27; Chancellorsville Camp., Apr. 27, 28, 29, 30; Bat. of Chancellorsville, May 1, 2, 3, 4; wounded at Chancellorsville, May 3; crosses Rappahannock R., May 5, 6; Lincoln confers with, May 7; Lincoln requests visit from, May 13; Lincoln to, May 14; Pleasonton replaces Stoneman, May 22; faces Lee, May 24; Lincoln to, May 27; on Rappahannock, May 31; Lincoln's opinion of, June 2; hears of Lee's movements, June 3; Gettysburg Camp., June 4, 5, 6, 8 (Bat. of Brandy Station), 10 (Lincoln to), 15 (to Lincoln), 16 (dispute with Halleck), 16 (Lincoln to), 23, 24 (asks for orders), 25, 26; replaced by Meade, June 27, 28; commands reinforcement of Rosecrans, Sept. 23, 24, 28, Oct. 1, 2; moves toward Chattanooga, Oct. 26; in Wauhatchie Valley, Oct. 28; offensive planned, Nov. 21; Bat. of Lookout Mt., Nov. 24; Bat. of Missionary Ridge, Nov. 25; (1864) Atlanta Camp., May 15, 25; resigns command, July 27

Hookertown, N.C.: (1865) sk., Mar. 31

Hoopa Valley, Calif.: (1863) sk. with Inds., Sept. 3

Hoover's Gap, Tenn.: (1863) sk. (Tullahoma Camp.), June 24

Hopefield, Ark.: (1863) burned, Feb. 17; (1864) sk., Mar. 14

Hopewell, Mo.: (1862) Fed. exped. against guerrillas, Oct. 24; (1863) sk., Aug. 25; aff. near, Oct. 21

Hopewell Gap, Va.: (1863) Fed. sc. to, Dec. 28

Hopkinsville, Ky.: (1861) sk., Sept. 29; (1864) Conf. raid to, Dec. 6

Hornersville, Mo.: (1862) Fed. exped. to, Mar. 9; sk., Sept. 20; (1864) sk., Sept. 8

Hornets' Nest: (1862) at Shiloh, Apr. 6

Horn Lake Cr., Miss.: (1862) sk., Aug. 16

Horn Lake Cr., Tenn.: (1863) sk., May 18

Hornsborough, S.C.: (1865) sk., Mar. 3

Horse Cave, Ky.: (1862) sk., Sept. 19

Horse Cr., Mo.: (1862) sk., May 7; (1863) sk., Sept. 17

Horse Head Cr., Ark.: (1864) sk., Feb. 17

Horses, swapping: (1864) quote by Lincoln, June 9

Horses, U.S.: (1861) 150 die in Wash. fire, Dec. 26; (1862) Lincoln on "fatigued horses," Oct. 25; (1863) concentrated food for, Jan. 15; (1864) White House stable fire, Feb. 10; Morgan steals 7000, June 10

Horseshoe Bottom, Ky.: (1863) act., May 10

Hospitals, Fed.: (1861) chaplains for, Oct. 21: (1862) Lincolns visit, Dec. 25

Hudson's Crossing, Neosho R., I.T.: (1864) aff., June 4
Hudson's Fd., Neosho R., Mo.: (1863) sk., June 30
Hudsonville, Miss.: (1862) Fed. recon. to, Nov. 8; sk., Dec. 1; (1863) Fed. sc.
   to, Mar. 2; sk., June 21; (1864) aff., Feb. 25
Huff's Fy., Tenn.: (1863) cav. sk., Nov. 14
Huger, Benjamin (C): (1862) eng. at Oak Grove, Va., June 25
Huger, Ft., Ala.: (1865) Mobile Camp., Apr. 9, 10, 11
Hughes, John Joseph: (1861) Lincoln to, Oct. 21
Humansville, Mo.: (1862) act., Mar. 26; (1863) aff. (Shelby's raid), Oct. 6;
   sk., Oct. 16
Humboldt, Kas.: (1863) exped. from, Apr. 10
Humboldt, Tenn.: (1862) sks., July 28, Sept. 5; aff., Oct. 9; Dec. 20
Humboldt, Mil. Dist. of, Calif.: (1863) oper. in, Sept. 3; (1864) Fed. oper. in,
   Jan. 1; Fed. oper. in (Ind.), Feb. 1, 29, May 1, 6, 23, 27, 28
Humboldt R., Nev. Terr.: (1864) Fed. exped. to, June 8
Humphreys, Andrew Atkinson (F): (1865) leads Second Army Corps, Ap-
   pomattox Camp., Mar. 29, 30, 31, Apr. 1, 6 (Sayler's Cr.), 8
Hundley's Corner, Va.: (1862) sk., June 26
Hungary Station, Va.: (1863) sk., May 4
Hunley, H. L. (C): (1863) dies in sinking of *Hunley*, Oct. 15
Hunley, C.S.S.: *See H. L. Hunley*
Hunnewell, Mo.: (1861) aff., Aug. 17; (1862) sk., Jan. 3; (1864) aff., Apr. 18
Hunter, David (F): (1861) sent to advise Frémont, Sept. 9; orders sent to
   supersede Frémont, Oct. 24; replaces Frémont, Nov. 2; commands Western
   Dept., Nov. 3; repudiates Frémont-Price prisoner agreement, Nov. 7; com-
   mands new Dept. of Kas., Nov. 9, 19, assumes command, Nov. 20; (1862)
   commands Dept. of the South, Mar. 15; orders slaves freed, Apr. 12, May 9;
   emancipation order disavowed by Lincoln, May 19; Pres. Davis orders
   treated as felon, Aug. 21; (1863) resumes command, Dept. of the South,
   Jan. 20; superseded, June 12; (1864) supersedes Sigel, May 21; movements
   of, May 26; Lynchburg Camp., May 30, June 2, 4, 5 (eng. at Piedmont), 6
   (occupies Staunton); Sheridan to join, June 7; force augmented, June 8;
   moves toward Lexington, Lynchburg, June 10; Sheridan trying to join, June
   11; sk. Lexington, Va. Mil. Institute burned, June 11; Sheridan not to join,
   June 12; Early against, June 13; invests Lynchburg, June 16, 18; retreats,
   June 19, 23; levy on Hagerstown, July 6; eng. at Snicker's Fy. or Parker's
   Fd., July 17; defense of Shenandoah, July 22; Lincoln warns of attack,
   July 23; retribution for depredations, July 30; replaced in command, Dept. of
   W. Va., Aug. 30; (1865) named to head commission to try Lincoln con-
   spirators, May 6
Hunter, Robert Mercer Taliaferro (C): (1861) Sec. of State, July 25; (1862)
   to Conf. Sen., Mar. 18; (1865) Hampton Rds. Peace Conference, Jan. 28,
   Feb. 2, 3
Hunter's Farm, Mo.: (1861) sk., Sept. 26
Hunter's Mill, Va.: (1861) Fed. recon. to, Oct. 20; (1862) exped., Feb. 7; (1863)
   aff., Dec. 21; (1864) aff., Apr. 23
Huntersville, Ark.: (1864) Fed. sc. from, June 4
Huntersville, W. Va.: (1862) desc., Jan. 3; (1863) sk., Aug. 22

Hunting I., S.C.: (1862) aff., Mar. 20

Huntington, Ind.: (1863) Copperheads seize arms, July 6

Huntington, Tenn.: (1863) sk., Dec. 27

Hunt's Mill, near Larkinsville, Ala.: (1863) sk., Sept. 26

Huntsville, Ala.: (1862) occup., Apr. 11; sks., June 4, July 2; disloyal ministers
to ride guerrilla-attacked trains, Aug. 8; (1863) Fed. exped. to, July 13;
(1864) sks., Oct. 1, 18; (1865) Fed. scs. from, Apr. 3, 5

Huntsville, Ark.: (1862) Van Dorn retreats through, Mar. 8; sk., Oct. 22;
Fed. exped. to, Dec. 21; (1863) Fed. exped. from, Jan. 9; Fed. sc. to, July
18; Fed. exped. to, Nov. 10; (1864) Fed. scs. to, Sept. 12, Nov. 11; (1865)
sk., Jan. 6

Huntsville, Ga.: (1864) sk., May 24

Huntsville, Mo.: (1862) sk., Nov. 9; (1864) guerrilla att., July 15; sks. near,
July 16, Aug. 7; aff., Sept. 25

Huntsville, Tenn.: (1862) sk., Aug. 13

Huntsville, Tex.: (1863) death of Houston, July 26

Hupp's Hill (or Strasburg), Va.: (1864) sk., Oct. 14

Hurlbut, Stephen Augustus (F): (1862) arrives at Pittsburg Ldg., Mar. 15;
commands Sixteenth Army Corps, Dec. 18; (1863) Lincoln to, Mar. 20;
(1864) Forrest occupies Memphis, Aug. 21; assumes command Dept. of the
Gulf, Sept. 23; Lincoln to on La. govt., Nov. 14

Hurricane Br., W. Va.: (1862) sk., Sept. 12; (1863) sk., Mar. 28; aff., Dec.
13; (1864) aff. near, Feb. 20

Hurricane Cr., Ark.: (1864) exped. from, Oct. 19

Hurricane Cr., Miss.: (1864) sks., Aug. 9, 13, 19

Hutchinson, Minn.: (1862) sk. with Inds., Sept. 4

Hutchinson's I., S.C.: (1862) Conf. recon. on, June 12

Huttonsville, W. Va.: (1862) sk., Aug. 18; (1863) sk., July 4; (1864) sk.,
Aug. 5; aff., Aug. 24

Hutton Valley, Mo.: (1863) sk., Sept. 6

Hyde County, N.C.: (1861) pro-Union meeting, Oct. 12

Iberia, Mo.: (1861) exped., Sept. 2; (1862) sk., Aug. 29

Ida, C.S.S. (steamer): (1864) capt., burned, Dec. 10

Ida, U.S.S.: (1865) sunk, Apr. 13

Idaho: (1862) exped. (Ind.), Aug. 19; (1863) made terr., Mar. 3

Ile à Vache, Haiti: (1862) plan for Negro colonization, Dec. 31; (1864) return of colonists, Feb. 1

Illinois: (1861) in Fed. Dept. of the Mo., Nov. 9; (1862) Democratic gains,
in, Nov. 4; (1865) ratifies Thirteenth Amendment, Feb. 1

Illinois Cr., Ark.: (1862) Bat. of Prairie Grove, Dec. 7

Illinois troops: (1861) arrive at Cairo, Ill., Apr. 22

Imboden, John Daniel (C): (1863) oper. in W. Va., Apr. 20; commands Valley
Dist., July 21; (1864) opposes Sigel in Valley, May 14

Immigration, Commissioner of: (1864) office instituted, July 4

Imperial Navy (Russian): (1863) arrival of in N.Y., San Francisco, Sept. 23

Imperial, U.S.S. (steamer): (1863) 1st down Miss. R. after Vicksburg, July 16

Inaugural ball: (1861) Lincoln's, Mar. 4; (1865) Lincoln's, Mar. 6

Inauguration, pres., U.S.: (1861) Lincoln's, Mar. 4; (1865) Lincoln's second, ment., Jan. 24

Income tax, Conf.: (1863) Apr. 24

Income tax, U.S.: (1861) first, Aug. 2; Lincoln signs bill, Aug. 5; (1862) Lincoln signs revised, July 1; (1864) base broadened, June 30

Independence, Miss.: (1863) sk., Dec. 7

Independence, Mo: (1861) sk., Nov. 26; (1862) sks., Feb. 18, 22, May 15; capt. by guerrillas, Aug. 11; Fed. exped. to, Aug. 12; Fed. exped. against guerrillas, Oct. 24; (1863) sks., Feb. 8, Mar. 22, Apr. 23, 26, Aug. 25; (1864) sks., Feb. 19, Apr. 23, Aug. 1; Fed. sc. from, Aug. 7; Fed. evac. of, Oct. 21; act., Oct. 22

Independence, W. Va.: (1863) aff. (Jones' raid), Apr. 27

Independence Day: (1862) July 4

Independence Hall: (1861) Lincoln speaks at, Feb. 22

Independent Hill, Prince William Co., Va.: (1863) sk., Mar. 4

Indiana: (1861) Nov. 9; (1862) Lincoln declines Negro regts. from, Aug. 4; Democratic gains in, Oct. 14; (1863) Morgan's raid, July 8, 9, 10, 11, 12; (1864) and Republican party, Sept. 19; Republicans win in, Oct. 11; Morton gov., Oct. 11; (1865) ratifies Thirteenth Amendment, Feb. 16

Indiana Home Guards: (1862) drive Conf. guerrillas from Hawesville, Oct. 10

Indianapolis, Ind.: (1861) Lincoln stops in, Feb. 11; (1863) Chickamauga court of inquiry, Sept. 28; Grant meets Stanton in, Oct. 17

Indiana State Democratic Convention: (1862) "Copperhead" used in reference to, July 30

Indian Bay, Ark.: (1864) sk., Feb. 16

Indian Bayou, La.: (1863) sk. near, Nov. 9; (1864) aff., June 8

Indian Bend, La.: (1863) sk., Apr. 13; (1865) Fed. exped. to, Mar. 25

Indian chiefs: (1862) meet with Fed. authorities, Feb. 1

Indian Cr., Va.: (1864) sks. on, Feb. 22

Indian Nations (*See also* names of tribes): (1863) C.S.A. Cong. authorizes delegates from, May 1

Indianola, Tex.: (1862) falls to Union gunboats, Oct. 26; (1864) aff. near, Feb. 22

Indianola, U.S.S. (ram): (1863) passes Vicksburg batteries, Feb. 13; meets with *New Era No. 5,* Feb. 14; posted at Red R. mouth, Feb. 17; surrenders, Feb. 24; scuttled, Feb. 26

Indian Ranch, Colo. Terr.: (1864) Fed. sc. from, May 9

Indian R., Fla.: (1863) U.S.S. *Sycamore* takes prizes off, Aug. 8

Indians (*See also* Five Civilized Tribes, Sioux uprising, and individual tribes): (1862) at Bat. of Pea Ridge, Mar. 7; (1863) Fed. oper. against, Jan. 4; Lincoln on progress of, Mar. 27; Lincoln on, Dec. 8; (1864) Fed. oper. against in Minn., July 1; Fed. oper. in N. Mex. Terr., July 23; fighting between units of, Sept. 11; (1865) Lincoln orders trial for sellers of arms to, Mar. 17; surrender of Stand Watie, June 23; tribes sign treaty with U.S., Sept. 14

Indians, Five Civilized Tribes (*See also* individual tribes): (1861) influenced by Confs., Apr. 30; some held slaves, Apr. 30; (1865) treaty of loyalty to U.S., Sept. 14

for, Oct. 4; first launched, Oct. 12; (1862) at Ft. Donelson, Feb. 14; (1863) fake, on Miss. R., Feb. 26; Lincoln on failure of at Charleston, Apr. 13; escape of from Alexandria, La., May 11

Iron Co., Mo.: (1861) M. Jeff Thompson on driving out Feds., Oct. 14; (1862) sk. on Black R., Sept. 13

Ironton, Mo.: (1861) Fed. recon. from, Aug. 2; Thompson's raiders advance, Oct. 12; Fed. oper. against Thompson, Oct. 18; Fed. anti-guerrilla oper., Oct. 20; Nov. 2; (1864) sks., Sept. 26, 27

Ironton, Mo., Dist. of: (1861) U. S. Grant commands, Aug. 8

Irvine, Ky.: (1863) sk., July 30

Irving's Plantation, Ark.: (1864) Fed. exped. to, Oct. 26

Irwinville, Ga.: (1865) capture of Davis, May 10

Isaac Smith, U.S.S. (gunboat): (1863) capt., Jan. 30

Isabella, U.S.S.: (1861) seized, Mar. 20

Isham's Fd., Ga.: (1864) sks., July 5, 8

Island Mount, Mo.: (1862) sk., Oct. 29

Island No. 10 (*See also* New Madrid Bend): (1862) oper., Feb. 28; Conf. troop concentration, Mar. 1; Miss. R. post, Mar. 2; Fed. capture of New Madrid, Mar. 14; Pope's drive on, Mar. 18; Mackall supersedes McCown in Conf. command, Mar. 31; Feds. land on, Apr. 1; Fed. canal near New Madrid, Apr. 4; Pope prepares ass. on, Apr. 6; surrender of, Apr. 7; news of, Apr. 8; sk., Oct. 17; (1863) sk. near, Oct. 16; Fed. exped. from, Nov. 21; (1864) aff., Mar. 6; Fed. sc. from, Mar. 18

Island No. 76: (1864) sk., Jan. 20

Island No. 82: (1863) sk., May 18

Island Queen (American excursion steamer): (1864) capt., burned, Sept. 19

"The Island," Vernon Co., Mo.: (1863) Mar. 30

Isle of Wight Co., Va.: (1864) Fed. exped. to, Apr. 13

Issaquena Co., Miss.: (1864) sks., Mar. 22, July 10, Aug. 17; Fed. oper. in, Oct. 24

Itasca, U.S.S.: (1862) breaches obstructions below New Orleans forts, Apr. 20; duels with Grand Gulf batteries, June 9

Iuka, Miss.: (1862) Fed. exped. to, May 22; sk., Sept. 13; recon. and sk., Sept. 16; Bat. of, Sept. 19; sks. near, Sept. 20, 27; (1863) sks., July 7, 14; (1865) Fed. recon. to, Jan. 9; Fed. exped. to, Feb. 17

Ives, Malcolm: (1862) arrest of on spying charges, Feb. 9

Ivey Hills, Miss.: (1864) eng. of (or Okolona or Ivey's Farm), Feb. 22

Ivey's Farm, Miss.: (1864) eng. of (or Okolona or Ivey Hills), Feb. 22

Ivey's Fd., Ark.: (1865) sk., Jan. 8

Ivy Mt., Ky.: (1861) eng., Nov. 8; sk., Nov. 9

J. D. Perry (U.S. steamer): (1864) att. on, Sept. 9

J. M. Chapman (Conf. privateer schooner): (1863) seized, Mar. 15

J. W. Wilder (Conf. schooner): (1862) run ashore, Jan. 20

Jacinto (or Glendale), Miss.: (1863) sks., Aug. 13, Sept. 7

Jacksborough, Tenn.: (1862) sk., Mar. 14; (1863) sk., Aug. 28

Jack's Cr., Tenn.: (1863) sk., Dec. 24

Jack's Fork, Mo: (1863) sk., Aug. 14; Fed. sc. to, Nov. 4

Jackson, Claiborne Fox (C): (1861) Davis promises aid to Mo. gov., Apr. 23; pro-Conf. statement, May 3; Camp Jackson aff., May 10; refuses to disband troops, May 24; Planter's House meeting, June 11; calls for militia, June 12; evac. of capital, June 14; withdraws toward Boonville, June 15; eng. at Boonville, June 17; retires forces to southwest Mo., June 17; eng. at Carthage, Mo., July 5; claims to represent state, July 22; replaced as Mo. gov. by Gamble, July 31; (1862) Davis to, Jan. 8

Jackson, Henry Rootes (C): (1861) commands W. Va. forces, July 14

Jackson, James (C): (1861) shoots Ellsworth, May 24; emotions high over death of, May 26

Jackson, Stonewall: *See* Jackson, Thomas Jonathan

Jackson, Thomas Jonathan (Stonewall) (C): (1861) assigned command, Apr. 27; ordered to Harper's Fy., May 1; seizes rolling stock, May 14; superseded, May 15; arrives at Manassas Junction, July 19; at Manassas, July 20; Bat. of 1st Bull Run, or Manassas, called "Stonewall," July 21; commands Shenandoah Valley Dist., Oct. 22; assumes command Shenandoah Valley Dist., Nov. 4; oper. along Potomac R., Dec. 17; (1862) exped. to Romney, Jan. 1; Romney Camp., Jan. 3; troops occupy Bath, W. Va., Jan. 4; bomb. of Hancock, Md., Jan. 5; toward Romney, Jan. 7; occup. of Romney, Jan. 10; resignation refused, feud with Loring, Jan. 10; Banks moves toward, Mar. 5; sk. at Winchester, Mar. 7; withdraws from Winchester, Mar. 11; moving up Shenandoah, Mar. 12; Shields advances against, Mar. 19; Feds. threatened by, Mar. 20; sk., Kernstown, Mar. 22; 1st Bat. of Kernstown, Mar. 23; falls back up Valley, Apr. 1; retires, Apr. 17; leaves for Elk Run Valley, Conrad's Store, Apr. 18; heads for Staunton, Apr. 30

Valley Camp., May 6; Bat. of McDowell, May 8; toward Franklin, May 9, 10; leaves Franklin, May 12; advances down Shenandoah, May 13; reaches main Shenandoah, May 15, 18; through New Market, Luray, May 20; troops move in Luray Valley, May 21; toward Front Royal, May 22; eng. at Front Royal, May 23; attempt to cut off Banks, May 24; Lincoln orders troops to Shenandoah Valley, May 24; Bat. of 1st Winchester, May 25; legend growing, May 25; occupies Winchester, May 26; toward Harper's Fy., May 27; successes cause consternation, May 27; sk. at Charles Town, May 28; Lincoln on attacking, May 28; demon. toward Harper's Fy., May 29; Lincoln controls oper. against, May 29; sk. at Front Royal, May 30; Lincoln urges commanders to destroy, May 30; at Strasburg, June 1; growing reputation, June 1; escapes Fed. pincers, June 2; withdrawal, sk. at Mt. Jackson, Tom's Brook, June 3; withdrawing, June 4; retreats toward Port Republic, June 6; Bat. of Cross Keys, June 8; Bat. of Port Republic, summary of Valley Camp., June 9; speculation on moves, June 11; reinforcements to, June 12; near Weyer's Cave, June 12; Lincoln warns Frémont of, June 12; Lincoln to Frémont re, June 15; to reinforce Lee, June 17; strategy conference, June 23; approaching Peninsula, June 25; Bat. of Mechanicsville, blamed for tardiness, June 26; delayed, Gaines' Mill, June 27; Savage's Station, June 29; White Oak Swamp, June 30; advance on Gordonsville, July 13; Bat. of Cedar Mt., Aug. 9; near Gordonsville, Aug. 11; offensive move, Aug. 25

2nd Manassas (Bull Run) Camp., Aug. 26, 27, 28; Bat. of 2nd Manassas (Bull Run), Aug. 29, 30; moves west of Chantilly, Aug. 31; Bat. of

Chantilly, Sept. 1; occup. of Frederick, Md., Sept. 6; Lee's Orders No. 191, Sept. 9; converging on Harper's Fy., Sept. 12; besieging Harper's Fy., Sept. 14; capture of Harper's Fy., Sept. 15; McLaws joins, Sept. 15; joins Lee, Sept. 16; Bat. of Antietam, Sept. 17; remains in Valley, Nov. 3; promoted, to command Second Army Corps, Nov. 6; in Winchester, Nov. 20; en route to Fredericksburg, Nov. 21, 24; into right of Lee, Dec. 1; at Guiney's Station, Dec. 11; orders at Fredericksburg, Dec. 12; Bat. of Fredericksburg, Dec. 13; (1863) Bat. of Chancellorsville, May 1; wounded, May 2; ment., May 4; at Guiney's Station, May 6; death of, May 10; praise of in England, June 3; (1864) ment., July 24, Sept. 22, Nov. 13

Jackson, Ark.: (1862) sk., Aug. 3

Jackson, Ky.: (1863) aff., Dec. 1

Jackson, La.: (1863) sk., Aug. 3; (1864) sk., Mar. 3; sk. near, Oct. 5; (1865) Fed. expeds. to, Mar. 1, Apr. 12

Jackson, Miss.: (1861) Davis stops at, Feb. 12; (1863) Vicksburg Camp., May 1, 3; Fed. move toward begins, May 7; Grant's strategy, May 12; Grant's forces move toward, May 13; eng. and occup. by Grant, May 14; Sherman moves toward, July 5, 6, 9; investment of, July 10, 11, 12, 15; Conf. evac. of, July 16; sk. at Brookhaven, July 18; (1864) Sherman to, Feb. 5; Sherman leaves, Feb. 6

Jackson, Mo.: (1861) sk., June 24; (1862) Fed. recon. to, Apr. 2; sks., Apr. 9, 26, 27; (1864) sk., Sept. 24

Jackson, N.C.: (1863) Fed. exped. toward, July 25; Fed. exped. to, Dec. 27

Jackson, Tenn.: (1862) Beauregard at, Mar. 5; taken by Feds., June 7; Conf. exped. to, July 25; Grant at, Bat. of Corinth, Oct. 3; Forrest att. on r.r. near, Dec. 19; (1863) Fed. expeds. from, Apr. 1, June 3; sks., July 13, 15; Fed. exped. to, Sept. 19; (1864) Forrest raid toward, Oct. 19; Forrest at, Oct. 22; Forrest moves from, Oct. 28, 30

Jackson, Camp, Mo.: (1861) May 10

Jackson, Camp, Tenn.: (1862) sk., Mar. 24

Jackson, C.S.S. (or *Muscogee*) (ironclad gunboat): (1865) destruction of, Apr. 17

Jackson, Ft., Ga.: (1861) seized, Jan. 25

Jackson, Ft., La.: (1861) seized, Jan. 10; (1862) Apr. 17; Fed. bomb. begins, Apr. 18; r. obstructions breached, Apr. 20; Farragut to run ships past, Apr. 23; Fed. fleet passes, Apr. 24; mutiny, Apr. 27; surrendered, Apr. 28; (1863) Negro troops mutiny, Dec. 9

Jackson, Miss., *Appeal:* (1863) on South meeting enemy, May 9

Jackson Campaign: *See* Sherman, W. T.

Jackson Co., Mo.: (1862) sk. on Little Blue, June 2; Fed. exped. through, Sept. 8; Nov. oper. in, Nov. 1; aff., Nov. 26; (1863) aff., Apr. 2; General Orders No. 11, Aug. 25; sk. in, Sept. 15; (1864) Fed. scs. in, Jan. 15, Mar. 20, Aug. 25, Sept. 2

Jackson Co., Tenn.: (1865) sk., Mar. 8

Jacksonport, Ark.: (1862) aff. near, June 2; sk., June 12; (1863) sc. to, June 11; aff., Nov. 21; sk., Dec. 23; (1864) Conf. att. on, Apr. 20; Fed. exped. from, Apr. 22

Jackson R.R., La.: (1863) Fed. exped. to, Mar. 21

Jackson's Br., near Pensacola, Fla.: (1864) aff., May 25
Jackson's Fy., Ala.: (1864) sk., May 12
Jackson's R., W. Va.: (1863) Conf. saltpeter works destroyed, Aug. 25
Jackson's R. Depot, Va.: (1862) raid on Va. Central R.R., May 20
Jacksonville, Ala.: (1864) Fed. exped. to, Aug. 11
Jacksonville, Fla.: (1862) occup. of, Mar. 12; Feds. evacuate, Apr. 9; (1863) Feds. reoccupy, Mar. 10; Fed. oper. near, Mar. 23; sk., Mar. 29; evac. by Feds., Mar. 31; (1864) Fed. Fla. exped., Feb. 5; occup. by Fed. troops, Feb. 7; Fed. advance from, Feb. 8, 9, 10; Fed. retreat to from Olustee, Feb. 20; Fed. exped. from, Apr. 26; sk. near, May 28; Fed. exped. from, July 15; Fed. raid from, July 23; (1865) exped. from, Mar. 7
Jacksonville, N.C.: (1862) Cushing captures schooners at, Nov. 23; sk. ment., Jan. 17
Jacksonville, Va.: (1863) sk., Mar. 25
Jacob Musselman (U.S. riverboat): (1863) capt., Jan. 6
James, George S. (C): (1861) signal shot at Sumter fired, Apr. 12
James, Jesse: *See* James boys
James boys: (1864) att. on Centralia, Mo., Sept. 27
James, Army of the (*See also* Benjamin F. Butler): (1864) assembled, May 4; south side James oper., May 5, 6, 7, 8, 9, 12, 13, 14, 15, 16 17, 18; delayed at Cold Harbor, June 1; eng. Fair Oaks, Darbytown Rd., Oct. 27; Lincoln to remove Butler from command of, Dec. 30; (1865) Grant asks Butler's removal, Jan. 6; Butler removed, Jan. 7; Appomattox Camp. begins, Mar. 29; occup. of Richmond, Apr. 3
James, Military Division of the: (1865) Halleck assigned to command, Apr. 19; Halleck assumes command, Apr. 22
James City, Va.: (1862) Fed. recon. to, July 22; (1863) sk. near, Oct. 8, 9, 10
James Cr., Mo.: (1865) aff. near, Apr. 27
James I., S.C.: (1862) aff. near Dixon's I., May 25; sk. on, June 3; sks., June 7, 10; eng. at Secessionville, June 16; Feds. abandon, June 28; (1863) aff. on, May 31; eng. near Grimball's Ldg., July 16; bomb. of Legar's Point, July 20; firing on, Aug. 11; magazine explosion, Sept. 15; bomb. of Sumter, Oct. 3; Davis visits, Nov. 4; (1864) Fed. exped. to, Feb. 6; demon., Apr. 8; May 21; sk., Fed. ldg. on, July 2, 3; act. on, July 4; Feds. driven off, July 7; sk., July 16; (1865) sk., Feb. 10
James' Plantation, La.: (1863) sk., Apr. 8
James R., Va.: (1861) boats seized in, Apr. 18; (1862) burial of Pres. Tyler, Jan. 18; Fed. threat from, Mar. 9; McClellan's Peninsula plan, Mar. 13; A. of P. embarks for, Mar. 17; May 1, 7; Fed. fleet moves up, Bat. of Drewry's Bluff, May 15; Fed. exped. from Bottom's Br. to, May 25; recon. to by Feds., June 3; aff. at Gill's Bluff on, June 20; McClellan's change of base to Harrison's Ldg. on, June 26, 27; Fed. naval exped., June 28; McClellan withdraws, July 1, 2; C.S.S. *Teaser* capt., July 4; Conf. att. on Fed. shipping, July 5; A. of P. on, July 6; armies resting on, July 7; Fed. recons. on, July 10, 16; Fed. recon. on south side of, Aug. 3; A. of P. ordered from, Aug. 9, 26; Aug. 27; (1863) threat of att. from, Feb. 18; Union control of, July 14; Fed. recon. on, Aug. 4; Fed. naval exped. on, Aug. 6; (1864) Fed. exped. up, Jan. 24; Jan. 31; Feds move from south of, Apr.

9; Butler to move on, May 4; Butler lands on, May 6; U.S.S. *Commodore Jones* sunk in, May 6; Butler moves south of, May 7; *Shawsheen* capt., May 7; torpedo station on destroyed, May 10; Bat. of Fort Darling or Drewry's Bluff, May 12; ment., May 17, 20, 21, 24; comb. on, Haxall's Ldg., May 18; Butler's command on, June 1; ment., June 3; Grant plans to cross, June 7, 9, 10, 11; movement to begins, June 12, 13; Grant orders Butler to obstruct, June 13; Grant's crossing begins, June 14, 15, 16; Lee realizes Grant has crossed, June 17; Sheridan to, June 24, 25, 26; Grant sends corps north of, July 25, 27; Fed. demon. on north bank of, Aug. 13; Fed. exped. north of, Aug. 15, 16, 20; Conf. left north of, Oct. 27; destruction of *Greyhound* on, Nov. 27; (1865) Dutch Gap explosion, Jan. 1; Conf. vessels head down, Jan. 23; Lee on position on, Feb. 21; evac. of Richmond, Apr. 2

James R. Canal, Va.: (1865) Grant orders destroyed, Feb. 27; Sheridan wrecks, May 19

James R. Rd., Va.: (1862) sk. on, June 29

James R. Squad., Conf.: (1865) Semmes named to command, Feb. 10

Jamestown, Ky.: (1863) sk., June 2

Jamesville, N.C.: (1864) *Otsego* sunk near, Dec. 9

Jamison, D. F. (C): (1860) Dec. 17

Japan: (1863) Bat. of Shimonoseki, July 16

Jarratt's Station, Va.: (1864) sk., May 8

Jasper, Tenn.: (1862) sks., June 4, 21; (1863) sk. near, Oct. 2

Jasper Co., Mo.: (1863) Fed. sc. in, Feb. 19; Fed. oper. in, Mar 5; Fed. scs. to, May 6, 21; sk. in, Nov. 18

Jayhawkers: (1861) raid on Osceola, Mo., Sept. 22; act. at Little Blue, Mo., Nov. 11

Jeanerette, La.: (1863) sk., Apr. 14

Jeff Davis: *See* Davis, Jefferson

Jefferson, Md.: (1862) sk., Sept. 13

Jefferson, Tenn.: (1862) sk., Dec. 30

Jefferson, Va.: (1862) sks., Nov. 11, 14

Jefferson, Ft., Dry Tortugas: (1860) moves to protect, Nov. 15; (1861) U. S. Army garrisons, Jan. 18; prison, Jan. 18; (1865) Lincoln conspirators sent to, July 7

Jefferson, Ft., Ky.: (1862) gunboat eng., Jan. 11

Jefferson City, Mo.: (1861) Mo. troops evacuate, June 14; Feds. occupy, June 15, 17; state convention at, July 22; Sept. 20; (1864) aff. near, Sept. 27; sks., Oct. 7, 8; Price near, Oct. 9

Jefferson Co., Mo.: (1861) sk., Sept. 1; Thompson calls for fight in, Oct. 14

Jefferson Pike, Tenn.: (1862) sk., Stewart's Cr. Br., Dec. 27

Jeffersonton, Va.: (1863) sks., Oct. 12, Nov. 8

Jeffersonville, Ark.: (1862) Fed. exped. to, Sept. 26

Jeffersonville, W. Va.: (1864) sk. (W. Va., Va., and Tenn. R.R. raid), May 8

Jenkins, Albert Gallatin (C): (1862) raids into O., Sept. 4

Jenkin's Fy., Ark.: (1864) eng. (Camden exped.), Apr. 30

Jenks' Br., Ogeechee R., Ga.: (1864) sk., Dec. 7

Jennie's Cr., Ky.: (1862) sk., Jan. 7

Johnson, Ft., Charleston Harbor, S.C.: (1861) seized by S.C., Jan. 2; signal shot fired from, Apr. 12; (1864) Fed. ass. on fails, July 3; Fed. att. on, July 10

Johnson Co., Ark.: (1863) sk., Oct. 26; (1865) sk. in, Jan. 7

Johnson Co., Mo.: (1862) Fed. oper. in, Jan. 5; oper., Mar. 18; Fed. exped., Sept. 8; (1863) sk. in on Bear Cr., Feb. 5; Fed. exped. into, Aug. 28; (1864) sk., Apr. 28; oper. in, July 20; Fed. sc. in, July 26; oper. in, Aug. 11; Fed. oper. in, Sept. 1

Johnson's Crook, Ga.: (1865) sk. in, Feb. 10

Johnson's Farm, Va.: (1864) comb., Oct. 7; sk., Oct. 29

Johnson's Fy. (or Hamilton's Fd.) on Rolling Fork, Ky.: (1862) sk., Dec. 29

Johnson's I., Lake Erie: (1864) plot to rescue Conf. prisoners, Sept. 19

Johnson's Ranch, N. Mex. Terr.: (1862) eng. at Apache Canyon near, Mar. 26; eng. at Glorieta or Pigeon's Ranch, Mar. 28

Johnson's Station, S.C.: (1865) sk., Feb. 10; Sherman on r.r. from, Feb. 11; act., Feb. 11

Johnsonville, Tenn.: (1864) sk., Sept. 25; Forrest moves toward, Nov. 1; eng., Nov. 4; Forrest's foray to ment., Nov. 10

Johnston, Albert Sidney (C): (1861) succeeded by Sumner in Dept. of Pacific, Apr. 25; appointed gen., Aug. 31; commands Tenn., Mo., Ark., Ky., Sept. 10; assumes command Conf. armies in West, Sept. 15; calls for Tenn. troops, Sept. 21; commands Army of Central Ky., Oct. 28; calls for arming of troops, Nov. 19; (1862) Beauregard under, Jan. 26; troops to Ft. Donelson, Feb. 7; confers on Tenn. situation, Feb. 7; arrives in Nashville, Feb. 15; commands at Nashville, Feb. 20; moves toward Corinth, Mar. 1; Fed. Tenn. R. exped., Mar. 5; movement to Corinth, Mar. 18, 24; Davis to, Mar. 26; commands Army of the Miss., Mar. 29; orders att. at Pittsburg Ldg., Apr. 2; delayed, Apr. 3, 4; readies att., Apr. 5; Bat. of Shiloh, death of, Apr. 6; Beauregard replaces, Apr. 7

Johnston, Joseph Eggleston (C): (1861) commands forces around Richmond, Apr. 26; commands troops near Harper's Fy., May 15; doubts Harper's Fy. can be held, June 13; evac. of Harper's Fy., June 15; plan to move toward Wash., July 2; falls back toward Winchester, July 3; Patterson opposes, July 14; ment., July 16; oper. before Manassas, July 17, 18, 19; commands at Manassas, July 20; Bat. of 1st Bull Run (Manassas), July 21; July 22; appointed gen., Aug. 31; disagreement with Davis, Sept. 14, 25; strategy conference, Oct. 1; relations with Davis, Oct. 20; commands Dept. of Va., Oct. 22; Davis to, Nov. 3, 10

    (1862) in command in Va., Jan. 26; Davis to, Feb. 19; difficulties with Davis, Mar. 4; Davis to, Mar. 6; McClellan's advance, Mar. 7; line on Rappahannock R., Mar. 9; Davis to, Mar. 10; Mar. 13, 15; orders to Jackson, Mar. 23; ordered to reinforce Peninsula, Mar. 27; toward Peninsula, Apr. 4, 5, 6; reinforces Magruder, Apr. 12; command extended, Apr. 12; siege against, Apr. 22; Davis to, May 1; pulls back toward Richmond, May 3; size of force, May 3; Davis to, May 10; pulls back of Chickahominy, May 15; Davis to, May 17; waits Fed. moves, May 20; Davis disappointed in, May 28; Bat. of Fair Oaks or Seven Pines, May 31; wounded, May 31;

ment., June 1; assigned major command in West, Nov. 24; assumes over-all Western command, Dec. 4; Davis on reinforcements, Dec. 7

(1863) Davis orders to investigate Bragg, Jan. 21; Davis to, on Bragg, Feb. 19; Davis to, on Pemberton, Apr. 30; to command all Miss. troops, May 9; at Jackson, Miss., May 12; Grant outmaneuvers, May 13; occup. of Jackson, May 14; can't unite with Pemberton, May 16; order to evacuate Vicksburg, May 18; Davis calls for att., May 18; Davis to Bragg on, May 22; Davis to, May 23, 24; Davis on, May 26, 31; forces probed, June 13; attempts to aid Vicksburg, June 25, July 1, 3; Sherman moves toward, July 5, 6, 9; Davis to, July 9; investment of Jackson, Miss., July 10, 11, 12, 15; Davis to, July 11, 16; evac. of Jackson, July 16; ment., Aug. 10; to command Dept. and Army of Tenn., Dec. 16; Davis to, Dec. 19, 23; assumes command, Dec. 27

(1864) Davis to, Jan. 13, 14, Feb. 11; reinforcements from to Miss., Feb. 17; ment., Feb. 21; Fed. demon. on Dalton, Feb. 22, 23, 25; Sherman against, Apr. 9; move against expected, May 1; outposts meet Sherman's, May 2; Sherman's march to Atlanta, May 7, 8, 9, 10; Atlanta Camp., May 12, 13, 14 (Resaca), 15 (Resaca), 17, 18, 19, 20, 21, 22, 23, 24, 28 (Dallas), 29, 30, June 1, 3, 4, 5, 6, 8, 9 (Davis to), 10, 11, 12, 13, 14, 16, 17, 18, 19, 20, 21, 23, 24, 25, 27 (Kennesaw Mt.), 28, 29, 30 (Davis to), July 2, 3, 4, 5; Davis to, July 7; Fed. flanking movements, July 8; crosses Chattahoochee, July 9, 10; Davis on relieving, July 12; Davis on "failure" of, July 13; plans att., July 16; to Davis, July 16; relieved of command, July 17; semi-retirement, July 18; ment., July 19; defense of Atlanta, July 20; ment., Sept. 1

(1865) Cong. advocates for command, Jan. 16; troops sent to, Jan. 23; over-all Carolina command, Feb. 13; restored to command, Feb. 22; assumes command, Feb. 25; to Lee, Feb. 25; gathering troops, Feb. 28; assumes command Dept. of N.C., Mar. 6; troops to Bragg, Mar. 8; mustering, Mar. 10; strategy against, Mar. 11; Lee ment., Mar. 14; opposes Sherman's advance, Mar. 18; weakness of forces, Mar. 18; Bat. of Bentonville, Mar. 19, 20, 21; Bentonville aftermath, Mar. 22; defense, Mar. 23; Lee to join, Mar. 26; surrender terms ment., Mar. 28; advance against, Apr. 12, 13; confers with Davis, Apr. 12; returns to Hillsborough, N.C., Apr. 13; asks terms, Apr. 14; meeting with Sherman scheduled, Apr. 16; meets with Sherman, Apr. 17; on Lincoln's assassination, Apr. 17; "memorandum" signed, Apr. 18; rejection of memorandum, Apr. 24; asks to reopen negotiations, Apr. 25; surrenders, Apr. 26; army disbanded, Apr. 27

Johnston-Sherman surrender negotiations: (1865) Mar. 28, Apr. 14, 15, 16, 17, 18, 24, 25, 26

Johnston, Ft., N.C.: (1861) occup. of, Jan. 9, 10; seized, Apr. 16

Johnston's Farm, Ark.: (1865) Fed. sc. to, May 15

Johnstown, Mo.: (1861) sk., Nov. 24; (1863) sk. (Shelby's raid), Oct. 16

Johnstown, Harrison Co., W. Va.: (1863) aff., Apr. 18

Joint Committee on the Conduct of the War: (1861) congressional approval of, Dec. 9, 10; (1862) Gen. Stone's arrest, Feb. 9; (1864) investigation of Ft. Pillow, Apr. 12

Jollification, Mo.: (1862) sk., Oct. 3

"Jonathan Fed": (1863) at Vicksburg, June 19

Jones, Catesby ap Roger (C): (1862) commands *Merrimack,* Mar. 8, 9

Jones, "Grumble": *See* Jones, William Edmonson "Grumble"

Jones, Samuel (C): (1862) assigned command Trans-Allegheny or Western Dept. of Va., Nov. 25; (1864) superseded, Feb. 25; supersedes Beauregard in Dept. of S.C., Ga., and Fla., Apr. 20; (1865) surrenders at Tallahassee, Fla., May 10

Jones, William Edmonson "Grumble" (C): (1863) raid, Apr. 21, 26, 27, 29, 30; (1864) in valley, May 26; opposes Hunter, June 2, 5; death of, June 5

Jones, Ft., Ky.: (1865) Conf. att. on, Feb. 18

Jonesboro, Mo.: (1861) sk., Aug. 21; (1862) sk., Aug. 2

Jonesborough, Ala.: (1862) act. near at Spangler's Mill, July 26

Jonesborough, Ga.: (1864) comb., Aug. 19; act., Aug. 22; Sherman's flank movements on, Aug. 25, 27; preparation for Sherman's advance on, Aug. 29, 30; Bat. of, Aug. 31, Sept. 1; Kilpatrick heads for, Nov. 14; sk., Nov. 15

Jonesborough, Mo.: (1863) sk., Oct. 12

Jonesborough, Tenn.: (1863) act., Sept. 21; sk., Sept. 28; (1864) sk., Sept. 29; (1865) ment., Mar. 20

Jones' Br., Va.: (1864) ment., May 12; sk., June 23

Jones Co., Miss.: (1864) oper. in, Mar. 14

Jones' Cross Roads, Md.: (1863) sk., July 10

Jones' Crossroads, Miss.: (1863) sk., May 3

Jones' Farm, Va.: (1864) comb., May 28

Jones' Fy., Miss.: (1863) sk. (Sherman's Jackson Camp.), July 6

Jones' Fd., Chickahominy R., Va.: (1862) Fed. recon. to, July 30

Jones' Hill, Tenn.: (1863) sk., Oct. 26

Jones' Plantation, near Birdsong Fy., Miss.: (1863) sk., June 22

Jones' raid: *See* Jones, William Edmonson "Grumble"

Jones' Station, Ark.: (1864) act., Aug. 24

Jonesville, Va.: (1863) sks., Jan. 2, Nov. 29, Dec. 1; (1864) act., Jan. 3; sk., Jan. 28; (1865) Fed. recon. toward, Mar. 3

Jordan's Store, Tenn.: (1863) sk., May 30

Jornada del Muerto, N. Mex. Terr.: (1863) sk. in, June 16

Joyner's Fy., Blackwater R., Va.: (1862) sk., Dec. 22

Juarez, Benito: (1864) opposes Maximilian, May 28

Judah (Conf. privateer): (1861) destroyed, Sept. 14

Jug Tavern, Ga.: (1864) eng., Aug. 3

Julesburg, Colo. Terr.: (1865) sk., Jan. 7; Fed. oper. (Ind.), Jan. 14; Overland Stage Station at burned by Inds., Feb. 2

Julian, George Washington (F): (1864) Lincoln interview with, July 2

Jumpertown, Miss.: (1862) sk., Nov. 5

Kabletown, W. Va.: (1864) sks., Mar. 10, June 10; aff., July 18; sks., July 19, Nov. 18, Nov. 30; (1865) Fed. scs. to, Mar. 16, 20

Kamehameha IV: (1861) proclaims Hawaiian Is. neutral, Aug. 26

Kanawha, state of (*See also* West Virginia): (1861) Aug. 20

Kanawha area, W. Va.: (1861) Oct. 19

Kanawha Gap, W. Va.: (1861) act., Sept. 25

Kenansville, N.C.: (1863) sk., July 5

Kenly, John Reese (F): (1862) eng. of Front Royal, Va., May 23

Kennedy, R. C. (C): (1864) hanged (plot to burn N.Y.), Nov. 25

Kennesaw Mt., Ga.: (1864) Thomas moves army toward, June 15; Johnston's line along, June 18; Bat. of, June 27; June 28; Johnston evacuates, July 2; Sherman moves past, July 3; Sherman's hdqrs. on, Oct. 4, 5

Kennesaw Water Tank, Ga.: (1864) sk., Oct. 3

Kennett, Mo.: (1863) Fed. exped. to, Mar. 9

Kent's Ldg., Ark.: (1864) Fed. exped., Aug. 11

Kentucky: (1861) urges national convention, Jan. 25; refuses troops to Union, Apr. 15; companies tender services to Union, May 3; neutrality of, May 14; proposes neutrality, May 16; to have both Union and Conf. govts., May 20; neutrality, June 12, July 10, 27; Lincoln on, Aug. 24, Sept. 2; U.S. flag raised in, Sept. 2; neutrality ended, Sept. 3, 4, 7; seizure of Paducah, Sept. 6; mountain people pro-Union, Sept. 7; legislature on Conf. troops, Sept. 11; unionists in control, Sept. 11; Lincoln on importance of, Sept. 29; Sept. 30; in Fed. Dept. of the Mo., Nov. 9; Conf. govt., Nov. 18; admitted to C.S.A., Dec. 10; (1862) Conf. defense line broken, Jan. 19; Lincoln calls for movement, Jan. 27; defense line useless, Feb. 11; state lost to C.S.A., Feb. 16; devoid of Conf. troops, Feb. 20; defense line gone, Mar. 2; Morgan's raid into, *See* Morgan, John Hunt; Bragg declares blow struck for freedom of, Sept. 5; Conf. gov. inaugurated, Oct. 4; Conf. invasion of ended, Oct. 8; Morgan's 2nd raid, Dec. 21; (1863) Confs. in, July 25; (1864) trade restrictions lifted, Jan. 23; Morgan raid into, May 30; habeas corpus suspended, July 5; Fed. exped. into, Aug. 16; (1865) citizens request Butler's assignment to, Feb. 2; rejects Thirteenth Amendment, Feb. 22; martial law in ends, Oct. 12

Kentucky, Army of, Conf.: (1862) crosses into Ky., Aug. 16

Kentucky, Army of, Fed.: (1862) Gordon Granger assumes command of, Oct. 7

Kentucky, Central Army of, Conf.: (1861) Hardee assumes command, Dec. 5; (1862) merges with Army of the Miss., Mar. 29

Kentucky, Central Division of: *See* Central Division of Kentucky

Kentucky, Dept. of, Fed.: (1865) under Thomas, Feb. 10

Kentucky defense line: *See* Kentucky

Kentucky Line: (1862) aff. at, Sept. 8

Kentucky raid of John Hunt Morgan: *See* Morgan, John Hunt

Kentucky R., Ky.: (1862) sk., Aug. 31

Kentucky State Guard: (1861) July 10

Kentucky-Tennessee state line: (1862) Feb. 4

Kentucky troops: (1861) Fed., Sept. 20; Conf., Oct. 16

Kernstown, Va.: (1862) sk., Mar. 22; 1st Bat. of, Mar. 23; (1864) sk., July 23; 2nd Bat. of, July 24; sk., Nov. 11; Fed. exped. from, Dec 19

Kershaw, Joseph Brevard (C): (1864) sent to reinforce Lee, Sept. 16; Bat. of Cedar Cr., Oct. 19

Kettle Run, Va.: (1862) eng. near Bristoe Station, Aug. 27

Key, John J. (F): (1862) dismissed from service, Sept. 27

Keyes, Erasmus Darwin (F): (1862) Bat. of Seven Pines or Fair Oaks, May 31

King William Court House, Va.: (1864) Kilpatrick-Dahlgren raid, Mar. 2

Kinston, N.C.: (1862) capt., Dec. 14; (1863) Fed. demon. on, Mar. 6; Fed. expeds. toward, Apr. 16, 27; demon., May 20; Fed. sc. to, Dec. 5; (1864) Pickett's exped. from, Feb. 1; (1865) Conf. forces reach, Mar. 7; Bat. of, Mar. 8, 9, 10; Cox occupies, Mar. 14

Kirby Smith, Edmund: *See* Smith, Edmund Kirby

Kirk's Bluff, S.C.: (1862) aff., Oct. 18

Kirksville, Mo.: (1861) Fed. oper., Aug. 16; (1862) act., Aug. 6

Kirkwood House: (1865) Apr. 14; Johnson takes oath of office in, Apr. 15

Kittredge's Sugar House, La.: (1865) sk., Feb. 10

Klapsford, Mo.: (1861) sk., Aug. 19

Kneeland's Prairie, Calif.: (1864) sk., May 2

Knight's Cove, Ark.: (1862) sk. near, June 19

"Knights of the Golden Circle": (1863) in Pa., Apr. 3; membership in forbidden, May 3; seize arms in Ind., July 6; leader arrested, July 18

Knob Cr., near Ripley, Tenn.: (1863) sk., Jan. 8

Knob Gap, Tenn.: (1862) sk., Dec. 26

Knobnoster, Mo.: (1862) sk., Jan. 22

Knoxville, Md.: (1863) Gettysburg Camp., June 27

Knoxville, Tenn. (*See also* Knoxville Camp.): (1861) riots in, May 7; (1862) E. Kirby Smith reaches, Mar. 8; Army of Tenn. retires toward, Oct. 26; (1863) sk., June 19; occup. by Feds., Sept. 2; East Tenn. Camp., Sept. 5; Burnside's hdqrs., Sept. 22; Conf. attempt to retrieve, Nov. 4; siege of, *See* Knoxville Camp.; (1864) sk., Jan. 26; Fed. exped. from, Feb. 1; Fed. sc. near, Feb. 13; sk., Feb. 20; pro-Union meeting in, Apr. 15; wire entanglements used at, ment., May 15; Stoneman's exped. into Va. from, Dec. 10, 12

Knoxville, Tenn., Camp.: (1863) Longstreet to oppose Burnside, Nov. 4, 5; sks., Nov. 14 (Huff's Fy., Maryville, Little R., Rockford); Longstreet nears Knoxville, Nov. 16; siege, Nov. 16 (eng. Campbell's Station, sk. at Kingston), 17, 22, 23, 24, 25, 27, 28, 29 (ass. on Ft. Sanders), 30 (aff. at Charleston), Dec. 1, 2; Longstreet withdraws, Dec. 3; sk. at Log Mt., Dec. 3; Dec. 4, 5; Sherman enters, siege ending, Dec. 6; sks., Dec. 6, 7, 9, 12, 13, 14 (eng. at Bean's Station, sks. Clinch Mt. Gap, Granger's Mill, Morristown), 15 (sk. Bean's Station), 16 (sk. Rutledge), 18 (sks. Bean's Station, Rutledge), 19 (sk. Stone's Mill), 21 (Clinch R.), 22 (scs. in east Tenn.); (1864) Fed. pickets capt. near, Jan. 24

Knoxville, Tenn., *Whig*: (1861) suppression, Oct. 24

Kossuth, Miss.: (1862) sk., Aug. 27

Labor: (1864) Lincoln on, Mar. 21

Lacey's Springs, Va.: (1864) Fed. exped. to, Dec. 19

Laclede, Mo.: (1864) Conf. desc. on, June 18

Laclede Co., Mo.: (1862) Fed. sc. in, Mar. 4

Ladd's House, Ala.: (1865) sk., Feb. 3

Ladiga, Ala.: (1864) sk., Oct. 28

La Fayette, Ga.: (1863) Bragg at, Sept. 9; Fed. recons. toward, Sept. 10, 13;

sks. near, Sept. 14, Dec. 12; (1864) Fed. recon. to, Apr. 11; Fed. sc. to, Apr. 24; sks., June 24, 30; sk., Oct. 12

La Fayette, Ky.: (1863) sk., Nov. 27

La Fayette, Tenn.: (1863) Fed. sc. to, Mar. 10; sks., May 11, Nov. 5, Dec. 4; (1864) sks., June 9, 29, Aug. 8

Lafayette, Ft., N.Y.: (1861) Md. political prisoners sent to, Sept. 20; (1862) Gen. Stone sent to, Feb. 9

La Fayette Co., Mo.: (1862) oper. in, Jan. 5; sk., Mar. 10, Fed. exped. through, Sept. 8; aff., Nov. 26; (1863) Fed. exped. to, Aug. 28; Fed. sc. to, Sept. 22; (1864) Fed. sc. in, Mar. 20; oper. in, July 20; Fed. sc. into, Aug. 7; Fed. oper. in, Aug. 13; (1865) sk. in, Jan. 30; Fed. scs. in, Feb. 3, May 8

La Fayette Ldg., Tenn.: (1862) aff., Oct. 3

La Fayette Rd., Ga.: (1863) sk. on near Chattooga R., Sept. 12

La Fayette Station, Tenn.: (1862) aff., June 25

La Fourche, Bayou: *See* Bayou La Fourche

La Fourche Crossing, La.: (1863) eng., June 20

La Fourche Dist., La.: (1862) oper. in, Oct. 24

La Grange, Ark.: (1862) Fed. exped. to, Sept. 26; sks., Nov. 1, 8, Dec. 30; (1863) sk., May 1

La Grange, Tenn.: (1862) Fed. exped. to, Sept. 20; Grant occupies, Nov. 4; Fed. recons. from, Nov. 5, 6, 8; Grant moves to, Dec. 20; (1863) Fed. sc. from, Jan. 28; Fed. exped. from, Feb. 13; Fed. sc. from, Mar. 2; Fed. exped. from, Mar. 8; Fed. sc. from, Mar. 21; sk., Mar. 24; Fed. exped. from, Mar. 28; Fed. scs. from, Apr. 5, 10, 11; Fed. exped. from, Apr. 15; Fed. sc. from, Apr. 29; Fed. cav. exped. from, May 11; Fed. scs. from, May 17, 19; Fed. expeds. fro.m. May 21, June 16, Sept. 11; (1864) sk., Jan. 2; Fed. sc. from, Jan. 23; sks., Jan. 25, Feb. 2; Fed. expeds. from, July 5, Aug 1, 9

"Laird Rams": (1863) held up by British, Sept. 5

Laird Shipyards, Liverpool: (1862) *Alabama* launched, May 15; (1863) rams held up, Sept. 5

Lake Borgne, La.: (1863) aff., Nov. 22

Lake Chicot (or Old River Lake), Ark.: (1864) eng., June 6

Lake City, Fla.: (1864) Fed. exped. toward, Feb. 10; sk., Feb. 11; Fed. troops march toward (Bat. of Olustee), Feb. 20

Lake Erie: *See* Erie, Lake

Lake Natchez, La.: (1864) Fed. exped. to, Sept. 7

Lake Providence, La.: (1863) Lincoln asks about, Mar. 20; sk., May 9; sks. near, May 24, 27; act. near, June 9; sk., June 24

Lake Saint Joseph, La.: (1863) Fed. exped. to, Apr. 24; aff., June 4

Lake Springs, Mo.: (1863) Fed. exped. from, Apr. 21; (1864) sk., Oct. 1

Lake Superior: *See* Superior, Lake

Lake Verrett, La.: (1865) Fed. expeds. to, Jan. 30, Feb. 10; Fed. sc. to, May 23

Lake Village, Ark.: (1864) sk., Feb. 10

Lamar, Lucius Quintus Cincinnatus (C): (1861) agent to Russia, Nov. 19

Lamar, Miss.: (1862) Fed. recon. toward, Nov. 6; (1863) Fed. exped. from, Feb. 13; (1864) sk., Aug. 14

Lamar, Mo.: (1862) sk. on Coon Cr., Aug. 24; act., Nov. 5; (1864) sk., May 20; sack of, May 28

Lamar, Tex.: (1864) Fed. desc. upon, Feb. 11

Lamb, William (C): (1864) defends Ft. Fisher, Dec. 24; (1865) notifies Bragg of Feds. arrival, Jan. 12; 2nd att. on Ft. Fisher, Jan. 13; call for help, Jan. 14; capture of Ft. Fisher, Jan. 15

Lamb's Cr. Church, Va.: (1863) sk., Sept. 1

Lamb's Fy., Ala.: (1862) sks., May 10, 13

Lamb's Fy., Va.: (1863) sk., Aug. 25

Lamb's Plantation, Ark.: (1864) sk., Aug. 1

La Mine Br., Mo.: (1863) aff. (Shelby's raid), Oct. 10

Lamon, Ward Hill (F): (1861) en route to Wash., Feb. 22; arrives, Feb. 23; confers with Gov. Pickens, Beauregard, Mar. 25

Lancaster, Ky.: (1862) sks., Oct. 13, 14; (1863) sk., July 31

Lancaster, Mo.: (1861) sk., Nov. 24; (1862) sk., Sept. 7

Lancaster, Ft., Tex.: (1861) surrender of, Mar. 19

Lancaster, U.S.S. (ram): (1863) sunk running Vicksburg batteries, Mar. 25

Land Grant colleges: *See* Morrill Act

Lane, "Jim" James Henry (F): (1861) "Frontier Guards" in White House, Apr. 18; raid on Osceola, Mo., Sept. 22

Lane, Joseph: (1860) Breckinridge's vice-pres. candidate, defeated, Nov. 6

Lane's Br., on Little Salkehatchie, S.C.: (1865) act. near, Feb. 6

Lane's Prairie, Maries Co., Mo.: (1864) aff., May 26

Langley's Plantation, Issaquena Co., Miss.: (1864) sk., Mar. 22

L'Anguille Fy., Ark.: (1862) sk., Aug. 3

Lanier's Mills, Ala.: (1865) sk., Apr. 6

Laramie, Ft., Dak. Terr.: (1865) Fed. oper., Apr. 1

Laredo, Tex.: (1864) Fed. att. on, Mar. 19

Larkin's Ldg., Ala.: (1864) Fed. exped. from, Mar. 2

Larkinsville, Ala.: (1863) sk. near, Sept. 26; (1864) aff. near, Feb. 14

Larned, Ft., Kas.: (1863) Fed. sc. to, Sept. 4; from, Sept. 13; (1864) sk. with Inds. near, Nov. 13; (1865) Fed. sc. from, Jan. 15; sk., Jan. 20; Fed. sc. from, Feb. 3; Fed. oper. about, Feb. 12; Fed. sc. from, Feb. 16; sk. with Inds. near, Mar. 7; Fed. sc. from, Mar. 9

La Salle, Tex.: (1865) port restrictions, May 22

". . . last best, hope of earth": (1862) Lincoln's State of Union message, Dec. 1

Last land engagement: (1865) sks. at Palmito Ranch, Tex., May 12, 13

Lattimer's Mills, Ga.: (1864) comb., June 20

Lauderdale Springs, Miss.: (1864) sk., Feb. 16

Laurel Br., Ky.: (1861) sk., Oct. 28

Laurel Co., Ky.: (1861) Sept. 26; Oct. 28

Laurel Cr., Fayette Co., W. Va.: (1861) sk. near, Nov. 12

Laurel Cr., Wayne Co., W. Va.: (1864) sk., Feb. 15

Laurel Cr. Gap, Tenn.: (1864) sk., Oct. 1

Laurel Fork Cr., W. Va.: (1861) sk., Aug. 20

Laurel Hill, Spotsylvania Co., Va.: (1864) comb., May 8

Laurel Hill, W. Va.: (1861) sk., July 7; Fed. troops move toward, July 10;

named to command Dept. of S.C., Ga., and East Fla., Nov. 5, 8; concern over Fed. incursions on coast, Nov. 9

(1862) Davis recalls to advise, Mar. 3; advisory post, Mar. 13; succeeds Johnston, May 31; orders withdrawal at Fair Oaks or Seven Pines, June 1; sends reinforcements to Jackson, June 12; Stuart reports to, June 15; confers on Peninsula offensive, June 23; Seven Days' Camp., June 25–July 1; Mechanicsville, June 26; Gaines' Mill, June 27; prepares offensive, June 28; Savage's Station, June 29; Frayser's Farm or White Oak Swamp, June 30; Bat. of Malvern Hill, July 1; defends Richmond, July 1; army condition, July 2; troops "thinned," July 5; troops move from Richmond, July 13; Davis to, July 31; Davis to, Aug. 1; advances into northern Va., Aug. 4; 2nd Bull Run Camp., Aug. 13; advances, Aug. 16; presses Pope, Aug. 18; sks., Aug. 20, 21; offensive, Aug. 25; Aug. 27; Bat. of Groveton or Brawner's Farm, Aug. 28; 2nd Bat. of Bull Run or Manassas, Aug. 29, 30; plans to turn Fed. right, Aug. 31; Bat. of Chantilly, Sept. 1; toward Potomac, Sept. 3; crossing Potomac, Sept. 4; moves toward Frederick, Sept. 5; Davis to, Sept. 7; proclamation, Sept. 8; field orders, Sept. 9; McClellan's pursuit of, Sept. 10; "Lost Order of Antietam," Sept. 13; Antietam Camp., Sept. 15; forces of gather, Sept. 16; Bat. of Antietam, Sept. 17; withdraws, Sept. 18, 19; McClellan pursues, Sept. 19, 20; withdraws to Opequon Cr. Valley, Sept. 20; Davis to, Sept. 28; suggests Stuart's Chambersburg raid, Oct. 9; in Shenandoah, Oct. 16; shifts south, Oct. 28; not pursued, Nov. 1; Longstreet's, Jackson's positions, Nov. 3; A. of P. movement, Nov. 16; arrives at Fredericksburg, Nov. 20; Jackson's troops to right, Dec. 1; faces Burnside, Dec. 2; Davis to, Dec. 8; Bat. of Fredericksburg, Dec. 13; criticized, Dec. 14; defense position, Dec. 15

(1863) Davis to, Jan. 7, 22, Feb. 4; announces achievements, Feb. 28; Chancellorsville Camp., Apr. 27, 28, 29, 30; Bat. of Chancellorsville, May 1, 2, 3, 4; recalls Longstreet, May 3; preparing attack, May 5; Hooker's withdrawal, May 6; on death of Jackson, May 10; at Fredericksburg, May 24; Davis to, May 26; army reorganized, May 30; on Rappahannock, May 31; Davis to, May 31; Gettysburg Camp., June 3, 4, 5, 6, 8, 9 (Bat. of Brandy Station), 10, 11, 12, 13, 14, 15, 16, 17, 18, 19, 21, 22, 23, 24, 25 (Stuart's ride begins), 27, 28, 29, 30; Bat. of Gettysburg, July 1, 2, 3; acknowledges defeat, July 4; retreat, July 4, 5, 6; to Davis, July 7, 8; increased action, July 10; north of Potomac, July 11, 12; to Davis, July 12; crosses into Va., July 13, 14; moves up Shenandoah, July 15; to Davis, July 16; at Harper's Fy. and Berlin, Md., Meade pursues, July 19; moves south, July 20, 21; Davis to, July 21; to Davis, July 24; Davis to, July 28, Aug. 2; offers to resign, Aug. 8; Davis to, Aug. 11, Sept. 8; weakened, withdraws, Sept. 13; Lincoln mentions, Sept. 15; Davis to, Sept. 15; Bristoe Camp., Oct. 9, 10, 11, 12, 13, 14, 16, 17, 18, 19, 20, 22; Lincoln calls for att. on, Oct. 24; withdraws, Nov. 7; strategy, Nov. 8; Mine Run Camp., Nov. 26, 27, 28, 29, 30, Dec. 1; Davis considers sending Lee west, Dec. 6; Davis requests visit, Dec. 8

(1864) Davis to, Jan. 4; Davis warns, Feb. 7; Longstreet to return to, Apr. 7; army of, Meade's objective, Apr. 9; to Davis, Apr. 12; ment., Apr. 15; moves to meet Grant's advance, May 4; Bat. of Wilderness, May 5, 6; Butler's ldgs., May 5; May 7; Bat. of Spotsylvania, May 8, 9, 10, 11, 12, 13,

Leesburg, Ala.: (1864) sk., Oct. 21

Leesburg, Tenn.: (1863) sk., Sept. 29

Leesburg, Va.: (1861) Ball's Bluff Camp., Oct. 20; Bat. of Ball's Bluff, Oct. 21; (1862) Fed. occup. of, Mar. 8; sk., Sept. 2; Lee edges toward, Sept. 3; A.N.Va. near, Sept. 4; sc., Sept. 12; Fed. recon. to, Sept. 16; recon. to, Oct. 1; sk. near, Dec. 12, 13; (1863) Fed. sc. to, Feb. 14; sk., Feb. 19; Fed. sc. to, Mar. 15; Fed. sc. to, May 27; Fed. exped. to, Aug. 30; sk., Sept. 1; Fed. sc. to, Dec. 25; (1864) aff., Apr. 19; in Early camp., July 13, 14, 15, 16

Lee's Cr., Ark.: (1864) sk., May 1

Lee's House, Va.: (1862) aff., Jan. 29

Lee's House on Cornersville Pike, Tenn.: (1864) aff., Jan. 28

Lee's Lost Order: (1862) Sept. 13

Lee's Mill, Va.: (1864) sk., Nov. 16

Leesville, Va.: (1863) sk., May 4

Leetown, W. Va.: (1864) sks., July 3, Aug. 28

Leet's Tanyard (or Rock Spring), Ga.: (1863) sk., Sept. 12; (1864) sk., Mar. 5

Leeward Is.: (1861) Nov. 25

Legare's Point on James I., S.C.: (1863) bomb. of, July 20

Legareville, S.C.: (1864) burned, Aug. 20

Leggett, Mortimer Dormer (F): (1864) July 21

Leggett's (or Bald) Hill, Ga.: (1864) engs., July 20, 21

Lehigh, U.S.S.: (1863) at Sullivan's I., Nov. 16

Leighton, Ala.: (1863) sk., Apr. 23; (1864) sk., Dec. 30

Leiper's Fy., Holston R., Tenn.: (1863) sks., Oct. 28, 30

Leitersburg, Md.: (1863) sk., July 10

Lenoir's Station, Tenn.: (1863) aff., June 19; sk., Nov. 15

Letcher, John (C): (1861) as gov. of Va. criticizes S.C., calls for convention, Jan. 7; on furnishing troops, Apr. 16; orders custom house, post office seized, Apr. 18; Davis promises aid to, Apr. 18; Davis asks to "sustain Baltimore," Apr. 22; nominates Lee, Apr. 22; volunteers ordered out, May 1; calls for volunteers, May 2; greets Davis, May 29; transfers Va. forces to C.S.A., June 8; Davis to, Sept. 13

Letters of marque, Conf.: (1861) Apr. 17, May 6

Levi, U.S.S. (steamer): (1864) capt., Feb. 3

Lewinsville, Va.: (1861) sk., Sept. 10; Fed. recons. to, Sept. 11, 25; (1863) sk., Oct. 3; affs., Dec. 9

Lewisburg, Ark.: (1863) Jan. 2; (1864) sks., Jan. 17, June 10; Fed. sc. from, Sept. 9; Fed. exped. from, Nov. 5; sk., Dec. 6; (1865) Fed. sc. from, Mar. 12

Lewisburg, W. Va.: (1862) sk., May 12; act., May 23; sk., May 30; (1863) sk., May 2; Fed. exped. toward, Nov. 1, 6, 7 (*See also* Beverly, W. Va., exped.); Fed. r.r. raid, Dec. 12; (1864) sk., May 24

Lewisburg Pike, Tenn.: (1863) sk., Apr. 4

Lewisburg Rd., Tenn.: (1863) Fed. recon., Feb. 21

Lewis Cass, U.S.S. (revenue cutter): (1861) surrender of, Jan. 30

Lewis Chapel, near Pohick Church, Va.: (1862) aff., Feb. 24

Lewis Co., Mo.: (1862) oper. in, Oct. 11

Lewis' Farm, Va.: (1865) sk., Mar. 29

Lewis' Fd., Va.: (1862) sk., Aug. 28

Lewisville, Va.: (1863) sk., Oct. 1

Lexington, Ky.: (1861) Camp Dick Robinson near, Aug. 6; (1862) fear of Morgan, July 12; Bat. of Richmond, Aug. 30; E. K. Smith occupies, Sept. 2; Morgan joins Smith at, Sept 4; Smith withdraws toward, Sept. 16; Morgan captures garrison, Oct. 18; (1863) Aug. 16; (1864) and Morgan raid, June 4, 10; (1865) Fed. scs., Apr. 13

Lexington, Miss.: (1865) sk., Jan. 2

Lexington, Mo.: (1861) sk., Aug. 29; siege of, Sept. 12, 13, 16, 19, 20; siege critized, Sept. 23; Price withdrawing from, Oct. 7; Feds. capture, Oct. 16; Fed. exped. to, Dec 23; (1862) sk., Oct. 17; (1863) oper., May 4; sk., July 30; Fed. exped. from, Aug. 28; sk., Nov. 4; Fed. sc. from, Dec. 20; (1864) Fed. sc. from, Mar. 19; sks., June 14, Sept. 18; Price approaching, Oct. 17; act., Oct. 19; situation, Oct. 20; act. on Little Blue R., Oct. 21; (1865) sks., Jan. 11, May 4

Lexington, N.C.: (1865) Conf. govt. at, Apr. 16

Lexington, S.C.: (1865) sk., Feb. 15

Lexington, Tenn.: (1862) sk., Dec. 18; eng., Dec. 31; (1863) Fed. exped. from, Feb. 17; Fed. sc. from, Mar. 31; sk. near, June 29; (1864) Fed. sc. near, Jan. 11

Lexington, Va.: (1863) Jackson's body at, May 10; (1864) Bat. of New Market, May 15; Hunter moves toward, June 10; sk., Va. Mil. Institute burned, June 11; Fed. sc. from, June 13

Lexington, U.S.S. (gunboat): (1861) at Cairo, Aug. 12; eng. at Lucas Bend, Mo., Sept. 10; eng. at Iron Bluffs, Ky., Oct. 7; (1863) eng. at Milliken's Bend, June 7; (1864) eng., June 15

Libby Prison: (1864) Fed. officers escape from, Feb. 9; (1865) Lincoln lands near, Apr. 4

Liberia: (1862) Fed. representatives to, June 5; (1863) treaty with U.S., Mar. 23

Liberty: (1864) Lincoln on, Apr. 18

Liberty, Mo.: (1861) Arsenal seized, Apr. 20; (1862) sk., Oct. 6; (1864) sk., July 23

Liberty, Tenn.: (1863) Fed. expeds. to, Feb. 3, 17; sk., Mar. 19; Fed. exped. to, Apr. 1; sk., Apr. 7; Fed. recon. toward, May 12

Liberty, Va.: (1863) sk., Oct. 24; aff., Nov. 21; (1864) sks., June 16, 19

Liberty Gap, Tenn.: (1863) sk., June 24

Liberty Mills, Va.: (1863) sk., Sept. 23; (1864) Dec. 19

Liberty Post Office, Ark.: (1864) sk. (Camden exped.), Apr. 16

Lick Cr., near Helena, Ark.: (1863) sk., Jan. 12; Fed. exped., Mar. 6

Lick Cr., Tenn.: (1862) sk., Apr. 24

Licking, Mo.: (1862) sk., May 26; (1864) Fed. exped. to, Nov. 5; (1865) Fed. exped. from, Feb. 23; oper. about, Mar. 7

Licking R., Ky.: (1864) act. on, Apr. 14

Licking Run Br., Va.: (1863) sk., Nov. 30

Lieutenant general: *See* Lincoln, Grant, Congress, U. S.

"Light Division" of A. P. Hill: (1862) at Antietam, Sept. 17

Light House Point, Va.: (1864) Fed. cav. raid to, June 22

Limestone Br., Ala.: (1862) oper., May 1

Limestone Ridge, Va.: (1864) aff., Sept. 17

Limestone Station, Tenn.: (1863) act., Sept. 8

Limestone Valley, Ark.: (1864) sk. in, Apr. 17

Lincoln, Abraham (F): (1860) elected Pres., Nov. 6; congratulated, Nov. 7; silence of, Nov. 10; office seekers, Nov. 14; won't "shift . . . ground," Nov. 16; Cabinet posts, Nov. 16; on secession, Nov. 18; re leaving states alone, Nov. 20; meets with Hamlin, Nov. 21; in Springfield, Nov. 26; re Buchanan's message to Cong., Dec. 5; on slavery, Dec. 10, 11; confers on Cabinet, Dec. 12; on slavery extension, Dec. 13, 15; on Charleston forts, Dec. 21; to Stephens on slavery, Dec. 22; denies compromise, Dec. 29; Cabinet appointments, Dec. 29, 30

(1861) threats of assassination, Jan. 2; Chase in Springfield, Jan. 4; concern over Cameron in Cabinet, Jan. 6; names Seward Sec. of State, Jan. 10; on breakup of govt., Jan. 11; preparing inaugural, Jan. 28; visits stepmother, Jan. 30; on "inflexibility," writing inaugural address, Feb. 2; electoral vote, Feb. 4; farewell reception, Feb. 6; moves to hotel, Feb. 8; farewell address, departs, Feb. 11; at Indianapolis, Feb. 11; at Cincinnati, O., Feb. 12; at Columbus, Feb. 13; leaves Columbus, Feb. 14; at Pittsburgh, Feb. 15; at Cleveland, O., Feb. 15; at Buffalo, Feb. 16, 17; at Albany, Feb. 18; at N.Y. City, Feb. 19, 20; at Trenton, Feb. 21; at Philadelphia, warned of plot, Feb. 21; on Declaration of Independence, Feb. 22; Southern papers' reaction to, Feb. 22; route revised, Feb. 22; arrives Wash., Feb. 23; sees Buchanan, Cabinet, Feb. 23; receptions at Capitol, visits Supreme Court, Feb. 25; confers with Cabinet, Feb. 26; approves slavery amendment, Feb. 28; offers Cameron War post, Mar. 1; Cabinet appointments, Mar. 2; dinner for Cabinet, appointments, Mar. 3; inauguration, Mar. 4; inaugural address, Mar. 4; office seekers, Mar. 4, 5, 6; confers with Gen. Scott, Cabinet meeting, Mar. 5; confers with Cabinet on Sumter, Mar. 7; reception, Mar. 8; appointments, Mar. 11; Conf. commissioners, Mar. 13; disacknowledges Confederacy, Mar. 13; resupplying of Sumter, Mar. 13, 15, 18; appoints ministers to Britain, France, Mar. 18; Cabinet meeting, Mar. 26; appointments to Sen., Mar. 28; state dinner, Mar. 28; resupplying of Sumter ordered, Mar. 29; relief exped. to Ft. Pickens, Mar. 31; to hold Sumter, Mar. 31; *Powhatan* orders, Apr. 1; Seward's "thoughts," reply to, Apr. 1; visits Wash. Navy Yard, Apr. 2; Cabinet meets on Sumter crisis, Apr. 3; Magruder to Richmond, Apr. 3; meets with Baldwin, Apr. 4; informs Fox of exped. to Sumter, drafts letter to Anderson, Apr. 4; confers on Sumter crisis, Apr. 6; sends messenger to S.C., Apr. 6, 8; sees John Minor Botts, Apr. 7; appointments, Apr. 9; confers on colonization, Apr. 10; confers on Md., Apr. 11; on govt. property, Apr. 13; gets news of Sumter, calls for 75,000 militia, special session of Cong., Apr. 14; proclamation on insurrection, calls out militia, calls Cong., Apr. 15; confers with Gen. Scott, Apr. 17; report to on Charleston, Apr. 18; offer of Army command to Lee, Apr. 18; declares blockade, Apr. 19; confers with Scott, Apr. 20; confers with Baltimore mayor, Apr. 21; on defending Wash., Apr. 22; impatience for troops, Apr. 23, 24; to Reverdy Johnson, Apr. 24; reviews Seventh N. Y. Inf., Apr. 21; considers interference with Md. legislature, Apr. 25; extends blockade, Apr. 27; habeas corpus suspension, Apr. 27; visits Seventh N. Y. Inf., Apr. 28; invites Anderson to White House, May 1; to G. V. Fox on Sumter, May 1; calls for volunteers, May 3; Md. protests Fed. troop movements, May 4; on occup. of Md., May 6; appoints Anderson recruiter, reviews Zouaves, May 7; on govt. right to maintain itself, May 7; reception, May 9; appointments, May 10; re arming Ky. unionists, May 14; orders removal of Harney order withheld, May 18; orders to Adams, May 21; Ellsworth's funeral, May 25; and *ex parte* Merryman, May 27; on suspension of habeas corpus, May 27; on Mo. citizens, May 27; ponders fugitive slave treatment, May 30; Davis castigates, June 1; mourns death of Douglas, June 3; Beauregard on, June 5; Douglas' funeral, June 7; approves Sanitary Commission, June 8; lends moral support, June 16; Prof. Lowe demonstrates balloons, June 17; watches weapon demonstration, June 24; Cabinet meeting, June 29; suspends habeas corpus, July 2; confers with Frémont, July 2; message to Cong., July 3, 4; on Sumter crisis, July 4; signs temperance declaration, July 4; message to Cong. read, July 5; empowered to collect customs, declares insurrection, July 13; approves loan, July 17; report on McDowell's army, July 20; re defeat at Bull Run, July 21; military policy memorandum, July 23, 27; gives McClellan command, July 27; approves militia act, July 29; appoints Grant brig. gen., July 31; confers on McClellan memorandum, Aug. 3; entertains Prince Napoleon, Aug. 3; signs congressional bills, Aug. 5, 6; and friction between McClellan and Scott, Aug. 10; proclaims day of "humiliation" and "prayer," Aug. 12; confers with McClellan, Anderson, Aug. 13; reinforcements for Frémont, Aug. 15; proclaims insurrection, bans commercial intercourse, Aug. 16; on Ky. neutrality, Aug. 24; disapproves Frémont's eman. proc., Aug. 30, Sept. 2; Ky. neutrality, Sept. 2; confers with Scott, Sept. 5; concerned about West, Frémont, Sept. 9; sends Hunter to Frémont, Sept. 9; interview with Mrs. Frémont, Sept. 10; to Frémont, Sept. 11; to Mrs. Frémont, Sept. 12; modifies Frémont's eman. proc., Sept. 12; Cabinet meets, Sept. 15; on coastal expeditions, Sept. 18; on Frémont's eman. proc., Sept. 22, 23; reviews troops, Sept. 24; meets with Cabinet, McClellan, Sept. 27; Lincoln to Morton, Sept. 29; Sept. 30; calls for military movements, Oct. 1; watches balloons, confers on Frémont, approves contracts, Oct. 4; sends Cameron west, Oct. 7; considers removal of Frémont, Oct. 7; Cabinet meets, Oct. 9; on habeas corpus, Oct. 14; on desire to work, Oct. 17; Cabinet meets, Oct. 18; and Edward Baker, Oct. 21; to J. J. Hughes, Oct. 21; to S. R. Curtis, Oct. 24; attends Baker's funeral, Oct. 24; confers with McClellan, Oct. 29; visits Scott, Nov. 1; Frémont-Price prisoner agreement, Nov. 1; McClellan parade, Nov. 11; McClellan snubs, Nov. 13; compensated eman., Nov. 26; to McClellan, Dec. 1; suspension of habeas corpus, Dec. 2; State of Union message, Dec. 3; on labor and capital, Dec. 3; Baker memorial services, Dec. 11; *Trent* Aff., Dec. 18, 23, 25, 26; confers with McClellan, Dec. 18; to Halleck, Dec. 31

(1862) New Year's reception, Jan. 1; seeks concerted action, Jan. 1; McClellan improved, Jan. 2; east Tenn. movement, Jan. 4; confers with McClellan, writes Buell, Jan. 6; to McClellan, Jan. 9; to Cameron on offensive, Jan. 10; Cameron's resignation, Jan. 11; military conference, Jan. 12; appoints Stanton Sec. of War, Cameron minister to Russia, Cabinet conference, Jan. 13; on concerted offensive, Jan. 13; relations with Stanton, Jan. 15; General War Order No. 1, Jan. 27; Special War Order No. 1, Jan. 31; refuses elephants, Feb. 3; to McClellan, urging Va. att., Feb. 3; Willie's illness, Feb. 7, 8; to McClellan, Feb. 8; Gen. Stone's arrest, Feb. 9; prisoner amnesty, Feb. 14; proclamation, Feb. 18; Willie's death, Feb. 20; order for movement of A. of P., Feb. 22; grief of, Feb. 22; names Johnson mil. gov. of Tenn., Feb. 23; confers with McClellan, Feb. 26; signs loan and treasury bill, Feb. 26; appointments of genls., Mar. 3; eman. plan, Mar. 6; confers with McClellan, Mar. 8; General War Order No. 2, Mar. 8; on A. of P., Mar. 10; visits Lieut. Worden, Mar. 10; relieves McClellan, Mar. 11; on security of Wash., Manassas Junction, Mar. 13; on compensated eman., Mar. 14; Atlantic fisheries commission, Mar. 15; to Greeley on compensated eman., Mar. 24; orders Blenker to Frémont, fears for Washington's safety, Mar. 31; to McClellan, Mar. 31; compensated eman. resolution, Apr. 2; holds back McDowell, Apr. 3; to McClellan, Apr. 6; Cabinet meets, Apr. 9; to McClellan, Apr. 9; size of armies, Apr. 9; approves resolution on eman., Apr. 10; rescinds Hunter's eman. orders, Apr. 12; signs D.C. eman. bill, Apr. 16; meets McDowell, Apr. 20; visits *Gassendi,* Apr. 26; to McClellan, May 1; goes to Ft. Monroe, May 5, 6; visits *Monitor,* May 7; on corps, May 9; at Hampton Rds., May 9; Hunter's eman. order, May 9; watches occup. of Norfolk, Portsmouth, May 10; to Halleck, May 11; opens ports, May 12; approves Dept. of Agriculture, May 15; confers with Stanton, May 17; on compensated gradual eman., disavows Hunter, May 19; Homestead Act, May 20; to McClellan, May 21; visits McDowell, May 22, 23; orders troops to Shenandoah, May 24; to McClellan, May 25, 26; to McDowell, May 28; Shenandoah oper., May 29, 30, 31; to McClellan, June 1; to McClellan, McDowell, June 2; representatives, Haiti, Liberia, June 5; orders to Frémont, June 9; to Frémont, June 12, 15; to McClellan, June 18; Eman. Proc. draft, June 18; signs slavery in territories bill, June 19; asks McClellan's views, June 21; confers with Scott, June 23, 24, 25; to McClellan on troops, June 26; Frémont's resignation on, June 27; McClellan blames for defeat, June 28; to Seward re McClellan, June 30; signs bills revising income tax, approves Union Pacific-Central Pacific R.R., July 1; asks govs. for troops, July 1; acts banning polygamy, requiring loyalty oaths, July 2; signs Morrill Act, July 2; "Harrison's Bar letter" of McClellan, July 7; confers with McClellan, July 8; names Halleck General-in-Chief, July 11; treaty with Britain suppressing slave trade, July 11; on compensated eman., July 12; doubts McClellan, July 13; on compensated eman., July 14; pension act, July 14; signs bills, July 16; approves Confiscation Act, July 17; signs bills, July 17; appoints mil. gov. of Ark., July 19; discusses use of Negro troops, July 21; 1st draft Eman. Proc., July 22; proclaims Confiscation Act, July 25; calls for militia draft, Aug. 4; refuses Negro enlistments from Ind., Aug. 4; on separation of races, Aug. 14; criticism of, Aug. 19; on saving Union, Aug. 22; to Burnside, Aug. 27; asks "What news?", Aug. 29, 30, 31; confers with McClellan, Halleck, Sept. 1; restores McClellan to full command, Sept. 2; "Meditations on the Divine Will," Sept. 2; confers with Pope, Sept. 3; asks about Bragg, Harper's Fy., Sept. 7; queries McClellan,

Sept. 8; asks military status, Sept. 12; to Gov. Curtin, Sept. 16; Preliminary Eman. Proc., Sept. 20, 22 (announced); on habeas corpus, Sept. 24; Cabinet on colonization, Sept. 26; dismissal of Key, Sept. 27; McClellan's inaction, Sept. 27; confers with McClellan, Oct. 1, 3, 4; memo of troops in A. of P., Oct. 2; "McClellan's bodyguard," Oct. 3; orders McClellan to fight, Oct. 6; congratulates Grant, Oct. 8; asks about Buell's follow-up, Oct. 12; urges McClellan movement, Oct. 13; orders Capitol bakeries removed, Oct. 14; appoints David Davis to Supreme Court, Oct. 17; on strength of A. of P., court in La., Oct. 20; orders to McClernand, Oct. 20; calls for Tenn. elections, Oct. 21; to McClellan, Oct. 25, 26; Mrs. Gurney, Oct. 26; to McClellan, Oct. 29; removes McClellan, Burnside to command A. of P., Nov. 5; to Banks on Miss., Nov. 8; reviews Sioux uprising records, Nov. 10; on Confiscation Act, Nov. 13; approves Burnside's plans, Nov. 14; on Sabbath, Nov. 15; on retracting Eman. Proc., Nov. 21; to Carl Schurz, Nov. 24; confers with Burnside, Nov. 26, 27; State of Union message, "we cannot escape history," Dec. 1; to Fernando Wood, Dec. 12; conference, Dec. 14; changes Sioux execution date, Dec. 16; rescinding of Grant's "Jew order," Dec. 17; McClernand machinations, Dec. 18; meets with senators, Dec. 18; Cabinet crisis, Dec. 19, 20; to Burnside, Dec. 19; confers with Burnside, Dec. 22; visits wounded, Dec. 25; prepares final Eman. Proc., Dec. 30; discusses Eman. Proc. with Cabinet; meets with Burnside, Dec. 31; approves W. Va. statehood, plan for Negro colonization, Dec. 31

(1863) Final Eman. Proc. issued, Jan. 1; Burnside offers to resign, Jan. 1, 5; New Year's reception, Jan. 1; revokes "Jew order," Jan. 4; thanks Rosecrans, Jan. 5; to Burnside, Jan. 7, 8; to McClernand on Eman. Proc., Jan. 8; to Curtis on slaves, Jan. 10; considers inventions, Jan. 15; signs bills, Jan. 17; to Manchester workingmen, Jan. 19; on Grant "Jew order," Jan. 21; orders F. J. Porter cashiered, Jan. 21; to McClernand, Jan. 22; unsent letter replacing Butler, Jan. 23; confers with Halleck, Jan. 24; appoints Hooker to command A. of P., replacing Burnside, Jan. 25; letter of advice to Hooker, Jan. 26; meets with Hooker, Jan. 26; concern over Charleston exped., Feb. 15; to Rosecrans, Feb. 17; signs national currency, bank system act, Feb. 25; calls special Sen. session, Feb. 28; confers on military appointments, Mar. 1; signs 1st Fed. Draft Act, Mar. 3; amnesty to deserters, Mar. 10; to Rosecrans, Mar. 17; to H. W. Davis., Mar. 18; to Hurlbut on Vicksburg, Mar. 20; to Seymour, Mar. 23; to Johnson on enlisting Negroes, Mar. 26; on Inds., Mar. 27; on interstate intercourse, Mar. 31; revokes trade exceptions, Apr. 2; visit to Hooker, Apr. 3, 4, 5, 6, 8, 10, 11; object of war statement, Apr. 6; confers with Halleck, Cabinet, Apr. 11; receives Hooker's plan, Apr. 12; orders Charleston positions held, Apr. 13, 14; to Hooker, Apr. 15; visits Aquia Cr., Apr. 19; proclamation on W. Va., Apr. 20; séance, Apr. 23; to Rosecrans, Apr. 23; to Hooker, Apr. 27; commutes death sentence, Apr. 28; inquiry on bat. progress, May 3, 4; to Hooker, May 6; visits A. of P., May 6, 7; on alien exemption, May 8; Chase offers resignation, May 11; requests visit from Hooker, May 13; to Hooker, May 14; banishes Vallandigham, May 19, 25; hears of Grant's Vicksburg Camp., May 22; and "One-Legged Brigade," May 22; confers on Charleston, May 23; visits hospitals, May 24; to Hooker, Rosecrans, May 27; refuses

Burnside's resignation, May 29; newspaper suppression, June 1; A. of P. command rumors, June 2; to Grant, June 2; on lifting ban on Chicago *Times,* June 4; to Hooker, June 5; Vicksburg siege, June 6, 8; to Hooker, June 10; concern over Lee, June 12; on arbitrary arrests, June 12; to Hooker, June 14; orders to Milroy, June 14; Hooker to, June 15; calls for 100,000 militia, June 15; to Halleck, June 16; replaces Hooker with Meade, June 27, 28; pressure to reinstate McClellan, June 30; concern over events, July 2; Davis peace feeler, July 2; at War Dept., July 3; announces victories, July 4; refuses peace negotiations, July 4, 6; to Halleck on Meade's inaction, July 6, 7; hears of fall of Vicksburg, July 7; serenaded, July 7; expects Gettysburg follow-up, July 11, 12; congratulates Grant, July 13; to Schofield, July 13; unsent to Meade on, July 14; sets day of praise and prayer, July 15; commutes sentences, July 18; writes doggerel, July 19; to O. O. Howard re Meade, July 21; raising of Negro troops, July 21; to Halleck, July 29; orders retaliatory punishment of prisoners, July 30; N.Y. gov. requests draft suspension, Aug. 3; to Banks on eman., Aug. 5; to Grant, Aug. 9; confidence in Rosecrans, Aug. 10; defends draft policy, Aug. 11; refuses McClernand command, Aug. 12; Meade confers with, Aug. 14; to Seymour on draft, Aug. 16; tests rifle, Aug. 18; to "unconditional Union men," Aug. 26; on Eman. Proc. legality, Sept. 2; refuses Burnside resignation, Sept. 11; asks Johnson to form Tenn. govt., Sept. 11; confers on Charleston, Sept. 11; suspends habeas corpus, Sept. 15; to Halleck, Sept. 15, 19; Rosecrans to, Sept. 20; mourns death of Gen. Helm, Sept. 22; confers on strategy, Sept. 23; to Mrs. Lincoln on Chickamauga, Sept. 24; promises Rosecrans reinforcements, Sept. 24; to Burnside, unsent, Sept. 25; N. Y. *Post* reveals troop movements, Sept. 26; to Burnside, Sept. 27; on intemperance, Sept. 29; news of Chattanooga, Oct. 1; to Schofield, Oct. 1; Thanksgiving proclamation, Oct. 3; to Rosecrans, Oct. 4; on responsibility of military, Oct. 5; asks news of Rosecrans, Oct. 7; to Meade, Oct. 10, 11, 12; to Rosecrans, Oct. 12; to Halleck, Oct. 16; calls for 300,000 volunteers, Oct. 17; to Halleck, Oct. 24; to Schofield on Mo., Oct. 28; accepts Gettysburg invitation, Nov. 2; on ridicule, Nov. 2; to Seward, Nov. 3; to Banks on La., Nov. 5; sees Booth on stage, Nov. 9; congratulates Meade, Nov. 9; attends Kate Chase's wedding, Nov. 12; to Burnside, Nov. 16; works on Gettysburg speech, Nov. 17; leaves for Gettysburg, Nov. 18; Gettysburg Address, Nov. 19; praise for address, Nov. 20; ill with varioloid, Nov. 21, 23, 26, 29, Dec. 1; proclamation of amnesty and reconstruction, Dec. 8; annual message to Cong., Dec. 8, 9; congratulates Grant, Dec. 8; on blockade, Dec. 9; health improved, Dec. 10; and Emily Helm, Dec. 13, 14; plans for Bureau of Emancipation, Dec. 17; to Stanton, Dec. 18; reception for Russians, Dec. 19; on Eman. Proc., Dec. 20; to Banks, Dec. 24; visits Conf. prisoner camp, Dec. 27

(1864) on bounties to volunteers, Jan. 5; commutes death sentence, Jan. 7; to Banks on La. govt., Jan. 13; to Gillmore on Fla. govt., Jan. 13; reconstruction, Jan. 15; suspends executions, Jan. 20; orders Ark. elections, Jan. 20; leaves Ark. administration to Gen. Steele, Jan. 22; favors owners freeing, hiring slaves, Jan. 23; "trading with enemy" regulations, suspends executions, Jan. 26; on Ark., Jan. 27; to Banks, Jan. 30; orders 500,000 draft, Feb.

Henry W. Hoffman on slavery, Oct. 10; election returns, Oct. 11; concern over election, Oct. 13; attends Taney's funeral, Oct. 15; serenaded, on govt., Oct. 19; issues thanksgiving proclamation, Oct. 20; praises genls., Oct. 21; on "rightness" of soldiers, Oct. 24; proclaims Nev. a state, Oct. 31; reelected Pres., Nov. 8; gains soldier vote, Nov. 8; on govt. and liberty, Nov. 10; on wartime election, Nov. 10; opens "sealed" document signed by Cabinet, Nov. 11; accepts McClellan's resignation, Nov. 14; names Sheridan maj. gen., Nov. 14; on La., Nov. 14; pleasure at election, Nov. 17; ends blockade in places, Nov. 19; writes "Bixby Letter," Nov. 21; confers with Grant, Stanton, Halleck, Nov. 23; Bates resigns, Nov. 24; offers Attorney Generalship to Holt, Nov. 26; names Speed Attorney General, Dec. 1; works on message to Cong., Dec. 3; names Chase Chief Justice, Dec. 6; message to Cong., Dec. 6; appoints western commissioners, Dec. 10; to Canby on govt. of La., Dec. 12; praises Thomas, Dec. 15; schism with Radicals, Dec. 18; calls for 300,000 volunteers, Dec. 19; Sherman's "Christmas gift" to, Dec. 22; to Sherman, Dec. 26; to Grant, Dec. 28

(1865) exasperation with Butler, Jan. 2; New Year's reception, Jan. 2; job seekers, Jan. 5; gives pass, Jan. 5; to Stanton, Jan. 5; exerts pressure for Thirteenth Amendment, Jan. 6; Grant to on Butler, Jan. 6; Butler relieved from command, Jan. 7; patronage to Odell, for Thirteenth Amendment stand, Jan. 9; Blair-Davis conference, Jan. 12; to Dodge on violence, Jan. 15; Blair reports on peace overtures, Jan. 16; to Blair, Jan. 18; speaks of one country, Jan. 18; asks Grant post for son, Jan. 19; meets with Stanton, Jan. 20; wires Johnson, Jan. 24; issues passes to Conf. commissioners, Jan. 30; Thirteenth Amendment, Jan. 31; sends Seward to confer with Conf. commissioners, Jan. 31; on restoration of nation, Jan. 31; signs Thirteenth Amendment resolution, Feb. 1; to Grant, Feb. 1; Hampton Rds. Conference, Feb. 3; disappointed in conference, Feb. 4; to Grant, Feb. 4; compensated emancipation, Feb. 5, signs act barring Southern states from Electoral College, Feb. 8; reports on Hampton Rds. Conference, Feb. 10; Electoral College vote, Feb. 12; on confiscated property, Feb. 12; on military interference in civil affairs, Feb. 13; Radical opposition to reconstruction plan of, Feb. 18; to gov. of Mo., Feb. 20; to Grant, Mar. 2; considers bills, Freedmen's bill, Mar. 3; to Grant, on policy, Mar. 3; second inauguration, Mar. 4; McCulloch Sec. of Treas., replaces Fessenden, Mar. 5; orders on trade, Mar. 7; accepts Usher's resignation, names Harlan to replace as Sec. of Interior, Mar. 9; proclaims pardon for deserters, Mar. 11; orders trial for selling arms to Inds., Mar. 17; on slavery, Mar. 17; to City Point, Mar. 23; at Ft. Monroe, Mar. 24; visits Grant, Mar. 25, 26, 27, 28; on reconstruction plan, Mar. 28; visits Grant, Mar. 29, 30, Apr. 1, 2, 3; in Richmond, Apr. 4, 5; confers with John A. Campbell, Apr. 4, 5; states peace aims, Apr. 5; on calling Va. legislature, Apr. 5; to Weitzel, Apr. 6; to Grant, Apr. 7; in Petersburg, Apr. 8; surrender of Lee, Apr. 9; serenaded, asks "Dixie" be played, Apr. 10; defends reconstruction policy, Apr. 11; on calling Va. legislature, Apr. 12; conference, Apr. 13; Cabinet meeting, tells of dream, Apr. 14; assassination of, Apr. 14; death of, Apr. 15; national mourning, Apr. 16; Southern reaction, Apr. 16; lies in state, Apr. 17, 18, 19; Wash. funeral, Apr. 19; funeral train, Apr. 21, 22, 24, 25, 27, 28, 29,

Sept. 2; Feds. pushed back to, Oct. 19; act. at, Oct. 21; (1865) aff. near, Mar. 11

Little Boston, Va.: (1863) sk., Nov. 24

Little Cacapon Br., W. Va.: (1862) oper., Oct. 2

Little Cacapon R., W. Va.: (1861) sk., Nov. 30

Little Coal R., W. Va.: (1863) Fed. sc. from Camp Piatt on, June 18

Little Compton, or Compton's Fy., Grand R., Mo.: (1862) sk., Aug. 11

Little Cr., N.C.: (1862) sk., Nov. 1

Little Folly I., S.C.: (1863) oper. on, June 11

Little Ft. Valley, Va.: (1865) Fed. exped. to, Feb. 13

"Little Giant": *See* Douglas, Stephen A.

Little Kennesaw Mt., Ga.: *See* Kennesaw Mt., Ga.

"Little Mac": *See* McClellan, George B.

Little Missouri R., Ark.: (1864) sk., Jan. 25; eng. on, Apr. 3; sk. (Camden exped.), Apr. 6

Little Missouri R., Dak. Terr.: (1864) Fed. sc. against Inds., Aug. 8

Little Ogeechee R., Ga.: (1864) sks., Dec. 4, 5

Little Osage R.: (1864) Shelby forms forces on, Oct. 25; eng. on, Oct. 25

Little Piney R., Mo.: (1865) sk., May 14

Little Red R., Ark.: (1862) sks., May 17, June 5, 7; (1863) Fed. exped. up, Aug. 13; (1864) sk., June 6

Little R., Ala.: (1864) sk., Oct. 20

Little R., Ark.: (1863) Fed. exped. up, Mar. 5

Little R., I.T.: (1865) Fed. exped. to, Mar. 18

Little R., Mo.: (1862) Fed. recon. to, Feb. 23; (1864) Fed. exped. to, Apr. 5; sk., Dec. 18

Little R., Tenn.: (1863) sk., Nov. 14

Little R., Va.: (1864) comb., May 27

Little R. Br., Mo.: (1862) sk., Aug. 31

Little R. Turnpike, Va.: (1861) sks., Aug. 31, Oct. 15; (1863) sk., Mar. 23

Little Rock, Ark.: (1863) Fed. advance on, Aug. 1; Steele's march to, Aug. 10, 17, 25, 30, Sept. 1; fall of, Sept. 10; ment., Sept. 22; Oct. 28; unionist conference in, Nov. 12; Fed. recon. from, Dec. 5; (1864) Dodd executed in, Jan. 8; pro-Union constitutional convention, Jan. 19; Steele's camp. starts, Mar. 23; Steele heads back for, Apr. 10; pro-Union govt., Apr. 11; sk. near, Apr. 26; Steele's exped. returns to, May 3, 13; sks., May 24, 28, July 10, 19; Fed. expeds. from, Aug. 6, 27; sk. near, Sept. 2; Fed. exped. from, Sept. 25; Fed. recon. from, Oct. 19; sk. near, Oct. 25; Fed. expeds. from, Oct. 26, Nov. 17; Fed. sc. from, Nov. 27; (1865) sk., Jan. 22; Fed. exped. from, Jan. 22; Fed. exped. near, Feb. 8; Fed. exped. from, Mar. 10; Fed. scs. from, Apr. 26, May 6

Little Rockcastle R., Ky.: (1862) sk., Oct. 18

Little Rock Rd., Ark.: (1863) sk., Apr. 2

Little Round Top: (1863) Bat. of Gettysburg, July 1, 2

Little Salkehatchie R., S.C.: (1865) act. on, Feb. 6

Little Sandy R., Ky.: (1862) Fed. exped. to, Jan. 24

Little Santa Fe, Mo.: (1861) sk., Nov. 20; (1862) sk., Mar. 22

Little Sewell Mt., W. Va.: (1863) sk., Nov. 6

Little Sni R., Mo.: (1862) sk., Apr. 1

Little Tennessee R., Tenn.: (1863) sk., Nov. 4; (1864) Fed. exped. up, Jan. 11

Little Washington, Va.: (1863) sks., Aug. 5, 27

Liverpool, England: (1862) launching of *Alabama,* May 15; trial run of *Alabama,* July 29; (1863) mass meeting supports Eman. Proc., Feb. 19; seizure of *Alexandria,* Apr. 6; detaining of "Laird Rams," Sept. 5; (1864) ment., Oct. 7; Conf. benefit held in, Oct. 18

Liverpool, Miss.: (1864) sk., Mar. 3

Liverpool Heights, on Yazoo R.: (1864) act., Feb. 3; sk., Feb. 4

Livingston, Miss.: (1863) sk., Oct. 17; (1864) sk., Mar. 27

Livington, Tenn.: (1862) Morgan at, July 22; (1863) sk., Dec. 15; (1865) sk., Mar. 18

Livingston, Ft., La.: (1862) surrenders, Apr. 27

Livingston Co., Mo.: (1862) July 27

Lizzard, Tenn.: (1862) sk., Dec. 29; (1863) May 1

Lobelville, Tenn.: (1864) sk., Sept. 27

Locke's Fd., Opequon Cr., Va.: (1864) aff., Sept. 13

Locke's Mills, near Moscow, Tenn.: (1863) sk., Sept. 27

Lockhart's Mill, Coldwater R., Miss.: (1863) Chalmers' raid, sk., Oct. 6

Lockwood, Henry Hayes (F): (1864) superseded, Mar. 22

Lockwood's Folly Inlet, N.C.: (1864) aff., Jan. 4; U.S.S. *Iron Age* lost off, Jan. 10; blockade-runners capt., burned off, Jan. 11

Locomotive chase: *See* Great locomotive chase

Locust Grove, I.T.: (1862) sk., July 3

Locust Grove, Va.: (1863) sk., Nov. 27

Logan, John Alexander ("Blackjack Logan") (F): (1864) commands Army of the Tenn., July 22; Bat. of Atlanta, July 22; replaced, July 27; ordered to replace Thomas, Dec. 13; en route during Bat. of Nashville, Dec. 15; (1865) resumes Fifteenth Corps command, Jan. 8

Logan Co., W. Va.: (1863) Fed. exped. through, Apr. 3

Logan Court House, W. Va.: (1862) Fed. expeds. to, Jan. 12, Dec. 1; (1864) Averell's cav. exped., May 5

Logan's Cross Roads, Ky., Bat of: *See* Mill Springs, Bat. of

Log Church, Ky.: (1862) sk., Sept. 10

Loggy Bayou, La.: (1864) Porter's gunboats at, Apr. 11

Log Mt., Tenn.: (1863) sk., Dec. 3

Lomax, Lunsford Lindsay (C): (1864) eng. at Tom's Brook, Oct. 9

London, England: (1863) ment., May 22; (1864) *Shenandoah* leaves, Oct. 8

London, Ky.: (1862) capt., Oct. 22; (1863) sk., July 26

London *Post:* (1861) backs recognition of C.S.A., Oct. 5

London *Times:* (1861) inclines to Union, Oct. 5

Lone Jack, Mo.: (1862) act., Aug. 16; (1865) aff., Mar. 12

Lone Star, emblem: (1861) Jan. 11

Long Branch Rd., Va.: (1862) Fed. recon. on, July 9

Long Br., Va.: (1864) act., June 12; ment., June 13; (1865) Fed. sc. to, Jan. 30

Long Br., Wash., D.C.: (1861) troops cross, May 24

Long Fd., Tenn.: (1863) sk., Dec. 10

Long I., N.Y.: (1861) Aug. 29

Lovell, Mansfield (C): (1861) commands in La. and Tex., Oct. 18; (1862) Conf. commander at New Orleans, Apr. 24; refuses to surrender, Apr. 25

Love's (or Blue's) Br., S.C.: (1865) sk., Mar. 8

Love's Hill, near Knoxville, Tenn.: (1864) Fed. pickets capture, Jan. 24

Lovettsville, Va.: (1861) sk., Aug. 8; (1862) oper., Sept. 3; Fed. recon. to, Oct. 21; (1865) aff., Jan. 18

Lowe, Thaddeus Sobieski Coulincourt: (1861) balloons of, June 17, 23, Nov. 11

Lower Post Fy. (or Toone's Station), Tenn.: (1862) aff., July 27

Lowndesborough, Ala.: (1865) sk., Apr. 10

Lowndes' Mill, Combahee R., S.C.: (1863) telegraph party capt. near, Sept. 13

Lowry's Fy., Tenn.: (1863) sk., Jan. 11

Loyalty oaths: *See* Oaths

Lubbock, F. R. (C): (1863) as gov. of Tex., asks arms, July 13

Lucas Bend, Mo.: (1861) eng., Sept. 8; Confs. battle *Lexington*, Sept. 10; Fed. gunboat recon. toward, Oct. 7

Lumpkin Co., Ga.: (1864) sk., Sept. 15

Lumpkin's Mill, Miss.: (1862) sk., Nov. 29

Lumpkin's Station, Ga.: (1864) Fourteenth Corps at, Dec. 3; sk., Dec. 4

Luna Ldg., Ark.: (1864) sk., Feb. 22

Lundy's Lane, Ala.: (1863) sk., Apr. 17

Lunenburg, Ark.: (1864) sk., Jan. 1

Luray, Va.: (1862) Jackson reaches, May 20; Fed. recon. to, June 29; Fed. occup. of, July 21; Fed. recon. from, July 22; (1863) Fed. exped. to, Dec. 21; (1864) sk., Sept. 24

Luray Valley, Va. (*See also* Shenandoah Valley): (1862) Jackson's moves in, May 20, 21, 22; (1863) Lee retreats through, July 23; (1864) Sheridan prevented from occupying, Sept. 21; sk., Oct. 8

Luzerne Co., Pa.: (1862) opposition to draft in, Oct. 17

Lynchburg, Tenn.: (1864) sk., Sept. 29

Lynchburg, Va.: (1864) Hunter's camp. against, May 30, June 2, 3, 10, 13 (*See also* Hunter, David); Fed. investment of, eng., June 16, 17, 18; Hunter withdraws from, June 18; Early advances from, June 23; (1865) Grant orders Sheridan to take, Feb. 27; supplies ordered, Apr. 5; Lee heads for, Apr. 8

Lynch's Cr., S.C.: (1865) sk., Feb. 26

Lynde, Isaac (F): (1861) sk. at Mesilla, N. Mex. Terr., July 25; surrenders Ft. Fillmore, July 26, 27; discharged, July 27; dismissed from U. S. Army, Nov. 25

Lynnville, Tenn.: (1864) sks., Nov. 24, Dec. 24

Lyon, Nathaniel (F): (1861) refuses to remove troops, May 6; Camp Jackson affair, May 10; sends troops to Wash. Co., May 15; opinion of Price-Harney pact, May 21; supersedes Harney in Dept. of West, May 31; Harney-Price agreement, May 31; Planter's House meeting, June 11; nears Jefferson City, June 14; occup. of Jefferson City, June 15; occup. of Boonville, June 17; warns against "treason," June 18; falls back on Springfield, Aug. 5; moves out, Aug. 9; Bat. of Wilson's Cr., death of, Aug. 10; funeral, Aug. 28

Lyon, Ft., Colo. Terr.: (1863) Fed. sc. from, Sept. 4; (1864) affs., Aug. 7, Nov. 6; Sand Creek massacre, Nov. 29

Lyon Co., Ky.: (1865) sk., Apr. 29
Lyons, Richard Bickerton Pemell, Lord: (1861) ment. as arbiter, Apr. 22;
   Trent Aff., Nov. 30, Dec. 18, 19, 21, 23, 26
Lytle's Cr., Tenn.: (1863) sk., Jan. 5

McAffee's Crossroads, Ga.: (1864) act., June 11
McAllister, Ft., Ga.: (1862) Fed. naval att. on, July 29; (1863) Fed. naval
   atts. on, Jan. 27, Feb. 1; *Montauk* destroys *Nashville* near, Feb. 28; Fed.
   att. fails, Mar. 3; (1864) Sherman recon. to, Dec. 10; preparations for att.
   on, Dec. 11, 12; fall of, Dec. 13
McCall, George Archibald (F): (1861) Ball's Bluff Camp., Oct. 20
McCauley, Charles Stewart (F): (1861) orders evac. of Gosport Navy Yard,
   Apr. 20
McCausland, John (C): (1864) levies $20,000 on Hagerstown, Md., July 6;
   crosses Potomac, July 29; capture, burning of Chambersburg, Penn., July
   30, 31; pursuit of, July 31; Conf. att. on Cumberland, Md., Aug. 1; sk. at
   Hancock, Md., Aug. 2; escapes into W. Va., Aug. 3
McClellan, George Brinton (F): (1861) commands Dept. of the Ohio, May 3;
   Scott advises, May 3; assumes command, May 13; orders W. Va. move,
   May 26; evac. of Harper's Fy., June 15; commands in W. Va., June 23;
   on prosecution of war, June 23; July 10; eng. at Rich Mt., July 11; occupies
   Beverly, July 12; W. Va. Camp., July 13; household word, July 15; order
   of congratulation, July 19; supersedes McDowell, July 22; commands Div.
   of the Potomac, July 27; re military affairs, Aug. 3; friction with Scott,
   Aug. 10; confers with Lincoln, Aug. 13; assumes command Dept. and the
   Army of the Potomac, Aug. 20; reviews troops, Sept. 24; meets with Lincoln,
   Cabinet, Sept. 27, Oct. 1, 9; squabble with T. W. Sherman, Oct. 18; Ball's
   Bluff Camp., Oct. 20, 21; believes Scott unfit, Oct. 31; General-in-Chief,
   replacing Scott, Nov. 1; procession in honor of, Nov. 11; snubs Lincoln,
   Nov. 13; Lincoln to, re movement, Dec. 1; confers with Lincoln, Dec. 18;
   illness, Dec. 31
      (1862) illness, Jan. 1; improving, Jan. 2, 4; move to remove, Jan. 6;
   Lincoln to on move, Jan. 9; conference, Jan. 12; keeps plans secret, Jan. 13;
   confers with Lincoln, Cabinet, Jan. 15; Special War Order No. 1 orders movement, Jan. 31; Lincoln to, re strategy, Feb. 3; Lincoln to, Feb.
   8; blame in Stone arrest, Feb. 9; confers with Lincoln, Feb. 26, 28; advance expected, Mar. 6; army moves, Mar. 7; confers with Lincoln, Mar. 8;
   "victory," Mar. 9; Lincoln to, Mar. 10; relieved as General-in-Chief, commands Dept. and A. of P., Mar. 11; Peninsula plans, Mar. 13; Lincoln to
   re security of Wash., Mar. 13; A. of P. embarks, Mar. 17; agreement to
   protect Wash. not kept, Mar. 23; to threaten Confs. on Peninsula, Mar. 27;
   troops to Frémont, Mar. 31; "denial" of troops to, Mar. 31, Apr. 3, 9;
   prepares assault, Apr. 1; Lincoln to, re Yorktown, Apr. 6; Yorktown siege
   lines, Apr. 7; size of armies, Apr. 9, 12; McDowell moving toward, Apr. 18;
   Apr. 21; reinforced, Apr. 22; siege of Yorktown, May 1; Lincoln to on
   procrastination, May 1; feels outnumbered, May 3; calls Yorktown success,
   May 4; Bat. of Williamsburg, May 5; Lincoln to re corps, May 9; nearer to
   Richmond, May 14; hdqrs. at White House, May 16; before Richmond,
   May 20; Lincoln to on McDowell's movement, May 21; along Chickahominy,

May 22; May 23; McDowell ordered to Shenandoah, May 24; blames Administration, May 24; inaction, May 26; Lincoln to, May 26; ment., May 28; Bat. of Seven Pines or Fair Oaks, May 31, June 1; Lincoln to, June 1, 2; on Chickahominy, near Richmond, June 4; rains delay, June 5; ment., June 9; Stuart's ride around, June 12, 13, 14, 15; Conf. strategy, June 17; Lincoln asks views of, June 21; inaction of, June 22; eng. at Oak Grove (start of 7 Days), June 25; Bat. of Mechanicsville, June 26; moves to Harrison's Ldg., June 26; Lincoln to on troops, June 26; Bat. of Gaines' Mill, June 27; blames Lincoln for defeat, June 28; Savage's Station, June 29; Bat. of Frayser's Farm or White Oak Swamp, June 30; Bat. of Malvern Hill, July 1; withdrawal, July 2, 3; July 5; "Harrison's Bar letter," July 7; Lincoln arrives, July 8; to Lincoln on strength, July 13; July 14; ordered to move wounded, July 30; protests order to defend Wash., Aug. 3; corps moved, Aug. 14; completes evacuation of Harrison's Ldg., Aug. 16; Aug. 18; to Aquia Cr., Aug. 20, 21, 22; 2nd Bull Run Camp., Aug. 26; 2nd Bat. of Bull Run, Aug. 29, 30; confers with Lincoln, Halleck, Sept. 1; restored to full command, Sept. 2; Pope makes charges against, Sept. 3; reorganizing army, Sept. 4, 5; pursuit of Lee, Sept. 7, 8, 10; to Lincoln on Lee, Sept. 12; Lee's lost order, Sept. 13; Bat. of Crampton's Gap, South Mt., Sept. 14; Sept. 15; no att. by, Sept. 16; Bat. of Antietam, Sept. 17; did not att. Lee, Sept. 18; pursues Lee, Sept. 19, 20; Lincoln perturbed with, Sept. 27; rumors of compromise on slavery rife, Sept. 27; Lincoln confers with, Oct. 1, 2, 3, 4; ordered to give bat., Oct. 6; Stuart's Chambersburg raid, Oct. 9, 10, 11, 12; Lincoln urges action, Oct. 13; launches recons., Oct. 16; Lincoln to on strength, Oct. 20; Lincoln to on horses, Oct. 25; crosses Potomac, Lincoln to, Oct. 26; moves into Va., Oct. 28; Lincoln to, Oct. 29; does not pursue Lee, Nov. 1; Snicker's Gap occup., Nov. 2; Longstreet in front of, Nov. 3; replaced by Burnside, Nov. 5; relieved of command, Nov. 7; reaction to dismissal, Nov. 8, 10; ment., Dec. 19

(1863) pressure to reinstate, June 30; (1864) ment., May 30; ment., Aug. 23; ment. as candidate at Democratic convention, Aug. 29; in nomination, Aug. 30; nominated for Pres., Aug. 31; accepts nomination, Sept. 8; disavows "peace plank," Sept. 8; Frémont's withdrawal, Sept. 17; defeated for President, Nov. 8; resigns from Army, Nov. 8; resignation accepted, Nov. 14; (1865) electoral vote, Feb. 12

McClellansville, S.C.: (1864) aff. at, Mar. 25

McClernand, John Alexander (F): (1862) recon. into Ky., Jan. 17; to Ft. Donelson, Feb. 11; att. on Donelson, Feb. 13; bat. at Ft. Donelson, Feb. 15; ordered to organize Vicksburg exped., Oct. 20; commands Thirteenth Corps, Dec. 18; (1863) Sherman's forces under, Jan. 2; unauthorized Ark. R. move, Jan. 4; assumes command Army of the Miss., Jan. 4; Lincoln to, Jan. 8; eng. at Arkansas Post, Jan. 10, 11; ordered to return to Vicksburg forces, Jan. 11; begins move, Jan. 17; reduced to corps commander, Jan. 22; ordered to New Carthage, La., Mar. 29; oper., Mar. 31, Apr. 5, 8, 15; Bat. of Port Gibson, May 1; sk. at Fourteen-Mile Cr., May 12; heads toward Clinton, Miss., May 13; on r.r., May 14; Bat. of Champion's Hill, May 16; siege of Vicksburg, May 19, 22; relieved of command, June 18; Lincoln refuses command to, Aug. 12

McConnellsburg, Pa.: (1863) sks., June 25, 29; (1864) McCausland moves to, July 30

McCook, Alexander McDowell (F): (1863) commands Twentieth Army Corps, Jan. 9; Chickamauga Camp., Sept. 16; Bat. of Chickamauga, Sept. 19; court of inquiry, relieved of command, Sept. 28; (1864) raids Ga. r.r., July 27

McCook, Robert Latimer (F): (1862) death of, Aug. 6

McCook, Ft., Tenn.: (1862) Fed. att. on, Aug. 27

McCooks, "Fighting": *See* McCook, Alexander McDowell, and McCook, Robert Latimer

McCown, John Porter (C): (1862) superseded in command, Mar. 31; assumes command, Dept. of East Tenn., Sept. 1

McCoy's Mill, W. Va.: (1861) sk., Nov. 14

McCulla's Store, Mo.: (1861) aff., July 26; sk., Aug. 3

McCulloch, Ben. (C): (1861) near Wilson's Cr., Aug. 9; Commands, Bat. of Wilson's Cr., Aug. 10; on Wilson's Cr. victory, destiny of Mo., Aug. 12; invasion by feared, Aug. 15; (1862) death of, Mar. 7

McCulloch, Hugh (F): (1865) offered Treasury post, Mar. 5; appointed Sec. of Treasury, Mar. 6

McDonald, Camp, W. Va.: (1862) sk., May 6

McDonough, Ga.: (1864) Kilpatrick heads for, Nov. 14

McDonough Rd., near Atlanta, Ga.: (1864) sk., Nov. 6

McDougal, David Stockton (F): (1863) Bat. of Shimonoseki, July 16

McDowell, Irvin (F): (1861) assumes command Dept. of Northeastern Va., May 28; plans for att., June 29; pressure for advance, July 14; moves toward Manassas, July 16, 17; eng. at Blackburn's Fd., July 18; prepares for att., July 19, 20; Bat. of 1st Bull Run, July 21; superseded by McClellan, July 22; replacement, July 27; (1862) corps to guard Wash., Mar. 23; corps withheld, Apr. 3; put into Dept. of the Rappahannock, Apr. 4; occupies Falmouth, Va., Apr. 18; meets Lincoln, Apr. 20; Apr. 21; to march on Richmond, May 17; Lincoln on, May 21; Lincoln confers with, May 22, 23; ordered to Shenandoah, May 24; moving to cut off Jackson, May 25, 26; Lincoln to, May 28; troop strength, May 29; Jackson falls back from, May 30; converges with Frémont, May 30; Lincoln to on destroying Jackson, May 30; McClellan to connect with, May 31; Jackson gets between, May 31; Shields at Front Royal, June 1; Lincoln to, June 2; Bat. of Cross Keys, June 8; Bat. of Port Republic, June 9; 2nd Manassas or Bull Run, Aug. 29; (1864) assumes command Dept. of the Pacific, July 1

McDowell, Va.: (1862) Jackson heads for, May 6; Bat. of, May 8; May 9, 13, 15

McGirt's Cr., Fla.: (1864) sk., Mar. 1

McGowan, John (F): (1861) captain, *Star of the West*, Jan. 9

McGuire's, Ark.: (1862) act., Oct. 28

McGuire's Fy., Ark.: (1862) sk., Sept. 23

McIntosh, James McQueen (C): (1862) killed at Pea Ridge, Mar. 7

McIntosh, Ft., Tex.: (1861) abandoned, Mar. 12

McKay's Farm, Mo.: (1862) aff., Mar. 21

McKee, William: (1863) arrest of, July 13

McKenzie's Cr., near Patterson, Mo.: (1865) sk., Apr. 15

McLane, Ft., N. Mex. Terr.: (1861) abandoned, July 3

McLaws, Lafayette (C): (1862) Bat. of Crampton's Gap, Sept. 14; besieging Harper's Fy., Sept. 14; joins Jackson, Sept. 15; to join Lee, Sept. 16; (1863) northern invasion, June 3

McLean, Wilbur, House: (1861) July 19; (1865) Lee surrenders in, Apr. 9

McLean Co., Ky.: (1861) Nov. 17

McLean's Fd., Va.: (1863) eng., Oct. 14; sk., Oct. 15

McLemore's Cove, Ga.: (1863) abortive Conf. att., Sept. 10; (1864) Fed. recon. to, Mar. 30; (1865) sk. in, Feb. 1

McLemoresville, Tenn.: (1863) Fed. exped. to, Sept. 20

McMilley's Farm, Ark.: (1865) Fed. exped. to, Feb. 26

McMinnville, Tenn.: (1862) Fed. exped. to, Mar. 25; (1863) Fed. exped. to, Apr. 20; aff., Oct. 3; sk. near, taken by Wheeler, Oct. 4; sk., Dec. 21; (1865) sk., Feb. 5

McNeil, John (F): (1863) assumes command Dist. of the Frontier, Nov. 2

McNutt's Hill, La.: (1864) sk., Apr. 26

McPherson, James Birdseye (F): (1862) commands Seventeenth Army Corps, Dec. 18; (1863) ordered to New Carthage, La., Mar. 29; eng. at Raymond, Miss., May 12; toward Jackson, May 13; occup. of Jackson, May 14; Bat. of Champion's Hill, May 16; siege of Vicksburg, May 19; (1864) assumes command Army of the Tenn., Mar. 26; Atlanta Camp., May 7, 8, 9, 10, 17, 18, 26, 28, 29, June 15, July 4, 8, 19, 20 (Bat. of Peachtree Cr.), 21, 22 (Bat. of Atlanta); death of, July 22

McPherson's Ridge, Pa.: (1863) in Bat. of Gettysburg, July 1

McPherson's Woods, Pa.: (1863) in Bat. of Gettysburg, July 1

McRee, Ft., Fla.: (1861) Fla. troops take, Jan. 12; bomb., Nov. 22

McWilliam's Plantation, Indian Bend, La.: (1863) sk., Apr. 13

Macarthy, Harry: (1861) author, "Bonnie Blue Flag," Jan. 9

Machodoc Cr., Va.: (1863) Fed. exped. to, Mar. 3

Mackall, William Whann (C): (1862) supersedes McCown, Mar. 31; surrenders to Pope, Apr. 7

Mackville Pike, Ky.: (1862) sk. on, Oct. 9

Macomb, William H. (F): (1864) capture of Plymouth, N.C., Oct. 31

Macomb, Ft., La.: (1861) occup. of, Jan. 28

Macon, Ga.: (1864) Stoneman's cav. raid toward, July 26, 27; comb., July 30; ment., Sept. 2; Davis in, Sept. 22; sk., Nov. 21; (1865) capt., Apr. 20

Macon, Mo.: (1864) sk., Feb. 12; (1865) sk., Feb. 12

Macon, Tenn.: (1863) Fed. exped. to, Mar. 28

Macon, Ft., N.C.: (1861) seized by Confs., Apr. 15; (1862) Feds. besiege, Mar. 23, Apr. 21; surrenders, Apr. 25; formal surrender, Apr. 26

Macon Co., Mo.: (1862) sk. at Stockton, Aug. 8.

Macon Fd., Big Black R., Miss.: (1863) sk., June 9

"Macon line": *See* Macon and Western R.R.

Macon R.R.: *See* Macon and Western R.R.

Macon and Western R.R.: (1864) McCook's raid on, July 27; Kilpatrick's raid, Aug. 18, 20; cut, Aug. 31; Sherman's troops move along, Nov. 18

Madison, Ark.: (1863) sks., Mar. 5, June 25; (1865) Fed. sc. to, Feb. 8

Madison Co., Ala.: (1864) oper. in, Aug. 12

Madison Co., Ark.: (1865) sk., Jan. 15

Madison Court House, Va.: (1862) Fed. recons. to, July 12, 22; act., Aug. 8; (1863) sk., Sept. 21; (1864) Fed. sc. to, Jan. 30; Fed. recon. near, Jan. 31; Fed. recon. to, Apr. 28; ment., Dec. 19

Madison Station, Ala.: (1864) aff., May 17

Madisonville, Ky.: (1862) sks., Aug. 25, Sept. 5

Madisonville, La.: (1862) sk., July 27; (1864) Fed. exped. from, Feb. 1; sks. near, Feb. 11

Madisonville, Miss.: (1864) aff., Feb. 27

Mad R., Calif.: (1861) sk., Apr. 14; Fed. sc. on, May 23

Magnolia, Fla.: (1864) sks., Sept. 24, Oct. 24

Magnolia, Md.: (1864) capture of Fed. trains, July 11

Magnolia, Tenn.: (1865) sk., Mar. 31

Magnolia Ldg., La.: (1864) June 16 att. on Fed. gunboats, June 15

Magoffin, Beriah: (1861) as Ky. gov., alerts defenses, convenes legislature, Apr. 24; proclamation on neutrality, May 20

Magrath, Andrew Gordon (C): (1865) Davis to, Jan. 17

Magruder, Allan B. (F): (1861) Lincoln sends to Richmond, Apr. 3

Magruder, John Bankhead (C): (1861) in command at Big Bethel, June 10; burns Hampton, Va., Aug. 7; (1862) Johnston ordered to reinforce, Mar. 27; commands on Peninsula, Apr. 1; Johnston to reinforce, Apr. 4, 12; holds Yorktown line, Apr. 6; Bat. of Williamsburg, May 5; Bat. of Gaines' Mill, June 27; assigned command, Oct. 10; assumes command, Dist. of Texas, N. Mex., and Arizona, Nov. 29; (1863) recaptures Galveston, Jan. 1; att. on Sabine Pass, Sept. 8

Magruder's Fy., Va.: (1861) sk., Sept. 16

Mahone, William (C): (1864) Petersburg Mine explosion, July 30; eng. of Burgess' Mill, Boydton Plank Rd., or Hatcher's Run, Oct. 27; (1865) eng. at Sayler's Cr., Apr. 6; guards crossing, Apr. 7

Maine: (1865) approves Thirteenth Amendment, Feb. 7

Maine troops: (1861) men of 2nd regt. mutiny, Aug. 15

Malacca, Straits of: (1863) *Alabama* takes prizes off, Dec. 26

Mallory, Robert (F): (1865) opposes Thirteenth Amendment, Jan. 9

Mallory, Stephen Russell (C): (1861) resigns from U. S. Sen., Jan. 21; Sec. of Navy, C.S.A., Feb. 19; officially appointed, Feb. 21; advocates ironclads, May 10; (1865) resigns, May 2

Malvern, U.S.S.: (1865) transports Lincoln, Apr. 4

Malvern Hill, Va.: (1862) Stuart's ride passes through, June 14; Fed. lines close in on, June 30; Bat. of, July 1; Fed. retreat, July 2; Fed. forces reoccupy, Aug. 2; eng., Aug. 5; sk., Aug. 6; Fed. forces withdraw, Aug. 7; (1864) Lee's line from, June 13; sk., June 15; acts., July 14, 16

Mammoth Cave, Ky.: (1862) sk. near, Aug. 17

"The man and the hour have met": (1861) Feb. 16

Manassas, Va.: (1861) Beauregard at, June 5; Fed. plan of att., June 29, July 2; Beauregard at, July 16, 18; Jackson arrives, July 19; 1st Bat. of, or 1st Bull Run, July 21; aftermath, July 22, 23; Aug. 20; Nov. 9; (1862) A. of P. moves toward, Mar. 7; A. of P. at, Mar. 11; 2nd Manassas or 2nd Bull Run Camp., Aug. 26, 27, 28; 2nd Bat. of, or 2nd Bull Run, Aug. 29,

30; (1863) Lee heads toward (Bristoe Camp.), Oct. 12, 13; Meade's lines near, Oct. 14; sk., Oct. 15; Lee withdraws from vicinity, Oct. 18; Bristoe Camp. ends, Oct. 20

Manassas, C.S.S. (ironclad ram): (1861) challenges Fed. squadron, Oct. 12; (1862) eng. before New Orleans, Apr. 24

Manassas, 1st Bat. of: *See* Bull Run, 1st

Manassas, 2nd Bat. of: *See* Bull Run, 2nd

Manassas Gap, Va.: (1863) cav. eng., July 21; Fed. att. in, July 22, 23

Manassas Gap R.R.: (1861) July 19

Manassas Junction, Va.: (1861) Beauregard arrives at, commands Conf. forces, June 3; Jackson arrives at, July 19; 1st Bull Run, Bat. of, July 21; July 27; (1862) A. of P. ordered to occupy, Jan. 31; Lincoln on security of, Mar. 13; Fitzhugh Lee captures, Aug. 26; sk., 2nd Bull Run Camp., Aug. 26; 2nd Bull Run or Manassas, Bat. of, Aug. 29, 30; sk., Oct. 24; (1863) sks., Oct. 17; (1864) Nov. 11

Manchester (U.S. grain ship): (1862) sunk by *Alabama,* Oct. 11

Manchester, England, workingmen: (1863) Lincoln to, Jan. 19

Manchester, Ky.: (1862) sk., Oct. 14; salt works near destroyed, Oct. 23; Carter's Fed. exped. leaves, Dec. 26

Manchester, Tenn.: (1862) Fed. recon. to, Mar. 25; (1863) Fed. occup. of, June 27; (1864) sk., Mar. 17

Manchester Pike, Tenn.: (1863) sks. on, Jan. 4, 5, Feb. 22; Fed. recons. on, Apr. 29, May 27

Mandeville, La.: (1865) Fed. exped. to, Jan. 15

Mankato, Minn. (*See also* Sioux uprising): (1862) Sioux uprising Indians' execution ment., Aug. 17; citizens attack Ind. prisoners, Dec. 4; 38 Inds. hanged, Dec. 26

Manley, Miss.: (1864) ment., Mar. 12

Mann, Ambrose Dudley (C): (1861) Davis names commissioner to Britain, Mar. 16; received by Lord Russell, May 3; (1863) special agent to Holy See, Sept. 24

Manning's Neck, N.C.: (1864) Fed. exped. to, July 28

Manpower, Conf. (*See also* Mobilization, Conf.): (1861) reported lack of, Oct. 29

Manpower, Fed. (*See also* Mobilization, Fed.): (1861) reported lack of, Oct. 29

Manscoe Cr., near Edgefield Junction, Tenn.: (1862) sk., Aug. 19

Man's Cr., Shannon Co., Mo.: (1863) sk., Oct. 14

Mansfield, Joseph King Fenno (F): (1861) assigned command Dept. of Wash., Apr. 27; commands at Hatteras Inlet, Oct. 5; superseded, Oct. 13

Mansfield, La.: (1864) Banks advances, Apr. 7; Bat. of (or Sabine Cross Roads), Apr. 8; Smith orders retreat to, Apr. 9, 10; eng. ment., Apr. 11

Mansura or Belle Prairie or Smith's Plantation, La.: (1864) eng., May 16

Mantapike Hill, Va.: (1864) Kilpatrick-Dahlgren raid, Mar. 2

Maple Cypress, N.C.: (1865) Confs. burn steamers, Apr. 5

Maple Leaf, U.S.S. (steamer): (1863) taken over by prisoners, June 10; (1864) sunk, Apr. 1

Maplesville, Ala.: (1865) sk., Apr. 1

Marais des Cygnes, Kas.: (1863) sk., Aug. 31; (1864) eng., Oct. 25

"Marble Heart, The": (1863) Lincoln sees, Nov. 9

Marblehead, U.S.S.: (1863) att. on, Dec. 25

March to the Sea: *See* Sherman, William T.

Marianna, Ark.: (1862) Fed. expeds. to, July 24, Sept. 26; eng., Nov. 7; sk., Nov. 8

Marianna, Fla.: (1864) Fed. exped. to, Sept. 18; sk., Oct. 2

Maries Co., Mo.: (1864) Fed. sc. in, July 30

Marietta, Ga.: (1862) great locomotive chase, Apr. 12; (1863) Davis at, Oct. 9; (1864) sk. near, June 1; Johnston's line near, June 5, 10; Sherman attacks at Mud Cr. near, June 17; Johnston moves lines closer to, June 18; Bat. of Kennesaw Mt., June 27; Sherman moves through, July 3; Rousseau's cav. raid, July 10

Marietta, Miss.: (1862) Fed. exped. to, Aug. 19; sk., Aug. 30

Marine band: (1864) concert, May 7

Marines, Fed.: (1863) oper. Bayport, Fla., Apr. 3; (1865) at Ft. Fisher, Jan. 15

Marion, Ark.: (1865) Fed. exped. to, Jan. 19

Marion, Va.: (1864) act., Dec. 16; sk., Dec. 17

Marion, Ft., St. Augustine, Fla.: (1861) Fla. takes, Jan. 7

Marion Co., Ala.: (1864) oper. against pro-unionists in, Apr. 19

Marion Co., Ark.: (1865) Fed. sc., Feb. 16

Marion Co., Fla.: (1865) Fed. exped., Mar. 7

Marion Station, Miss.: (1864) sk., Feb. 15

Marks' Mills, Ark.: (1864) sk. (Camden exped.), Apr. 5; act. (Camden exped.), Apr. 25

Marksville Prairie, La.: (1864) sk. (Red R. Camp.), Mar. 15; sk., May 15

Marlborough Point, Va.: (1861) act. against, July 29

Marling's Bottom, W. Va.: (1864) aff., Apr. 19

Marling's Bottom Br., Va.: (1863) sk., Dec. 11

Marmaduke, John Sappington (C): (1862) defeated at Cane Hill, Ark., Nov. 28; raid into Mo., Dec. 31; (1863) into Mo., Jan. 2; sk. at Ft. Lawrence, Mo., Jan. 6; capture of Ozark, moves to Springfield, Jan. 7; Springfield resists att. by, Jan. 8; surrender of Hartville garrison, Jan. 9; eng. at Hartville, Jan. 11; takes Patterson, Mo., Jan. 20; at Batesville, Ark., Jan. 25; sk. at Batesville, Feb. 4; goes to Mo., Apr. 17; sk. at Patterson, Mo., Apr. 20; sk. at Fredericktown, Apr. 22; sk. at Mill or Middle Cr. Brs., Mo., Apr. 24; act. at Cape Girardeau, Apr. 26; sk. at Jackson, Mo., Apr. 27; sk. at Castor R., Apr. 29; sk. at Bloomfield, Apr. 30; sk. at Chalk Bluff, May 1; att. on Pine Bluff, Ark., Oct. 25; (1864) eng. at Poison Springs, Ark., Apr. 18; Price plans to att. Army of the Border, Oct. 22; Bat. of Westport, Oct. 23

Marmiton R., Mo.: (1864) eng., Oct. 25

Marmora, U.S.S.: (1863) guerrillas fire upon, June 14

Marr, John Q. (C): (1861) killed, June 1

Marrowbone, Ky.: (1863) sk. (Morgan), July 2

Marrow Bone Cr., Ky.: (1863) sk., Sept. 22

Marshall, Humphrey (C): (1862) eng. at Middle Cr., Ky., Jan. 10

Marshall, Ky.: (1864) sk., Jan. 12

Marshall, Mo.: (1862) sks. near, Mar. 15, 16; (1863) sks., July 28, 30; act., Oct. 13

Marshall, Tex.: (1865) Conf. govs., officers confer, May 13

Marshall House, Alexandria, Va.: (1861) Ellsworth, Jackson killed, May 24

Marshfield, Mo.: (1862) sks., Feb. 9, Oct. 20

Martial law: (1861) in St. Louis, Aug. 14; Frémont declares in Mo., Aug. 30; in St. Louis, on Mo. r.r.'s, Dec. 26; (1862) Davis puts cities under, Feb. 27; in Richmond, Mar. 1; in southeast Va., Mar. 14; in San Francisco, Mar. 16; in southwest Va., May 3; in Charleston, S.C., May 13; in Cincinnati, Ohio, Covington, and Newport, Ky., Sept. 2

Martin Cr., Tenn.: (1863) sk. on, July 10

Martinsburg, Mo.: (1861) sk., July 18

Martinsburg, W. Va.: (1861) Feds. move toward, July 2; occup., July 3; Fed. advance from, July 15; (1862) sk., Feds. occupy, Mar. 3; sk., Sept. 3; Fed. garrisons cut off, Sept. 7; cav. sk., Oct. 1; sk., Nov. 6; Fed. recon. from, Dec. 25; (1863) sk., occup. of, June 14, 15; sk., July 18; Conf. cleanup oper. around, July 21; Belle Boyd's arrest in, Aug. 1; Fed. expeds. from, Sept. 2; Fed. sc. from, Nov. 14; (1864) sks., July 3, 25; Early att. on r.r. near, July 26; sk., Aug. 31; Early advances toward, Sept. 17, 18; Sheridan at, Oct. 19

Martinsburg Pike, Va.: (1864) 3rd Bat. of Winchester, Sept. 19

Martin's Cr., Ark.: (1864) sk., Jan. 7

Martin's House, Ind. Terr.: (1863) sk., May 6

Martinsville, N.C.: (1865) act., Apr. 8

Marvin, William: (1865) provisional gov. of Fla., July 13

Marye's Heights, Fredericksburg, Va.: (1862) Bat. of Fredericksburg, Dec. 13; (1863) Bat. of 2nd Fredericksburg, May 3; bat. ment., May 4

Maryland: (1861) Baltimore riots, Apr. 19, 20; tends toward Union, Apr. 27; House of Delegates votes against secession, Apr. 29; pro-Union, pro-Conf. meetings, May 3; passage of troops through, May 4; Lincoln on military use of state, May 6; tends to Union, May 8; legislature resolves to ask Lincoln to stop war, May 10; Davis on "self-government," May 25; arrest of legislators, Sept. 12; held in Union, Sept. 12; disloyalty arrests, Sept. 15; legislature doesn't assemble, Sept. 17; possible invasion of, Oct. 20; (1862) fear of Conf. invasion of, Sept. 8, 10; (1863) gov. rallies citizens, June 10; fear of Lee's invasion, June 15; Lincoln fears violence in, Nov. 2; (1864) Lincoln on eman. in, Mar. 17; Constitutional Convention meets in, Apr. 27; abolishes slavery, June 24; militia called, July 5; Conf. cav. enters, July 29; Early threatens invasion of, Aug. 25; adopts constitution, Sept. 6; voters approve constitution, Oct. 13; Lincoln on reconstruction in, Dec. 6; (1865) ratifies Thirteenth Amendment, Feb. 3

Maryland Camp.: *See* Lee, R. E.; Antietam; Crampton's Gap; South Mt.; Harper's Fy.

Maryland Heights, Md.: (1862) McLaws withdraws from, Sept. 15; (1863) Hooker wants to evacuate, June 26; Fed. reoccup. of, July 7

Maryland troops, C.S.A.: (1861) leave for Va., May 9

Maryville, Tenn.: (1863) sk., Nov. 14; (1864) Fed. expeds. from, Jan. 11, Jan. 31; Fed. recon. from, Feb. 1; Fed. sc., Feb. 8; sk., Feb. 18

Mayfield Cr., Ky.: (1861) sk., Sept. 22

Maynardville, Tenn.: (1863) sk., Dec. 1

May R., S.C.: (1862) Fed. recon. on, Mar. 19

Maysville, Ala.: (1863) sk., Aug. 21; sk. (Wheeler's raid), Oct. 13; sk., Nov. 4; Fed. exped. from, Nov. 14; (1864) sk., Nov. 17; (1865) Fed. sc. to, Apr. 5

Maysville, Ark.: (1863) sk., Sept. 5; (1864) sk., May 8

Maysville, Ky.: (1862) Smith occupies, Sept. 11; (1863) sk., June 16

Mezeppa (U.S. steamer): (1864) Forrest captures, Oct. 30

Meade, George Gordon (F): (1861) exped. to Gunnell's Farm, Dec. 6; (1862) Bat. of Fredericksburg, Dec. 13, (1863) given corps command, Feb. 5; Bat. of Chancellorsville, May 2; commands A. of P., June 27; receives orders, June 28; moves forward, June 29; orders Gettysburg occupied, June 30; Bat. of Gettysburg, July 1, 2, 3; lack of pursuit, July 4, 5, 6; Lincoln on lack of follow-up, July 6, 7; mounting att., July 11, 12; finds Lee across Potomac, July 13; Lincoln to (unsent), July 14; crosses Potomac, July 19; pursues Lee, July 20, 21; Lincoln expresses confidence in, July 21; finds Confs. gone, July 24; Mosby's oper., July 28; Lincoln on, July 29; confers with Lincoln, Aug. 14; Aug. 24; moves to Rapidan, Sept. 13; Lincoln to, Sept. 15; Bristoe Camp., Oct. 9, 10, 11, 12, 13, 14; to Lincoln, Oct. 10; on attacking Lee, Oct. 16; to Lincoln, Oct. 24; advance, Nov. 7; strategy of, Nov. 8; Lincoln congratulates, Nov. 9; Mine Run Camp., Nov. 26, 27, 28, 29, 30, Dec. 1, 2; (1864) Grant visits, Mar. 10; removal of urged, Mar. 23; Lincoln dissuades from court of inquiry, Mar. 29; Lee's army to be objective, Apr. 9; A. of P. to move, May 3; at Bat. of Spotsylvania, May 12, 18; movement to left, May 20; Bat. of North Anna, May 26; moves toward Richmond, May 29; Bat. of Cold Harbor, June 3; moves to James R., June 12; ass. on Petersburg, June 17; siege of Petersburg, June 18, 21, July 9, Sept. 14, 29, Oct. 2; (1865) stops att. at Amelia Court House, Apr. 5; pursues Lee, Apr. 8; not at surrender, Apr. 9; visits Lee, Apr. 10

Meade Co., Ky.: (1864) Fed. sc. in, May 5

Meadow Bluff, W. Va.: (1861) Fed. exped., Dec. 15; (1862) Fed. sc. from, Aug. 2; (1863) sks., Dec. 4, 11, 14; (1864) r.r. raid reaches, May 19; Crook starts from, May 30

Meadow Br., Chickahominy R., Va.: (1862) Bat. of Mechanicsville, June 26; (1864) sk., May 12

Mechanicsburg, Miss.: (1863) sk., May 24; Fed. expeds. to, May 26, June 2; (1865) sk., Jan. 3

Mechanicsburg Gap, W. Va.: (1861) Sept. 23

Mechanicsville, Va.: (1862) sks., May 23, 24, June 24; Bat. of, (or Beaver Dam Cr. or Ellerson's Mill), June 26; (1864) comb., May 12; Lee's forces at, May 28

Mechump's Cr., Va.: (1864) comb., May 31

Medicine Cr., Mo.: (1862) sk., Apr. 8

Medley, W. Va.: (1864) cav. sk., Jan. 29; capture of wagon train, Jan. 30

Medoc, Mo.: (1861) sk., Aug. 23

Medon, Tenn.: (1862) sk., Aug. 13

Medon Station, Tenn.: (1862) sk., Oct. 10

Meffleton Lodge, Ark.: (1864) sk., June 29

Melbourne, Australia: (1865) *Shenandoah* at, Jan. 25

Melville, Mo.: (1864) Conf. raid on, June 14

Memminger, Christopher Gustavus (C): (1861) resolution for Southern Confederacy, Feb. 5; heads Committee of Twelve to form C.S.A. govt., Feb. 7; Sec. of Treasury, C.S.A., Feb. 19; (1864) resigns, June 21; Trenholm replaces, July 18

Memphis, Mo.: (1862) sk., July 18

Memphis, Tenn.: (1861) Lincoln ment., July 27; (1862) state capital moved to, Feb. 20; undefended, Apr. 7; Conf. gunboats withdraw to, May 10; Conf. mass meeting for defense of city, June 2; jeopardized by fall of Corinth, Miss., June 3; Fed. gunboats push toward, June 5; Bat. of, surrender, June 6; sks., Sept. 2, 23; Davis on recapture of, Oct. 21; Sherman's exped. from, Dec. 24, 26; (1863) Fed. exped. against guerrillas, Feb. 17; sk. near, Apr. 4; Fed. expeds. from, May 23, 26, 27; Fed. scs. from, May 28, June 16, July 3, 20; sk. near, July 18; Fed. exped. from, July 23; Fed. exped. to, Aug. 10; Fed. exped. from, Aug. 12; Fed. sc. from, Aug. 16; troops move toward Chattanooga, Oct. 5; Fed. exped. from, Oct. 10; Fed. sc. from, Nov. 19; (1864) cold wave in, Jan. 1; Fed. sc. from, Jan. 3; Smith's cav. exped. from, Jan. 10; Smith's Meridian Camp., Feb. 6, 11, 18, 21; Fed. exped. from, Apr. 30; Sturgis leaves from, June 1; Fed. retreat to after Brice's Cross Roads, June 10; Fed. exped. from, July 4; Forrest occupies, Aug. 21; sks. near, Sept. 12, Oct. 4, 20, 25; Fed. exped. from, Nov. 9; Fed. sc. around, Nov. 10; sk. near, Dec. 14; Fed. exped. against the Mobile and Ohio, Dec. 21; (1865) Fed. expeds. from, Jan. 19, 26; sk. near, Feb. 9; Fed. expeds. from, Mar. 3, Apr. 19

Memphis, Tenn., *Argus:* (1862) Jan. 2

Memphis, U.S.S.: (1864) att. on, Mar. 6

Memphis and Charleston R.R.: (1862) occup. of Huntsville on, Apr. 11; sk. on, May 3; Fed. raid on, May 13; sk. on, May 14; act. along, May 15; broken by fall of Corinth, June 3; (1863) Conf. cav. oper. against, Nov. 3; Forrest's oper. against, Nov. 28

Mercedita, U.S.S. (blockader): (1863) damaged in Conf. att., Jan. 31

Mercersburg, Pa.: (1863) sk. near, July 5; (1864) sk., July 29

Merchants, Conf.: (1861) repudiate U.S. debts, Apr. 20

Mercier, M.: (1863) offers French mediation in war, Feb. 3

Meridian, Miss. (*See also* Meridian, Miss., Camp.): (1863) Davis in, Oct. 23; (1864) Fed. cav. exped. to, Jan. 10; occup., destruction of, Feb. 14; Sherman withdraws from, Feb. 20; (1865) Maury's forces reach, Apr. 12

Meridian, Miss., Camp.: (1864) Sherman leads, Feb. 3, 4, 5, 6, 7, 8, 9, 10, 11, 12, 13, 14, 15, 16, 17, 18, 19, 20, 21, 22 (Okolona), 23, 24, 25, 26, 27, 28, 29, Mar. 1, 4; ment., Mar. 12

Meriwether's Fy., Bayou Boeuf, Ark.: (1863) sk., Dec. 13

Meriwether's Fy., Obion R., Tenn.: (1862) sk., Aug. 16; (1863) sk., Nov. 19

Merrill & Thomas gun factory: (1861) taken by U.S. marshal, June 5

Merrill's Crossing, Mo.: (1863) sk., Oct. 12

Merrimack, U.S.S. (C.S.S. *Virginia*): (1861) sunk, Apr. 20; raised by Confs., May 30; converted to C.S.S. *Virginia,* Nov. 25; (1862) Fed. squad. anticipates att. from, Mar. 6; eng. with Union fleet, Mar. 8; bat. with *Monitor,* Mar. 9; press covers bat., Mar. 10; Washington astir over bat., Mar. 10; captures Fed. vessels, causes uproar, Apr. 11; left without a port, May 9; scuttled, May 11; May 15; foundering of *Monitor*, Dec. 30

Merritt, Wesley (F): (1864) eng. at Tom's Brook, Va., Oct. 9; (1865) moves south from Winchester, Feb. 27; Appomattox Camp., Mar. 30

Merritt's Plantation, La.: (1863) oper. about, May 18

Merryman, John: (1861) arrest, *ex parte* Merryman, May 27

Merry Oaks, Ky.: (1862) sk., Sept. 17

Mescalero Apaches: (1861) ambush Conf. troops, Aug. 12

Mesilla, N. Mex. Terr.: (1861) sk., July 25; surrender, Ft. Fillmore, July 26; sk., Aug. 3

Messinger's Fy., Big Black R., Miss.: (1863) sks., June 29, July 4, 6 (Jackson Camp.)

Mexico: (1861) C.S.A. sends agent to, May 17; (1863) shipping into C.S.A. through, Feb. 25; aff. with Zapata's banditti, Sept. 2; French occupying, Sept. 4; ment., Nov. 6; (1864) Conf. envoy to named, Jan. 7; Fed. troops sent to Matamoros, Jan. 12; U. S. House of Representatives resolves to bar monarchy in, Apr. 4; Maximilian lands in, May 28; (1865) plan for conquest of, Jan. 16; talk of U.S. movement against, Feb. 3; Conf. troops seek refuge in, May 26, 29

Mexico, Mo.: (1861) sk., July 15

Miami, Mo.: (1862) Fed. oper. around, May 25; sc., June 4; (1865) Fed. sc. to, Jan. 12; sk., Apr. 24

Mibres, Camp, N. Mex. Terr.: (1864) Fed. sc. from, Feb. 24

Michigan: (1861) Nov. 9; (1862) war resolution presented, Feb. 3; Republican victories in, Nov. 4; (1865) ratifies Thirteenth Amendment, Feb. 2

Michigan, U.S.S.: (1864) plot to free Johnson's I. prisoners, Sept. 19

Middlebrook, Va.: (1864) sk., June 10

Middleburg, Tenn.: (1862) sk., Dec. 24

Middleburg, Va.: (1862) oper., Mar. 27; Fed. recon., Oct. 13; (1863) sks., Jan. 26, June 17; act., June 19; Fed. scs. against guerrillas, Dec. 18; (1864) Fed. sc. to, Mar. 28; sk., May 29; (1865) Fed. sc. to, Feb. 15

Middle Cr., Ky.: (1862) eng., Jan. 10

Middle (or Mill) Cr. Br., Mo.: (1863) sk., Apr. 24

Middle Dept., Fed.: (1864) Wallace commands, Mar. 22; merged into Middle Military Division, Aug. 7

Middle Fork Br., W. Va.: (1861) July 6

Middle Military Dept., Fed.: (1862) created, Dix commands, Mar. 22; John A. Wool assigned to command, June 1

Middle Military Division, Fed.: (1864) Sheridan assigned to command, Aug. 7

Middlesex Co., Va.: (1862) Fed. recon. in, Dec. 11; (1863) oper. in, May 20; (1864) Fed. exped. into, Mar. 17

Middle Tennessee Camp.: *See* Tullahoma Camp.

Middleton, Tenn.: (1862) sk., Oct. 4; (1863) Jan. 31; Fed. exped. to, May 21; Tullahoma Camp., sk., June 24; (1864) sk., Jan. 14

Middleton Pike, Tenn.: (1863) Fed. sc. on, June 10

Middletown, Md.: (1862) sk., Sept. 13; (1863) sk., June 20; Gettysburg Camp., June 27; (1864) sk., July 7

Middletown, N.J.: (1861) "Peace" meeting fails, Aug. 29

Middletown, Va.: (1862) sks., Mar. 18, May 24, July 15; (1863) sk., June 12; (1864) sk. near, Apr. 24; sk., Sept. 20; Bat. of Cedar Cr., Oct. 19; act., Nov. 12

Middleway, W. Va.: (1864) sk., Aug. 21

Mid-South states: (1861) committee to consider compromise, Jan. 3

Midway, S.C.: (1865) Sherman on r.r. from, Feb. 11

Midway, Va.: (1864) sk. near, June 11

Midway Station, Neb. Terr.: (1864) sks., Oct. 22, 28; (1865) Fed. sc. to, May 8

Mier, Mex.: (1863) aff. with Zapata's banditti, Sept. 2

Mifflin, Tenn.: (1864) sk., Feb. 18

Miles, Dixon S. (F): (1862) mortally wounded, Sept. 15

Milford, Mo. (or Blackwater Cr. or Shawnee Mound): (1861) Fed. sc., Dec. 18

Milford, Va.: (1864) aff. near, Apr. 15; sk., Oct. 25

Milford Haven, Va.: (1864) naval act., Sept. 24

Military Division of the West: *See* West, Military Division of the

Militia: *See* Mobilization

Mill Cr., Mo.: (1864) sk., May 30

Mill Cr., N.C.: (1862) sk., July 26; (1865) sk., Mar. 22

Mill Cr., Tenn.: (1862) sk., Nov. 27, Dec. 6; (1863) aff., Jan. 8; sk., Jan. 25

Mill (or Middle) Cr. Br., Mo.: (1863) sk., Apr. 24

Mill Cr. Br., N.C.: (1865) Bat. of Bentonville, Mar. 21

Mill Cr. Gap, Ga.: (1864) demon. on (or Buzzard Roost), May 8

Milledgeville, Ga.: (1861) state secession convention meets in, Jan. 19; (1864) Slocum occupies, Nov. 22; sk. near, Nov. 23; Sherman moves from, Nov. 24

Millen, Ga.: (1864) Sherman approaching, Dec. 1; Sherman at, Dec. 3

Miller, U.S.S. (steamer): (1864) capt., Aug. 17

Miller's Station, Mo.: (1864) aff., Oct. 3

Milligan, Lambdin P.: (1864) case against, Oct. 5; (1865) reprieved, June 2

Milligan, *ex parte*: (1864) Oct. 5; (1865) Milligan, Bowles reprieved, gets life imprisonment, June 2

Milliken's Bend, La.: (1862) Fed. gunboat exped., Aug. 16; aff., Aug. 18; Fed. exped., Dec. 25; (1863) McClernand moves toward, Jan. 17; Grant orders corps from, Mar. 29; oper. from, Mar. 31; sk. at Richmond, La., Apr. 4; oper. succeeding, Apr. 5; Fed. oper., Apr. 8, 15; Sherman joins Grant from, May 7; Conf. att. at, June 7; sk., June 25

Mill Point, W. Va.: (1863) sk., Nov. 5

Mill Springs, Ky.: (1861) oper., Dec. 1; Fed. sc. to, Dec. 18; (1862) Zollicoffer at, Jan. 16; Thomas converges on, Jan. 18; Bat. of (or Logan's Cross Roads), Jan. 19; Confs. withdraw, Jan. 20; Jan. 21; (1863) sks., May 24, 29

Mill Springs, Ky., Bat. of (or Logan's Cross Roads, Fishing Creek, Somerset, or Beech Grove): (1862) Conf. defeat dents Conf. defense line in Ky., Jan. 19; Conf. retreat, Jan. 20; Jan. 21

Mill Springs Gap, Ga.: (1864) sk., May 19

Millwood, Va.: (1863) sk., Feb. 6

Millwood Rd., near Winchester, Va.: (1863) sk., Apr. 8

Milroy, Robert Huston (F): (1861) eng. at Camp Alleghany, Dec. 13; (1863) Bat. of 2nd Winchester, Va., June 14; Lincoln orders out too late, June 14

Milton, Fla.: (1862) Fed. exped. to, June 14; Fed. recon. to, Aug. 7; (1864) sks., Aug. 29, Oct. 18; (1865) Fed. expeds. to, Feb. 19, 22

Milton, Tenn.: (1863) eng. at Vaught's Mill, Mar. 20

Mimms Mills, Tobesofkee Cr., Ga.: (1865) sk., Apr. 20

Mine, at Petersburg, Va.: (1864) July 25, 29; explosion of, July 30; July 31; ment., Aug. 18

Mine Cr. (or Little Osage R.), Kas.: (1864) eng., Oct. 25

Mineral Point, Mo.: (1864) sk., Sept. 27

Mine Run, Va.: (1863) Meade heads for, Nov. 27

Mine Run Camp.: (1863) Nov. 26, 27, 28, 29, 30, Dec. 1, 2

Mingo Cr., N.C.: (1865) sk., Mar. 18

Mingo Cr., near St. Francisville, Mo.: (1862) sk., Feb. 24

Mingo Swamp, Mo.: (1863) scs. and sks., Feb. 2

Ministers: *See* Clergy

Mink Springs, near Cleveland, Tenn.: (1864) sk., Apr. 13

Minna (Brit. blockade-runner): (1863) taken off Charleston, Dec. 9

Minnesota (*See also* Sioux Uprising): (1862) included in Dept. of the Northwest, Sept. 6

Minnesota, U.S.S. (wooden frigate): (1862) opposes *Merrimack*, aground, Mar. 8

Minnesota, Valley of the: (1862) Sioux Uprising, Aug. 19

Missionary Ridge, Tenn.: (1863) sk., Sept. 22; Fed. offensive planned, Nov. 21; Buckner sent to reinforce Longstreet, Nov. 22; Bat. of Chattanooga, Nov. 23–25; Bat. of Lookout Mt., Nov. 24; Bat. of Missionary Ridge, Nov. 25; (1864) Bragg's conduct at ment., Feb. 24; ment., June 27

Mississippi: (1861) state convention meets, Jan. 7; votes to secede, Jan. 9; Representatives withdraw from U. S. Cong., Jan. 12; legislature calls for convention of seceded states, Jan. 19; takes Ft. Massachusetts, Jan. 20; Jefferson Davis leaves U. S. Sen., Jan. 21; ratifies Conf. constitution, Mar. 29; call for troops, Sept. 22; (1862) Conf. defense of, Apr. 10, 11; (1865) William L. Sharkey appointed provisional gov. of, June 13; imprisonment, parole of Gov. Clark, Oct. 11; rejects Thirteenth Amendment, Dec. 4

Mississippi, Army of, Conf.: (1863) Polk commands, Dec. 16

Mississippi, Army of the Conf.: (1862) Beauregard assumes command, Mar. 5; Army of Ky. merges with, Mar. 29; A. S. Johnston commands, Mar. 29; ordered to Chattanooga, July 21; Bragg resumes command of, Nov. 7

Mississippi, Army of the, Fed.: (1862) Pope assumes command of, Feb. 23; included in Dist. of West Tenn., Grant to command, July 16; Grant assumes command of, July 17; (1863) McClernand commands, Jan. 4

Mississippi, Dept. of the, Fed.: (1862) Halleck given command, Mar. 11; Halleck assumes command, Mar. 13; Halleck relinquishes command, July 16; Grant assumes command, July 17

Mississippi, Military Dist. of, Conf.: (1862) created, Van Dorn commands, July 2

Mississippi, Military Division of the, Fed.: (1863) created, Grant to command, Oct. 16; Grant given orders to command, Oct. 17; Grant assumes command, Oct. 18; (1864) Sherman assigned to command, Mar. 12; Sherman assumes command, Mar. 18

Mississippi, U.S.S.: (1862) bat. for New Orleans, Apr. 24; set afire, Apr. 25; (1863) destruction of, Mar. 14

trabands along, Feb. 28; eng. at Ratliff's Ldg., May 16; Greene raid along, May 24, June 1; Conf. att. on *White Cloud,* Aug. 29; (1865) *Sultana* disaster, Apr. 27

Mississippi Sound: (1861) Oct. 19

Mississippi Springs, Miss.: (1863) sk., May 13

Mississippi Squadron, Fed.: (1862) Porter commands, Oct. 1

Mississippi Valley: (1862) Pope brought from, June 17; Davis on defense of, Apr. 3; (1863) loss of to Confs., Dec. 31

Missouri: (1861) sen. plans State Convention, Jan. 5; State Convention meets, Feb. 28; convention moved to St. Louis, Mar. 4; shows pro-Union sentiment, Mar. 7; committee on Fed. relations reports no cause to leave Union, Mar. 9; refuses militia to U.S., Apr. 17; pro-secession militia gather, May 6; Lincoln on, May 18; to have Union and Conf. govts., May 20; Price-Harney sign proclamation on order, May 21; Planters' House meeting, June 11; pro-Union govt., troops evacuate Jefferson City, June 12, 14, 15, 17; Gamble named Fed. gov., July 22; Jackson's Conf. govt. claims to represent state, July 22; Gamble inaugurated, July 31; McCulloch on "destiny" of, Aug. 12; "admitted" into C.S.A., Aug. 19; C.S.A. Cong. authorizes aid to, Aug. 21; depredations, Sept. 22; legislature remnant votes state into C.S.A., Oct. 31; Gamble organizes militia, Nov. 8; in Fed. Dept. of the Mo., Nov. 9; 2 govts., Nov. 18; admitted officially to C.S.A., Nov. 28; Dec. 10; Conf. argument over command in, Dec. 13; Davis to Price on welfare of, Dec. 20; charges of Conf. neglect of, Dec. 20; martial law in St. Louis, on r.r., Dec. 26; (1862) effects of Pea Ridge on Conf. hold in, Mar. 8; in Conf. Trans-Miss. Dept., May 26; gov. asks Davis for aid, July 28; (1863) State Convention votes to end slavery, July 1; Lincoln on pacification of, Oct. 1; (1864) Fed. trade restrictions in lifted, Jan. 23; public opinion in, Oct. 5; (1865) Constitutional Convention abolishes slavery, Jan. 11; Lincoln on violence in, Jan. 15; ratifies Thirteenth Amendment, Feb. 10; reports of sale of confiscated property in, Feb. 12; Lincoln on depredations in, Feb. 20; constitution ratified, June 6

Missouri, Army of, Conf.: (1864) heads toward St. Louis, Sept. 26

Missouri, Dept. of, Fed.: *See* Missouri, Dept. of the

Missouri, Dept. of the, Fed.: (1861) created, Nov. 9; Halleck commands, Nov. 19; suspension of habeas corpus in, Dec. 2; (1862) Halleck in command, Mar. 11; reestablished, Sept. 19; Curtis assumes command of, Sept. 24; (1863) Schofield replaces Curtis, May 24; Lincoln to Stanton on removal of Schofield, Dec. 18; (1864) Rosecrans named commander of, Jan. 22; Rosecrans supersedes Schofield, Jan. 30; troops of ordered from Curtis, Oct. 28; Dodge given command, Dec. 1

Missouri, Military Division of the, Fed.: (1861) Pope assigned command of, Jan. 30

Missouri Compromise Line, 36° 30′: (1860) Crittenden Compromise and, Dec. 18

Missouri Democrat: (1863) editor arrested, July 13

Missouri-Kansas state line: (1864) Price retreats down, Oct. 23, 24

Missouri R.: (1861) control of, June 17; surrender of Lexington on, Sept. 20; (1862) Ind. fight with miners, Oct. 10; (1863) capture of Boonville on, Oct. 11; (1864) Wash. occup., Oct. 2; act. at Lexington, Oct. 19, 20; (1861) sks. on, May 3

Mitchel, John C. (C): (1864) mortally wounded at Sumter, July 20

Mitchel, Ormsby MacKnight (F): (1861) commands Dept. of the Ohio, Sept. 21; east Tenn. exped., Oct. 10; (1862) occupies Huntsville, Ala., Apr. 11; occupies Decatur, Ala., Apr. 13; occupies Rogersville, Ala., May 13; threatens Chattanooga, June 4; att. on Chattanooga, June 7; assigned to command Dept. of the South, Sept. 1; assumes command, Dept. of the South, Sept. 17; death of, Oct. 30

Mitchel, Ft., Ky.: (1862) sk., Sept. 10

Mitchell's Cr., Fla.: (1865) sk., Mar. 25

Mitchell's Cross Roads, Miss.: (1862) sk. near, Dec. 1; (1864) sk., July 4

Mitchell's Fd., Va.: (1861) sk., July 18; (1863) sks., Oct. 7, 15

Mobile and Mobile Bay, Ala.: (1861) Fts. Morgan, Gaines taken by state, Jan. 5; *Lewis Cass* surrenders, Jan. 30; blockade, May 26; (1862) Davis on Fed. moves, Jan. 3; (1863) women march on supply stores in, Sept. 4; (1864) rumors of att. on, Jan. 9; Davis on sending troops, Jan. 14; Fed. recon., Jan. 20; att. on urged, Jan. 20; ment., Feb. 14, 15; Fed. oper. near, Feb. 16; Davis concerned over defense of, Feb. 19; Fed. preparation for att., June 16, July 27, Aug. 2; investment of Ft. Gaines, Aug. 3; Bat. of Mobile Bay, Aug. 5; Ft. Powell evac., Aug. 6; Ft. Gaines surrenders, Aug. 7, 8; siege of Mobile, Ft. Morgan, Aug. 9; news of victory at, Aug. 11; Ft. Morgan falls, Aug. 23; Farragut requests leave, Aug. 27; torpedo explosion, Aug. 29; Lincoln proclaims day of celebration for victory at, Sept. 3; salt works destroyed, Sept. 8; Fed. exped. from, Sept. 9; (1865) Mobile Camp., Mar. 17, 18, 20, 21, 25 (siege begins), 26, Apr. 1, 2, 7, 8 (Spanish Ft. evac.), 9 (Ft. Blakely taken), 10, 11, 12 (surrender of city); U.S.S. *Ida* sunk, Apr. 13; Fed. ship sunk, Apr. 13; gunpowder explosion in, May 25

Mobile and Ohio R.R.: (1862) raid, Apr. 29; raid, near Bethel, Tenn., May 4; sk., near Corinth, May 14; Fed. raid on, Dec. 13; Fed. exped. against, Dec. 14; (1864) Fed. expeds. against, Nov. 27, Dec. 21; (1865) Jan. 2, 3, 4

Mobile Point, Ala.: (1865) Mobile Camp., Mar. 17

Mobilization, Conf. (*See also* Conscription, C.S.A.): (1861) call for Va. volunteers, Apr. 17; volunteer forces ordered out, May 1; call for Va. volunteers, May 3; Davis signs bill to enlist volunteers, May 9; appointments, recruiting, May 30; progress of, June 16; act for raising troops in Ky., Mo., Md., Del., Aug. 8; in Tenn., Sept. 21; call for troops from Ark., Miss., Sept. 22; Davis concerned about, Oct. 10; state-consciousness causes difficulties, Oct. 16; Davis to Johnston on, Nov. 10; call for 10,000 Miss. volunteers, Nov. 21; (1862) appeal for reenlistments, Feb. 4; Davis approves draft act, Apr. 16; Davis calls for troops, June 4; 2nd conscription act, Sept. 27; (1863) Cong. bans substitutes, Dec. 28; (1864) Cong. authorizes men 18–19, 45–50 years old, June 10

Mobilization, Fed. (*See also* Conscription, U.S.): (1861) call, Apr. 15; troops raised, Apr. 17; volunteers aided monetarily, Apr. 18; troops leave for Wash., Apr. 19; Lincoln calls for 3-year volunteers, May 3; appointments, recruiting, May 30; progress of, June 16; Tenn., Ky. troops, July 1; Ky. troops, Sept. 20; Dept. of New England, Oct. 1; (1862) call for troops, May 25; Lincoln asks govs. for 300,000 men, July 1; Lincoln authorizes

9-month men, July 17; meetings to encourage enlistments, July 19; Lincoln calls for 300,000 draft, Aug. 4; recruiting, Aug. 5; recruiting, draft evaders, Aug. 8, 9; draft begins in states, Oct. 16; opposition to draft, Oct. 17; (1863) Conscription Act passed by Sen., Feb. 16; Cong. passes Conscription Act, Feb. 25; Fed. Draft Act approved, Mar. 3; substitutes, Mar. 3; enrolling officers pelted, June 15; Lincoln calls for 300,000 volunteers, Oct. 17; (1864) Lincoln orders 500,000 draft, Feb. 1; act compensating for enlisting slaves, Feb. 24; Navy draft order, Mar. 14; Lincoln urges 100-day troops, May 21; call for N.Y. and Pa. volunteers, July 5; D.C. militia called up, July 11; Lincoln calls for 500,000 troops, July 18; Lincoln calls for 300,000 volunteers, Dec. 19

Moccasin Cr., N.C.: (1865) sk., Mar. 24

Moccasin Gap, Tenn.: (1862) Carter's exped. passes, Dec. 29

Moccasin Swamp, N.C.: (1865) sk., Apr. 10

Mockabee Farm, Mo.: (1864) act., Oct. 22

Mocksville, N.C.: (1865) sk., Apr. 11

Moffat's Station, Franklin Co., Ark.: (1863) sk., Sept. 27

Mojave, Ft., Ariz. Terr.: (1864) Fed. sc. to, May 9

Molino, Miss.: (1863) sk., Nov. 28

Monagan Springs, Mo.: (1862) sks., Apr. 25, May 27

Monarch, U.S.S.: (1864) eng. with Greene's raiders, June 2

Monday Hollow, Mo.: *See* Wet Glaize, Mo.

Monett's Fy., La.: (1864) sk. (Red R. Camp.), Mar. 29; eng. (or Cane R. Crossing), Apr. 23

Money order system, postal: *See* Postal money order system

Moniteau Co., Mo.: (1862) Fed. exped. in, Mar. 25; (1864) Fed. sc. in, Sept. 11

Monitor, U.S.S.: (1861) contract for, Oct. 4; keel laid, Oct. 25; (1862) launched, Jan. 30; trials, Feb. 27; leaves for Ft. Monroe, Mar. 6; arrives at Hampton Rds., Va., Mar. 8; bat. with *Merrimack,* Mar. 9; press covers bat., Mar. 10; Washington astir, Mar. 10; expects encounter with *Merrimack,* Apr. 11; Lincoln visits, May 7; May 11; at Bat. of Drewry's Bluff, May 15; founders, Dec. 30, 31; (1863) ment., Feb. 28

Monitors, U.S.: *See* individual names of

Monocacy, Md.: (1862) sk., Sept. 4; (1864) Bat. of, July 9

Monocacy Aqueduct, Md.: (1862) sk., Sept. 4

Monocacy Church, Md.: (1862) sk., Sept. 9

Monocacy Junction, Md.: (1864) sk., July 30

Monocacy R., Md.: (1862) Sept. 10; cav. sk. near mouth, Oct. 12; (1864) Bat. of, Early's ride, July 9

Monocacy Valley, Md.: (1862) Stuart's Chambersburg raid, Oct. 9

Monongahela, Dept. of the, Fed.: (1864) merged into Dept. of the Susquehanna, Apr. 6

Monongahela, U.S.S.: (1863) damaged passing Port Hudson batteries, Mar. 14

Monongahela Co., W. Va.: (1861) pro-Northern citizens meet, Apr. 21

Monroe, John: (1862) as mayor, on authority to surrender New Orleans, Apr. 25; negotiations with Farragut, Apr. 26

Monroe, La.: (1863) Fed. exped. to, Aug. 20

Monroe, Ft., Va.: (1861) Ft. Pickens reinforcements sail from, Jan. 24; Fourth Mass. Inf. arrives, Apr. 20; Butler takes command of, May 15; Fed. recon.

Montpelier Springs, Ala.: (1865) sk., Apr. 20

Montrose, Va.: (1865) Conf. supply base destroyed, Mar. 16

Moon's Station, Ga.: (1864) sk., Oct. 4

Moore, A. B. (F): (1862) Morgan captures men of at Hartsville, Tenn., Dec. 7

Moore, Andrew B. (C): (1861) as gov. of Ala., issues proclamation against high prices, Oct. 2

Moore, Thomas Overton (C): (1861) bans cotton shipments, Oct. 3; (1862) Davis to gov. of La., Apr. 17; (1864) sks. at plantation of (Red R. Camp.), May 1

Moore, Camp, La.: (1864) Fed. exped. to, Oct. 5

Moorefield, W. Va.: (1862) sks., Feb. 12, Apr. 3; aff., June 29; sks., Aug. 23, Dec. 3; (1863) Fed. exped. to, Jan. 2; sks., Jan. 3; Conf. raid, Jan. 5; (1863) sks., Aug. 6, 26, Sept. 4; affs., Sept. 11, 21; sk., Dec. 28; (1864) sk., Feb. 4; Fed. sc. to, Feb. 21; sk., June 6; eng. near, Aug. 7; Fed. exped. to, Nov. 6; sks., Nov. 27; (1865) Fed. exped. to, Feb. 4; Fed. sc. to, Mar. 14

Moorefield Junction, W. Va.: (1864) sk., Jan. 8

Moore's Bluff, Tenn.: (1864) sk., Sept. 29

Moore's Mill near Fulton, Mo.: (1862) sk., July 24

Moore's Plantation, Ala.: (1864) sks. at home of Gov. Moore, May 1

Mooresville, Ala.: (1862) oper., May 1

Moreau Cr., Mo.: (1864) sk., Oct. 7

Moreauville, La.: (1864) act., May 17

Morgan, George Washington (F): (1862) assigned to command Seventh Div., to capture Cumberland Gap, Mar. 28; occup. of Cumberland Gap, June 18; evacuates Cumberland Gap, Sept. 17

Morgan, John Hunt (C): (1862) raids Nashville suburbs, Mar. 8; oper. around Gallatin, Tenn., Mar. 15; starts 1st Ky. raid, July 4; capture of Tompkinsville, Ky., July 9; calls on Kentuckians to "rise and arm," July 10; capture of Lebanon, July 12; raid causes consternation in Northern cities, July 12; raids to Cynthiana, Ky., July 14; takes Cynthiana, July 17; sk. near Paris, Ky., July 19; arrives at Livingston, Tenn., July 22; captures Gallatin, Tenn., Aug. 12; joins Smith at Lexington, Ky., Sept. 4; captures garrison at Lexington, Oct. 18; captures garrison at Hartsville, Tenn., Dec. 7; Davis to Seddon, ment., Dec. 18; "Christmas raid" into Ky., Dec. 21; crosses Cumberland R., Dec. 22; occupies Glasgow, Ky., Dec. 24; sks., Green's Chapel, Bear Wallow, Bacon Cr., Nolin, Dec. 25, 26; captures garrison, Elizabeth, Ky., Dec. 27; destroys br., Muldraugh's Hill, Ky., Dec. 28; sks. on Rolling Fork, captures stockade at Boston, Ky., Dec. 29; withdraws, Dec. 30; (1863) completes camp., Jan. 2; capture of Mt. Sterling, Ky., Mar. 22; sk. at Danville, Ky., Mar. 24; raid into Ky., O., Ind., July 2, 3, 4, 5, 6, 7, 8, 9, 10, 11, 12, 13, 14, 15, 16, 17, 18, 19, 20, 22, 23, 24, 25, 26 (surrenders, imprisoned); escapes from prison, Nov. 27; (1864) reception held in Richmond for, Jan. 8; raid into Ky., May 30, 31, June 1, 4, 8 (Mt. Sterling), 9, 10 (raids Lexington, Georgetown, Frankfort), 11 (captures Cynthiana), 12 (retreat, defeat); assumes command Dept. of Western Va. and Eastern Tenn., June 22; Fed. oper. against, Aug. 29; death of, Sept. 4; Stoneman defeats remnants of old command of, Dec. 13

Morgan, Ft., Ala.: (1861) taken by Ala., Jan. 5; (1864) Fed. recon. of, Jan. 20;

ment., Aug. 3; Bat. of Mobile Bay, Aug. 5; still in Conf. hands, Aug 7; Fed. siege of, Aug. 9; falls to Feds., Aug. 23

Morgan Co., Ind.: (1863) arrest of deserters resisted, Jan. 31

Morgan Co., Mo.: (1863) Fed. exped. to, Nov. 23; (1864) Fed. sc. in, Sept. 11

Morgan Co., Tenn.: (1862) sk., Feb. 2; Conf. exped., Mar. 28; (1863) sk., Oct. 6

Morganfield, Ky.: (1862) sk., Aug. 3; (1864) sks., May 6, June 25

Morgan's Fy., Atchafalaya R., La.: (1863) sk., Sept. 7; (1864) sk., Aug. 25; Fed. exped. to, Dec. 13

Morgan's Fy. Rd., La.: (1864) sk. on, near Morganza, July 28

Morgan's Mill, Spring R., Ark.: (1864) sk., Feb. 9

Morgantown, Ky.: (1861) sk., Oct. 31

Morgantown, N.C.: (1865) act., Apr. 17

Morgantown, W. Va.: (1863) Jones' raid, aff. at, Apr. 27

Morganza, La.: (1863) sk., Sept. 12; (1864) sk., May 24; Fed. exped. from, May 30; Fed. forces organized at, June 16; Fed. scs. from, Aug. 10; Fed. expeds. from, Sept. 6, 13; Fed. oper. near, Sept. 16; Fed. exped. from, Oct. 3; sk., Oct. 16; sks., Nov. 23; sk., Dec. 4; Fed. exped. from, Dec. 13; Fed. oper. near, Dec. 14; Fed. exped. from, Dec. 16; (1865) Fed. expeds. from, Jan 12, 31; Fed. sc. from, Feb. 7

Morganza Bend, La.: (1865) sk., Mar. 12

Moro, Ark.: (1862) oper. to, Nov. 5

Moro Bottom, Ark.: (1864) sk., Apr. 25

Morocco: (1862) seizure of Conf. officers at Tangier, Feb. 21

Morrill, Justin Smith (F): (1861) tariff act approved, Mar. 2; (1862) Morrill Act approved, July 2

Morrill Act: (1862) Lincoln signs, July 2

Morrill Tariff Act: (1861) approved, Mar. 2

Morris, Thomas Armstrong (F): (1861) Philippi Races, June 3; moves toward Laurel Hill, July 10; eng. of Rich Mt., July 11; pursues Garnett, July 12; act. at Corrick's Fd., July 13

Morris I., Charleston Harbor, S.C.: (1861) battery fires on *Star of the West,* Jan. 9; battery fires on *Rhoda H. Shannon,* Apr. 3; in bomb. of Sumter, Apr. 12; (1863) mayor warns of Fed. attacks at, July 9; 1st ass. on Battery Wagner, July 11; Conf. sortie from Battery Wagner, July 14; 2nd ass. on Battery Wagner, July 18; bomb. of Battery Wagner on, July 24, Aug. 4; Fed. att. on Conf. steamer *Chesterfield,* Aug. 2; Fed. offensive preparations, Aug. 8; Conf. firing on Fed. work parties, Aug. 11; Fed. offensive from, Aug. 12; practice firing on Sumter, Aug. 13, 16; 1st great bomb. of Sumter, Aug. 17; Gillmore demands evac. of, Aug. 21; ass. on rifle pits at Battery Wagner, Aug. 25; capture of rifle pits, Aug. 26; Sept. 1, 2; boat attacks on Cummings Point, Sept. 5; evacuated, Sept. 6; batteries occupied by Fed. troops, Sept. 7; bomb. of Sumter from ceases, Oct. 3; *Weehawken* founders near, Dec. 6; (1864) Fed. ass. on Ft. Johnson from, July 3

Morris' Mills, W. Va.: (1863) sk., July 31

Morris's Fd., Tenn.: (1863) sk., July 2

Morristown, Tenn.: (1861) sk., Dec. 1; (1863) sks., Dec. 10, 14; (1864) Fed. sc. near, Mar. 12; raid from, June 13; act., Oct. 28

Morrisville, N.C.: (1865) sks., Apr. 13, 14

Morse's Mills, Mo.: (1861) sk., Aug. 29

Mortar flotilla, Fed.: (1861) Porter ordered to organize, Nov. 18; (1862) below New Orleans, Apr. 17; bomb. of fts., Apr. 18; Apr. 19; bomb. of fts., Apr. 21, 23; fleet passes fts., Apr. 24; bomb. of gun positions at Vicksburg, June 26, 27

Morton, Oliver Perry (F): (1861) as gov. of Ind. greets Lincoln, Feb. 11; Sept. 29; (1862) calls for militia, Sept. 5; (1863) protests Vallandigham's arrest, May 29; (1864) reelected, Oct. 11

Morton, Miss.: (1864) sks., Feb. 7, 8, 10

Morton, Ft., Va.: (1864) sk., Oct. 27; Nov. 5

Morton's Fd., Va.: (1863) sks., Oct. 10, 11, Nov. 26; (1864) eng., Feb. 6

Mosby, John Singleton (C): (1863) capture of Stoughton, Mar. 8; active in Va., July 28; capture of wagon train, Aug. 6; oper. in Va., Aug. 24, Nov. 5; (1864) raids in Va., Aug. 9; r.r. robbery, Oct. 13; (1865) disbands rangers, Apr. 21

Moscow, Ark.: (1864) act. (Camden exped.), Apr. 13

Moscow, Ky.: (1864) Fed. sc. to, Mar. 30

Moscow, Tenn.: (1863) affs. near, Feb. 9, 18; Fed. sc. to, Mar. 10; Fed. exped. to, Mar. 28; aff., Mar. 29; sks., Sept. 27, Nov. 5; act. near, Dec. 3; sk., Dec. 27; (1864) sk., June 15; Fed. exped. to, Nov. 9

Moselle Br., near Franklin, Mo.: (1864) aff., Dec. 7

Mosely Hall, N.C.: (1865) sk., Mar. 30

"Mosquito" fleet, Conf.: (1862) destroyed at Elizabeth City, N.C., Feb. 10

Mossy Cr., Tenn.: (1863) sk., Dec. 26; act., Dec. 29; (1864) sks., Jan. 10, 12, Oct. 15, 27

Mossy Cr. Station, Tenn.: (1863) sk., Dec. 24

Motley's Fd., Little Tenn. R., Tenn.: (1863) sk., Nov. 4; (1864) Fed. exped. from, Feb. 17

Moulton, Ala.: (1864) aff., Mar. 8; sk., Mar. 21; cav. eng., May 26; act., May 29

Moultrie, Ft., Charleston Harbor, S.C.: (1860) Nov. 7; Robert Anderson ordered to, Nov. 15; Gardner relieved of command, Nov. 15; Anderson reports undefendable, Nov. 23; status of fts., Dec. 10; Buell sent to Charleston, Dec. 11; S.C. leaders ban reinforcements, Dec. 19; Secession Convention resolves it is under state control, Dec. 22; Anderson transfers garrison to Sumter, Dec. 26; S.C. seizes, fortifies, Dec. 26, 27; (1861) *Star of the West* fired on, Jan. 9; (1863), Fed. naval att., Apr. 7; troop transport fired on in error, Aug. 30; monitors engage, Sept. 7; (1864) fires on U.S. tug *Geranium*, Apr. 14

Mound City, Ark.: (1863) guerrilla center burned, Jan. 15

Mound City, U.S.S. (gunboat): (1862) sunk temporarily at Plum Run Bend, May 10

Mound Plantation, La.: (1863) sks., May 24, June 24, 29

Mountain Dept., Fed.: (1862) Frémont in command, Mar. 11; Frémont assumes command, Mar. 29; Blenker's div. sent to, Mar. 31; merged into Army of Va., June 26

Mountain Fork, Ark.: (1864) sk., Feb. 4

Mountain Gap, Ky.: (1862) sk., Oct. 16

Mountain Gap, Tenn.: (1863) sk., near Smith's Cross Roads, Oct. 1

Muddy Cr., Ala.: (1865) sk., Mar. 26
Muddy Cr., near Culpeper, Va.: (1863) sk., Nov. 8
Muddy Cr., W. Va.: (1862) sk., June 8; (1863) sk., Nov. 7
Muddy R., Ky.: (1861) sk., Sept. 26
Muddy Run, Va.: (1863) sks., Aug. 5, Sept. 13
Mud Lick Springs, Ky.: (1863) sk., June 13
"Mud March": (1863) Jan. 19, 20, 21, 22, 23, 24
Mud Springs, Neb. Terr.: (1865) act., Feb. 4
Mudtown, Ark.: (1862) sk., Dec. 9
Mulberry Cr., Ga.: (1864) eng., Aug. 3
Mulberry Cr., Kas.: (1864) Fed. sc. to, Aug. 8
Mulberry Gap, Tenn.: (1863) sk., Nov. 19; (1864) sk., July 28
Mulberry Point, James R., Va.: (1862) Fed. recon. to, May 7
Mulberry Springs, Ark.: (1863) sk., Jan. 26
Mulberry Village, Tenn.: (1863) sk., Dec. 23
Muldraugh's Hill, Ky.: (1862) sk., Dec. 28; aff., Dec. 31
Mule meat: (1863) eaten at Vicksburg, July 3
Mullahla's Station, Neb.: (1864) sk., Oct. 13
Mulligan, James F. (F): (1861) siege of Lexington, Mo., begins, Sept. 12; not relieved by Frémont, Sept. 13; siege of Lexington, Sept. 16; surrender of Lexington, Sept. 20
Mumford, William B. (C): (1862) removes U.S. flag from New Orleans mint, Apr. 26; hanged, June 7
Munford's Station, Ala.: (1865) act., Apr. 23
Munfordville, Ky.: (1862) Conf. siege of, Sept. 14, 15; Feds. surrounded, Sept. 16; Wilder surrenders to Bragg, Sept. 17; act. near, Sept. 20; Feds. reoccupy, Sept. 21; (1864) Fed. sc. from, July 13
Mungo Flats, W. Va.: (1862) sk., June 25
Munitions: *See* Ordnance
Munson's Hill, Va.: (1861) sk., Aug. 31; Conf. evac., Sept. 28
Murfreesboro, Tenn.: (1862) Conf. army pulls back to, Feb. 20; A. S. Johnston moves from, Mar. 1; Mar. 5; A. S. Johnston moves to Corinth, Mar. 18; A. S. Johnston's army moves from, Mar. 24; Fed. recon. from, Mar. 25; city, Fed. garrison capt. by Forrest, July 13; sk. near, Aug. 27; Buell withdraws to, Sept. 5; Bragg bypasses, Sept. 7; sk., Sept. 7; Army of Tenn. moves toward, Nov. 13, 24; Davis at, Dec. 13; Dec. 18; Bragg at, Dec. 26, 27; Rosecrans moves toward, Dec. 28; sks. near, Dec. 29; Rosecrans near, Dec. 30; Bat. of (or Stone's R.), Dec. 31; (1863) respite in bat., Jan.1; Bat. of resumes, Jan. 2; sk., Bragg withdraws, Jan. 3, 4; Fed. troops enter, aftermath of bat., Jan. 5; Fed. recon. from, Jan. 13; Fed. forage train taken, Jan. 21; Fed. recon. from, Jan. 21; Davis orders investigation of Bragg's retreat from, Jan. 21; sk. on Brandyville Pike near, Jan. 23; Fed. recon. from, Jan. 25; Fed. expeds. from, Jan. 31, Feb. 3; sks. near, Feb. 4, 7; Fed. expeds. from, Feb. 17, Mar. 3, 4, 10, 22; Fed. recon. from, Mar 26; Fed. exped. from, Apr. 1; Fed. recon. from, Apr. 2; Fed. exped. from, Apr. 20; Fed. recons. from, Apr. 29, May 1, 12; Fed. exped. from, May 21; Rosecrans regrouping, May 24; Fed. recon. from, May 27; Lincoln to Rosecrans, May 27; Rosecrans faces Bragg, May 31; sk., June 3; Conf. oper.

Memphis, Feb. 20; evac., Feb. 23; Feds. approach, Feb. 24; occupied by Buell, Feb. 25; Conf. sc. toward, Feb. 26; Mar. 1; Morgan raids suburbs, Mar. 8; sk. near, Mar. 9; Mar. 15; Fed. troops from, Mar. 26; mayor, city official suspended, Apr. 5; Apr. 6; May 4; pro-Union meeting, May 12; Forrest captures Murfreesboro, July 13; Confs. capture Fed. pickets near, July 21; sk. near, Sept. 2; Sept. 5; Bragg bypasses Fed. forces at, Sept. 7; sk. at Davis' Br. near, Oct. 1; sk. at Ft. Riley, near, Oct. 5; Forrest repulsed near, Oct. 20; Davis on recapture of, Oct. 21; act., Nov. 5; sk. near, Nov. 13; Bragg concentrates at Tullahoma, Nov. 14; armies concentrating on, Nov. 18; sks. near, Dec. 3, 11; att. on Fed. forage train near, Dec. 14; sks. near, Dec. 23, 24; Rosecrans moves out from, Dec. 26; (1863) Fed. recon. from, Jan. 13; sk. near, Jan. 28; Union meeting in, Feb. 23; Streight's raid moves south from, Apr. 17; aff. near, May 4; disloyalists sent South, May 6; Wheeler near, Oct. 5; Grant at, Oct. 20; Fed. exped. from, Dec. 28; (1864) pro-Northern citizens meet, favor abolition, Jan. 21; sk. near, May 24; Thomas sent to, Oct. 3; Thomas building forces, Oct. 21, 28; Smith's divisions heading for, Nov. 1; ment., Nov. 4; Twenty-third Corps goes to, Nov. 9; Thomas building defenses, Nov. 14; Conf. advance toward, Nov. 22, 24; troop alignment at, Dec. 1; Hood's forces arriving at, Dec. 2; lines established at, Dec. 3; Thomas ordered to attack, Hood approaches, Dec. 2; troops dug in, Dec. 3, Dec. 5; Thomas ordered again to attack, Dec. 6; pressure on Thomas, Dec. 7, 8; Grant replaces Thomas, suspends order, Dec. 9; sleet storm delays Thomas, Dec. 10, 11, 12; Grant orders Logan to supersede Thomas, unless Thomas had moved, Dec. 13; Thomas orders advance, Dec. 14; Bat. of Nashville, Dec. 15, 16; pursuit of Hood, Dec. 17, 18, 19, 20, 21, 22; follow-up opers. lessen, Dec. 24; (1865) Jan. 4; ment., Jan. 23; Fed. sc. from, Feb. 15; Fed. exped. from, Feb. 20

Nashville, Bat. of: *See* Nashville, Tenn.

Nashville, C.S.S. (later privateer *Rattlesnake*): (1861) ment., Oct. 12; seizes *Harvey Birch*, Nov. 19; (1863) destroyed by *Montauk*, Feb. 28

Nashville and Chattanooga R.R.: (1863) Wheeler raids, Apr. 7; (1864) Conf. raid on, Mar. 16

Nashville and Northwestern R.R., Tenn.: (1864) Conf. raids on, Aug. 15, Oct. 18

Nassau, Bahama Is.: (1861) blockade-runner from, Dec. 1; (1862) C.S.S. *Florida* sails for, Mar. 22, Apr. 28; blockade-runners from, May 20; (1863) blockade-runner capt. off, May 20

Nassau R., Fla.: (1864) Fed. exped. up, Feb. 9

Natchez, Miss.: (1862) Fed. occup., May 12; (1863) Feb. 14; Farragut off, Mar. 17; Fed. occup., July 13; Fed. exped. from, July 26; sk., July 31; Fed. exped. from, Sept. 1; Fed. exped. from, Oct. 14; sk. near, Nov. 11; oper. about, Dec. 1; (1864) oper. near, Jan. 24; sk. near, Apr. 25; Fed. expeds. from, Aug. 4, Sept. 19, 26, Oct. 5

Natchez Bayou, La.: (1864) Fed. exped. to, Aug. 30

Natchez and Liberty Rd., Miss.: (1864) sk. on, Sept. 6

Natchitoches, La.: (1864) sks. (Red R. Camp.), Mar. 31, Apr. 5, 20, May 5

National Cemetery, Gettysburg, Pa.: *See* Gettysburg National Cemetery

National Union Party Convention: (1864) meets in Baltimore, June 7, 8; Lincoln notified of nomination, June 9

Sen. approves, Mar. 8; Lee to Davis on, Mar. 10; approval of, Mar. 13; troops raised, Mar. 13; Davis on, Apr. 1

Negro Soldiers, Fed.: (1862) Hunter orders, May 9; "free papers" for, Aug. 1; Lincoln declines offer of regts. of, Aug. 4; Butler enlists in New Orleans, Aug. 22; authorized in Southern Dept., Aug. 25; 1st S. C. Volunteers (African descent) organizing, Nov. 3; (1863) S. C. Volunteer Inf. authorized, Higginson to command, Jan. 13; S. C. Volunteer Inf. organized, Jan. 25; at reoccupation of Jacksonville, Fla., Mar. 10; Lincoln on, Mar. 26; C.S.A. authorizes punishment of officers of, May 1; bureau for organizing established, May 22; at Port Hudson, May 27; Fifty-fourth Mass. Volunteers leave Boston, May 28; at Port Royal, S.C., June 3; at Milliken's Bend, June 7; at Honey Springs, I.T., July 17; Fifty-fourth Mass. in 2nd ass. on Battery Wagner, July 18; Lincoln asks recruiting of, July 21; Lincoln on, July 30, Aug. 9; enlistment of ordered, Oct. 3; meeting of, Dec. 9; (1864) Eighth U. S. Colored Troops at Olustee, Fla., Feb. 20; Fed. bill subjects to draft, Feb. 24; as prisoners, Mar. 7; Ft. Pillow massacre, Apr. 12; Davis on, Apr. 22; at Crater, July 30; exped. by to Kent's Ldg., Ark., Aug. 11; recruiting detachment att., Oct. 11; (1865) at burning of Columbia, Feb. 17, Mar. 3; in Richmond, Apr. 3; Tex. exped., May 11

Nelson, Thomas A. R.: (1861) discharged from arrest, Aug. 13

Nelson, William "Bull" (F): (1861) occupies Prestonburg, Ky., Nov. 5; (1862) commands units arriving at Savannah, Tenn., Apr. 6; Bat. of Richmond, Ky., Aug. 30; mortally wounded by Jefferson C. Davis, Sept. 29

Nelson, Camp, Ky.: (1863) Burnside leaves, Aug. 16

Nelson's Br., near New Iberia, La.: (1863) aff., Oct. 4

Nelson's Crossroads, Va.: (1862) Bat. of (or White Oak Swamp or Frayser's Farm), June 30

Nelson's House, Marietta Rd., Ga.: (1864) Johnston at, July 17

Neosho, Mo.: (1861) legislature remnant votes Mo. into Confederacy at, Oct. 31; (1862) sks., Apr. 26, May 31, Aug. 21, Sept. 1, 5, Dec. 15; (1863) sk., Mar. 2; Fed. sc. near, Apr. 19; act., Oct. 4; sks., Nov. 4, 5; (1864) Fed. sc. near, May 18; sk. near, June 3; sk., Nov. 10

Neosho R., Mo.: (1863) sk. near Hudson's Fd., June 30

Netherlands Consulate, New Orleans, La.: (1862) Butler seizes gold, May 10

Neuse R.: (1862) Fed. exped. to mouth of, Mar. 12; Burnside lands on, Mar. 13; Feds. advance, Mar. 14; Fed. naval oper. on, Dec. 12; (1863) blockade-runner capt. off, May 20; *Shawsheen* captures schooner on, July 20; (1864) U.S.S. *Underwriter* capt., burned in, Feb. 2; (1865) Conf. forces on, Mar. 7; sk. on, Mar. 19

Neuse R. Br., N.C.: (1865) sk., Mar. 19

Neuse Rd., N.C.: (1863) Fed. recon. on, Jan. 27

Neutrality of Ky.: *See* Kentucky

Nevada: (1864) gains statehood, Oct. 31; (1865) ratifies Thirteenth Amendment, Feb. 16

Nevada Territory: (1861) established, Mar. 2; (1863) proposed constitution rejected, Sept. 2; (1864) Cong. passes enabling act for, Mar. 21; becomes state, Oct. 31

New Iberia, La.: (1863) Conf. salt works destroyed, Apr. 18; Bayou Teche Camp., Oct. 3, 4; Franklin retires to, Nov. 1

New Inlet, N.C.: (1864) *Condor* run aground off, Oct. 1

New Ironsides, U.S.S.: (1863) att. on, Aug. 21; *David* attacks, Oct. 5; (1864) bomb. of Ft. Fisher, Dec. 24

New Jersey: (1862) Democratic election gains, Nov. 4; (1865) rejects Thirteenth Amendment, Mar. 1

New Kent Court House, Va.: (1862) sk. near at Baltimore Crossroads, May 13; oper. about, June 23; (1863) Fed. exped. to, Nov. 9; (1864) Kilpatrick's Richmond exped., Mar. 2

New Lisbon, O.: (1863) capture of John Hunt Morgan, July 26

New London, Va.: (1864) sk., June 16

New Madrid, Mo.: (1861) Confs. occupy, July 28; (1862) sk., Feb. 24; Pope's troops move on, Feb. 28; troops concentrate on, Mar. 1; sk., Mar. 2; siege of, Mar. 3; bomb., Mar. 13; Feds. occupy, Mar. 14; Mar. 23; tornado, Apr. 2; canal near, Apr. 4; Fed. exped. from, Dec. 17; Fed. evac. of, Dec. 28; (1863) Fed. reoccupation of, Jan. 2; sk., Aug. 7; (1864) Fed. sc. to, Mar. 18; Fed. expeds. from, Apr. 5, July 5; sk. near, Dec. 3

New Madrid Bend, Tenn. (*See also* Island No. 10): (1862) Mackall supersedes McCown, Mar. 31; surrenders to Pope, Apr. 7; Apr. 8; (1863) sk., Oct. 22

New Madrid Co., Mo.: (1864) sk. in on Little R., Dec. 18

Newman, Ga.: (1864) act. near, July 30

New Market, Ala.: (1862) sk., Aug. 5; (1863) sks., Oct. 12; (1864) Nov. 17; (1865) Fed. sc. to, Apr. 5; Fed. exped. to, May 5

New Market, Ky.: (1865) aff., Feb. 8

New Market, Mo.: (1864) Fed. raid near, June 1

New Market, Tenn.: (1863) sks., Dec. 24

New Market, Va.: (1861) sk., Dec. 22; (1862) Feds. occupy, Apr. 17; Feds. fall back toward, May 6; Confs. pass through, May 20; sk., June 13; Fed. recon. near, June 15; (1863) Fed. exped. to, Nov. 15; (1864) Bat. of, May 15; Early retreats to, Sept. 23; sk., Sept. 23; Early moves north from, Nov. 10

New Market Br., Va.: (1861) aff., July 19; sk., Nov. 11

New Market Rd., Va.: (1862) sk. on, June 8; Bat. of (also Frayser's Farm or White Oak Swamp), June 30; (1864) Fed. advance on, July 27; eng., July 27; comb., Aug. 13; comb. at Ft. Gilmer on, Sept. 29; eng. on, Oct. 7

New Mexico, Dept. of, Fed.: (1861) Canby takes command, June 11; Nov. 9; (1862) Carleton in command, Sept. 18

New Mexico Territory (*See also* Apache Canyon; Glorieta; Navajo Indians): (1861) July 3; Conf. efforts to control, July 8; open to Conf. invasions, July 27; Terr. claimed by Confs., Aug. 1; pro-unionists of, Aug. 1; Sibley commands Conf. forces in, Dec. 14; (1862) Conf. Ariz. Terr. formed from, Jan. 18; Sibley's invasion of, Mar. 2; (1863) Fed. oper. against Inds. in, Jan. 4; Ariz. Terr. organized separately, Feb. 24; (1864) Fed. oper. in, Feb. 1, July 23

New Orleans, La.: (1861) forts below city, Jan. 10; Ft. Pike, seized by state, Jan. 14; Ft. Macomb, near, seized by state, Jan. 28; U.S. revenue cutter surrenders, Jan. 29; U. S. Mint and Customs House seized, Jan. 31; U.S. revenue schooner taken, Jan. 31; U.S. paymaster's office seized, Feb. 19;

blockaded, May 26; recruiting for New Orleans Camp., Oct. 1; cotton shipments to banned, Oct. 3; Oct. 4; exped. planned, Nov. 18; Nov. 27; preparation for Fed. move against, Dec. 3; (1862) Davis on Fed. moves against, Jan. 3; powder mills explode, Mar. 9; Fed. build-up for att. on, Mar. 20; in danger of att., Apr. 17; bomb. of fts., Apr. 18, 19, 20, 21; Farragut to pass fts., Apr. 23; Feds. pass fts., Apr. 24; Farragut enters, Apr. 25; negotiations with mayor, Apr. 26; U.S. flag removed from mint, Apr. 26; fts. surrender, Apr. 27; Apr. 28; U.S. flag raised, Apr. 29; Butler takes over, May 1; Netherlands' gold seized, May 10; May 12; commerce opened to, May 12; Butler's "women order" No. 28, May 15; Butler closes *Bee,* takes over *Delta,* May 16; Mumford hanged, June 7; July 1; "cleaner," July 12; Farragut heads fleet toward, July 24; Butler confiscates bells, July 30; Butler's assessments for poor, Aug. 4; registration of foreigners, Sept. 13; 1st Negro regt. mustered in, Sept. 27; Butler replaced by Banks, Nov. 8; proclamation on election of U.S. congressmen, Nov. 14; Butler leaves, Dec. 15; Banks assumes command, Dept. of the Gulf, Dec. 16; (1863) Fed. exped. from to mouth of Rio Grande, Mar. 2; Banks moves north from, Mar. 7; Fed. exped. from, Mar. 21; public gatherings forbidden, curfew, July 3; *Imperial* reaches, July 16; Grant injured in, Sept. 4; Bayou Teche Camp., Oct. 3; Grant ment., Oct. 21; Banks' Rio Grande exped. starts, Oct. 27; Butler's rule ment., Nov. 11; Negro mutiny at Ft. Jackson, Dec. 9; (1864) Red R. Camp. readying, Mar. 10; Lincoln on freedom of churches in, Mar. 15; La. constitutional convention meets in, Apr. 6; (1865) Lincoln on Butler at, Jan. 2; Fed. exped. from, Jan. 15

New Orleans Camp.: *See* New Orleans

New Orleans and Jackson R.R.: (1863) Fed. raid on, May 11

Newport, Ky.: (1862) martial law in, Sept. 2

Newport, N.C.: (1862) Fed. exped., Apr. 7; Fed. recons. from, July 26, Aug. 14

Newport, Tenn.: (1864) sk. near, Jan. 23

Newport, Va.: (1864) sk., May 12; aff., June 10

Newport Barracks, N.C.: (1863) Fed. expeds. from, Mar. 7, July 13; Dec. 27; (1864) sk., Feb. 2; sk. near, Feb. 6; Fed. exped. from, Apr. 29

Newport Br., Fla.: (1865) sk., Mar. 5

Newport Crossroads, La.: (1864) sk., June 15

Newport News, Va.: (1861) Butler's troops approach, May 27; recon. from Yorktown, June 7; Fed. troops march out from, June 9; sk., July 5; Oct. 21; sk. near, Dec. 22; (1863) Ninth Corps transferred to, Feb. 6; Ninth Corps troops embark from, Mar. 19; (1864) C.S.S. *Squib* damages U.S.S. *Minnesota* off, Apr. 9

New R., La.: (1863) Fed. exped. to, Sept. 24; (1864) sk., Feb. 9; Fed. exped. to, Oct. 2

New R., N.C.: (1862) Lieut. Cushing captures schooners on, Nov. 23

New R., W. Va.: (1861) Oct. 19; (1862) sk. at Pack's Fy., Aug. 6

New R. Br., La.: (1864) May 10

New Rds., La.: (1865) Fed. exped. to, Jan. 31

New Smyrna, Fla.: (1863) Fed. vessels shell, July 28

Newspapers, C.S.A.: (1861) Knoxville *Whig* suppressed, Oct. 24; clamor for military act., Dec. 4; (1863) pro-Union Raleigh, N.C., *Standard* pillaged, Sept. 10

Newspapers, U.S., suppression of: (1861) in St. Louis, Aug. 14; N.Y. papers, Brooklyn *Eagle* charged with disloyalty, Aug. 16; West Chester and Easton, Pa., papers raided, Aug. 19; Haverhill, Mass., publisher attacked, Aug. 19; N.Y. papers confiscated, mailing of banned, Aug. 21; in N.Y., Canton, O., Phila., Aug. 22; raids on, Aug. 24; Louisville *Courier* banned, Sept. 18, 19; (1862) Grant orders newspapers inspected, Jan. 9; (1863) Phila. *Journal* proprietor arrested, Jan. 27; Chicago *Times* restricted, Feb. 8; restriction of *Times* lifted, Feb. 17; Columbus, O., *Crisis* office damaged, Mar. 5; Chicago *Times* suppressed, June 4; (1864) arrests for spurious Lincoln proclamation, May 18

New Tex. Rd., near Morganza, La.: (1864) sk. on, Dec. 4

Newton, Long I., N.Y.: (1861) "peace" meeting fails, Aug. 29

Newton, W. Va.: (1863) sk., Jan. 17

Newton Co., Ark.: (1863) sk., Nov. 15

Newton Co., Mo.: (1863) Fed. oper. in, Mar. 5; Fed. sc. into, May 21

Newtonia, Mo.: (1862) sks., Aug. 8, Sept. 13; eng., Sept. 30; sks., Oct. 4, 7; (1863) Fed. sc. from, May 13; Fed. sc. from, July 28; sk., Sept. 27; (1864) eng., Oct. 28

Newtown, La.: (1863) sk., Apr. 16

Newtown, Va.: (1862) sk., Nov. 24; (1863) sks., June 12, Aug. 2; (1864) sks., May 21, 29, July 20, 22, Oct. 28; act., Nov. 12

New Ulm, Minn.: (1862) Sioux Uprising, Aug. 17, 19; att., evac., Aug. 25

New Windsor, Md.: (1863) Gettysburg Camp., June 29

New York, N.Y.: (1861) Mayor Wood proposes free city, Jan. 6; guns seized in, Jan. 22; triumphal march by Sixth Mass. Inf., Apr. 18; Maj. Anderson arrives, Apr. 18; merchants pledge loyalty to Union, Apr. 19; pro-Union mass meeting, Apr. 20; troops leave, June 25; (1862) cotton auction held in, Jan. 10; slave trader hanged, Feb. 21; Mar. 6; excitement over Jackson's success, May 27; Lincoln leaves for, June 23; Mrs. Lincoln visits, Nov. 2; (1863) discontent over draft, July 7; Draft riots, July 13, 14, 15, 16; merchants plan relief of Negro draft riot victims, July 20; estimates of shipping loss to raiders, July 22; draft resumed, Aug. 19; arrival of Russian fleet, Sept. 23; Mrs. Lincoln visits in, Sept. 24; (1864) John Hay sent to, July 16; Seward warns mayor of conspiracy, Nov. 2; Conf. attempt to burn city, Nov. 25; (1865) Lincoln lies in state in, Apr. 24

New York *Daily News:* (1861) charged with disloyalty, Aug. 16; banned in mails, Aug. 21

New York *Day Book:* (1861) charged with disloyalty, Aug. 16; banned in mails, Aug. 21

New York draft riots: *See* Draft riots

New York Fire Zouaves: (1861) in Washington, May 2; reviewed by Lincoln, May 7

New York *Freeman's Journal:* (1861) charged with disloyalty, Aug. 16; banned in mails, Aug. 21

New York *Herald:* (1861) on Lincoln's inaugural address, Mar. 4; (1862) correspondent arrested, Feb. 9

New York *Journal of Commerce:* (1861) charged with disloyalty, Aug. 16; banned in mails, Aug. 21; (1864) spurious Lincoln proclamation, May 18

New York newspapers: (1861) charged with disloyalty, Aug. 16; banned in mails, Aug. 21; suppression of, Aug. 22

New York *Post:* (1863) reveals troop movements, Sept. 26

New York Sanitary Commission Fair: (1864) Apr. 4

New York State: (1861) legislature adopts pro-Union resolutions, Jan. 11; legislature pledges support to Union, Jan. 21; (1862) Seymour elected gov., Nov. 4; (1864) Fed. call for militia, July 5; C.S.S. *Tallahassee* takes prizes off, Aug. 12; (1865) ratifies Thirteenth Amendment, Feb. 3

New York *Tribune* (*See also* Greeley, Horace): (1860) Nov. 9; (1861) on Lincoln's inaugural, Mar. 4; "Forward to Richmond," July 14; July 29; (1862) prints "Prayer of Twenty Millions," Aug. 19; (1864) Greeley and Canadian peace feelers, July 5; Wade-Davis Manifesto, Aug. 5

New York Workingman's Democratic Republican Assoc.: (1864) Lincoln to, Mar. 21

New York *World:* (1864) spurious Lincoln proclamation, May 18

New York Yacht Club: (1861) offers vessels to U.S., Apr. 30

Niagara, U.S.S.: (1861) patrol off Charleston, May 10; bombards Pensacola, Nov. 22, 23

Niagara Falls, N.Y.: (1864) Greeley and "peace conference," July 18

Niblett's Bluff, La.: (1863) Fed. exped. toward, Apr. 26

Nichol's Mills, N.C.: (1863) recon. to, June 28

Nickajack Cr., Ga.: (1864) Johnston's lines along, July 3; sks., July 6, 9

Nickajack Gap, Ga.: (1864) sks., Mar. 9, May 7

Nickajack Trace, Ga.: (1864) att. on Fed. pickets, Apr. 23

Nicolay, John George (F): (1861) buys executive office sofa, Sept. 25; (1864) Lincoln sends west, Oct. 5; (1865) confirmed as U.S. consul in Paris, Mar. 11

Nightingale (slave ship): (1861) capt., Apr. 21

Nine Mile Br., Kas.: (1865) sk., Jan. 20

Nine Mile Ordinary, Va.: (1863) sk., June 14

Nine months militia, Fed.: (1862) Lincoln authorizes, July 17

Nineteenth Corps, U. S. Army: (1864) units of defend D.C., July 11; pursuit of Early, July 13

Ninevah, Va.: (1864) act., Nov. 12

Ninth Corps, U. S. Army: (1862) Burnside takes command, July 22; (1863) under W. F. Smith, transferred to Newport News from A. of P., Feb. 6; 2 divs. of head for Dept. of the Ohio, Mar. 19; ordered to Vicksburg, June 3; ordered for Ky. service, Aug. 3; 1st div. en route to Tenn., Aug. 12; (1864) movement of, May 4; at Spotsylvania, May 9; Bat. of the North Anna, May 24; ass. on Petersburg, June 16, 17; Petersburg Mine explosion, July 30; Bat. at Poplar Spring Church, Va., Sept. 30; Bat. of Cedar Cr., Va., Oct. 19

Niobrara, Neb. Terr.: (1863) sk. (Ind.), Dec. 4

Niphon, U.S.S.: (1864) runs *Condor* aground, Oct. 1

Nixonton, N.C.: (1863) sk., Apr. 6

Noble's Farm, Ark.: (1865) Fed. sc. to, May 4

Noconah Cr., Tenn.: (1862) sk., Aug. 3

Nokesville, Va.: (1864) aff. near, Apr. 13

Nola Chucky Bend, near Morristown, Tenn.: (1864) Fed. sc. to, Mar. 12

Noland's Fy., Md.: (1864) aff., July 5

Nolensville, Tenn.: (1862) sks., Dec. 1, 26, 30; (1863) Fed. recon. from Murfreesboro to, Jan. 13; sk., Feb. 15

Nolensville Pike, Tenn.: (1865) Fed. sc. on, Feb. 15

Nolin, Ky.: (1862) sk., Dec. 26

Nomini Bay, Va.: (1863) Fed. exped. to, Feb. 12

Nonconnah Cr., Tenn.: (1863) sk., Apr. 4; (1864) sk., Oct. 29

Noonday Church, Ga.: (1864) act., June 20

Noonday Cr., Ga.: (1864) acts., June 15, 19; comb., June 20; act., June 21

Norfleet House, Va.: (1863) engs., Apr. 14, 15

Norfolk, Mo.: (1861) sk., Sept. 27

Norfolk, Va.: (1861) Apr. 18; abandoned by Feds., Apr. 20; (1862) Davis
puts under martial law, Feb. 27; threatened, Mar. 9; plans by Confs. to
evacuate navy yard, May 1; Confs. evacuate, May 9; Lincoln tours area,
May 9; Fed. occup., May 10; Davis on, May 13; (1863) Negroes parade
for Eman. Proc., Jan. 1; aff., Mar. 25; sk., May 2; Feds. evacuate Suffolk,
July 3; exped. from, Dec. 5; (1864) Fed. exped. from, Apr. 13, July
27; Lincoln lifts blockade at, Nov. 19

Norfolk, Va., *Day-Book:* (1862) on drinking among Conf. officers, Mar. 21

Norfolk, Dept. of, Conf.: (1862) J. E. Johnston commands, Apr. 12

Norfolk and Petersburg R.R.: (1863) oper. on, May 15

Norristown, Ark.: (1864) Shelby's Conf. cav. near, May 10; Fed. sc. to, Sept. 9

North Anna R., Va.: (1864) comb., May 9–10; Lee plans to withdraw to, May
21; Grant moves toward, May 22; Bat. of, May 23, 24, 25, 26; Grant
moves from, May 27, 28; Trevilian raid, June 7

North Atlantic Blockading Squad. (*See also* Blockade): (1861) Goldsborough
commands, Sept. 19; (1862) Goldsborough relieved, Sept. 2; (1864) D. D.
Porter assumes command, Oct. 12

North Carolina: (1860) commissioners meet at Raleigh, Dec. 18; state sen.
bill to arm state, Dec. 18; (1861) legislature votes for state convention,
Jan. 24; voters reject secession convention, Feb. 28; refuses troops to Union,
Apr. 15; legislature votes secession convention, May 1; Davis signs bill
admitting to Confederacy conditionally, May 17; secedes, May 20; U. S.
Sen. expels Sens., July 11; Hatteras convention votes pro-Union govt.,
Nov. 18; (1862) Edward Stanly named Fed. mil. gov., May 2; (1863) gov.
warns of Fed. invasion, Jan. 21; Gov. Vance to Davis re discontent, Dec.
30; (1864) opposition to conscription, Jan. 18; (1865) W. W. Holden named
provisional gov., May 29; ratifies Thirteenth Amendment, Dec. 4

North Carolina, Dept. of, Conf.: (1862) D. H. Hill assigned command, July
17; (1863) Hill assumes command all troops in N.C., Feb. 25; in Longstreet's command, Apr. 1; W. H. C. Whiting named to command, July 14;
Pickett assigned command, Sept. 23; (1865) Johnston assumes command
of, Mar. 6

North Carolina, Dept. of, Fed.: (1862) constituted, Jan. 7; Burnside commands
Jan. 13; (1865) Schofield assumes command of, Feb. 9

North Carolina, Dist. of: (1864) oper. in, Jan. 20

North Carolina and Southern Virginia, Dept. of, Conf.: (1864) Beauregard commands, Apr. 18

North Dakota: (1861) part Dak. Terr., Mar. 2

Northeastern Virginia, Dept. of, Fed.: (1861) Irvin McDowell assumes command, May 28; merged into Dept. of the Potomac, Aug. 17

Northeast Fy., N.C.: (1865) sk., Feb. 22

North Edisto, S.C.: (1861) blockade-runner taken, Nov. 25

North Edisto R., S.C.: (1864) att. on U.S.S. *Memphis,* Mar. 6; (1865) sks., Feb. 12, 14

Northern cities: (1861) contribute money to volunteers, Apr. 18

Northern Democratic party: (1860) Nov. 6

Northern Neck, Va.: (1863) oper., May 20; (1864) Fed. raid, Jan. 12

Northern Pacific R.R.: (1864) U. S. Cong. charters, July 2

Northern Virginia, Army of, Conf. (*See also* Lee, R. E.; individual camps. and bats. including Peninsula; Seven Days; 2nd Bull Run or Manassas; Antietam or Sharpsburg; Fredericksburg; Chancellorsville; Gettysburg; Bristoe Station; Mine Run; Wilderness; Spotsylvania; Cold Harbor; Petersburg; Appomattox Camp.): (1862) R. E. Lee takes command, June 1; J. E. B. Stuart assigned command all cav., Aug. 17; command changes in, Nov. 6; (1863) reorganized, May 30; (1864) Davis on food for, Jan. 4; soap in, Aug. 10; Lee's concern over strength, Sept. 2; (1865) surrender of, Apr. 9; paroling of, Apr. 10; Lee's General Orders No. 9, Apr. 10; ceremony, Apr. 12

North Mt., W. Va.: (1862) Fed. recon. from, Dec. 12; (1864) sk., July 3

North Mt. Station, W. Va.: (1863) sk., July 17

North Platte R.: (1865) Fed. oper. against Inds., Feb. 2, 8

North R., N.C.: (1862) Fed. exped. from, Feb. 13

North R., Va.: (1864) sk., Oct. 3

North R. Mills, W. Va.: (1864) sk., July 3

Northwest, Dept. of the, Fed.: (1862) Pope heads, Sept. 5, 6

Northwest conspiracy: (1864) June 8; Johnson's I., Sept. 10; Chicago conspirators arrested, Nov. 6

Norwood's Plantation (or Yellow Bayou, Bayou De Glaize, or Old Oaks), La.: (1864) sk., May 17; eng., May 18

Nottoway Court House, Va.: (1864) sk., June 23

Nova Scotia: (1863) capture of *Chesapeake* off, Dec. 8

"Now he belongs to the ages": (1865) re Lincoln, attributed to Stanton, Apr. 15

Noyes Cr., Ga.: (1864) comb., June 19; sks., June 20, Oct. 2

Nueces R., Tex.: (1862) aff., Aug. 10

Nursing: (1861) Dorothea Dix offers assistance, accepted by Feds., May 29; pay, rations ordered, Aug. 17

Nutter's Hill, W. Va.: (1864) sk., Aug. 27

Oak Grove, Calif.: (1861) Fed. exped. to, Sept. 25; Oct. 5

Oak Grove (or King's School House, French's Field, the Orchard), Va.: (1862) eng., June 25; (1863) sk., Apr. 26

Oak Hill, Va.: (1863) sk., Oct. 15

Oak Hills, Mo. *See* Wilson's Creek, Bat. of: (1861) bat., Aug. 10

Oakland, Miss.: (1862) sk., Dec. 3
Oakland, Md.: (1863) sk., Apr. 26
Oakland Station, Ky.: (1862) sk., Sept. 16
Oak Ridge, Miss.: (1864) sk., Jan. 16
Oak Ridge, Gettysburg, Pa.: (1863) Bat. of Gettysburg, July 1
Oak Shade, Va.: (1863) sk., Sept. 2
Oaths, loyalty: (1862) political prisoners to take, Feb. 14; govt. officers required to take, July 2; Fed. Gen. Pope forces, July 23; (1863) allegiance to U.S., Dec. 8; Mrs. Helm takes, Dec. 14; (1864) Conf. deserters take, Feb. 2; Lincoln on, Mar. 26; in Wade-Davis bill, July 4; (1865) Johnson's amnesty proclamation, May 29
Obey's R., Tenn.: (1864) sk., Mar. 28; Fed. exped. to, Apr. 18
Obion Plank Rd. Crossing, Tenn.: (1863) sk., May 5
Obion R., Tenn.: (1862) sk., Aug. 16; (1863) sk., Apr. 9
Occoquan, Va.: (1862) Fed. recon. to, Feb. 3; Confs. withdraw, Mar. 7; sk., Dec. 20; (1863) aff., Mrs. Violett's, Mar. 22
Occoquan R., Va.: (1861) Fed. recon. toward, Oct. 18; Fed. recon. to, Nov. 12; (1862) aff., Lee's House, Jan. 29; sk., Dec. 19
Ocean Eagle: (1861) capt. by privateer *Calhoun,* May 15
Ocean Pond (or Olustee), Fla.: (1864) Bat. of, Feb. 20
Ocklockonnee Bay, Fla.: (1863) aff., Mar. 24
Ocmulgee R.: (1864) re March to the Sea, Nov. 18
Oconee R.: (1864) March to the Sea, Nov. 18; sk., Nov. 23
Ocracoke Inlet, N.C.: (1861) closed to blockade-runners, Sept. 17
Odell, Moses (F): (1865) vote in House Thirteenth Amendment, Jan. 9
Offutt's Cross Roads, Md.: (1863) sk., June 28
Ogeechee Canal, Ga.: (1864) sk., Dec. 9
Ogeechee R., Ga.: (1862) att., Ft. McAllister, July 29; (1863) att., Ft. McAllister, Jan. 27; destruction C.S.S. *Nashville,* Feb. 28; Fed. att., Ft. McAllister, Mar. 3; (1864) sk., Dec. 7; Fed. recon. to, Dec. 10; fall of Ft. McAllister, Dec. 13
Oglethorpe Barracks, Savannah, Ga.: (1861) seized by state troops, Jan. 26
Ohio: (1861) legislature supports Union, Jan. 12; Nov. 9; (1862) Jan. 13; Democratic gains in Cong., Oct. 14; (1863) Morgan's raid, July 13, 14, 15, 16; (1864) election, Oct. 11; (1865) ratifies Thirteenth Amendment, Feb. 10
Ohio, Army of the, Fed. (*See also* Ohio, Dept. of the; McClellan, George B.; Mitchel, O. M.; Buell, Don Carlos; Wright, H. G.; Burnside, A. E.; Foster, John; Schofield, John M.): (1862) G. W. Morgan commands Seventh Div., Mar. 28; at Shiloh under Buell, Apr. 7; (1864) Atlanta Camp., May 7, July 19, 20, Aug. 16, 27, 31
Ohio, Dept. of the, Fed.: (1861) formed, McClellan commands, May 3, May 13; O. M. Mitchel assumes command, Sept. 21; Nov. 9; Buell assumes command, Nov. 15; (1862) Halleck commands part of, Mar. 11; enlarged, Aug. 19; H. G. Wright assumes command, Aug. 23; (1863) Ninth Corps in, Mar. 19; Burnside in command, Mar. 25; re Conf. sympathizers, Apr. 13; suppression Chicago *Times,* June 1; merged into Military Dept. of the Miss., Oct. 16; Burnside continues command, Oct. 17; John S. Foster supersedes Burnside, Dec. 9; (1864) distilling prohibited in, Jan. 21; Schofield to

command, Jan. 22; Schofield takes command, Feb. 9; Sherman in over-all command, Mar. 12

Ohio R.: (1861) line of attack on, June 3; July 11, 12; Paducah, Ky., Sept. 6; (1862) Ft. Henry exped., Feb. 2; Ft. Donelson Camp., Feb. 6; gunboats on, Feb. 7; Conf. troops cross, Newburg, Ind., July 18; Jenkins' raid crosses, Sept. 4; militia to protect, Sept. 5; Sept. 10; E. K. Smith withdraws, Sept. 16; Sept. 25; cities on defended by Buell, Oct. 1; Oct. 3; Bragg's drive to, ment., Nov. 1; (1863) J. H. Morgan heads for, July 6; Morgan crosses, July 8; Morgan raid, July 15; (1864) Forrest's exped. toward, Mar. 25, 27; Conf. oper., Ill. side of, Aug. 13; Grant fears Hood might reach, Dec. 8

Ohio State Penitentiary, Columbus, O.: (1863) J. H. Morgan imprisoned, July 26; Morgan escapes, Nov. 27

Oiltown, W. Va.: (1863) works destroyed, May 9

Oil Trough Bottom, Ark.: (1864) sk., Mar. 24

Oja de Anaya, N. Mex. Terr.: (1865) Fed. sc. from, May 1

Okolona, Ark.: (1864) sks., Apr. 2

Okolona, Miss.: (1863) sk., Dec. 9; (1864) sk., Feb. 18; eng., Feb. 22; sk., June 23; sk., Dec. 27

O'Laughlin, Michael: (1865) Lincoln conspirator, imprisoned, May 1; found guilty, life sentence, June 30; July 7

Old Antietam Forge, Md.: (1863) sk., July 10

Old Bahama Channel, off Cuba: (1861) *Trent* Aff., Nov. 8

Old Capitol Prison, Washington, D.C.: (1862) Belle Boyd in, July 29, Aug. 28

Old Chesterfield, Va.: (1864) Bat. of the North Anna, May 23

Old Church, Va.: (1862) sk., June 13; (1864) comb., May 30; sk., June 10

Old Cold Harbor, Va.: (1864) Bat. of Cold Harbor, June 1

Oldfield's, Moorefield, W. Va.: (1864) eng., Aug. 7

Old Hen and Chickens I.: (1865) *Sultana* disaster, Apr. 27

Old Lamar, Miss.: (1862) sk., Nov. 6

Old Oaks (or Yellow Bayou, Bayou De Glaize, or Norwood's Plantation), La.: (1864) sk., May 17; eng., May 18

Old Penitentiary bldg., Washington: (1865) hanging of Lincoln conspirators, July 7

Old Randolph, Mo.: (1861) sk., Sept. 14

Old R., La.: (1863) sk., Feb. 10

Old R. Lake (or Lake Chicot), Ark.: (1864) eng., June 6

"Old Straight": *See* Stewart, Alexander Peter

Old Town, Ark.: (1862) Fed. exped. to, July 28

Old Town, Md.: (1864) sk., Aug. 2

Old Town Cr., Miss.: (1864) act., July 15

Old Wilderness Tavern, Va.: (1864) Bat. of Wilderness, May 5

Olive Branch, La.: (1864) sk., Aug. 5

Olive Branch Bayou, La.: (1864) sk., May 3

Olive Branch Church, Va.: (1863) sks., Feb. 5, 7

Oliver's Prairie, Mo.: (1863) sc., July 28

Olley's Cr., Ga.: (1864) comb., June 26

Olmstead, Charles Hart (C): (1862) commands Ft. Pulaski during bomb., Apr. 10; surrenders Ft. Pulaski, Apr. 11

Olustee (or Ocean Pond), Fla.: (1864) Bat. of, Feb. 20
Olustee, C.S.S. (formerly C.S.S. *Tallahassee*): (1864) runs blockade, Oct. 30
Olympian Springs, Ky.: (1863) Fed. recon. to, Oct. 8
Onandaga Co., N.Y., Cav.: (1861) Aug. 1
189th New York Volunteers: (1864) Lincoln to, Oct. 24
"One-Legged Brigade": (1863) Lincoln greets, May 22
169th Ohio Volunteers: (1864) Lincoln to, Aug. 22
Onslow, N.C.: (1863) Fed. recon. to, Jan. 17
"On to Richmond": *See* Horace Greeley and "Forward to Richmond"
Ooltewah, Tenn.: (1864) Fed. sc. to, Jan. 21; Fed. sc. from, Feb. 18
Oostenaula R., Ga.: (1864) act., May 15
Opelika, Ala.: (1865) sk., Apr. 16
Opelousas, La.: (1863) Fed. exped. to, Apr. 17; occup., Apr. 20; Fed. exped.
    from, Apr. 21, 26, 29; Fed. occup., Oct. 21; aff., Oct. 30; Feds. retire from,
    Nov. 1
Opequon Cr., Va.: (1862) Lee moves to, Sept. 20; (1863) sk., June 13; (1864)
    sks., Aug. 18, 19, 20; Early toward, Aug. 26; eng. Smithfield Crossing of,
    Aug. 29; sk., Sept. 1; Early retreats, Sept. 4; sk., Sept. 5; aff., Sept. 13;
    Bat. of (or 3rd Winchester), Sept. 19
Opothleyahola (F): (1861) Creek chief, Dec. 9; leads pro-Union Creeks, Dec. 26
Orange, N.J.: (1864) McClellan accepts 1864 nomination, Sept. 8
Orange and Alexandria R.R.: (1862) sk., Mar. 28; oper. along, Nov. 10
Orangeburg, S.C.: (1865) sk., Feb. 11
Orangeburg Br., on North Edisto, S.C.: (1865) sk., Feb. 12
Orange Court House, Va.: (1862) Fed. recon. to, July 12, 24, 29; sk., Aug.
    2; Fed. advance toward, Aug. 9; Fed. recon. toward, Aug. 13; (1863) sk.,
    Sept. 22; Conf. chaplains meet, Dec. 18; (1864) Lee moves from, May 4
Orange Grove, near Donaldsonville, La.: (1864) aff., July 31
Orange Plank Rd., Va.: (1864) Bat. of Wilderness, May 5, 6
Orange Turnpike, Va.: (1863) Bat. of Chancellorsville, May 2; (1864) Bat. of
    the Wilderness, May 5, 6
Orchard, The, Va.: *See* Oak Grove, Va.
Orchard Knob, Tenn.: (1863) Bat. of Chattanooga, Nov. 23
Ord, Edward Otho Cresap (F): (1862) Bat. of Iuka, Miss., Sept. 19; inter-
    cepts Van Dorn at Hatchie R., Oct. 5; (1863) commands Thirteenth Army
    Corps, June 18; (1865) to command Dept. of Va. and N.C., replacing
    Butler, Jan. 7; assumes command, Army of the James, Dept. of Va. and
    N.C., Jan. 8; Appomattox Camp., Apr. 6, 8, 9
Order No. 28; (1862) "woman order" of New Orleans, Butler, May 15
Orders No. 11, Grant: (1862) Grant orders "Jew" peddlers from army, Dec. 17
Orders No. 11, Mo.: (1863) evac. western Mo. counties, Aug. 25
Ordnance, C.S.A.: (1861) purchase of guns abroad, Aug. 24; Davis on, Nov.
    10; (1862) saltpeter for powder, Feb. 4; congressmen ask for more, Mar.
    4; New Orleans powder mills explode, Mar. 9
Oregon: (1861) Oct. 21
Oregon (or Bowers' Mill), Mo.: (1863) sk., Oct. 4
Oregon Co., Mo.: (1862) Fed. oper., June 1; (1863) Fed. exped. to, Sept. 29;
    sk., Nov. 4

Oreto (British steamer): *See* C.S.S. *Florida*

Orient Fy., Black R., Ark.: (1862) sk., July 8

Orton Pond, N.C.: (1865) act., Feb. 18

Osage, Mo.: (1864) sk., Nov. 26

Osage, U.S.S.: (1865) sunk, Mar. 29

Osage Branch, King's R., Ark.: (1864) aff. on, Apr. 16

Osage Indians: (1865) treaty of loyalty with U.S., Sept. 14

Osage Mission, Kas.: (1864) sk., Sept. 26

Osage R., Mo.: (1862) sk., Apr. 25; (1864) sk., Oct. 5

Osage Springs, Ark.: (1862) aff., Feb. 28

Osborne's Cr., Miss.: (1862) sk., June 4

Osceola, Mo.: (1862) sk., May 27; (1863) raid, Aug. 21

Ossabaw I., Ga.: (1863) Fed. exped. to, July 3

Ossabaw Sound, Ga.: (1864) capture of *Water Witch,* June 3; aff., June 4

Osterhaus, Peter Joseph (F): (1865) superseded command Fifteenth Corps, Jan. 8; takes surrender of Army of Trans-Miss., May 26

Otsego, U.S.S.: (1864) sunk by torpedoes, Dec. 9

Otter Cr., Va.: (1864) sk., June 16

Otto, William (F): (1865) as Asst. Sec. of Interior takes over Sec. office temporarily, Mar. 9

Ouachita R., La.: (1863) Ft. Beauregard att., May 10; (1864) Fed. naval recon., Feb. 29; sk., Apr. 29

Our American Cousin: (1865) play at Lincoln's assassination, Apr. 14

Outer Banks of N.C.: (1861) att. on Hatteras, Aug. 27; (1862) Fed. vessels over Hatteras Inlet bar, Feb. 7

Overall's Cr., Tenn.: (1862) sk., Dec. 31

Overland Stage Rd., Colo. Terr.: (1865) Fed. oper., Jan. 14

Owen Co., Ky.: (1862) guerrilla activity, June 20; oper. against Conf. guerrillas, Oct. 15

Owensborough, Ky.: (1862) sk., Sept. 18; (1864) sk., Aug. 27; guerrilla raid on, Sept. 2

Owen's Cross Roads, Tenn.: (1864) act., Dec. 1

Owens R. Valley, Calif.: (1863) Fed. oper. (Ind.), Apr. 24

Oxford, Miss.: (1862) sk., Dec. 1; aff., Dec. 4; Grant moves back from, Dec. 20; (1864) Fed. expeds. to, Aug. 1, 9; sk., Aug. 9

Ox Fd., Va.: (1864) comb., May 24

Oxford Bend, White R., Ark.: (1862) act., Oct. 28

Ox Hill, Va.: (1862) Bat. of Chantilly, Sept. 1

Oyster Bayou, La.: (1865) Fed. exped. to, Mar. 25

Ozark, Mo.: (1862) sk., Aug. 1; sc. to, Aug. 7; Fed. exped. from, Aug. 14, Oct. 12, Dec. 9; (1863) Fed. sc. from, Jan. 4; Marmaduke captures, Jan. 7; sk., Oct. 29; (1864) Fed. sc. from, Aug. 23

Ozark Co., Mo.: (1864) Fed. sc., June 5; (1865) Fed. oper., Feb. 6; Fed. sc., Feb. 16

Ozark Mts., Mo.: (1862) Fed. exped. from, Nov. 30

Pace's Fy., Ga.: (1864) sk., July 5; act., Aug. 26

Pacific, Dept. of the, Fed.: (1861) E. V. Sumner commands, Apr. 25; com-

mand change, Oct. 20; George Wright assumes command, Oct. 26; Wright formally assigned, Nov. 19; (1864) McDowell assumes command, July 1
Pacific Northwest: (1864) r.r., telegraph land granted, July 2
Pack's Fy., New R., W. Va.: (1862) sk., Aug. 6
Padre I., Tex.: (1862) aff., Dec. 7
Paducah, Ky.: (1861) steamers seized, Aug. 22; Grant heads for, Sept. 5; Grant seizes, Sept. 6; Sept. 25; sk., Oct. 10; Fed. demon. from, Nov. 7; (1862) Fed. transports move to, Feb. 3; Feb. 11; Mar. 8; (1863) Fed. expeds. from, Sept. 1, 20; (1864) Forrest attacks, Mar. 25; sk., Apr. 14; Fed. exped. from, July 26
Pagan Cr., Va.: (1864) Fed. exped. to, Dec. 15
Paine, Lewis: *See* Payne, Lewis
Paine's Cross Roads, Va.: (1865) sk., Apr. 5
Paint Lick Br., Ky.: (1863) sk., July 31
Paint Rock, Ala.: (1865) sk., Jan. 26
Paint Rock Br., Ala.: (1862) sk., Apr. 28; (1864) sk., Apr. 8, Dec. 7; aff., Dec. 31
Paint Rock R., Ala.: (1864) sk., Nov. 19
Paint Rock Station, Ala.: (1864) sk., July 30
Paintsville, Ky.: (1862) sk., Jan. 7; (1864) sk., Apr. 13
Palatka, Fla.: (1863) sk., Mar. 27; (1864) sks., Mar. 16, 31; Fed. exped. from, Apr. 1; Fed. exped. from, Aug. 13
Palmer, Innis Newton (F): (1864) defends New Berne, N.C., Feb. 1
Palmer, John McCauley (F): (1864) demon. Dalton, Ga., Feb. 23, 25
Palmer, Camp, N.C.: (1864) Fed. sc. from, Oct. 11
Palmerston, Viscount Henry John Temple (Lord): (1862) states Britain's strict neutrality, Aug. 8
Palmetto, Ga.: (1864) Davis, Hood confer at, Sept. 25
Palmetto State, C.S.S.: (1863) gunboat att. on Charleston blockade, Jan. 31
Palmito Ranch, Tex.: (1865) sk., May 12, 13
Palmyra, Mo.: (1861) aff., Aug. 17; act., Nov. 18
Palmyra, Tenn.: (1863) destruction of, Apr. 3; sk., Nov. 13
Palo Alto, Miss.: (1863) sk., Apr. 21
Pamlico R., N.C.: (1863) sk. Rodman's Point, Mar. 30; eng. Hill's Point, Apr. 2; (1864) Feds. capture Conf. boats, June 16
Pamlico Sound, N.C.: (1861) *Fanny* capt., Oct. 1; (1862) Burnside exped. moves into, Jan. 25; Bat. of Roanoke I., Feb. 8; destruction Conf. "Mosquito" fleet, Feb. 10
Pamunkey R., Va.: (1862) eng. Eltham's Ldg., May 7; White House, May 16; Fed. exped. up, May 17; White House burned, June 28; Lincoln's plan, Nov. 27; (1863) aff. near West Point, Apr. 16; (1864) Grant moves to cross, May 26, 27; Grant south of, May 29; Feds. move down, June 12
Panama: (1861) Chiriqui Improvement Co., Apr. 10
Panda, Miss.: (1863) Fed. exped. to, May 11, June 16; sk., June 19
Panther Cr., Mo.: (1862) sk., Aug. 8
Panther Gap, W. Va.: (1864) sk., June 4
Panther Springs, Tenn.: (1864) sks., Mar. 5, Oct. 27
Paola, Kas.: (1863) sk., Aug. 21

Papinsville, Mo.: (1861) sk., Sept. 5; (1863) sk., June 23

Parajé, N. Mex. Terr.: (1862) aff., May 21

Paris, France: (1865) John Nicolay confirmed U.S. consul, Mar. 11

Paris, Ky.: (1862) sk., July 19; (1863) aff., Mar. 11; sks., Apr. 16, July 29

Paris, Mo.: (1864) surrender of, Oct. 15

Paris, Tenn.: (1862) sk., Mar. 11; (1864) Conf. raid from, Dec. 6

Paris, Va.: (1862) Fed. recon., Oct. 13

Parke, John Grubb (F): (1862) besieges Ft. Macon, Mar. 23; Ft. Macon surrenders, Apr. 25; (1864) commands Ninth Corps, Poplar Spring Church, Va., Sept. 30

Parkersburg, W. Va.: (1863) sc. from, May 15

Parker's Cross Roads, or Store, Tenn.: (1862) eng., Dec. 31

Parker's Fd., Va.: (1864) eng., July 17

Parker's Store (or Cross Roads), Tenn.: (1862) eng., Dec. 31

Parker's Store, Va.: (1863) act., Nov. 29

Park Hill, I.T.: (1862) Fed. recon. to, July 14

Parkville, Mo.: (1864) Conf. guerrilla att., July 7

Parliament, British: (1861) May 6; (1863) Queen's address, Feb. 5; Debates U.S. seizure of vessels, Apr. 25, June 15

Parrott guns: (1863) on Morris I., Aug. 12; fired on Ft. Sumter, Sept. 1

Parsons, Lewis E.: (1865) provisional gov. Ala., June 21

Pasquotank, N.C.: (1863) sk., Aug. 18

Passaic, U.S.S.: (1863) att. on Charleston, Apr. 7

Pass Cavallo, Tex.: (1864) Fed. evac. of, June 15

Pass Christian, Miss.: (1862) Fed. exped. to, Apr. 3

Pass Manchac, La.: (1862) sk., June 17; Fed. exped. to, July 25, Sept. 13

Patapsco, U.S.S.: (1863) att. on Charleston, Apr. 7; (1865) sunk, Jan. 15

Patent Office, U. S.: (1861) site inaugural balls, Mar. 4; (1865) Mar. 6

Patrick Henry, C.S.S.: (1861) damaged in act., Dec. 2

Patterson, Robert (F): (1861) assigned command Del., Pa., Md., D.C., Apr. 19; evac. Harper's Fy., June 15; into Shenandoah, July 2; to Martinsburg, W. Va., July 3; stalled, July 14; sk., July 15; reluctance to attack, July 15; disobeys orders, July 17; superseded in Dept. of the Shenandoah, July 21, 25

Patterson, Mo.: (1863) Marmaduke takes, Jan. 20; sk., Apr. 20; Conf. sc. to, Aug. 2; (1864) Fed. sc. from, Jan. 23, May 6; Fed. exped. from, May 16; aff., Sept. 22; Fed. exped., Nov. 16; (1865) sk., Apr. 15

Patterson's Cr., W. Va.: (1861) sk., June 26; (1865) aff., Mar. 30

Patterson's Cr. Br., W. Va.: (1864) sk., July 4

Patterson's Cr. Station, W. Va.: (1865) sk., Mar. 22

Pattersonville, La.: (1863) eng., Mar. 28; sk., Apr. 11; (1864) Fed. recon. to, Aug. 2

Pawnee, U.S.S.: (1861) ordered to provision Ft. Sumter, Apr. 5; leaves for Charleston, Apr. 10; fails to provision Sumter, Apr. 13; in Wash., Apr. 23; June 28; (1863) at John's I., S.C., Dec. 25

Pawnee Agency, Neb. Terr.: (1863) att. on, June 23

Pawnee Cr., South Fork, Kas.: (1865) Fed. sc. to, Feb. 3

Pawnee Fork, Kas.: (1865) Fed. sc. to, Jan. 15

Pelham, John (C): (1863) killed, Kelly's Fd., Va., Mar. 17

Pelham, Tenn.: (1863) sk., July 2

Pelton's Plantation, La.: (1865) Fed. exped. to, Apr. 19

Pemberton, John Clifford (C) (*See also* Vicksburg): (1862) assumes command Dept. of S.C., Ga., and East Fla., Mar. 4; Mar. 14; Beauregard supersedes, Aug. 29; Sept. 24; commands Dept. of Miss. and East La., Oct. 1; assumes command, Oct. 14; J. E. Johnston to supervise, Nov. 24; Davis to, Dec. 7; Forrest's raid to aid, Dec. 15; troops to Vicksburg, Dec. 27; thwarts Chickasaw Bayou ass., Dec. 29; (1863) Davis to, Jan. 29, Mar. 10; orders Ft. Pemberton built, Mar. 11; Davis on, Apr. 2; on Vicksburg defense, Apr. 30; Davis to, May 7; between Jackson and Vicksburg, May 12; Grant's army, May 13; prevented from joining Johnston, May 14; Champion's Hill, May 16; Big Black R. Br., May 17; pulls back to Vicksburg, May 17; siege begins, May 18; Davis calls for att., May 18; att. on Vicksburg, May 19; siege of Vicksburg, May 20, 21, 22; Davis to, May 23; Davis on, May 24, 26, June 10; Davis to Johnston, July 1, 2; discusses terms with Grant, July 3; surrender of Vicksburg, July 4; parole of forces, July 5; Aug. 13; (1864) Davis to, Mar. 11

Pemberton, Ft., Miss.: (1863) ordered constructed, Mar. 11; repels Fed. att., Mar. 11; bomb. of, Mar. 13; Yazoo Pass exped., Mar. 16

Pemiscot Co, Mo.: (1864) Fed. sc., Oct. 10, Nov. 13

Pender, William Dorsey (C): (1863) Bat. of Gettysburg, July 3

Pendleton, Alexander S. (C): (1864) mortally wounded, Sept. 22

Pendleton, George H. (F): (1864) Democratic nominee for Vice-Pres., Aug. 31; defeated, Nov. 8

Pendleton Co., W. Va.: (1862) oper., Nov. 5; (1865) Fed. exped., June 1

Peninsula, Va.: (1862) McClellan's plans, Mar. 8, 9; A. of P. embarks for, Mar. 17; troops withheld from, Mar. 23; Mar. 31; preparations for ass., Apr. 1; McDowell withheld, Apr. 3; Fed. move toward Yorktown, Apr. 4; siege of Yorktown begins, Apr. 5; Lincoln to McClellan, Apr. 6, 9; siege of Yorktown, Apr. 11, 18; Davis to Johnston, May 1; Lincoln to McClellan, May 1; Conf. evac. of Yorktown, May 3; Feds. enter Yorktown, May 4; Bat. of Williamsburg, May 5; Feds. enter Williamsburg, May 6; eng. Eltham's Ldg., May 7; May 9; Davis to J. E. Johnston, May 10; Davis to wife, May 13; May 23; McDowell diverted, May 24; inaction, May 26, 30; Bat. of Seven Pines or Fair Oaks, May 31, June 1; Feds. on Chickahominy, June 4; rains, June 5; reinforcements kept from Feds., June 9; June 10; Stuart's ride around McClellan, June 12, 13, 14, 15; Jackson's men moving toward Richmond, June 17; sk., Fair Oaks, June 18; Lincoln asks McClellan when can attack, June 18; sk., Charles City Rd., June 19; sk., Fair Oaks, June 21; stalemate on, June 22; oper. New Kent Court House, June 23; sk., Mechanicsville, June 24; *See* Seven Days' Camp.; eng. at Oak Grove or French's Field opens Seven Days, June 25; Bat. of Mechanicsville, Beaver Dam Creek, or Ellerson's Mill, June 26; Bat. of Gaines' Mill, 1st Cold Harbor, or Chickahominy, June 27; McClellan withdraws toward James, June 28; Bat. of Savage's Station, June 29; Bat. of Frayser's Farm or White Oak Swamp, June 30; Bat. of Malvern Hill, losses of Seven Days, July 1; Fed. withdrawal continues, July 2; Fed. recon., July 3; sk., Westover,

July 3; Davis, Lee agree no att., July 5; reinforcements A. of P., July 6; act. quiet on James, July 7; Lincoln arrives, July 8; Fed. recon., July 11; Lincoln doubts McClellan, July 13; A. of P. ordered back to defend Wash., Aug. 3; eng. Malvern Hill, Aug. 5; sk., White Oak Swamp Br., Aug. 5; Fed. forces withdraw Malvern Hill again, Aug. 7; Lee's army moves, Aug. 13; McClellan's army moves away, Aug. 20; sk., Gloucester Point, Nov. 16; Fed. recon., Dec. 17; (1863) threat of att., Feb. 18; Mar. 21; West Point occup., May 7; evac. West Point, May 31; sc. on, June 18; act. on, July 1; (1864) Kilpatrick's Richmond raid, Mar. 1; *See* Cold Harbor; Grant's move to the James, June 11, 12, 13, 14

Peninsula, Dept. of the, Conf.: (1862) J. E. Johnston commands, Apr. 12

Penguin, U.S.S.: (1861) capture of *Albion* off Charleston, Dec. 1

Pennsylvania: (1861) Jan. 11; legislature pledges to support Union, Jan. 24; (1862) apprehension over Conf. invasion, Sept. 8, 10; Gov. Curtin calls for 50,000 men, Sept. 11; state treasure sent north, Sept. 12; Democratic gains in Cong., Oct. 14; draft opposition, Oct. 17; (1863) anxiety over Lee's Gettysburg invasion, June 15; (1864) Fed. request for militia, July 5; threatened invasion, Aug. 25; Republican gain in election, Oct. 11; (1865) ratifies Thirteenth Amendment, Feb. 8

Pennsylvania, Dept. of, Fed.: (1861) Robert Patterson assigned command, Apr. 27

Pensacola (and Pensacola Bay), Fla. (*See also* Pickens, Ft.): (1861) Fed. fire, Jan. 8; Fla. troops take fts., Jan. 12; U.S.S. *Brooklyn* arrives off Ft. Pickens, Feb. 9; U.S.S. *Isabelle* seized, Mar. 20; Bragg asks permission to fire, Apr. 7; Lieut. Worden arrives, Apr. 10; Ft. Pickens reinforced, Apr. 12; harbor blockaded, Apr. 13; Sept. 14; Oct. 9; Nov. 22, 23; (1862) Fed. bomb., Conf. bomb., Jan. 1; Confs. evacuate, May 9; Feds. occupy, May 10; Fed. exped. from, June 14; Farragut at, Oct. 15; (1864) sk., Apr. 2; (1865) Mobile Camp., Mar. 17

Pensacola Navy Yard: (1861) taken by Feds., Jan. 12; bomb. of, Nov. 22, 23

Pensions, Fed.: (1862) for disabled, dead service men, July 14

Peosi R., Tex.: (1861) Conf. sk. (Ind.), Nov 1

Peralta, N. Mex. Terr.: (1862) Apr. 13; sk., Apr. 15

Perche Hills, Mo.: (1865) Fed. sc. to, Mar. 7; sk. in, May 5

Perkins' Mill, Tenn.: (1862) raid, Dec. 26

Perry Co., Ark.: (1864) sks., May 13, Dec. 3

Perryville, I.T.: (1863) sk., Aug. 26

Perryville, Ky.: (1862) Feds. near, Oct. 7; sk., Oct. 7; Bat. of, or Chaplin Hills, Oct. 8; Oct. 9; Bragg retreats, Oct. 13, 22

Perryville, Tenn.: (1863) Fed. exped. to, Mar. 12

Pest House, La.: (1864) sk., May 28

Pet (Brit. blockade-runner): (1864) capt., Feb. 16

Peterhoff (Brit. steamer): (1863) Feds. seize, Feb. 25

Petersburg, Tenn.: (1863) Mar. 2

Petersburg, Va. (*See also* individual battles): (1864) May 4; Butler's advance, May 5; Fed. raids toward, May 5; Feds. can see, May 6; Butler's camp. against, May 9, 12, 13, 14, 15, 16, 17; front quiet, May 21; Butler fails to take, June 9; Davis on threat, June 9; Eighteenth Fed. Corps ordered to, June 14; Fed. att. fails, June 15; ass. continues, June 16, 17, 18; siege of, June 18, 19, 20, 21; Fed. att. Weldon R.R., June 22, 23; siege, June 23, 25, 27, July 1, 6, 7, 9, 12, 15; Lincoln on, July 17; Grant moves troops north of James, July 25; mining, July 25, 27, 29; Fed. mine explosion, July 30; aftermath, July 31; Conf. r.r. threatened, Aug. 1; Conf. mine blast, Aug. 5; Aug. 9; Davis on, Aug. 11; Aug. 13, 16; Lincoln on, Aug. 17; Bat. of Weldon R.R. or Globe Tavern, Aug. 18, 19, 20, 21; Hancock destroys part of r.r., Aug. 23; Aug. 24; Bat. of Ream's Station, Aug. 25; act., Sept. 2; Sept. 14; quiet, Sept. 15, 28; Bat. of Peebles' Farm, Sept. 29, 30, Oct. 1; siege continues, Oct. 1, 2, 8, 15; eng. Burgess' Mill or Boydton Plank Rd., Oct. 27; siege of continues, Oct. 27, Nov. 13, Dec. 8, 9, 10, 19; (1865) Jan. 1; siege, Jan. 17, Feb. 5; Bat. of Hatcher's Run, Feb. 5, 6, 7; Confs. to attack Ft. Stedman, Mar. 24; att. Ft. Stedman, Mar. 25; siege, Mar. 26, 27, 28; Appomattox Camp., Mar. 29, 30, 31; Bat. of Five Forks, Apr. 1; Feds. break Petersburg lines, Apr. 2; Fed. occup., Apr. 3; Lincoln in, Apr. 3

Petersburg, W. Va.: (1861) sk., Sept. 12; (1863) Fed. exped. to, Jan. 2; sk., Sept. 6; (1864) sks., Jan. 10, 15; Fed. exped. to, Feb. 29; sks., Mar. 3, Oct. 11

Petersburg Gap, W. Va.: (1863) sk., Sept. 4

Petersburg and Weldon R.R.: *See* Weldon R.R.

Peterson, William, house of: (1865) wounded Lincoln taken to, Apr. 14; Lincoln dies in, Apr. 15

Petersville, Md.: (1862) sk., Sept. 14

Petigru, James Louis: (1860) S.C. pro-unionist on secession, Dec. 20; (1863) death of, Mar. 9

Petite Anse I., La.: (1862) aff., Nov. 22

Petit Jean, Ark.: (1864) sk., July 10

Petrel, U.S.S.: (1864) capt., Apr. 19

Pettigrew, James Johnston (C): (1863) Pickett's charge, Gettysburg, July 3

Pettis Co., Mo.: (1862) Fed. sc., July 28

Pettus, John J. (C): (1862) Davis to gov. of Miss., June 19

Peytona, W. Va.: (1861) sk., Sept. 12

Peyton's Mill, Miss.: (1862) sk., Sept. 19

Phelps, John Smith: (1862) Lincoln names mil. gov. of Ark., July 19

Phelps, John Wolcott (F): (1862) Davis declares outlaw, Aug. 21

Phelps Co., Mo.: (1864) Fed. sc., July 30

Philadelphia, Pa.: (1861) Lincoln speaks at, Feb. 21, 22; Feb. 23; Fed. troops embarked, Apr. 19; suppression of press, Aug. 21; Aug. 22; (1862) mayor to defend city, Sept. 12; (1863) protest Vallandigham's arrest, June 1; (1864) Lincoln and Sanitary Fair, June 16; (1865) Lincoln funeral train, Apr. 22

Philadelphia, Tenn.: (1863) sk., Sept. 27; act., Oct. 20; sks., Oct. 25, Dec. 2; (1865) sk., Mar. 1

Philadelphia *Journal:* (1863) proprietor arrested, Jan. 27

Philippi, W. Va.: (1861) act., "Philippi Races," June 3; June 8; McClellan's troops at, July 10; (1862) sk., Mar. 20; (1865) Fed. sc., Mar. 14

Philippi, U.S.S.: (1864) destroyed, Mobile Bay, Aug. 5

Phillips, Mrs. Philip (C): (1861) arrested by Butler, Aug. 24

Phillips, Wendell (F): (1861) as abolitionist glad for disunion, Jan. 21; (1862) pelted in Cincinnati, Mar. 24

Phillips' Cr., Miss.: (1862) sk., May 21

Phillips' Cross Roads, N.C.: (1865) sk., Mar. 4

Phillips' Fd., Red Bird Cr., Ky.: (1863) sk., May 10

Philomont, Va.: (1862) sks., Nov. 2, 19; (1864) sk., July 20

Philo Parsons (U.S. steamer): (1864) capt., Lake Erie, Sept. 19

Phoenix Iron Works, Gretna, La.: (1861) May 4

Piankatank R., Va.: (1864) Fed. exped. to, Mar. 9

Piatt, Camp, W. Va.: (1863) Fed. sc. from, Feb. 5; Fed. sc. from, Mar. 12, Sept. 11

Picacho Pass, Ariz. Terr.: (1862) sk., Apr. 15

Pickens, Francis Wilkinson (C) (*See also* Charleston; Sumter, Ft.; South Carolina): (1860) declares state independent, Dec. 24; (1861) Fed. protests to, Jan. 9; back pay, Jan. 13; temporary "truce" with Ft. Sumter, Jan. 13; Washington's Birthday speech, Feb. 22; to Davis, Feb. 27; Davis to, Mar. 18; confers with Ward Hill Lamon, Mar. 25; need of men, Mar. 28; R. S. Chew delivers Lincoln's message, Apr. 8; sends representatives to Ft. Sumter, Apr. 11

Pickens, Ft., Fla. (*See also* Pensacola, Fla.): (1861) Fed. garrison transferred to, Jan. 10; Fla. state troops demand surrender, Jan. 12; Feds. refuse surrender, Jan. 15; surrender demand again refused, Jan. 18; Fed. reinforcements sail, Jan. 24; U.S.S. *Brooklyn* off, Feb. 9; Confederacy forbids resupplying, Mar. 18; exped. to resupply, Mar. 29; U.S.S. *Powhatan* sent to reinforce, Apr. 1; *Powhatan* incident, Apr. 6; Worden arrives, Apr. 10; Fed. Navy reinforces, Apr. 12; harbor blockaded, Apr. 13; reinforced, Apr. 17; Oct. 9; bombards Confs., Nov. 22, 23; (1862) Conf. bomb. of, Jan. 1; May 9

Pickett, George Edward (C): (1862) breaks line at Gaines' Mill, June 27; (1863) charge at Gettysburg, July 3; commands Dept. of N.C., Sept. 23; (1864) leads exped. against New Berne, N.C., Feb. 1; exped. unsuccessful, Feb. 7; at Bermuda Hundred, May 6; Beauregard succeeds, May 12; (1865) Appomattox Camp., Mar. 29, 30; eng. Dinwiddie Court House, Mar. 31; Bat. of Five Forks, Apr. 1

Pickett, John T. (C): (1861) Conf. agent to Mexico, May 17

Pickett's charge, Gettysburg: (1863) July 3

Pickett's Mills, Ga.: (1864) comb., May 27

Piedmont, Augusta Co., Va.: (1864) eng., June 5

Piedmont, Fauquier Co., Va.: (1864) Fed. sc. to, Feb. 17; sk., Oct. 9

Piedmont, W. Va.: (1864) r.r. raid, May 5

Piedmont Station, Va.: (1863) sk., May 16

Pierce, Ebenezer W. (F): (1861) at Big Bethel, June 10

Pierce, Franklin (F): (1864) withdraws nomination Democratic convention, Aug. 30

Pierce, L. (F): (1864) U.S. consul in Mexico, Jan. 12

Pierpoint, Francis Harrison (name often variously spelled): (1861) provisional gov. of Fed. Va., June 19; (1865) recognized as gov. of Va., May 9

Pigeon Cr., Mo.: (1863) sc. to, Nov. 24

Pigeon Hill, Tenn.: (1863) sk., Nov. 26

Pineville, Mo.: (1862) sk., June 23, Nov. 19; (1863) sks., Aug. 9, 13

Pine Wood, Tenn.: (1865) Fed. exped. to, Feb. 20

Piney Branch Church, Va.: (1864) sk., May 15

Piney Factory, Tenn.: (1862) sk., Nov. 2

Piney Green, N.C.: (1864) Fed. sc. from, June 22

Piney Mt., Ark.: (1864) sk., Apr. 6

Piney R., Mo.: (1864) aff., Feb. 18

Pin Hook (or Bayou Macon), La.: (1863) sk., May 10

Pinkerton, Allan (F): (1861) detective with Lincoln to Wash., Feb. 23

Pink Hill, Mo.: (1862) sks., Mar. 31, June 4, 11; oper., June 23

Pinney, Ft., Ark.: (1865) Fed. exped. from, Jan. 27

Pinola, U.S.S.: (1862) below New Orleans, Apr. 20

Pinos Altos, Ariz. Terr.: (1864) sk., Feb. 27

Pioneer battalions, Fed.: (1865) on Carolina Camp., Feb. 1

Pisgah, Mo.: (1864) sk., Sept. 10

Pitman's Cross Roads, Ky.: (1862) sk., Oct. 21

Pitman's Fy., Ark.: (1862) sk., Nov. 25

Pitt R., Calif.: (1861) sc. from, Aug. 15

Pittsburg, U.S.S.: (1862) at Island No. 10, Apr. 7

Pittsburg Ldg., Tenn. (*See also* Shiloh, Bat. of): (1862) Conf. battery silenced, Mar. 1; Fed. build-up, Mar. 10; Sherman toward, Mar. 14; sk., Mar. 16; Mar. 17; Grant at, Mar. 24; Fed. exped. on Tenn. R., Apr. 1; A. S. Johnston orders Conf. att., Apr. 2; Conf. att. delayed, Apr. 3; sk., Monterey, Tenn., Apr. 3; Conf. advance delayed, Apr. 4; Apr. 5; Bat. of Pittsburg Ldg. or Shiloh, Apr. 6, 7; aftermath, Apr. 8; Fed. relief aid, Apr. 9; Halleck arrives, Apr. 11; Apr. 17; Fed. army enlarges, Apr. 19; sk., Apr. 27; Halleck prepares to march, Apr. 29; Fed. army leaves, May 3; May 6

Pittsburgh, Pa.: (1863) alarm over Lee's invasion, June 15

Pitt's Cross Roads, Tenn.: (1863) sk., Oct. 2

Plains Store, La.: (1863) act., May 21

Plains Store Rd., La.: (1863) sk., May 23

Planter (steamer): (1862) Conf. vessel taken by Negroes, May 13

Plantersville, Ala.: (1865) sk., Apr. 1

Plaquemine, La.: (1862) aff., Dec. 29, 31; (1863) sk., June 18; (1864) sk., Aug. 6; (1865) Fed. exped. from, Jan. 26, Feb. 17

Platform, Democratic: (1864) Aug. 30; Sept. 8

Platform, National Union party: (1864) June 7, 8, 9

Platform, Republican: *See* Platform, National Union party

Platte City, Mo.: (1864) aff., July 10

Platte Co., Mo.: (1862) sk., Rocky Bluff, Aug. 7, (1864) sk., July 3; Fed. sc., Aug. 25

Platte Valley, Neb. Terr.: (1864) Ind. att., near Alkali Station, Oct. 20

Plattsburg, Mo.: (1864) Conf. att., July 21

Pleasant Grove, La.: (1864) Bat. of, or Sabine Cross Roads or Mansfield, Apr. 8

Pleasant Hill, Ga.: (1865) sk., Apr. 18

Pleasant Hill, La.: (1864) Feds. near in Red R. Camp., sk., Apr. 7; Bat. of Sabine Cross Roads, Apr. 8; eng. Pleasant Hill, Apr. 9; Confs. ordered to retreat from, Apr. 10; Apr. 11

Pleasant Hill, Mo.: (1861) Feds. capt. near, Nov. 16; (1862) sks., July 8, 11; (1863) sks., May 15, Aug. 22; (1864) May 28, July 25; (1865) aff., May 3

Pleasant Hill Ldg. (or Blair's Ldg.), La.: (1864) eng., Apr. 12

Pleasant Hill Ldg., Tenn.: (1864) sk., Apr. 12

Pleasant Valley, Md.: (1862) Bat. of Crampton's Gap, Sept. 14

Pleasonton, Alfred (F): (1862) Bat. of South Mt., Sept. 14; (1863) assumes command, A. of P., cav., May 22; Bat. of Brandy Station, June 9; (1864) superseded by Gregg, sent to Mo., Mar. 25; Apr. 4; act. Lexington, Mo., Oct. 20; opposes Price, Oct. 22; Bat. of Westport, Mo., Oct. 23; pursuit of Price, Oct. 24; Marais des Cygnes, Kas., Mine Cr., Mo., Oct. 25; to Ft. Scott, Kas., Oct. 26

Pleasureville, Ky.: (1864) aff., June 9

Plentytude, Miss.: (1864) sk., July 10

Plum Cr., Neb. Terr.: (1864) aff., Sept. 29

Plum Cr. Station, Neb. Terr.: (1864) sks., Nov. 19, 25, 26; (1865) Fed. sc. from, May 8

Plummer, Joseph Bennett (F): (1861) eng. Fredericktown, Mo., Oct. 21

Plum Point Bend, Tenn.: *See* Plum Run Bend, Tenn.

Plum Run Bend, Tenn.: (1862) gunboat eng., May 10

Plymouth, N.C.: (1862) sk., Aug. 30; Confs. seize, Dec. 10; (1863) Fed. exped. to, Feb. 1; Conf. demon., Mar. 10; Fed. exped. from, July 26; sk., Nov. 26; (1864) sk., Apr. 1; Conf. att. on, Apr. 17, 18, 19; Conf. capture of, Apr. 20; Apr. 26; sinking of *Albemarle,* Oct. 27; Feds. capture, Oct. 31

Pocahontas, Ark.: (1862) sk., Apr. 21; (1863) Conf. sc. from, Aug. 2; exped. to, Aug. 17; Fed. exped. to, Oct. 26; (1864) sk., Feb. 10

Pocahontas, Tenn.: (1862) act., on Hatchie R., Oct. 5; (1863) Fed. expeds. from, June 8, 12, 17

Pocahontas, U.S.S.: (1861) sent to provision Ft. Sumter, Apr. 5

Pocahontas Co., W. Va.: (1862) oper. Nov. 5; (1863) sk., Jan. 22; Fed. exped. into, Feb. 10; (1864) Fed. exped. into, May 15; (1865) Fed. sc. in, Apr. 15; Fed. exped. in, June 1

Pocotaligo, S.C.: (1862) sk., May 29; Fed. demon., July 9; eng., Pocotaligo or Yemassee, Oct. 22; (1865) Fed. move to, Jan. 14; Fed. recon. from, Jan. 20; sk., Jan. 26

Pocotaligo Rd., S.C.: (1864) sk., Dec. 20

Pohick Church, Va.: (1861) sk., Aug. 18; Fed. occup., Oct. 3; Fed. recon. to, Nov. 12; Fed. sc. toward, Dec. 18; (1862) aff. near, Feb. 24; sk., Mar. 5; (1863) sk., Oct. 17

Pohick Run, Va.: (1862) sk., Jan. 9

Poindexter's Farm (Malvern Hill), Va. (*See* Malvern Hill, Bat. of): (1862) July 1

Point Isabel, Tex.: (1863) capt. by Feds., Nov. 6

Point Lookout, Md.: (1863) Lincoln visits prisoner camp at, Dec. 27; (1864) Fed. exped. from, May 11, June 11

Point Pleasant, La.: (1864) aff., June 25

Point Pleasant, Mo.: (1862) eng., Mar. 7, Mar. 18; Fed. exped. from, Mar. 23

Point Pleasant, O.: (1862) Jenkins' raid near, Sept. 4

Point Pleasant, W. Va.: (1862) Fed. exped. from, Sept. 26; (1863) sk., Mar. 30; sk., Apr. 22

Point of Rocks, Kas.: (1865) sk., Jan. 20

Point of Rocks, Md.: (1861) Feds. obstruct, June 15; sks., Aug. 5, Sept. 17, 24; Feds. break up Conf. camp near, Nov. 14; sk., Dec. 19; (1862) sk., Sept. 4; (1863) sk., June 17; (1864) sk., July 5

Point of Rocks, Va.: (1862) eng., June 26

Point Washington, Fla.: (1864) sk., Feb. 9

Poison Cr., Id. Terr.: (1865) sk., Mar. 8

Poison Springs, Ark.: (1864) eng., Apr. 18

Poland: (1863) Russian suppression of revolt, Sept. 23, Dec. 19

Pole Cat Cr., Va.: (1864) comb., May 27

Political prisoners: *See* Disloyalty, Union arrests for

Polk, Leonidas (C): (1861) commands along Miss. R., Tenn., Ark., and Mo., Sept. 2; orders Ky. neutrality ended, Sept. 3; Sept. 4; superseded by A. S. Johnston, Sept. 15; assigned to Johnston's dept., Sept. 21; eng. Belmont, Mo., Nov. 7; wounded, Nov. 11; (1862) evacuates Columbus, Ky., Mar. 2; commands corps, Army of the Miss., Mar. 29; Bragg gives corps command to, Nov. 7; corps commander, Army of Tenn., Nov. 20; (1863) Chickamauga Camp., Sept. 13; Bat. of Chickamauga, Sept. 19, 20; controversy with Bragg, Oct. 3; relieved corps command, Oct. 23; commands Army of Miss., Dec. 16; (1864) opposes Sherman's Meridian Camp., Feb. 3, 7, 14; reinforcements, Feb. 17, 23; Davis to, Apr. 22; Atlanta Camp., May 9, 10, 13, 19, 25; death of at Pine Mt., Ga., June 14

Polk, Trusten (C): (1862) U. S. Sen. expels Mo. sen., Jan. 10

Polk Co., Mo.: (1862) Union sc., July 19; (1864) sks., Aug. 28, Sept. 28

Polk's Plantation, near Helena, Ark.: (1863) sk., May 25

Pollock's Mill Cr. (White Oak Run or Fitzhugh's Crossing), Va.: (1863) oper., Chancellorsville Camp., Apr. 29

Pollacksville, N.C.: (1862) sks., Apr. 27, May 15, 22; Fed. exped. to, July 24; sk., July 26; (1863) Fed. recon., Jan. 17

Pollard, James (C): (1864) foils Dahlgren's Richmond raid, Mar. 2

Pollard, Ala.: (1864) Fed. exped. to, Dec. 13; (1865) Fed. troops enter, Mar. 26

Pomeroy, Samuel C. (F): (1864) U.S. sen. Kas., and "Pomeroy Circular," Feb. 22

Pomeroy, O.: (1863) Morgan raid, July 18

"Pomeroy Circular": (1864) Feb. 22, 23

Pomme de Terre R., Mo.: (1861) sk., Oct. 12

Ponchartrain, Lake, La.: (1862) Fed. exped. to, July 25; (1863) Conf. sc. to, Sept. 13

Ponchatoula, La.: (1862) Fed. exped. from, July 5; Fed. exped. to, Sept. 13; (1863) Fed. exped. to, Mar. 21

Pond Cr., Pike Co., Ky.: (1864) sk., May 16

Pond Cr., Union Co., Ky.: (1863) July 6

Ponder's Mill, Little Black R., Mo.: (1864) sk., Sept. 20

Ponds, The, Miss.: *See* The Ponds, Miss.

Pond Springs, Ala.: (1864) sks., May 27, Dec. 29

Pon Pon R., S.C.: (1863) eng., July 10

Pontotoc, Miss.: (1863) sk., Apr. 19; Fed. exped. toward, June 17; (1864) sks., Feb. 17, July 11

Atlantic Blockading Squad., Oct. 12; commands Navy 1st Ft. Fisher exped., Dec. 23; bomb. Ft. Fisher, Dec. 24; failure of exped., Dec. 25; (1865) commands 2nd Ft. Fisher exped., Navy, Jan. 4; arrives Beaufort, N.C., Jan. 8; off Ft. Fisher, Jan. 12; attack on Ft. Fisher, Jan. 13, 14, 15; accord with Gen. Terry, Jan. 15; confers with Lincoln, Grant, Sherman, Mar. 27, 28; escorts Lincoln into Richmond, Apr. 4

Porter, Fitz John (F): (1862) Bat. of Mechanicsville, Va., June 26; Bat. of Gaines' Mill, June 27; disputed action at 2nd Bull Run, Aug. 29, 30; Pope charges against, Sept. 3; crosses Potomac, Sept. 19; replaced by Hooker, Nov. 5; charge of disobedience, 2nd Bull Run, Nov. 5; Hooker takes command Fifth Corps, Nov. 10; (1863) cashiered from Army, Jan. 10

Porterfield, George A. (C): (1861) at Philippi, June 3, 8

Porter's Plantation, Indian Bend, La.: (1863) sk., Apr. 13

Port Gibson, Miss.: (1863) Bat. of, May 1; Fed. move from, May 2; sk., Oct. 10; Dec. 26; (1864) Fed. exped. to, Sept. 29; (1865) Fed. exped. to, May 3

Port Hudson, La.: (1862) Confs. fortify, Aug. 5; eng. with Fed. ship, Aug. 29; U.S.S. *Essex* duel, Sept. 7; Davis on, Dec. 21, 31; (1863) Davis on, Jan. 28; Fed. move toward, Mar. 7; sk., Mar. 9; Farragut's fleet passes batteries, Mar. 14; Banks demon., Mar. 14; Davis on, Apr. 2, May 7; Banks en route, May 14; Feds. in position opposite, May 17; Feds. gather, May 20; siege of, May 21, 22, 23, 24, 25, 26; first ass. on, May 27; siege continues, June 1, 2, 3; Lincoln on, June 8; outposts capt., June 11; ass., June 14; siege continues, June 26, 28, July 1, 2, 3; unconditional surrender, July 8; ceremony, July 9; Davis on, July 10; sk., Nov. 30; (1864) sk., Apr. 7; att. on Pest House, May 28; Conf. att. near, Aug. 29; (1865) Fed. exped. from, Apr. 12

Port Isabel, Tex.: (1863) aff., May 30; (1865) restrictions on maintained, May 22

Portland, Me.: (1863) descent on, June 26

Portland, Mo.: (1862) sk., Oct. 16

Portland, W. Va.: (1863) sk., Apr. 26

Port Republic, Va.: (1862) Jackson at, June 8; Bat. of, June 9; Frémont withdraws, June 11; (1864) aff., June 4; sk., Sept. 26, 27, 28

Port Royal, S.C.: (1861) oper. ment., Oct. 1; Fed. exped. to planned, Oct. 12; exped. leaves, Oct. 29; storm, Nov. 1; citizens warned, Nov. 2; U.S. vessels assemble, Nov. 4; Fed. vessels battle Conf. flotilla, Nov. 5; Bat. of Port Royal Sound, Nov. 7; effect Fed. victory, Nov. 8; (1862) cotton auctioned, Jan. 10; commerce opened to, May 12; (1863) Fifty-fourth Mass. arrives, June 3; (1864) Sherman at, Dec. 22

Port Royal, Va.: (1862) Fed. exped. to, Aug. 15; eng. near, Dec. 4; (1863) Fed. exped. to, Apr. 22

Port Royal Fy., S.C.: (1861) Fed. exped. around, Dec. 6; (1862) eng., Jan. 1; sks., June 6, July 4

Port Royal Sound, S.C. (*See also* Port Royal): (1861) U.S. vessels prowl area, Nov. 4; Feds. battle Conf. flotilla, Nov. 5; Bat. of Port Royal Sound, Nov. 7; Nov. 10; confiscation of crops, Nov. 28; investigation of rivers, towns, Dec. 12

Portsmouth, N.H.: (1863) draft riot in, July 13

Portsmouth, Va.: (1862) under martial law; Fed. occup., May 10; (1863) Fed. exped. from, July 25, Aug. 11; (1864) Conf. demon., Mar. 4; Fed. recon. from, Apr. 13

Port Tobacco, Md.: (1865) J. W. Booth near, Apr. 17

Postage stamps, U.S.: (1862) authorized as money, July 17; issued for currency, Aug. 21

Postal money order system: (1864) U. S. Cong. passes act for, May 17

Post Oak Cr., Mo.: (1862) sk., Mar. 22; act., Mar. 26

Post Office Dept., U.S.: (1860) Postmaster General Joseph Holt opposes secession, Nov. 9; (1861) Horatio King appointed, Feb. 1; Lincoln names Montgomery Blair Postmaster General, Mar. 3; service with South ends, May 26; (1864) Blair asked to resign, Sept. 23; Dennison replaces, Sept. 24

Potomac, Army of the, Conf.: (1861) Beauregard takes command, June 2

Potomac, Army of the, Fed. (*See also* McDowell, Irvin; McClellan, George B.; Burnside, A. E.; Hooker, Joseph; Meade, George G.; Grant, Ulysses S.; camps. and bats. including Peninsula Camp.; Seven Days; 2nd Bull Run or Manassas; Antietam or Sharpsburg; Fredericksburg; Chancellorsville; Gettysburg; Mine Run; Wilderness; Spotsylvania; Cold Harbor; Petersburg; Appomattox Camp.): (1861) established, Aug. 17; McClellan assumes command, Aug. 20; plans of, Oct. 29; Cong. dissatisfied, Dec. 2; (1862) Gen. War Order No. 1, Jan. 27; President's Special War Order No. 1, Jan. 31; had not moved, Feb. 22; Lincoln on, Mar. 10; conference on plans, Mar. 13; McClellan reorganizes after 2nd Bull Run, Sept. 4; Army of Va. consolidated with, Sept. 5, 12; Burnside ordered to replace McClellan, Nov. 5; McClellan relieved, Nov. 7; impact of McClellan's dismissal, Nov. 8; Burnside assumes command, Nov. 9; McClellan leaves, Nov. 10; Burnside reorganizes into Grand Divisions, Nov. 14; (1863) Hooker replaces Burnside in command, Jan. 25, 26; Grand Divisions eliminated, Feb. 5; Meade named to replace Hooker, June 27; Meade assumes command before Gettysburg, June 28; pressure to reinstate McClellan, June 30; two corps sent west, Sept. 22, 24, Oct. 2; (1864) Grant visits, Meade still commands, Mar. 10; Grant announces hdqrs. to be with army, congressmen press for Meade's removal, Mar. 23; Grant establishes hdqrs. with, Mar. 26; Sheridan made cav. commander, Apr. 4; (1865) surrender of Lee, Apr. 9; parole of A.N.Va., Apr. 10; Grand Review, May 23

Potomac, Dept. of the, Fed.: (1861) formed, Aug. 17; *See* Potomac, Army of the

Potomac, Dist. of the, Conf.: (1861) Beauregard commands, Oct. 22; (1862) Beauregard leaves, Jan. 26

Potomac batteries, Conf.: (1861) control river, Oct. 22

Potomac Cr., Va.: (1861) steamers engage Conf. batteries, Aug. 23; (1862) Fed. exped. from, Dec. 30

Potomac Cr. Br., Va.: (1862) Fed. recon. from, Dec. 21

Potomac flotilla, Fed.: (1861) shell Conf. batteries Aquia Cr., May 31; duel with Conf. batteries, July 29

Potomac R.: (1861) Ft. Washington on, Jan. 5; Apr. 18; Feds. cross, May 24; May 31, June 21; Aug. 27, Sept. 30; Conf. schooner burned on at Dumfries Cr., Oct. 11; Oct. 20; Ball's Bluff, Oct. 21; Oct. 22, 28; balloon-boat, Nov. 11;

act. on Lower Potomac, Dec. 15; Conf. oper. along, Dec. 17, 19; (1862) Hancock, Md., bomb., Jan. 5; Jan. 7; Fed. canal boats, Feb. 8, 24; Feb. 28; Apr. 1; May 24; Banks on, crosses, May 26, 27; two steamers collide, Aug. 13; Lee toward, Sept. 3; Lee's army crosses, Sept. 4; A.N.Va. north of, Sept. 6; Sept. 9, 15; Lee withdraws to south, Sept. 18, 19; pursuit, Sept. 20; Oct. 4; Stuart's Chambersburg raid, Oct. 9, 10, 11, 12; A. of P. crosses, Oct. 26; sk. near Williamsport, Md., Oct. 29; sk. South Fork, Nov. 9; Lincoln at Belle Plain, Nov. 26; (1863) concern over Lee's moves north of, June 10; Fed. patrols, June 11; A.N.Va. crosses to north, June 24; high water, July 10; Lee to cross, July 12; Lee crosses to south, July 13, 14; (1864) Early plans to cross, July 4; Early crosses to north, July 5, 6; Early heads for, July 12, 13; Early retires south of, July 14; ment., July 15; Aug. 2; Aug. 21

Potomac Valley: (1861) Banks commands area, Oct. 20

Potosi, Mo.: (1861) Lyon aids unionists, May 15; Oct. 15

Pott's Hill, Sugar Cr., Ark.: (1862) act., Feb. 16

Pound Gap, Ky.: (1862) act., Mar. 16; (1864) sks., May 9, June 1

Powder Springs, Ga.: (1864) comb., June 20; sk., Oct. 2

Powder Springs Gap, Tenn.: (1863) sk., June 21; recon. to, Dec. 23

Powell, L. W. (F): (1864) withdraws nomination at Democratic convention, Aug. 30

Powell, Ft., Ala.: (1864) Fed. bomb. of, Feb. 16; evacuated, Aug. 6

Powell Co., Ky.: (1862) guerrilla camp att., Dec. 26

Powell R., Tenn.: (1862) aff., June 30

Powell Valley, Tenn.: (1863) sk., June 22

Powell's Big Ft. Valley, Va.: (1862) sk., July 1; Fed. recon., July 2

Powell's Br., Tenn.: (1864) sk., Feb. 22

Powell's R., Va.: (1863) sk., Dec. 13

Powhatan, Va.: (1865) sk., Jan. 25

Powhatan, Ft., Va.: (1863) Feds. capture, July 14; (1864) sk., May 21

Powhatan, U.S.S.: (1861) under sealed orders, Apr. 1; to Ft. Pickens, Apr. 5; re orders to Ft. Pickens, Apr. 6; arrives Ft. Pickens, Apr. 17; on blockade, Mobile, May 26

Powhatan Co., Va.: (1861) Dec. 26

Prairie D'Ane, Ark.: (1864) sks., Apr. 9, 10

Prairie Chapel, Mo.: (1862) sk., Sept. 4

Prairie Grove, Ark.: (1862) bat., Dec. 7; (1864) sk., Apr. 6

Prairie du Rocher, Ill.: (1864) aff., Apr. 6

Pratt, Camp, La.: (1863) sk., Nov. 20; aff., Nov. 25

Pratt's Ldg., Va.: (1863) Fed. exped. from, Feb. 12

"Prayer of Twenty Millions": (1862) printed by N. Y. *Tribune,* Aug. 19

Prentiss, Benjamin Mayberry (F): (1862) holds Hornets' Nest, Shiloh, Apr. 6

Prentiss, Miss.: (1862) sk., Sept. 19

Presidential election, Conf.: (1861) Davis chosen Provisional Pres., Feb. 9; elected regular Pres., Nov. 6

Presidential election, U.S.: (1860) Lincoln, Hamlin win, Nov. 6; (1861) electoral vote, Feb. 4; official count, Feb. 13; (1863) Lincoln fears violence at, Nov. 2; (1864) Republican party split, May 31; Frémont nominated, May 31; Lincoln nominated, June 8; Lincoln on, July 25; Lincoln has Cabinet sign pledge, Aug. 23; McClellan nominated by Democrats, Aug. 31; Frémont withdraws, Sept. 17; Lincoln urges soldiers return to vote, Sept. 19; Lincoln concerned over, Oct. 13; soldier vote, Oct. 13; attention on, Nov. 6; Lincoln reelected, Nov. 8; assessment of results, Nov. 9

President's General War Order No. 1: (1862) by Lincoln, Jan. 27

President's Special War Order No. 1: (1862) orders McClellan to take offensive, Jan. 31

Preston, William (C): (1864) envoy to Mexico, Jan. 7

Preston, Mo.: (1864) aff., June 16

Prestonburg, Ky.: (1861) occup. by Feds., Nov. 5; (1862) eng., Jan. 10; Confs. capture supply boats, Dec. 4

Price, Sterling "Pap" (C): (1861) signs proclamation with Feds., May 21; refuses to disband troops, May 24; Planters' House meeting, June 11; near Wilson's Cr., Aug. 9; Bat. of Wilson's Cr. or Springfield, Aug. 10; invasion by feared, Aug. 15; proclaims Northern defeat, Aug. 20; siege of Lexington, Mo., begins, Sept. 12; siege of Lexington, Sept. 16, 19; surrender of Lexington, Sept. 20; withdraws from Lexington, Oct. 7, 25; Oct. 27; Nov. 2; prisoner exchange, Nov. 1, 7; Davis to, Dec. 20; (1862) Mar. 5; at Pea Ridge or Elkhorn Tavern, Ark., Mar. 7, 8; assumes command Army of the West, July 3; assumes command Dist. of the Tenn., July 21; occupies Iuka, Miss., Sept. 14; Bat. of Iuka, Sept. 19; Bat. of Corinth, Miss., Oct. 3, 4; commands corps, Dec. 7; (1863) ordered to Trans-Miss., Feb. 27; evac. Little Rock, Ark., Sept. 10; (1864) assumes command Dist. of Ark., Mar. 16; eng. Poison Springs, Ark., Apr. 18; commands exped. to recover Mo., Aug. 29; camp. to Mo., Sept. 19, 20, 22, 23, 24, 25, 26, 27, 28, 29, Oct. 1, 2, 3, 4, 5, 7, 8, 9, 11, 14, 15, 16, 17; act. at Lexington, Oct. 19; exped. continues, Oct. 20, 21, 22; Bat. of Westport, Mo., Oct. 23; retreats, Oct. 23, 24; eng. Marais des Cygnes, Mine Cr., Oct. 25; retreat continues, Oct. 26; eng. Newtonia, Mo., Oct. 28; sk., Oct. 29; Nov. 1; sk., Cane Hill, Ark., Nov. 6; command at Laynesport, Ark., Dec. 25

Price's Ldg., Mo.: (1861) Fed. exped. to, Aug. 7; seizure of Fed. steamer, Nov. 18

Prim's Blacksmith Shop, Edmondson Pike, Tenn.: (1862) sk., Dec. 25

Prince George Court House, Va.: (1864) sk., Nov. 24

Princess Anne Court House, Va.: (1863) Fed. oper., Sept. 21

Princeton, Ark.: (1863) Fed. recon. to, Dec. 5; (1864) sk., Apr. 28; Price's exped. to Mo., Aug. 29; Fed. recon. to, Oct. 19

Princeton, W. Va.: (1861) sk., Sept. 16; (1862) sk., May 5, 11, 15; (1864) sk., May 6

Prince William Co., Va.: (1863) sk., Mar. 4; (1865) Fed. sc., Feb. 18

Prisoner exchange: (1862) cartel signed, July 31; (1864) Grant refuses exchange, Apr. 17, Aug. 18; (1865) Grant agrees to, Jan. 24

Prisoners, Conf. (in U.S. hands): (1861) Frémont-Price agreement on, Nov. 1, 7; (1862) crews of privateers to be prisoners, Feb. 3; (1863) Lincoln orders on, July 30; Lincoln visits camps of, Dec. 27; (1864) statistics on, Apr. 16; Grant refuses exchange of, Aug. 18; (1865) Grant agrees to exchange, Jan. 24; Johnson orders release of, May 27

Prisoners, U.S. (in Conf. hands): (1861) Frémont-Price agreement, Nov. 1,

7; (1862) 2000 Fed. prisoners released, Feb. 19; capt. officers as felons, July 31; (1864) Fed. raid to Richmond to free, Feb. 6; Kilpatrick-Dahlgren raid to Richmond, Feb. 28; Negro prisoners in Richmond, Mar. 7; Grant restricts exchange, Apr. 17; Davis on Negro prisoners, Apr. 22; Grant refuses exchange of, Aug. 18; (1865) Henry Wirz hanged for Andersonville cruelties, Nov. 10

Pritchard's Mill, Va.: (1861) sk., Sept. 15

Privateers, Conf.: (1861) Apr. 17, May 6; active, July 31; burned, Oct. 5; Oct. 12; (1862) crews as prisoners, Feb. 3; (1863) *J. P. Chapman* seized, Mar. 15

Prize Courts: (1863) May 18

Prophet Br., Miss.: (1862) sk., Dec. 3

Protestant Episcopal Church in the U.S.: (1861) Ala. diocese withdraws, May 10

Pro-Union sentiment: (1860) Judge J. L. Petigru, Dec. 20; (1861) Mar. 1; meetings in England, Oct. 29; (1862) in N.C., Mar. 14; in east Tenn., Apr. 8; Nashville, May 12; Cumberland Gap, June 18; Ala., July 12; east Tenn., Oct. 23; Ky. delegation to Lincoln, Nov. 21; Dec. 18; (1863) in Southern cities, Feb. 23; death of Judge Petigru, Mar. 9; in Wash., N.C., Aug. 11; Ark., Oct. 30; Little Rock, Nov. 12; (1864) Ark., Jan. 19; Tenn., Jan. 21; Knoxville meeting, Apr. 15; Ala., Apr. 19

Providence, Lake, La.: *See* Lake Providence

Providence Church, Va.: (1862) sks., Nov. 12, Dec. 28

Providence Church Rd., Va.: (1863) sk., Apr. 12

Provincetown, Mass.: (1862) Mason and Slidell sail, Jan. 1

Provost marshal general, U.S.: (1862) Sec. of War creates office, Sept. 24

Pryor's Cr., I.T.: (1864) act., Sept. 19

Public Domain: (1862) Lincoln signs Homestead Act, May 20

Pueblo Colorado, N. Mex. Terr.: (1863) sk., Aug. 18; oper. against, Aug. 20

Puget Sound, Wash.: (1864) telegraph, r.r. lines land granted, July 2

Pulaski, Tenn.: (1862) sk., May 1, 4, 11, Aug. 27; (1863) sk., July 15; sc. toward, Oct. 27; Fed. sc. from, Dec. 1, Dec. 11; aff., Dec. 15; (1864) sks., May 13, Sept. 26, 27; Fourth Fed. Corps heads for, Oct. 30; Fourth Corps at, Nov. 3; Twenty-fourth Corps reinforces, Nov. 9; Schofield at, Nov. 14; Schofield moves north from, Nov. 22, 23, 24; Conf. march toward, Dec. 21; (1865) Fed. sc. from, Apr. 23; Fed. exped. from, May 5

Pulaski, Ft., Ga.: (1861) seized by Ga. troops, Jan. 3; Fed. threat, Nov. 24; Nov. 26; (1862) bomb. of by Fed., Apr. 10; fall of, Apr. 11; freeing slaves around, Apr. 12; Conf. steamer capt. near, Aug. 10; (1863) Fed. exped. from, June 4; July 18

Pumpkin Vine Cr., Ga.: (1864) New Hope Church Camp., May 25

Pungo Ldg., N.C.: (1863) aff., Oct. 16

Purcellville, Va.: (1864) Conf. wagon train capt., July 16

Purdy, Tenn.: (1862) Fed. probe toward, Mar. 9; occup. by Feds., Apr. 29; sk., May 7

Purdy Rd., Tenn.: (1862) sk., Mar. 31; Fed. recon., Apr. 13

Purgitsville, W. Va.: (1863) sk., Apr. 6

Putnam, Mo.: (1862) sk., Sept. 1

Putnam Co., Tenn.: (1864) Fed. sc., Feb. 1
Pyramid Lake, Nev.: (1865) Fed. exped. to, Mar. 12

Quaker City, U.S.S.: (1863) captures blockade-runner, Jan. 4
Quaker guns: *See* Wooden guns
"Quaker" (fake) ironclads: (1863) Feb. 26, Mar. 9
Quaker Rd., Va.: (1865) sk., Mar. 29
Quakers: *See* Friends, Society of
Quallatown, N.C.: (1864) Fed. exped. to, Jan. 31
Quantrill, William Clarke (C): (1863) nears Lawrence, Kas., Aug. 20; sack of Lawrence, Aug. 21; withdraws, Aug. 22; (1865) mortally wounded, May 10; death, June 6
Quapaw Indians: (1865) treaty with U.S., Sept. 14
Queen City, U.S.S.: (1864) destroyed, June 24
Queen's Hill, Miss.: (1863) sk., July 7
Queen of the West, U.S.S.: (1862) Bat. of Memphis, June 6; att. on, Sept. 19; (1863) runs Vicksburg, Feb. 2; captures vessels, Feb. 3; oper. on Miss. R., Feb. 10; destroys wagons, Feb. 12; abandoned to Confs., Feb 14; as Conf. vessel attacks *Indianola*, Feb. 24; and fake ironclad, Feb. 26; destroyed, Apr. 14
Quiberon Bay, France: (1865) *Sphinx* sails to, Jan. 7
Quicksand Cr., Ky.: (1864) sk., Apr. 5
Quincy, Mo.: (1863) aff., Sept. 4
Quinn and Jackson's Mill, Miss.: (1863) sks., Oct. 12, Nov. 1, 3
Quinn's Mills, Coldwater R., Miss.: (1863) sk., June 16
Quitman, Ark.: (1864) sks., Mar. 26, Sept. 2
Quitman, Ft., La.: (1862) surrenders, Apr. 27
Quitman, Ft., Tex.: (1861) Fed. surrender, Apr. 5

Raccoon Bottom, Ga.: (1864) sk., June 2
Raccoon Cr., Ga.: (1864) sk., June 6
Raccoon Fd., Ala.: (1864) sk., Oct. 30
Raccoon Fd., Va.: (1862) Fed. recon. to, July 28; sk., Aug. 20; (1863) sks., Apr. 30, Sept. 14, 17, 19, 22, Oct. 10, Nov. 26, 30, Dec. 5
Raccourci, La.: (1864) aff., Nov. 25
Radical Republican Convention: (1864) nominates Frémont, May 31; favors confiscation, June 8
Radical Republicans: (1860) Committee of Thirteen, Dec. 20; (1862) request McClellan's removal, Jan. 6; support Confiscation Act, July 17; (1864) oppose Lincoln, Feb. 22; Cleveland Convention nominates Frémont, May 31; and National Union Convention, June 7; back Chase for Pres., June 30; Wade-Davis bill, July 4; Wade-Davis Manifesto, Aug. 5; Aug. 30; Lincoln seeks support, Sept. 22; influence re Blair's ouster, Sept. 23; Bates's opposition, Nov. 24; (1865) favor Thirteenth Amendment, Jan. 6; on states' return to U.S., Jan. 31; treating South as conquered territory, Apr. 16; opinion on secession, Apr. 21
Ragland Mills, Bath Co., Ky.: (1864) sk., Jan. 13

Raiders, Conf. (*See also* individual ships): (1863) estimate of vessels taken, July 22; (1865) Johnson orders arrest of crews, May 10

Raiford's Plantation, near Byhalia, Miss.: (1864) aff., Feb. 11

Railroad redoubt at Vicksburg: (1863) May 22

Railroads, Conf. (*See also* various military camps.): (1861) Oct. 10; (1862) guerrilla att., Aug. 8; (1863) condition, Sept. 9; raid on, Dec. 10, 11, 12, 13, 16, 19, 25; (1864) disruption of, Feb. 18; raids, May 11

Railroads, U.S.: (1861) protection of, July 13; martial law on in Mo., Dec. 26; (1862) Lincoln gets power of seizure, Jan. 31; Administration takes possession, May 25; trans-continental line bill approved, July 1; (1863) reinforcements for Rosecrans, Sept. 23, Oct. 1, 2

Rainbow Bluffs, N.C.: (1864) Feds. clear torpedoes, Dec. 20

Raleigh, N.C.: (1860) secession crisis, Dec. 18; (1861) volunteers, May 5; (1863) pro-Union paper pillaged, Sept. 10; (1865) Sherman heads for, Apr. 10; Feds. near, Apr. 12; act., Apr. 12; sk., Apr. 13; Feds. occupy, Apr. 13

Raleigh, N.C., *Standard:* (1863) office pillaged, Sept. 10

Raleigh, Tenn.: (1863) Fed. exped. to, July 23; (1864) sks., Apr. 3, 9

Raleigh, W. Va.: (1861) sk., Nov. 14

Raleigh, C.S.S.: (1864) destruction of, May 7

Raleigh Court House (or Beckley), W. Va.: (1861) Feds. take, Dec. 28

Ralls Co., Mo.: (1862) Fed. sc., Sept. 15; (1864) oper., Sept. 11

Ramer's Crossing, Miss.: (1862) sk., Oct. 2

Ram fleet, Fed.: (1862) under Navy, Nov. 7; (1863) at Vicksburg, Mar. 25

Rams (*See also* Ram fleet): (1863) "Laird Rams," Sept. 5

Ramseur, Stephen Dodson (C): (1864) eng., Stephenson's Depot, July 20; 2nd Kernstown, July 24; 3rd Winchester, Sept. 19; mortally wounded, Oct. 19

Rancho Las Rinas, Tex.: (1864) sk., June 25

Randolph, George Wythe (C): (1862) appointed Conf. Sec. of War, Mar. 18; Davis accepts resignation, Nov. 15; Nov. 17

Randolph, Ala.: (1865) sk., Apr. 1

Randolph, Tenn.: (1862) burning of, Sept. 23

Randolph, Ft., Tenn.: (1862) Fed. exped. to, Sept. 28; (1864) guerrilla att., Oct. 27

Randolph Co., Mo.: (1864) oper., July 23, Sept. 15

Randolph Co., W. Va.: (1865) Fed. sc., Apr. 15

Rankin's Fy., Tenn.: (1862) sk., June 21

Ransom, Robert, Jr. (C): (1864) command Dept. of Richmond, Va., Apr. 25; ordered to protect Richmond, June 1; command Dept. of Western Va., June 13

Rapidan Line: (1863) Longstreet's corps detached, Sept. 9

Rapidan R., Va.: (1862) r.r. br. destroyed by Feds., July 13; Aug. 9; Jackson withdraws from, Aug. 11; (1863) Union position, May 3; A. of P. to, Sept. 13, 14, 15; sk., Sept. 17; Fed. recon., Sept. 21; sk., Sept. 23; Bristoe Camp., Oct. 9, 10, 11; Lee withdraws toward, Nov. 7; Mine Run Camp., Nov. 26, 27, 30, Dec. 1, 2; (1864) Feb. 28, 29; A. of P. crosses, May 3, 4; June 3; Grant's move from, summary, June 18

appointed Sec. of Treasury, Apr. 27; capt. by Feds., May 10; paroled, Oct. 11

Reams' Station, Va.: (1864) sk., June 22; act., Aug. 23; sk., Aug. 24; bat., Aug. 25

Rear admiral: (1862) U.S. grade created, July 16

Recognition of Confederacy: (1861) argued in Britain, Mar. 12; Lincoln eschews acknowledgment, Mar. 13; Britain recognizes as belligerent, May 6, 13, 28, June 1; Spain recognizes as belligerent, June 17; Brazil recognizes as belligerent, Aug. 1; attempts to obtain, Aug. 24; cotton, Oct. 3; London *Post* on, Oct. 5; Mason and Slidell sail, Oct. 12; hopes of raised, Dec. 17; *Trent* Aff. ends, Dec. 26; (1862) meeting England advocates, Aug. 7; Gladstone statement, Oct. 7; (1863) Davis on, Jan. 12; Mason strives for, Feb. 11

Reconstruction (*See also* Restored State Governments): (1862) Confiscation Act, July 17; (1863) Lincoln's Proclamation of Amnesty and Reconstruction, Dec. 8; Lincoln on, Dec. 24; (1864) Lincoln on La., Fla. govt., Jan. 13; Lincoln on, Jan. 15; Ark. ratifies constitution, Jan. 19; elections ordered in Ark., Jan. 20; La. election, Feb. 22; Johnson mil. gov. of Tenn., Mar. 4; Lincoln on, Mar. 15; Ark., Mar. 18; Wade-Davis bill, May 4, July 4, 8; tensions in Cong., July 4; Wade-Davis Manifesto, Aug. 5; (1865) at Hampton Rds. Conference, Feb. 3; Lincoln on, Mar. 28; re Va. legislature, Apr. 5, 6; Lincoln on La., Apr. 11; misunderstanding re Va. legislature, Apr. 12; Johnston-Sherman memo, Apr. 17, 18; Johnson denies states left Union, Apr. 21; pro-Union govt. Va., May 23; Johnson's amnesty proclamation, May 29

Recruiting: *See* Mobilization, Conscription

Rector, Henry M. (C): (1861) orders U. S. Arsenal Little Rock taken, Feb. 8; refuses Lincoln's call for troops, Apr. 22

Rector's Farm, Ark.: (1864) sk., Dec. 19

Rectortown, Va.: (1862) McClellan relieved command at, Nov 7; (1864) sk., Oct. 10

Red Bank Cr., S.C.: (1865) sk., Feb. 15

Red Bird Cr., Ky.: (1862) sk., Aug. 25

Red Bone, Miss.: (1864) sk., Apr. 21

Red Chief, C.S.S.: (1863) capt., May 25

Red Clay, Ga.: (1864) sk., May 3

Red House, W. Va.: (1861) act., July 13

Red Mount, Ark.: (1864) sk., Apr 17

Red Mt., Calif.: (1864) sk., Mar. 17

Red Oak, Ga. (or Red Oak Station): (1864) comb., Aug. 19; Thomas reaches, Aug. 28; act., Aug. 28; sk., Aug. 29

Red R. (*See also* Red R. Camp.): (1863) Feb. 2; *Queen of the West* oper., Feb. 10, 12, 14; *Indianola,* Feb. 17; Ft. De Russy, May 4, 5; Alexandria occupied, May 6; steamers burned, Oct. 7; Fed. exped., Oct. 14; (1864) recon. on, Feb 29; destruction *Eastport,* Apr. 15; Fed. gunboats trapped, Apr. 26; (1865) Conf. surrender, June 3

Red R. Camp. (*See also* Banks, Nathaniel P.; Camden exped.; Steele, Frederick): (1864) Mar. 10, 11, 12 (under way), 14 (Ft. De Russy), 15 (at Alexandria), 16 (Alexandria occupied), 21, 23 (Steele's Camden exped.), 28, 29 (Monett's

Rheatown, Tenn.: (1863) sks., Sept. 12, Oct. 11; (1864) sks., Apr. 16, Sept. 28

Rhett, Robert Barnwell (C): (1861) considered for Conf. Pres., Feb. 9

Rhoda H. Shannon (schooner): (1861) fired on, Morris I., Apr. 3

Rhode Island: (1865) ratifies Thirteenth Amendment, Feb. 2

Rhode Island, U.S.S.: (1862) foundering of *Monitor*, Dec. 30-31

Rice Station, Va.: (1865) Longstreet at, Apr. 6

Richards' Fd., Va.: (1862) Fed. exped. to, Dec. 30; (1863) sk., Sept. 26

Rice, Ft., Dak. Terr.: (1864) Fed. exped. to, Sept. 11

Rice fields: (1864) near Savannah, Dec. 10

Richardson, Israel Bush (F): (1861) eng. Blackburn's Fd., July 18

Richfield, Mo.: (1863) sk., May 19

Rich Hill, Md.: (1865) Booth reaches, Apr. 16

Richland, Ark.: (1864) sks., Apr. 11, Sept. 6; sc. to, Dec. 24

Richland Cr., Ark.: (1864) sks., Apr. 13, May 3, Sept. 26

Richland Cr., Tenn.: (1862) sks., Aug. 27, Oct. 23; (1864) act., Dec. 24; sk., Dec. 25

Richland Station, Tenn.: (1863) sk., Mar. 19

Richmond, Ky.: (1862) bat., Aug. 29, 30; (1863) act., July 28

Richmond, La.: (1863) sks., Jan. 29, Apr. 4, June 6; act., June 15

Richmond, Mo.: (1864) sk., July 8; "Bloody Bill" Anderson, Sept. 27

Richmond, Va.: (1861) U.S. property seized, Apr. 18; C.S.A. Cong. votes to move capital to, May 20, 21; Davis arrives, May 29; Cong. convenes, Nov. 18; (1862) ex-Pres. Tyler dies in, Jan. 18; discouraged, Jan. 21; Davis inaugurated, Feb. 22; Feb. 25; martial law, Mar. 1; Mar. 8; threatened, Mar. 9; Mar. 10; McClellan plan to reach, Mar. 13; Mar. 15; church bell makes cannon, Apr. 1; Fed. drive toward, Apr. 4, Apr. 21, May 3, 7, 9; Davis on threat, May 13; Fed. threat, May 14, 15, 16; McDowell orders march on, May 17; McClellan in front of, May 17; Davis on threat, May 19; Feds. near city, May 21, 23, 24, 25, 26; Lincoln on, May 26; fighting near, May 27; May 28; Bat. of Seven Pines or Fair Oaks, May 31, June 1; armies rest near, June 2, 4; June 7; Fed. recon., June 7; McDowell toward, June 8; and Jackson, June 11; Stuart's ride from, June 12, 13, 14, 15; Lincoln on, June 15; sk. near, June 18; Lincoln to McClellan on, June 18, sk. near, June 19; stalemate on Peninsula, June 22; Lee confers near, June 23; June 24; Seven Days' Camp., June 25-July 1; Feds. retreat from, July 3; part of Lee's army leaves, July 13; news of McClellan reaches, Aug. 9; Cong. convenes, Aug. 18; relieved, Aug. 30; re Negroes to work on forts, Oct. 10; Burnside plans drive to, Nov. 14; (1863) high prices, shortages, Jan. 2; Wash. civilians sent to, Jan. 7; Cong. convenes, Jan. 12; threat to, Feb. 6; moves to protect, Feb. 18; explosion, Mar. 13; bread riot, Apr. 2; Lincoln on, Apr. 6; Apr. 12; May 1; June 10; July 1; Sept. 9; Longstreet in, Sept. 10; in Mine Run Camp., Nov. 26; Belle Boyd sent to, Dec. 1; (1864) reception for John Hunt Morgan, Jan. 8; fire, Jan. 25; Fed. attempt to free prisoners, Feb. 6, 7, 9; buyer's panic, Feb. 23; Kilpatrick raid, Feb. 28-Mar. 1; Negro prisoners arrive, Mar. 7; snowfall, Mar. 22; Butler to move against, Apr. 9, May 4; Cong. convenes, May 2; Bat. of Wilderness, May 5-6; *See* Bat. of Spotsylvania; Bat. of Yellow Tavern, May 11; Butler threat, May 12, 16; Sheridan near, May 13; threat, May 17; holds out, May 31; Cold

Harbor, June 3; final camp. for under way, June 13; June 14; *See* Petersburg, Va.; demons. north of James, Aug. 13; Weldon R.R. lost, Aug. 21; Petersburg-Richmond Camp., Sept. 29, 31; Fed. troops near, Oct. 7; siege of, Oct. 27; Early detached to, Nov. 13, Dec. 19; (1865) A.N.Va. pinned at, Jan. 1; siege continues, Jan. 17; act. near, Jan. 23; *See also* Grant and Lee; Appomattox Camp., Mar. 29, 30, 31, Apr. 1; evacuated by Confs., Apr. 2; occupied by Feds., Apr. 3; Lincoln in, Apr. 4, 5; Fed. exped. from, May 6; "loyal" Va. govt. established, May 23

Richmond, Va., *Dispatch:* (1861) "Yankee books," Nov. 20; (1863) on criticism of govt., Dec. 18

Richmond, Va., *Enquirer:* (1863) on Eman. Proc., Jan. 7; (1864) favors Negro enlistments, Oct. 6

Richmond, Va., *Examiner:* (1861) "need a dictator," May 8; (1862) "necessity of exertion," Feb. 4; (1863) diplomacy of battlefield, Nov. 24; on 1863 action, Dec. 31; (1864) on contest in Va., Apr. 15

Richmond, Va., *Whig:* (1862) on Eman. Proc., Oct. 1

Richmond, Dept. of, C.S.A.: (1863) A. Elzey commands, Apr. 1; (1864) Robert Ransom commands, Apr. 25; Ewell commands, June 13

Richmond, U.S.S.: (1861) *Manassas* rams, Oct. 12; bombards Pensacola, Nov. 22, 23; (1863) damaged at Port Hudson, Mar. 14

Richmond Co., Va.: (1863) oper., Feb. 10

Richmond and Danville R.R.: (1864) Kautz raid against, May 12

Richmond and Fredericksburg R.R.: (1863) sk. at South Anna Br., July 4

Richmond-Petersburg front: *See* Petersburg and Grant, U. S.

Richmond and Petersburg R.R.: (1864) Butler attempts advance on, May 6; Feds. seize, May 7

Richmond and York R. R.R.: (1862) sk. at Dispatch Station, June 28; bat. at Savage's Station, June 29

Rich Mt., W. Va.: (1861) sk., July 10; eng., July 11; July 12, 14

Richwoods, Mo.: (1864) sk., Oct 4

Riddell's Shop, Va.: (1864) sk., June 13

Riddle's Point, Mo.: (1862) sk., Mar. 17

Ridgeley, Mo.: (1864) sk., June 11; Price captures, Oct. 16

Ridgely, Daniel Bowly (F): (1861) seizes Conf. agent, Dec. 7

Ridgely, Ft., Minn.: *See* Fort Ridgely

Rienzi, Miss.: (1862) aff., June 2; Fed. exped. from, July 27, Aug. 19; sks., Aug. 6, Sept. 9, 19; Fed. recon. from, Sept. 30; sk., Aug 8

Righter, W. Va.: (1861) sk., June 23

Riley, Ft., Kas.: (1865) Fed. oper., Feb. 12

Riley, Ft., Tenn.: (1862) sk., Oct. 5

Rinaldo, H.B.M.S.: (1862) takes Conf. commissioners to Europe, Jan. 1

Ringgold, Ga.: (1863) sk., Sept. 11; Bragg moves from, Sept. 18; pursuit of Bragg, Nov. 26; Fed. recon. to, Dec. 5; sk., Dec. 13; (1864) sk., Feb. 18; Fed. sc. from, Apr. 24; att., Apr. 27; Fed. recon. from, Apr. 29; Army of the Cumberland at, May 4; (1865) sk., Mar. 20

Ringgold Barracks, Tex.: (1861) abandoned by Fed. forces, Mar. 7

Ringgold Gap, Ga.: (1863) eng., Nov. 27; (1864) sk., May 2

Rio de las Animas, N. Mex. Terr.: (1863) sk. with Inds., July 19

Rio Grande: (1861) July 25; Sibley commands Confs. on, Dec. 14; (1862) Sibley moves toward Ft. Craig, Feb. 21; Mar. 2; Sibley retreats on, Mar. 28, Apr. 8; (1863) blockade-runners capt. off, Nov. 5; (1864) F. J. Herron commands Feds. on, Jan. 3; (1865) oper. on, May 29

Rio Grande exped. (*See also* Nathaniel P. Banks): (1863) Oct. 27, Nov. 2, 6, 16, 22, 23

Rio Hondo, N. Mex. Terr.: (1863) sk., July 18

Riots (*See also* Draft riots): (1861) Baltimore, Md., Apr. 19–20; Knoxville, Tenn., May 7; (1863) Richmond, Va., Apr. 2; Mobile, Ala., Sept. 4

Ripley, Roswell Sabine (C): (1861) commands Dept. of S.C., Aug. 21

Ripley, Miss.: (1862) Fed. exped. to, July 27; Army of West Tenn. from, Sept. 29; sk., Oct. 7; Fed. exped. to, Nov. 19; sk., Dec. 25; (1863) Fed. sc. to, Jan. 25, 28; sk., Apr. 18; Fed. exped. to, June 8, 12; sks., July 7, Aug. 3, Dec. 1; aff., Dec. 4; (1864) Fed. sc. to, Jan 23; Fed. exped. to, Apr. 30; Feds. head for, June 1; sk., June 7; act., June 11; sk., July 7

Ripley, Tenn.: (1863) sk., Jan. 8

Rising Sun, Tenn.: (1862) sk., June 30

River Defense Fleet, Conf.: (1862) Bat. of Plum Run Bend, May 10

River gunboats: *See* Gunboats, river

River Queen (Fed. steamer): (1865) Lincoln, Seward meet on, Feb. 2; at Hampton Rds. Conference, Feb. 3; Lincoln, Grant confer on, Mar. 27, 28; Lincoln goes to Richmond on, Apr. 4

Rivers' Br., Salkehatchie R., S.C.: (1865) sks., Feb. 2, 3

Rixey's Fd., Va.: (1863) sk., Sept. 2

Rixeyville, Va.: (1863) sk., Nov. 8

Roane Co., W. Va.: (1861) sk., Dec. 15; (1863) sk., Sept. 12

Roanoke, Mo.: (1862) sk., Sept. 6

Roanoke, U.S.S.: (1862) Fed. frigate opposes *Merrimack*, Mar. 8

Roanoke I., N.C.: (1862) Fed. exped. to begins, Jan. 11; Wise commands Confs., Jan. 22; Fed. exped. lands, Feb. 7; bat., Feb. 8; Fed. operations, Feb. 9, 12; Fed. exped. from, Mar. 12; Mar. 14; May 7

Roanoke I., N.C., Bat. of: (1862) Feb. 8; cleanup oper., Feb. 9

Roanoke R., N.C.: (1864) C.S.S *Albemarle* on, May 4; *Albemarle* engages Fed. fleet on, May 5; Feds. capture *Plymouth* on, Oct. 31

Roanoke Station, Va.: (1864) sk., June 25

Roan's Tan-Yard, Mo.: (1862) act., Jan. 8

Roaring Spring, Ky.: (1864) sk., Aug. 22

Robert McClelland: (1861) U.S. revenue cutter surrenders, Jan. 29

Roberts' Fd., La.: (1863) sk., May 2

Robertson's Fd., Va.: (1863) sk., Sept. 14, 23

Robertson's R., Va.: (1863) sks., Oct. 8, 10

Robertson's Tavern, Va.: (1863) sk., Nov. 27

Robertsville, S.C.: (1865) sk., Jan. 29

Robinette, Battery, at Corinth, Miss.: (1862) Bat. of Corinth, Oct. 4

Robinson, Charles (F): (1861) as gov. Kas., calls militia, June 20

Robinson's Mills, near Livingston, Miss.: (1863) sk., Oct. 17

Robledo, Camp, N. Mex. Terr.: (1861) oper., Sept. 20

Rocheport, Mo.: (1863) sks., June 1, 18; (1864) Aug. 28; sk., Sept. 3; (1865) sk., May 24

Rochester, N.Y.: (1861) abolitionist meeting broken up, Jan. 12; (1865) Lincoln funeral train at, Apr. 27

Rockcastle Hills (or Camp Wildcat), Ky.: (1861) sk., Oct. 18; act., Oct. 21

Rock Cr., Miss.: (1863) sk., June 23

Rock Cr. Fd., Tenn.: (1863) sk., July 2

Rock Cut, near Tuscumbia, Ala.: (1863) act., Apr. 22

Rockfish Gap, Va.: (1864) sk., Sept. 28

Rock Fd., Miss.: (1863) sc. to, Jan. 7

Rockford, Tenn.: (1863) sk., Nov. 14

Rock Gap, W. Va.: (1863) eng. at, Aug. 26

Rock Hill, Ky.: (1862) sk., Oct. 17

Rock House Cr., W. Va.: (1864) Fed. exped. to, May 9

Rockingham, N.C.: (1865) sk., Mar. 7

"Rock of Chickamauga" *See* Thomas, George H.: (1863) earns sobriquet, Sept. 20

Rock I. Fy., Tenn.: (1863) Fed. recon. to, Aug. 4

Rockport, Ark.: (1863) Confs. withdraw to, Sept. 10; (1864) sk., Mar. 25

Rock Spring, Tenn.: (1862) sk., Dec. 30

Rockville, Md.: (1862) McClellan at, Sept. 8; (1863) sk., June 28, Sept. 22; (1864) sk., July 10; aff., July 13

Rockville, O.: (1863) sk., Morgan's raid, July 23

Rockville, S.C.: (1861) evacuated by Confs., Dec. 17

Rockville exped.: (1861) begins, June 10

Rocky Bluff, Platte Co., Mo.: (1862) sk., Aug. 7

Rocky Cr. Br., Ga.: (1865) sk., Apr. 20

Rocky Cr. Church, Ga.: (1864) sk., Dec. 25

Rocky Face Gap, Ga.: *See* Rocky Face Ridge, Ga.

Rocky Face Ridge, Ga.: (1864) Fed. move to, Feb. 22; sk., Feb. 24; Fed. demon. against, May 7, 8, 9

Rocky Gap, Ky.: (1863) aff., June 9

Rocky Hock Cr., N.C.: (1863) sk., Mar. 24

Rocky Mount, N.C.: (1863) Fed. exped. to, July 18, 21

Rocky Mount, S.C.: (1865) U. S. Twentieth Corps reaches, Feb. 22; sk., Feb. 28

Rocky Point, Tampa Bay, Fla.: (1864) Fed. naval exped., Dec. 3

Rocky Run, N.C.: (1863) sc. from, June 17; sk., Nov. 4; Fed. sc. from, Dec. 21

Rodes, Robert Emmett (C): (1863) captures Martinsburg, W. Va., June 14; moves to Chambersburg, Pa., June 15; (1864) mortally wounded, Sept. 19

Rodgers, John (F): (1861) Western river naval command, May 16; replaced by Foote, Aug. 26

Rodgers Plantation, Ark.: (1865) Fed. sc. to, Apr. 25

Rodney, Miss.: (1865) Fed. exped. from, May 3

Rodolph, U.S.S.: (1865) tinclad sunk, Apr. 1

Rodman's Point, N.C.: (1863) sk., Mar. 30; eng., Apr. 1, 4; aff., Apr. 16

Rodney, Miss.: (1863) crew of Fed. *Rattler* seized, Sept. 13; sks., Dec. 17, 24; (1864) sk., Mar. 4

Roebuck Lake, Miss.: (1863) exped. to, Nov. 18

Rogers' Gap, Tenn.: (1862) sks., June 10, Aug. 31; oper., Sept. 10

Rogersville, Ala.: (1862) Feds. occupy, May 13; (1865) Fed. sc. to, Apr. 23

Rogersville, Ky.: (1863) sk., July 27

Rogersville, Tenn.: (1863) act., Nov. 6; (1864) sks., Oct. 8, Dec. 12

Rolla, Mo.: (1861) Feds. withdraw to, Aug. 10; Fed. oper., Nov. 1; Fed. recon. from, Dec. 18; (1862) oper., Mar. 8; Fed. exped. from, Nov. 30; (1864) Fed. scs. from, Feb. 1; Fed. exped. from, Feb. 29; sks., Aug. 1, Nov. 1; Fed. exped. from, Nov. 5; (1865) Fed. sc. to, Mar. 5; aff., Mar. 24; Fed. sc. from, Apr. 21

Rolling Fork, Miss.: (1864) Fed. exped. to, Sept. 21

Rolling Prairie, Ark.: (1864) sks., Jan. 23, Feb. 4; Fed. exped. from, Mar. 19

Roman, André B. (C): (1861) Conf. commissioner to Wash., Feb. 27, Mar. 8

Roman Catholic Church: (1861) Lincoln on, Oct. 21; (1863) on Knights of Golden Circle, May 3; Conf. special agent named, Sept. 24

Rome, Ga.: (1863) Streight's raid, Apr. 26; Fed. recon. to, Sept. 10, 11; (1864) Fed. exped. toward, Jan. 25; sk., May 15; act., May 17; Fed. exped. from, Aug. 11; sk., Oct. 10; Feds. near, Oct. 11; sk., Oct. 12; destruction property, Nov. 11

Rome, Italy: (1863) Dudley Mann Conf. special agent to Holy See, Sept. 24

Rome, Tenn.: (1862) sk., Nov. 28

Romney, W. Va.: (1861) raid to, June 13, 15; Fed. desc. on, Sept. 23; Fed. drive on, Oct. 25; taken, Oct. 26; sks., Nov. 13, Dec. 8; (1862) exped. to, Jan. 1; Jan. 3; Jackson toward, Jan. 7; Feds. evacuate, Jan. 10; Feds. reoccupy, Feb. 7; sk., Dec. 1; (1863) aff., Feb. 16

Romney Camp.: (1862) Jackson moves toward, Jan. 1, 3, 7; Feds. evacuate, Jan. 10

Rose, Thomas E. (F): (1864) leads Libby Prison escape, Feb. 9

Rosecrans, William Starke (F): (1861) sk., July 10; eng. Rich Mt., July 11; commands Dept. of the O., July 23; moves in W. Va., Sept. 9; eng. Carnifix Fy., Sept. 10; Sept. 21; in Kanawha, Sept. 25; commands Dept. of Western Va., Oct. 11; (1862) Bat. of Iuka, Sept. 19; Bat. of Corinth, Oct. 3, 4, 5; assigned command Dept. of the Cumberland, Oct. 24; assumes command, Oct. 30; Nov. 1; moves to Nashville, Nov. 7; Dec. 1; to Murfreesboro, Dec. 26, 27, 28, 30; Bat. of Murfreesboro, Dec. 31; (1863) respite in bat., Jan. 1; Bat. of Murfreesboro continues, Jan. 2; Lincoln thanks, Jan. 5; reorganizes army, Jan. 9; Lincoln to, Feb. 17, Mar. 17, Apr. 23; regrouping, May 24; Lincoln to, May 27; faced Bragg, May 31; Tullahoma Camp., June 23, 24, 27, 29, July 1, 2, 3, 7, 11; exped. to Huntsville, July 13; Lincoln's confidence, Aug. 10; Chickamauga Camp., Aug. 16, 20, 21, 29, Sept. 1, 2, 3, 4, 5, 8, 9, 10, 11, 12, 13, 14, 15, 16, 17 (corps concentrate), 18, 19–20 (Bat. of Chickamauga); to Lincoln, Sept. 20; Lincoln to, Sept. 21; reinforcements, Sept. 22, 23, 24, 25; Lincoln to, Sept. 24; entrenched Chattanooga, Sept. 26; Sept. 27; Wheeler's raid, Sept. 30, Oct. 1; food short, Oct. 2; Lincoln to, Oct. 4; troops en route, Oct. 5; Lincoln inquires re, Oct. 7; Lincoln to, Oct. 12; relieved command Dept. of the Cumberland, Oct. 17; rumors of retreat, Oct. 18; confers with Grant, Oct. 21; re Burnside, Dec. 9; Lincoln on, Dec. 18; (1864) named commander Fed. Dept. of Missouri, Jan. 22; assumes command, Jan. 30; troops of, Oct. 28; replaced, Dec. 2

St. Stephen's Church, Va.: (1863) sk., Oct. 14

St. Thomas, West Indies: (1863) seizure of *Peterhoff,* Feb. 25

Salem, Ark.: (1864) Fed. wagon train capt., May 29

Salem, Ind.: (1863) Morgan's raid, July 10

Salem, Ky.: (1864) sk., Aug. 8

Salem, Miss.: (1863) Fed. sc. to, Mar. 2; sk., June 11

Salem, Mo.: (1861) act., Dec. 3; (1862) sks., July 6, Aug. 9; Fed. sc. from, Aug. 24; (1863) Fed. sc. from, Apr. 18; sk., Sept 13; Fed. sc. from, Nov. 24, Dec. 26; (1865) Fed. sc. from, Feb. 23

Salem, Tenn.: (1863) Fed. recon. to, Mar. 9; sks., Mar. 21, May 20

Salem, Va.: (1862) sks., Apr. 1, Aug. 27; (1863) sk., Dec. 16; (1864) sk., June 21; (1865) Fed. oper., Mar. 3

Salem Church, Hanover Co., Va.: (1864) comb., May 27

Salem Church (or Salem Heights), Spotsylvania Co., Va.: (1863) bat., May 3

Salem Depot, Va.: (1863) Stuart's ride begins from, June 25

Salem Heights (or Salem Church), Va.: (1863) bat., May 3, 4

Salem Pike, Tenn.: (1863) Fed. sc., June 12

Salina, Kas.: (1864) Fed. sc., Aug. 8

Saline, I.T.: (1862) sk., Dec. 2

Saline Bottom, Ark.: (1864) sk., Apr. 29

Saline Co., Mo.: (1862) oper., Mar. 7; Fed. oper., July 29; (1864) Fed. sc., Aug. 6; Fed. oper., Aug. 13; (1865) Fed. sc., May 8

Saline R., Ark.: (1864) sk., Feb. 15; (1865) Fed. sc., Apr. 26

Salineville, O.: (1863) capture of Morgan, July 26

Salisbury, Mo.: (1864) Fed. exped. to, Nov. 16

Salisbury, N.C.: (1865) eng., Apr. 12

Salkehatchie River, S.C.: (1865) Fed. recon., Jan. 20, 25; Sherman's right on, Feb. 2; sk., Feb. 2; act., Feb. 3

Salmon Falls, Id. Terr.: (1864) Fed. exped. to, Aug. 27

Salt: *See* Salt Works

Salt House Point, Mobile Bay, Ala.: (1864) salt works destroyed, Sept. 8

Salt Lick Br., W. Va.: (1863) sk., Oct. 14

Saltpeter: (1862) Conf. speculators, Feb. 4; (1863) works destroyed, Aug. 19, 25; (1864) works destroyed, Feb. 29

Salt Ponds (or Salt Pond Mt.), Va.: (1864) sks., May 12

Salt R., Ky.: (1862) act., Oct. 9

Salt R., Mo.: (1862) sk., May 31

Salt Springs, Ga.: (1864) sk., Oct. 1

Saltville, Va.: (1864) Fed. exped. to, Oct. 2; Feds. destroy salt works, Dec. 20, 21

Salt Works, Conf., destroyed or attacked by Feds.: (1862) Mathews Co., Va., Nov. 22; (1863) St. Joseph's, Fla., Jan. 9; Wale's Head, N.C., Feb. 2; New Iberia, La., Apr. 18; Darien, Ga., Sept. 22; Back Bay, Va., Sept 30; Bear Inlet, N.C., Dec. 25; (1864) Goose Cr., Fla., Feb. 27; Masonborough Inlet, N.C., Apr. 21; Cane Patch, S.C., Apr. 21; Tampa, Fla., July 11; Salt House Point, Ala., Sept. 8; Rocky Point, Fla., Dec. 3; southeast Va., Dec. 10, 20; Saltville, Va., Dec. 20, 21; (1865) St. Andrews Bay, Fla., Feb. 1

Santa Fe Rd., Mo.: (1862) sk., Apr. 14; (1863) exped., May 3; guerrillas on, May 21

Santa Fe Trail: (1862) ment., Mar. 26

Santa Rosa, Tex.: (1864) sk., Mar. 16

Santa Rosa I. (Ft. Pickens), Fla.: (1861) Fed. troops to, Jan. 10; Ft. Pickens reinforced, Apr. 12; Conf. landing attempt, Oct. 9; (1862) recon., Mar. 27

Santee R., S.C.: (1865) Fed. exped., Apr. 5

Santiago de Cuba, U.S.S.: (1861) seizes Conf. agent, Dec. 7; (1862) captures *Columbia,* Aug. 3

Sapello R. (or Spaulding's), Ga.: (1862) sk., Nov. 7

Saratoga, Ky.: (1861) *Conestoga* attacks, Oct. 26

Saratoga, U.S.S.: (1861) captures slave ship, Apr. 21

Sarcoxie Prairie, Mo.: (1863) sk., Feb. 10

Sassacus, U.S.S.: (1864) disabled by *Albemarle,* May 5

Satan: (1864) Garfield on, Jan. 12

Satartia, Miss.: (1863) Fed. exped. to, June 2; sk., Oct. 17; (1864) sk., Feb. 7

Satellite, U.S.S.: (1863) Fed. gunboat captured, Aug 23; Feds. wreck, Sept. 2

Saulsbury, Tenn.: (1862) sk., Aug. 11; (1863) Fed. recon., Feb. 2; Fed. sc. to, Mar. 2; Fed. sc. to, Mar. 21, Apr. 5, 11; Fed. exped. to, Apr. 15; Conf. desc. on, Dec. 2

Saunders, Fla.: (1865) sk., Mar. 19

Savage's Station, Va.: (1862) bat., June 29; losses at, July 1

Savannah, Ga.: (1861) Ft. Jackson, barracks seized by state, Jan. 26; port blockaded, May 28; Oct. 29; Nov. 4; Feds. near, Nov. 7; Lee commands area, Nov. 8; C.S.S. *Fingal* arrives, Nov. 12; defended by Ft. Pulaski, Nov. 24; act. with blockaders, Nov. 26; cotton burned, Nov. 29; (1862) fall of Ft. Pulaski, Apr. 11; Fed. naval att. Ft. McAllister, July 29; Conf. *Gen. Lee* capt., Aug. 10; (1863) Fed. att. Ft. McAllister, Jan. 27, Feb. 1; *Montauk* destroys C.S.S. *Nashville,* Feb. 28; Fed. att. Ft. McAllister, Mar. 3; Davis in, Nov. 1; (1864) women demonstrate, Apr. 17; Sherman march to begins, Nov. 16; Feds. converge on, Dec. 3; Sherman's march to, Dec. 5, 6, 7, 8, 9; arrives at, Dec. 10; investment, Dec. 11, 12, 13, 16, 17; Sherman demands surrender, Dec. 17; Hardee refuses surrender, Dec. 18; Conf. evac., Dec. 20; Fed. occup., Dec. 21; Sherman to Lincoln, Dec. 22; Lincoln to Sherman, Dec. 26; (1865) Jan. 1; Sherman moves north, Jan. 3, 5, 19, 20, 21, 22; Carolina Camp., Feb. 1

Savannah, Tenn.: (1862) Feds. arrive, Mar. 5; Fed. oper., Mar. 9; build-up, Mar. 10; Sherman exped., Mar. 14; Fed. gunboat exped., Apr. 3; Grant's hdqrs., Apr. 6; Apr. 25

Savannah Cr., S.C.: (1865) sk., Feb. 15

Savannah Harbor, Ga.: (1861) Nov. 24; Feds. sink hulks, Dec. 17; (1862) Ft. Pulaski, Apr. 10

Savannah R., Ga.: (1861) seizure of Ft. Pulaski, Jan. 3; Nov. 24; Confs. displace blockade, Dec. 26; (1862) recon., Mar. 7; Apr. 10; fall of Ft. Pulaski, Apr. 11; Fed. recon., Sept. 30; (1864) *Ida* capt., Dec. 10; C.S.S. *Resolute* capt., Dec. 12; crossed in evac., Dec. 20; (1865) Carolina Camp., Feb. 1, 2, 4

Savior, the: (1864) Lincoln mentions, Sept. 7

Saybrook, Conn.: (1861) peace meeting, Aug. 16

Sayler's Cr., Va.: (1865) eng., Apr. 6

Scarey Cr., W. Va.: (1861) act., July 17

Scatterville, Ark.: (1862) sk., Aug. 3

Schenck, Robert Cumming (F): (1862) Bat. of McDowell, May 8

Schimmelfennig, Alexander (F): (1865) surrender of Charleston, Feb. 18

Schofield, John McAllister (F): (1862) assumes command Dist. of St. Louis,
    Feb. 15; (1863) superseded command Army of the Frontier, Apr. 1; ordered
    to command Dept. of the Missouri, May 24; Lincoln to, July 13, Oct. 1; re-
    moval asked, Oct. 5; Lincoln to, Oct. 28; Lincoln dissatisfied with, Dec. 18;
    (1864) removed from Dept. of the Mo., soon to head Dept. of the O., Jan.
    22; superseded by Rosecrans, Jan. 30; commands Dept. of the O., Feb. 9;
    Atlanta Camp., May 7, 9, 17, 18, 20, 25, 26, June 15, July 8, 9, 19, 20,
    Aug. 5, 6, 18, 26, 28, 31; Bat. of Jonesboro, Sept. 1; commands at Pulaski,
    Tenn., Nov. 14; pulls back, Nov. 22, 23, 24, 25, 26, 27, 28; Spring Hill aff.,
    Nov. 29; Bat. of Franklin, Nov. 30; at Nashville, Dec. 1; Dec. 8; Grant
    replaces Thomas with, rescinds order, Dec. 9; (1865) moves to N.C., Jan.
    15; commands Dept. of N.C., Feb. 9; reaches Ft. Fisher, Feb. 9; drive
    on Wilmington, N.C., Feb. 22; Battle of Kinston or Wise's Forks, N.C.,
    Mar. 8, 9, 10; re Sherman's plans, Mar. 11; sks., Mar. 19

Schooner Channel, S.C.: (1862) Feb. 23

Schooners: (1863) seizure of, Aug. 25

Schultz' Mill, Cosby Cr., Tenn.: (1864) sk., Jan. 13

Schurz, Carl (F): (1862) Lincoln to, Nov. 24; (1863) superseded by Howard
    command Eleventh Corps, Apr. 2

Schuyler Co., Mo.: (1862) sk., June 26; oper., Oct. 11

Scotland Co., Mo.: (1862) oper., Oct. 11

Scott, Dred: *See* Dred Scott case

Scott, Winfield (F): (1860) advises Buchanan, Nov. 9, 20; opposes evacuating
    Sumter, Dec. 28; to Buchanan, Dec. 30; (1861) recommends steamer to Ft.
    Sumter, Jan. 2; advises sending *Star of the West* to Sumter, Jan. 5; im-
    practical to relieve Sumter, Mar. 3; confers with Lincoln on Sumter, Mar. 5;
    relief of Sumter naval problem, Mar. 6; Lincoln to, Mar. 9; views on relief
    Sumter, Mar. 11; recommends evac. of fts., Mar. 28; confers with Lincoln,
    Apr. 17, 20; discretion as to habeas corpus, Apr. 27; "Anaconda Plan,"
    May 3; proposes Miss. R. exped., June 29; suspension of habeas corpus,
    July 2; and Gen. Patterson, July 2, 21; friction with McClellan, Aug. 10;
    confers with Lincoln, Sept. 5; confers with Cabinet, Oct. 1; possible retire-
    ment, Oct. 18; resigns, Oct. 31; superseded by McClellan, Nov. 1; (1862)
    Lincoln confers with, June 23, 24, 25; (1864) lieut. gen. by brevet, Feb. 29

Scott, Ft., Kas.: (1861) sk., Sept. 1; (1862) Fed. exped. from, Nov. 6; (1863)
    Fed. sc. from, May 5; aff., June 8; sk., Sept 6; (1864) Pleasonton to, Oct 26

Scott Co., Tenn.: (1862) Conf. exped., Mar. 28

Scott Co., Va.: (1864) aff., Oct. 26

Scottsborough, Ala.: (1864) Fed. exped. from, Jan. 25

Scott's Cross Roads, Va.: (1865) act., Apr. 2

Scott's Farm, Washita Cove, Ark.: (1864) sk., Feb. 14

Scott's Fd., Mo.: (1863) sk., Oct. 14

Scottsville, Ky.: (1863) aff., June 11

Scottsville Rd., Ky.: (1862) sk., Sept. 9
Scuppernong R., N.C.: (1864) act., Sept. 29
Scupperton, N.C.: (1863) sk., July 22
Scurry, William Read (C): (1862) eng. Glorieta, Mar. 28
Sea, March to the: *See* Sherman, William T.
Seaboard and Roanoke R.R.: (1863) Fed. oper., May 12
Sea Bride, U.S.S.: (1863) bark capt. by *Alabama,* Aug. 6
Seabrook Island, S. C.: (1862) Fed. recon., Apr. 14
Sea King: See *Shenandoah,* C.S.S.
Seal of Confederacy: (1862) adopted by Sen., Sept. 24
Séance: (1863) at White House, Apr. 23
Searcy, Ark.: (1862) Fed. exped. to, May 27; (1864) aff., May 18; sk., June 3;
    Fed. sc. to, July 26; Fed. exped. to, Aug. 27; sks., Sept. 6, 13; Fed. sc.
    to, Nov. 9
Searcy Co., Ark.: (1863) sk., Dec. 31; (1864) sk., July 4; (1865) Fed. sc.,
    Mar. 12
Searcy Ldg., Ark.: (1862) sk., May 19; Fed. exped. from, May 27; (1864)
    Fed. sc. to, Jan. 30; Mar. 15
Sears' Fd., Mo.: (1862) sk., Aug. 9
Sears' House, Mo.: (1862) sk., July 11
Seceded states, Montgomery, Ala., convention: *See* Conf. States of America;
    Congress, C.S.A. (1861) Feb. 4
Secession conventions (*See* also individual states; Secession of states): (1860)
    S.C., Nov. 10, Dec. 17, 18, 19; S.C. secedes, Dec. 20; (1861) caucus of
    Southern sens., Jan. 5; Miss. and Ala. conventions, Jan. 7; Miss. secedes,
    Jan. 9; Fla. secedes, Jan. 10; Ala. secedes, Jan. 11; Ark. legislature calls for
    referendum, Jan. 16; Ga. secedes, Jan. 19; La. secedes, Jan. 26; Tex. con-
    vention votes secession referendum, Feb. 1, 11; Montgomery convention of
    seceded states begins, Feb. 4; Va. convention meets, Feb. 13; Tex. ref-
    erendum votes secession, Feb. 23; Mo. convention, Feb. 28; N.C. votes reject
    convention, Feb. 28; Mo. convention moves, Mar. 4; Ark. convention votes
    referendum, Mar. 18; Va. convention rejects secession, Apr. 4; secessionists
    meet in Baltimore, Apr. 17; Va. convention adopts secession referendum,
    Apr. 17; Tenn. votes commissioners to Confederacy, May 1; N.C. legislature
    votes secession convention, May 1
Secession of states: (1860) S.C., Dec. 20; (1861) Miss., Jan. 9; Fla., Jan. 10;
    Ala., Jan. 11; Ga., Jan. 19; La., Jan. 26; Tex., Feb. 1; Tex. referendum,
    Feb. 23; Va., Apr. 17; Ark., May 6; Tenn., May 6; N.C., May 20; Va.
    referendum, May 23; Tenn. referendum, June 8
Secessionville, S.C.: (1862) eng., June 16; (1864) sk., July 2
Second Baptist Church, Richmond: (1862) bell cast into cannon, Apr. 1
Second Bull Run: *See* Bull Run, 2nd
Second Corps, A.N.Va., Conf.: (1864) Bat. of Wilderness, May 5
Second Corps, Army of Tennessee, Conf.: (1863) Hill supersedes Hardee,
    July 19; Breckinridge commands, Nov. 8
Second Corps, A. of P., Fed.: (1862) 2nd Bull Run Camp., Aug. 26; (1863)
    Warren assumes command, Aug. 16; (1864) crosses Rapidan, May 4; Bat. of
    North Anna, May 23, 24; Cold Harbor, June 1; reaches, crosses James,

June 13, 14; att. on Petersburg, June 15; Birney in command, June 17; siege Petersburg, June 21, 22, 23; Bat. of Reams' Station, Aug. 25; eng. Burgess' Mill, Oct. 27; (1865) Bat. of Hatcher's Run, Feb. 5, 6, 7; Appomattox camp., Mar. 29, 30, 31, Apr. 6, 8

Second Cr., W. Va.: (1863) sk., Nov. 8

Second Fredericksburg: (1863) bat., May 3

Second Me. Inf.: (1861) mutiny, Aug. 15

Second Manassas: *See* Bull Run, 2nd

Second Winchester: *See* Winchester

Securities, Conf.: (1861) reported weak on European markets, May 22

Sedalia, Mo.: (1862) sk., June 5; (1863) sk., Apr. 9; Fed. sc. from, Aug. 25; exped. from, Oct. 7; (1864) Fed. sc. from, June 3; aff., Oct. 15

Sedalia and Marshall Rd., Mo.: (1864) aff., June 26

Seddon, James A. (C): (1862) Davis names Sec. of War, Nov. 21; Davis to, Dec. 18; (1863) report, Dec. 11; (1864) Davis to, Dec. 18; (1865) recommends Lee as General-in-Chief, Jan. 28; resigns, Feb. 1; Breckinridge replaces, Feb. 6

Sedgwick, John (F): (1863) commands Sixth Army Corps, Feb. 4, 5; at Chancellorsville, May 1, 3, 4; sk., June 5; (1864) crosses Rapidan, May 4; Bat. of Wilderness, May 5, 6; Bat. of Spotsylvania, May 8; death of, May 9

Sedgwick, Ft., Va.: (1864) sk., Oct. 27

Seleeman's Fd., Va.: (1863) aff., Mar. 22

Selma, Ala.: (1863) Davis in, Oct. 18; (1865) Fed. drive to, Feb. 19; camp. of, Mar. 22, 28, 30, 31, Apr. 1; fall of, Apr. 2

Selma, C.S.S.: (1864) surrenders, Aug. 5

Seminary Ridge at Gettysburg: (1863) bat., July 1, 2, 3, 4

Seminoles: (1861) Apr. 30; oppose Creeks, Dec. 29; (1865) treaty with U.S., Sept. 14

Semmes, Raphael (C) (*See also Alabama,* C.S.S.): (1861) resigns U.S.N., Feb. 15; runs blockade in *Sumter,* June 30; *Sumter* captures whaler, Dec. 8; (1863) *Alabama* sinks U.S.S. *Hatteras,* Jan. 11; (1864) *Alabama* sunk by U.S.S. *Kearsarge,* June 19; (1865) commands James R. Squad., Feb. 10; named rear adm., Feb. 10

Senate, C.S.A. (*See also* Congress, C.S.A.): (1862) R. M. T. Hunter goes to, Mar 18; passes conscription, Apr. 9; Conf. seal, Sept. 24; (1865) resolution on Lee, Jan. 16; approves appointment Lee General-in-Chief, Jan. 31; approves Negro soldiers, Mar. 8

Senate, U.S. (*See also* Congress, U.S.): (1860) Southern sens. resign, Nov. 10; Committee of Thirteen, Dec. 18, 20; Crittenden Compromise, Dec. 18; Seward proposes amendment on slavery, Dec. 24; (1861) caucus of Southern members, Jan. 5; Crittenden speaks for compromise, Jan. 7; compromise killed, Jan. 16; 5 Southern sens. resign, Jan. 21; Lincoln visits, Feb. 25; rejects Peace Convention amendment, Mar. 2; Hamlin inaugurated Vice-Pres., Mar. 4; confirms Lincoln's Cabinet, Mar. 5; expels Southern sens., July 11; passes Crittenden resolution, July 25; debates insurrection-sedition bill, Aug. 1; confirms commissions, Aug. 3; expels Breckinridge, Dec. 4; creates Joint Committee on the Conduct of the War, Dec. 9; (1862) expels Missouri sens., Jan. 10; resolution on prosecution of war, Feb. 3; confirmation of A. Johnson, mil. gov. Tenn., Feb. 23; on compensated emancipation, Apr. 2; W. Va. state bill, Dec. 10; sens. meet with Lincoln, Dec. 18; Republican sens. meet with Lincoln, Dec. 19; (1863) conscription act, Feb. 16; (1864) amendment abolishing slavery, Jan. 11; lieut. gen. act, Feb. 24; confirm Grant as lieut. gen., Mar. 1, 2; confirm Johnson, mil. gov. Tenn., Mar. 4; joint resolution on Thirteenth Amendment, Apr. 8; (1865) failure of Thirteenth Amendment, Jan. 6; repudiates Conf. debt, Feb. 17; blocks admission of La., Feb. 18; special session, Mar. 4; adjourns, Mar. 11

Senate Chamber, U.S.: (1861) Sixth Mass. quartered, Apr. 19

Senatobia, Miss.: (1863) Fed. exped. to, May 21; (1864) sk., Feb. 8

Seneca, Md.: (1863) sk., June 28

Seneca Cr., Md.: (1861) sks., Sept. 16, 20

Seneca Indians: (1861) treaty with C.S.A., Oct. 4; (1865) treaty with U.S., Sept. 14

Seneca Mills, Md.: (1861) sk., June 14

Seneca Trace Crossing, Cheat R., W. Va.: (1863) sk., Sept. 25

Sequatchie Valley, Tenn.: (1863) sk., Oct. 2; (1864) sk., Feb. 27

Service organizations, North: *See* Sanitary Commission, U. S. Christian Commission

Seven Days' Camp., Va. (*See also* individual battle names): (1862) eng. Oak Grove or French's Field, June 25; Bat. of Mechanicsville, Beaver Dam Cr., or Ellerson's Mill, June 26; sk. in area, June 26; Bat. of Gaines' Mill, 1st Cold Harbor, or the Chickahominy, June 27; McClellan withdraws toward James R., June 28; act. Golding's and Garnett's farms, June 28; Bat. of Savage's Station, June 29; Bat. of Frayser's Farm or White Oak Swamp, June 30; Bat. of Malvern Hill, July 1; losses in camp., July 1; (1864) ment., June 1

Seven Pines or Fair Oaks, Va.: (1862) sks., May 24, 29; bat., May 31; conclusion of bat., June 1; Davis on, June 1; armies rest, June 2; sk., June 15

Seventeenth Corps, Fed.: (1862) James B. McPherson commands, Dec. 18; (1864) Sherman's right wing, Nov. 9; at Millen, Ga., Dec. 3; (1865) Carolina Camp., Feb. 1

Seventh Corps, Fed.: (1863) discontinued, Aug. 1

Seventh N.H. Inf., Fed.: (1864) Bat. of Olustee, Fla., Feb. 20

Seventh N.Y. Inf., Fed.: (1861) arrives Annapolis, Apr. 22; "is a myth," Lincoln says, Apr. 24; reviewed by Lincoln, Apr. 25; relieves tension at Wash., Apr. 27

Seventy-ninth N.Y. Inf., Fed.: (1861) mutinied, Aug. 14

Sevierville, Tenn.: (1864) aff., Jan. 13; sk., Jan. 26; Fed. recon. to, Feb. 1; sk., Feb. 18

Sevierville Rd., Tenn.: (1864) sk., Feb. 20

Seward, Frederick W. (F): (1862) Asst. Sec. of State, Dec. 17

Seward, William Henry (F): (1860) on Sen. Committee of Thirteen, Dec. 20; proposes amendment on slavery, Dec. 24; (1861) accepts post Sec. of State, Lincoln Cabinet, Jan. 10; Sen. speech, Jan. 12; Lincoln to, Feb. 1; asks to withdraw, Mar. 2; Lincoln asks to stay in Cabinet, Mar. 4; and Conf. commissioners, Mar. 8, 20; on provisioning Sumter, Mar. 15; favors giving up Sumter, Mar. 29; *Powhatan* incident, Apr. 1, 6; thoughts for Lincoln,

Shawnee Indians: (1861) treaty with C.S.A., Oct. 4; (1865) treaty with U.S., Sept. 14

Shawnee Mound (or Blackwater Cr., or Milford), Mo.: (1861) Fed. sc., Dec. 18

Shawneetown, Ill.: (1864) Conf. oper., Aug. 13

Shawneetown, Kas.: (1863) sk., June 6

Shawsheen, U.S.S.: (1863) captures 5 schooners, July 20; (1864) capt., May 7

Sheffield, England: (1863) meeting praises Stonewall Jackson, June 3

Shelbina, Mo.: (1861) sk., Sept. 4; (1864) Conf. att., July 26

Shelby, Joseph O., "Jo" (C): (1863) raid into Ark. and Mo., Sept. 22, 27, Oct. 4, 5, 6, 7, 9, 10, 11, 12, 13, 14, 15, 16, 17, 18, 24, 26; (1864) oper. north of Ark. R., May 13, 15, 17, 19, 25; assumes command Confs. north of Ark. R., May 27; eng. riverboats, June 24; *See* Sterling Price for 1864 Mo. Camp.; aff., Sedalia, Mo., Oct. 15; Price's strategy, Oct. 22; Bat. of Westport, Mo., Oct. 23; eng. Little Osage R., Kas., and Marmiton R., Mo., Oct. 25; eng. Newtonia, Mo., Oct. 28; (1865) threat to arrest E. K. Smith, May 13; troops of refuse to surrender, May 26

Shelby Co., Mo.: (1864) sk., Sept. 3

Shelbyville, Ky.: (1862) sk., Sept. 4

Shelbyville, Tenn.: (1862) Fed. recon. to, Mar. 25; (1863) act., June 27; sk., Oct. 7; (1864) sk., Nov. 28

Shelbyville Pike, Tenn.: (1863) sks., Jan. 5, Feb. 20, Apr. 23; Conf. oper., June 4; sk., June 6

Shelbyville Rd., Tenn.: (1862) sk., Apr. 24

Sheldon, Camp, Miss.: (1863) aff., Feb. 8, 10

Sheldon's Place, near Barren Ft., I.T.: (1863) sk., Dec. 18

Shellmound, Tenn.: (1863) act., Aug. 21; sk., Aug. 28; Fed. recon. from, Aug. 30; Fed. Army of the Cumberland crosses Tenn. R., Sept. 4

Shell's Mill, Ark.: (1862) sk., Oct. 16

Shenandoah, Army of the, Fed.: (1864) Sheridan named to command, Aug. 1, 7

Shenandoah, C.S.S.: (1864) leaves London for Madeira, Oct. 8; commissioned, Oct. 19; (1865) reaches Melbourne, Australia, Jan. 25; captures whalers, Apr. 1; in Pacific, Apr. 14; in Bering Sea, June 22, 26, 28; learns war over, Aug. 2; surrenders to Brit. authorities, Nov. 6

Shenandoah, Dept. of the, Fed.: (1861) N. P. Banks takes command, July 21; merged into Dept. of the Potomac, Aug. 17; (1862) Banks' Fifth Corps put into, Apr. 4; merged into Army of Va., June 26

Shenandoah Co., W. Va.: (1863) Fed. sc., Dec. 7

Shenandoah Fy., W. Va.: (1865) Fed. sc. to, Mar. 16

Shenandoah R. (*See also* Shenandoah Valley): (1861) Harper's Fy. on, Apr. 18; (1862) Feb. 24; Jackson on south fork, May 20; Feds. follow Jackson, June 6

Shenandoah R., north fork, Va.: (1864) May 15; Bat. of Cedar Cr., Oct. 19

Shenandoah Valley, Va.: (1861) Conf. troops fall back to, June 15; Patterson's Feds. in, July 2; Feds. stalled in, July 14; sk., north of Winchester, July 15; July 21, 23, 27; Dec. 13

(1862) Banks advances, Mar. 5; sk., Stephenson's Depot, Mar. 11; Mar.

17; sk., Shields and Jackson, Mar. 19; Mar. 20, 22; 1st Bat. of Kernstown, Mar. 23; Banks follows Jackson, Apr. 1; sk., Stony Creek, Apr. 2; Feds. occupy New Market, Apr. 17; Jackson leaves valley, Apr. 18; Banks at Harrisonburg, New Market, Apr. 26; Apr. 30; May 6; Bat. of McDowell, May 8; Jackson heads to valley, May 12; Jackson advances north, May 13, 15, 18; Jackson moves through New Market, Luray, May 20; Jackson goes north in Luray Valley, May 21, 22; eng. Front Royal, May 23; Jackson tries to cut Banks' retreat, May 24; Lincoln orders Frémont, McDowell to valley, May 24; 1st Bat. of Winchester, May 25; Lincoln to McClellan on, May 25; Jackson occupies Winchester, May 26; excitement in North, May 27, 28; Lincoln to McDowell on, May 28; Fed. strength, May 29; Lincoln in control, May 29; Lincoln urges capture of Jackson, May 30; Jackson between Frémont and McDowell, May 31; Lincoln awaits news, May 31; at Front Royal, June 1; sk. Strasburg, Woodstock, Jackson escapes pincers, June 2; Jackson withdraws, June 3, 4; Turner Ashby killed, June 6; Bat. of Cross Keys, June 8; Bat. of Port Republic, June 9; summary, June 9; speculation on Jackson, June 11; Lee sends reinforcements to, June 12; Feds. leave Harrisonburg, June 12; sk. New Market, June 13; Lincoln to Frémont on, June 15; sk., Mt. Jackson, June 16; Jackson leaves valley, June 17, 23; Fed. sc., from Strasburg, June 22; Fed. recon. from Front Royal, June 29; Pope's order on depredations, July 10; Feds. occupy Luray, July 21; Lee's army in, Oct. 16; Jackson's march from to Fredericksburg, Dec. 1; recon. in, Dec. 12

(1863) 2nd Bat. of Winchester, June 14–15; Lee's army moves south in, July 15; Fed. advance into, July 21, 22; Lee's retreat through, July 23; Meade moves into, July 24; Fed. demon., Dec. 8

(1864) Sigel ordered to move to, Apr. 9; act. begins in, May 14; Bat. of New Market, May 15; Fed. command change, May 21; Hunter's Feds. move in, May 26; Lynchburg Camp., June 3, 4, 5, 6, 8, 10; Trevilian raid, June 7; comb. at Trevilian Station, June 11, 12; Va. Mil. Institute burned, June 11; Lee reinforces, June 13; *See also* Hunter, Early; aff. New Glasgow, June 14; Early defends Lynchburg, June 17; Hunter withdraws, June 18, 19, 20, 21; Early advances in, June 23, 28, July 15, 16; Feds. consolidate in, July 17; engs., July 19; Stephenson's Depot, July 20; act. in, July 22, 23; Bat. 2nd Kernstown, July 24; July 25, 26; Early wrecks r.r.'s, July 27; Lincoln on Fed. failures in, Aug. 3; Fed. oper. coordinated against Early, Aug. 7, 9; Early moves south in, Aug. 10, 11; Confs. entrench on Cedar Cr., Aug. 12, 13; Sheridan withdraws slightly, Aug. 14; sks., Cedar Cr., Strasburg, Va., Charles Town, W. Va., Aug. 15; Sheridan moves toward Charles Town, W. Va., Aug. 16; Early toward Bunker Hill, Aug. 17, 18, 19; sk., Aug. 20; Early attacks, Aug. 20; valley largely free of Feds., Aug. 21; demon. against Sheridan, Aug. 22, 23; Early-Sheridan movements, Aug. 24, 25, 26, 27, 28, 29, 30, 31, Sept. 1, 2, 3, 4, 5, 6, 7, 12, 13, 14, 15, 16, 17, 18; 3rd Winchester, Sept. 19; Sept. 20; Bat. of Fisher's Hill, Sept. 21, 22; victories aid to Lincoln's camp., Sept. 22; Early retreats, Sept. 23; Sheridan depredations in, Sept. 24, 25; Sept. 26, 27; movements, Sept. 28; Sept. 29; Oct. 1, 2, 3, 6, 8; eng. Tom's Brook, Oct. 9; movements, Oct. 10, 12, 13, 14, 15,

18; Bat. of Cedar Creek, Oct. 19; Oct. 20; movements, Nov. 12, 13; Early and Sheridan reinforce Richmond-Petersburg front, Dec. 19

(1865) Some Fed. troops pull out, Jan. 7; Fed. movement in, Feb. 27; Mar. 1; eng. Waynesborough, Mar. 2; Fed. prisoner escort att., Mar. 3; oper. in, Apr. 26

Shenandoah Valley Dist., Conf.: (1861) Jackson commands, Oct. 22; Nov. 4; (1863) Early assigned to command, Dec. 15

Shepherdstown, W. Va.: (1861) sk., Sept. 9; (1862) sk., Sept. 19; eng., Sept. 20; Fed. recon. from, Sept. 25; sk., Oct. 1; Fed. exped. to, Nov. 24; (1863) Gettysburg aftermath, July 15, 16; (1864) Sigel escapes across Potomac at, July 3; Early crosses Potomac, July 5, 6; sk., July 30; Early sends troops to, Aug. 25; act., Aug. 25

Shepherdsville, Ky.: (1862) Fed. outpost surrenders, Sept. 7; sk. at Cedar Church, Oct. 3; (1863) sk., July 7

Shepherdsville Rd., Ky.: (1862) sk., Oct. 2

Sheridan, Philip Henry (F): (1862) act., Booneville, Miss., July 1; Bat. of Perryville, Ky., Oct. 8; (1863) Bat. of Chattanooga, Nov. 23; Bat. of Missionary Ridge, Nov. 25; (1864) heads cav. A. of P., Apr. 4; cav. exped., *See also* Yellow Tavern, May 8, 9, 10, 11, 12, 13, 15, 17, 18, 21, 24, 26, 27; Bat. of Cold Harbor, June 1, 3; Trevilian raid, June 7, 11, 12, 20, 21, 22, 23; eng. St. Mary's Church, June 24; on James, June 25, 26; July 27, 28, 29; named command Army of the Shenandoah, Aug. 1; in Wash., Aug. 3; assigned command Middle Mil. Div., Aug. 7; prepares move toward Early, Aug. 9; moves south in Shenandoah, Aug. 10, 11, 12; movements in Shenandoah, Aug. 13, 14, 15, 16, 17, 18, 20; Early attacks, Aug. 21; Early demon., Aug. 23, 24; Early threat, Aug. 25, 26, 27; Sheridan advances, Aug. 28, 29, 30, Sept. 1, 2; eng. Berryville, Sept. 3; advances, Sept. 4, 5; sks. Brucetown, Winchester, Sept. 7; Lincoln's concern, Sept. 12; Sept. 14; Grant meets with, Sept. 15, 16; 3rd Winchester Camp., Sept. 18, 19, 20; assigned permanent command Middle Mil. Dist., Sept. 21; Bat. of Fisher's Hill, Sept. 21, 22, 23; begins depredations, Sept. 24, 25; sks. with Early, Sept. 26, 28, 29; at Harrisonburg, Oct. 1; harassed, Oct. 3; eng. Tom's Brook, Oct. 9; position on Valley Pike, Oct. 10; at Cedar Cr., Oct. 13, 18; Bat. of Cedar Cr., Oct. 19; "Sheridan's Ride," Oct. 19; Early moves toward, Nov. 10; act. Newtown or Middletown, Cedar Cr., Ninevah, Nov. 12; summary of camp., Nov. 13; reinforcements to Richmond-Petersburg, Dec. 19; detaches Torbert, Dec. 19; Davis on, Dec. 20; (1865) movement in Shenandoah, Feb. 27; pursuing Early, Mar. 1; defeats Early at Waynesborough, Mar. 2; occupies Charlottesville, Mar. 3; en route to Petersburg, Mar. 9; moves toward junction with Grant, Mar. 13, 14, 15, 19, 26; talks with Grant, Mar. 26; Appomattox Camp., Mar. 29, 30; eng. Dinwiddie C. H., Mar. 31; Bat. of Five Forks, Apr. 1; Appomattox Camp., Apr. 3, 4, 5, 6, 7; Lee at Appomattox Station, Apr. 8; at surrender, Apr. 9; assigned to command west of Miss. R., south of Arkansas R., May 17

Sherman, F. C. (F): (1863) mayor of Chicago and Chicago *Times* suppression, June 1

Sherman, Thomas West (F): (1861) dispute with McClellan, Oct. 18; commands Port Royal exped., Oct. 29; Bat. of Port Royal Sound, Nov. 7

Sherman, William Tecumseh (F): (1861) Camp Jackson aff., May 10; command, Dept. of the Cumberland, Oct. 8; concern over Conf. advance, Oct. 23; superseded by Buell, nervous breakdown, Nov. 9

(1862) assigned command Dist. of Cairo, Feb. 14; embarks up Tenn. R., Mar. 8; returns, Mar. 14; at Pittsburg Ldg., Tenn., Mar. 15; Shiloh, Apr. 6, 7; nears Corinth, May 4; commands Fifteenth Corps, Dec. 18; exped. leaves Memphis, Dec. 20; nears Vicksburg, Dec. 24; near Milliken's Bend, Dec. 25; advances on Walnut Hills, Dec. 26; aff. Snyder's Mill, Dec. 27; approaches Vicksburg, Dec. 28; ass. Chickasaw Bayou, Dec. 29; at Chickasaw Bayou, Dec. 30, 31

(1863) Jan. 1; withdraws from bluffs, Jan. 2; with McClernand's army, Jan. 4; Steele's Bayou exped., Mar. 16, 21; Black Bayou exped., Mar. 24; Grant orders move down west side Miss. R., Mar. 29; demon. against Haynes' and Drumgould's bluffs, Apr. 29, 30; sk., Fourteen-Mile Cr., May 12; moves toward Jackson, Miss., May 13; occupies Jackson, May 14; 1st ass. Vicksburg, May 19; 2nd ass. Vicksburg, May 22; *See also* Vicksburg Camp.; Jackson Camp., July 5, 6, 7, 8, 10, 11, 12, 15, 16, 18, 19; to command Dept. of the Tenn., Oct. 17; assumes command, Army of the Tenn., Oct. 24; re Grant's concern, Nov. 5; at Chattanooga, Nov. 15; offensive under way, Nov. 21; Bat. of Chattanooga, Nov. 23–25; att., Nov. 24; Missionary Ridge, Nov. 25; pursuit of Bragg, Nov. 26; to reinforce Burnside, Nov. 28; enters Knoxville, Dec. 6

(1864) Meridian, Miss., Camp., Feb. 3, 4, 5, 6, 7, 8, 9, 10, 11, 12, 13, 14, 15, 16, 17, 18, 20, 21, 22, 26; to be commander in West, Mar. 11; assigned command Mil. Div. of the Miss., Mar. 12; Mar. 14; Grant confers with, Mar. 17; assumes command West, Mar. 18; Mar. 23; Grant orders into Ga., Apr. 9; expects move against Johnston, May 1; outpost action, May 2; Atlanta Camp., May 2, 4, 7, 8, 9, 10, 12, 13, 14, 15, 17, 18, 19, 20, 21, 22, 23, 24, 25, 26, 27, 28, 29, 30, 31, June 1, 2, 3, 4, 5, 6, 8, 9, 10, 11, 12, 13, 14, 15, 16, 17, 18, 19, 20, 21, 23, 24; Bat. of Kennesaw Mt., June 27; Johnston evacuates Kennesaw, July 2; camp. continues, July 3, 4, 5, 7, 8, 9, 10, 13, 15, 16, 19; Bat. of Peachtree Cr., July 20; July 21; Bat. of Atlanta July 22; July 25; Lincoln to, July 26; command problems, July 27; Bat. of Ezra Church, July 28; camp. around Atlanta, July 29, 30, Aug. 1, 3, 4, 5, 6, 9, 14, 15, 18; supply lines threatened, Aug. 21; moves on Jonesborough, Aug. 25; camp. around Atlanta continues, Aug. 26, 27, 28, 29, 30; Bat. of Jonesborough, Aug. 31–Sept. 1; Confs. evacuate Atlanta, Sept. 1; Fed. troops enter Atlanta, Sept. 2; occup. Atlanta, Sept. 3, 4; orders evac., Sept. 7; Forrest operates on communications, Sept. 16; Sept. 18; soldiers vote, Sept. 19; harassed by cav., Sept. 20; Davis on, Sept. 22; Hood threatens supply lines, Oct. 1, 2, 3, 4; hdqrs. Kennesaw Mt., Oct. 4, 5; eng. at Allatoona, Ga., Oct. 5; sk., near Rome, Oct. 10; concentrates Rome, Oct. 11; Oct. 12; holds Resaca, Oct. 13; Hood harasses lines, Oct. 15, 16, 17; halts pursuit, Oct. 21; Hood heads for Tenn., Oct. 22; Sherman decides to head for coast, Oct. 28; on Forrest, Nov. 4; orders for March to Sea, Nov. 9; destruction of property, Nov. 10, 11; destroys portions Atlanta, Nov. 12, 14, 15; preparation for march, Nov. 14; March to the Sea begins, Nov. 16; March to the Sea, Nov. 17, 18, 19, 20, 21, 22, 23, 24, 25, 26, 29, 30, Dec. 1, 3, 7, 8, 9; before Savannah, Dec. 10; investment Savannah, Dec. 11, 12; captures Ft. McAllister, Dec. 13; siege continues, Dec. 14; resupplied from sea, Dec. 16; demands Hardee surrender, Dec. 17; surrender refused, Dec. 18; Confs. evacuate Savannah, Dec. 20; Fed. occupation Savannah, Dec. 21: "Christmas gift" message to Lincoln, Dec. 22; Lincoln congratulates, Dec. 26

(1865) prepares to move north, Jan. 3; Jan. 5; Jan. 11; Davis on, Jan. 12; troops move to Pocotaligo, S.C., Jan. 14; preparation and orders, Jan. 17, 18, 19, 20; embarks for Beaufort, S.C., Jan. 21, 22, feints toward Charleston, Jan. 26; Carolina Camp., Jan. 28, 29, Feb. 1, 2, 3, 5, 6, 7, 9, 11, 12, 14, 15, 16; Columbia, S.C., burns, Feb. 17; Carolina Camp. continues, Feb. 18, 19, 21, 22, 23, 24, 25, 26, 27, 28, March 2, 3, 4, 5, 6, 7, 8, 9, 10, 11, 12, 13, 14; Bat. of Averasboro, N.C., Mar. 16; Mar. 18; Bat. of Bentonville, N.C., Mar. 19, 20, 21; Mar. 22; joins Schofield at Goldsborough, N.C., Mar. 23; confers with Lincoln, Grant on *River Queen,* Mar. 27, 28; on reconstruction, Mar. 28; returns to Goldsborough, Mar. 29; reorganizes forces, Apr. 1; moves toward Raleigh, N.C., Apr. 10; Apr. 11; hears news of Lee's surrender, Apr. 11; Johnston asks terms, Apr. 14; meeting scheduled, Apr. 16; meets Johnston near Durham Station, Apr. 17; "Memorandum" signed, Apr. 18; Grant brings Pres. Johnson's disapproval of terms, Apr. 24; agrees to reopen negotiations, Apr. 25; signs terms with Johnston, Apr. 26; confers with Grant, Apr. 27; leaves for Savannah, Apr. 28; rumored to favor Davis' escape, May 10; Grand Review in Wash., May 24

Sherwood, Mo.: (1863) Fed. sc. to, May 5; destruction of, May 6; sk., Aug. 14

Shields, James (F): (1862) advances against Jackson, Mar. 19; sk., Kernstown, Va., Mar. 22; 1st Kernstown, Mar. 23; sk., Front Royal, May 30; at Front Royal, June 1; pursues Jackson, June 6; Bat. of Cross Keys, June 8; Bat. of Port Republic, June 9; ordered toward Fredericksburg, June 9

Shiloh, Mo.: (1862) sk., Apr. 11

Shiloh, N.C.: (1862) oper., Sept. 17

Shiloh, Bat. of, Tenn. (*See also* Pittsburg Ldg., Tenn.): (1862) sk., Monterey, Apr. 3; Conf. att. delayed, Apr. 4; more delay, Apr. 6; bat., Apr. 6, 7; aftermath, Apr. 8; relief aid, Apr. 9; Apr. 10

Shiloh Church or Meeting House: (1862) sk., Apr. 2; Apr. 3; Apr. 5; in Bat. of Shiloh, Apr. 6, 7; aftermath, Apr. 8

Shimonoseki, Straits of: (1863) naval bat., July 16

Ship I., Miss.: (1861) Miss. forces take, Jan. 20; evacuated by Confs., Feds. occupy, Sept. 16, 17; Oct. 19; Fed. exped. to, Nov. 27; Feds. reoccupy, Dec. 3; Fed. attack on Biloxi, Dec. 31; (1862) Butler assumes command Dept. of the Gulf at, Mar. 20; Fed. exped. to Biloxi, Pass Christian, Apr. 3; Fed. build-up, Apr. 17

Shippensburg, Pa.: (1863) anxiety over Conf. invasion, June 20

Shipping, U.S. (*See also* Blockade; *Alabama,* C.S.S.; Cruisers; Raiders; individual ships such as *Florida, Shenandoah, Sumter, Tacony*): (1862) Conf. att. on, James R., July 5; (1863) *Tacony* marauding, June 15

Ship's Gap, Ga.: (1864) sk., Oct. 16

Shirley, Va.: (1862) Conf. att., July 31

Shirley's Fd., Spring R., Mo.: (1862) sk., Sept. 20

Shoal Cr., Ala.: (1864) sk., Jan. 14; sk., Oct. 31, Nov. 5, 9, 11, 16

Shoal Cr., Jasper Co., Mo.: (1863) sk., Nov. 18

Showalter, Daniel (C): (1861) leads pro-Conf. group in Calif., pursued, capt., Nov. 20, 29

Shreveport, La.: (1863) Conf. move to, May 6; (1864) Banks' advance on, Apr. 8, 9; *See* Red R. Camp.

Shut-in-Gap, Mo.: (1864) sk., Sept. 26

Shy's Hill, Tenn.: (1864) in Bat. of Nashville, Dec. 16

Siam, King of: (1862) Lincoln refuses elephants, Feb. 3

Sibley, Henry Hastings (F): (*See also* Sioux uprising): (1862) Aug. 17; relieves Ft. Ridgely, Minn., Aug. 28; relieves Birch Coulee siege, Sept. 2; defeats Sioux at Wood Lake, Minn., Sept. 23

Sibley, Henry Hopkins (C): (1861) ordered to Tex., July 8; assumes command Conf. forces upper Rio Grande, N. Mex. Terr., Dec. 14; (1862) eng., Valverde, Feb. 21; N. Mex. Terr. invasion, Mar. 2; occupies Santa Fe, Mar. 4; eng. of Glorieta or Pigeon's Ranch, Mar. 28; retreat, Apr. 8

Sibley, Mo.: (1862) oper., June 23; sk., Oct. 6; (1863) destruction of, June 23

Sickles, Daniel Edgar (F): (1863) given corps command, Feb. 5; Bat. of Gettysburg, July 1, 2

Sierra Bonita, N. Mex. Terr.: (1864) sk., Apr. 7

Sierra del Datil, N. Mex. Terr.: (1865) Fed. sc., Jan. 11

Sigel, Franz (F): (1861) eng., Carthage, Mo., July 5; Bat. of Wilson's Creek, Aug. 10; (1862) in Army of Va., June 17; (1863) corps command, Feb. 5; (1864) commands Dept. of W. Va., Mar. 10; ordered into Shenandoah, Apr. 9; movement in Shenandoah, May 14; Bat. of New Market, May 15; superseded by David Hunter, May 21; re Early camp., July 3

Sikeston, Mo.: (1862) sk., Mar. 1; (1864) aff., June 7; sk., Sept. 22

Silver Cr., Mo.: (1862) sk., Jan. 8

Silver Run Cr., N.C.: (1865) Fed. recon, Mar. 14

Silver Spring, Md.: (1864) Early burns Blair home, July 11

Silver Springs, Tenn.: (1862) sk., Nov. 9

Simmons' Bluff, S.C.: (1862) sk., June 21

Simms, William E. (C): (1862) on Conf. defense to end, Feb. 26

Simpsonville, Shelby Co., Ky.: (1865) sk., Jan. 25

Sims' Cove on Cedar Cr., Mo.: (1862) sk., Oct. 5

Sims' Farm, Shelbyville, Tenn.: (1863) sk., Oct. 7

Simsport, La.: (1863) eng., June 3; (1864) eng., June 8

Singleton, James W. (F): (1865) unofficial peace envoy, Jan. 5

Sinking Cr., Mo.: (1862) Fed. sc., Aug. 4; (1863) Fed. sc. to, Apr. 18

Sioux Indians (*See also* Sioux uprising): (1862) sk. with miners Ft. Berthold, Dak. Terr., Oct. 10; (1863) Fed. exped. in Dak., June 16; act. Dead Buffalo Lake, Dak. Terr., July 26; (1864) Fed. exped., Dak. Terr., July 25, 28

Sioux uprising (Minn.): (1862) begins (lasting till Sept. 23), Aug. 17; murder, arson continues, Aug. 18, 19, 20; Inds. repulsed, Ft. Ridgely, Aug. 22; New Ulm, Aug. 25; relief Ft. Ridgely, Aug. 28; relief Birch Coulee, Sept. 2; sk., Hutchinson, Minn., Sept. 4; Pope assigned command Dept. of the Northwest, Sept. 5, 6; Sioux defeated Wood Lake, Sept. 23; Lincoln asks record of condemned Inds., Nov. 10; Lincoln orders 39 Sioux executed; Dec. 6; execution date changed, Dec. 16; 38 Inds. hanged, Dec. 26

Sipsey Cr., Ala.: (1865) sk., Apr. 6

Sir John's Run, W. Va.: (1862) sk., Jan. 4; (1864) sk., July 6

Sir William Wallace (U.S. steamer): (1864) att. on, Jan. 29

Sister's Fy., Ga.: (1864) Dec. 7; (1865) Feds. cross Savannah R., Feb. 1

Sisters of Charity: (1862) arrive Ft. Monroe as nurses, June 22

Six-Mile Cr., Ala.: (1865) act., May 31

Sixteenth Corps, Fed.: (1862) S. A. Hurlbut commands, Dec. 18; (1864) heads for Nashville, Nov. 1

Sixth Corps, Fed.: (1863) Sedgwick succeeds W. F. Smith, Feb. 4; (1864) crosses Rapidan, May 4; death of Sedgwick, May 9; Bat. of North Anna, May 23, 24; Bat. of Cold Harbor, June 1; June 16; siege Petersburg, June 21, 23; div. of goes to Baltimore, July 7, 8; leaves for Wash., July 9; defense of Wash., July 11; ordered to pursue Early, July 13; to Wash., July 22, Oct. 10; Bat. of Cedar Cr., Oct. 19; (1865) ass. Petersburg lines, Apr. 2; eng. Sayler's Cr., Apr. 6; blocks Lee, Apr. 8; parade in Wash., June 8

Sixth Mass. Inf., Fed.: (1861) march in N.Y., Apr. 18; Baltimore riots, Apr. 19

Skipwith's Ldg., Miss.: (1863) Fed. exped. from, Nov. 10, 18

Skull Cr., S.C.: (1862) aff., Sept 24

Slane's Cross Roads, W. Va.: (1862) sk., Jan. 4

Slash Church, Va.: (1862) sk., May 27

Slatersville, Va.: (1862) sk., May 9

Slaughter Mt., Bat. of: (1862) Aug. 9

Slaughter's House, Va.: (1862) sk., Aug. 8

Slavery (*See also* Colonization of Negroes; Emancipation; Negroes, employment of, Conf., U.S.; Negro soldiers, Conf., U.S.; Negroes; Slavery, extension of; Slavery as a war issue; Slaves; Slaves, fugitive; Slave trade; Thirteenth Amendment): (1860) Buchanan says "on way out," Dec. 4; Crittenden Compromise, Dec. 18; (1861) Crittenden resolution, July 22, 25; bills in U. S. Cong. to abolish, Dec. 5; (1862) slave trader hanged, Feb. 21; U. S. Cong. discusses, Mar. 10; Sen. abolishes in D.C., Apr. 3; treaty with Britain on trade, Apr. 7; House abolishes in D.C., Apr. 11; prohibited in U.S. territories, June 19; treaty with Britain, July 11; Lincoln urges compensated emancipation, July 12; Lincoln approves Confiscation Act, July 17; preliminary Eman. Proc., Sept. 22; (1863) Eman. Proc., Jan. 1; reaction, Jan. 2; Cherokees abolish, Feb. 26; W. Va. votes gradual emancipation, Mar. 26; Lincoln on, Aug. 5; (1864) Ark. abolishes, Mar. 18; Lincoln on, Apr. 4; La. abolishes, Apr. 6, July 23; Sen. approves Thirteenth Amendment, Apr. 8; House defeats Thirteenth Amendment, June 15; Lincoln on, July 8, 9; abolished in La., Sept. 5; abolished in Md., Sept. 6; Lincoln on, Oct. 10; Lincoln on Thirteenth Amendment, Dec. 6; (1865) Ashley on amendment, Jan. 6; Mo. convention, Jan. 11; Cong. on, Jan. 9, 10; Thirteenth Amendment passes House, Jan. 31; Lincoln again favors compensated emancipation, Feb. 5; Mo. abolishes, June 6; Chickasaws, Choctaws abolish, Sept. 14; Thirteenth Amendment declared in effect, Dec. 18

Slavery, extension of: (1860) Lincoln on, Dec. 10; Crittenden Compromise, Dec. 18; (1861) Crittenden in Sen., Jan. 7; Lincoln on, Feb. 1; (1862) act prohibiting in U.S. territories, June 19

Smith's Cross Roads, Ga.: (1864) act., July 29
Smith's Cross Roads, Tenn.: (1863) sk., Oct. 1
Smith's Mills, Black R., N.C.: (1865) sk., Mar. 15
Smith's Shoals, Cumberland R., Ky.: (1863) sk., Aug. 1
Smith's Station, Neb. Terr.: (1864) sk., May 12
Smith's Store, Va.: (1864) sk., June 15
Smithville, Ark.: (1862) sk., June 17
Smithville, Mo.: (1864) burned, Oct. 17
Smithville, N.C.: (1861) citizens occupy Fts. Johnston, Caswell, Jan. 10; (1865) abandoned by Confs., Jan. 16; sk., Feb. 17
Smithville, Tenn.: (1863) Fed. sc. to, June 4
Smoky Hill, Kas.: (1864) act., May 16
Smoky Hill Crossing, Kas.: (1864) sk. (Ind.), Aug. 16
Smoky Hill R., Kas.: (1865) Fed. sc. to, Jan. 15
Smuggling: (1861) Nov. 30
Smyrna, Fla.: (1862) aff., Mar. 23
Smyth Co., Va.: (1863) sk., Sept. 14
Snake Cr. Gap, Ga.: (1864) Atlanta Camp., May 7, 8, 9, 10, 11, 12; sks., Sept. 15, Oct. 15
Snake Indians: (1862) Fed. exped., Aug. 19; (1863) Fed. exped., May 4
Snake R., Wash. Terr.: (1864) Fed. exped. to, Feb. 16
Snapfinger Cr., Ga.: (1864) sk., July 27
Snead's Fy., N.C.: (1864) Fed. sc., June 22
Sneedville, Tenn.: (1864) sk., Oct. 21
Snibar Hills, Mo.: (1865) Fed. sc., Jan. 18
Snicker's Fy., Va.: (1863) sk., Apr. 13; Fed. scs. from, May 12, 27; (1864) eng., July 17
Snicker's Gap, Va.: (1862) McClellan occupies, Nov. 2; (1863) sk., June 1; in Gettysburg Camp., June 15; sk., July 17, 21, 23; (1864) Fed. recon. toward, Mar. 16; sk., Sept. 16; oper., Oct. 28; sk., Nov. 30
Snickersville, Va.: (1862) Fed. recon., Oct. 13; sk., Oct. 22; (1864) sk., Mar. 6
Sni Hills, Mo.: (1864) Fed. sc., Feb. 6; sk., Apr. 29
Snodgrass Hill, Ga.: (1863) Bat. of Chickamauga, Sept. 20
Snow Hill, N.C.: (1865) sk., Mar. 28, Apr. 1
Snow Hill, Tenn.: (1863) sk., Apr. 2, June 4
Snow's Pond, Ky.: (1862) sk., Sept. 25
Snyder's Bluff, Miss.: (1863) Fed. exped. from, June 25; (1864) Conf. att., Mar. 30
Snyder's Mill, Miss.: (1862) aff., Dec. 27; (1863) Fed. demon., Apr. 29
Soap Cr., Ga.: (1864) Schofield crosses Chattahoochee, July 8
Socorro, N. Mex. Terr.: (1862) aff., Apr. 25
Soda Springs, Id. Terr.: (1863) Fed. exped. to, May 5
Soldier vote: (1864) Lincoln's concern over, Oct. 13; goes to Lincoln, Nov. 8
Soldiers' Home: (1863) Lincoln at, July 6; (1864) Lincoln at, July 10, 14
Solemn Grove, S.C.: (1865) eng. Monroe's Cross Roads, Mar. 9, 10
Solomon's Gap, Md.: (1864) aff., July 5
Somerset, Ky.: (1861) oper., Dec. 1; sk., Dec. 8; sc., Dec. 18; (1862) sk., Jan. 8; Bat. of Mill Springs, Jan. 19; *See* Mill Springs

Somerset, Tenn.: (1863) Fed. recon. toward, Nov. 5

Somerton Rd., Va.: (1863) sk., Apr. 12

Somerville, Tenn.: (1862) sk., Nov. 26; (1863) act., Jan. 3; Fed. exped. to, May 26; sk., Dec. 26

Somerville, Va.: (1863) sk., Feb. 9, Sept. 14

Somerville Heights, Va.: (1862) act., May 7

Sons of Temperance: (1863) Lincoln receives, Sept. 29

South, Dept. of the, Fed.: (1862) David Hunter commands, Mar. 15; Hunter assumes command, Mar. 31; Hunter orders emancipation, Apr. 12; O. M. Mitchel assigned command, Sept. 1; assumes command, Sept. 17; (1863) Hunter resumes command, Jan. 20; Gillmore in command, June 12; (1864) Hatch assumes command, May 1; (1865) Jan. 18; Gillmore reassumes command, Feb. 9

South Africa: (1864) *Alabama* arrives at Capetown, Mar. 20

Southampton, England: (1862) Conf. commissioners arrive, Jan. 30

South Anna Br., Va.: (1863) sk., May 3; Fed. exped. to, June 23; sk., July 4; (1865) sk., Mar. 14

South Anna R., Va.: (1862) destruction r.r. br., May 28; Fed. oper., May 29; Stuart camped on, June 12; Stuart leaves, June 13; (1863) Fed. exped. to, July 1; (1864) ment., May 10

South Atlantic Blockading Squadron (*See also* Blockade, U.S.): (1861) Du Pont commands, Sept. 18, 19; (1863) John A. Dahlgren commands, July 6

South Atlantic coast: (1861) citizens warned of invasion, Nov. 2; crops to be seized, Nov. 28; planters burn cotton, Nov. 29, Dec. 9

South Branch Br., W. Va.: (1861) sk., Oct. 26; (1864) sk., July 4

South Carolina: (1860) call for secession convention, Nov. 10; legislature resolves raising volunteers, Nov. 13; delegation to Buchanan, Dec. 8, 10; secession convention, Dec. 17, 18, 19; secedes from Union, Dec. 20; others approve, representatives resign from House, Dec. 21; resolve forts belong to S.C., Dec. 22; convention on rights, Dec. 24; reaction to transfer of garrison to Sumter, Dec. 26; seizes Ft. Moultrie, Castle Pinckney, Dec. 26, 27; commissioners in Wash., Dec. 26; U.S. revenue cutter taken, Dec. 27; Ga., Ala. offer troops, Dec. 27; commissioners see Buchanan, Dec. 28; (1861) setting up govt., prepare for war, Jan. 1; commissioners and Buchanan, Jan. 2; seizes Ft. Johnson, Jan. 2; secession convention adjourns, Jan. 5; demands surrender Ft. Sumter, Jan. 11; Buchanan refuses surrender, Jan. 13; State Convention ratifies C.S.A. Constitution, Apr. 3; *See also* Sumter, Ft.; (1862) law on Negro defense labor, Dec. 18; *See also* Charleston, S.C., and Charleston Harbor for military events in area; (1865) Sherman orders march through, Jan. 19: *See* Sherman, William T.; Johnson names Benjamin F. Perry provisional gov., June 30; ratifies Thirteenth Amendment, Nov. 13

South Carolina, Dept. of, Conf.: (1861) Ripley heads, Aug. 21

South Carolina, U.S.S.: (1861) captures blockade-runners, Oct. 4

South Carolina and Georgia, Dept. of, Conf.: *See* South Carolina, Georgia, and East Florida, Dept. of

South Carolina, Georgia, and East Florida, Dept. of, Conf.: (1861) Lee named to command, Nov. 5; Lee takes command, Nov. 8; (1862) Lee recalled to

Southwest, Army of the, Conf.: (1863) E. K. Smith assigned command, Jan. 14; extended, Feb. 9

Southwest, Army of the (or Army of Southwest Mo.), Fed.: (1862) Frederick Steele assumes command of, Aug. 29; E. A. Carr assumes command, Oct. 7

Southwest Cr., N.C.: (1862) sk., Dec. 13; (1864) Fed. sc. to, Dec. 10; (1865) sk., Mar. 7

Southwest Mo., Army of the, Fed.: *See* Southwest, Army of the

Southwest Mt., Bat. of (or Cedar Mt.): (1862) Aug. 9

Southwest Pass, La.: (1861) blockade-runners capt. off, Oct. 4

Southwest Virginia Camp. of Stoneman: *See* Stoneman, George

Spain: (1861) proclaims neutrality, June 17

Spangler, Edward (*See also* Lincoln, assassination of): (1865) Lincoln conspirator, imprisoned, May 1; found guilty, receives life, June 30; sent to Dry Tortugas, July 7

Spangler's Mill, Jonesborough, Ala.: (1862) act., July 26

Spangler's Spring at Gettysburg: (1863) Bat. of Gettysburg, July 1, 3

Spanish Fork Cañon, Ut. Terr.: (1863) Fed. exped., Apr. 11

Spanish Ft., Ala.: (1865) Feds. near, Mar. 25, 26; siege of, Apr. 2; Confs. evacuate, Apr. 8

Sparta, N.C.: (1863) sk., July 20

Sparta, Tenn.: (1862) sks., June 28, Aug. 5; Fed. exped. from, Nov. 17; (1863) Bragg's forces at, May 24; sks., Aug. 17, Nov. 20, 24; (1864) oper., Jan. 4, Mar. 11

Spaulding's or Sapello R., Ga.: (1862) sk., Nov. 7

Spavinaw, Ark.: (1864) sk., May 13

Speaker of House, U.S.: (1861) Galusha A. Grow, July 4

Special Orders No. 191 of Lee (lost order of Antietam): (1862) Sept. 9, 13

Specie payment: (1861) suspension in U.S., Dec. 30

Speed, James (F): (1864) appointed Attorney General by Lincoln, Dec. 1

Spencer, W. Va.: (1864) sk., June 16

Spencer rifle: (1863) Lincoln tests, Aug. 18

Spencer's Ranch, N. Mex. Terr.: (1864) sk., Apr. 15

Sperryville, Va.: (1864) Fed. sc. to, Jan. 10; Fed. recon. to, Mar. 17

Sphinx (Danish ironclad) (*See also Stonewall*, C.S.S.): (1865) leaves Denmark for France, Jan. 7

Spies (*See also* individuals): Rose Greenhow (1861) July 17, 24, (1862) Apr. 2; Belle Boyd, (1862) arrested, July 29; (1863) Feds. hang two spies, June 9

Spirit Lake, Minn.: (1864) aff. with Inds., May 16

Spiritualism: (1863) at White House, Apr. 23

Sporting Hill, Pa.: (1863) sk., Gettysburg Camp., June 30

Spotsylvania Court House, Va.: (1863) sk., Apr. 30; (1864) Grant moves toward, May 7; Bat. of, May 8, 9, 10, 11, 12, 13, 14, 15, 17, 18, 19

Sprague, Kate Chase (F): (1863) marries, Nov. 12

Sprague, William (F): (1863) R.I. sen. marries Kate Chase, Nov. 12

Spring Cr., Ark.: (1864) aff., Mar. 18

Spring Cr., Ga.: (1863) sk., Sept. 18

Spring Cr., Neb. Terr.: (1864) sk., Nov. 26

Spring Cr., Tenn.: (1862) sk., Dec. 19

Spring Cr. or Wayman's Mill, Mo.: (1862) sk., Aug. 23

Spring Dale Br., Miss.: (1862) sk., Dec. 3

Springfield, Ill.: (1860) Election Day scene, Nov. 6; Lincoln thronged by office seekers, Nov. 14; Lincoln returns to, Nov. 26; (1861) Lincoln farewell reception, Feb. 6; Lincoln departs, Feb. 11; (1864) fire at Camp Butler, Jan. 17; (1865) funeral of Lincoln, May 4

Springfield, Ky.: (1862) sk., Oct. 6; aff., Dec. 30

Springfield, Mo.: (1861) Fed. exped. from, July 20; July 25; Lyon falls back to, Aug. 5; Lyon moves out of, Aug. 9; Bat. of Wilson's Cr., Aug. 10; *See* Wilson's Cr.; Aug. 11; Price at, Aug. 20; Frémont moves toward, Oct. 7; act., Oct. 13; Zagonyi's charge, Oct. 25; Oct. 27; Nov. 1; Frémont's removal, Nov. 2, 3; (1862) sk., Feb. 12; Fed. occup., Feb. 13; (1863) Conf. move to, Jan. 7; Feds. resist att., Jan. 8; Fed. exped. from, Sept. 7, Nov. 10, 23; sk., Dec. 16; (1864) Fed. sc. from, Feb. 23; Fed. exped. from, Nov 5; Fed. sc. from, Nov. 11

Springfield, O.: (1863) sk., Morgan's raid, July 25

Springfield, Tenn.: (1862) oper., Nov. 26

Springfield, W. Va.: (1861) sk., Aug. 23; sk., Oct. 26; (1864) sk., June 26

Springfield Ldg., La.: (1863) aff., July 2; (1864) Porter's gunboats at, Apr. 11

Springfield Rd., La.: (1863) sk., May 23

Springfield Station, Va.: (1861) sk., Oct. 2, 3

Spring Hill, Ala.: (1865) Fed. exped. from, May 8

Spring Hill, Ga.: (1865) sk., Apr. 20

Spring Hill, Mo.: (1861) sk., Oct. 27; (1862) Fed. exped. to, May 24

Spring Hill, or Thompson's Station, Tenn.: (1863) Feds. surrender, Mar. 4; sks., Mar. 19; Mar. 23, May 2; (1864) sk., Mar. 13; Spring Hill Aff., Nov. 29; eng., Nov. 29; Hood withdraws to, Dec. 17; sk., Dec. 18

Spring I., S.C.: (1864) aff., Mar. 31

Spring Place, Ga.: (1864) sk., June 25; (1865) sk., Feb. 27; Fed. exped. to, Apr. 1

Spring R., Ark.: (1862) act., Mar. 13; (1863) sc., Oct. 7; (1864) sks., Feb. 9, Apr. 13

Spring R., Mo.: (1862) sks., Sept. 1, 20

Spring R. Mills, Ark.: (1865) Fed. exped. to, Feb. 23

Squib, C.S.S.: (1864) damages U.S.S. *Minnesota,* Apr. 9

Squirrel Cr. Crossing, Colo. Terr.: (1863) sk., Apr. 11

"Squirrel hunters": (1862) Cincinnati home guard, Sept. 10

Squirrel Level Rd., Va.: (1864) Bat. of Peebles' Farm, Sept. 30; Fed. recon. on, Oct. 8

Stafford Court House, Va.: (1862) Fed. recon. from, Dec. 21; (1863) sk., Aug. 22

Stafford Heights, Va.: *See* Fredericksburg, Va. (1862) A. of P. on, Dec. 16

"Stainless Banner": (1863) Cong. C.S.A. adopts, May 1

Stanard's Mill, Va.: (1864) comb., May 21

Stanardsville, Va.: (1864) sk., Feb. 29

Stanbery, Henry (F): (1864) named Trans-Miss. commissioner, Dec. 10

Standing Stone, W. Va.: (1862) sk., Sept. 28

Stanford, Ky.: (1863) sk., July 31

Stanley, David Sloane (F): (1864) protects road to Franklin, Tenn., Nov. 29

Stanly, Edward (F): (1862) mil. gov. N.C., May 2

Stannard, George Jerrison (F): (1864) Bat. of Ft. Harrison, Va., Sept. 29

Stanton, Edwin McMasters (F): (1860) Attorney General under Buchanan, Dec. 20; Dec. 27; opposes Floyd on Sumter, Dec. 28; joint document to Buchanan, Dec. 30; (1862) Lincoln names Sec. of War, Jan. 13; appointment confirmed, Jan. 15; introduces efficiency in War Dept. Jan. 16; arrest of Gen. Stone, Feb. 9; security of Wash., Mar. 13; re McDowell's corps, Apr. 3; size of Peninsula armies, Apr. 9; with Lincoln at Aquia Cr., Apr. 20; sails for Ft. Monroe, May 5; confers with Lincoln re troops, May 17; confers with Lincoln, May 24; calls on states for troops, May 25; authorizes Negro soldiers, Aug. 25; opposes McClellan, Sept. 2; creates provost marshal general, Sept. 24; discharges political prisoners, Nov. 22; (1863) Burnside on, Jan. 1; séance at White House, Apr. 23; commutation for Vallandigham, May 19; re Chicago *Times,* June 4; re Negro troops, July 21; Lincoln confers with, Sept. 11; strategy conference, Sept. 23; rail reinforcements to Rosecrans, Sept. 23; en route to visit Grant, Oct. 16, 17; confers with Grant, Oct. 20; Lincoln to, Dec. 18; visits prisoners, Dec. 27; (1864) re Negro colonists, Feb. 1; confers with Lincoln, Aug. 7; pressure to remove, Sept. 17; confers with Lincoln, Grant, Halleck, Nov. 23; re Nashville, Dec. 7; (1865) Lincoln to, Jan. 5; removal of Butler, Jan. 7; reports on Savannah visit, Jan. 20; message to Grant, Feb. 4, Mar. 3; halts draft, purchasing, Apr. 13; confers with Lincoln, Apr. 13; pursuit of Booth, Apr. 14, 22; "Now he belongs to the ages" attributed to, Apr. 15; Sherman angry with, Apr. 24; secrecy over Booth's capture, Apr. 26; Sherman allegedly snubs, May 24

Stanton, Ft., N. Mex. Terr.: (1861) July 26, Aug. 2; Conf. oper. against Inds., Aug. 25

Star House, near Lexington, Mo.: (1865) sk., May 4

Starlight, C.S.S.: (1863) capt., May 25

"Stars and Bars": (1861) first flew over Conf. Capitol, Mar. 4; (1863) "Stainless Banner" supersedes, May 1

Star of the West: (1861) leaves N.Y. for Ft. Sumter, Jan. 5; Charleston told vessel coming, Jan. 8; en route, Jan. 8; fired upon in Charleston Harbor, Jan. 9; arrives N.Y., Jan. 12; capt., Apr. 17; becomes Conf. receiving ship, May 4

State, Dept. of, Conf. (*See also* Cabinet, C.S.A.; Toombs, Robert; Hunter, R. M. T.; Benjamin, Judah P.): (1861) Robert Toombs, Feb. 19; R. M. T. Hunter, July 25; (1862) Judah P. Benjamin, Mar. 18

State, Dept. of, U.S. (*See also* Cabinet, U.S.; Cass, Lewis; Black, J. S.; Seward, William H.): (1860) Cass favors Union, Nov. 9; Cass resigns, Dec. 12; J. S. Black appointed, Dec. 20; document of advice on crisis, Dec. 30; (1861) Seward accepts post, Jan. 10; officially appointed, Mar. 4, 5

State line, Mo.: (1864) act., Oct. 22

Statesborough, Ga.: (1864) sk., Dec. 4

States' rights, Conf.: (1861) mobilization difficulties over, Oct. 16; (1862) correspondence from Davis on, May 29

States' rights, Fed. control of: (1860) Dec. 24

Station Four, Fla.: (1865) act., Feb. 13

Stonewall, C.S.S.: (1865) sails for France as ironclad *Sphinx,* Jan. 7; leaves Ferrol, Spain, Mar. 24; arrives in Havana, Cuba, May 11; surrenders in Cuba, May 19

"Stonewall" Jackson: *See* Jackson, Thomas Jonathan

Stonewall Jackson (blockade-runner): (1863) forced ashore, Apr. 11

Stono R., S.C.: (1863) U.S.S. *Isaac Smith* capt. in, Jan. 30; U.S.S. *Marblehead* att., Dec. 25; (1864) Fed. forces driven to, July 3; Fed. drive from, July 7

Stony Cr., Va.: (1862) sk., Apr. 2; (1864) Fed. recon. toward, Nov. 7

Stony Cr. Station, Va.: (1864) sk., May 7; Fed. sc. to, Oct. 11; sk., Dec. 1

Stony Lake, Dak. Terr.: (1863) act., July 28

Stony Point, Ark.: (1864) sk., May 20

Stoughton, Edwin Henry (F): (1863) capt. in bed by Mosby, Mar. 8

Strahl, Otho French (C): (1864) killed, Bat. of Franklin, Nov. 30

Strasburg, Va.: (1861) July 27; (1862) sk., Mar. 19; Mar. 20; Apr. 1; May 6, 13; sk., May 24; sks., June 1, 2; Fed. sc. from, June 22; sk., Dec. 21; (1863) sk., Feb. 25; recon., Apr. 20; sk., June 2; aff., Sept. 2; sks., Dec. 12, 13; (1864) sk., Feb. 2; aff., May 12; May 15, 26, July 20, 22, 23; sks., Aug. 13, 14, 15; 3rd Winchester, Sept. 19; sks., Sept. 20; Sept. 21; Oct. 7; act., Oct. 12; sk., Oct. 14

Strawberry Cr., Ark.: (1864) Fed. exped. to, Mar. 10

Strawberry Hill, Va.: (1864) comb., May 12

Strawberry Plains, Tenn.: (1864) Fed. withdrawal to, Jan. 16; sk., Jan. 21, Feb. 20; Fed. sc. from, Aug. 1; Feds. driven to, Nov. 4; sk., Nov. 16; (1865) Fed. exped. from, Jan. 28

Street's Fy., N.C.: (1863) sk., July 21

Strawberry Plains, Va.: (1864) eng., July 27

Streight, Abel D. (F): (1863) raid, Apr. 11, 17, 26, 30, May 1, 2; surrenders to Forrest, May 3; (1864) escapes from prison, Feb. 9

Stringham, Silas Horton (F): (1861) leads Hatteras exped., Aug. 27

Strong, Ft., Fla.: (1865) sk., Feb. 21

Strother fork of Black R., Mo.: (1862) sk., Sept. 13

Stroud's Mill, S.C.: (1865) sk., Feb. 26

Stroud's Store, Ark.: (1863) Dec. 16; sk., Dec. 23

Stuart, James Ewell Brown, "Jeb" (C): (1862) begins ride around McClellan, June 12; ride continues, June 13, 14; arrives in Richmond, June 15; exped. to near Fredericksburg, Aug. 4; commands cav. A.N.Va., Aug. 17; recon. after 2nd Manassas, Aug. 31; Lost Order, Sept. 13; Chambersburg raid begins, Oct. 9; enters Chambersburg, Pa., Oct. 10; destruction, Chambersburg, Oct. 11; completes 2nd ride around McClellan, Oct. 12; (1863) Bat. of Chancellorsville, May 1, 2, 3; cav. review Brandy Station, June 8; Bat. of Brandy Station, June 9; ride around A. of P., Gettysburg Camp. begins, June 25; ride continues June 27, 29; Bat. of Gettysburg, July 3; act. Buckland Mills, Oct. 19; (1864) Bat. of Spotsylvania, May 8; Sheridan's exped. against, May 9, 10; mortally wounded, Yellow Tavern, May 11; Lee hears of death, May 12

Stumptown, Mo.: (1863) sk., Aug. 2

Sturgeon, Mo.: (1865) sk., Feb. 27

Sturgis, Samuel Davis (F): (1861) at Wilson's Cr., Aug. 10; (1864) moves against Forrest, June 1, 4, 7; Bat. of Brice's Crossroads, June 10; retreat, June 12; sk., Collierville, June 13

Subligna, Ga.: (1864) aff., Jan. 22

Substitutes: (1862) Conf., Apr. 16; (1863) in U.S., Mar. 3; Conf. Cong. bans, Dec. 28

Sudley Fd., Va.: (1861) 1st Bull Run or Manassas, July 20, 21

Sudley Springs, Va.: (1862) 2nd Bat. of Bull Run or Manassas, Aug. 29

Suffolk, Va.: (1862) Fed. exped. from, Sept. 2; oper. around, Nov. 12, 15; Fed. recon. from, Dec. 8; sk., Dec. 28; (1863) Fed. exped. from, Jan. 8; sk., Jan. 27, 30; Fed. recon., Mar. 7; Conf. siege, Apr. 11; eng., Apr. 14, 15; sk., Apr. 17; capture of Battery Huger, Apr. 19; Feds. capture Hill's Point, Apr. 20; aff. Chuckatuck, Apr. 23; sk., Edenton Rd., Apr. 24; Longstreet at, May 1, 2; sk., May 1; Longstreet abandons siege, May 3; camp. concluding, May 4; Fed. sc. from, June 8; sc., June 10; Fed. exped. from, June 12; Fed. evac. of, July 3; Conf. raid, Nov. 11; (1864) sk., Mar. 9; (1865) Fed. exped. from, Mar. 10

Sugar Cr., Ark.: (1862) act., Feb. 16, 17; Curtis at, Mar. 6; sk., Oct. 17

Sugar Cr., Tenn.: (1863) sk., Oct. 9; (1864) sk., Dec. 26

Sugar Cr. Hills, Mo.: (1862) oper., Dec. 23

Sugar Loaf, N.C.: (1865) act., Feb. 11

Sugarloaf Mt., Md.: (1862) sk., Sept. 10

Sugar Loaf Prairie, Ark.: (1865) aff. near, Jan. 12

Sugar Loaf Prairie, Mo.: (1864) Fed. sc., Aug. 23

Sugar Valley, Ga.: (1864) comb., May 9, 11

Sullivan's I., S.C.: (1863) bomb. Ft. Sumter, Oct. 3; eng. with Fed. monitors, Nov. 16

Sulphur Branch Trestle, Ala.: (1864) act., surrender of, Sept. 25

Sulphur Springs, Ark.: (1864) sk., Jan. 25

Sulphur Springs, Tenn.: (1863) sk., Oct. 21; (1864) sk., Feb. 26

Sulphur (or Warrenton) Springs, Va.: (1862) acts., Aug. 23; sks., Aug. 25, 26, Nov. 13, 15; (1863) sk., Oct. 11; (1865) Fed. oper., Mar. 3

Sulphur Springs Rd., Ala.: (1864) aff., Apr. 11

Sultana (river steamer): (1865) disaster, Apr. 27

Summertown, Tenn.: (1863) sk., Sept. 23

Summerville, Ga.: (1863) Fed. recon., Sept. 10; sks., Sept. 10, 13, 15; (1864) act., July 7; sk., Oct. 18; (1865) sk., May 5

Summerville, W. Va.: (1861) act., Aug. 26; (1862) aff., July 25; Fed. exped. from, Nov. 24

Summit Point, W. Va.: (1864) sk., Aug. 21; (1865) Fed. sc. from, Mar. 16

Sumner, Charles (F): (1861) protests *Trent* Aff., Nov. 16, Dec. 23

Sumner, Edwin Vose (F): (1861) commands Dept. of Pacific, Apr. 25; relinquishes command, Oct. 20; superseded by G. Wright, Oct. 24; (1862) Seven Pines or Fair Oaks, May 31; commands Right Grand Div., A. of P., Nov. 14; at Falmouth, Va., Nov. 17; Nov. 22; occup. Fredericksburg, Dec. 11; Bat. of Fredericksburg, Dec. 13; (1863) Lincoln removes, Jan. 25; dies, Mar. 21

Sumner, Ft., N. Mex. Terr.: (1863) against Navajos, Aug. 20; (1864) sk., Jan. 5; Fed. sc., Aug. 3; (1865) Fed. sc., Mar. 15

Sump's Tannery, Va.: (1863) Fed. exped., Apr. 17

Susquehanna, Dept. of the, Fed.: (1864) Dept. of the Monongahela merged into, Apr. 6; merged into Middle Military Division, Aug. 7

Susquehanna R.: (1863) Meade mentions, June 28

Sutherland's Station, Va.: (1865) eng., Apr. 2

Sutton, W. Va.: (1863) sks., Aug. 26, Sept. 8; (1864) sk., Aug. 24

"Swamp Angel" (Fed. mortar): (1863) on Morris I., S.C., July 18; Aug. 4; major bomb. Ft. Sumter, Aug. 17; explodes, Aug. 22

Swampy Toe, Miss.: (1862) Fed. exped., to dig canal across, June 20; Fed. exped. arrives, June 25; digging continues, June 27; canal apparent failure, July 22; (1863) Grant resumes digging efforts, Jan. 22

Swan Lake, Ark.: (1864) aff., Apr. 23

Swan Quarter, N.C.: (1863) Fed. exped. to, Mar. 1

Swansborough, N.C.: (1862) Fed. recon. to, Aug. 14; (1863) Fed. exped. to, Mar. 6, Dec. 27; (1864) Fed. recon. toward, Feb. 9, Apr. 29; Fed. sc. to, June 22

Sweden's Cove, near Jasper, Tenn.: (1862) sk., June 4

Sweet Sulphur Springs, W. Va.: (1864) sk., June 23

Sweetwater, Ga.: (1864) sk., July 23

Sweet Water, Tenn.: (1863) sks., Sept. 6, Oct. 10, 26; (1864) sk., Jan. 25; (1865) Conf. att., Feb. 16

Sweetwater Br., Ga.: (1864) act., July 3

Sweetwater Cr., Ga.: (1864) sk., Oct. 2

Swift Cr., N.C.: (1865) act., Apr. 12

Swift Cr. (or Arrowfield Church), Va.: (1864) eng., May 9

Swift Cr. Village, N.C.: (1863) Fed. exped. to, Apr. 13, July 17

Swift Run Gap, Va: (1862) Apr. 30

Switzerland, U.S.S.: (1863) ram attempts to run Vicksburg, Mar. 25; passes Grand Gulf batteries, Mar. 31

Switzler's Mill, Mo.: (1862) sk., Aug. 10; (1863) sk., July 12; (1865) aff., Feb. 24; sk., May 27

Sycamore Church, Va.: (1862) sk., Aug. 3; Fed. recon. to, Aug. 4; (1864) aff., Sept. 3; Fed. recon. to, Sept. 5; Hampton's Conf. cattle raid, Sept. 16

Sykes, George (F): (1864) superseded, Fifth Army Corps, Mar. 23

Sylamore, Ark.: (1864) sk., Jan. 1

Syracuse, Mo.: (1863) sks., Oct. 5, 10

Tabernacle Church (or Beaver Pond Cr.), Va.: (1865) sk., Apr. 4

Taberville, Mo.: (1862) sks., July 20, Aug. 2, 11

Tabo Cr., Mo.: (1865) Fed. sc. to, Feb. 1

Tacony (U.S. bark): (1863) capt. by Conf. Charles Read, June 12; U. S. Navy hunts, June 15; captures schooners, June 22; exploits of, June 26

Tahkahokuty Mt., Dak. Terr.: (1864) Fed. act. against Sioux, July 28

Tahlequah, I.T.: (1862) Fed. recon. to, July 14; (1863) sk., Mar. 30

Talbot, Theodore: (1861) sent by Lincoln to S.C., Apr. 6

Talbot's Fy., Ark.: (1862) sk., Apr. 19; (1865) sk., Mar. 20

Talbott's Station, Tenn.: (1863) sks., Dec. 27, 29

Talladega, Ala.: (1865) occup., Apr. 22

Tallahassa Mission, I.T.: (1865) Fed. sc. from, Apr. 12

Tallahassee, Fla.: (1861) Fla. State Convention approves secession, Jan. 10; (1865) Samuel Jones surrenders forces, May 10

Tallahassee, C.S.S.: (1864) leaves Wilmington, Aug. 6; takes prizes, Aug. 10, 12, 15, 16; runs blockade at Wilmington, Aug. 25; changed to C.S.S. *Olustee,* which *see*

Tallahatchie R., Miss.: (1862) sks., Nov. 28, 30; (1863) Yazoo Pass exped., Feb. 24; Davis re, Apr. 2; (1864) sks., Aug. 7, 10

Tallulah Court House, Miss.: (1863) exped. to, Nov. 10

Tampa, Fla.: (1864) aff., May 6; salt works destroyed, July 11

Taney, Roger Brooke (F): (1861) as Chief Justice administers oath to Lincoln, Mar. 4; and *ex parte* Merryman, habeas corpus, May 27; (1864) death of, Oct. 12; funeral, Oct. 15; Chase succeeds, Dec. 6

Taneytown, Md.: (1863) Meade at, July 1

Tangier, Morocco: (1862) seizure of C.S.S. *Sumter* officers, Feb. 21

Tannery, The, near Little Rock, Ark.: (1864) sk., Sept. 2

Taos, Mo.: (1864) Fed. sc. to, July 19

Tarborough, N.C.: (1863) Fed. expeds. to, July 18, 21; sk., July 20

Tariffs, U.S.: (1861) Mar. 2; higher, Aug. 2, 5; (1862) increased, July 16; (1864) increased, Apr. 29

Taxes, Conf. (*See also* Income Tax, Conf.): (1863) tax in kind, Apr. 24; Commissioner of Taxes, May 1; use of force authorized to collect, Nov. 14; tax in kind changes, Dec. 28

Taxes, Fed. (*See also* Income Tax, U.S.; Tariffs, U.S.): (1861) $20,000,000 tax measure, Aug. 5

Taylor, Richard (C): (1862) assigned command Dist. West La., Aug. 20; (1864) opposes Fed. R. Camp., Mar. 28; draws back, Apr. 7; Bat. of Sabine Crossroads or Mansfield, La., Apr. 8; eng. Pleasant Hill, Apr. 9; orders, Apr. 10; att. Dunn's Bayou, May 5; assigned command Dept. of Ala., Miss., and East La., Aug. 15; assumes command, Sept. 6; Oct. 2; (1865) Davis on, Jan. 2; Davis to, Jan. 12; named command Army of Tenn., Jan. 13, 14; assumes command, Jan. 23; fall of Selma, Ala., Apr. 2; Apr. 26; truce with Canby, Apr. 30; May 2; surrender of army, May 4; parole of troops, May 8

Taylor, Ft., Fla.: (1860) Fed. move to protect, Nov. 15; (1861) Fed. garrison, Jan. 14

Taylor's Bayou, Tex.: (1862) aff., Sept. 27

Taylor's Cr. (or Crowley's Ridge), Ark.: (1863) sk., May 11

Taylor's Farm, Little Blue R., Mo.: (1863) sk., Aug. 1

Taylor's Hole, N.C.: *See* Averasborough, N.C.

Taylor's Ridge, Ga.: (1863) eng., Nov. 27; (1864) sk., Apr. 14; att., Apr. 27

Taylorsville, Ky.: (1865) sk., Apr. 18

Taylorsville, Va.: (1864) sk., Feb. 29

Tazewell, Tenn.: (1862) sks., July 26, Aug. 2; (1863) sk., Sept. 5; (1864) sks., Jan. 19, 24; Fed. sc. to, Aug. 3

Teaser, C.S.S.: (1862) gunboat capt., July 4

Tebb's Bend, Green R., Ky.: (1863) eng., Morgan, July 4

Teche, Bayou: *See* Bayou Teche; Teche Country oper.

Teche Country, La., oper.: (1863) Oct. 3, 4, 15, 16, 18, 21, 24, 27, 30, 31, Nov. 1, 2; eng. Bayou Bourbeau, Nov. 3; Nov. 5, 11, 12, 18, 23, 25

Teche Rd., La.: (1863) oper., May 21

Tecumseh, U.S.S.: (1864) sunk, Bat. of Mobile Bay, Aug. 5

Telegraph: (1861) U.S. confiscates dispatches, May 20; Oct. 22; trans-continental completed, Oct. 24; (1862) Fed. authority to take over, Jan. 31; U. S. War Dept. takes control, Feb. 25; intercepted, July 22; (1863) Fed. telegraph party capt., S.C., Sept. 13

Telford's Station, Tenn.: (1863) act., Sept. 8

Temecula Ranch, Calif.: (1861) exped. to, Sept. 25; Oct. 5

Temperance: (1861) meeting in N.Y., Aug. 4

Ten-Mile Run, Camp Finegan, Fla.: (1864) sk., Feb. 8

Tennessee: (1861) special session legislature, Jan. 7; convention, Jan. 19; voters reject secession convention, Feb. 9; refuse militia to Union, Apr. 17; legislature votes commissioners re Confederacy, May 1; legislature votes secession referendum, May 6; Gov. Harris leagues state to Confederacy, May 7; officially admitted Confederacy, May 16; voters approve secession, June 8; east Tenn. opposes secession, June 8, 17, 21; U. S. Sen. expels sen., July 11; T. A. R. Nelson opposes state action, Aug. 13; east Tenn., Sept. 7; Oct. 1, Nov. 8, 9; (1862) oper. east Tenn., Jan. 10; opened up by surrender Ft. Donelson, Feb. 16; capital moves to Memphis, Feb. 20; Lincoln names A. Johnson U.S. mil. gov., Feb. 23; Sen. confirms Johnson, Mar. 4; Davis proclaims martial law east Tenn., Apr. 8; Bragg proclaims restoration of, Sept. 5; Davis on, Oct. 21; (1864) pro-Union meeting, Jan. 21; Mar. 4; Breckinridge in east Tenn., Nov. 4; (1865), constitutional convention adopts anti-slavery amendment, Jan. 9; Lincoln on east Tenn., Feb. 13; ratifies constitution abolishing slavery, Feb. 22; W. G. Brownlow elected gov., Mar. 4; ratifies Thirteenth Amendment, Apr. 7

Tennessee, Army of, Conf. (*See also* camps. and bats. such as Perryville; Murfreesboro or Stone's R.; Tullahoma Camp.; Chickamauga; Chattanooga; Lookout Mt.; Missionary Ridge; Atlanta Camp.; Franklin, Tenn.; Nashville; commanders, Bragg, Braxton; Johnston, J. E.; Hood, J. B.; Taylor, R.): (1862) advance into Tenn., Aug. 28, Sept. 2; constituted, Nov. 20; Davis reviews, Dec. 13; (1863) Davis visits, Oct. 6, 9, 10; Oct. 13, 14, 23, Nov. 8; Bragg asks to resign, Nov. 28; Hardee temporary commander, Nov. 30, Dec. 2; Dec. 6; J. E. Johnston to command, Dec. 16; J. E. Johnston assumes command, Dec. 27; (1864) concern over Johnston, July 9, 12, 13, 16; Johnston relieved of command, Hood takes over, July 17, 18; army broken at Nashville, Dec. 15, 16; (1865) Jan. 9, 11, 12; Hood resigns, Jan. 13; R. Taylor named to command, Jan. 13; Jan. 14, 16; efforts to send to coast, Feb. 1; J. E. Johnston assumes command of army, Feb. 25

Tennessee, Army of the, Fed. (*See also* camps. and bats. such as Shiloh; Vicksburg; Chattanooga; Atlanta; March to the Sea; commanders, Grant, U. S.; Sherman, W. T.; McPherson, J. B.; Logan, J. A.; Howard, O. O.): (1862) Grant assumes command, July 17; Dept. constituted under Grant. Oct. 16, 25; (1863) Sherman appointed to command, Oct. 17; assumes command, Oct. 24; (1864) McPherson replaces Sherman, Mar. 12; death of McPherson, Atlanta, July 22; John A. Logan temporary commander, July 22; O. O. Howard assumes command, July 27

Tennessee, C.S.S.: (1864) surrender of, Mobile Bay, Aug. 5

Tennessee, Dept. of, Conf. (*See also* Tennessee, Army of): (1863) Dept. of East Tenn. merged into, July 25; Johnston to command vice Bragg, Dec. 16, 27; (1864) Johnston relieved, Hood commands, July 27

Tennessee, Dept. of the, Fed. (*See also* Tennessee, Army of the): (1862) constituted, Grant named to command, Oct. 16; Grant assumes command, Oct. 25; (1863) merged into Mil. Div. of the Miss., Oct. 16; Sherman to command, Oct. 17; (1864) Sherman replaced by McPherson, Mar. 12; John A. Logan replaces deceased McPherson, July 22; O. O. Howard commands army, July 27

Tennessee, Dist. of the, Conf.: (1862) Price assumes command, July 21

Tennessee and Georgia, Dept. of, Conf.: (1865) Johnston ordered to command, Feb. 22

Tennessee ironworks: (1862) destroyed by U.S.S. *St. Louis,* Feb. 16

Tennessee R.: *See* individual camps. and bats. such as, Henry, Ft.; Shiloh or Pittsburg Ldg.; Tullahoma Camp.; Chickamauga Camp.; Chattanooga Camp.; Johnsonville, Tenn.; and Forrest, N. B.

Tennessee troops, Conf.: (1861) Polk commands, Sept. 2; Nov. 19

Tennessee Valley: (1862) exped. into, Dec. 26

Tenth Corps, U. S. Army: (1864) bat. Ft. Harrison, Ft. Gilmer, Sept. 29

Terman's Fy., Ky.: (1864) sk., Jan. 9

Terre Bonne, La.: (1864) Fed. exped. from, Nov. 19; (1865) Fed. exped. from, Apr. 19

Terre Noir Cr. (or Antoine), Ark.: (1864) sk., Apr. 2

Terrell's Tex. Cav., Conf.: (1863) mutiny put down, Sept. 11

Territories, U.S. (*See also* individual territories): (1862) slavery prohibited in, June 19

Terry, Alfred Howe (F): (1865) leads 2nd Ft. Fisher-Wilmington exped., Jan. 4; at rendezvous, Jan. 8; off Ft. Fisher, Jan. 12; att. on, Jan. 13; bomb. Ft. Fisher continues, Jan. 13, 14; capture of Ft. Fisher, Jan. 15

Texas (*See also* individual military oper. and camps.): (1861) secession convention votes to secede, Feb. 1; convention elects delegates to Conf. Cong., Feb. 11; U.S. Arsenal seized, Feb. 16; referendum approves secession, Feb. 23; admitted to Confederacy, Mar. 2; ratifies Conf. Constitution, Mar. 23; U. S. Sen. expels sens., July 11; Nov. 20; (1862) included in Conf. Trans-Miss. Dept., May 26; gov. writes Davis for aid, July 28; (1863) Gov. Lubbock asks arms, July 13; (1865) Andrew J. Hamilton named provisional gov., June 17; (1866) Pres. Johnson declares insurrection over, except in Tex., Apr. 2; Johnson proclaims insurrection ended in, Aug. 20

Texas, Dept. of, Conf.: (1861) Paul O. Hébert commands, Sept. 18

Texas, Dist. of, Conf.: (1862) Magruder assigned command, Oct. 10; Magruder assumes command, Nov. 29

Texas, New Mexico, and Arizona, Dist. of, Conf.: *See* Texas, Dist. of

Texas, the: (1862) Great Locomotive Chase, Apr. 12

Texas Co., Mo.: (1861) Fed. exped., Nov. 13; (1863) aff. at, Sept. 12; (1864) Fed. exped. to, Nov. 5; (1865) sk., Jan 9

"Texas Invasion," of N. Mex. Terr.: (1861) Aug. 1

Texas Prairie, Mo.: (1863) sk., Aug. 29; (1865) Fed. sc. to, Jan. 12

Thanksgiving, day of: (1861) observed Confederacy, July 28; U.S., Nov. 28;

(1863) Lincoln sets Aug. 6 as, July 15; proclaimed, Oct. 3; (1864) Lincoln sets day of, Oct. 20

Theodora (steamer): (1861) Mason and Slidell sail on, Oct. 12

The Park, La.: (1865) Fed. expeds. to, Jan. 26, Feb. 17, Apr. 2

The Ponds, Miss.: (1865) sk., Jan. 4

Thibodeaux, La.: (1865) Fed. expeds. from, Jan. 30, Feb. 10, Apr. 2; Fed. sc. from, May 23

Third Army Corps, Fed.: (1863) at Gettysburg, July 2; at Manassas Gap, July 22, 23; moves to Front Royal, July 24

Thirteenth Amendment (frees slaves): (1864) U. S. Sen. approves, Apr. 8; U. S. House defeats, June 15; Lincoln for, Dec. 6; (1865) in House, Jan. 6; Representative Odell, Jan. 9; debate, Jan. 10, 12; passed by House, Jan. 31; ratified by Ill., Feb. 1; R.I., Mich., Feb. 2; Md., N.Y., W. Va., Feb. 3; Me., Kas., Feb. 7; Mass., Pa., Feb. 8; Va., Feb. 9; Mo., O., Feb. 10; Ind., Nev., La., Feb. 16; Minn., Feb. 23; Wis., Mar. 1; Vt., Mar. 9; Tenn., Apr. 7; Ark., Apr. 20; Conn., May 5; N.H., July 1; S.C., Nov. 13; Ala., Dec. 2; N.C., Dec. 4; Ga., Dec. 5; Ore., Dec. 11; states rejecting—Del., Feb. 7; Ky., Feb. 22; N.J., Mar. 1; Miss., Dec. 4; amendment in effect, Dec. 18

Thirteenth Army Corps, Fed.: (1862) Grant assumes command, Oct. 25; McClernand commands, Dec. 18; (1863) Ord to command, McClernand relieved, June 18; sent to Carrollton, La., Aug. 10

Thomas, George Henry (F): (1861) named brig. gen., Aug. 19; commands Camp Dick Robinson, Ky., Sept. 10; demon., east Tenn., Nov. 23; (1862) reports Ky. advance, Jan. 16, 18; Bat. of Mill Springs, Ky., Jan. 19; Bat. of Murfreesboro or Stone's R., Dec. 31; (1863) heads Fourteenth Corps, Jan. 9; Chickamauga Camp., Sept. 16, 18; Bat. of Chickamauga, Sept. 19, 20; at Rossville, Ga., Sept. 21; supersedes Rosecrans command Army of the Cumberland, Oct. 17; resists siege of Chattanooga, Oct. 22; Grant confers with, Oct. 23; offensive planned, Nov. 21, 22; Bat. of Chattanooga, Nov. 23–25; Orchard Knob, Nov. 23; Missionary Ridge, Nov. 25; pursues Bragg, Nov. 26; (1864) *See* Atlanta Camp.; demon. Dalton, Ga., Feb. 22, 23; Atlanta Camp., May 7, 9, 17, 18, 25, June 15, July 19, 20 (Peachtree Cr.) July 20, 27, Aug. 28, Sept. 1; sent to Nashville, Oct. 3; at Nashville, Oct. 21, 28, Nov. 1, 4, 9, 12; troops in position, Nov. 14; Hood's plan, Nov. 21; defense lines, Dec. 1; ordered to attack Hood, Dec. 2; Dec. 3; preparations, Dec. 4; Grant orders att., Dec. 6; pressure on to attack, Dec. 7, 8; Grant removes and rescinds order, Dec. 9; storm delays att., Dec. 9, 10, 11, 12; Grant orders Logan to replace, Dec. 13; tells of plans, Dec. 14; Bat. of Nashville, Dec. 15, 16; pursues Hood, Dec. 17, 18, 20, 21, 22, 23, 25; Lincoln on victory, Dec. 26; (1865) Davis on, Jan. 12; Depts. Ky., the Cumberland under, Feb. 10

Thomas, Philip F.: (1860) named Sec. of Treasury by Buchanan, Dec. 8

Thomas' House, Trinity R., Calif.: (1864) sk., May 27

Thomas' Station, Ga.: (1864) sk., Dec. 3

Thomasville, Mo.: (1864) sk., Sept. 14; (1865) Fed. sc. toward, Apr. 21

Thompson, Jacob: (1860) Sec. of Interior opposes force, Nov. 9; (1861) resigns Buchanan's Cabinet, Jan. 8; tells Charleston Feds. coming, Jan. 8; (1864) named Conf. commissioner to Canada, Apr. 27

Thompson, M. Jeff (C): (1861) raid in Ironton, Mo., area, Oct. 12; burns Big R. Br., Oct. 15; Fed. oper. against, Oct. 18; oper. in southeast Mo., Nov. 2; seizes Fed. vessel, Nov. 18; destroys Commerce, Mo., Dec. 29; (1865) surrender negotiations, May 9; surrenders forces, May 11

Thompson's Cr., La.: (1863) sk., May 25; (1864) sk., Oct. 5

Thompson's Cr., S.C.: (1865) sk., Mar. 2, 3

Thompson's Hill, Miss.: *See* Port Gibson

Thompson's Plantation, La.: (1865) sk., Jan. 23

Thompson's Station, Tenn.: *See* Spring Hill, Tenn.

Thorn (U.S. transport): (1865) destroyed, Mar. 4

Thorn, Ft., N. Mex. Terr.: (1861) sk., Sept. 26

Thornburg (or Massaponax Church), Va.: (1862) sk., Aug. 5; act., Aug. 6

Thorn Hill, Ala.: (1865) sk., Jan. 4

Thorn Hill, Tenn.: (1864) sk., Oct. 10

Thornton Station, Va.: (1861) Fed. recon. to, Oct. 20

Thoroughfare Gap, Va.: (1862) 2nd Bull Run Camp., Aug. 26; Bat. of Groveton or Brawner's Farm, Aug. 28; Fed. recon. toward, Sept. 16; Fed. exped. to, Oct. 17; (1863) sks., June 17, 21; Fed. exped. to, Nov. 21

Thoroughfare Mt., Va.: (1864) aff., Jan. 27

Three-top Mt., Va.: (1864) Bat. of Cedar Cr., Oct. 19

Threlkeld's Fy., Ark.: (1863) Fed. sc., Feb. 5

Thumb, Tom: (1863) entertained by Mrs. Lincoln, Feb. 13

Tickfaw Br., La.: (1863) sk., May 16

Tilghman, Lloyd (C): (1861) commands Fts. Henry, Donelson, Nov. 21; (1862) defends Ft. Henry, Feb. 5; surrender Ft. Henry, Feb. 6

Tilghman, William: (1861) capture of *S. J. Waring,* July 16

Tilton, Ga.: (1864) sk., May 13; surrender of, Oct. 13

Timberville (or Forest Hill), Va.: (1864) sk., Sept. 24

Tippah R., Miss.: (1864) sk., Feb. 24

Tipton, Mo.: (1863) aff., Oct. 10

Tiptonville, Tenn.: (1862) Pope prepares ass., Island No. 10 Camp., Apr. 6; Confs. surrender, Apr. 7; (1863) Fed. exped. to, Nov. 21

Tishomingo Cr., Miss.: *See* Brice's Crossroads (1864) Bat. of, or Brice's Crossroads, Guntown, June 10

Tobesofkee Cr., Ga.: (1865) sk., Apr. 20

Tod, David (F): (1864) former Ohio gov. declines Sec. of Treasury, June 30

Todd, George (C): (1864) att. Centralia, Mo., Sept. 27

Todd's Tavern, Va.: (1864) comb., Wilderness, May 6, 7, 8

Tolbert's Mill, Ark.: (1865) Fed. oper., Feb. 16

Toll-Gate near White Post, Va.: (1864) act., Aug. 11

Tomahawk, Ark.: (1864) sk., Jan. 22

Tomahawk Gap, Ark.: (1864) sk., Feb. 9

Tompkinsville, Ky.: (1862) sk., June 6; capture of, Morgan, July 4, 9

Tom's Brook, Va.: (1862) sk., June 3; (1864) sk., Oct. 8; eng., Oct. 9

Toombs, Robert Augustus (C): (1860) Ga. sen. on Committee of Thirteen, Dec. 20; (1861) considered for Conf. Pres., Feb. 9; Sec. of State, C.S.A., Feb. 19; resigns, July 25

Toone's Station (or Lower Post Fy.), Tenn.: (1862) aff., July 27; (1863) Fed. exped. to, Sept. 11

Torbert, Alfred Thomas Archimedes (F): (1864) eng. Tom's Brook, Oct. 9; exped. to Gordonsville, Dec. 19

Tornadoes: (1862) Apr. 2

Torpedo, C.S.S.: (1863) gunboat carries Confs. to Hampton Rds., July 4

Torpedo boats: (1863) C.S.S. *David* attacks *New Ironsides,* Oct. 5; (1864) C.S.S. *Squib* damages U.S.S. *Minnesota,* Apr. 9

Totopotomoy R.: (1864) comb., May 28; Feds. along, May 30; Bat. of Cold Harbor, June 3

Totten, James (F): (1861) evacuates U. S. Arsenal, Little Rock, Feb. 8

Totten's Plantation, Coahoma Co., Miss.: (1862) sk., Aug. 2

Toucey, Isaac: (1860) Sec. of Navy under Buchanan favors convention, Nov. 9

Towaliga Br., Ga.: (1864) aff., Nov. 17

Town Cr., Ala.: (1863) sks., Apr. 6, 27; act., Apr. 28

Town Cr., N.C.: (1865) sk., Feb. 19

Township, Fla.: (1863) sk., Jan. 26

Towson, Ft., I.T.: (1865) surrender of Confs., June 23

Tracy, Ft., Ala.: (1865) Mobile Camp., Apr. 9, 10, 11

Tracy City, Tenn.: (1863) Fed. exped. from, Aug. 22; (1864) sk., Jan. 20; Aug. 4

Trade, regulation of: (1864) restrictions lifted in Ky., Mo., Jan. 23; Lincoln's order on, May 20; (1865) Johnson lifts restrictions, June 2, Aug. 29

Trade with enemy (*See also* Cotton): (1863) Fed. regulations tightened, Nov. 15; (1864) Lincoln approves new regulations, Jan. 26; Lincoln order, May 20; Lincoln authorizes, Sept. 24

Trans-Allegheny or Western Dept. of Va., Conf.: (1862) Samuel Jones assigned command, Nov. 25; (1864) J. C. Breckinridge assigned command, Feb. 25; Breckinridge assumes command, Mar. 5

Trans-Mississippi (*See also* individual bats. and camps.): (1861) charges of Conf. neglect, Dec. 20; (1862), Davis and govs. re, May 20, July 28, Sept. 12; (1863) Davis concern for, Feb. 26, May 7; (1864) Lincoln names commissioners to, Dec. 10; (1865) resistance continues in, May 8

Trans-Mississippi, Army of, Conf.: (1865) surrenders, May 26; Shelby's men refuse terms, May 26

Trans-Mississippi Dept., Conf.: (1862) command extended, May 26; T. H. Holmes assigned, July 16; Holmes assumes command, July 30; Aug. 20; (1863) Jan. 28; in Southwestern Army, Feb. 9; Price ordered to, Feb. 27; (1864) Davis on, Apr. 28, Dec. 24; (1865) surrender suggested, Apr. 19; surrender of, May 26

Trans-Mississippi Dist., Conf.: (1862) Van Dorn commands, Jan. 10; assumes command, Jan. 29; T. C. Hindman assumes command, May 31; (1863) Davis on aid to Vicksburg, July 2

Tranter's Cr., N.C.: (1862) sks., May 30, June 2; act., June 5; Fed. recon. to, June 24

Travisville, Tenn.: (1861) Sept. 29

Treadwell's Plantation, Miss.: (1863) sks., Oct. 16, 20

Treasury, Comptroller of the, Fed.: (1864) post established, June 3

Treasury Dept., Conf.: (1861) Memminger named Sec., Feb. 18; (1864) Memminger resigns, June 21; Trenholm appointed Sec., July 18; (1865) Trenholm resigns, Apr. 28

Triune, Tenn.: (1862) sks., Dec. 27, 29; (1863) sk., Mar. 21; Fed. sc. from, May 3; sks., June 8, 9; act., June 11; sk., June 19; (1864) sk., Aug. 3; (1865) aff., Feb. 10

Troublesome Cr., Ky.: (1864) sk., Apr. 27

Troy, N.Y.: (1863) draft riots, July 13

Trumbull, Lyman: (1860) Lincoln to, Dec. 10

Tucson, Ariz. Terr.: (1862) evac., Apr. 15, May 4; Fed. occup., May 20

Tulip, Ark.: (1863) sks., Oct. 10, 12, 27

Tullahoma, Tenn.: (1862) Fed. recon. to, Mar. 25; Bragg concentrates, Nov. 13; armies converge on, Nov. 18; (1863) Confs. withdraw toward, Jan. 3; Bragg at, May 22; Rosecrans north of, May 31; Tullahoma Camp., June 23, 24, 26, 27, 28, 29, 30; occup. of, July 1; camp. continues, July 2, 3, 4; aftermath, July 11; (1864) Conf. raid, Mar. 16

Tulsey Town (Tulsa), I.T.: (1861) Dec. 9

Tumbling Run, Va.: (1864) Sept. 20; Bat. of Fisher's Hill, Va., Sept. 22

Tunica Bend (or Bayou Tunica), La.: (1863) sk., Nov. 8; (1864) aff., Apr. 21

Tunica Ldg., Miss.: (1864) Fed. exped. from, Oct. 5

Tunnel at Petersburg, Va.: *See* Petersburg

Tunnel Hill, Ga.: (1864) Fed. move toward, Feb. 22; sks., Feb. 23, 24; eng. Tunnel Hill or Buzzard's Roost, Feb. 25; Fed. recon. toward, Apr. 29; sks., May 2, 5, 6, 7, June 28; Hood's troops seize, Oct. 13; (1865) sk., Mar. 3

Tunnel Hill, Ky.: (1862) sk., Nov. 19

Tunnel Hill, Tenn.: (1863) Nov. 24; Missionary Ridge, Nov. 25

Tunstall, Thomas T. (C): (1862) seized by U.S. consul, Tangier, Feb. 21

Tunstall's Station, Va.: (1862) Fed. train escapes, June 13; (1863) May 4; (1864) sk., June 21

Tupelo, Miss.: (1862) Confs. move toward, May 29, 30; June 3; Confs. in, June 17; Sept. 19; Fed. raid to, Dec. 13; (1863) act., May 5; (1864) Forrest at, June 1; act., July 13; Bat. of Tupelo or Harrisburg, July 14, 15; Fed. retreat, July 16; Hood heads for, Dec. 27; (1865) Hood reaches, Jan. 9

Turkey Br., Va.: (1862) Bat. of (known as White Oak Swamp or Frayser's Farm), June 30

Turkey Cr., Jasper Co., Mo.: (1863) sk., Nov. 18

Turkey Cr., Va.: (1864) aff., Jan. 16; sk., July 12

Turkey I., Va.: (1864) *Shawsheen* capt., May 7

Turkey I. Cr. Br., Va.: (1862) recon. to, May 23

Turkeytown, Ala.: (1864) sk., Oct. 25

Turnback Cr., Mo.: (1862) sk., Apr. 26

Turner's Farm, Va.: (1864) comb., May 31

Turner's Fy., Ga.: (1864) sk., July 5; feint at, July 8; sk., July 16; oper., Aug. 26; sk., Oct. 19

Turner's Gap, Md.: (1862) bat., Sept. 14

Turner's Mills, Va.: (1863) sk., Jan. 30

Tuscumbia, Ala.: (1862) Fed. occup., Apr. 16; sks., Apr. 24, 25; Fed. exped. toward, Dec. 9; (1863) att. on, Feb. 22; act., Apr. 22; sk., Apr. 23; capt., Apr. 24; Streight's raid, Apr. 26; sk., Oct. 24; (1864) Confs. reach, Oct. 30; Hood at, Oct. 31; Forrest at, Nov. 16; (1865) Fed. exped. to, Feb. 19

Tuscumbia, Mo.: (1864) aff., Dec. 8

Tuscumbia Br., Miss.: (1862) Confs. burn, May 30

Tuscumbia Cr., Miss.: (1862) sk., May 31

Tuskegee, Ala.: (1865) sk., Apr. 14

Twelfth Army Corps, Fed.: (1863) sent to Rosecrans, Sept. 23; reaches Nashville, Oct. 1

Twelfth N. Y. Inf.: (1861) at White House, June 29

Twentieth Corps, Fed.: (1863) under A. McD. McCook, Jan. 9; (1864) Hooker resigns command, July 27; lines at Atlanta, Aug. 28; enters Atlanta, Sept. 1, 2; part of Sherman left wing, Nov. 9; March to the Sea, Nov. 14, Dec. 3; enters Savannah, Dec. 21; (1865) Carolina Camp., Feb. 22, 23, 26, Mar. 2

Twenty-first Army Corps, Fed.: (1863) T. L. Crittenden commands, Jan. 9

Twenty-first Ga. Cav., Conf.: (1864) aff., Waccamaw Neck, S.C., Jan. 7

Twenty-third Corps, Fed.: (1864) Nov. 9; at Franklin, Nov. 30; (1865) to N.C., Jan. 15; at Ft. Fisher, Feb. 9

Twiggs, David Emanuel (C): (1861) surrenders U.S. military posts, Feb. 18; dismissed U. S. Army, Mar. 1; superseded in Conf. command, Oct. 18

Two League Cross Roads, S.C.: (1865) sk., Feb. 15

290 (first name of C.S.S. *Alabama*): *See Alabama*

Tybee I., Ga.: (1861) Feds. land, Nov. 24; (1862) Feds. fire on Ft. Pulaski, Apr. 10, 11

Tyler, Daniel (F): (1861) eng. Blackburn's Fd., July 18

Tyler, Erastus Barnard (F): (1862) June 8; Bat. of Port Republic, June 9

Tyler, John: (1861) former Pres. presides at Peace Convention, Feb. 4; for patriotism, Feb. 5; (1862) death, Jan. 18

Tyler, U.S.S.: (1861) at Cairo, Ill., Aug. 12; eng. Iron Bluffs, Ky., Oct. 7

Tyler's Mills, Big R., Mo.: (1864) sk., Oct. 7

Tyler Mt., W. Va.: (1861) July 24

Typhoid: (1862) Feb. 8

Tyree Springs, Tenn.: (1862) sk., Nov. 7

Tyson's Cross Roads, Va.: (1863) sk., Nov. 14

"Unconditional surrender": (1862) Grant to Buckner, Ft. Donelson, Feb. 16; Grant new hero, Feb. 17

"Unconditional Union Men": (1863) Lincoln to, Aug. 26

Underwood's Farm, Mo.: (1861) sk., Oct. 14

Underwriter, U.S.S.: (1864) capt., Feb. 2

Undine, U.S.S.: (1864) damaged at Eastport, Miss., Oct. 10; Forrest captures, Oct. 30; damaged, Nov. 2; as Conf., Nov. 3; abandoned, Nov. 4

Union, U.S.S.: (1861) blockades Savannah, May 28; June 18

Union, Miss.: (1864) sk., Feb. 21

Union, Mo.: (1864) sk., Oct. 1

Union, Tenn.: (1862) capt., Dec. 30

Union, W. Va.: (1863) sk., Nov. 8

Union, Ft., N. Mex. Terr.: (1862) Feds. retire to, Mar. 4; Colo. volunteers move from, Mar. 26; Fed. exped. from, Oct. 9

Union Brigade, Corinth, Miss.: (1862) att., Oct. 5

Union Church, Miss.: (1863) sk., Apr. 28

Union City, Tenn.: (1862) Fed. desc., Mar. 30, 31; Confs. capture, Dec. 21; (1863) capture of Fed. outpost, July 10; Fed. exped. from, Sept. 1; sk., Nov. 19; (1864) sk., Mar. 12; Forrest captures, Mar. 24; sk., Sept. 2

Union Convention, National: (1864) *See* National Union Party Convention
Union Co., Ky.: (1864) sk., July 14
Union Co., Tenn.: (1864) Conf. raid, Aug. 7
Unionists: *See* Pro-Union sentiment
Union League: (1862) organized, June 25
Union League Council: (1864) and National Union Party Convention, June 8
Union League delegation: (1864) Lincoln addresses, June 9
Union Mills, Mo.: (1861) sk., Dec. 9; (1864) sk., July 22
Union Mills, Va.: (1863) aff., Feb. 14
Union Pacific-Central Pacific R.R.: (1862) Lincoln signs bill, July 1; (1864) Lincoln sets starting point of, Mar. 7
Union Party Convention, National: (1864) meets, June 7, 8, 9
Union Springs, Ala.: (1865) Fed. exped. to, Apr. 17
Union Station, Tenn.: (1864) sk., Nov. 1
Uniontown, Mo.: (1862) sk., Oct. 18
Unionville, Tenn.: (1863) sks., Jan. 31, Mar. 4, June 23
United States, U.S.S.: (1861) abandoned, Apr. 20
U.S. armory, Harper's Fy.: (1861) abandoned, burned, Apr. 18
U. S. Branch Mint and Customs House, New Orleans: (1861) seized, Jan. 31
U. S. Christian Commission: (1861) organized, Nov. 15
U. S. Coast Survey: (1861) vessels off Port Royal, Nov. 4
U. S. Ford, Va.: (1862) aff., Nov. 16; (1863) A. of P. moves toward, Jan. 19; in Chancellorsville Camp., Apr. 29; Bat. of Chancellorsville, May 2, 3
U. S. Marine Hospital: (1861) La. troops possess, Jan. 11
U. S. Naval Academy: (1861) transferred to Newport, R.I., Apr. 25, May 9
U. S. Sanitary Commission: *See* Sanitary Commission, U. S.
University Depot, Tenn.: (1863) sk., July 4
Upperville, Va.: (1863) Fed. sc. to, May 12; sk., June 2; eng., June 21; sk., Dec. 16; (1864) sk., Feb. 20; Fed. sc., Apr. 28
Upshaw's Farm, Barry Co., Mo.: (1864) sk., Oct. 29
Upton, Emory (F): (1864) at Spotsylvania, May 10
Upton's Hill, Ky.: (1861) sk., Oct. 12
Upton's Hill, Va.: (1862) Fed. recon., Sept. 16
Urbanna, Va.: (1862) Mar. 13
Urbanna Cr., Va.: (1861) U.S.S. *Rescue* captures schooner, Nov. 8
Usher, John Palmer (F): (1863) as Sec. of Interior, Jan. 8; (1865) offers resignation, Lincoln accepts, to take effect May 15, Mar. 9
Utah Cr., N. Mex. Terr.: (1862) Fed. exped. to, Oct. 9
Utah Territory: (1861) Ind. att., Aug. 8; (1863) Fed. exped., Apr. 11; Fed. sc. to Bear R., May 5
Utica, Miss.: (1863) sk., May 9
Utoy Cr., Ga.: (1864) Fed. troops cross, Aug. 3, 4; comb., Aug. 5; ass., Aug. 6; Sherman toward, Aug. 15; Schofield at, Aug. 18
Utz's Fd., Va.: (1863) sk., Oct. 7

Vache Grass, Ark.: (1864) sk., Sept. 26
Valhermoso Springs, Ala.: (1864) Fed. sc. to, Aug. 15
Vallandigham, Clement Laird: (1861) stoned, July 7; commends Wilkes in

House, Dec. 16; (1863) arrested, May 5; banished by Lincoln, May 19; O. protests arrest, May 23; turned over to Confederacy, May 25; Burnside resigns over arrest, May 29; Democrats protest arrest, May 30; Philadelphia meeting protests arrest, June 1; Davis rejects, June 2; nominated for O. gov., June 11; defeated for gov., Oct. 13; (1864) returns to O., June 15; backs McClellan, Aug. 31

Valley Br. (or Williston, White Pond, or Walker's), S.C.: (1865) sk., Feb. 8

Valley Dist., Conf.: (1863) Imboden named to command, July 21

Valley Mines, Mo.: (1865) sk., May 22

Valley of the Rio Grande: (1862) Sibley moves toward Ft. Craig, Feb. 21

Valley Rd., near Jasper, Tenn.: (1863) sk., Oct. 2

Valley Station, Colo. Terr.: (1864) sk., Oct. 10; (1865) sk., Jan. 7

Valley Turnpike (or Pike), Shenandoah Valley, Va. (*See also* Shenandoah Valley): (1862) Fed. retreat on, May 23, 24; Jackson moves south on, June 1; (1864) Bat. of New Market, May 15; Early goes north on, July 23; 2nd Kernstown, July 24; 3rd Winchester, Sept. 19; Sheridan on, Oct. 10

Valley Woods, Ky.: (1862) sk., Oct. 17

Valverde, N. Mex. Terr.: (1862) eng., Feb. 21

Van Buren, Martin: (1862) former Pres. dies, July 24

Van Buren, Ark.: (1862) Van Dorn retreats to, Mar. 8; Fed. recon. toward, Nov. 20; Hindman advances from, Dec. 7; sk., Dec. 21; Fed. capture of, Dec. 28; (1863) Fed. sc. to, Jan. 23, Feb. 5; (1864) sks., Apr. 12, July 7, Aug. 12; (1865) sk., Apr. 2

Van Buren, Mo.: (1862) sks., Aug. 12, Oct. 22

Van Buren, Tenn.: (1862) sk., Sept. 21

Van Buren Co., Ark.: (1864) sk., Mar. 25

Vance, Zebulon B. (C): (1862) as gov. N.C. asks supplies, Oct. 15; (1863) anxiety over desertion, May 13; on submission, Nov. 24; to Davis, Dec. 30; (1864) Davis to, Jan. 8

Vanceburg, Ky.: (1864) Conf. att., Oct. 28

Vanderbilt, U.S.S.: (1863) seizure of *Peterhoff*, Feb. 25

Vanderburgh's House, Va.: (1861) aff., Sept. 28

Van Dorn, Earl (C): (1862) command Trans-Miss. Dist., Dept. No. 2, Jan. 10; assumes command, Jan. 29; joins Price, Mar. 5; before Pea Ridge or Elkhorn Tavern, Mar. 6; Bat. of Pea Ridge, Mar. 7, 8; unable to aid at Shiloh, Apr. 7; assumes command Dept. of Southern Miss. and East La., June 20; Davis to, June 24; commands new Dist. of Miss., July 2; re Iuka, Miss., Sept. 19; toward Corinth, Sept. 29; replaced by Pemberton head Dept. of Miss. and East La., Oct. 1; Bat. of Corinth, Oct. 3, 4; pursued, Oct. 5; Oct. 12; commands First Corps, Dept. of Miss. and East La., Dec. 7; Holly Springs raid, Dec. 20; (1863) captures Feds. near Spring Hill, Tenn., Mar. 4; eng., Franklin, Tenn., Apr. 10; death of, May 7

Van Dorn, C.S.S.: (1862) Bat. of Memphis, June 6

Van Dusen's Cr., Calif.: (1861) sk., Apr. 14

Van Wert, Ga.: (1864) sk., Oct. 9

Varina Reach, James R., Va.: (1864) Fed. squad. bombards, June 21

Varioloid: (1863) Lincoln ill with, Nov. 21, 24, 26

Varnell's Station, Ga.: (1864) sk., May 4, 7; comb., May 9
Varuna, U.S.S.: (1862) sunk at New Orleans, Apr. 24
Vaughan Rd., Va.: (1864) act., Aug. 24; comb., Sept. 29; Fed. recon., Oct. 8;
    (1865) *See* Bat. of Hatcher's Run, Feb. 5, 6, 7; sk., Mar. 29
Vaughan Rd. Crossing, Va.: (1865) Bat. of Hatcher's Run, Feb. 7
Vaught's Mill, Milton, Tenn.: (1863) eng., Mar. 20
Velasco, Tex.: (1862) Conf. att., July 4; aff., Aug. 11
Venus (Fed. steamer): (1864) driven ashore, Nov. 2
Venus Point, Ga.: (1862) act., Feb. 15
Vera Cruz, Mexico: (1864) Maximilian lands, May 28
Vera Cruz, Mo.: (1864) sk., Nov. 3
Verde, Camp, Tex.: (1861) Col. C. A. Waite commands posts; abandoned by
    U.S. forces, Mar. 7
Verdon, Va.: (1862) sk., July 22
Vermillion Bayou, La.: (1863) sks., Oct. 9, Nov. 25, 30
Vermillionville, La.: (1863) sks., Nov. 5, 8
Vermont: (1864) St. Albans raid, Oct. 19
Vernon, Ind.: (1863) Morgan raid, July 12
Vernon Co., Mo.: (1863) sk., Mar. 30; General Orders No. 11, Aug. 25; oper.,
    Oct. 3
Vernon R., Ga.: (1864) naval atts., Dec. 14
Verona, Miss.: (1864) Forrest leaves from, Sept. 16; eng., Dec. 25
Versailles, Ky.: (1862) Morgan toward, Oct. 18
Versailles, Mo.: (1864) aff., July 13
Versailles, Tenn.: (1863) Fed. recon. to, Jan. 13, Mar. 9
Via's House, Va.: (1864) sk., June 3
Vice-admiral: (1864) U. S. Cong. establishes rank, Dec. 21
Vice-President, Conf.: *See* Stephens, Alexander
Vice-President, U.S. (*See also* Hamlin, Hannibal; Johnson, Andrew): (1864)
    choice of, June 7
Vicksburg, Miss.: (1861) Miss. orders artillery to, Jan. 12; Feb. 10; Davis at,
    Feb. 11; (1862) Union fleet at, surrender refused, May 18; Vicksburg
    fortifies, June 18; Fed. canal Swampy Toe, June 20; Earl Van Dorn assumes
    Conf. command of area, June 20, June 24; canal exped. arrives, June 25;
    bomb. by mortars, June 26, 27; Farragut's fleet passes, June 28; fleet north
    of, July 1; bomb. continues, July 3, 4; att. on Fed. fleet, July 15; Fed. att.
    Arkansas, canal fails, July 22; gunboats guard river, July 24; Confs. regain
    stretch Miss., Aug. 5; J. C. Pemberton replaces Van Dorn, Oct. 1; Lincoln
    authorizes McClernand exped., Oct. 20; Fed. moves toward Grand Junction,
    Oct. 31; Grant prepares overland camp., Nov. 1; Grant's progress, Nov. 4;
    Fed. probes, Nov. 19; Johnston to supervise Pemberton's defense, Nov. 24;
    Fed. build-up, Nov. 28; Forrest's raids to aid Vicksburg, Dec. 15; McCler-
    nand-Lincoln plans, Dec. 18; Confs. wreck Holly Springs, Miss., halt over-
    land march, Dec. 20; Davis at, Dec. 21; Davis on importance, Dec. 21; more
    guns for, Dec. 23; Sherman nears, Dec. 24, 25, 26, 27, 28; Sherman's as-
    sault Chickasaw Bayou, Dec. 29; Sherman halted, Dec. 30, 31
    (1863) Jan. 1; Sherman withdraws, Jan. 2; Jan. 11; McClernand toward
    Milliken's Bend, Jan. 17; Grant resumes canal efforts, Jan. 22; Davis on,

Vienna, Va.: (1861) act., June 17; sks., July 9, 17, Nov. 26; act., Dec. 3; (1862) exped. to, Feb. 22; sk., Sept. 2; (1863) Fed. recon. from, Nov. 18; Fed. scs. from, Dec. 18, 25, 28; (1864) Fed. sc. from, Apr. 28; (1865) Fed. sc. from, Apr. 8

Village Cr., Ark.: (1862) sk., May 21, June 12

Vincennes, U.S.S.: (1861) burns *Alvarado,* Aug. 5; goes aground, Oct. 12

Vincent's Cr., S.C.: (1863) aff., Aug. 4

Vincent's Cross Roads, Miss.: (1863) sk., Oct. 26

Vine Prairie, Ark.: (1863) sk., Feb. 2

Vining's Station, Ga.: (1864) eng., July 4; sks., July 7, 9, 17

Violett's, Mrs., Va.: (1863) aff. near, Mar. 22

Virginia (*See also* West Virginia; Virginia unionists; individual military camps. and bats. for war in Va.): (1861) Va. gov. on situation, Jan. 7; Va. invites states to Peace Convention, Jan. 19; Peace Convention in Wash., Feb. 4; refuses troops to Union, Apr. 16; convention passes ordinance of secession, Apr. 17; call for volunteers, Apr. 17; recruiting, Apr. 18; invites Conf. govs. to Richmond, Apr. 27; volunteers, May 3; Cong. votes capital to Richmond, May 20; May 21; referendum favors secession, May 23; gov. transfers troops to Confederacy, June 8; U. S. Sen. expels sens., July 11; Davis on defense, Sept. 13; West Va. constitution adopted, Nov. 26; (1864) Restored State of Va., Apr. 11; (1865) Va. unionists ratify Thirteenth Amendment, Feb. 9; Lincoln on calling legislature of, Apr. 5, 6, 12; "loyal" gov. established, May 23

Virginia, Army of, Fed. (*See also* Pope, John): (1862) Pope to command, June 17, 26; assumes command, June 27; controversial order, July 10; moves between Confs. and Wash., July 14; depredations order, July 18; hdqrs. in field, July 29; Conf. offensive, Aug. 3; Bat. of Cedar or Slaughter Mt., Aug. 9; reinforcements, Aug. 18; McClellan moves to support, Aug. 20; 2nd Bull Run or Manassas Camp., Aug. 26–31; Chantilly, Sept. 1; charges against Porter, McClellan, Sept. 3; consolidated with A. of P., Sept. 5, 12

Virginia, Dept. of, Conf.: (1861) organized, J. E. Johnston commands, Oct. 22

Virginia, Dept. of, Fed.: (1861) Wool succeeds Butler in command, Aug. 17; (1862) extended, June 1

Virginia, Restored State of: (1864) votes constitution, Apr. 11

Virginia, western: *See* West Virginia

Virginia, C.S.S., Conf.: *See Merrimack*

Virginia Central R.R.: (1862) raid on, May 20; Feds. destroy br., May 28; (1864) Fed. raids on, May 10; Fed. exped. toward, Dec. 19; (1865) Grant orders destroyed, Feb. 27; wrecked, Mar. 19

Virginia City (Alder Gulch), Mont. Terr.: (1863) gold discovered, May 26

Virginia House of Delegates: (1862) on enrolling free Negroes, Feb. 4

Virginia Military Institute: (1864) Bat. of New Market, May 15; Feds. burn buildings, June 11

Virginia and North Carolina, Dept. of, Conf.: (1863) Longstreet assumes command of, Feb. 26; reorganized, Apr. 1

Virginia and North Carolina, Dept. of, Fed.: (1863) Foster assumes command, July 18; Butler commands, Nov. 11; (1865) Butler relieved command, Jan. 7; E. O. C. Ord in command, Jan. 7

Warwick R., Va.: (1862) McClellan approaches, Apr. 4; Yorktown-Warwick R. line, Apr. 6

Warwick Swamp, Va.: (1864) sk., July 12

Washburn, Cadwallader Colden (F): (1864) Forrest occupies Memphis, Aug. 21

Washburne, Elihu Benjamin (F): (1860) Lincoln to, Dec. 21; (1861) greets Lincoln, Feb. 23

Washington (U.S. revenue cutter): (1861) seized New Orleans, Jan. 31

Washington, Ark.: (1864) sk., May 28; (1865) sk., Mar. 11

Washington, D.C. (*See also* District of Columbia): (1861) rumors of plot to capture, Jan. 3; defenses, Jan. 5; concern over att., Mar. 1; defenses, Apr. 17; Pa. troops arrive, Apr. 18, 20; guarding of, Apr. 19; Baltimore riots, Apr. 19; isolated, Apr. 21; fears att., Apr. 24; crisis over, Apr. 27; more troops, May 9; after 1st Manassas or Bull Run, July 21, 23; habeas corpus suspension authorized, Oct. 14; (1862) Feb. 22; defenses, Mar. 8; news, *Monitor-Merrimack*, Mar. 9; Lincoln to McClellan on security, Mar. 13; protection of, Mar. 17, 19, 20, 23, Apr. 3; slavery abolished in D.C., Apr. 3, 16; Lincoln to McClellan, Apr. 9; McDowell defending, Apr. 18, May 1; fears of Jackson, May 23; May 24; Lincoln to McClellan, May 26; May 30; Army of Va. to protect, June 26, July 14; A. of P. ordered back to defend, Aug. 3; McClellan at, Aug. 27; Aug. 29; Conf. armies near, Aug. 30; Sept. 1; troops into entrenchments, Sept. 2; McClellan forces around, Sept. 5, 7; Heintzelman commands defenses, Sept. 9, Oct. 26; (1863) civilians sent south, Jan. 7; pro-Union meeting, Aug. 11; Russian Navy visit, Sept. 23; Conf. threat, Bristoe Camp., Oct. 9, 12, 13, 14; (1864) concern over Early's threat, July 3, 5, 6, 7, 8, 9, 10; Early at, July 11, 12; Early's retreat, July 13, 14, 15; Halleck commands defenses, July 27; Sixth Corps toward, Oct. 10; (1865) Grand Review, May 23, 24

Washington, D.C., Dept. of, Fed.: (1861) Joseph K. F. Mansfield assigned, Apr. 27; merged into Dept. of the Potomac, Aug. 17; (1863) re-created, Feb. 7; C. C. Augur commands, Oct. 14; (1864) Halleck commands, July 27; merged into Middle Military Division, Aug. 7

Washington, La.: (1863) Fed. occup., Apr. 20; sks., Apr. 22, May 1, Oct. 24, 31

Washington, Mo.: (1864) Conf. occup., Oct. 2

Washington, N.C.: (1862) Feds. capture, Mar. 20; Fed. recon. from, June 24; eng., Sept. 6; (1863) sk., Feb. 13; Conf. siege of, Mar. 30; eng., Apr. 4; end siege, Apr. 15; Fed. exped., Apr. 17; sk., Aug. 14; Fed. exped. from, Dec. 17; (1864) Fed. evac., Apr. 26

Washington, O.: (1863) sk., Morgan, July 24

Washington, Tenn.: (1864) Conf. capture of, Feb. 26

Washington, Ft., Md.: (1861) Jan. 5

Washington Arsenal, D.C.: (1864) explosion, June 17; (1865) conspirators hanged in, July 7

Washington Co., Ark.: (1865) sk., Feb. 17

Washington Co., Miss.: (1864) Fed. oper., Oct. 24

Washington Co., Mo.: (1861) Oct. 14

Washington Navy Yard: (1861) Lincoln visits, Apr. 2; Cabinet on, Apr. 18; John A. Dahlgren commands, Apr. 22; (1862) Lincoln visits French vessel, Apr. 26; (1865) Booth's body taken to, Apr. 26

Washington Observatory: (1861) Dec. 26

Washita, Ft., I.T.: (1861) Fed. troops concentrate, Apr. 16; abandoned, Apr. 30; Texas militia occupies, May 1

Wassaw Sound, Ga.: (1863) Fed. *Weehawken* captures *Atlanta,* June 17

Watauga R., Tenn.: (1862) br. destroyed, Dec. 30; (1864) Fed. exped. to, Apr. 25

Wateree R., S.C.: (1865) sk., Feb. 22

Waterford, Miss.: (1862) sk., Nov. 29

Waterford, Va.: (1862) sks., Aug. 27, Dec. 14; (1863) sk., Aug. 8

Waterhouse's Mill, Tenn.: (1864) sk., Apr. 19

Waterloo, La.: (1863) demon., June 16; (1864) sk., Oct. 20

Waterloo, Va.: (1862) sk., Nov. 14

Waterloo Br., Va.: (1862) act., Aug. 24

Waterproof, La.: (1864) Fed. exped. to, Jan. 29; sk., Apr. 20; Fed. exped. to, Sept. 26

Water Valley, Miss.: (1862) sks., Dec. 4, 18

Water Witch, U.S.S.: (1864) capt., June 3

Watie, Stand (C): (1865) surrender of, June 23

Watkins Fy., Ga.: (1862) sk., May 3

Watkins House, Va.: (1865) act., Mar. 25

Watts, Thomas Hill (C): (1862) Conf. Attorney General, Mar. 18; (1863) resigns, becomes gov. Ala., Sept. 8

Watuga R., Tenn.: (1864) sk., Sept. 29

Waugh's Farm, near Batesville, Ark.: (1864) captures wagon train, Feb. 19

Wauhatchie, Tenn.: (1863) eng., Oct. 28

Wauhatchie Valley, Tenn.: (1863) Fed. advance to, Oct. 27

Waverly, Mo.: (1862) Fed. oper., May 25; June 4; (1863) aff., June 1

Wayman's Mill or Spring Cr., Mo.: (1862) sk., Aug. 23

Wayne, Ft., I.T.: (1862) sk., Oct. 22

Wayne Co., Mo.: (1862) Fed. sc., Aug. 20; (1864) sk., Apr. 26; (1865) Fed. sc. in, Mar. 9

Wayne Co., W. Va.: (1864) Fed. sc., Mar. 16

Wayne Court House, W. Va.: (1861) sk., Aug. 26

Waynesborough, Ga.: (1864) act., Nov. 27; sk., Nov. 28; eng., Dec. 4

Waynesborough, Va.: (1864) sk., June 10; Sheridan toward, Sept. 25; sk., Sept. 29; (1865) eng., Mar. 2

Waynesville, Mo.: (1862) sk., May 31; Fed. sc. from, July 6; (1863) Fed. sc. from, June 20; sk., Aug. 25; sk., Oct. 26; Fed. sc., Nov. 25; (1864) sks., Sept. 30, Nov. 1; oper., Dec. 1; (1865) oper., Jan. 16; Fed. sc. from, Mar. 5, 29; sk., May 23

Weaverville, Va.: (1863) sk., Aug. 27

Webber's Falls, I.T.: (1863) sks., Apr. 11, 25, Sept. 9, Oct. 12

Webster, Washington Co., Mo.: (1864) Conf. att., July 19; aff., Aug. 23

Webster Co., Ky.: (1864) sk., July 14

Webster Co., W. Va.: (1861) sk., Dec. 29; (1864) Fed. sc., May 15

Weed, Thurlow (F): (1864) re Lincoln election, Aug. 12

Weehawken, U.S.S.: (1863) att., Charleston, Apr. 7; aground, Sept. 7; founders, Dec. 6

Weem's Springs, Tenn.: (1863) sk., Aug. 19

Wetumpka, Ala.: (1865) sks., Apr. 13, May 4
Weyer's Cave, Va.: (1864) sks., Sept. 26, 27
Whaley's Mill, Mo.: (1862) sk., Sept. 13
Wheatfield: (1863) at Gettysburg, July 2
Wheatley Farm, Va.: (1863) Bat. of Kelly's Fd., Mar. 17
Wheeler, Joseph (C): (1862) captures London, Ky., Oct. 22; at Murfreesboro or Stone's R., Dec. 31; (1863) raid, Jan. 8; captures U.S.S. *Slidell,* Jan. 13; raids in Tenn., Apr. 7; raid, Sept. 30, Oct. 1, 2, 3, 4, 5, 6, 7, 9, 12, 13; (1864) Atlanta Camp., May 24; Ga. and Tenn. raid, Aug. 10; Waynesborough, Ga., Nov. 27, Dec. 4; (1865) eng. Monroe's Cross Roads, Mar. 10; Bat. of Bentonville, Mar. 19, 20, 21
Wheeling, W. Va. (*See also* West Virginia): (1861) Union meetings, May 11, June 19; convention, Aug. 20; new state ratified, Oct. 24; constitution adopted, Nov. 26; (1862) convention bans Negroes, Feb. 13
Whippoorwill Cr., Ky.: (1861) sk., Dec. 1
Whippy Swamp, S.C.: (1865) sk., Feb. 2
Whippy Swamp Cr., S.C.: (1865) sk., Feb. 1
Whisky Bayou, La.: (1865) Fed. exped. to, Jan. 16
Whistler (or Eight-Mile Cr.), Ala.: (1865) sk., Apr. 13
White, Moses J. (C): (1862) surrenders Ft. Macon, N.C., Apr. 25
White Cloud, U.S.S.: (1864) Conf. att., Aug. 29
White Co., Ark.: (1862) sk., May 27; (1864) sk., Feb. 9
White Co., Tenn.: (1864) sk., Jan. 15; Fed. sc., Feb. 1
White Hall, N.C.: (1862) eng., Dec. 16
White Hall Br., N.C.: (1862) aff., Dec. 15
White Hare, Mo.: (1864) sk., June 15
White House, C.S.A.: (1864) New Year's Day reception, Jan. 1; Davis' son killed, Apr. 30
White House, U.S.: (1861) reception, Jan. 1; Lincoln calls, Feb. 23; "Frontier Guards" in, Apr. 18; Ellsworth's funeral, May 25; Twelfth N.Y. on grounds, June 29; lack of ceremony at, Aug. 3; (1862) ball, Feb. 5; Willie Lincoln ill, Feb. 7, 8; Willie Lincoln dies, Feb. 20; (1863) New Year's reception, Jan. 1; reception, Feb. 21; séance in, Apr. 23; Emily Todd Helm guest, Dec. 13; (1864) New Year's ceremonies, Jan. 1; levee, Feb. 9; fire in stables, Feb. 10; Lincoln meets Grant, Mar. 8; Grant given commission, Mar. 9; (1865) New Year's reception, Jan. 2; Lincoln lies in state, Apr. 17, 18; Lincoln funeral service, Apr. 19
White House, on the Pamunkey, Va. (or White House Ldg.): (1862) McClellan hdqrs. at, May 16; McClellan moves, June 26; evacuated, burned, June 28; (1863) Fed. exped. to, Jan. 7; Fed. exped. from, July 1, 2; (1864) May 12; Sheridan at, May 21; May 30; June 1; sks., June 12, 20, 21; Sheridan leaves, June 22, 23, 24; (1865) Sheridan at, Mar. 19
White House Fd., Va.: (1862) Fed. recon. to, July 22
Whitemarsh I., Ga.: (1862) aff., Mar. 30; sk., Apr. 16; (1864) sk., Feb 22
White Oak Bayou, Miss.: (1862) sk., July 23, 24
White Oak Cr., Ark.: (1864) sks., Apr. 14, Aug. 11
White Oak Cr., N.C.: (1863) sk., Jan. 17
White Oak Cr., Tenn.: (1865) sk., Apr. 1
White Oak Ridge, Mo.: (1862) sk., oper., Aug. 18

Wildcat, Camp, Ky. (*See also* Rockcastle Hills): (1861) act., Oct. 21

Wilder, John T. (F): (1862) surrenders Munfordville, Ky., Sept. 17

Wilderness, The, Va.: (1863) in Chancellorsville Camp., Apr. 28, 29, 30, May 1, 2, 3, 4; (1864) Bat. of, May 5, 6; aftermath, May 7; Feds. move to Spotsylvania, May 8; Lee entrenched in, May 9; May 13; bat. losses, May 19

Wilderness Church, Va.: (1863) wagon train capt., Nov. 27

Wilderness Tavern, Va.: (1864) May 7

Wild Haws, Ark.: (1864) Fed. exped., Mar. 10

Wilkerson's Cross Roads, Tenn.: (1862) sk., Dec. 29

Wilkes, Charles (F): (1861) *Trent* Aff., Nov. 8; arrives Ft. Monroe, Nov. 15; honored, Nov. 26, Dec. 16; (1863) *Peterhoff* seizure, Feb. 25

Wilkesborough, N.C.: (1865) sk., Mar. 29

Willard's Hotel, Wash.: (1861) Lincoln at, Feb. 23, Mar. 4

William Aiken: (1860) U.S. revenue cutter surrenders, Dec. 27

Williams, Thomas (F): (1861) N.C. Fed. comm., Oct. 13; (1862) leads Fed. exped. to Vicksburg, June 20; opposite Vicksburg, June 25; commands eng. Baton Rouge, killed, Aug. 5

Williams' Br., La.: (1863) on Grierson raid, sk., May 2

Williamsburg, Ky.: (1863) sk., July 25

Williamsburg, Va.: (1862) J. E. Johnston pulls back through, May 3; sk., Mar. 4; Bat. of, May 5; Fed. occup., May 6; May 7; Aug. 14; Conf. att., Sept. 9; (1863) Fed. sc. from, Jan. 19; sks., Mar. 29, Apr. 11; Fed. expeds. from, Aug. 26, Nov. 9, Dec. 12; (1864) Fed. sc., Jan. 19; Fed. exped., Apr. 27; (1865) aff., Feb. 11

Williamsburg Rd., Va.: (1864) Oct. 27

Williamsport, La.: (1864) aff., Raccourci, Nov. 25

Williamsport, Md.: (1861) Feds. cross Potomac, July 2; (1862) May 24; May 26; Banks crosses Potomac, May 27; sks., Sept. 19, 20, Oct. 29; (1863) Confs. cross Potomac, June 15; act., July 6, 8; Lee gathers forces after Gettysburg, July 10; Meade prepares att., July 12; sk., July 14; (1864) sk., July 25; Confs. at, July 29; sk., Aug. 5; Confs. in, Aug. 25; aff., Aug. 26

Williamsport, Tenn.: (1862) sk., Aug. 11

Willis' Church, Va.: (1862) sk., June 29; Bat. of (also Frayser's Farm or White Oak Swamp), June 30

Williston, S.C.: (1865) sk., Feb. 8

Willoughby Run, Pa.: (1863) Bat. of Gettysburg, July 1

Willow Cr., Calif.: (1863) sk., Nov. 17

Willow Springs, Miss.: (1863) sk., May 3

Will's Cr., Ala.: (1863) sk., Sept. 1

Will's House, Gettysburg, Pa.: (1863) Lincoln at, Nov. 18, 19

Willstown, S.C.; (1862) eng., Apr. 29

Willstown Bluff, S.C.: (1863) eng., July 10

Will's Valley, Ala.: (1863) sk., Aug. 31

Wilmington, N.C.: (1861) occup. Fts. Johnston, Caswell, Jan. 10; blockade begins, July 14; (1863) *Britannia* runs blockade, Mar. 15; June 2; Davis at, Nov. 6; (1864) capture of blockade-runner, Feb. 16; Aug. 2; C.S.S. *Tallahassee* leaves, Aug. 6; last major Conf. port, Aug. 23; Aug. 25; Fed. plans, Oct. 12; blockade tightens, Oct. 22; C.S.S. *Olustee* (formerly *Tallahassee*) runs blockade, Oct. 30; Fed. fleet sails for, Dec. 18; Davis on, Dec. 20; Fed.

Ft. Fisher exped., Dec. 23, 24, 25, 28, 30; (1865) 2nd. Fed. exped., readying, Jan. 3; Feds. off Ft. Fisher, Jan. 12; 2nd att. Ft. Fisher, Jan. 13, 14, 15; Fed. att. Wilmington prepared, Feb. 9; drive on, Feb. 18, 19, 20; evac., Feb. 21; capt., Feb. 22; Fed. march from, Mar. 18

Wilmington I., Ga.: (1862) aff., Mar. 30

Wilmington Narrows, Ga.: (1862) Fed. naval recon., Jan. 26

Wilmington R., Ga.: (1863) *Atlanta* vs. *Weehawken*, June 17

Wilmington and Weldon R.R., N.C.: (1863) Fed. raid, July 3, 6

Wilson, James Harrison (F): (1864) exped., June 22, 23; Nov. 27; Bat. of Nashville, Dec. 16; pursuit of Hood, Dec. 17; (1865) Selma Camp., Mar. 22; sks., Mar. 28, 30, 31, Apr. 1; fall of Selma, Apr. 2; act. Northport, Apr. 3; takes Tuscaloosa, Apr. 4; sks., Apr. 7, 10; occup. Montgomery, Ala., Apr. 12; sk., Apr. 14; captures West Point, Columbus, Ga., Apr. 16; Apr. 17; sks., Apr. 18, 19; occup. Macon, Ga., Apr. 20; occup. Talladega, Ala., Apr. 22

Wilson Cr. Pike, Tenn.: (1862) sks., Dec. 21, 25

Wilson's Cr., Mo.: (1861) Aug. 9; Bat. of (or Springfield or Oak Hills), Aug. 10; aftermath, Aug. 11, 12; Nov. 2; (1862) Fed. advance from, Dec. 7

Wilson's Gap, Tenn.: (1862) sks., June 10, 18

Wilson's Ldg., La.: (1864) sks., May 2, 14

Wilson's Plantation, La.: (1864) sk., Apr. 7

Wilson's Store, S.C.: (1865) sk., Mar. 1

Wilson's Wharf, Va.: (1864) act., May 24

Wilsonville, Tenn.: (1864) Fed. wagons capt., Jan. 22

Winans, Ross: (1861) seized by Butler, May 14

Winans steam gun: (1861) capt. by Feds., May 10

Winchester, Ky.: (1863) sk., July 29; (1864) Morgan retreats, June 9

Winchester, Tenn.: (1862) sks., May 22, 24, June 10, 16; (1863) sks., July 3, Sept. 26; sc. from, Oct. 29; sk., Nov. 22; (1864) aff., May 10; guerrillas, May 29

Winchester, Va.: (1861) June 15; Confs. fall back to, July 3; sk., July 15; July 17; (1862) Romney Camp., Jan. 3; Confs. pull back, Feb. 7; exped. toward, Mar. 5; sks., Mar. 7, 11; Jackson withdraws, Mar. 11; Feds. in, Mar. 12; Mar. 20; Bat. of 1st Kernstown, Mar. 23; Jackson attempts to cut off Banks from, May 23; Banks' retreat, May 24; Bat. of 1st Winchester, May 25; Jackson occupies, May 26; sk., June 18; Aug. 23; Feds. evacuate, Sept. 2; Conf. occup., Sept. 3; Nov. 20, 21; sk., Nov. 22; Fed. recon. to, Dec 2; (1863) sk., Feb. 25; sks., Mar. 19, Apr. 8; Fed. recon. from, Apr. 12; Fed. exped. from, Apr. 17; Fed. recon. from, Apr. 20; Fed. sc. from, May 4; Lee moves toward, June 12; sk., June 13; Bat. of 2nd Winchester, June 14, 15; July 20, 21; Fed. cav. exped. from, Aug. 5; Fed. sc. to, Aug. 14; Fed. sc. from, Oct. 29; sk., Nov. 13; (1864) aff., Feb. 5; aff., Mar. 22; sk., Apr. 8; aff., Apr. 26; Early at, July 2; Early leaves, July 3; Early retreats toward, July 19; eng. Stephenson's Depot, July 20; Feds. near, July 22; 2nd Kernstown, July 24; Aug. 9; Early near, Aug. 10; Early moves south, Aug. 11; sks., Aug. 11; Aug. 12; Aug. 15, 16; act., Aug. 17; Aug. 18; Early moves north, Aug. 19; Aug. 27; Aug. 30, Sept. 1; act., Sept. 5; sk., Sept. 7; Sept. 12, 17; bat. expected, Sept. 18; Bat. of 3rd Winchester, Sept.

19; aftermath, Sept. 20, 23; Oct. 19; (1865) Fed. exped. from, Feb. 4, 13; Fed. scs. from, Mar. 17, 27, Apr. 11

Winder, Camp, Richmond, Va.: (1864) hospital burns, Jan. 25

Windmill Point, Va.: (1864) Feds. cross Potomac, June 14

Windsor, N.C.: (1864) sk., Jan. 30

Windsor, Va.: (1862) sk., Dec. 22; (1863) Fed. recon., Mar. 7

Winfield, N.C.: (1863) sk., Mar. 23

Winfield, W. Va.: (1864) sk., Oct. 26

Wingate, Ft., N. Mex. Terr.: (1864) Fed. exped. from, May 25, Nov 23; (1865) Fed. sc. from, Jan. 11

Winslow, John Ancrum (F): (1864) *Kearsarge-Alabama* duel, June 19

Winstead Hills, Tenn.: (1864) Bat. of Franklin, Nov. 30

Winston Farm, Va.: (1862) in Stuart's ride, June 12

Winston's Gap, Ala.: (1863) sk., Sept. 8

Winter's Gap, Tenn.: (1863) sk., Aug. 31

Winthrop, Theodore (F): (1861) killed, June 10

Winton, N.C.: (1862) Fed. exped. to, Feb. 18; (1863) Fed. exped. to, July 25

Wire: (1864) entanglements, May 15

Wire Br., W. Va.: (1862) sk., Aug. 16; (1864) sk., June 26

Wirz, Henry (C): (1865) execution of Andersonville Prison commander, Nov. 10

Wisconsin: (1861) legislature pro-Union, Jan. 22; (1862) in Dept. of the Northwest, Sept. 6; Democrats gain in, Nov. 4; (1865) ratifies Thirteenth Amendment, Mar. 1

Wise, Henry A. (C): (1861) commands Confs. in Kanawha Valley, June 6; Feds. move against, July 12; act. Scarey Cr., W. Va., July 17; retreats, July 24; relations with Floyd, Aug. 11; relieved, Sept. 25; assigned to N.C., Dec. 21; (1862) command Roanoke I., Jan. 22; ill Bat. of Roanoke I., Feb. 8

Wise, John S. (C): (1865) informs Davis of situation, Apr. 8

Wise's Crossroads, N.C.: (1863) sk., Apr. 27

Wise's Forks, N.C.: (1865) Bat. of (or Kinston), Mar. 8, 9, 10

Wissahickon, U.S.S.: (1862) at Grand Gulf, June 9

Witteburg, Ark.: (1863) Fed. cav. oper. from, Aug. 1

Wolf Cr., Ark.: (1864) sk., Apr. 2

Wolf Cr., W. Va.: (1862) sk., May 15

Wolf Cr., Br., near Memphis, Tenn.: (1862) sk., Sept. 23

Wolf R., Ky.: (1864) sk., May 18

Wolf R. Br., Moscow, Tenn.: (1863) act., Dec. 3

Wolf's Cr., Miss.: (1862) sk., June 4

Wolf's Plantation, S.C.: (1865) sk., Feb. 14

Wolftown, Va.: (1862) sk., Aug. 7

Women, assist war effort, C.S.A.: (1861) Apr. 26, May 4

Women, Conf.: (1863) Richmond, bread riot, Apr. 2; Mobile, Sept. 4; (1864) bread demon. Savannah, Ga., Apr. 17

Women Order of New Orleans: (1862) issued by Gen. Butler, May 15

Wood, Fernando: (1861) propose N. Y. City free city, Jan. 6; meets Lincoln, Feb. 20; (1863) peace meeting, June 3; (1865) opposes Thirteenth Amendment, Jan. 10

Wood, John Taylor (C): (1863) captures Fed. gunboats, Aug. 23; (1864) raid Cherrystone Point, Va., Mar. 5

Wright Co., Mo.: (1861) Fed. exped., Nov. 13; (1862) Fed. sc., Mar. 4; (1863) Fed. exped. to, Nov. 23; (1864) sk., July 22

Wright R., S.C.: (1862) Fed. recon. to, Feb. 6

Wrightsville, Pa.: (1863) sk., June 28

Writ of habeas corpus: *See* Habeas corpus, privilege of writ of

Wyandotte Constitution: (1861) Kas. admitted to Union with, Jan. 29

Wyatt, Miss.: (1863) act., Oct. 13; (1864) sk., Feb. 13

Wyatt's Farm, Va.: (1864) comb., Sept. 29

Wyerman's Mill, Va.: (1864) sk., Feb. 22

Wyoming: (1861) part Dak. Terr., Mar. 2

Wyoming, U.S.S.: (1863) Bat. of Shimonoseki, Japan, July 16

Wyoming Co., W. Va.: (1862) Fed. sc., July 24

Wyoming Court House, W. Va.: (1862) oper., Aug. 2; sk., Aug 5

Wytheville, Va.: (1863) Fed. exped., to, July 13; cav. eng., July 17; Feds. enter, July 18; (1864) eng., May 10; Feds. capture, Dec. 16; (1865) act., Apr. 6

Yalobusha R., Miss.: (1863) Mar. 11; bomb. Ft. Pemberton, Mar. 13; Yazoo Pass exped., Mar. 16

Yancey, William Lowndes (C): (1861) considered for Conf. Pres., Feb. 9; proclaims, "The man and the hour have met," Feb. 16; Davis names commissioner to Britain, Mar. 16; received by Lord Russell, May 3; (1863) death, July 27

Yankee, U.S.S.: (1861) exchanges shots, May 9; engages Confs., Aug. 23

Yankee "bummers": (1864) on March to the Sea, Nov. 22

Yankeetown, Tenn.: (1863) sk., Nov. 25

Yazoo City, Miss.: (1863) Fed. exped. to, May 20; Fed. flotilla to, May 21; Fed. exped. to, July 12; Feds. take, July 13; Fed. exped. to, Sept. 27; sk., Oct. 31; (1864) Fed. occup., Feb. 9; sk., Feb. 28; att. on, Mar. 5; Feds. abandon, Mar. 6; Fed. expeds. to, May 4, Nov. 23

Yazoo Pass (*See also* Pemberton, Ft.; Yazoo City; Yazoo R.): (1863) Davis on, Jan. 29; levee opened by Feds., Feb. 3; sk., Feb. 16; Fed. exped., Feb. 24, Mar. 11, 16; Lincoln asks about, Mar. 20

Yazoo R., Miss.: (1862) burning cotton, June 4; *Arkansas* attacks Fed. fleet, July 15; oper. on, Dec. 12; Sherman's exped. on, Dec. 26, 28; (1863) Sherman withdraws, Jan. 2; Feb. 3; sk., Feb. 19; Steele's Bayou exped., Mar. 16; Fed. mortar att., Vicksburg, May 19; Fed. Yazoo exped., Confs. destroy boats, May 21; Fed. exped., May 24; (1864) Fed. exped. up, Apr. 19; sk., May 29

Yeadon, Robert (C): (1863) offers reward for Ben Butler, Jan. 1

Yell Co., Ark.: (1864) sk., Aug. 22; (1865) Fed. sc., Mar. 12

Yellow Bayou (or Bayou De Glaize, Norwood's Plantation, or Old Oaks), La.: (1864) sk., May 17; eng., May 18

Yellow Cr., Mo.: (1862) sk., Aug. 13

Yellow Cr., Tenn.: (1863) sks., May 22, July 5

Yellow House, Va.: (1864) comb., Aug. 18

Yellow Medicine, Minn.: (1862) Sioux defeated, Wood Lake, Sept. 23

Yellow R., Fla.: (1864) oper., June 25

Yellow Tavern, Henrico Co., Va.: (1864) bat., mortal wounding Jeb Stuart, May 11; oper., Sept. 2

Yellow Tavern, Weldon R.R., Va.: (1864) Sept. 2

Yellville, Ark.: (1862) sk., June 25; Fed. exped. to, Nov. 25; (1863) Fed. sc. to, Apr. 3; (1864) Fed. sc. from, Mar. 13; Fed. sc. to, Nov. 11

Yerby's, Va.: (1862) Confs. at, Dec. 11

Yocknapatalfa R., Miss.: (1862) sks., Dec. 1, 3

Yocum Cr., Mo.: (1862) sk., Nov. 15

Yokohama, Japan: (1863) Bat. of Shimonoseki, July 16

York, Pa.: (1863) Early marches toward, June 26; surrenders to Confs., June 27; Early at, June 28, 30

York Plantation, La.: (1864) Fed. exped. to, Oct. 26

York R.: (1862) McClellan's Peninsula plan, Mar. 13; A. of P. embarks for, Mar. 17; May 7

Yorktown, Va.: (1861) Conf. recon. from, June 7; possible att. on, Oct. 24; (1862) Conf. lines, Apr. 1; McClellan moves toward, Apr. 4; siege of begins, Apr. 5; siege, Apr. 6, 7, 11, 12, 18, 19, 21, 22, May 1; J. E. Johnston withdraws from, May 3; A. of P. enters, May 4; May 7; Fed. recon. from, July 7; Oct. 10; Fed. recon. from, Dec. 11; (1863) Fed. Army-Navy exped. from, Jan. 7; Fed. expeds. from, Jan. 13, Apr. 27, June 4, June 23, Oct. 4; fire in, Dec. 16; (1864) Fed. expeds. from, Feb. 6, Mar. 17; (1865) Fed. exped. from, Feb. 23

Yorkville, S.C.: (1865) Davis reaches, Apr. 29

Yorkville, Tenn.: (1863) sk., Jan. 28

Young, Bennett H. (C): (1864) organizes raiders, June 16; St. Albans, Vt., raid, Oct. 19

Young Men's Christian Association: (1861) Lincoln to, Apr. 22; organizes U. S. Christian Commission, Nov. 15

Young's Cross Roads, N.C.: (1862) sk., May 15; Fed. recon. to, July 26; (1863) Fed. recon. to, Jan. 17; Fed. exped. to, Dec. 27

Young's Mill, Va.: (1861) sk., Oct. 21

Yulee, David Levy (C): (1861) Fla. sen. resigns, Jan. 21

Zacharie, J. W.: (1861) seized, Dec. 7

Zagonyi, Charles (F): (1861) occup. Springfield, Mo., Oct. 25

Zapata: (1863) aff. with, Sept. 2

Zarah, Ft., Kas.: (1864) sks., Nov. 20, Dec. 4; (1865) aff., Apr. 23

Zion Church, Ga.: (1864) att., June 22

Zoar Church, Va.: (1863) sk., Mar. 30

Zollicoffer, Felix Kirk (C): (1861) command east Tenn., July 26; act., Barboursville, Ky., Sept. 19; Oct. 23; Nov. 8; (1862) north of Cumberland R., Jan. 16; position vulnerable, Jan. 18; death at Bat. of Mill Springs, Ky., Jan. 19

Zollicoffer, Tenn.: (1863) act., Sept. 20; sks., Sept. 24, Oct. 19

Zouaves: (1861) N. Y. Fire Zouaves, May 2; Lincoln reviews, May 7; (1865) in Grand Review, May 23

Zuni, Va.: (1862) sks., May 30, Oct. 3, 25, Nov. 14, Dec. 8

INDEX TO SPECIAL STUDIES

The following index is to the section of Special Studies following the chronology, and is by pages.

V

Value of annual product: 726
Van Buskirk, Capt., tallest soldier: 707
Vermont: 1860 pop., 701
Virginia: 1860 pop., 702; desertion sanctuary, 715; number of military events in, 719; 721; railroads, 723, 724; industrial establishments, 726; value annual product, 726
Virginia, C.S.S., or C.S.S. *Merrimack:* 721

W

Wagon trains: 724
War Department, U. S.: telegraph office, 725
War of 1812: casualties in, 711
Washington, D.C.: pop. 1860, 703
Washington Territory: 1860 pop., 701
Welles, Gideon: 720

West Point: graduates who went South, 709
West Virginia: number of military events in, 719; 721
Wheat: 721
Whites: pop. South 1860, 700; 1860 by states, 701–2; military pop., 704
Wiley, Bell Irvin: 712
Wilmington, N.C.: 720
Wilson's Creek or Springfield, Mo., Battle of: 717
Wisconsin: 1860 pop., 701
Wool: 722
World War I: casualties in, 711
World War II: casualties in, 712
Wounded: mortally, U.S. Negro troops, 708; mortally, U. S. Army, 710; wounded, U. S. Army, 710; U. S. Navy, 710; mortally, Conf. Army, 711; Conf. Army wounded, 711; total, U.S. and Conf., 711; chances of being wounded, 713

Other DA CAPO titles of interest